MODERN PRACTICAL BOTANY

VOLUME – II

Including: **Diversity of Seed Plants and their Systematics and Structure, Development and Reproduction of Flowering Plants**

Dr. B.P. PANDEY

M.Sc., Ph.D., FPSI

Former Head

Department of Botany

J.V. College, Baraut, Uttar Pradesh

S Chand And Company Limited

(ISO 9001 Certified Company)

S Chand And Company Limited

(ISO 9001 Certified Company)

Head Office: D-92, Sector–2, Noida – 201301, U.P. (India), Ph. 91-120-4682700

Registered Office: A-27, 2nd Floor, Mohan Co-operative Industrial Estate, New Delhi – 110 044, Phone: 011-49731800

www.**schandpublishing.com**; e-mail: **info@schandpublishing.com**

Marketing Offices:

Chennai : Ph: 23632120; chennai@schandpublishing.com
Guwahati : Ph: 2738811, 2735640; guwahati@schandpublishing.com
Hyderabad : Ph: 40186018; hyderabad@schandpublishing.com
Jalandhar : Ph: 4645630; jalandhar@schandpublishing.com
Kolkata : Ph: 23357458, 23353914; kolkata@schandpublishing.com
Lucknow : Ph: 4003633; lucknow@schandpublishing.com
Mumbai : Ph: 25000297; mumbai@schandpublishing.com
Patna : Ph: 2260011; patna@schandpublishing.com

First Edition 1979
Subsequent Editions and Reprints 1982, 86, 88, 95, 96, 99, 2001, 2003, 2005, 2007, 2008
Revised Edition 2010
Reprints 2012, 2013, 2014, 2015, 2016 (Twice), 2019, 2020 (Twice), 2021, 2022

Reprint 2024

ISBN: 978-81-219-0920-4 **Product Code:** H6BOP68BOTN10ENAE10R

PRINTED IN INDIA

By Vikas Publishing House Private Limited, Plot 20/4, Site-IV, Industrial Area Sahibabad, Ghaziabad – 201 010 and Published by S Chand And Company Limited, A-27, 2nd Floor, Mohan Co-operative Industrial Estate, New Delhi – 110 044.

PREFACE TO THE FIFTH EDITION

I feel really delighted in presenting the thoroughly **Revised** and **Enlarged Fifth** edition of **'Modern Practical Botany' Volume II.** This volume includes, **1. Diversity of Seed Plants and Their Systematics** (Gymnosperms and Angiosperms) and **2. Structure, Development and Reproduction in Flowering Plants.** Laboratory methods, Preparing and caring for a herbarium collection, System of classification of angiosperms, How to describe an angiospermic plant, Structure of angiosperms, Description of angiospermic plants in semitechnical language, Plant physiology experiments, Anatomy of angiosperms, Ecological anatomy, Special modes of reproduction, Dormant and non-dormant seeds and some other topics of practical value have been added. In end of text, a general glossary of technical and medical terms has been added that will make study of *viva-voce* easy and graspable.

This volume covers the syllabus of UGC Model Curriculum and the syllabus prescribed in different Indian Universities, situated in different parts of country.

The text has been thoroughly revised. Several new descriptions and laboratory exercises have been added. However, general plan of manual remains unchanged. I hope, this 'practical manual' would be useful for degree and postgraduate students of botany.

I am thankful to my publisher S. Chand & Company Ltd., New Delhi especially CMD, Mrs. Nirmala Gupta, the JMD, Mr. Himanshu Gupta and other Directors, and the Vice-President (Publishing), Mr. Navin Joshi, Mr. R.S. Saxena (Advisor), Mr. Shishir Bhatnagar (Pre-press Manager) for their cooperation for print this edition.

Dr. B.P. Pandey

PREFACE TO THE FIRST EDITION

The practical study of the subject is of immense value. The theoretical class room knowledge remains meaningless and incomplete unless and until is supplemented with the practical work either in the field or inside the laboratory. The laboratory work always adds to the knowledge and discipline. The practical work develops confidence and scientific outlook which makes the most essential part of life. The science subjects can only be understood well when a student works in the laboratory and makes the rational approach based on the facts and figures. Laboratory is the only place where a student learns and makes clear cut demarcation between right and wrong. A student always needs some guide lines to facilitate his work in the laboratory. The present text will fulfil this need. The first edition of 'Modern Practical Botany' Vol II is just published and it is hoped that this will serve those well for whom it is intended.

In conclusion, I wish to express my deep sense of gratitude and indebtedness to those who helped me directly or indirectly during the preparation of the manuscript of this text. Especially I am indebted to Dr. N.P. Saxena, D.N. College, Meerut who allowed the diversion from research to this work. I also wish to express my appreciation to Dr. Ashok Kumar who gave the time to review the manuscript. I am really grateful to Sri T.N. Goel, my publisher, who managed to bring out the book in this shape. I am also thankful to Mr. Onkar Saran, the artist, who has drawn most of the drawings of the text. My son Sanjeeva deserves highest appreciation for his help and assistance he sponsored to me in several ways.

Suggestions and healthy criticisms for improvement of the book will be most welcomed and thankfully acknowledged.

AUTHOR

CONTENTS

1. DIVERSITY OF SEED PLANTS AND THEIR SYSTEMATICS

MONOCOTYLEDONS

2. STRUCTURE, DEVELOPMENT AND REPRODUCTION IN FLOWERING PLANTS

UNIT–1
DIVERSITY OF SEED PLANTS AND THEIR SYSTEMATICS

1
CHAPTER

Laboratory Methods

The practical study of the subject is of immense value. The theoretical knowledge is always incomplete unless and until is supplemented with laboratory work. The laboratory work always adds to the knowledge and discipline. The practical work develops the scientific outlook which is most essential part of life. The science subjects can only be understood when a student works in the laboratory and makes the rational approach based on the facts and figures. The confusions are removed only by practical study of a subject. The practical aspect of the science subject is more essential than other theoretical aspects. Here a student makes the clear cut demarcation between right and wrong.

When one enters in the laboratory to work one should be most disciplined. The student while at working table should follow the laboratory rules. The student is expected to work silently and carefully. If one feels some difficulty in proceeding the work, he should immediately consult the teacher-in-charge. The most essential instruction about the practical work is that things should be signed by the teacher-in-charge, the same day. The cleanliness seems to be most important for practical work. The implements which are provided to you in the laboratory and the instruments which you possess should be clean and in working order. When you leave the laboratory after work, the things should be properly arranged by you.

PRESERVING BOTANICAL SPECIMENS

Preserving specimens for laboratory study. Such specimens may be preserved in alcohol or in formalin, but the latter is by far the most satisfactory. A comparatively weak solution of formalin is suitable for plant tissues. For most plant specimens 4% solution of formalin is recommended, although certain very large, fleshy forms may require a 5 or 6% solution. Plant material preserved in this way will be kept indefinitely and will be available whenever needed for laboratory study.

Green leaves placed in 4% formalin soon lose their green colouring matter (chlorophyll) and become yellowish or whitish. Alcohol presents the same difficulty, but the following solution will preserve the natural green colour in plants :

Phenol	...	*20 gms.*
Lactic acid	...	*20 gms.*
Glycerine	...	*40 gms.*
Distilled water	...	*20 gms.*
Cupric chloride	...	*0.2 gms.*

Cupric acetate ... *0.2 gms.*

The specimens are merely dropped into this fluid and left there until needed. Usually from 3 to 10 days are required for complete preservation.

Preserving specimens for microscopic examination. For general use the most useful fixative is "F.A.A." This solution is made as follows :

50% Alcohol ... *100 ml*
40% Formalin ... *6½ ml.*
Glacial acetic acid ... *2½ ml.*

This fixative is excellent for most plant tissues. Its usefulness is also due to the fact that tissues may be left in it indefinitely without harm.

A solution which will preserve **green algae** in good natural colour is made as follows :

Potassium chrome alum ... *10 gms.*
40% formalin ... *5 ml.*
Water ... *500 ml.*

This fixative will not plasmolyse such forms as *Vaucheria*, and most algae fixed in it will be well preserved for microscopic examination.

Preserving specimens for display purposes. Green plants intended for display purposes may be preserved in the "ever green" solution mentioned above. After being fixed in this solution the specimens may be mounted in fluid (4% formalin) in glass display jars, or they may be pressed and mounted on standard herbarium sheets.

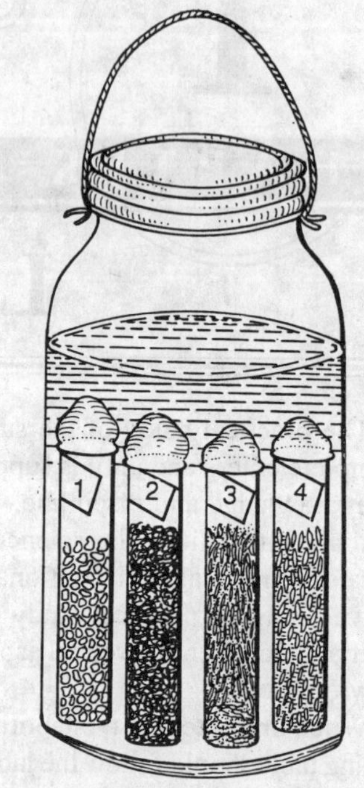

Fig. 1.1. Preservation of small specimens in a larger bottle.

Fruits and Flowers

The natural colours of some of the fruits and flowers may be preserved to some extent, however, by adding 10% of pure cane sugar to the usual (4%) formalin solution.

Fruits such as apples may be preserved in a solution made as follows :

Distilled water ... *400 ml.*
Zinc chloride ... *200 gms.*
Formalin (40%) ... *100 ml.*
Glycerine ... *100 ml.*

It is best to dissolve the zinc chloride in hot (distilled) water and filter while hot. Add formalin and glycerine.

INSTRUMENTS

The students while working in the laboratory must possess the following instruments and accessories with them :

1. Practical record book.
2. Pencils (HB, 2H, 4H, etc.)
3. Rubber (pencil eraser)
4. Foot scale
5. Camel-hair brush (No. 3)
6. Dropper

7. Razor with hollow-ground blade
8. Forceps
9. Needles with plastic handles (two)
10. Muslin cloth.

The slides, cover glasses, stains, reagents, mounting media, hone, strop, watch glasses, petri dishes, other glassware and a compound student microscope will be provided in the laboratory.

The following instruments are required, while one is in the field to collect plant materials for laboratory work and to make herbarium of dried specimens.

1. Vasculum
2. Pen knife.
3. Magnifying lens (10 X)
5. Trowel or pick
6. Tough and fair book and pencil
7. Pruning shears
8. Plant presses
9. Blotting papers or waste newspapers
10. Walking stick
11. First aid outfit (Iodine or Burnol)

SECTION CUTTING

In order to reveal the cellular structure of the plant material sections are being cut in various planes.

1. Cross section. Here the section passes at right angle to the material. It is of two types.

(*a*) *Transverse section.* Here the section is cut at right angle to vertical axis of the plant such as stem and roots..

(*b*) *Vertical section.* In case of thallus, leaf, etc., the section is cut in transverse plane and is known as vertical section. It is generally applied to the dorsiventral leaf and thallus growing prostrate.

2. Longitudinal section. The section is cut at right angles to the transverse axis. It is of two types :

(*a*) *Radial longitudinal section* (*R.L.S.*). It is the section that passes through the radius.

(*b*) *Tangential longitudinal section* (*T.L.S.*). It is the section that passes through the tangent, this does not pass through central region, it is transverse to medullary ray.

Method. To cut the thin sections suitable pith material should be used. In case of thalli and leaves, etc., the pith is first divided longitudinally into two equal halves with the help of scalpel and the material is placed in between the two halves of pith. In case of stems, roots, etc., a hole is made in the pith and the material is being fitted in the hole.

During the process of section cutting the students should be cautious so that the material does not dry up in whole operation of section cutting. To avoid this a few drops of water may be put now and then on the material. For cutting the sections the pith is being held in between the fingers and thumb of the left hand and the razor in the right hand. The first two fingers remain at the back of the razor and the thumb remain pressed against the milled surface of thick shank of the blade. The cutting edge of the razor blade should be kept always in horizontal position so that the uniform and thin sections are cut. The sections should be cut by sliding the razor over the material repeatedly. This process should be repeated several times and then the sections thus cut are transferred with the help of camel's hair brush to a watch glass containing water. With the help of camel's hair brush the thinnest and perfect sections are being selected for staining.

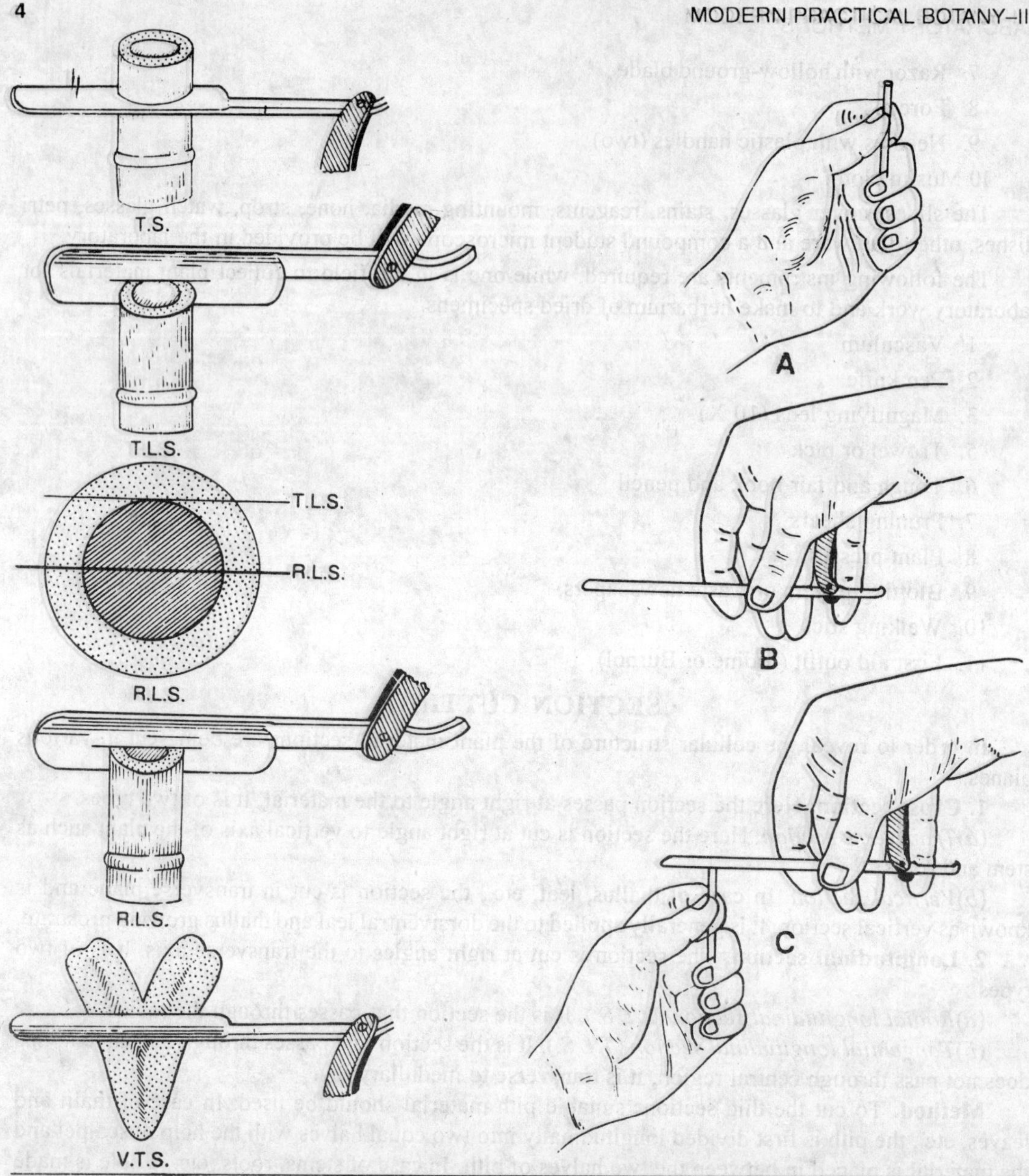

Fig. 1.2. Section cutting. Three planes of a block transverse, radial longitudinal and tangential longitudinal, and vertical transverse sections.

Fig. 1.3. Section cutting. *A*, holding of pith; *B*, holding of razor; *C*, section cutting material is being inserted in the pith.

HOW TO PREPARE MICROSCOPE SLIDES OF SIMPLE OBJECTS

Whole Mounts

As the name indicates, whole mounts are preparations of the object entire. Many interesting mounts may be made without cutting sections, and without staining. Fibres of cotton, fern sporangia, the fruiting heads of mosses (if dried first) and pine pollen, may be dropped directly into xylol, placed in a drop of balsam on a slide, and covered.

Free-hand Sections

Free-hand sections of cork, pith and the stems and roots of many of the common plants may be cut. For this purpose the razor must be sharp and free from nicks. Only thinnest sections should be used and they may be placed into 95% alcohol as cut. Subsequent treatment of sections is as follows. Handling should be gentle as possible, using section lifter and camel's hair brush.

1. *95% alcohol - 1/2 hour.*
2. *50% alcohol - 5 minutes.*
3. *Water - 5 minutes.*
4. *Safranin - 4 hours (1% solution in water).*
5. *Water to rinse.*
6. *50% alcohol - 5 minutes.*
7. *95% alcohol - 5 minutes.*
8. *Absolute alcohol - 5 minutes.*
9. *95% alcohol containing 1% light green 1-3 minutes.*
10. *Absolute alcohol - 3-5 minutes.*
11. *Clove oil - 5 minutes.*
12. *Xylol-indefinite.*
13. *Mount in balsam : cover with cover glass.*

The time values given are approximate, and will vary somewhat with the kind of section being stained. Practice on a few sections will teach whether to hasten or retard the process.

MACERATION TECHNIQUE

The various parts of the plants consist of several types of tissues. Such tissues can be studied well by a special technique known as *maceration.* This process involves the separation of a particular cell from a mass of cells. This type of dissociation is brought about by chemical treatment of the plant organ that dissolves the middle lamella and the cells are separated from each other.

Usually three undermentioned methods are employed for the purpose.

1. Jeffrey's method. Take the dried or fresh plant material and make very thin slices of it. Boil the material in water by keeping it in a test tube. After some time when the material becomes air free and settles down in the bottom of the test tube, it is macerated in a solution. The maceration solution may be prepared as follows :

(*i*) 10% Nitric acid (*i.e.*, 90 ml. water + 10 ml. nitric acid).
(*ii*) 10% Chromic acid (*i.e.*, 90 ml water + 10 ml. chromic acid)
Mix (*i*) and (*ii*) acids.

Now take the material in this maceration solution in a test tube. Heat this solution and separate the material in small pieces by piercing a needle to the material. Stop heating as soon as the material becomes soft and pulp like. Now transfer this pulpy material to a watch glass. Drain out all the maceration fluid. Wash the material several times with water, so that the acid traces are removed completely. Now strain the material with aqueous safranin and mount it in glycerine or glycerine jelly. The material may also be passed through alcohol series for making permanent slides.

2. Harlow's method. Treat the sliced and boiled material with chlorine water for two hours. Now wash the material with water. After proper washing boil the material in sodium sulphite for fifteen minutes. Now transfer this fluid to a watch glass. Drain out the water. Tease the material with the help of a needle for the separation of tissues. Prepare temporary or permanent mounts.

3. Schultze's method. Make thin slices of the material and boil it in water in a test tube. Now fill the test tube with concentrated nitric acid, and add a few crystals of potassium chlorate to it. Heat it gently till material becomes white. Now transfer the fluid to the watch glass and drain out the liquid leaving material alone. Wash the material with water. Tease the material with the help of a needle, so that the cells may be separated from each other. Stain the material and make temporary or permanent mounts.

STAINING

The tissue differentiation is possible only by staining the different tissues with different stains. The stains are the chemical dyes having different reactions with the cell wall of the tissue and thus giving a particular stain to a particular tissue. For example, the acidic dye stains unlignified tissue while the basic one stains lignified tissue.

Single staining. The plant materials having no differentiation of tissues (*e.g.*, algae, fungi, bryophytes) are stained by this process.

Double staining. The plant materials having highly differentiated tissues (*e.g.*, Pteridophyta, Gymnosperms, Angiosperms, etc.) are stained by this process. Double staining involves the use of two dyes, one acidic and other basic. The acidic dye stains unlignified tissues while the basic one stains the lignified tissues. Some important dyes are as follows :

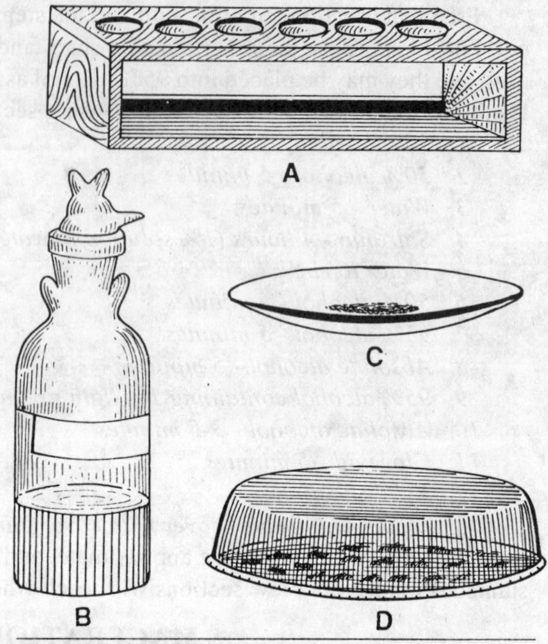

Fig. 1.4. Some laboratory requirements *A*, staining rack; *B*, dropping bottle; *C*, watch glass; *D*, petri dish (petri plate).

1. Safranin :

Alcoholic :

Safranin ... *1 gm.*
Alcohol 95% ... *50 c.c.*
Distilled water ... *50 c.c.*

Aqueous :

Safranin ... *1 gm.*
Distilled water ... *10 c.c.*

This is mainly used to stain lignified tissues.

2. Crystal violet or Gentian violet:

Crystal violet ... *1 gm*
Distilled water ... *100 c.c*

It is basic violet dye and stains lignified tissues.

3. Aniline blue :

Aniline blue ... *1 gm.*
Alcohol (95%) of
distilled water ... *100 c.c.*

It stains cellulose walls.

4. Erythrosine:

Erythrosine ... *1 gm.*
Absolute alcohol ... *5 c.c.*
Clove oil ... *95 c.c.*

It is used to stain gelatinous sheath, e.g., Algae.

5. Eosine :

Eosine ... *1 gm*
Water ... *100 c.c.*

It stains cytoplasm.

6. Light green

Light green	...	*0.5 gm.*
Alcohol 95%	...	*100 c.c.*

OR

Light green	...	*1 gm*
Absolute alcohol	...	*2.5 c.c.*
Clove oil	...	*75 c.c.*

It is used to stain cellulose and lignified cell walls.

7. Fast green :

Fast green	...	*0.5 gm.*
Alcohol 95%	...	*100 c.c.*

OR

Fast green	...	*0.5 gm.*
Absolute alcohol	...	*25 c.c.*
Clove oil	...	*75 c.c.*

8. Cotton blue :

Aniline blue	...	*0.1 gm.*
Phenol	...	*25 gms.*
Glycerine	...	*25 c.c.*
Lactic acid	...	*25 c.c.*
Distilled water	...	*25 c.c.*

This is used for staining various fungi.

9. Basic fuchsin :

Solution A

Basic fuchsin	...	*0.3 gm.*
Alcohol 95%	...	*10 c.c.*

Solution B

Phenol (melted)	...	*5 gms.*
Distilled water	...	*95 c.c.*

Mix solutions A and B.

This is a nuclear stain and also used to stain bacteria.

10. Hematoxylins :

Heidenhain's hematoxylin.

Hematoxylin	...	*0.5 gm.*
Warm distilled water	...	*100 c.c.*

Store in a dark place to ripen at least for four days before use.

Delafield's hematoxylin.

1. Saturated aqueous solution (100 c.c.) of ferric ammonium sulphate.

2. 1 gm. Hematoxylin + 6 c.c. absolute alcohol.

3. Mix 1 and 2 solutions.

The prepared solution is kept for sufficient time and then used. The solution becomes dark red in colour. It is good nuclear stain.

11. Acetocarmine :

Carmine	...	*1 gm.*
Glacial acetic acid	...	*45 c.c.*

Dissolve 1 gm. of carmine in 100 c.c. of boiling 45% acetic acid. Cool this mixture and decant. Add few drops of ferric acetate aqueous solution in the mixture. Cool the mixture abruptly by keeping it in ice. Filter the mixture and stock it in a cool place.

MOUNTING MEDIA AND MOUNTING

Mounting Media for Temporary Preparations

1. Glycerine. Prepare the mounting medium as follows – 30 ml. pure glycerine + 70 ml. water. This medium is quite good for the mounting purpose of algae and stained sections.

2. Glycerine jelly. It is prepared by dissolving one part of the gelatin with six parts of water by boiling. Add to it seven parts of glycerine. Also add 10% phenol which acts as preservative. This is a good mounting medium for algae. The slides become semipermanent and can be kept for long.

3. Lacto-phenol. This mounting medium can be prepared by adding equal amounts of phenol, lactic acid, glycerine and distilled water. This makes a good mounting medium to mount various fungi.

Mounting Media for Permanent Preparations

1. Canada balsam. This medium is used for permanent slide preparations. According to need this may be diluted by adding xylene in it. This medium is somewhat yellowish in colour.

2. D.P.X. mountant. This is a good mounting medium for permanent slide preparations. This is perfectly transparent and gives good results.

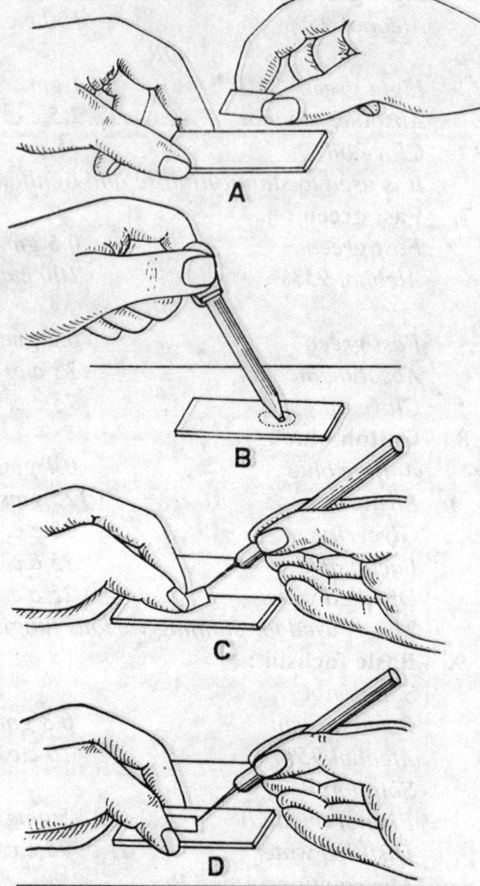

Fig. 1.5. Mounting material after section cutting and proper staining (A—D).

Method of mounting. The stained sections or materials are generally mounted in any one of the media mentioned above. While mounting one should be watchful that the object is being mounted in the centre of the slide. Put a drop of mounting medium in the centre of the slide with the help of a dropper and the material is being transferred in this drop of medium with the help of a fine brush. With the help of forceps or needle the cover glass is kept on the material in such a way that the air bubbles are avoided. The mounting fluid should not flow outside the coverslip. The extra amount of fluid can be removed with the help of a blotting paper.

Labelling. After making the preparation neat and clean it should be properly labelled. The labels should be uniformly pasted on the left side of the slide. Usually the generic and specific names, name of the part and plane of the section are being written on the label. One should also write his name on the bottom of the label.

Ringing. Usually the temporary and semipermanent slides are sealed by cementing material with the help of a ringing machine. By this method only those slides can be sealed which possess round cover-glasses.

HOW TO MAKE LABORATORY DRAWINGS

Accurately made drawings are a very important part of laboratory work. An accurate drawing made in the laboratory from the specimen itself, is a very good indication of the student's grasp of the subject. Every teacher of Biology has heard students say : "I can't draw." However, any student who can follow laboratory directions intelligently and who can be taught to see accurately can make a drawing that will demonstrate his observations. Too often students feel that because their drawings do not look artistic their work is inferior, when as a matter of fact an artistic drawing may be decidedly unsatisfactory from a scientific standpoint. A good drawing is often spoiled by trying to make it look artistic. A laboratory drawing should be as simple as possible, with clean, clear cut lines showing what has been seen and neatly labelled.

Preliminary Study

The most important prerequisite in making a drawing is careful observation. If a laboratory outline is being used, all parts called for in the drawing must be identified in the specimen, and the student must understand the work that he is doing before pencil is put to the drawing paper.

Materials

1. The drawing paper should be heavy enough to permit a good deal of erasing and should have a smooth, hard surface. A heavy, white paper size 8 × 10½ inches, with holes punched to fit the laboratory note book.
2. A hard drawing pencil, 6H preferred. The pencil should not be softer than 4H.
3. A soft rubber eraser.
4. A ruler with the English system on one edge and the metric system on the other. Six-inch celluloid rulers are satisfactory for most work.
5. A very fine sand paper for putting a good point on the drawing pencil.

Size of Drawings

The most common mistake made by beginning students is to make their drawing too small. Since it is almost impossible in every instance for the teacher or for the manual to give the size that every drawing should be, the simplest rule to follow is to have the drawing large enough to show all parts without crowding. If the drawing is one showing a single cell it must be large enough to show clearly and to label all of its parts. Obviously such a drawing need not cover a whole page. The student must learn to judge for himself how large to make the drawing, remembering, roughly speaking, that the greater the number of parts to be shown the larger the drawing should be and also that the tendency is to make drawing too small.

Laying Out the Drawing

The punched holes in the paper should be to the left. Draw on the one side of the paper. The student's name should appear on each sheet, usually at the upper right hand corner. The title of the drawing should be directly over it.

First, determine the size of the drawing and its arrangement on the page. Keep far enough to the right of the punched holes so that no part of the drawing will be obscured when it is placed in the note book. Leave enough margin for labels, one both sides if necessary.

Draw a very faint guideline down the centre of the drawing field. On either side of this line mark the natural divisions of the specimen by means of light dots. Then carefully outline the drawing with very light lines connecting the dots until the proportions are accurately portrayed. Compare the faint outline sketch with the specimen, and erase and sketch until it is accurate. Having obtained an accurate outline erase the guideline and the superfluous light lines, leaving only the faint traces of the outline to be used. Then tracing over this outline makes a sharp, clear-cut line. In doing this use a normal, continuous movement of the hand or finger. The general outline having been completed, the details should then be filled in, sketching lightly at first where necessary to obtain proportion, continually comparing with the specimen to insure accuracy in proper relationship of parts. When the drawing has been completed, every line should be clear and sharp. Any traces of the light lines used in making the outline should be removed by erasing lightly. Every line in the drawing should be there for the purpose of indicating some part of the specimen. Extra line for artistic effect may spoil an otherwise good drawing.

Labelling

When a student has completed his drawing he often feels that the important part has been finished. However, he should give just as careful attention to the labelling as to the drawing. Careless labelling can spoil a good drawing. If possible, all labels should be in a column to the right of the drawing. If there are a great many parts to be labelled, another column to left of the drawing may be necessary.

Neatness

The finished drawing should be neat and clean. Clean hands, and careful procedure at all time will enable the student to make a neat and scientific drawing, against a clean, white background. If the drawing has proved difficult and becomes slightly soiled from much handling, diligent use of the eraser before labelling will usually result in a clean page.

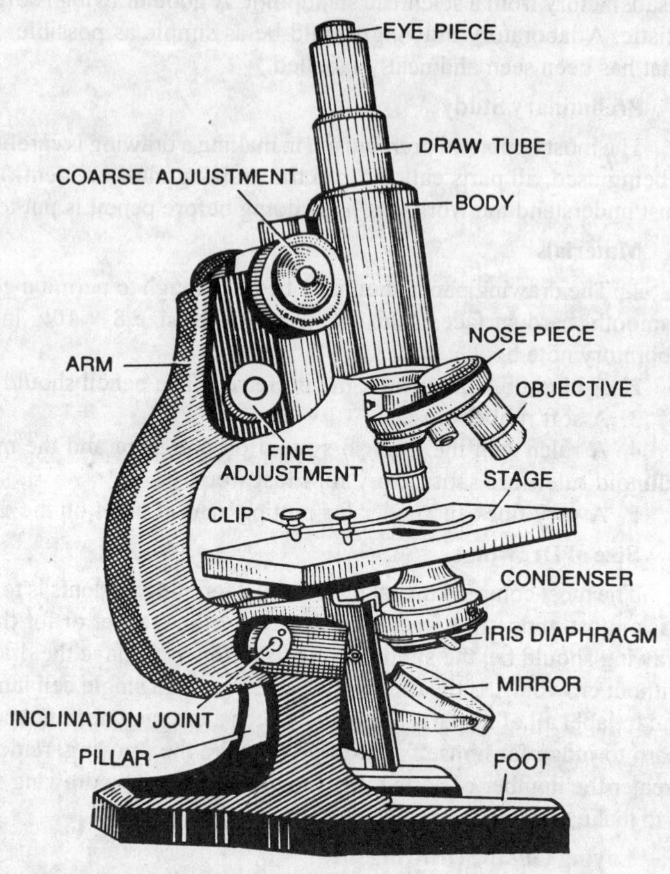

Fig. 1.6. Compound student microscope.

PRACTICAL MICROSCOPY

Illumination

Artificial light is preferable because of its uniformity and availability. For direct observation through the microscope, a desk lamp placed about six inches from the microscope.

Eye Care

Both eyes must be kept open and used alternately while working with the monocular microscope to avoid eye-strain. Microscope illumination may be modified for eye comfort by exchanging the light bulb of the lamp for one of lower or higher watt value, or by interposing a ground glass screen (near the lamp) between the light source and substage condenser. Do not

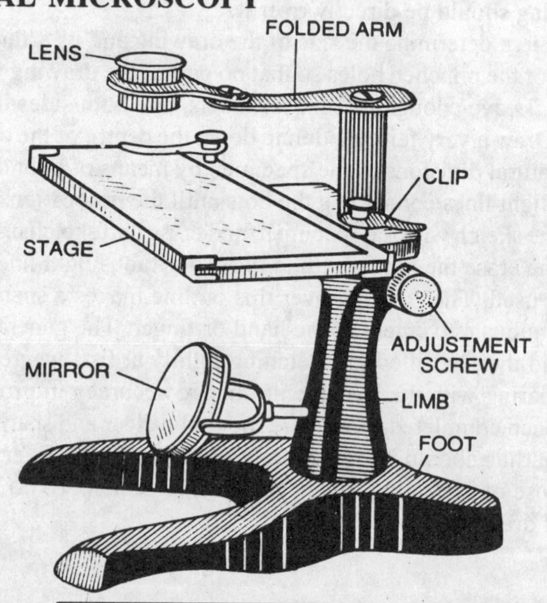

Fig. 1.7. Dissecting microscope.

alter the correct position of the substage condenser or the correct opening of the substage diaphragm to reduce light intensity.

To Illuminate the Low Power Objective

(*a*) Place a suitable object on the stage and while matching from the level of the stage, lower the objective within an eighth of an inch of the slide.

(*b*) Then, looking, through the 10 X eye piece, direct the light through the condenser with the plane mirror until the field or view is illuminated. Elevate the tube with the coarse adjustment until the object appears in focus. Complete focussing with the fine adjustment.

To Illuminate the High Power Objective

(*a*) Revolve the high dry-objective into position. If the objectives are parfocal, the image will be approximately in focus. If the objectives are not parfocal, lower the high dry objective until it nearly touches the cover glass.

(*b*) Then, looking through the eyepiece, focus up. Use the fine adjustment only for delicate focussing.

To Illuminate the Homogeneous oil Immersion Objective

(*a*) Place a suitable object slide on the stage. Locate the desired field with a low power objective and centre the light with the plane mirror.

(*b*) Elevate the microscope tube and place a drop of cedarwood immersion oil on the area to be observed. (Avoid air bubbles)

(*c*) Lower the oil immersion objective with the coarse adjustment to contact with the drop of immersion oil. Control this operation from the level of the stage.

(*d*) Raise the objective slightly with the coarse adjustment without breaking the immersion contact.

(*e*) Then, looking through the eyepiece, focus down carefully with the coarse adjustment until the image comes into view. Complete the focussing with the fine adjustment.

(*f*) Immersion oil should be removed once a day from objectives when the day's work is complete. It is undesirable to subject the lens surface to excessive polishing. To clean an objective wipe across the lens front with a dry portion of lens paper removing the bulk of oil, then follow with lens paper moistened with xylol, and finally with dry lens paper.

Care of the Microscope

Carry the instrument by the arm - supporting it at the same time by placing the other hand under it. Do not subject the microscope to rapid changes of temperature. The slides of the rack and pinion may be lubricated and cleaned occasionally by applying a small amount of paraffin oil or light grease and wiping it off. Do not lubricate the fine adjustment nor the teeth of either rack or pinion of the coarse adjustment. Keep the microscope covered and protected from dust when not in use. Dust may be removed from lenses with a clean camel's hair brush. Should the front lens of the objective be soiled, wipe it gently with lens paper moistened with distilled water - do no rub.

MEASURING WITH THE MICROSCOPE (MICROMETRY)

The micrometry is the subject in which we have some measurement of the dimensions of an object being observed use under the microscope. The method employs some special types of measuring devices which are so oriented that these can well be attached to or put into the microscope and observed. The object to be measured is calibrated against these scales.

Once an object is being observed under a microscope by the 10 X objective the 10 X eye piece; this way, the image that is perceived is 100 times of the object. We get the magnified view no doubt and also that it is perfect coordination of the dimensions but to find out the absolute size of the object will need precision and which is achieved through the application of micrometers. Usually the micrometers are or two types - the ocular micrometer disc and the stage micrometer.

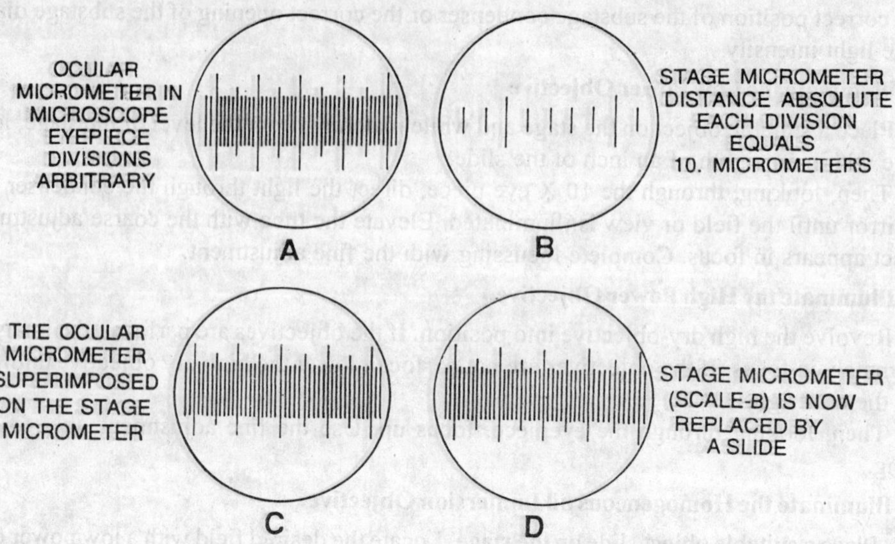

Fig. 1.8. Micrometry. Standardization of the ocular micrometer and its use in measuring bacterial cells.

The ocular micrometer disc. Before inserting the disc, clean it gently with distilled water and wipe it with a soft lifeless tissue. Examine the disc with a hand magnifier by light reflected from each surface to detect adhering particles and removed them with a clean camel's hair brush. Select the ocular (preferably not stronger than 10 X) and unscrew the eyelens mount. Position the disc over the eyepiece diaphragm with the engraved side down (figures should appear erect), and replace the eyelens. With the micrometer disc in place, insert the ocular into the illuminated microscope and bring the lines into sharp focus unscrewing the upper eyelens for a sufficient distance. There are usually 50 or 100 divisions in the ocular meter which are engraved on the glass.

The stage micrometer. The scale, mounted like a microscope specimen on a glass slide which is generally thicker than a specific slide. The micrometer has a amount of very finely graduated scale. The scale measures only one millimeter and has a least count of .01 mm, *i.e.,* 1 millimeter region is divided into 100 divisions. As 1 mm has 1000 μ–one division of stage micrometer is equal to 10 μ.

Method. The stage micrometer is kept in low power under microscope and is observed through the eye piece hang ocular micrometer disc. Suppose we have 10 X objective and 5 X eye piece in the microscope with a tube of 170 mm. length. At this magnification the number of ocular divisions coinciding the stage micrometer are observed and then calculated for microns per ocular division, *e.g.,* 6 ocular divisions coincide 8 stage micrometer divisions

i.e., 6 ocular divisions = 8 stage micrometer divisions

or 6 ocular divisions = .08 mm.

(since 1 division of stage micrometer is equal to .01 mm.)

$$1 \text{ ocular division} = \frac{.08}{6} \text{ mm.}$$

$$= \frac{.08 \times 1000}{6}$$

$$= 13.3\ \mu$$

Thus the microscope is calibrated for different combinations of eye pieces and objective lens and is kept for record.

Measurement of an object. When the microscope is calibrated, then the object to be measured is kept on the stage of the microscope and is observed through eye piece of ocular. The object is measured in the particular magnification by ocular divisions and then is being changed into micron by multiplying ocular division with calibrated value of one ocular division in that particular magnification, *e.g.*, the length of a bacterial cell is equal to five divisions of ocular that means the length in microns will be 5 ocular divisions X 13.3 = 66.5 μ.

This way the object can be measured in any of the magnification.

COMMON STAINS AND MOUNTING MEDIA

For Algae — Temporary preparations

Stains : (*i*) *Aniline blue (.1% aqueous)*
(*ii*) Fast *green (.5 aqueous)*
(*iii*) *Safranin (.5% aqueous)* } *Single staining*

Mounting media (*i*) Glycerine 10%
(*ii*) Glycerine jelly.

For Fungi — Temporary preparations

Stains : (*i*) *Cotton blue*
(*ii*) *Aniline blue* } *Single staining*

Mounting media : (*i*) *Lactophenol*
(*ii*) *Glycerine 10%*

For Bryophytes — Temporary preparations

Stains : (*i*) *Safranin.*
(*ii*) *Fast green.* } *Single staining*

Mounting media (*i*) *Glycerine 10%*
(*ii*) *Glycerine jelly.*

For Pteridophytes

(*Temporary and permanent preparations*)

Primary stains :	**Secondary stains :**	
(*i*) *Safranin*	*Fast green*	} *Double staining*
(*ii*) *Crystal violet*	*Erythrosine*	

Mounting media :

(*i*) *Glycerine 10% (for temporary preparations)*
(*ii*) *Canada Balsam or D.P.X. mountant (for permanent preparations)*

For Gymnosperms :

(*Temporary and permanent preparations*)

Primary stains :	**Secondary stains :**	
(*i*) *Safranin*	*Fast green*	} *Double staining*
(*ii*) *Crystal violet*	*Erythrosine*	

Mounting media :

(*i*) *Glycerine 10% (for temporary preparations)*
(*ii*) *Canada Balsam or D.P.X. mountant (for permanent preparations)*

Gymnosperms

The gymnosperms have long been considered as a group of seed-bearing plants.

Together with the angiosperms they are known as phanerogams or spermatophytes. They are distinguished from the angiosperms by having naked ovules and seeds. The ovules are not enclosed in an ovary and the seeds are not enclosed in a pericarp.

The Gymnospermae comprises trees and shrubs which are characterized by xeromorphic acicular or fern-like leaves and unisexual inflorescence.

The ovules lie exposed on the megasporophylls which are open and therefore, devoid of a style and stigma.

The pollen grains are spherical or oval, often with a bladder-like extension of the exine. The pollination is direct in the sense that the pollen grains or at least the pollen tubes reach the nucellus of the ovule without the intervention of the stigma and styles through which the pollen tubes have to penetrate in angiosperms.

The pollen grains possess a prothallus of two or more cells, one of which produces two non-motile or rarely motile male gametes or spermatozoids. (*e.g.*, *Cycas, Ginkgo*).

The pollen grains are disseminated by wind. They directly settle upon the micropyle.

The embryosac (female gametophyte) contains a tissue before fertilization which is known as rudimentary prothallium, and two or more archegonia are formed in it, each consisting of large egg cell and a short neck. Only one embryo usually develops to maturity, the embryo consists of an axis bearing two to several cotyledons and ending in a radicle. The whole embryo remains enclosed in amass of endosperm which represents a continuation of the gametophytic tissue. The sporophylls are usually arranged in a cone-like structure.

Key to the identification of gymnosperms :

Trees or shrubs usually resinous; ovules naked, not enclosed in an ovary; flowers unisexual, rarely bisexual; leaves needle-shaped, scale like, linear pinnate, rarely fan-shaped or oblong elliptic, mostly evergreen.

Classification of Gymnosperms

Bierhorst (1971)
GYMNOSPERMS

Classes :

1. Cycadopsida

Orders :

1. Pteridospermales
2. Ciytoniales
3. Cycadeoideales
4. Cycadales
5. Pentoxylales
6. Glossopteridales

2. Coniferopsida

1. Cordaitales
2. Protopityales
3. Ginkgoales
4. Coniferales
5. Taxales

3. Gnetopsida

1. Ephedrales
3. Gnetales
3. Welwitschiales

CYCAS

Habit and Occurrence

The genus includes about sixteen species which are found wild or cultivated in the tropics and sub-tropics of the world. In India, *Cycas* is represented by the following six species which may be identified by the characters given below.

Margins of leaflet flat.

Trunk not swollen at the base.

Leaflets 5 mm to 10 mm broad, blade of megasporophyll broadly orbicular, long, acuminate and deeply pectinate. 1. *C. pectinata Griff.*

Leaflets usually not more than 12 mm broad, megasporophylls spinous, toothed along the margin. 2. *C. circinnalis* Linn.

Leaflets 12 mm to 16 mm broad, blade of megasporophyll ovate to ovate-lanceolate, densely villous, teeth small. 3. C. *rumphii* Miq.

Trunk conspicuously swollen at the base.

Leaflets not more than 8 mm broad, megasporophyll ovate. 4. C. *siamensis* Miq.

Margins of leaflets revolute

Small palm-like tree, blade of megasporo-phyll pectinate. 5. C. *revoluta* Thunb.

Small shrubs, stem about 15 cm. high, blade of megasporophyll dentate lobate. 6. C. *beddomei* Dyer.

In general, the plants are low and palm like. The normal size of the plant ranges from 4 to 8 feet in height. *Cycas media* is the tallest species upto 20 feet in height.

Generally the stem is unbranched, columnar and covered with persistent leaf bases. The leaves are pinnately compound and aggregated in terminal crown.

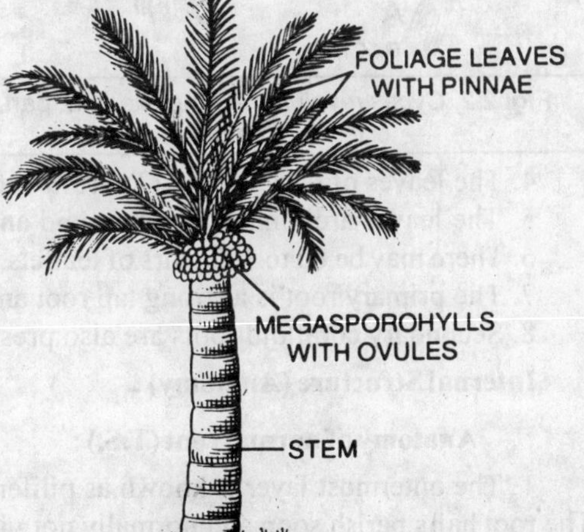

Fig. 2.1. *Cycas circinnalis* The plant with megasporophylls and a crown of foliage leaves.

Proposed Laboratory Work :

(*i*) Study of external structure of sporophyte.

(*ii*) Study of internal structure (Anatomy).

(*a*) Anatomy of normal and coralloid root (T.S.).
(*b*) Anatomy of stem (T.S. and R.L.S.).
(*c*) Anatomy of rachis (T.S.).
(*d*) Anatomy of leaflet (T.S.).

(*iii*) Study of reproductive structures.
(*a*) Vegetative propagation.
(*b*) Spore producing organs.
(*c*) The gametophyte.
(*d*) The sex organs.

External Structure :

1. In general, the plant is unbranched and bearing a crown of large fern-like leaves. The branches are rarely seen.

2. The stem is tuberous when young but in some species the tuberous body passes into the columnar stem.

3. When the leaves fall off, their bases remain on the stem in the form of a protective armour of leaf-base.

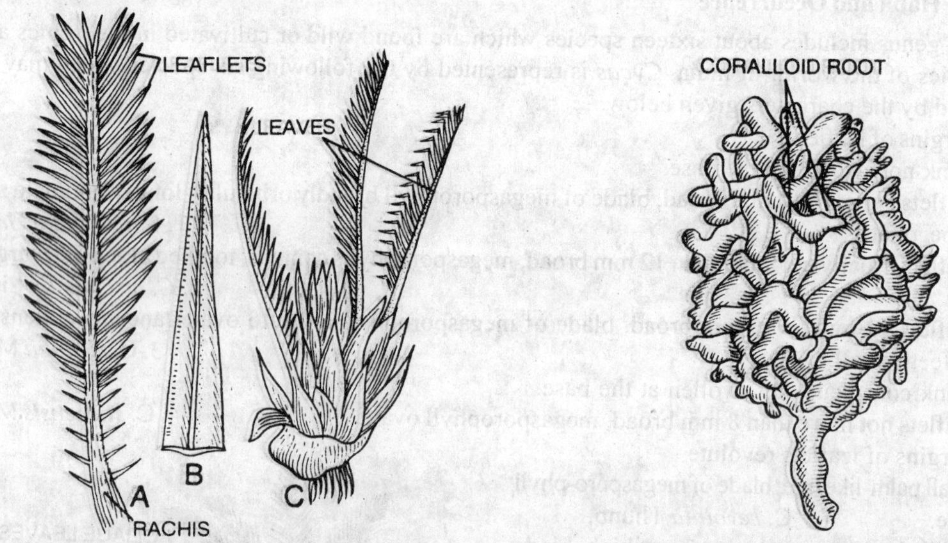

Fig. 2.2. *Cycas revoluta* : A, single leaf; B, part, of leaflet; C, a bulbil.

Fig. 2.3. *Cycas revoluta.* Coralloid roots.

4. The leaves of *C. revoluta*, *C. media* and *C. circinnalis* are more or less hairy in the bud.

5. The leaves are pinnately compound and possess circinate vernation when young.

6. There may be 80 to 100 pairs of leaflets.

7. The primary root is a strong tap root and bears less laterals.

8. Secondary coralloid roots are also present in abundance.

Internal Structure (Anatomy) :

Anatomy of normal root (T.S.) :

1. The outermost layer is known as piliferous layer possessing numerous unicellular root hairs. The root hairs perish soon and normally not visible in T.S.

2. The root is diarch, triarch or tetrarch

3. The bundles are radially arranged and the xylem is exarch.

4. In young roots the pith is present but soon disappears or becomes smaller as soon as the secondary xylem develops due to secondary growth.

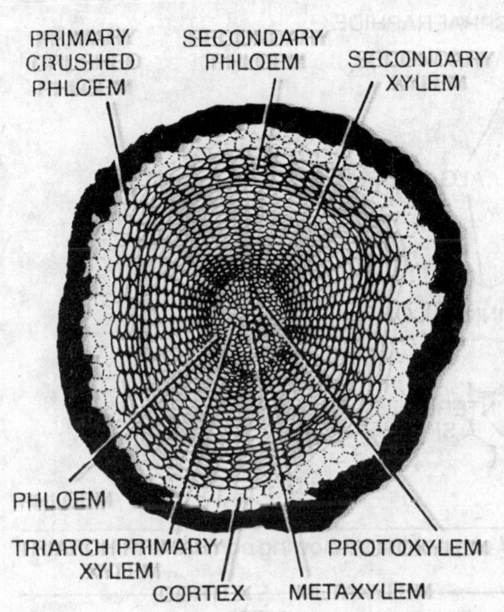

Fig. 2.4. *Cycas revoluta.* T.S. of root showing triarch condition and secondary growth.

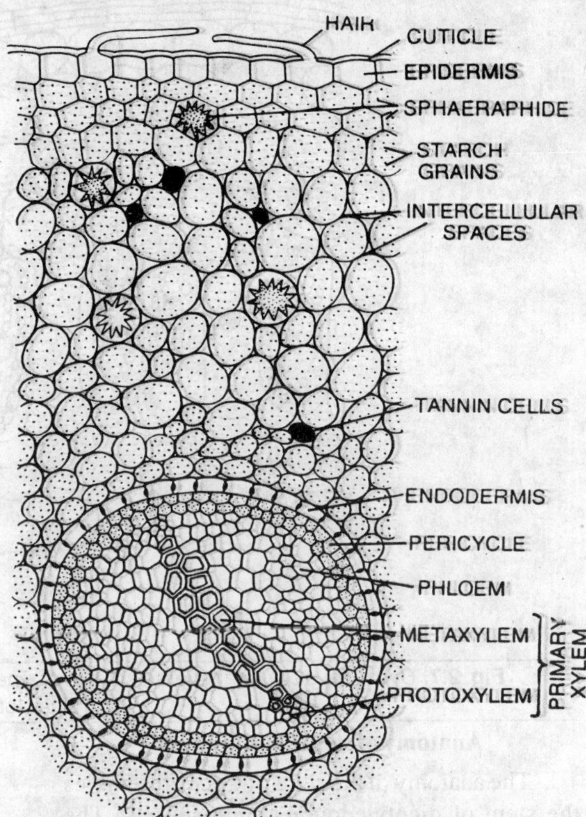

Fig. 2.5. *Cycas revoluta.* Transverse section showing details of primary root (diarch).

5. The secondary xylem remains traversed by many parenchymatous rays.
6. Outside the root the cork is developed; the cork cambium develops from the pericycle region.

Anatomy of Coralloid root (T.S.) :

The anatomy of the coralloid root is similar to that of normal root. The differences are as follows.

1. In coralloid root the cortex is divided into three zones — the outer cortex, middle cortex and the inner cortex.

2. The outer and inner cortical regions comprise parenchyma; the middle cortical zone harbours the blue-green *alga Anabaena cycadaeae* and is termed algal zone.

3. The stele is diarch, triarch or tetrarch and surrounded by an endodermis which is followed by pericycle.

4 In the outermost region the cork is developed by cork cambium.

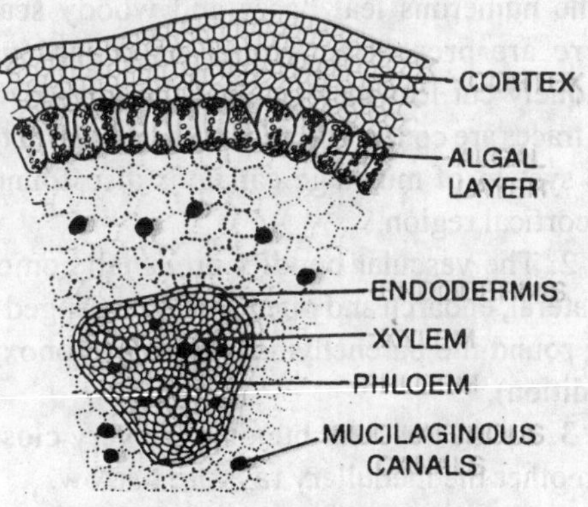

Fig. 2.6. *Cycas revoluta.* T.S. of a coralloid root showing triarch xylem and algal layer in the cortical region.

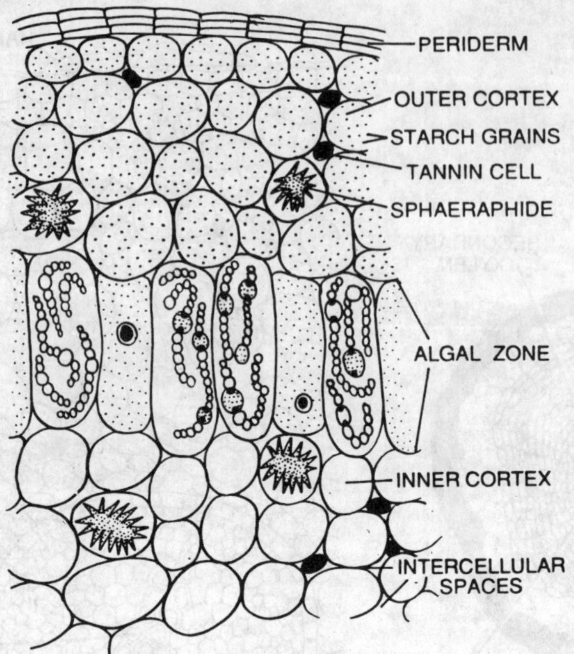

Fig. 2.7. *Cycas revoluta.* Transverse section of a part of coralloid root showing cortical region and algal zone.

Anatomy of stem (T.S.)

The anatomy of the stem of *Cycas* resembles the stem of dicotyledonous angiosperms. The most characteristic feature that distinguishes the stem of *Cycas* from other gymnosperms is the presence of a large pith, broad cortex and a narrow zone of conducting tissue.

1. The cortex is thickly clothed on the outside of the numerous leaf bases and woody scales. There are present a number of conspicuous obliquely cut leaf traces called the girdles. The leaf traces are concentric and mesarch in structure. The system of mucilage canals is also found in the cortical region.

2. The vascular bundles are small conjoint, collateral, endarch and open and are arranged in a ring round the parenchymatous pith (monoxylic condition).

3. As the vascular bundles are very close to each other the medullary rays are narrow.

4. The pericycle and endodermis are not distinct.

5. The pith region also contains the mucilage canals which remain joined to those of cortex by canals running through the medullary rays of the stem.

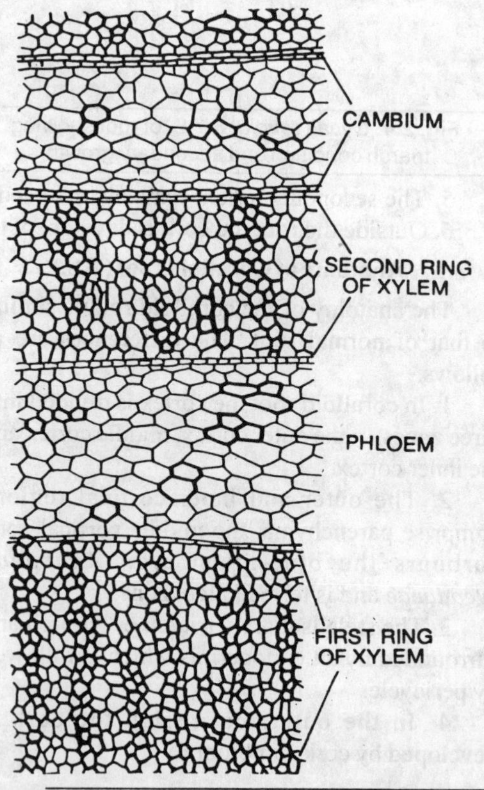

Fig. 2.8. *Cycas* sp. T.S. of a portion of old stem showing two rings of secondary xylem.

Anatomy of Old Stem (T.S.)

An old stem of *Cycas* in T.S. shows 3 to 4 or even more concentric zones of xylem and phloem (polyxylic condition), few scattered concentric bundles in the inner layers of the cortex, prominent leaf traces in the different parts of the cortex and an armour of persistent leaf bases. Both in the cortical region and pith are present a number of mucilage canals. (See Fig. 2.12)

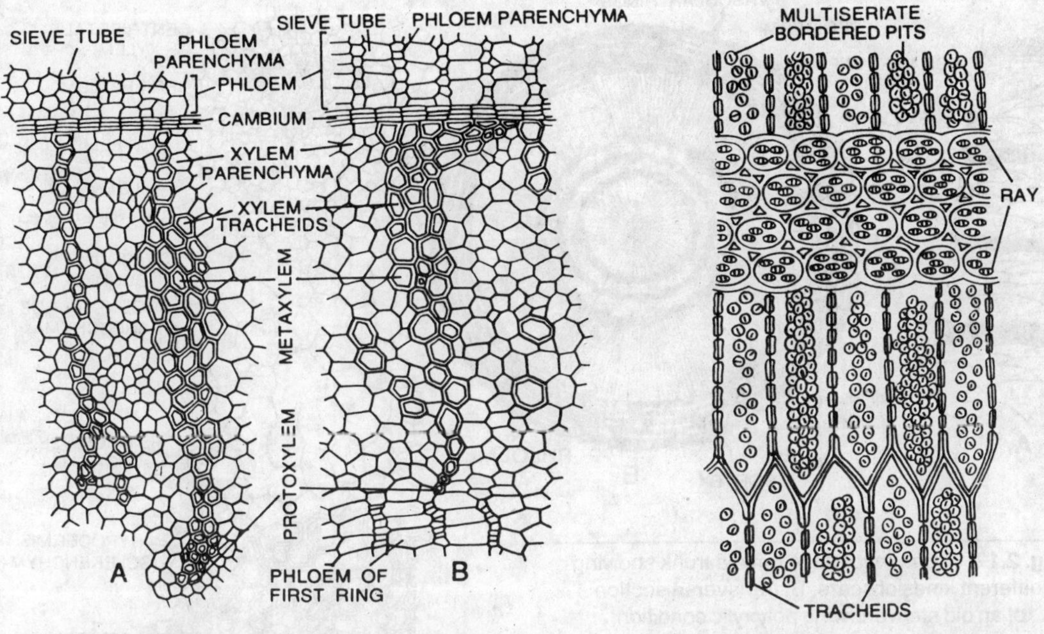

Fig. 2.9. *Cycas revoluta.* Anatomy of stem. A, transverse section of a part of vascular bundle of first ring; B, T.S. of a part of vascular bundle of second ring.

Fig. 2.10. *Cycas.* R.L.S. of wood showing medullary, ray and multiseriate bordered pits.

Anatomy of Wood (R.L.S.) :

1. In older plants all the primary xylem consists of scalariform tracheids.

2. The secondary xylem consists of tracheids with the multiseriate bordered pits.

3. True vessels are absent from the xylem.

4. The cells of the medullary rays and also the thin-walled cells of the xylem which remain in contact with the medullary ray cells contain a large amount of starch. (See Fig. 2.10).

Anatomy of Rachis (T.S.) :

1. The outermost layer is the single layered epidermis covered by a thick cuticle.

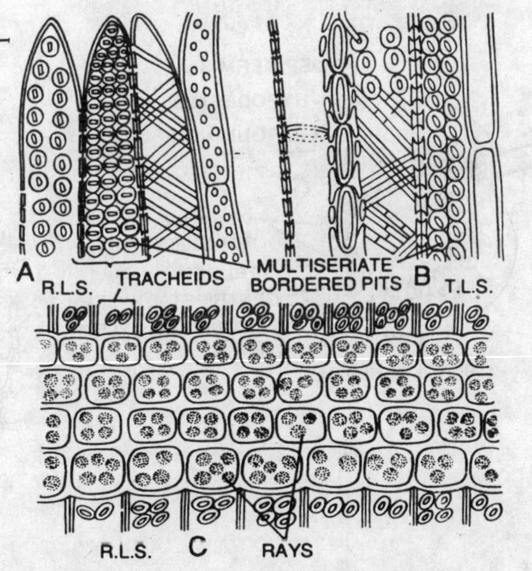

Fig. 2.11. *Cycas.* A-C, portions of secondary wood in longitudinal sections showing multiseriate bordered pits.

2. Just beneath the epidermis there is a hypodermis which is two or three layers in thickness on the adaxial side and many layered on the abaxial surface. The cells of the hypodermis are sclerenchymatous.

3. The ground tissue which follows the hypodermis is parenchymatous.

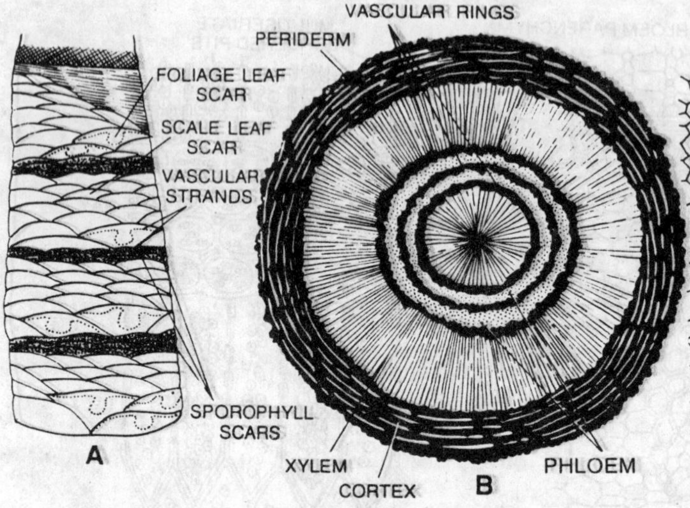

Fig. 2.12. *Cycas revoluta.* A, an old trunk showing different kinds of scars; B, transverse section of an old stem showing polyxylic condition.

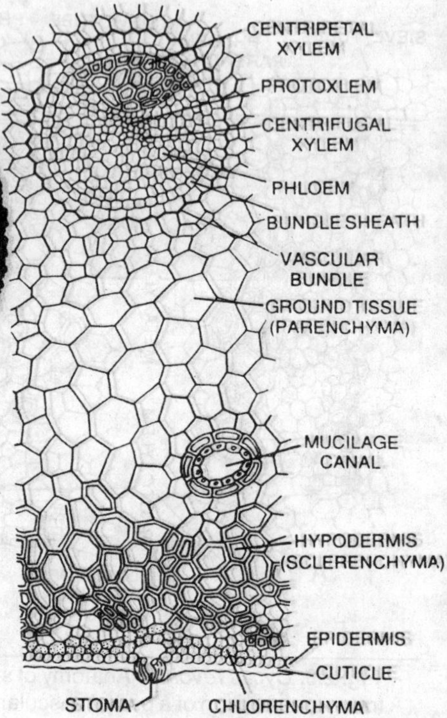

Fig. 2.14. *Cycas revoluta.* Transverse section of a part of petiole showing one vascular bundle and other tissues.

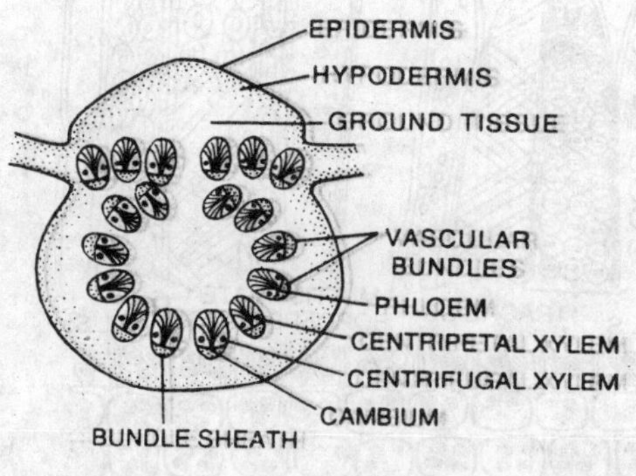

Fig. 2.13. *Cycas.* T.S. of rachis (diagrammatic).

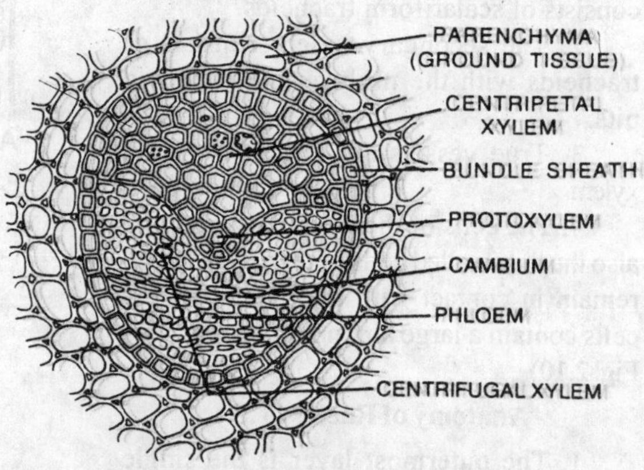

Fig. 2.15. *Cycas revoluta.* A vascular bundle of rachis with centripetal xylem and mesarch protoxylem.

4. The most characteristic features of the rachis is the arrangement of vascular bundles in a omega-shaped (υ) outline.

5. The vascular bundles vary in their structure at the base, centre and at the apex of the rachis.

6. Each vascular bundle remains ensheathed by a single layered sclerenchymatous sheath.

7. The vascular bundles are open and collateral.

8. A single layered endodermis and one to multilayered pericycle surround the vascular bundle.

9. The condition of xylem is mesarch.

CENTRIPETAL XYLEM
EPIDERMIS (UPPER)
MID RIB
HYPODERMIS
SPONGY PARENCHYMA
PALISADE
STOMA
WING
TRANSFUSION TISSUE
CAMBIUM
BUNDLE SHEATH
HYPODERMIS
PHLOEM
EPIDERMIS (LOWER)
CENTRIFUGAL XYLEM
PARENCHYMA

Fig. 2.16. *Cycas revoluta.* T.S. of leaflet (diagrammatic).

10. Centripetal and centrifugal xylem patches are clearly distinguished.

Anatomy of Leaflet (V.S.)

1. The vertical section of the leaflet shows strong xerophytic features. The cells of the epidermis are thick-walled and heavily cutinized. The stomata are confined only to the lower epidermis and are greatly sunken, each having a sub-stomatal cavity below it.

2. Beneath the upper epidermis there is a layer of hypodermis which becomes several cells thick in the midrib region. The cells of the hypodermis are thick-walled.

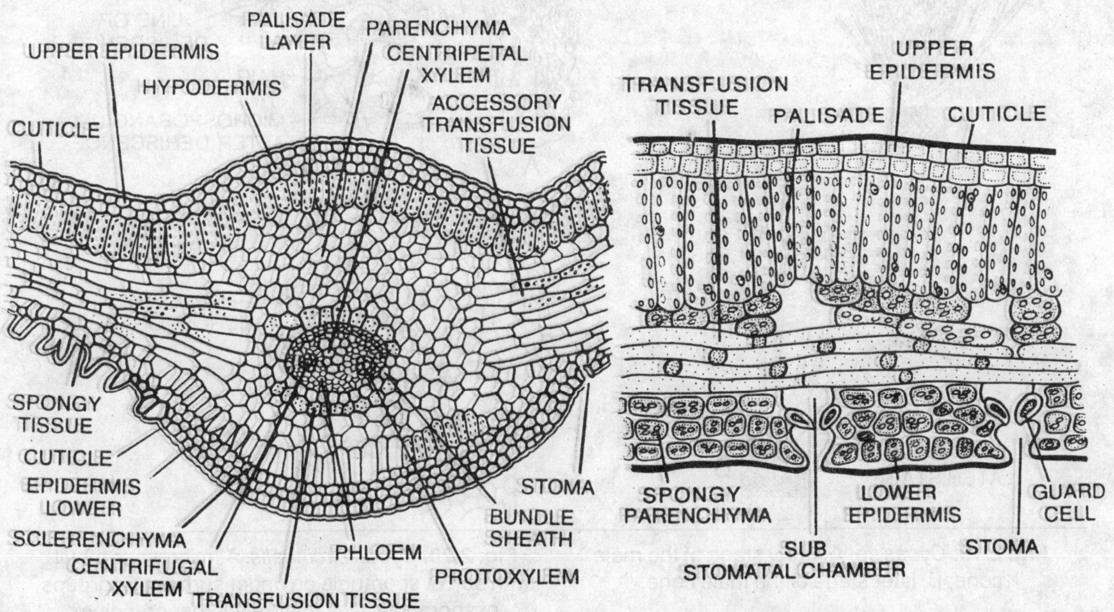

Fig. 2.17. *Cycas revoluta.* T.S. of leaflet (detailed structure).

Fig. 2.18. Cycoy *revoluta.* T.S. of a part of pinna showing palisade, sunken stomata and transfusion tissue.

3. The mesophyll is differentiated into the palisade (towards the upper side) and spongy parenchyma (towards the lower side), are both rich in chloroplasts. The palisade tissue remains continuous even in the midrib portion.

4. In between the palisade and the spongy tissues there are present colourless cells elongated parallel to the leaf surface. This is the transfusion tissue and it extends upto the margin of the leaflet.

5. In the midrib the vascular bundle is mesarch. The metaxylem (centripetal xylem) is fan-shaped and is towards the upper side. The protoxylem points towards the lower side.

6. Below the protoxylem there are present a few layers of tracheids, the centrifugal xylem. This centrifugal xylem may be primary or secondary in origin.

7. Below the xylem is present a large patch of phloem.

8. Cambium is absent.

9. A sclerenchymatous sheath is present round the vascular bundle.

10. On both the lateral sides of the xylem there are present few transfusion tissue cells which are cut transversely.

Reproductive Structures :

Vegetative Propagation

The vegetative propagation takes place by means of bulbils which develop in the crevices of the scales. Each bulbil possesses a few scales and foliage leaves. [See Fig. 2.2(*c*)]

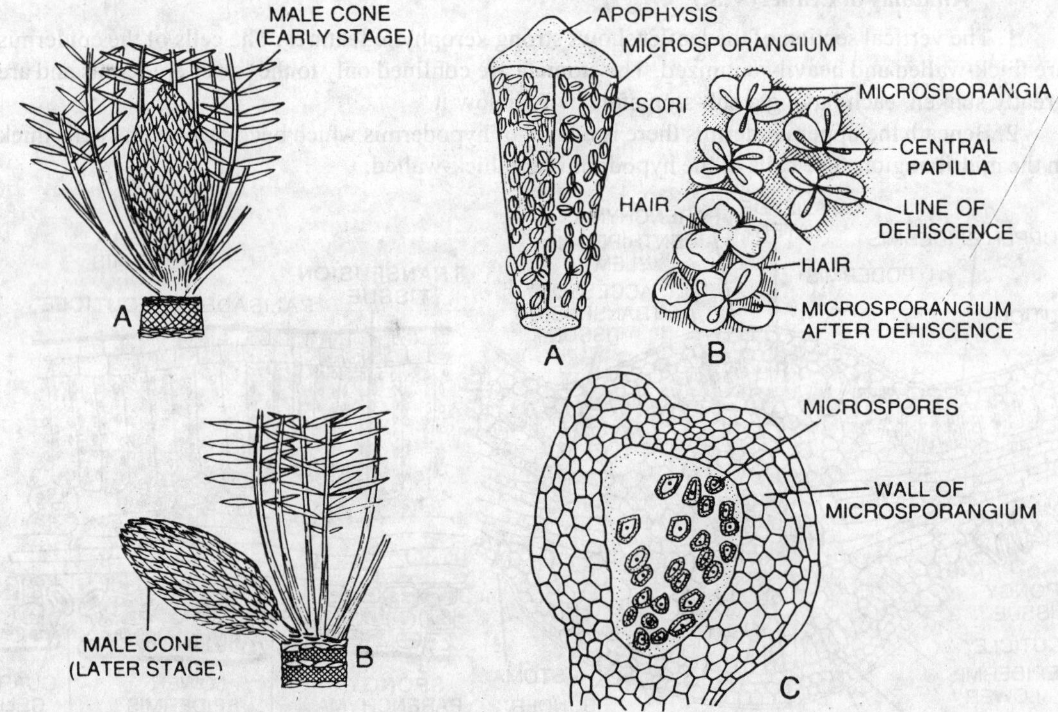

Fig. 2.19. *Cycas* sp. A, early stage of the male cone; B, later stage of the male cone.

Fig. 2.20. *Cycas circinnalis.* A, microsporophyll with sori of sporangia on under surface; B, groups of sporangia; C, a mature microsporangium containing microspores and surrounded by thick wall.

Sexual Reproduction

The *Cycas* is strictly dioecious plant, *i.e.*, male and female sex organs are found on two separate plants.

The microspores (male) and megaspores (female) develop in micro and megasporangia respectively. In India, the male plants of *Cycas* are rare. The cones or strobili are found at the apex of the trunk concealed at first among the bases of the leaves. The male flowers are found to be arranged in erect cones. Usually a single male cone develops at the apex of male plant. The megasporophylls or female strobili are found in crowded whorls around the apex of the female plant alternating with whorls of foliage leaves.

Male Cone :

1. Usually the male cone is about more than 50 cms in length. Normally a single male cone develops at the apex of the plant.

2. The sporophylls are closely imbricate and spirally arranged in a compact cone.

3. Some of the sporophylls of the base and apex of the cone are sterile.

4. Each microsporophyll is narrow below and broad above terminating into a projection called the 'apophysis'.

5. The microsporangia are confined to the abaxial (lower) surface of the microsporophyll, the upper surface is sterile. The sporangia may number upto one thousand in certain species.

6. The sporangia occur on two flanks of the microsporophyll differentiated by a median sterile ridge. They are usually found in definite sori each consisting of two to six sporangia. The sporangia are more or less united at base.

7. The wall of sporangium is four to seven layered.

8. The sori of microsporangia are inter-mingled with hairs.

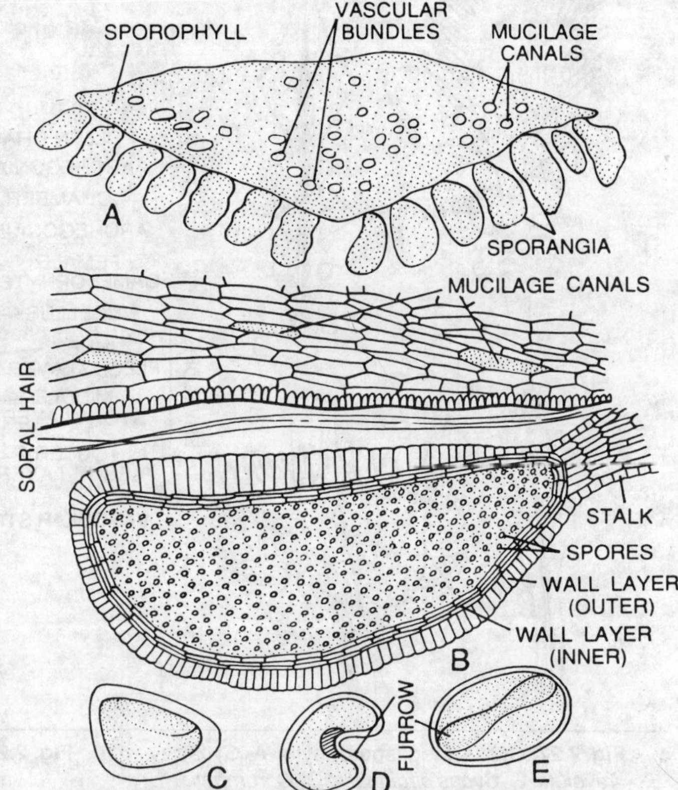

Fig. 2.21. *Cycas.* A, transverse section of microsporophyll showing sporangia on its lower side; B, enlarged view of microsporangium showing its details; C-E, mature microspores released from microsporangium.

9. Each spore mother cell divides meiotically and four microspores or pollens are produced.

10. A mature microspore possesses two sharply distinguished coats known as exine and intine.

11. A large number of microspores are produced in each sporangium.

Female Strobilus :

1. The female strobilus is made up of a whorl of spirally arranged megasporophylls which remain situated among the crown of vegetative leaves.

2. The megasporophylls are not arranged in definite cones. They resemble the foliage leaves.

3. Each megasporophyll is leaf-like, its upper portion bears pinnae while the lower part bears the ovules.

4. Megasporophylls remain densely covered with brown hairs.

5. In *Cycas revoluta* and *C. circinnalis* several ovules develop on the margins of the megasporophyll whereas in *C. siamensis* only two ovules are found. In *C. rumphii* the megasporophyll bears two to five ovules. The ovules of *Cycas* are quite large in size. In *C. circinnalis,* the largest

ovules are formed. The ovules of C. *circinnalis* are smooth and dark green, whereas of C. *revoluta* are densely hairy and orange-red in colour.

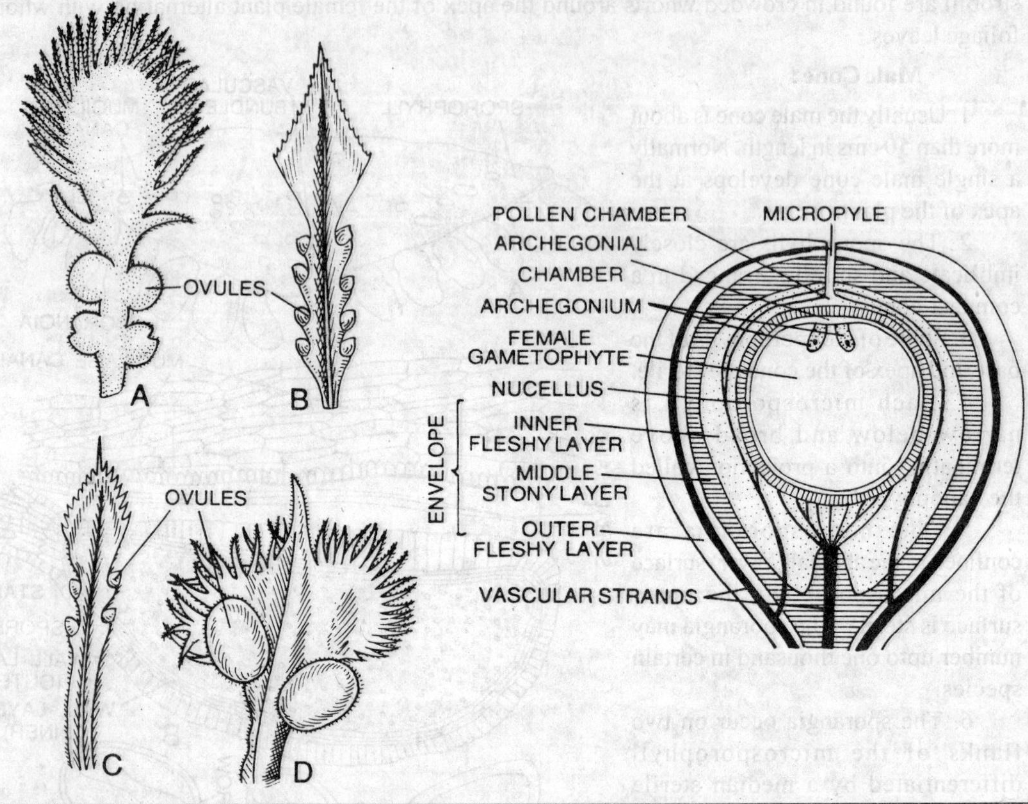

Fig. 2.22. *Cycas*. Megasporophylls. A, *Cycas revoluta;* B, *Cycas circinnalis;* C, *C. rumphii,* D, *C. pectinata.*

Fig. 2.23. *Cycas* sp. L.S. of the ovule with mature gametophyte showing two archegonia.

6. The ovules are sessile and orthotropous in their position. They are ovoid or spherical and vary in size.

L.S. of Mature Ovule :

1 . Each ovule has a single thick integument which is differentiated in three layers. The inner and outer fleshy layers of the integument remain separated from each other by a hard stony layer in between the two. The inner fleshy layer remains more prominent in young ovule. On the ripening of the ovule into the seed this layer disappears.

2. There is a mass of nucellar tissue or nucellus within the integument.

3. The nucellus remains fused with the inner fleshy layer of the integument except at the top portion.

4. In the top portion of the ovule in the integument forms a long micropyle.

5. In the apical portion the nucellus forms a nucellular beak. The beak forces its way into the micropyle, while the centre of the beak and below it cells break down and form the pollen chamber.

6. The ovule is well supplied with vascular bundles. True bundles serve the base of the ovule. Each vascular bundle divides into two branches, each serving the outer and inner fleshy layers. These branches further divide for proper vascular supply.

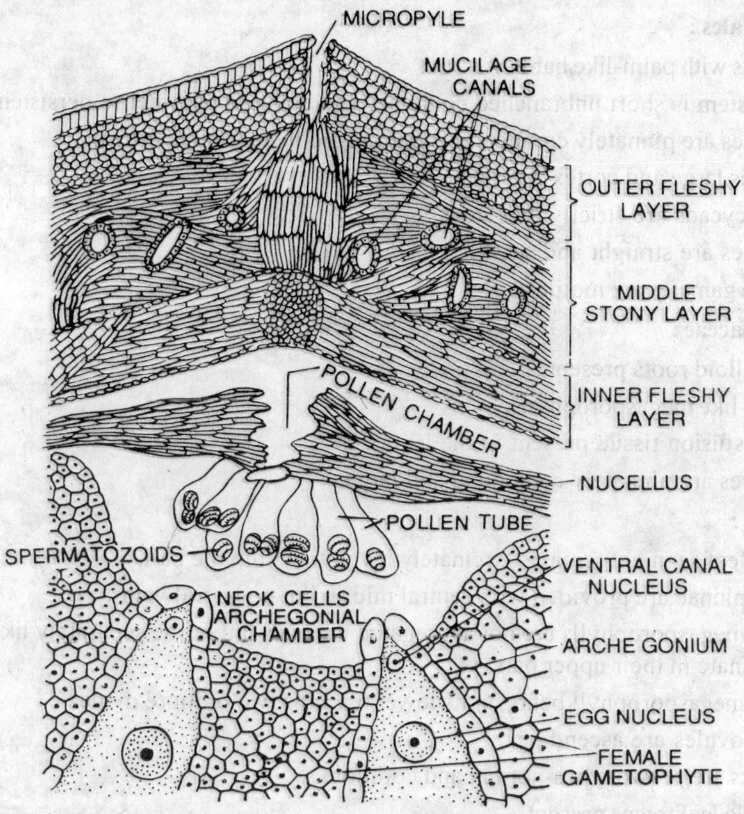

Fig. 2.24. *Cycas revoluta.* Vertical section of a mature ovule. (After Swamy)

7. Towards the micropylar end, just at the base of micropyle a small depression appears at the place where the archegonia are developed.

8. The mature archegonia open into a cavity, the archegonial chamber.

L.S. of Seed :

1. The mature seed has a fleshy outer coat which is developed from the outer portion of the three-layered integument of the ovule.

2. The inner stony coat of seed is developed from the middle stony layer of the integument within the stony layer there lies a thin dry membranous layer of the integument which contains the vascular supply of the ovule. The membrane develops partly from the nucellus and partly from the inner fleshy layer of the integument.

3. Within the seed coat there lies a straight embryo, which consists of two unequal cotyledons.

4. The axis of the embryo is differentiated into hypocotyl and radicle.

Identification and Systematic Position

Gymnosperms :

(*i*) Tress or shrubs usually resinous.

(*ii*) Ovules naked, not enclosed in an ovary.

(*iii*) Flowers unisexual, rarely bisexual.

(*iv*) Leaves needle-shaped, linear, pinnate, rarely fan-shaped or oblong elliptic, mostly evergreen.

(*v*) Vessels absent.

Cycadales :

(*i*) Plants with palm-like habit.

(*ii*) The stem is short unbranched columnar and covered with dense persistent leaf bases.

(*iii*) Leaves are pinnately compound and arranged in a terminal crown.

(*iv*) Pith is large and cortex is broad.

(*v*) The cycads are strictly dioecious.

(*vi*) Ovules are straight and sessile.

(*vii*) Male gametes are motile.

Cycadaceae :

(*i*) Coralloid roots present.

(*ii*) Leaf-like megasporophylls.

(*iii*) Transfusion tissue present in the leaflets.

(*iv*) Leaves are pinnately compound and large.

Cycas :

(*i*) The leaf segment remains circinately involute within the bud.

(*ii*) The pinnae are provided with central midrib but no lateral veins.

(*iii*) The megasporophylls are not aggregated in cones but borne separately like foliage leaves pectinate in their upper part.

(*iv*) The megasporophyll bears on its lower margins two or more ovules.

(*v*) The ovules are ascending.

(*vi*) Roots are of two types-normal and coralloid.

(*vii*) Girdle leaf traces present.

(*viii*) Embryo is straight and contains two cotyledons.

PINUS

Occurrence and Geographical Distribution :

The genus *Pinus* is widely distributed in the Northern hemisphere. There are about 75 species of this genus. About six species have been recorded from different parts of India. The blue pine, *Pinus wallichiana* (syn. *P. excelsa*) is largely found in North-West Himalayan region at 1,800 metres to 3,700 metres elevation. The chir pine, *P.roxburghii* (syn. *P. longifolia*) occurs from Afghanistan to Bhutan in the outer ranges of the Himalayas. This species is also commonly found in the Indian plains. The chilgoza pine, *P.gerardiana* is found in the inner arid valleys of the Himalayas at 1,800 m to 3,000 m elevation. The khasi pine *P.insularis* is distributed in the Khasi Naga hills and Manipur region at elevation of 750 m to 1950 m.

Proposed Laboratory Work :

(*i*) Study of external morphology.

(*ii*) Study of internal structure (anatomy).

(*a*) Anatomy of root (T.S.).

(*b*) Anatomy of stem (T.S., R.L.S., and T.L.S.)

(*c*) Anatomy of leaf (T.S.)

(*iii*) Study of reproductive structures.

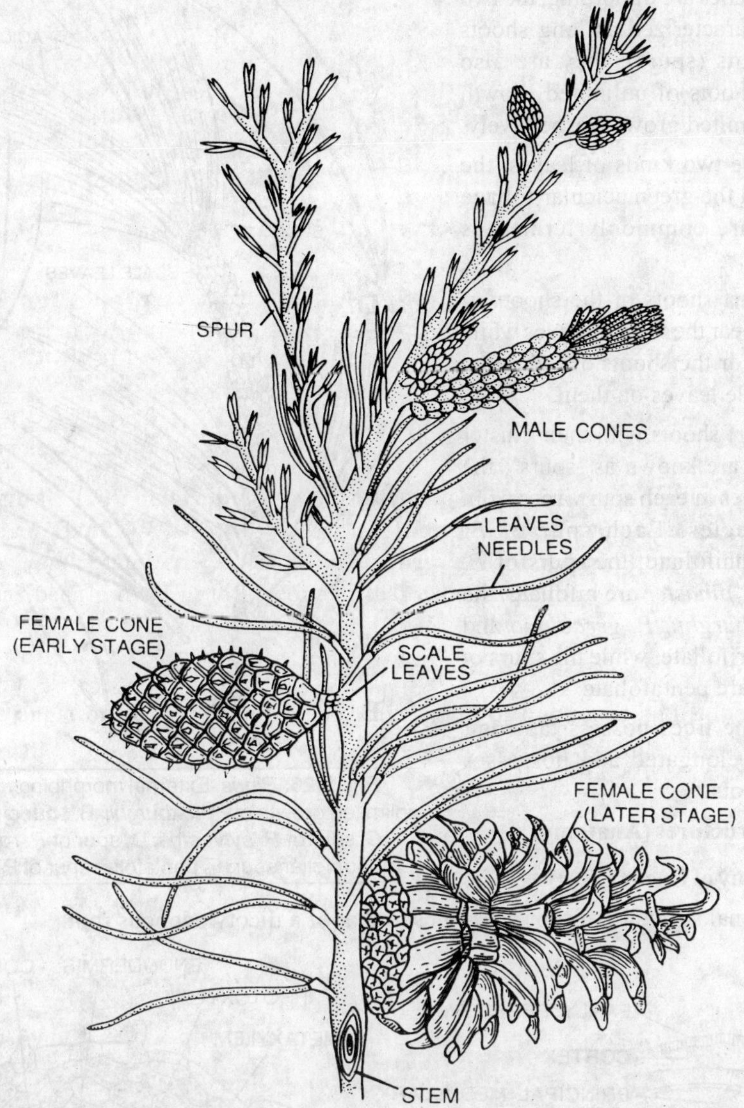

Fig. 2.25. *Pinus* sp. A twig with male and female cones, scale leaves and foliage leaves.

External Morphology :

1. The adult plant is a large tree giving rise to a series of wide spread branches.

2. In most of pine trees a whorl of branches is produced each year; sometimes two such whorls may be produced in one year.

3. The whorls are formed in the axils of scale leaves every year.

4. The main shaft is cylindrical and covered with a rough scaly bark.

5. The branching is confined to the upper part of the stem, giving a pyramid-like appearance to the plant.

6. The branches are dimorphic, the two forms being characterized as long shoots and dwarf shoots (spurs); they are also known as the shoots of unlimited growth and shoots of limited growth respectively.

7. There are two kinds of leaves, the scale leaves and the green acicular foliage leaves which are commonly termed as needles.

8. The dwarf shoots or the shoots of limited growth bear the foliage leaves while the long shoots or the shoots of unlimited growth bear scale leaves on them.

9. The dwarf shoots with their cluster of green leaves are known as 'spurs'; the number of needles in each spur varies from species to species. Each spur of *P. monophylla* is unifoliate; the spurs of *P. sylvestris* and *P. pinaster* are bifoliate; the spurs of *P. roxburghii, P. geradiana* and *P. insularis* are trifoliate, while the spurs *of P. wallichiana* are pentafoliate.

10. The pine trees possess tap root; the tap root is elongated and possesses strong lateral roots.

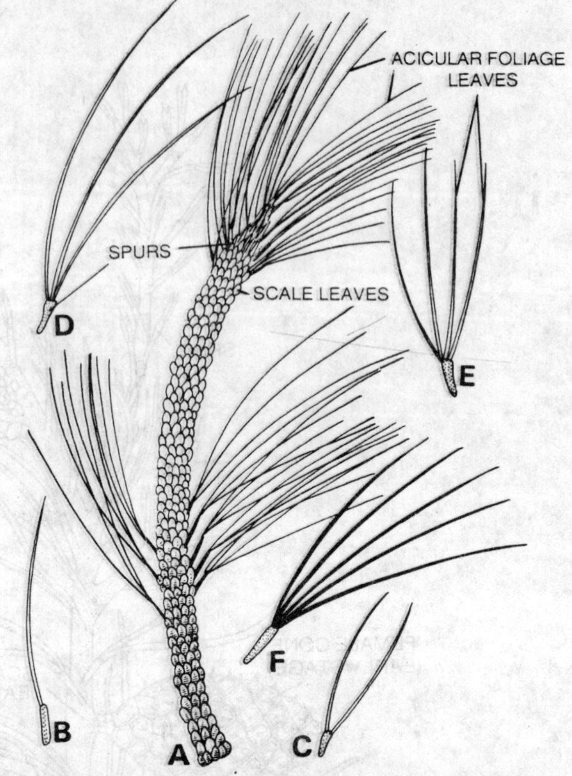

Fig. 2.26. *Pinus.* External morphology. A, shoot of unlimited growth of *P. roxburghii*; B, spur of *P. monophylla*; C, spur of *P. sylvestris;* D, spur of *P. roxburghii*; E, quadrifoliar spur; F, pentafoliar spur of P. wallichiana.

Internal Structures (Anatomy)

Anatomy of Root-(T.S.) :

1. The internal structure of root resembles to that of a dicotyledonous root.

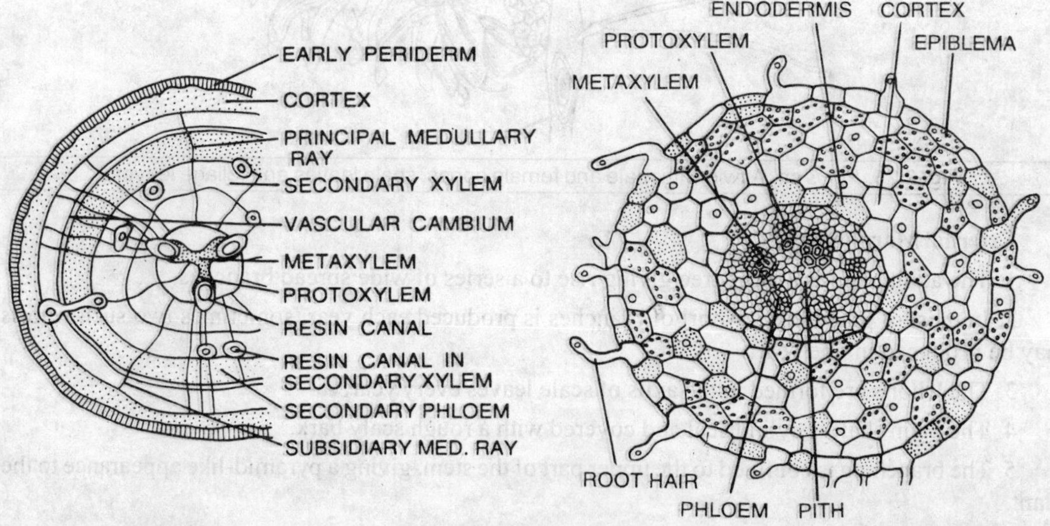

Fig. 2.27. *Pinus.* T.S. of root (diagrammatic).

Fig. 2.28. *Pinus.* T.S. of young root showing triarch condition.

2. In a T.S. the root shows a piliferous layer bearing unicellular root hairs; the root hairs are found only in the young roots and root tips.

3. In young roots there is fungal growth of ectophytic mycorrhiza; with the appearance of this fungus the root hairs disappear.

4. Just beneath the piliferous layer there lies a broad cortex consisting of 4 to 5 layers of thin walled parenchymatous cells.

5. The innermost layer of the cortex is single layered endodermis consisting of brown suberized cells containing tannin in them.

6. Just below the endodermis there is multilayered pericycle tannin and starch grains.

7. In the centre of the stele there are two to six Y-shaped xylem bundles, and an equal number of phloem alternating with them.

8. The xylem has no true vessels and consists of tracheids.

9. The phloem consists of sieve tubes and phloem parenchyma; companion cells are altogether absent.

10. In between the arms of a Y-shaped xylem bundle there lies a resin canal.

11. In the centre there is a small pith.

12. The secondary growth resembles to that of a dicotyledonous root.

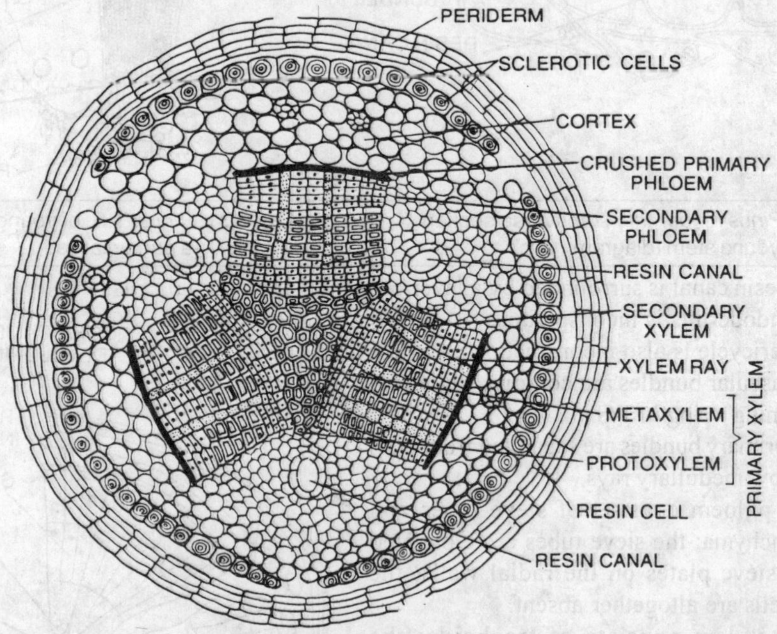

Fig. 2.29. *Pinus.* Transverse section of an old triarch root with secondary growth.

13. A cambial strip develops in between the phloem and metaxylem.

14. The cambium cuts secondary xylem towards the inner side and the secondary phloem towards the outside.

15. Cork develops towards the outside.

Anatomy of young stem (T.S.)

1. The young stem is somewhat wavy in outline.

2. It remains surrounded by a single layered cuticularized epidermis.

3. Just beneath the epidermis there is multilayered hypodermis consisting of lignified sclerenchymatous cells.

4. The hypodermis constitutes the outer region of the cortex.

5. Underneath the hypodermis there lies the inner cortex consisting of thin walled parenchymatous cells containing chloroplasts and resin canals.

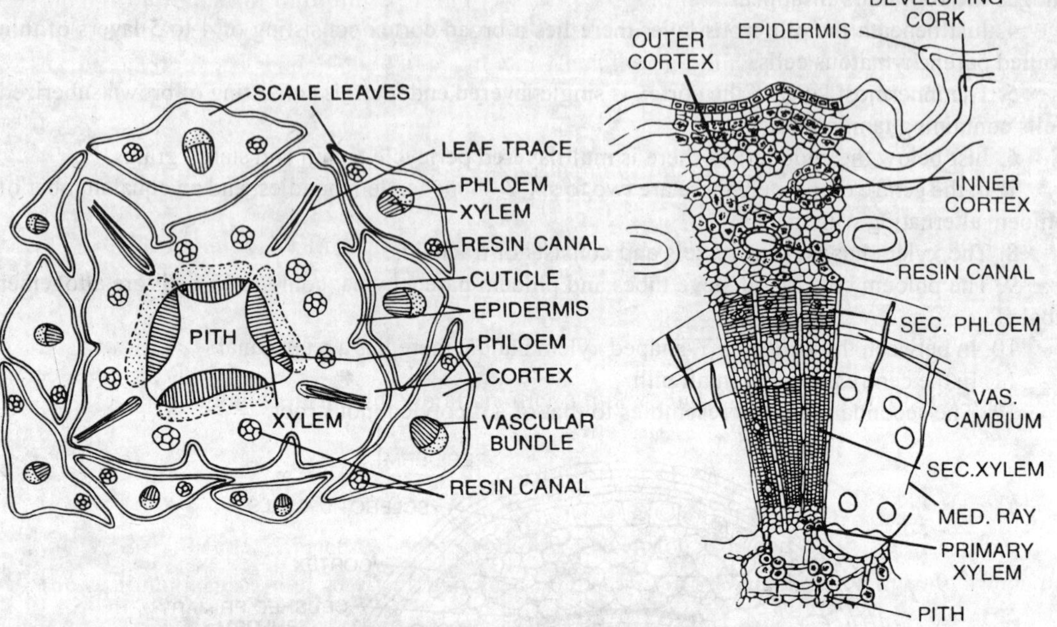

Fig. 2.30. *Pinus roxburghii.* Transverse section of young stem (diagrammatic).

Fig. 2.31. *Pinus.* T.S. of young stem (a part enlarged)

6. Each resin canal is surrounded by a layer of glandular epithelial cells.

7. The endodermis is inconspicuous.

8. The pericycle is also inconspicuous.

9. The vascular bundles are conjoint, collateral and open forming a ring in T.S.

10. The primary bundles are separated from each other by narrow medullary rays.

11. The phloem consists of sieve tubes and phloem parenchyma; the sieve tubes are elongated and possess sieve plates on the radial walls; the companion cells are altogether absent.

12. The xylem consists of tracheids; the protoxylem consists of annular and spiral tracheids.

Anatomy of Old Stem (T.S.)

1. The cambium present in the vascular bundles initiates secondary growth in the same way as in dicotyledons.

2. The cambium forms secondary xylem on its inner and secondary phloem on its outer sides.

3. These xylem and phloic zones are traversed by secondary medullary rays (xylem rays).

4. The secondary wood shows well marked growth rings.

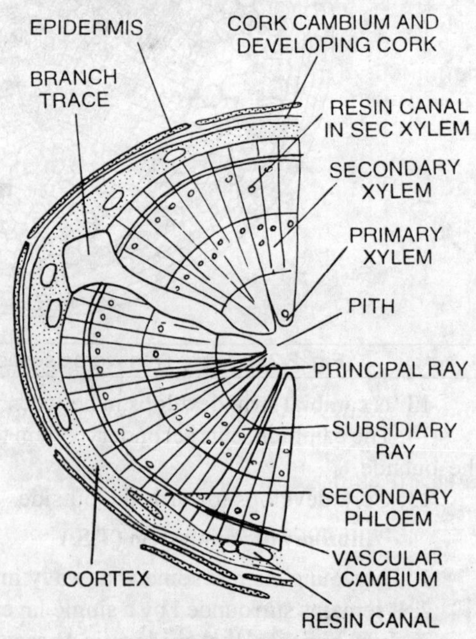

Fig. 2.32. *Pinus.* T.S. of old stem (diagrammatic).

5. Each ring possesses thin walled spring wood with wide tracheids and large bordered pits. The autumn wood has thick walled narrow tracheids and small bordered pits.

6. The secondary wood consists of tracheids with typical bordered pits.

7. Primary xylem groups are endarch and .lie near the pith.

8. The metaxylem consists of tracheids with typical bordered pits.

9. The protoxylem consists of annular and spiral tracheids.

10. The resin canals are present both in primary and secondary wood. Each resin canal is surrounded by the epithelial cells. The resin canals are also found in the cortical region opposite each primary vascular bundle.

11. The secondary phloem consists of sieve tubes and phloem parenchyma. The companion cells are altogether absent.

12. The cork cambium (phellogen) originates in the outer cortical region near the surface. The phellogen cuts off additional cortical cells (phelloderm) towards the inner side and forming the cork towards outside. This cork surrounds the stem.

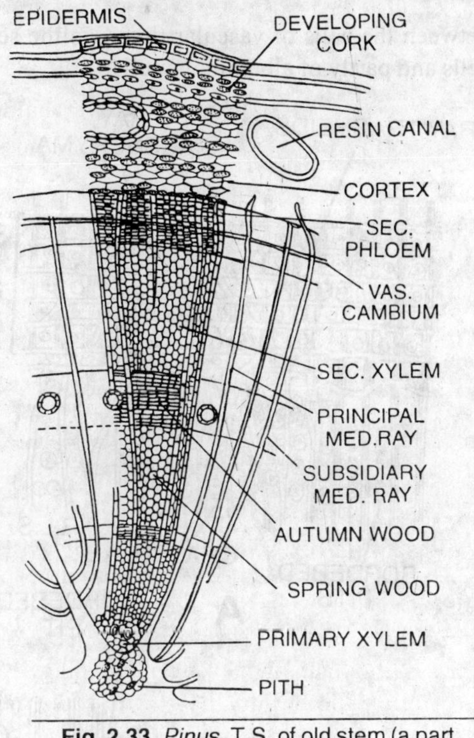

Fig. 2.33. *Pinus.* T.S. of old stem (a part enlarged)

13. The pith is small and consists of parenchyma. Many cells are filled up with tannin.

Radial Longitudinal Section (R.L.S.) of the wood.

1. The R.L.S. of *Pinus* wood shows the secondary xylem, ray teacheids and medullary rays.

2. The secondary xylem is composed of tracheids with typical bordered pits. The bordered pits are found on the radial walls. In R.L.S. the bordered pits are seen in surface view.

3. The secondary xylem and secondary phloem zones are traversed by secondary medullary rays. These vascular rays also develop from the cambial cells to replace the original primary rays.

4. These rays run horizontally and are usually uniseriate.

5. Each ray is composed of rectangular cells with thick walls and numerous simple pits. The cells contain cytoplasm, a nucleus and many starch grains.

6. The upper and lower margins of the medullary rays are constituted of one or two rows of marginal ray-tracheids which run horizontally and resemble short tracheids of the xylem from which they have been derived.

7. In the cambium and phloem zones instead of marginal ray-tracheids, large thin walled cells develop which extend upwards and downwards in

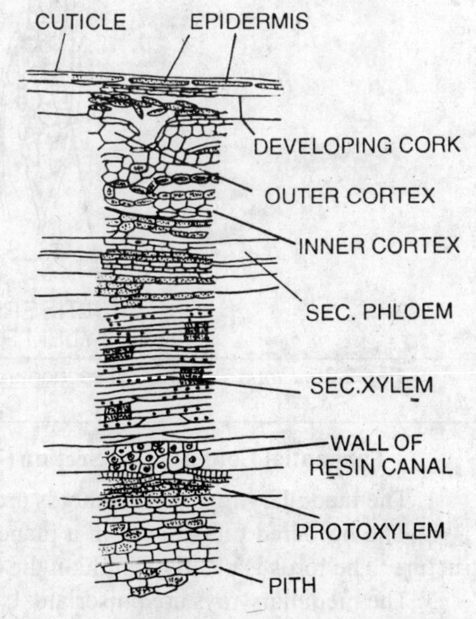

Fig. 2.34. *Pinus.* R.L.S. of young stem (a part).

between the cells of vascular tissue, in the secondary phloem cells and partly of starch containing cells and partly of albuminous cells.

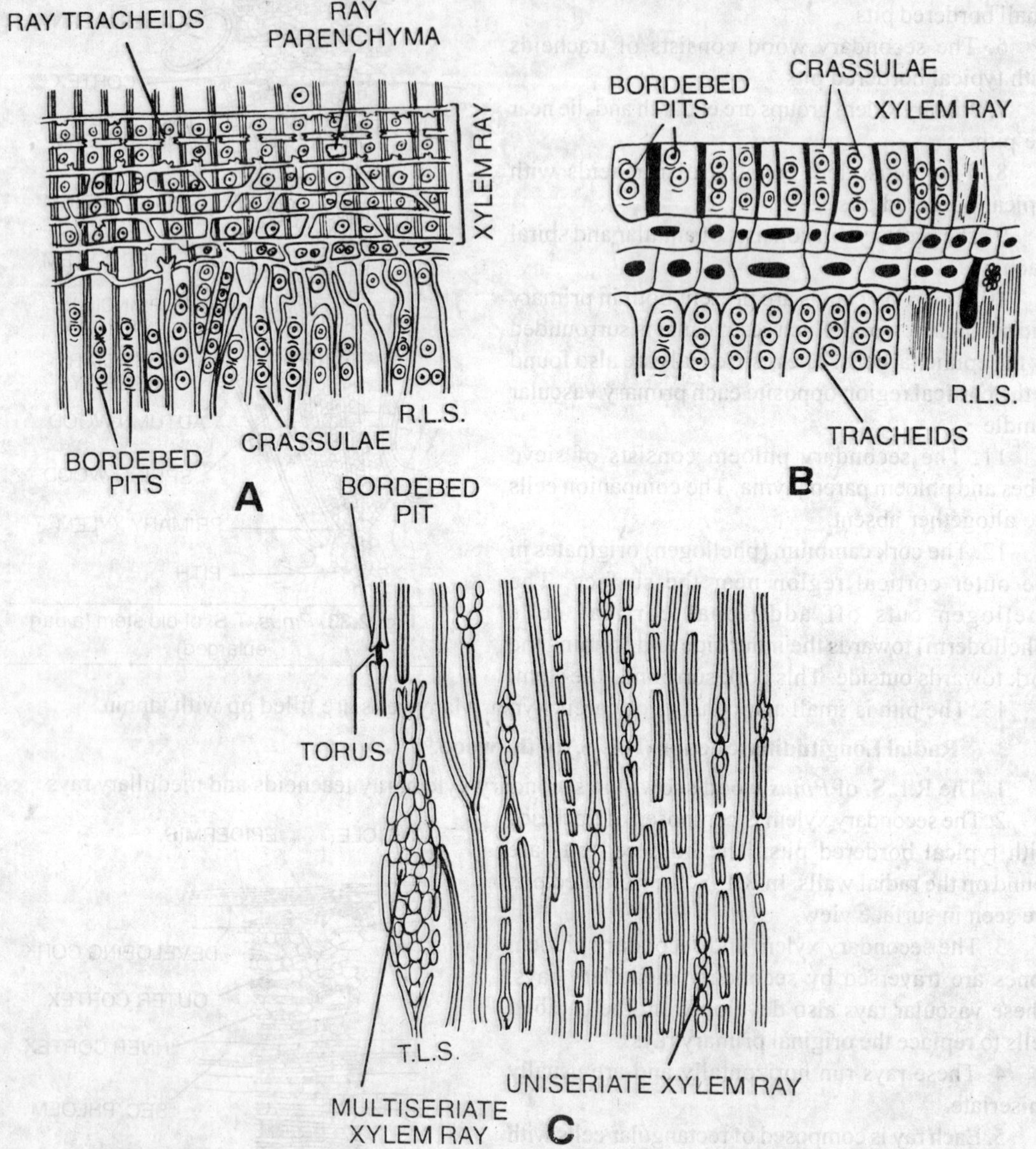

Fig. 2.35. *Pinus.* A, R.L.S. of secondary wood; B, R.L.S. showing details of ray parenchyma; C, T.L.S. of wood.

Tangential Longitudinal Section (T.L.S.) of the wood.

1. The medullary rays and tracheids are cut transversely in the plane.

2. The bordered pits are cut in a plane to show over arching borders which form a dome like structure. The torus is clearly visible in the centre of border.

3. The medullary rays are uniseriate. Usually they are only one cell broad and less than a dozen cells in height.

4. The medullary ray consists of centrally placed thin walled and living cells albuminous cells in phloem region and ray cells in xylem region.

5. The medullary rays remain surrounded on the lower and upper side by dead cells of ray tracheids.

Anatomy of Leaf (T.S.)

The outline of the needle (foliage leaf) in a transverse section depends on the number of needles in the dwarf short (spur). In *P. monophylla* the spur bears a single-needle and therefore, the outline of needle is circular. In *P. sylvestris* each spur consists of two needles and the outline of each needle is semi circular. In *P. roxburghii* each spur consists of three needles and therefore, the two flat faces of each needle are towards the inner side and the curved face towards the outside. In this species the outline of the needle is somewhat triangular.

1. The outermost layer is the epidermis which consists of extremely thick-walled and cuticularized cells. A number of depressions are found over the epidermis.

2. The stomata are developed all over the epidermis in these depressions. The guard cells are sunken in depressions below the level of the epidermis.

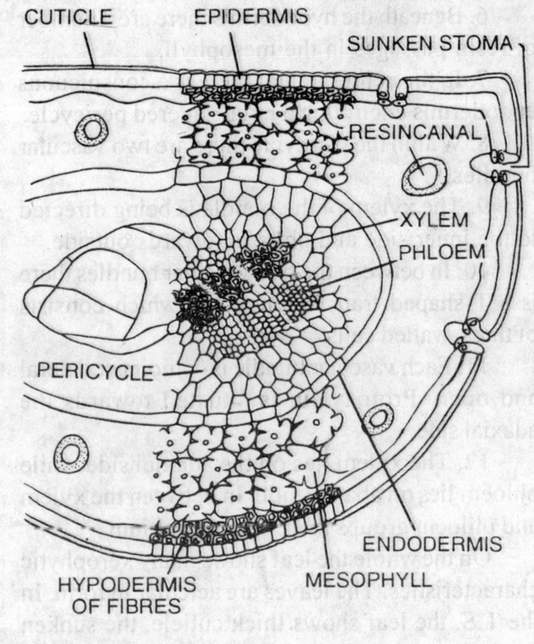

Fig. 2.36. *Pinus sylvestris.* T.S. leaf (a part)

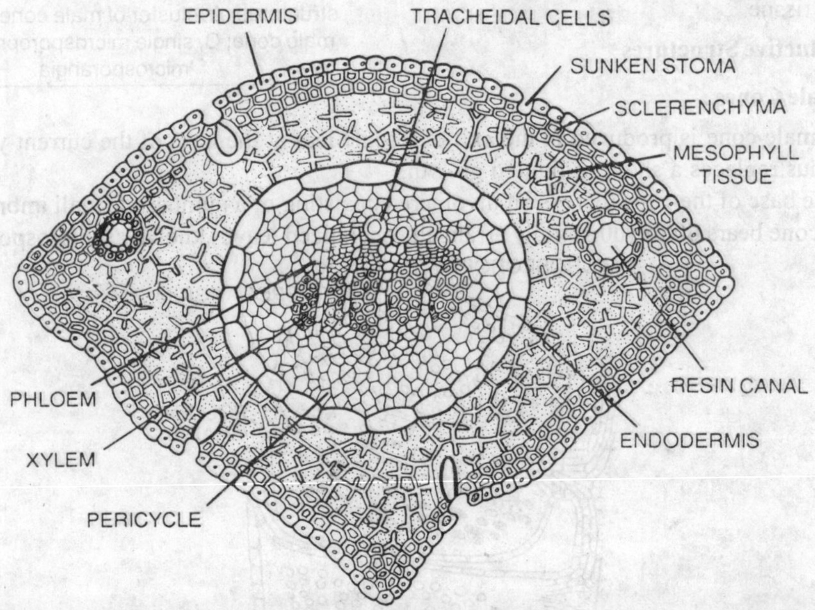

Fig. 2.37. *Pinus roxburghii.* T.S. of needle showing mesophyll with peg-like in foldings.

3. Just beneath the epidermis there is hypodermis which is composed of one or two layers of sclerenchymatous cells. The hypodermis is several layered at the corners.

4. The hypodermis is interrupted by air spaces beneath each stoma.

5. The parenchymatous mesophyll is not differentiated into palisade and spongy tissues; it consists of thin-walled cells containing a large number of chloroplasts and starch grains. These thin-walled cells have peg-like infoldings of cellulose projecting into their cavities.

6. Beneath the hypodermis there are a number of resin passages in the mesophyll.

7. In the centre of leaf there is a conspicuous endodermis encircling a many layered pericycle.

8. Within the pericycle there are two vascular bundles.

9. The xylem of the bundle is being directed to the inner side and phloem towards outside.

10. In between the two vascular bundles there is a T-shaped transfusion tissue which consists of thick-walled cells.

11. Each vascular bundle is conjoint collateral and open. Protoxylem is situated towards the adaxial side.

12. The xylem lies on the adaxial side while phloem lies on abaxial side. In between the xylem and phloem groups there lies a cambium.

On the whole the leaf shows many xerophytic characteristics. The leaves are acicular in form. In the T.S. the leaf shows thick cuticle, the sunken stomata, sclerenchymatous hypodermis, the simple vascular system and the peculiar transfusion tissue.

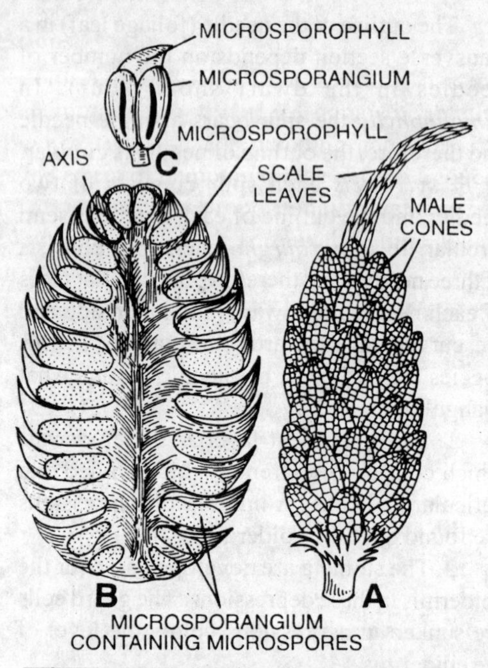

Fig. 2.38. *Pinus* sp. Male reproductive structures. A, cluster of male cones; B, L.S. of male cone; C, single microsporophyll with two microsporangia.

Reproductive Structures

Male Cones :

1. The male cone is produced in the axil of a scale leaf at the base of the current year's young shoot and thus replaces a shoot of limited growth.

2. At the base of the cone there is an involucre consisting of a number of small imbricate scales.

3. The cone bears 60 to 100 spirally arranged specialized leaves known as microsporophylls.

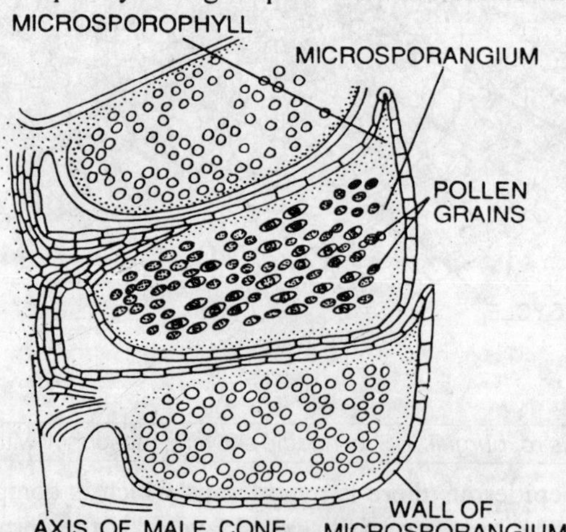

Fig. 2.39. *Pinus.* L.S. of male cone (a part).

4. Each microsporophyll bears two microsporangia or pollen sacs on its under side.

5. The sporangial wall consists of four layers. These four layers are — the epidermis, two middle layers and a glandular tapetum.

6. The central archesporial tissue forms a number of microspore mother cells. Each microspore mother cell divides meiotically producing four haploid (n) microspores.

The Microspore :

1. The microspore is surrounded by a three-layered wall.

2. The exine is heavily cuticularized and is found only on one side of the microspore; it does not completely cover the mature spore.

3. The exo-intine or the middle layer covers the rest of the spore; it projects outward into two large balloon-like air sacs or wings.

4. The intine or the inner layer of the spore is very thin.

The Female Cone :

1. The female cones develop laterally in the axil of scale leaves.

2. They are formed in clusters in place of long shoots, *i.e.*, shoots of unlimited growth.

3. They are produced on the different branches from those of the male cones.

4. There may be one to four cones on each long shoot.

5. The young cones are dark reddish purple in colour.

6. Each cone consists of central axis bearing spirally arranged scales.

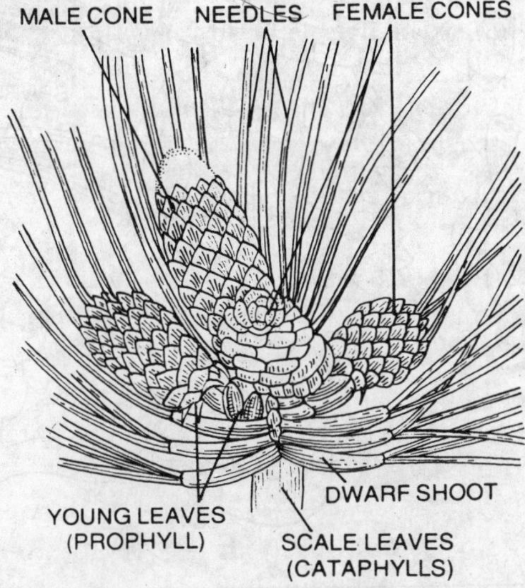

Fig. 2.40. *Pinus roxburghii.* A long shoot with male and female strobili (cones), prophylls and cataphylls.

7. At the base of the cone certain sterin scales are also found.

8. Each fertile scale consists of two structures — (*a*) bract scales or cover scales which are spirally arranged and directly developed from the cone axis, and (*b*) the ovuliferous scale which develops on the upper surface of bract scales.

9. The bract scale is leathery while the ovuliferous scale is woody in structure.

10. Each ovuliferous scale bears two ovules on its upper surface.

11. The bract scales are concealed under the ovuliferous scales and therefore, not visible from outside.

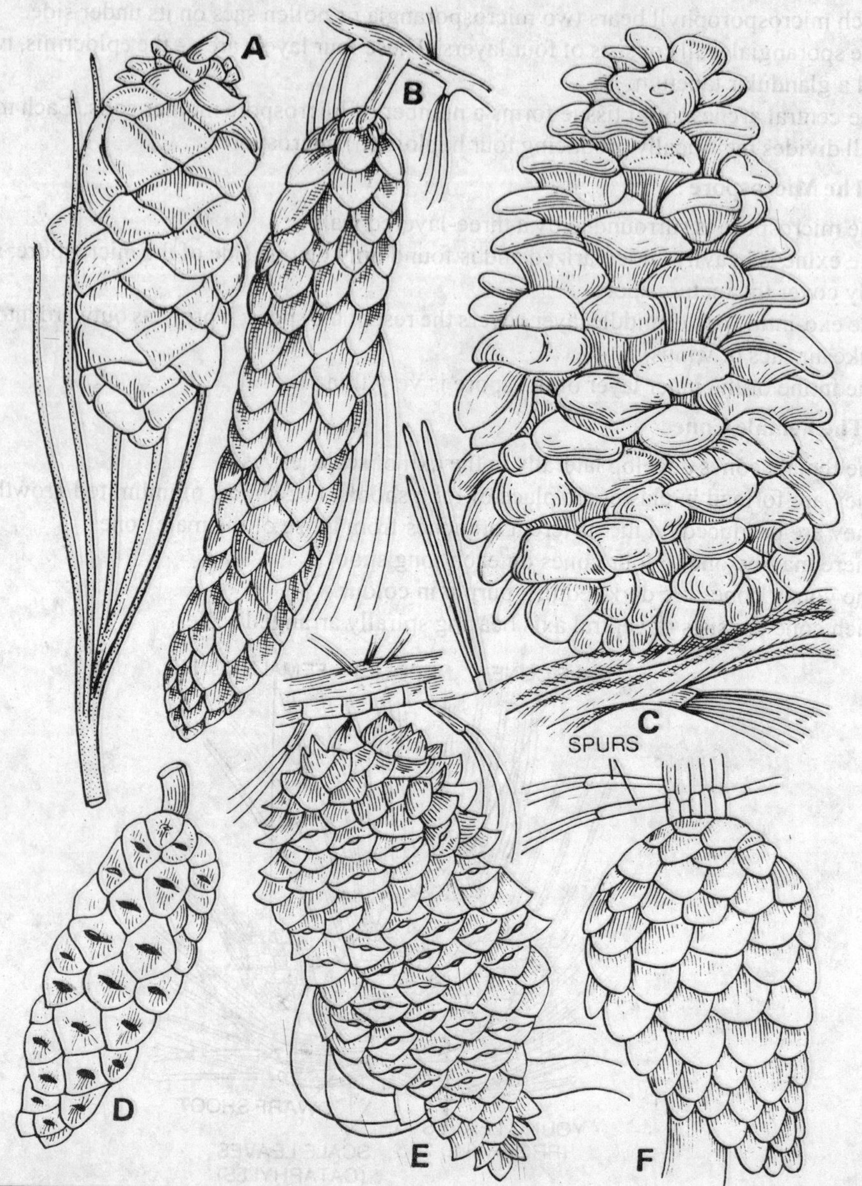

Fig. 2.41. *Pinus* sp. Female cones of different species. A, *P. armandi*; B, *P. wallichiana*; C, *P. gerardiana;* D, *P. merkusii*; E, *P. roxburghii*; F, *P. insularis.*

The Ovule (L.S.) :

1. The ovules are found side by side on the upper surface of the ovuliferous scale.
2. Each ovule consists of a group of cells forming a tissue, the nucellus.
3. The ovule is surrounded by a twolipped covering known as integument. The integument develops up around the ovule. It starts from the abaxial or outer end of the nucellus and grows inwards towards the base of the ovuliferous scale.
4. The integument completely surrounds the nucellus except at the inner and where a wide aperture lies, known as micropyle.
5. The integument is fused to the nucellus except for a short distance near the micropyle.

6. In the nucellar region there lies a small cavity just opposite the micropyle. This is known as pollen chamber.

7. Female gametophyte is differentiated from nucellus. About 2-5 archegonia are situated in this region.

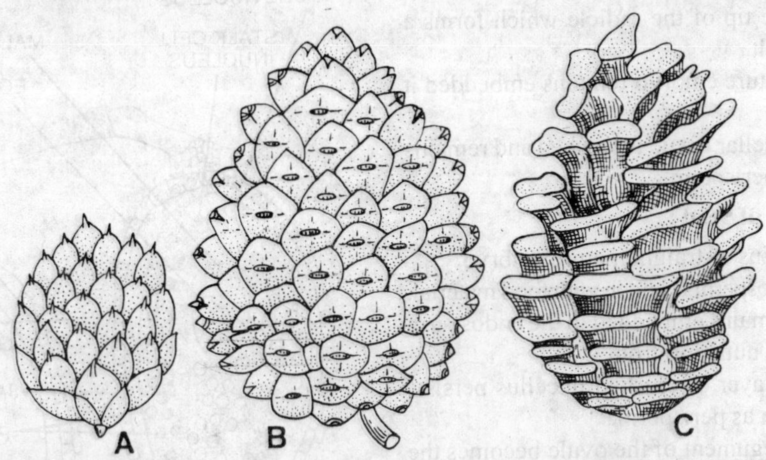

Fig. 2.42. *Pinus* sp. Female cones. A, first year; B, second year and C, third year female cones.

Structure of Embryo :

1. The mature embryo consists of a short axis with the radicle towards the micropylar end a small plumule downwards.

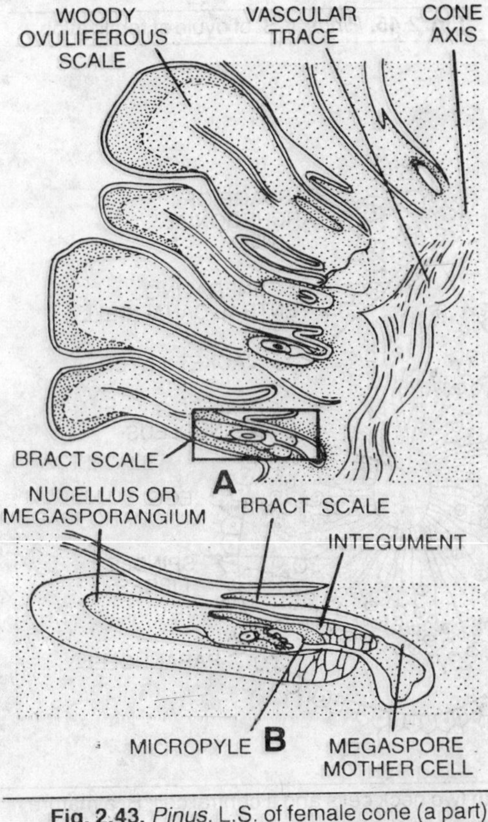

Fig. 2.43. *Pinus*. L.S. of female cone (a part).

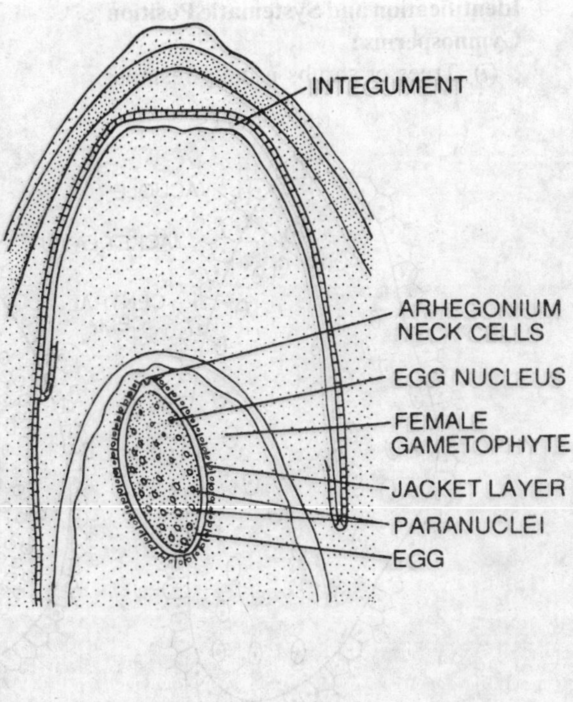

Fig. 2.44. *Pinus*. L.S. of archegonium.

2. The plumule is surrounded by a number of minute leaves, the cotyledons; they are about ten in number.

3. The suspensor remains attached as a small thin coil to the tip of the radicle which forms a thick cap over it.

4. The mature embryo remains embedded it the endosperm.

5. The nucellar tissue is crushed and remains in the form of perisperm.

Structure of Seed :

1. It contains a straight mature embryo.

2. The endosperm is laid in with food material. The embryo remains embedded in the endosperm and absorbs its nutrition from it.

3. A thin layer of crushed nucellus persists which is known as perisperm.

4. The integument of the ovule becomes the seed coat or testa.

5. The testa is hard and stony as it develops from the middle stony layer of the integuments.

6. The seed has a thin membranous wing which is derived from the surface of the ovuliferous scale.

Identification and Systematic Position
Gymnosperms :

(*i*) Trees or shrubs usually resinous.

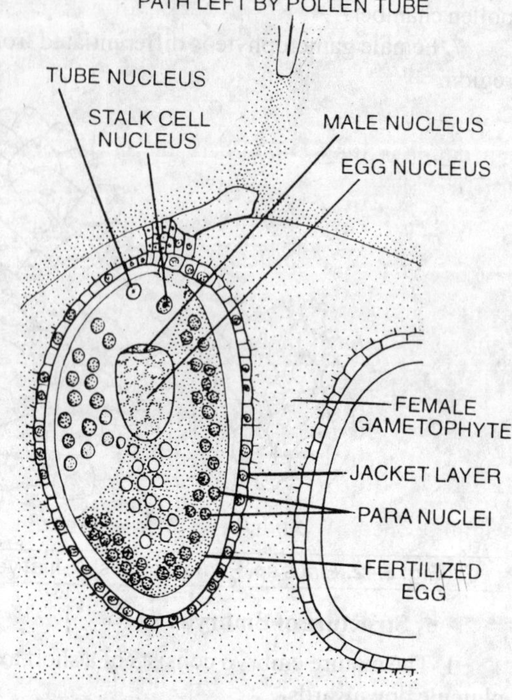

Fig. 2.45. *Pinus*. L.S. of ovule at fertilization.

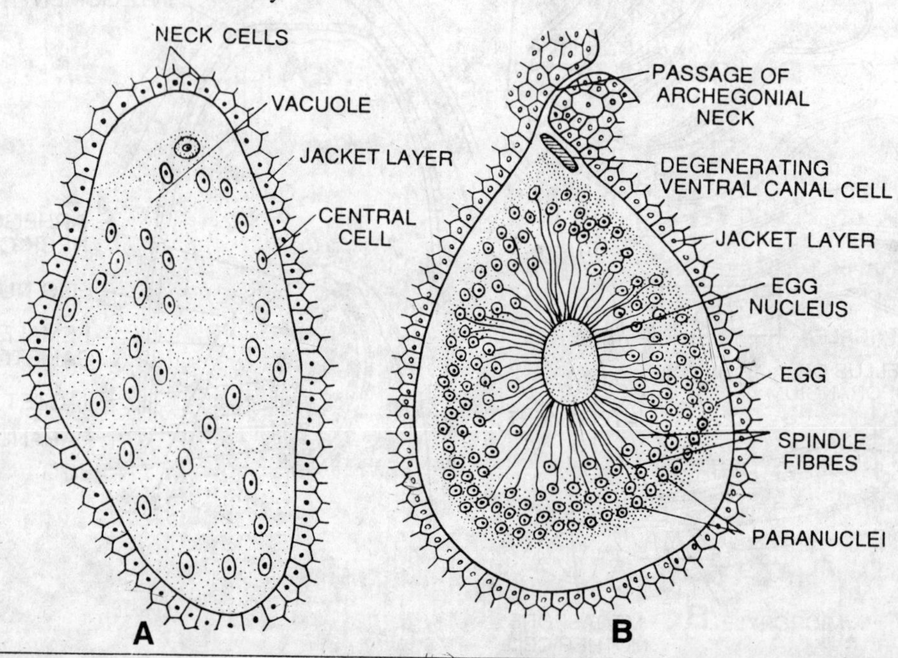

Fig. 2.46. *Pinus roxburghii*. A, a young archegonium with two neck cells and a central cell; B, a mature archegonium with degenerating ventral canal cell.

(*ii*) Ovules naked, not enclosed in an ovary.
(*iii*) Flowers unisexual, rarely bisexual.
(*iv*) Leaves needle-shaped, linear, pinnate, rarely fan-shaped or oblong elliptic, mostly evergreen.
(*v*) Vessels absent.

Coniferales :

(*i*) Mostly evergreen trees with branched stems.
(*ii*) The leaves are needle or scale-like.
(*iii*) Resin canals present frequently.
(*iv*) Wood is pycnoxylic and xylem possesses bordered pits.
(*v*) Male and female cones are compact.
(*vi*) Non-motile sperms.

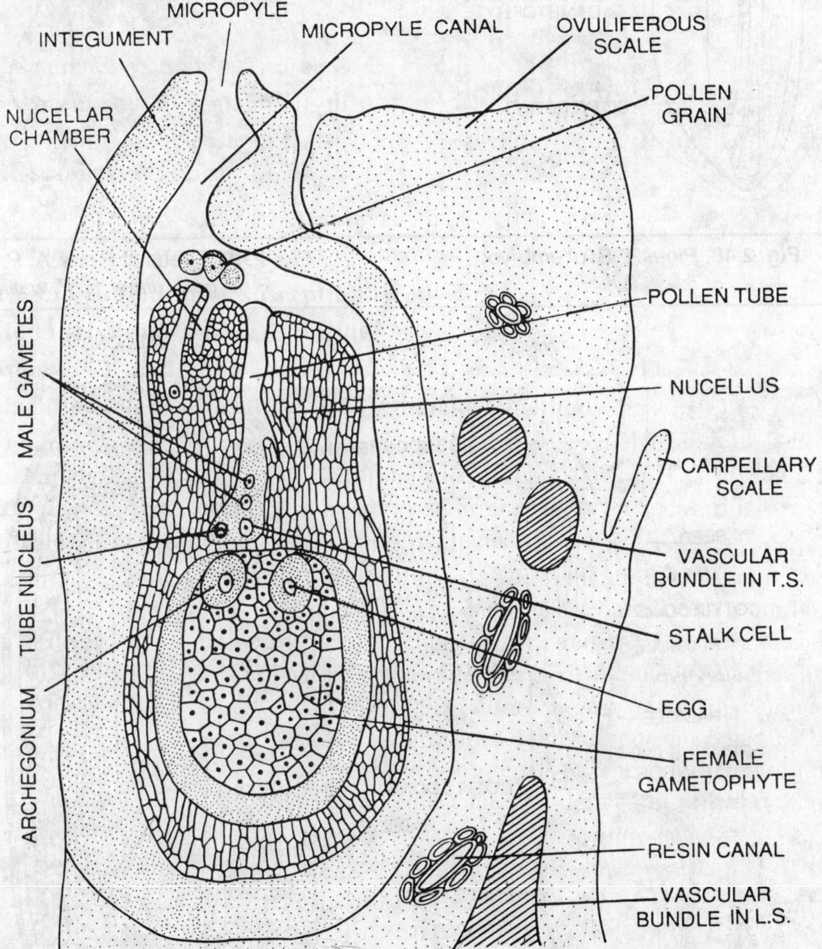

Fig. 2.47. *Pinus roxburghii.* Longitudinal section of mature ovule.

Pinaceae :

(*i*) Plants monoecious.
(*ii*) Resin canals present in wood.
(*iii*) Sporophylls spirally arranged.

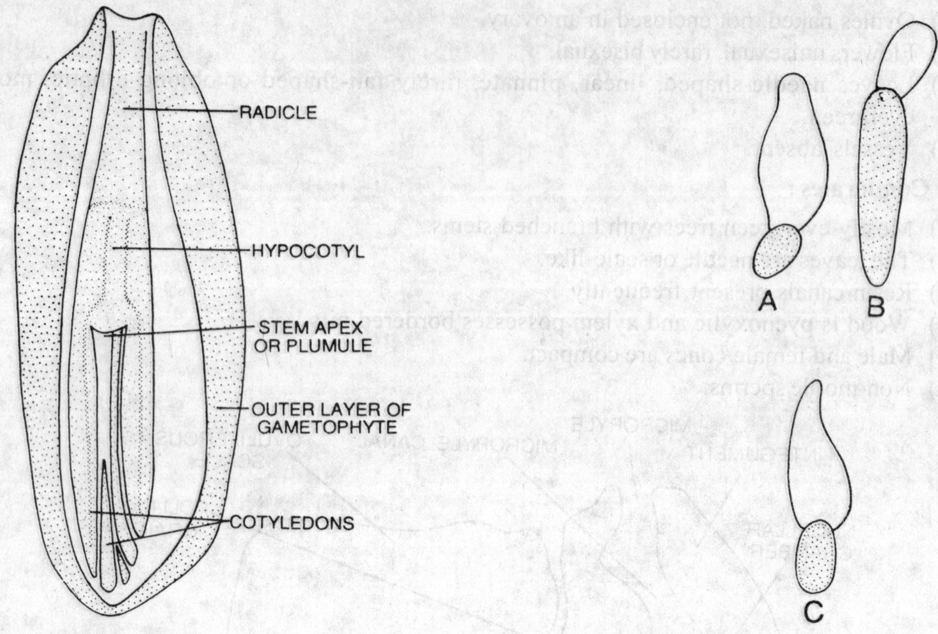

Fig. 2.48. *Pinus*. L.S. of embryo.

Fig. 2.49. Seeds of *Pinus*. A, *P. roxburghii*; B, *P. gerardiana*; C, *P. wallichiana*.

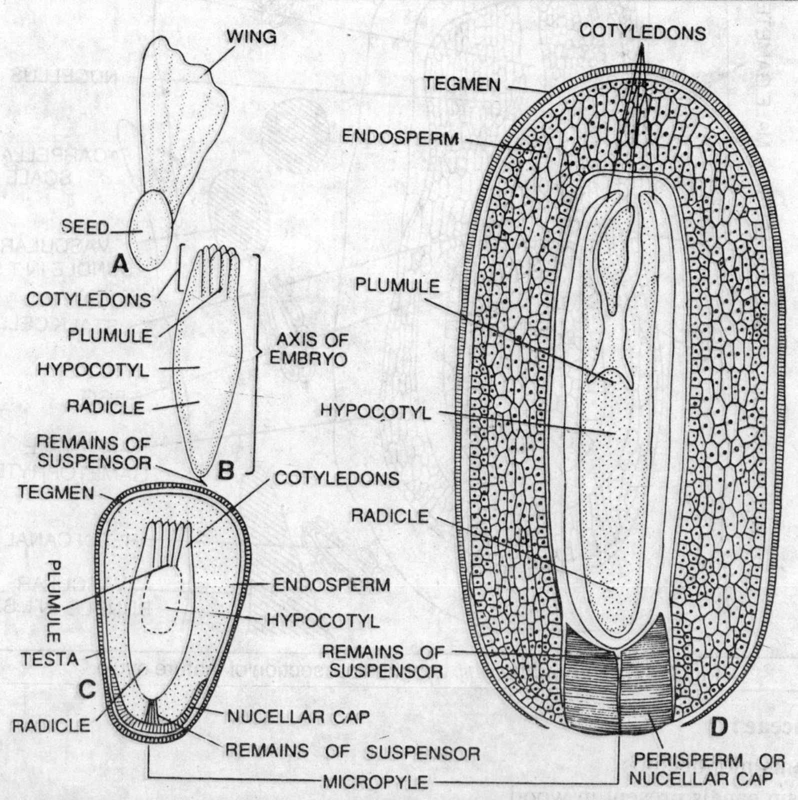

Fig. 2.50. *Pinus roxburghii*. A, winged seed; B, the embryo removed from the seed; C, longitudinal section of seed; D, longitudinal section of seed; seed showing details.

(*iv*) Each microsporophyll with two microsporangia.
(*vi*) Seeds are winged.
(*vii*) Female cone woody.

Pinus :

(*i*) The leaves are needle and scale-like and xeromorphic.
(*ii*) Wood consists of long tracheids with bordered pits.
(*iii*) Resin canals present.
(*iv*) The plants are sporophytic and monoecious.
(*v*) Branches are dimorphic.
(*vi*) Pollen grains winged.
(*vii*) Each female flower consists of a bract and a scale.
(*viii*) The ovuliferous scale bears two naked ovules on its abaxial side.
(*ix*) Seeds are winged and dry.

TAXUS

Habit and Occurrence :

Taxus with about 8 or 9 species has the widest distribution being found in America, Europe, Asia, Malayasia and Mexico. In India it is distributed in various ranges of Himalayas. It is commonly found above 10,000 feet in the Himalayas. The most common species is *T. baccata.* The sporophyte is profusely branched evergreen small tree sometimes reaching a height of about 20 metres with a strong root system. The main trunk may become 7 metres or more in girth.

Proposed Laboratory Work :

(*i*) Study of External Features.
(*ii*) Study of Internal Structure.
(*a*) Anatomy of stem. (*b*) Anatomy of leaf. (*c*) Anatomy of root.
(*iii*) Study of reproductive structures.

External Features :

1. It is a slow-growing evergreen tree reaching a height of 10-12 metres. Sometimes *T. baccata* (the yew) attains a height of 30 metres and a girth of five metres.

Fig. 2.51. *Taxus baccata.* A twig with leaves and seeds.

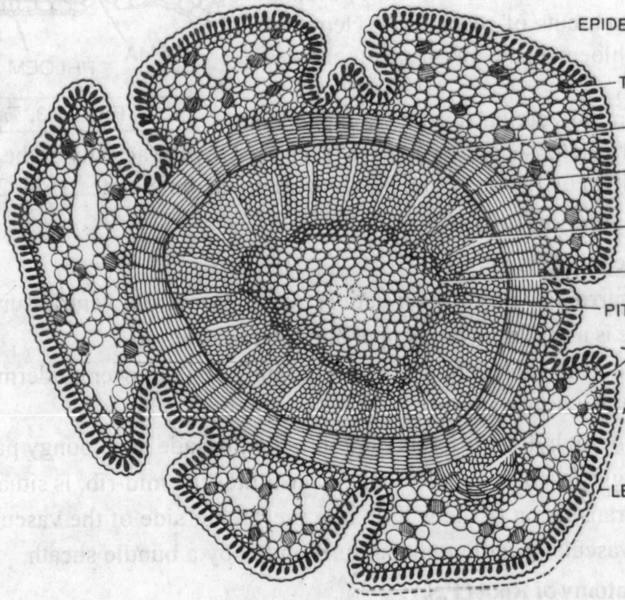

Fig. 2.52. *Taxus baccata.* T.S. of stem showing secondary growth and leaf trace.

2. The general habit of the plant body of *Taxus* resembles *Pinus*. The branches grow horizontally and form a very dense canopy.

3. There are no foliar spurs.

4. During its growth branching occurs from the base, and the branches fuse together to form the compound columnar trunk which is characteristic of the tree.

5. The plant possesses a long tap root.

6. The trunk remains covered by a red-dish-brown scaly bark.

7. The branches are spreading and remain covered by scales at their bases.

8. The spirally arranged foliage leaves are 2 to 3 cm long, narrow, flat with prominent mid-rib and recurved margins. The upper surface is shining and dark-green in colour while the lower surface is pale or rusty red in colour.

9. The scale leaves on the fertile shoots are opposite and decussate and they are shortly petioled.

10. Leaf bases are persistent and they appear of form ridges on the shoot.

Internal Structure

Anatomy of Stem (T.S.) :

1. Anatomically the stem of *Taxus* resembles with that of *Pinus* in many respects.

2. There is complete absence of resin passages.

3. It possesses a thick cuticle, a single cell thick epidermis, sclerenchymatous hypodermis and multilayered cortex.

4. Vascular bundles are arranged in a ring, they are conjoint, collateral and open.

5. Protoxylem is endarch and is made up of tracheids.

6. Phloem consists of sieve cells and phloem parenchyma.

7. Pith is small and is situated in the centre.

8. Secondary growth is initiated by the activity of the cambium present in the vascular bundles, which cuts of secondary xylem and secondary phloem on the inner and outer sides respectively.

9. Xylem rays are narrow and homogeneous.

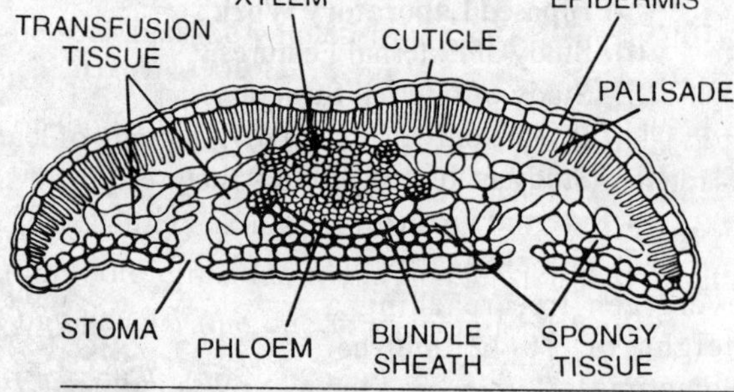

Fig. 2.53. *Taxus baccata.* T.S. of leaf.

10. Extra-stelar secondary growth takes place by the activity of the phellogen or cork cambium. It cuts off phellem on the outer and phelloderm on the inner sides. (Fig. 2.52).

Anatomy of Leaf (T.S.) :

1. The leaf is dorsiventral.

2. It is surrounded by a thick cuticle on the dorsal and ventral surfaces.

3. There is a single-layered upper and lower epidermis.

4. Stomata are sunken in pits and occur only on the lower epidermis.

5. Resin canals are absent.

6. The mesophyll is differentiated into the plaisade and spongy parenchyma.

7. A single vascular bundle, which constitutes the mid-rib, is situated in the centre of the leaf.

8. The transfusion tissue is found on the "either side of the vascular bundle.

9. The vascular bundle remains surrounded by a bundle sheath.

Anatomy of Root (T.S.) :

1. The resin passages are absent.

2. It possesses the diarch structure.

3. The pith is absent.

4. The pericycle is multilayered and consists of parenchymatous cells.

5. It resembles the root of *Pinus* in other respects.

Reproductive Structure

The plants of *Taxus* are dioecious, *i.e.*, the staminate strobili and the ovules arise on two different plants. The strobili are monosporangiate. The male and female cones develop on different trees in the axils of leaves of the previous year.

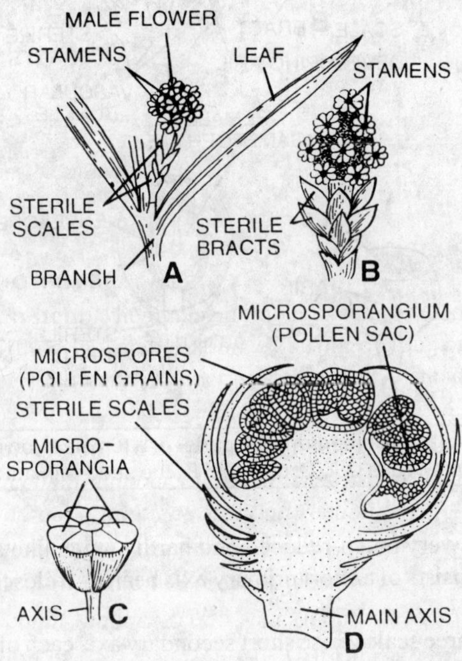

Fig. 2.54. *Taxus baccata.* Male reproductive organs. A, a branch with a male flower having stamen and sterile scales; B, a male flower detached from the plant; C. a stamen (microsporangiophore) with pendant microsporangia; D, V.S. of male flower.

Male Strobilus :

1. The staminate strobili are borne upon short stalks in the axils of the foliage leaves on the undersides of the branchlets of the previous year.

2. The male flowers are arranged in globose heads.

3. At the base of strobilus there are ten decussate sterile scales which at first cover over and protect the young sporophylls.

4. These sterile bract scales are spirally arranged on the axis and increase in size upwards.

5. The upper portion of the central axis bears 6-14 stamens or microsporophylls of the peltate type, that is, the stalk is capped by a peltate expansion from the underside of which are situated the pendant sporangia. The number of sporangia is generally 6-8.

6. The microsporangia (pollen sacs) remain united with one another and attached to the stalk of the sporophyll.

7. The microsporangia contain a number of microspore mother cells which divide meiotically to produce haploid microspores or pollen grains. Each microsporangium contains numerous small microspores.

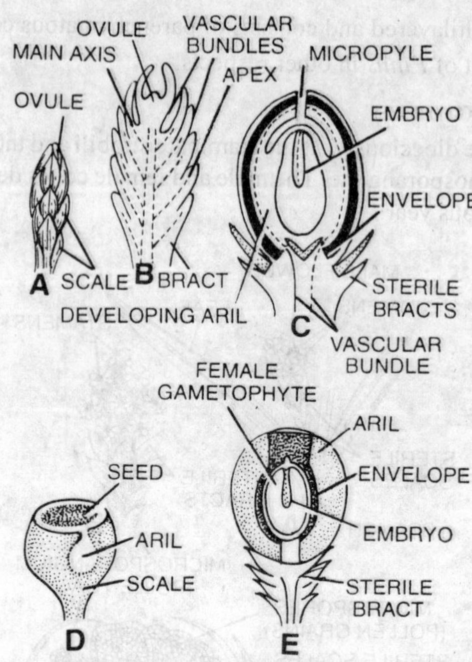

Fig. 2.55. *Taxus baccata*. Seed and female reproductive parts. A, a female strobilus with terminal ovule; B, L.S. of female strobilus showing terminal ovule; C, L.S. of ovule; D, the seed with aril and scales; E, L.S. of seed.

Female Strobilus :

1. The ovulate strobilus is very much-reduced and hardly looks like a strobilus.

2. The female strobilus consists of a short primary axis bearing a closely imbricated succession of sterile scale leaves.

3. From the axil of upper three scales arise short secondary axis each of which consists of 2-3 pairs of scale leaves and a terminal ovule.

4. Ultimately only one ovule matures in the strobilus.

The Ovule :

1. The ovule is more or less rounded to slightly oval in shape.

2. There is a single thick integument which remains free from the nucellus in its apical part forming a long micropyle.

3. From the base of the ovule two vascular strands enter the integument and run upto the tip.

4. On the maturity of the ovule the integument develops a thick strong layer outer to the vascular supply.

5. Just below the integument there is a ring-like swelling, the aril, correctly known as cupule.

6. The integument of ovule is differentiated into an outer fleshy, middle very hard stony and an inner fleshy layers.

7. The ovule does not have a nucellar beak or pollen chamber. The nucellus becomes conical upward.

Seed :

1.. The mature seed is dicotyledonous and non endospermic.

2. It is surrounded by a three-layered seed coat.

3. The middle layer is hard and stony while the inner layer is fleshy and the outermost is a thin membranous covering.

4. The whole seed is enclosed in a cup like structure, the cupule.

Identification and Systematic Position

Gymnosperms :

(*i*) Trees or shrubs usually resinous.

(*ii*) Ovules naked, not enclosed in an ovary.

(*iii*) Flowers unisexual rarely bisexual.

(*iv*) Leaves needle-shaped, linear, pinnate, rarely fan-shaped or oblong elliptic mostly evergreen.

(*v*) Vessels absent.

Taxales :

(*i*) Evergreen slow growing, profusely branched shrubs or small trees.

(*ii*) Leaves acute, arranged spirally on the branches.

(*iii*) Secondary wood pycnoxylic and compact.

(*iv*) Tertiary spirals on the wall of tracheids.

(*v*) Resin canals absent.

(*vi*) Male flowers found singly in the leaf axils.

(*vii*) Female flowers develop in the leaf on secondary fertile dwarf or long shoots.

(*viii*) Ovules are freely exposed and solitary.

(*ix*) Cupule develops on the seed.

(*x*) Pollens do not bear wings.

(*xi*) Embryo is dicotyledonous.

Taxaceae

N.B. single family. Characteristics of the order.

Taxus :

(*i*) Complete absence of resin passages.

(*ii*) Secondary wood is compact and pycnoxylic possessing tertiary spirals on the wall of tracheids.

(*iii*) Male flowers found singly in the axil of leaves or bracts.

(*iv*) The female strobilus is much reduced and not strobilus like.

(*v*) Ovules are freely exposed and solitary.

(*vi*) Fleshy cupule develops on the seed.

(*vii*) Pollens do not bear wings.

(*viii*) Embryo is dicotyledonous.

EPHEDRA

Occurrence :

There are about 35 species of *Ephedra* growing in the arid region about the Mediterranean, and in tropical to temperate Asia, North America and South America. A few species are found in India. They are *E. intermedia, E. gerardiana, E. foliata* and *E. nebrodensis.*

E. intermedia occurs in the natural state in Kashmir and North-West Himalayas at an altitude of about 2,500 to 4,200 metres above sea level. *E. foliata* occurs in the wild state in the Punjab and certain parts of Rajasthan. *E. gerardiana* occurs along the length of the Himalayas at an altitude of about 3,050 metres above sea level.

Proposed Laboratory Work :

(*i*) Study of habit and external features of the plant (sporophyte).

(*ii*) Study of internal structure (anatomy) of stem.

(*iii*) Study of reproductive structures.

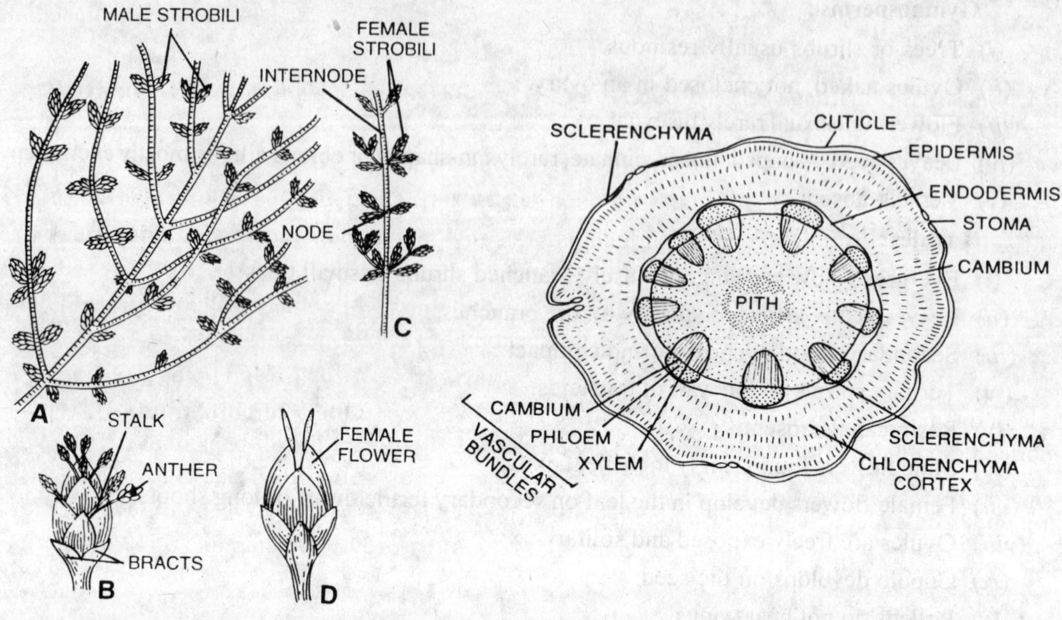

Fig. 2.56. *Ephedra* sp. A, male (staminate) branches : B, staminate strobilus; C, female (ovulate) branch; D, ovualate; strobilus.

Fig. 2.57. *Ephedra foliata.* Transverse section of young stem showing primary structure (diagrammatic).

External Features :

1. Commonly the plants are low straggling shrubs reaching the height of one metre or so.
2. The green, long jointed, slender branches bear minute leaves.
3. The scaly leaves are opposite and connate in a two-toothed sheath.
4. The whole aspect of the plant is xeromorphic.

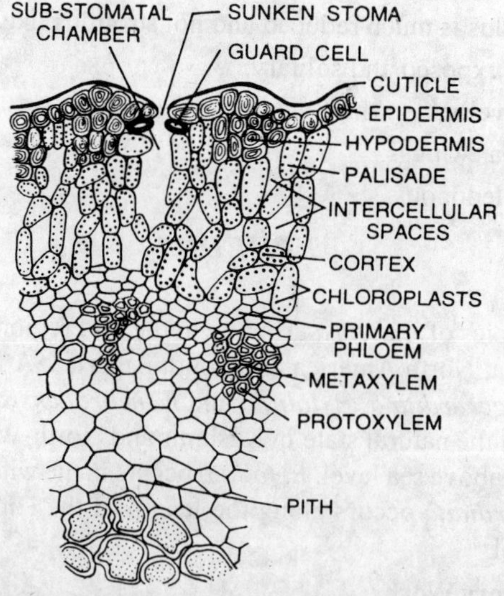

Fig. 2.58. *Ephedra* sp. T.S. of young photosynthetic stem.

5. True foliage leaves are generally lacking and the whole habit is suggestive of a shrubby *Equisetum.*

6. The leaves also occur in the whorls of trees and rarely of fours, at each node.

Internal Structure (Anatomy)

Anatomy of the stem (T.S.) :

1. The outline of the stem as shown by its transverse section is ridged (Fig. 2.57.)

2. The epidermis is quite thick and provided with cuticle and sunken stomata.

3. Just beneath the ribs there are groups of fibre cells.

4. The stomata occur in furrows between the ribs and each stoma is situated in a circular pit.

5. The cortex remains differentiated into a loose outer palisade layer and an inner spongy tissue. The cells of both spongy and palisade tissue contain chloroplasts. (Fig. 2.58)

6. The innermost layer of the cortex is known as endodermis.

7. The pericycle is indistinct.

8. The endodermis encircles the ring of collateral and endarch vascular bundles.

9. The large and small bundles are grouped into pairs of threes.

10. Each small bundle is represented by a leaf trace.

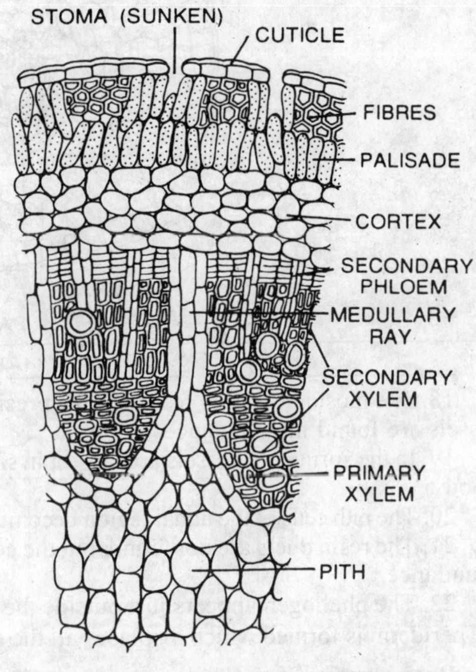

Fig. 2.59. *Ephedra* sp. T.S. of old stem.

11 . Each vascular bundle runs through two internodes and thereafter passes out in pairs into the leaves and hence there is a double leaf trace.

12. The cambium is present and sometimes the older stems become greatly thickened due to secondary growth.

13 . In the course of the formation of secondary wood the annual rings are formed.

14. The young stem contains uniseriate medullary rays, whereas in older stem these rays become very broad and long (Fig. 2.59)

15. The rays are composed of lignified cells and therefore, the wood texture is very hard.

16. The xylem elements, *i.e.,* the tracheids possess single rows of scattered bordered pits arranged on the radial and tangential walls.

17. Bars of sanio and trabeculae are also present across the tracheids.

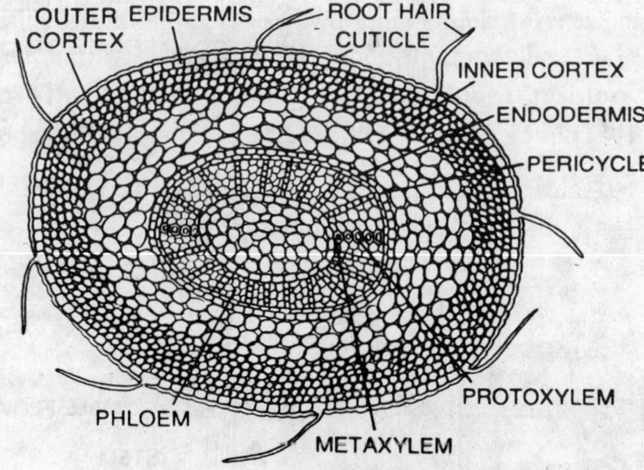

Fig. 2.60. *Ephedra foliata.* Transverse section of young root.

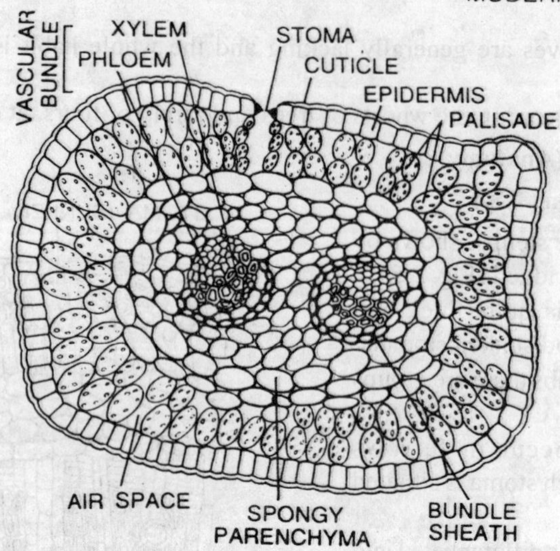

Fig. 2.61. *Ephedra foliata.* Vertical section of leaf.

18. The most interesting feature is the presihce of vessels, resembling those of angiosperms. The vessels are found in abundance.

19. In the spring the vessels are largest in size but they decrease in size and number in the autumn wood.

20. The pith cells of the nodal region become lignified resulting in the formation of transverse plates.

21. The resin ducts are not found, but the cells with large crystals of calcium oxalate are found in abundance.

22. The phellogen appears just outside the phloem in the third or fourth year and with the result the periderm is formed which displaces all the outer tissues.

Reproductive Structures

The plants are usually dioecious and the strobili are monosporangiate. Sometimes the plants may be monoecious bearing both male and female strobili. The scales of strobili are arranged in decussate pairs forming a short membranous strobilus. In rare cases hermaphrodite flowers are found. Such bisporangiate strobili produce stamens at the base and ovules above.

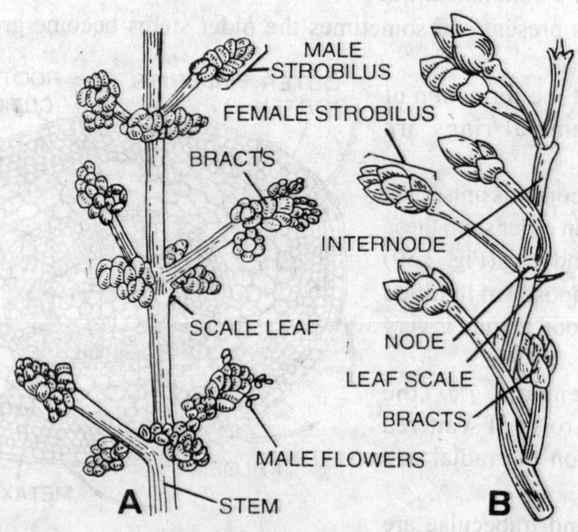

Fig. 2.62. *Ephedra* sp. A, a twig with male strobili (staminate branch); B, a twig with female strobili (ovulate branch).

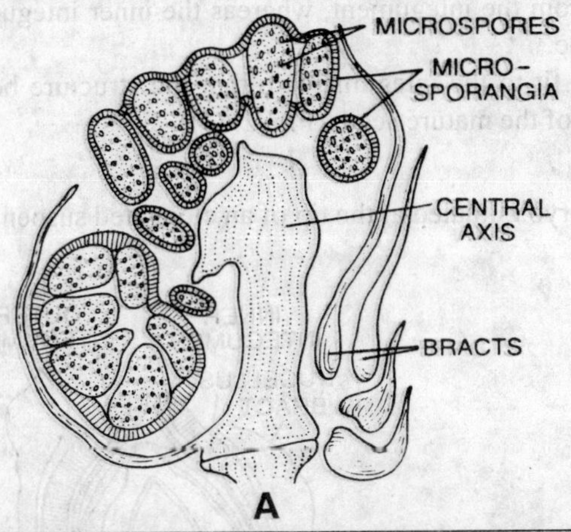

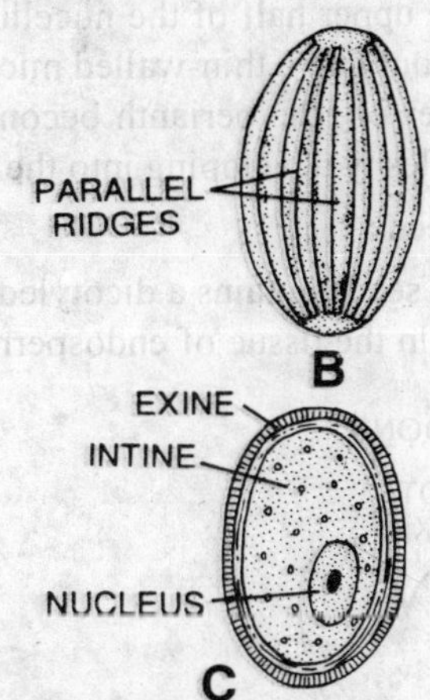

Fig. 2.63. *Ephedra foliata*. A, longitudinal section of male strobilus; B, pollen grain showing parallel ridges on its exine; C, pollen grain in sectional view.

The Male Strobilus :

1. Each male strobilus arises from the axil of a leaf. (Fig. 2.62A).

2. It consists of a short axis which bears a number of thick and closely arranged bracts found in decussate pairs.

3. The pairs of bracts vary from two to twelve in number.

4. A single male flower stands in the axil of each bract.

5. Eadrmale flower consists of a perianth of two scales and a stalked stamen srises from between the two scales of the perianth and bears two to several anthers (sporangia) at its top.

6. The simple stamen bears two sporangia and when it becomes branched it bears several sporangia.

7. The anther is two or three lobed.

8. Each lobe opens by an apical slit and the pollens are released.

9. The pollens are elliptical in shape. (Fig. 2.63)

The Female Strobilus

1. The female strobili like the male strobili also develop in groups of two to four at each node in the axils of scale leaves; (Fig. 2.62B).

2. Each strobilus consists of an axis bearing two to four or sometimes more pairs of bracts which are opposite.

3. All the bracts of a strobilus except one or two at the apex, are sterile.

4. The fertile bract develops a single female flower in the axil.

The Ovule :

1. Each ovule consists of a nucellus with envelopes.

2. The inner envelope consists of two segments while the outer of four segments.

3. The inner envelope is a true ovular integument, and the outer envelope is perianth.

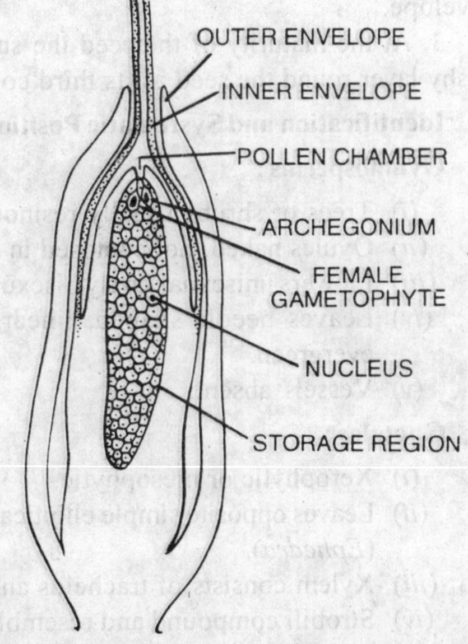

Fig. 2.64. *Ephedra* sp. L.S. of a mature ovule with long micropylar canal and two archegonia in the gametophyte.

4. The upper half of the nucellus is free from the integument, whereas the inner integument is prolonged out into a thin-walled micropylar tube.

5. Later on, the perianth becomes closely fit to the integument so that the structure becomes woody or fleshy developing into the outer coat of the mature seed. (Fig. 2.64).

The seed :

1. The seed contains a dicotyledonous embryo rsituated at the tip of an elongated suspensor and embedded in the tissue of endosperm.

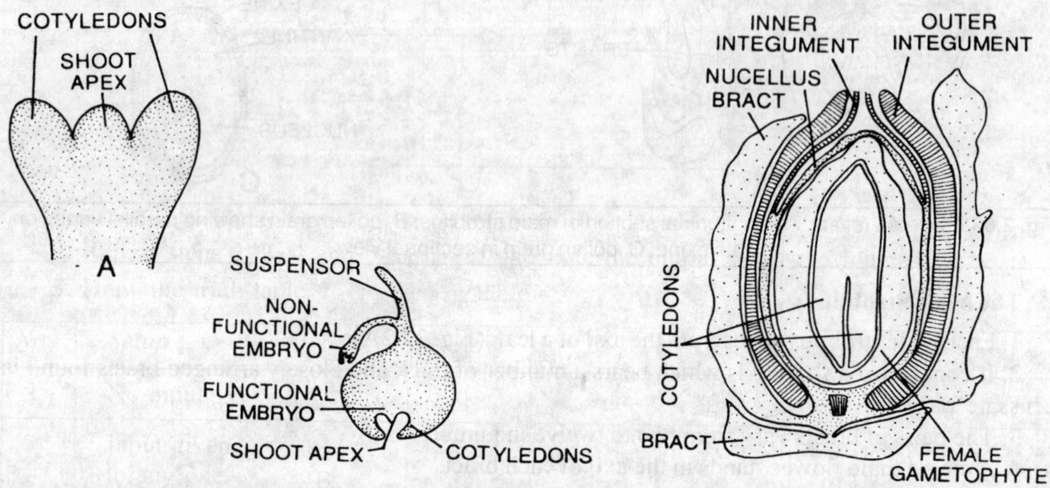

Fig. 2.65. *Ephedra foliata.* A, embryo; B, functional and non-functional embryos; C, longitudinal section of seed.

2. The seed coat consists of two distinct layers which are derived from the two layers of the envelope.

3. At the maturity of the seed the subtending bracts of the strobilus develop into a thick and fleshy layer round the seed as its third covering.

Identification and Systematic Position

Gymnosperms :

(*i*) Trees or shrubs usually resinous.
(*ii*) Ovules naked, not enclosed in an ovary.
(*iii*) Flowers unisexual rarely bisexual.
(*iv*) Leaves needle-shaped, linear, pinnate, rarely fan-shaped or oblong elliptic, mostly evergreen.
(*v*) Vessels absent.

Gnetales :

(*i*) Xerophytic or mesophytic.
(*ii*) Leaves opposite simple elliptical (*Gnetum*), strap-shaped (*Welwitschia*) or reduced to scales (*Ephedra*).
(*iii*) Xylem consists of tracheids and true vessels.
(*iv*) Strobili compound and resemble angiospermous inflorescence.
(*v*) Male flowers possess perianth and anthers.
(*vi*) Perianth occurs in one or two whorls.
(*vii*) Female flower a single erect ovule.
(*viii*) The embryo possesses two cotyledons.

Ephedraceae

(*i*) Xerophytic shrubs.
(*ii*) Scaly leaves opposite and connate in a two-toothed sheath.
(*iii*) Vessels present resembling those of angiosperms.
(*iv*) Strobili compound and resemble angiospermous inflorescence.
(*v*) Male flowers resemble the stamens of angiosperms.
(*vi*) Archegonia present.
(*vii*) Embryo sac monosporic.

Ephedra :

N.B. Single senus. Characteristics of the family.

GNETUM

Habit and Occurrence

There are about 40 species in this genus. They are mainly distributed in the tropical and humid regions of the world. Out of that total species about nineteen species are common to the Eastern and Western hemispheres. In India, the genus is represented by six species -*G.gnemon* grows in Assam, Naga hills, Golaghat area, etc. G. *montanum* grows in Sikkim, Assam, Orissa, etc. G. *ula* grows in Western and Eastern coasts of India, near Khandala, Kanara, Coorg, Kerala, Nilgiris, Godavari district and Orissa, etc. G. *contraction* grows in Kerala, the Nilgiri hills and Coonoor and G. *oblongum* occurs in Bengal and Burma. G. *latifolium* var. *macropodum* occurs in the Andaman and Nicobar Islands.

Most of species are climbing or trailing plants. Only few species are either trees or shrubs. The adult plant is a sporophyte and resembles a dicotyledonous angiosperm in appearance.

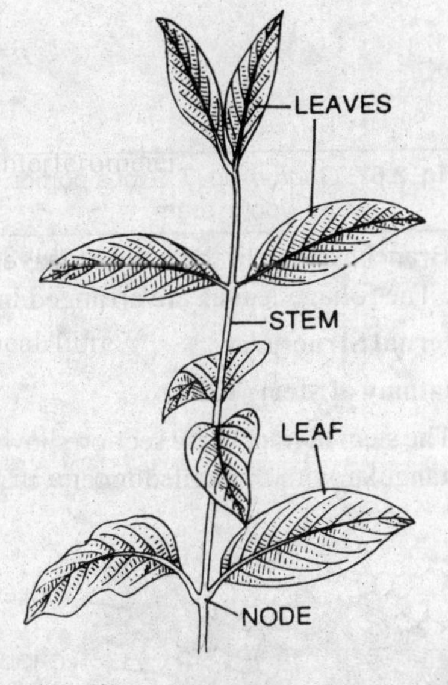

Fig. 2.66. *Gnetum.* A twig.

Proposed Laboratory Work :

(*i*) Study of external features of sporophyte.
(*ii*) Study of internal structure (anatomy).
(*a*) Anatomy of stem (T.S.)
(*b*) Anatomy of leaf (T.S.)
(*c*) Anatomy of root (T.S.)

External Structure :

1. The adult plant is a sporophyte resembling angiosperms in appearance.

2. G. *neglectum,* G. *latifolium* var. *funiculars,* G. *africanum, G. ula are* woody climbers with twining stems.

3. G. *gnemon* is a woody tree.

4. The lower portions of the climbers are generally devoid of leaves.

5. In some species branches are dimorphic, *i.e.,* they are of limited and unlimited growth.

6. In many species the stem is articulated.

7. In climbing species foliage leaves occur on short unbranched shoots.

8. The leaves are net-veined, large, oval and entire.

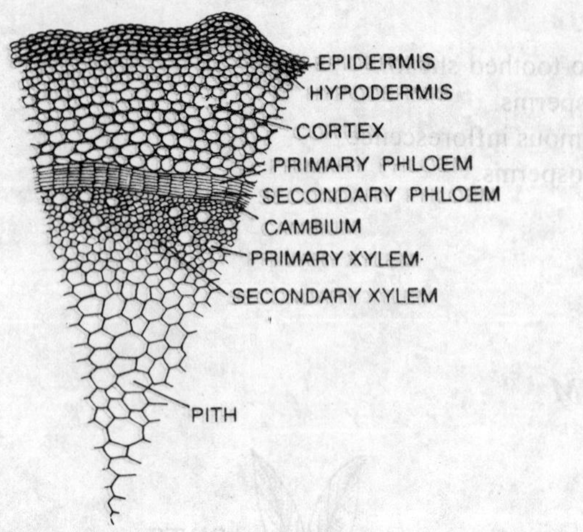

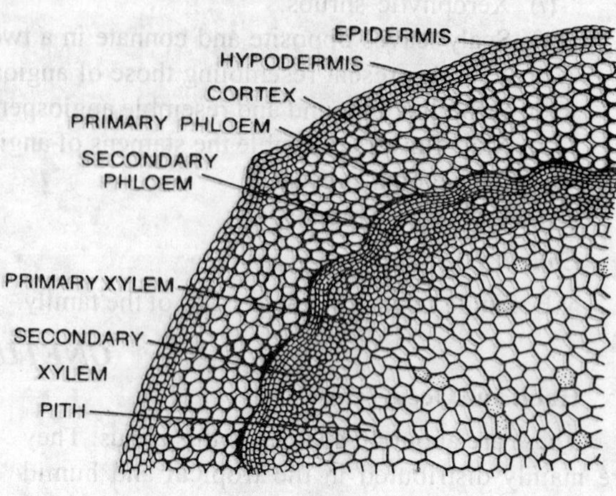

Fig. 2.67. *Gnetum* sp. T.S. of a portion of young stem.

Fig. 2.68. *Gnetum gnemon.* A portion of T.S. of young stem.

9. Branches arise in the axils of leaves and the stems are usually jointed.

10. The foliage leaves are arranged in decussate pairs.

Internal Structures

Anatomy of Stem (T.S.) :

1. The stem in transverse section shows a single-layered epidermis, the cells of which are papillate and rectangular with thickened outer walls. Cuticle is thick and the stomata are sunken.

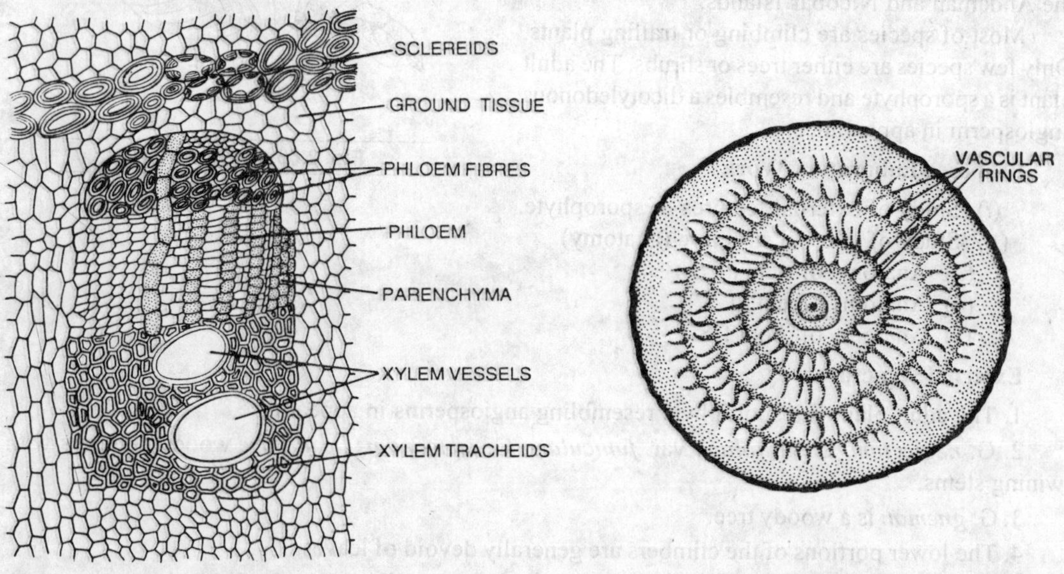

Fig. 2.69. *Gnetwn* sp. A portion of T.S of stem showing xylem vessels, xylem tracheids, phloem and sclereids.

Fig. 2.70. *Gnetum* sp. T.S. of an old stem showing vascular rings.

2. The multi-layered cortex in older stems develops an irregular ring of sclerenchymatous tissue.

3. Endodermis and pericycle are inconspicuous.

4. There is a ring of 20 to 24 conjoint, collateral and endarch vascular bundles separated from one another by broad medullary or xylem rays.

5. The wood is composed of a large number of tracheids and a few vessels.

6. The phloem is composed of sieve cells and phloem parenchyma.

7. The pith consists of round or polygonal parenchymatous cells. Some of the cells of pith in older stems become lignified and pitted.

8. Protoxylem elements possess spiral, annular or reticulate thickenings while the metaxylem elements possess bordered pits as well.

Secondary Growth :

1. The secondary growth begins in a normal manner but after a short time an extra fascicular cambium develops and it produces a normally oriented ring of vascular bundles.

2. In G. *ula* and G. *africanum* there is anomalous type of secondary growth. Here several successive rings of cambia develop one after the other in different parts of cortical region.

3. These rings gradually become incorporated into a continuous xylem cylinder possessing wedge-shaped vascular bundles.

4. The growth of the first ring ceases and thereafter the growth of second ring begins and hence the rings are formed successively one after another.

5. Some of the rings remain incomplete and become in eccentric position with regard to pith.

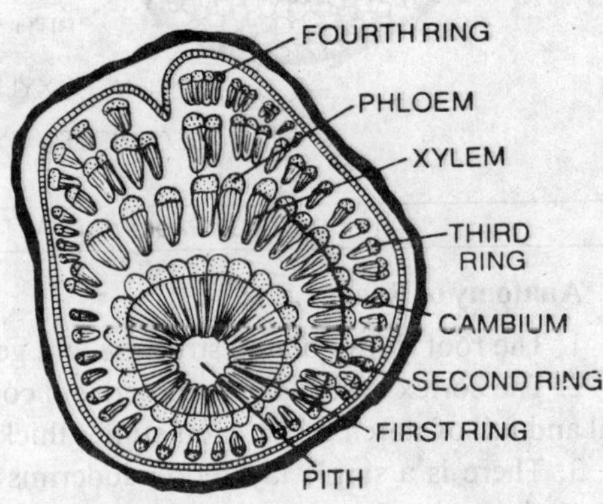

Fig. 2.71. *Gnetum* sp. T.S. of stem showing eccentric secondary growth.

6. Secondary phloem is composed of sieve cells and parenchyma cells.

7. In G. *ula* sclerenchymatous fibres occur in the phloem.

8. The vessels of secondary xylem have simple pits on their radial walls. These vessels in *Gnetum* are more advanced than seen in *Ephedra*.

9. Sometimes the cortex and the pith both possess laticiferous elements.

10. Periderm is generally thin, it develops from the hypodermal region. It also possesses lenticels.

Anatomy of Leaf (T.S.)

1. The epidermis on the upper and lower surface of the leaf is undulate.

2. It possesses a well developed cuticle upon its upper side.

3. The stomata are found only in the lower surface.

4. The mesophyll tissue is differentiated into palisade and spongy tissues.

5. Mixed with spongy parenchyma occur branched and lignified sclerotic cells, fibres and latex tubes.

6. Vascular bundles in the midrib region are arranged in the form of an arch followed by patches of stone cells on their lower side.

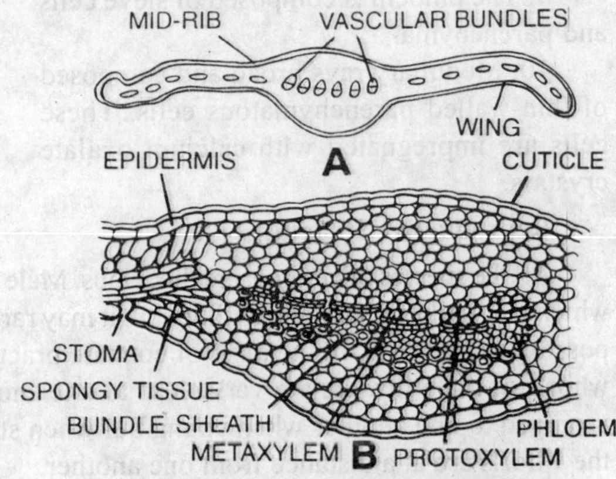

Fig. 2.72 *Gnetum ula*. T.S. of leaf A, diagrammatic; B, detailed structure.

7. The bundles are conjoint, collateral and endarch; protoxylem is found towards upper side.

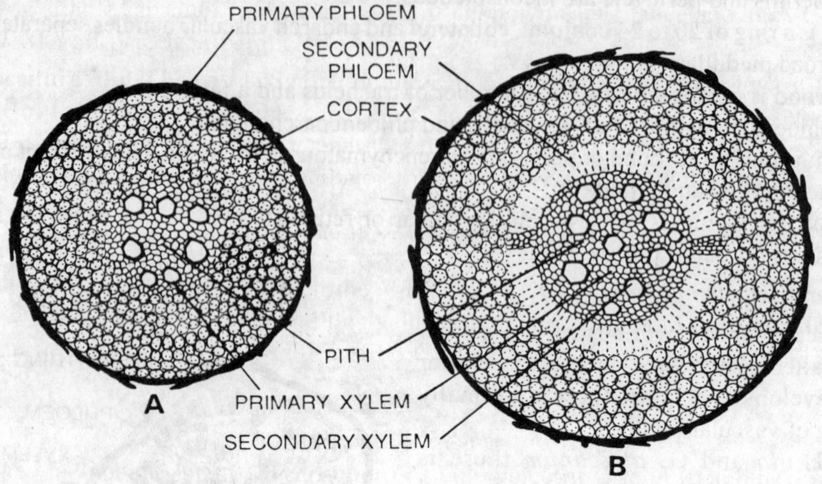

Fig. 2.73. *Gnetum* sp. A, T.S. of young root; B, T.S. of old root.

Anatomy of Root (T.S.) :

1. The root shows diarch structure and generally resembles with the root of angiosperms.

2. The cortex is sufficiently broad and consists of parenchymatous cells which are polygonal or oval and full of starch grains. Sometimes thick-walled fibres are also present in the cortex.

3. There is a single layered endodermis around the pericycle.

4. The primary xylem cannot be differentiated after secondary growth.

5. Secondary growth is of normal type.

6. The secondary xylem consists of tracheids possessing uniseriate bordered pits.

7. The vessels are also present.

8. The pits which occur on the vessels may be bordered or simple, small and multiseriate.

9. The phloem is composed of sieve cells and parenchyma.

10. Medullary rays broad and composed of thin-walled parenchymatous cells. These cells are impregnated with calcium oxalate crystals.

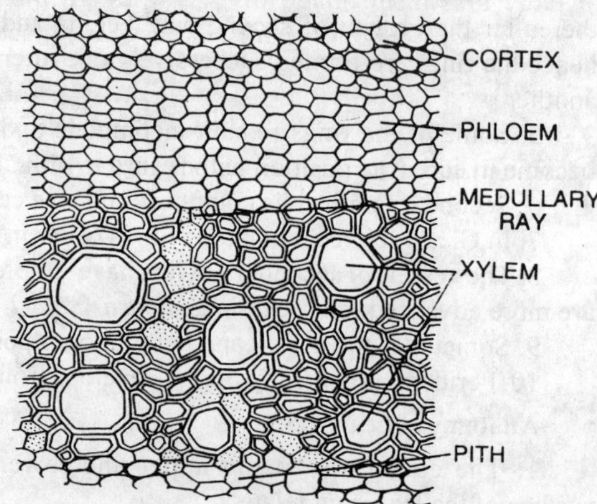

Fig. 2.74. *Gnetum gnemon.* A portion of the T.S. of root.

Reproductive Structures :

All the species of *Gnetum* are dioecious. Male and female strobili are organised like an inflorescence which is usually solitary and axillary but it may rarely be terminal. The strobili, whether male or female, possess a short axis. In the axils of connate bracts arise the strobili. In the case of male strobilus the whorls of male flowers are very close to one another but not overlapped. In female they are closely arranged to one another when young but when strobilus becomes ripe and reaches the fruiting stage the whorls are at a distance from one another.

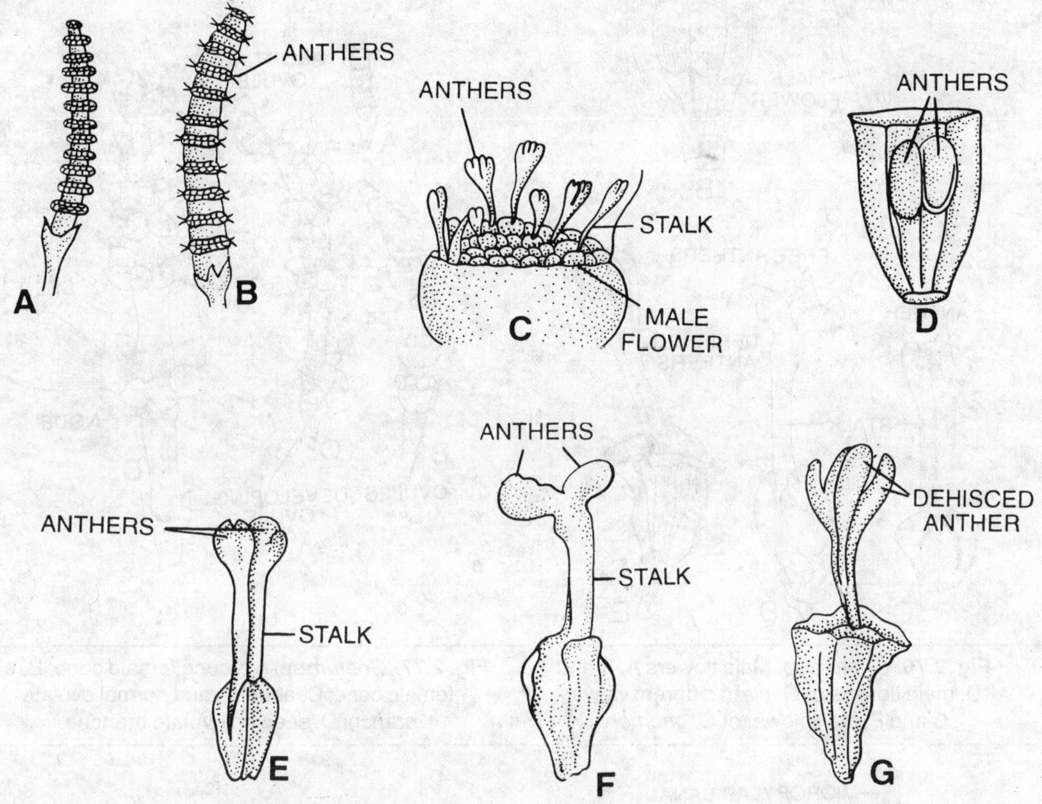

Fig. 2.75. *Gnetum ula.* A, young male cone; B, mature male cone; C, portion of male cone with dehiscing male flowers; D, L.S. of male flower; E-F, male flowers with anthers; G, dehisced male flowers.

Male Strobilus :

1. It has a long slender axis which bears numerous decussating pairs of bracts.

2. These bracts are practically fused along their margins, so round the axis at short interval. There are cup-shaped structures (collars) formed by the fusion of these bracts.

3. In the axils of these are whorls of staminate flowers, 3-5 in each whorl.

Male flower :

1. Each male flower when young is enclosed within a sheath-like perianth.

2. It consists of a stalk which at its apex usually bears two unilocular anthers or microsporangia.

3. On the maturation of the anthers the stalks elongate and push the anthers beyond the collars through a slit which is formed in the perianth.

4. Young microsporangia are enclosed with in the anthers.

5. The pollen mother cells divide meiotically and form the pollen grains.

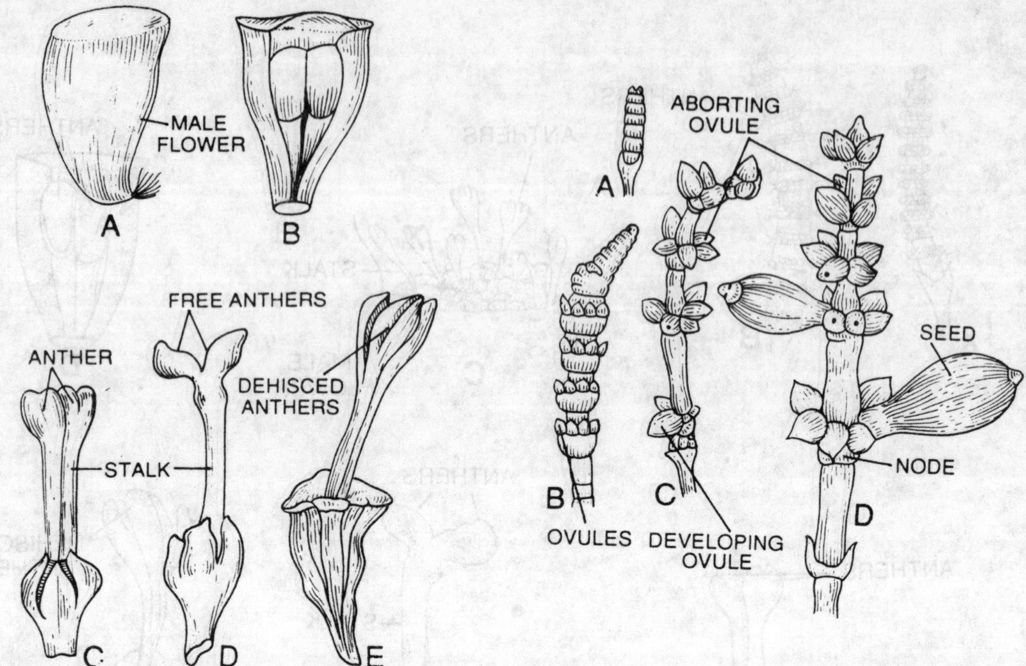

Fig. 2.76. *Gnetum* sp. Male flowers A, B and D, male flowers of *G. ula* in different views; C and E, male flower of *G. gnemon*.

Fig. 2.77. *Gnetum* sp. A, young female cone; B, old female cone; C, aborting and normal ovulate branch; D, seed on ovulate branche.

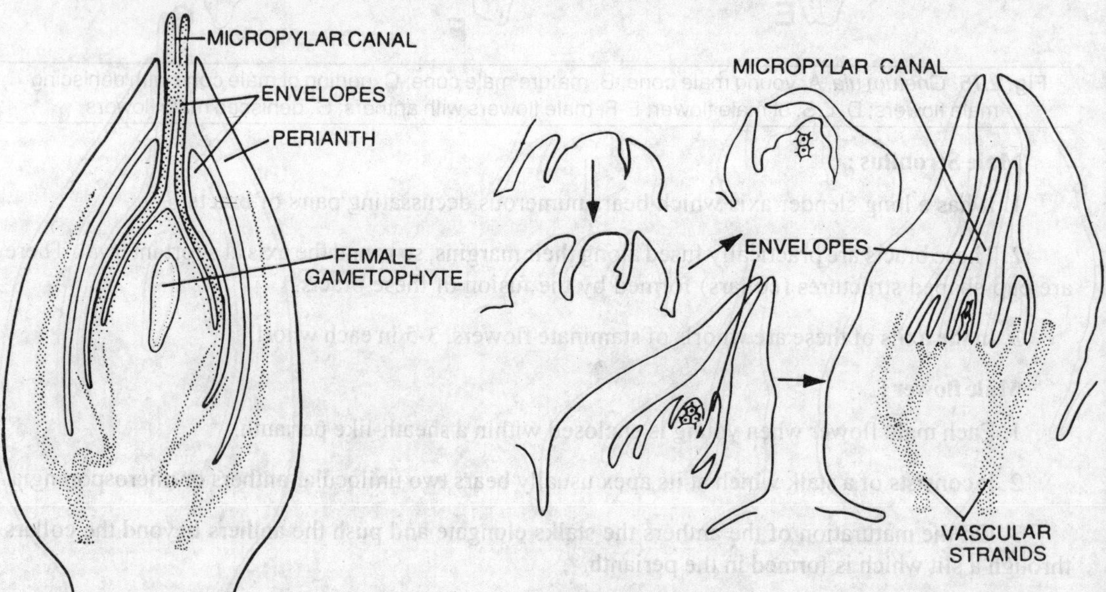

Fig. 2.78. *Gnetum* sp. L.S. of the ovule with mature gametophyte and vascular supply.

Fig. 2.79. *Gnetum* sp. Successive stages in the development of ovule. The ovule shows different layers of the envelope and micropylar canal.

Female Strobilus :

1. Like the male strobilus the female strobilus also possesses an axis which bears collars arranged one above the other.

2. Above each collar about 4-10 ovules are found arranged in a ring.

3. The ovules are dimorphic. The smaller ovules ultimately degenerate.

4. Each female-flower is represented by a single ovule.

Female flower (The Ovule) :

1. Each of the ovule represents a female flower.

2. The ovule is usually short stalked and rarely sessile.

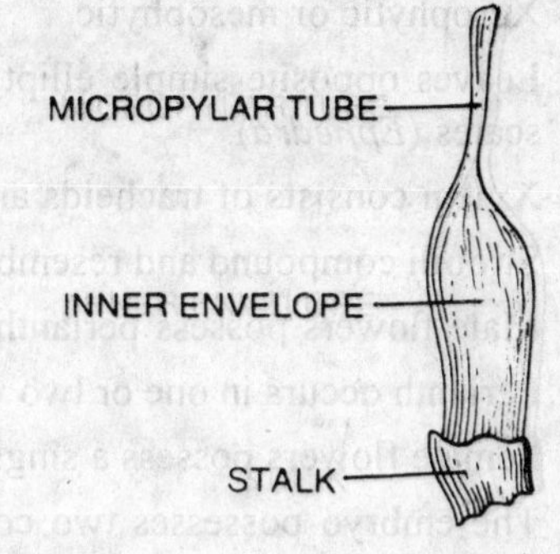

Fig. 2.80. *Gnetum* sp. Structure of ovule.

3. Each ovule consists of nucellus and remains surrounded by a three-layered envelope.

4. The inner two coverings are the outer and inner integuments while the outermost covering is perianth. Here the perianth is quite large in size and encloses the ovule, hence the ovule is completely invested by three coverings.

5. The innermost layer (inner integument) of the envelope gets prolonged above the ovule to form a long micropylar canal.

6. The middle covering in the outer integument in the ripe ovule which becomes differentiated into an inner stony and outer fleshy layer.

7. Two sets of vascular bundles are found in the outer fleshy layer of the outer integument, and one set in the inner integument is seen to be running along the length of integuments.

8. The outermost covering, the perianth has its own vascular supply.

Structure of Seed :

1. The mature seed is oval or slightly elongated and green to red in colour.

2. The seed remains surrounded by three-layered envelope.

3. The outermost layer of the envelope is free from base at apex. It is composed of parenchymatous cells. It possesses scattered fibres, sclereids and stomata.

4. The middle layer is hard and protective. This layer is traversed by numerous branched vascular strands. It also possesses distinct palisade and parenchymatous cells.

5. The innermost layer of the envelope is composed of parenchymatous cells and remains united with the nucellus upto two third of its length.

6. It projects out beyond the nucellus. Numerous vascular bundles also traverse through this layer. The endosperm lies within the innermost layer.

Identification and Systematic Position

Gymnosperms :

(*i*) Trees or shrubs; usually resinous.

(*ii*) Ovules naked, not enclosed in an ovary.

(*iii*) Flowers unisexual rarely bisexual.

(*iv*) Leaves needle-shaped, linear, pinnate, rarely fan-shaped or oblong elliptic, mostly evergreen.

Gnetales :

(*i*) Xerophytic or mesophytic.

(*ii*) Leaves opposite simple elliptical (*Gneturn*), strap-shaped (*Welwitschid*) or reduced to scales (*Ephedra*).

(*iii*) Xylem consists of tracheids and true vessels.

(*iv*) Strobili compound and resemble angiospermous inflorescence.

(*v*) Male flowers possess perianth and anthers.

(*vi*) Perianth occurs in one or two whorls.

(*vii*) Female flowers possess a single erect ovule.

(*viii*) The embryo possesses two cotyledons.

Gnetaceae :

(*i*) Climbing or trailing plants; few species trees or shrubs.

(*ii*) Leaves are net-veined, large, oval and entire; opposite decussate.

(*iii*) Vessels are more angiosperm like in having a single large perforation on their end walls.

(*iv*) The axis of male strobilus bears cupule like structures 'the collar' at each node; each collar bearing several male flowers.

(*v*) Archegonia are absent.

(*vi*) Embryo sac is tetrasporic.

Gnetum :

N.B. single genus. Characters of the family.

Fossil Plants

MAIN EVENTS OF EARTH'S HISTORY

GEOLOGICAL ERA AND TIME IN MILLIONS OF YEARS BEFORE THE PRESENT	PERIODS	DURATION IN MILLIONS YEARS	MAIN GVMNOSPERM GROUPS
0	QUATERNARY RECENT		
CENOZOIC 70	TERTIARY	62	
MESOZOIC	CRETACEOUS	72	
200	JURASSIC	45	
	TRIASSIC	50	
PALAEOZOIC	PERMIAN	50	
	CARBONI FEROUS	65	
	DEVONIAN	60	
	SILURIAN	20	
	ORDOVICIAN	75	
600	CAMBRIAN	100	
PROTEROZOIC 2000 ARCHAEOZOIC 3000	PRE-CAMBRIAN		
5000			ORIGIN OF EARTH

CAYTONIALES, CYCADALES, PTERIDOSPERMALES, CYCADEOIDALES, CORDAITALES, GINKGOALES, CONIFERALES, TAXALES, GNETALES

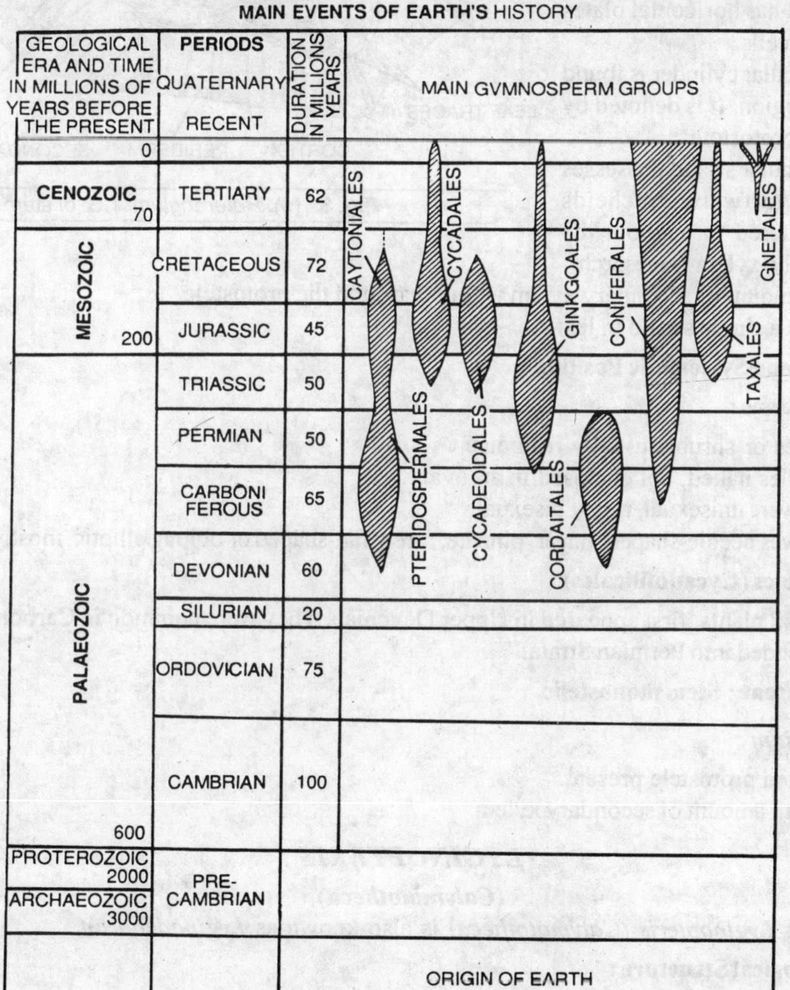

Fig. 3.1. Main events of earth's history.

HETERANGIUM

The best known species *Heterangium grievii* was found in the upper and lower Carboniferous beds.

Anatomy (T.S. of Stem) :

1. The outline of the stem in transverse section appears somewhat angular because of the presence of large decurrent bases on it.

2. The T.S. of stem exhibits an outer epidermal layer (epidermis), outer and inner cortex and a vascular cylinder.

3. The outer cortex shows radially elongated fibrous bands and the inner cortex has horizontal plates of thick walled cells.

4. The vascular cylinder is found in the central region. It is denoted by a terete mixed protostele.

5. The vascular strand possesses groups of six to twelve tracheids uniformly scattered throughout the parenchyma. The xylem is mesarch.

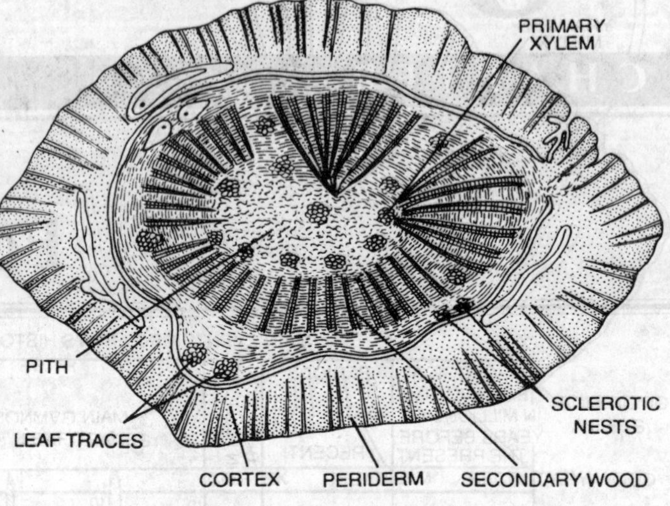

Fig. 3.1(*a*). *Heterangium.* T.S. of stem.

6. Small amount of secondary xylem is found around the protostele.

7. There is a single strand in leaf.

Identification and Systematic Position :

Gymnosperms :

(*i*) Trees or shrubs; usually resinous.
(*ii*) Ovules naked, not enclosed in an ovary.
(*iii*) Flowers unisexual, rarely bisexual.
(*iv*) Leaves needle-shaped, linear, pinnate, rarely fan-shaped or oblong elliptic, mostly evergreen.

Pteridospermales (Cycadofilicales) :

(*i*) Fossil plants; first appeared in Upper Devonian. They were common in Carboniferous and extended into Permian Strata.

Lyginopteridaceae : Stem monostelic.

Heterangium :

(*i*) Mixed protostele present.
(*ii*) Small amount of secondary xylem.

LYGINOPTERIS

(*Calymatotheca*)

The genus *Lyginopteris (Calymatotheca)* is also known as *Lyginodendron.*

Morphological Structure :

1. The stem was slender and covered with large scaly leaves.
2. Near the base of the plant adventitious roots were developed.
3. The plant seems to have been a climber.

Anatomical Structure :

1. The primary structure was an ectophloic siphonostele with large pith surrounded by a number of primary mesarch bundles.

2. Older plants showed normal secondary growth.

3. In some specimens, however the xylem portion of primary vascular bundles was in a continuous ring.

4. Mesarch vascular bundles, 5-10 in number, surrounded the pith in the form of a ring.

5. The bulk of the primary wood was centripetal, but centrifugal xylem was also well developed the primary xylem, therefore, had mesarch structure.

6. Secondary wood formed a continuous ring round the primary xylem, while at places was interrupted by leaf traces.

7. It consisted of large tracheids with multiseriate bordered pits on radial walls along with a large number of broad, many celled high, medullary rays.

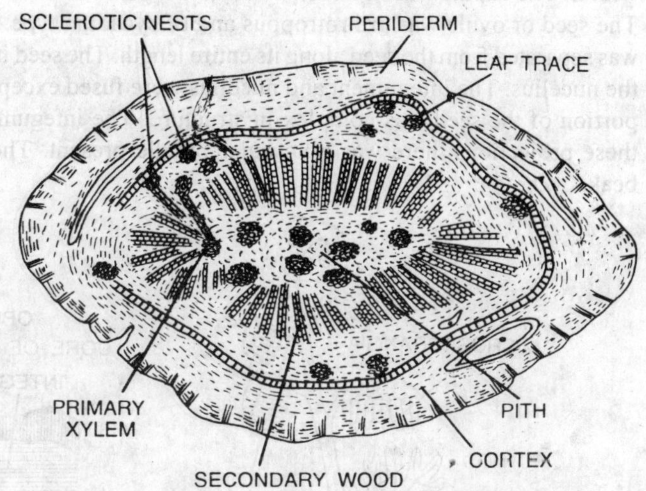

Fig. 3.2. *Lyginopteris oldhamia (Calymatotheca hoeninghausi).* T.S. of stem showing well develoepd secondary wood and leaf traces.

8. Secondary wood on its outer side was surrounded by phloem and pericycle.

9. Phellogen probably developed from the outer layers of pericycle and produced the periderm.

10. The pericycle like the pith, possessed a large number of sclerotic cells.

Reproductive structure. Some of these palaeozoic leaves bore microsporangia on them. The fertile pinnules were more or less peltate in form and on their underside they bore usually six sporangia. These sporangia are usually bilocular. Such a type has been described as *Crossotheca* type. The microspores seem to have formed a male prothallus. The sperms seem to have been like those of present day cycads.

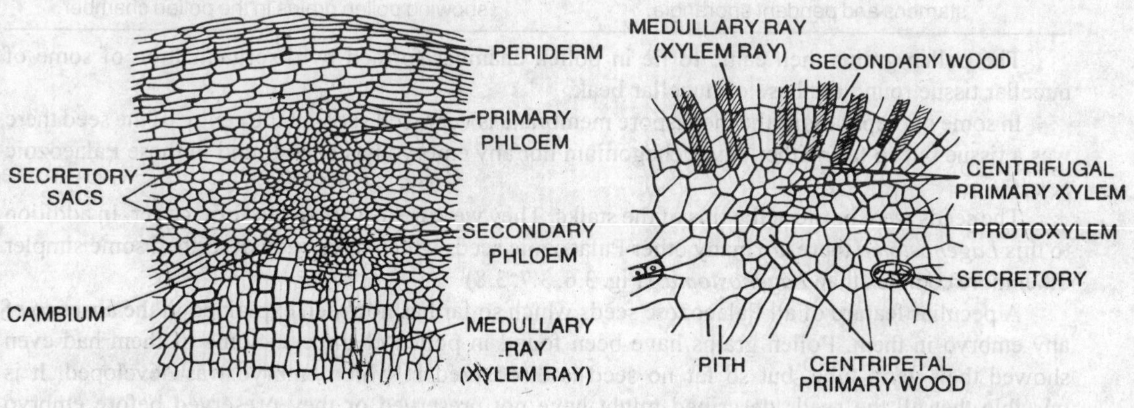

Fig. 3.3. *Lyginopteris Oldhamia.* A part of T.S. of stem showing the outer portion of the stele.

Fig. 3.4. *Lyginopteris oldhamia.* A part of T.S. of stem showing primary and secondary xylem, medullary rays and pith.

Seed. The best known seed has been described under the name *Lagenostoma.* These seeds were small in size, only about 1 /4" but they were highly organized. It was barrel shaped and whole seed enclosed in cupule. This cupule opened out when seed was mature.

Each seed was borne at the tip of stalk. The cupule rose from the base of the seed but not fused with it. The cupule was in three main lobes. These lobes were divided in the upper parts of the seeds. The seed or ovule was orthrotropous and of cycadian type. It was radially symmetrical. The cupule was separated from the seed along its entire length. The seed itself had an integument which surrounded the nucellus. The integument and nucellus were fused except at the top. The integument in the upper portion of the seed was complex in structure. The integument formed nine projections. In each of these projections there was a vascular bundle present. These projections surrounded the nucellar beak.

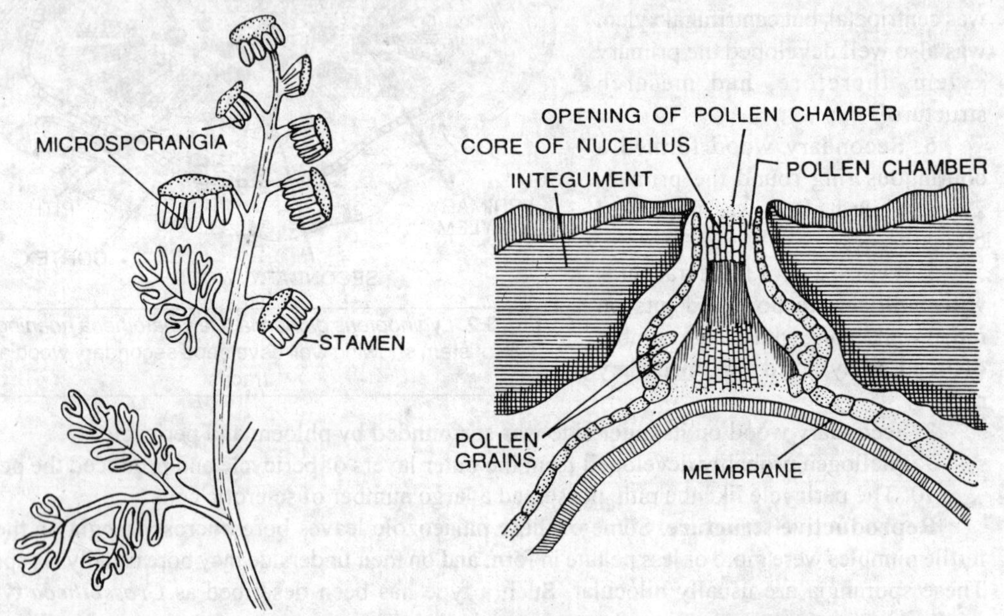

Fig. 3.5. *Crossotheca* sp. The male reproductive structures of *Lyginopteris oldhamia* with few stamens and pendant sporangia.

Fig. 3.6. *Lagenostoma lomaxi.* L.S. through the apex of the seed of *Lyginopteris oldhamia* showing pollen grains in the pollen chamber.

The pollen grains then came to lie in pollen chamber formed by disorganization of some of nucellar tissue round the base of nucellar beak.

In some of preparations the megaspore membrane is very well seen. In the centre of the seed there was a tissue but so far neither any archegonium nor any embryo has been found in these Palaeozoic seeds.

The seeds were borne at the tips of the stalks. They were not organized to form cover. In addition to this *Lagenostoma* there are many other Palaeozoic seeds which have been described some simpler other more complex than *Lagenostoma.* (Fig. 3.6, 3.7, 3.8)

A peculiar feature of all Palaeozoic seeds which so far has not been explained in the absence of any embryo in them. Pollen grains have been found in pollen chambers. Some of them had even showed their germ tube, but so far no seed is discovered in which embryo was developed. It is possible that all the seeds described might have not preserved or they preserved before embryo formation.

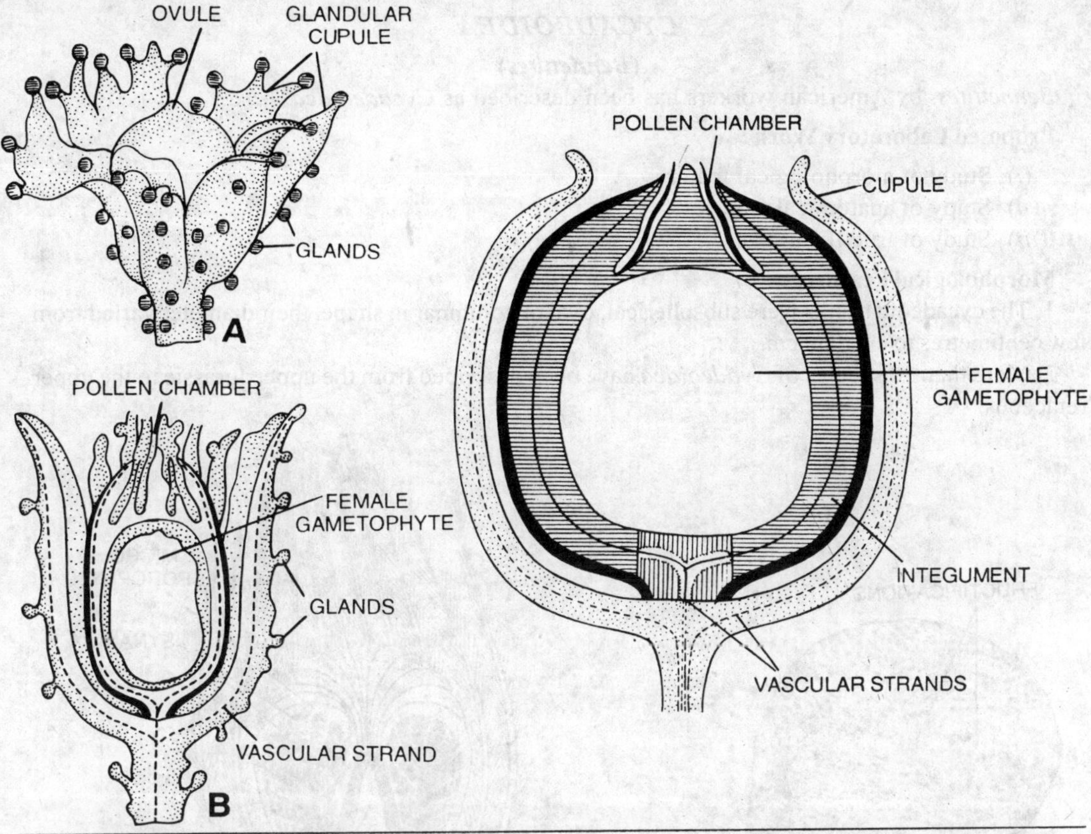

Fig. 3.7. *Lagenostoma lomaxi.* A, the seed of *Lyginopteris oldhamia* enclosed in a glandular cupule; B, L.S. of seed showing details of cupule.

Fig. 3.8. *Lagenostoma lomaxi.* Longitudinal section of the ovule with the investing cupule.

Identification and Systematic Position :

Gymnosperms :

(*i*) Trees or shrubs usually resinous.
(*ii*) Ovules naked, not enclosed in an ovary.
(*iii*) Flowers unisexual, rarely bisexual.
(*iv*) Leaves needle shaped, linear, pinnate, rarely fan-shaped or oblong elliptic, mostly ever green.

Pteridospermales (Cycadofilicales) :

(*i*) Fossil plants first appeared in Upper Devonian; they were common in Carboniferous and extended into Permian strata.
(*ii*) Tree or small plants with fern-like leaves.
(*iii*) Sporangia borne on frond-like leaves never formed a cone.

Lyginopteris (Calymatotheca) :

(*i*) Primary structure was ectophloic siphonostele with large pith round which a number of primary mesarch bundles.
(*ii*) Older plants showed normal secondary growth.
(*iii*) Normally primary wood was centripetal.
(*iv*) Secondary wood was interrupted by leaf traces.

CYCADEOIDEA

(*Bennettites*)

Bennettites, by American workers has been described as *Cycadeoidea.*

Proposed Laboratory Work :

(*i*) Study of morphological features.
(*ii*) Study of anatomical features.
(*iii*) Study of fructifications.

Morphological Features :

1. The cycadeoid trunks were subspherical, oval or columnar in shape, their diameter varied from a few centimetres to even 60 cm.

2. More than 30 species of *Cyadeoidea* have been described from the upper Jurassic to the upper Cretaceous.

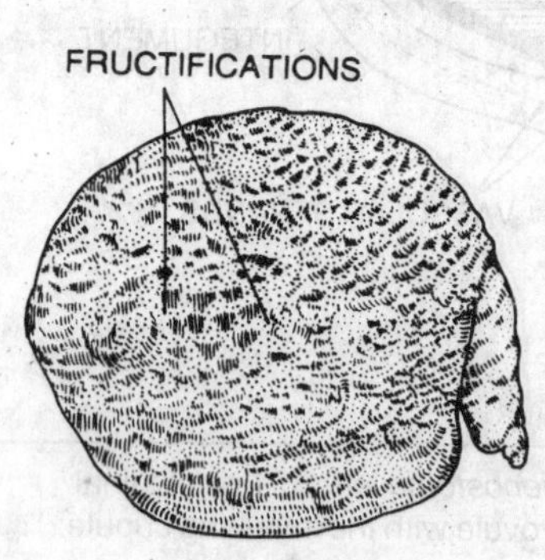

Fig. 3.9. *Cycadeoidea* sp. Lateral view of an unbranched trunk.

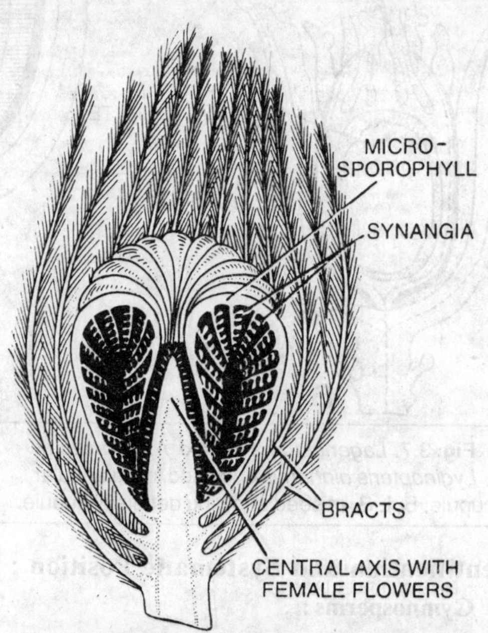

Fig. 3.10. *Cycadeoidea* sp. Young strobilus showing unexpanded microsporophylls covered with bracts.

3. Some of them attained a height of 3.0 to 3.6. meters.

4. In *Cycadeoidea* the stem was un-branched with a single crown of pinnate leaves at the tops, but some species had branched stem with a multiple crown.

5. In some cases the stem was tuberous.

6. In all cases the stem was covered up by persistent leaf bases as we find in *Cycas.*

Anatomical Features :

1. The stem possessed centrally situated large, parenchymatous pith which was surrounded by a thin zone of xylem.

2. The xylem cylinder was punctuated by radially extending, parenchymatous, medullary rays.

3. The protoxylem was endarch and the metaxylem was situated towards the cortex.

4. The thick cortex possessed a number of gum canals and leaf traces.

5. There was small amount of secondary growth.

6. The xylem had scalariform thickenings, pitted thickenings rather rare.

Reproductive Structure (Fructifications) :

1. The fructification was bisporangiate.

2. The strobili were developed in the upper part of the plant in large numbers.

3. The whole of the strobilus and the bases of leaves were covered up by large sized scales; strobili so were axillary and borne at the tip of axillary stalk.

4. Each strobilus was made up of a number of heavy imbricate reduced leaves or bracts; these bracts completely surrounded the strobilus. (Fig. 3.10.)

5. The second whorl was made up of a number of leaf like sporophylls, all of which were united at the base to form a cup-shaped structure round the central part of strobilus.

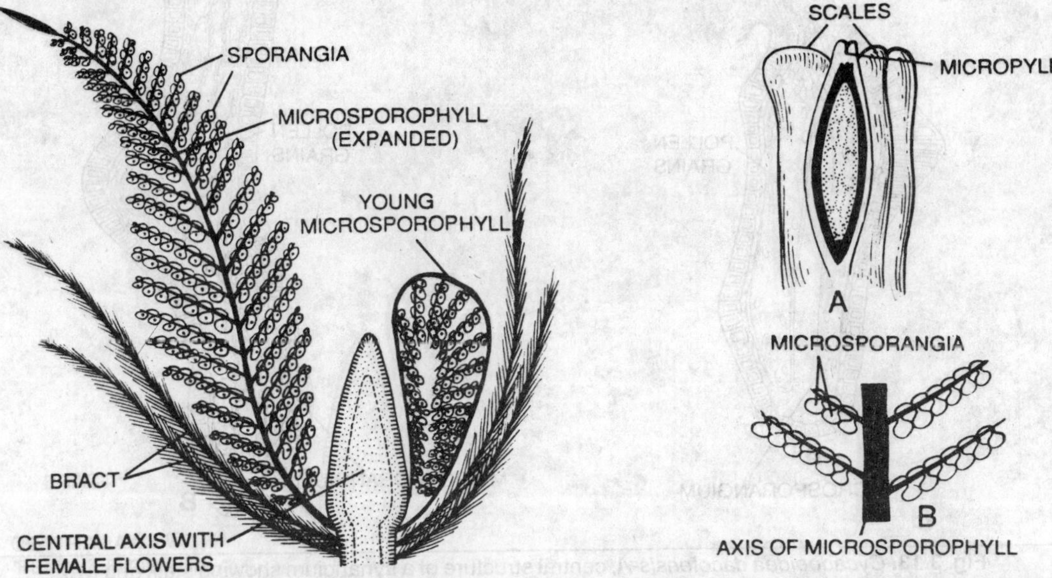

Fig. 3.11. *Cycadeoidea dacotensis.* Apical portion with expanded and curved microsporophylls; the conical central axis possesses female reproductive structures.

Fig. 3.12. *Cycadeoidea* sp. A, L.S. of seed with micropyle above, the seed remains surrounded by scales on either side; B, axis of microsporophyll with microsporangia.

6. The third central portion was hemispherical or dome-shaped in appearance bearing ovules on the stalks; ovule was orthrotropous and terminal.

7. The central part was made up of a number of ovulate sporophylls; these megasporophylls were simply stalked; at the tip of the stalk was developed an ovule; some stalks were sterile and their tips were flattened.

8. The microsporophylls or the stamens were 10 or 20 in number.

9. The microphylls or stamens were all united at the base and each stamen was pinnate in form and on each stamen there were about twenty slender pinnae on either side; under the pinnae were developed two rows of fused sporangia or synangium had a short stalk and two pollen sacs in it; so each stamen was pinnate in structure.

Identification and Systematic Position

Gymnosperms :

(*i*) Tress or shrubs; usually resinous.

(*ii*) Ovules naked, not enclosed in an ovary.

(*iii*) Flowers unisexual rarely bisexual.

(*iv*) Leaves needle-shaped, linear, pinnate, rarely fan-shaped or oblong elliptic, mostly green.

Cycadeoidales (Bennettitales) :

(*i*) Fossil plants of Palaezoic age.

(*ii*) Trees with stems covered with an armour of persistent leaf bases.

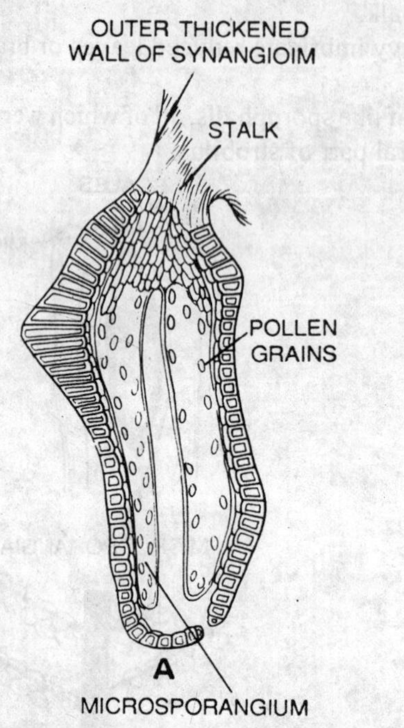

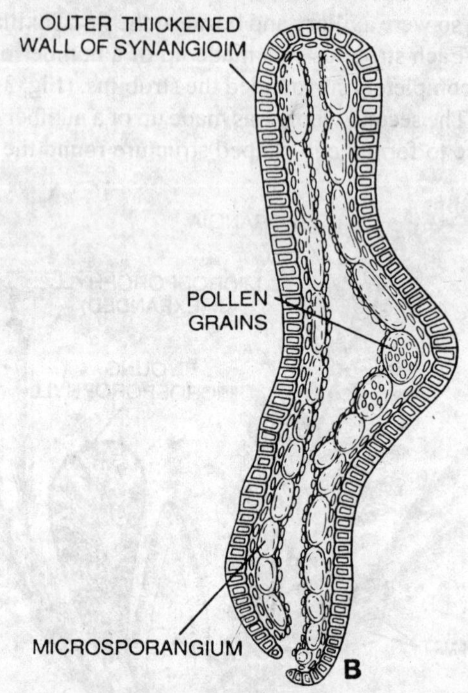

Fig. 3.13. *Cycadeoidea dacotensis-A,* central structure of a synangium showing stalk and two microsporangia in longitudinal section; B, T.S. of the synangium showing thickened outer wall and inner parenchymatous layer.

(*iii*) Male sporophylls formed a loose crown.

(*iv*) Female sporophylls found in a dome-shaped cone-like structure, no longer leaf-like.

***Cycadeoidea (Bennettites)* :**

(*i*) Stem was unbranched with a single crown of pinnate leaves at the top; in some stem was tuberous.

(*ii*) Fructification was bisporangiate.

(*iii*) The microsporophylls were united at the base to form a cup-like structure round the central part of strobilus.

(*iv*) The central female part was dome-shaped bearing ovules on the stalks.

(*v*) Ovule was orthrotropous and terminal.

WILLIAMSONIA

(*Williamsonia sewardiana* Sahni)

Systematic Position. Gymnosperms

Class. Cycadopsida

Order. Cycadeoideales

Family. Williamsoniaceae

Genus. *Williamsonia*

The second type of Cycadeoideales (Bennettitales) are known as Williamsonias cycads. This group of plants was more ancient than *Cycadeoidea* (*Bennettites*). The group differs both from *Cycadeoidea* and cycads in some important features, in the stem anatomy and also in the form and structure of fructification.

An Indian type *Williamsonia sewardiana* Sahni has been described from the Jurrasic period. It was found in a silicified condition in Rajmahal Hills (Bihar) which is made up of upper Gondwana rocks.

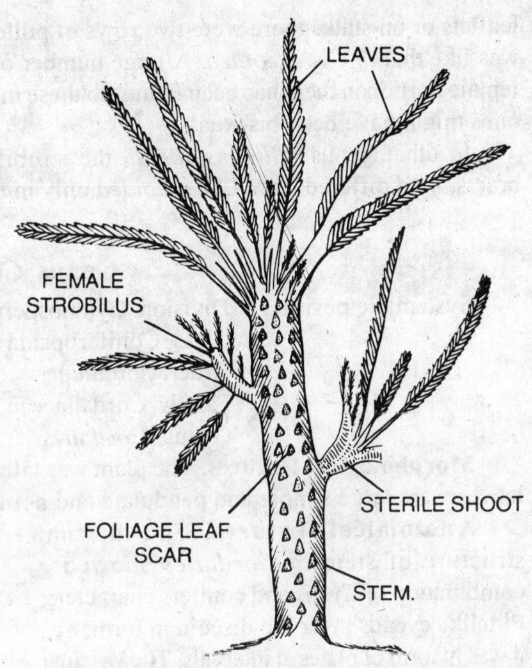

Fig. 3.14. *Williamsonia sewardiana* Sahni. Reconstruction showing a female strobilus and a sterile shoot.

The stem was erect; cylindrical and branched. The branches were covered up by scales and also the leaf bases.

The stem anatomy of this type was more like those of conifers. The pith, however, was large, dense compact mass of xylem and phloem and the cortex was comparatively narrow.

The strobili were borne on short branched lateral shoots. They differ from those of *Cycadeoidea* in that they were monosporangiate. In this *Williamsonia sewardiana* only the female has so far been described but Dr. Sahni himself was of opinion that this Indian form might have been bisporangiate. The specimen got separated from the strobilus. The structure of female portion was practically like that of *Cycadeoidea (Bennettites)*. The ovules were borne on short stalks which has interstaminal scales in between. The ovule structure was again that of *Cycadeoidea (Bennettites)*.

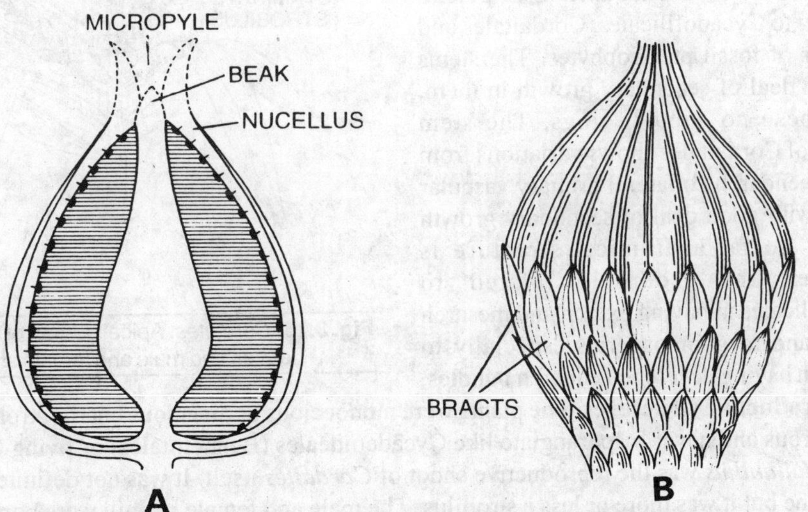

Fig. 3.15. *Williamsonia gigas*. A, V.S. of ovuliferous flower; B, floral bud.

The male strobilus rather which has been described in some other species of *Williamsonia* had a number of stamens which fused together to form a cup or disc shaped structure. The free parts of stamens had two rows of slender leaflets were absent and only stalks were present. So either on leaflets or on stalks there were two rows of pollen sacs. This way, the male portion of *Williamsonia* was like that *of Cycadeoidea.* A large number of male strobili have been described, but no trace of female portion in them has been found, so these male strobili were evidently unisexual while the female ones might have been bisexual.

In other genus *Williamsoniella,* the strobilus was bisexual but round it there were no basal bracts, so it differed from *Cycadeoidea* only in the absence of bracts,

Genus *CORDAITES*

Systematic position : Division. Gymnospermae
Class. Coniferopsida
Order. Cordaitales
Family. Cordaitaceae
Genus. *Cordaites.*

Morphological features. The plant was tall and slender, it had a crown of branches near the top, leaves were large simple and pendulate and not found on any living gymnosperms.

Anatomical features. The internal structure of stem in *Cordaites* showed a combination of *Cycas* and conifers characters. Pith like cycads layer but discoid in form, *i.e.*, it was in form of plates at intervals. The vascular cylinder was like those of conifers. It was made up of thick collateral endarch primary bundles which sometimes however, seem to have been mesarch as in *Mesoxylon.* There was good deal of normal secondary growth. Secondary xylem was made up of living pitted tracheids with pits on radial walls. In fact it is clear that majority of plants found in Carboniferous period belonging to Cycadofilicales, Cordaitales and a number of fossil pteridophytes. The stems had good deal of secondary growth in them, but in these no annular rings. The stem anatomy of Cordaitales shows variations from exarch to endarch collateral primary vascular bundles with good deal of secondary growth in stem. So far anatomical structure is concerned the group is related to Cycadofilicales in having exarch and mesarch bundles and to gymnosperms especially to conifers in having developed endarch bundles.

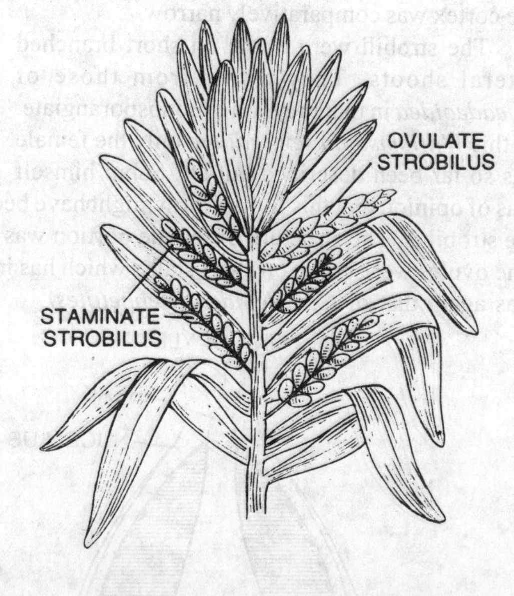

Fig. 3.16. *Cordaites.* Apical portion of the stem with leaves and male and female strobili.

Reproductive structures. The plants were monoecious or dioecious but the strobili were always monosporous and never bisporangiate like Cycadeoideales (Bennettitales) or living Gnetales.

Cordaitanthus was the reproductive shoot of *Cordaites* itself. It was not definitely organized to form a cone but it was more or less a strobilus. The male and female strobili were borne separately in lateral sides of short simple axis. The strobili were enclosed when young by bracts so outwardly they could not be distinguished unless sections were cut and examined. Both were usually of small size.

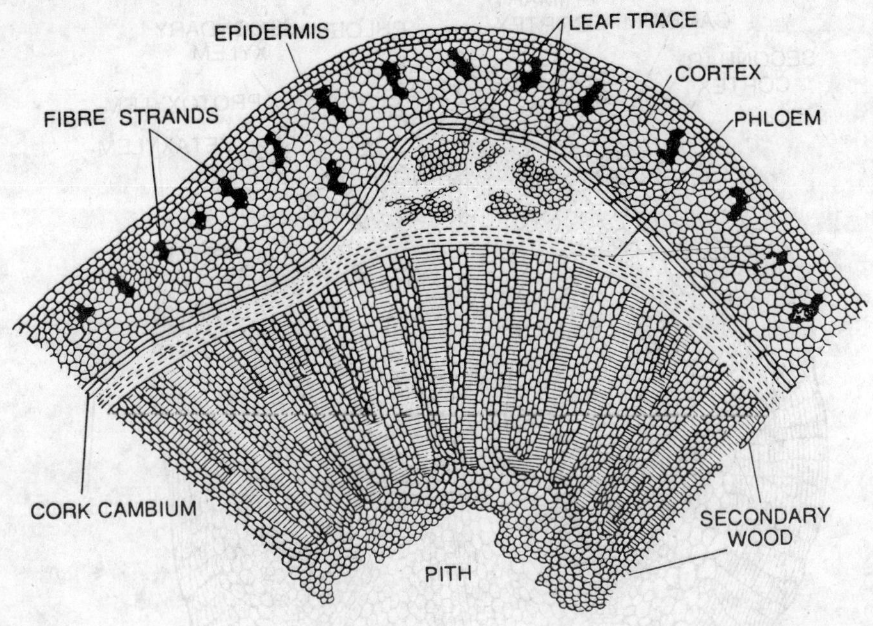

Fig. 3.17. *Cordaites.* Portion of transverse section of stem showing well developed secondary wood.

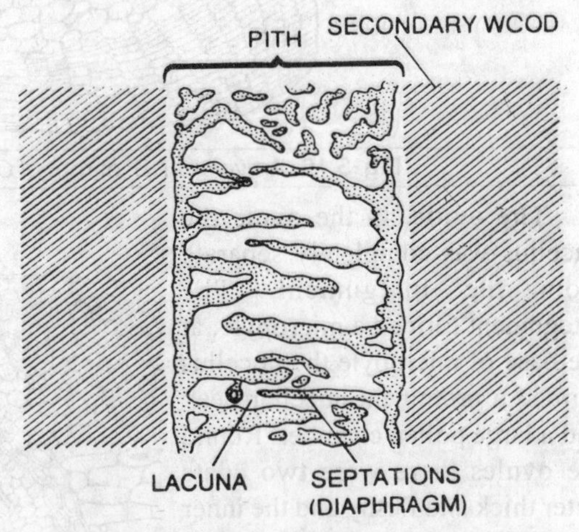

Fig. 3.18. Cordaites. R.L.S. of stem showing secondary wood and discoid pith.

Male strobilus. The male strobilus had a thick axis bearing spirally arranged bracts with stamens on them, the stamens themselves were either solitary or grouped near the apex and in between the stamens there were sterile bracts present. These bracts might have been sterile microsporophylls. Each individual stamen was peculiar in form, in that it had a cluster of three to six terminal sporangia similar types of stamens have also sometimes described belonging to Cycadofilicales, but the important difference was that at the tips were borne synangia and separate or individual sporangia. If in this male catkin of *Cordaites* there were no sterile bracts the structure would by very much like the staminate strobilus *of Ginkgo* but there is a very important difference and that in the *Cordaitanthus* the sporangia were terminal while in *Ginkgo* they were pendant and only two in number. In fact the morphology of this male strobilus *of Cordaites* is not quite clear. Different interpretations are put on male catkin *of Cordaites.* Some think that whole of strobilus acting as single male flower in which there are large number of stamens, the stalk being the filamentous bearing a number of pollen sacs were simply sterile filaments. Other workers described this male catkin as inflorescence, each catkin bearing a flower itself, the filament is stalk of flower, the pollen sacs the stamens.

Female strobilus. The female , strobilus when young was enclosed by bracts. It had a thick conical axis bearing a number of spirally arranged bracts. In the axils of some of these bracts there were dwarf shoots present. These dwarf shoots in turn had minute bracts. On the tip of dwarf shoot there was a terminal ovule.

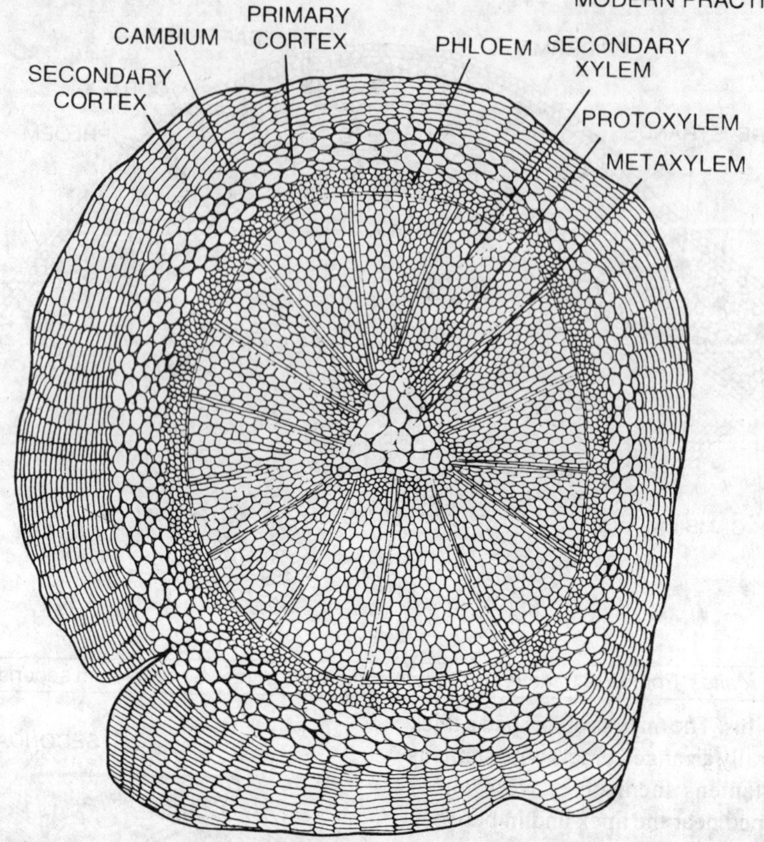

Fig. 3.19. *Amyelon.* T.S. of root *of Cardaites* showing various structures.

The ovule. In the ovule the nucellus was completely separate from the integument. The integument formed a micropyle; at the base of micropyle the nucellus formed a prominent nucellar beak and a large pollen chamber. Round the ovules there were two coats outer thick and fleshy and the inner one delicate in young ovule but hard in older ovules. Both these coats were separate below but more or less united above. So these coats may be interpreted as two separate integuments which are formed at upper part or a case of single integument which differentiated into three coats one of which not preserved.

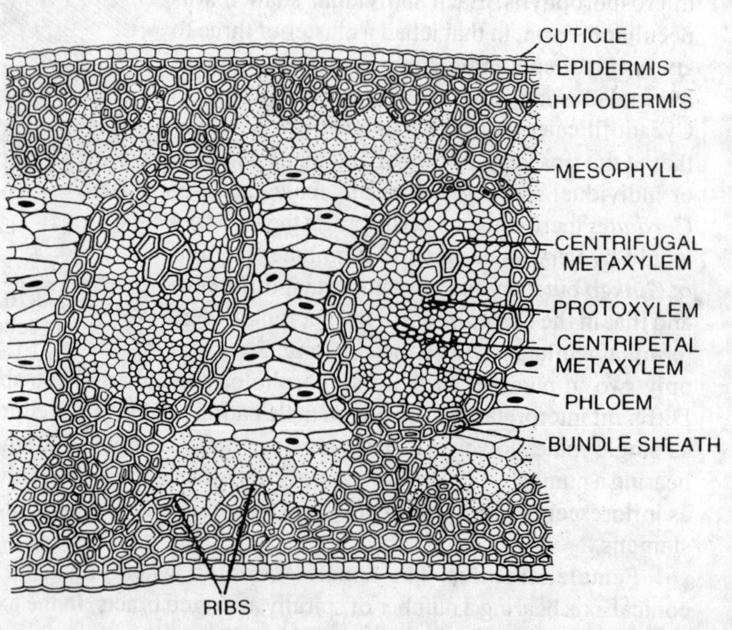

Fig. 3.20. *Cordaites angulostriatus.* V.S. of leaf.

The female strobilus is distinctly compound in form as compared to male strobilus. The ovule bearing stalks were distinctly axillary in position just like those of present day conifers. In Cycadofilicales, Cycadeoideales (Bennettitales) and the living cycads the ovule bearing structures are not axillary in position and the ovules in these groups were borne on leaves while in Cordaiteles and the Coniferales the ovules are borne on stem structure. Dr. Sahni according to the position of ovules recognized two groups.

1. Phyllosperms and 2. Stachysperms.

1. Phyllosperms. The ovules borne on leaves as seen in pteridosperms and *Cycas*.

2. Stachysperms. The ovules as seen in Cordaitales, *Ginkgo* and the Coniferales.

A large number of detached seeds have been described from Palaeozoic times and when they separated from branches they can not definitely be assigned to Cycadofilicales and to Cordaitales. Generally according to Dr. Sahni those belonging to Cordaitales were flat and described as platysperms and more or less heart shaped in appearance and no embryo in them like those Cycadofilicales.

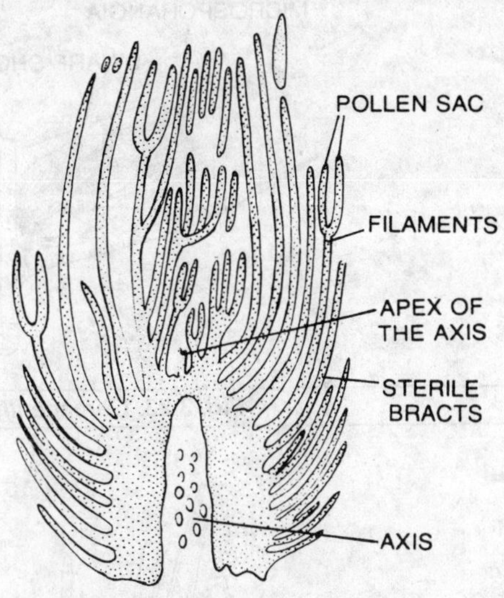

Fig. 3.21. *Cordaitanthus.* The staminate strobilus of *Cordaites*, showing sterile bracts and stalked stamens.

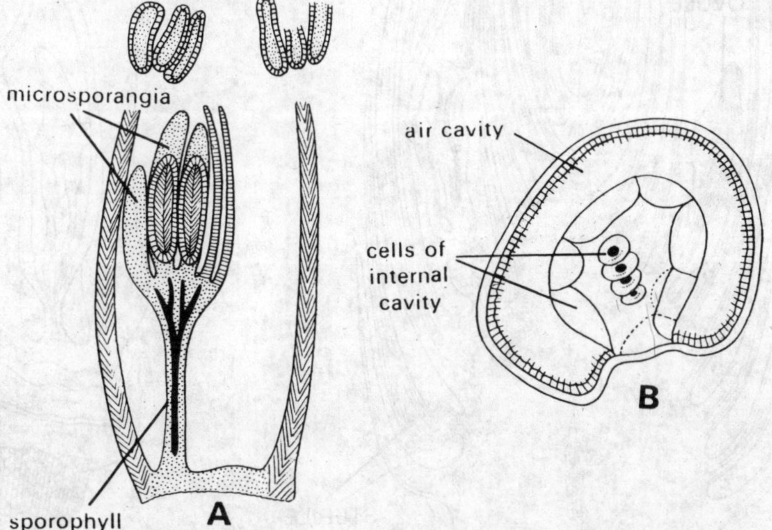

Fig. 3.22. *Cordaitanthus.* A, microsporophylls and microsporangia; B. pollen grain.

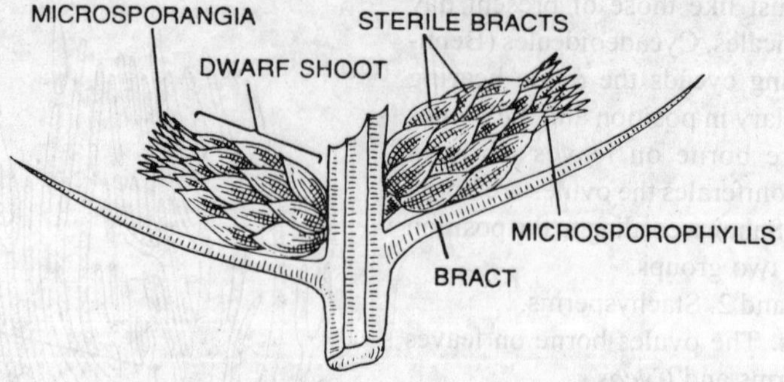

Fig. 3.23. *Cordaitanthus.* Two male strobili of *Cordaites.*

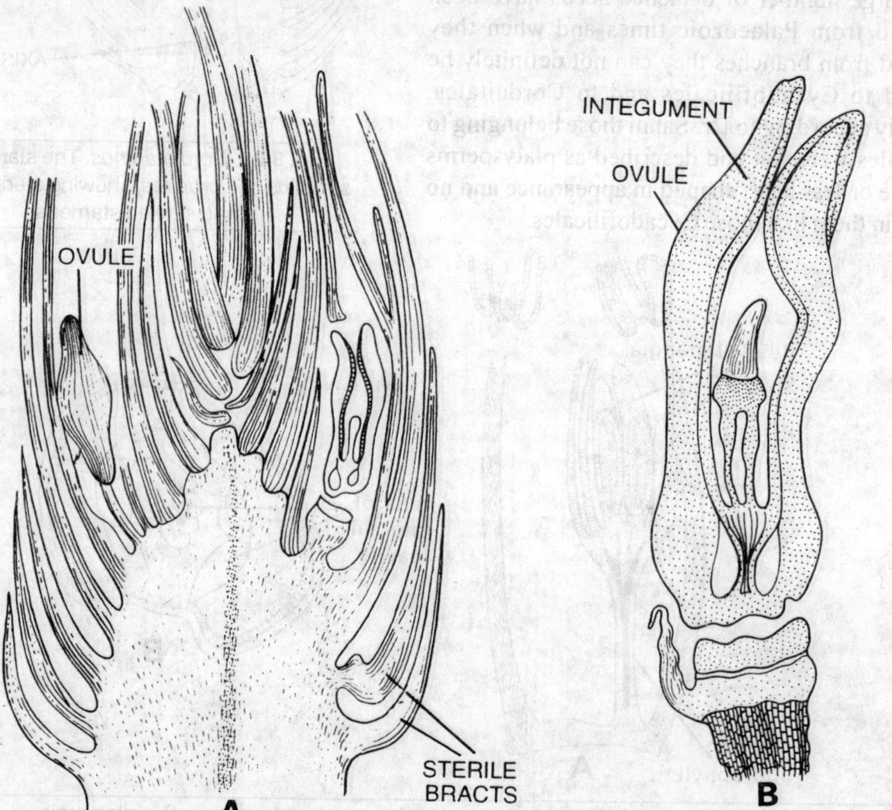

Fig. 3.24. *Cordaitanthus.* The female reproductive organs of *Cordaites.* A, longitudinal section of female strobilus; B, longitudinal section of an ovule.

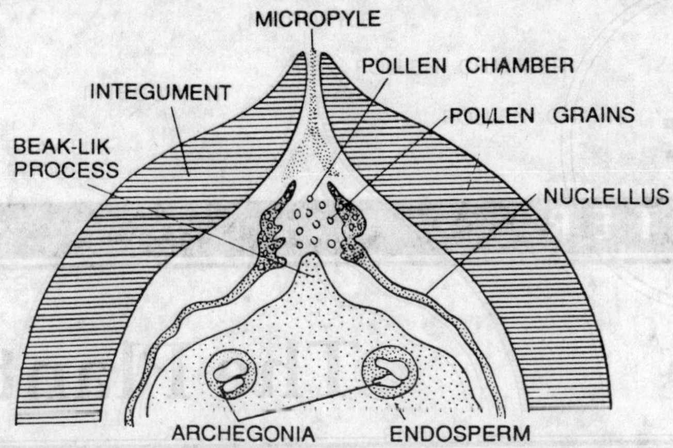

Fig. 3.25. *Cycadinocarpus.* Longitudinal section of the apical portion of a mature ovule showing parts and pollen grains within pollen chamber.

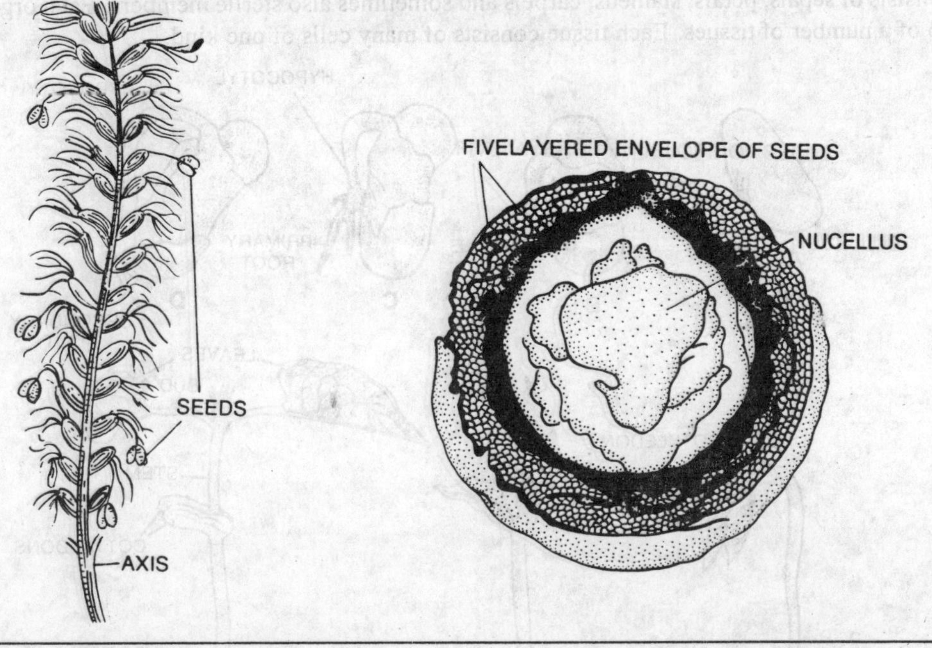

Fig. 3.26. *Cordaitanthus.* A portion of axis bearing seeds.

Fig. 3.27. *Cardiocarpus.* The seed of *Cordaites* with five layered envelope.

The Plant Body

THE PLANT BODY AND ITS DEVELOPMENT

The plant body consists of a number of organs, *i.e.*, root, stem, leaf and flower. The flower consists of sepals, petals, stamens, carpels and sometimes also sterile members. Each organ, is made up of a number of tissues. Each tissue consists of many cells of one kind.

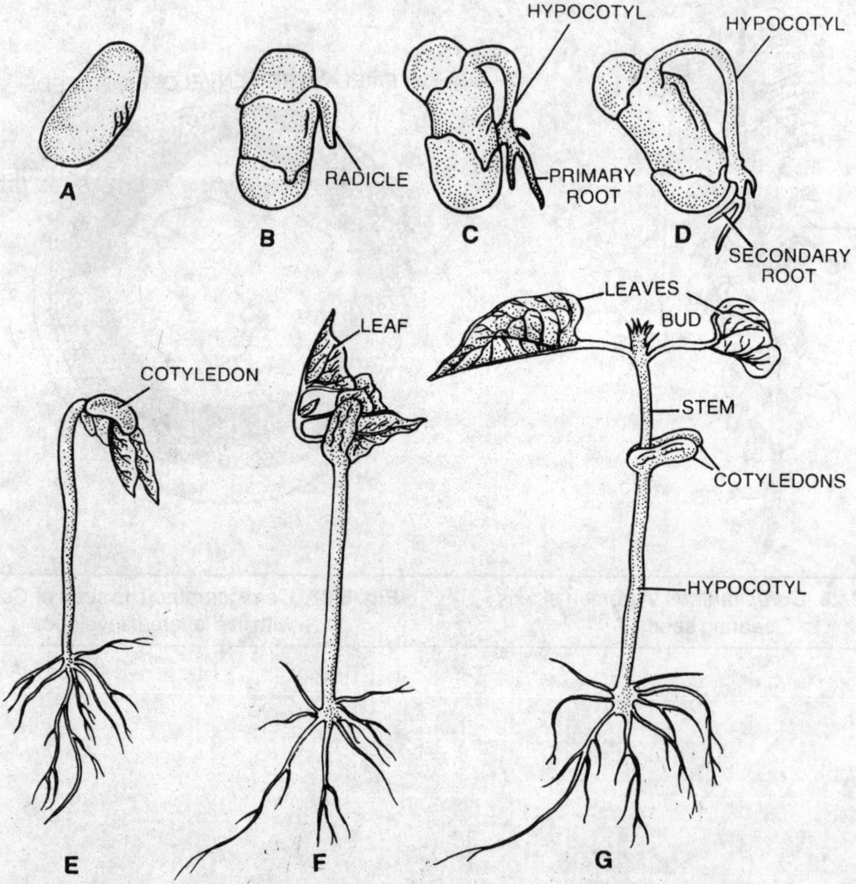

Fig. 4.1. Different stages in the germination of the seed leading to the formation of young seedling (A-G); G, seedling with well developed roots, two young leaves, hypocotyl, cotyledons, stem and young apical bud.

The complex multicellular body of the seed plant is a result of evolutionary specialization of long duration. This specialization has given rise to the establishment of morphological and physiological differences between the various parts of the plant body and also caused the development of the concept *of plant organs.*

The organization of the plant body of the oldest known land plants, the Psilophytales, suggests that the differentiation of the vegetative plant into leaf, stem and root is a result of evolutionary development from an originally simple axial structure (Arnold, 1947; Eames, 1936).

As regards the morphologic nature of the flower it is thought that the flower is homologous with a shoot and the floral parts with leaves.

Fundamental parts of the plant body. The axis, consists of two parts — that portion which is normally aerial is know as the *stem*, and the portion which is subterranean is called the *root.* There are three types of appendages arising from the axis. 1. *Leaves*—The strands of vascular tissue pass through the leaves. The leaves are characteristic of the stem and do not occur on the root. The leaves are found to be arranged on the stem in a definite manner, and bear an intimate structural relation to the skeleton of the axis. The leaf is looked upon as the lateral expansion of the stem, continuous with it. All fundamental parts of the stem are concerned with the formation of the leaf. 2. *Emergences*—In the appendages of the second rank only the outermost layers of stem, the cortex and the epidermis, are usually present which are known as emergences. The prickles of the rose make a good example of it. 3. *Hairs*—The appendages of the third rank are hairs. These are projections of the outermost layer of the cells. The emergences and hairs occur on both axis and leaves, usually without definite arrangement.

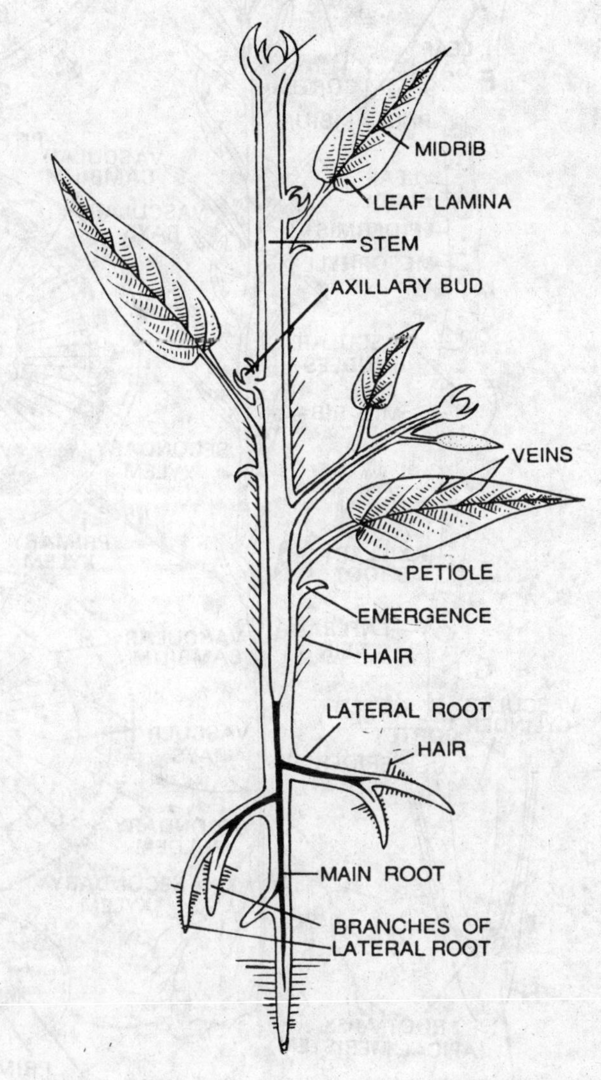

Fig. 4.2. The plant body, showing fundamental parts.

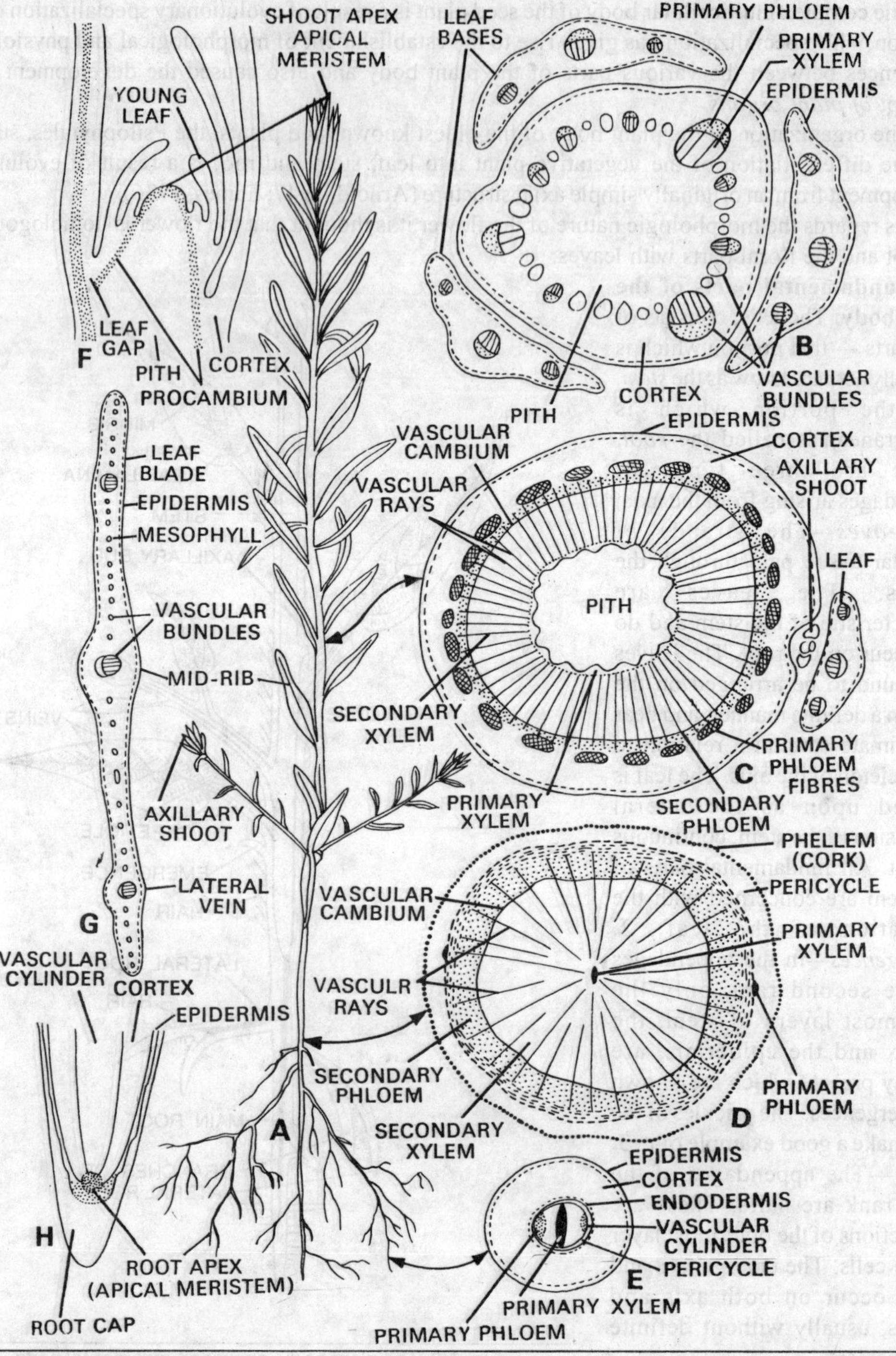

Fig. 4.3. Organization of a vascular plant. A, habit sketch of linseed plant (*Linum usitatissimum*) in vegetative state; B-C, transverse sections of stem; D-E, transverse sections of root; F, L.S. of shoot apex with apical meristem and developing leaves; G, transection of leaf lamina; H, L.S. of root apex with apical meristem and other root regions.

STOMATA

The stomata are minute pores which occur in the epidermis of the plants. Each stoma remains surrounded by two kidney or bean shaped epidermal cells the *guard cells.* The stomata may occur on any part of a plant except the roots. The epidermal cells bordering the guard cells are called *accessory cells* or *subsidiary cells.* Generally the term stoma is applied to the stomatal opening and the guard cells. The guard cells are living and contain chloroplasts in them. They also contain a larger proportion of protoplasm than other epidermal cells. Usually in the leaves of dicotyledons the stomata remain scattered whereas in the leaves of monocotyledons they are arranged in parallel rows. The number of stomata may also range on the surface of a single leaf from a few thousand to hundreds of thousands per square centimetre. Stomata occur on both upper and lower surfaces of leaf, but especially they are confined to the lower surface. In floating leaves stomata are confined only on the upper surface of the leaf. Under normal conditions the stomata remain closed in the absence of light or in night or remain open in the presence of light or in day time. Structurally the stomata may be of different types. The four main types of stomata which occur in dicotyledons are known as 1. Ranunculaceous or anomocytic type — type A; 2. Cruciferous or anisocytic — type B; 3. Caryophyllaceous or diacytic — type C; 4. Rubiaceous or paracytic— type D. the fifth type of stomata is commonly found in monocotyledons are known as —gramineous type.

1. Ranunculaceous or anomocytic. Type A — (*Anomocytic* = irregular celled). In this type the stoma remains surrounded by a limited number of subsidiary cells which are quite alike the remaining epidermal cells. The accessory or subsidiary cells are five in number.

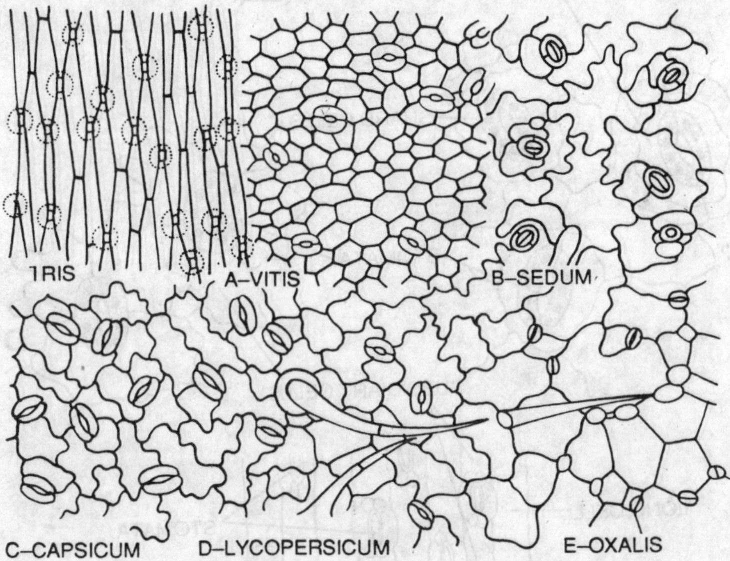

Fig. 4.4. *Stomata.* Surface views of abaxial leaf epidermis. Upper figure on left side of *Iris*, sunken stomata in longitudinal rows. A, dispersed stomata of *Vitis*; B, anisocytic stomata of *Sedum*; C, raised stomata of *Capsicum;* D, raised stomata of *Lycopersicon*; E, sunken stomata of *Oxalis*.

2. Cruciferous or anisocytic. Type B — (*Anisocytic* = unequal celled). In this type stoma remains surrounded by three accessory or subsidiary cells of which one is distinctly smaller than the other two.

3. Rubiaceous or paracytic. Type C — (*Paracytic* = parallel celled). In this type, the stoma remains surrounded by two subsidiary or accessory cells which are parallel to the long axis of the pore and guard cells.

4. Caryophyllaceous or diacytic. Type D—(*Diacytic* = cross celled)—In this type the stoma remains surrounded by a pair of subsidiary or accessory cells and whose common wall is at right angles to the guard cells.

Gramineous. The gramineous stoma possesses guard cells of which the middle portions are much narrower than the ends so that the cells appear in surface view like dump-bells. They are commonly found in Gramineae and Cyperaceae of monocotyledons.

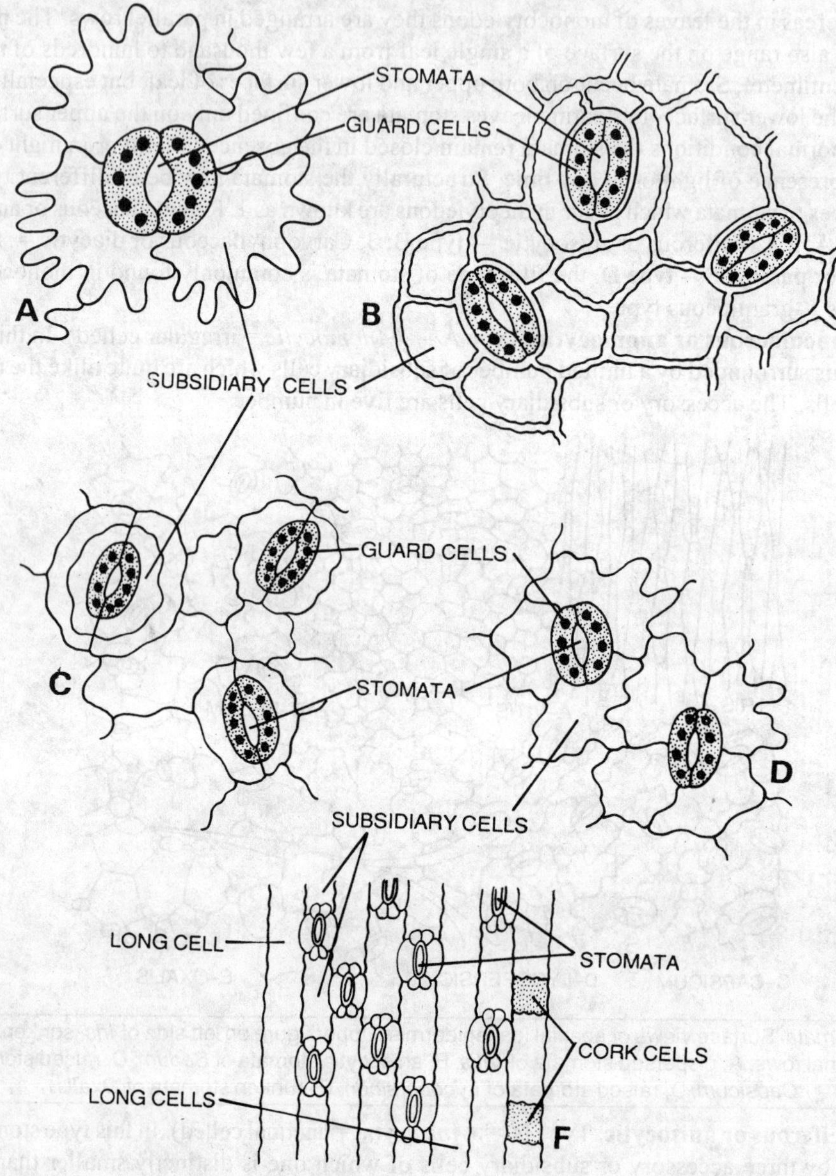

Fig. 4.5. Stomata—types of stomata. A, anomocytic or irregular celled type (ranunculaceous type); B, anisocytic or unequal celled type (cruciferous type); C, paracytic or parallel celled type (rubiaceous type); D, diacytic or cross-celled type (caryophyllaceous type); E, gramineous type.

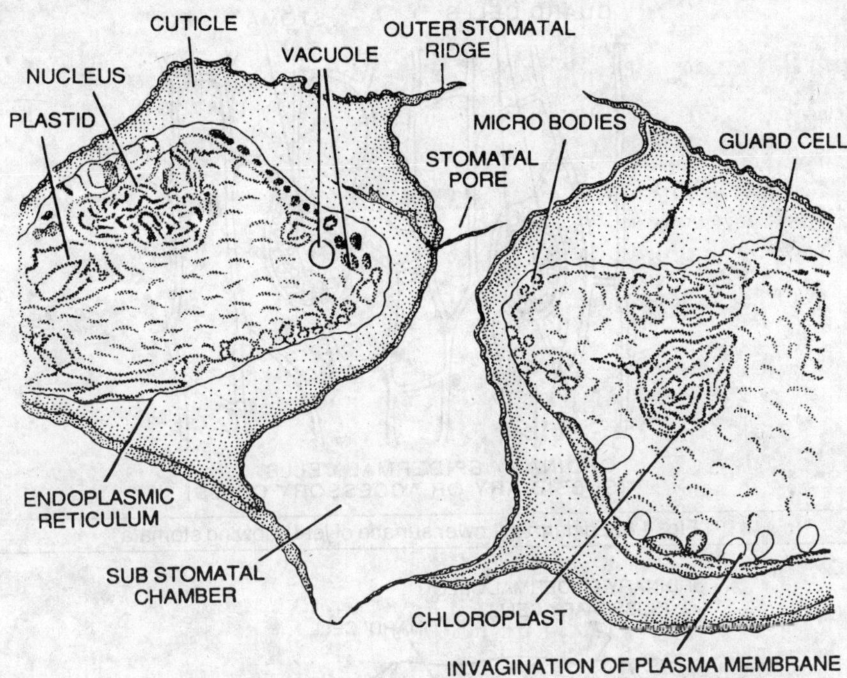

Fig. 4.6. Guard cells of *Vicia faba* as seen in electron microscope.

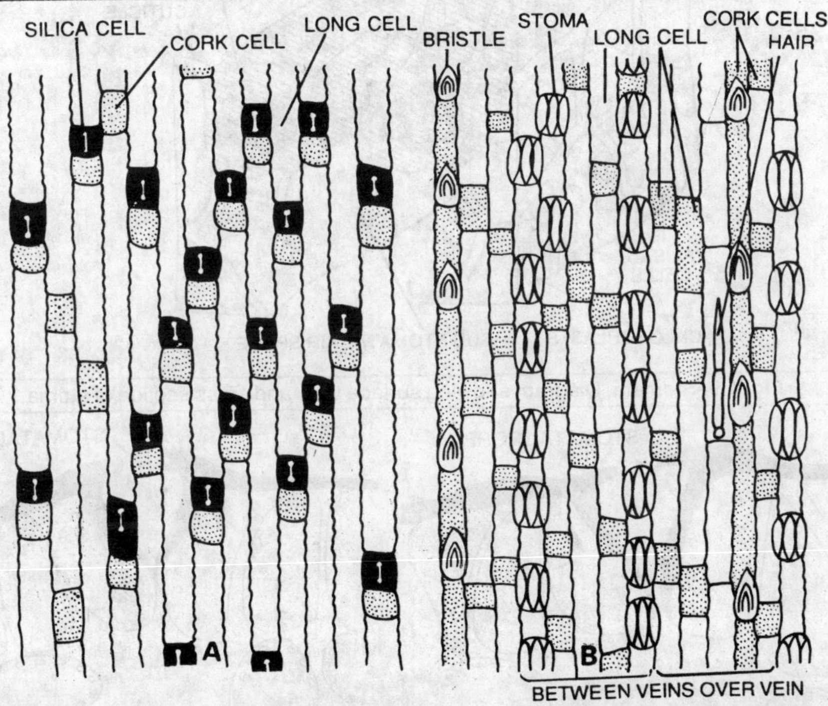

Fig. 4.7. Epidermis. A, epidermis of sugarcane stem showing alternation of long cells with pairs of short cells, the cork cells and silica cells; B, lower epidermis from leaf blade of sugarcane, showing distribution of stomata and their epidermal cells (After Artschwager).

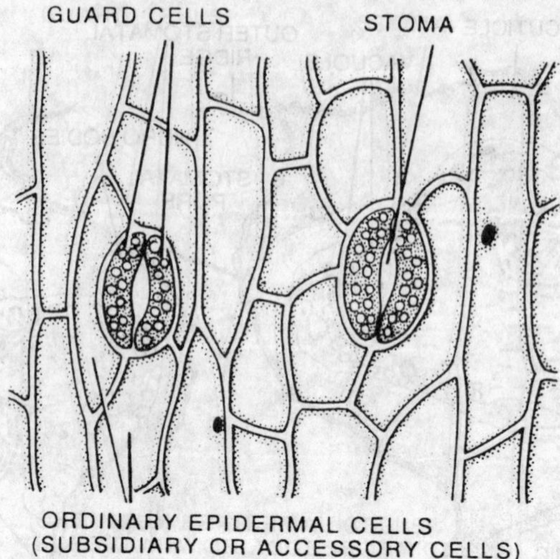

Fig. 4.8. Epidermis. Lower surface of leaf showing stomata.

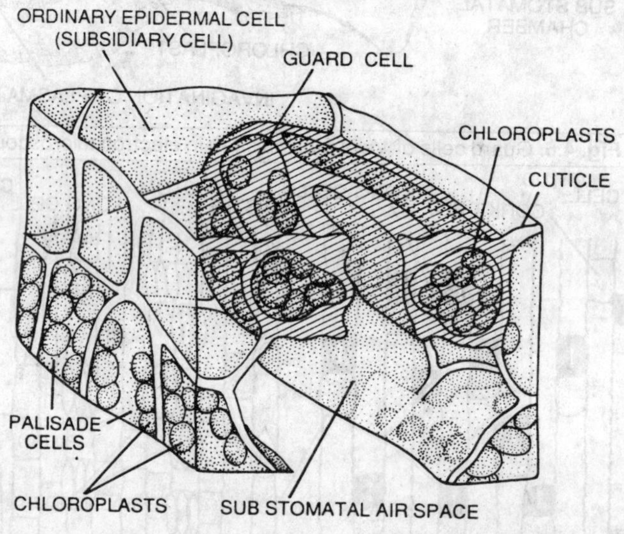

Fig. 4.9. Stomata. Diagram showing surface view and cross section of stoma.

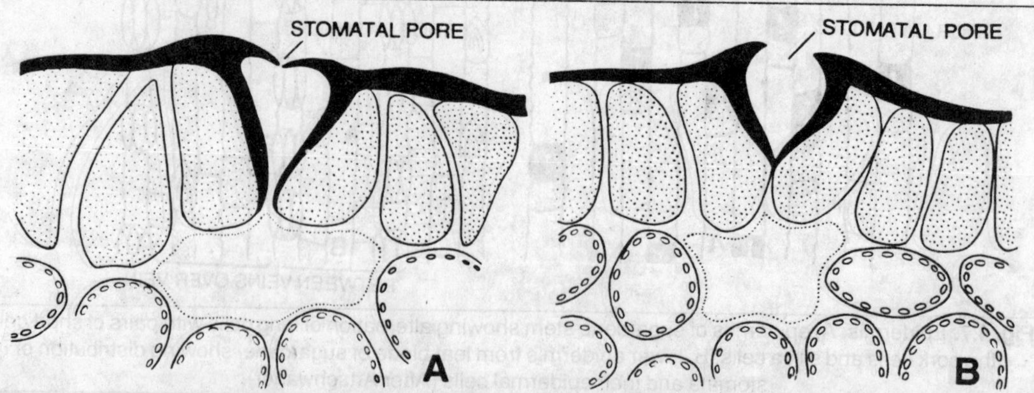

Fig. 4.10. Stomata. A—B, closed and open stomatal pores.

VEGETATIVE SHOOT APEX

The vegetative shoot apices vary in shape, size and cytohistologic structure, and in their relation to the lateral organs. The shoot apex of *Pinus* and other conifers are commonly narrow and conical in form. In *Cycas* (cycads) and *Ginkgo* they are usually broad and flat on the other hand the apical meristem of a grass and some other monocotyledons remains elevated above the youngest leaf primordium. In many dicotyledons the apical meristem rises above the primordia, and in other cases it appears to be sunken beneath them. The diameters of apices range from 90μ in some angiosperms to 3.5 mm in *Cycas revoluta* (Foster, 1949). The size and shape of the apex marked by change during the plant development.

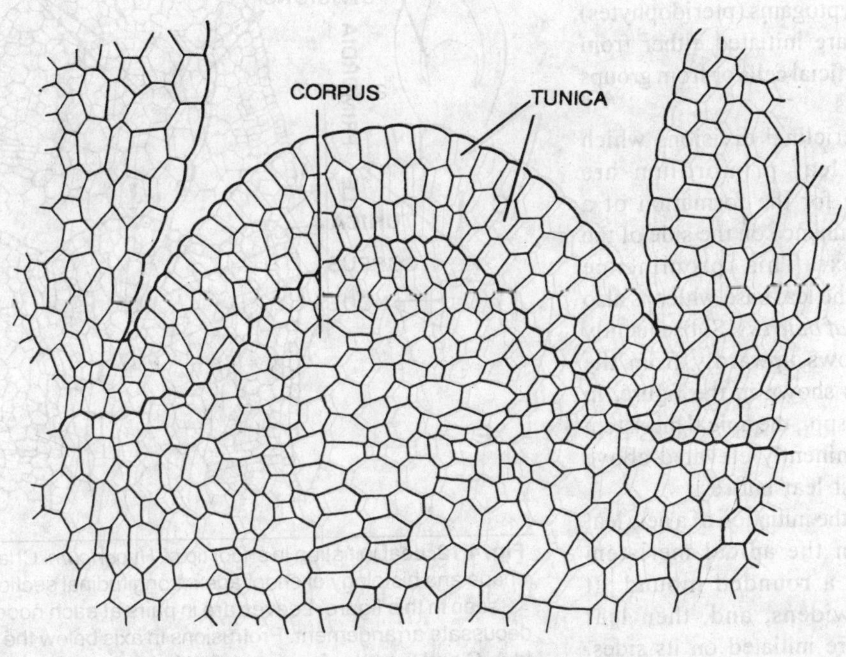

Fig. 4.11. Tunica and Corpus organization.

Angiosperms. There is *tunica-corpus organization* in the shoot apex of angiosperms. One to five layers tunica have been observed in the dicotyledons, and one to three-layered in the monocotyledons. However, tunica-corpus organization is not found in *Saccharum officinarum.* To draw a clear cut demarcation line in between tunica and corpus is not simple matter. In angiosperms, the number of parallel periclinal layers in the shoot apex may vary during the ontogeny of the plant body and under the influence of seasonal growth changes.

In the angiosperms the segregation of apical-meristem zones is more definite than in lower groups. There are two sets of initials, one above the other, which give rise to *tunica* and *corpus.* The tunica has no or only rare periclinal divisions and ranges in thickness from several layers to one with two or three layers probably most frequent. The number of layers in the tunica may vary even in an individual plant.

ORIGIN OF LEAVES

A leaf initiates by periclinal divisions in a small group of cells at the side of an apical meristem. In angiosperms, the tunica and the corpus are responsible for leaf initiation. In the dicotyledonous plants the periclinal divisions initiating the leaves occur, not in the surface layer, but in one or more layers beneath it. If the tunica is single-layered, such divisions take place within the corpus, otherwise they occur both in tunica and corpus or in the tunica only. In certain monocotyledonous plants the superficial tunica layer undergoes periclinal divisions and gives rise to some or most of the tissue. In the case of gymnosperms the leaves initiate from the peripheral tissue zone. In the vascular cryptogams (pteridophytes) the leaves are initiated either from single superficial cells or from groups of such cells.

The periclinal divisions which initiate a leaf primordium are responsible for the formation of a lateral prominence on the side of the shoot apex. This prominence constitutes the leaf base which is also known as *leaf buttress*. Subsequently the leaf grows upwardly from the buttress. As shown in the figure, in *Hypericum* spp., the apical meristem is less prominently elevated above the youngest leaf buttress.

Before the initiation of a new leaf primordium the apical meristem appears as a rounded mound. It gradually widens, and, then leaf buttresses are initiated on its sides. While the new leaf primordia grow upward from the buttresses, the apical meristem again becomes like a small mound.

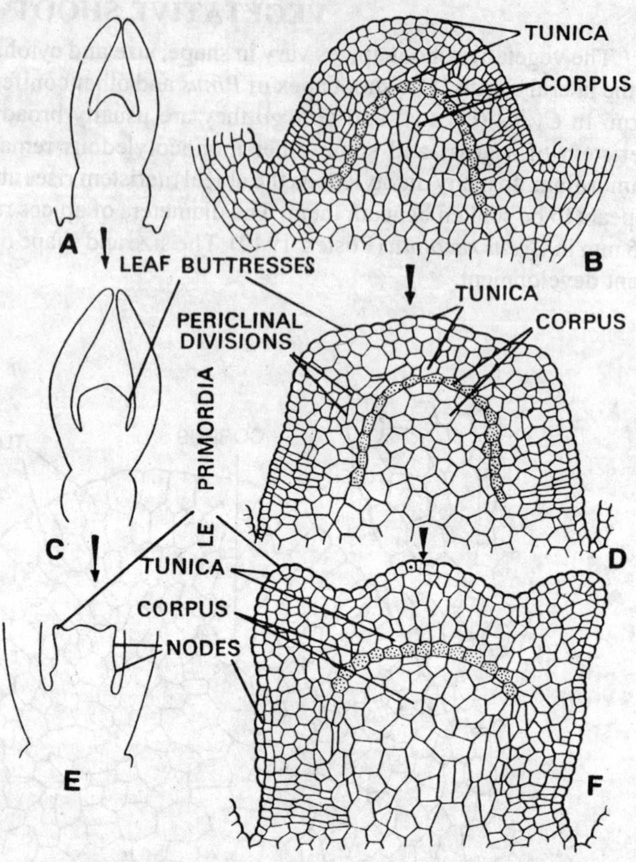

Fig. 4.12. Leaf initiation in shoot tip of *Hypericum*. Change in shape and histology of shoot apex. Longitudinal sections are seen in this figure. Leaves are in pairs at each node, in decussate arrangement. Protrusions in axis below the leaves in A, C and E are leaf bases of next lower pair of leaves; B, D and F, stippling indicates outer-boundary cells of corpus and their immediate derivatives; F, four sided figure indicates the presumptive place of origin of an axillary bud.

ORIGIN OF BRANCHES

In angiosperms, branches commonly are initiated in close association with the leaves — They originate in the axils of the leaves, and in their nascent state they are known as *axillary buds*. The axillary buds commonly initiate somewhat later than the leaves subtending them and therefore, it is not always clear whether the meristem of the axillary bud is derived directly from the apical meristem of the main shoot or whether it originates from partly differentiated tissue of the internode. Both situations may occur because plants vary with regard to time of appearance of axillary buds. On the one hand, the axillary buds may be directly related to the apical meristem of the parent shoot; on the other hand they may intergrade, ontogenetically with the adventitious buds which arise in obviously differentiated tissue regions.

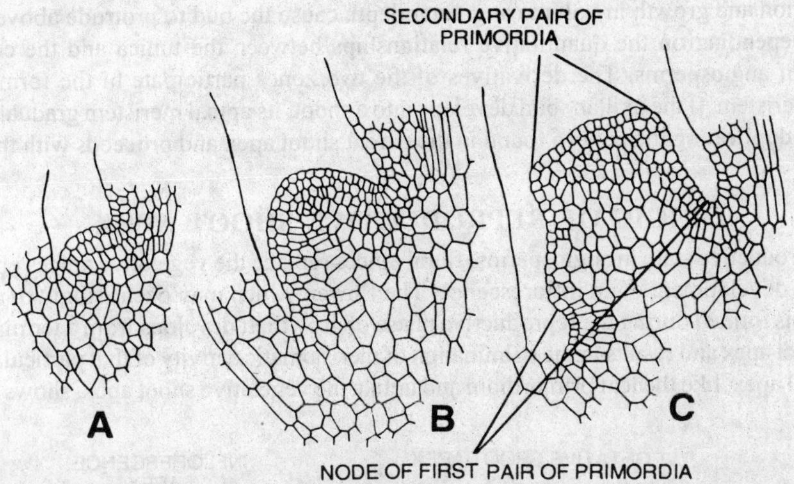

Fig. 4.13. Initiation of axillary bud in *Hypericum.* It is developed by derivatives of three layers of tunica of bud (A - C). Third layer divides periclinally and gives rise to third and fourth layers of tunica and to corpus of bud, C, second pair of leaf primordia is being initiated.

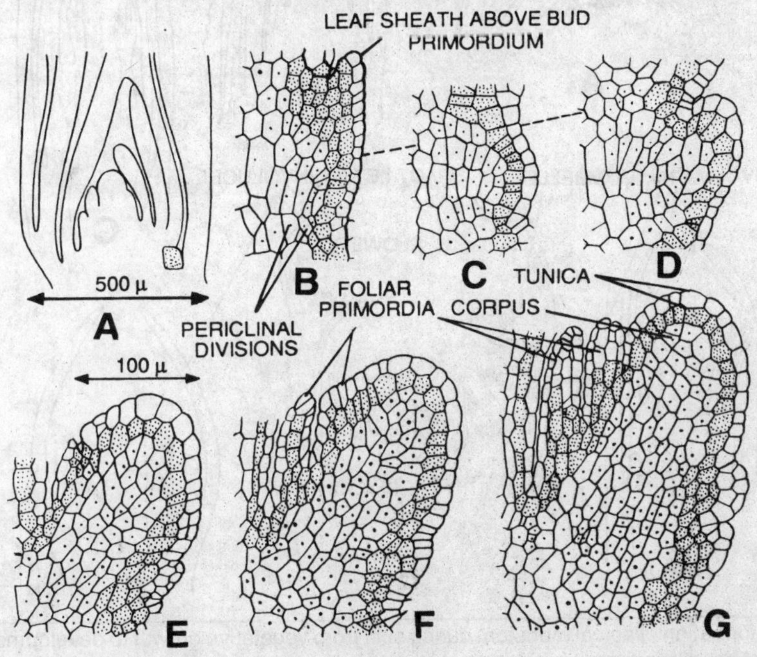

Fig. 4.14. Initiation of lateral bud in *Agropyron.* A, low-power view of shoot tip with several leaf primordia; stippled part indicates position of bud; it is developed by derivatives of the two-layered tunica and the corpus. B - G derivatives of second layer of tunica are stippled, and those of corpus indicated by a single dot in each cell. Bud is initiated by periclinal divisions in corpus derivatives (B, C). Anticlinal divisions occur in tunica derivatives; bud emerges above surface of stem (D). Tunica derivatives remain in a biseriate arrangement at apex of bud and form its two-layered tunica (E, G). Foliar primordia arise on bud (E-G).

The initiation of the axillary bud in seed plants is characterized by a combination of anticlinal divisions, in one or more of the superficial layers of the young axis, and of various divisions, sometimes predominantly periclinal, in the deeper layers (see Fig. 4.13). This coordinated growth in surface of the peripheral region and growth in volume at greater depth cause the bud to protrude above the surface of the axis. Depending on the quantitative relationships between the tunica and the corpus in the shoot apices of angiosperms. The derivatives of the two zones participate hi the formation of the axillary bud meristem. If the axillary bud develops into a shoot, its apical meristem gradually organizes — commonly duplicating the pattern found in the parent shoot apex and proceeds with the formation of leaves.

ORIGIN OF REPRODUCTIVE SHOOT APEX

In the reproductive state in angiosperms, floral apices replace the vegetative apices either directly or through the development of an inflorescence. The flower, which may occur singly or as part of an inflorescence, is formed during the reproductive phase of growth. It develops from a terminal or lateral vegetative shoot apex and results in the culmination of meristematic activity of that particular meristem. Thus, the floral apex, like the leaf primordium and unlike the vegetative shoot apex, shows determinate growth.

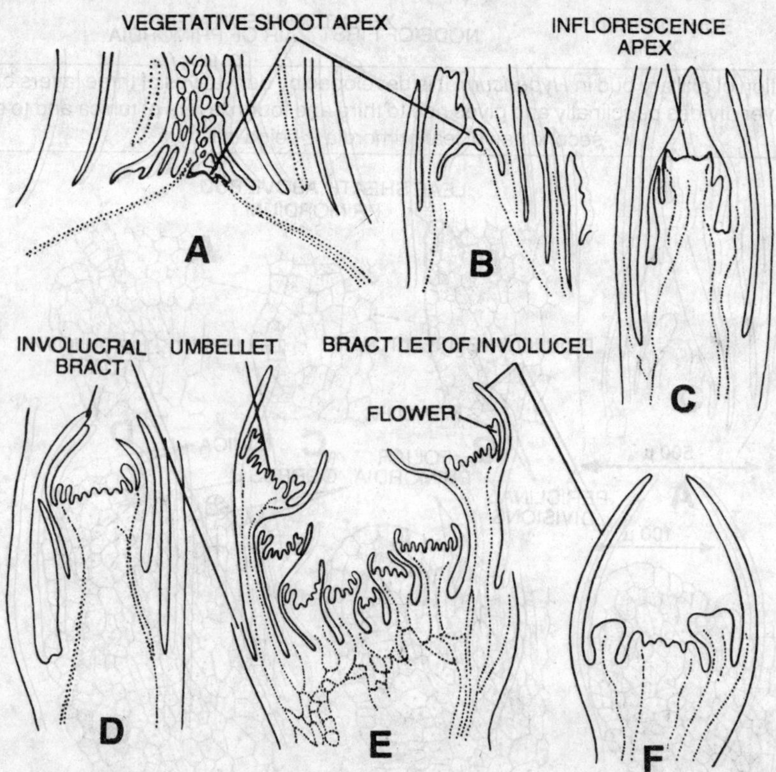

Fig. 4.15. Transformation of apical meristem during shift from vegetative growth to development of floral apices in carrot. The inflorescence is a compound umbel. A, vegetative shoot apex at base of rosette of leaves; B, shoot apex at approach of reproductive stage by internodal elongation. C, D, flattened inflorescence apices producing bracts and umbel primordia; E, compound umbel in young state; F, each flower develops a flat apex and forms floral organs.

5 CHAPTER

Preparing and Caring for a Herbarium Collection

Equipment

There are, however, several items which each collector of botanical specimens should have. These are as follows :

1. Trowel or pick.
2. Gardener's knife.
3. Vasculum or portfolio type field plant press.
4. Heavy laboratory plant press.
5. Blotting papers or plant driers.
6. Corrugated board.
7. Collecting sheets.
8. Mounting sheets.
9. Glue, gummed tape, labels, note-book, waterproof ink, pen and pencil.

The trowel or pick is used to take the roots of plants which can be taken whole. This pick should have a handle about a foot long and be equipped with a head at least five inches in length. One end of the head must be pointed to enable the collector to dig around crevices in rocks or to take roots from stony soil.

If a large number of specimens are to be collected on each field trip, the collector will find a light weight field press most practical for bringing them back to the laboratory. A simple collecting press or portfolio may be made by taking two pieces of heavy binder's board, size 12 × 17 inches, and holding these together by two pieces of heavy cord, light rope or straps. These may be tied together and the press thrown over the shoulder for carrying.

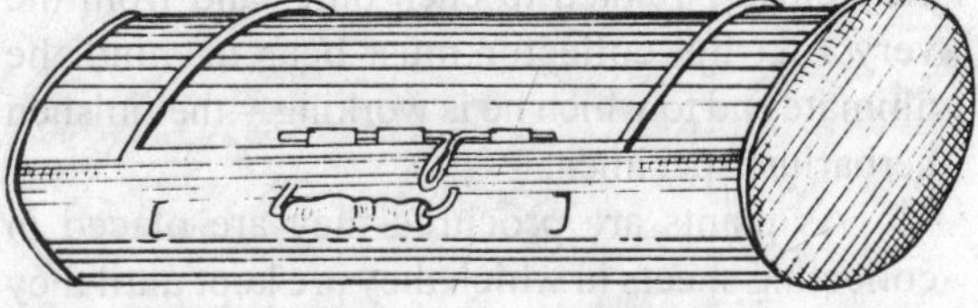

Fig. 5.1. A typical vasculum for botanical collections.

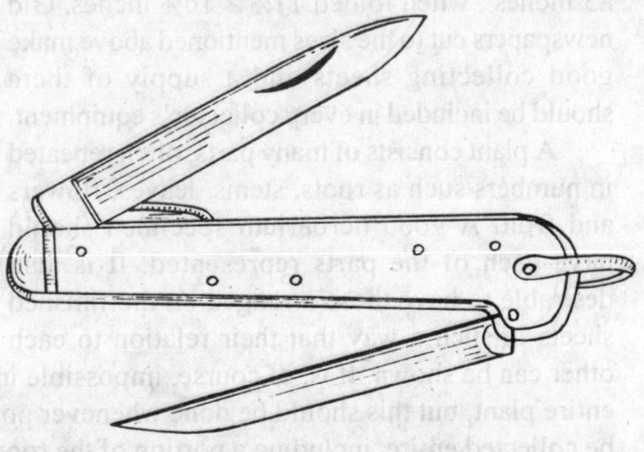

Fig. 5.2. Gardener's knife-one should carry such knife in field trips.

If a comparatively small number of plants are to be taken on each field trip, a vasculum may be used to take the specimens to the laboratory. If several persons are collecting together, it is well to take both the portfolio press and vasculum, as both of these items will be found extremely useful.

A heavy plant press which will take sheets at least 11½ by 17 inches should be used in pressing the specimens when they are brought to the laboratory. This press should be very durable and made of materials which will stand continued strain without warping.

Mounting sheets, gummed tape, pencils, labels, etc., will be selected according to the preference of the collector. It must be remembered, however, that the herbarium collection is to be more or less permanent, and this part of the equipment should be uniform in size and colour and of a uniformly high quality.

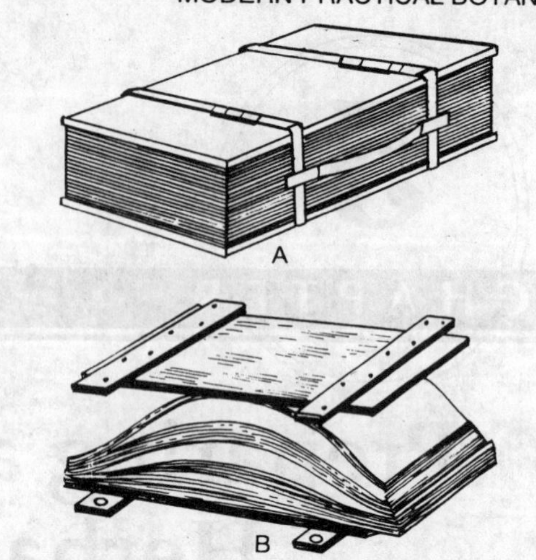

Fig. 5.3. Pressing of specimens in press boards : A, the right way of packing the press ; B, the wrong way of packing the press.

Collecting Specimens

The preparation of herbarium specimens for botanical study may be divided into two main processes : (1) Collecting and (2) Preservation by drying and pressing. These two processes are very closely related to each other and from the very first the collector must bear in mind the ultimate end to which he is working—the finished herbarium specimen.

As plants are procured they are placed in collecting sheets in which they are kept until they have been pressed and are ready for the mounting sheets. These collecting sheets are folders of unglazed paper. The most practical size is 16½ by 23 inches ; when folded 11½ × 16½ inches. Old newspapers cut to the sizes mentioned above make good collecting sheets and a supply of them should be included in every collector's equipment.

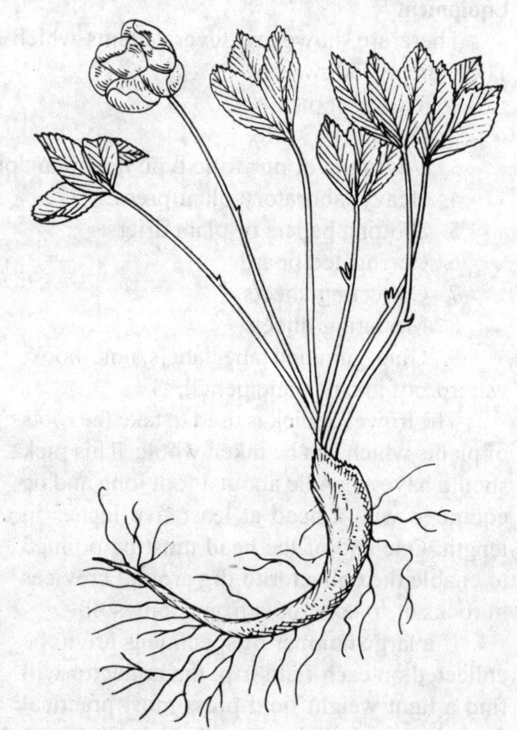

Fig. 5.4. The wrong method of pressing plants. Here the parts of the plant are folded.

A plant consists of many parts, often repeated in numbers such as roots, stems, leaves, flowers and fruit. A good herbarium specimen should have each of the parts represented. It is also desirable to have these arranged on the finished sheets in such a way that their relation to each other can be shown. It is, of course, impossible in the case of many of the larger plants to collect the entire plant, but this should be done whenever possible. Herbaceous plants 2 feet high or less should be collected entire, including a portion of the root and bent in a V or N shape, when necessary, to get them on the collecting sheet. In taking parts of shrubs or trees, a branch about a foot long should be collected which contains representative leaves, flowers and fruits, when possible. It is desirable to have both the staminate and pistillate flowers, although these may be found on different parts of the same plant or on different plants. In addition to the leaves which are found on the terminal branches, leaves should be collected from the lower parts of the branches. Also a portion of the bark should be taken.

If the fruits of woody plants are too thick to be placed in a press they should be put in a separate container and labelled for future reference. In the case of large herbs where the entire plant cannot be folded to the size of a herbarium sheet it is advisable to collect the flowering and fruiting portions, leaves from the upper and lower parts of the stem and representative portions of the root.

When it is necessary to bend the stem of a plant to make it fit the collecting sheet a small piece of cardboard about the weight of a postal card may be used for holding the stem in position and keeping it from springing outward and extending beyond the edge of the collecting sheet. The card is prepared by cutting a small slit in it. Place the V-shaped bent portion of the stem through this slit. In this way a neat specimen is obtained.

Many delicate flowers will collapse even if perfectly fresh when placed in the press ; but it is possible to get perfect specimens of these by applying bits of moist paper to the fresh flower and spreading the petals when the plants are placed in the portfolio. It will be found that some parts are placed in the portfolio. It will be found that some parts of herbaceous plants are too thick to be placed in the collecting sheet in the usual way. In cases of this kind it is best to split these before placing them in the collecting sheet. After this is done they may be dried in the usual manner.

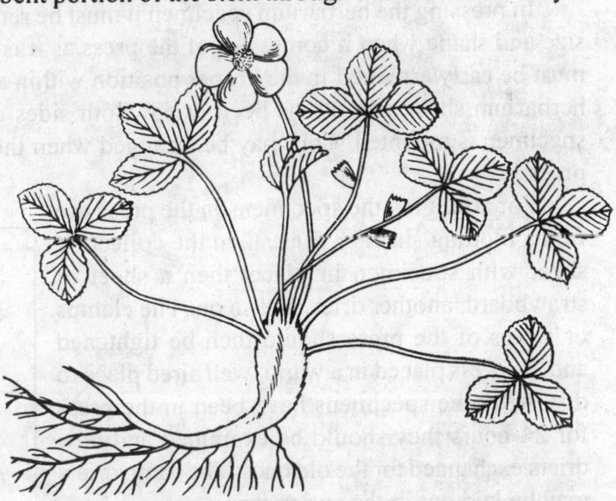

Many of the fine-leaved water plants will collapse entirely if dried by the usual method. These should be rolled up in wet paper when in the field and brought back in this condition. After they are in the laboratory they should be placed in water and floated out on sheets of white paper. These sheets should then be carefully taken from the water so that the fine divisions of the leaves do not cohere. These white sheets may then be placed in the collecting sheets and the specimens treated exactly as others.

Fig. 5.5. The right method of pressing plants. Here every part of the plant is unfolded.

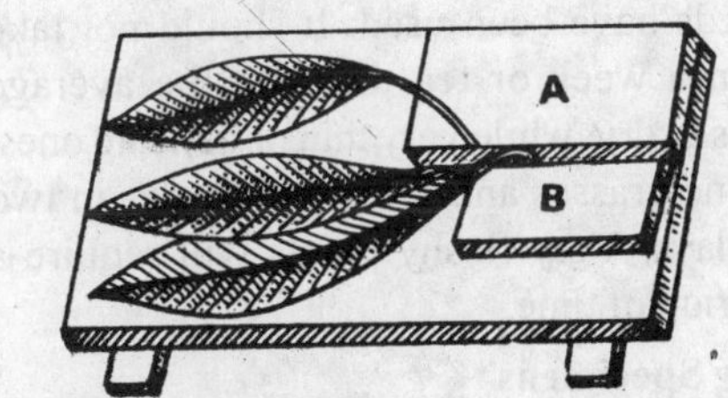

Fig. 5.6. Pressing of specimens with stout branches ; A and B, newspaper cushions supporting the stout branch.

After the specimen has been collected and placed in the collecting sheet, put it in the collecting press or portfolio. For the proper arrangement in the portfolio, first place a sheet of blotting paper or plant drier in the portfolio, then your collecting sheet, then another plant drier, etc. As soon as your portfolio is full it is strapped up and if you have several portfolios each one should be numbered.

It is of first importance in making a herbarium collection, that notes regarding the date, locality, habitat, height, method of branching, colour of flower parts, common name, etc., should be kept. These should either be keyed with the collecting sheet or placed in the collecting sheet with the specimen until they can be recorded on the permanent record. It is also highly desirable to secure photographs of individual plants if possible. These are not only interesting, but are also of great value for future reference to the herbarium collection.

It is necessary to make some arrangements whereby the specimens may be associated with its data. This may easily be done by giving your herbarium specimen a number and placing this number in your field note-book opposite the information regarding that particular specimen. This number should, of course, appear with all of the parts to the plant in question. After your specimen is permanently mounted on a herbarium sheet this information can be rewritten and possibly added to, a certain extent, and placed in the permanent note-book.

Pressing the Specimens

Specimens should be taken from the portfolio and placed in the laboratory press as soon as possible after returning from the collecting trip. This is particularly true in hot weather. In some cases they may be left overnight if the portfolio is strapped up tightly, but as a rule, this is inadvisable.

In pressing the herbarium specimen it must be remembered that the specimen will be of the same size and shape when it comes out of the press as it is when it goes in. This means that the specimen must be early arranged in the proper position within a space which will allow it to be fastened to the herbarium sheet after it has been dried. Both sides of leaves of plants should be shown when the specimen is mounted. This may be arranged when the specimens are limp after their first day in the press.

For arranging the specimens in the press use first a blotting sheet or drier, then the collecting sheet with specimen in place, then a sheet of strawboard, another drier, and so on. The clamps or straps of the press should then be tightened and the press placed in a warm, well aired place to dry. After the specimens have been in the press for 24 hours they should be examined and now driers exchanged for the old ones. The damp driers may be laid out in the sun to dry.

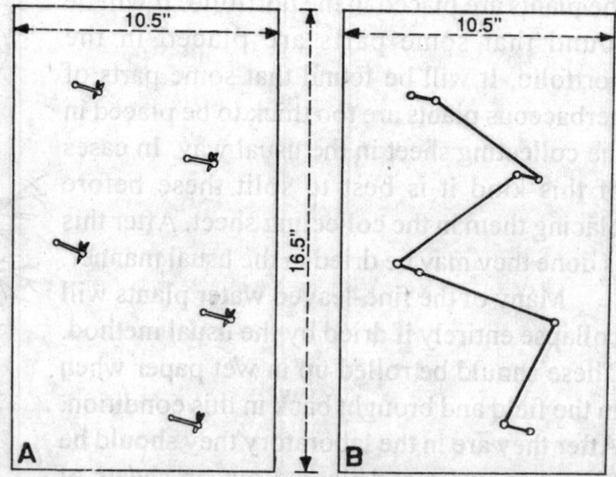

Fig. 5.7. Sticking of specimen on herbarium sheet : A, the right way (back view) ; B, the wrong way (back view).

For average specimens two or three changes of driers should be sufficient if plenty of strawboards have been used. It should not take more than a week or ten days for the average specimens to dry, while very thin or delicate ones, such as fine grasses and ferns will be dry in two or three days. Very fleshy plants will require a longer period of time.

Mounting Specimens

When dried, the specimens in their collecting sheets should be neatly stacked and each specimen identified. The specimen is then ready for mounting.

The standard size mounting paper is 10½ × 16½ inches (H. Santapau, Botanical Collector's Manual, 1955). This size be used throughout a collection. This paper should be of a good weight and not too flexible. It should also be of a quality which will not readily turn yellow with age.

Three methods are used for attaching the specimens to the herbarium sheets. (1) The glue is spread on a glass plate, the specimen laid on the glue and lifted as soon as all parts have come in contact with the glue, then transferred to the paper. (2) The specimen is inverted on the paper where it has been stored, painted with glue by means of a brush and then transferred to the mounting sheet. (3) The specimen is laid on the mounting sheet and fastened there by means of small strips of gummed tape which are used in large enough quantity to securely affix the stems, petioles, flower stocks, leaf tips and other parts. If either of the first two methods are used it is also well to use some of the small strips of gummed tape to fasten the specimen more securely to the sheet.

After the specimens are mounted the label, which was made out when the specimen was identified, should be placed in the lower right-hand corner. This label should contain as much information as possible regarding the specimen, including the name, date, collector, collector's number, etc.

The teaching collection of herbarium mounts is usually handled quite frequently and is subjected to a certain amount of unavoidable abuse. For this reason the mounted specimen should be covered in cellophane covering. Cellophane is perfectly transparent, flexible and does not interfere with detailed study. The covers protect the specimens from dust and in handling them there is less chance for the sheets to become spoiled by finger prints or the specimens broken or rubbed off. Cellophane sheets, 12¼ × 17½ inches, are placed over the specimen and the upper edge folded under the edge, about one inch, is glued to the back side of the herbarium sheet. The lower corners of the cellophane are then fastened to the corners of the herbarium sheets by means of paper clips. This makes it possible for the cellophane to be rolled back should it become necessary. Specimens protected by cellophane covers will last much longer than the unprotected specimens and, therefore, these covers be used in the teaching collection.

Arranging and Storing the Collection

After the specimens have been mounted they should be arranged according to their classification so that any specimen may readily be located when reference is made to it in the class work. In doing this it is well to divide the specimens into groups according to species, genus or family. Each group should then be placed in a folder slightly large than the herbarium sheets : 12 × 17 inches. If a large number of specimens of one group are later obtained, the material can be divided into smaller taxonomic divisions. Each folder must be labelled in one of the lower corners where the label may readily be seen without removing the folder from the file. These folders should be arranged in the case of file in which they are to be kept in their proper taxonomic order.

Fig. 5.8. Holding of specimen for poisoning.

Herbarium specimens, like many other parts of the teaching collection, are often attacked by museum pests. To guard against the collection being ruined by these pests, the specimens should be fumigated with carbon bisulphide three or four times per year. Some botanists prefer to poison the specimens (at the time they are mounted) with mercuric bichloride to guard against museum beetles.

CHAPTER

System of Classification of Angiosperms

In the present text the system of classification by Bentham and Hooker published in *'Genera Plantarum'* (1862 - 1883) has been followed with minute alterations. This system is preferred here for its simplicity and for its wide use in arranging the herbaria of the world.

Bentham and Hooker, the well known English systematists, established an important system of classification which appeared in the last half of the nineteenth century. **George Bentham** (1800 - 1884) and **Sir Joseph Dalton Hooker** (1817 - 1911), two English botanists, whose researches were carried over at the great herbarium of the Royal botanical garden at Kew. After the death of his father Sir W.J. Hooker, Sir Joseph Dalton Hooker was director of the Kew gardens for twenty years. Bentham and Hooker published a joint system of classification, containing 202 orders (families) in a monumental work "*Genera Plantarum*" (1862 - 1883) which became most popular classification in European countries except France for many years.

The plane adopted for presenting the diagnose of the natural orders (families) in this text follows very closely Sir Joseph Hooker's arrangement.

The following tabulated list of the larger and more important groups of flowering plants is given so as to bring into focus the general plane of the classification of the natural orders (families).

Class I. DICOTYLEDONS

Division 1. *Polypetalae*

Sub-division 1. Thalamiflorae

Sub-division 2. Disciflorae

Sub-division 3. Calyciflorae

Division 2. *Gamopetalae*

Division 3. *Monochlamydeae*

Class II. GYMNOSPERMS

Class III. MONOCOTYLEDONS

Division 1. Petaloideae

Division 2. Glumiferae.

System of Classification by Bentham and Hooker (1862 - 1883)

PHANEROGAMS OR SEED PLANTS

Dicotyledons | Gymnospermae | Monocotyledones

Polypetalae | Gamopetalae | Monochlamydeae or incompletae

1. **Polypetalae.** Petals separate.

Series (A) Thalamiflorae. Hypogynous, stamens and pistils many, indefinite, mostly free, distinct sepals free from ovary.

Order 1. **Ranales**

Families. 1. Ranunculaceae, 2. Dilleniacease, 3. Calycanthaceae, 4. Magnoliaceae, 5. Annonaceae, 6. Menispermaceae, 7. Berberidaceae, 8. Nymphaeaceae.

Order 2. **Parietales**

Families. 1. Sarraceniaceae, 2. Papaveraceae, 3. Cruiciferae, 4. Capparidaceae, 5. Resedaceae, 6. Cistineae, 7. Violaceae, 8. Canellaceae, 9. Bixineae.

Order 3. **Polygalineae**

Families. 1. Pittosporeae, 2. Tremandreae, 3. Polygaleae, 4. Vochysiaceae.

Order 4. **Caryophyllineae**

Families. 1. Frankeniaceae, 2. Caryophyllaceae, 3. Portulacaceae, 4. Tamariscineae.

Order 5. **Guttiferales**

Families. 1. Elatineae, 2. Hypericineae, Guttiferae, 3. Ternstroemiaceae, 4. Dipte-rocarpeae, 6. Chlaenaceae.

Order 6. **Malvales**

Families. 1. Malvaceae, 2. Sterculiaceae, 3. Tiliaceae.

Series (B) Disciflorae. Hypogynous, calyx consists of free or united sepals which are usually free from ovary. A prominent cushion shaped disc present below the ovary. Ovary free or embedded in the receptacular disc. Stamens usually definite in number.

Order 7. **Geraniales**

Families. 1. Lineae, 2. Humiriaceae, 3. Malpighiaceae, 4. Zygophylleae, 5. Geraniaceae, 6. Rutaceae, 7. Simarubeae, 8. Ochnaceae, 9. Burseraceae, 10. Meliaceae, 11. Chailletiaceae.

Order 8. **Olacales**

Families. 1. Olacineae, 2. Ilicineae, 3. Cyrilleae.

Order 9. **Celastrales**

Families. 1. Celastrineae, 2. Stackhousieae, 3. Rhamneae, 4. Ampelideae.

Order 10. **Sapindales**

Families. 1. Sapindaceae, 2. Sabiaceae, 3. Anacardiaceae, 4. Coriarieae, 5. Moringeae.

Series (C) Calyciflorae. Calyx consists of united sepals rarely free and adnate to ovary. Perigynous or epigynous. Ovary enclosed by the axis sometimes inferior.

Order 11. **Rosales**

Families. 1. Connaraceae, 2. Leguminosae, 3. Rosaceae, 4. Saxifrageae, 5. Crassulaceae, 6. Droseraceae, 7. Hamamelideae. 8. Brunia-ceae, 9. Halorageae.

Order 12. **Myrtales**

Families. 1. Rhizophoraceae, 2. Combretaceae, 3. Myrtaceae, 4. Melastomaceae, 5. Lythrarieae, 6. Onagrarieae.

Order 13 **Passiflorales**

Families. 1. Samydaceae, 2. Loaseae, 3. Turneraceae, 4. Passifloreae, 5. Cucurbitaceae, 6. Begoniaceae, 7. Datisceae.

Order 14. **Ficoidales**

Families. 1. Cactaceae, 2. Ficoideae.

Order 15. **Umbellales**

Families. 1. Umbelliferae, 2. Araliaceae, 3. Cornaceae.

2. Gamopetalae : Petals united.

Series (A) Inferae. Ovary inferior, stamens as many as corolla lobes or fewer.

Order 1. **Rubiales**

Families. 1. Caprifoliaceae, 2. Rubiaceae.

Order 2. **Asterales**

Families. 1. Valerianeae, 2. Dipsaceae, 3. Calycereae, 4. Compositae.

Order 3. **Campanales**

Families. 1. Stylidieae, 2. Goodenovieae, 3. Campanulaceae.

Series (B) Heteromerae. Ovary usually superior, carpels more than two, stamens as many as corolla lobes or fewer, epipetalous or free.

Order 4. **Ericales**

Families. 1. Ericaceae, 2. Vaccinieae, 3. Monotropeae, 4. Epacrideae, 5. Diapensiaceae, 6. Lennoaceae.

Order 5. **Primulales**

Families. 1. Plumbagineae, 2. Primulaceae, 3. Myrsineae.

Order 6. **Ebenales**

Families. 1. Sapotaceae, 2. Ebenaceae, 3. Styraceae.

Series (C) Bicarpellatae. Ovary usually superior, carpels usually two, rarely 1 or 3, stamens alternate with the corolla lobes and equal in number or fewer.

Order 7. **Gentianales**

Families. 1. Oleaceae, 2. Salvadoraceae, 3. Apocynaceae, 4. Asclepiadaceae, 5. Loganiaceae, 6. Gentianaceae.

Order 8. **Polemoniales**

Families. 1. Polemoniaceae, 2. Hydro-phyllaceae, 3. Poragineae, 4. Convolvulaceae, 5. Solanaceae.

Order 9. **Personales**

Families. 1. Scrophularineae, 2. Orobanch-aceae, 3. Lentibularieae, 4. Columelliaceae, 5. Gesneraceae, 6. Bignoniaceae, 7. Pedalineae, 8. Acanthaceae.

Order 10. **Lamiales**

Families. 1. Myoporineae, 2. Selagineae, 3. Verbenaceae, 4. Labiatae, 5. Plantagineae.

3. Monochlamydeae or Incompletae. Flowers with simple perianth which is usually sepaloid and sometimes altogether absent.

Series 1. Curvembryae

Families. 1. Nyctagineae, 2. Illecebraceae, 3. Amarantaceae, 4. Chenopodiaceae, 5. Phytolaccaceae, 6. Batideae, 7. Polygonaceae.

Series 2. Multivulatae Aquaticae

Family. Podostemaceae.

Series 3. Multivulatae Terrestres

Families. 1. Nepenthaceae, 2. Cytinaceae and 3. Aristolochieae.

Series 4. Micrembryae

Families. 1. Piperaceae, 2. Chloranthaceae, 3. Myristiceae, 4. Monimiaceae.

Series 5. Daphnales

Families. 1. Laurineae, 2. Proteaceae, 3. Thymelaceae, 4. Penaeaceae, 5. Elaeagn-aceae.

Series 6. Achlamydosproeae

Families. 1. Loranthaceae, 2. Santalaceae. 3. Balanophoreae.

Series 7. Unisexuales

Families. 1. Euphorbiaceae, 2. Balanopseae, 3. Urticaceae, 4. Plantanaceae, 5. Leitnerieae, 6. Juglandeae, 7. Myricaceae, 8. Casurineae, 9. Cupuliferae.

Series 8. Ordines anomali (*Anomalous Families*)

Families. 1. Salicaceae, 2. Lacistemaceae, 3. Empetraceae, 4. Ceratophylleae.

Gymonospermae.

Families. 1. Gnetaceae, 2. Coniferae 3. Cycadaceae.

Monocotyledones.

Series 1. Microspermae. Ovary superior tricarpellary. Seeds very minute and many. Inner perianth leaves petaloid.

Families. 1. Hydrocharideae, 2. Burmanniaceae, 3. Orchideae.

Series 2. Epigynae. Ovary inferior.

Families. 1. Scitamineae, 2. Bromeliaceae, 3. Haemodraceae, 4. Irideae, 5. Amaryllideae, 6. Taccaceae, 7. Dioscoreaceae.

Series 3. Coronarieae. Ovary superior, albuminous.

Families. 1. Roxburghiaceae, 2. Liliaceae, 3. Pontederiaceae, 4. Philydracee, 5. Xyrideae, 6. Mayacaceae, 7. Commelinaceae, 8. Rapateaceae.

Series 4. Calycineae. Ovary superior, albumen copious, perianth inconspieuous, sepaloid, stiff or herbaceous.

Families. 1. Flagellarieae, 2. Juncaceae, 3. Palmae.

Series 5. Nudiflorae. Ovary superior, Perianth absent or reduced to scales.

Families. 1. Pandaneae, 2. Cyclanthaceae, 3. Typhaceae, 4. Aroideae, 5. Lemnaceae.

Series 6. Apocarpae. Ovary superior, carpels separate or single.

Families. 1. Triurideae, 2. Alismaceae, 3. Najadaceae.

Series 7. Glumaceae. Ovary single celled, single ovuled. Flowers in spikelets or heads. Perianth scale-like

Families. 1. Eriocauleae, 2. Centrolepideae, 3. Restiaceae, 4. Cyperaceae, 5. Gramineae.

CHARACTERISTICS OF SOME SELECTED FAMILIES

Class I. DICOTYLEDONS

Herbs, shrubs or trees. Leaves net-veined, usually disarticulating. Whorls of perianth 4 or 5-merous. Ovules enclosed in an ovary. Embryo with 2 cotyledons.

Division **1. Polypetalae.** Flowers with both calyx and corolla. Petals free.

Sub-division **1. Thalamiflorae.** Flowers mostly regular and 2-sexual. Calyx inferior, of distinct or connate sepals. Petals distinct or united at the very base only, hypogynous. Stamens hypogynous. Ovary superior.

Ranunculaceae. Sepals deciduous, often petaloid. Petals sometimes absent. Stamens indefinite. Herbs with alternate leaves, or climbing shrubs (*Clematis*) with opposite leaves, stipules 0 or adnate to petioles.

Papaveraceae. Flowers regular or irregular. Sepals 2 or 3, caducous. Petals twice the sepals. Stamens indefinite, free, or (in *Fumaria*) 6 and diadelphous. Ovary 1-celled; ovules 2 or more on parietal placentas. Fruit a capsule, or an indehiscent 1-seeded nut. Herbs with milky or coloured juice (except in *Fumaria*). Leaves alternate, exstipulate.

Cruciferae. Sepals 4, imbricate. Petals 4, rarely 0. Stamens 6, the 4 inner longest (tetradynamous). Ovary usually 2-celled by a membrane from the placenta, or 1-celled. Fruit a 2-valved pod, rarely indehiscent or transversely septate. Herbs with alternate exstipulate leaves.

Capparidaceae. Trees shrubs or herbs, with alternate, simple or compound leaves; stipules spinescent in *Capparis.* Sepals 4. Petals usually 4, rarely 0. Stamens 4-many, at the base or on the sides of an elongated torus. Ovary sessile or stalked, 1-celled; ovules many, on 2-5 parietal placentas. Fruit capsular or a berry.

Violaceae. Herbs or shrubs, with alternate usually stipulate leaves. Flowers regular or irregular. Sepals 5; imbricate, persistent. Petals and stamens 5; connective of two anthers appendaged. Disc annular in *Alsodeia.* Ovary 1-celled, with 3 parietal placentas. Capsule 3-valved.

Caryophyllaceae. Herbs with opposite simple leaves; stipules rare or 0. Flowers regular. Sepals 4-5, free or connote. Petals 4-5. Stamens usually twice the petals, rarely fewer. Styles 2-5. Capsule 2-6 valved. Embryo curved round mealy endosperm ; free-central.

Malvaceae. Trees, shrubs or herbs. Leaves alternate simple or rarely compound, stipulate. Flowers regular, usually 2-sexual. Sepals 5, valvate, free or connate. Petals 5, imbricate, twisted. Stamens usually many 1-adelphous, the tube adnate to base of petals; anther 1-celled. Ovary 2-many celled; ovules 1 or more in each cell, axile. Fruit of distinct carpels or capsular. Embryo curved.

Sub-division **2. Disciflorae.** Sepals distinct or connate, rarely superior to ovary. Petals distinct or connate at the very base. Torus generally expanded into a pulvinate or cupular disc between the petals and ovary, rarely of glands or 0.

Linaceae. Usually herbs or shrubs with alternate simple leaves. Flowers regular and bisexual. Sepals usually 5; free or connate below, imbricate, Petals 5, imbricate, often contorted. Stamens usually with interposed staminodes; filaments more or less connate. Disk of glands, or obscure. Ovary 3-5 celled; cells 1-2 ovuled; styles 3 or 5. Fruit a capsule or drupe. Endosperm scanty.

Rutaceae. Usually trees or shrubs. Leaves simple or compound, exstipulate, pelucid punctate. Flowers 2-or 1-sexual. Sepals 4-5, imbricate. Petals 4-5, distinct, imbricate or valvate. Disk large or small. Stamens usually definite (many in *Citrus* and *Aegle*). Carpels 4-5, free or connate; ovules 1-2 or many in each cell. Fruit various.

Meliaceae. Usually trees with alternate compound exstipulate leaves. Flowers regular, 1- or 2-sexual. Calyx 3-6 lobed, Petals 3-6, usually imbricate. Stamens 4-12, 1-adelphous except in *Cedrela* and *Chloroxylon.* Disk annular (absent in *Amoora*). Ovary 2-5 celled; cells 1-2 many-ovuled, style simple. Fruit a capsule or drupe.

Anacardiaceae. Trees or shrubs, with alternate simle or compound exstipulate leaves. Flowers 1 or 2-sexual. Calyx 3-5, partite. Petals free 3-5, rarely 0. Disk annular. Ovary of 5 distinct 1-ovuled carpels, or carpels combined into a 2.5 celled ovary. Drupe with a 1 celled 1-seeded stone (2-5 celled in *Spondias*). Embryo large, endosperm absent.

Sub-division **3. Calyciflorae.** Flowers regular or irregular, 1 or 2-sexual. Calyx superior or inferior. Petals distinct or united at the base perigynous, disk rarely present. Stamens perigynous or epigynous.

Leguminosae. Trees, shrubs or herbs, often climbing. Leaves alternate usually compound stipulate. Flowers usually irregular and 2-sexual. Calyx-lobes usually connate, often 2-lipped. Petals 5 or fewer, rarely 0 or connate, usually very unequal (papilionaceous). Stamens normally 10, diadelphous or monadelphous, and declinate, or many, rarely all distinct. Ovary free, 1-celled; ovules 1 or more, on the ventral suture. Fruit a dehiscent or indehisent 1-many seeded pod. Cotyledons large; endosperm usually absent.

Rosaceae. Herbs, shrubs or trees. Leaves alternate, simple or compound, stipulate. Flowers regular and 2-sexual, rarely polygamous. Petals 5, stamens many distinct. Ovary of 1 or more free or connate carpels; ovules 1 or 2 in each carpel. Fruit various. Endosperm absent.

Myrtaceae. Trees or shrubs, with simple usually gland dotted leaves; stipules small or absent. Flowers regular, 2-sexual, Calyx superior; limb short, 4-5 lobed. Petals 4 or 5, free or united in a cap. Stamens many, epigynous. Ovary 2-4 celled, cells many-ovuled, style simple. Fruit indehiscent, 1-many seeded; endosperm absent.

Cucurbitaceae. Herbs with spiral tendrils. Leaves alternate, simple, lobed or compound. Flowers regular, 1-sexual. MALE : Calyx-tube short, 5-lobed. Petals 5, usually connate. Stamens 3, rarely 5, on the calyx tube; anthers free or connate, cells usually conduplicate. FEMALE: Calyx-tube wholly adnate to ovary (except in *Actinostemma*), limb 5-fid. Staminodes 3 or 5. Ovary 1-celled; placentas 3, fleshy, often meeting in the centre, stigmas 3, ovules usually many. Fruit fleshy, rarely dehiscent.

Umbelliferae. Herbs with alternate simple or compound exstipulate leaves; petiole usually dilated at base. Flowers in umbels, usually regular, 2-sexual or polygamous. Calyx superior; limb 5-fid or 0. Petals 5, often inflexed, free valvate or imbricate. Stamens 5 epigynous. Ovary 2-celled, crowned with a large epigynous disk; cells with 1 pendulous ovule, styles 2. Fruit of 2 indehiscent carpels pendulous from the summit of the carpophore, each 5-ridged and often traversed by oil canals.

Division **2. Gamopetalae.** Flowers usually 2-sexual, regular or irregular. Calyx superior or inferior. Petals connate, forming an entire or cleft corolla, rarely free to a little above the base. Stamens inserted on corolla rarely hypogynous or epigynous.

Rubiaceae. Herbs, shrubs or trees. Leaves opposite with interpetiolar stipules, or (in Tribe Galieae) whorled and exstipulate. Flowers usually 4-5 cleft, corolla tubular to rotate, usually 4-5 lobed. Stamens as many as corolla lobes, inserted on the tube alternate to lobes, ovary 2-or more-celled, rarely 1-celled, inferior; ovules 1 or more in each cell; style simple. Disk epigynous. Fruit a berry drupe or capsule, or of distinct cocci, 2-many-seeded. Endosperm horny.

Compositae. Herbs or shrubs, rarely trees. Leaves mostly alternate; stipules absent. Flowers regular or irregular, 1 or 2-sexual arranged in a head on a common receptacle and surrounded by an involucre of bracts, all tubular (head discoid), or the outer or all ligulate (flowers rayed). Calyx superior; limb of hairs (pappus) or scales or 0. Corolla of ray flowers with the lobes eonnate in a strap, of disk flowers with 4 or 5 valvate spreading lobes. Stamens on the corolla tube, filaments free, anthers connate (in *Xanthium* the filaments are connate and anther free). Ovary inferior; 1-celled; ovule 1, erect. Disk epigynous. Fruit an achene with or without pappus.

Apocynaceae. Trees, shrubs or herbs, with usually milky juice. Leaves opposite or whorled, entire exstipulate. Flowers 2-sexual. Calyx inferior, 5-parted, often with scales or glands within. Corolla salver-shaped or rotate, lobes 5, contorted. Stamens 5, inserted on corolla tube free or adnate to the stigma, pollen granular, disk various or 0. Carpels 2, distinct, 1 or 2-celled, few or many-ovuled, style 1, stigma 2-fid. Fruit a berry or drupe, or of 2 distinct or connate follicles. Seeds often compressed at one or both ends.

Asclepiadaceae. Herbs or shrubs, usually twining, leaves opposite, exstipulate, entire, rarely 0. Calyx inferior; lobes 5, imbricate. Corolla tube with often a ring of scales in the throat ; lobes 5, valvate or contorted. Stamens 5, on base of corolla, filaments usually connate in a fleshy tube ; anthers adnate by a broad connective to the stigma, 2-celled ; pollen in 1 or 2 erect or pendulous granular masses in each cell, the masses of contiguous cells of different anthers attached to glands at the angles of the stigma. Carpels 2, distinct, enclosed in the staminal tube, many-ovuled; styles 2; stigma 1, adnate to the anther. Follicles 2, seeds many, crowned with a long pencil of hairs, endosperm copious.

Convolvulaceae. Herbs or shrubs often twining. Leaves alternate (0 in *Cuscuta*). Flowers usually cymose. Calyx inferior persistent, 5-parted or of 5 imbricate sepals. Corolla campanulate, or funnel-shaped; lobes 5, plaited or contorted in bud. Stamens 5, on the corolla tube, filaments free. Ovary often surrounded by an annular disk, 2-celled and with 1 ovule in each cell, styles simple or 2-fid, stigmas 2, Fruit dry or fleshy, indehiscent or 2-4 valved, 1-4 seeded, endosperm absent; cotyledon plaited (0 in *Cuscuta*).

Solanaceae. Herbs or shrubs with alternate simple or binate leaves; stipules 0. Flowers in axillary or terminal cymes. Calyx inferior, often persistent and enlarged, 5-eleft. Corolla campanulate funnel-shaped or rotate, lobes 5, plaited or valvate in bud. Stamens 5, on corolla tube; anther cells sometimes opening by pores. Ovary 2-celled or imperfectly 4-celled, style and stigmas simple; ovules many, on large placentas. Fruit a berry or capsule, many seeded. Embryo curved, round fleshy endosperm.

Scrophulariaceae. Herbs. Leaves opposite or whorled or the upper rarely alternate; stipules 0. Flowers in racemes or spikes. Calyx inferior, 5-lobed. Corolla 4-5 lobed, usually 2-lipped, lobes imbricate. Stamens 4, didynamous, rarely 2 or 5. Ovary 2-celled styles simple, stigmas 2. Capsule 2-valved, usually many seeded. Seeds small, endosperm fleshy.

Pedaliaceae. Herbs with opposite or alternate leaves. Flowers axillary, large. Calyx 5-lobed. Corolla ventricose, sub-2-lipped; lobes 5, imbricate in bud. Stamens 4, didynamous, of 5. Ovary 1-celled or 2-

4 celled by confluence of parietal placentas; ovules 2 or more, superposed, stigmas 2. Fruit dehiscent (beaked with spines in *Martynia*).

Acanthaceae. Herbs or shrubs, with opposite simple exstipulate leaves, Inflorescence various; flowers often with conspicuous bracts. Calyx 4-5 partite, or (in *Thunbergia*) many-partite. Corolla 2-lipped, or upper lip absent; lobes imbricate or contorted. Stamens 4 or 2; anthers 2 or 1-celled. Ovary 2-celled; ovules one or more, superposed in each cell, style usually bifid. Capsules loculicidal. Seeds usually compressed and often hairy.

Verbenaceae. Herbs, shrubs or trees, with opposite or ternate simple or compound leaves; stipules 0. Flowers in heads, spikes or racemes. Flowers regular or not. Calyx 2- or 4-6 partite, 2-lipped or not persistent. Corolla 4-6 lobed, 2-lipped or not. Stamens 4, didynamous, rarely more or 2. Disk present. Ovary 2-4 celled (1-celled in *Verbena*), cells 1-2 ovuled. Fruit usually a drupe, rarely capsular.

Labiatae. Herbs or undershrubs, usually aromatic. Stem usually 4-gonous. Leaves opposite or whorled, stipules 0. Flowers in cymes or fascicles or whorled. Flowers irregular; calyx 5 rarely 6 - 10 cleft, persistent. Corolla 2-lipped or upper lip 0, rarely nearly regular, 4-5 lobed. Stamens 4, didynamous; anthers 1 or 2-celled. Disk present. Ovary 4 lobed, or of two 2-celled. carpels; ovules solitary and erect in each cell; style slender, usually bifid. Fruits of 4 small indehiscent nutlets.

Division **3. Monochlamydeae :** Perianth single, rarely 0. Lobes or segments 1-seriate or if 2-seriate both usually calycine.

Nyctaginaceae. Herbs with opposite leaves; stipules O. flowers panicled, umbelled or capitate. Flowers 2-sexual. Perianth inferior, 5-lobed, coloured, imbricate, plaited in bud, tube persistent. Stamens 1-5, hypogynous exerted. Ovule erect, style slender. Fruit membranous. Cotyledons large, folded round the endosperm.

Amarantaceae. Herbs or shrubs with opposite or alternate exstipulate leaves. Flowers 1-2 sexual. Sepals inferior, 5, scarious or herbaceous, imbricate, persistent. Stamens 1-5, opposite sepals; filaments distinct, or connate with the interposed staminodes. Ovary 1-ovuled (2 or more in *Celosia)*, ovules basal. Fruits usually an indehiscent utricle, rarely a berry. Seeds erect.

Chenopodiaceae. Herbs or undershrubs. Leaves usually alternate. Flowers small, axillary. Flowers 1 or 2 sexual. Perianth inferior; segments 3-5, or in female flowers often 0, distinct or connate, imbricate, persistent. Stamens usually 5, opposite perianth lobes, hypogynous or prigynous. Ovary 1-celled, 1-ovuled, stigmas 2-5. Fruit a membranous utricle. Seed horizontal or vertical; endosperm mealy, or scanty or 0.

Polygonaceae. Herbs with alternate leaves and sheathing stipules. Flowers axillary, in heads spikes or cymes, bracteate. Flowers 2-sexual. Perianth inferior 4-6 cleft, often coloured, imbricate, persistent. Stamens 4-8, perigynous. Styles 2 or 3. Ovule basal. Fruit a 3-gonous or biconvex nutlet. Embryo lateral, endosperm floury.

Euphorbiaceae. Herbs, shrubs or trees often with milky juice. Leaves alternate, simple, rarely opposite or compound, usually stipulate. Perianth inferior, single, rarely double or 0. Disk often present. Stamen 1, or more. Ovary 2-3 celled, cells 1-2 ovuled, ovules pendulous. Fruit of 2-3 loculicidal cocci, or a drupe or berry. Endosperm fleshy.

Class 2. GYMNOSPERMS

Class 3. MONOCOTYLEDONS

Herbs, rarely shrubs or trees. Leaves usually parallel veined. Whorls of perianth 3-merous. Ovules enclosed in an ovary. Embryos with 1-cotyledon; radicle not elongating to form a tap root, but emitting secondary roots from its crown.

Division **1. Petaloideae.** Perianth usually of 6 free or connate segments in 2 series, the inner or both series more or less coloured petal-like.

Sub-division **1. Microspermae.** Flowers 1 or 2-sexual. Perianth superior; segments usually 2-seriate, inner or both corolline. Ovary 1-celled, or placentas parietal. Seeds many, minute.

Orchidaceae. Herbs or shrubs often epiphytic. Flowers irregular, 2-sexual. Perianth 6-parted;

segments in 2 series, inner or both corolline. Stamens usually 1, confluent with the style in a column; anther 2-celled, pollen grains cohering in waxy or powdery masses. Ovary 1-celled, with 3-parietal placentas, usually twisted. Capusules loculicidal.

Sub-division **2. Epigyneae.** Flowers 2-sexual. Perianth superior in 2-series, one or both corolline. Ovary 1-3 celled. Endosperm copious.

Musaceae. Perennial herbs with penninerved leaves. Inflorescence usually spicate. (In *Musa* the flower 2-sexual the inner perianth is represented by one short petal and there are five fertile stamens). Flowers irregular, bisexual. Perianth biseriate; inner or both petaloid, limb spreading. Stamen only one fertile. Ovary unitrilocular, style long, stigma often ciliate round the margin.

Amaryllidaceae. Rootstock bulbous or tuberous. Leaves linear or lanceolate Scape few or many flowered. Perianth superior, petaloid limb 6-lobed or parted in two series. Stamens six, on base of perianth segments, filaments distinct or connate, anthers erect or versatile. Ovary tri-locular, locules many-ovuled. Fruit indehiscent, or a capsule opening loculicidally or bursting irregularly.

Sub-division **3. Coronariae.** Flowers rarely unisexual (dioecious in *Smilax)*. Perianth inferior, 6-lobed, in two series, one or both corolline. Ovary superior, trilocular.

Liliaceae. Herbs rarely shrubs. Flowers bisexual. Perianth petaloid 6-merous, segments free or connate below. Stamens 6, on the perianth or hypogynous, filaments usually free. Ovary trilocular, locules 2-or more ovuled. Fruit a 3-celled berry or capsule. Seeds subglobose or flattened; endosperm horny or fleshy, embryo terete.

Sub-division **4. Calycinae.** Perianth inferior, lobes or segments biseriate, inner series rarely corolline. Ovary superior, 1-3 celled. Endosperm copious.

Palmae. Shrubs or trees, armed or not. Stem erect, scandent or decumbent. Leaves alternate, variously compound. Inflorescence various, at first enclosed in a woody or coriaceous spathe. Flowers usually small, green or yellowish. Flowers mostly unisexual. Perianth inferior, 6-lobed, in two series. Stamens usually six, on base of perianth, anthers versatile. Ovary 1-3 celled, or of three distinct or connate carpels, cells 1-2 ovuled.

Araceae. Terrestrial or aquatic herbs with radical leaves, or suffruticose climbers. Leaves various. Spathe herbaceous, convolute. Flowers small unisexual (bisexual in *Acorus*), usually on a 2-sexual spadix, with the female flowers below. Perianth 0. (of 6 orbicular sepals in *Acorus*). *Male Flower :* Anthers 2-4 celled, free or connate. *Female Flower :* Ovary sessile, 1-3 celled ; cells 1-or more ovuled. Fruit a 1-or few seeded berry. Embryo small, in copious endosperm, or macropodous and without endosperm.

Division **2. Glumiferae.** Flowers in the imbricating bracts of heads, or spikelets, 1- or 2-sexual. Perianth 0, or of minute scales or bristles, rarely with sheathing bracteoles. Ovary superior, 1-celled and 1-ovuled.

Cyperaceae. Grasslike herbs (sedges) with terete or 3-angled stems. Leaves narrow, sheaths entire. Flowers in spikelets of imbricate bracts (glumes). 1 or 2-sexual. Perianth 0, or of hypogynous scales or bristles. Stamens 1-3, anthers basifixed. Ovary superior (included in an utricle in *Carex*), style 1, stigmas 2-3, ovule erect. Fruit indehiscent. Embryo in base of copious endosperm.

Gramineae. Grasses, mostly herbs (shrubby or arboreous in Bambuseae). Stem terete or compressed. Leaves usually narrow; sheath split to the base, distinct from the blade and with a membrane or ridge of hairs (ligule) at the junction. Flowers in spikelets of imbricate bracts (glumes) 1- or 2-sexual. Perianth of 2 or more minute hypogynous scales (lodicules), or 0. Stamens 3, rarely 1, 2 or more, anthers versatile. Ovary superior; styles 2, rarely 1, distinct or united below, stigmas penicillate or feathery, ovule erect. Fruit indehiscent. Seed usually adherent to the membranous or coriaceous pericarp ; embryo towards the base and side of copious endosperm.

How to Describe an Angiospermic Plant

1. Habitat. The natural abode or locality of plant, *i.e.*, whether cultivated as an ornamental plant, a food crop or occurs in a wild state.

2. Habit. (*a*) Herb, undershrub, shrub or tree.

(*b*) annual, biennial or perennial.

(*c*) Any special feature, *e.g.*, parasite, epiphyte, mesophyte, xerophyte or hydrophyte.

3. Root. (*a*) Tap or adventitious.

(*b*) Branched or unbranched.

(*c*) Any special modification, *i.e.*, fibrous, prop, stilt, aerial, climbing, respiratory, tuberous, parasitic, conical, fusiform, napiform, fasciculated, beeded, nodulated, etc.

4. Stem. (*a*) Nature of stem, *i.e.*, crect, prostrate, twining or climbing; if climbing, write mode of climbing whether by leaf tendrils, leaflet tendrils, stem tendrils or stipular tendril or by hooks or some other means.

(*b*) Any special modification, *i.e.*, rhizome, bulb, corm, tuber, offset, stolon, runner, sucker, phylloclade, etc.

(*c*) Branched or unbranched. If branched, write the mode of branching, *i.e.*, whether racemose or cymose. If cymose, whether uniparous or multiparous.

(*d*) Texture, *i.e.*, herbaceous.

(*e*) Solid or fistular.

(*f*) Cylindrical (terete), angular flattened or reduced.

(*g*) Hairy, glabrous, waxy or spiny.

(*h*) Colour. Whether green, grey, etc.

5. Leaf. (*a*) Insertion. Radical, cauline or ramal.

(*b*) Arrangement. Alternate, opposite or whorled (verticillate). If opposite, whether superposed or decussate.

(*c*) Petiolate, sessile or subsessile.

(*d*) Stipulate or exstipulate. If stipulate, describe the nature of stipules, *i.e.*, leafy (foliaceous), spiny, tendrillar, petiolar, etc.

(*e*) Leaf base. Sheathing connate or ligulate or amplexicaul.

(*f*) Kind. Simple or compound.

(*g*) If simple, write about form of lamina, *i.e.*, acicular, linear, lanceolate, oval, ovate, obovate, cordate, obcordate, spathulate, orbicular, rotund, reniform, sagittate, hastate, lyrate, etc.

(*h*) If compound, whether pinnate or palmate, paripinnate, imparipinnate, bifoliate, trifoliate, etc.

(*i*) Incision of lamina. Pinnatifid or palmatified, pinnatisect or palmatisect.

(*j*) Margin of lamina. Entire dentate, serrate, hairy, spiny, convolute, etc.

(*k*) Apex. Acute, obtuse, acuminate, emarginate, truncate, mucronate, cuspidate, etc.

(*l*) Surface. Hairy, glaucous, spiny.

(*m*) Venation. Reticulate or parallel, unicostate or multicostate.

(*n*) Texture. Coriaceous, fleshy, succulent etc.

(*o*) Colour. Green or pigmented.

Note. In a compound leaf, the leaflets should be described in the manner as a simple leaf.

6. Inflorescence. Simple mixed, compound and special. If simple, racemose or cymose. If racemose, whether raceme, corymb, spike, catkin, spadix, umbel, hypanthodium, capitulum, etc. If cymose, uniparous, biparous or multiparous cyme, helicoid or scorpioid, or solitary axillary. Compound and mixed, compound spike, compound umbel, compound corymb, spike of spikelets, panicle and panicle of spikelets etc. Special verticillaster, cyathium, etc.

7. Flower. (*a*) Pedicellate or sessile.

(*b*) Bracteate or ebracteate; if bracteate, the nature of the bract should be described.

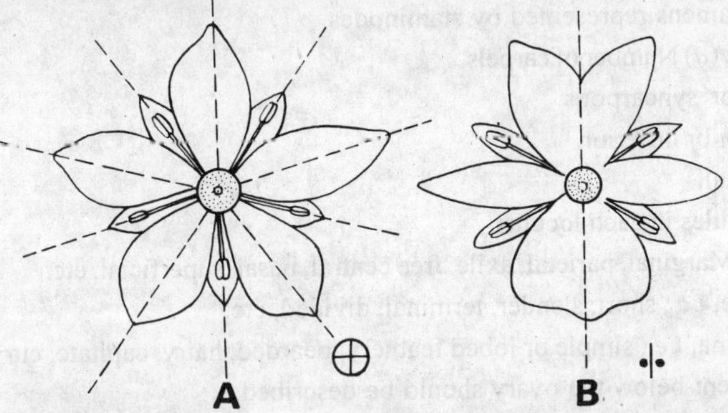

Fig. 7.1. Symmetry of flower. A, regular or actinomorphic; B, Zygomorphic or irregular.

(*c*) Actinomorphic or zygomorphic.

(*d*) Unisexual or hermaphrodite (bisexual).

(*e*) Complete or incomplete.

(*f*) Regular or irregular.

(*g*) Hypogynous, perigynous or epigynous.

(*h*) Colour of the flowers.

8. Calyx. (*a*) Number of sepals.

(*b*) Polysepalous or gamosepalous. If polysepalous, describe the nature and form of sepals, *i.e.* deciduous, caducous, persistent, etc. If gamosepalous, give special forms, *e.g.*, tubular, campanulate, bilabiate, etc.

(*c*) Sepaloid (green) or petaloid (coloured).

(*d*) Inferior or superior.

(*e*) Aestivation of the calyx, *e.g.*, imbricate, valvate, quincuntial, etc.

9. Corolla. (*a*) Number of petals.

(*b*) Poly or gamopetalous, if polypetalous, one should describe the form and nature of

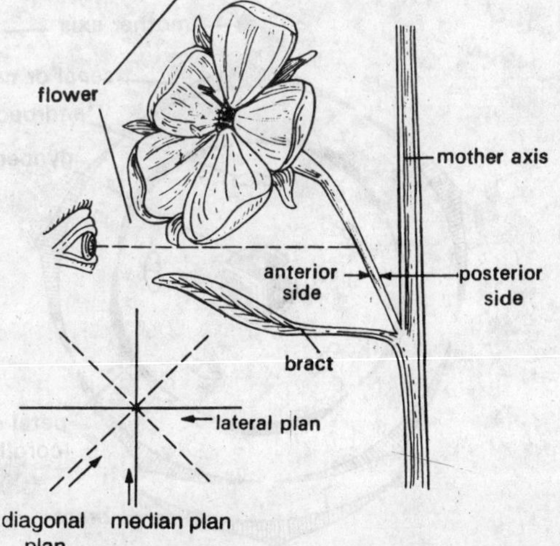

Fig. 7.2. A, Relation of a flower to the mother axis or the peduncle; B, it shows antero-posterior, lateral and diagonal planes of the flower.

petals, *i.e.*, rosaceous, papilionaceous, etc. If gamopetalous, given special form, *e.g.*, campanulate, tubular, bilabiate, spurred, ligulate, etc.

(*c*) Colour of the petals.

(*d*) Inferior or superior.

(*e*) Aestivation of the corolla.

10. Androecium. (*a*) Number of stamens; 1 to 10 or indefinite.

(*b*) Free or fused; if fused, adelphous or syngenesious; if adelphous, mono, di or polyadelphous. If free, any special form, *e.g.*, didynamous, tetradynamous, etc.

(*c*) Epipetalous, epiphyllous or free from petals or tepals.

(*d*) Filament long, short or flattened.

(*e*) Fixation of anthers. Adnate, basifixed, dorsifixed or versatile.

(*f*) Anthers. Monothecous or dithecous (single-celled or bicelled).

(*g*) Dehiscence of anthers. Longitudinal transverse, porous, extrorse, introrse.

(*h*) Colour of the anthers.

(*i*) Sometimes stamens represented by staminodes.

11. Gynoecium. (*a*) Number of carpels.

(*b*) Apocarpous or syncarpous.

(*c*) Ovary superior or infferior.

(*d*) Number of loculi.

(*e*) Number of ovules in each loculus.

(*f*) Placentation. Marginal, parietal, axile, free central, basal, superficial, etc.

(*g*) Nature of style, *i.e.*, short, slender, terminal, divided, etc.

(*h*) Nature of stigma, *i.e.*, simple or lobed feathery, bearded, hairy, capitate, curved, etc.

(*i*) Any disc present below the ovary should be described.

12. Fruit. Whether it is simple, aggregate, multiple; pod, legume, follicle, lomentum, capsule, siliqua, silicula, achene, cypsela, cremocarp, caryopsis, samara, nut, pome, drupe, berry, carcerule, hesperidium, etaerio of achenes, drupes, follicles or berries, sorosis, syconus.

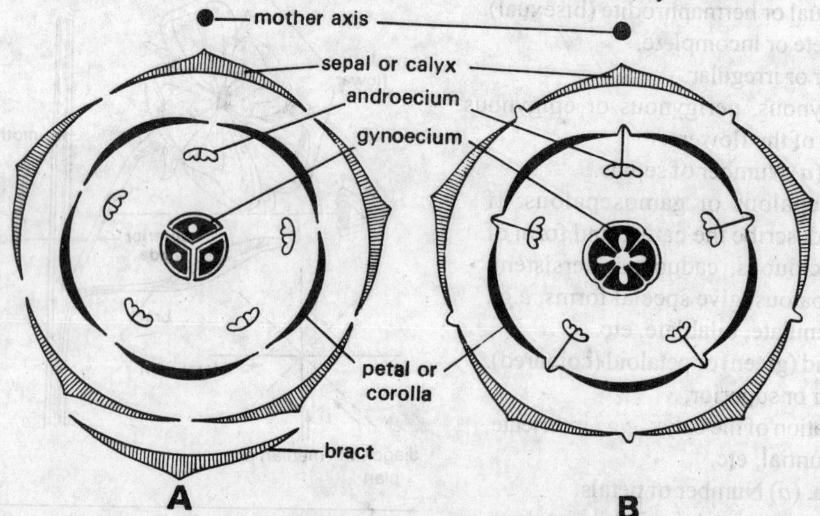

Fig. 7.3. Floral diagrams of polypetalous (A) and gamopetalous (B) flowers, with apocarpous and syncarpous gynoecia respectively.

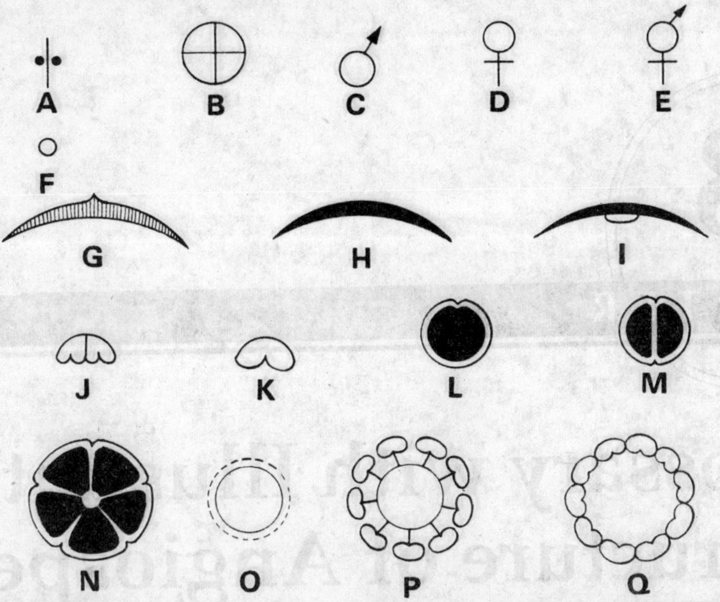

Fig. 7.4. Various symbols used in writing a floral formula. A, zygomorphic ; B, actinomorphic ; C, male; D, female ; E, bisexual; F, mother axis; G, calyx; H, corolla; I, coralla with pocket nectary; J, dithecous stamen; K, monothecous stamen; L, monocarpellary gynoecium; M, bicarpellary gynoecium; N, polycarpellary syncarpous; O, nectar secreting disc around carpel; P, monadelphous androecium.

13. Seed. (*a*) Albuminous or exalbuminous.

(*b*) Single or two cotyledons.

(*c*) Position, shape and size of the embroyo.

(*d*) Cotyledons straight or curved.

14. Floral formula. The floral formula must be given in the end of plant description, *e.g.*, *Solanum* :

$$\oplus \ ⚥ \ K(5), \ \overset{\frown}{C(5), \ A5}, \ G(\underline{2}).$$

15. Floral diagram

16. Generic characters. The distinguishing characters of the genus should be underlined in the description.

17. Systematic position. In the end of the description the systematic position of the genus should be given with the help of key. In the present text, Benthen and Hooker's system of classification has been followed for its simplicity.

CHAPTER 8

Glossary with Illustrations Structure of Angiosperms

HABITAT

The natural abode or locality of plant, *i.e.*, whether cultivated as an ornamental plant, a food crop or occurs in a wild state.

HABIT

Herb. Plant with no persistent parts above ground, as distinct from shrubs and trees, *e.g., Ranunchulus* or Ranunculaceae.

Shrub. Perennial woody plant, typically with several stems arising from or near the ground, *e.g., Capparis* of Capparidaceae.

Tree. A perennial woody plant with a single trunk, *e.g., Melia* of Meliaceae.

Annual. Plant that completes its life-cycle, from seed germination to seed production, followed by death within a single season, *e.g., Brassica* or Cruciferae.

Biennial. Plant that continues its growth from year to year. In *herbaceous* perennials serial parts die away in autumn, replaced by new shoots in the following year from underground structures, *e.g., Delphinium;* in *woody* perennials, permanent woody stems above ground from starting point for each new years's growth, a characteristic that enables some of them to reach a large size, *e.g.,* shrubs and trees.

Parasite. Plant living in or on another plant (its host) from which it obtains food, *e.g., Cuscuta* of Convolvulaceae.

Epiphyte. Plant attached to another plant, not growing parasitically upon it but merely using it for support, *e.g., Vanda* (an orchide) or Orchidaceae.

Mesophyte. Plant growing under average conditions of water supply.

Hydrophyte. Plant whose habitat is water or very wet places, *e.g., Ranunculus aquatilis* of Ranunculaceae; *Neptunia oleracea* of Mimosoideae.

Xerophyte. Plant of dry havitate able to endure conditions of prolonged drought, *e.g., Capparis decidua* of Capparidaceae.

Saprophyte. Plant which obtains organic matter in solution from dead and decaying tissues of plants (or animals), *e.g., Monotropa.*

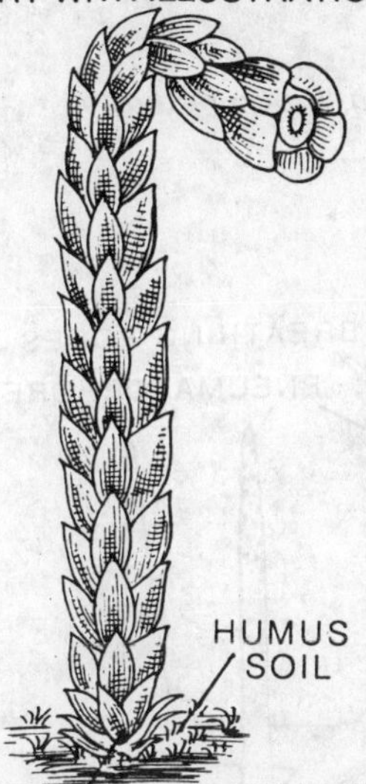

Fig. 8.1. Saprophyte. *Monotropa*.

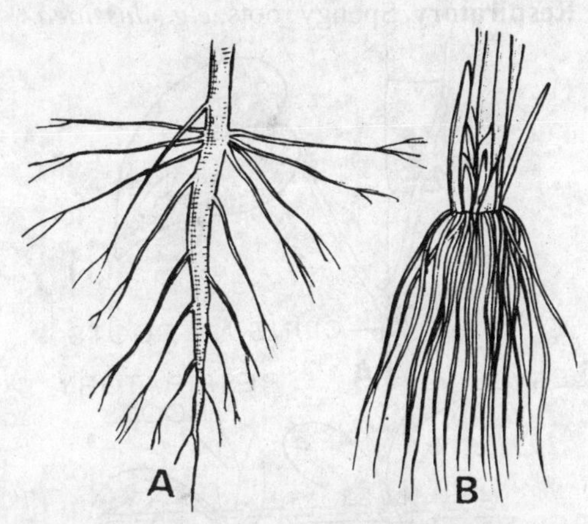

Fig. 8.2. Roots A, tap and lateral roots of a dicotyledon; B, fibrous roots of a monocotyledon.

Root. That part of vascular plants that usually grows downwards into the soil, anchoring plant and absorbing water and nutrient salts.

Tap. Root system with a prominent main root, directed vertically downwards and bearing smaller lateral roots, *e.g.*, most of dicots; *Cajanus* of Papilionatae.

Adventitious. Root developing from part of plant other than roots, *e.g.*, from stem or leaf cutting; of buds, developing from part of plant other than in axil of leaf, *e.g.*, from root, most of monocots.

Branched. Roots possessing branches.

Unbranched. Roots without branches.

Fibrous. A fibrous root system consists of a tuft of adventitious roots of more of less equal diameter, arising from stem base or hypocotyl and bearing smaller lateral roots, *e.g.*, wheat, strawberry.

Prop. Hanging aerial roots of *Ficus*.

Stilt. Such roots arise from the nodes of the stem above the soil, *e.g.*, *Saccharum*.

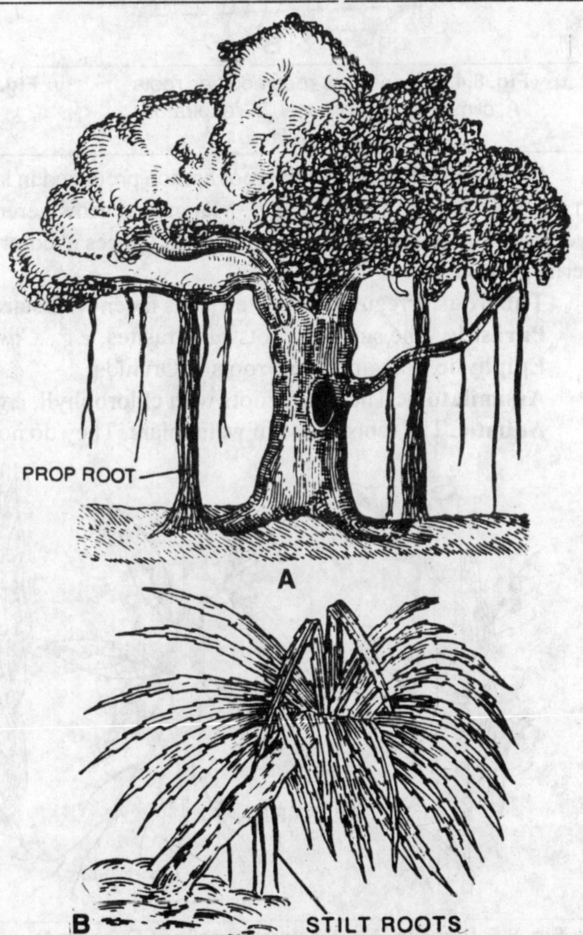

Fig. 8.3. Adventitious modified roots. A, prop roots of banyan; B, stilt roots of **Keora**.

Aerial. Hanging aerial roots, *e.g.*, Orchids.

Climbing. The roots that help in climbing of plants, *e.g., Tecoma, Piper, Pothos.*

Respiratory. Spongy roots, *e.g., Jussiaea.*

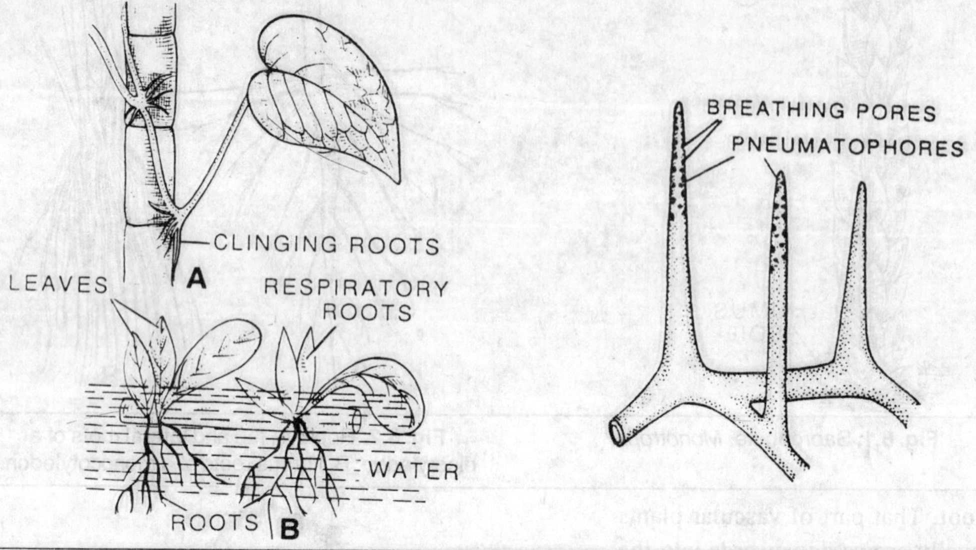

Fig. 8.4. Adventitious root modified roots. A, climbing roots of betel, B, respiratory roots of *Jussiaea*.

Fig. 8.5. Roots. Pneumatophores arising vertically upwards from an underground root.

Pneumatophores. Special root branch produced in large numbers by some vascular plants growing in water or in tidal swamps, *e.g.*, Mangrove; grows erect, projecting into the air above and contains well developed intercellular system of air spaces in communication with atmosphere through pores on aerial portion.

Tuberous. Irregularly swollen roots laden with starch, *e.g., Ipomoea batatas* of Convolvulaceae.

Parasitic. The sucking roots of parasites, *e.g., Cuscuta, Dendrophthoe, Viscum, Orobanche.*

Epiphytic. Hanging aerial roots of Orchids.

Assimilatory. The aerial roots with chlorophyll, *e.g., Tinospora.*

Aquatic. The roots found in water plant. They do not possess root caps and root hairs, *e.g., Pistia.*

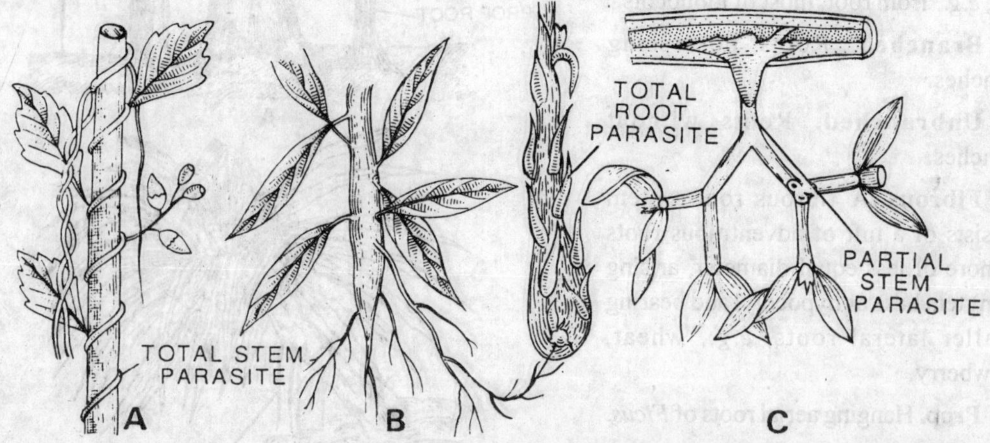

Fig. 8.6. Parasite. A, total stem parasite of *Cuscuta*; B, total root parasite of *Orobanche*; C, partial stem parasite of *Viscum*.

Conical. Cone like fleshy roots, *e.g.,* carrot.

Fusiform. *e.g.,* fleshy root of radish (*Raphanus sativus* of Cruciferae).

Napiform. *e.g.,* fleshy root of turnip.

Fasciculated. Clusters of fleshy roots, *e.g., Asparagus.*

Nodulated. The nodules of the roots contain bacteria, *e.g.,* Leguminous roots; *Cicer, Arachis, Trifolium.*

Beaded or Moniliform. The roots possessing beaded structures, *e.g., Vitis.*

Annulated. When the root has a series of ring-like swellings on its body, *e.g.,* ipecacuanha.

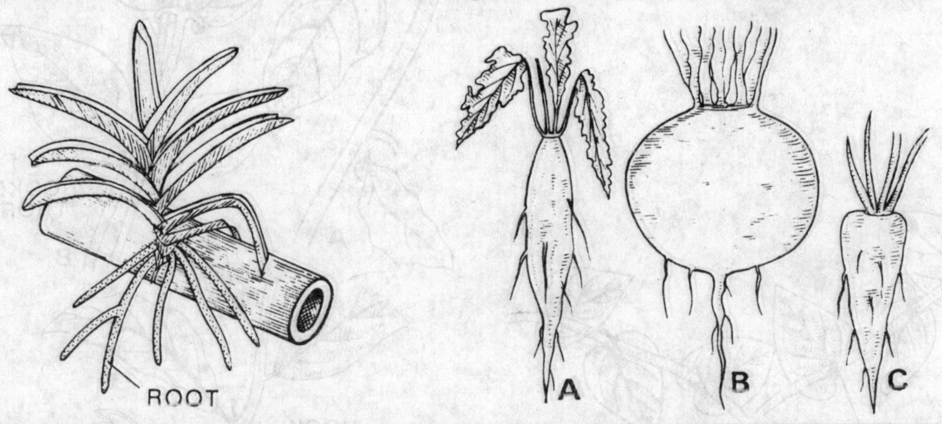

Fig. 8.7. Epiphytic roots of an orchid (*Vanda*).

Fig. 8.8. Modified roots. A, fusiform roots of radish; B, napiform root of turnip; C, conical root of carrot.

Nodulose. When the slinder root becomes suddenly swollen near the apex, *e.g., Curcuma amada* **(Am-haldi).**

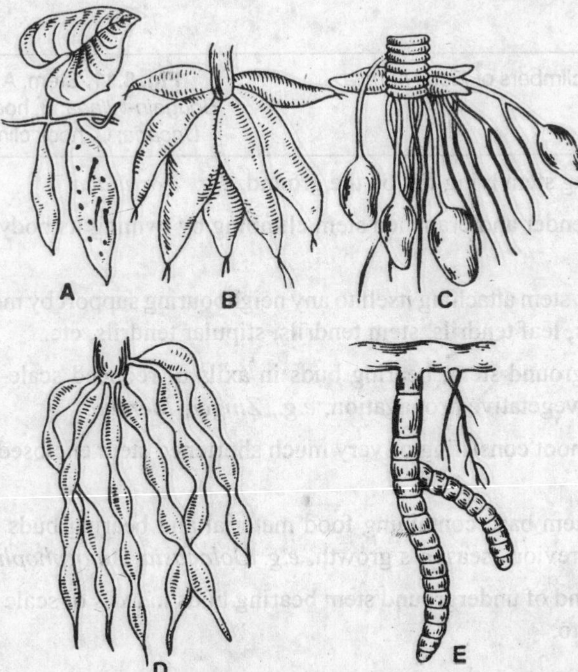

Fig. 8.9. Adventitious modified roots. A, tuberous roots of sweet potato; B, fasciculated tuberous roots of *Dahlia*; C, nodulated roots of mango ginger; D, moniliform roots of *Momordica*; E, annulated roots.

STEM

Stem. Normally aerial part of axis of vascular plants, bearing leaves and buds at definite positions (nodes) and reproductive structures, *e.g.,* flowers.

Erect. Rigid, strong and upright stem.

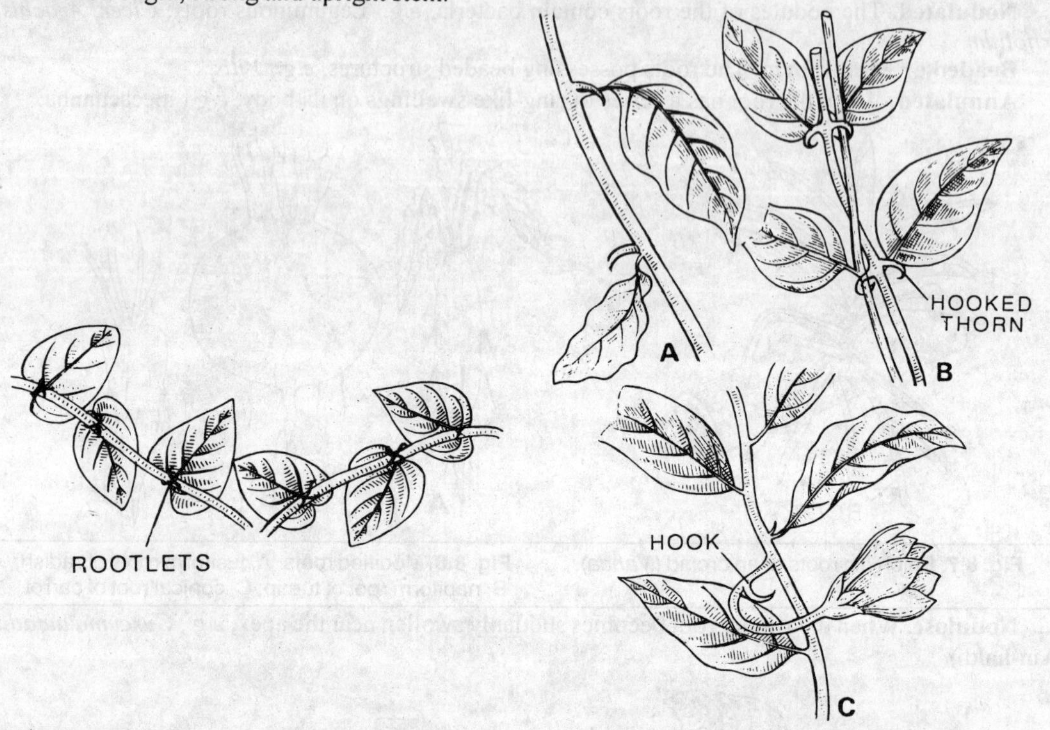

Fig. 8.10. Rootlet climbers of *Ficus pumila.*

Fig. 8.11. Stem. A, thorn climber of *Bougain-villaea*; B, hooked thorn climber of *Uncaria*; C, hook climber of *Artabotrys.*

Prostrate. Trailing stem lying flat on the ground, *e.g., Portulaca.*

Twiner. Long, slender and branched stem climbing by twining its body round the support, *e.g., Cuscuta.*

Climbers. A weak stem attaching itself to any neighbouring support by means of special structures such as rootlets, hooks, leaf tendrils, stem tendrils, stipular tendrils, etc.

Rhizome. Underground stem, bearing buds in axils of reduced scale-like leaves; saving as a means of perennation vegetative propagation, *e.g., Zinger, Mentha.*

Bulb. Modified shoot consisting of very much shortened stem enclosed by fleshy, scale leaves, *e.g., Allium cepa.*

Corm. Swollen stem base containing food material and bearing buds in the axils of scalelike remains of leaves of previous season's growth, *e.g. Colocasia, Amorphophallus, Gladiolus.*

Tuber. Swollen end of underground stem bearing buds in axils of scale-like rudimentary leaves (stem tuber), *e.g.*, potato.

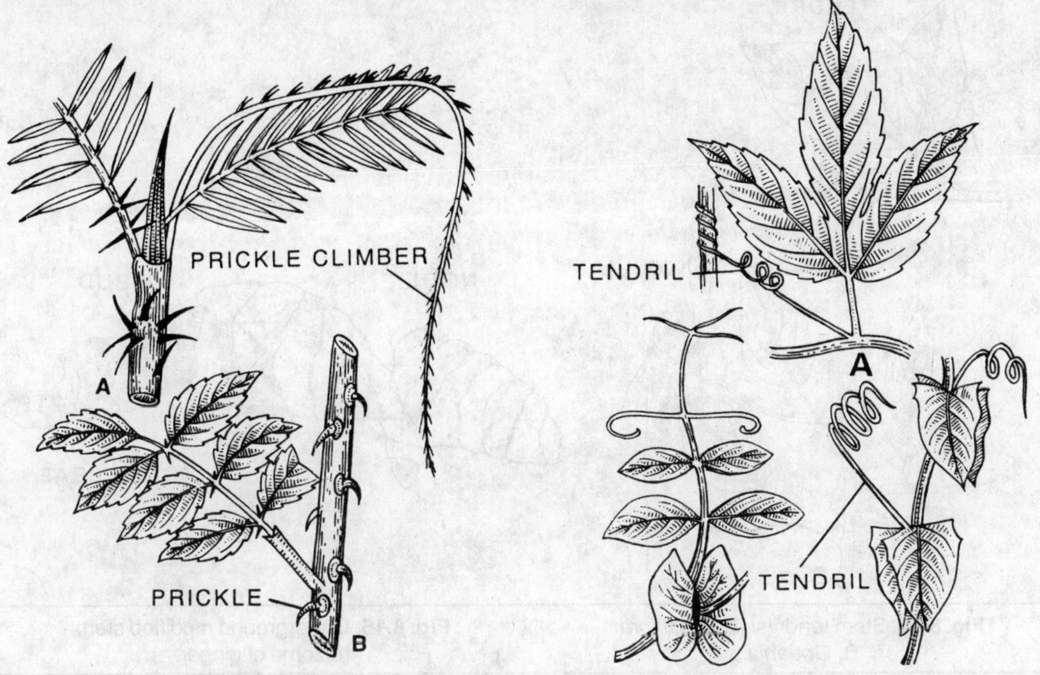

Fig. 8.12. Stem. A, prickle climber of cane; B, prickle climber of rose.

Fig. 8.13. Tendril climbers. A, stem tendril climber of passion flower; B, leaf tendril climber of pea; C, leaf tendril climber of *Lathyrus*.

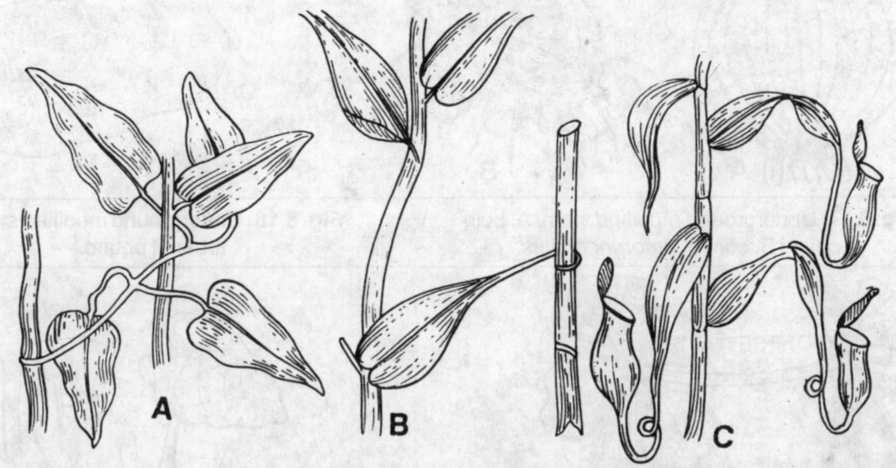

Fig. 8.14. Leaf climbers. A, leaf climber of *Clematis*; B, leaf climber of *Gloriosa*; C, leaf climber of pitcher plant.

Offset. A horizontal, short, more or less thickened, prostrate branch producing at the apex a tuft of leaves above and a cluster of small roots beneath, *e.g., Pistia.*

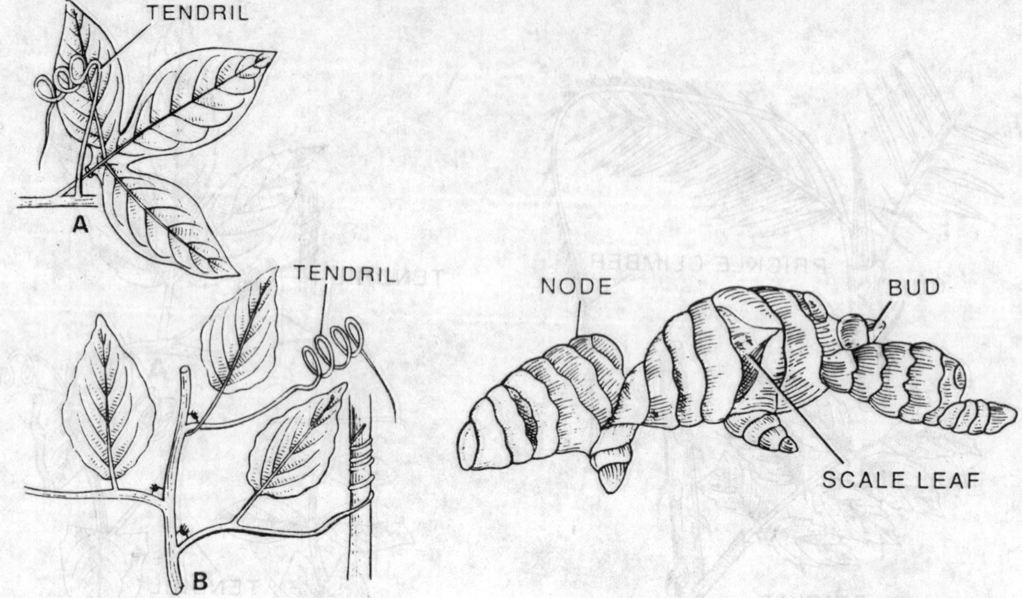

Fig. 8.15. Stem tendrils. A, *Passiflora*; B, *Gouania*.

Fig. 8.16. Underground modified stem rhizome of ginger.

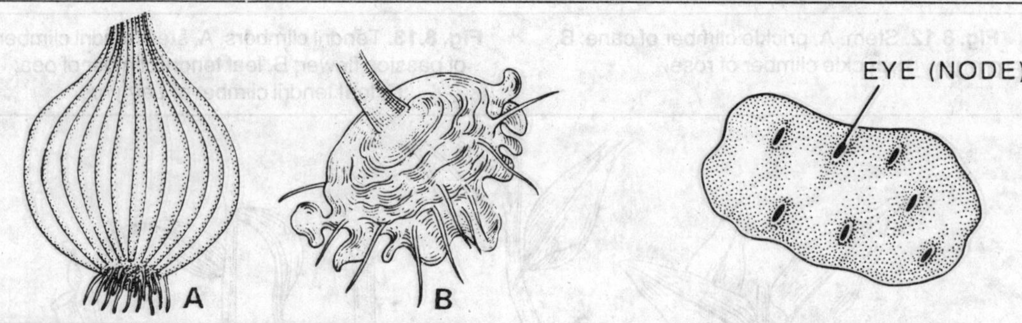

Fig. 8.17. Underground modified stem. A, bulb of onion; B, corn of *amorphophalus*.

Fig. 8.18. Underground modified stem; tuber of potato.

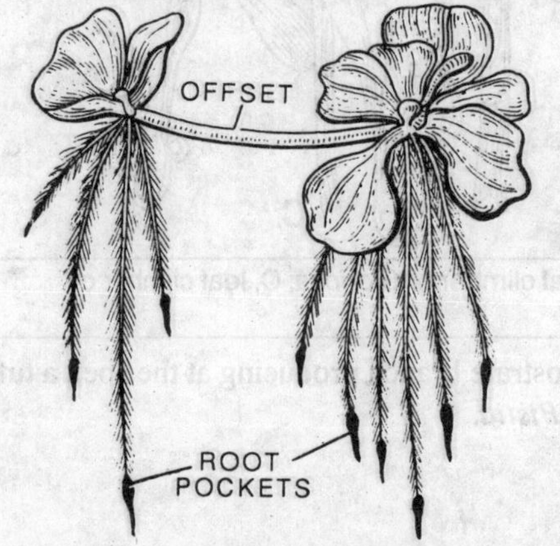

Fig. 8.19. Sub-aerial modification of stem. Offset of *Pistia*.

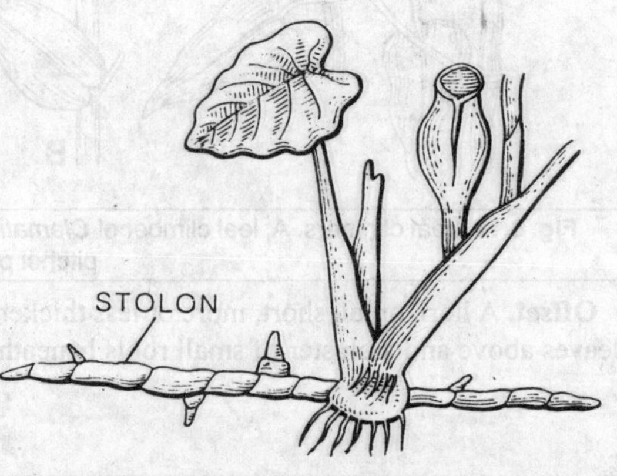

Fig. 8.20. Sub-aerial modification of stem. Stolon of *Colocasia*.

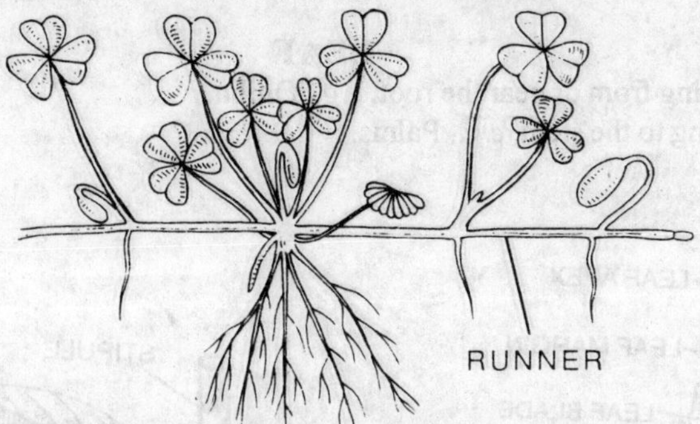

Fig. 8.21. Sub-aerial modification of stem. Runner of *Oxalis*.

Stolon. Horozontally growing stem that roots at nodes, *e.g.*, strawberry runner, *Colocasia.*

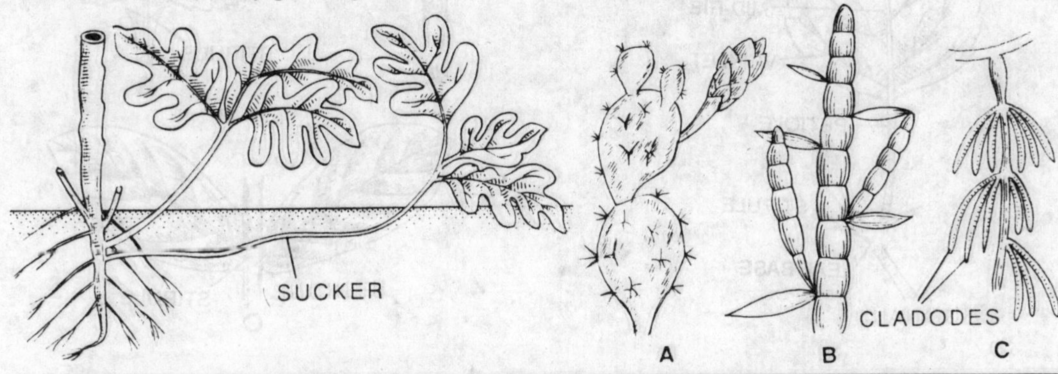

Fig. 8.22. Sub-aerial modification of stem. Suckers of *Chrysanthemum*.

Fig. 8.23. Aerial modification of stem. A, phylloclade of *Opuntia*; B, phylloclade of Cocoloba; C, cladodes of *Asparagus*.

Runner. Stolon that roots at tip forming new plant that eventually is freed from connection with parent by decay of runner, *e.g.*, *Oxalis*.

Sucker. A creeping stem but growing obliquely upwards directly giving rise to a leafy shoot, *e.g.*, *Chrysanthemum.*

Phylloclade. Modified stem having appearance and function of a leaf, *e.g.*, *Ruscus,* Cocoloba.

Cladode. A phylloclade of single internode, *e.g.*, *Asparagus.*

Branched. Stem possessing branches, *e.g.*, Nim tree.

Unbranched. Stem having no branches, *e.g.*, Palm.

If branched whether recemose or cymose type of branching. If cymose whether uniparous, biparous or multiparous.

Herbaceous. Having the characters of a herb, *e.g.*, *Ranunculus.*

Woody. Heaving the characters of a shrub and tree, *e.g.*, *Capparis, Melia.*

Solid. Interior portion of the stem is filled up with matter.

Fistular. A stem having hollow interior, *e.g.*, wheat, bamboo.

Cylinderical (terete). Circular stem as seen in T.S.

Angular. A stem shows many angles in T.S., *e.g.*, *Cucurbita.*

Flattened. Flat stem in T.S.

Hairy. Stem possessing hairs on its surface.

Glabrous. Smooth stem.

Waxy. Stem having wax coating, *e.g.*, *Calotropis.*

Spiny. Stem having spines.

Colour. Whether green, grey, etc.

LEAF

Radical. Proceeding from or near the root, *e.g.*, Onion.

Cauline. Pertaining to the stem, *e.g.*, Palms.

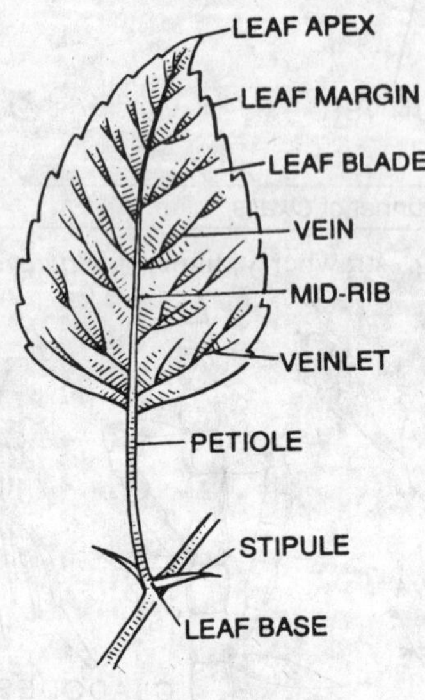

Fig. 8.24. Leaf. Parts of a leaf

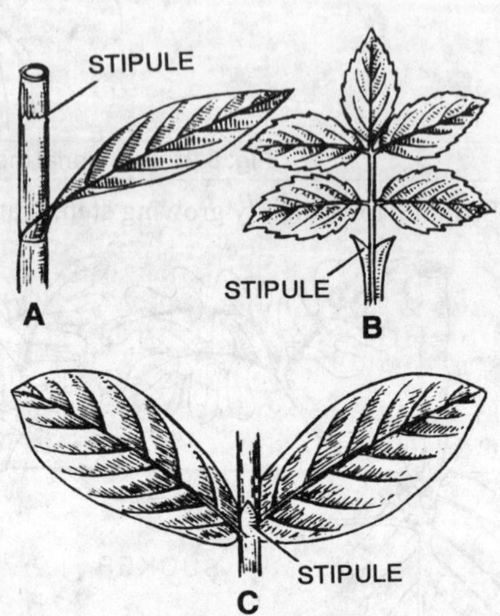

Fig. 8.26. Stipules. A, ochreate stipule of *Polygonum*; b, interpetiolar stipule of *Ixora*; C, adnate stipule of rose.

Cauline and ramal. Pertaining to the main stem as well as its branches, *e.g.*, Mango.

Alternate. A single leaf arising at each node, *e.g.*, *Hibiscus rosa-sinensis*.

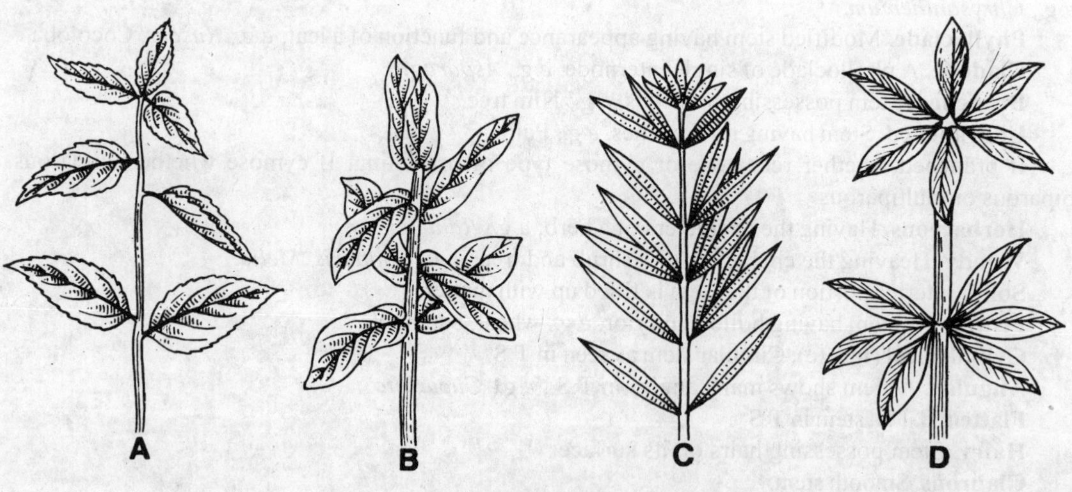

Fig. 8.25. Phyllotaxy of leaves. A, alternate; B, opposite decussate; C, whorled leaves of *Nerium*; D, whorled leaves of *Alstonia*.

Opposite. On different sides of the axis with the bases at the same level.

Opposite decusate. In pairs at right angles to one another, *e.g., calotropis.*

Opposite superposed. A pair of leaves that stands directly over the lower pair in the same plant, *e.g.,* Guava.

Whorled. More than two leaves arranged in a circle round an axis, *e.g., Spergula.*

Petiolate. The leaf blade is situated on the petiole.

Sessile. Without a petiole or stalk.

Sub-sessile. Having short petiole.

Stipulate. With stipules, *e.g.,* rose.

Extipulatc. Having no stipules, *e.g., Ipomoea.*

Stipules. An appendage of the leaf. Normally two stipules are developed at base of a leaf petiole, they may be leafy (foliaeous), *e.g., Lathyrus*; free lateral, *e.g.,* China rose; adnate, *e.g.,* rose; interpetiolar, *e.g., Ixora*; *Spergula*; spiny, *e.g., Acacia*; tendrilar, *e.g., smilax.*

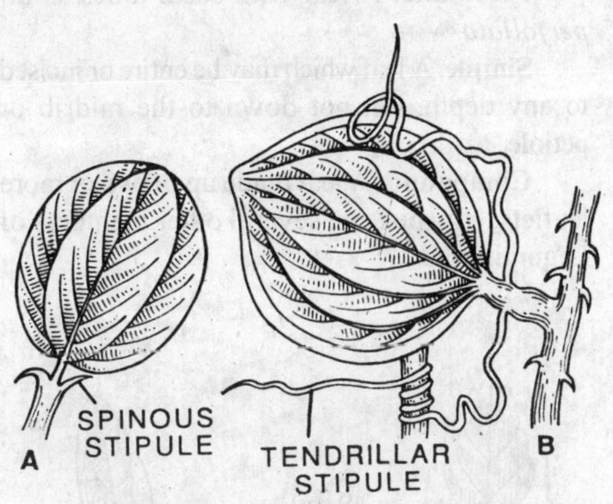

Fig. 8.27. Stipules, A, spinous stipules of *Zizyphus*; B, tendrilar stipules of *Smilax.*

Leaf Base

Connate. Two sessile opposite leaves meeting each other across the stem and fusing together, *e.g., Lomicera flava.*

Amplexicaul. Clasping or surrounding the stem, as base of leaf, *e.g., Sonchus.*

Auriculate. Leaf with expanded bases surrounding stem, *e.g., calotropis.*

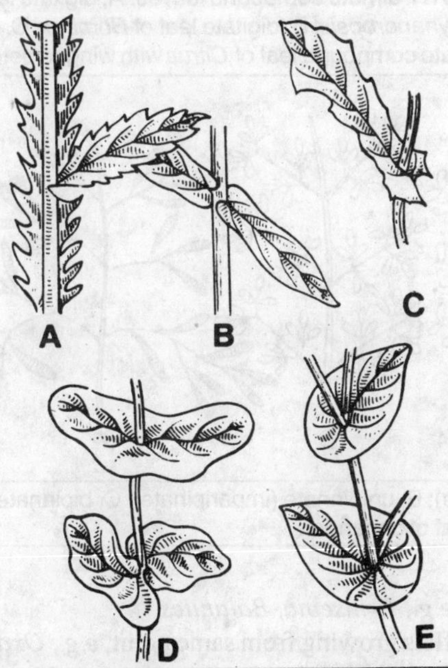

Fig. 8.28. Leaf base of sessile leaves. A, decurrent leaf of *Laggera*; B, auriculate leaf of *Calotropis*; C, amplexicaul leaf of *Emilia*; D, connate leaf of *Lomicera*; E, perfoliate leaves.

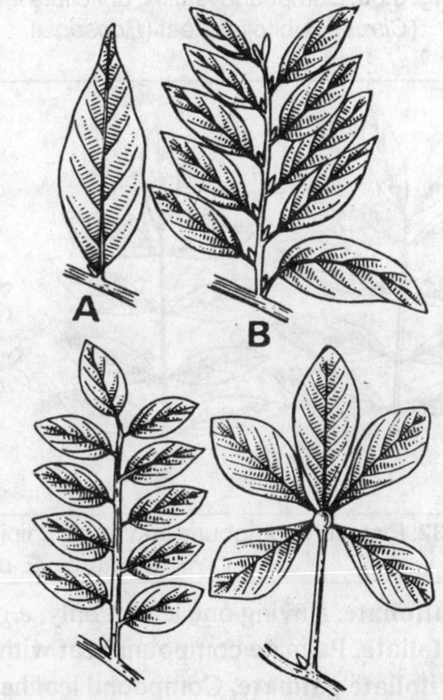

Fig. 8.29. Simple and compound leaves. A, simple leaf; B, a branch; C, pinnately compound loaf; D, palmately compound leaf.

Decurrent. Having leaf base prolonged down stem as a winged expansion or rib, *e.g.*, *Laggera pterodonta.*

Perfoliate. A leaf with basal lobes so united as to appear as if stem ran through it, *e.g.*, *Aloe perfoliata.*

Simple. A leaf which may be entire or incised to any depth, but not down to the midrib or petiole.

Compound. A leaf made up of two or more leaflets, *e.g.*, pea and several other members of Leguminosae.

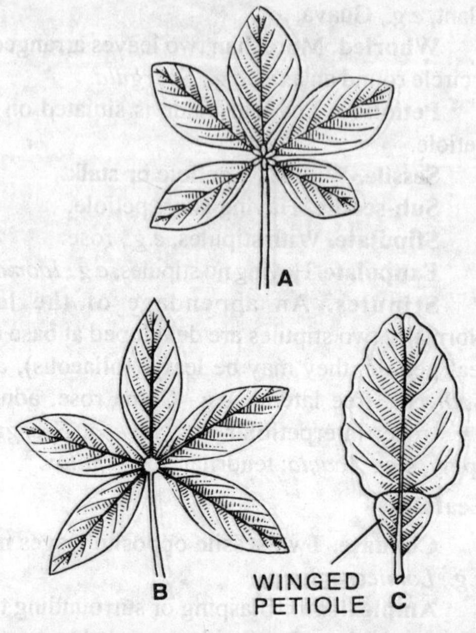

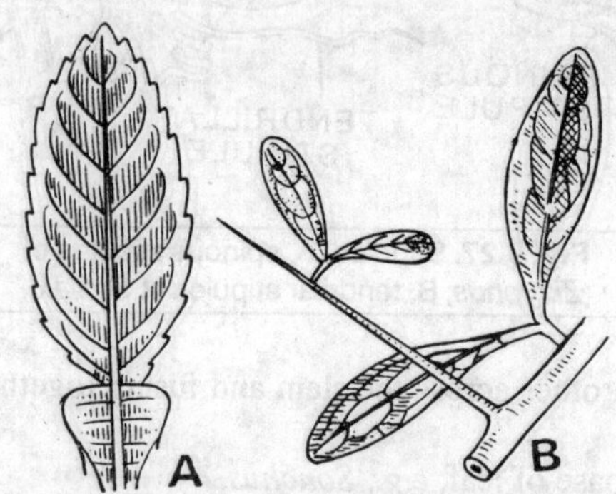

Fig. 8.30. Compound leaf. A, unifoliate leaf (*Citrus*); B, bifoliate leaf (*Prinsepia*).

Fig. 8.31. Palmate compound leaves. A, digitate leaf of *Gynandropsis*; B, digitate leaf of *Bombax;* C, unifoliate compound leaf of *Citrus* with winged petiole.

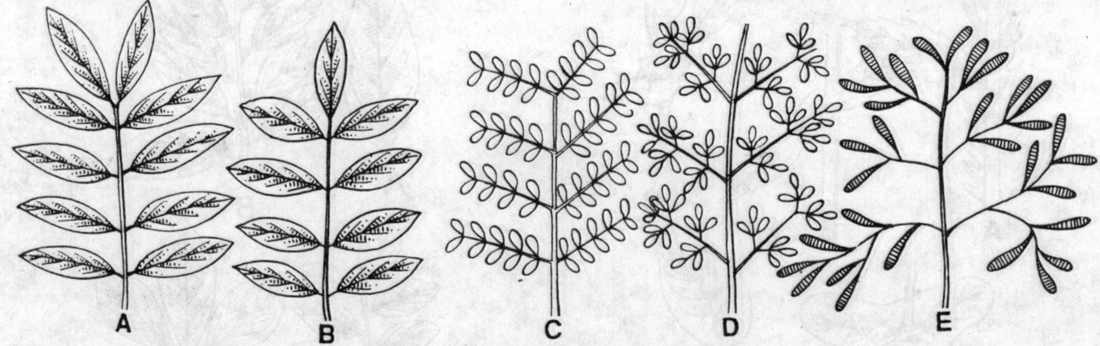

Fig. 8.32. Pinnately compound leaves. A, unipinate (paripinate); B, unipinnate (imparipinate); C, bipinnate; D, tripinnate; E, decompound leaf of coriander.

Unifoliate. Having one leaflet only, *e.g.*, *Citrus.*

Bifoliate. Palmate compound leaf with two leaflets, *e.g.*, *Prinsepia, Balanites.*

Trifoliate palmate. Compound leaf having three leaflets growing from same point, *e.g.*, *Oxalis.*

Quadrifoliate. Compound palmate leaf, with four leaflets arising at a common point, *e.g.*, *Marsilea.*

Multifoliate. Compound palmate leaf with five or more leaflets arising at a common point, *e.g.*, *Gynandropsis pentaphylla.*

Pinnate. A compound leaf having leaflets on each side on an axis or mid-rib.

Unipinnate. Having leaflets on each side of an axis, *e.g.*, *Cassia.*

Bipinate. The central axis produces secondary axis which bears the leaflets, *e.g.*, *Acacia.*

The secondary axes produce the tertiary axes which bears the leaflets, *e.g., Acacia.*

The secondary axes produce the tertiary axes which bear the leaflets, *e.g., Moringa.*

Decompound. More than thrice pinnate, *e.g.,* old leaves of coriander.

Paripinnate. Pinnately compound without a terminal leaflet, *e.g., Cassia.*

Imparipinate. Pinnately compound leaf with an odd terminal leaflet, *e.g.,* Pea.

Incision of Lamina

Pinnatifid. Leaves lobed half-way to midrib.

Pinnatisect. With leaves lobed almost to base or midrib.

Palmatifid. Leaves divided into lobes to about the middle, at acute angles to each other, *e.g.,* Castor.

Palmatisect. Palmate with division nearly to base.

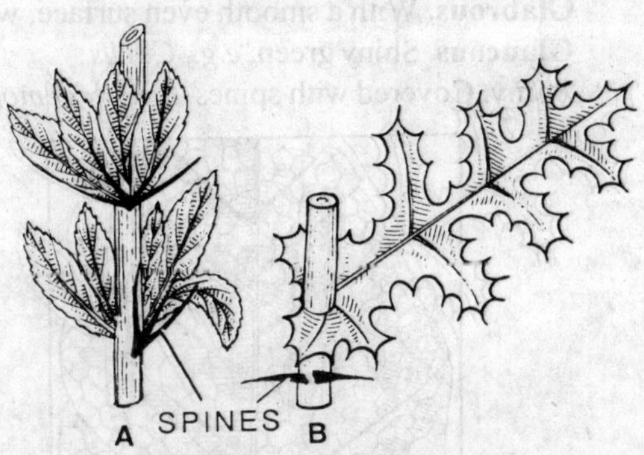

Fig. 8.33. Modified leaves. A, leaves modified into spines; B, leaf of *Argemone* with spines.

Margin of Lamina

Entire. With continuous margin, *e.g., Psidium.*

Dentate. With large saw-like teeth on the margin.

Serrate-dentate. With serrate edges themselves toothed.

Undulate. Many, *e.g., Polyalthia.*

Convolute. Rulled together.

Crenate. With scalloped margain, *e.g., Bryophyllum.*

Lacerate. Having margin or apex deeply cut into irregular lobes, *e.g.,* many members of Ranunculaceae.

Laciniate. Irregularly incised; fringed.

Laciniolate. Minutely incised or fringed.

Ciliate. Bearing fine hairs on the margin.

Crispate. Curled or extremely undulate margin.

Spinous. Bearing many spines, *e.g., Argemone.*

Pectinate. Comb-like.

Lobed. Leaf margin divided into many lobes, *e.g., Ranunculus.*

Leaf Apex

Acute. Ending in a sharp point forming an acute angle, *e.g.,* mango.

Acuminate. Drawn out into long point; tapering; pointed, *e.g., Ficus religiosa.*

Obtuse. With blunt or rounded end, *e.g.,* Banyan.

Emarginate. Having a notch at apex, *e.g., Bauhinia.*

Truncate. Terminating abruptly, as if tapering end were cut off, *e.g., caryota urens.*

Mucronate. Abruptly terminated by a sharp spine, *e.g.,* apex of leaflet of *Cassia obtusifolia.*

Cuspidate. Terminating in a point.

Aristate. Provided with awns, or with a well developed bristle.

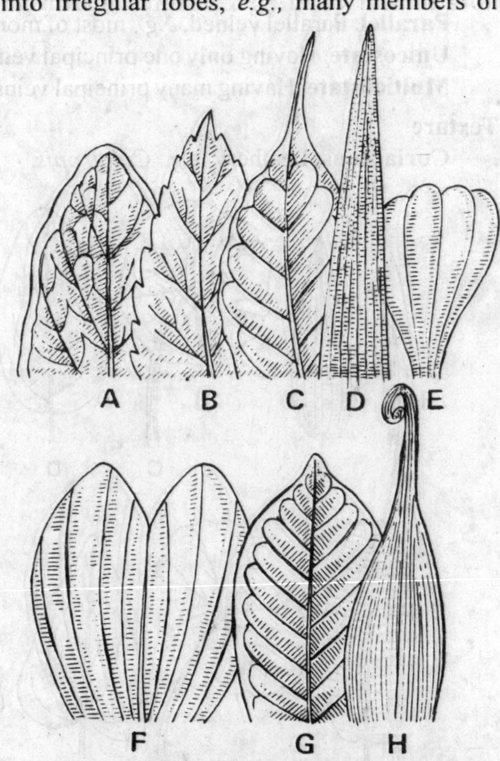

Fig. 8.34. Leaf apex. A, obtuse; B, acute; C, acuminate; D, cuspidate; E, retuse; F, emarginate; G, mucronate; H, cirrhose.

Retuse. Obtuse with a broad shallow notch in middle, *e.g., Oxalis.*

Cirrhose. Leaf with prolongation of midrib forming a tendril, *e.g., Gloriosa.*

Apiculate. Forming abruptly to a small tip, *e.g. Dalbergia.*

Leaf Surface

Hairy. Leaf surface covered with fine hair. The hairs are of various types.

Glabrous. With a smooth even surface, without hairs, *e.g.,* China rose.

Glaucous. Shiny green, *e.g., Citrus.*

Spiny. Covered with spines, *e.g., Argemone.*

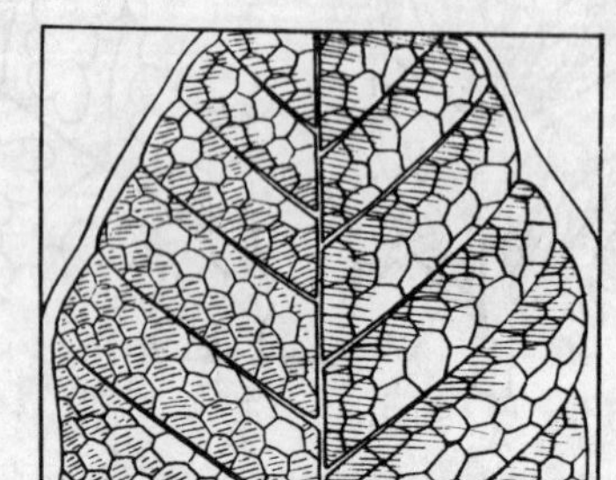

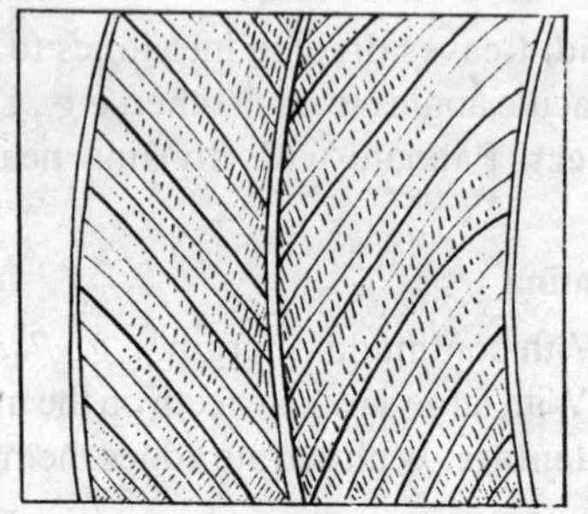

Fig. 8.35. Leaf venation. A, reticulate in a dicot leaf; b, parallel in a monocot leaf.

Venation. System or disposition of veins.

Reticulate (net veined). Like net work, *e.g.,* most of dicots.

Parallel. Parallel veined, *e.g.,* most of monocots.

Unicostate. Having only one principal vein.

Multicostate. Having many principal veins.

Texture

Coriaceous. Leathery, *e.g., Calotropis.*

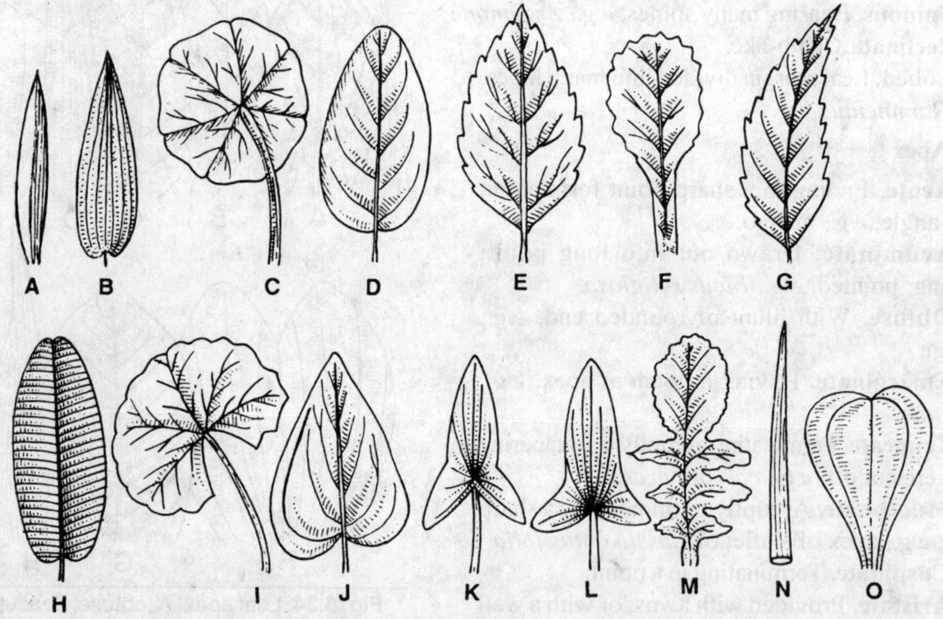

Fig. 8.36. Shape of leaf. A, linear; B, lanceolate; c, rotund; D, oval or elliptical; E, ovate; F, spathulate; G, oblique; H, oblong; I, reniform; J, cordate; K, sagittate; L, hastate; M, lyrate; N, acicular; O, cuneate.

Fleshy. Soft and thick, *e.g., Spergula.*

Succulent. Full of juice or sap, *e.g., Aloe.*

Colour

Green. Usually the leaves are green in colour.

Pigmented. In certain leaves the pigments are developed, *e.g., Aerva.*

Note. In a compound leaf the leaflet should be described in the manner as a simple leaf.

Shape of the Leaf

Linear. Long and narrow leaf, *e.g.,* many grasses.

Lanceolate. Lance-shaped leaf, *e.g.,* bamboo, *Nerium,* etc.

Round or orbicular. Leaf with a circular leaf blade, *e.g.,* lotus, garden nasturtium, etc.

Elliptical. An ellipse-shaped leaf, *e.g.,* guava, jack, etc.

Ovate. Leaf with an egg-shaped leaf blade, *i.e.,* slightly broader at the base than at the apex, *e.g.,* banyan, China rose, etc.

Spathulate. Spatula-shaped leaf, *i.e.,* broad and round at the top and narrower towards the base, *e.g., Calendula* and *Drosera.*

Oblique. Leaf with two unequal halves *e.g., Begonia.*

Oblong. Leaf with wide and long leaf blade. Here the two margins run more or less straight up, *e.g.,* banana.

Reniform. Kidney-shaped leaf, *e.g.,* Indian pennywort.

Cordate. Leaf with heart-shaped leaf blade, *e.g.,* betel (inversely heart-shaped leaf called as obcordate, *e.g.,* wood-sorrel).

Sagittate. Leaf with an arrow-shaped leaf blade, *e.g.,* arrowhead and some ariods.

Hastate. Sagittate leaf with its two lobes directed outside, *e.g.,* water bindweed and *Typhonium.*

Lyrate. Lyre-shaped leaf, *i.e.,* with a large terminal lobe and some smaller lateral lobes, *e.g.,* radish, mustard, etc.

Acicular. Long narrow and cylindrical leaf, *i.e.,* needle shaped, *e.g.,* pine.

Cuneate. Wedge shaped leaf, *e.g.,* water lettuce.

Modified Leaves

Leaves of many plants are often modified into some specified structures to do various specialized functions. **Leaf tendril** is one of these structures.

Leaf-tendrils. Leaf or part of the leaf modified as a slender, branched or unbranched, thread like structure, used by many climbing plants for attachment to a support in various ways.

In the leaf of pea upper leaflets modify into tendrils while in *Gloriosa* leaf-apex modifies into a tendril. In *Naravelia* the terminal leaflet modifies into a tendril. Likely in *Bignonia unguis-cati* these leaflets are modified into the hooks. *Lathyrus aphaca* is an example of whole leaf modification into a single tendril.

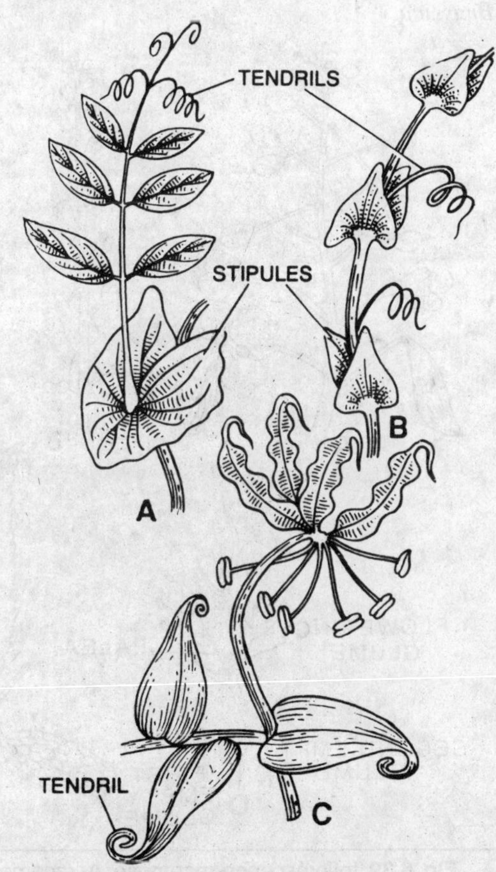

Fig. 8.37. Modified leaves. A, leaf tendrils of pea; B, leaf tendrils of *Lathyrus*; C, leaf tendrils (cirrhose) of *Gloriosa*.

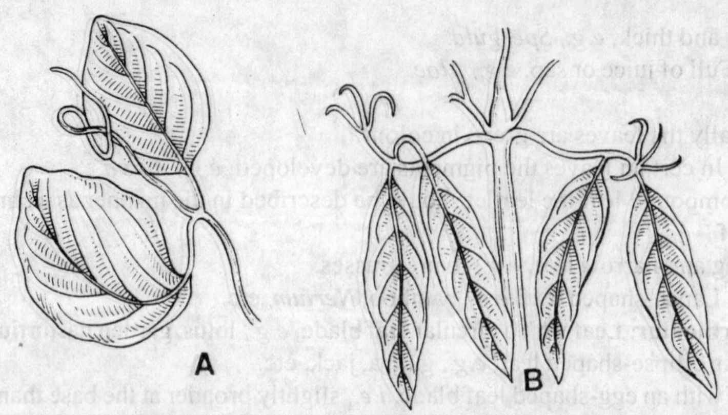

Fig. 8.38. Modified leaves. A, leaf of *Naravelia* with the terminal leaflet modified into a tendril; B, leaflet modified into hooks (*Bignonia*).

INFLORESCENCE

Inflorescence. Method in which flowers are arranged on an axis.

Racemose. Inflorescence with monopodial branching.

Raceme. Inflorescence having a common axis and stalked flowers in acropetal succession, *e.g.*, *Brassica.*

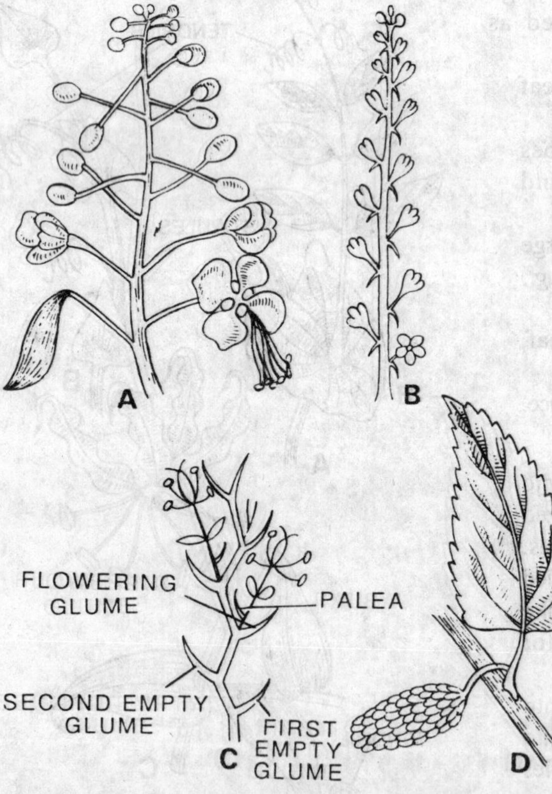

Fig. 8.39. Inflorescence-recemose. A, raceme of **gul-mohur**; B, spike; C, spikelet of a grass; D, female catkin of mulberry.

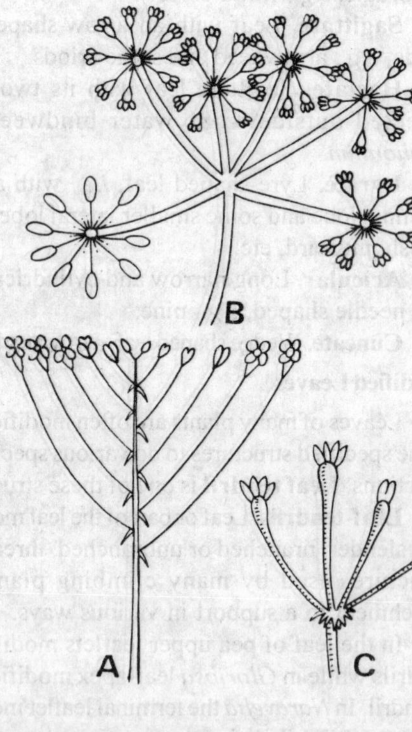

Fig. 8.40. Inflorescence. a, Corymb; B, compound umbel (umbel of umbels); C, simple umbel.

Corymb. A raceme with lower pedicels elongated so that the top is nearly flat, *e.g.*, Candytuft.

Spike. Inflorescence with sessile flowers along axis, *e.g., Achyranthes.*

Catkin. A spike with unisexual flowers and pendulous rachis, *e.g., Morus.*

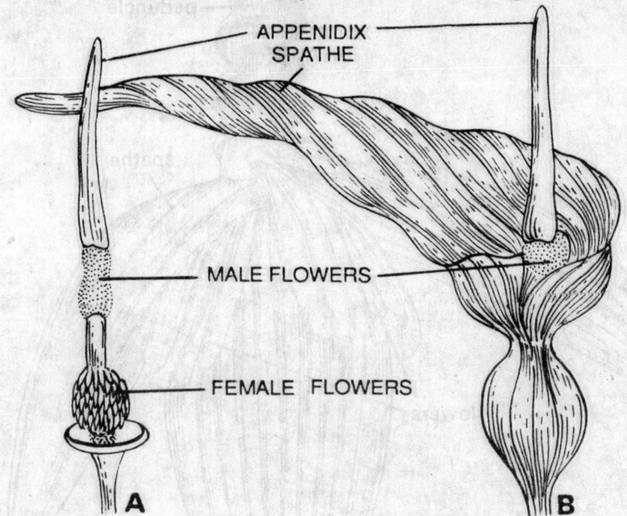

Fig. 8.41. Inflorescence-spadix. A, apadix of an aroid without spathe; B, same with spathe.

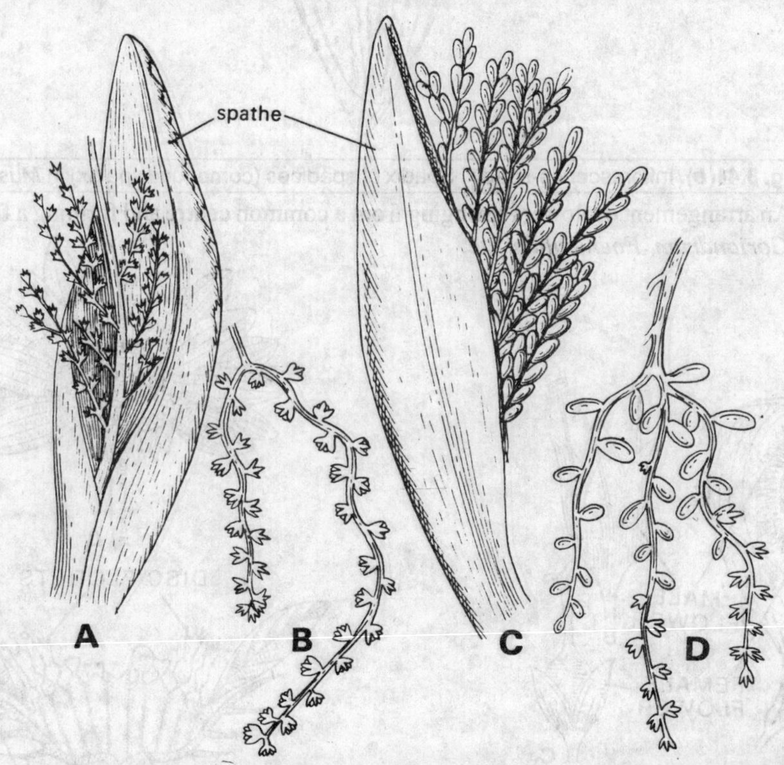

Fig. 8.41(*a*). Inflorescence. Spadix of spadices (compound spadix) in coconut palm; A, male spadix of spadices; B, male flowers on the branched peduncle; C, female spadix of spadices; D, female flowers on branched peduncles.

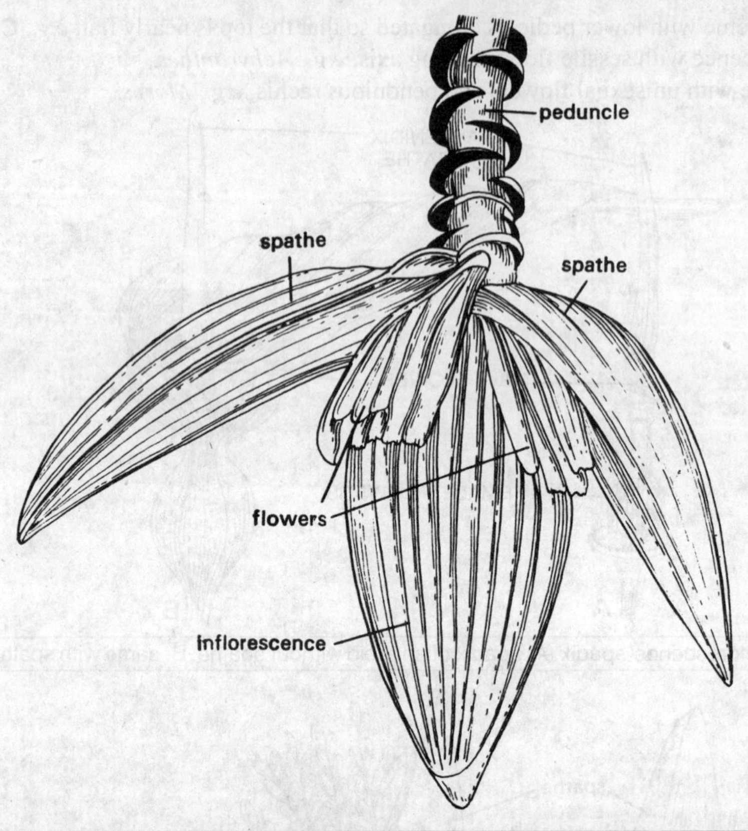

Fig. 8.41(*b*). Inflorescence-spadix. Spadix of spadices (compound spadix) in *Musa*.

Umbel. An arrangement of flowers springing from a common centre and forming a flat or rounded cluster, *e.g., Coriandrum, Foeniculum,* etc.

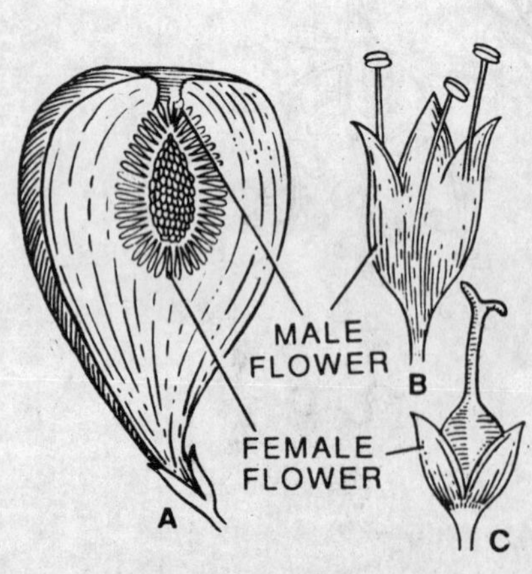

Fig. 8.42. Inflorescence. A, hypanthodium of *Ficus*; B, male flower; C, female flower.

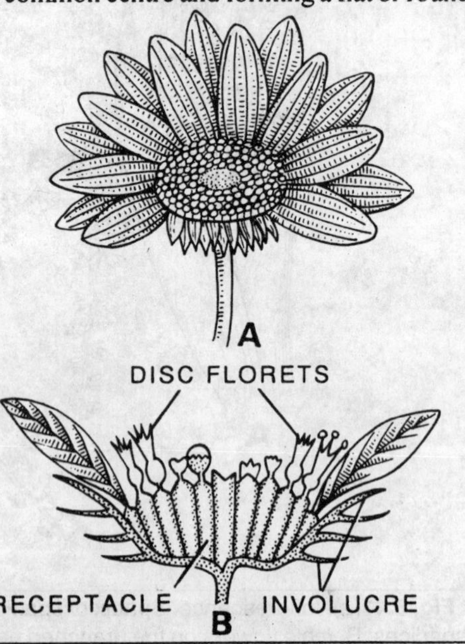

Fig. 8.43. Inflorescence. Head (capitulum). A, a head; B, a head in L.S.

Spadix. A racemose inflorescence with elongated axis, sessile flowers, and an enveloping spathe, *e.g., Colocasia, Alocasia,* Palm, *Musa,* etc.

Hypanthodium. An inflorescence with concave capitulum on whose walls the flowers are arranged, *e.g., Ficus.*

Capitulum. An inflorescence of sessile flowers or florets crowded together on a receptacle and usually surrounded by an involucre.

Cymose. Sympodially branched.

Uniparous (monochasial). Having a cymose inflorescence with one axis at each branching.

Biparous (dichasial). Dichotomously branched cymose inflorescence, *e.g., Ixora, Saponaria.*

Helicoid cyme. An uniparous inflorescence produced by suppression of successive axes on same side, thus causing the sympodium to be spirally twisted, *e.g., Begonia, Juncus.*

Scorpioid. An uniparous inflorescence in which the lateral branches develop on alternate sides evidently forming a zigzag, *e.g., Heliotropium*

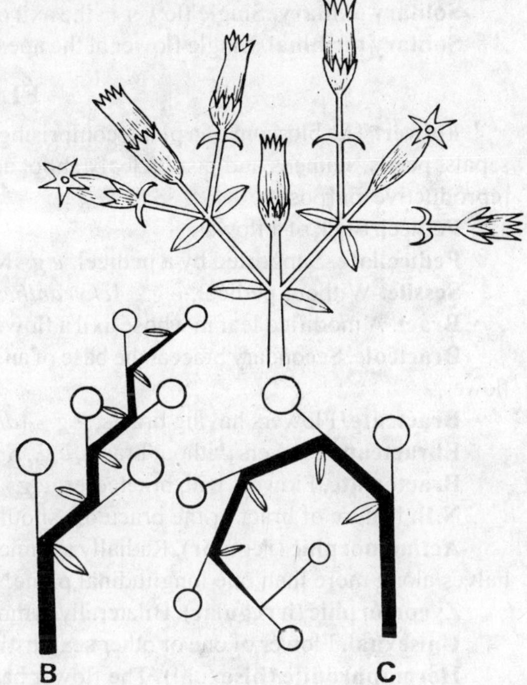

Fig. 8.44. Inflorescence. Cymose. A, Biparous (dichasial) cyme; B, scorpioid cyme; C, helicoid cyme.

Special Types

Cyathium. The peculiar inflorescence in *Euphorbia,* a cup-shaped involucre with stamens and stalked gynoecium, each stamen and the gynoecium being a separate flower.

Verticillaster. A much condensed cyme with appearance of whorl, but in reality arising in axils of opposite leaves, *e.g.,* characteristic of Labiatae.

Panicle. A compound branched raceme, *e.g.,* Mengo, *Melia.*

Spikelet. A secondary spike of grasses, bearing few flowers.

Compound umbel. Umbel of umbels.

Compound corymb. Corymb of corymbs.

Solitary flower. Single flower.

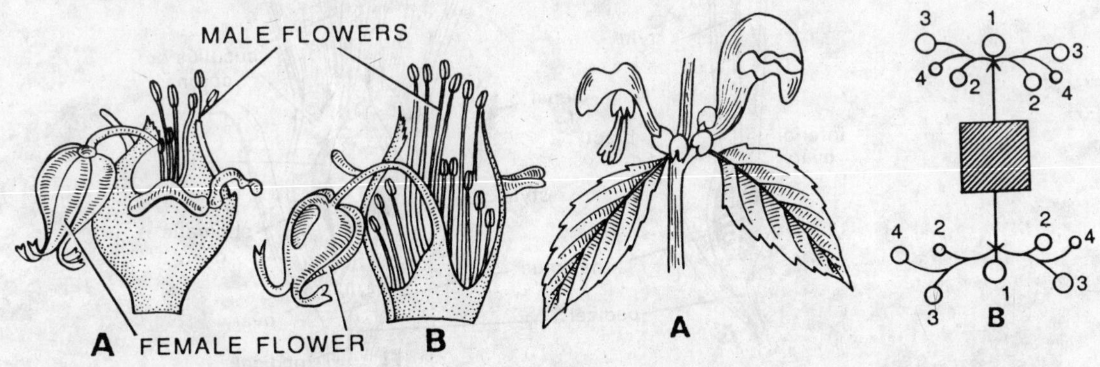

Fig. 8.45. Inflorescence. Special. Cyathium. A, cyathium of *Euphorbia*; B, L.S. of same.

Fig. 8.46. Inflorescence. Special verticillaster. A, verticillaster of Labiatae; B, diagram of same.

Solitary axillary. Single flower in the axil of leaf, *e.g., Cucrubita.*

Solitary terminal. Single flower at the apex, *e.g.,* Poppy.

FLOWER

Flower. The blossom of a plant, comprising generally sepals, petals, stamens and pistil a leafy shoot adapted for reproductive purposes.

Pedicel. Stalk of a flower.

Pedicellate. Supported by a pedicel, *e.g.,* Mustard.

Sessile. Without pedicel, *e.g., Achyranthes.*

Bract. A modified leaf in whose axil a flower arises.

Bracteole. Secondary bract at the base of an individual flower.

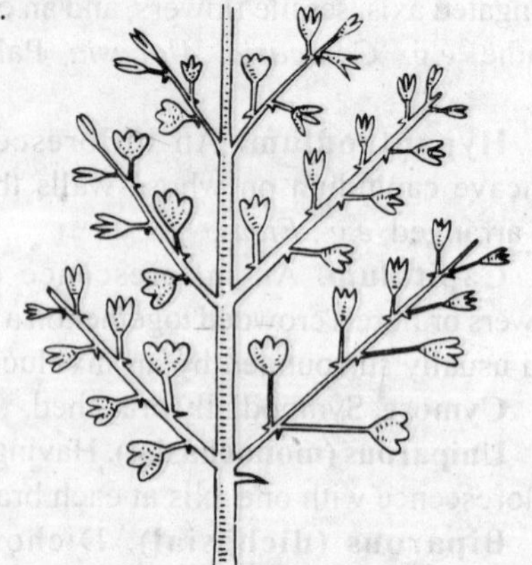

Fig. 8.47. Inflorescence. Panicle.

Bracteate. Flowers having bracts, *e.g., Adhatoda.*

Ebracteate. Flowers without bracts, *e.g., Solanum.*

Bracteolate. Flowers with bracteoles, *e.g., Ruellia.*

N.B. Nature of bract or the bracteole should be described separately.

Actinomorphic (regular). Radially symmetrical flower; the flower can be divided into two equal halves along more than one longitudinal plane, *e.g., Vinca.*

Zygomorphic (irregular). Bilaterally symmetrical, with only one plane of symmetry, *e.g., Pisum.*

Unisexual. Flower of one or other sex; distinctly male or female, *e.g., Morus.*

Hermaphrodite (bisexual). The flower having both male and female reproductive organs, *e.g., Brassica.*

Complete. The flower with all the four whorls, *i.e.,* calyx, corolla, androecium and gynoecium, *e.g., Hibiscus.*

Incomplete. The flower lacking any one of the four whorls, *e.g., Lagenaria, Luffa, Cucurbita.*

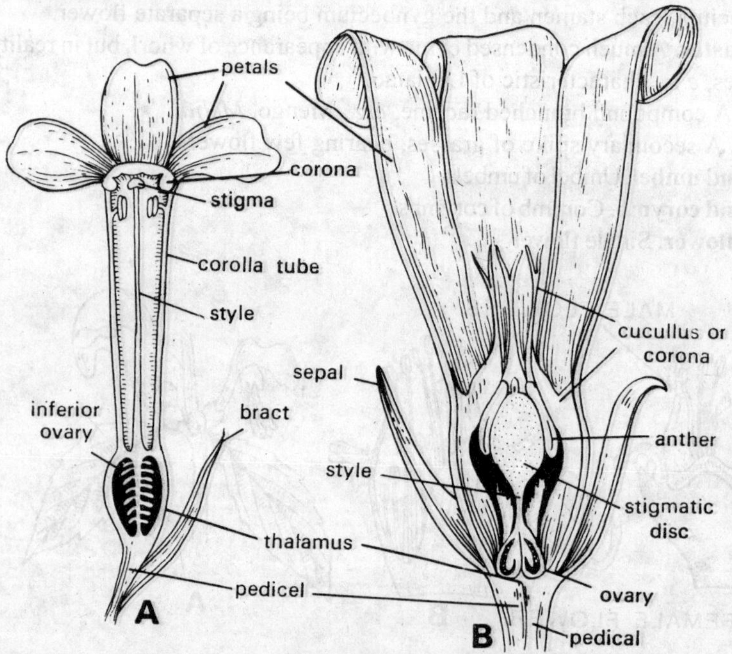

Fig. 8.48. Flower. A, Parts of a flower with inferior ovary; B, L.S. of flower showing position of whorls on the thalamus with superior ovary.

Regular. Actinomorphic. *e.g., Brassica.*

Irregular. Zygomorphic, *e.g.,* Pea.

Hypogynous. The other whorls inserted below the gynoecium, and not adherent; ovary superior, *e.g., Solanum.*

Perigynous. Having sepals, petals, stamens, round the gynoecium; ovary half superior, *e.g., Prunus.*

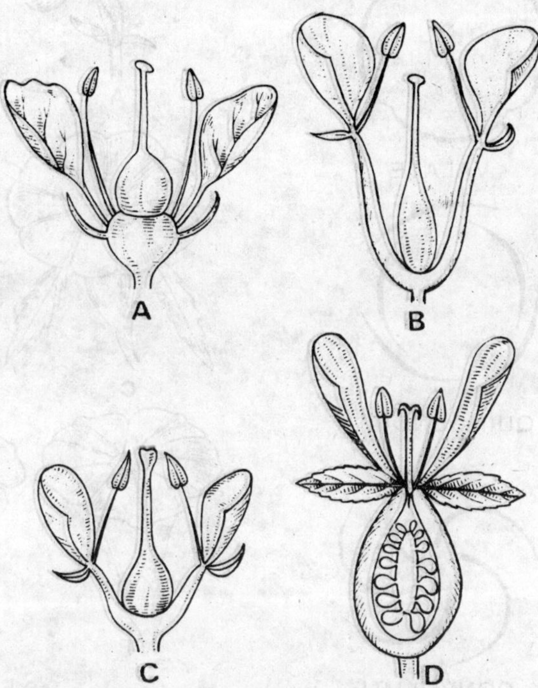

Fig. 8.49. Position of floral leaves on the thalamus. A, hypogyny; B and C, perigyny, D, epigyny.

Epigynous. Having the various whorls adnate to ovary, thus apparently inserted in ovary; inferior ovary, *e.g., Hamelia; Coriandrum.*

Acyclic. Flowers with floral leaves arranged in a spiral, *e.g., Ranunculus.*

Cyclic. Having parts of flowers arranged in whorls, *e.g., Solamum.*

Colour. Variously coloured.

CALYX

Calyx. The outer whorl of floral leaves (sepals).

Sepal. A leaf-like division of calyx.

Sepaloid. Like a sepal; green in colour.

Petaloid. Like a petal; coloured.

Number of Sepals

Polysepalous. Having free or distinct sepals, *e.g.,* Mustard.

Gamosepalous. With coherent sepals, *e.g.,* China rose.

Aestivation. The mode in which sepals are disposed in flower bud.

Valvate. Meeting at edges, *e.g., Solanum.*

Induplicate. In aestivation having bud sepals folded inwards at points of contact, *e.g., Ipomoea.*

Contorted (twisted). Aestivation in which one sepal overlaps the next with one margin, and is overlapped by the previous on the other.

Imbriate. Having sepals overlapping each other, one sepal completely internal, one completely external and the remaining three partly internal and partly external.

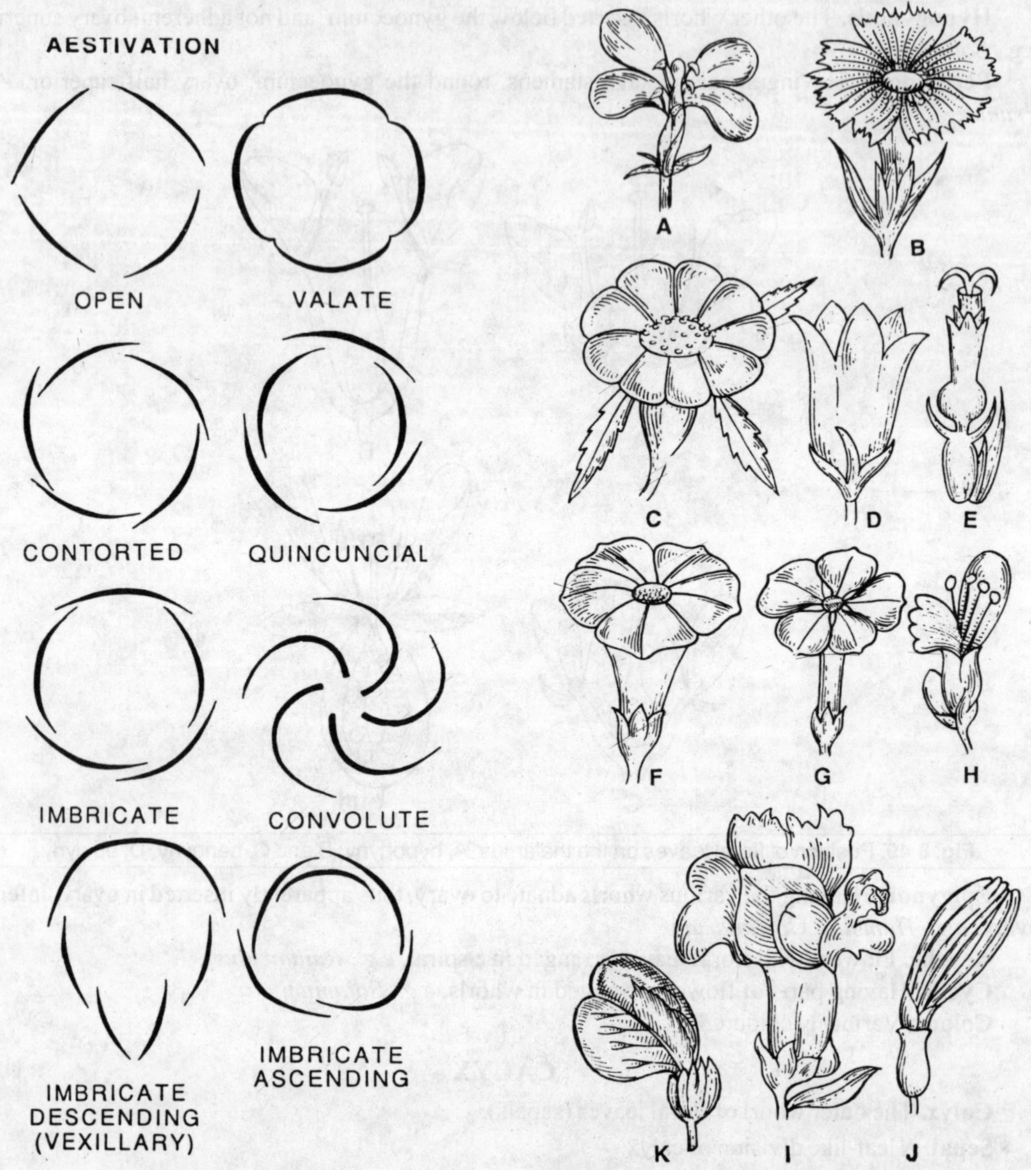

Fig. 8.50. Aestivation of corolla.

Fig. 8.51. Forms of corolla. A, cruciform; B, caryophyllaceous; C, rosaceous; d, campanulate; E, tubular; F, funnel-shaped; G, rotate; H, bilabiate, I, personate; J, ligulate K, papilionaceous.

Quincuncial (quincunx). Arrangement of five sepals, of which two are exterior, two interior and the fifth partly interior, partly exterior.

Caducous. The sepals that fall off early, *e.g., Argemone, Papaver*.

Deciduous. Falling at maturity.

Persistent. Remaining attached till maturation, *e.g., Solanum* and other members of Solanaceae.

COROLLA

Corolla. The whorl of petals.

Petal. One of the floral leaves of corolla.

Polypetalous. With free petals, *e.g., Brassica, rosa.*

Gamopetalous. United petals, *e.g., Ipomoea, Petunia.*

Aestivation. The arrangement of the parts of the floral envelopes in bud.

Valvate. An aestivation when the segments of corolla are so placed that their edges touch each other, not overlap, *e.g., Solanum.*

Valvate induplicate. Valvate aestivation with the margins of the petals folded inwards, *e.g., Ipomoea.*

Twisted. Also known as contorted; one margin of the petal overlaps that of the next one, and the next margin overlaps the third one.

Imbricate. A mode of aestivation in which one member of whorl is outside all the others (*i.e.,* its margins are free) and one inside all the others (*i.e.,* both margins are overlapped), the others overlap by one margin only.

Quincuncial. An imbricate (aestivation with 5 petals out of which two are exterior, two interior and the fifth has one margin exterior and one interior.

Vexillary. An imbricate (descending imbricate), in which out of the five petals the posterior one is the largest and covers the two lateral petals, and the lateral petals (wings) overlap the two anterior and smallest petals (keels), *e.g.,* in Papilionaceae.

Shape of Corolla

Cruciform. The corolla with four free petals arranged in the form of a cross; each petal is being differentiated into a *claw* and a *limb, e.g., Brassica.*

Caryophyllaceous. The corolla with 5 free petals; the petals are with long claws and with limbs placed at right angles to the claws, *e.g., Dianthus.*

Rosaceous. The corolla with five or more free petals, not distinguished into limbs and claws and spreading regularly outwards, *e.g., Rosa.*

Campanulate. Bell-shaped; the petals are fused to each other, *e.g., Ipomoea, Cuscuta.*

Infundibuliform. Funnel-shaped corolla; *e.g., Ipomoea, Petunia.*

Salver-shaped (hyporcrateriform). A gamopetalous corolla with a long tube horizontal limb, *e.g., Mussaenda.*

Rotate. Wheel-shaped gamopetalous coroll, *e.g., Solanum;* the gamopetalous corolla with a flat and circular limb at right angles to the short tube.

Papilionaceous. Butterfly-like, as corolla of pea family; the corolla possesses one large posterior *standard,* two lateral *wings* and two innermost and smallest *keels.*

Bilabiate. Two lipped; zygomorphic gamopetalous corolla, *e.g., Justicea, Ocimum Salvia.*

Personate. Zygomorphic, gamopetalous corolla with two lips, as in *Antirrhinum.*

Ligulate. Zygomorphic, gamopetalous corolla forming a short, narrow tube below and ligule-like flat structure above, *e.g., sonchus.*

Tubular. Tube-like, gamopetalous corolla, *e.g., Helianthus, Ageratum.*

Spur. A sac-like or tubular projection of a petal, *e.g., Viola, Tropaeolum.*

Nectary. A nectar-secreting gland in petals, *e.g., Salvia, Ramunculus.*

Corona. The appendages found in between corolla and stamens, or on the corolla, *e.g., Calotropis, Asclepias.*

PERIANTH

Perianth. The floral envelopes including both calyx and corolla, no differentiation, into calyx and corolla.

Tepal. A segment of perianth.

Polytepalous. With free tepals.

Gamotepalous. With united tepals.

Sepaloid. Green resembling sepals.

Petaloid. Coloured resembling petals.

Aestivation. The arrangement of the tepal in bud.

ANDROECIUM

Androecium. Collective term for all the stamens and staminodes.

Androphore. A stalk bearing the androecium.

Stamen. A modified leaf in flowering plants bearing pollen sacs. It consists of filaments and anthers.

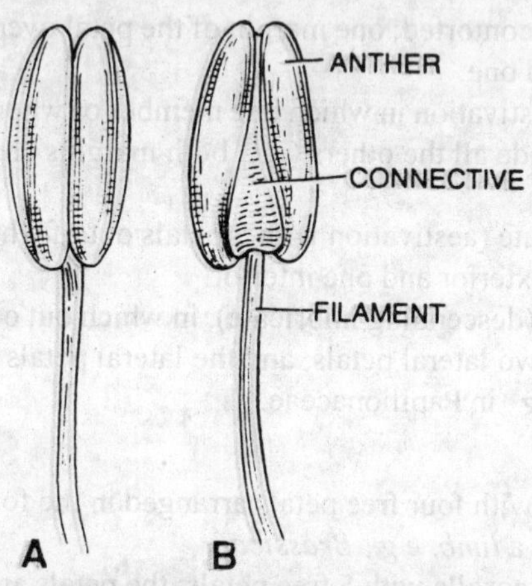

Fig. 8.52. Stamens. A, face; B, back.

Staminode. Rudimentary stamens which do not bear fertile pollen, *e.g.*, *Stellaria.*

Polyandrous. Androecium that consists of free stamens, *e.g.*, Poppy.

Monadelphous. United into one bundle by the filaments, *e.g.*, *Hibiscus.*

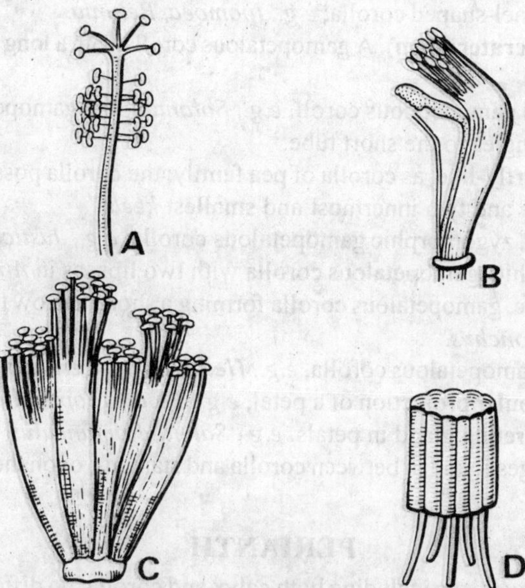

Fig. 8.53. Cohesion of stamens. A, monadelphous; B, diadelphous; C, polyadelphous; D, syngenesious.

Diadelphous. Stamens arranged in two bundles, *e.g.*, many members of Papilionaceae.

Polyadelphous. Stamens united in many bundles, *e.g., Citrus, Bombax.*

Syngenesious. With anther cohering in a ring, *e.g.*, many members of Compositae, (*e.g., Helianthus*).

Epipetalous. Stamens born on the petals or corolla tube, *e.g., Convolvulus, Ipomoea, Justicea, Solanum,* etc.

Epipetalous. Stamens born on the tepals, *e.g., Asphodelus.*

Gynandrous. Stamens adhering to the carpels, *e.g., Calotropis.*

Obdiplostemonous. Stamens found in two alternating whorls and that of the outer whorl opposite the petals, *e.g., Murraya, Geranium.*

Tetradynamous. With four long and two short stamens, *e.g., Brassica, Raphanus, Eruca,* etc.

Didynamous. In an androecium four stamens in two pairs one pair shorter than the other, *e.g., Ocimum.*

Inserted. Stamens shorter than the corolla tube, *e.g., Ixora, Mussaenda.*

Exerted. The stamens projecting beyond the petals, *e.g.*, passion flower.

Monothecous. Single-celled anther, *e.g., Hibiscus.*

Dithecous. Two-celled anther, *e.g., Papaver.*

Basifixed. Fixed to the filament (stalk) at the base, *e.g., Brassica, Papaver.*

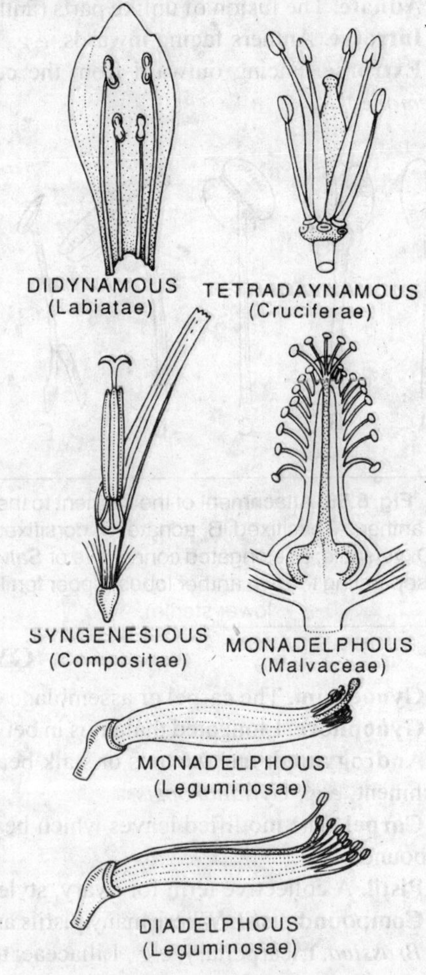

Fig. 8.53 (*a*). Cohesion of stamens.

Dorsifixed. Filament attached to the dorsal side of the anther, *e.g., Bauhinia.*

Versatile. The anther can move in any way, *e.g.*, Gramineae.

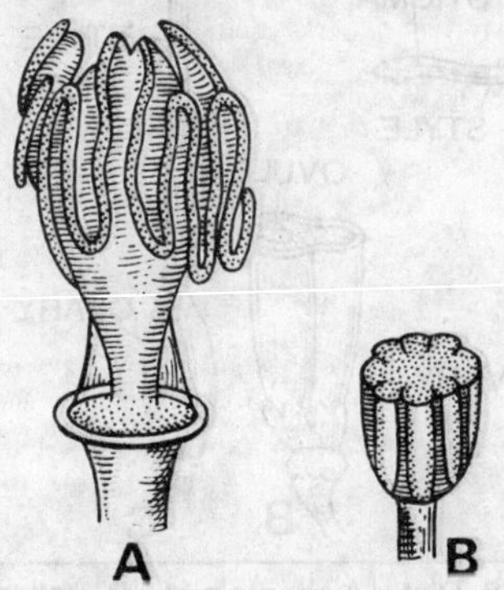

Fig. 8.54. Stamens. Synandrous. A, *Cucurbita;* *B, Colocasia.*

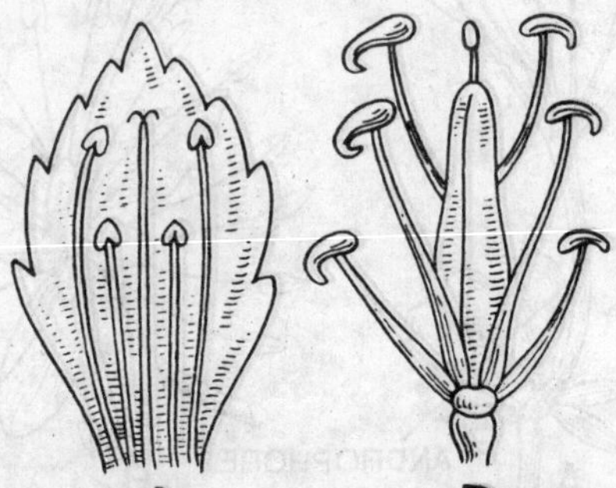

Fig. 8.55. Length of stamens. A, didynamous; b, tetradynamous.

Adnate. The fusion of unlike parts (anther and filament), *e.g., Michelia.*

Introrse. Anthers facing inwards, *e.g., hibiscus, Solanum, Stellaria,* etc.

Extrorse. Facing outward from the centre of the flower referred for anthers, *e.g., Papaver, Argemone.*

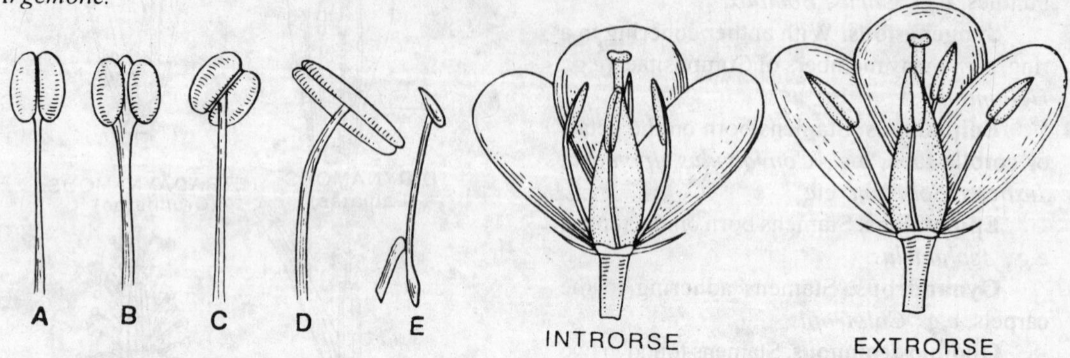

Fig. 8.56. Attachment of the filament to the anther. A, basifixed; B, adnate; C, dorsifixed; D, versatile; E, elongated connective of *Salvia,* separating the two anther lobes (upper fertile, lower sterile).

Fig. 8.56 (*a*). Facing of stamens.

GYNOECIUM

Gynoecium. The carpel or assemblage of carpels; collective name for the carpels of a flower.

Gynophore. Elongated thalamus in between androecium and gynoecium, *e.g., Cleome.*

Androgynophore. An axis or stalk bearing both stamens and pistil above the point of perianth attachment, *e.g., Gynandropsis.*

Carpel. The modified leaves which bear the ovules, a simple pistil or one of the segments of a compound pistil.

Pistil. A collective term for ovary, style and stigma.

Compound pistil. Where many pistils are aggregated together; the condition may be bicarpellary, *e.g., Brassica*; tricarpellary, *e.g.,* Liliaceae; tetracarpellary, *e.g., Datura;* pentacarpellary, *e.g., Melia*; polycarpellary, *e.g., Sida, Papaver,* etc.

Apocarpous. Carpels in a flower free from each other, *e.g., Ranunculus, Nigella, clematis,* etc.

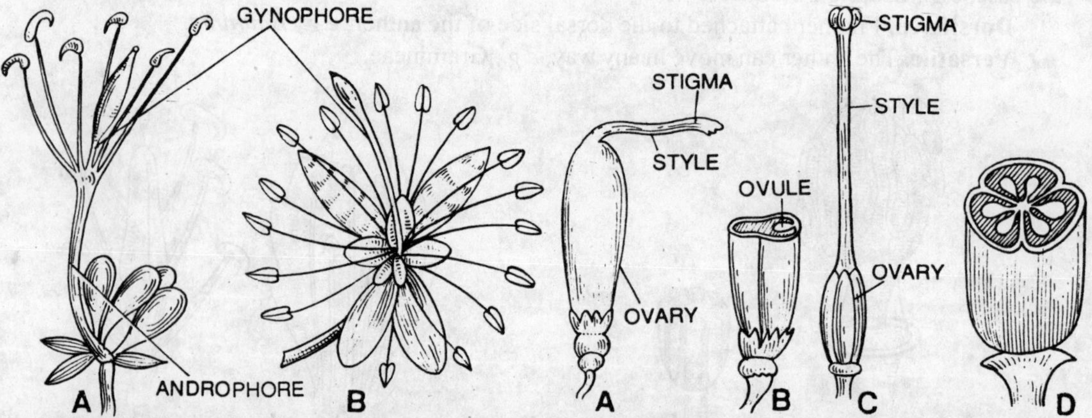

Fig. 8.57. Thalamus. A, Flower of *Gynandropsis* showing androphore and gynophore; B, flower of *Capparis* showing gynophore.

Fig. 8.58. Pistil. A simple pistil; B, unilocular ovary of simple pistil; C, syncarpous pistil; D, trilocular ovary of syncarpous pistil.

Syncarpous. United carpels, compound ovary, *e.g., Citrus.*

Superior. Situated above another member, a superior ovary has its base above the insertion of calyx; a superior calyx or corolla is inserted above the ovary, *e.g., Brassica.*

Inferior. Epigynous condition; the ovary is borne below attachment of all other floral envelopes and adnate to them, *e.g., Coriandrum, Ixora, Pyrus,* etc.

Semi-inferior. Intermediate condition between superior and inferior, *e.g.,* Pea.

Locule. Chamber; the ovary may be unilocular (single chambered), *e.g., Delphinium*; bilocular (two-chambered), *e.g., solanum*; trilocular (three-chambered), *e.g., Allium, Asphodelus;* tetralocular (four-chambered), *e.g., Ocimum*; pentalocular (five-chambered), *e.g., Hibiscus rosa-sinensis*; multilocular (many chambered), *e.g., Citrus.*

Ovule. Minute bodies found inside the ovary, which after fertilization develop into seeds.

Placenta. The organs to which ovules are attached.

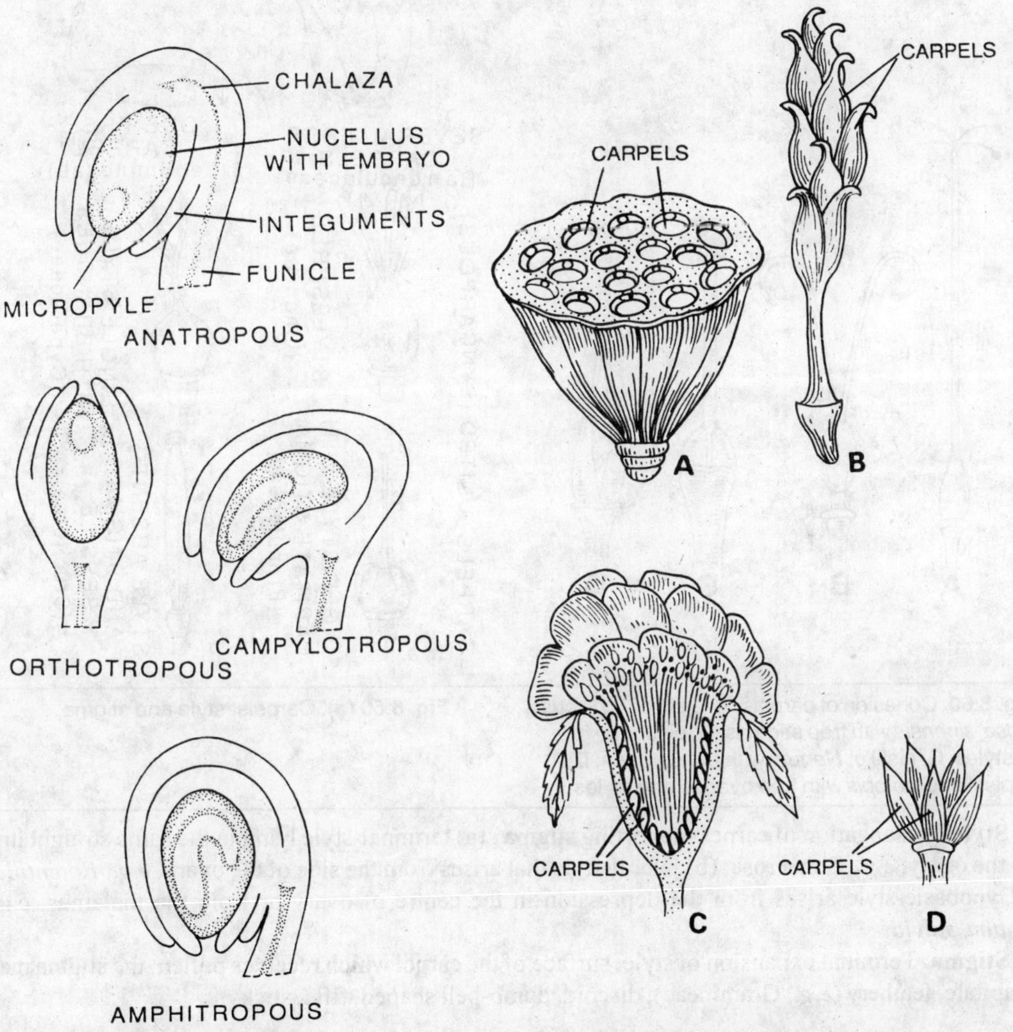

Fig. 8.58 (*a*). Ovules.

Fig. 8.59. Apocarpous pistil. A, lotus; B, *Michelia*; C, Rose; *D*, Sedum.

Placentation. Type of arrangement of placentas in a syncarpous ovary; (*a*) **parietal;** carpels are fused only by their margins, placentas then appearing as internal ridges on ovary wall, *e.g., Argemone, Viola, Brassica,* etc. (*b*) **axile;** margins of carpels fold inwards, fusing together in centre of ovary to form a single, central placenta; ovary is divided into as many compartments (loculi) as there are carpels, *e.g., Asphodelus, Hibiscus*; (*c*) **freecentral;** placenta arising as a central upgrowth from ovary base, *e.g., Stellaria*; (*d*) **marginal;** placenta develops along the junction of two carpels, in a unilocular ovary, *e.g.,* pea; (*e*) **basal;** the ovules are few or reduced to one and are borne at the base of ovary, the ovules when solitary often filling the cavity, the ovary is unilocular, *e.g., Compositae; (f)* **superficial;** carpels numberous, the placentae develop all round the inner surface of the partition wall, ovary multilocular, *e.g., Nymphaea*; (g) **lamellate;** this is modified partietal placentation, *e.g., Papaver* (Fig. 8.61).

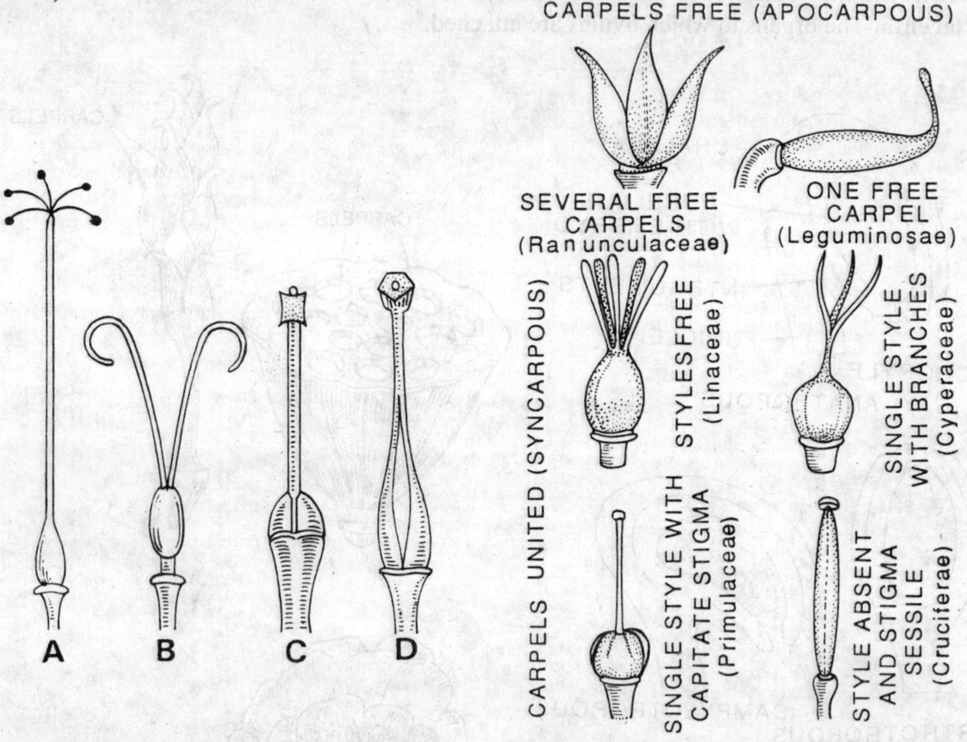

Fig. 8.60. Cohesion of carpels. A, pistil of *Hibiscus rosa-sinensis* with free stigmas; B, pistil with free styles; C, pistil of *Nerium* with free ovaries; D, pistil of *Calotopis* with free ovaries and styles.

Fig. 8.60 (*a*). Carpels, style and stigma.

Style. Prolongation of carpel supporting stigma : (a) terminal-style lying in the same straight line with the ovary, *e.g.,* China rose; (b) lateral-style that arises from the side of the ovary, *e.g., Potentilla*; (c) Gynobasic-style arises from the depression in the centre of ovary or from the thalamus, *e.g., Ocimum, salvia.*

Stigma. Terminal expansion of style, surface of the carpel which receives pollen; the stigma may be capitate, feathery (*e.g.,* Gramineae), discoid, dumb-bell shaped, fifid, sticky.

FRUIT

Fruit. Ripened ovary of the flower, enclosing seeds.

Simple fruit. When a single fruit develops from the ovary of a flower with or without accessory parts, it is said to be a simple fruit.

Legume or *Pod.* A dry monocarpellary fruit developing from a superior, one chambered ovary and dehiscing by both the sutures, *e.g.,* pea, bean, pulses.

Follicle. A dry, Monocarpellary, superior one-chambered fruit like the legume, but it dehisces by one sutre only, *e.g., Calotropis, Asclepias, Vinca, Michelia.*

Siliqua. A long, narrow many seeded fruit developing from a superior, bicarpellary ovary with two parietal placentae, dehiscing from below upwards by both the sutures, *e.g., Brassica, Raphamus.*

Silicula. When a siliqua is much shorter and contains only a few seeds, *e.g., Capsella,* candytuft.

Capsule. A many-seeded, uni or multilocular fruit developing from a superior, bi or polycarpellary ovary, and dehiscing in various ways, A capsule may dehisce by pores, as in poppy; or transversely, as in cock's comb; or loculicidally, as in cotton, lady's finger and *Hibiscus mutabilis.*

Caryopsis. A very small, dry one-seeded fruit developing from a superior, monocarpellary ovary, with the pericarp fused with the seedcoat, *e.g.,* Gramineae.

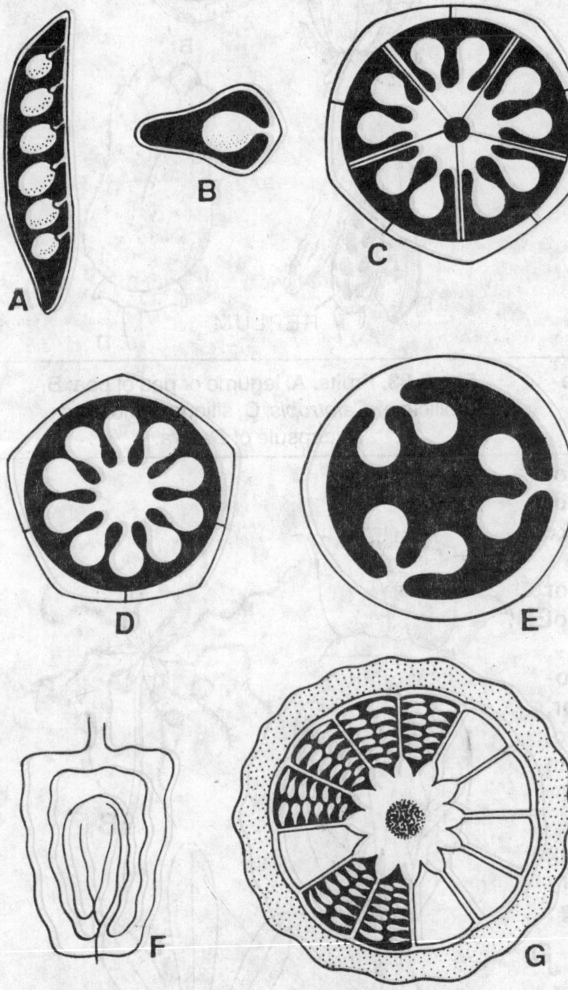

Fig. 8.61. Types of placentation. A, marginal in L.S.; B, marginal in T.S.; C, axile; D, free-central; E, parietal; F, basal; G, superficial.

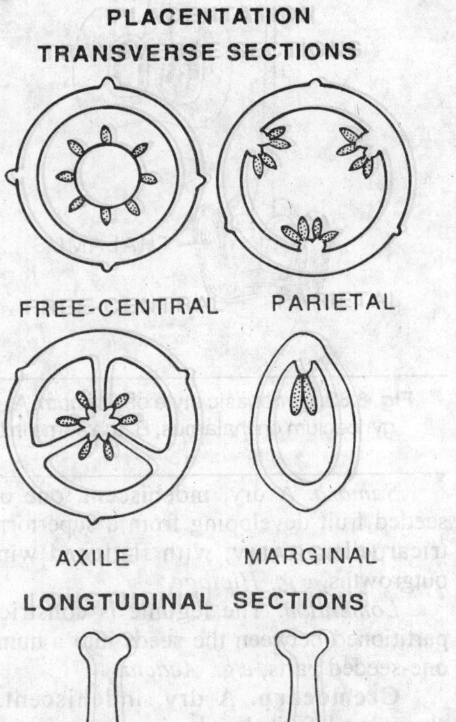

Fig. 8.61(*a*). Placentation.

Achene. A small, dry, one-chambered and one-seeded fruit developing from a superior, monocarpellary ovary; but unlike the previous one, the pericarp is free from the seed coat; commonly developing an apocarpous pistil and, therefore, a single flower produces an aggregate of achenes, *e.g., Clematiis, Naravelia.*

Cypsela. A dry, one-chambered and oneseeded fruit developing from an inferior, bicarpellary ovary with the pericarp and the seed-coat free, *e.g.,* Sunflower, marigold, *Cosmos.*

Nut. A dry, one chambered and one-seeded fruit developing from a superior, bi or polycarpellary ovary, with the pericarp hard and woody, *e.g.,* chestnut, oad, etc.

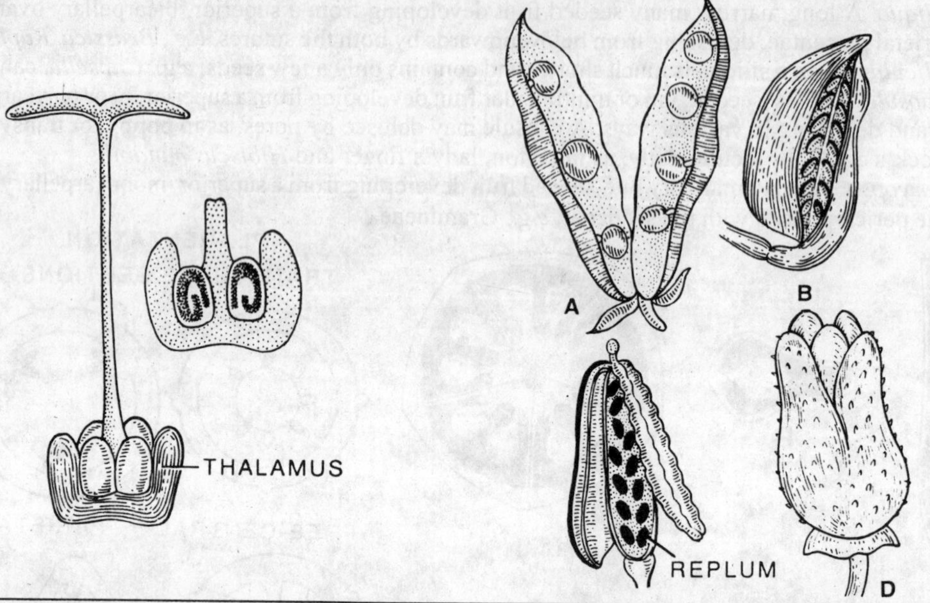

Fig. 8.62. Gynobasic style of *Ocimum.* A, entire gynoecium on thalamus; B, the same in L.S.

Fig. 8.63. Fruits. A, legume or pod of pea; B, follicle of *Calotropis*; C, siliqua of mustard; D, capsule of *Datura.*

Samara. A dry, indehiscent, one or two-seeded fruit developing from a superior, bi- or tricarpellary ovary, with flattened wing-like outgrowths, *e.g., Hiptage.*

Lomentum. The legume is constricted or partitioned between the seeds into a number of one-seeded parts, *e.g., Acacia.*

Cremocarp. A dry, indehiscent, two-chambered fruit developing from an inferior, bicarpellary ovary; when ripe splits into two, indehiscent, one-seeded mericarps which remain attached to the prolonged end (carpophore) or the axis, *e.g.,* Umbelliferae.

Regma. A dry schizocarpic fruit developing from a tricarpellary, syncarpous, superior ovary and splitting at maturity into three cocci, *e.g., ricinus.*

Carcerulus. The fruit develops from a bicarpellary pistil with a superior ovary which becomes quadrilocular owing to the formation of two false septa; at maturity the four mericarps separate from each other towards the middle, *e.g.,* Labiatae (*Ocimum*) and Boraginaceae. In the carcerulus of *Malva* the superior ovary of the polycarpellary pistil splits into a large number of mericarps.

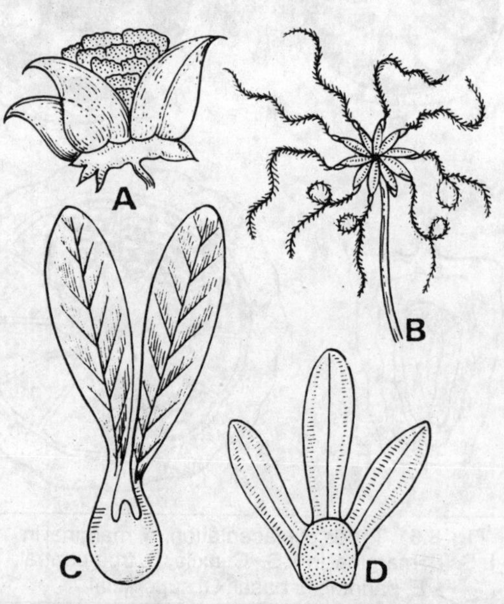

Fig. 8.64. Fruits. A, capsule of cotton; B, achenes of *Naravelia* with persistent feathery styles; C, samara of *Dipterocarpus*; D, samara of *Hiptage.*

Double samara. It consists of two, three or four samaras, *e.g., Acer* and Sapindancae.

Drupe. A fleshy, one or more-chambered and one or more-seeded fruit developing from a monocarpellary or syncarpous pistil, with the pericarp differentiated into the *epicarp* which forms the skin of the fruit, the *mesocarp* which is often fleshy, and the *endocarp* which is hard and stone, *e.g.,* mango, peach, plum, coconut-palm, plamyra-palm, almond, etc.

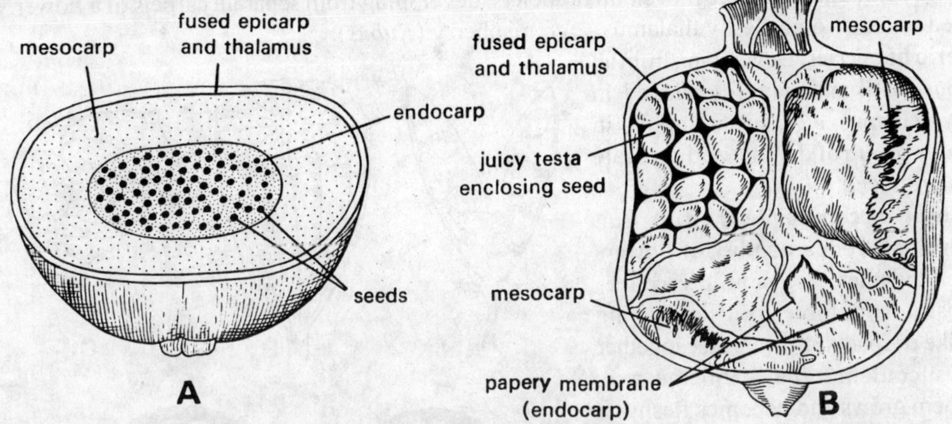

Fig. 8.65. Fruits (inferior berries), A, T.S. of inferior berry of guava; B, L.S. of infeior berry of balusta of pomegranato (*Punica granatum*).

Berry. A superior (rarely inferior) indehiscent, usually many-seeded, fleshy or pulpy fruit developing from a single carpel or more commonly from a syncarpous pistil, with axile or parietal placentation, *e.g.,* tomato, grapes, brinjal, guava.

Pepo. A fleshy, many-seeded fruit developing from an inferior, one-celled or three-celled, syncarpous pistil with parietal plantation, *e.g.,* cucurbitaceae.

Pome. An inferior, two or more-called fleshy syncarpous fruit surrounded by the thalamus, *e.g.,* Apple, Pear.

Hesperidium. A superior, many-celled, fleshy fruit developing from a syncarpous pistil with axile placentation; the endocarp projecting inwards forming distinct chambers and the epicarp and mesocarp, fused together, forming the separable rind of the fruit, *e.g., Citrus.*

Aggregate fruit. It develops from a single flower with an apocarpous pistil, carpels being free, each of them develops into a simple fruitlet; an aggregate fruit, therefore, consists of a collection of simple fruitlets as may as the number of free carpels, borne by a single flower; an aggregate of simple fruitlets born by a

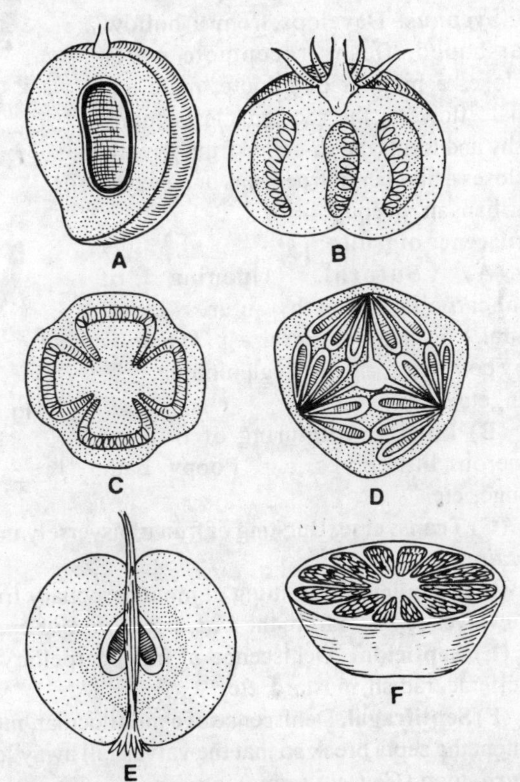

Fig. 8.66. Fruits. A, drupe of mango, B, berry of tomato, C, same in T.S., D, pepo of cucumber in T.S., E, pome of apple, F, hesperidium of orange.

single flower is known as an *etaerio.* Each fruitlet of an etaerio may be a follicle, an achene, a drupe or a berry.

Etaerio of follicles. Each etaerio consists of two or more follicles, *e.g., Calotropis, Asclepias, Aconitum, Michelia.*

Etaerio of achenes. Aggrellgate of achenes, *e.g., Clematis, Naravelia,* strawberry, etc.

Etaerio of drupes. A number of small drupelets, developing from separate carpels of a flower, are aggregated together on a fleshy thalamus, *e.g.,* raspberry (*Rubus*).

Etaerio of berries. Developing from an apocarpous pistil and lying embedded in the fleshy thalamus, *e.g.,* custard apple; in *Artabotrys* a group of distinct and separate berries is produced.

Multiple of composite fruit. A fruit which develops from a number of flowers juxtaposed together, from a inflorescence.

Sorosis. A multiple fruit developing from a spike or spadix; flowers fuse together by their succulent sepals and the axis bearing them grows and becomes fleshy or woody, and the whole inflorescence becomes a compact mass, *e.g.,* pineapple, jack-fruit, mulberry.

Syconus. Develops from a hollow, pearshaped, fleshy receptacle which encloses a number of minute, male and female flowers; the recepatacle becomes fleshy and forms the so-called fruit; it really encloses a number of true fruits or achenes, *e.g.,* banyan, peepul.

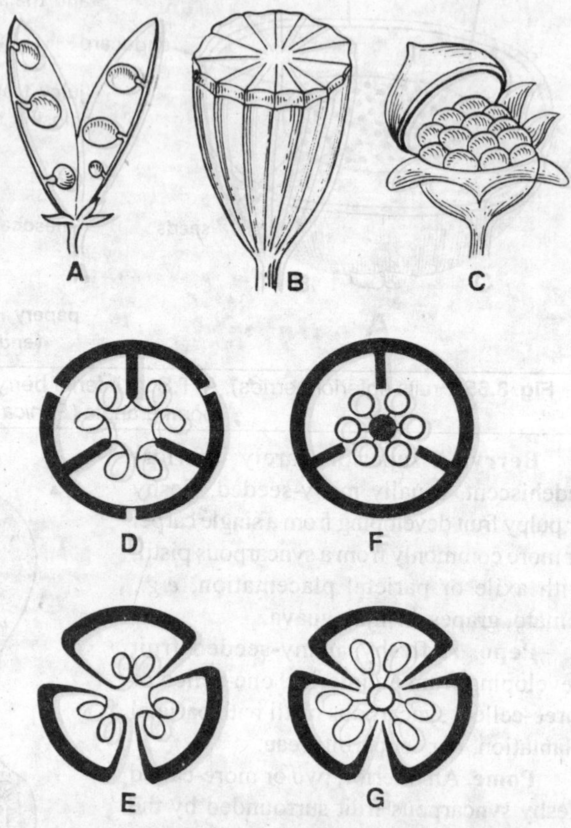

Fig. 8.67. Dehiscence of fruits. A, sutural, B, porous, C, transverse, D, loculicidal E, septicidal, F and G, septifragal.

Dehiscence of fruits :

(A) Sutural. Opening of monocarpellary fruit by sutures, either ventral, *e.g.,* madar or dorsal, *e.g., Magnolia* or by both sides, *e.g.,* in Leguminosae, pea, bean, etc.

(B) Porous. Rupturing of fruit by numerous little pores, *e.g.,* Poppy, bath sponge, etc.

(C) Transverse. Bursting of fruit transversely in the way of unhinged lid of a box, *e.g.,* in *Celosia, Portulaca,* etc.

(D) Loculicidal. Splitting of monocarpellary fruit through the back of the loculus (or chamber). Here valves separate from the axis, *e.g., Hibiscus mutabilis* and Acanthaceae, *Adhatoda, Ruellia,* etc.

(E) Septicidal. Dehiscence of monocarpellary fruit through septa, *e.g.,* in mustard family or Cruciferae, radish, mustard, etc.

(F) Septifragal. Dehiscence of a multilocular, monocarpellary fruit loculicidally. Here at the same moment the septa break so that the valves fall away leaving the seeds attached to the central axis, *e.g., Datura,* toon (*Cedrela toona*), etc.

CHAPTER 9

Description of Angiospermic Plants in Semitechnical Language

DICOTYLEDONS

FAMILY—RANUNCULACEAE (Crowfoot family)

RANUNCULUS

1. Ranunculus sceleratus. Linn.; Verna. **Shim;** Eng. The water celery.

Ranunculus sceleratus Linn is abundant throughout the area in wet ground. Distribution - Punjab and Bengal plains, and warm valleys of the Himalayas up to 5,000 feet.

Habit : Annual herb.

Root : Tap, branched.

Stem : Erect, reduced in early stages, herbaceous, green, glabrous, solid, branched, aerial with nodes and internodes.

Leaf : Simple, petiolate, radical with long petioles, tripartite or trilobed, each lobe further divided with obovate, cuneate segments, stipulate, membranous stipules fused with the leaf base, multicostate reticulate venation.

Inflorescence : Cymose, dichasial cyme.

Flower : Pedicellate, bracteate, bracteolate, hermaphrodite, complete, spirocyclic, actinomorphic, pentamerous, yellow and hypogynous, thalamus prominent and convex.

Calyx : Five, polysepalous, petaloid, quincuncial, *i.e.,* imbracate in bud condition, boat shaped.

Corolla : Five, polypetalous, yellow, oblong, pocket-shaped nectary present at the base of each petal, imbricate.

Androecium : Indefinite, the stamens arranged spirally, polyandrous, filaments long, dithecous, anthers extrorse, elongated, yellow and basifixed.

Gynoecium : Indefinite (Polycarpellary), apocarpous, ovary superior unilocular, one ovule in each locule, basal placentation, style reduced, stigma simple and sticky, carpels arranged spirally.

Fruit : An etaerio of single seeded achenes.

Floral formula : Br. Brl. ⊕ ⚥ K 5, C 5, A $\propto$, G $\underline{\propto}$.

Identification and Systematic Position :

(*i*) Leaves net-veined.
(*ii*) Flowers 4- or 5-merous. *Dicotyledons.*
(*iii*) Petals separate. *Polypetalae.*
(*vi*) Flowers hypogynous; ovary superior. *Thalamiflorae.*

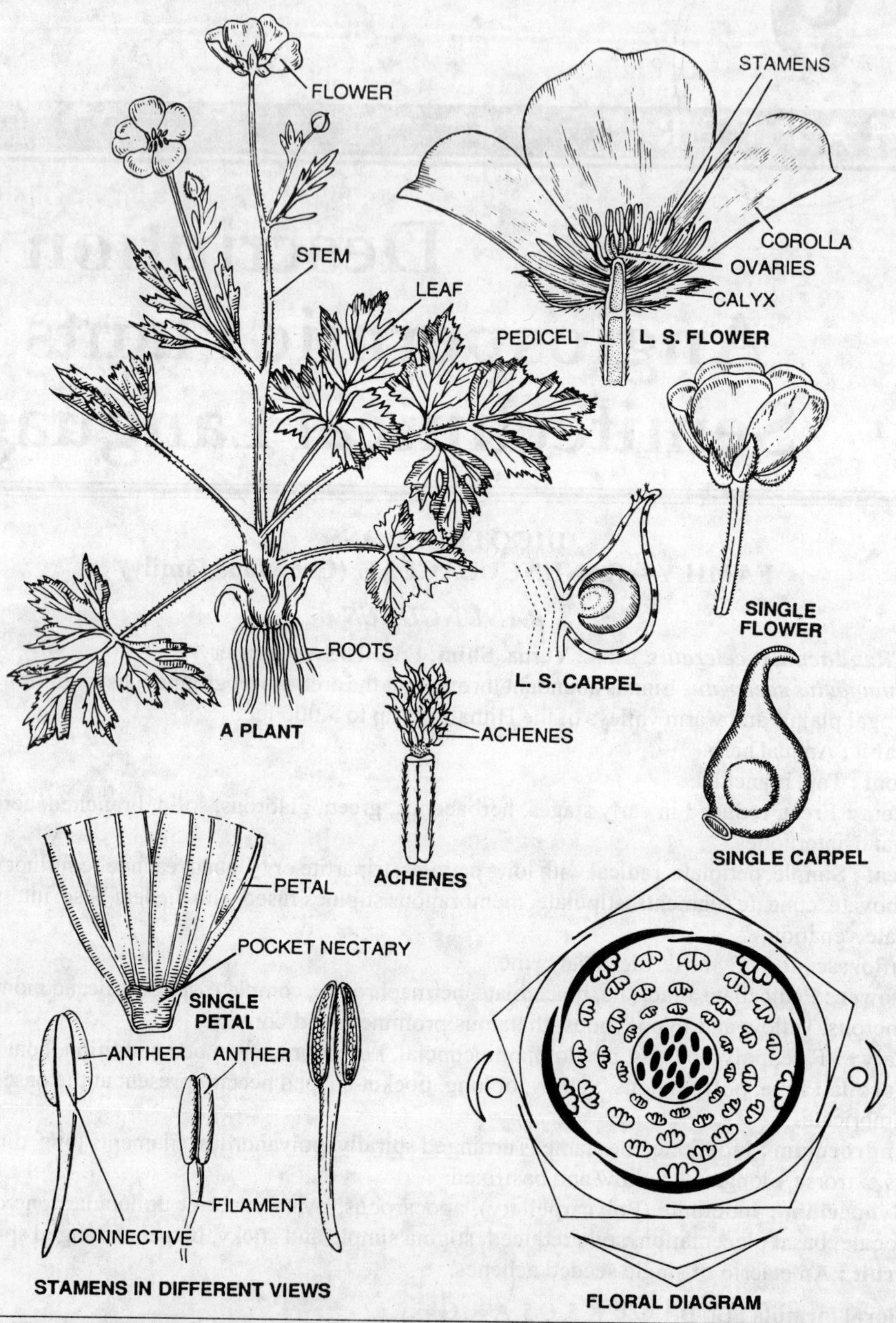

Fig. 9.1. Ranunculaceae. *Ranunculus sceleratus* Linn.; Eng., the water lily; Verna. **Shim.**

(*i*) Stamens usually many.
(*ii*) Gynoecium apocarpous; carpels usually many (rarely reduced to one). — *Ranales.*
(*iii*) Sepals deciduous, often petaloid.
(*iv*) Stamens indefinite, extrorse.
(*v*) Usually herbs with alternate and dissected leaves. — *Ranunculaceae.*

Bentham & Hooker (*1862*)	*Engler & Prantl* (*1931*)	*Hutchinson* (*1959*)
Dicotyledons	Dicotyledoneae	Dicotyledones
Polypetalae	Archichlamydeae	Herbaceae
Ranales	Ranales	Ranales
Ranunculaceae	Raunculaceae	Ranunculaceae.

Economic value. The plant is used as vegetable by tribal people, when boiled. It is poisonous, and a powerful vesicant when uncooked. The plant is emmenagogue, galactagogue and poisonous.

DELPHINIUM

2. ***Delphinium ajacis*** Linn.; Eng. Rocket larkspur.

Habit : Annual herb.

Root : Tap, branched.

Stem : Erect, herbaceous, aerial, green, branched, cylinderical, glabrous and fistular.

Leaf : Simple, cauline, much dissected, entire, lobes linear with acute apex, sessible, exstipulate, multicostate reticulate venation.

Inflorescence : Racemose, typical raceme.

Flower : Pedicellate, bracteate, bracteolate (two bracteoles), hermaphrodite, complete, pentamerous, zygomorphic, hypogynous, cyclic and violet coloured.

Calyx : Five, polysepalous, petaloid, violet coloured, posterior sepal forms a long spur, quincuncial aestivation.

Corolla : Four, gamopetalous, the two posterior petals are smaller and produced into a long spur which enters into the spur of posterior sepal and the remaining two lobes which are large in size enclose the essential organs, imbricate, blue or violet.

Androecium : Indefinite or 15 stamens arranged spirally in five groups of three stames each alternating with the petals, polyandrous, filaments flattened at base, basifixed anthers, dehisce by lateral slits, dithecous, extrorse.

Gynoecium : One (monocarpellary), ovary superior, unilocular, pubescent, marginal placentation, style reduced, stigma simple.

Fruit : A follicle

Floral formula : Br. Brl. •|• ⚥ K 5, C (4), A ∞, or 15, G$\underline{1}$.

Identification and Systematic Position :

(*i*) Leaves net-veined.
(*ii*) Flowers 4- or 5-merous. — *Dicotyledons.*
(*i*) Petals separate. — *Polypetalae.*
(*i*) Flowers hypogynous; ovary superior. — *Thalamiflorae.*
(*i*) Stamens usually many.
(*ii*) Gynoecium apocarpous; carpels usually many (rarely reduced to one). — *Ranales.*
(*i*) Sepals deciduous, often petaloid.
(*ii*) Stamens indefinite, extrorse.
(*iii*) Usually herbs with alternate and dissected leaves. — *Ranunculaceae.*

Other important members of the family. *Aconitum heterophyllum* Wall., Verna. **Atis;** *Nigella sativa* Linn., Verna., **Kalonji;** *Thalictrum foliolosum* DC., Verna, **Mamira.**

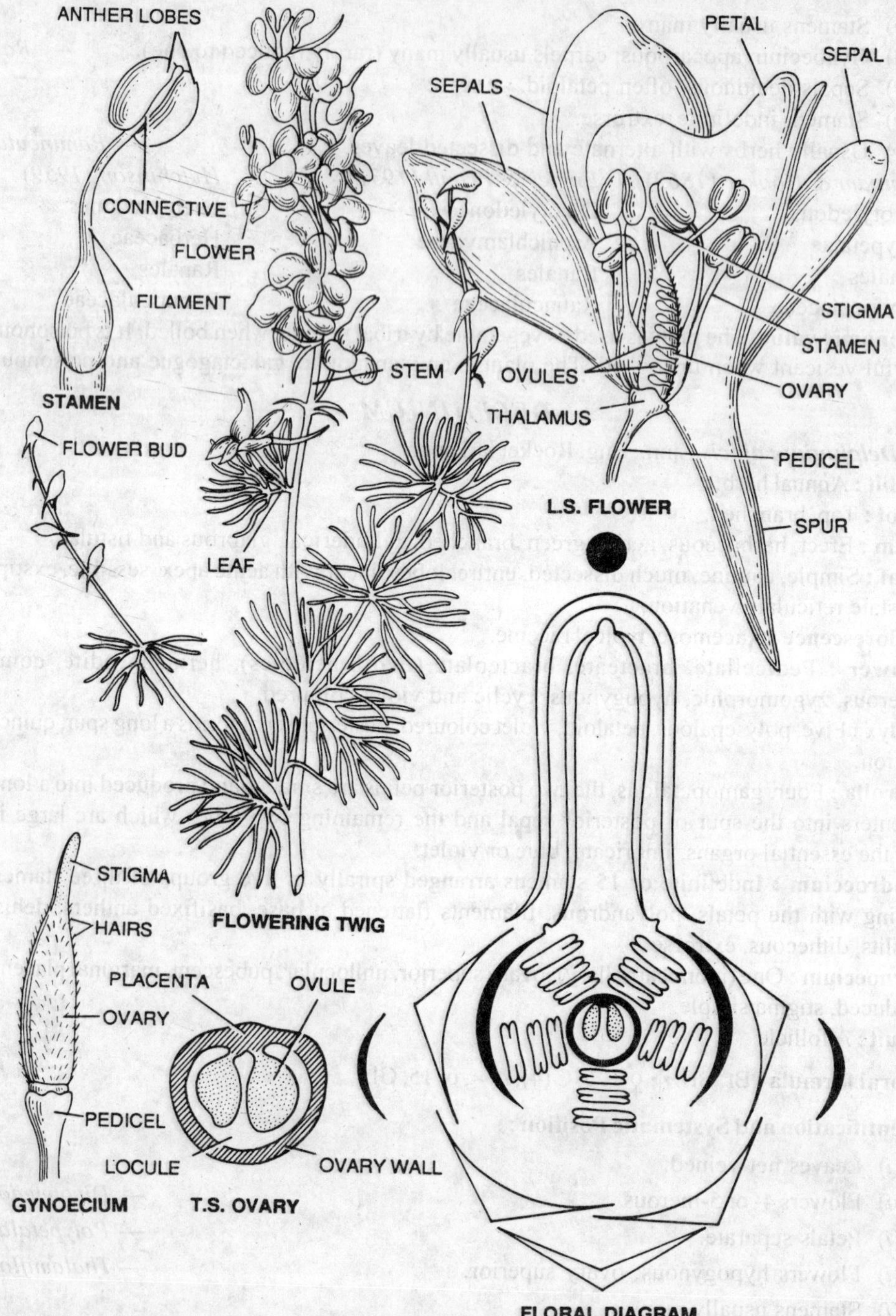

Fig. 9.2. Ranunculaceae. *Delphinium ajacis* Linn.; Eng., rocket larkspur.

Economic value. Grown as an ornamental. The seeds are insecticidal, in form of a tincture applied externally for the destruction of lice in hair.

AQUILEGIA

3. *Aquilegia vulgaris* Linn.

Habit : Annual or perennial herbs.

Root : Tap and branched.

Stem : Erect, herbaceous, aerial green, branched, cylinderical glabrous.

Leaf : Cauline and ramal, simple, petiolate, much dissected, entire, lobes with acute apices, stipulate, membranous stipules fused with leaf base, multicostate reticulate venation.

Inflorescence : Cymose.

Flower : Pedicellate, bracteate, hermaphrodite, complete, zygomorphic, hypogynous, nectar secreted in spurs of petals, pentamerous.

Calyx : 5 petals, polysepalous, petaloid, imbricate aestivation.

Corolla : 5 petals, polypetalous imbricate aestivation, nectar secreted in spurs of petals.

Androecium : Indefinite, polyandrous, filament long, anthers dithecous, extrorse, basifixed.

Gynoecium : 5 carpels, apocarpous, carpels are connate in a five-chambered ovary, ovary superior.

Fruit : Follicle, made up of 5 loose follicles.

Floral formula : Br. Brl. •|• ⚥ K 5, C 5, A ∞, $\underline{G}$ 5.

Identification and Systematic Position :

(*i*) Leaves net-veined.
(*ii*) Flowers 4- or 5-merous. — *Dicotyledons.*
(*i*) Petals separate. — *Polypetalae.*
(*i*) Flowers hypogynous; ovary superior. — *Thalamiflorae.*
(*i*) Stamens usually many.
(*ii*) Gynoecium apocarpous; carpels usually many (rarely reduced to one). — *Ranales.*
(*i*) Sepals deciduous, often petaloid.
(*ii*) Stamens indefinite, extrorse.
(*iii*) Usually herbs with alternate and dissected leaves. — *Ranunculaceae.*

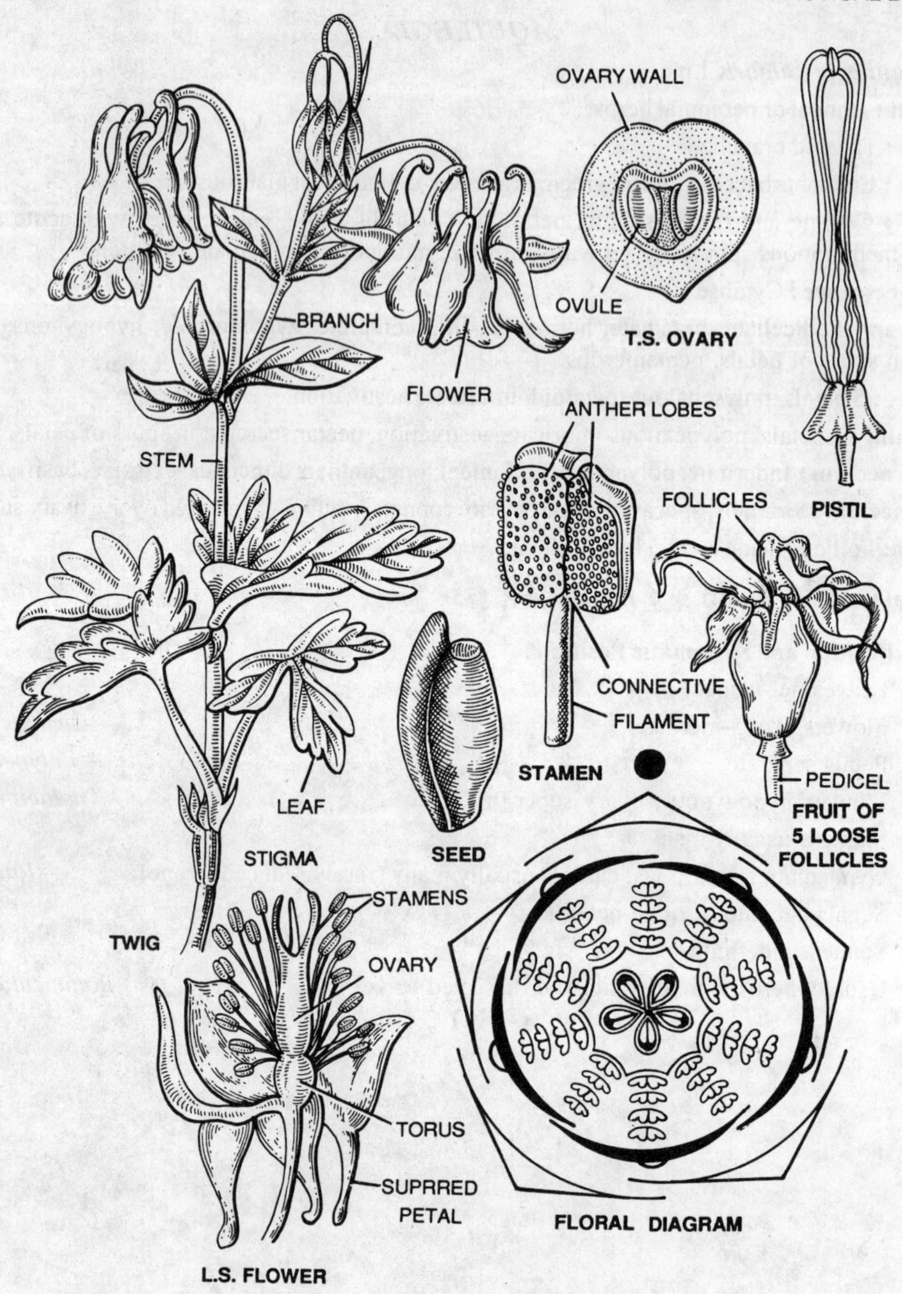

Fig. 9.3. Ranunculaceae. *Aquilegia vulgaris* Linn.

Economic value. Grown as on ornamental. It is poisonous.

CLEMATIS

4. Clematis paniculatea Thunb.

Habit : A climber, annual or perennial.

Root : Tap and branched.

Stem : Herbaceous, aerial, weak, climbing with the help of tendrilar petioles, branched, solid, smooth and green.

Leaf : Cauline and ramal, simple, petiolate, petiole tendrilar, exstipulate, opposite decussate, ovate, acute, entire, glabrous, unicostate reticulate, coriaceous.

Inflorescence : Cymose, dichasial cyme.

Flower : Pedicellate, bracteate, bracteolate, complete, actinomorphic, hermaphrodite, tetramerous, hypogynous, hemicyclic and scented.

Calyx : 4 sepals, polysepalous, valvate, petaloid, white.

Corolla : Absent.

Androecium : Indefinite, polyandrous, filaments long, monothecous, extrorse, basifixed.

Gynoecium : 4-6 carpels, apocarpous, ovary superior, unilocular, basal placentation, style short, stigma simple, hairy outgrowths arise from ovary.

Fruit : Achene.

Floral formula : Br. Brl. ⊕ ⚥ K 4, C 0, A ∞, G $\underline{4\text{-}6}$.

Identification and Systematic Position :

(*i*) Leaves net-veined.
(*ii*) Flowers 4- or 5-merous. — *Dicotyledons.*
(*i*) Petals separate. — *Polypetalae.*
(*i*) Flowers hypogynous; ovary superior. — *Thalamiflorae.*
(*i*) Stamens usually many.
(*ii*) Gynoecium apocarpous; carpels usually many (rarely reduced to one). — *Ranales.*
(*i*) Sepals deciduous, often petaloid.
(*ii*) Stamens indefinite, extrorse.
(*iii*) Usually herbs with alternate and dissected leaves. — *Ranunculaceae.*

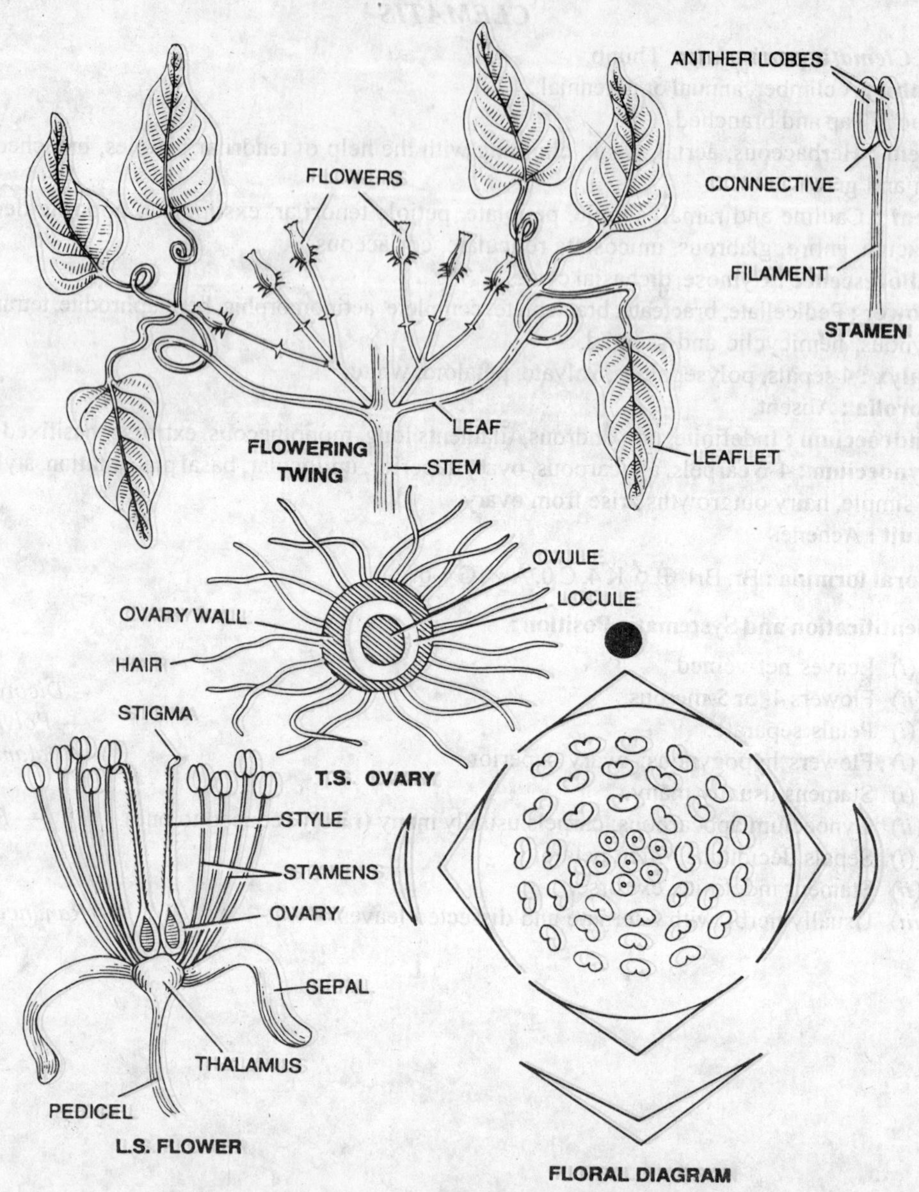

Fig. 9.4. Ranunculaceae. *Clematis paniculata* Thunb.

Economic value. A shrub, grown as an ornamental.

FAMILY—PAPAVERACEAE (Poppy family)

ARGEMONE

*1. **Argemone mexicana*** Linn. Verna. **Shialkanta;** Eng. Mexican prickly poppy.

Argemone mexicana Linn. (Mexican or prickly poppy) is a common weed on waste ground.

Distribution. Throughout India.

Habit : An annual prickly herb with yellowish latex.

Root : Tap, branched.

Stem : Erect, herbaceous, woody below, cylinderical solid, branched, spiny, greens\ish, yellow latex.

Leaf : Simple, alternate, cauline and ramal, sessile, exstipulate, prickly, deeply cut, with spiny teeth, unicostate reticulate venation.

Inflorescence : Cymose, solitary axillary.

Flowers : Pedicellate, ebracteate, large, yellow, hermaphrodite, actinomorphic, complete, hypogynous, trimerous, cyclic.

Calyx : Three, polysepalous, green, caducous, horned at the top, valvate or twisted aestivation.

Corolla : Six, polypetalous, petals arranged in two whorls, of three each (petals of inner whorl slightly smaller), yellow, inferior, imbricate aestivation.

Androecium : Indefinite, polyandrous, stamens arranged in several alternating whorls, filaments long, anthers extrorse, bicelled, basifixed.

Gynoecium : Four to six carpels (tetracarpellary to hexacarpellary), syncarpous, ovary superior, unilocular, parietal placentation, several ovules on each placentation, several ovules on each placenta, style absent, or reduced, stigmas as many as the number of carpels, stigma hood-like.

Fruit : A spiny capsule.

Floral formula : ⊕ ⚥ K 3, C 3+3, A ∝, G $\underline{(4\text{-}6)}$.

Identification and Systematic Position :

(*i*) Leaves net-veined.

(*ii*) Flowers 4- or 5-merous. — *Dicotyledons.*

(*i*) Petals separate. — *Polypetalae.*

(*i*) Flowers hypogynous; ovary superior. — *Thalamiflorae.*

(*ii*) Carpels unite to form a 1-celled ovary with parietal placentation. — *Parietales.*

(*i*) Sepals caduous.

(*ii*) Petals double the number of sepals.

(*iii*) Flowers actinomorphic, 2- or 3-merous.

(*iv*) Herbs with milky juice (latex).

(*v*) Stamens many, extrorse.

(*vi*) Fruit capsule.

Other important members of the family. *Papaver rhoeas* Linn., **Lalpost,** an ornamental.

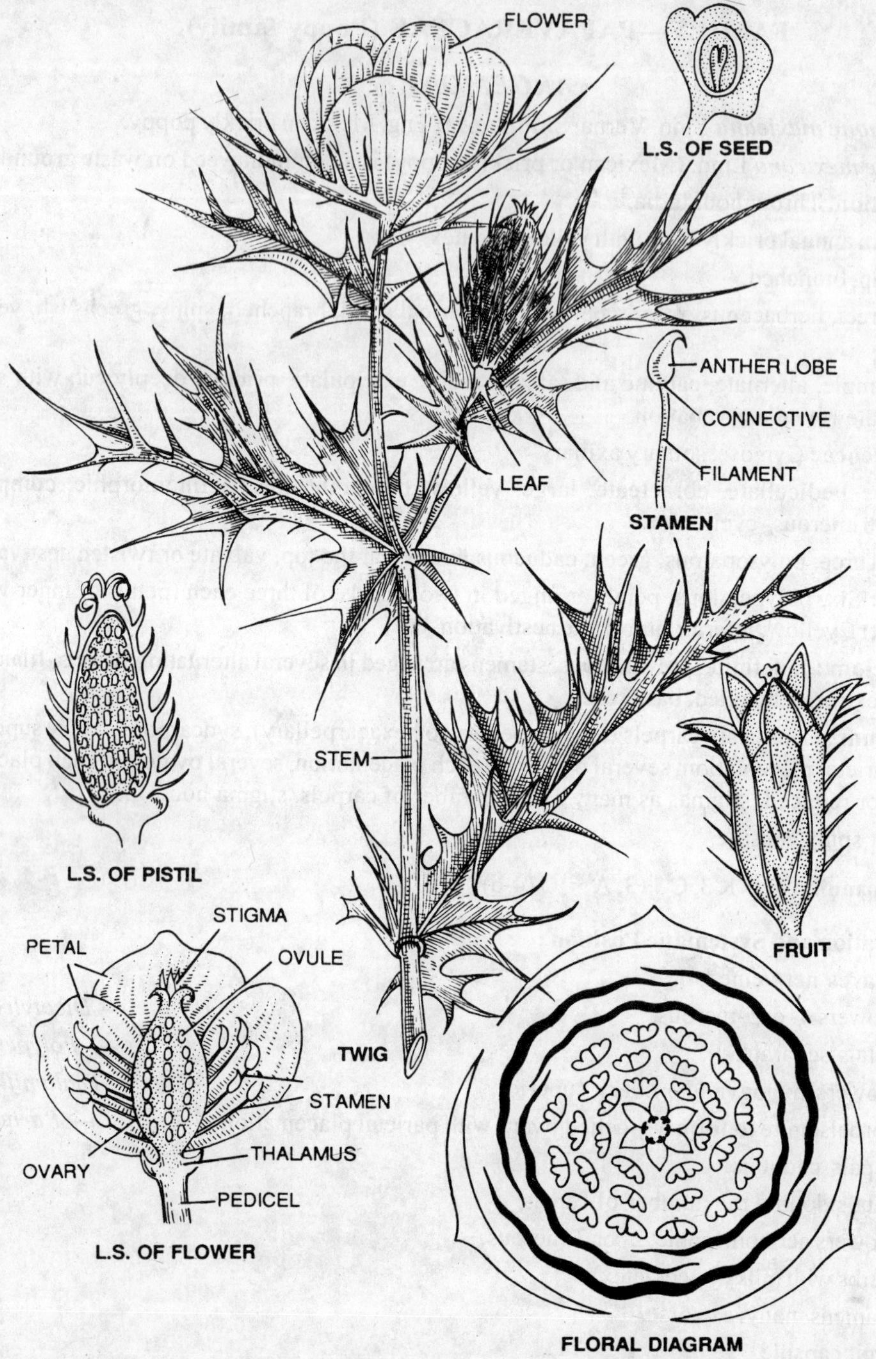

Fig. 9.5. Papaveraceae. *Argemone mexicana* Linn.

Economic value. Seeds are the source of a semi-drying oil, which is used as an illuminant and lubricant. The plant is being used to reclaim '*usar*' land. The root is alterative and used in chronic skin diseases. The seeds are laxative, emetic, expectorant and demulcent. The plant juice is used for dropsy, jaundice and cutaneous affections.

PAPAVER

2. ***Papaver somniferum*** Linn. Verna. **Afim, Post;** Eng. Opium poppy.

Habit : An annual herb with latex.

Root : Tap, branched.

Stem : Erect, herbaceous, green sometimes branched, cylinderical, hairy and fistular, latex.

Leaves : Simple, alternate, sessile, sheathing base, exstipulate, lobed, unicostate reticulate venation.

Inflorescence : Cymose, solitary or terminal.

Flower : Pedicellate (long pedicels), ebracteate, actinomorphic, hermaphrodite, complete, hypogynous, red or white, large, showy, dimerous, cyclic.

Calyx : Two sepals, polysepalous, caducous, hairy, inferior, imbricate aestivation.

Corolla : Four petals, polypetalous, arranged in two whorls of two each, inferior, often crumpled or rolled in the bud, aestivation imbricate.

Androecium : Indefinite stamens arranged in several whorls, polyandrous, anthers extrorse, basifixed, bi-celled, dehisce by longitudinal slits.

Gynoecium : Polycarpellary, syncarpous, ovary superior unilocular, parietal placentation, many ovules on each placenta, stigma persistent, discoid with stigmatic rays.

Fruit : A capsule dehiscing by minute pores.

Floral formula : ⊕ ⚥ K 2, C 2+2, A $\propto$, G $(\underline{\propto})$.

Identification and Systematic Position :

(*i*) Leaves net-veined.
(*ii*) Flowers 4- or 5-merous. — *Dicotyledons.*
(*i*) Petals separate. — *Polypetalae.*
(*i*) Flowers hypogynous; ovary superior. — *Thalamiflorae.*
(*i*) Gynoecium syncarpous.
(*ii*) Carpels unite to form a 1-celled ovary with parietal placentation. — *Parietales.*
(*i*) Sepals caducous.
(*ii*) Petals double the number of sepals.
(*iii*) Flowers actinomorphic, 2- or 3-merous.
(*iv*) Herbs with milky juice (latex).
(*ii*) Stamens many, extrorse.
(*iii*) Fruit capsule. — *Papaveraceae.*

Bentham & Hooker (1862)	*Engler & Prantl (1931)*	*Hutchinson (1959)*
Dicotyledons	Dicotyledoneae	Dicotyledones
Polypetalae	Archichlamydeae	Herbaceae
Parietales	Rhoeadales	Rhoeadales
Papaveraceae	Papaveraceae	Papaveraceae

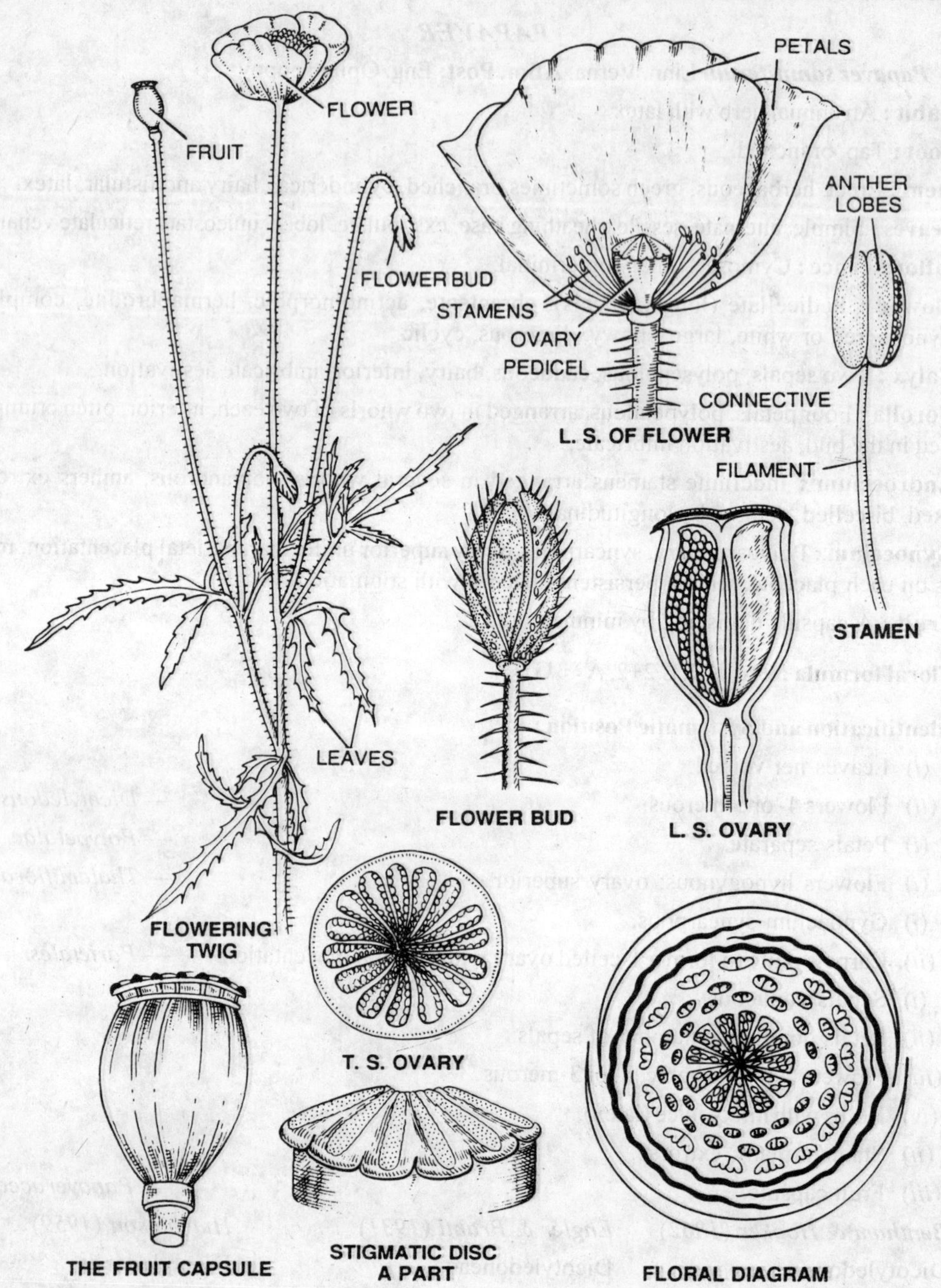

Fig. 9.6. *Papaver somniferum* Linn.

Economic value. The latex, obtained from the immature fruits, is the source of opium, which is used to induce sleep, relieve pain and relax spasms.

ESCHSCHOLTZIA

3. Eschscholtzia californica Chamb.

Habit : An annual herb.

Root : Tap, branched.

Stem : Erect, herbaceous, aerial, branched, solid, green, watery, juice present.

Leaf : Cauline and ramal, simple, much dissected, alternate, sessile, exstipulate, sheathing at base, acute, glabrous, unicostate reticulate.

Inflorescence : Cymose, solitary axillary.

Flower : Pedicellate, ebracteate, complete, actinomorphic, hermaphrodite, hypogynous, yellow, dimerous, cyclic.

Calyx : 2 sepals, arise from a cup-like structure of floral axis, fused together (gamosepalous), caducous.

Corolla : 4 petals (2+2), polypetalous, imbricate, yellow.

Androecium : Indefinite, polyandrous, filaments short, anthers dithecous, basifixed, extrorse.

Gynoecium : 2 carpels, syncarpous, ovary half superior - half inferior, unilocular, parietal placentation, style short, stigma 2, each bifid and linear, one is shorter than the other.

Fruit : Capsule.

Floral formula : ⊕ ⚥ K 2, C 2+2, A ∝, G ($\underline{2}$).

Identification and Systematic Position :

(*i*) Leaves net-veined.

(*ii*) Flowers 4- or 5-merous. — *Dicotyledons.*

(*i*) Petals separate. — *Polypetalae.*

(*i*) Flowers hypogynous; ovary superior. — *Thalamiflorae.*

(*i*) Gynoecium syncarpous.

(*ii*) Carpels unite to form a 1-celled ovary with parietal placentation. — *Parietales.*

(*i*) Sepals caducous.

(*ii*) Petals double the number of sepals.

(*iii*) Flowers actinomorphic, 2- or 3-merous.

(*iv*) Herbs with milky juice (latex).

(*v*) Stamens many, extrorse.

(*vi*) Fruit capsule. — *Papaveraceae.*

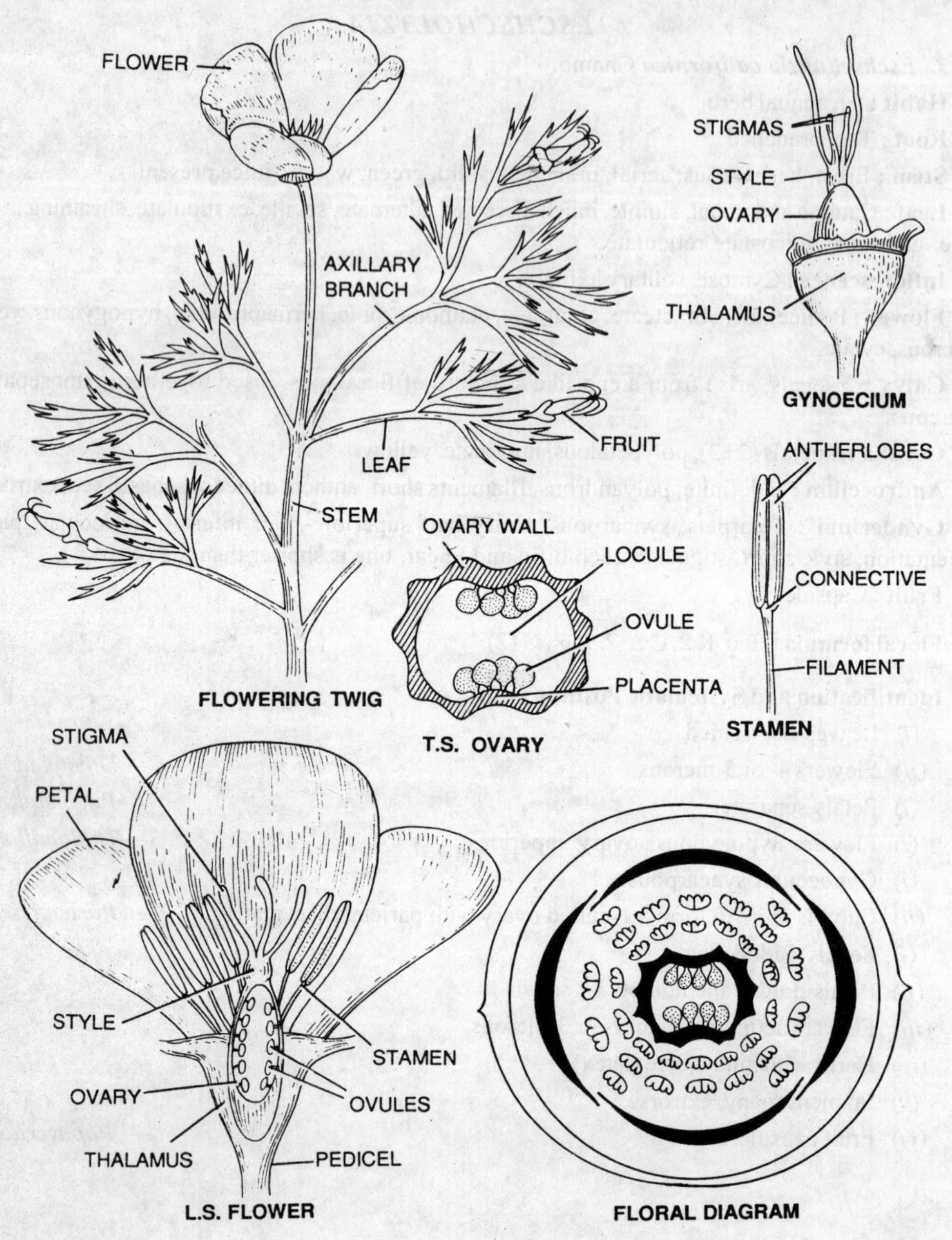

Fig. 9.7. Papaveraceae. *Eschscholtzia californica* Chamb.

Economic value. A popular annual ornamental herb with beautiful yellow or orange coloured flowers.

FAMILY—FUMARIACEAE (Fumitory family)

FUMARIA

1. Fumaria parviflora Lamk.; Verna. **Pitpapra.**

Fumaria parviflora Lamk. Common throughout area as a weed of cultivation; flowering and fruiting during the cold season. Distribution : over the greater part of India, ascending to 8,000 feet on the Himalayas.

Habit : An annual herb, wild, weed.

Root : Tap, branched.

Stem : Herbaceous, aerial, branched, glabrous, solid or fistular, scandent, watery juice, pale green.

Leaves : Cauline and ramal, simple, alternate, much dissected, pale green, exstipulate, leaf base sheathing, entire, acute, glabrous.

Inflorescence : Racemose, raceme.

Flower : Small, bracteate, pedicellate, zygomorphic, hermaphrodite, hypogynous, complete, purplish, dimerous.

Calyx : Two sepals, caducous, polysepalous, membranous, placed anterio-posteriorly.

Corolla : Four petals, polypetalous, two petals of outer whorl dissimilar, one of them flat or concave and other spurred, remaining inner petals winged or keeled at the base, the spurred petal contains nectary, petals of inner whorl smaller and placed anterio-posteriorly.

Androecium : According to Lawrence and Hutchinson six stamens, united into two bundles one on each side of the pistil. According to other authors two stamens, each stamen three-partite, middle segment of complete anther, and two lateral segments bear half anther each. The stamen towards the spurred petal produces a nectariferious spur which runs into the spur of the petal; basifixed, extrorse.

Gynoecium : Two carpels (bicarpellary), syncarpous, ovary superior, unilocular, two ovules on each placenta, parietal placentation, style slender, stigma lobed.

Fruit : A capsule or a single seeded nut.

Floral formula : Br. •|• ⚥ K 2, C 2+2, A (½ + 1 + ½) (½ + 1 + ½), G($\underline{2}$).

Identification and Systematic Position :

(*i*) Leaves net-veined.
(*ii*) Flowers 4- or 5-merous. — *Dicotyledons.*
(*i*) Petals separate. — *Polypetalae.*
(*i*) Flowers hypogynous; ovary superior. — *Thalamiflorae.*
(*i*) Gynoecium syncarpous.
(*ii*) Carpels unite to form a 1-celled ovary with parietal placentation. — *Parietales.*
(*i*) Herbs with water juice (latex).
(*ii*) Leaves usually lobed or dissected.
(*iii*) Flowers irregular; racemose.
(*iv*) Petals 2+2, 2 outer larger.
(*v*) 6 stamens in two bundles opposite the outer petals or (½ + 1 + ½) (½ + 1 + ½).
(*vi*) Ovary 1-celled with parietal placentation. — *Fumariaceae.*

Bentham & Hooker (1862)	*Engler & Prantl (1931)*	*Hutchinson (1959)*
Dicotyledons	Dicotyledoneae	Dicotyledones
Polypetalae	Archichlamydeae	Herbaceae
Parietales	Rhoeadales	Rhoeadales
Papaveraceae	Papaveraceae	Fumariaceae
	Fumariaceae	

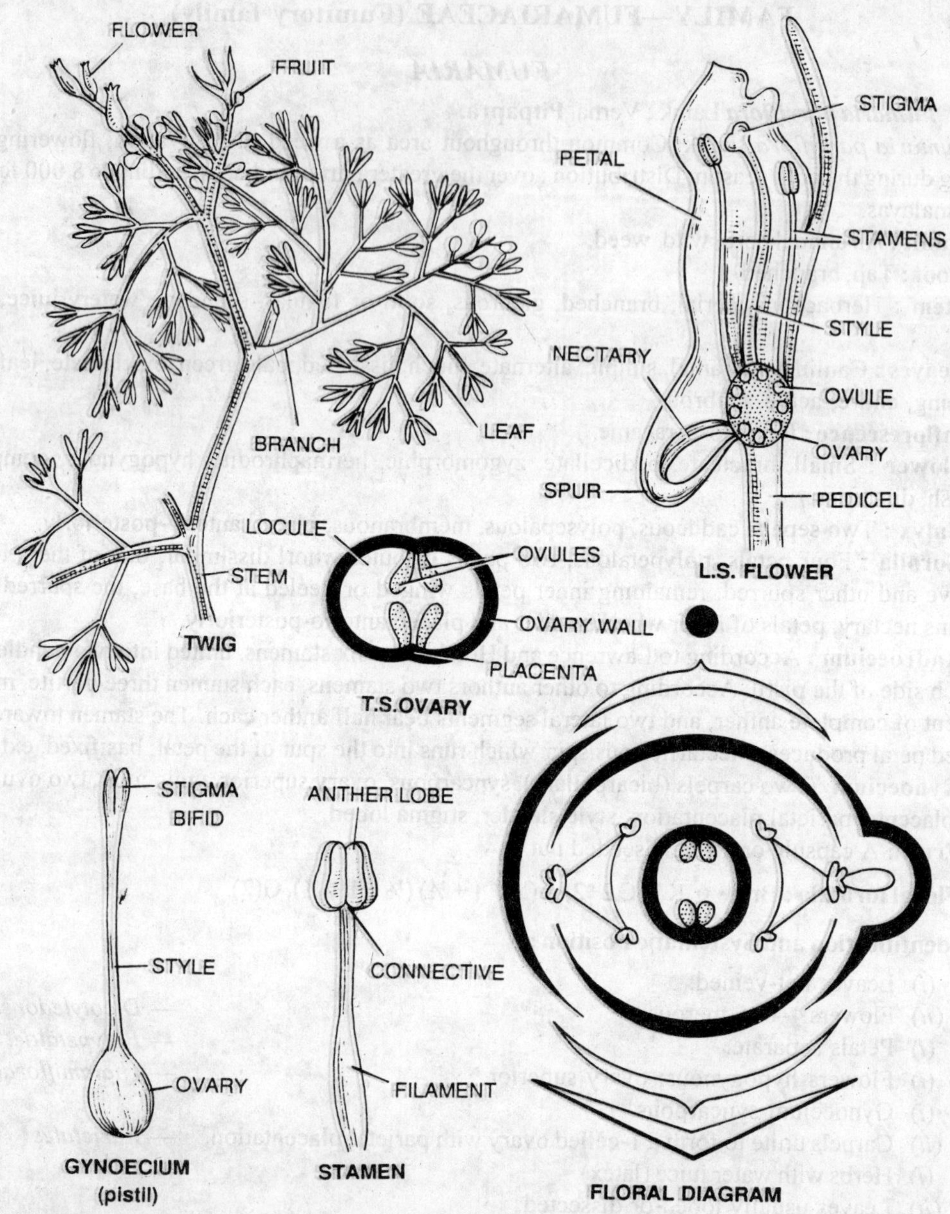

Fig. 9.8. Fumariaceae (Papaveraceae). *Fumaria parviflora* Lamk.; Verna. Pitpapra.

Economic value. Fumitory, has long been regarded as laxative, diuretic, alterative, tonic, and febrifuge. The drug is also useful in leprous affections.

CORYDALIS

2. ***Corydalis cava*** (Linn.) Schweigg.; Verna. **Bhutkesi.**

Habit : Annual herbs.

Root : Tap, branched.

Stem : Herbaceous, aerial, branched, glabrous, solid, cylinderical, scandent, watery juice present, green.

Leaf : Alternate, petiolate, simple, much dissected, each lobe acute at apex, entire, glabrous, exstipulate, leaf base sheathing.

Inflorescence : Racemose, raceme.

Flower : Bracteate, bracteolate, pedicellate, hermaphrodite, zygomorphic, hypogynous, complete, dimerous.

Calyx : 4 sepals, minute, caducous, placed anterio-posteriorly.

Corolla : 4 petals, polypetalous, two petals of out whorl dissimilar, one flat or concave other saccate or spurred, inner hooded and envelop the stamens like a cap, the spurred petal contains nectary, petals of inner whorl are smaller and placed anterio-posteriorly.

Androecium : 6 stamens, arranged in two series, outer two with dithecous anthers, inner four with monothecous anthers; each stamen branches off into three, two of the lateral branches bear monothecous anthers; stamens are coherent in two bundles; one or two nectar glands at the base of androecium, or stamens in two groups and each group consists of ½ + 1 + ½ stamens, basifixed, extrorse.

Gynoecium : 2, bicarpellary, syncarpous, ovary superior, unilocular, parietal placentation, two ovules on each placenta, style slender, stigma lobed.

Fruit : Capsule or nut.

Floral formula : Br. Brl. •|• ⚥ K 2, C 4, A 6, G $(\underline{2})$ OR Br. Brl. •|• ⚥ K 2, C 2+2, A (½ + 1 + ½) (½ + 1 + ½), G $(\underline{2})$.

Identification and Systematic Position :

(*i*) Leaves net-veined.
(*ii*) Flowers 4- or 5-merous. — *Dicotyledons.*
(*i*) Petals separate. — *Polypetalae.*
(*i*) Flowers hypogynous; ovary superior. — *Thalamiflorae.*
(*i*) Gynoecium syncarpous.
(*ii*) Carpels unite to form a 1-celled ovary with parietal placentation. — *Parietales.*
(*i*) Herbs with water juice (latex).
(*ii*) Leaves usually lobed or dissected.
(*iii*) Flowers irregular; racemose.
(*iv*) Petals 2+2, 2 outer larger.
(*v*) 6 stamens in two bundles opposite the outer petals or (½ + 1 + ½) (½ + 1 + ½).
(*vi*) Ovary 1-celled with parietal placentation. — *Fumariaceae.*

Other important members of the family. *Dicentra officinalis* Linn., an ornamental; *Fumaria indica* Pugsley, diuretic, diaphoretic; *Corydalis gavaniana* Wall, **Bhutkesi,** tonic, diuretic, alterative.

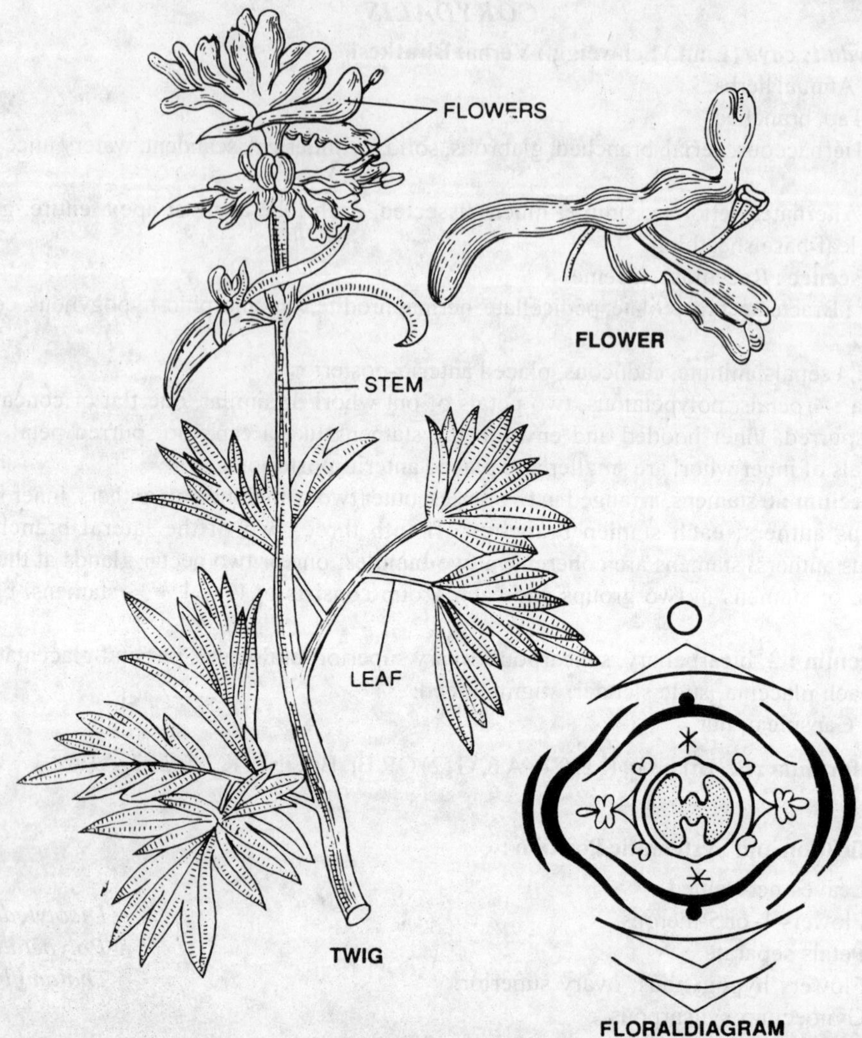

Fig. 9.9. Fumariaceae (Papaveraceae). *Corydalis cava* (Linn.) Schweigg.; Verna., **bhutkesi**.

Economic value. A medicinal plant. The root contains a principle, *Corydalia.* The roots are supposed to be tonic, diuretic, and alterative, and are prescribed in syphilitic and cutaneous affections.

FAMILY—CRUCIFERAE (Mustard Family)

BRASSICA

1. ***Brassica campestris*** Linn.; Verna. **Sarson;** Eng. Yellow mustard.

Brassica campestris Linn., very largely grown during the cold season, especially in Uttar Pradesh. The oil (**Karwa tel**) is yielded from its seeds.

Habit : Annual herb, cultivated.

Root : Tap, branched.

Stem : Erect, herbaceous, cylinderical, slightly hairy, branched, smooth and green.

Leaf : Cauline and ramal, simple, alternate, sessile, glabrous, upper leaves entire, lower leaves lyrate, exstipulate, unicostate reticulate venation.

Inflorescence : Racemose, typical raceme.

Flower : Pedicellate, ebracteate, hermaphrodite, actinomorphic, yellow, hypogynous, complete, tetramerous, cyclic.

Calyx : Four sepals, polysepalous, arranged in two whorls of two each, the sepals of inner whorl are longer, imbricate aestivation.

Corolla : Four petals, polypetalous, each petal consists of a limb and claw, cruciform alternating the sepals, imbricate or valvate.

Androecium : Six stamens, polyandrous arranged in two whorls, the two stamens of outer whorl are smaller than the four stamens of inner whorl (*i.e.,* tetradynamous condition) anthers bicelled, basifixed, introrse.

Gynoecium : Two carpels (bicarpellary), syncarpous, ovary superior, unilocular but becomes bilocular because of the development of false septum (replum) parietal placentation, style short and stigma bilobed.

Fruit : Siliqua.

Floral formula : ⊕ ⚥ K 2+2, C 4, A 2+4, G $(\underline{2})$.

Identification and Systematic Position :

(*i*) Leaves net-veined.
(*ii*) Flowers 4- or 5-merous. — *Dicotyledons.*
(*i*) Petals separate. — *Polypetalae.*
(*i*) Flowers hypogynous; ovary superior. — *Thalamiflorae.*
(*i*) Gynoecium syncarpous.
(*ii*) Carpels unite to form a 1-celled ovary with parietal placentation. — *Parietales.*
(*i*) Herbs with exstipulate alternate leaves.
(*ii*) Petals cruciform; 4.
(*ii*) Stamens tetradynamous; rarely 2 or 4 stamens.
(*vi*) Ovary 2 carpels, septate longitudinally by a replum; fruit siliqua or silicula. — *Cruciferae.*

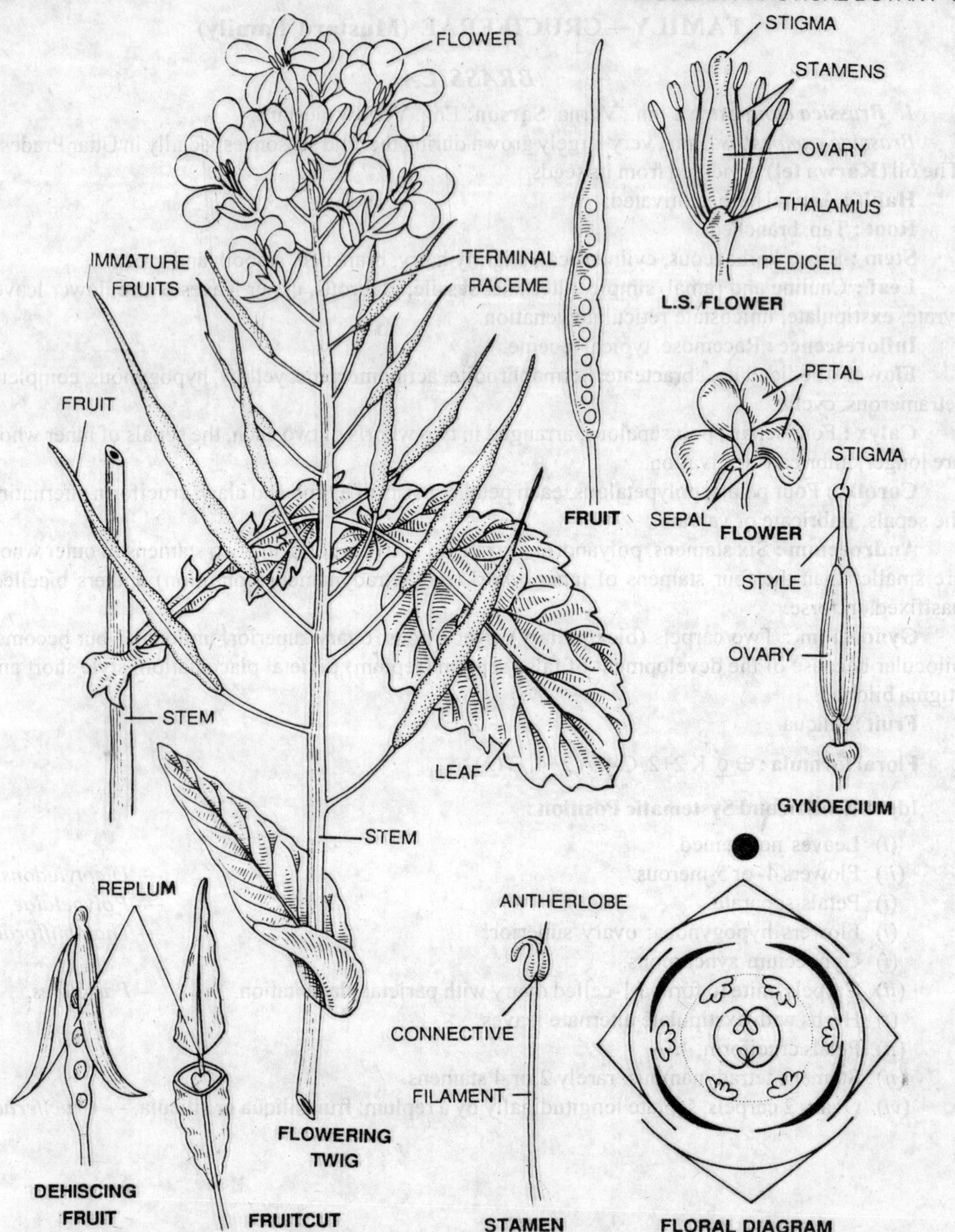

Fig. 9.10. Cruciferae (Brassicaceae). *Brassica campestris* Linn.; Eng., yellow mustard; Verna., **sarson.**

Economic value. The tender leaves, and shoots are used as vegetable. Ground mustard seeds are used as a condiment. The seeds yield a fatty oil, which is generally used for cooking purposes.

SENEBIERA

2. ***Senebiera didyma*** Pers.

Senebiera didyma Pers. (Lesser Wart-cress). An established weed of cultivation during the cold season. Distribution-plains of N. India.

Habit : Annual herb, wild, weed.

Root : Tap, branched.

Stem : Prostrate, aerial, weak, trailing, cylindrical, branched, branches arranged in rosettes, green glabrous, herbaceous, solid.

Leaf : Radical, cauline and ramal compound, exstipulate, unipinnate and imparipinnate, pinnae with cut margins, petiolate, petiole base hairy, alternate, leaf surface glabrous, reticulate venation.

Inflorescence : Racemose, leaf opposed typical raceme.

Flower : Minute, greenish, pedicellate, ebracteate, hermaphrodite, actionomorphic, hypogynous, complete, tetramerous, cyclic.

Calyx : Four sepals, polysepalous, arranged in two whorls of two each, sepals spreading, short, larger than petals, inferior, valvate aestivation.

Corolla : Very much reduced (rudimentary), represented by four minute whitish scaly structures alternating the sepals, valvate.

Androecium : Two stamens, polyandrous, median, anterior-posterior, anthers basifixed, filaments long tapering at apex and broad at base, dithecous, introrse.

Gynoecium : Two carpels (bicarpellary), syncarpous, ovary superior, unilocular but becomes bilocular due to formation of replum, parietal placentation, one ovule on each locule, style reduced, stigma discoid.

Fruit : Compressed silicula.

Floral formula : ⊕ ⚥ K 2+2, C 4, A 2, G $\underline{(2)}$.

Identification and Systematic Position :

(*i*) Leaves net-veined.
(*ii*) Flowers 4- or 5-merous. — *Dicotyledons.*
(*i*) Petals separate. — *Polypetalae.*
(*i*) Flowers hypogynous; ovary superior. — *Thalamiflorae.*
(*i*) Gynoecium syncarpous.
(*ii*) Carpels unite to form a 1-celled ovary with parietal placentation. — *Parietales.*
(*i*) Herbs with exstipulate alternate leaves.
(*ii*) Petals cruciform; 4.
(*iii*) Stamens tetradynamous; rarely 2 or 4 stamens.
(*iv*) Ovary of 2 carpels, septate longitudinally by a replum; fruit siliqua or silicula.
— *Cruciferae.*

Bentham & Hooker (1862)	*Engler & Prantl (1931)*	*Hutchinson (1959)*
Dicotyledons	Dicotyledoneae	Dicotyledons
Polypetalae	Archichlamydeae	Herbaceae
Parietales	Rhoeadales	Cruciales (Brassicales)
Cruciferae	Cruciferae	Cruciferae (Brassicaceae).

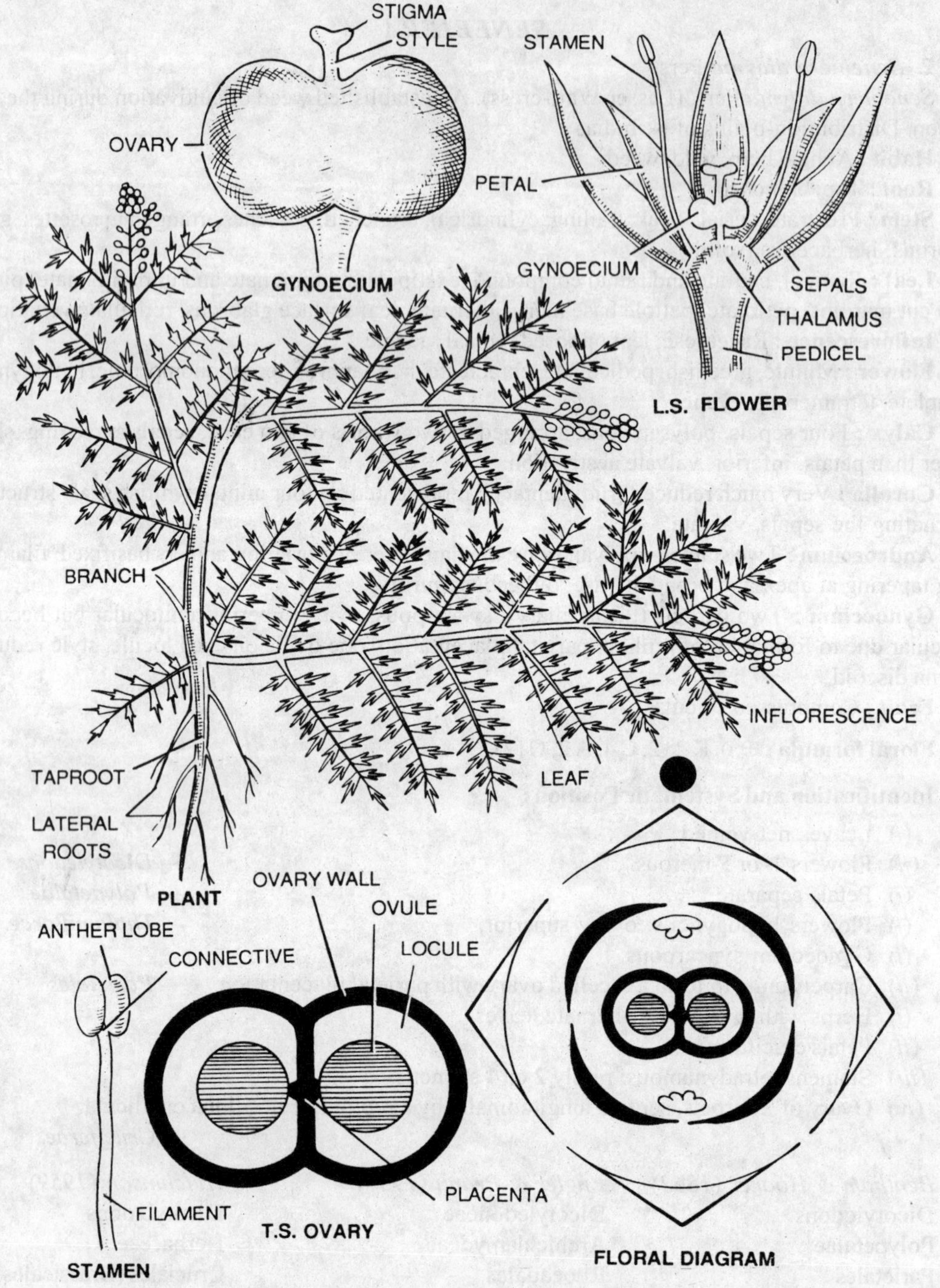

Fig. 9.11. Cruciferae (Brassicaceae). *Senebiera didyma* Pers.; Eng. lesser wart cress.

IBERIS

*3. **Iberis amara*** Linn.; Eng. Candytuft.

Habit : Annual ornametal herb, cultivated.

Stem : Herbaceous, erect, aerial, branched, green, solid, rough surface.

Leaf : Cauline and ramal, alternate, sometimes opposite, sessile, exstipulate, simple, margin somewhat dissected, acute, glabrous, unicostate reticulate.

Inflorescence : Racemose, corymb.

Flower : Ebracteate, pedicellate, complete, irregular (zygomorphic), hermaphrodite, tetramerous, hypogynous, white, cyclic.

Calyx : 4, polysepalous, in two whorls of 2 each, imbricate, petaloid, boat shaped.

Corolla : 4, polypetalous, valvate, 2 anterior petals large, 2 posterior petals small, each petal consists of a claw and limb, cruciform.

Androecium : 6, free stamens (polyandrous), tetradynamous -2 outer lateral short, remaining 4 anterio-posterior long, dithecous, dorsifixed, intorse.

Gynoecium : Bicarpellary, syncarpous, ovary superior, unilocular when young, at maturity becomes bilocular because of the development of false septum, parietal placentation, style long, stigma globular.

Fruit : Silicula.

Floral formula : •|• ⚥ K 2+2, C 4, A 2+4, G $(\underline{2})$.

Identification and Systematic Position :

(*i*) Leaves net-veined.
(*ii*) Flowers 4- or 5-merous. — *Dicotyledons.*
(*i*) Petals separate. — *Polypetalae.*
(*i*) Flowers hypogynous; ovary superior. — *Thalamiflorae.*
(*i*) Gynoecium syncarpous.
(*ii*) Carpels unite to form a 1-celled ovary with parietal placentation. — *Parietales.*
(*i*) Herbs with exstipulate alternate leaves.
(*ii*) Petals cruciform; 4.
(*iii*) Stamens tetradynamous; rarely 2 or 4 stamens.
(*iv*) Ovary of 2 carpels, septate longitudinally by a replum; fruit siliqua or silicula.
— *Cruciferae.*

Other important members of the family. *Capsella bursa-pastoris* Medic., astringent, antiscorbutic; *Cheiranthus cheiri* Linn., **Todrisurkh** - flowers cardiac, emmenagogue, used in paralysis and impotency; *Lepidium sativum* Linn. **Halim** - used in asthma, cough and bleeding piles; *Raphanus sativus* Linn., **Muli** - common vegetable, diuretic and laxative.

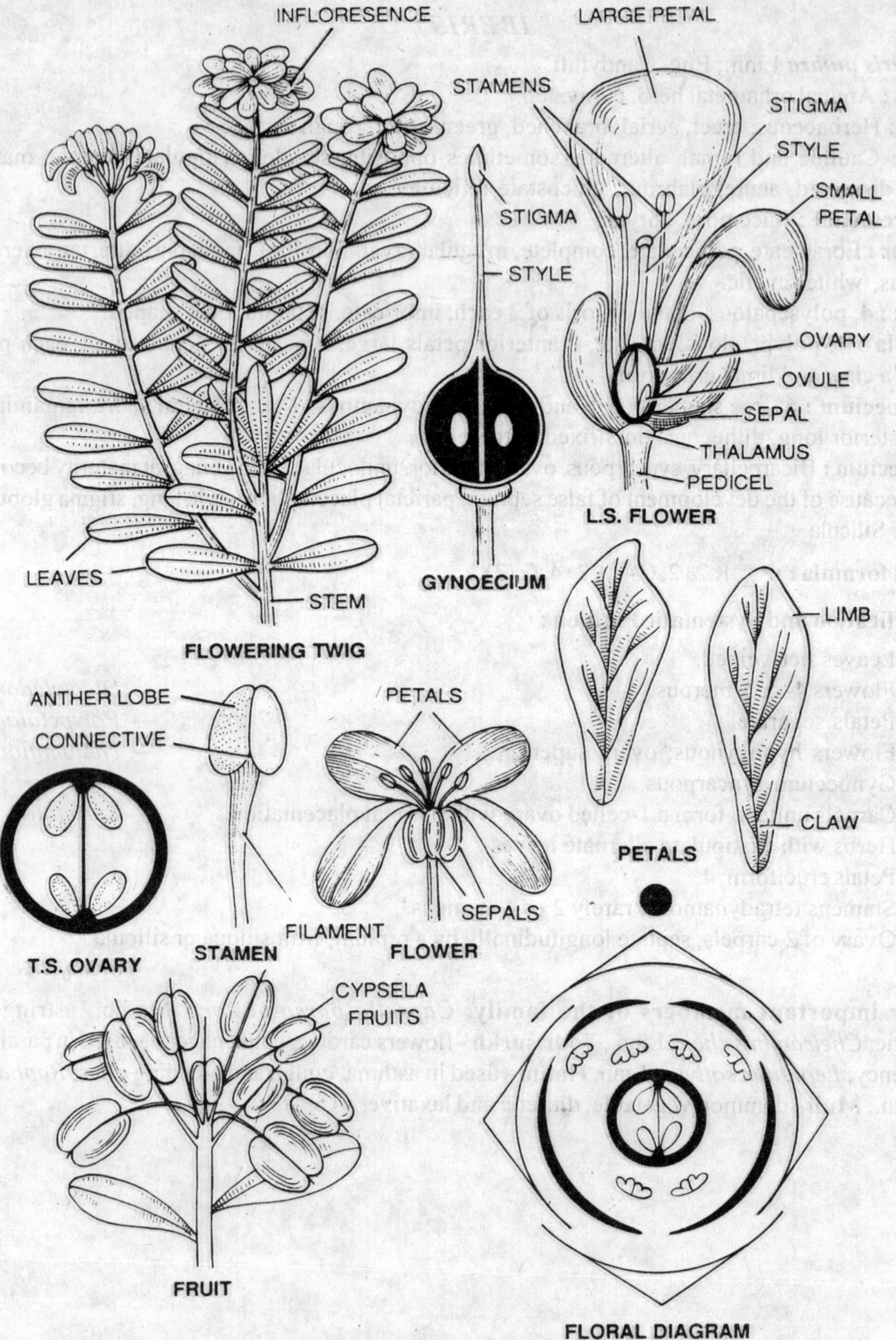

Fig. 9.12. Cruciferae (Brassicacae). *Iberis amara* Linn.; Eng., candytuft.

Economic value. A common ornamental herb. The plants are used in rheumatism and gouts. Seeds are used in asthma and bronchitis.

FAMILY—CAPPARIDACEAE (Caper family)

CAPPARIS

1. Capparis spinosa Linn.; Verna. **Kabra.**

Capparis aphylla Linn. (Verna. **Karil**). A leafless shrub. Abundant in the drier portions of Indian plains, associated with *Salvadora, Acacia* and other desert shrubs. Distribution - Punjab, Haryana, Uttar Pradesh, Rajasthan, M.P. and South India.

Capparis sepiaria Linn. Commonly found in dry places; leaves present; flowers in May, fruit ripens in July. Distribution - throughout India.

Habit : Erect or climbing shrubs, sometimes small trees.

Root : Tap and branched.

Stem : Erect, branched, solid, rough, woody, spiny, usually armed with a pair of stipular thorns at the base of petioles.

Leaves : Cauline and ramal, simple, rarely altogether absent alternate, stipulate, stipules spiniscent, acute apex, reticulate venation.

Inflorescence : Cymose or racemose. In *C. aphylla* many-flowered corymbs, *C. sepiaria* many flowered umbels or umbellate corymbs, *C. horrida* solitary axillary cyme.

Flower : Pedicellate, hermaphrodite, actinomorphic or zygomorphic, ebracteate, tetramerous, hypogynous, complete, cyclic.

Calyx : Four sepals, arranged in two series, polysepalous, imbricate aestivation, interior. In *C. aphylla,* the sepals unequal, the inner being saccate.

Corolla : Four petals, polypetalous, sessile, imbricate.

Androecium : Many, polyandrous, inserted on the disk at the base of the long gynophore, anthers dorsifixed, introrse, dithecous, inferior.

Gynoecium : Two carpels (bicarpellary), syncarpous, ovary superior, unilocular, parietal placentation, many ovules on each placenta, ovary being situated on a long stalk (gynophore), stigma sessile.

Fruit : A berry.

Floral formula : •|• or ⊕ ⚥ K 2+2, C 4, A ∝, G $\underline{(2-6)}$.

Identification and Systematic Position :

(*i*) Leaves net-veined.
(*ii*) Flowers 4- or 5-merous. — *Dicotyledons.*
(*i*) Petals separate. — *Polypetalae.*
(*i*) Flowers hypogynous; ovary superior. — *Thalamiflorae.*
(*i*) Gynoecium syncarpous.
(*ii*) Carpels unite to form a 1-celled ovary with parietal placentation. — *Parietales.*
(*i*) Woody or herbaceous.
(*ii*) Stamens 4-indefinite.
(*iii*) Ovary usually on a gynophore; 1-celled (unilocular) with 2-4 parietal placenta.
(*iv*) Fruit capsule or berry. — *Capparidaceae.*

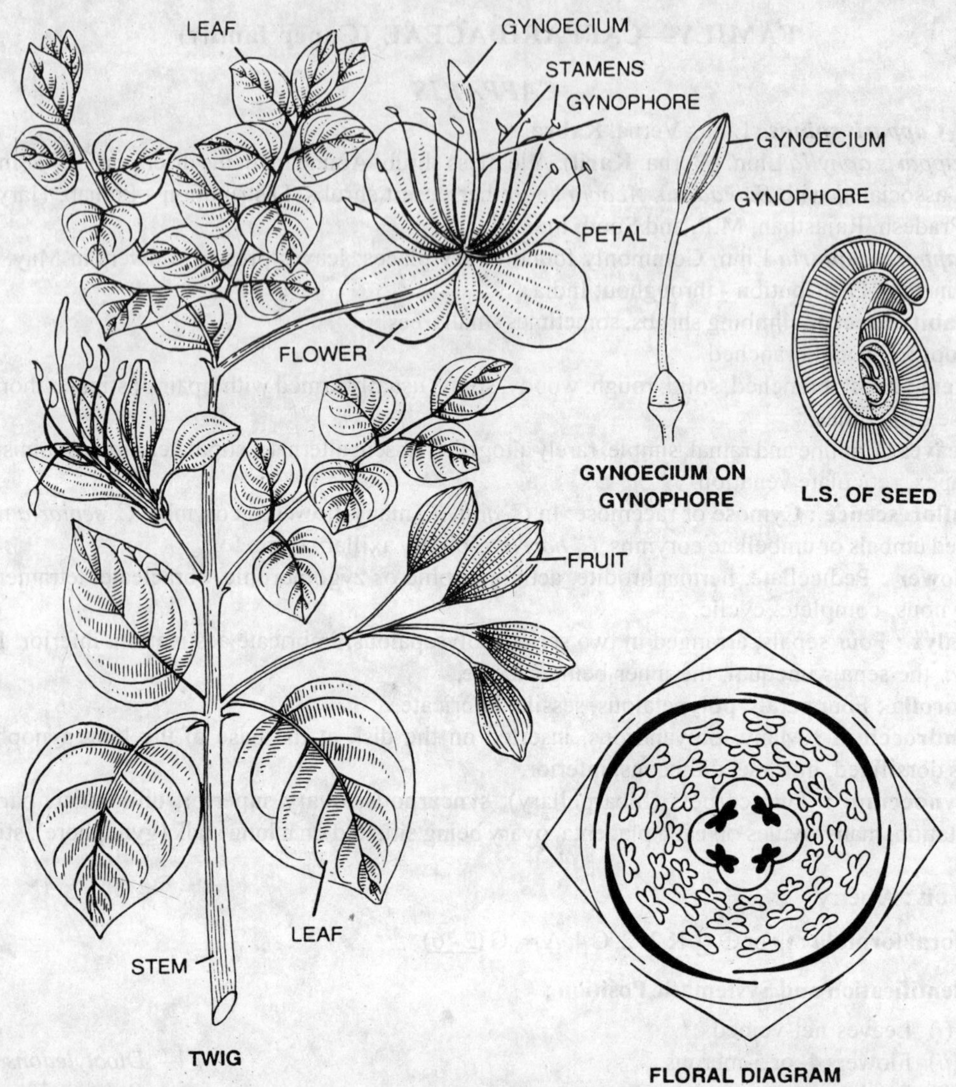

Fig. 9.13. Capparidaceae. *Capparis spinosa* Linn.; Verna., **kabra.**

Economic value. The flower buds, known as capers, are used as condiment. The root bark is used as tonic, diuretic, expectorant, anthelmintic, emmenagogue, analgesic, in rheumatism, paralysis, enlarged spleen and tubercular glands. The pultice of leaves is used in gout.

CLEOME

2. *Cleome viscosa* Linn.; Verna. **Hulhul.**

Cleome viscosa Linn. (verna. **Hulhul**). A common weed, especially in cultivated ground; flowering during the rainy season. Distribution - warmer parts of India.

Habit : An annual rainy season herb, weed, 1-3 feet high.

Root : Tap, branched.

Stem : Erect, aerial, glandular pubescent, branched, solid, herbaceous, cylinderical and green.

Leaves : Cauline and ramal, 3-5 foliate leaflets, sessile, ovate or obuvate or obovate, alternate, exstipulate, acute, hairy, unicostate reticulate.

Inflorescence : Racemose, typical receme or corymbo-raceme.

Flower : Pedicellate (long pedicels), ebracteate, hermaphrodite, yellow, actinomorphic, complete, hypogynous, tetramerous and cyclic.

Calyx : Four sepals, arranged in two whorls of two each, polysepalous, ovate, acute, inferior, imbricate.

Corolla : Four petals, polypetalous, two approximate and two spreading, obtuse, clawed, yellow, inferior, valvate aestivation.

Androecium : Many stamens (12-24), polyandrous, filaments long, inferior, anthers introse, basifixed, dithecous.

Gynoecium : Two carpels (bicarpellary), syncarpous, ovary superior, sessile or subsessile, unilocular, placentation parietal, many ovules on two parietal placentas, short style, stigma round, gynophore short.

Fruit : Oblong or linear capsule.

Floral formula : $\oplus$ ⚥ K 2+2, C 4, A ∞, G $(\underline{2})$.

Identification and Systematic Position :

(*i*) Leaves net-veined.
(*ii*) Flowers 4- or 5-merous. — *Dicotyledons.*
(*i*) Petals separate. — *Polypetalae.*
(*i*) Flowers hypogynous; ovary superior. — *Thalamiflorae.*
(*i*) Gynoecium syncarpous.
(*ii*) Carpels unite to form a 1-celled ovary with parietal placentation. — *Parietales.*
(*i*) Woody or herbaceous.
(*ii*) Stamens 4-indefinite.
(*iii*) Ovary usually on a gynophore; 1-celled (unilocular) with 2-4 parietal placenta.
(*iv*) Fruit capsule or berry. — *Capparidaceae.*

Bentham & Hooker (*1862*)	*Engler & Prantl* (*1931*)	*Hutchinson* (*1959*)
Dicotyledons	Dicotyledoneae	Dicotyledons
Polypetalae	Archichlamydeae	Lignosae
Parietales	Rhoeadales	Capparidales
Capparidaceae	Capparidaceae	Capparidaceae

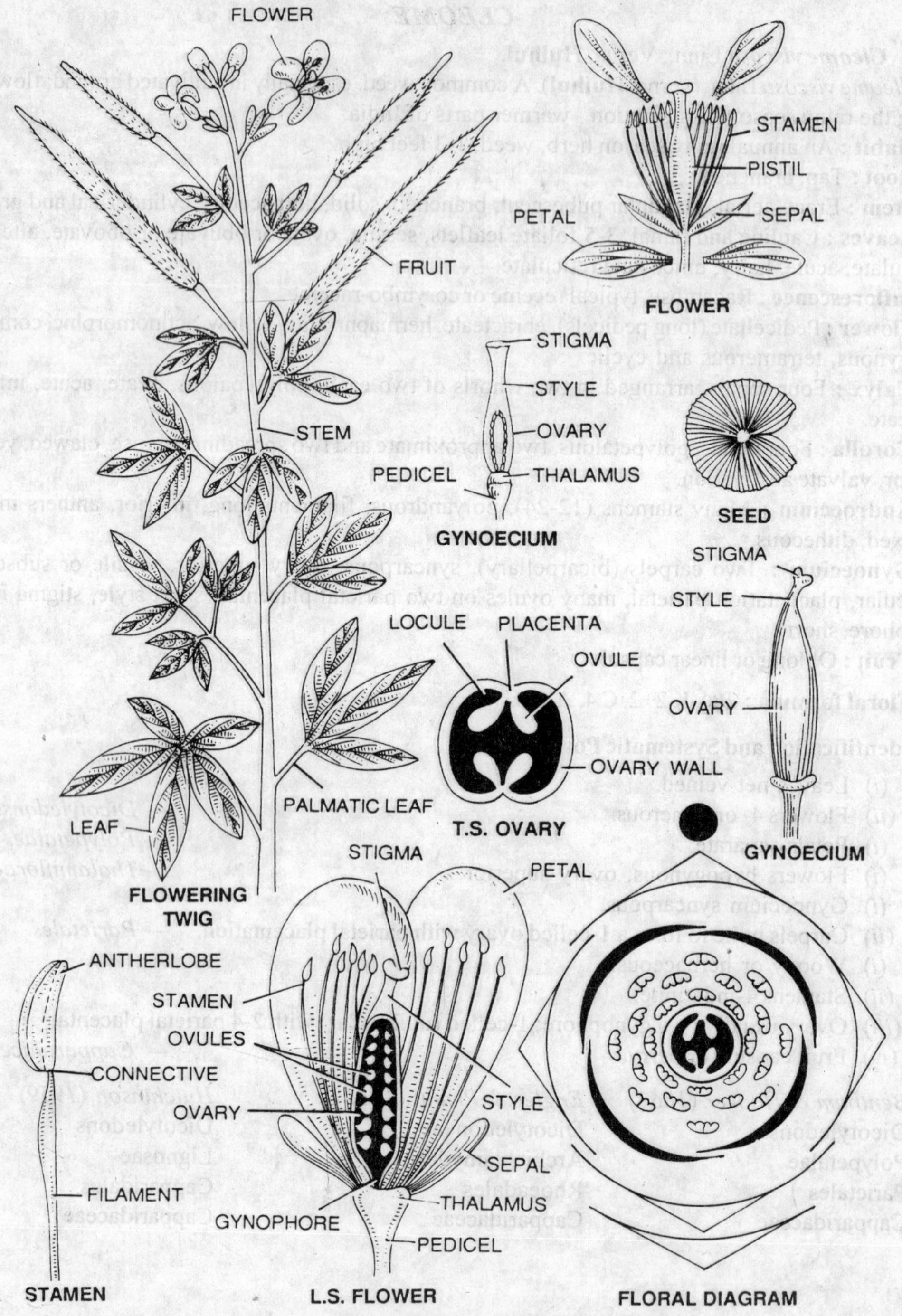

Fig. 9.14. Capparidaceae. *Cleome viscosa* Linn.; Verna. **Hulhul**

Economic value. Seeds are used in curries. The leaves are rubifacient, vesicant, sudorific and externally applied for wounds and ulcers. The juice of leaves is used to remove earache. The seeds are carminative, anthelmintic, rubifacient and vesicant.

CRATAEVA

3. *Crataeva religiosa* Linn.; Verna. **Barna.**

Crataeva religiosa Linn. (Verna. **Barna**). Occurs generally as a planted tree in N. India, flowering in April and May.

Habit : A small spreading unarmed tree.

Stem : Erect, woody, branched, cylinderical, solid.

Leaves : Compound, alternate, deciduous, appearing with the flowers, petiolate (long petioles), 3-foliate, leaflets 3 – 6" long, ovate or ovate lanceolate, acuminate, entire, glabrous, pale beneath.

Inflorescence : Racemose, flowers arranged in corymbose clusters at the ends of the new growths.

Flower : Large, yellow or purplish, hermaphrodite, actinomorphic (regular), pedicellate, hypogynous, complete, tetramerous, cyclic.

Calyx : Four sepals, polysepalous, inferior, inserted on the edge of large lobed disk, valvate or imbricate.

Corolla : Four petals, polypetalous, long clawed, open in bud, claw half as long as the limb, ovate or oblong, obtuse or acute, imbricate.

Androecium : Stamens many, polyandrous, adnate to the base of the gynophore, stamens longer than the petals, filaments long, anthers bicelled, introrse, dithecous, basifixed.

Gynoecium : Two carpels (bicarpellary), ovary superior, on a slender stalk (gynophore), unilocular, parietal placentation, ovules many on two parietal placentas, style short, stigma capitate.

Fruit : Berry, 1-2" diameter, situated on a thick woody gynophore, pericarp hard.

Floral formula : ⊕ ⚥ K 4, C 4, A ∝, G $(\underline{2})$.

Identification and Systematic Position :

(*i*) Leaves net-veined.
(*ii*) Flowers 4- or 5-merous. — *Dicotyledons.*
(*i*) Petals separate. — *Polypetalae.*
(*i*) Flowers hypogynous; ovary superior. — *Thalamiflorae.*
(*i*) Gynoecium syncarpous.
(*ii*) Carpels unite to form a 1-celled ovary with parietal placentation. — *Parietales.*
(*i*) Woody or herbaceous.
(*ii*) Stamens 4-indefinite.
(*iii*) Ovary usually on a gynophore; 1-celled (unilocular) with 2-4 parietal placenta.
(*iv*) Fruit capsule or berry. — *Capparidaceae.*

Other important members of the family. *Capparis sepiaria* Linn., **Kanthari** - febrifuge, alterative, tonic, useful in skin diseases; *Cleome brachycarpa* Vahl ex DC., **Panwar** - bitter, used for scabies and rheumatism; *Maerua arenaria* Hook., **Vika** - alterative, tonic and stimulant.

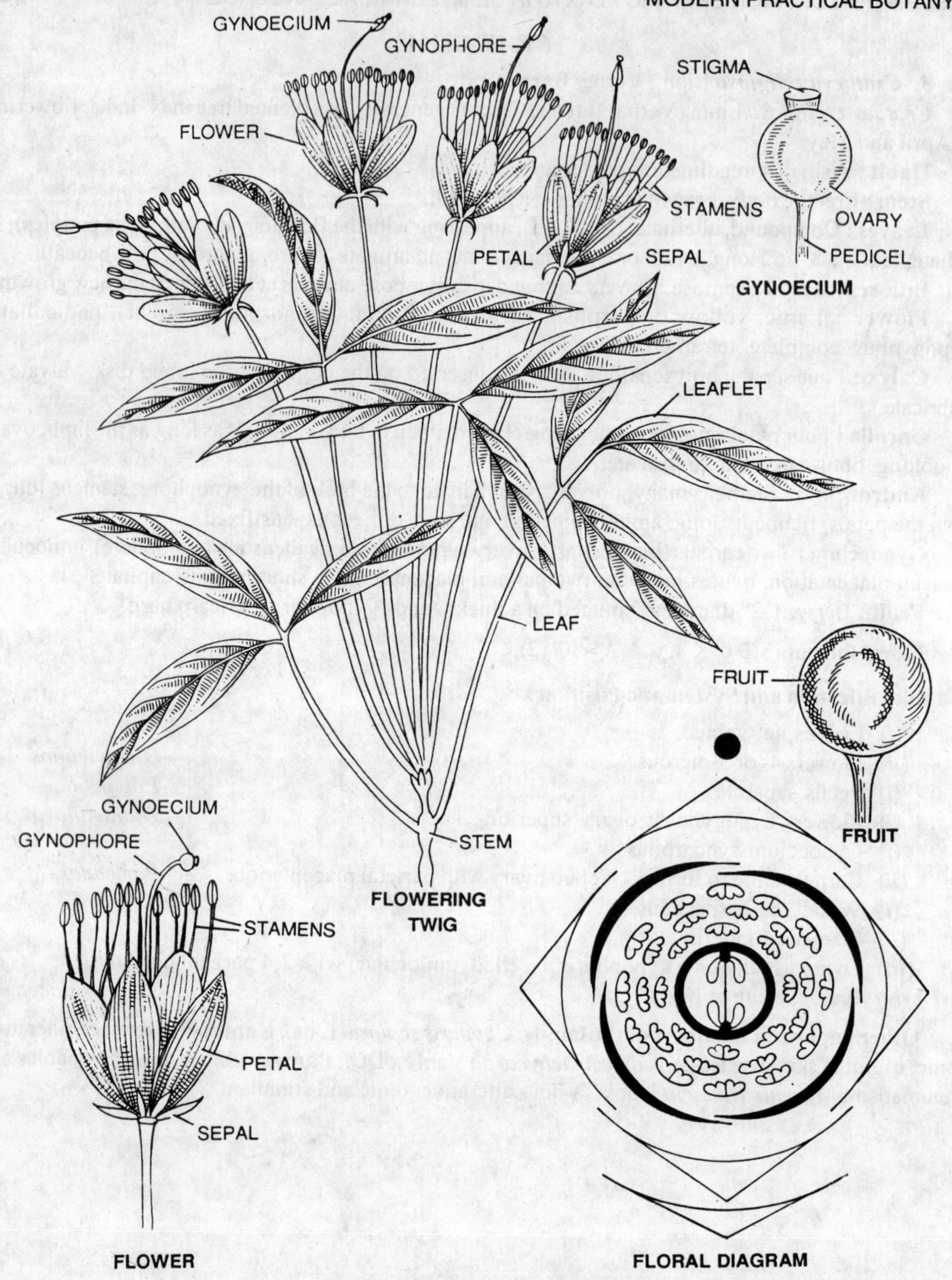

Fig. 9.15. Capparidaceae. *Crataeva religiosa* Linn.; Verna., **berna.**

Economic value. An ornamental tree cultivated in gardens for its white and plae-yellow flowers in lax terminal corymbs. Usually planted near Muslim tombs. The bark is demulcent, stomachic, laxative, diuretic, antipyretic, alterative, tonic, useful in calculus affections, disorders of urinary organs and used in snake-bite.

CLEOME

4. Cleome gynandra Linn.; Syn. *Gynandropsis pentaphylla* DC.

Habit : An annual rainy season herb.

Root : Tap, branched.

Stem : Erect, aerial, herbaceous, branched, solid, cylindric, hairy, green.

Leaf : Cauline and ramal, exstipulate, alternate, petiolate, palmately compound, pentafoliate, leaflet elliptic-ovate, acute, hairy, entire, unicostate reticulate.

Inflorescence : Racemose, corymbose raceme.

Flower : Pedicellate (long pedicels), ebracteate, hermaphrodite, actinomorphic, tetramerous, hypogynous, complete, cyclic, purplish white.

Calyx : 4 sepals, arranged in two whorls, polysepalous, acute, inferior, imbricate.

Corolla : 4 petals, polypetalous, valvate, obtuse, each petal distinguished into a claw and limb, inferior, white.

Androecium : 6 stamens, polyandrous, stamens present on the androphore, dithecous, dorsifixed, introrse.

Gynoecium : 2 carpels, syncarpous, ovary superior, unilocular with many ovules, parietal placentation, hairy, style short, stigma globular, gynophore present.

Fruit : Oblong or linear capsule.

Floral formula : ⊕ ⚥ K 2+2, C 4, A 6, G $\underline{(2)}$.

Identification and Systematic Position :

(*i*) Leaves net-veined.
(*ii*) Flowers 4- or 5-merous. — *Dicotyledons.*
(*i*) Petals separate. — *Polypetalae.*
(*i*) Flowers hypogynous; ovary superior. — *Thalamiflorae.*
(*i*) Gynoecium syncarpous.
(*ii*) Carpels unite to form a 1-celled ovary with parietal placentation. — *Parietales.*
(*i*) Woody or herbaceous.
(*ii*) Stamens 4-indefinite.
(*iii*) Ovary usually on a gynophore; 1-celled (unilocular) with 2-4 parietal placenta.
(*iv*) Fruit capsule or berry. — *Capparidaceae.*

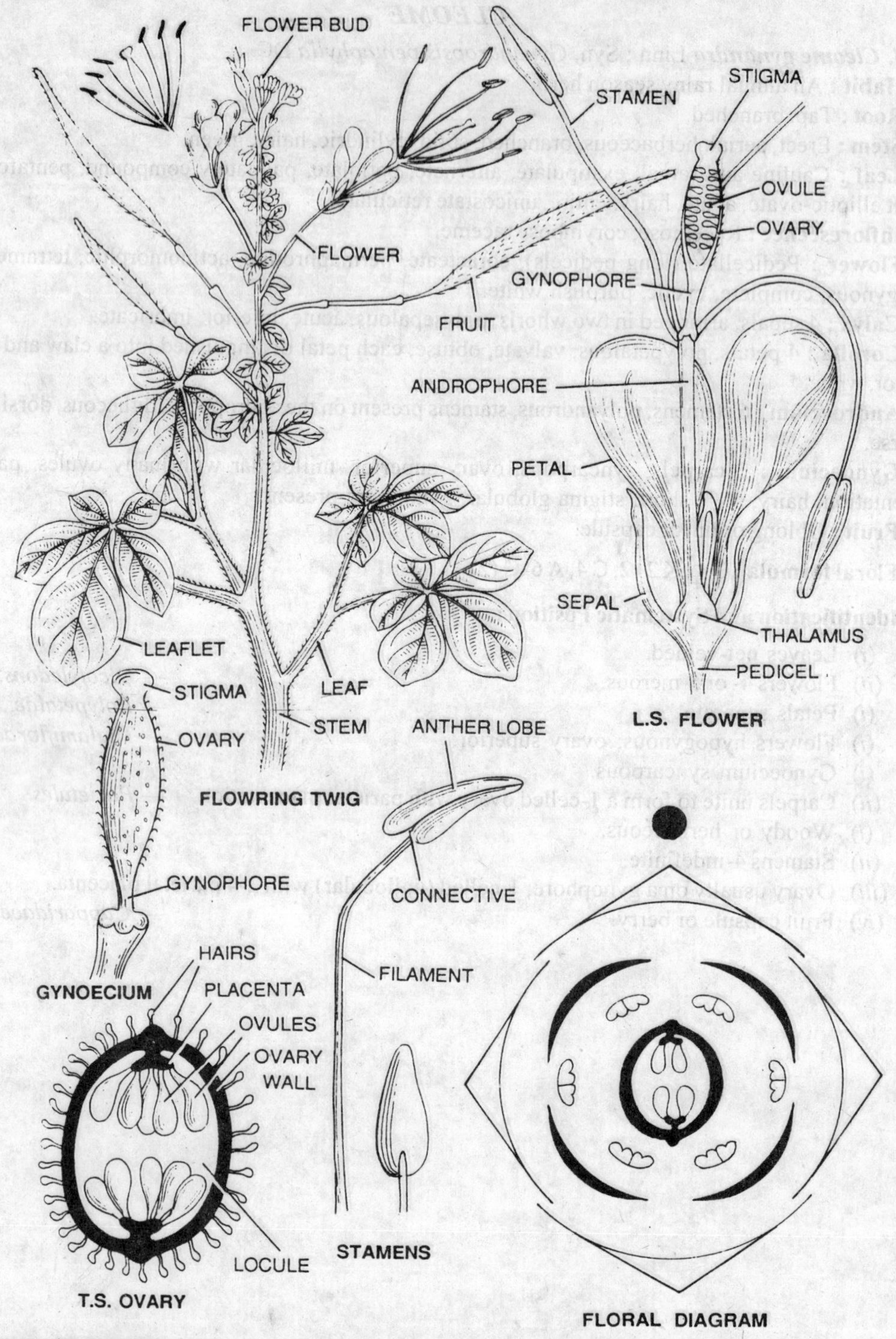

Fig. 9.16. Capparidaceae. *Cleome gynandra* Linn. Syn. *Gynandropsis pentaphylla* DC.

Economic value. Decoction of root is used in fever. The leaves are used in rheumatism. The plant is used in scorpion-sting and snake-bite.

FAMILY—VIOLACEAE (Pansy family)

VIOLA

Viola tricolor Linn.; Eng. Pansy.

Habit : Annual herb. ornamental, cultivated.

Root : Tap, branched.

Stem : Erect, branched, glabrous, angular, green, herbaceous, fistular.

Leaf : Simple, cauline and ramal, alternate, stipulate (foliaceous stipules), petiolate, oblong, margins with rounded teeth, unicostate reticulate venation.

Inflorescence : Cymose, solitary axillary.

Flower : Large, showy (violet), pedicellate, bracteate, bracteolate (two bracteloes), hermaphrodite, zygomorphic, hypogynous, complete.

Calyx : Five sepals. polysepalous, green, lanceolate, appendiculate, quincuncial aestivation, inferior.

Corolla : Five petals, polypetalous, petals unequal, violet, dark streaks present, the anterior or lower petal is produced backward into a spur and collects honey, imbricate aestivation.

Androecium : Five stamens, alternating with the petals, the stamens form a ring like structure round the ovary and style, filaments short, anthers introrse, connate, connectives of the two lower often spurred at the base which project into the spur of the anterior petal.

Gynoecium : Three carpels, syncarpous, ovary superior, unilocular, parietal placentation, many ovules attached to parietal placentas, style short, tip straight or oblique, stigma lobed.

Fruit : 3-valved loculicidal capsule.

Floral formula : Br. Brl. •|• ⚥ K 5, C 5, A 5, G ($\underline{3}$).

Identification and Systematic Position :

(*i*) Leaves net-veined.
(*ii*) Flowers 4- or 5-merous. — *Dicotyledons.*
(*i*) Petals separate. — *Polypetalae.*
(*i*) Flowers hypogynous; ovary superior. — *Thalamiflorae.*
(*i*) Gynoecium syncarpous.
(*ii*) Carpels unite to form a 1-celled ovary with parietal plscentation. — *Parietales.*
(*i*) Flowers bisexual, zygomorphic, hypogynous.
(*ii*) Fove [ersostemt se[a; s; 5 petals, lowermost spurred.
(*iii*) Stamens 5; connivent around ovary.
(*iv*) Ovary superior, unilocular, pariental placentation; fruit loculicidal capsule.
— *Violaceae.*

Bentham & Hooker (*1862*)	*Engler & Prantl* (*1931*)	*Hutchinson* (*1959*)
Dicotyledons	Dicotyledoneae	Dicotyledones
Polypetalae	Archichlamydeae	Lignosae
Parietales	Parietales	Violales
Violaceae	Violaceae	Violaceae

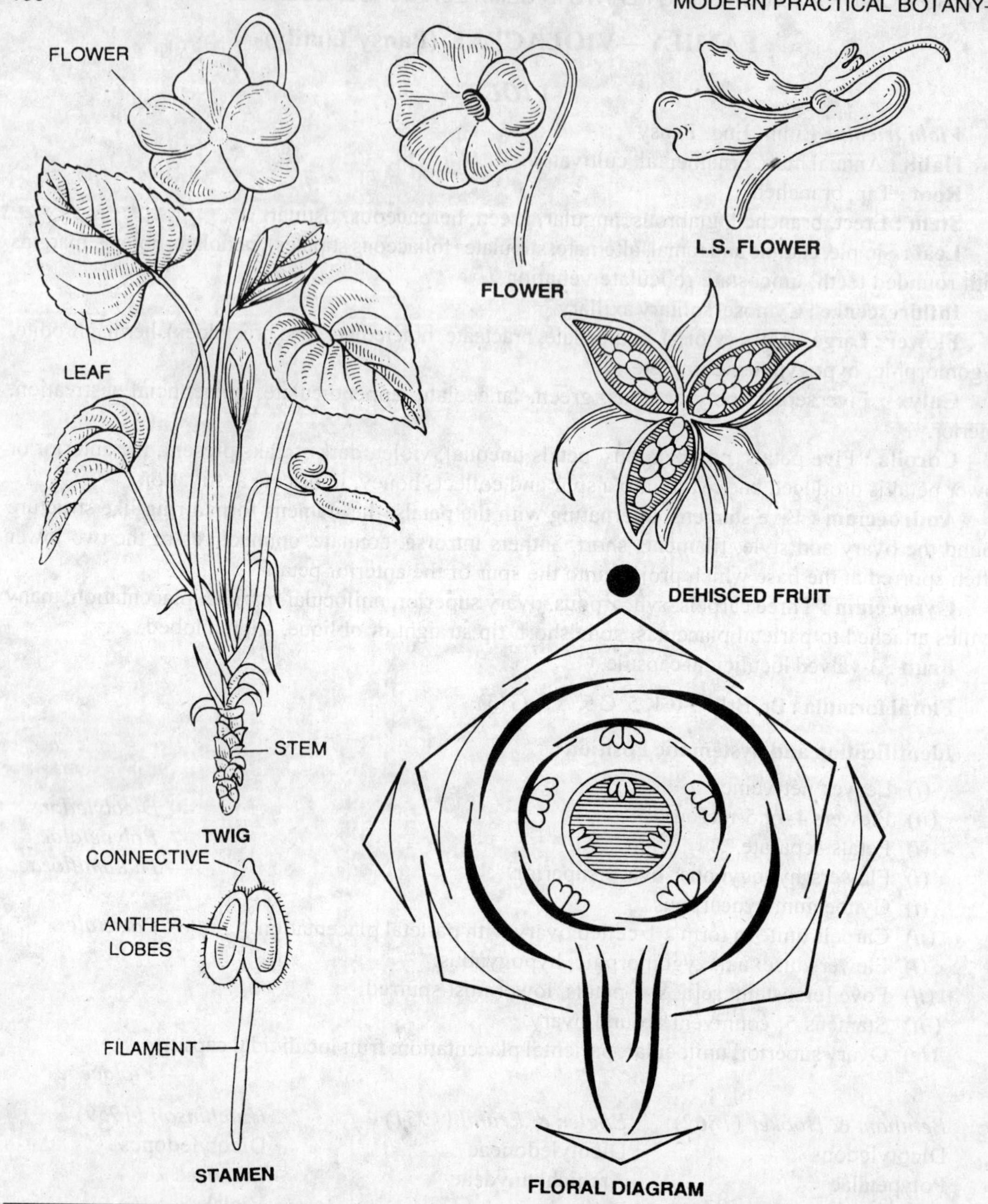

Fig. 9.17. Violaceae. *Viola tricolor* Linn. Eng., pansy.

Economic value. Grown as an ornamental. The plant is considered stimulant and used in rheumatism and in skin diseases. The infusion of root is useful in dysentery of children.

Other important members of the family. *Viola odorata* Linn., **Banafshah :** plant - antipyretic, diaphoretic, febrifuge; flowers - emollient, demulcent, used in lung troubles. *Hybanthus enneaspermus* Muell., **Ratan purus :** plant - tonic diuretic; leaves and tender stalks demulcent; root is used in bowel complaints of children; fruit is used in scorpion-sting.

FAMILY—CARYOPHYLLACEAE (Pink family)

STELLARIA

1. ***Stellaria media*** Linn.; Verna. **Morolia;** Eng. Chickweed.

Stellaria media Linn. (Eng. Chickweed). A common weed. Distribution : throughout N. India.

Habit : An annual herb, weed, six inches to two feet high.

Root : Tap, branched.

Stem : Erect, aerial, herbaceous, cylinderical, branched, green, glabrous, solid, nodes swollen.

Leaves : Cauline and ramal, simple, opposite decussate, exstipulate, ½ to 1 inch long, lower petiolate, upper sessile, entire, ovate, acuminate, smooth, unicostate reticulate venation.

Inflorescence : Cymose, axillary dichasial or terminal cyme.

Flower : Minute, pedicellate, bracteate, bracteolate (two bracteoles), hermaphrodite, complete, actinomorphic, hypogynous, pentamerous, cyclic.

Calyx : Five sepals, polysepalous hairy, glandular, obtuse or sub-acute, inferior, quincuncial aestivation.

Corolla : Five petals, polysepalous, petals shorter than sepals, deeply bilobed, inferior, immbricate aestivation, white.

Androecium : Ten stamens, arranged in two whorls of five each, polyandrous, obdiplostemonous (two alternating whorls of stamens, the stamens of outer whorl being arranged opposite the petals), generally outer three or all five stamens reduced to staminodes, filaments long and slender, dithecous, basifixed, introrse.

Gynoecium : Three carpels, syncarpous, ovary superior, unilocular, free-central placentation, styles three, each with its own stigma.

Fruit : An unilocular capsule.

Floral formula : Br. Brl. ⊕ ⚥ K 5, C 5, A 5+5, G $\underline{(3)}$.

Identification and Systematic Position :

(*i*) Leaves net-veined.
(*ii*) Flowers 4- or 5-merous. — *Dicotyledons.*
(*i*) Petals separate. — *Polypetalae.*
(*i*) Flowers hypogynous; ovary superior. — *Thalamiflorae.*
(*i*) Usually herbs, with simple exstipulate leaves
(*ii*) Stamens usually 5-10, obdiplostemonous, sometimes many.
(*iii*) Gynoecium of 2-5 carpels, 1-celled ovary with free-central placentation.
— *Caryophyllales.*

(*i*) Herbs with stems often tumid at the node and opposite exstipulate leaves.
(*ii*) Stamens normally diplostemonous, inserted with the petals in a perigynous ring.
(*iii*) Ovary free 1-celled or 3-5 celled, at the base, with 2-5 free or connate styles.
(*iv*) Free central placentation.
(*v*) Fruit capsule or berry. — *Caryophyllaceae*

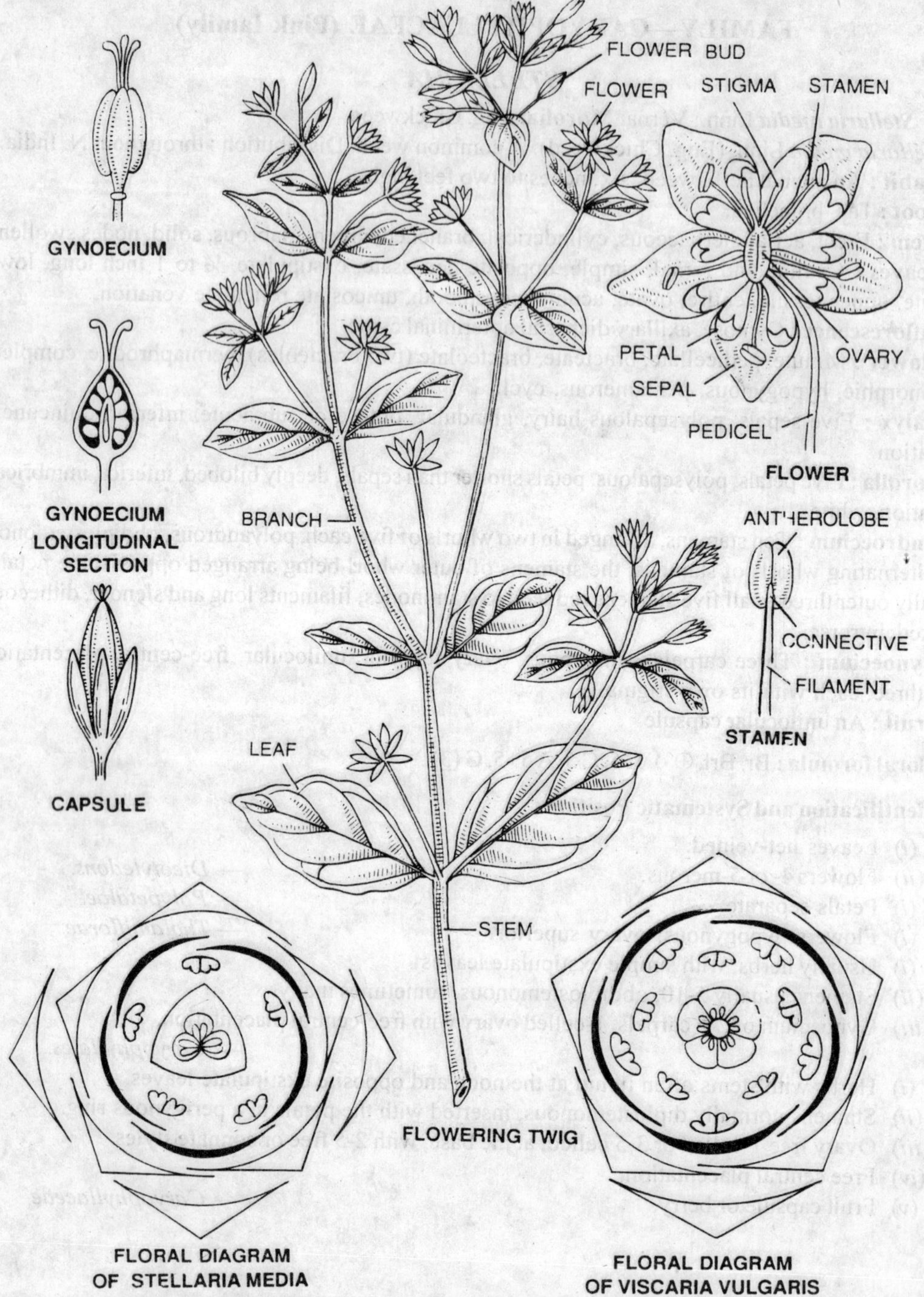

Fig. 9.18. Caryophyllaceae. *Stellaria media* Linn.; Eng. chickweed; Verna, **Morolia.**

Economic value. The natives of Assam eat the leaves and tender stalks, boiled in *Khar* water, either by themselves or with fish. It is used also as vegetable by the natives of the Nilgiris. The plant is employed in plaster for broken bones and swellings, as it is supposed to be cooling and binding.

SPERGULA

2. ***Spergula arvensis*** Linn.; Eng. Corn spurrey.

Spergula arvensis Linn. (Eng. Corn spurrey), plentiful in cultivated ground, flowering during the cold season. Distribution : throughout N. India.

Habit : Annual herb.

Root : Tap, branched.

Stem : Erect, cylindrical, branched, solid or fistular, green, herbaceous, thickened at the joints, glabrous.

Leaf : Cauline and ranal, simple, opposite, linear, sessile, fleshy, leafy buds in their axils and looking apparently whorled, lanceolate, acute, stipulate (stipules small).

Inflorescence : Cymose, dichasial cyme with suppression of branches on one side, *i.e.,* cincinnus.

Flower : Pedicellate, bracteate, bracteolate (two bracteoles), hermaphrodite, complete, actinomorphic, hypogynous, greenish white, pentamerons, cyclic.

Calyx : Five speals, oily green, inferior, quincuncial aestivation, persistent.

Corolla : Five petals, polypetalous, white, inferior, entire, imbricate aestivation.

Androecium : Ten stamens, arranged in two whorls of five each obdiplostemonous, anthers bicelled, introrse, dorsifixed.

Gynoecium : 3 or 5 carpels, syncarpous, ovary superior, unilocular, free-central placentation. styles three or five, stigmas 3 or 5.

Fruit : An ovoid capsule.

Floral formula : Br. Brl. ⊕ ⚥ K 5, C 5, A 5, G ($\underline{3}$ or $\underline{5}$).

Identification and Systematic Position :

(*i*) Leaves net-veined.
(*ii*) Flowers 4- or 5-merous. — *Dicotyledons.*
(*i*) Petals separate. — *Polypetalae.*
(*i*) Flowers hypogynous; ovary superior. — *Thalamiflorae*
(*i*) Usually herbs, with simple exstipulate leaves.
(*ii*) Stamens usually 5-10, obdiplostemonous, sometimes many.
(*iii*) Gynoecium of 2-5 carpels, 1-celled ovary with free-central placentation.
— *Caryophyllales.*

(*i*) Herbs with stems often tumid at the nodes and opposite exstipulate leaves.
(*ii*) Stamens normally dipolostemonous, inserted with the petals in a perigynous ring.
(*iii*) Ovary free 1-celled or 3-5 celled, at the base, with 2-5 free or connate styles.
(*iv*) Free central placentation.
(*v*) Fruit capsule or berry. — *Caryophyllaceae*

Bentham & Hooker (*1862*)	*Engler & Prantl* (*1931*)	*Hutchinson* (*1959*)
Dicotyledons	Dicotyledoneae	Dicotyledones
Polypetalae	Archichlamydeae	Herbaceae
Caryophyllales	Centrospermae	Caryophyllales
Caryophyllaceae	Caryophyllaceae	Caryophyllaceae

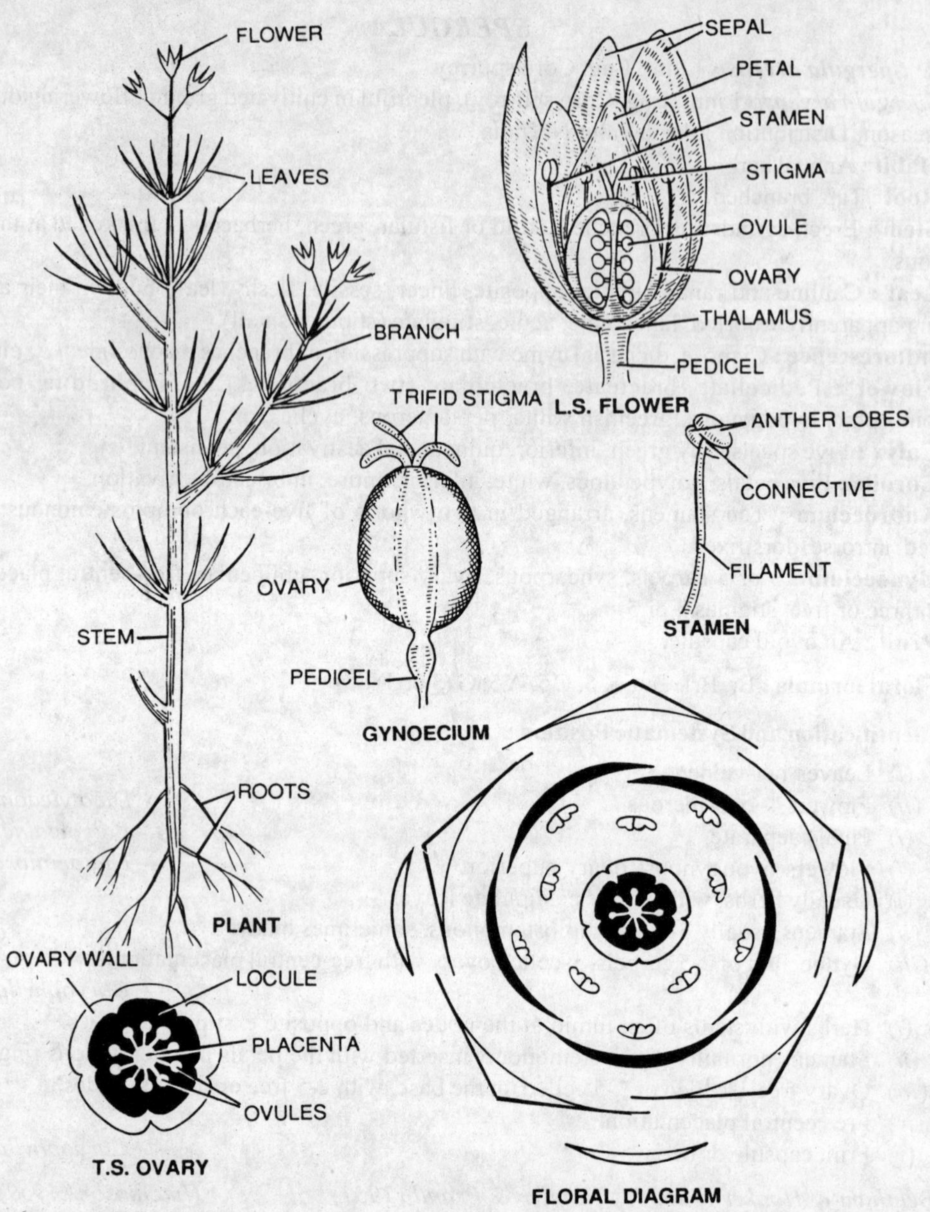

Fig. 9.19. Caryophyllaceae. *Spergula arvensis* Linn.; Eng., corn spurrey.

Economic value. Cultivated in Europe as a fodder plant. Used as a diuretic.

DIANTHUS

3. ***Dianthus caryophyllatus*** Linn.; Eng. Carnation plant.

Habit : An annual herb, ornamental, cultivated.

Root : Tap, branched.

Stem : Erect, aerial, herbaceous, branched, green smooth, solid.

Leaf : Cauline and ramal, simple, opposite, decussate, sessile, exstipulate, sessile, lanceolate, entire, acute, glabrous, unicostate reticulate venation, leaf-base sheathing.

Inflorescence : Cymose, axillary or terminal dichasial cyme.

Flower : Pedicellate, ebracteate, hermaphrodite, actinomorphic, complete, hypogynous, pentamerous, cyclic.

Epicalyx : 4, in two whorls of 2 each, outer whorl anterio-posterior.

Calyx : Five sepals, polysepalous, inferior, quincuncial aestivation.

Corolla : Five petals, polypetalous, petals fimbriate, inferior, imbricate aestivation, variously coloured, caryophyllaceous, each petal possesses a claw and limb.

Androecium : Ten stamens arranged in two whorls of fie each, obdiplostemonous, polyandrous, anthers bicelled, dorsifixed, introrse.

Gynoecium : Two-five carpels, syncarpous, ovary superior, unilocular, free-central placentation, ovules many, styles two, stigmas two, coiled and feathery.

Fruit : A capsule.

Floral formula : ⊕ ⚥ Epi K 2+2, K 5, C 5, A 5+5, G $(\underline{2}\text{-}\underline{5})$.

Identification and Systematic Position :

(*i*) Leaves net-veined.
(*ii*) Flowers 4- or 5-merous. — *Dicotyledons.*
(*i*) Petals separate. — *Polypetalae.*
(*i*) Flowers hypogynous; ovary superior. — *Thalamiflorae.*
(*i*) Usually herbs, with simple exstipulate leaves.
(*ii*) Stamens usually 5-10, obdiplostemonous, sometimes many.
(*iii*) Gynoecium of 2-5 carpels, 1-celled ovary with free-central placentation.
— *Caryophyllales.*

(*i*) Herbs with stems often tumid at the nodes and opposite exstipulate leaves.
(*ii*) Stamens normally dipolostemonous, inserted with the petals in a perigynous ring.
(*iii*) Ovary free 1-celled or 3-5 celled, at the base, with 2-5 free or connate styles.
(*iv*) Free central placentation.
(*v*) Fruit capsule or berry. — *Caryophyllaceae*

Other important members of the family. *Arenaria serpyllifolia* Linn., used for bladder diseases, calculus troubles and chronic cystitis. *Lychnis coronaria* Desr., used for lung and liver diseases. *Saponaria vaccaria* Linn., **Musna** - sap of plant is considered febrifuge and tonic in long-continued fevers.

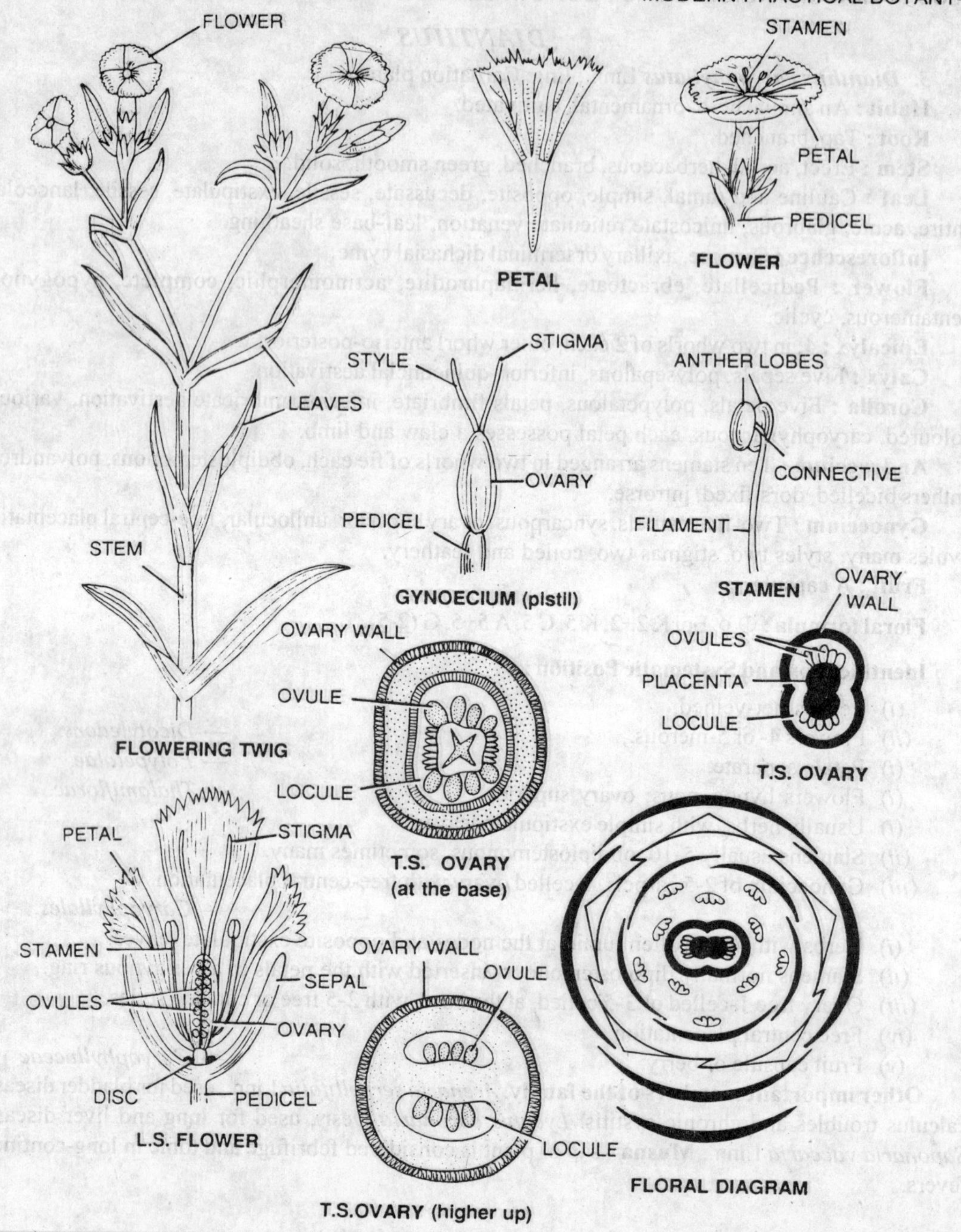

Fig. 9.20. Caryophyllaceae. *Dianthus caryophyllatus* Linn.; Eng., carnation plant.

Economic value. Grown as an ornamental in the gardens. The flowers are considered cardiotonic, diaphoretic, nervine and antiseptic.

SILENE

4. Silene conoidea Linn.

Habit : An annual herb.

Root : Tap, branched.

Stem : Erect, herbaceous, aerial, branched, solid, cylindrical, flat at the nodes, hairy and green.

Leaf : Cauline and ramal, exstipulate, simple, sessile, opposite decussate, leaf base semiamplexicaul, linear, entire, acute, hairy, leathery, unicostate reticulate.

Inflorescence : Cymose, solitary axillary.

Flower : Pedicellate, ebracteate, hermaphrodite, actinomorphic, complete, cyclic, pentamerous, hypogynous.

Calyx : 5 sepals, gamosepalous, forming a flask-like structure, acute, inferior, green.

Corolla : 5 petals, polypetalous, twised, caryophyllaceous, pink, inferior.

Androecium : 10 stamens in two whorls, 5 in each whorl, polyandrous, obdiplostemonous, dithecous, basifixed, introrse.

Gynoecium : 3 carpels, syncarpous, ovary superior, upper region of the ovary possesses free central placentation while the lower region possesses axile placentation, many ovules, style three, stigmas three and globular.

Fruit : A capsule.

Floral formula : ⊕ ⚥ K (5), C 5, A 5+5, G $\underline{(3)}$.

Identification and Systematic Position :

(*i*) Leaves net-veined.
(*ii*) Flowers 4- or 5-merous. — *Dicotyledons.*
(*i*) Petals separate. — *Polypetalae.*
(*i*) Flowers hypogynous; ovary superior. — *Thalamiflorae.*
(*i*) Usually herbs, with simple exstipulate leaves.
(*ii*) Stamens usually 5-10, obdiplostemonous, sometimes many.
(*iii*) Gynoecium of 2-5 carpels, 1-celled ovary with free-central placentation.
— *Caryophyllales.*

(*i*) Herbs with stems often tumid at the nodes and opposite exstipulate leaves.
(*ii*) Stamens normally dipolostemonous, inserted with the petals in a perigynous ring.
(*iii*) Ovary free 1-celled or 3-5 celled, at the base, with 2-5 free or connate styles.
(*iv*) Free central placentation.
(*v*) Fruit capsule or berry. — *Caryophyllaceae.*

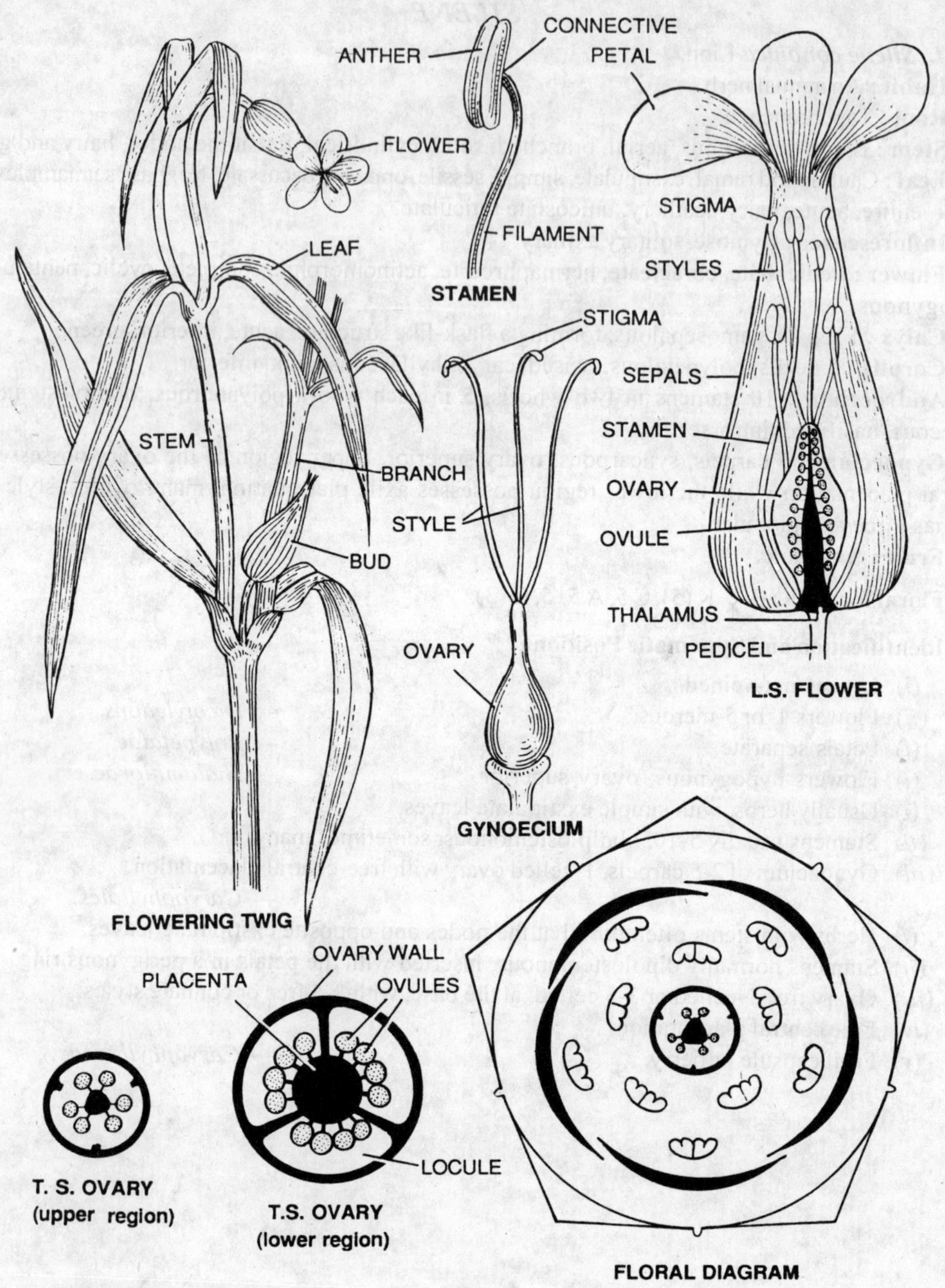

Fig. 9.21. Caryophyllaceae, *Silene conoidea* Linn.

Economic value. The plant is considered emollient and used in baths or as a fumigant. The plant juice is used in opthalmia.

FAMILY—MALVACEAE (Mallow family)

HIBISCUS

1. ***Hibiscus rosa-sinensis*** Linn.; Verna. **Gurhal;** Eng. China shoe flower.

Hibiscus rosa-sinensis Linn. (Eng. China shoe flower). Cultivated in many gardens of N. India.

Habit : Ornamental perennial shrub.

Root : Tap, branched.

Stem : Erect, aerial, woody, branched, cylinderical, glabrous, green and solid.

Leaf : Cauline and ramal, simple, alternate, petiolate, stipulate, free lateral, ovate, serrate, glabrous, appex acuminate, multicostate reticulate venation.

Inflorescence : Solitary axillary.

Flower : Pedicellate, ebracteate, hermaphrodite, large, showy, pentamerous, actinomorphic, complete, hypogynous, cyclic.

Epicalyx : 5-7 bracteoles constitute epicalyx below calyx.

Calyx : Five sepals, gamosepalous, greem inferior, valvate aestivation.

Corolla : Five petals, polypetalous, slightly united below, adnate to the staminal tube, inferior, twisted aestivation, red or pink.

Androecium : Stamens indefinite, monadelphous, stamens forms a staminal tube round the style, epipetalous, anthers monothecous, reniform, basifixed, extrorse.

Gynoecium : Five carpels (pentacarpellary), syncarpous, ovary superior, pentalocular, with many ovules, axile placentation, style long and passing through the staminal tube ending in five distinct rounded stigmas.

Fruit : In other species of *Hibiscus,* loculicidal capsule.

Floral formula : $\oplus$ ⚥ K (5), C 5, A ($\propto$), G ($\underline{5}$).

Identification and Systematic Position :

(*i*) Leaves net-veined.
(*ii*) Flowers 4- or 5-merous. — *Dicotyledons.*
(*i*) Petals separate. — *Polypetalae.*
(*i*) Flowers hypogynous; ovary superior. — *Thalamiflorae.*
(*i*) Woody or herbaceous with usually alternate, simple or plamately compound, stipulate leaves.
(*i*) Usually herbs, with simple exstipulate leaves.
(*ii*) Bracteoles often present as an epicalyx.
(*iii*) Stamens many, monadelphous; or polyadelphous anthers 1-2 celled.
(*iv*) Ovary of 2-many carpels with axile placentation. — *Malvales.*
(*i*) Calyx usually persistent and gamosepalous; epicalyx present.
(*ii*) Stamens many united into a tube; anthers one-celled, reniform.
(*iii*) Gynoecium of 5-many carpels with axile placentation.
(*iv*) Fruit usually capsule. — *Malvaceae.*

Bentham & Hooker (*1862*)	*Engler & Prantl* (*1931*)	*Hutchinson* (*1959*)
Dicotyledons	Dicotyledoneae	Dicotyledones
Polypetalae	Archichlamydeae	Lignosae
Malvales	Malvales	Malvales
Malvaceae	Malvaceae	Malvaceae

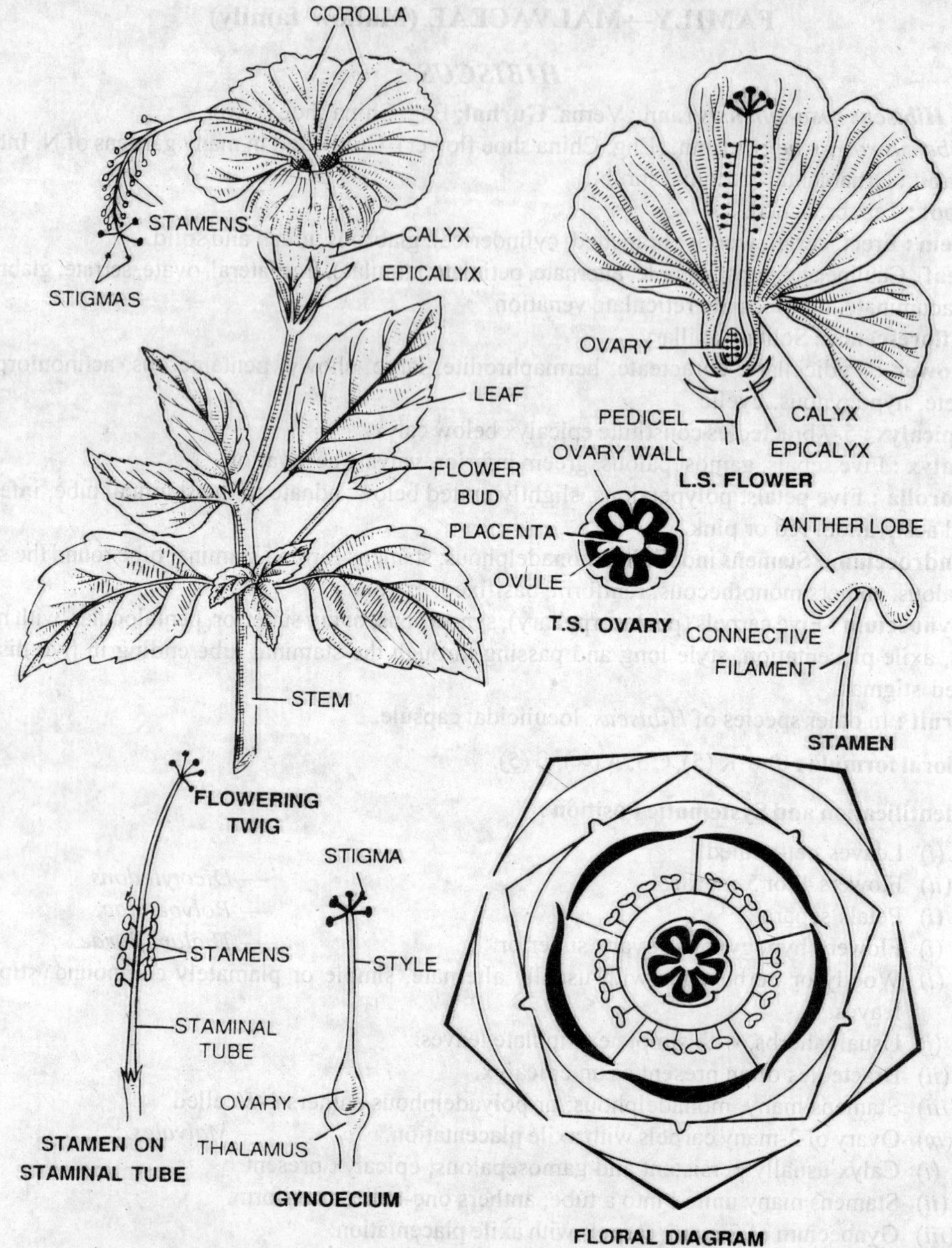

Fig. 9.22. Malvaceae. *Hibiscus rosa-sinensis* Linn.; Eng. China shoe flower; Verna., **gurhal.**

Economic value. A common ornamental shrub. The flowers yield a dark purplish dye, which is used for making shoe polishes. The leaves and flowers are emollient. Infusion of petals is given as a demulcent and refrigerant drink in fevers.

ABUTILON

2. Abutilon indicum Gaertn.; Verna. **Kangi;** Eng. Country mallow

Abutilon indicum Gaertn. A common weed flowering during the greater part of the year.

Distribution : Hotter parts of India.

Habit : Annual or perennial herb or undershrub.

Root : Tap, branched.

Stem : Erect, aerial, branched, herbaceous, solid, cylinderical, hairy, green.

Leaves : Cauline and ramal, simple, alternate, petiolate (petiole usually longer than blade), broadly cordate, acute or acuminate apex, irregularly toothed, pale, minutely pubescent on both surfaces, entire, multicostate reticulate venation.

Inflorescence : Cymose, solitary axillary.

Flower : Bracteate, pedicellate (pedicels longer than the petioles and jointed near the top), one inch diameter, hermaphrodite, actinomorphic, complete, hypogynous, pentamerous, cyclic.

Calyx : Five sepals, gamosepalous, shallow, ovate, acute, persistent, valvate aestivation.

Corolla : Five petals, polypetalous, free above, connate below and adnate to the staminal tube, orange yellow, petals spreading, imbricate aestivation.

Androecium : Indefinite stamens, staminal tube dividing at the top into numerous anther bearing filaments, monadelphous, anthers one-celled, basifixed, dehisce longitudinally, extrorse.

Gynoecium : 15-20 carpels (polycarpellary), carpels longer than the calyx, with short spreading awns, hair, syncarpous, ovary superior, multilocular, axile placentation, many ovules in each locule, style long, stigmas short and as many as carpels in number.

Floral formula : ⊕ ⚥ K (5), C 5, A ∞, G $(\underline{\infty})$.

Identification and Systematic Position :

(*i*) Leaves net-veined.
(*ii*) Flowers 4- or 5-merous. — *Dicotyledons.*
(*i*) Petals separate. — *Polypetalae.*
(*i*) Flowers hypogynous; ovary superior. — *Thalamiflorae.*
(*i*) Woody or herbaceous with usually alternate, simple or plamately compound, stipulate leaves.
(*ii*) Bracteoles often present as an epicalyx.
(*iii*) Stamens many, monadelphous; or polyadelphous anthers 1-2 celled.
(*iv*) Ovary of 2-many carpels with axile placentation. — *Malvales.*
(*i*) Calyx usually persistent and gamosepalous; epicalyx present.
(*ii*) Stamens many united into a tube; anthers one-celled, reniform.
(*iii*) Gynoecium of 5-many carpels with axile placentation.
(*iv*) Fruit usually capsule. — *Malvaceae.*

Other important members of the family. *Gossypium herbaceum* Linn., *G. arboreum* L., *G. barbadense* L., *G. hirsutum* L., **Kapas** - The fibre obtained from the seeds is used in making cloth; seed oil is edible; seed cake is used as cattle feed. *Hibiscus cannobinus* Linn., **Patsan** - The fibre obtained from stem is used for making cordage and ropes.

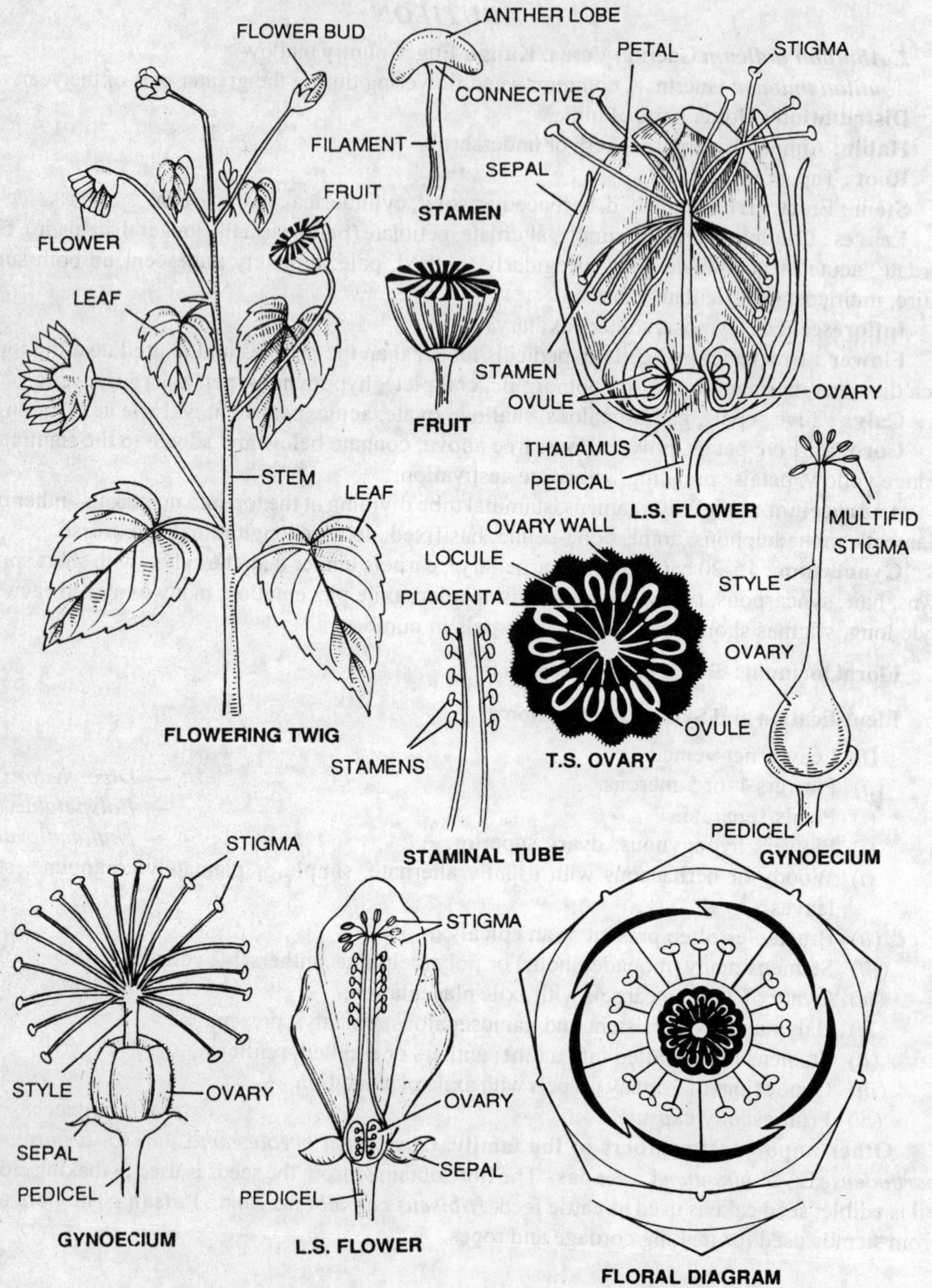

Fig. 9.23. Malvaceae. *Abutilon indicum* (Linn) Sweet.; Eng. Country mallow; Verna. **Kangi.**

Economic value. The stems, on retting, yield a fibre, which is used for making ropes. The leaves are demulcent. The bark is astringent and diuretic. The infusion of roots is given in fevers. The seeds are aphrodisiac, laxative and demulcent.

MALVA

Malva sylvestris Linn.; Verna. **Vilayati Kangi;** Eng. Common mallow.

Habit : Annual, 3-5 feet high herb.

Root : Tap and branched.

Stem : Erect aerial, branched, glabrous, herbaceous, solid, cylinderical, green.

Leaves : Cauline and ramal, simple, alternate, cordate, round with 5-7 obtuse lobes; petiolate, petioles as long as the leaves, stipulate, stipules oval, acute; multicostate reticulate venation.

Inflorescence : Cymose, flowers in axillary tufts.

Flower : Pedicellate, bracteate, peduncles several, axillary much shorter than the petiole, 1-1½ inches in diameter, pale rose streaked with purple, actinomorphic, bisexual, complete, hypogynous, pentamerons, cyclic.

Calyx : 5 sepals, polysepalous, connate at base, valvate aestivation.

Corolla : 5 petals, polypetalous connate at the external base, petals notched, claw bearded, valvate aestivation, adnate to the staminal tube.

Androecium : Indefinite stamens, staminal tube antheriferous to the top without sterile teeth, monadelphous, anthers monothecous, filament short, basifixed, dehiscing longitudinally, introrse.

Gynoecium : Many carpels, ploycarpellary, syncarpous, carpels wrinkled on the back, glabrous, ovary many-celled, styles as many as the carpels, stigmas linear, ovules on the each locule, axile placentation.

Fruit : Capsule.

Floral formula : Br. ⊕ ⚥ K 5, C 5, A ∞, G $(\underline{\infty})$.

Identification and Systematic Position :

(*i*) Leaves net-veined.
(*ii*) Flowers 4- or 5-merous. — *Dicotyledons.*
(*i*) Petals separate. — *Polypetalae.*
(*i*) Flowers hypogynous; ovary superior. — *Thalamiflorae.*
(*i*) Woody or herbaceous with usually alternate, simple or plamately compound, stipulate leaves.
(*ii*) Bracteoles often present as an epicalyx.
(*iii*) Stamens many, monadelphous; or polyadelphous anthers 1-2 celled.
(*iv*) Ovary of 2-many carpels with axile placentation. — *Malvales.*
(*i*) Calyx usually persistent and gamosepalous; epicalyx present.
(*ii*) Stamens many united into a tube; anthers one-celled, reniform.
(*iii*) Gynoecium of 5-many carpels with axile placentation.
(*iv*) Fruit usually capsule. — *Malvaceae.*

Other important members of the family. *Althaea rosea* Cav., **Gulkhera** - an ornamental; seeds demulcent, diuretic, febrifuge; flower cooling, diuretic, used in rheumatism. *Abelmoschus esculentus* Moench., **Bhindi** - Fruit used as vegetable; Fibre obtained from stalks; mucilage from fruits and seed- emollient, demulcent, useful in gonorrhoea. *Urena lobata* Linn., **Bachata** - diuretic, used for rheumatism.

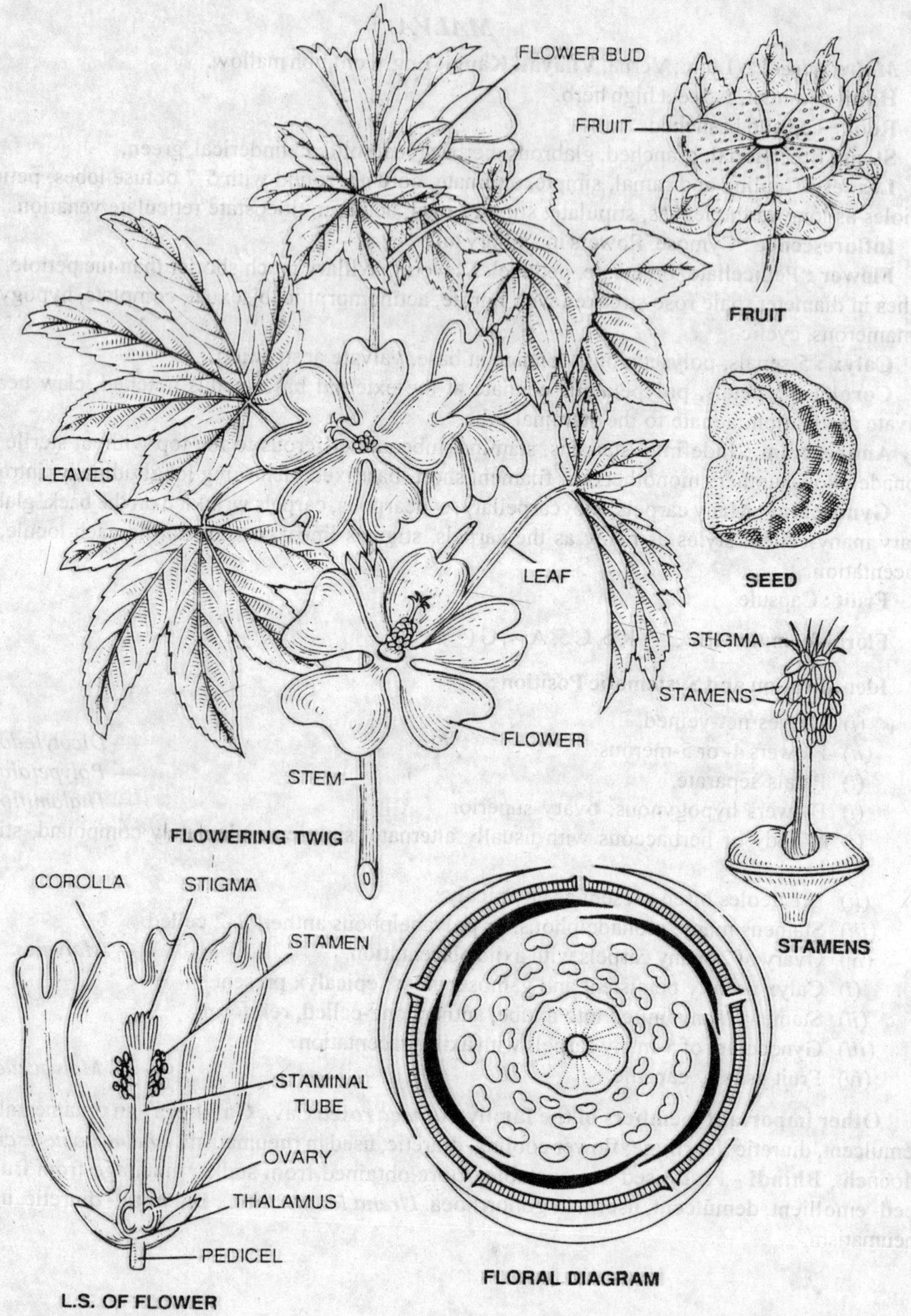

Fig. 9.24. Malvaceae. *Malva sylvestris* Linn.; Eng. Common mallow; Verna. **Vilayati Kangi.**

Economic value. The plant yields a fibre; this is described as a valuable emollient and demulcent, also diuretic.

MALVASTRUM

Malvastrum tricuspidatum A. Gray.

Habit : An annual or perennial herb.

Root : Tap, branched.

Stem : Erect, aerial, herbaceous, cylinderical, branched, solid, hairy, green.

Leaf : Cauline and ramal, petiolate, stipulate, stipules small and free-lateral, alternate, simple, ovate-lanceolate, serrate, acute, glabrous, unicostae reticulate.

Inflorescence : Cymose, solitary axillary.

Flower : Bracteate, bracteolate, 3 small bracteoles, pedicellate, actinomorphic, hermaphrodite, hypogynous, pentamerous, cyclic.

Calyx : 5 sepals, gamosepalous, valvate aestivation, persistent.

Corolla : 5 petals, polypetalous, twisted, yellow.

Androecium : Indefinite, monadelphous, a staminal tube is formed around the style, epipetalous, monothecous, reniform, basifixed, extrorse.

Gynoecium : Many carpels, syncarpous, ovary superior, multilocular, axile placentation, stigmas as many as carpels, style within staminal tube.

Fruit : A capsule.

Floral formula : Br. Brl. ⊕ ⚥ K (5), C 5, A ∞, G $(\underline{\infty})$

Identification and Systematic Position :

(*i*) Leaves net-veined.
(*ii*) Flowers 4- or 5-merous. — *Dicotyledons.*

(*i*) Petals separate. — *Polypetalae.*

(*i*) Flowers hypogynous; ovary superior. — *Thalamiflorae.*

(*i*) Woody or herbaceous with usually alternate, simple or plamately compound, stipulate leaves.
(*ii*) Bracteoles often present as an epicalyx.
(*iii*) Stamens many, monadelphous; or polyadelphous anthers 1-2 celled.
(*iv*) Ovary of 2-many carpels with axile placentation. — *Malvales.*

(*i*) Calyx usually persistent and gamosepalous; epicalyx present.
(*ii*) Stamens many united into a tube; anthers one-celled, reniform.
(*iii*) Gynoecium of 5-many carpels with axile placentation.
(*iv*) Fruit usually capsule. — *Malvaceae.*

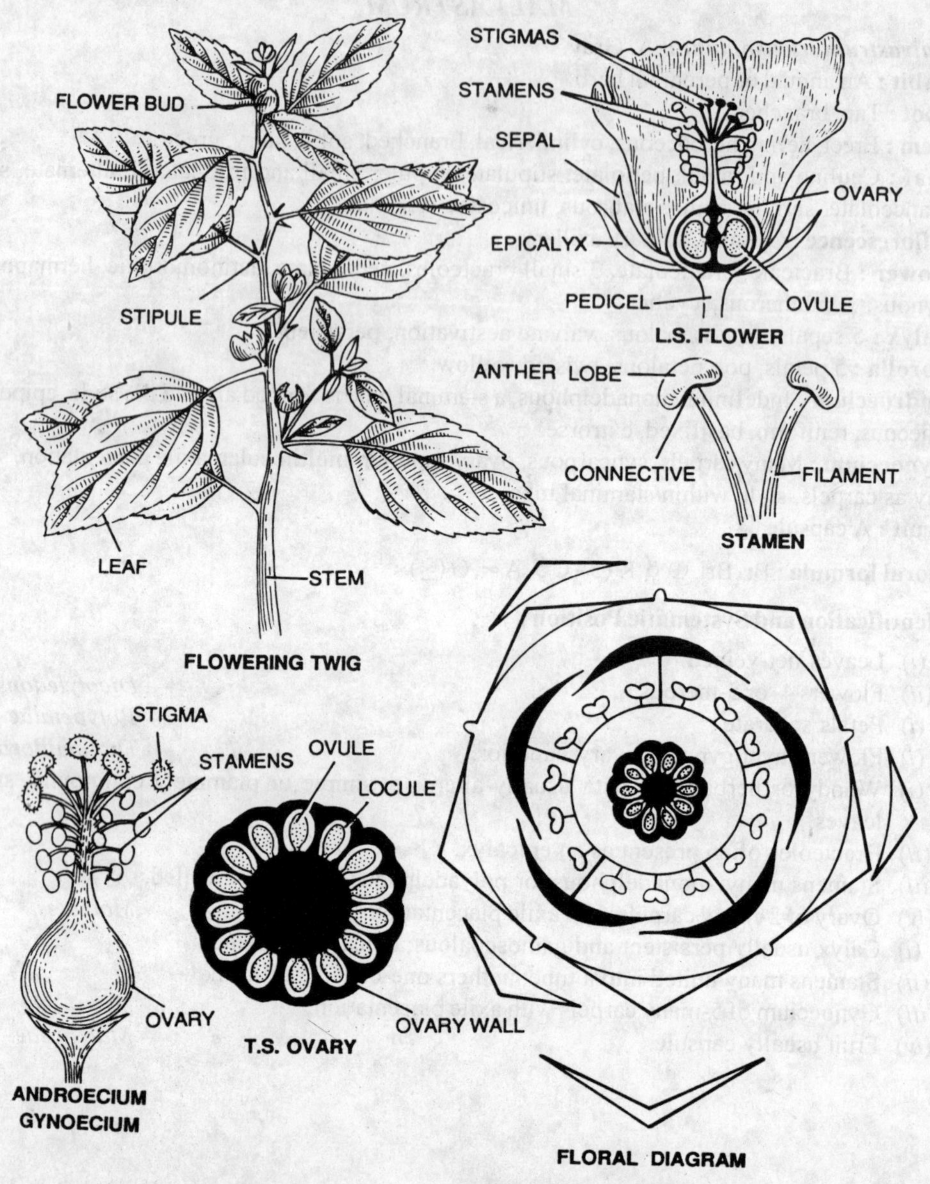

Fig. 9.25. Malvaceae. *Malvastrum tricuspidatum* A. Gray.

BOMBAX

5. ***Bombax ceiba*** Linn.; Verna. **Semal;** Eng. Silk cotton tree.

Habit : A large handsome deciduous soft-wooded tree.

Root : Tap and branched.

Stem : Erect, straight buttressed trunk, wide spreading branches in whorls, woody; young stem and branches covered with hard conical prickles.

Leaves : Petiolate, petiole longer than leaflets, large, palmately compound, glabrous; leaflets 5-7, lanceolate acuminate, tapering below, 6-12 inches long, entire; stipulate, stipules small, caducous; deciduous.

Inflorescence : Cymose, clustered towards the ends of the branches.

Flower : Large, ebracteate, pedicellate, on short thick pedicels, crimson red, hermaphrodite, actinomorphic, regular, hypogynous; pentamerous; flowers appearing before the leaves, cyclic.

Calyx : 5 sepals, gamosepalous, leathery, cup-shaped, smooth outside, silky within margin slightly lobed, deciduous.

Corolla : 5 petals, polypetalous, oblong recurved above, fleshy, twice as long as the stamens, deciduous, red.

Androecium : Indefinite, pentadelphous, antepetalous, divided above into numerous filaments, filaments pink, anthers reniform, monothecous (1-celled), brown basifixed, introrse.

Gynoecium : 5 carpels, syncarpous, ovary superior, pentalocular, many ovules in each loculus, style clavate, stigmas five, style longer than stamens.

Fruit : Loculicidal capsule, 5-valved, oblong, valves silky within.

Seeds : Many, obovate, smooth, enveloped in dense silky hairs.

Floral formula : $\oplus$ ⚥ K (5), C 5, A ∞, G $(\underline{5})$.

Identification and Systematic Position :

(*i*) Leaves net-veined.
(*ii*) Flowers 4- or 5-merous. — *Dicotyledons.*
(*i*) Petals separate. — *Polypetalae.*
(*i*) Flowers hypogynous; ovary superior. — *Thalamiflorae.*
(*i*) Woody or herbaceous with usually alternate, simple or plamately compound, stipulate leaves.
(*ii*) Bracteoles often present as an epicalyx.
(*iii*) Stamens many, monadelphous; or polyadelphous anthers 1-2 celled.
(*iv*) Ovary of 2-many carpels with axile placentation. — *Malvales.*
(*i*) Calyx usually persistent and gamosepalous; epicalyx present.
(*ii*) Stamens many united into a tube; anthers one-celled, reniform.
(*iii*) Gynoecium of 5-many carpels with axile placentation.
(*iv*) Fruit usually capsule. — *Malvaceae.*

Bentham & Hooker (*1862*)	*Engler & Prantl* (*1931*)	*Hutchinson* (*1959*)
Dicotyledons	Dicotyledoneae	Dicotyledones
Polypetalae	Archichlamydeae	Lignosae
Malvales	Malvales	Tiliales
Malvaceae	Bombacaceae	Bombacaceae

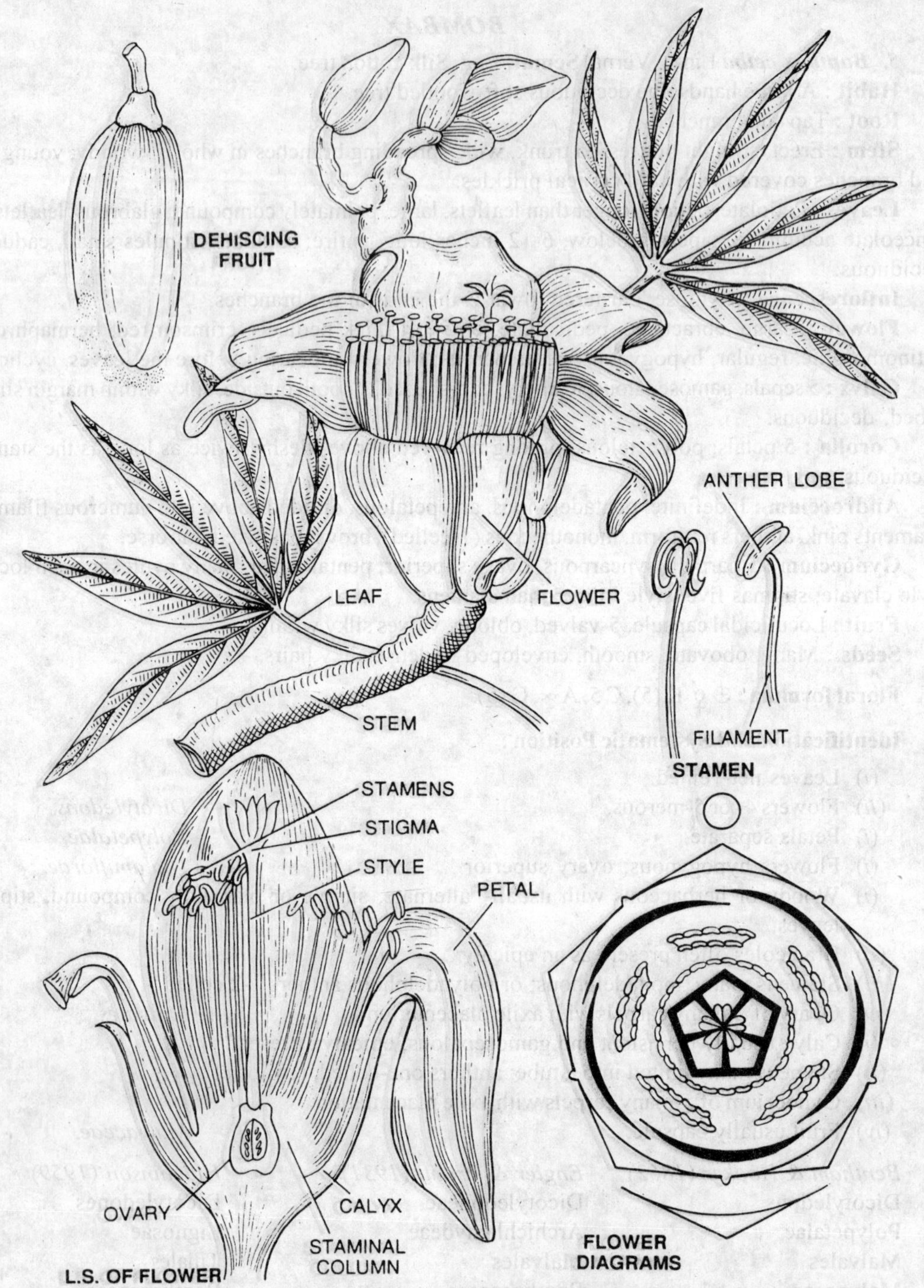

Fig. 9.26. Malvaceae (Bombacaceae). *Bombax ceiba* Linn.; Eng., silk cotton tree; Verna. **Semal.**

Economic value. The flowers and fleshy calyx are cooked as vegatable. The seeds are used as fooder. The silky floss obtained from the inner wall of the fruit, is used for stuffing pillows and mattresses. The gum obtained from the trunk is used as adhesive.

FAMILY—LINACEAE (Flax family)

LINUM

Linum usitatissimum Linn. Verna. **Alsi;** Eng. Flax.

Linum usitatissimum Linn. (Verna. **Alsi;** Eng. Flax). (Linseed is extensively grown within the area in Bundelkhand and in the Sub-Himalayan tract.)

Habit : Annual herb 2-4 feet high, cultivated for the seeds and fibres.

Root : Tap and branched.

Stem : Erect, aerial, usually corymbosely branched towards the upper side, herbaceous, cylinderical,

Leaves : Cauline and ramal, green, simple, alternate, exstipulate, linear or lanceolate, sub 3-nerved, entire, unicostate reticulate.

Inflorescence : Cymose, flowers arranged in broad cymes.

Flower : Pedicellate, hermaphrodite, complete, actinomorphic, hypogynous, blue or sometimes white, one inch across, pentamerous, cyclic.

Calyx : 5 sepals, ovate acuminate, 3-nerved, glandular, margins white, ciliate or not, aestivation quincuncial.

Corolla : 5 petals, polypetalous, free, contorted aestivation, arranged alternately to sepals, claw-shaped, blue or white.

Androecium : 5 stamens alternating with 5 minute staminodes; filaments connate at the base, nectar secreting glands are present on the ring below the ovary, the anthers dithecous, introrse, versatile, basifixed.

Gynoecium : 5 carpels, syncarpous, ovary pentalocular, two ovules in each locule; styles usually free; stigmas linear, clavate.

Fruit : Septicidal capsules, capsule hardly exceeding the sepals, edges of valves ciliate.

Floral formula : ⚥ ⊕ K 5, C 5, A 5, G $(\underline{5})$.

Generic characters : Herbs, perfect stamens 5, styles 5, capsule 5-celled.

Identification and Systematic Position :

(*i*) Leaves net-veined.
(*ii*) Flowers 4- or 5-merous. — *Dicotyledons.*
(*i*) Petals separate. — *Polypetalae.*
(*i*) Flowers hypogynous; ovary superior.
(*ii*) Cupular disc present between petals and ovary. — *Disciflorae.*
(*i*) Torus raised in centre into the centre of ovary, or disc well developed and hypogynous, annular or of glands only.
(*ii*) Stamens inserted outside the disc, diplostemonous, or obdiplostemonous.
(*iii*) Ovary of 3-5 or more carpels, syncarpous, axile placentation. — *Geraniales.*
(*i*) Herbs or shrubs with alternate, simple, entire leaves.
(*ii*) Alternate stamens usually reduced to staminodes; filaments united to the base into a hypogynous or perigynous ring.
(*iii*) Ovary 3-5 celled; styles 3-5; fruit septicidally separating into 3-5 coci. — *Linaceae.*

Bentham & Hooker (*1862*)	*Engler & Prantl* (*1931*)	*Hutchinson* (*1959*)
Dicotyledons	Dicotyledoneae	Dicotyledones
Polypetalae	Archichlamydeae	Lignosae
Geraniales	Geraniales	Malpighiales
Linaceae	Linaceae	Linaceae

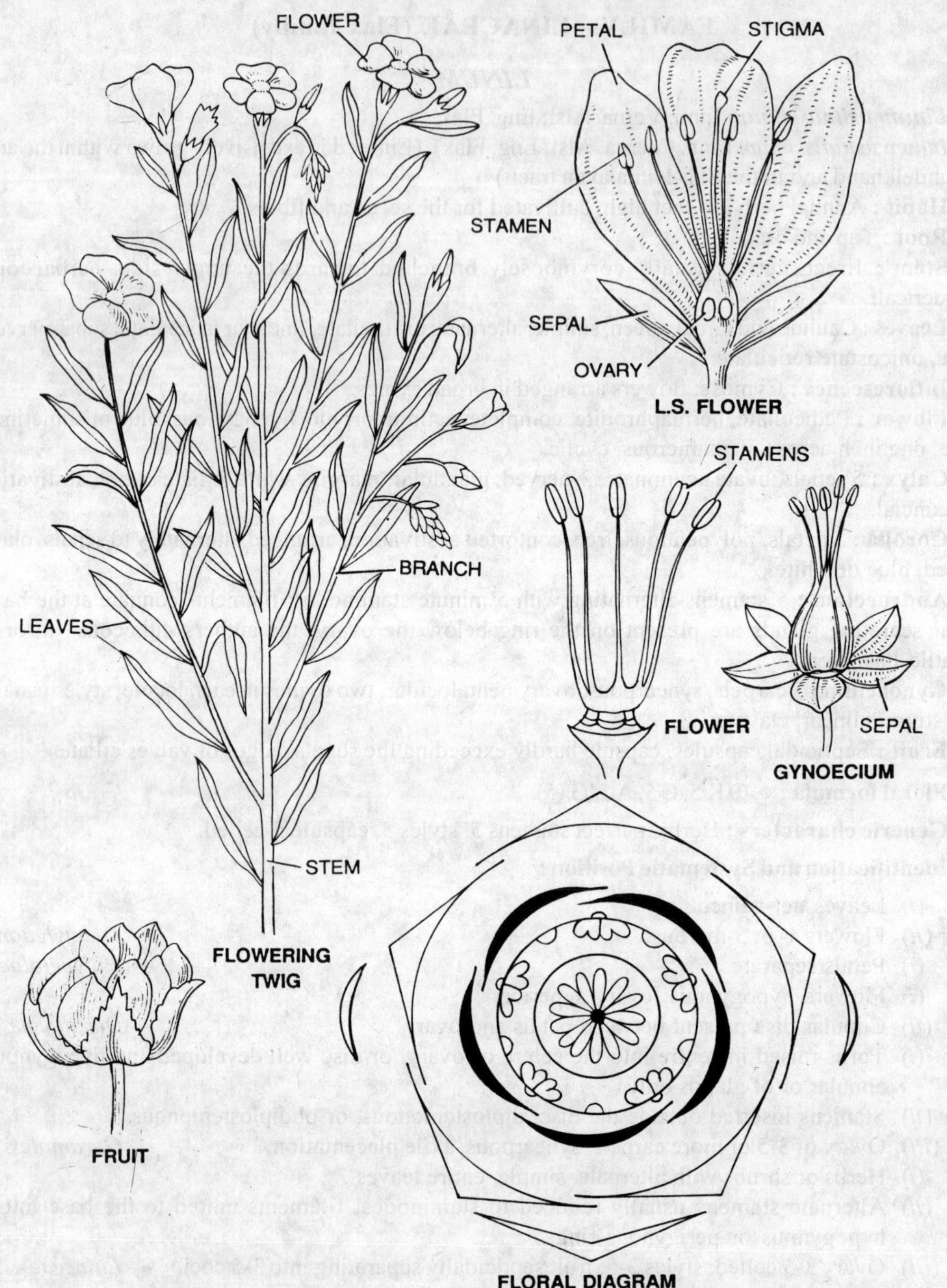

Fig. 9.27. Linaceae. *Linum usitatissimum* Linn.; Eng., flax; Verna., **alsi.**

Economic value. The stem fibre is used for making cloth, twines and wrapping paper. The seed oil is utilized in making paints, varnishes, soap and printer's ink. The green fruits are edible.

FAMILY—RUTACEAE (Rue family)

CITRUS

1. ***Citrus aurantium*** Linn,; Verna. **Narangi;** Eng. Orange.

Citrus aurantium Linn., usually a small tree, with the young shoot glabrous and greenish white. Largely grown in the neighbourhood of Delhi, and also in the Nagpur district of Maharashtra. The oranges grown in Bhutan, Nepal and Garhwal belong also to this class.

Habit : A small tree.

Root : Tap and branched.

Stem : Erect, aerial, woody, branched, cylinderical, glabrous, solid.

Leaf : Cauline, alternate, petiolate (petiole winged and flattened); stipulate, coriacious, persistent; more or less serrate, acute or obtuse, glabrous, unicostate reticulate venation.

Inflorescence : Cymose, solitary axillary or in small cymes.

Flower : Pedicellate, bracteate, hermaphrodite, white or pinkish, scented, actinomorphic, complete, hypogynous, pentamerous, cyclic.

Calyx : Five sepals, gamosepalous, inferior, quincunical aestivation.

Corolla : Five petals, polypetalous, white, scented, inferior, imbricate aestivation, linear oblong.

Androecium : Indefinite, stamens (15-60), inserted round, a large cupular or annular disk, polyadelphous, filaments variously connate, compressed at the base, anthers oblong basifixed, introrse, dithecous.

Gynoecium : Polycarpellary, syncarpous, ovary superior, multilocular, nectar secreting disc present below ovary, axile placentation, style stout, deciduous, stigma capitate.

Fruit : Berry (hesperidium).

Floral formula : ⊕ ⚥ K (5), C 5, A $\propto$, G $(\underline{\propto})$.

Identification and Systematic Position :

(*i*) Leaves net-veined.
(*ii*) Flowers 4- or 5-merous. — *Dicotyledons.*
(*i*) Petals separate. — *Polypetalae.*
(*i*) Flowers hypogynous; ovary superior.
(*ii*) Cupular disc present between petals and ovary. — *Disciflorae.*
(*i*) Torus raised in centre into the centre of ovary, or disc well developed and hypogynous, annular or of glands only.
(*ii*) Stamens inserted outside the disc, diplostemonous, or obdiplostemonous.
(*iii*) Ovary of 3-5 or more carpels, syncarpous, axile placentation. — *Geraniales.*
(*i*) Small trees or shrubs; leaves contain aromatic oil glands; leaves simple or usually 1-foliolate compound, exstipulate.
(*ii*) Stamens 2-5 or many and obdiplostemonous, inserted around a disc.
(*iii*) Fruit hesperidium. — *Rutaceae.*

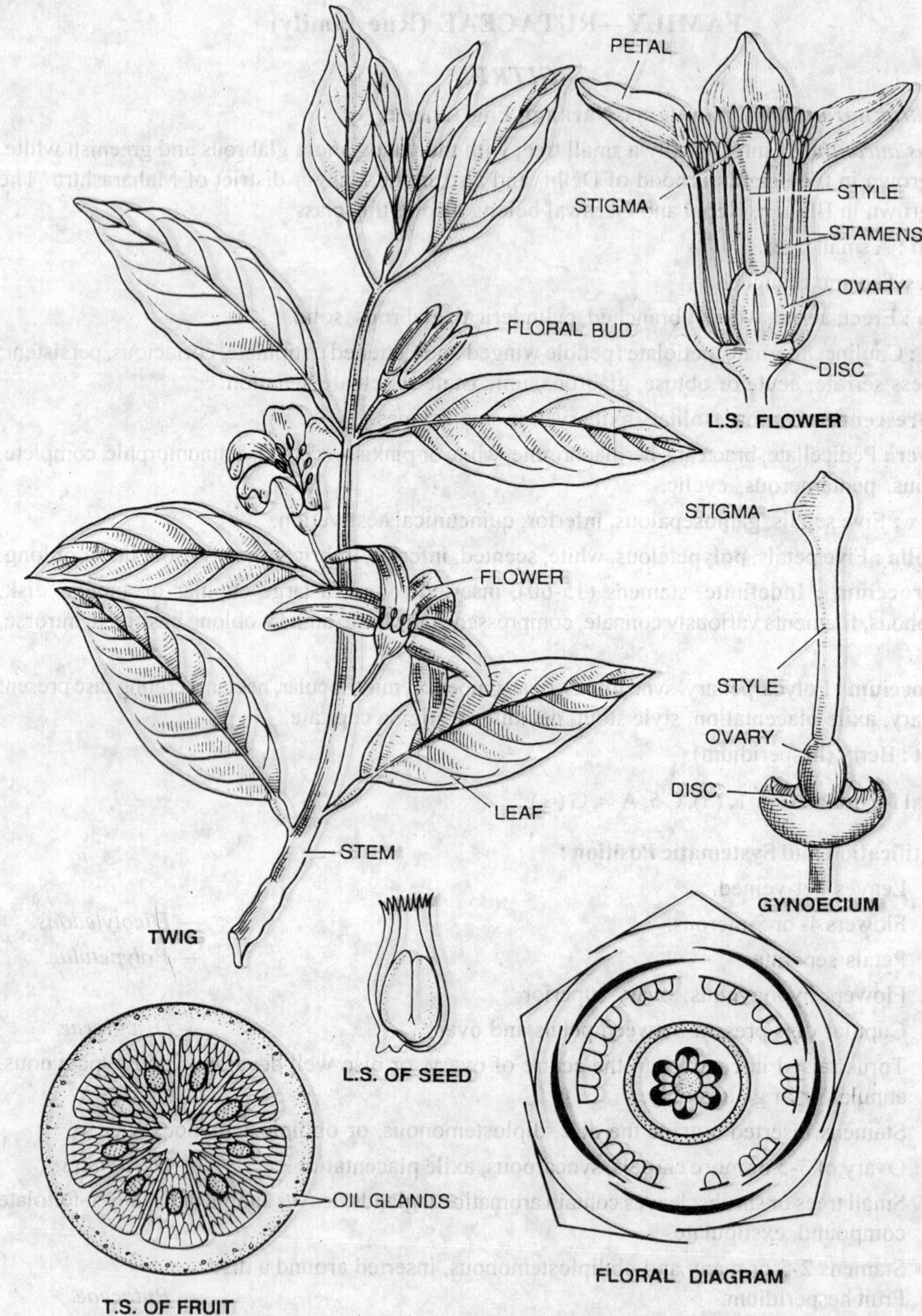

Fig. 9.28. Rutaceae. *Citrus aurantium* Linn.; Eng., orange; Verna. **Narangi.**

Economic value. The fruit is a rich source of vitamin C. The leaves are the source of an essential oil, which is used in confectionery, cosmetics and perfumery.

MURRAYA

*2. **Murraya exotica*** Spreng.; Verna. **Kamini;** Eng. Orange Jessamine.

Murraya exotica Spreng. An evergreen shrub or small tree with ash-coloured bark. Distribution : N. India, Outer Himalayas up to 4,500 feet.

Habit : Evergreen large shrub.

Root : Tap, branched.

Stem : Erect, aerial, branched, cylinderical, woody, green, solid.

Leaf : Cauline and ramal, compound, pinnate, exstipulate, alternate, leaflets 3-7, oval, entire, smooth, coriaceous, alternate, petioled, unicostate reticulate venation, notched at the tip, dark green, shining above, oblique at the base, gland dotted, aromatic oil present in glands.

Inflorescence : Cymose, short terminal and axillary corymbocymes or dichasial cyme.

Flower : Pedicellate, bracteate, pentamerous, hermaphrodite, complete, hypogynous, white, very fragrant, ½ diameter, cyclic.

Calyx : Five sepals, polysepalous, minute, acute, inferior, valvate aestivation.

Corolla : Five petals, polypetalous, white, fragrant, oblong-lanceolate, spreading above, inferior, imbricate aestivation.

Androecium : Ten stames, inserted round an elongated disk, alternate filaments thick, flat and short, obdiplostemonous, anthers bi-celled, introrse, polyandrous, dorsifixed.

Gynoecium : Two or three carpels, syncarpous, ovary, superior, two or three locular, axile placentation, two ovules in each chamber, style filiform stigma capitate, bilobed and sticky, disk present below ovary.

Fruit : Ovoid berry, orange red when ripe.

Floral formula : Br. ⊕ ⚥ K (5), C 5, A 5+5, G ($\underline{2}$-$\underline{3}$).

Identification and Systematic Position :

(*i*) Leaves net-veined.
(*ii*) Flowers 4- or 5-merous. — *Dicotyledons.*
(*i*) Petals separate. — *Polypetalae.*
(*i*) Flowers hypogynous; ovary superior.
(*ii*) Cupular disc present between petals and ovary. — *Disciflorae.*
(*i*) Torus raised in centre into the centre of ovary, or disc well developed and hypogynous, annular or of glands only.
(*ii*) Stamens inserted outside the disc, diplostemonous, or obdiplostemonous.
(*iii*) Ovary of 3-5 or more carpels, syncarpous, axile placentation. — *Geraniales.*
(*i*) Small trees or shrubs; leaves contain aromatic oil glands; leaves simple or usually 1-foliolate compound, exstipulate.
(*ii*) Stamens 2-5 or many and obdiplostemonous, inserted around a disc.
(*iii*) Fruit hesperidium. — *Rutaceae.*

Bentham & Hooker (*1862*)	*Engler & Prantl* (*1931*)	*Hutchinson* (*1959*)
Dicotyledons	Dicotyledoneae	Dicotyledones
Polypetalae	Archichlamydeae	Lignosae
Geraniales	Geraniales	Rutales
Rutaceae	Rutaceae	Rutaceae.

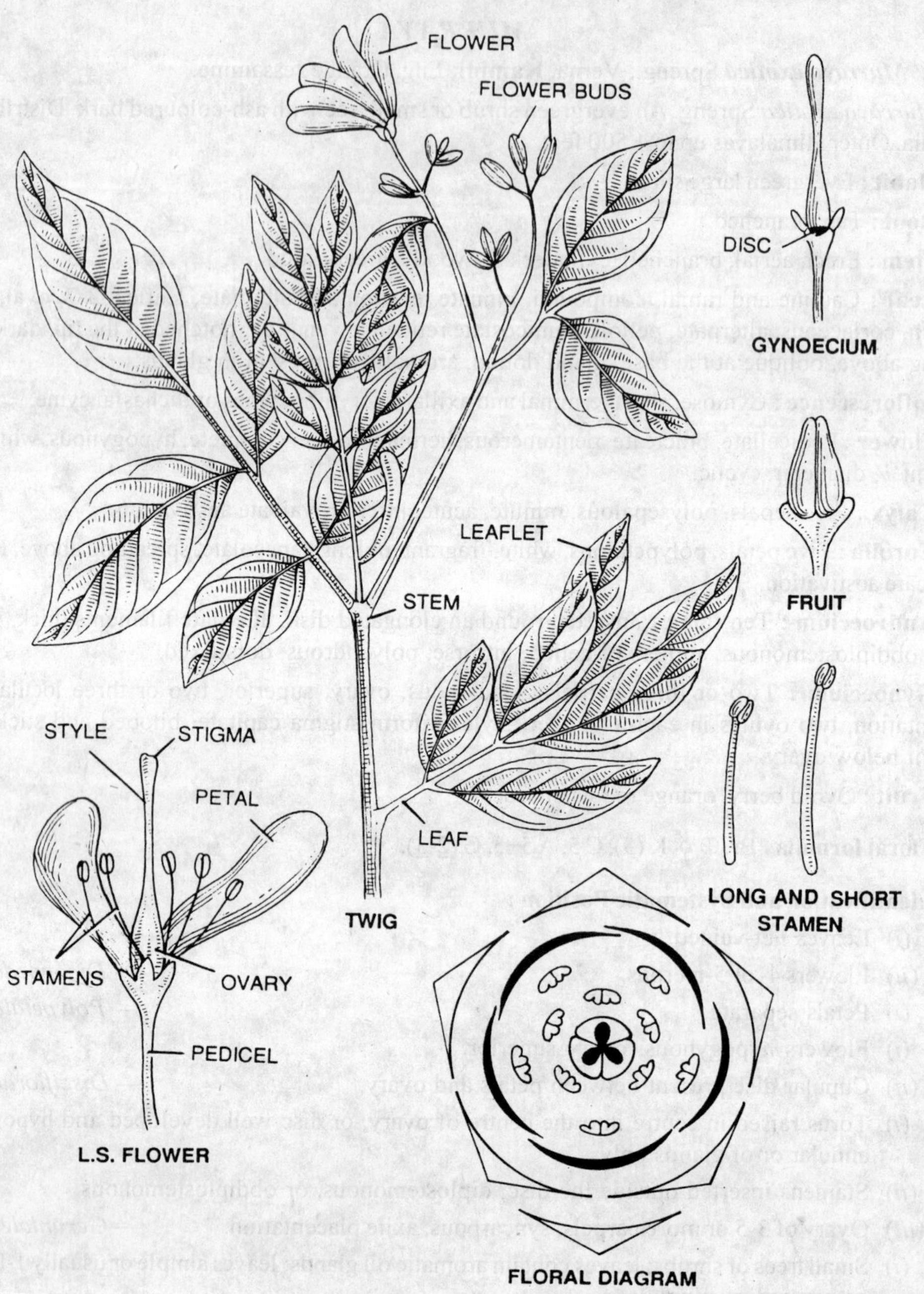

Fig. 9.29. Rutaceae. *Murraya exotica* Spreng.

Economic value. A fragrant shrub. Cultivated as a hedge plant. The fruits are edible. A glucoside has also been separated from the flowers.

AEGLE

3. Aegle marmelos Corr.; Verna. **Bel;** Eng. Bael, Bengal quince.

Habit : Large spinous tree.

Root : Tap and branched.

Stem : Erect, aerial, branched woody, cylinderical, solid, strong thorns present.

Leaf : Palmately compound, trifoliate, exstipulate, petiolate, alternate, gland dotted, each leaflet ovate-lanceolate, acute, entire, glabrous, net-veined, unicostate reticulate, lateral sessible, terminal stalked, gland dotted.

Inflorescence : Cymose, axillary panicles.

Flower : Pedicellate, bracteate, hermaphrodite, actinomorphic, complete, hypogynous, yellowish white, disc present beneath ovary, pentamerous, sweet scented, cyclic.

Calyx : 5 sepals, polysepalous, valvate or imbricate, pubescent, deciduous.

Corolla : 5 petals, polypetalous, imbricate, yellowish white.

Androecium : Indefinite, stamens, polyadelphous, polyandrous, filaments short, fascicled, basifixed, anther dithecous, introrse, elongate.

Gynoecium : 10, indefinite carpels, syncarpous, axile placentation, ovary superior, multilocular, each locule contains one or more ovules, style short and stout stigma capitate, sticky.

Fruit : Berry, large, globose oblong or pyriform, rind woody, grey or yellow, pulp orange-coloured, sweet.

Floral formula : Br. ⊕ ⚥ K 5, C 5, A ∞, G $(\underline{\infty})$.

Identification and Systematic Position :

(*i*) Leaves net-veined.

(*ii*) Flowers 4- or 5-merous. — *Dicotyledons.*

(*i*) Petals separate. — *Polypetalae.*

(*i*) Flowers hypogynous; ovary superior.

(*ii*) Cupular disc present between petals and ovary. — *Disciflorae.*

(*i*) Torus raised in centre into the centre of ovary, or disc well developed and hypogynous, annular or of glands only.

(*ii*) Stamens inserted outside the disc, diplostemonous, or obdiplostemonous.

(*iii*) Ovary of 3-5 or more carpels, syncarpous, axile placentation. — *Geraniales.*

(*i*) Small trees or shrubs; leaves contain aromatic oil glands; leaves simple or usually 1-foliolate compound, exstipulate.

(*ii*) Stamens 2-5 or many and obdiplostemonous, inserted around a disc.

(*iii*) Fruit hesperidium. — *Rutaceae.*

Other important members of the family. *Feronia limonia* (Linn.) Swingle, **Kavitha** - edible fruit; it is astringent, stimulant, stomachic. *Luvunga scandens* Buch. - Ham., **Lavangalata** - fruits yield an essential oil which is used in perfumery and pharmaceuticals. *Ruta graveolens* Linn., **Sadab** - plant is antiseptic, stimulant, emmenagogue, abortifacient. *Taddalia asiatica* lam., **Kanj** - yields yellow dye; root bark bitter, aromatic, tonic, stimulant and antiperiodic.

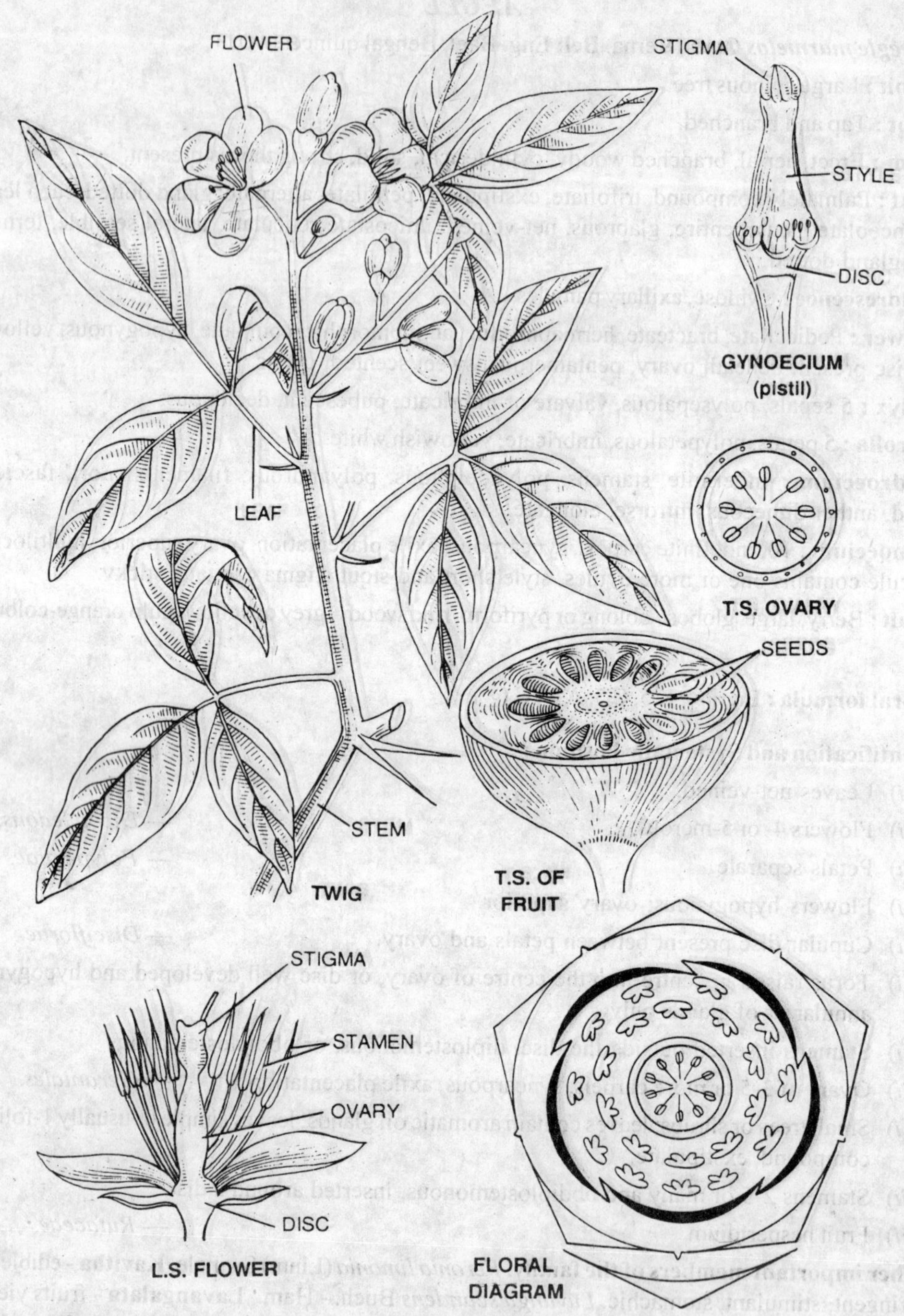

Fig. 9.30. Rutaceae. *Aegle marmelos* Corr.; Eng. Bengal quince; Verna., **bell.**

Economic value. The ripe fruits are edible. The unripe fruits are used as an astringent, stomachic, and also in the treatment of diarrhoea. The mucilaginous substance, secreted round the seeds, is used as a cement and is also employed as a varnish.

FAMILY—MELIACEAE (Melia family)

AZADIRACHTA

1. Azadirachta indica Juss.; Syn. *Melia azadirachta;* Eng. Margosa tree; Verna. **Neem.**

The Neem tree is found to be distributed in tropical regions. Common shade giving tree of N. India with antiseptic medicinal properties.

Habit : A large tree with blackish bark.

Root : Tap and branched.

Stem : Erect, aerial, branched, solid, woody with characteristic smell.

Leaves : Cauline and ramal, alternate, petiolate, compound, bipinnate and imparipinnate, unicostate reticulate, leaflet coarsely serrate.

Inflorescence : Axillary cymose panicle.

Flower : Bracteate, bracteolate, pedicellate, complete, actinomorphic, hermaphrodite, pentamerous, hypogynous, cyclic.

Calyx : Sepals 5, polysepalous, sepals connate at the base, small, aestivation valvate or imbricate.

Corolla : Petals 5, polypetalous, aestivation imbricate.

Androecium : Stamens 10, monadelphous, forming a cylinderical staminal tube, anthers dithecous, introrse, basifixed.

Gynoecium : Carpels 5-7, syncarpous, ovary superior, 5-7, loculed one or two ovules in each locule, placentation axile, ovule pendulous and anatropous, style long and slender, capitate stigma.

Fruit : Drupe.

Floral formula : Br. Brl. ⊕ ⚥ K 5, C 5, A (10), G $(\underline{5\text{-}7})$.

Identification and Systematic Position :

(*i*) Leaves net-veined.
(*ii*) Flowers 4- or 5-merous. — *Dicotyledons.*
(*i*) Petals separate. — *Polypetalae.*
(*i*) Flowers hypogynous; ovary superior.
(*ii*) Cupular disc present between petals and ovary. — *Disciflorae.*
(*i*) Torus raised in centre into the centre of ovary, or disc well developed and hypogynous, annular or of glands only.
(*ii*) Stamens inserted outside the disc, diplostemonous, or obdiplostemonous.
(*iii*) Ovary of 3-5 or more carpels, syncarpous, axile placentation. — *Geraniales.*
(*i*) Leaves alternate, usually pinnately compound, exstipulate.
(*ii*) Flowers in axillary panciles.
(*iii*) Stamens 4-12, usually diplostemonous, more or less united into a petaloid tube outside the disc, disc frequently tubular. — *Meliaceae*

Bentham & Hooker (1862)	*Engler & Prantl (1931)*	*Hutchinson (1959)*
Dicotyledons	Dicotyledoneae	Dicotyledones
Polypetalae	Archichlamydeae	Lignosae
Geraniales	Geraniales	Meliales
Meliaceae	Meliaceae	Meliaceae

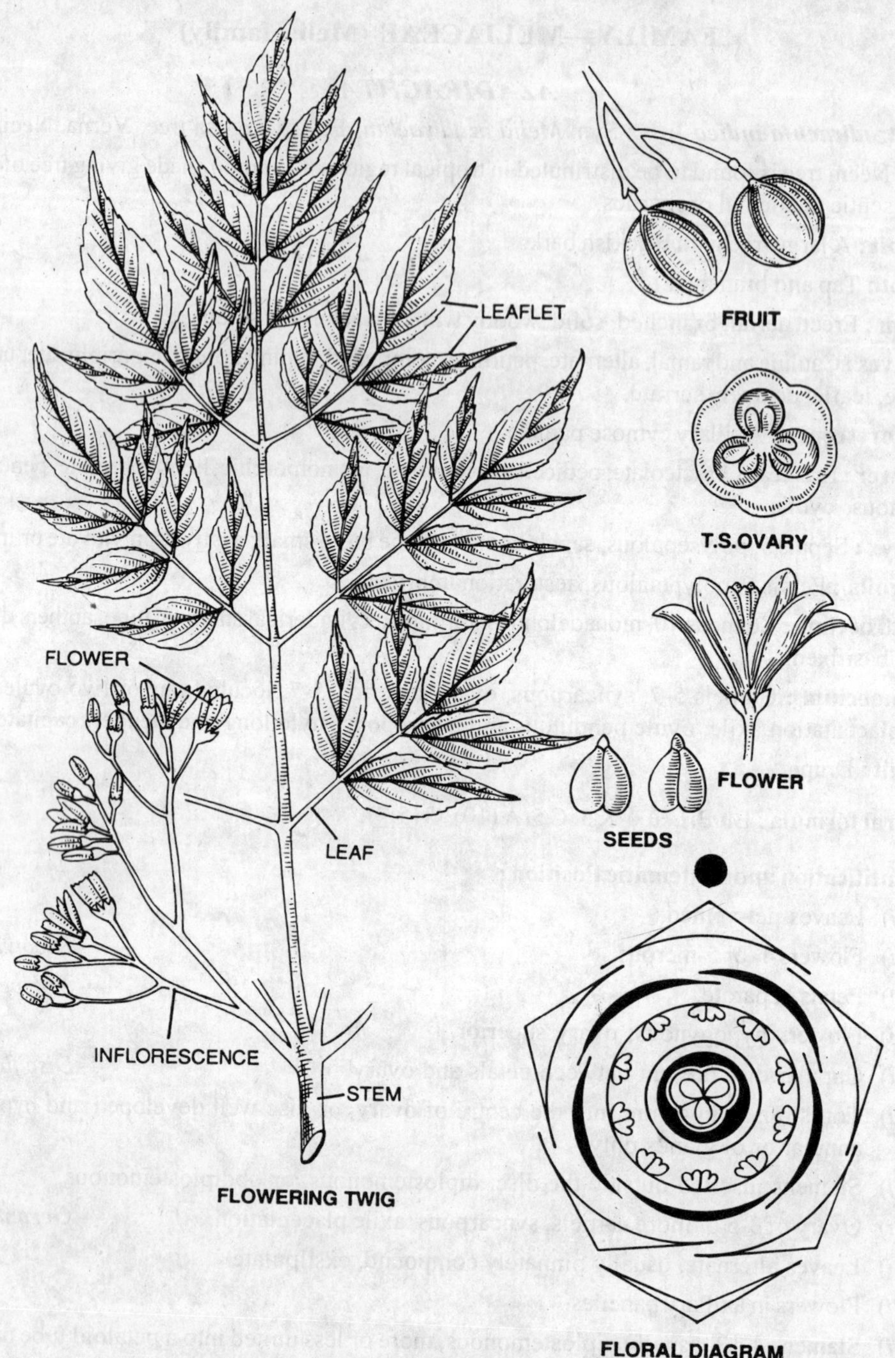

Fig. 9.31. Meliaceae. *Azadirachta indica* Juss.; Eng. Margosa tree; Verna., **neem.**

Economic value. All parts of the plant used medicinally. The leaves are placed in suit-cases to repel insects and to preserve woollens. An extract of the leaves is used in tooth-pastes and soaps. The seed-oil is used as an antiseptic and for burning purposes. The oilcake, obtained from the seeds, is used as a fertilizer and manure.

MELIA

2. *Melia azedarach* Linn.; Eng. Pride of India; Verna. **Bakain.**

Habit : A tree

Root : Tap, branched.

Stem : Erect, aerial, woody, solid, cylinderical, branched, smooth and green.

Leaf : Cauline and ramal, exstipulate, leaf base pulvinus, alternate, compound, bipinnate, imparipinnate, pinnae ovate-lanceolate, serrate, acute, oblique, glabrous, pinna unicostate reticulate.

Inflorescence : Cymose, axillary panicle cyme.

Flower : Pedicellate, bracteate, bracteolate, actinomorphic, hermaphrodite, complete, pentamerous, hypogynous, cyclic.

Calyx : 5 sepals, polysepalous, connate at base, valvate, acute, hairy, green.

Corolla : 5 petals, polypetalous, imbricate or quincuncial aestivation, purple white.

Androecium : 10, monadelphous, a staminal tube encloses the ovary, tube cylindric dialated at apex and base, ten-toothed at apex, anthers inserted near apex, anthers inserted near apex, dithecous (bicelled), basifixed, introrse.

Gynoecium : 5-8 carpels, syncarpus, ovary superior, 5-8 loculed, one to two ovules in each locule, axile placentation, style slender and long, stigma capitate, 5-lobed, nectariferous disc present beneath the ovary.

Fruit : A drupe.

Floral formula : Br. Brl. ⊕ ⚥ K 5, C 5, A (10), G $(\underline{2}\text{-}\underline{8})$.

Identification and Systematic Position :

(*i*) Leaves net-veined.
(*ii*) Flowers 4- or 5-merous. — *Dicotyledons.*
(*i*) Petals separate. — *Polypetalae.*
(*i*) Flowers hypogynous; ovary superior.
(*ii*) Cupular disc present between petals and ovary. — *Disciflorae.*
(*i*) Torus raised in centre into the centre of ovary, or disc well developed and hypogynous, annular or of glands only.
(*ii*) Stamens inserted outside the disc, diplostemonous, or obdiplostemonous.
(*iii*) Ovary of 3-5 or more carpels, syncarpous, axile placentation. — *Geraniales.*
(*i*) Leaves alternate, usually pinnately compound, exstipulate.
(*ii*) Flowers in axillary panciles.
(*iii*) Stamens 4-12, usually diplostemonous, more or less united into a petaloid tube outside the disc, disc frequently tubular. — *Meliaceae*

Other important members of the family. *Toona ciliata* Roem., **Toon.** flowers yield a yellow red dye; wood is used for construction work and furniture, bark yields a tan. *Swietenia mahagoni* (Linn.) Jacq., **Mahogani** - a timber tree; also grown as a hedge plant. *Soymida febrifuga* A. Juss., **Rohan** - bark yields a fibre for ropes; bark astringent, bitter tonic, febrifuge, used in diarrhoea and dysentery.

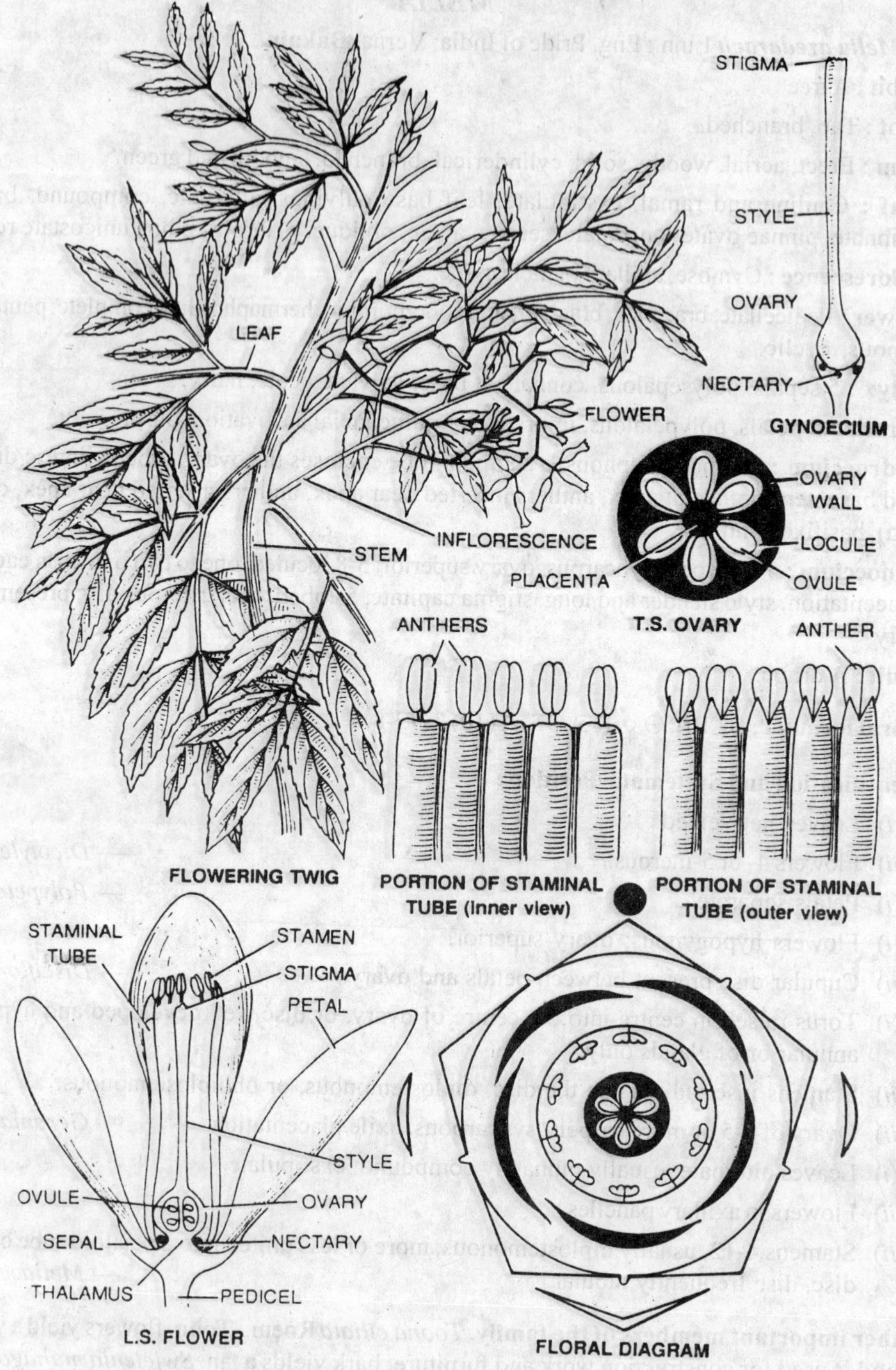

Fig. 9.32. Meliaceae. *Melia azedarach* Linn.; Eng. Pride of India; Verna. **Bakain.**

Economic value. Root bark, fruit flowers and leaves are used medicinally. Flowers and leaves are applied as poultice to relieve nervous headaches. Juice of leaves is used internally as anthelmintic, diuretic and emmenagogue. Seeds are prescribed in rheumatism. Oil is used as antiseptic.

FAMILY—ANACARDIACEAE (Mango family)

MANGIFERA

Mangifera indica Linn. Verna. **Aam;** Eng. Mango tree.

Mangifera indica Linn. (Vern. **Aam;** Mango tree). A large evergreen tree with widely spreading branches and dark coloured bark. Distribution : Tropical Himalayas from Garhwal to the Bhutan and Khasia hills, up to 3,000 feet, Bihar and on the hills of Central and south India cultivated throughout the greater part of India, and in most tropical countries. Flowers during March and April, and the fruit ripens during the early part of the rainy season.

Habit : Medium or large tree; resin canals present in wood.

Root : Tap and branched.

Stem : Erect, aerial, branched, woody, cylinderical and solid.

Leaves : Simple, alternate, petiolate, exstipulate, acute, entire, unicostate reticulate, glabrous, thick or coriaceous, young leaves soft and purple.

Inflorescence : Flowers arranged in panciles.

Flower : Pedicellate, bracteate, hermaphrodite, actinomorphic, regular, complete, pentamerous, hypogynous, cyclic, yellowish white.

Calyx : 5 sepals, gamosepalous, sepals adnate to the ovary wall.

Corolla : 5 petals, polypetalous, quincuntial or imbricate aestivation.

Androecium : 5 stamens, one functional or perfect stamen, antisepalous, stamens arise from the edge of an intrastaminal disc; anthers dithecous, introrse, dehiscence by longitudinal slits, basifixed.

Gynoecium : 3 carpels (tricarpellary), syncarpous, only one carpel functional; ovary superior, placentation basically axile; each locule contains a single pendulous ovule; style short, stigma lobed.

Fruit : Drupe.

Seed : Exalbuminous, embryo bears fleshy cotyledons.

Floral formula : Br. Brl. •|• ⊕ ⚥ K 5, C 5, A 1, G $\underline{(1)}$.

Identification and Systematic Position :

(*i*) Leaves net-veined.
(*ii*) Flowers 4- or 5-merous. — *Dicotyledons.*
(*i*) Petals separate. — *Polypetalae.*
(*i*) Flowers hypogynous; ovary superior.
(*ii*) Cupular disc present between petals and ovary. — *Disciflorae.*
(*i*) Torus raised in centre into the centre of ovary, or disc well developed and hypogynous, annular or of glands only.
(*ii*) Stamens inserted outside the disc.
(*iii*) Ovary of 3-5 or more carpels, syncarpous, axile placentation. — *Sapindales.*
(*i*) Woody plants with resin canals and tannin sacs.
(*ii*) Flowers polygamous, perfect stamens few (1 in *Mangifera*).
(*iii*) Fruit usually a 1-celled and 1-seeded often oblique drupe. — *Anacardiaceae.*

Bentham & Hooker (*1862*)	*Engler & Prantl* (*1931*)	*Hutchinson* (*1959*)
Dicotyledons	Dicotyledoneae	Dicotyledones
Polypetalae	Archichlamydeae	Lignosae
Sapindales	Sapindales	Sapindales
Anacardiaceae	Anacardiaceae	Anacardiaceae

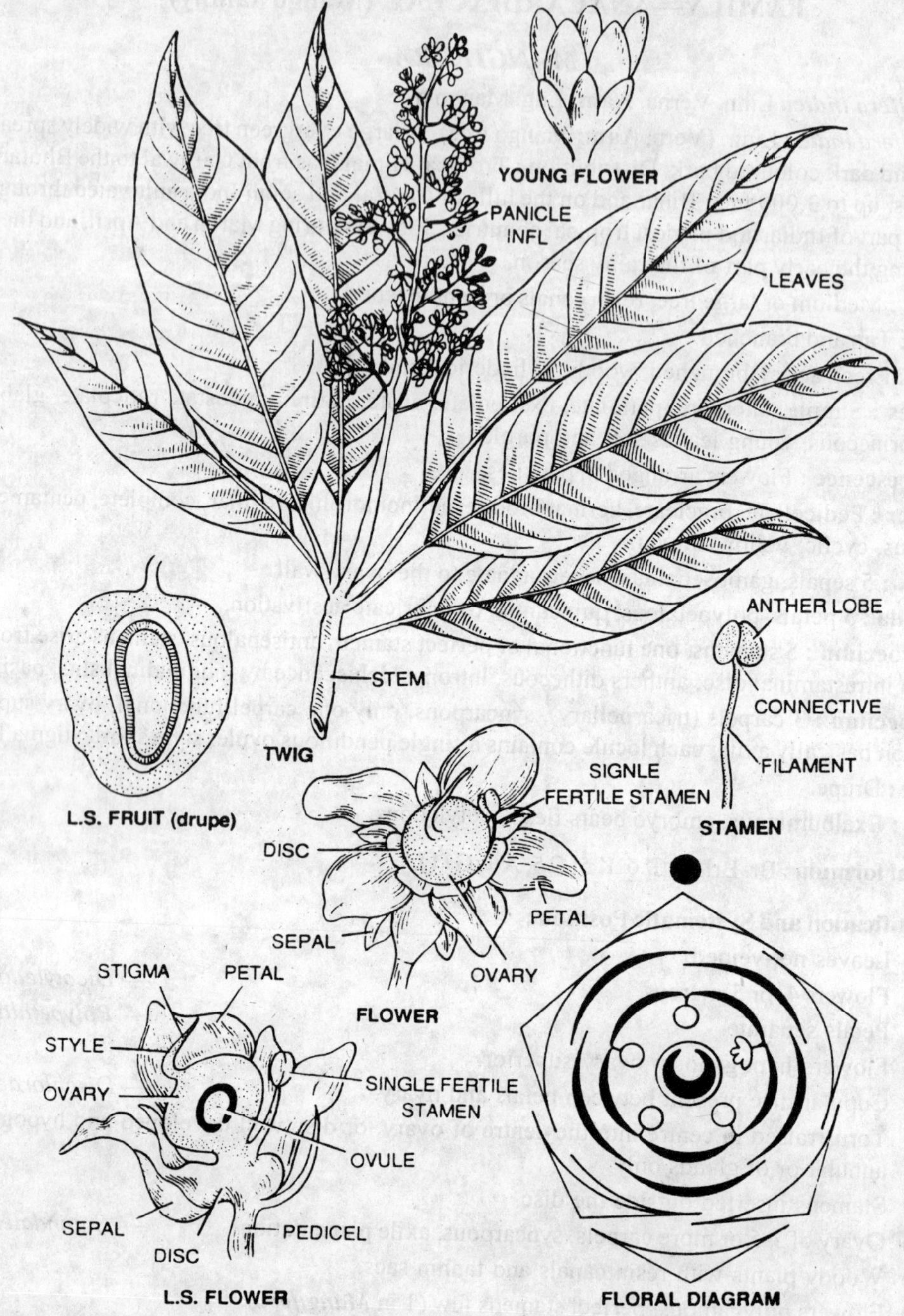

Fig. 9.33. Anacardiaceae. *Mangifera indica* Linn.; Eng., mango tree; Verna., **aam.**

Economic value. The mango fruit is one of the most highly prized dessert fruits of the tropics. It has a rich, luscious, aromatic flavour and a delicious taste in which sweetness and acidity are delightfully blended. Ripe fruits constitute a rich source of vitamin A. Young and unripe fruits are usually acidic and used in pickles, chutney, *amchur* and culinary preparations.

FAMILY—PAPILIONACEAE (Pea family)

PISUM

1. ***Pisum sativum*** Linn.; Verna. **Matar;** Eng. Garden Pea.

Pisum sativum Linn. a smooth glaucous annual. Largely grown as a cold-weather crop in many districts of N. Indian plains.

Habit : Annual herb; cultivated.

Root : Tap, branched, with nodules containing nitrogen fixing bacteria (*Rhizobium radicicola*).

Stem : Herbaceous, weak, climbing with the help of leaf tendrils, cylindrical, branched, smooth, glaucous.

Leaves : Cauline and ramal, alternate, compound, imparipinnate, stipulate (stipules large foliaceous, ovate, semicordate, irregularly toothed at the base), leaflets 4 or 6, the common rachis ends in a branched tendril; the leaflets entire, smooth, net veined, oval to oblong, mucronate tips, green and glaucous, the terminal leaflet is always a tendril.

Inflorescence : Racemose, flowers arranged in axillary racemes or solitary.

Flower : Bracteate, pedicellate, zygomorphic, irregular, hermaphrodite, papilionaceous, white or pink, complete, hypogynous or perigynous.

Calyx : 5 sepals, gamosepalous, campanulate calyx tube teeth long or the upper short; sepaloid, ascending imbricate aestivation.

Corolla : 5 petals, 1 standard, 2 wings, 2 keels united, keels shorter than wings and enclose the pistil and stamens; corolla papilionaceous, white or pink in colour; descending imbricate (vexillary) aestivation; inferior.

Androecium : 10 stamens in two bundles (diadelphous) or 9+1, nine stamens unite at the base and form a tube around ovary, tenth is posterior and free; anthers bi-lobed, basifixed, introrse, dehiscence by longitudinal splitting.

Gynoecium : Carpel one (monocarpellary); ovary superior, unilocular; marginal placentation; ovules many; style bent and long, stigma simple; terminal and hairy; ovary also hairy.

Fruit : A legume (pod), broad.

Seeds : Rounded, uniform, white.

Generic characters : Leaflets are even in number; terminal leaflet is represented by a tendril; stamens diadelphous (9+1); pods normal, flattened, nor partitioned; style dialated from the base towards the apex, hairy on one side; calyx lobes leafy.

Floral formula : •|• ⊕ ⚥ K (5), C 1+2+(2), A (9)+1, **G** $\underline{1}$.

Identification and Systematic Position :

(*i*) Leaves net-veined.
(*ii*) Flowers 4- or 5-merous. — *Dicotyledons.*
(*i*) Petals separate. — *Polypetalae.*
(*i*) Flowers regular or irregular, 1 or 2-sexual.
(*ii*) Petals distinct or united at the base, perigynous.
(*iii*) Stamens peri or epigynous. — *Calyciflorae.*
(*i*) Woody or herbaceous with alternate, stipulate compound leaves.
(*ii*) Flowers perigynous; rarely hypogynous, with a disc lining the hypanthium.
(*iii*) Ovary apocarpous reduced to 1 usually elongate, declinate carpel; marginal placentation; fruit a legume (pod). — *Leguminosae.*
(*i*) Simple, digitate or pinnate leaves.
(*ii*) Flowers zygomorphic and papilionaceous.
(*iii*) Descending imbricate aestivation of corolla; 1 standard, 2 wings and 2 keels.
(*iv*) Stamens 10 monadelphous or diadelphous, *i.e.*, 5+5 or 9+1. — *Papilionaceae.*

Other important members of the family. *Phaseolus mungo* Roxb., **Urd;** *P. aureus* Roxb., **Mung;** *Cajanus cajan* (Linn.) Millsp., **Arhar;** *Arachis hypogaea* Linn., **Mungphali;** *Cicer arietinum* Linn., **Chana;** *Dalbergia sisoo* Roxb., **Shisham.**

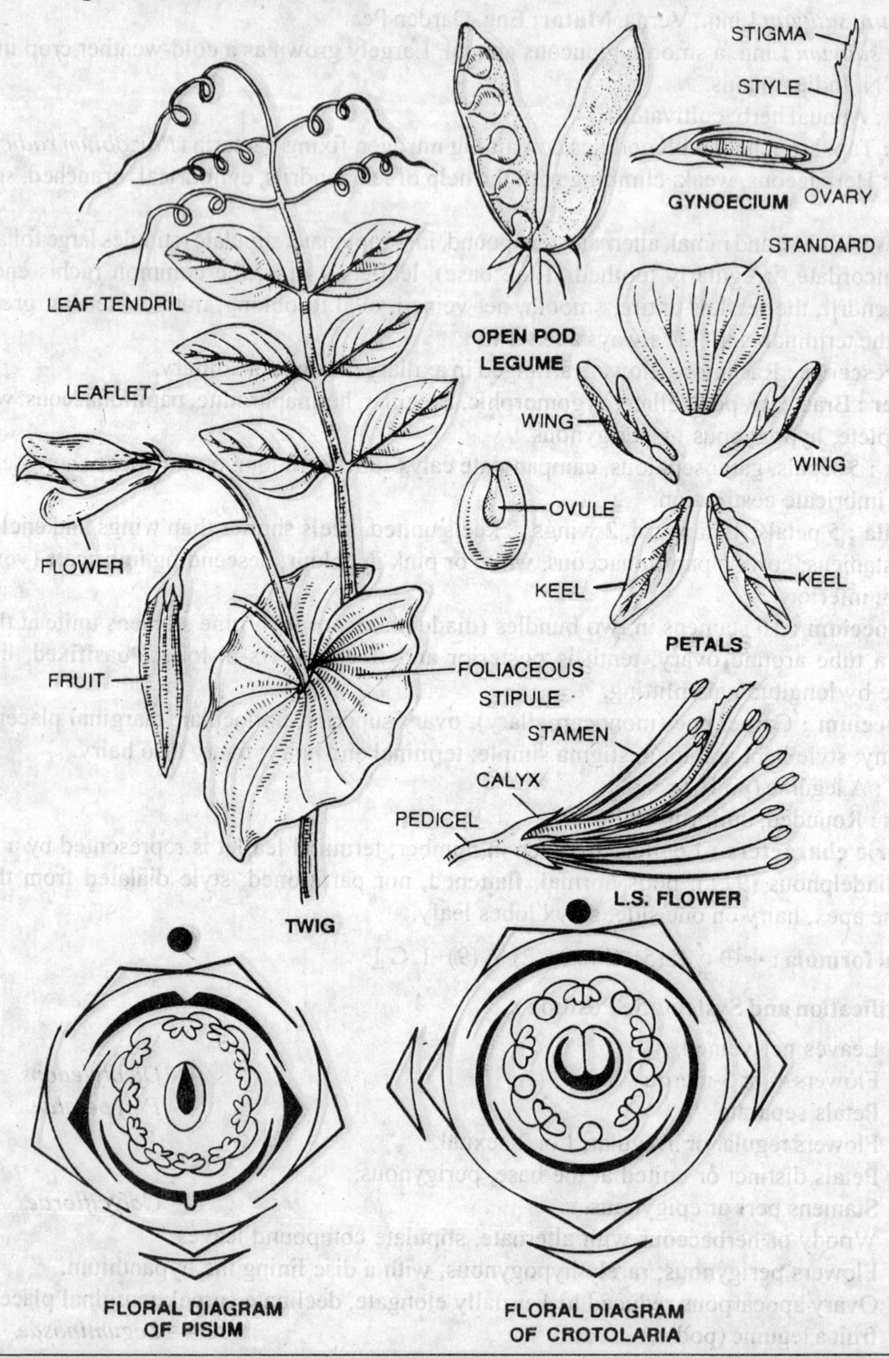

Fig. 9.34. Papilionaceae (Leguminosae). *Pisum sativum* Linn.; garden pea; Verna., **matar.**

Economic value. The garden pea seeds are eaten green or are used for canning. The seed is also used for human consumption in the form of pea meal or split peas. The peas are used as pulses, and they are good source of proteins. The plants are used for forage and green manuring.

LATHYRUS

*2. **Lathyrus aphaca*** Linn.; Eng. Yellow vetchling; Verna. **Jangli Mattar.**

Habit : An annual herb; wild.

Root : Tap, branched, with nodules containing nitrogen fixing bacteria (*Rhizobium radicicola*).

Stem : Herbaceous, weak, aerial, climbing with the help of leaf tendrils, cylinderical branched, smooth, glaucous, green.

Leaf : Cauline and ramal, alternate, modified into a tendril, stipulate, stipules foliaceous and in pairs, hastate, entire, acute.

Inflorescence : Cymose, solitary axillary.

Flower : Pedicellate, bracteate, zygomorphic, hermaphrodite, complete, pentamerous, hypo- or perigynous, papilionaceous, cyclic.

Calyx : 5 sepals, gamosepalous, valvate, green.

Corolla : 5 petals, 1 standard, 2 wings, 2 keels united, keels shorter than wings and enclose the pistil and stamens, vexillary (descending imbricate), papilionaceous, inferior, white or whitish yellow.

Androecium : 10 stamens in two bundles (diadelphous) of 9+1, nine stamens unite at the base and form a tube around ovary, tenth is posterior and free; anthers dithecous, basifixed, introrse.

Gynoecium : Carpel one (monocarpellary), ovary superior, unilocular, marginal placentation; ovules many; style bent and long, stigma simple, terminal and hairy.

Fruit : Legume.

Floral formula : Br. •|• ⚥ K (5), C 1+2+(2), A (9)+1, G $\underline{1}$.

Identification and Systematic Position :

(*i*) Leaves net-veined.
(*ii*) Flowers 4- or 5-merous. — *Dicotyledons.*
(*i*) Petals separate. — *Polypetalae.*
(*i*) Flowers regular or irregular, 1 or 2-sexual.
(*ii*) Petals distinct or united at the base, perigynous.
(*iii*) Stamens peri or epigynous. — *Calyciflorae.*
(*i*) Woody or herbaceous with alternate, stipulate compound leaves.
(*ii*) Flowers perigynous; rarely hypogynous, with a disc lining the hypanthium.
(*iii*) Ovary apocarpous reduced to 1 usually elongate, declinate carpel; marginal placentation; fruit a legume (pod). — *Leguminosae.*
(*i*) Simple, digitate or pinnate leaves.
(*ii*) Flowers zygomorphic and papilonaceous.
(*iii*) Descending imbricate aestivation of corolla; 1 standard, 2 wings and 2 keels.
(*iv*) Stamens 10 monadelphous or diadelphous, *i.e.*, 5+5 or 9+1. — *Papilionaceae.*

Bentham & Hooker (*1862*)	*Engler & Prantl* (*1931*)	*Hutchinson* (*1959*)
Dicotyledons	Dicotyledoneae	Dicotyledones
Polypetalae	Archichlamydeae	Lignosae
Rosales	Rosales	Leguminales
Leguminosae	Leguminosae	Papilionaceae

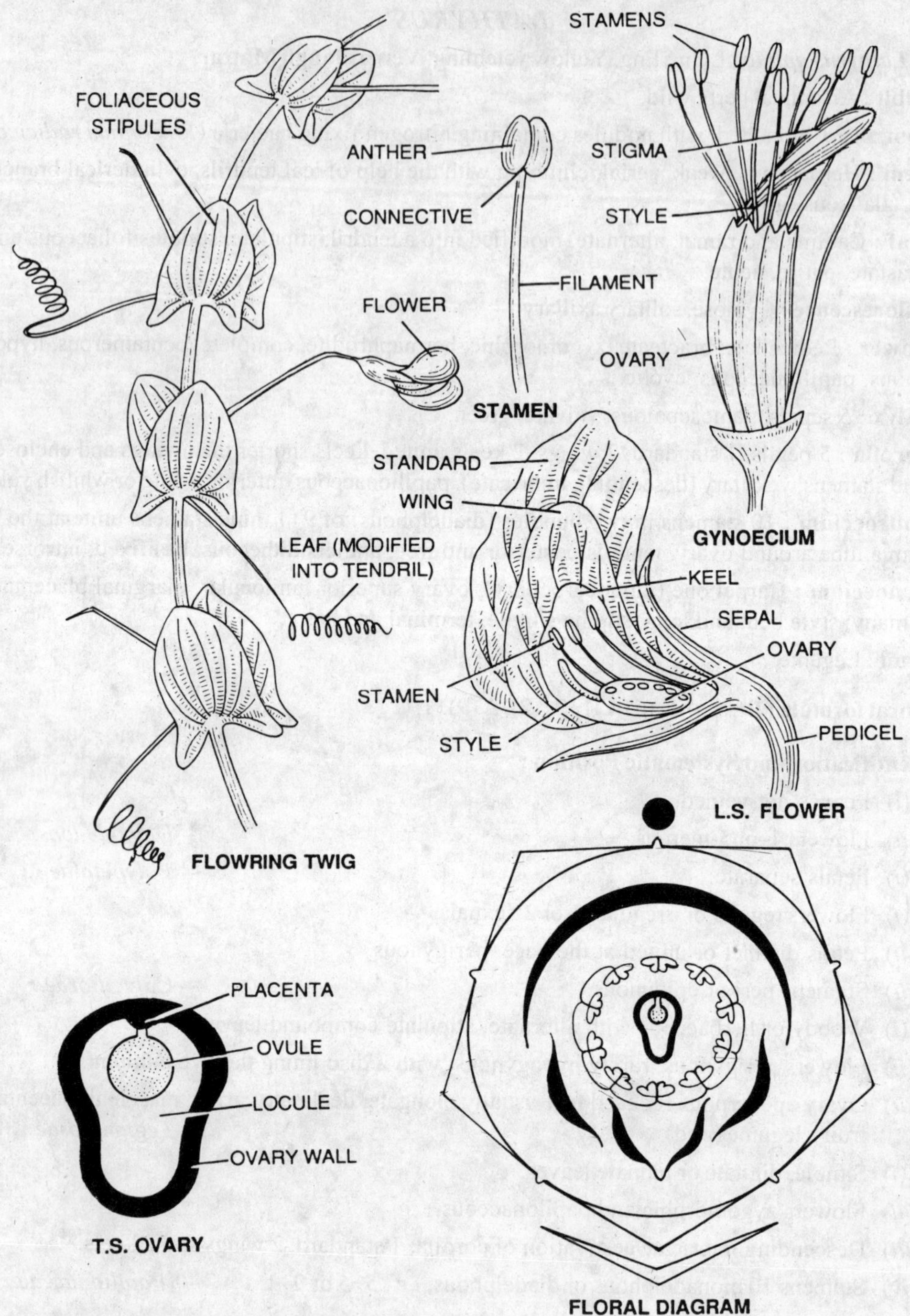

Fig. 9.35. Papilionaceae. *Lathyrus aphaca* Linn.; Eng. Yellow vetchling; Verna. **Jangli mattar.**

Economic value. The plant is used as cattle fodder. The ripe seeds are said to be narcotic.

FAMILY—CAESALPINIACEAE (Cassia family)

CASSIA

*1. **Cassia tora*** Linn. Verna. **Pamaar, Chakunda;** Eng. Sickle senna.

Habit : A medium size tree or shrub.

Root : Tap, branched.

Stem : Erect, aerial, woody, branched, cylinderical, glabrous, solid.

Leaves : Cauline and ramal, compound, alternate, paripinnate, pulvinus at the base, petiolate, stipulate (stipules caducous), leaflets 4-8 pairs, ovate, entire, acute, glabrous, venation unicostate reticulate.

Inflorescence : Racemose, typical raceme.

Flower : Pedicellate (long pedicels), bracteate (bracts minute and caducous) or ebracteate, hermaphrodite, actinomorphic, complete, hypogynous, yellow, pentamerous, cyclic.

Calyx : Five sepals, polysepalous, more or less petaloid (yellowish green), inferior, quincuncial aestivation, odd sepals anterior.

Corolla : Five petals, polypetalous, yellow, clawed, ascending imbricate aestivation, inferior.

Androecium : Ten stamens, polyandrous, unequal in length, three posterior stamens reduced to staminodes, basifixed anthers with abortive and indehiscent lobes, dithecous, introrse.

Gynoecium : One carpel (monocarpellary), ovary superior, unilocular, marginal placentation, style short, stigma terminal, hairy.

Fruit : A legume, black when ripe.

Floral formula : Br. •|• ⚥ K 5, C 5, A 7 + 3, G $\underline{1}$.

Identification and Systematic Position :

(*i*) Leaves net-veined.
(*ii*) Flowers 4- or 5-merous. — *Dicotyledons.*
(*i*) Petals separate. — *Polypetalae.*
(*i*) Flowers regular or irregular, 1 or 2-sexual.
(*ii*) Petals distinct or united at the base, perigynous.
(*iii*) Stamens peri- or epigynous. — *Calyciflorae.*
(*i*) Woody or herbaceous with alternate, stipulate compound leaves.
(*ii*) Flowers perigynous, rarely hypogynous, with a disc lining the hypanthium.
(*iii*) Ovary, apocarpous reduced to 1 usually elongate, declinate carpel; marginal placentation; fruit a legume (pod). — *Leguminosae.*
(*i*) Pinnate or 2-pinnate leaves (simple or 2 connate leaflets in *Bauhinia*).
(*ii*) Petals usually 5 with ascending imbricate aestivation.
(*iii*) Stamens definite, diplostemonous or usually fewer by reduction.
(*iv*) Fruit often indehiscent. — *Caesalpiniaceae.*

Bentham & Hooker (*1862*)	*Engler & Prantl* (*1931*)	*Hutchinson* (*1959*)
Dicotyledons	Dicotyledoneae	Dicotyledones
Polypetalae	Archichlamydeae	Lignosae
Rosales	Rosales	Leguminales
Leguminosae	Leguminosae	Caesalpiniaceae

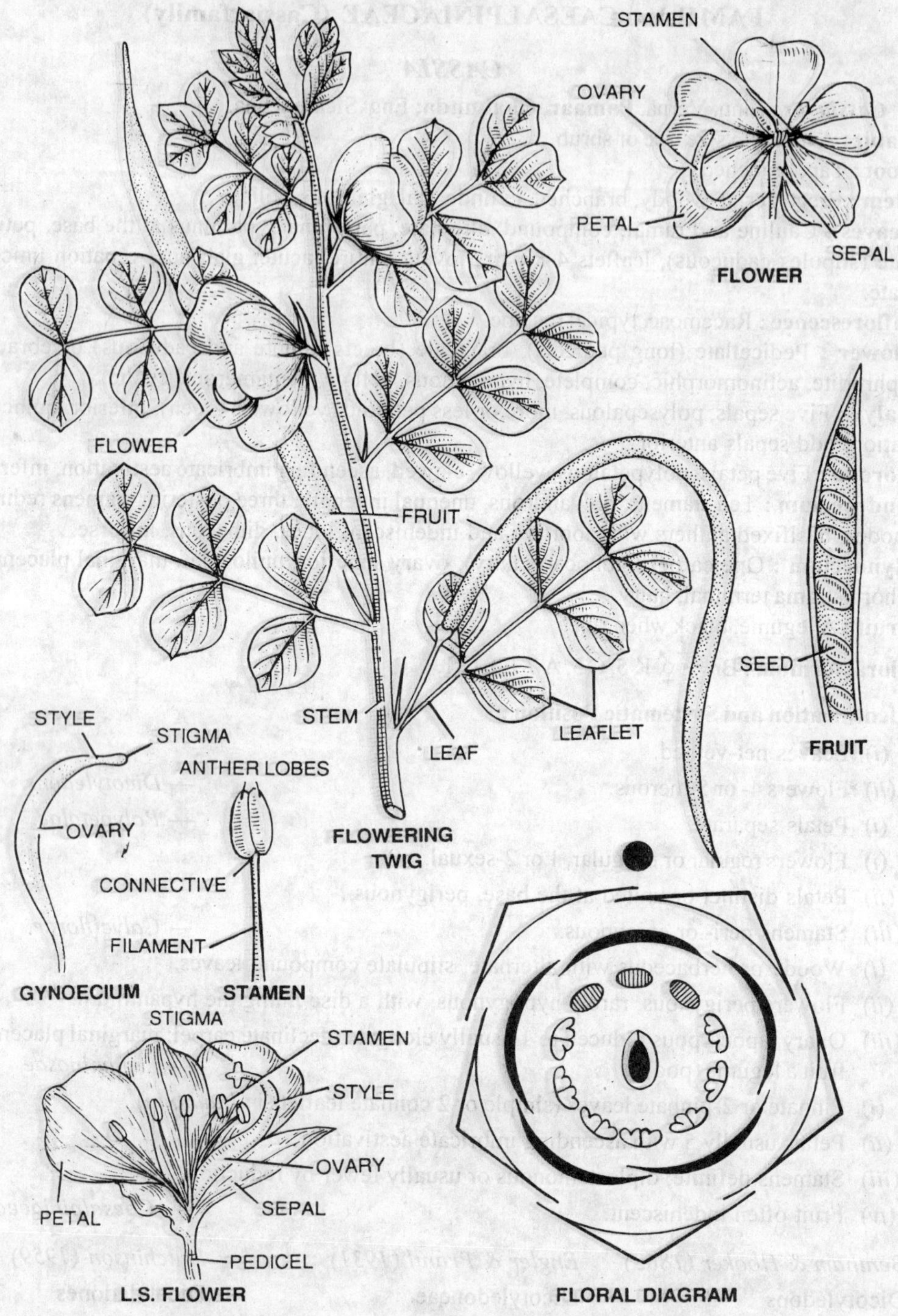

Fig. 9.36. Caesalpiniaceae (Leguminosae). *Cassia tora* Linn.; Eng. Sickle senna; Verna. **Pamaar, chakunda.**

Economic value. The seeds are used in the preparation of sweets and the tender young leaves are used as vegetable. Decoction of leaves is laxative. Leaves and seeds are used in skin diseases, for ringworm and itch. Root is used in snake-bite.

CASSIA FISTULA

2. Cassia fistula Linn.; Eng. Golden shower; Verna. **Amaltas.**

Habit : A medium-size tree.

Root : Tap, branched.

Stem : Erect, woody, aerial, cylinderical, branched, solid glabrous, green.

Leaves : Cauline and ramal, exstipulate, alternate, pulvinus at base, compound, unipinnate, paripinnate, petiolate, leaflet ovate, entire, acute, glabrous, coriaceous, unicostate reticulate.

Inflorescence : Racemose, raceme.

Flower : Bracteate, pedicellate, complete, zygomorphic, hermaphrodite, actinomorphic, complete, hypogynous, yellow, pentamerous, cyclic.

Calyx : 5 sepals, polysepalous, yellowish-green, inferior, quincuncial, inferior.

Corolla : 5 petals, polypetalous, imbricate, inferior, yellow.

Androecium : 10 stamens, polyandrous, unequal in length, three posterior stamens reduced to staminodes, dorsifixed anthers with abortive and indehiscent lobes, dithecous, introrse.

Gynoecium : One carpel (monocarpellary), ovary superior, sickle shaped, unilocular, many ovules, marginal placentation, style short, stigma terminal, capitate, hairy.

Fruit : A legume, 1-2 feet long, cylinderical green when young, black when ripe.

Floral formula : Br. •|• ⚥ K 5, C 5, A 7+3, G $\underline{1}$.

Identification and Systematic Position :

(*i*) Leaves net-veined.

(*ii*) Flowers 4- or 5-merous. — *Dicotyledons.*

(*i*) Petals separate. — *Polypetalae.*

(*i*) Flowers regular or irregular, 1 or 2-sexual.

(*ii*) Petals distinct or united at the base, perigynous.

(*iii*) Stamens peri- or epigynous. — *Calyciflorae.*

(*i*) Woody or herbaceous with alternate, stipulate compound leaves.

(*ii*) Flowers perigynous, rarely hypogynous, with a disc lining the hypanthium.

(*iii*) Ovary, apocarpous reduced to 1 usually elongate, declinate carpel; marginal placentation; fruit a legume (pod). — *Leguminosae.*

(*i*) Pinnate or 2-pinnate leaves (simple or of 2 connate leaflets in *Bauhinia*).

(*ii*) Petals usually 5 with ascending imbricate aestivation.

(*iii*) Stamens definite, diplostemonous or usually fewer by reduction.

(*iv*) Fruit often indehiscent. — *Caesalpiniaceae.*

Other important members of the family. *Bauhinia variegata* Linn., **Kachnar** - flower buds eaten as vegetable; bark alterative, tonic, astringent, useful in skin diseases and ulcers. *Caesalpinia crista* Linn. **Karanja** - seeds antiperiodic, antipyretic, tonic, febrifuge in asthma; *Saraca indica* Linn., **Ashok** - bark astringnt, used in uterine affection. *Tamarindus indica* Linn., **Imli** - fruit refrigerant, digestive, carminative, laxative.

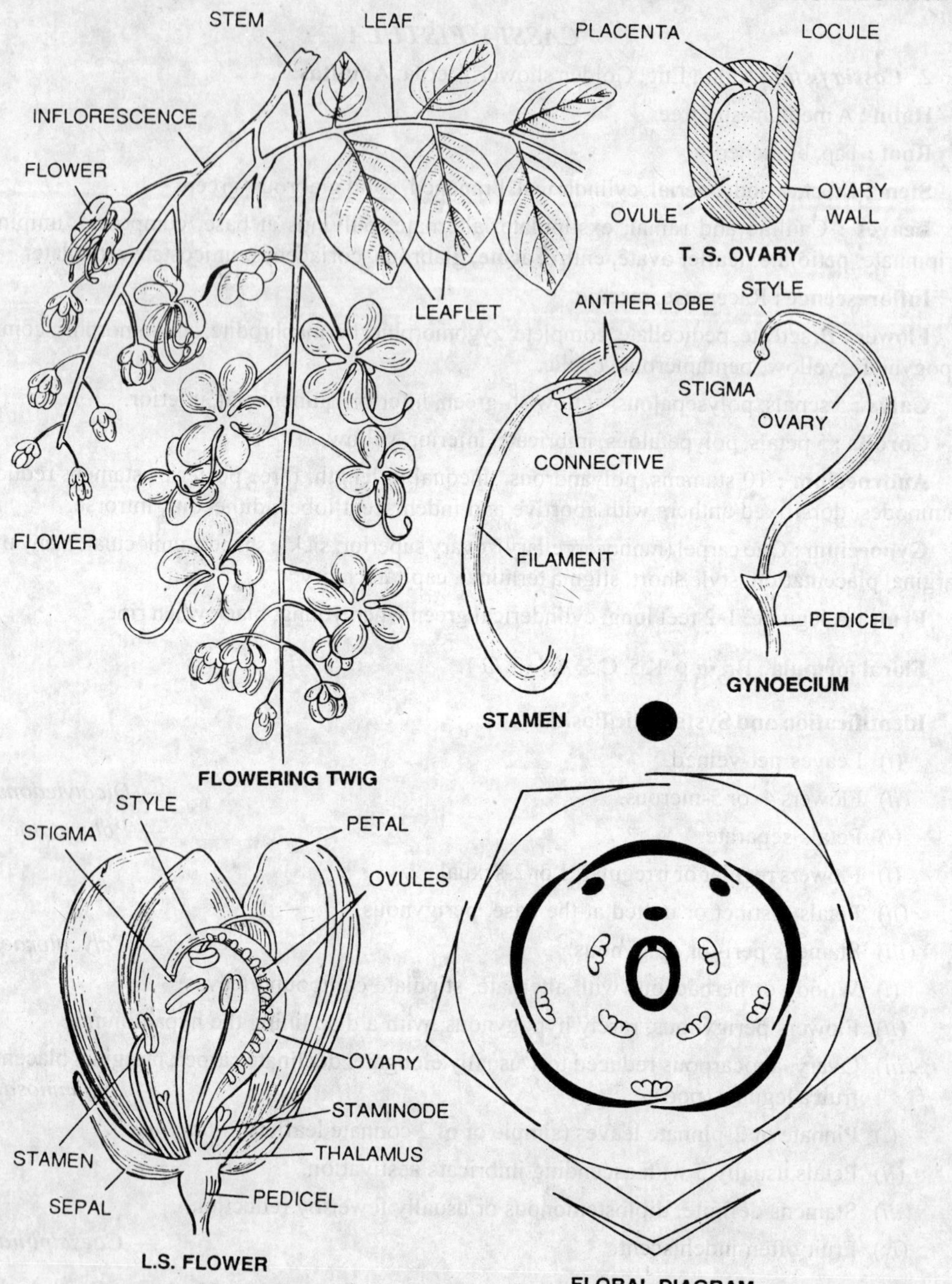

Fig. 9.37. Caesalpiniaceae. *Cassia fistula* Linn.; Eng., golden shower; Verna., **amaltas.**

Economic value. Often grown as an ornamental tree. Root bark, seeds and leaves are laxative. The fruit is used in rheumatism and snake-bite. The seeds are emetic. The root is astringent, tonic, febrifuge and purgative. Juice of leaves is used in skin diseases.

FAMILY—MIMOSACEAE (Acacia family)

ACACIA

1. Acacia nilotica (Linn.) Del.; Verna., **babul, kikar;** Eng. Babul Acacia.

A. Nilotica (L.) Del. A medium sized evergreen tree with dark-brown bark. Distribution. Throughout the greater part of India.

Habit : A medium size spiny tree.

Root : Tap, branched.

Stem : Erect, aerial, woody, solid, cylinderical, branched.

Leaf : Cauline and ramal, compound, bipinnate, stipulate, stipules modified into spines, petiolate, rachis possesses glands, leaflet oval alternate, sub-sessile, entire, obtuse, unicostate reticulate venation, glabrous, leaf base pulvinus.

Inflorescence : The flowers are arranged in compound cymose heads, yellow.

Flower : Sessile, bracteate, actinomorphic, hermaphrodite, hypogynous, complete, fragrant, small, yellow, tetra - or pentamerous, cyclic.

Calyx : Sepals 4 or 5, minute, gamosepalous, campanulate, membranous, valvate aestivation, inferior.

Corolla : Petals 4 or 5, gamopetalous, valvate aestivation, inferior.

Androecium : Stamens indefinite, polyandrous, long filaments, minute anthers, introrse, yellow, dithecous, dorsifixed.

Gynoecium : Monocarpellary, ovary superior, unilocular, many ovules, marginal placentation, style long, stigma minute, capitate.

Fruit : A lomentaceous pod.

Floral formula : Br ⊕ ⚥ K (4-5), C (4-5), A ∝, G $\underline{1}$.

Identification and Systematic Position :

(*i*) Leaves net-veined.
(*ii*) Flowers 4- or 5-merous. — *Dicotyledons.*
(*i*) Petals separate. — *Polypetalae.*
(*i*) Flowers regular or irregular, 1 or 2-sexual.
(*ii*) Petals distinct or united at the base, perigynous.
(*iii*) Stamens peri- or epigynous. — *Calyciflorae.*
(*i*) Woody or herbaceous with alternate, stipulate compound leaves.
(*ii*) Flowers perigynous, rarely hypogynous, with a disc lining the hypanthium.
(*iii*) Ovary, apocarpous reduced to 1 usually elongate, declinate carpel; marginal placentation; fruit a legume (pod). — *Leguminosae.*
(*i*) Bipinnate leaves.
(*ii*) Flowers arranged in dense heads or spikes; flowers small, regular 4-5 merous.
(*iii*) Stamens free diplostemonous or indefinite.
(*iv*) Fruit usually lomentum. — *Caesalpiniaceae.*

Bentham & Hooker (1862)	*Engler & Prantl* (1931)	*Hutchinson* (1959)
Dicotyledons	Dicotyledoneae	Dicotyledones
Polypetalae	Archichlamydeae	Lignosae
Rosales	Rosales	Leguminales
Leguminosae	Leguminosae	Mimosaceae

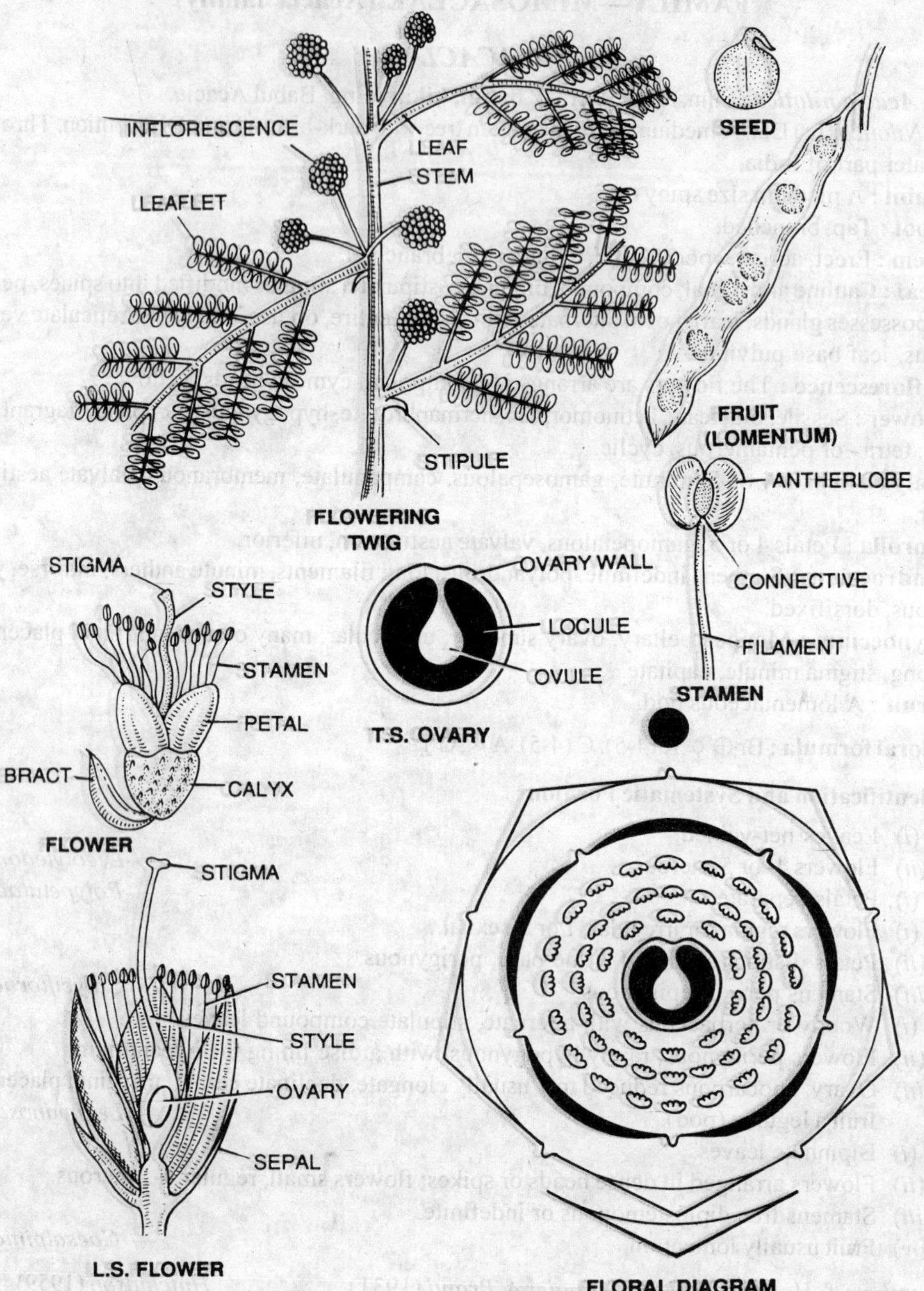

Fig. 9.38. Mimosaceae (Leguminosae). *Acacia nilotica* (Linn.) Del.; Eng., babul acacia; Verna., **babul, kikar.**

Economic value. The pods are used as fodder. The bark is used as a tan. The gum, obtained from the bark, is used in confectionery. Baskets are made of young, green twigs. Gum is used in diarrhoea and dysentery. Bark is astringent and demulcent.

MIMOSA

2. ***Mimosa pudica*** Linn., Verna. **Chhui-mui, lajvanti;** Eng. Touch me not.

Mimosa pudica Linn. A widely spreading diffuse undershrub. Distribution. Throughout the hotter parts of India. Dehradun and in the sub-himalayan tracts eastward, naturalized as a need in waste land; often cultivated.

Habit : Perennial herb or shrub.

Root : Tap, branched.

Stem : Erect or prostrate, aerial, woody, solid, cylindrical, branched, prickly, densely clothed with deflexed bristles.

Leaf : Cauline and ramal, compound bipinnate, very sensitive, rachis best with ascending bristles, stipulate, stipules lanceolate, striate, margins bristly, pinnae usually, 2½ to 3½ inches long, leaflet, 12 to 20 pairs, ½ inch long, sessile, oblong, acute, subcoriaceous, glabrous above, appressed-bristly beneath.

Inflorescence : Heads usually in pairs.

Flower : Small, sessile, bracteate, hermaphrodite, actinomorphic, complete, tetramerous, hypogynous, cyclic.

Calyx : 4 sepals, minute, gamosepalous, campanulate, shortly toothed.

Corolla : 4 petals, polypetalous, connate towards the base, small, inconspicuous, purple, valvate aestivation, inferior.

Androecium : 4 stamens, conspicuous, brightly coloured, free, filaments filiform, anthers small, bicelled, not gland crested, basifixed, introrse.

Gynoecium : 1, monocarpellary, ovary superior, unilocular, many ovules, marginal placentation, style filiform, stigma minute, terminal.

Fruit : Pod, flat, membranous, joints 3-5, falling away when ripe from the sutures which are armed with weak spreading yellowish bristles.

Floral formula : ⊕ ⚥ K (4), C 4, G $\underline{1}$.

Identification and Systematic Position :

(*i*) Leaves net-veined.
(*ii*) Flowers 4- or 5-merous. — *Dicotyledons.*
(*i*) Petals separate. — *Polypetalae.*
(*i*) Flowers regular or irregular, 1 or 2-sexual.
(*ii*) Petals distinct or united at the base, perigynous.
(*iii*) Stamens peri- or epigynous. — *Calyciflorae.*
(*i*) Woody or herbaceous with alternate, stipulate compound leaves.
(*ii*) Flowers perigynous, rarely hypogynous, with a disc lining the hypanthium.
(*iii*) Ovary, apocarpous reduced to 1 usually elongate, declinate carpel; marginal placentation; fruit a legume (pod). — *Leguminosae.*
(*i*) Bipinnate leaves.
(*ii*) Flowers arranged in dense heads or spikes; flowers small, regular 4-5 merous.
(*iii*) Stamens free diplostemonous or indefinite.
(*iv*) Fruit usually lomentum. — *Mimosaceae.*

Other important members of the family. *Acacia catechu* wild; **Khair, kattha** - bark astringent; Kattha is obtained from heart wood and used as masticatory and in medicine. *Albizia lebbeck* (Linn.) Benth. **Siris** - a good timber tree. *Xylia xylocarpa* (Roxb.) Taub., **jambu** - a timber tree.

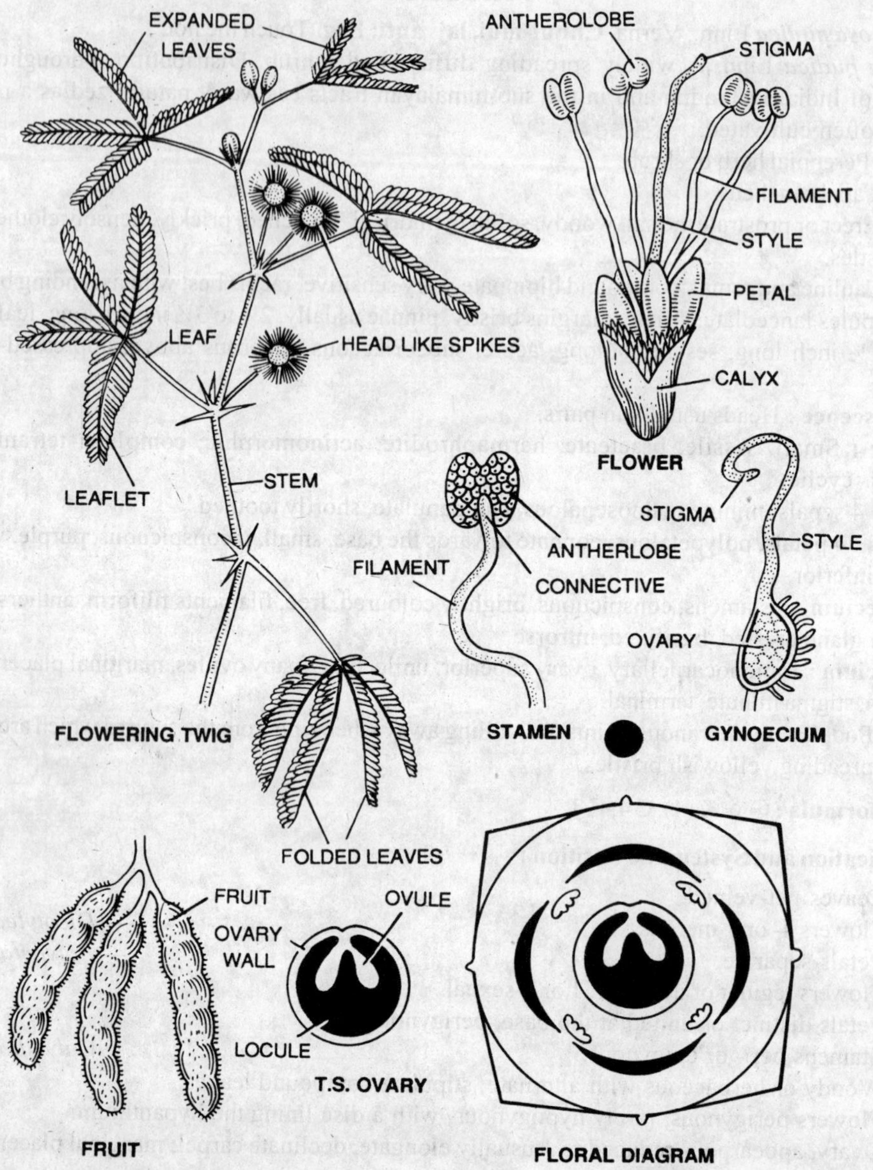

Fig. 9.39. Mimosaceae. *Mimosa pudica* Linn.; Eng., touch me not; Verna. **Chhui-mui, lajvanti.**

Economic value. Grown as an ornamental. The roots and leaves are prescribed in cases of piles and fistula. The juice of the leaves is also applied externally to the fistulous sores.

FAMILY-ROSACEAE (Rose family)

PRUNUS

1. ***Prunus persica*** (L.) Stokes; Verna. **Aru;** Eng. Peach.

Habit : Either shrubs or small trees, usually grown in the gardens for their delicious fruits.

Root : Tap and branched.

Stem : Erect, aerial, branched, woody, cylinderical and glabrous.

Leaf : Cauline and ramal, alternate, simple, stipulate, petiolate, or sub-sessile, entire or toothed, very frequently two glands present on the petiole. In *Prunus persica* the leaves are oblong lanceolate or oblong oblanceolate, 4 to 6 inches long, finely serrate, short petioles, fimbriate stipules, acute, unicostate reticulate.

Inflorescence : Cymose, flowers are solitary or in fascicles.

Flower : Bisexual (hermaphrodite), pedicellate (small or long pedicels), actinomorphic, regular perigynous, complete, pink, pentamerous, cyclic.

Calyx : Five sepals, gamosepalous, sepaloid, imbricate or deciduous in fruit, calyx-tube bell shaped, 5-lobed, inferior.

Corolla : 5 polypetalous (petals free), petals large, arranged on hypanthium, conspicuous, pink, inferior, imbricate aestivation.

Androecium : Stamens indefinite (15-60), perigynous, inserted on the hypanthium, anthers bi-celled, dorsifixed, reddish or brown dehiscence by longitudinal split, introrse, filaments free, bent in bud.

Gynoecium : One carpel (monocarpellary), ovary situated within the hypanthium (calyx tube), ovary unilocular with two pendulous ovules, marginal placentation, style terminal, stigma broad, capitate.

Fruit : Single seeded drupe, fleshy, enclosing an indehiscent or two valved furrowed stone.

Seeds : Exalbuminous, pendulous.

Generic charaters : Ripe carpels not enclosed within the calyx tube (hypanthium), carpels free; carpel one, fruit a drupe with a hard furrowed stone; shrubs or trees with simple leaves, calyx 5 lobed, petals large.

Floral formula : $\oplus$ ⚥ K (5), C 5, A $\propto$, G1—.

Identification and Systematic Position :

(*i*) Leaves net-veined.
(*ii*) Flowers 4- or 5-merous. — *Dicotyledons.*
(*i*) Petals separate. — *Polypetalae.*
(*i*) Flowers regular or irregular, 1 or 2-sexual.
(*ii*) Petals distinct or united at the base, perigynous.
(*iii*) Stamens peri- or epigynous. — *Calyciflorae.*
(*i*) Herbaceous or woody with simple or compound leaves often with adnate stipules.
(*ii*) Flowers regular, cyclic, perigynous to epigynous; stamens many to definite.
(*iii*) Ovary, apocarpous of 2 to many carpels; placentation axile or on ventral sutures of carpels.
(*iv*) Fruits achenes or follicles. — *Rosales.*
(*i*) Petals free, usually 5, rosaceous.
(*ii*) Indefinite stamens on the disc lining the hypanthium, often in curved or circinate in bud.
(*iii*) Ovary with 5-many free carpels (apocarpous).
(*iv*) Fruit-achenes, drupelets, a drupe or a pome. — *Rosaceae.*

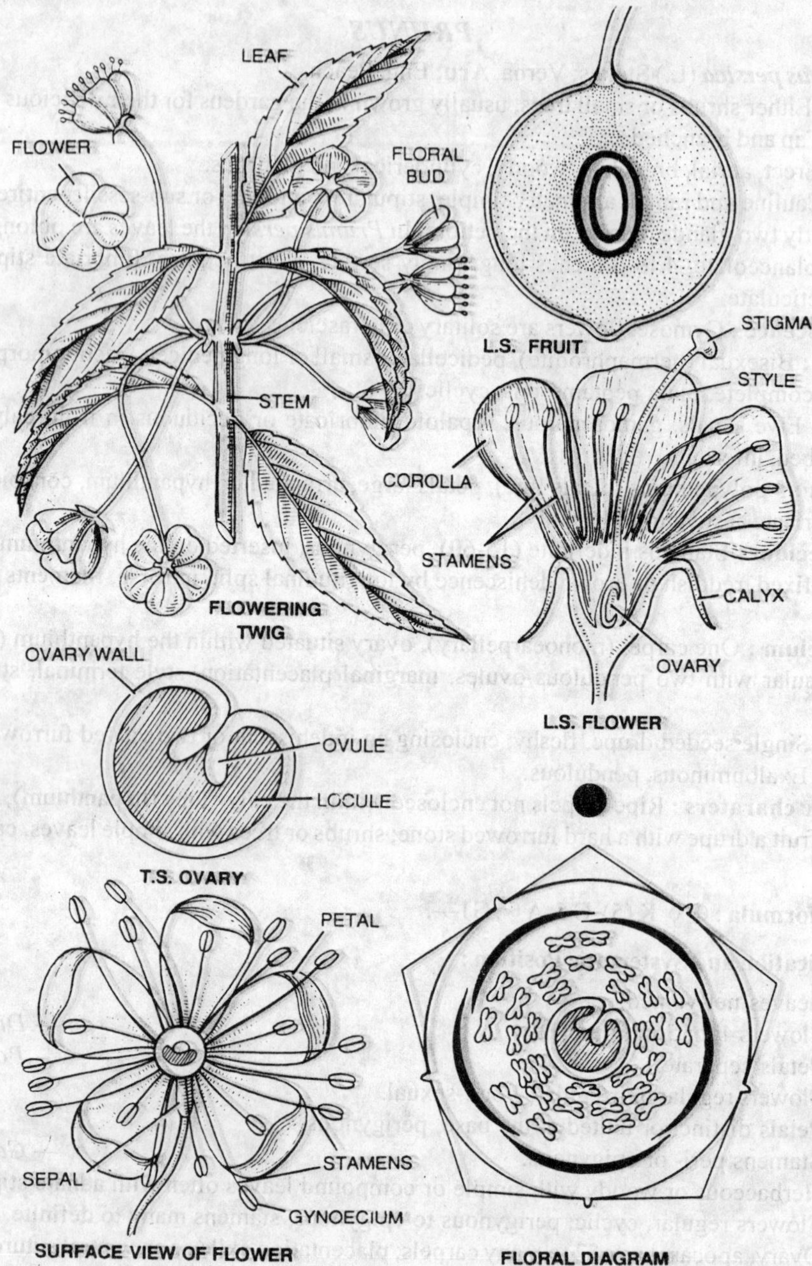

Fig. 9.40. Rosaceae. *Prunus persica.* (L). Stokes; Eng., peach; Verna., **aru.**

Economic value. The fruits are edible. They are the most popular fruit for canning. The oil, obtained from the seeds, is used for cooking and as an illuminant. Flowers are diuretic and purgative. Fruit is demulcent, antiscorbutic; considered to be useful as ascaricide.

MALUS

2. ***Malus sylvestris*** (Linn.) Mill.; Syn. *Pyrus malus* Linn.; Vrena. **Seb;** Eng. Apple.

Pyrus Linn. Trees or shrubs. Found chiefly in North temperate and mountain regions.

Habit : Small tree or large shrub.

Stem : Erect, aerial, woody, branched, cylinderical, solid.

Leaves : Cauline and ramal, simple or pinnate, deciduous, petiolate, stipulate (stipules deciduous), glabrous, acute, ovate, unicostate reticulate venation.

Inflorescence : Cymose, terminal cymes or corymbs.

Flower : Pedicellate, bracteate (bracts linear), bracteolate (two bracteoles), hermaphrodite, actinomorphic; complete, epigynous, pentamerous, cyclic.

Calyx : Five sepals, gamosepalous, calyx-tube obconical lobes erect or reflexed, persistent or deciduous, valvate.

Corolla : Five petals, polypetalous, quincuncially imbricate in bud.

Androecium : Indefinite stamens (20 or more), filaments long, connate at the base, anthers dorsifixed, introrse; dehisce longitudinally, dithecous.

Gynoecium : Two to five carpels, connate and adnate to calyx-tube, syncarpous, ovary inferior, 2-5 locular, axile placentation, styles 2-5, free or connate below, stigmas truncate; ovules 2 in each loculus.

Fruit : A pome, fleshy.

Floral formula : Br ⊕ ⚥ K (5), C 5, A ∞, G (2-5).

Identification and Systematic Position :

(*i*) Leaves net-veined.
(*ii*) Flowers 4- or 5-merous. — *Dicotyledons.*
(*i*) Petals separate. — *Polypetalae.*
(*i*) Flowers regular or irregular, 1 or 2-sexual.
(*ii*) Petals distinct or united at the base, perigynous.
(*iii*) Stamens peri- or epigynous. — *Calyciflorae.*
(*i*) Herbaceous or woody with simple or compound leaves often with adnate stipules.
(*ii*) Flowers regular, cyclic, perigynous to epigynous; stamens many to definite.
(*iii*) Ovary, apocarpous of 2 to many carpels; placentation axile or on ventral sutures of carpels.
(*iv*) Fruits achenes or follicles. — *Rosales.*
(*i*) Petals free, usually 5, rosaceous.
(*ii*) Indefinite stamens on the disc lining the hypanthium, often incurved or circinate in bud.
(*iii*) Ovary with 5-many free carpels (apocarpous).
(*iv*) Fruit-achenes, drupelets, a drupe or a pome. — *Rosaceae.*

Bentham & Hooker (1862)	*Engler & Prantl* (1931)	*Hutchinson* (1959)
Dicotyledons	Dicotyledoneae	Dicotyledones
Polypetalae	Archichlamydeae	Lignosae
Rosales	Rosales	Leguminales
Rosaceae	Rosaceae	Rosaceae.

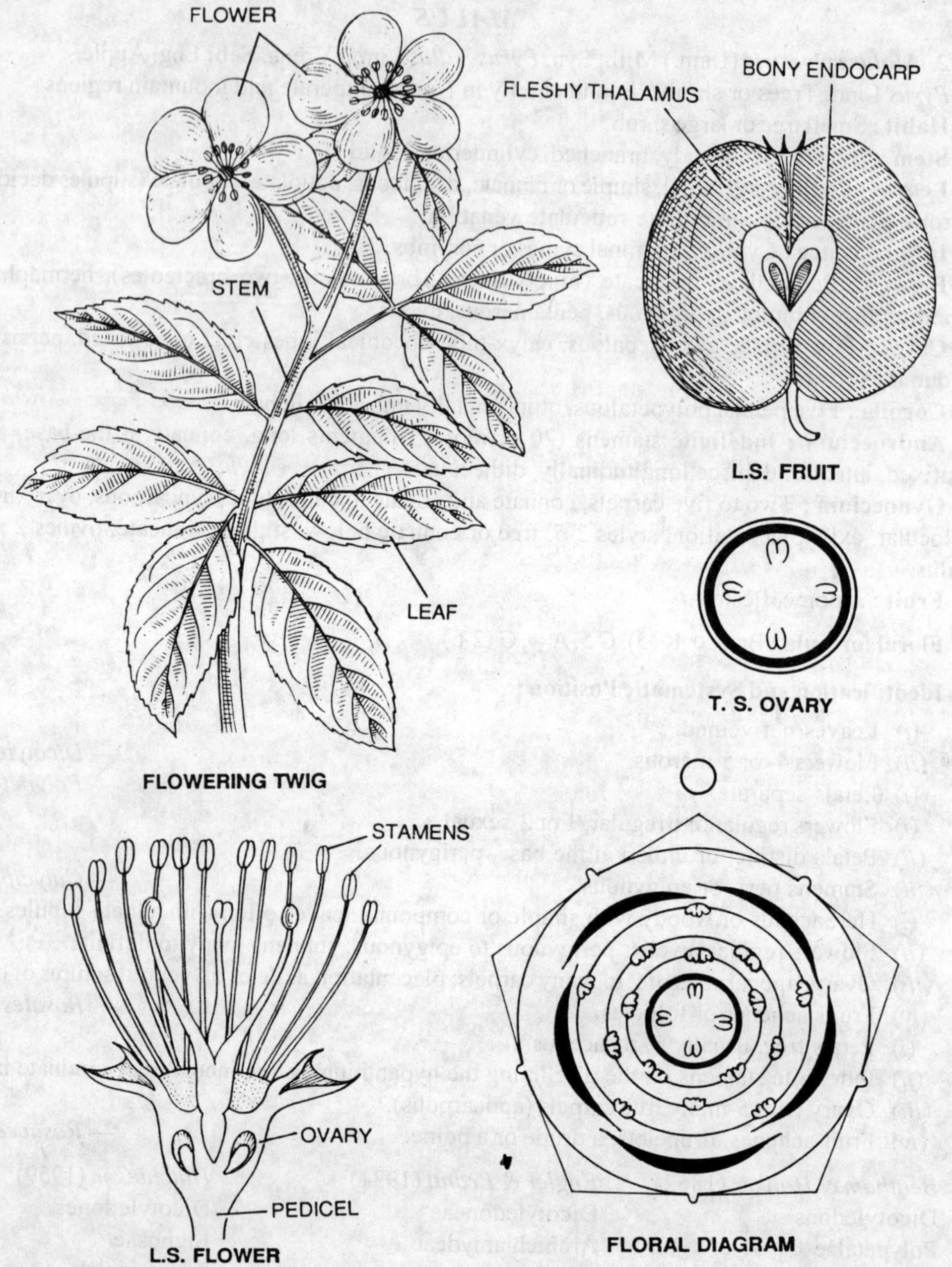

Fig. 9.41. Rosaceae. *Malus sylvestris* (L.) Mill.; Syn. *Pyrus malus* Linn.; Eng., apple; Verna., **seb.**

Economic value. Apples are valued mainly as dessert fruits. They are also canned and jams and jellies are made from them. Apples are rich in pectin and are used in diarrhoea. Apple *murabba* is regarded as a stimulant for the heart. Infusion of bark is given in intermittent fevers. Root is anthelmintic and refrigerant.

POTENTILLA

*3. **Potentilla supina*** Linn.

Potentilla Linn. Perennial herbs, rarely shrubs, species about 130, chiefly confined to the North temperate, Arctic and Alpine regions. Distribution : up to 8,500 feet on N.W. Himalayas and South to the Nilgiris. Also on river banks in North Indian plains.

Habit : Perennial herbs, rarely shrubs.

Stem : Erect or diffusely spreading, aerial, branched, woody or herbaceous, pubescent, cylinderical, solid.

Leaves : Cauline and ramal, compound, petiolate, stipulate (stipules adnate to the petiole), leaflets mostly serrate, reticulate venation.

Inflorescence : Cymose, solitary axillary or corymbose cymes.

Flower : Ebracteate, bracteolate, pedicellate, hermaphrodite, actinomorphic, complete, hypogynous, white or yellow rarely red, pentamerous and spirocyclic.

Epicalyx : Five bracteoles, rarely four bracteoles, alternating with sepals.

Calyx : Five sepals, rarely four sepals, persistent, valvate in bud.

Corolla : Five petals, rarely four petals, white, yellow or rarely red, polypetalous, valvate.

Androecium : Indefinite stamens, rarely few (5-10), polyandrons, filaments slender, anthers dithecous, basifixed, introrse.

Gynoecium : Many carpels (polycarpellary), on a small dry receptacle, ovary superior with single ovule, basal placentation, style persistent or deciduous, lateral, short, stigma minute.

Fruit : An etaerio of achenes.

Floral formula : ⊕ ⚥ K 5, C 5, A ∞, G $\underline{\infty}$.

Identification and Systematic Position :

(*i*) Leaves net-veined.
(*ii*) Flowers 4- or 5-merous. — *Dicotyledons.*

(*i*) Petals separate. — *Polypetalae.*

(*i*) Flowers regular or irregular, 1 or 2-sexual.
(*ii*) Petals distinct or united at the base, perigynous.
(*iii*) Stamens peri- or epigynous. — *Calyciflorae.*

(*i*) Herbaceous or woody with simple or compound leaves often with adnate stipules.
(*ii*) Flowers regular, cyclic, perigynous to epigynous; stamens many to definite.
(*iii*) Ovary, apocarpous of 2 to many carpels; placentation axile or on ventral sutures of carpels.
(*iv*) Fruits achenes or follicles. — *Rosales.*

(*i*) Petals free, usually 5, rosaceous.
(*ii*) Indefinite stamens on the disc lining the hypanthium, often incurved or circinate in bud.
(*iii*) Ovary with 5-many free carpels (apocarpous).
(*iv*) Fruit-achenes, drupelets, a drupe or a pome. — *Rosaceae.*

Other important members of the family. *Prunus amygdalus* Batsch, **Badam;** *P. armeniaca* Linn., **Khubani;** *P. domestica* Linn. **Alu bokhara;** *Pyrus communis* Linn., **Nakh;** *Rubus ellipticus* Smith, **Lalanchu;** *R. fruticosus,* **Vilaiti anchu;** *Eriobotrya japonica* (Thunb). Lindl., **Lokat.** Temperate or hill fruits belong to this family.

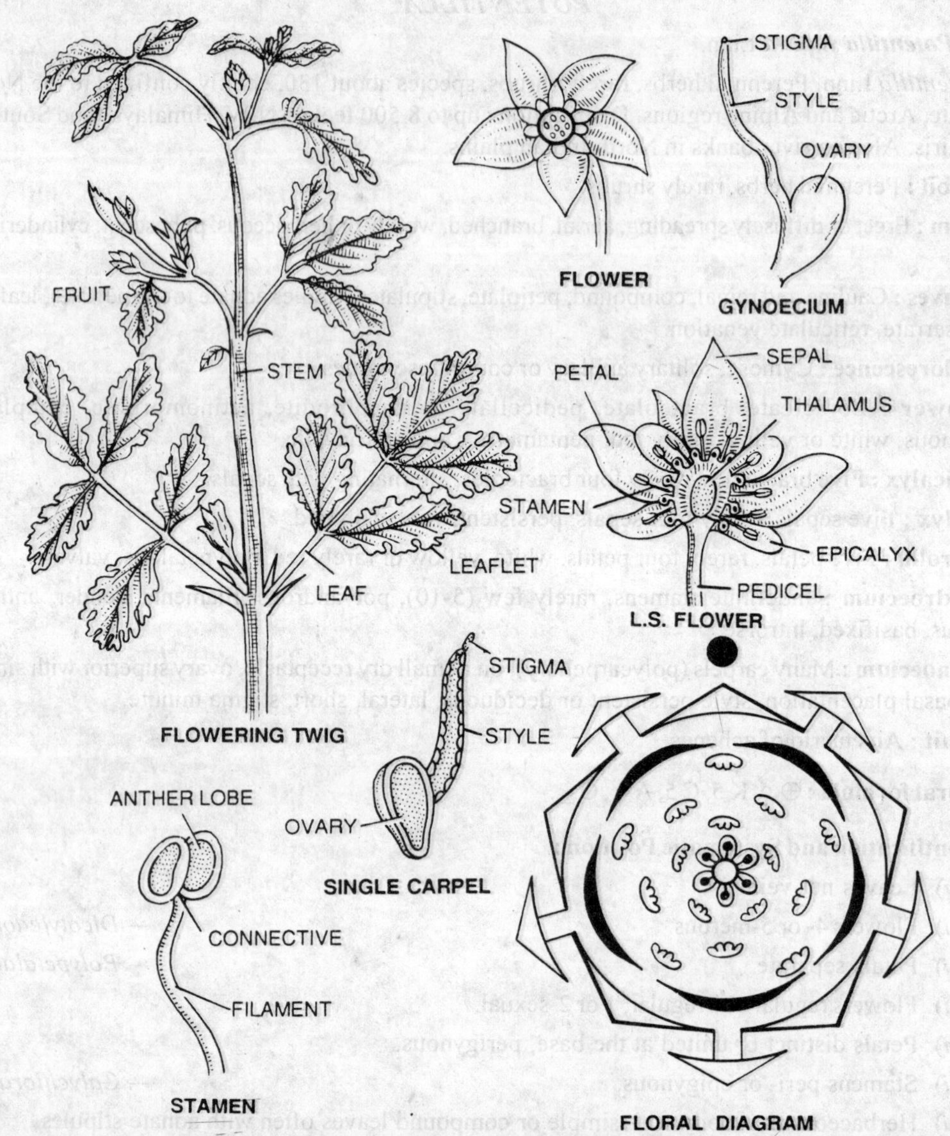

Fig. 9.42. Rosaceae. *Potentilla supina* Linn.

Economic value. The root is employed as a febrifuge. It is rich in tannin, and is probably astringent and tonic.

ROSA

4. *Rosa indica* Linn. Eng., Rose; Verna. **Gulab, Jangli Gulab.**

Rosa Linn. Erect, sarmentose or climbing shrubs, usually prickly. Species widely diffused over the temperate regions of the N. hemisphere, rarely extending to the tropics, except in mountain districts.

Habit : Erect or climbing perennial shrubs, usually prickly.

Root : Tap, branched.

Stem : Erect, aerial, branched, prickly, woody, cylinderical, green.

Leaf : Cauline and ramal, compound, imparipinnate, petiolate, stipulate (stipules adnate to the petiole), leaflets serrate, ovate, acute, unicostate reticulate venation.

Inflorescence : Cymose, flowers terminal, solitary.

Flower : Pedicellate, ebracteate (bracts rarely present), hermaphrodite, actinomorphic, complete, perigynous, white, yellow, red or pink, pentamerous, cyclic, inferior.

Calyx : Five sepals, gamosepalous, narrowly lanceolate, inferior, quincuncial aestivation, calyx-tube persistent, globose ovoid or pitcher shaped.

Corolla : Five to indefinite petals, polypetalous, large, showy, scented, quincuncial or imbricate aestivation in bud, rosaceous.

Androecium : Stamens many, inserted on the disk, polyandrous, petals are modified into stamens, anthers bicelled, introrse, basifixed.

Gynoecium : Many carpels, apocarpous, found in the bottom of calyx-tube, styles subterminal, free or connate above, stigma thickened, ovule one, basal placentation.

Fruit : An etaerio of achenes.

Floral formula : Br. ⊕ ⚥ K (5), C 5, A ∝, G∝.

Identification and Systematic Position :

(*i*) Leaves net-veined.

(*ii*) Flowers 4- or 5-merous. — *Dicotyledons.*

(*i*) Petals separate. — *Polypetalae.*

(*i*) Flowers regular or irregular, 1 or 2-sexual.

(*ii*) Petals distinct or united at the base, perigynous.

(*iii*) Stamens peri- or epigynous. — *Calyciflorae.*

(*i*) Herbaceous or woody with simple or compound leaves often with adnate stipules.

(*ii*) Flowers regular, cyclic, perigynous to epigynous; stamens many to definite.

(*iii*) Ovary, apocarpous of 2 to many carpels; placentation axile or on ventral sutures of carpels.

(*iv*) Fruits achenes or follicles. — *Rosales.*

(*i*) Petals free, usually 5, rosaceous.

(*ii*) Indefinite stamens on the disc lining the hypanthium, often incurved or circinate in bud.

(*iii*) Ovary with 5-many free carpels (apocarpous).

(*iv*) Fruit-achenes, drupelets, a drupe or a pome. — *Rosaceae.*

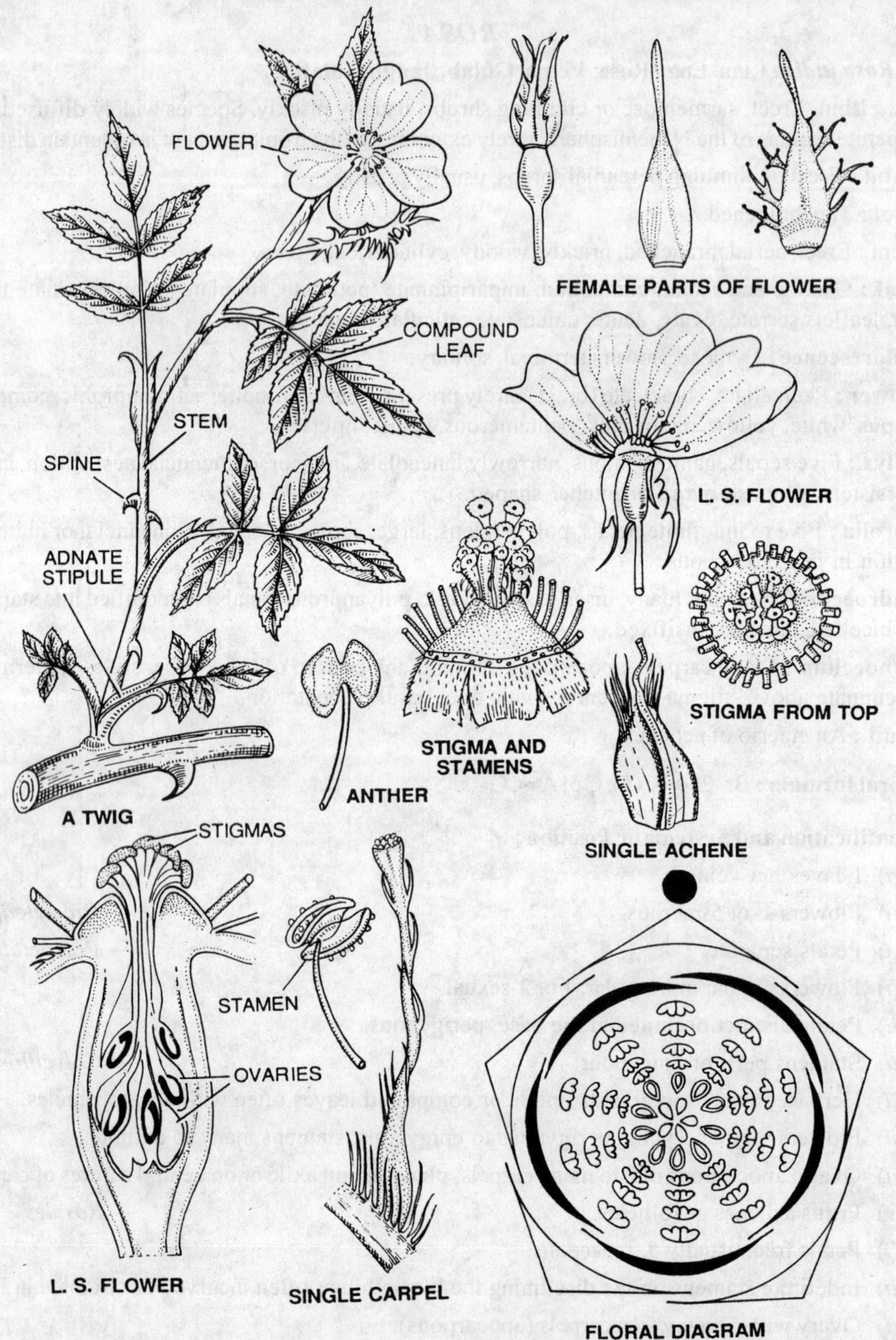

Fig. 9.43. Rosaceae. *Rosa indica* L.; Eng., rose; Verna. **Gulab, jangli gulab.**

Economic value. The rose flowers are a source of an essential oil, known as *oil of roses.* The other rose products are : rose water, *attar, gulkand* and *pankhuri.* Gulkand is a good tonic and laxative. The dried rose petals are known as *Pankhuri,* which is used for preparing cold drinks.

FAMILY—MYRTACEAE (Myrtle family)

CALLISTEMON

1. Callistemon citrinus (Curtis) Skeels; Eng. Bottle-brush tree; Verna. **Botal brush.**

Habit : A small or large tree.

Root : Tap, branched.

Stem : Erect, aerial, woody, cylinderical, branched, hairy, solid.

Leaf : Simple, alternate at 2/5, cauline and ramal, petiolate, petiole very short, lanceolate, entire, acute apex, unicostate reticulate venation, inframarginal veins, gland dotted, coriaceous.

Inflorescence : Spike.

Flower : Sessile, bracteate, bracts leafy, green, bracteolate, two bracteoles, hermaphrodite, actinomorphic, complete, epigynous, pentamerous, cyclic, red.

Calyx : 5, gamosepalous, green, superior, imbricate aestivation.

Corolla : 5, polypetalous, superior, whitish green, quincuncial aestivation.

Androecium : Indefinite stamens, monadelphous, scarlet red, filaments very long, slightly connate at the base, anthers dorsifixed, bicelled, dark brown, dehisce longitudinally, introrse.

Gynoecium : The number of carpels varies from 2-4 even in the different flowers of the same spike, syncarpous, ovary inferior, 3 or 4 chambered according to the number of carpels, axile placentation, many ovules in each locule, style long, stigma capitate.

Floral formula : Br Brl •|• ⊕ ⚥ K (5), C 5, A $\propto$, G (2-4).

Identification and Systematic Position :

(*i*) Leaves net-veined.
(*ii*) Flowers 4- or 5-merous. — *Dicotyledons.*
(*i*) Petals separate. — *Polypetalae.*
(*i*) Flowers regular or irregular, 1 or 2-sexual.
(*ii*) Petals distinct or united at the base, perigynous.
(*iii*) Stamens peri- or epigynous. — *Calyciflorae.*
(*i*) Usually woody; leaves simple entire, usually opposite or whorled, frequently gland dotted, exstipulate.
(*ii*) Flowers 4-5 merous and diplostemonous or polystemonous; gynoecium syncarpous 2-many celled with axile placentation; ovary inferior. — *Myrtales*
(*i*) Tree or shrubs with opposite (rarely alternate) simple entire leaves, supplied with lysigenous oil glands appearing as translucent dots in the leaves.
(*ii*) Flowers epigynous, with numerous stamens often in 4-5 bundles.
(*iii*) Ovary 2-many celled with axile placentation; fruit berry or drupe. — *Myrtaceae.*

Bentham & Hooker (1862)	*Engler & Prantl* (1931)	*Hutchinson* (1959)
Dicotyledons	Dicotyledoneae	Dicotyledones
Polypetalae	Archichlamydeae	Lignosae
Myrtales	Myrtiflorae	Myrtales
Myrtaceae	Myrtaceae	Myrtaceae

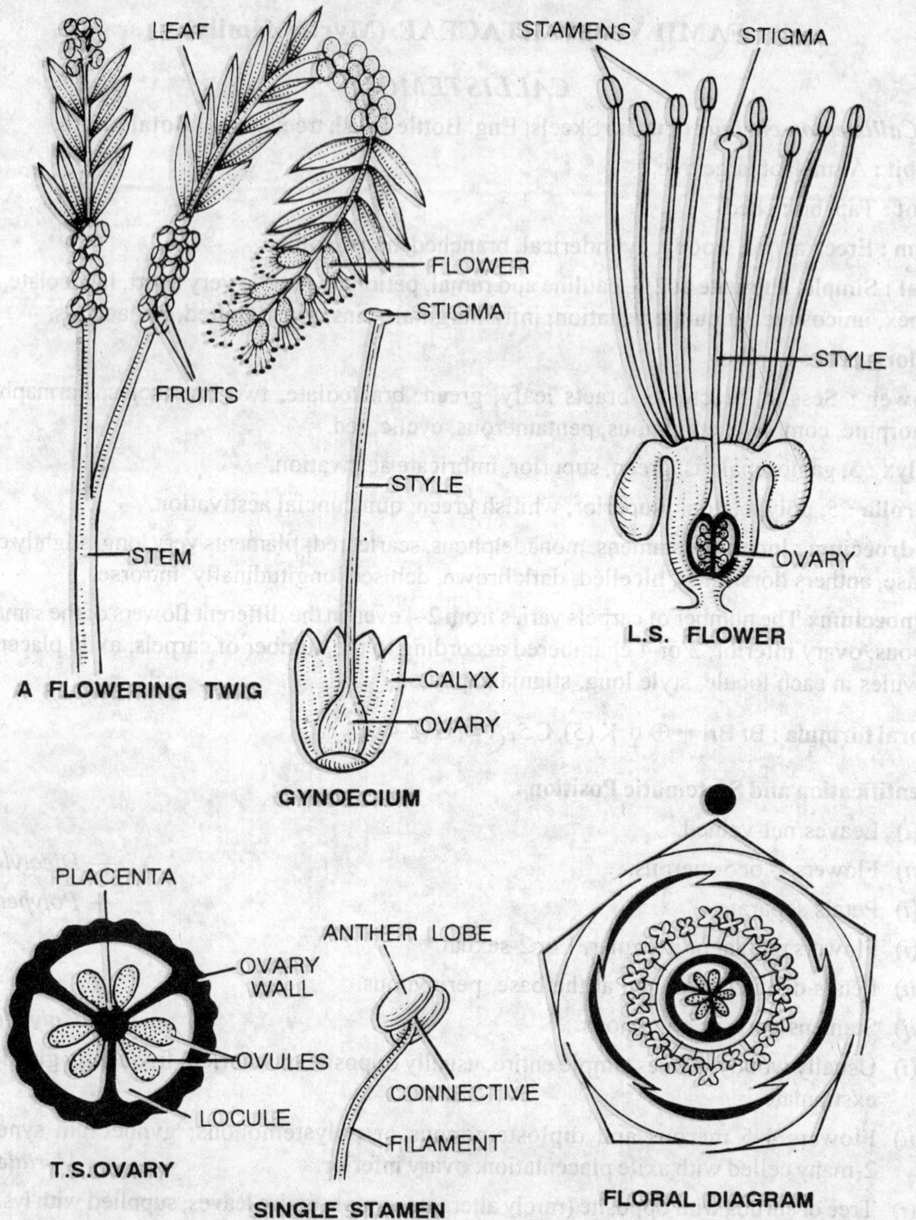

Fig. 9.44. Myrtaceae. *Callistemon citrinus* (Curtis) Skeels.; Eng., bottle brush tree; Verna., **botal brush.**

Economic value. Grown as an ornamental avenue tree.

PSIDIUM

2. ***Psidium guajava*** Linn.; Verna. **Amrood;** Eng. Guava.

Habit : Medium sized tree with whitish bark.

Root : Tap, branched.

Stem : Erect, aerial, woody, branched, cylinderical, solid, glabrous, white or brown.

Leaves : Simple, cauline, alternate, petiolate, exstipulate, gland dotted, aromatic, entire, glaucous, apex ovate, unicostate reticulate venation.

Inflorescence : Cymose, solitary axillary.

Flower : Pedicellate, bracteate, complete, hermaphrodite, actinomorphic, epigynous, pentamerous, cyclic, white.

Calyx : 5 sepals, gamosepalous, reduced, fused.

Corolla : 5 petals, gamopetalous, forming a corolla cap covered by calyx cap, the so formed calyptra falls off when flower opens, superior.

Androecium : Stamens indefinite, polyandrous, attached on the rim of calyx cap, folded inwards in bud condition, anthers dorsifixed, versatile, bicelled, small, dehisce longitudinally.

Gynoecium : Penta-carpellary, syncarpous, ovary_inferior, pentalocular, style single, stigma minute, terminal, axile placentation

Fruit : Berry.

Floral formula : Br ⊕ ⚥ K (5), C 5, A ∝, G (5).

Identification and Systematic Position :

(*i*) Leaves net-veined.
(*ii*) Flowers 4- or 5-merous. — *Dicotyledons.*
(*i*) Petals separate. — *Polypetalae.*
(*i*) Flowers regular or irregular, 1 or 2-sexual.
(*ii*) Petals distinct or united at the base, perigynous.
(*iii*) Stamens peri- or epigynous. — *Calyciflorae.*
(*i*) Usually woody; leaves simple entire, usually opposite or whorled, frequently gland dotted, exstipulate.
(*ii*) Flowers 4-5 merous and diplostemonous or polystemonous; gynoecium syncarpous 2-many celled with axile placentation; ovary inferior. — *Myrtales*
(*i*) Tree or shrubs with opposite (rarely alternate) simple entire leaves, supplied with lysigenous oil glands appearing as translucent dots in the leaves.
(*ii*) Flowers epigynous, with numerous stamens often in 4-5 bundles.
(*iii*) Ovary 2-many celled with axile placentation; fruit berry or drupe. — *Myrtaceae.*

Other important members of the family. *Syzygium aromaticum* (Linn). Merr. & Perry, **Laung** - dried flower buds are used as spice, and are also used medicinally as stimulant, carminative and in flatulence; *S. cumini* (Linn.) Skeels, **Jamun** - fruits edible, vinegar made from fruit juice is used as stomachic, carminative and diuretic.

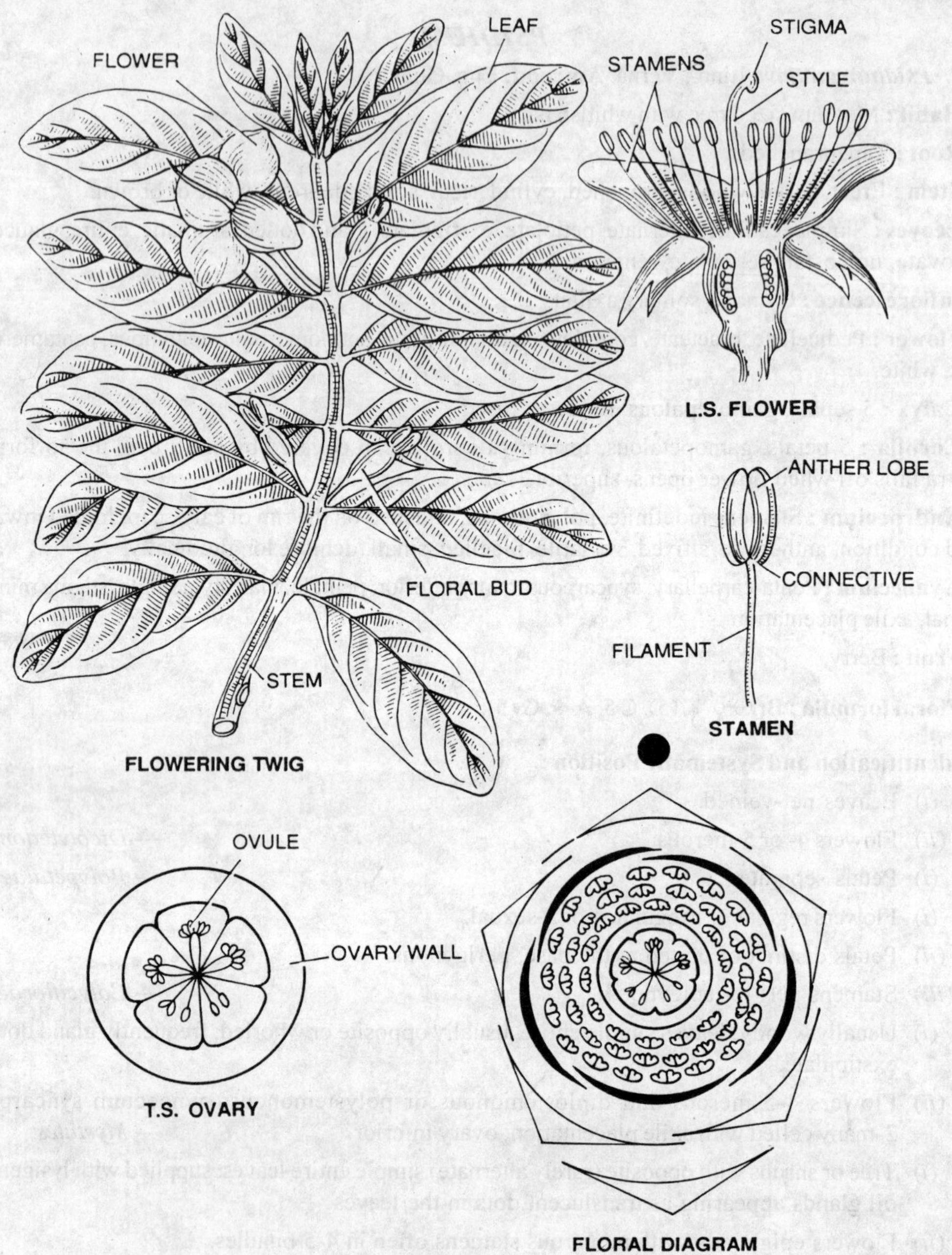

Fig. 9.45. Myrtaceae. *Psidium guajava* Linn.; Eng., guava; Verna., **amrood.**

Economic value. The fruits are edible. It is aromatic, sweet, juicy and highly flavoured. It contains acid, sugar and pectin. It is one of the richest sources of vitamins A, B, C and of ascorbic acid. It is commonly used for making jams, jellies and pastes. Bark of root is astringent and used in diarrhoea of children, fruit is laxative. Leaves are astringent and used for bowels and for wounds and ulcers.

EUCALYPTUS

*3. **Eucalyptus citriodora*** Hook.; Eng. Lemon-secented gum, Verna. **Safeda.**

Habit : A large tree with whitish bark.

Root : Tap, branched.

Stem : Erect, aerial woody, branched, cylinderical, solid, glabrous, white.

Leaf : Cauline and ramal, simple, alternate, petiolate, exstipulate, falcate, gland dotted, aromatic, entire, glaucous, acute, unicostate reticulate.

Inflorescence : Cymose, umbellate clustered cyme.

Flower : Ebracteate, pedicellate, actinomorphic, hermaphrodite, pentamerous, complete, epigynous, cyclic, regular.

Calyx : 5 sepals, gamosepalous, reduced, fused forming a cap-like structure on the corolla, superior.

Corolla : 5 petals, gamopetalous, forming a corolla cap covered by calyx cap, the so formed calyptra falls off when flower opens, superior.

Androecium : Stamens indefinite, polyandrous, attached on the rim of calyx cap, folded inwards in bud condition, anthers dorsifixed, dithecous, small, introrse.

Gynoecium : 3 carpels, syncarpous, ovary trilocular, inferior, style single, stigma minute, terminal, axile placentation, many ovules in each locule, ovary wall gland-dotted.

Fruit : A loculicidal capsule.

Floral formula : ⊕ ⚥ K (5), C (5), A ∝, G (3).

Identification and Systematic Position :

(*i*) Leaves net-veined.
(*ii*) Flowers 4- or 5-merous. — *Dicotyledons.*
(*i*) Petals separate. — *Polypetalae.*
(*i*) Flowers regular or irregular, 1 or 2-sexual.
(*ii*) Petals distinct or united at the base, perigynous.
(*iii*) Stamens peri- or epigynous. — *Calyciflorae.*
(*i*) Usually woody; leaves simple entire, usually opposite or whorled, frequently gland dotted, exstipulate.
(*ii*) Flowers 4-5 merous and diplostemonous or polystemonous; gynoecium syncarpous 2-many celled with axile placentation; ovary inferior. — *Myrtales*
(*i*) Tree or shrubs with opposite (rarely alternate) simple entire leaves, supplied with lysigenous oil glands appearing as translucent dots in the leaves.
(*ii*) Flowers epigynous, with numerous stamens often in 4-5 bundles.
(*iii*) Ovary 2-many celled with axile placentation; fruit berry or drupe. — *Myrtaceae.*

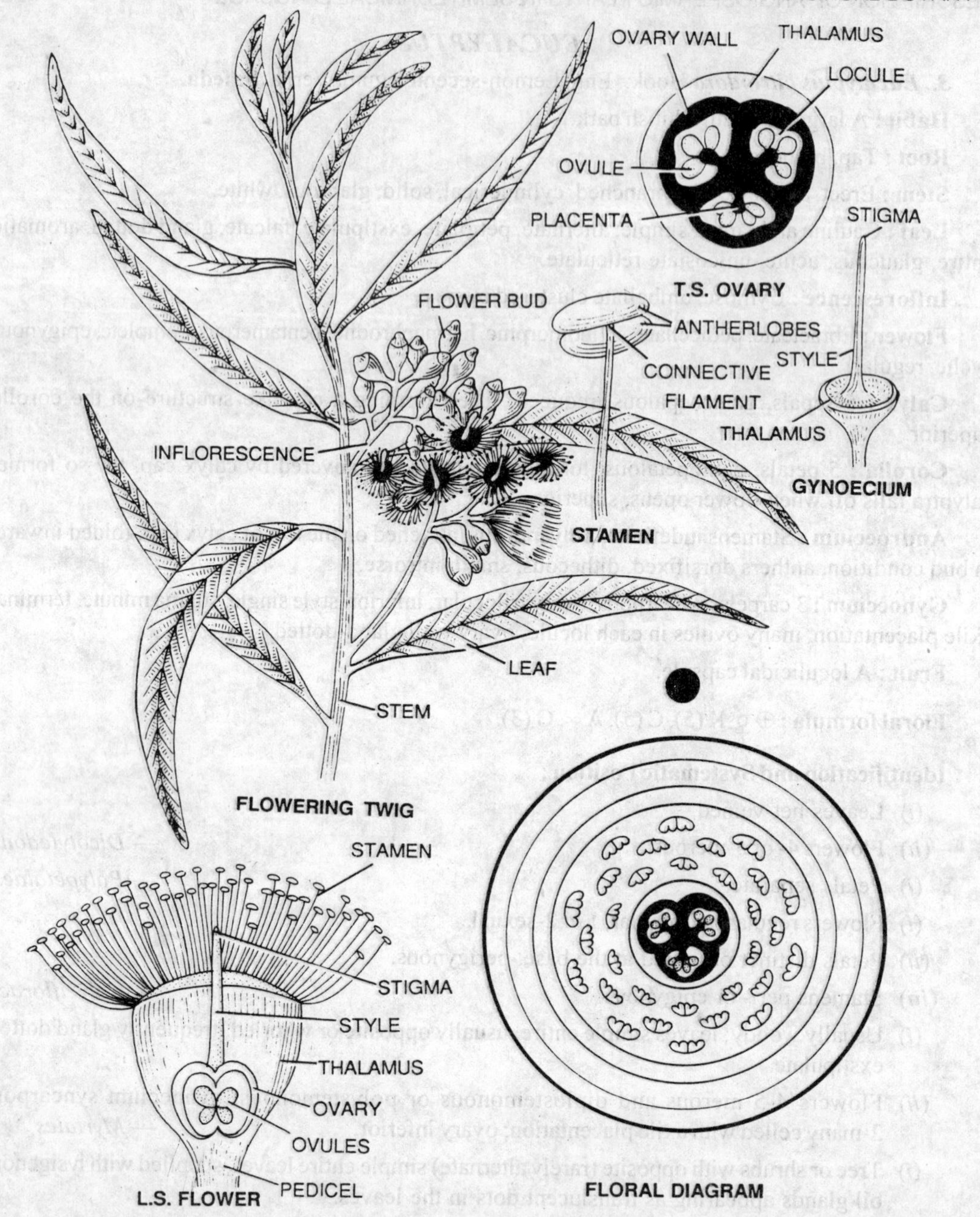

Fig. 9.46. Myrtaceae. *Eucalyptus citriodora* Hook.; Eng., lemon-scented gum; Verna., **Safeda.**

Economic value. The leaves yield an essential oil which is used medicinally. The wood is used for making paper pulp.

FAMILY—CUCURBITACEAE (Gourd family)

CITRULLUS

1. ***Citrullus vulgaris*** Schrad. ex Eckl. & Zeyh; Verna. **Tarbooz;** Eng. Water melon.

Citrullus Linn. Large climbing herbs, annual or perennial, hispid or hairy. Cultivated throughout India.

Habit : Large climbing herbs, annual or perennial, hispid or hairy.

Leaves : Cauline and ramal, petiolate, cordate, ovate, 5-angular or lobed, 2 to 4 fid tendril, multicostate reticulate venation, coriaceous.

Flowers : Bracteate, pedicellate, large, yellow, solitary, monoecious, unisexual, pentamerous, epigynous (female flower), cyclic.

Male flower : Staminate flowers (male) generally long pedicellate; calyx tube campanulate, 5-lobed, linear or foliaceous; corolla gamopetalous, campanulate, 5-lobed hardly half way down, stamens apparently 3 in number, inserted on the calyx tube, filaments free, anthers connate, linear and united, one 1-celled, two 2-celled, cells conduplicate, ovary rudimentary.

Female flower : Pistillate flowers (female) are short peduncled; calyx and corolla as in male; ovary oblong; 1-celled with 3 to 5 or many ovuled placentae; style short and thick with 3 to 5 stigmas; large epigynous cushion shaped 5-lobed disc.

Fruit : A large pepo.

Seeds : Ovoid or oblong flattened smooth, margin present or absent.

Generic characters : Fruit a pepo with hard firm rind, indehiscent; corolla campanulate (bell-shaped), 5-lobed to, or just below the middle; anthers connate.

Floral formula :

Male : ⊕ ⚥ K (5), C (5), A (2) + (2) + 1, G 0.

Female : ⊕ ⚥ K (5), C (5), A 0, G (3).

Identification and Systematic Position :

(*i*) Leaves net-veined.

(*ii*) Flowers 4- or 5-merous. — *Dicotyledons.*

(*i*) Petals separate. — *Polypetalae.*

(*i*) Flowers regular or irregular, 1 or 2-sexual.

(*ii*) Petals distinct or united at the base, perigynous.

(*iii*) Stamens peri- or epigynous. — *Calyciflorae.*

(*i*) Climbing by means of tendrils.

(*ii*) Ovary syncarpous, tricarpellary, inferior, unilocular with parietal placentation. — *Passiflorales.*

(*i*) Climbing by tendrils; leaves simple, palmately lobed; venation palmate.

(*ii*) Flowers monoecious or dioecious; calyx and corolla inserted on elongate hypanthium.

(*iii*) Stamens 5, 2 pairs connate; anthers sigmoid, cells usually conduplicate.

(*iv*) Fruit a berry (pepo). — *Cucurbitaceae.*

Bentham & Hooker (1862)	*Engler & Prantl* (1931)	*Hutchinson* (1959)
Dicotyledons	Dicotyledoneae	Dicotyledones
Polypetalae	Sympetalae	Lignosae
Passiflorales	Cucurbitales	Cucurbitales
Cucurbitaceae	Cucurbitaceae	Cucurbitaceae

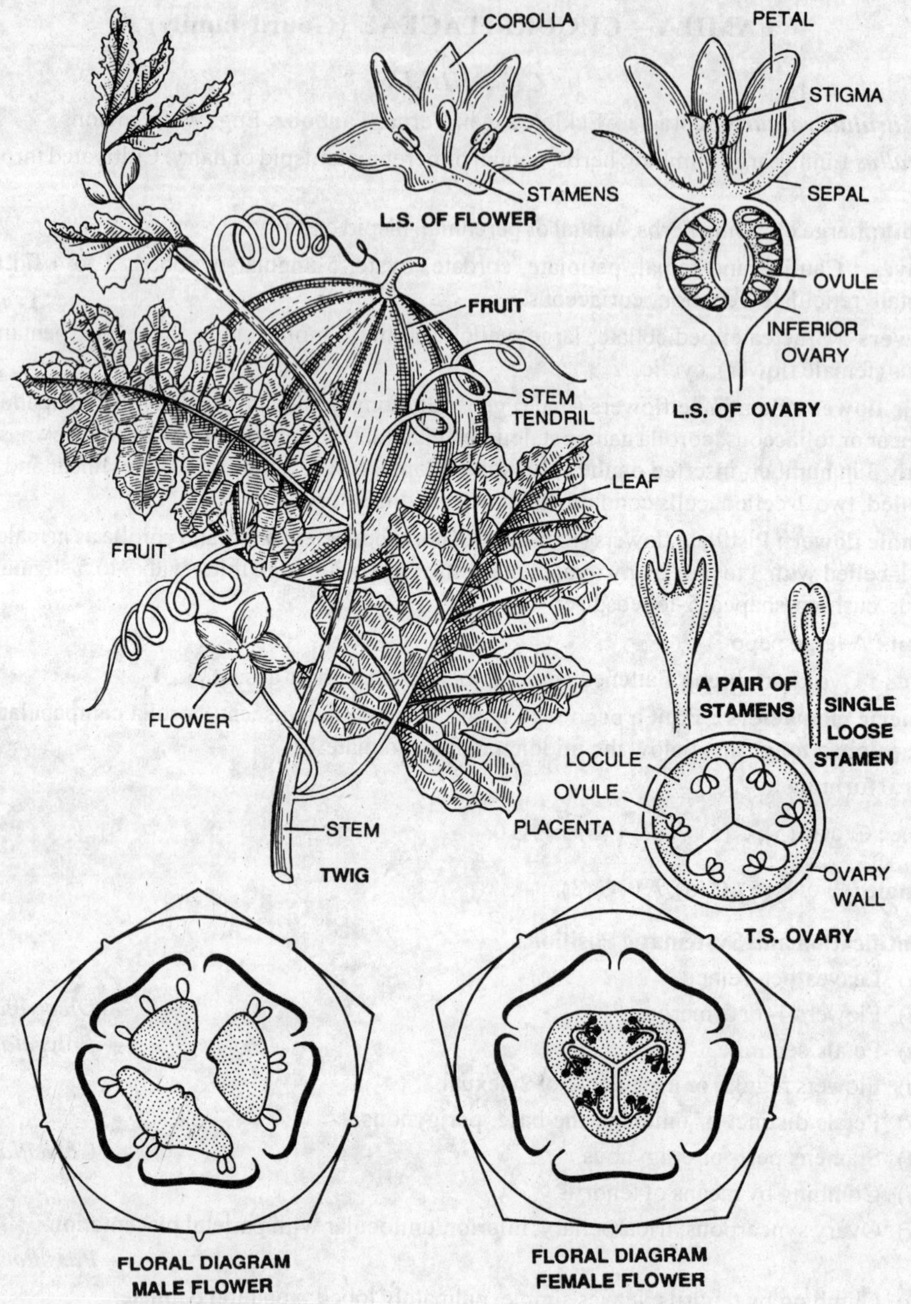

Fig. 9.47. Cucurbitaceae. *Citrullus vulgaris* Schr. ex. Eckl. & Zeyh.; Eng., water melon; Verna. **Tarbooz.**

Economic value. The red pulp of the fruit is eaten. The white solid flesh of the fruit is used for making jams, jellies and preserves, Fruit is cooling and diuretic. Seeds are cooling, aphrodisiac, tonic and diuretic.

COCCINIA

2. ***Coccinia indica*** W. & A.; Verna. **Kandoori;** Eng. Kovai fruit.

Habit : Usually climbing herbs, annual, wild.

Root : Tap, branched.

Stem : Prostrate, weak, aerial, herbaceous, climbing with unbranched tendrils, tendrils leaf opposed, branched, pubescent or nearly glabrous, sap present, usually angular, green, solid.

Leaves : Cauline and ramal, alternate, exstipulate, simple, large, cordate, denticulate, acute, petiolate (long petiole), multicostate reticulate, 4-7 lobed, nearly glabrous to slightly scabrid, coriaceous.

Inflorescence : Solitary axilary, monoecious.

Male flower (staminate flower) : Pedicellate, actinomorphic, regular, unisexual, incomplete, pentamerous, cyclic.

Calyx : Five sepals, gamospepalous, campanulate, lobes spreading, superior, valvate, acute.

Corolla : Petals five, free but united below, spreading, obovate or obcordate, yellow or white, superior, valvate.

Androecium : Stamens three, rarely five, filaments three or 5, free or connate, anthers extrorse, one 1-celled and the remaining two 2-celled, anther cells sigmoid, often the margin of the broad connective, stamens inserted on the mouth of the calyx.

Gynoecium : Absent.

Female flower (pistillate flower) : Pedicellate, actinomorphic, regular, unisexexual, epigynous, incomplete, pentamerous, cyclic.

Calyx : Calyx tube produced shortly above the ovary, 5 sepals, gamosepalous, valvate.

Corolla : As in male flower.

Androecium : Absent, sometimes staminodes present.

Gynoecium : Three carpels (tricarpellary), syncarpous; ovary inferior, elongated angled or grooved, unilocular; placentation parietal, style cylindric; ovules many; stigma, three, lobed.

Fruit : Berry, pepo, red on maturity.

Floral formula :

Male : ⊕ ⚥ K (5), C (5), A 3, G 0.

Female : ⊕ ⚥ K (5), C (5), A 0, G (3).

Identification and Systematic Position :

(*i*) Leaves net-veined.
(*ii*) Flowers 4- or 5-merous. — *Dicotyledons.*

(*i*) Petals separate. — *Polypetalae.*

(*i*) Flowers regular or irregular, 1 or 2-sexual.
(*ii*) Petals distinct or united at the base, perigynous.
(*iii*) Stamens peri- or epigynous. — *Calyciflorae.*

(*i*) Climbing by means of tendrils.
(*ii*) Ovary syncarpous, tricarpellary, inferior, unilocular with parietal placentation. — *Passiflorales.*

(*i*) Climbing by tendrils; leaves simple, palmately lobed; venation palmate.
(*ii*) Flowers monoecious or dioecious; calyx and corolla inserted on elongate hypanthium.
(*iii*) Stamens 5, 2 pairs connate; anthers sigmoid, cells usually conduplicate.
(*iv*) Fruit a berry (pepo). — *Cucurbitaceae.*

Other important members of the family. *Cucurbita maxima* Duch., **Sitaphal;** *C. pepo* Linn., **Safed Kaddu, Kumra;** *Cucumis melo* Linn., **Kharbuza;** *Momordica charantia* Linn., **Karela;** *Lagenaria siceraria* (Mol.) Standl., **Lauki;** all are used as vegetable.

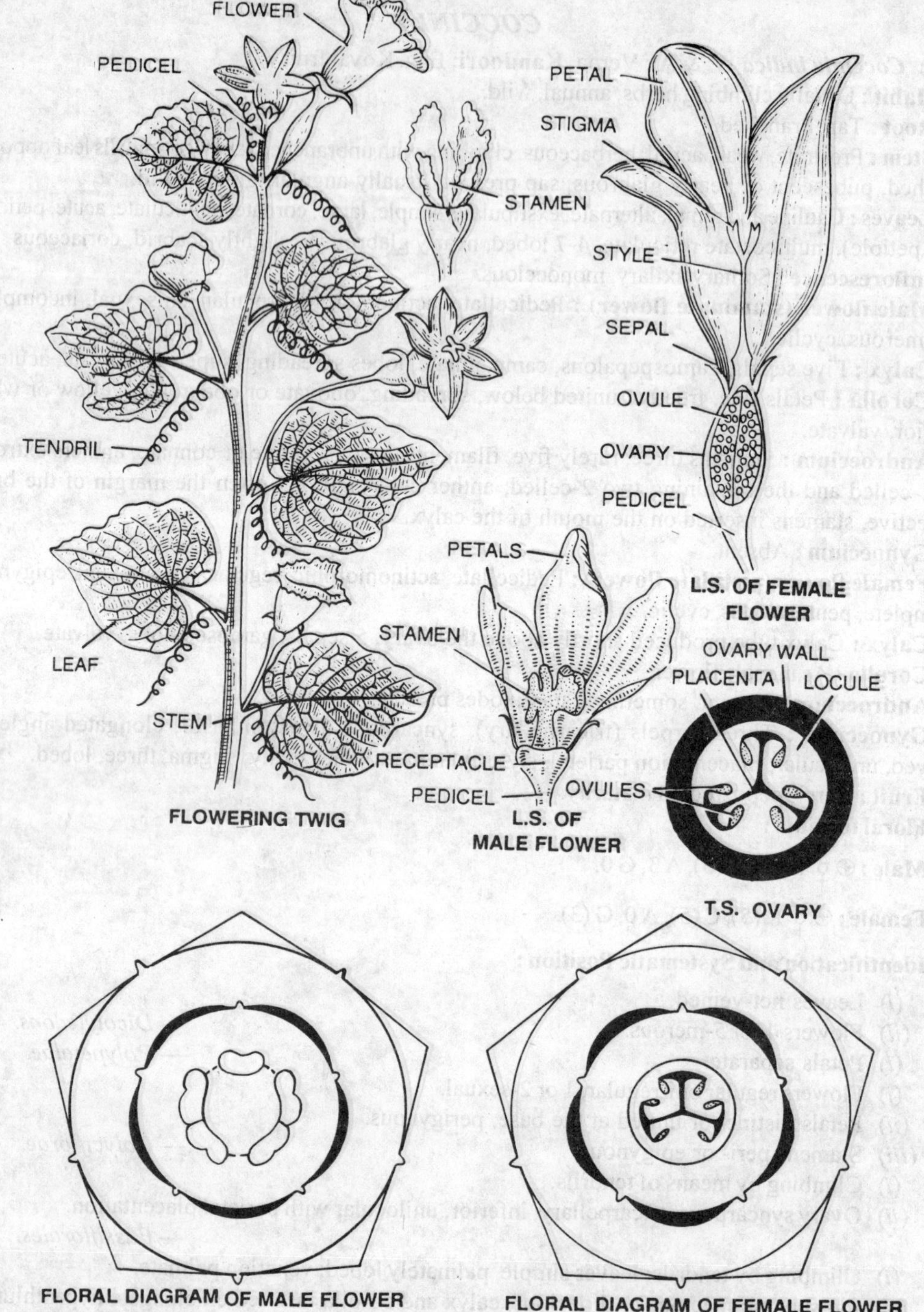

Fig. 9.48. Cucurbitaceae. *Coccinia indica* W & A.; Eng. Kovai fruit; Verna. **Kandoori.**

Economic value. The fruits are used as vegetable. The root yields a gum, which is very astringent. The bark of the root is a good cathartic. The green fruit is chewed to cure sores on the tongue.

LUFFA

3. ***Luffa cylindrica*** Linn.; Syn. *L. aegyptiaca* Mill; Eng. Vegetable sponge; Verna. **Ghia tori.**

Habit : Climbing herb, annual, cultivated as vegetable.

Root : Tap, branched.

Stem : Prostrate, aerial, weak, herbaceous, climbing with 2-5 fid tendrils, pubescent or nearly glabrous, sap present, angular, branched, green.

Leaf : Cauline and ramal, simple, large, cordate, petiolate, long petiole, 5-7 lobed, acute, nearly glabrous to slightly scabrid, multicostate reticulate.

Inflorescence : Male flowers arranged in racemes or in clusters on the top of peduncles; female flowers are solitary; monoecious.

Male flower (staminate flower) : Bracteate, pedicellate, actinomorphic, regular, unisexual, incomplete, pentamerous, cyclic.

Calyx : 5 sepals, gamosepalous, campanulate, lobes spreading, valvate, superior.

Corolla : 5 petals, polypetalous, united below, spreading, obovate or obcordate, yellow quincuncial aestivation.

Androecium : Stamens 3, rarely five, filaments 3 or 5, free or connate, anthers extrorse, one 1-celled and the remaining two 2-celled, anther cells sigmoid, margin of the connective broad, stamens inserted on the mouth of the calyx.

Gynoecium : Absent.

Floral formula : Br. ⊕ ⚥ K (5), C 5, A 3, G 0.

Female flower (pistillate flower) : Bracteate, pedicellate, actinomorphic, regular, unisexual, incomplete, epigynous, pentamerous, cyclic.

Calyx : 5 sepals, gamosepalous, valvate, calyx tube produced shortly above the ovary.

Corolla : 5 petals, polypetalous, imbricate, yellow, superior.

Androecium : Absent.

Gynoecium : 3 carpels (tricarpellary), syncarpous; ovary inferior, elongated, angled or grooved, unilocular, parietal placentation; style cylindric; stigma three-lobed; ovules many.

Fruit : Pepo, elongated, the rind becomes dry and paper like on maturity.

Floral formula : Br ⊕ ⚥ K (5), C 5, A 0, G (3).

Identification and Systematic Position :

(*i*) Leaves net-veined.
(*ii*) Flowers 4- or 5-merous. — *Dicotyledons.*
(*i*) Petals separate. — *Polypetalae.*
(*i*) Flowers regular or irregular, 1 or 2-sexual.
(*ii*) Petals distinct or united at the base, perigynous.
(*iii*) Stamens peri- or epigynous. — *Calyciflorae.*
(*i*) Climbing by means of tendrils.
(*ii*) Ovary syncarpous, tricarpellary, inferior, unilocular with parietal placentation. — *Passiflorales.*
(*i*) Climbing by tendrils; leaves simple, palmately lobed; venation palmate.
(*ii*) Flowers monoecious or dioecious; calyx and corolla inserted on elongate hypanthium.
(*iii*) Stamens 5, 2 pairs connate; anthers sigmoid, cells usually conduplicate.
(*iv*) Fruit a berry (pepo). — *Cucurbitaceae.*

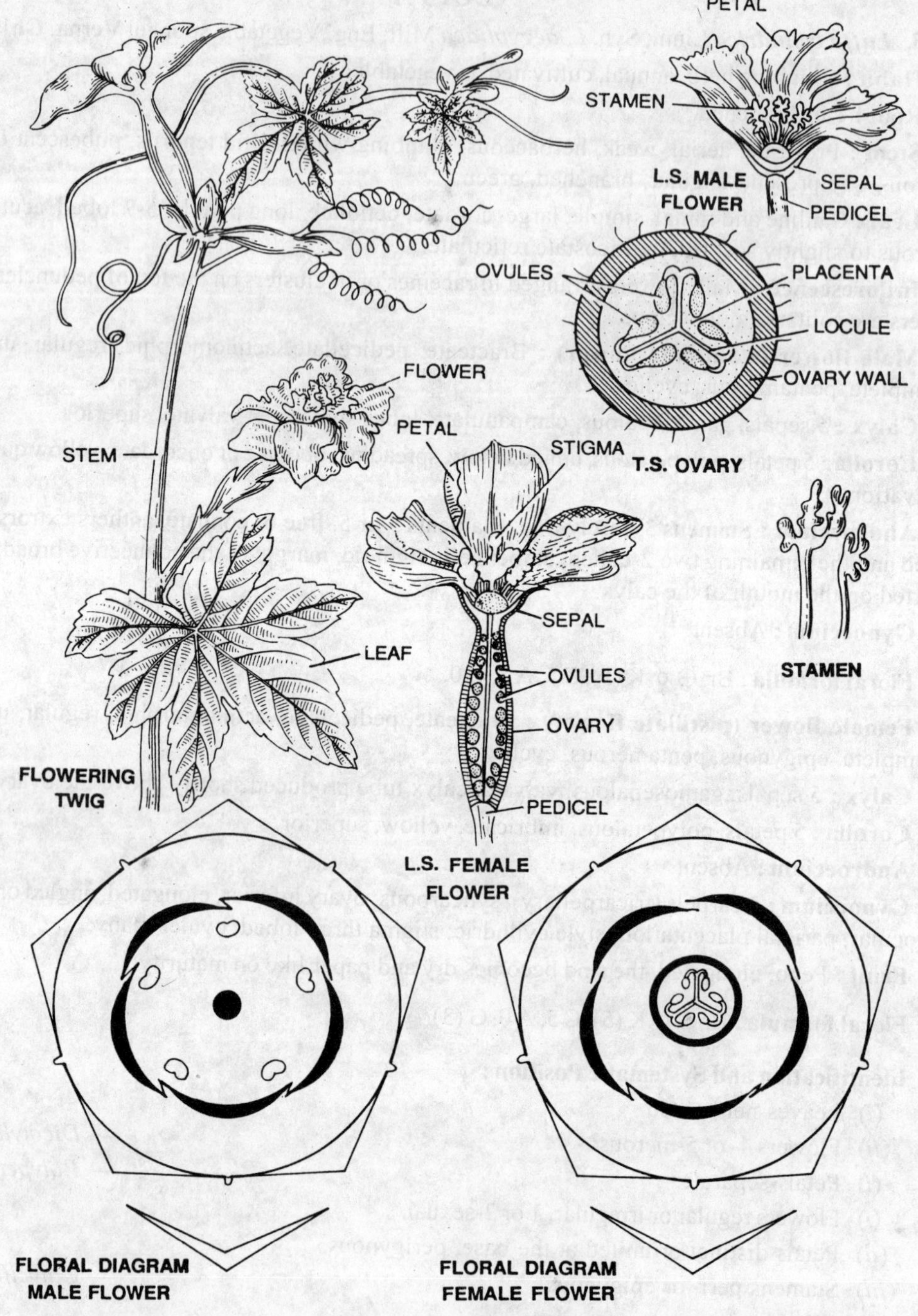

Fig. 9.49. Cucurbitaceae. *Luffa cylindrica*; Eng., vegetable sponge; Verna., **ghiatori.**

Economic value. The fruit is used as vegetable. Dried fruit is used as bath sponge. The seeds are emetic and cathartic.

FAMILY—UMBELLIFERAE (APIACEAE) (Parsley family)

CORIANDRUM

*1. **Coriandrum sativum*** Linn.; Verna. **Dhaniya;** Eng. Coriander.

Habit : An aromatic, annual, cultivated herb.

Root : Tap and branched.

Stem : Erect, herbaceous, green, solid, fistular when old, branched, cylinderical, aromatic, ribbed, glabrous, nodes slightly swollen.

Leaf : Cauline and ramal, decompound, much branched, when old, petiolate, base slightly sheathing, unicostate reticulate venation, pinnae narrow, entire, acute, aromatic.

Inflorescence : Compound umbel with involucre of bracts and involucel.

Flower : Pedicellate, bracteate, hermaphrodite, complete, epigynous, the outer flowers of the inflorescence are zygomorphic, *i.e.,* with large and unequal petals, whereas the central flowers are actinomorphic with equal and small petals.

Calyx : 5 sepals, gamosepalous, free at tips, green, acute, valvate aestivation, superior, calyx tube adnate to the ovary wall.

Corolla : 5 petals, polypetalous, in peripheral flowers two posterior petals bilobed and smallest, one anterior deeply bilobed and largest, two lateral large, bilobed, one lobe very small and the other large, zygomorphic, imbricate aestivation, purplish white; the petals of central flowers are small and equal in size, each petal consists of two equal lobes.

Androecium : 5 stamens, polyandrous, alternating with petals, filaments long, anthers dorsifixed, introrse, yellow, dithecous.

Gynoecium : 2 carpels, bicarpellary, syncarpous, ovary inferior, bilocular, one pendulous ovule in each loculus, axile placentation, epigynous disc (stylopodium) present at the top of ovary prolonged in two short styles, vittae (oil glands) present in ovary wall.

Fruit : Cremocarp splitting in two mericarps.

Floral formula : Br •|• ⚥ K (5), C (5), A 5, G $\overline{(2)}$ (zygomorphic flowers).

Br ⊕ ⚥ K (5), C (5), A 5, G $\overline{(2)}$ (actinomorphic flowers).

Identification and Systematic Position :

(*i*) Leaves net-veined.
(*ii*) Flowers 4- or 5-merous. — *Dicotyledons.*
(*i*) Petals separate. — *Polypetalae.*
(*i*) Flowers regular or irregular, 1 or 2-sexual.
(*ii*) Petals distinct or united at the base, perigynous.
(*iii*) Stamens peri- or epigynous. — *Calyciflorae.*
(*i*) Inflorescence simple or compound umbel; leaves alternate mostly compound.
(*ii*) 5-stamens alternating with the petals.
(*iii*) Ovary completely inferior of 2-5 carpels and as many cells. — *Umbellales.*
(*i*) Herbs with compound (simple in *Hydrocotyle*) and often much dissected leaves with sheathing petiole.
(*ii*) Flowers in simple or compound umbels; petals 5, inserted under the large epigynous disc (stylopodium).
(*iii*) Ovary 2-celled, syncarpous, inferior; fruit cremocarp with two separate mericarps; 1 seed in each mericarp; oil canals (vittae) in the pericarp. — *Umbelliferae.*

Bentham & Hooker (1862)	*Engler & Prantl* (1931)	*Hutchinson* (1959)
Dicotyledons	Dicotyledoneae	Dicotyledones
Polypetalae	Archichlamydeae	Herbaceae
Umbellales	Umbelliflorae	Umbellales
Umbelliferae	Umbelliferae	Umbelliferae (Apiaceae)

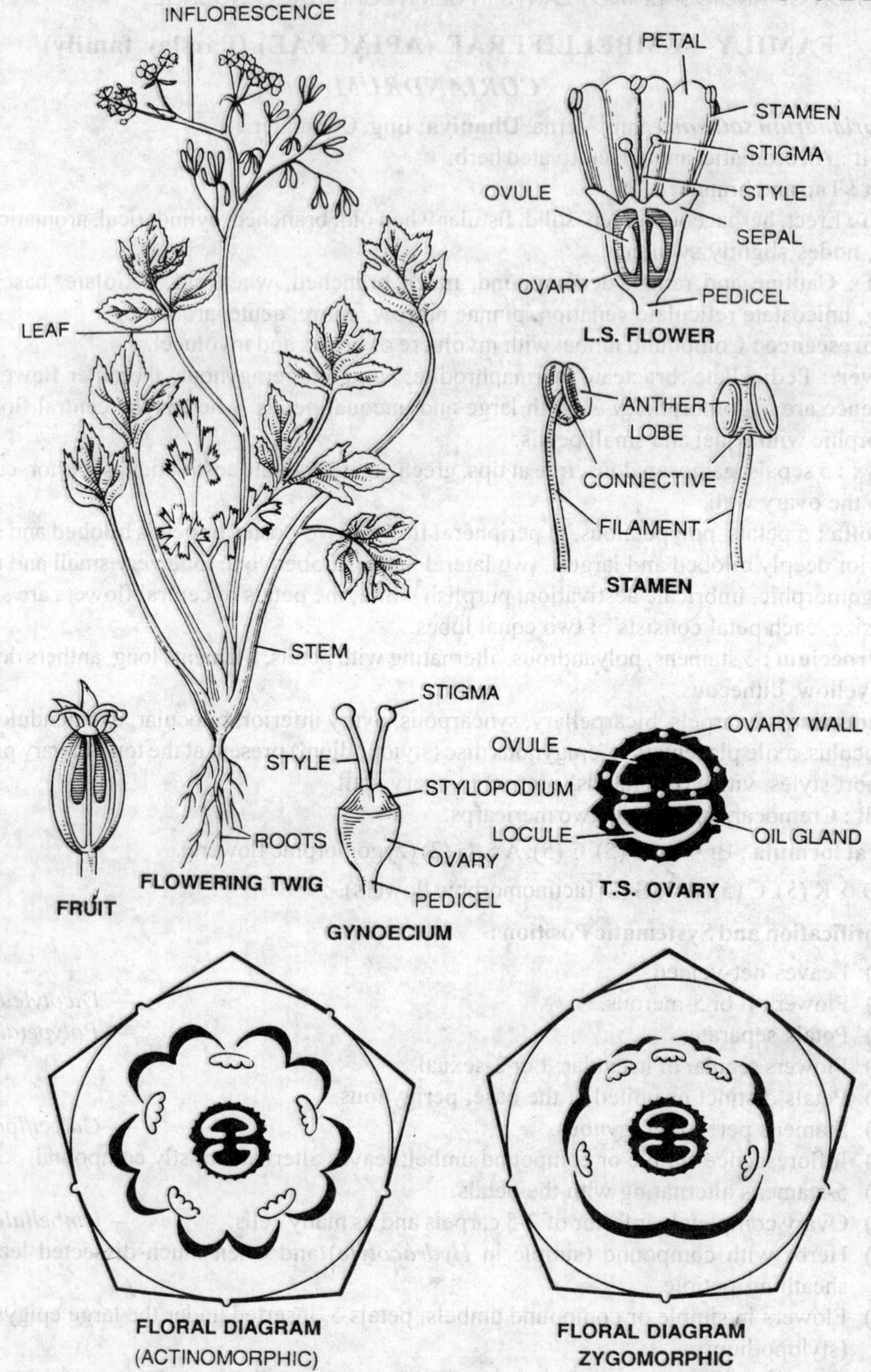

Fig. 9.50. Umbelliferae (Apiaceae). *Coriandrum sativum* Linn.; Eng., coriander; Verna., **dhaniya.**

Economic value. The fruit and leaves are aromatic and used as flavouring materials. The fruits are used as spice and condiment. The fruits are also used as stimulant, carminative, stomachic and tonic. Oil of coriander is used in medicine and in flavouring beverages, such as gin, whisky and various liquors.

TRACHYSPERMUM

*2. **Trachyspermum ammi*** (Linn.) Sprague. Verna. **Ajwain;** Eng. Lovage, Ammi.

Habit : Annual, aromatic, cultivated herb.

Root : Tap and branched.

Stem : Erect, branched, glabrous, fistular, ribbed, nodes slightly swollen.

Leaf : Cauline and ramal, compound 2, 3-4 pinnate, ultimate segments linear, alternate, petiolate, petiole sheathing at the base, exstipulate, aromatic.

Inflorescence : Racemose, compound umbel, primary umbels with an involucre of bracts at the base and the secondary umbel with an involucel of bracteoles.

Flower : Pedicellate, ebracteate, hermaphrodite, actinomorphic, complete, yellow, epigynous.

Calyx : 5 sepals, gamosepalous, calyx tube adnate to the ovary wall, calyx teeth 0.

Corolla : 5 petals, polypetalous, emarginate, yellow, valvate aestivation, superior, yellow.

Androecium : 5 stamens, polyandrous, alternating with petals, filaments long, anthers introrse, bicelled, basifixed.

Gynoecium : 2 carpels, bicarpellary, syncarpous, ovary inferior, bilocular, one ovule in each loculus, axile placentation, style extremely short, stigma bilobed, vittae present in ovary wall.

Fruit : Cremocarp splitting into two mericarps.

Floral formula : ⊕ ⚥ K (5), C 5, A 5, $\overline{G}$ (2).

Identification and Systematic Position :

(*i*) Leaves net-veined.

(*ii*) Flowers 4- or 5-merous. — *Dicotyledons.*

(*i*) Petals separate. — *Polypetalae.*

(*i*) Flowers regular or irregular, 1 or 2-sexual.

(*ii*) Petals distinct or united at the base, perigynous.

(*iii*) Stamens peri- or epigynous. — *Calyciflorae.*

(*i*) Inflorescence simple or compound umbel; leaves alternate mostly compound.

(*ii*) 5-stamens alternating with the petals.

(*iii*) Ovary completely inferior of 2-5 carpels and as many cells. — *Umbellales.*

(*i*) Herbs with compound (simple in *Hydrocotyle*) and often much dissected leaves with sheathing petiole.

(*ii*) Flowers in simple or compound umbels; petals 5, inserted under the large epigynous disc (stylopodium).

(*iii*) Ovary 2-celled, syncarpous, inferior; fruit cremocarp with two separate mericarps; 1 seed in each mericarp; oil canals (vittae) in the pericarp. — *Umbelliferae.*

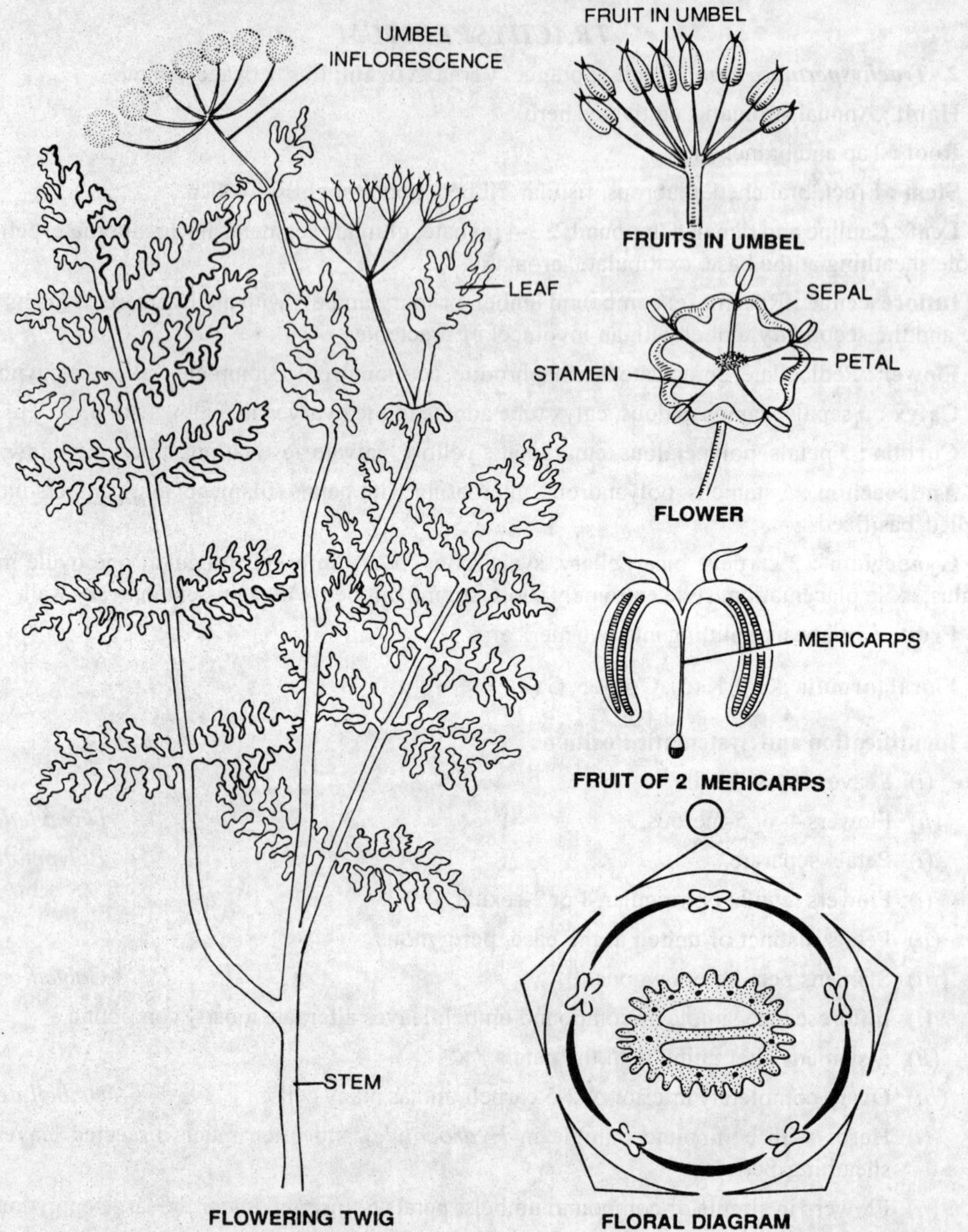

Fig. 9.51. Umbelliferae (Apiaceae). *Trachyspermum ammi* (Linn.) Sprague. (Syn. *Carum copticum*); Eng., lovage ammi, Verna. **Ajwain.**

Economic value. The fruits are used as spice. They are also used medicinally as carminative, stimulant, tonic and in indigestion.

CENTELLA

3. Centella asiatica (Linn.) Urb. (Syn. *Hydrocotyle asiatica* Linn.) Verna. **Brahmi;** Eng. Asiatic pennywort.

Habit : Prostrate herbs, rooting at nodes.

Root : Adventitious roots.

Stem : Prostrate, herbaceous, weak, cylinderical, stolon, leaves and roots at nodes.

Leaves : Simple, arising in groups from nodes, orbicular or reniform, crenate and often lobed; glabrous, shining, petiolate, long petioled; stipulate, stipule, adnate to petioles.

Inflorescence : Racemose, simple umbels, 3-6 flowers in each group.

Flower : Pedicellate, small pedicels, bracteate, bracts small, ovate, embracing the flowers, hermaphrodite, actinomorphic, regular, complete, epigynous.

Calyx : 5 sepals, minute, connate, valvate.

Corolla : 5 petals, polypetalous, valvate.

Androecium : 5 stamens, polyandrous, alternate to petals, filament short, anther dithecous, introrse.

Gynoecium : 2 carpels, syncarpous, ovary inferior, 2-celled, disk 2-lobed, vittae present in ovary wall, axile placentation, one ovule in each locule.

Fruit : Cremocarp, laterally compressed.

Floral formula : Br ⊕ ⚥ K (5), C 5, A 5, G (2).

Identification and Systematic Position :

(*i*) Leaves net-veined.
(*ii*) Flowers 4- or 5-merous. — *Dicotyledons.*
(*i*) Petals separate. — *Polypetalae.*
(*i*) Flowers regular or irregular, 1 or 2-sexual.
(*ii*) Petals distinct or united at the base, perigynous.
(*iii*) Stamens peri- or epigynous. — *Calyciflorae.*
(*i*) Inflorescence simple or compound umbel; leaves alternate mostly compound.
(*ii*) 5-stamens alternating with the petals.
(*iii*) Ovary completely inferior of 2-5 carpels and as many cells. — *Umbellales.*
(*i*) Herbs with compound (simple in *Hydrocotyle*) and often much dissected leaves with sheathing petiole.
(*ii*) Flowers in simple or compound umbels; petals 5, inserted under the large epigynous disc (stylopodium).
(*iii*) Ovary 2-celled, syncarpous, inferior; fruit cremocarp with two separate mericarps; 1 seed in each mericarp; oil canals (vittae) in the pericarp. — *Umbelliferae.*

Other important members of the family. *Cuminum cyminum* Linn. **Zira;** *Ferula assafoetida* Linn., **Hing** - used for flavouring food products and medicinally; *Foeniculum vulgare* Mill., **Saunf** - fruits used as spice and condiment and medicinally; *Anethum graveolens* Linn.; **Soya** - fruits used as spice and condiments and as carminative.

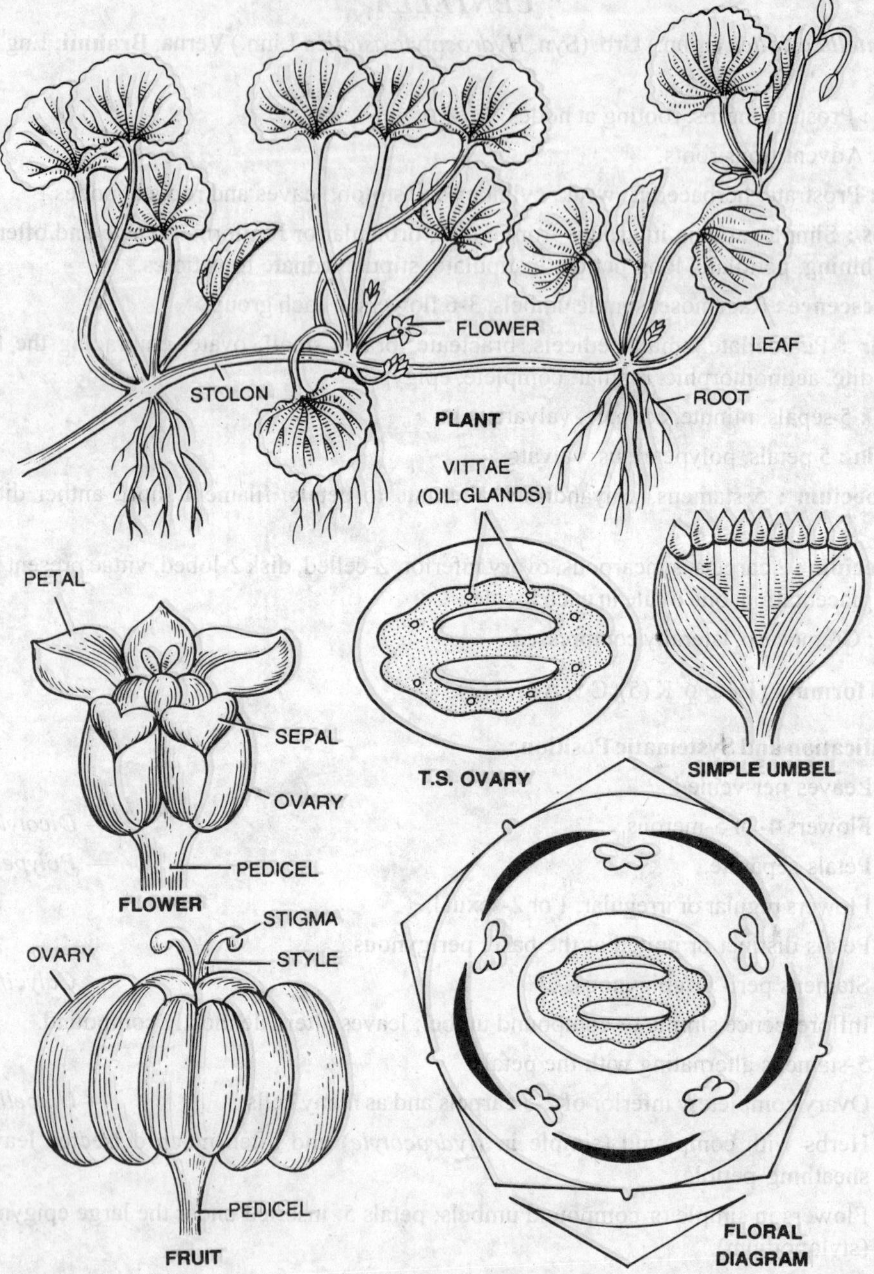

Fig. 9.52. Umbelliferae (Apiaceae). *Centella asiatica* (Linn.) Urb. (Syn. *Hydrocotyle asiatica* L.); Eng. Asiatic pennywort; Verna. **Brahmi.**

Economic value. The weed is alterative, tonic, diruetic, antiphlogistic, blood purifier and local stimulant. It is a remedy for skin diseases, like chronic eczema, chronic ulcers, etc., enlargement of glands, chronic rheumatism, chronic nervous diseases, madness, cholera, amenorrhoea and piles. An ointment made of leaf juice and lanoline is of great value in elephantiasis.

FAMILY—RUBIACEAE (Madder family)

IXORA

*1. **Ixora coccinea*** Linn.; Verna. **Rangan, Rookmini**; Eng. Jungle flame *Ixora.*

Habit : A large cultivated ornamental shrub.

Stem : Erect, branched, solid, cylinderical, green, herbaceous or somewhat woody.

Leaves : Cauline and ramal, simple, opposite, sessile, stipulate, ovate, smooth entire, acute, unicostate reticulate venation.

Inflorescence : Cymose, corymbose cyme.

Flower : Bisexual, actinomorphic, pedicellate, bracteate, bracteolate, complete, epigynous, tetramerous,

Calyx : 4 sepals, gamosepalous, superior, valvate aestivation.

Corolla : 4 petals, gamosepalous, corolla tubular, twisted aestivation.

Androecium : 4 stamens, epipetalous, inserted at the mouth of corolla, polyandrous, sessile, anthers bicelled, introrse, dorsifixed.

Gynoecium : 2 carpels (bicarpellary), syncarpous, ovary inferior, bilocular, single ovule in each loculus, axile placentation, style very long, stigma single, bifid.

Fruit : Berry.

Floral formula : Br ⊕ ⚥ K (4), C (4), A 4, G (2).

Identification and Systematic Position :

(*i*) Leaves net-veined.
(*ii*) Flowers 4- or 5-merous. — *Dicotyledons.*
(*i*) Petals united.. — *Gamopetalae.*
(*i*) Ovary inferior.
(*ii*) Stamens as many as corolla lobes. — *Inferae.*
(*i*) Leaves opposite or whorled.
(*ii*) Stamens epipetalous, free.
(*iii*) Ovary inferior, usually 2 (2-8) celled. — *Rubiales.*
(*i*) Woody or herbaceous with opposite or whorled leaves and inter or intrapetiolar stipules.
(*ii*) Corolla tubular, 4-5 lobed; stamens as many as corolla lobes, epipetalous, alternate to corolla lobes.
(*iii*) Ovary inferior 2- or more-celled, syncarpous; ovules 1 or more in each cell; fruit a berry, drupe or capsule. — *Rubiaceae*

Bentham & Hooker (1862)	*Engler & Prantl* (1931)	*Hutchinson* (1959)
Dicotyledons	Dicotyledoneae	Dicotyledones
Gamopetalae	Sympetalae	Lignosae
Rubiales	Rubiales	Rubiales
Rubiaceae	Rubiaceae	Rubiaceae

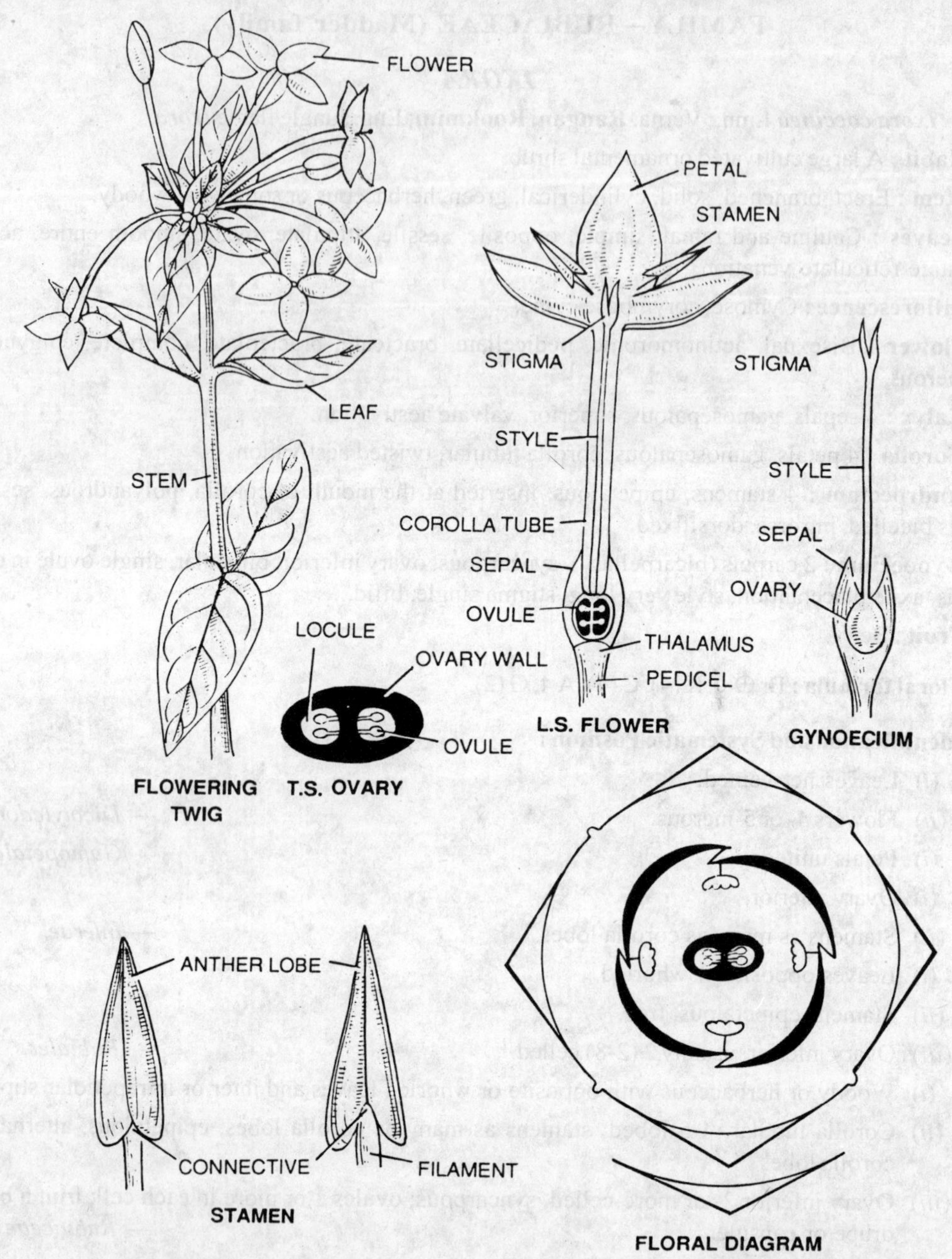

Fig. 9.53. Rubiaceae. *Ixora cocinea* Linn.; Eng. Jungle flame ixora; Verna. **Rangan, rookmini.**

Economic value. Grown as a hedge plant.

MUSSAENDA

2. ***Mussaenda luteola*** Delile; Eng. Advertising flag plant.

Habit : A cultivated ornamental shrub.

Stem : Erect, branched, solid, cylinderical, green herbaceous or somewhat woody, nodes and internodes prominent, hairy.

Leaf : Cauline and ramal, simple, opposite decussate, stipulate, stipules inerpetiolar, subsessile, elliptic-lanceolate, entire, acute, hairy, unicostate reticulate.

Inflorescence : Cymose, dichasial cyme.

Flower : Bracteate, bracteolate, pedicellate, complete, younger flowers actinomorphic, older flowers zygomorphic, hermaphrodite, pentamerous, epigynous, cyclic.

Calyx : 5 sepals, polysepalous, valvate, persistent, in older flowers one of the sepals becomes modified into a yellow leaf like structure, giving rise to zygomorphic condition.

Corolla : 5 petals, gamopetalous, valvate, tubular, hairy at mouth.

Androecium : 5 stamens, epipetalous, polyandrous, filament short, dithecous, dorsifixed, introrse.

Gynoecium : 2 carpels, bicarpellary, syncarpous, ovary inferior, bilocular, many ovules on T-shaped placenta, placentation axile, style long, stigma bifid.

Fruit : A berry.

Floral formula : Br Brl. ⊕ ⚥ K 5, $C\,\overbrace{(5), A\,5}$, $G\,\overline{(2)}$.

Identification and Systematic Position :

(*i*) Leaves net-veined.

(*ii*) Flowers 4- or 5-merous. — *Dicotyledons.*

(*i*) Petals united. — *Gamopetalae.*

(*i*) Ovary inferior.

(*ii*) Stamens as many as corolla lobes. — *Inferae.*

(*i*) Leaves opposite or whorled.

(*ii*) Stamens epipetalous, free.

(*iii*) Ovary inferior, usually 2 (2-8) celled. — *Rubiales.*

(*i*) Woody or herbaceous with opposite or whorled leaves and inter or intrapetiolar stipules.

(*ii*) Corolla tubular, 4-5 lobed; stamens as many as corolla lobes, epipetalous, alternate to corolla lobes.

(*iii*) Ovary inferior 2- or more-celled, syncarpous; ovules 1 or more in each cell; fruit a berry, drupe or capsule. — *Rubiaceae*

Other important members of the family. *Cinchona calisaya* Wedd., **Cinchona** - quinine is obtained from the bark of tree; *Coffea arabica* Linn., **Kafi** - the seeds are the source of famous nonalcoholic beverage "Coffee"; *C. robusta* Lind., seeds are also source of coffee; *Oldenlandia umbellata* Linn. **Saya** - the root bark is the source of a red dye.

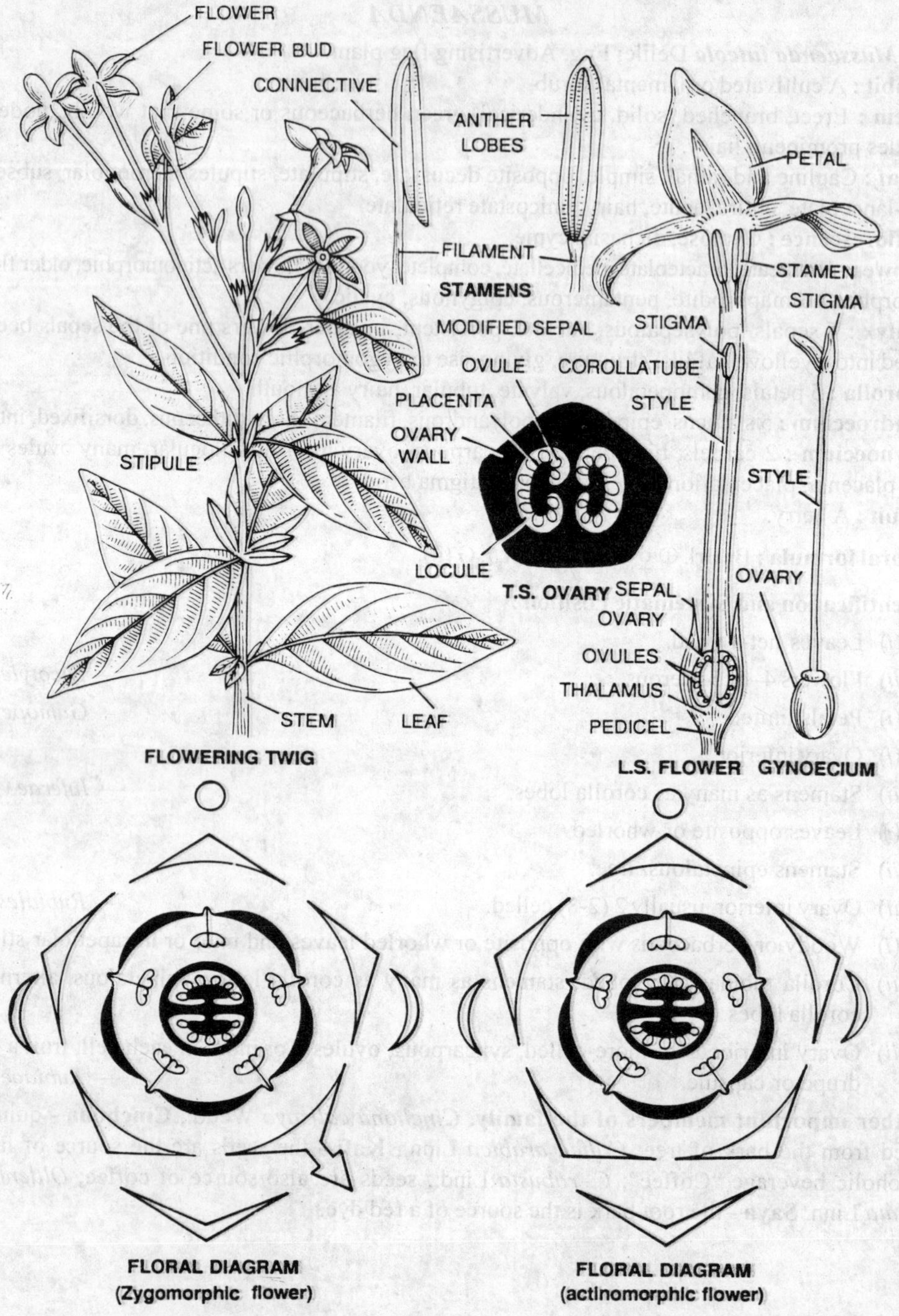

Fig. 9.54. Rubiaceae. *Mussaenda luteola* Delile.; Eng., advertising flag plant.

Economic value. The plant is grown in gardens as an ornamental.

FAMILY—COMPOSITAE (ASTERACEAE - Aster family)

HELIANTHUS

1. ***Helianthus annuus*** Linn.; Verna. **Surajmukhi;** Eng. Sunflower.

Habit : An annual large cultivated herb.

Root : Tap and branched.

Stem : Erect, herbaceous, branched, cylinderical, somewhat hairy.

Leaf : Simple, alternate, petiolate, exstipulate, ramal and cauline, persistent, large, ovate, serrate, acute, unicostate reticulate venation.

Inflorescence : Racemose, head or capitulum, consisting of ray and disc florets, involucre 3-seriate.

Ray-floret : Ebracteate, sessile, ligulate, zygomorphic, unisexual, incomplete, pistillate or neuter, epigynous.

Calyx : Either absent or represented by 2 or 3 scales, superior.

Corolla : 2-5, gamopetalous, ligulate, superior, yellow.

Androecium : Absent.

Gynoecium : 2, bicarpellary, syncarpous, ovary inferior, unilocular, single ovule, basal placentation, style single, stigma bifid.

Disc floret : Bracteate, sessile, actinomorphic, hermaphrodite, complete, epigynous.

Calyx : As in ray floret.

Corolla : 5, syngenesious, epipetalous, alternate to petals, filaments free, anthers bicelled, introrse, superior.

Androecium : 5, syngenesious, epipetalous, alternate to petals, filaments free, anthers bicelled, introrse, superior.

Gynoecium : 2, bicarpellary, syncarpous, ovary inferior, unilocular, single base ovule, basal placentation, style single, stigma bifid.

Fruit : Cypsela.

Floral formula : Ray Floret : •|• ⊕ ⚥ K 0(2-5 scales), C (5), A 0, G (2).

Disc Floret : Br ⊕ ⚥ K 0(2-5 scales), C (5), $\widehat{A\ (5),\ G\ (2)}$.

Identification and Systematic Position :

(*i*) Leaves net-veined.
(*ii*) Flowers 4- or 5-merous. — *Dicotyledons.*
(*i*) Petals united. — *Gamopetalae.*
(*i*) Ovary inferior.
(*ii*) Stamens as many as corolla lobes. — *Inferae.*
(*i*) Herbs or shrubs rarely trees; leaves alternate, simple or compound, exstipulate. — *Asterales.*
(*ii*) Ovary unilocular with single ovary. — *Asterales.*
(*i*) Leaves alternate, exstipulate.
(*ii*) Inflorescence a centripetal head of sessile flowers enclosed in an involucre of whorled bracts.
(*iii*) Calyx usually of hairs (pappus) or scales.
(*iv*) Stamens epipetalous and syngenesious.
(*v*) Ovary inferior 1-celled with basal placentation; style slender, bifid; fruit dry indehiscent (cypsela). — *Compositae*

Bentham & Hooker (1862)	*Engler & Prantl* (1931)	*Hutchinson* (1959)
Dicotyledons	Dicotyledoneae	Dicotyledones
Gamopetalae	Sympetalae	Herbaceae
Asterales	Campanulales	Asterales
Compositae	Compositae	Compositae (Asteraceae)

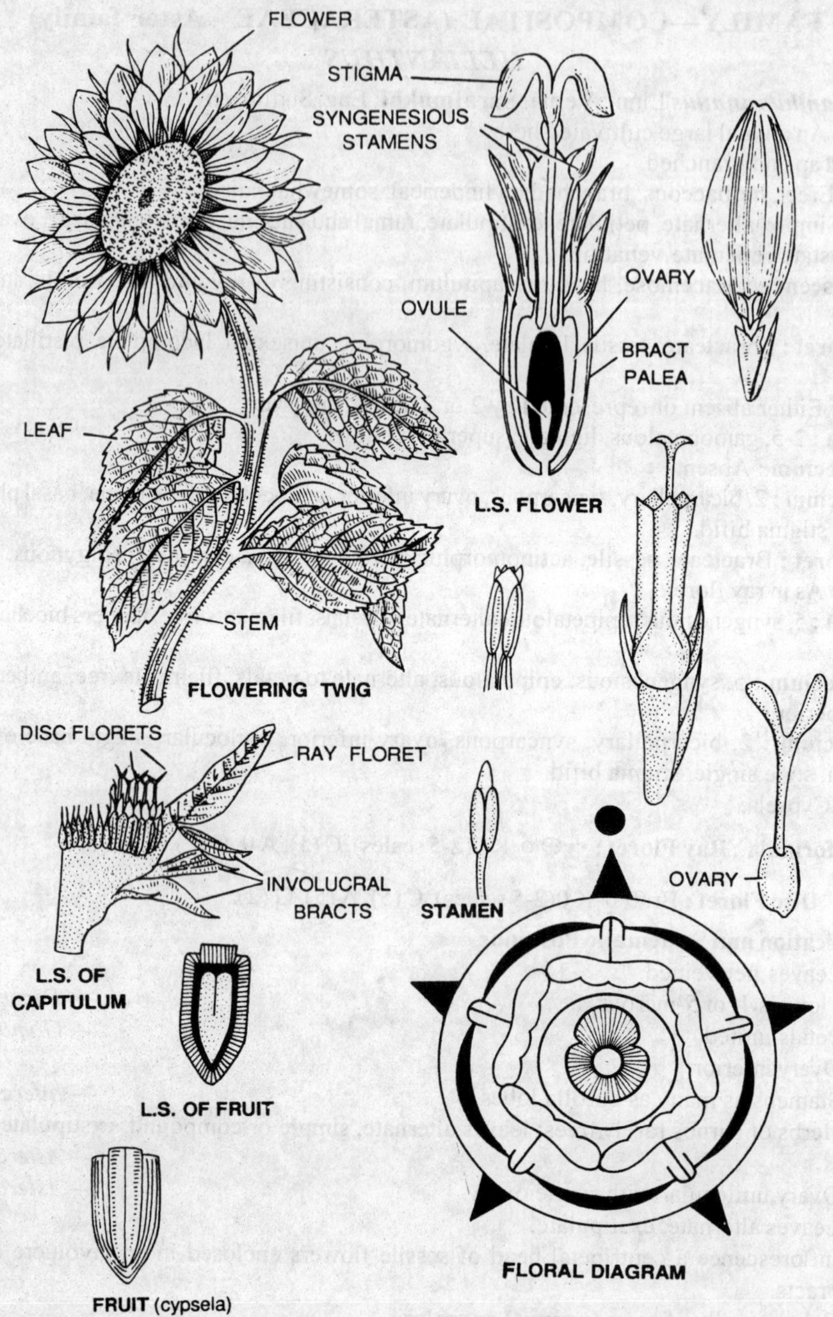

Fig. 9.55. Compositae (Asteraceae). *Helianthus annuus* Linn.; Eng., Sunflower; Verna., **surajmukhi.**

Economic value. The seeds are the source of an oil, which is used in foods, salads and for burning purposes. It can be used in place of groundnut oil in the preparation of *Vanaspati.* It can be safely used by heart patients. The oil does not raise the cholesterol level in the blood. It contains proteins, vitamins A, D and E. The oil is easily digested. Seeds are diuretic, expectorant, used in bronchial, laryngeal, pulmonary affections, coughs and colds, and in scorpion sting.

AGERATUM

*2. **Ageratum conyzoides*** Linn.; Verna. **Uchunti.**

Habit : Wild, annual herb.

Root : Tap and branched.

Stem : Erect, herbaceous, aerial, branched, cylinderical, solid, hairy, purple-green.

Leaf : Cauline and ramal, simple, petiolate, lower leaves opposite, upper leaves alternate, exstipulate, ovate, serrate, acute, hairy, unicostate reticulate.

Inflorescence : Compound capitulum, capitula arranged in cymose way, all flowers of a capitulum are tubular (homozygous), involucre of bracts present.

Flower : Bracteate, sessile, complete, actinomorphic, regular, hermaphrodite, pentamerous, epigynous and cyclic.

Calyx : 5 sepals, polysepalous, valvate, reduced to pappus.

Corolla : 5 petals, gamopetalous, valvate, tubular, violet coloured.

Androecium : 5 stamens, syngenesious, epipetalous, dithecous, basifixed, introrse.

Gynoecium : 2 carpels (bicarpellary), syncarpous, ovary inferior, unilocular, basal placentation, single basal ovule, style simple, long, stigma bifid.

Fruit : cypsela.

Floral formula : Br ⊕ ⚥ K 5 (pappus), $\overline{C (5), A (5)}$, G (2).

Identification and Systematic Position :

(*i*) Leaves net-veined.
(*ii*) Flowers 4- or 5-merous. — *Dicotyledons.*
(*i*) Petals united. — *Gamopetalae.*
(*i*) Ovary inferior.
(*ii*) Stamens as many as corolla lobes. — *Inferae.*
(*i*) Herbs or shrubs rarely trees; leaves alternate, simple or compound, exstipulate.
(*ii*) Ovary unilocular with single ovary. — *Asterales.*
(*i*) Leaves alternate, exstipulate.
(*ii*) Inflorescence a centripetal head of sessile flowers enclosed in an involucre of whorled bracts.
(*iii*) Calyx usually of hairs (pappus) or scales.
(*iv*) Stamens epipetalous and syngenesious.
(*v*) Ovary inferior 1-celled with basal placentation; style slender, bifid; fruit dry indehiscent (cypsela). — *Compositae*

Other important members of the family. *Carthamus tinctorius* Linn. **Kusum** - an edible oil is obtained from the seeds; *Artemisia absinthium* Linn., **Vialaity afsantin** - flowers are the source of a dry santonin; *Lactuca sativa* Linn., **Salad** - the leaves are vegetable; *Tagetes erecta* Linn., **Genda** - an ornamental.

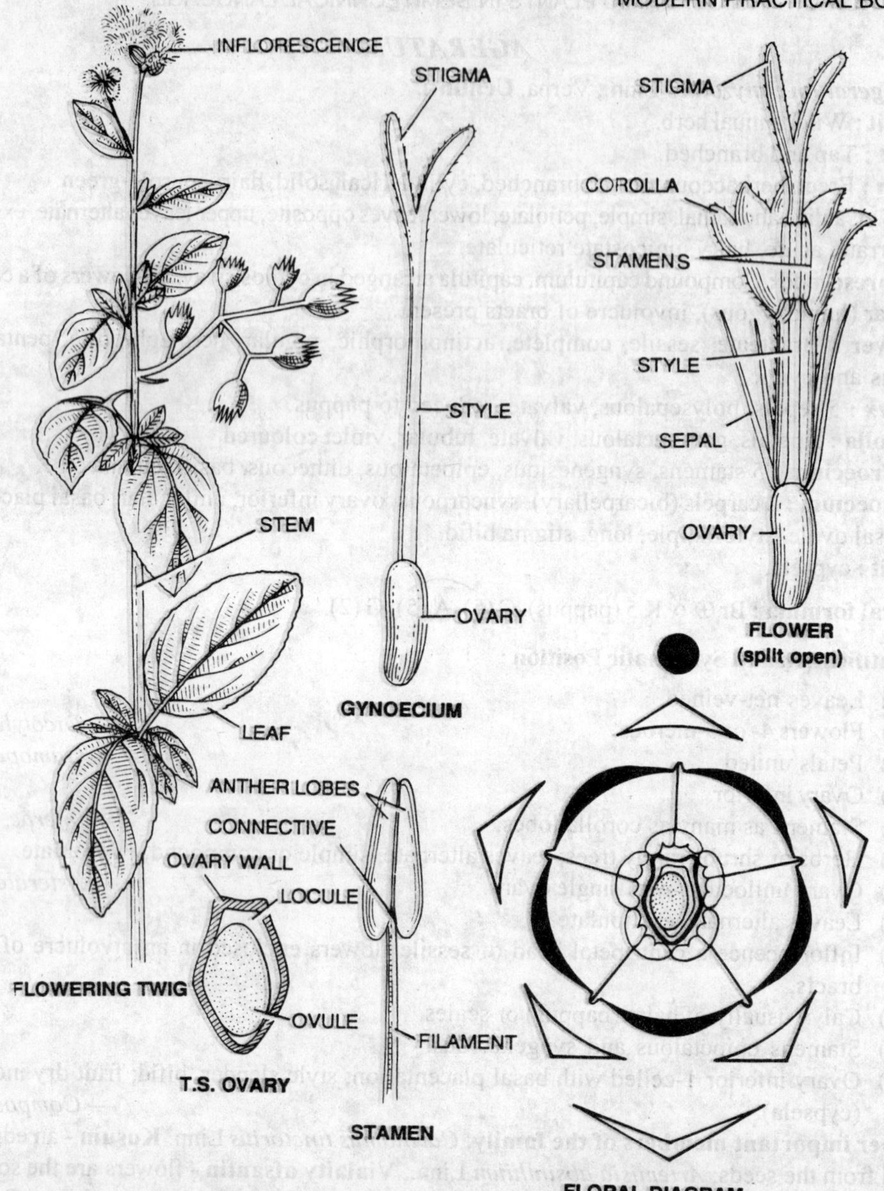

Fig. 9.56. Compositae (Asteraceae). *Ageratum conyzoides* Linn. Verna. **uchunti.**

Economic value. The juice of leaves is antilithic. The leaves are applied to cuts and sores.

FAMILY—APOCYNACEAE (Oleander family)

LOCHNERA

*1. **Lochnera rosea*** (L.) Reichb. Syn.; *Vinca rosea* L., *Catharanthus roseus* G. Don.; Verna. **Sadabahar;** Eng. Madagascar periwinkle.

Habit : A perennial herb.

Stem : Erect, cylinderical, branched, solid, reddish green, glabrous, latex present.

Leaf : Cauline and ramal, simple opposite decussate, petiolate, exstipulate, obovate, entire, glabrous, mucronate apex, unicostate reticulate venation, latex present.

Inflorescence : Cymose, flowers arranged in axillary pairs or solitary axillary.

Flower : Pedicellate, ebracteate, hermaphrodite, actinomorphic, complete, pink or white, hypogynous, pentamerous, cyclic.

Calyx : 5, polysepalous, glandular, green, inferior, valvate aestivation, persistent.

Corolla : 5, gamopetalous forming corolla tube, throat of corolla tube hairy forming a corona, contorted aestivation, purple or white.

Androecium : 5, free, epipetalous, alternate to petals, almost sessile, anthers dorsifixed, connivent round the stigma, yellowish, dithecous, introrse.

Gynoecium : 2 carpels (bicarpellary), syncarpous, carpels united above in the region of style and stigma, ovaries free (apocarpous below), with single style and stigma, ovaries superior, nectar secreting disc present beneath ovaries, unilocular, marginal placentation, glands present alternating with the carpels, style filiform, stigma thickened, dumb-bell shaped.

Fruit : A pair of elongated follicles.

Floral formula : $\oplus$ ⚥ K 5, C $\overparen{5, \text{ A } 5}$, G ($\underline{2}$).

Identification and Systematic Position :

(*i*) Leaves net-veined.
(*ii*) Flowers 4- or 5-merous. — *Dicotyledons.*
(*i*) Petals united. — *Gamopetalae.*
(*i*) Ovary usually superior, carpels usually 2, rarely 1 or 3.
(*ii*) Stamens alternate with the corolla lobes and equal in number or fewer. — *Bicarpellatae.*
(*i*) Corolla sympetalous, actinomorphic.
(*ii*) Stamens epipetalous, alternate with the corolla lobes.
(*iii*) Ovary superior, carpels-2, free or becoming free in fruit.
(*iv*) Leaves opposite, simple, no stipules. — *Gentianales.*
(*i*) Herbs, shrubs, trees with latex; leaves simple, opposite or whorled.
(*ii*) Flowers regular, bisexual, hypogynous, arranged in cymes, funnel-shaped, often with corona.
(*iii*) Stamens epipetalous, anthers usually connate around the stigma.
(*iv*) Carpels 2, apo- or syncarpous, superior, when apocarpous each ovary with marginal placentation; when syncarpous-parietal placentation; fruit a pair of follicles, berries or drupes. — *Apocynaceae*

Bentham & Hooker (1862)	*Engler & Prantl* (1931)	*Hutchinson* (1959)
Dicotyledons	Dicotyledoneae	Dicotyledones
Gamopetalae	Sympetalae	Lignosae
Gentianales	Contortae	Apocynales
Apocynaceae	Apocynaceae	Apocynaceae

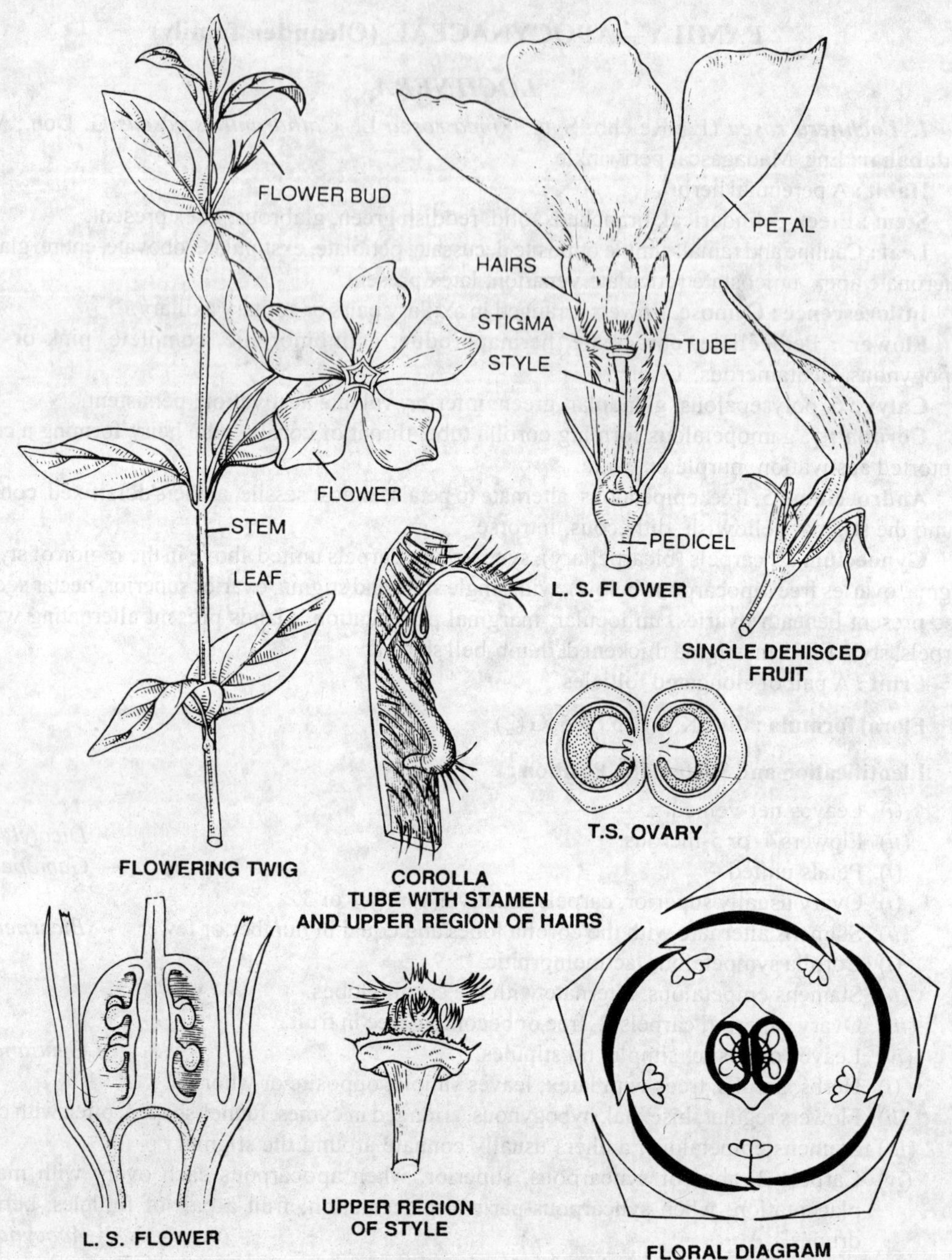

Fig. 9.57. Apocynaceae. *Lochnera rosea* (L.) Reichb.; Syn, *Vinca rosea*, Linn., (*Catharanthus roseus* G. Don.; Verna. **sadabahar.**

Economic value. The root is considered toxic and stomachic. The alkaloids possess hypotensive, sedative and tranquilizing properties. The alkaloids inhibit the growth of bacteria. Leaf extracts form a useful anti-bacterial agent.

TABERNAEMONTANA

*2. **Tabernaemontana divaricata*** (Linn); R. Br.; Verna. **Chandni;** Eng. Crape jasmine.

Habit : A large shrub.

Stem : Erect, solid, branched, woody, latex present, glabrous, green, cylinderical.

Leaf : Cauline and ramal, simple, opposite, petiolate, margin smooth, apex acute, unicostate reticulate venation.

Inflorescence : Cymose, terminal cyme.

Flower : Pedicellate, bracteate, bracteolate, hermaphrodite, actinomorphic, complete, hypogynous, pentamerous, cyclic, white.

Calyx : 5, gamosepalous, valvate or imbricate aestivation.

Corolla : 5, gamopetalous, forming a corolla tube, twisted aestivation.

Androecium : 5, free, epipetalous, included in the corolla tube, introrse, two-celled, basifixed.

Gynoecium : 2 (bicarpellary), syncarpous, ovary superior or partly inferior, bilocular, axile placentation, style one, stigma simple, bifid, several ovules in each locule.

Floral formula : Br ⊕ ⚥ K 5, C $\overset{\frown}{5, \text{ A } 5}$, G $(\underline{2})$.

Identification and Systematic Position :

(*i*) Leaves net-veined.
(*ii*) Flowers 4- or 5-merous. — *Dicotyledons.*
(*i*) Petals united.. — *Gamopetalae.*
(*i*) Ovary usually superior, carpels usually 2, rarely 1 or 3.
(*ii*) Stamens alternate with the corolla lobes and equal in number or fewer. — *Bicarpellatae.*
(*i*) Corolla sympetalous, actinomorphic.
(*ii*) Stamens epipetalous, alternate with the corolla lobes.
(*iii*) Ovary superior, carpels -2, free or becoming free in fruit.
(*iv*) Leaves opposite, simple, no stipules. — *Gentianales.*
(*i*) Herbs, shrubs, trees with latex; leaves simple, opposite or whorled.
(*ii*) Flowers regular, bisexual, hypogynous, arranged in cymes, funnel-shaped, often with corona.
(*iii*) Stamens epipetalous, anthers usually connate around the stigma.
(*iv*) Carpels 2, apo- or syncarpous, superior, when apocarpous each ovary with marginal placentation; when syncarpous-parietal placentation; fruit a pair of follicles, berries or drupes. — *Apocynaceae.*

Other important members of the family. *Carissa carandas* Linn., **Karaunda** - fruits are edible; *Rauvolfia serpentina,* (Linn.) Benth. ex Kurz., **Sarpagandha** - the roots are used in medicine in the treatment of mental disorders; *Beaumontia grandiflora* (Roxb.) Wall., a climbing ornamental.

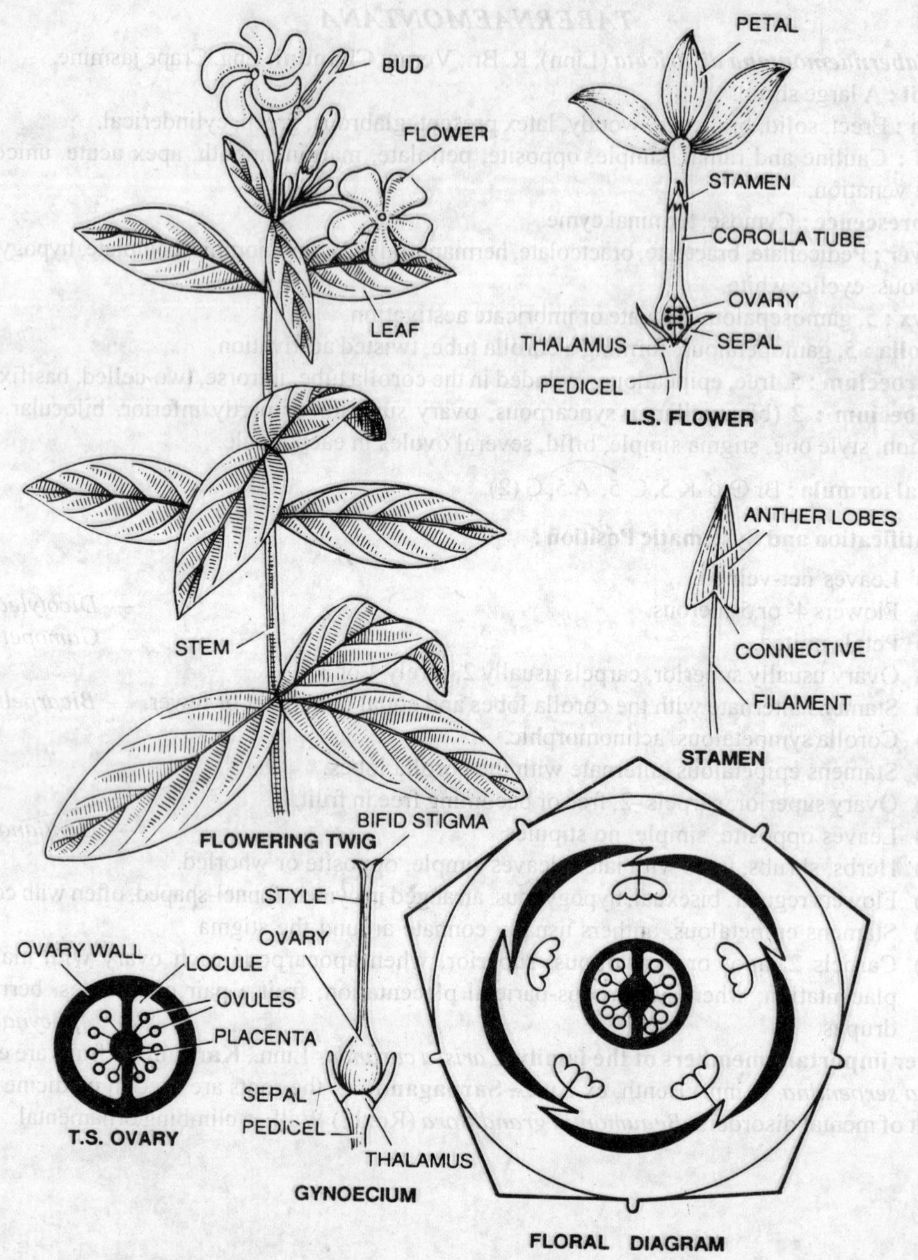

Fig. 9.58. Apocynaceae. *Tabernaemontana divaricata* (Linn.) R. Br. Syn. *Ervatamia coronaria* Stapf.; Eng., crape jasmine; Verna., **chandni.**

Economic value. Grown as an ornamental. The red pulp around seed is used as a dye. Wood is refrigerant. Milky juice is used for diseases of eye. Root is acrid, bitter, used as local anodyne and chewed for relief of toothache.

NERIUM

3. Nerium indicum Mill.; Verna. **Kaner;** Eng. Oleander.

Habit : A large shrub or small tree.

Stem : Erect, aerial, solid, woody, cylinderical, glabrous, branched, nodes swollen, milky latex present.

Leaf : Cauline and ramal, simple, whorled with three leaves in each whorl, sub-sessile, exstipulate, linear-lanceolate; unicostate reticulate venation, latex present.

Inflorescence : Cymose, terminal dichasial cyme.

Flower : Pedicellate, bracteate, bracteolate, hermaphrodite, actinomorphic, complete, yellow, hypogynous, pentamerous, cyclic, pink.

Calyx : 5, polysepalous, quincuncial aestivation, purple red.

Corolla : 5, gamopetalous, campanulate, corolla tube expanding above, throat of corolla tube hairy forming a corona, yellow, contorted aestivation, red or white.

Androecium : 5, epipetalous included in the corolla tube, alternating with the petals, polyardrous, filaments short, anthers connivent round the stigmatic head, basifixed, long hair appendages present on their apices, dithecous, introrse, protruded feathery connective present.

Gynoecium : Bicarpellay, syncarpous, ovary superior, bilocular, many ovules in each loculus, axile placentation, a nectar secreting disc present beneath the ovary, style long filiform, stigma thickened and dumb-bell shaped.

Floral Formula : Br Brl $\oplus$ ⚥ $K\,5, \overbrace{C\,(5), A\,5}, G\,(\underline{2})$.

Identification and Systematic Position :

(*i*) Leaves net-veined.
(*ii*) Flowers 4- or 5-merous. — *Dicotyledons.*
(*i*) Petals united. — *Gamopetalae.*
(*i*) Ovary usually superior, carpels usually 2, rarely 1 or 3.
(*ii*) Stamens alternate with the corolla lobes and equal in number or fewer. — *Bicarpellatae.*
(*i*) Corolla sympetalous, actinomorphic.
(*ii*) Stamens epipetalous, alternate with the corolla lobes.
(*iii*) Ovary superior, carpels -2, free or becoming free in fruit.
(*iv*) Leaves opposite, simple, no stipules. — *Gentianales.*
(*i*) Herbs, shrubs, trees with latex; leaves simple, opposite or whorled.
(*ii*) Flowers regular, bisexual, hypogynous, arranged in cymes, funnel-shaped, often with corona.
(*iii*) Stamens epipetalous, anthers usually connate around the stigma.
(*iv*) Carpels 2, apo- or syncarpous, superior, when apocarpous each ovary with marginal placentation; when syncarpous-parietal placentation; fruit a pair of follicles, berries or drupes. — *Apocynaceae.*

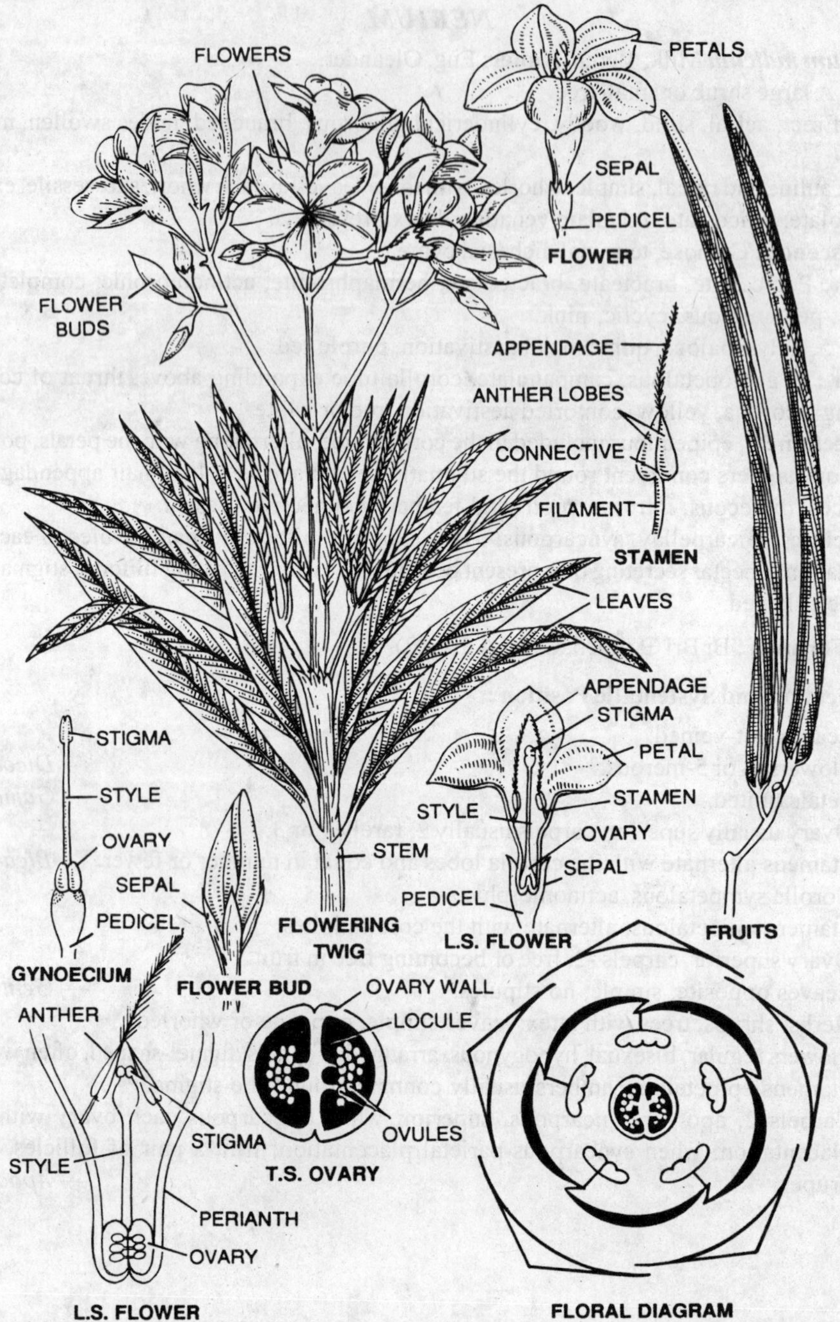

Fig. 9.59. Apocynaceae. *Nerium indicum* Mill.; Eng., oleander; Verna. **kaner.**

Economic value. A beautiful shrub; grown as a hedge plant. Plant is poisonous. Root is powerful resolvent and attenuant; used externally. Oil prepared from root bark is used in skin diseases and leprosy.

THEVETIA

4. *Thevetia peruviana* Pers.; Syn. *T. neriifolia* Juss.; Verna. **Pili kaner;** Eng. Yellow oleander.

Habit : Large shrub or small tree.

Root : Tap, branched.

Stem : Erect, aerial, solid, woody (old) or herbaceous (young), cylindrical, smooth, milky latex present.

Leaf : Cauline and ramal, exstipulate, sub-sessile, spiral, linear-lanceolate, entire, acute, glabrous, unicostate reticulate, latex present.

Inflorescence : Cymose, axillary dichasial cyme.

Flower : Bracteate, bracteolate, pedicellate, complete, actinomorphic, regular, hermaphrodite, pentamerous, hypogynous, cyclic.

Calyx : 5 sepals, polysepalous, quincuncial aestivation, persistent, green.

Corolla : 5 petals, gamopetalous, twisted aestivation, bell-shaped (infundibuliform), yellow fringed coronary outgrowths present.

Androecium : 5 stamens, polyandrous, epipetalous, stamens inserted at the throat of corolla, filament short, anther sagittate, dithecous, basifixed and introrse.

Gynoecium : 2 carpels (bicarpellary), syncarpous, ovary superior, bilocular, two ovules in each locule, axile placentation, style long, stigma umbrella-shaped, 5-lobed nectar secreting disc present.

Fruit : Drupe.

Floral Formula : Br Brl ⊕ ⚥ K 5, C (5), A 5, G $(\underline{2})$.

Identification and Systematic Position :

(*i*) Leaves net-veined.
(*ii*) Flowers 4- or 5-merous. — *Dicotyledons.*
(*i*) Petals united. — *Gamopetalae.*
(*i*) Ovary usually superior, carpels usually 2, rarely 1 or 3.
(*ii*) Stamens alternate with the corolla lobes and equal in number or fewer. — *Bicarpellatae.*
(*i*) Corolla sympetalous, actinomorphic.
(*ii*) Stamens epipetalous, alternate with the corolla lobes.
(*iii*) Ovary superior, carpels-2, free or becoming free in fruit.
(*iv*) Leaves opposite, simple, no stipules. — *Gentianales.*
(*i*) Herbs, shrubs, trees with latex; leaves simple, opposite or whorled.
(*ii*) Flowers regular, bisexual, hypogynous, arranged in cymes, funnel-shaped, often with corona.
(*iii*) Stamens epipetalous, anthers usually connate around the stigma.
(*iv*) Carpels 2, apo- or syncarpous, superior, when apocarpous each ovary with marginal placentation; when syncarpous-parietal placentation; fruit a pair of follices, berries or drupes. — *Apocynaceae.*

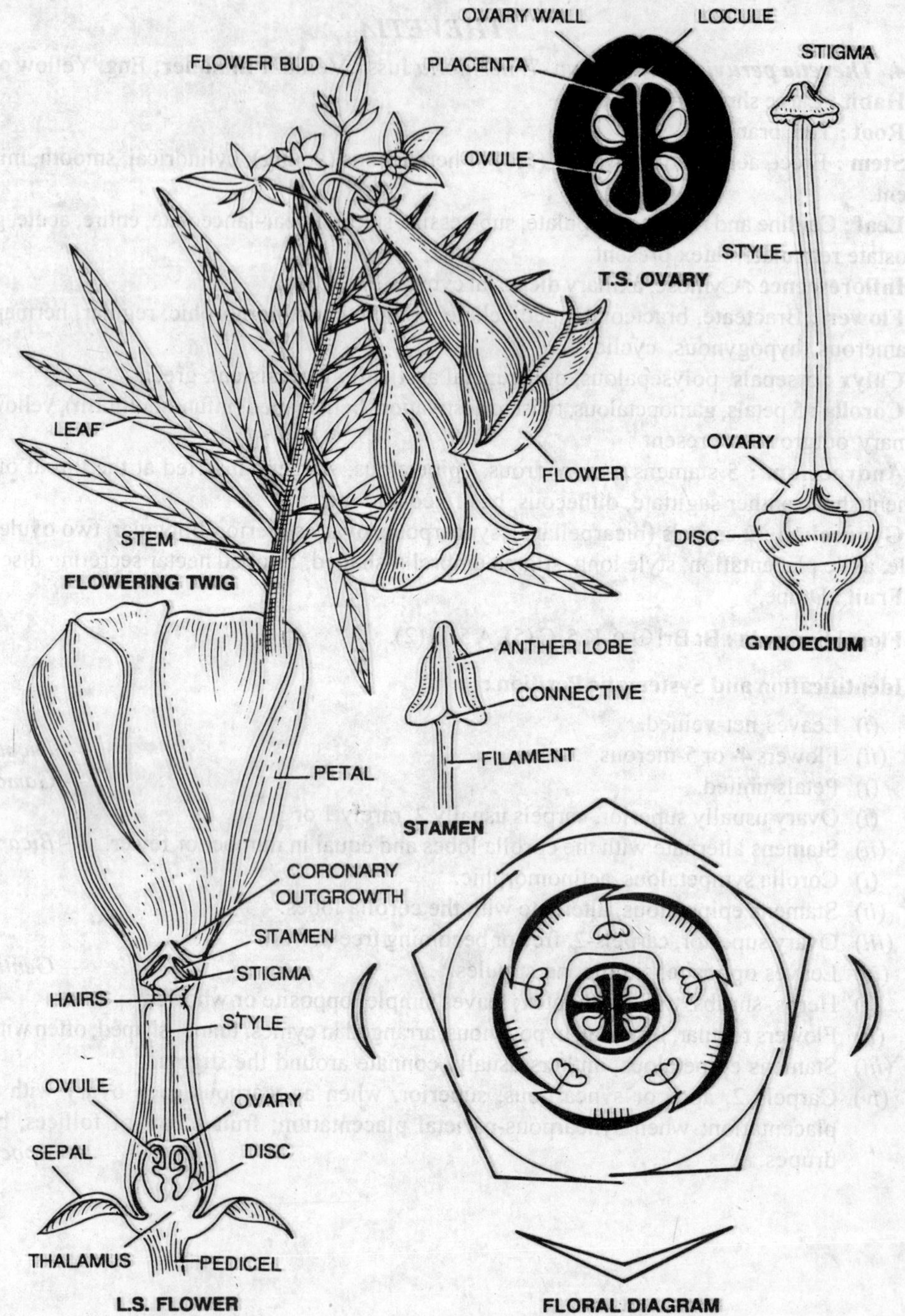

Fig. 9.60. Apocynaceae. *Thevetia peruviana* Pers., Syn. *T. neriifolia*. Juss.; Eng., yellow oleander; Verna., **pili kaner.**

Economic value. The bark is bitter, cathartic, febrifuge and useful in different kinds of intermittent fevers. Milky juice and seeds are poisonous.

FAMILY—ASCLEPIADACEAE (Milkweed family)

CALOTROPIS

*1. **Calotropis procera*** (Ait) R. Br.; Verna. **Ak**; Eng. Swallow-wart.

Habit : A shrub. about 3 to 6 feet high, younger parts and the under surface of the leaves covered with white waxy secretion, all parts contain milky latex.

Stem : Erect, branched, glabrous, woody below and herbaceous above, tomentose, solid, cylinderical.

Leaf : Simple, cauline and ramal, sessile, opposite decussate, exstipulate, 2-5 in., long thick, glaucous-green, elliptical or obovate oblong with cordate or often amplexicaul base, acute or shortly acuminate, unicostate reticulate venation.

Inflorescence : Cymose, umbellate, dichasial cyme.

Flower : Pedicellate, bracteate, bracteolate, hermaphrodite, actinomorphic, regular, complete, pentamerous except pistil, hypogynous and cyclic.

Calyx : 5 sepals, polysepalous or connate at the base, greenish, lobes lanceolate, acute apex, interior quincuncial aestivation.

Corolla : 5 petals, gamopetalous, pink or whitish with purple spots, lobes spreading, inferior, twisted aestivation.

Androecium : Five stamens, filaments connate in a fleshy staminal tube around the ovary, the apex of the staminal tube united with the much-dilated stigmatic head to which the anthers are also coherent, forming the pentagonal gynostegium; anthers short, broad tipped with inflexed membranous flaps, bi-celled, the pollen grains of each cell aglutinated into sac like pollinium; the pollinia of each anther are united together by means of short stalks or caudicles to a distinct dark coloured dot-structure, the corpusculum, which lies at the angle of the gynostegium, thus forming a translator apparatus.

Gynoecium : 2 carpels (bicarpellary), syncarpous; the pistil free below and fused above; two distinct ovaries end in two styles forming a pentangular stigmatic head to the sides of which the anthers are coherent; ovary superior, unilocular, many ovules, marginal placentation.

Fruit : A pair of follicles.

Seed : Many, broadly ovate, flat tomentose with tuft of silky hairs.

Floral Formula : Br Brl ⊕ ⚥ K 5, $\widehat{C\ 5, A\ (5)}$, G $(\underline{2})$.

Identification and Systematic Position :

(*i*) Leaves net-veined.
(*ii*) Flowers 4- or 5-merous. — *Dicotyledons.*
(*i*) Petals united. — *Gamopetalae.*
(*i*) Ovary usually superior, carpels usually 2, rarely 1 or 3.
(*ii*) Stamens alternate with the corolla lobes and equal in number or fewer. — *Bicarpellatae.*
(*i*) Corolla sympetalous, actinomorphic.
(*ii*) Stamens epipetalous, alternate with the corolla lobes.
(*iii*) Ovary superior, carpels-2, free or becoming free in fruit.
(*iv*) Leaves opposite, simple, no stipules. — *Gentianales.*
(*i*) Herbs, shrubs, or twiners with latex; leaves simple opposite.
(*ii*) Stamens (5), connate in a hollow tube, with horn like appendages known as staminal corona, epipetalous; anthers coherent laterally united with the style and stigma forming gynostegium; pollen cohering into two pollen masses-pollinia.
(*iii*) Gynoecium of 2-carpels free, superior, styles 2, free but united above forming 5-angled stigma; ovaries 2, free or united at the base only, each unilocular with marginal placentation; fruit a pair of follicles. — *Asclepiadaceae.*

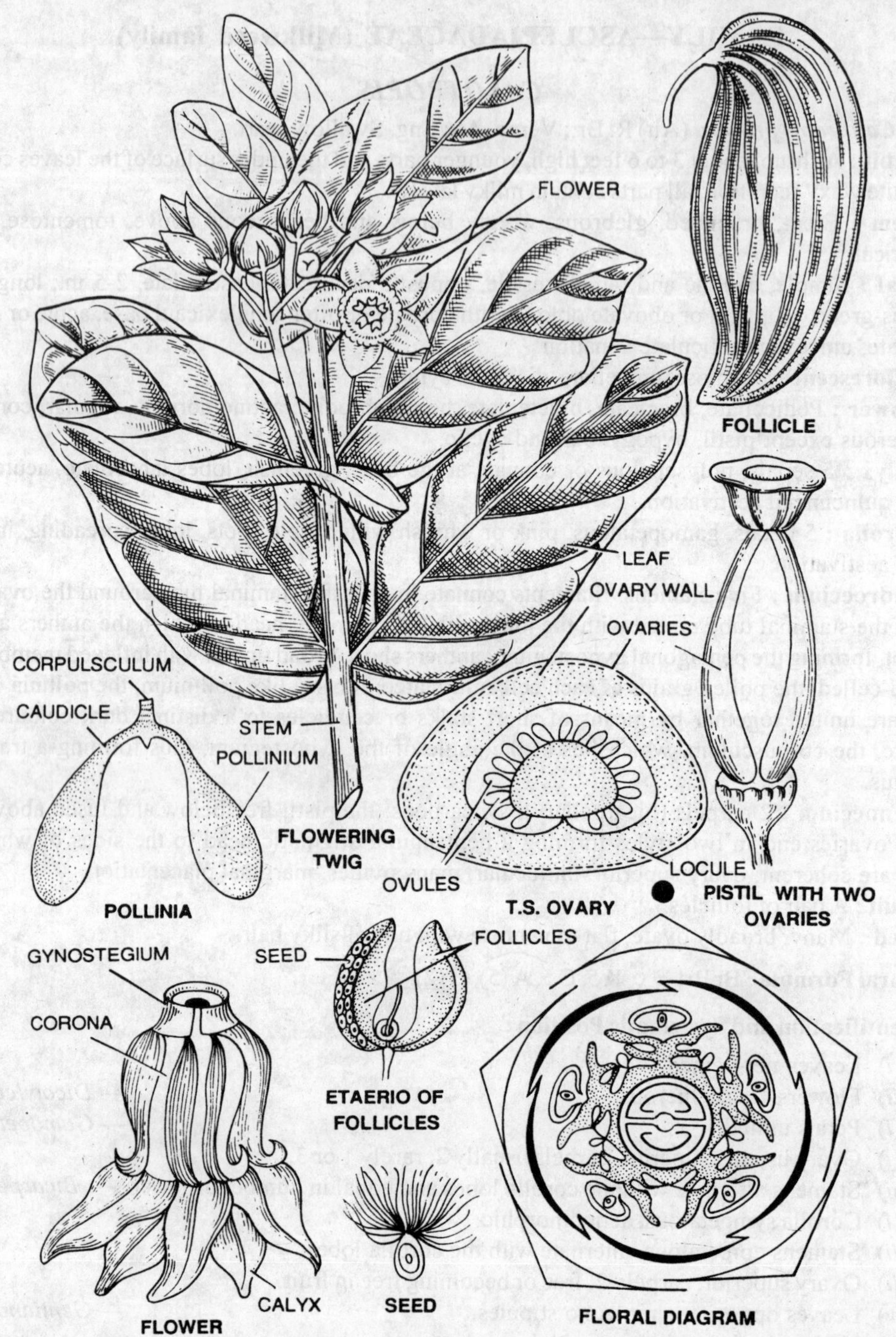

Fig. 9.61. Asclepiadaceae. *Calotropis procera* (Ait.) R. Br.; Eng., swallow wart; Verna., **aak.**

Economic value. The floss obtained from the seeds is used as stuffing material. The stem fibre is made into cordage. All parts of the plant are used medicinally. The flowers are given in cough, cold and asthma.

ASCLEPIAS

*2. **Asclepias curassavica*** Linn.; Verna. **Kakatundi;** Eng. Blood flower.

Habit : An erect perennial herb.

Stem : Erect, branched, herbaceous, solid, cylinderical.

Leaves : Simple, opposite, short petiolate, exstipulate, linear lanceolate, entire, acute, unicostate reticulate venation.

Inflorescence : Cymose, umbellate cyme.

Flower : Pedicellate, bracteate, purple-yellow, small, bisexual, actinomorphic, hypogynous, pentamerous, cyclic.

Calyx : 5 sepals, polysepalous, imbricate or valvate aestivation.

Corolla : 5 petals, gamopetalous, twisted aestivation, brightly coloured.

Androecium : Similar to that of *Calotropis procera.* The filaments attached to the base of the corolla are united to form a column around the pistil, the anthers being pressed close to the styles; each stamen bears on the side away from the pistil and appendage which enfolds the anther like a hood; these appendages collectively form a corona.

Gynoecium : 2 carpels (bicarpellary), syncarpous, ovary superior, placentation marginal.

Fruit : Follicle.

Floral formula : Br ⊕ ⚥ K 5, $\overparen{\text{C (5), A 5}}$, G $(\underline{2})$.

Identification and Systematic Position :

(*i*) Leaves net-veined.
(*ii*) Flowers 4- or 5-merous. — *Dicotyledons.*

(*i*) Petals united. — *Gamopetalae.*

(*i*) Ovary usually superior, carpels usually 2.
(*ii*) Stamens alternate with the corolla lobes and equal in number or fewer. — *Bicarpellatae.*

(*i*) Corolla sympetalous, actinomorphic.
(*ii*) Stamens epipetalous, alternate with the corolla lobes.
(*iii*) Ovary superior, carpels -2, free or becoming free in fruit.
(*iv*) Leaves opposite, simple, no stipules. — *Gentianales.*

(*i*) Herbs, shrubs, or twiners with latex; leaves simple opposite.
(*ii*) Stamens (5), connate in a hollow tube, with horn like appendages known as staminal corona, epipetalous; anthers coherent laterally united with the style and stigma forming gynostegium; pollen cohering into two pollen masses-pollinia.
(*iii*) Gynoecium of 2-carpels free, superior, styles 2, free but united above forming 5-angled stigma; ovaries 2, free or united at the base only, each unilocular with marginal placentation; fruit a pair of follicles. — *Asclepiadaceae.*

Bentham & Hooker (1862)	*Engler & Prantl* (1931)	*Hutchinson* (1959)
Dicotyledons	Dicotyledoneae	Dicotyledones
Gamopetalae	Sympetalae	Lignosae
Gentianales	Contortae	Apocynales
Asclepiadaceae	Asclepiadaceae	Asclepiadaceae

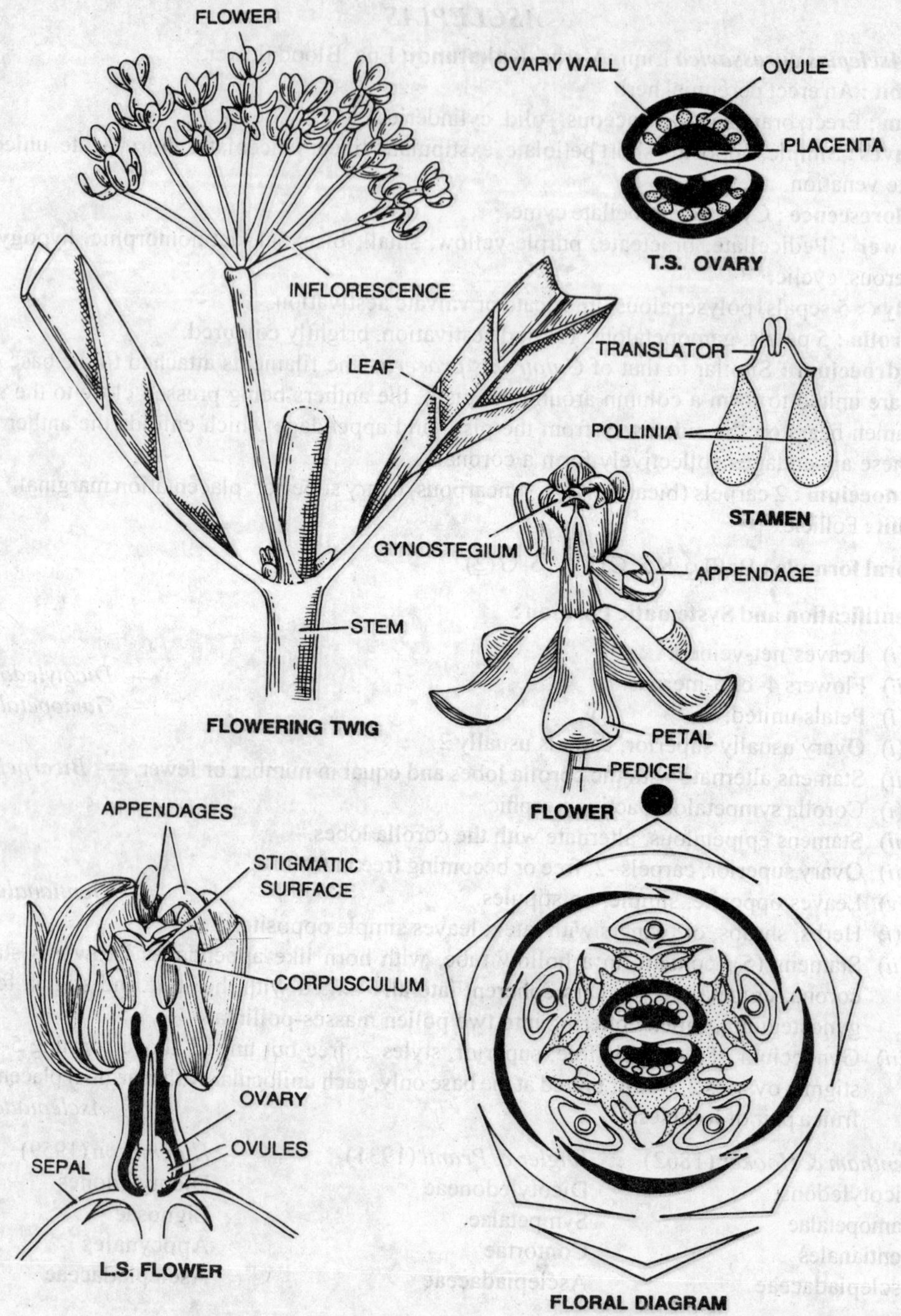

Fig. 9.62. Asclepiadaceae. *Asclepias curassavica* Linn.; Eng. Blood flower; Verna., **Kakatundi.**

Economic value. Grown as an ornamental. Root is emetic, purgative; remedy in piles and gonorrhoea. Juice of leaves is anthelmintic and sudorific for arresting haemorrhages and gonorhoea.

CRYPTOSTEGIA

*3. **Cryptostegia grandiflora*** R. Br.; Verna. **Vilayati vakhandi;** Eng. Rubber vine.

Habit : A perennial twiner.

Root : Tap and branched.

Stem : Herbaceous, lower part woody, aerial, weak, climbing, branched, twiner, solid, cylinderical, rough, green, latex present, nodes and internodes prominent.

Leaf : Ramal and cauline, opposite decussate, exstipulate, simple, petiolate elliptic ovate, entire, acute, coriaceous, glaucous, unicostate reticulate.

Inflorescence : Cymose dichasial cyme.

Flower : Bracteate, bracteolate, pedicellate, actinomorphic, regular, hermaphrodite, pentamerous, hypogynous, cyclic.

Calyx : 5 sepals, polysepalous, quincuncial aestivation, green, margins membranous.

Corolla : 5 petals, gamopetalous, twisted, coronary outgrowths present, violet.

Androecium : 5 stamens, polyandrous, epipetalous, dithecous, introrse; pollen grains are being shed from each anther lobe and are deposited in the translator. Each spoon-shaped translator is found to be situated in between two stamens.

Gynoecium : 2 carpels (bicarpellary), ovary superior, ovaries free but style and stigma fused, many ovules in each locule, marginal placentation, style short, stigma globular.

Floral formula : Br, Brl ⊕ ⚥ K 5, $\widehat{C\,(5), A\,5}$, G $\underline{(2)}$.

Identification and Systematic Position :

(*i*) Leaves net-veined.
(*ii*) Flowers 4- or 5-merous. — *Dicotyledons.*
(*i*) Petals united. — *Gamopetalae.*
(*i*) Ovary usually superior, carpels usually 2.
(*ii*) Stamens alternate with the corolla lobes and equal in number or fewer. — *Bicarpellatae.*
(*i*) Corolla sympetalous, actinomorphic.
(*ii*) Stamens epipetalous, alternate with the corolla lobes.
(*iii*) Ovary superior, carpels-2, free or becoming free in fruit.
(*iv*) Leaves opposite, simple, no stipules. — *Gentianales.*
(*i*) Herbs, shrubs, or twiners with latex; leaves simple opposite.
(*ii*) Stamens (5), connate in a hollow tube, with horn like appendages known as staminal corona, epipetalous; anthers coherent laterally united with the style and stigma forming gynostegium; pollen cohering into two pollen masses-pollinia.
(*iii*) Gynoecium of 2-carpels free, superior, styles 2, free but united above forming 5-angled stigma; ovaries 2, free or united at the base only, each unilocular with marginal placentation; fruit a pair of follicles. — *Asclepiadaceae.*

Other important members of the family. *Ceropegia tuberosa* Roxb., **Patalatumbi -** tubers used in the bowel complaints of children; *Leptadenia pyrotechnica* (Forsk.) Decne., fruits are edible; *Tylophora asthmatica* W. & A, **Antamul -** leaves emetic, diaphoretic and expectorant.

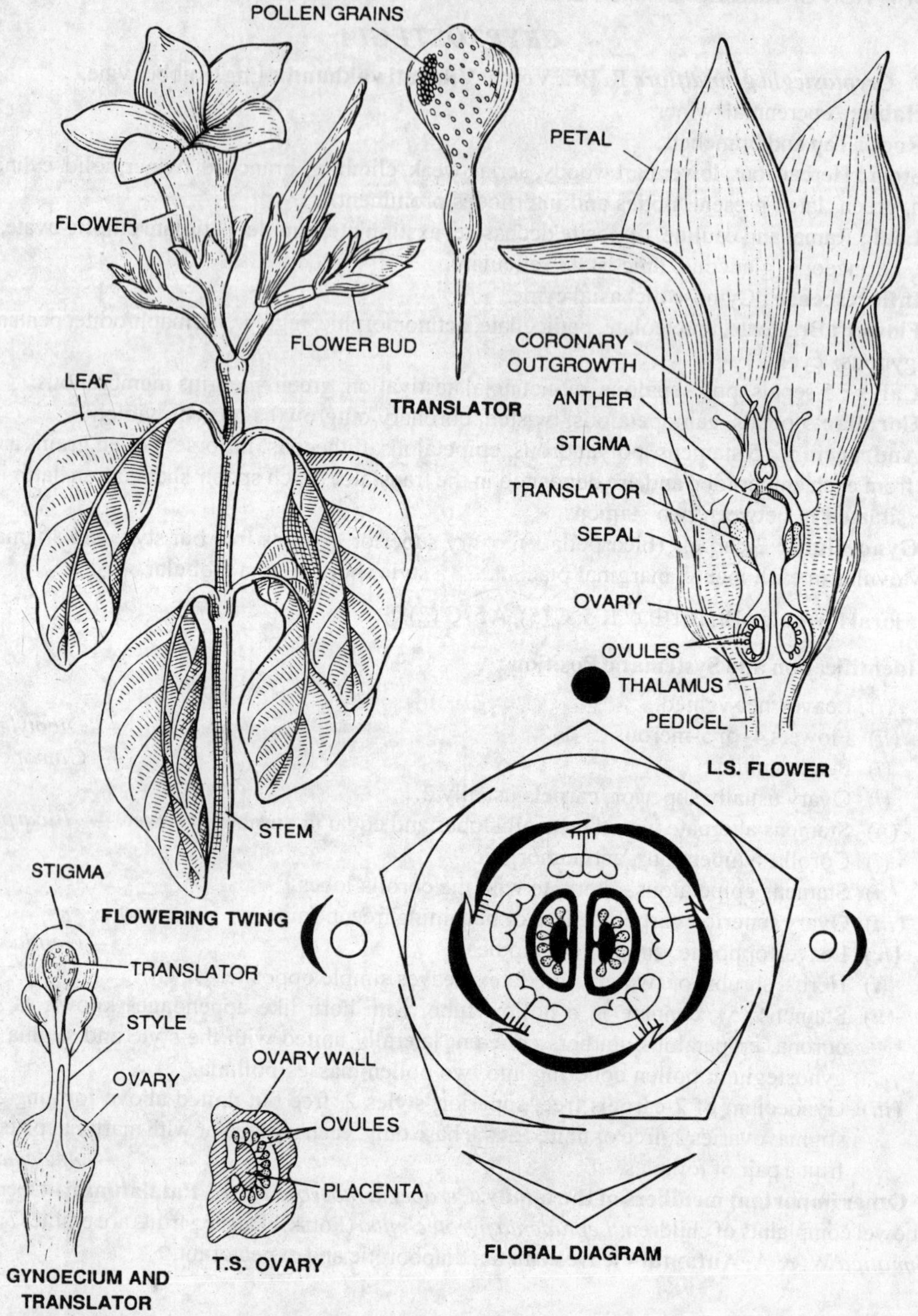

Fig. 9.63. Asclepiadaceae. *Cryptostegia grandiflora* R. Br., rubber vine; Verna., **vilayati vakhandi.**

Economic value. Grown as an ornamental for its beautiful violet-coloured flowers. The leaves are toxic.

FAMILY—CONVOLVULACEAE (Morning-glory family)

IPOMOEA

*1. **Ipomoea tropica*** Santapau & Patel.

Habit : A perennial twiner.

Stem : Prostrate, twining, branched, herbaceous, solid, glabrous and green.

Leaf : Simple, cauline and ramal, entire alternate, petiolate, stipulate, stipules small in size unicostate reticulate venation.

Inflorescence : Cymose, solitary axillary or in small cymes.

Flower : Pedicellate, pedicel long, campanulate, bracteate, bracteolate, hermaphrodite, actinomorphic, complete, hypogynous, violet coloured, pentamerous and cyclic.

Calyx : 5 sepals, polysepalous, sepaloid, quincuncial aestivation, inferior.

Corolla : 5 lobed, gamopetalous, campanulate, in duplicate valvate aestivation, inferior, violet coloured.

Androecium : 5 stamens, polyandrous, epipetalous, filaments long, of different lengths, two long and three short, hair at the base, anther bicelled, introrse, basifixed.

Gynoecium : 2 carpels (bicarpellary), syncarpous, nectar secreting disc present below the ovary, superior, bilocular, axile placentation, two ovules in each loculus, style long, stigma bifid.

Floral formula : Br, ⊕ ⚥ K 5, $\widehat{C\ (5),\ A\ 5}$, G $(\underline{2})$.

Identification and Systematic Position :

(*i*) Leaves net-veined.
(*ii*) Flowers 4- or 5-merous. — *Dicotyledons.*

(*i*) Petals united. — *Gamopetalae.*

(*i*) Ovary superior, carpels usually 2.
(*ii*) Stamens alternate with the corolla lobes and equal in number or fewer. — *Bicarpellatae.*

(*i*) Herbs or twiners; leaves alternate, exstipulate.
(*ii*) Flowers actinomorphic.
(*iii*) Stamens epipetalous, alternate with the corolla lobes.
(*iv*) Ovary superior, 2-carpels, 2-locular, with few or numerous ovules on axile placentas. — *Polemoniales.*

(*i*) Flowers hypogynous, often large and showy; petals (5), united, funnel-shaped, twisted in bud, sometimes imbricate.
(*ii*) Carpels (2), syncarpous; ovary superior, with a disc at the base, 2-celled with 2 ovules in each cell; placentation axile; fruit berry or capsule. — *Convolvulaceae.*

Bentham & Hooker (1862)	*Engler & Prantl* (1931)	*Hutchinson* (1959)
Dicotyledons.	Dicotyledoneae	Dicotyledones
Gamopetalae	Sympetalae	Herbaceae
Polemoniales	Tubiflorae	Solanales
Convolvulaceae	Convolvulaceae	Convolvulaceae

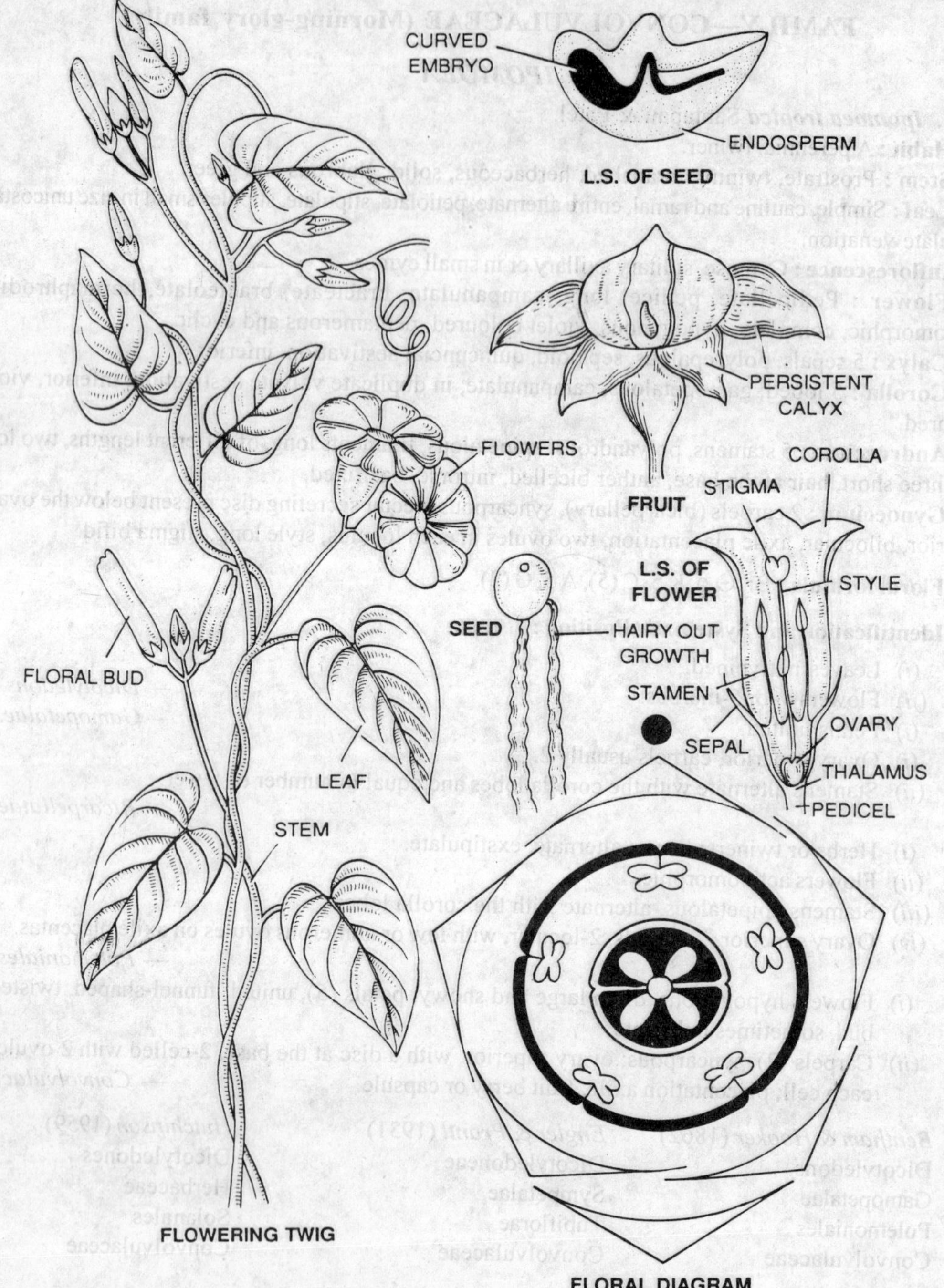

Fig. 9.64. Convolvulaceae. *Impomoea tropica* Santapau & Patel; Syn. *I. calycina* Clarke.

Economic value. A twiner; grown as an ornamental.

IPOMOEA FISTULOSA

*2. **Ipomoea fistulosa*** Mart ex Choisy.

Habit : Perennial shrub.

Stem : Erect, woody, branched, cylinderical, solid, glabrous and green.

Leaf : Cauline and ramal, simple, alternate, petiolate, exstipulate, entire, acute, glabrous, unicostate reticulate venation.

Inflorescence : Cymose, dichasial cyme.

Flower : Pedicellate, bracteate, hermaphrodite, actinomorphic, regular, pentamerous except gynoecium, hypogynous.

Calyx : 5 sepals, polysepalous, imbricate aestivation, inferior.

Corolla : 5 petals, gamopetalous, infundibuliform, corolla tube long, limbs, spreading, inferior.

Androecium : 5 stamens, polyandrous, epipetalous, inferior, filaments long, anthers bicelled, introrse, basifixed.

Gynoecium : 2 carpels (bicarpellary), syncarpous; ovary superior, bilocular, axile placentation, two ovules in each loculus, style dividing near its top into two linear stigmas, honey secreting disc present beneath the ovary.

Fruit : A capsule dehiscing by four valves.

Floral Formula : Br ⊕ ⚥ K 5, $\overline{\text{C (5), A 5}}$, G $(\underline{2})$.

Identification and Systematic Position :

(*i*) Leaves net-veined.
(*ii*) Flowers 4- or 5-merous. — *Dicotyledons.*

(*i*) Petals united. — *Gamopetalae.*

(*i*) Ovary superior, carpels usually 2.
(*ii*) Stamens alternate with the corolla lobes and equal in number or fewer.
— *Bicarpellatae.*

(*i*) Herbs or twiners; leaves alternate, exstipulate.
(*ii*) Flowers actinomorphic.
(*iii*) Stamens epipetalous, alternate with the corolla lobes.
(*iv*) Ovary superior, 2-carpels, 2-locular, with few or numerous ovules on axile placentas.
— *Polemoniales.*

(*i*) Flowers hypogynous, often large and showy; petals (5), united, funnel-shaped, twisted in bud, sometimes imbricate.
(*ii*) Carpels (2), syncarpous; ovary superior, with a disc at the base, 2-celled with 2 ovules in each cell; placentation axile; fruit berry or capsule. — *Convolvulaceae.*

Other important members of the family. *Ipomoea aquatica* Forsk., **Kalmisag, nari** - the tender twigs are used as vegetable; *I. batatas* (Linn.) Poir., **Shakarkand** - the roots are edible; *Evolvulus alsinoides* Linn., **Sankhapushpi** - plant bitter, tonic, febrifuge, vermifuge in dysentery, leaves made into cigarettes smoked in chronic bronchitis and asthma.

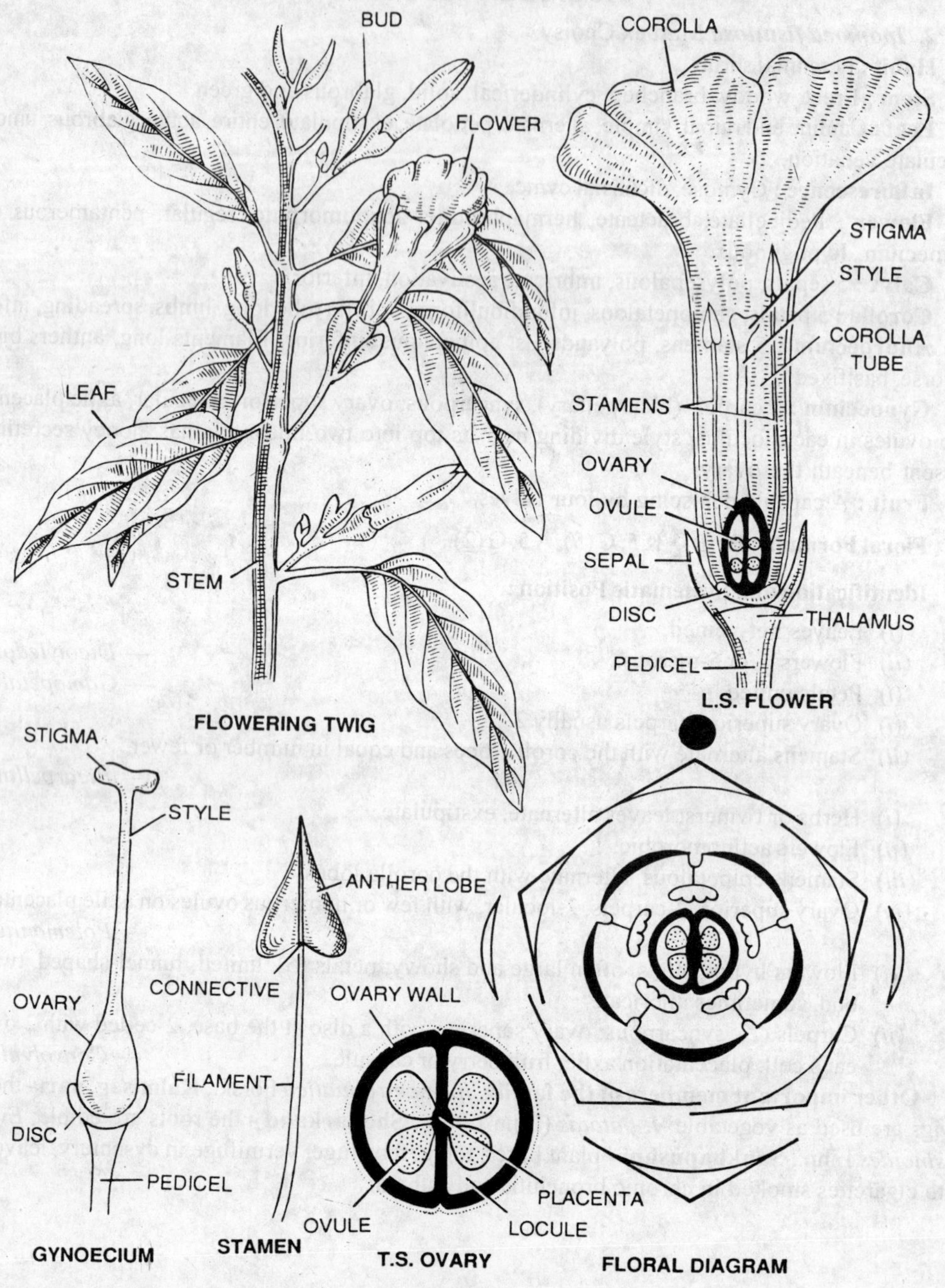

Fig. 9.65. Convolvulaceae. *Ipomoea fistulosa* Mart. ex Choisy; Syn. *I.carnea*, Jacq.

Economic value. A shrub; grown as an avenue plant.

CONVOLVULUS

3. Convolvulus pluricaulis Choisy; Verna. **Shankhapushpi.**

Habit : Annual herb.

Root : Tap and branched.

Stem : Erect, aerial, herbaceous, branched, cylinderical solid, hairy, green.

Leaf : Cauline and ramal, exstipulate, sessile, alternate, simple, lanceolate, entire, hairy, acute, coriaceous, unicostate reticulate venation.

Inflorescence : Cymose, dichasial cyme.

Flower : Bracteate, bracteolate, pedicellate, actinomorphic, regular, hermaphrodite, complete, pentamerous, hypogynous, cyclic.

Calyx : 5 sepals, polysepalous, quincuncial aestivation, hairy, green.

Corolla : 5 petals, gamopetalous, valvate, corolla infundibuliform, purple coloured.

Androecium : 5 stamens, polyandrous, epipetalous, filaments unequal, dithecous, dorsifixed, introrse.

Gynoecium : 2 carpels (bicarpellary), syncarpous, ovary superior, bilocular, 2 ovules in each locule, axile placentation, nectary present beneath the ovary, style short, stigma bifid.

Fruit : A capsule.

Floral formula : Br, Brl ⊕ ⚥ K 5, $\widehat{C\,(5), A\,5}$, G $(\underline{2})$.

Identification and Systematic Position :

(*i*) Leaves net-veined.
(*ii*) Flowers 4- or 5-merous. — *Dicotyledons.*
(*i*) Petals united. — *Gamopetalae.*
(*i*) Ovary superior, carpels usually 2.
(*ii*) Stamens alternate with the corolla lobes and equal in number or fewer. — *Bicarpellatae.*
(*i*) Herbs or twiners; leaves alternate, exstipulate.
(*ii*) Flowers actinomorphic.
(*iii*) Stamens epipetalous, alternate with the corolla lobes.
(*iv*) Ovary superior, 2-carpels, 2-locular, with few or numerous ovules on axile placentas. — *Polemoniales.*
(*i*) Flowers hypogynous, often large and showy; petals (5), united, funnel-shaped, twisted in bud, sometimes imbricate.
(*ii*) Carpels (2), syncarpous; ovary superior, with a disc at the base, 2-celled with 2 ovules in each cell; placentation axile; fruit berry or capsule. — *Convolvulaceae.*

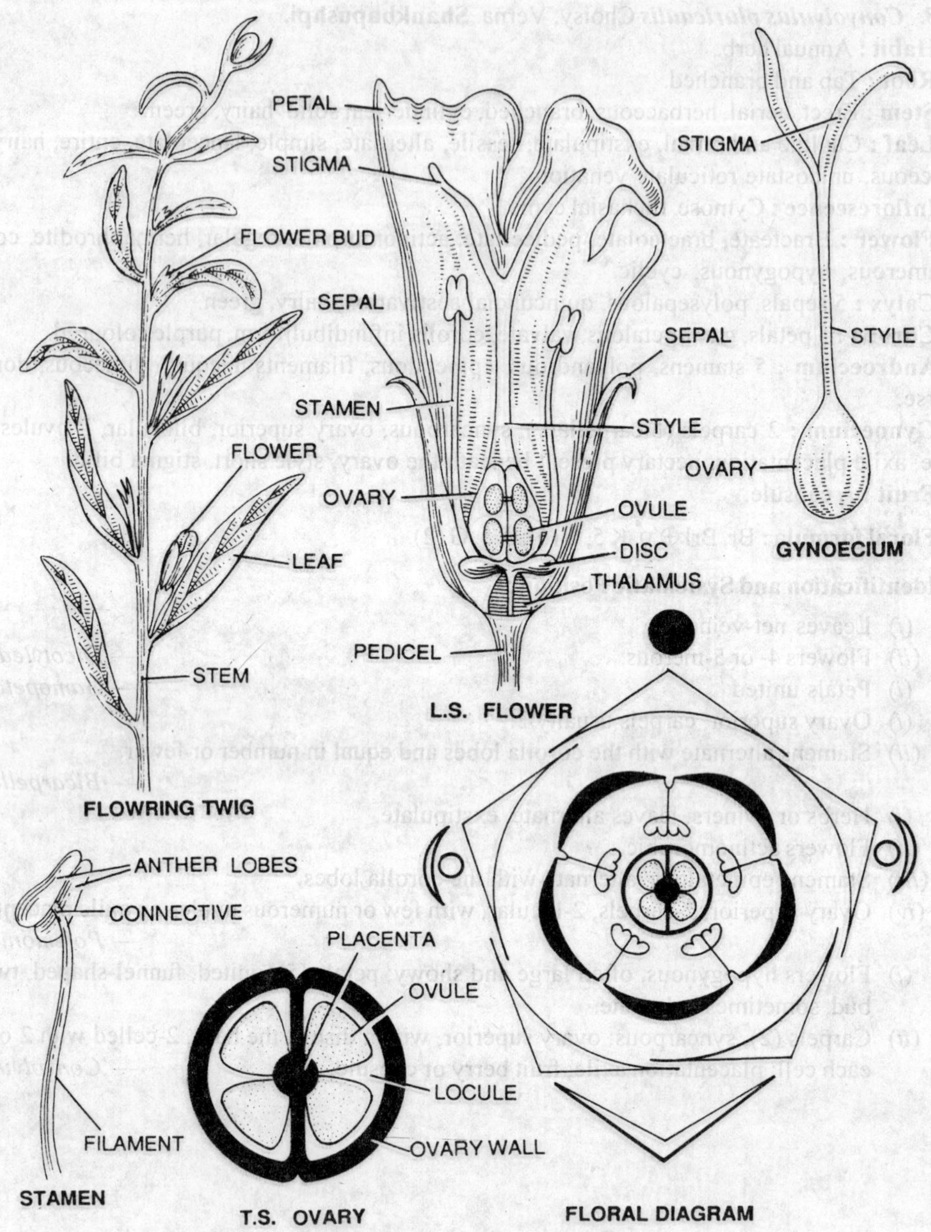

Fig. 9.66. Convolvulaceae. *Convolvulus pluricaulis* Choisy.; Verna., **shankhapushpi.**

CUSCUTA

4. Cuscuta reflexa Roxb.; Verna. **Amar bel;** Eng. Dodder.

Habit : A leafless twining total stem parasite, perennial herb.

Stem : Weak, twiner, branched, cylinderical, solid, glabrous yellowish green in colour.

Leaf : Absent.

Inflorescence : Fascicled, or racemose.

Flower : Pedicellate (short pedicels), bracteate, bracteolate (two lateral bracteoles). hermaphrodite, actinomorphic, complete, hypogynous.

Calyx : 5 sepals, slightly connate at the base, partly polysepalous, greenish white, quincuncial aestivation, inferior.

Corolla : 5 petals, gamopetalous, bracteolate, corolla lobes short, campanulate, acute, triangular spreading out scales, present at the base of the corolla tube, white, imbricate aestivation.

Androecium : 5 stamens, polyandrous, epipetalous, filaments short, anthers bilobed, dorsifixed.

Gynoecium : 2 carpels (bicarpellary), syncarpous, ovary-superior, bilocular, axile placentation, two ovules in each loculus, style very much reduced, stigma bifid.

Fruit : A capsule.

Floral formula : Br, ⊕ ⚥ K 5, C (5), A 5, G $(\underline{2})$.

Identification and Systematic Position :

(*i*) Leaves net-veined.
(*ii*) Flowers 4- or 5-merous. — *Dicotyledons.*

(*i*) Petals united. — *Gamopetalae.*

(*i*) Ovary superior, carpels usually 2.
(*ii*) Stamens alternate with the corolla lobes and equal in number or fewer. — *Bicarpellatae.*

(*i*) Herbs or twiners; leaves alternate, exstipulate.
(*ii*) Flowers actinomorphic.
(*iii*) Stamens epipetalous, alternate with the corolla lobes.
(*iv*) Ovary superior, 2-carpels, 2-locular, with few or numerous ovules on axile placentas. — *Polemoniales.*

(*i*) Flowers hypogynous, often large and showy; petals (5), united, funnel-shaped, twisted in bud, sometimes imbricate.
(*ii*) Carpels (2), syncarpous; ovary superior, with a disc at the base, 2-celled with 2 ovules in each cell; placentation axile; fruit berry or capsule. — *Convolvulaceae.*

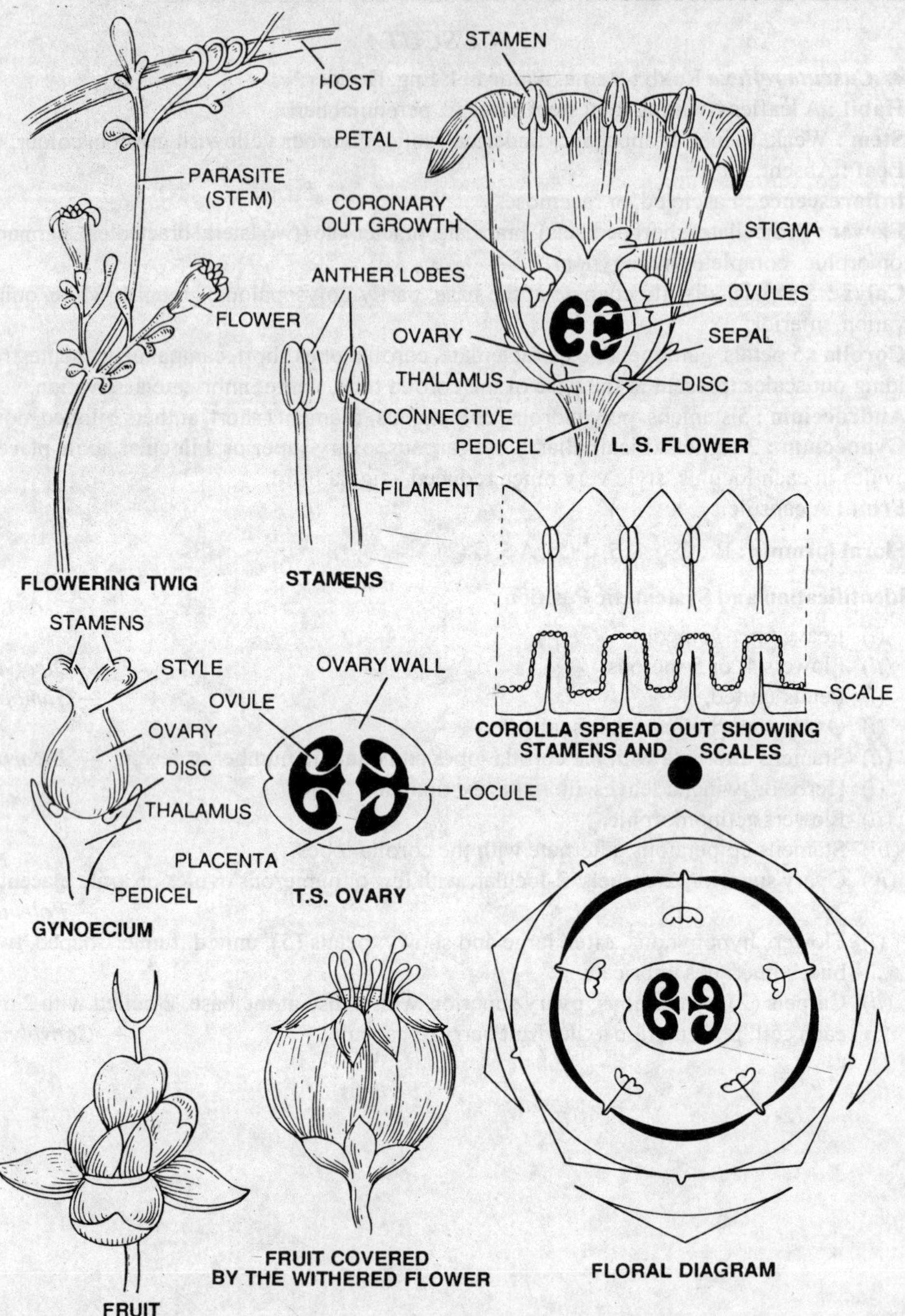

Fig. 9.67. Convolvulaceae. *Cuscuta reflexa* Roxb.; Eng., dodder; Verna., **amar bel.**

Economic value. The plant is sometimes used as a dye. The seeds are regarded as carminative. The seeds are alterative, and are used to purify the blood. The plant is purgative; used externally against itch, internally in protracted fevers. Infusion of plant is used as a wash for sores. The stems are useful in bilious disorders.

FAMILY—SOLANACEAE (Nightshade family)

SOLANUM

1. ***Solanum nigrum*** Linn. **Makoi;** Eng. Black nightshade.

Habit : An annual small wild herb.

Root : Tap and branched.

Stem : Erect, branched, herbaceous, cylinderical, solid, glabrous or somewhat hairy.

Leaf : Simple, alternate, cauline, petiolate or sub-sessile, exstipulate, ovate, dentate, acute, unicostate reticulate venation.

Inflorescence : Cymose, extra-axillary subumbellate cyme.

Flower : Pedicellate, ebracteate, hermaphrodite, actinomorphic, pentamerous except pistil, complete, small, white, hypogynous.

Calyx : 5 sepals, gamosepalous, lobes small, oblong, acute, green, hairy, valvate or imbricate aestivation.

Corolla : 5 petals, gamopetalous, rotate, lobes oblong, acute, white, twisted or valvate aestivation.

Androecium : 5 stamens, alternate to petals, polyandrous, epipetalous, filaments short, anthers oblong, connivent in a cone like structure, bicelled, introrse, yellow, dehiscence by apical pores.

Gynoecium : 2 carpels (bicarpellary), syncarpous, ovary obliquely placed in the flower, ovary superior, globose, bilocular, axile placentation, many shining ovules present on swollen placenta, style simple, hairy at the base, stigma one.

Fruit : Berry, with persistent calyx.

Floral formula : $\oplus$ ⚥ K (5), $\overparen{C\ (5), A\ 5}$, G $(\underline{2})$.

Identification and Systematic Position :

(*i*) Leaves net-veined.
(*ii*) Flowers 4- or 5-merous. — *Dicotyledons.*

(*i*) Petals united. — *Gamopetalae.*

(*i*) Ovary superior, carpels usually 2.
(*ii*) Stamens alternate with the corolla lobes and equal in number or fewer. — *Bicarpellatae.*

(*i*) Herbs or twiners; leaves alternate, exstipulate.
(*ii*) Flowers actinomorphic.
(*iii*) Stamens epipetalous.
(*iv*) Ovary superior, 2-carpels, 2-locular, with few or numerous ovules on axile placentas. — *Polemoniales.*

(*i*) Herbs and shrubs, leaves simple sometimes pinnate, alternate.
(*ii*) Sepals united, persistent; corolla usually funnel- or cup-shaped, 5-lobed valvate or twisted in bud.
(*iii*) Stamens 5, epipetalous, anthers connate.
(*iv*) 2-carpels, syncarpous; ovary superior, 2-loculed, sometimes 4-celled due to the formation of false septum; many ovules in each locule; swollen axile placentation; ovary obliquely placed in the flower; fruit a berry or capsule. — *Solanaceae.*

Bentham & Hooker (1862)	*Engler & Prantl* (1931)	*Hutchinson* (1959)
Dicotyledons	Dicotyledoneae	Dicotyledones
Gamopetalae	Sympetalae	Herbaceae
Polemoniales	Tubiflorae	Solanales
Solanaceae	Solanaceae	Solanaceae

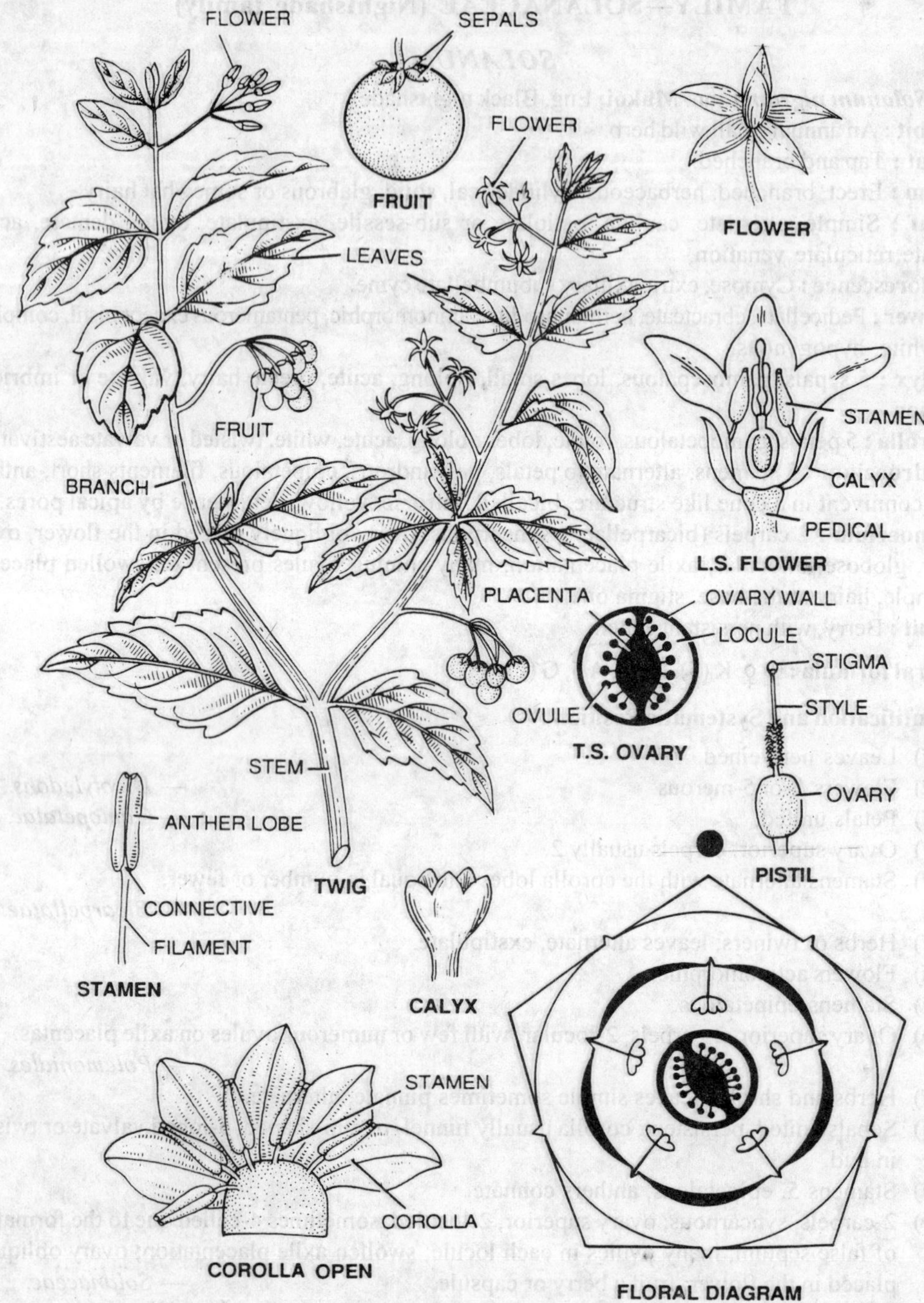

Fig. 9.68. Solanaceae. *Solanum nigrum* Linn.; Eng., black nightshade; Verna., **makoi.**

Economic value. A medicinal plant. The herb is a cardiac tonic, alterative diuretic, sedative, diaphoretic, cathartic and expectorant. It is used as decoction in enlargement of the liver and jaundice. The leaf juice is given in inflammation of the kidneys and bladder and in gonorrhoea, dropsy, heart diseases, piles and enlargement of spleen.

CESTRUM

*2. **Cestrum nocturnum*** Linn.; Verna. **Rat-ki-Rani;** Eng. Night jessamine.

Habit : An ornamental perennial shrub.

Stem : Erect, branched, woody, solid, glabrous and green.

Leaf : Simple, cauline and ramal, alternate, short petioled, exstipulate, entire, acute, unicostate reticulate venation.

Inflorescence : Cymose, axillary cymes.

Flower : Pedicellate, short pedicels, bracteate, hermaphrodite, actinomorphic, white, fragrant, complete, hypogynous, pentamerous and cyclic.

Calyx : 5 sepals, gamosepalous, green, valvate aestivation, inferior.

Corolla : 5 petals, gamopetalous, tubular, white, fragrant, valvate aestivation, inferior.

Androecium : 5 stamens, polyandrous, epipetalous, alternate to the petals, filaments long, anthers bicelled, introrse.

Gynoecium : 2 carpels (bicarpellary), syncarpous, ovary superior, obliquely placed in the flower, bilocular, axile placentation, many ovules in each loculus.

Floral formula : Br, ⊕ ⚥ K (5), $\overbrace{\text{C (5), A 5}}$, G $(\underline{2})$.

Identification and Systematic Position :

(*i*) Leaves net-veined.

(*ii*) Flowers 4- or 5-merous. — *Dicotyledons.*

(*i*) Petals united. — *Gamopetalae.*

(*i*) Ovary superior, carpels usually 2.

(*ii*) Stamens alternate with the corolla lobes and equal in number or fewer. — *Bicarpellatae.*

(*i*) Herbs or twiners; leaves alternate, exstipulate.

(*ii*) Flowers actinomorphic.

(*iii*) Stamens epipetalous, alternate with the corolla lobes.

(*iv*) Ovary superior, 2-carpels, 2-locular, with few or numerous ovules on axile placentas. — *Polemoniales.*

(*i*) Flowers hypogynous, often large and showy; petals (5), united, funnel-shaped, twisted in bud, sometimes imbricate.

(*ii*) Carpels (2), syncarpous; ovary superior, with a disc at the base, 2-celled with 2 ovules in each cell; placentation axile; fruit berry or capsule. — *Solanaceae.*

Other important members of the family. *Solanum tuberosum* Linn., **Alu;** *S. melongena* Linn., **Baigun;** *S. xanthocarpum* Schrad. & Wendl., **Kateli;** roots are used in cough, asthma and leaves for rheumatism; *Capsicum frutescens* Linn., **Lal-mirch;** *Lycopersicon esculentum* Mill., **Tamatar;** *Atropa belladona* Linn., **Sagangur** - roots used as sedative, stimulant and antispasmodic; *Nicotiana tabacum* Linn. **Tambaku** - fumitory.

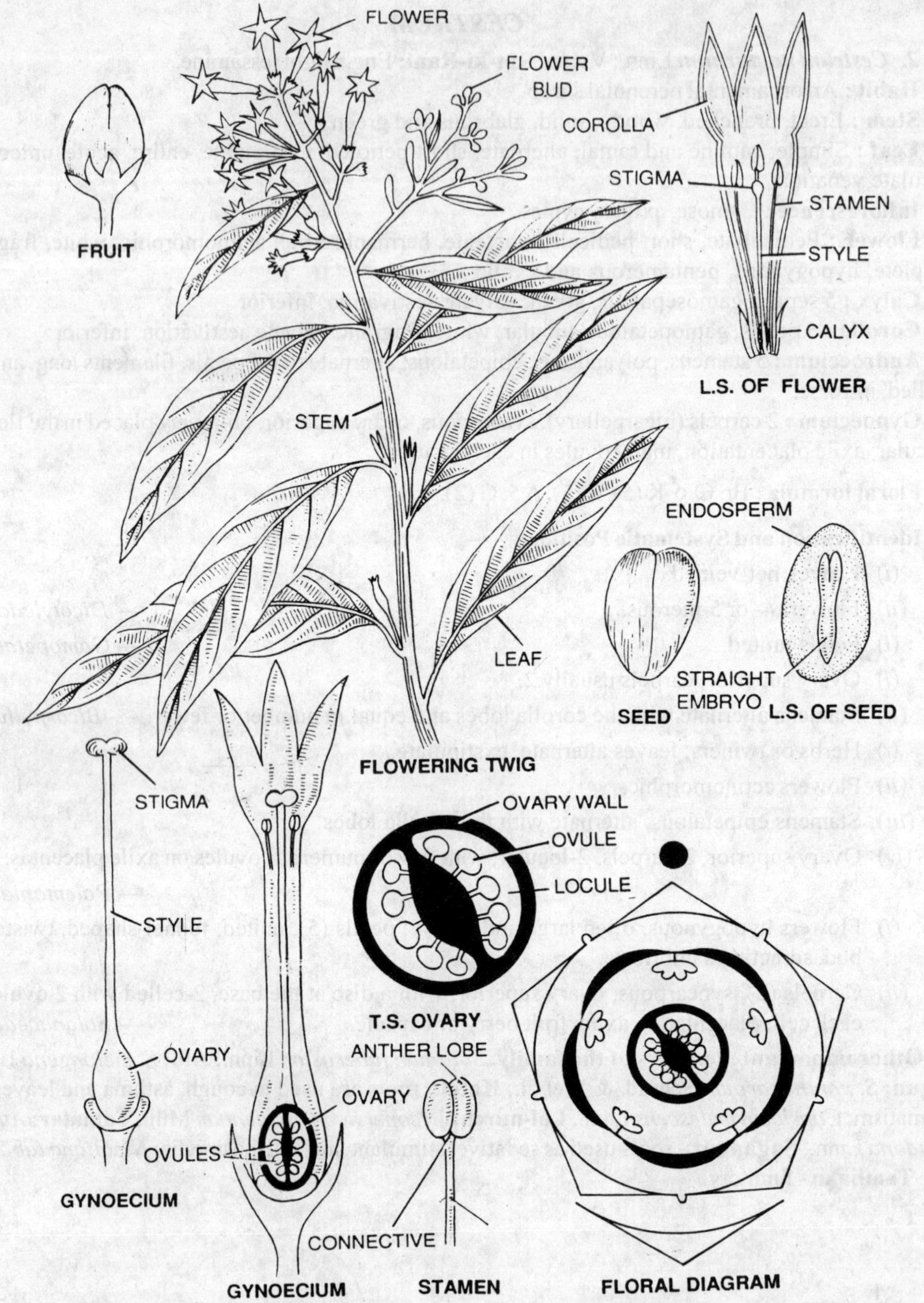

Fig. 9.69. Solanaceae. *Cestrum nocturnum* Linn.; Eng., night jessamine; Verna., **raat-ki-rani.**

Economic value. Grown for its flowers, which are scented at night.

PETUNIA

3. Petunia nyctaginifolia Juss.

Habit : Annual cultivated ornamental herb.

Root : Tap and branched.

Stem : Erect, aerial, herbaceous, branched, cylinderical, solid, hairy and green.

Leaf : Cauline and ramal, alternate in basal part and opposite decussate in upper part, exstipulate, sessile, simple, ovate, entire, acute, hairy, coriaceous, unicostate reticulate.

Inflorescence : Cymose, axillary dichasial cyme.

Flower : Bracteate, pedicellate, actinomorphic, regular, hermaphrodite, pentamerous, hypogynous, complete, cyclic.

Calyx : 5 sepals, gamosepalous, deeply lobed, persistent, hairy, inferior, green.

Corolla : 5 petals, gamopetalous, in duplicate, valvate, infundibuliform, white or purple coloured, inferior.

Androecium : 5 stamens, polyandrous, epipetalous, filaments unequal, dithecous, basifixed, introrse.

Gynoecium : 2 carpels (bicarpellary), syncarpous, ovary superior, bilocular, many ovules in each locule, axile placentation, septum oblique, placenta swollen, style long, stigma capitate.

Fruit : Capsule.

Floral formula : Br, $\oplus$ ⚥ K (5), $\widehat{C\,(5),\ A\,5}$, G $(\underline{2})$.

Identification and Systematic Position :

(*i*) Leaves net-veined.
(*ii*) Flowers 4- or 5-merous. — *Dicotyledons.*

(*i*) Petals united. — *Gamopetalae.*

(*i*) Ovary superior, carpels usually 2.
(*ii*) Stamens alternate with the corolla lobes and equal in number or fewer. — *Bicarpellatae.*

(*i*) Herbs or twiners; leaves alternate, exstipulate.
(*ii*) Flowers actinomorphic.
(*iii*) Stamens epipetalous, alternate with the corolla lobes.
(*iv*) Ovary superior, 2-carpels, 2-locular, with few or numerous ovules on axile placentas. — *Polemoniales.*

(*i*) Flowers hypogynous, often large and showy; petals (5), united, funnel-shaped, twisted in bud, sometimes imbricate.
(*ii*) Carpels (2), syncarpous; ovary superior, with a disc at the base, 2-celled with 2 ovules in each cell; placentation axile; fruit berry or capsule. — *Solanaceae.*

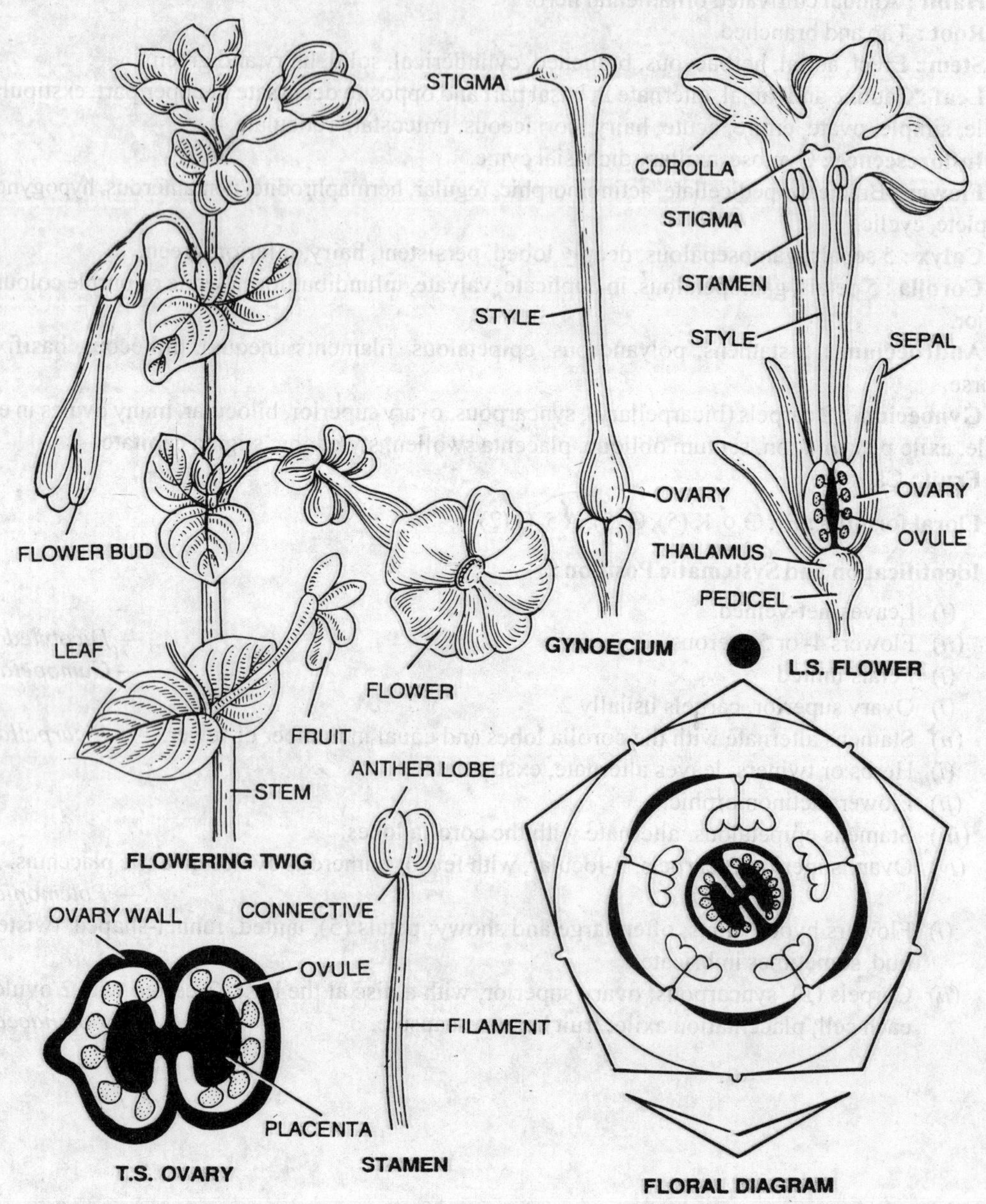

Fig. 9.70. Solanaceae. *Petunia nyctaginifolia* Juss.

Economic value. The plant is grown as an ornamental for its variously coloured funnel-shaped flowers.

WITHANIA

4. Withania somnifera Dunal; Verna. **Ashwagandha**.

Habit : A perennial shrub.

Root : Tap and branched.

Stem : Erect, aerial, basal part woody, terminal part herbaceous, branched, cylinderical, solid, hairy, green.

Leaf : Cauline and ramal, exstipulate, petiolate, alternate, simple, ovate, entire, acute, glabrous, coriaceous, unicostate reticulate.

Inflorescence : Cymose, axillary umbellate cyme.

Flower : Ebracteate, pedicellate, actinomorphic, regular, hermaphrodite, pentamerous, hypogynous, complete, cyclic.

Calyx : 5 sepals, gamosepalous, valvate, persistent, hairy, green, inferior.

Corolla : 5 petals, gamopetalous, valvate, campanulate, whitish-yellow, inferior.

Androecium : 5 stamens, polyandrous, epipetalous, anthers connivent, dithecous, basifixed, introrse.

Gynoecium : 2 carpels (bicarpellary), syncarpous, ovary superior, bilocular, many ovules in each locule, axile placentation, ovary obliquely placed in the flower, placenta swollen, style long, stigma capitate.

Fruit : Berry

Floral Formula : $\oplus$ ⚥ $K(5), \overparen{C(5), A(5)}, G(\underline{2})$

Identification and Systematic Position :

(*i*) Leaves net-veined.
(*ii*) Flowers 4- or 5- merous. — *Dicotyledons.*
(*i*) Petals united. — *Gamopetalae.*
(*i*) Ovary superior, carpels usually 2.
(*ii*) Stamens alternate with the corolla lobes and equal in number or fewer. — *Bicarpellatae.*
(*i*) Herbs or twiners; leaves alternate, exstipulate.
(*ii*) Flowers actinomorphic.
(*iii*) Stamens epipetalous.
(*iv*) Ovary superior, 2-carpels, 2-locular, with few or numerous ovules on axile placentas. — *Polemoniales.*
(*i*) Herbs and shrubs, leaves simple sometimes pinnate, alternate.
(*ii*) Sepals united, persistent; corolla usually funnel- or cup-shaped, 5-lobed valvate or twisted in bud.
(*iii*) Stamens 5, epipetalous, anthers connate.
(*iv*) 2-carpels, syncarpous, ovary superior, 2-loculed, sometimes 4-celled due to the formation of false septum; many ovules in each locule; swollen axile placentation; ovary obliquely placed in the flower; fruit a berry or capsule. — *Solanaceae.*

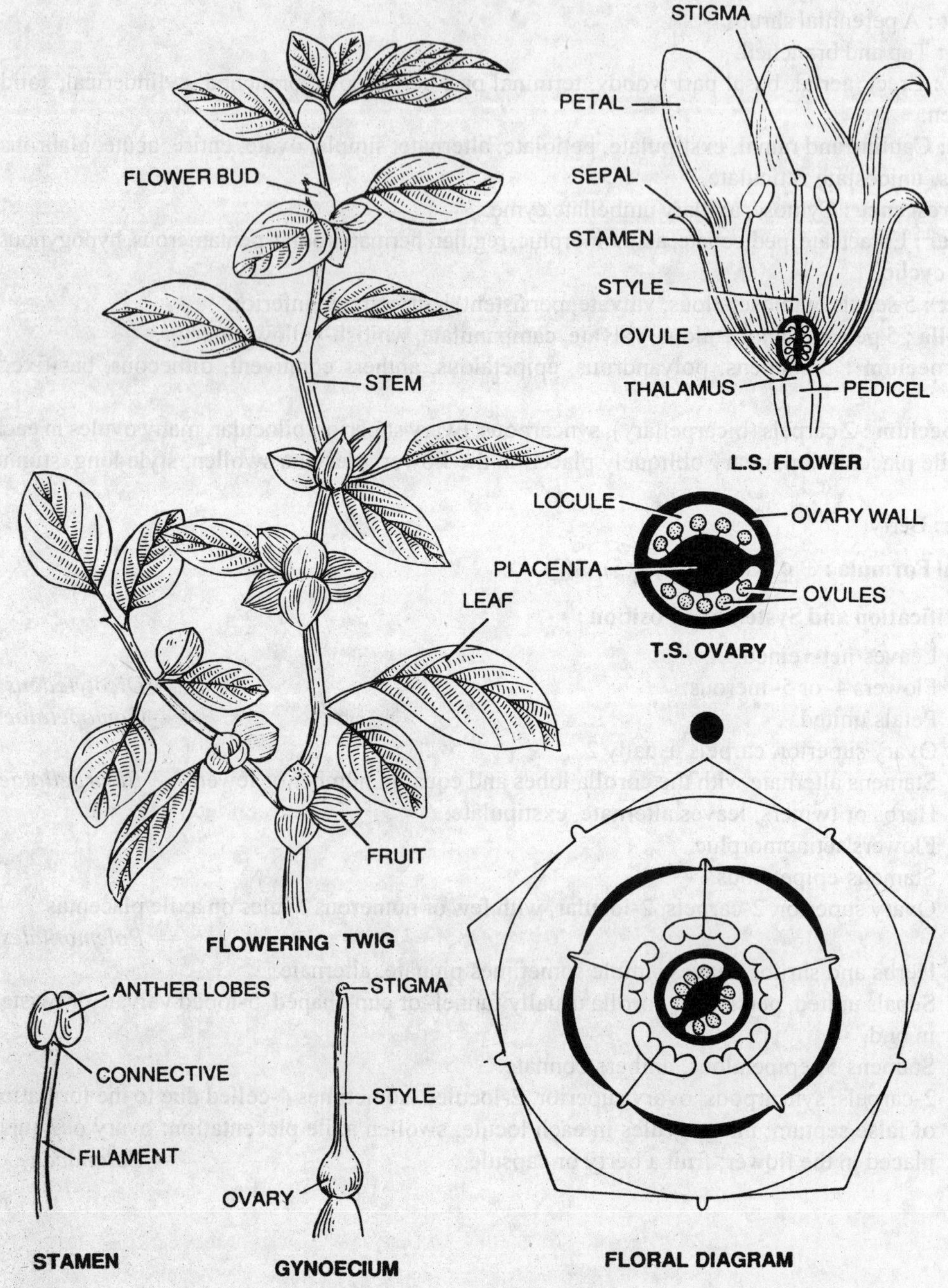

Fig. 9.71. Solanaceae. *Withania somnifera* Dunal.; Verna., **ashwagandha.**

Economic value. The root is considered alterative, aphrodisiac, tonic, deobstruent, diuretic, narcotic, abortifacient; used in rheumatism, constipation, debility from old age, emaciation of children, etc.

FAMILY - SCROPHULARIACEAE (Figwort family)

LINDENBERGIA

1. ***Lindenbergia indica*** (Linn.) O. Ktze.

Habit : Herb.

Root : Tap and branched.

Stem : Aerial, erect, herbaceous, cylinderical, branched, solid, green, hairy.

Leaves : Cauline and ramal, simple, opposite, petiolate, ovate, serrate, acute, unicostate reticulate, hairy.

Inflorescence : Cymose, solitary axillary.

Flower : Bracteate, pedicellate, hermaphrodite, zygomorphic, complete, pentamerous, hypogynous.

Calyx : 5 sepals, gamosepalous, imbricate.

Corolla : 5 petals, gamopetalous, zygomorphic, united in (2) + (3) lobes, yellow.

Androecium : 4 stamens, polyandrous, epipetalous, didynamous, filaments long, anther dithecous, introrse, basifixed, dehisce by longitudinal slits, anthers are separated from each other by the elongated connective.

Gynoecium : Bicarpellary, syncarpous, gynoecium situated on nectar secreting disc, ovary superior, bilocular, many anatorpous ovules arranged on a thick axile placenta (axile placentation); style simple, stigma bilobed.

Fruit : Capsule.

Floral formula : Br | ⚥ K(5), $\widehat{C(2/3),\ A\,2+2}$, $G(\underline{2})$

Identification and Systematic Position :

(*i*) Leaves net-veined.
(*ii*) Flowers 4- or 5- merous. — *Dicotyledons.*

(*i*) Petals united. — *Gamopetalae.*

(*i*) Ovary superior, carpels usually 2.
(*ii*) Stamens alternate with the corolla lobes and equal in number or fewer. — *Bicarpellatae.*

(*i*) Mostly herbaceous; leaves alternate to opposite.
(*ii*) Corolla nearly always zygomorphic with stamens fewer than the corolla-lobes; stamens 2 or 4, epipetalous.
(*iii*) Ovary superior, many ovules; axile placentation. — *Personales.*

(*i*) Flowers zygomorphic, 2-lipped, sometimes spurred or saccate.
(*ii*) Stamens 4, didynamous, sometimes 2; posterior stamen absent or a staminode.
(*iii*) Gynoecium - carpels (2), syncarpous, overy superior, bilocular, anteroposterior, placentation axile, ovules many; fruit a capsule or berry. — *Scrophulariaceae.*

Bentham & Hooker (1862)	*Engler & Prantl (1931)*	*Hutchinson (1959)*
Dicotyledons	Dicotyledoneae	Dicotyledones
Gamopetalae	Sympetalae	Herbaceae
Personales	Tubiflorae	Personales
Scrophulariaceae	Scrophulariaceae	Scrophulariaceae.

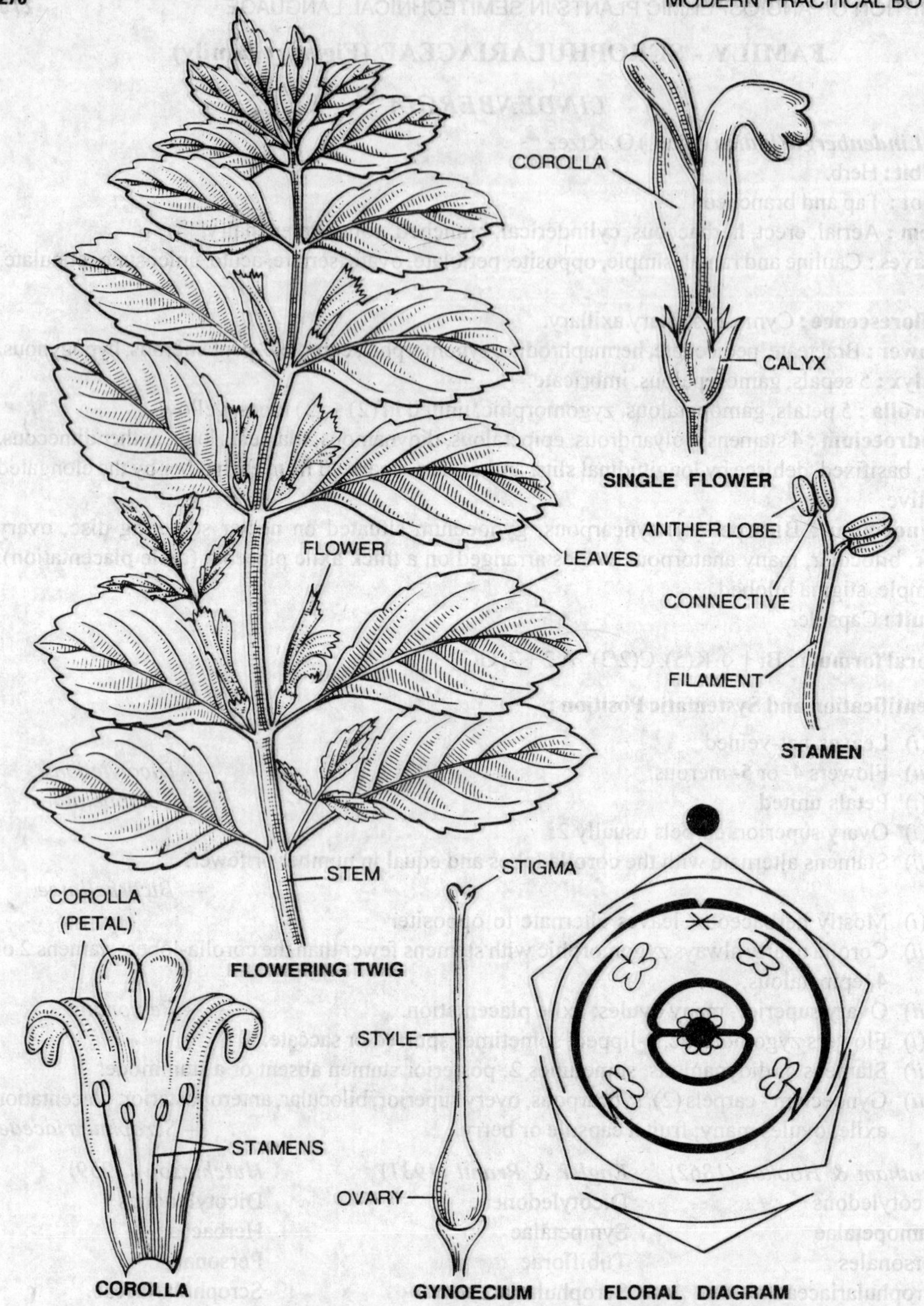

Fig. 9.72. Scrophulariaceae. *Lindenbergia indica* (Linn.) O. Ktze.

Economic value. The plant juice is given in chronic bronchitis and mixed with that of coriander applied to skin eruptions.

VERONICA

2. ***Veronica anagalis*** Linn.

Habit : Annual shade and moist loving herb.

Root : Tap and branched.

Stem : Erect, aerial, herbaceous, solid, cylinderical, branched, pubescent, green.

Leaves : Cauline and ramal, semi-amplexicaul, exstipulate, sessile, simple, entire, acute, unicostate reticulate, pubescent.

Inflorescence : Racemose, terminal raceme.

Flower : Bracteate, pedicellate, zygomorphic, hermaphrodite, complete, tetramerous, small. white, hypogynous and cyclic.

Calyx : 4 sepals, polysepalous, imbricate or quincuncial.

Corolla : 4 petals, gamopetalous, imbricate.

Androecium : Stamens 2, epipetalous, free, filaments long, anther dithecous, dorsifixed, introrse.

Gynoecium : Bicarpellary, syncarpous, ovary superior, bilocular, axile placentation, several anatropous ovules in each locule on swollen placenta, style simple, stigma lobed.

Fruit : Capsule.

Floral formula : Br | ⚥ K4, $\overparen{C(1/3), A2,}$ G($\underline{2}$)

Identification and Systematic Position :

(*i*) Leaves net-veined.
(*ii*) Flowers 4- or 5- merous. — *Dicotyledons.*
(*i*) Petals united. — *Gamopetalae.*
(*i*) Ovary superior, carpels usually 2.
(*ii*) Stamens alternate with the corolla lobes and equal in number or fewer. — *Bicarpellatae.*
(*i*) Mostly herbaceous; leaves alternate to opposite.
(*ii*) Corolla nearly always zygomorphic with stamens fewer than the corolla-lobes; stamens 2 or 4, epipetalous.
(*iii*) Ovary superior, many ovules; axile placentation. — *Personales.*
(*i*) Flowers zygomorphic, 2-lipped, sometimes spurred or saccate.
(*ii*) Stamens 4, didynamous, sometimes 2; posterior stamen absent or a staminode.
(*iii*) Gynoecium - carpels (2), syncarpous, overy superior, bilocular, anterioposterior, placentation axile, ovules many; fruit a capsule or berry. —*Scrophulariaceae.*

Other important members of the family. *Digitalis lanata* Ehrh., leaves are the source of a drug, which is used as a cardiac stimulant and tonic; *D. purpurea* Linn., leaves cardiac, stimulant and tonic in heart diseases; *Verbascum thapsus* Linn., **Bantamakhu, Gidar-tamakhu** - herb employed for treatment of asthma and other pulmonary complaints.

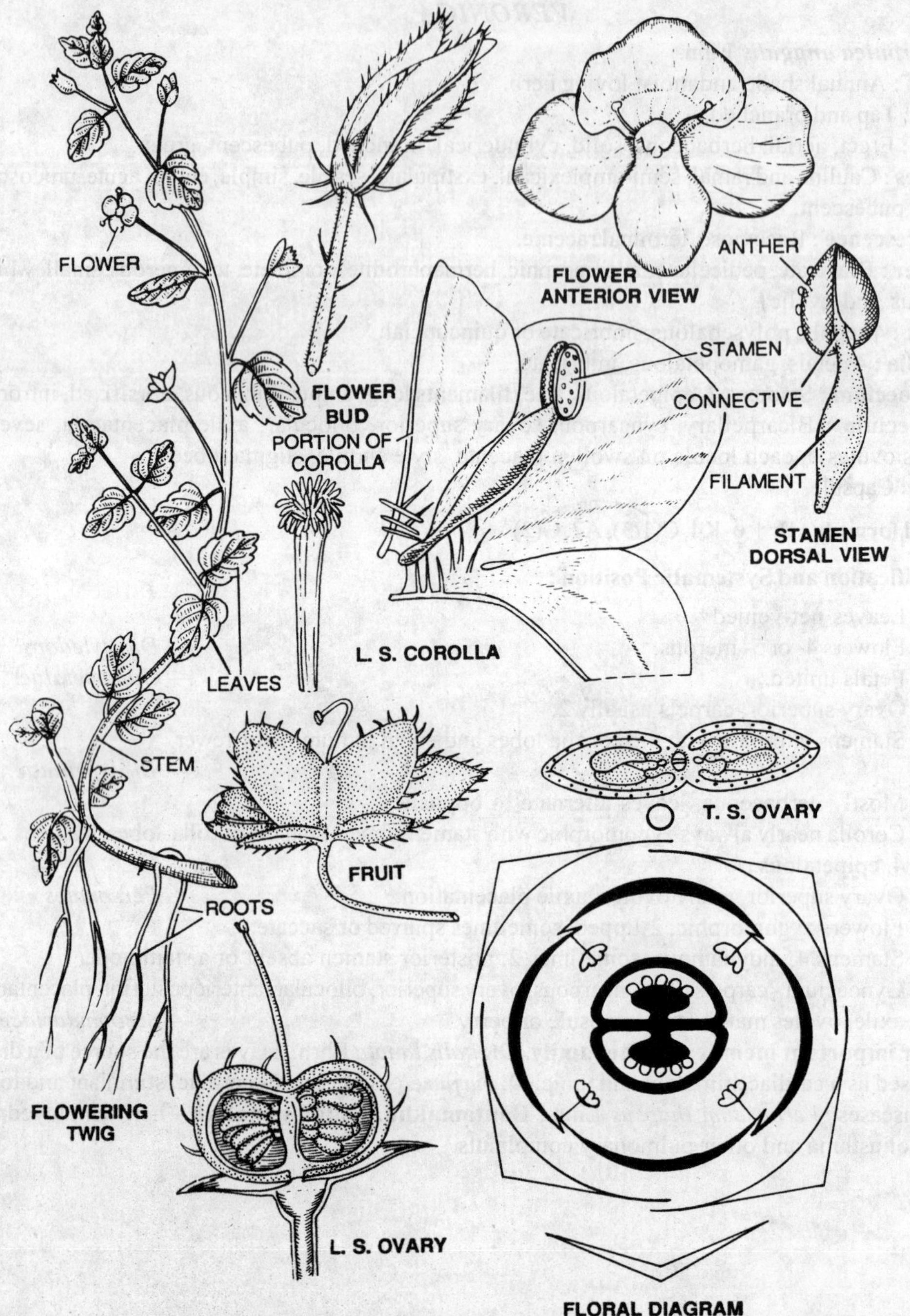

Fig. 9.73. Scrophulariaceae. *Veronica anagalis* Linn.

Economic value. The plant is used medicinally. It is alterative, diuretic, antiscorbutic, given, in scurvy, impurity of blood, etc. Used as a remedy for scrofulous affections, especially of the skin bruised and applied externally for healing burns and ulcers.

FAMILY - PEDALIACEAE (Pedalium family)

SESAMUM

Sesamum indicum Linn.; Verna. **Til;** Eng. sesame.

Habit : Annual herb 1-2 feet high, cultivated.

Root : Tap and branched.

Stem : Erect, pubescent, profusely branched from the base, angular.

Leaves : Cauline and ramal, oblong or ovate, 3-5 inches, lower leaves opposite, lobed, with serrated margins upper leaves alternate, narrow, oblong, the upper surface glabrous, the lower surface pubescent.

Inflorescence : Cymose, solitary axillary.

Flower : Pedicellate (small pedicels), bractcate, hermaphrodite, zygomorphic, hypogynous, complete, pinkish in colour, pentamerous, cyclic.

Calyx : 5 sepals (small in size about 1/4 inches long), gamosepalous, sepals lanceolate, acute, hairy, aestivation imbricate or valvate.

Corolla : 5 petals, gamopetalous, 2-lipped, pinkish in colour with yellow markings, each petal about 1½ inches long, corolla 5-lobed, the upper lip consists of two equal sized lobes while the lower lip includes three petals out of which the central one is largest, corolla tubular-ventricose with subgibbous throat which is hairy outside.

Androecium : 4 stamens, didynamous, epipetalous, instead of fifth stamen usually a staminode is present, anthers 2-celled (dithecous), sagittate, introrse and dehisce by longitudinal slit.

Gynoecium : 2-carpels (bicarpellary), syncarpous, ovary superior, bilocular (four locules formed due to false sepatation), placentation axile, style filiform, stigmas 2 and lobed.

Fruit : Loculicidal capsule, one inch long, erect, hispid, beak short, valves separating half way down.

Floral formula : | ⚥ K(5), $\overbrace{\text{C(5), A2+2}}$, G($\underline{2}$)

Identification and Systematic Position :

(*i*) Leaves net-veined.
(*ii*) Flowers 4- or 5- merous. — *Dicotyledons.*
(*i*) Petals united. — *Gamopetalae.*
(*i*) Ovary superior, carpels usually 2.
(*ii*) Stamens alternate with the corolla lobes and equal in number or fewer. — *Bicarpellatae.*
(*i*) Mostly herbaceous; leaves alternate to opposite.
(*ii*) Corolla nearly always zygomorphic with stamens fewer than the corolla-lobes; stamens 2 or 4, epipetalous.
(*iii*) Ovary superior, many ovules; axile placentation. — *Personales.*
(*i*) Herbs with glandular hairs and opposite leaves.
(*ii*) Flowers arranged in axillary cymes or racemes.
(*iii*) Gynoecium bicarpellary, 2-4 celled; axile placentation; fruit loculicidal capsule; seeds small, smooth. — *Pedaliaceae.*

Bentham & Hooker (1862)	*Engler & Prantl (1931)*	*Hutchinson (1959)*
Dicotyledons	Dicotyledoneae	Dicotyledones
Gamopetalae	Sympetalae	Lignosae
Personales	Tubiflorae	Bignoniales
Pedaliaceae	Pedaliaceae	Pedaliaceae

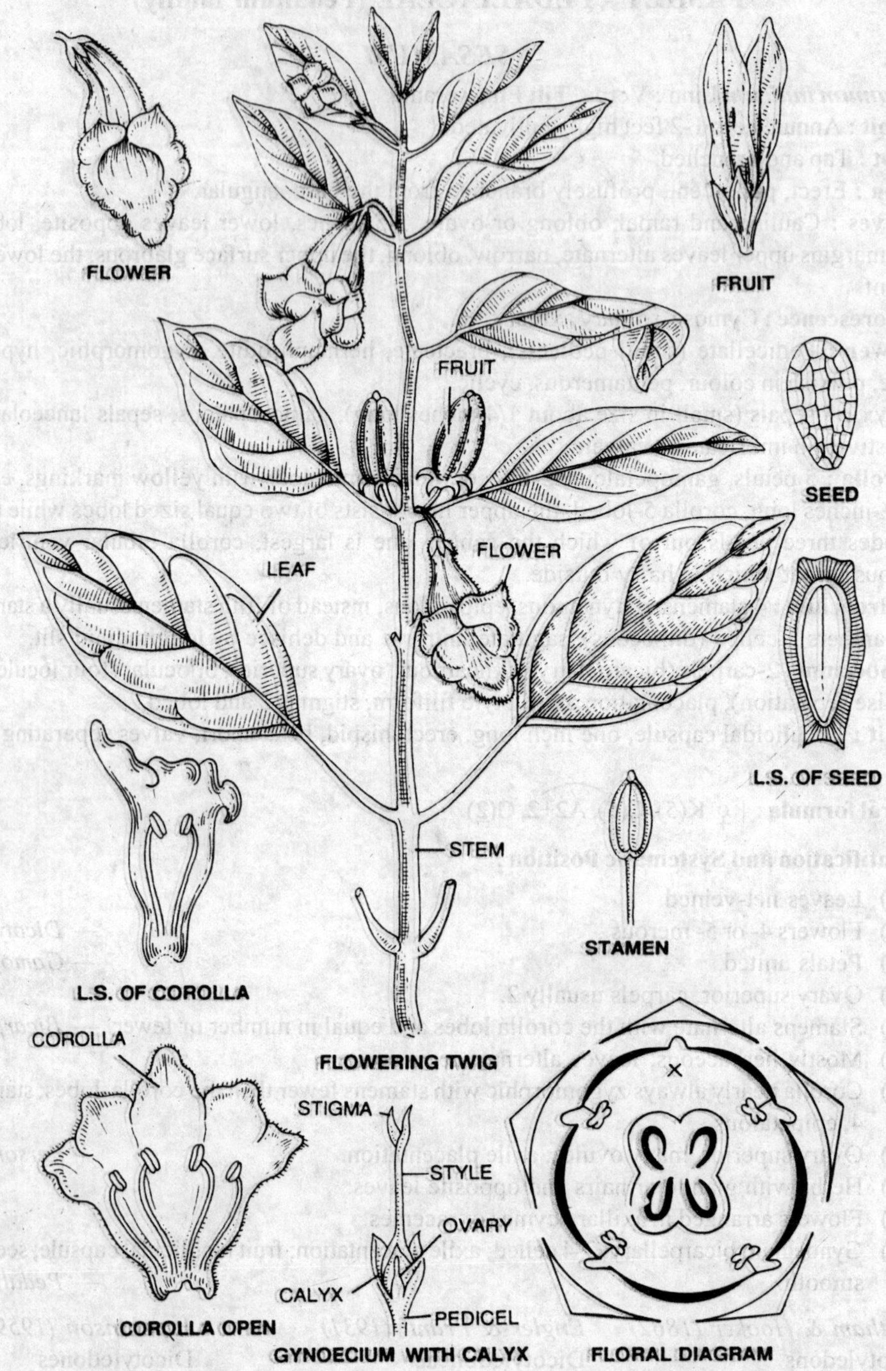

Fig. 9.74. Pedaliaceae. *Sesamum indicum* Linn.; Eng., sesame; Verna. **til**.

Economic value. The seed oil is edible, and is also used in the manufacture of soap and cosmetics. The oil-cake is used as fodder and the seeds are used in confectionery. The morning dew found on the flowers is used for curing eye diseases.

FAMILY - ACANTHACEAE (Acanthus family)

ADHATODA

1. Adhatoda vasica Nees.; Verna. **Arusa;** Eng. Malabar nut.

Habit : A busby shrub.

Root : Tap and branched.

Stem : Erect, branched, woody, cylinderical, solid, glabrous, green.

Leaf : Cauline and ramal, simple, opposite, decussate, upper leaves short petioled, lower leaves long petioled, ovate - lanceolate, entire acute, unicostate reticulate venation, coriaceous, glabrous.

Inflorescence : A terminal spike, lower flowers arranged in cymes.

Flower : Sessile, bracteate (leaf bracts), bracteolate, bracteoles - two, large, hermaphrodite, zygomorphic, hypogynous, pentamerous, cyclic.

Calyx : 5 sepals, polysepalous, slightly connate at the base, sepaloid, arranged in two whorls of two each, two outer bigger and inner smaller, inferior, imbricate aestivation.

Corolla : 5 petals, gamopetalous, slightly bilabiate, upper lip consisting of four lobes and the lower of single lobe, inferior, imbricate aestivation, yellowish in colour.

Androecium : 2 stamens, epipetalous, sometimes three stamens represented by staminodes anthers bicelled, dorsifixed, introrse.

Gynoecium : 2 carpels (bicarpellary), syncarpous, ovary superior, bilocular, axile placentation, one ovule in each loculus, style terminal, stigma slightly elongated, ovary situated on a honey secreting disc.

Fruit : Capsule.

Floral formula : Br, Brl | ⚥ K5, $\overparen{C(4+1), A2}$, G($\underline{2}$)

Identification and Systematic Position :

(*i*) Leaves net-veined.
(*ii*) Flowers 4- or 5- merous. — *Dicotyledons.*
(*i*) Petals united. — *Gamopetalae.*
(*i*) Ovary superior, carpels usually 2.
(*ii*) Stamens alternate with the corolla lobes and equal in number or fewer. — *Bicarpellatae.*
(*i*) Mostly herbaceous; leaves alternate to opposite.
(*ii*) Corolla nearly always zygomorphic with stamens fewer than the corolla-lobes; stamens 2 or 4, epipetalous.
(*iii*) Ovary superior, many ovules; axile placentation. — *Personales.*
(*i*) Herbs shrubs or climbers with opposite leaves.
(*ii*) Inflorescence a spike or a cyme; flowers zygomorphic, often bilabiate often with bracts and bracteoles.
(*iii*) Stamens 2 or 4, if 4 didynamous, epipetalous.
(*iv*) Carpels 2, syncarpous, ovary 2-celled, superior, 2 to many ovules in each cell; stigmas 2, placentation axile; fruit 2 valved capsule; seeds supported on curved hooks (jaculators).
— *Acanthaceae.*

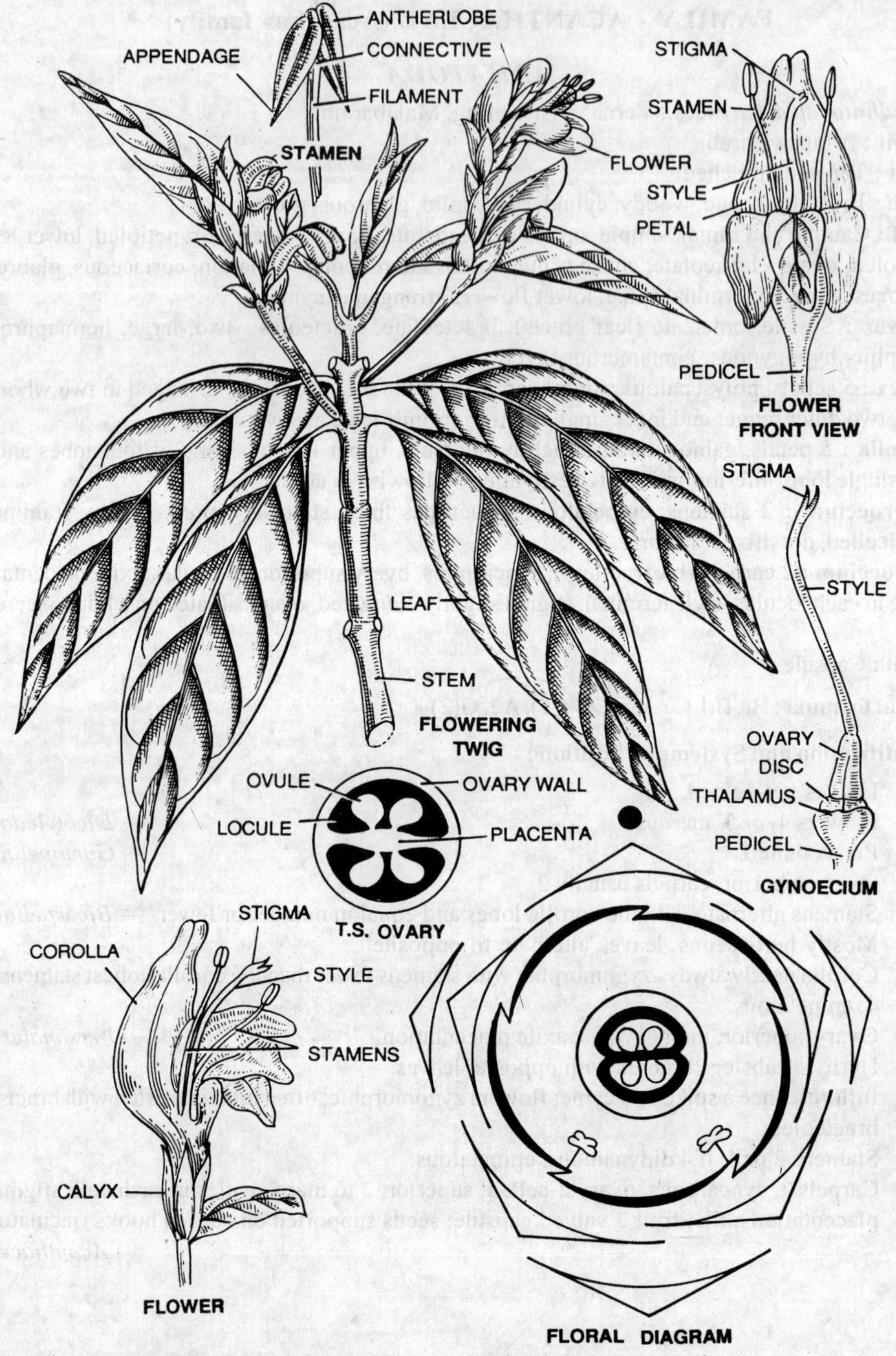

Fig. 9.75. Acanthaceae. *Adhatoda vasica* Nees.; Eng. Malabar nut; Verna. **arusa.**

Economic value. The leaves contain the alkaloid *vascine*; they are a powerful expectorant and antispasmodic; they are commonly used in chest diseases. A decoction of the leaves is given for chronic bronchitis and asthma.

RUELLIA

*2. **Ruellia prostrata*** Lamk.; Verna. **Kalighavani**.

Habit : An erect wild annual herb, common in the gardens near moist places.

Stem : Erect, branched, herbaceous, cylinderical, solid, green.

Leaf : Cauline and ramal, simple, opposite, decussate, subsessile, ovate, entire, acute, glabrous, unicostate reticulate venation, coriaceous.

Inflorescence : Cymose, dichasial cyme.

Flower : Pedicellate, bracteate, bracteolate, hermaphrodite, zygomorphic, funnel shaped, bluish pink, complete, hypogynous, pentamerous, cyclic.

Calyx : 5 sepals, gamosepalous (connate at the base), acute, sepaloid, valvate aestivation, inferior, persistent.

Corolla : 5 lobes, funnel shaped, gamopetalous, bluish-pink, twisted aestivation, inferior, infundibuliform corolla.

Androecium : 4 stamens, polyandrous, epipetalous, anthers bicelled, basifixed, introrse.

Gynoecium : 2 carpels (bicarpellary), syncarpous, ovary superior, bilocular, axile placentation, one ovule in each loculus, style slender, stigma single.

Fruit : An elongated capsule with tapering end, jaculators present.

Floral formula : Br, Brl | ⚥ K(5), $\widehat{C(5), A4}$, G($\underline{2}$)

Identification and Systematic Position :

(*i*) Leaves net-veined.
(*ii*) Flowers 4- or 5-merous. — *Dicotyledons.*
(*i*) Petals united. — *Gamopetalae.*
(*i*) Ovary superior, carpels usually 2.
(*ii*) Stamens alternate with the corolla lobes and equal in number or fewer. — *Bicarpellatae.*
(*i*) Mostly herbaceous; leaves alternate to opposite.
(*ii*) Corolla nearly always zygomorphic with stamens fewer than the corolla-lobes; stamens 2 or 4, epipetalous.
(*iii*) Ovary superior, many ovules; axile placentation. — *Personales.*
(*i*) Herbs shrubs or climbers with opposite leaves.
(*ii*) Inflorescence a spike or a cyme; flowers zygomorphic, often bilabiate often with bracts and bracteoles.
(*iii*) Stamens 2 or 4, if 4 didynamous, epipetalous.
(*iv*) Carpels 2, syncarpous, ovary 2-celled, superior, 2 to many ovules in each cell; stigmas 2, placentation axile; fruit 2 valved capsule; seeds supported on curved hooks (jaculators). — *Acanthaceae.*

Bentham & Hooker (1862)	*Engler & Prantl (1931)*	*Hutchinson (1959)*
Dicotyledons	Dicotyledoneae	Dicotyledones
Gamopetalae	Sympetalae	Herbaceae
Personales	Tubiflorae	Personales
Acanthaceae	Acanthaceae	Acanthaceae

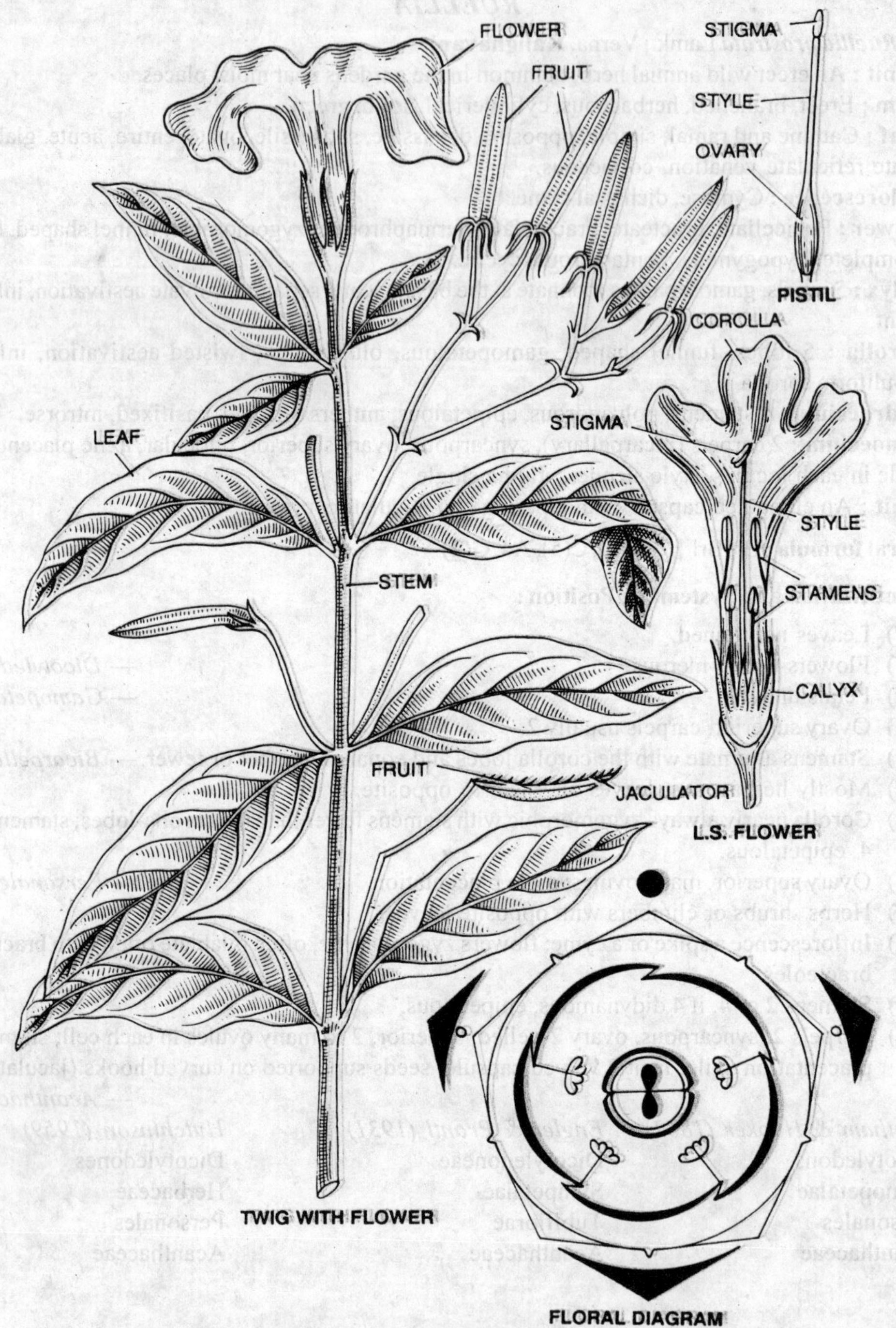

Fig. 9.76. Acanthaceae. *Ruellia prostrata* Lamk.; Verna. **kalighavani.**

Economic value. The leaves are given with liquid copal as remedy for gonorrhoea. Also used as a remedy for ear diseases.

JUSTICEA

*3. **Justicea gandarussa*** Brum. f. verna. **Bili-nargandi.**

Habit : An undershrub, commonly grown as hedge plant.

Stem : Erect, branched, cylinderical, solid, herbaceous or somewhat woody, glabrous.

Leaf : Cauline and ramal, simple, opposite, decussate, petiolate, lanceolate, entire, acute, glabrous, unicostate reticulate venation.

Inflorescence : Racemose and cymose mixed, dichasial cyme, arranged in a racemose fashion.

Flower : Sessile, bracteate (bracts lanceolate), bracteolate, hermaphrodite, zygomorphic, complete, hypogynous, pentamerous, cyclic.

Calyx : 5 sepals, gamosepalous, connate at the base and free above, green, inferior, valvate.

Corolla : 5 petals, gamopetalous, bilabiate, upper lip consists of two lobes, lower of three lobes, personate, yellowish white with pink or violet dots, imbricate aestivation inferior.

Androecium : 2 stamens, free, epipetalous, inserted on the upper part of the corolla, filaments long, anthers bicelled, basifixed.

Gynoecium : 2 carpels (bicarpellary), syncarpous, ovary superior, bilocular, axile placentation, two ovules in each loculus, style filiform, stigma bifid.

Fruit : A capsule.

Floral formula : Br, Brl | ⚥ $K(5), \overparen{C(2+3), A2}, G(\underline{2})$

Identification and Systematic Position :

(*i*) Leaves net-veined.
(*ii*) Flowers 4- or 5-merous. — *Dicotyledons.*
(*i*) Petals united. — *Gamopetalae.*
(*i*) Ovary superior, carpels usually 2.
(*ii*) Stamens alternate with the corolla lobes and equal in number or fewer.
— *Bicarpellatae.*
(*i*) Mostly herbaceous; leaves alternate to opposite.
(*ii*) Corolla nearly always zygomorphic with stamens fewer than the corolla-lobes; stamens 2 or 4, epipetalous.
(*iii*) Ovary superior, many ovules; axile placentation. — *Personales.*
(*i*) Herbs shrubs or climbers with opposite leaves.
(*ii*) Inflorescence a spike or a cyme; flowers zygomorphic, often bilabiate often with bracts and bracteoles.
(*iii*) Stamens 2 or 4, if 4 didynamous, epipetalous.
(*iv*) Carpels 2, syncarpous, ovary 2-celled, superior, 2 to many ovules in each cell; stigmas 2, placentation axile; fruit 2 valved capsule; seeds supported on curved hooks (jaculators).
Acanthaceae.

Other important members of the family. *Barleria prionitis* Linn., **Katsareya** - used in cough and asthma; *Asteracantha longifolia* Nees., **Tal-makhana** - leaves, roots and seeds - diuretic, employed for jaundice, dropsy and rheumatism; *Ecbolium linneanum* Kurz., **Udajati** - root are used in jaundice and rheumatism.

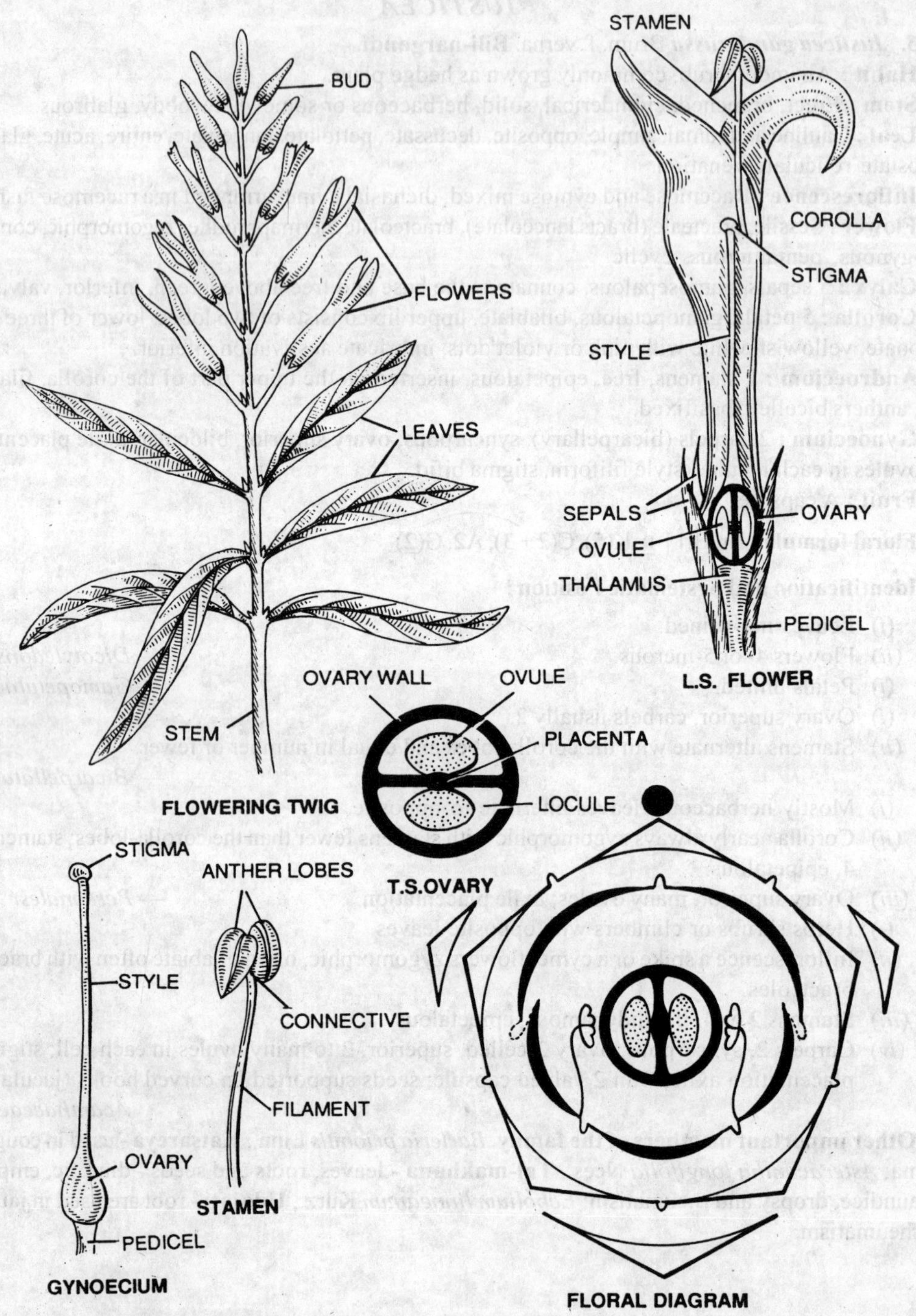

Fig. 9.77. Acanthaceae. *Justicea gandarussa* Brum.; Verna., **nili-nargandi.**

Economic value. Grown as a hedge plant. Leaves and tender shoots are diaphoretic, given in form of decoction in chronic rheumatism. Infusion of leaves is given internally in cephalalgia, hemiplegia and facial paralysis. Juice of leaf is used for earache. Plant is a febrifuge and emetic.

FAMILY - VERBENACEAE (Verbena family)

DURANTA

1. ***Duranta repens*** Linn.; Eng. Pigeon berry.

Habit : Shrub, largely grown as hedge plants.

Root : Tap and branched.

Stem : Erect, herbaceous to woody, branched, soid, cylinderical, glabrous, spiny.

Leaves : Cauline and ramal, opposite decussate, exstipulate, sub-sessile, simple, leaf base swollen, dentate, acute, ovate, unicostate reticulate, glabrous.

Inflorescence : Panicled terminal and axillary racemes.

Flower : Bracteate, bracteolate, sub-sessile, hermaphrodite, zygomorphic, complete, pentamerous, hypogynous, cyclic.

Calyx : 5 sepals, gamosepalous, valvate.

Corolla : 5 petals, gamopetalous, imbricate, tubular, violet coloured.

Androecium : 5 stamens, free, epipetalous, didynamous; anthers dithecous, basifixed, introrse, dehiscing longitudinally.

Gynoecium : 4 carpels, syncarpous, ovary superior, tetralocular, axile placentation, style simple, stigma lobed.

Fruit : Drupe.

Floral formula : Br, Brl | ⚥ K(5), $\widehat{\text{C(5), A4}}$, G($\underline{4}$)

Identification and Systematic Position :

(*i*) Leaves net-veined.
(*ii*) Flowers 4- or 5-merous. — *Dicotyledons.*
(*i*) Petals united. — *Gamopetalae.*
(*i*) Ovary superior, carpels usually 2.
(*ii*) Stamens alternate with the corolla lobes and equal in number or fewer. — *Bicarpellatae.*
(*i*) Leaves mostly opposite or whorled.
(*ii*) Corolla zygomorphic; bilipped.
(*iii*) Stamens 4, didynamous, or 2.
(*iv*) Ovary 2-4 celled; fruit drupe or schizocarpic. — *Lamiales*
(*i*) Trees, shrubs, rarely herbs; branches usually quadrangular possessing spines; leaves opposite or whorled.
(*ii*) Inflorescence racemose or cymose, very often dichasial cymes; axillary cymes aggregated in panicles.
(*iii*) Gynoecium usually bicarpellary, but becomes tetracarpellary due to formation of false septum.
(*iv*) Fruit usually drupe. — *Verbenaceae.*

Bentham & Hooker (1862)	*Engler & Prantl (1931)*	*Hutchinson (1959)*
Dicotyledons	Dicotyledoneae	Dicotyledones
Gamopetalae	Sympetalae	Lignosae
Lamiales	Tubiflorae	Verbenales
Verbenaceae	Verbenaceae	Verbenaceae.

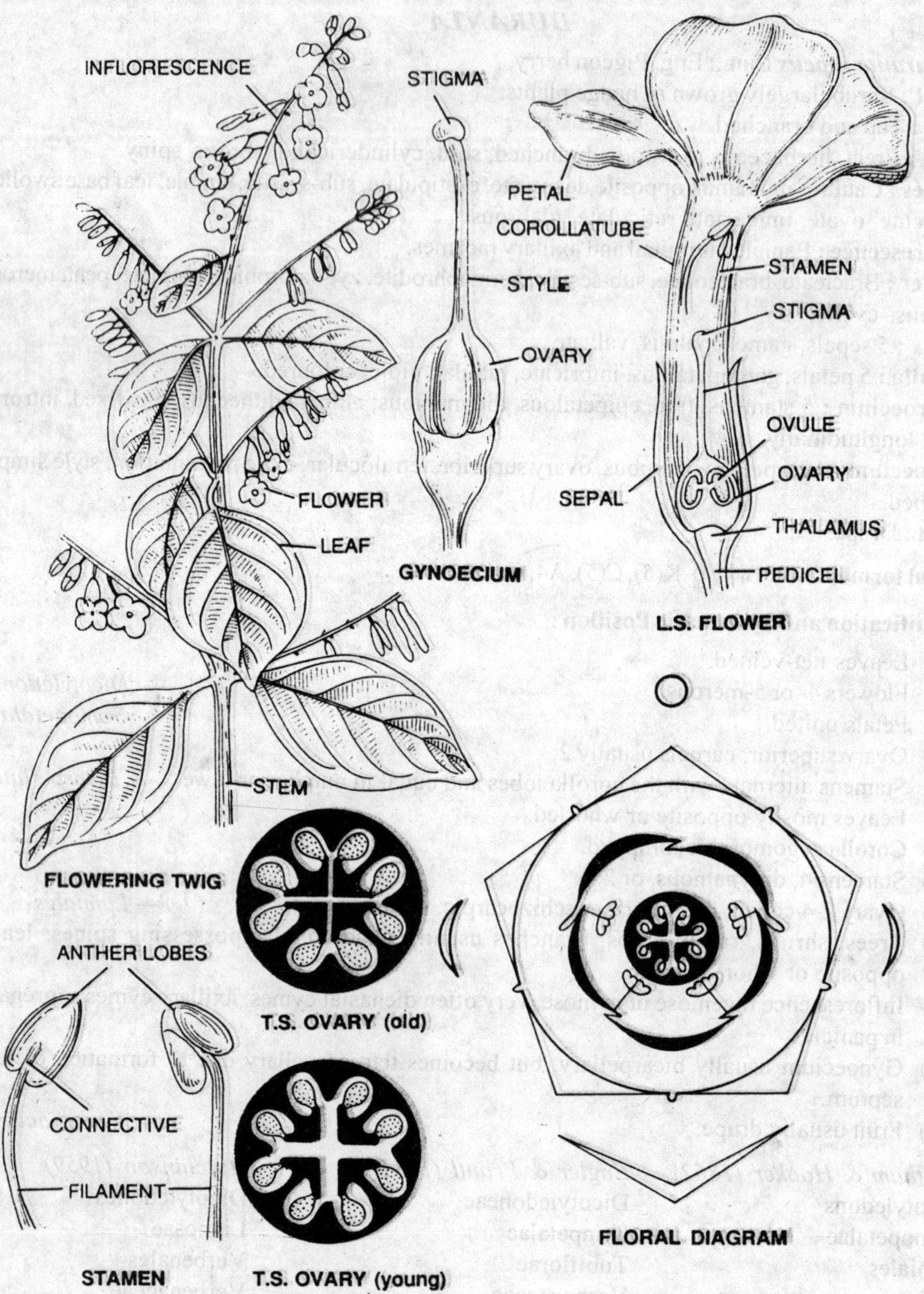

Fig. 9.78. Verbenaceae. *Duranta repens* Linn.; Eng., pigeon berry.

Economic value. Grown as a hedge plant. Juice of fruits is used to kill mosquito larvae. The juice can be used as a larvicide in ponds and swamps.

LANTANA

2. ***Lantana indica*** Roxb.; Verna. **Kuri.**

Habit : A perennial shrub.

Root : Tap and branched.

Stem : Erect, aerial, lower part woody, terminal branches herbaceous, branched, quadrangular, solid, hairy (stiff hairs), green.

Leaf : Cauline and ramal, exstipulate, opposite, decussate, simple, ovate, crenate, acute, rough surface, coriaceous, unicostate reticulate.

Inflorescence : Umbellate cyme.

Flower : Bracteate, bracteolate, sessile, zygomorphic, irregular, hermaphrodite, pentamerous, hypogynous, complete, cyclic.

Calyx : 5 sepals, gamosepalous, valvate, green.

Corolla : 5 petals, gamopetalous, quincuncial aestivation, 4/1 bilipped, one anterior petal large, variously coloured.

Androecium : 4 stamens, found in the throat of corolla, polyandrous, epipetalous, didynamous, dithecous, introrse.

Gynoecium : 2 carpels (bicarpellary), syncarpous, ovary superior, bilocular, one ovule per locule, axile placentation, style simple, stigma globular.

Fruit : Drupe.

Floral formula : Br, Brl | ⚥ K(5), $\widehat{\text{C(4 + 1), A2 + 2}}$, G($\underline{2}$)

Identification and Systematic Position :

(*i*) Leaves net-veined.
(*ii*) Flowers 4- or 5-merous. — *Dicotyledons.*
(*i*) Petals united. — *Gamopetalae.*
(*i*) Ovary superior, carpels usually 2.
(*ii*) Stamens alternate with the corolla lobes and equal in number or fewer. — *Bicarpellatae.*
(*i*) Leaves mostly opposite or whorled.
(*ii*) Corolla zygomorphic; bilipped.
(*iii*) Stamens 4, didynamous, or 2.
(*iv*) Ovary 2-4 celled; fruit drupe or schizocarpic. — *Lamiales*
(*i*) Trees, shrubs, rarely herbs; branches usually quadrangular possessing spines; leaves opposite or whorled.
(*ii*) Inflorescence racemose or cymose, very often dichasial cymes; axillary cymes aggregated in panicles.
(*iii*) Gynoecium usually bicarpellary, but becomes tetracarpellary due to formation of false septum.
(*iv*) Fruit usually drupe. — *Verbenaceae.*

Other important members of the family. *Clerodendrum fragrans* Vent., **Attardana -** an ornamental; *Tectona grandis* Linn., **Sagwan -** wood is used for construction, furniture and cabinet work, bark yields yellow dye; *Verbena officinalis* Linn., an ornamental.

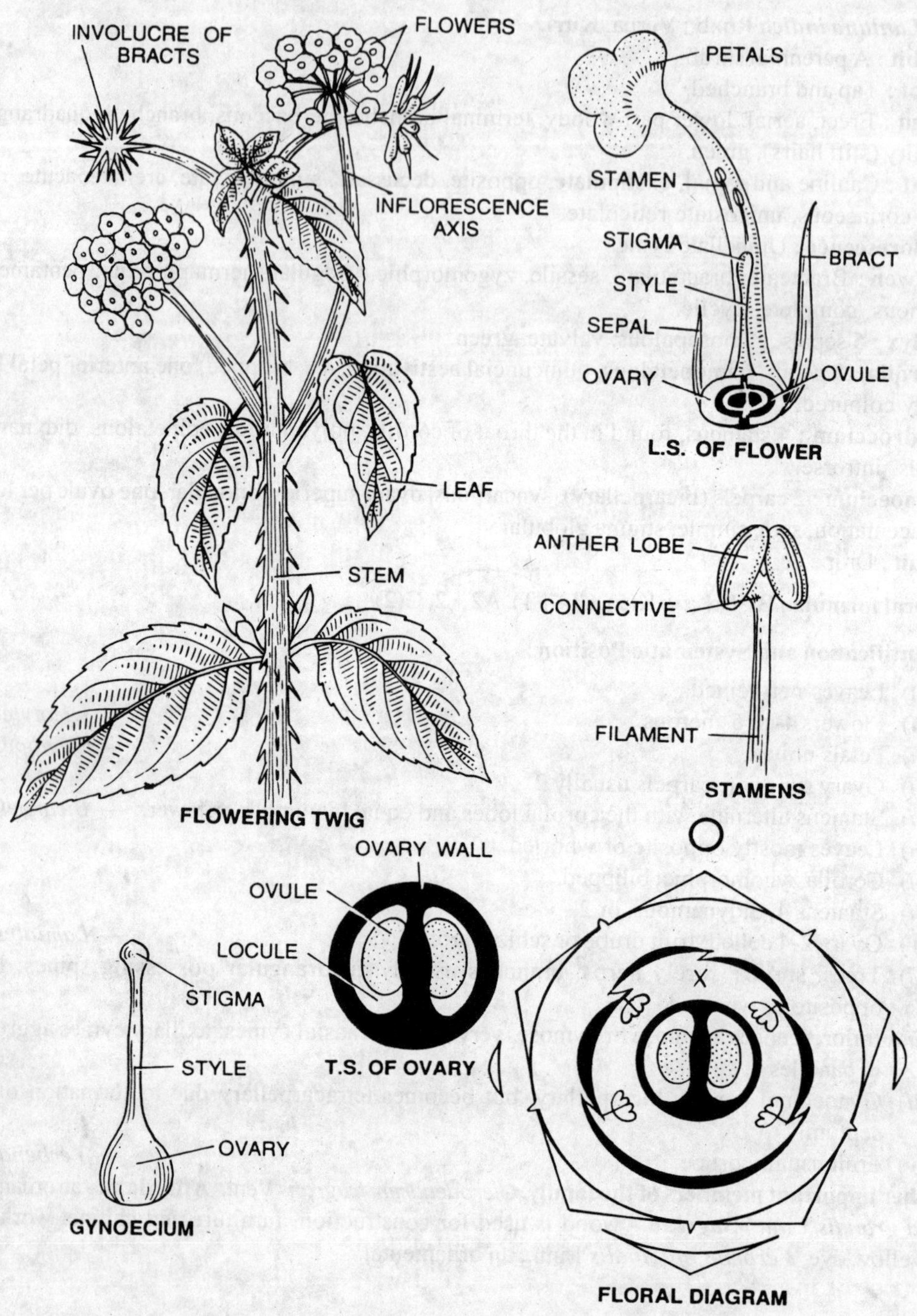

Fig. 9.79. Verbenaceae. *Lantana indica* Roxb.; Verna. **Kuri.**

Economic value. The leaves are used as a cure for snake-bite.

FAMILY - LABIATAE - LAMIACEAE (Mint family)

OCIMUM

1. ***Ocimum sanctum*** Linn.; Verna. **Tulsi;** Eng. Holy basil.

Habit : A perennial herb with typical aromatic smell.

Stem : Erect, aerial, branched, quadrangular, somewhat woody, solid, branches covered with soft hairs, green.

Leaf : Cauline and ramal, simple, opposite, short petioled, exstipulate, ovate, serrate, acute, gland dotted, aromatic smell, unicostate reticulate venation.

Inflorescence : Verticillaster, 6-10 flowered whorls present, emitting fine smell.

Flower : Pedicellate, bracteate, bracts small and caducous, hermaphrodite, zygomorphic, complete, purple, hypogynous, pentamerous, cyclic.

Calyx : 5 sepals, gamosepalous, bilabiate (1/4), petaloid (purple coloured), posterior lip broad and boat shaped, anterior lip with 4 small lobes possessing mucronate teeth, gland dotted, imbricate aestivation, inferior.

Corolla : 5 petals, gamopetalous, bilabiate (1/4), corolla tube short, upper lip four lobed, lower lip large, imbricate aestivation, inferior, white or purple.

Androecium : 4, stamens, polyandrous, didynamous, epipetalous, fifth posterior stamen completely suppressed, anthers bicelled, introrse, dorsifixed.

Gynoecium : 2 carpels (bicarpellary), syncarpous, ovary bilocular in early stage but becomes tetralocular in later stage, ovary superior, four chambered, axile placentation, single ovule in each loculus, gynobasic style (*i.e.*, it arises from the base of the ovary), stigma bifid.

Fruit : Schizocarpic, carcerulus, 4 nutlets developed.

Floral formula : Br $+$ ⚥ K(1 + 4), $\overset{\frown}{C(4+1), A2+2}$, G(2)

Identification and Systematic Position :

(*i*) Leaves net-veined.
(*ii*) Flowers 4- or 5-merous. — *Dicotyledons.*
(*i*) Petals united. — *Gamopetalae.*
(*i*) Ovary superior, carpels usually 2.
(*ii*) Stamens alternate with the corolla lobes and equal in number or fewer. — *Bicarpellatae.*
(*i*) Leaves mostly opposite or whorled.
(*ii*) Corolla zygomorphic; bilipped.
(*iii*) Stamens 4, didynamous, or 2.
(*iv*) Ovary 2-4 celled; fruit drupe or schizocarpic. — *Lamiales*
(*i*) Herbs and shrubs with square stem; leaves simple, opposite or whorled, exstipulate with oil glands.
(*ii*) Inflorescence verticillaster.
(*iii*) Gynoecium - carpels 2, syncarpous; disc prominent; ovary 4-lobed and 4-celled, with one ovule in each cell, when 2-celled two ovules in each cell; style gynobasic; fruit - a group of 4 nutlets each with one seed. — *Labiatae.*

Bentham & Hooker (1862)	*Engler & Prantl (1931)*	*Hutchinson (1959)*
Dicotyledons	Dicotyledoneae	Dicotyledones
Gamopetalae	Sympetalae	Herbaceae
Lamiales	Tubiflorae	Lamiales
Labiatae	Labiatae	Lamiaceae

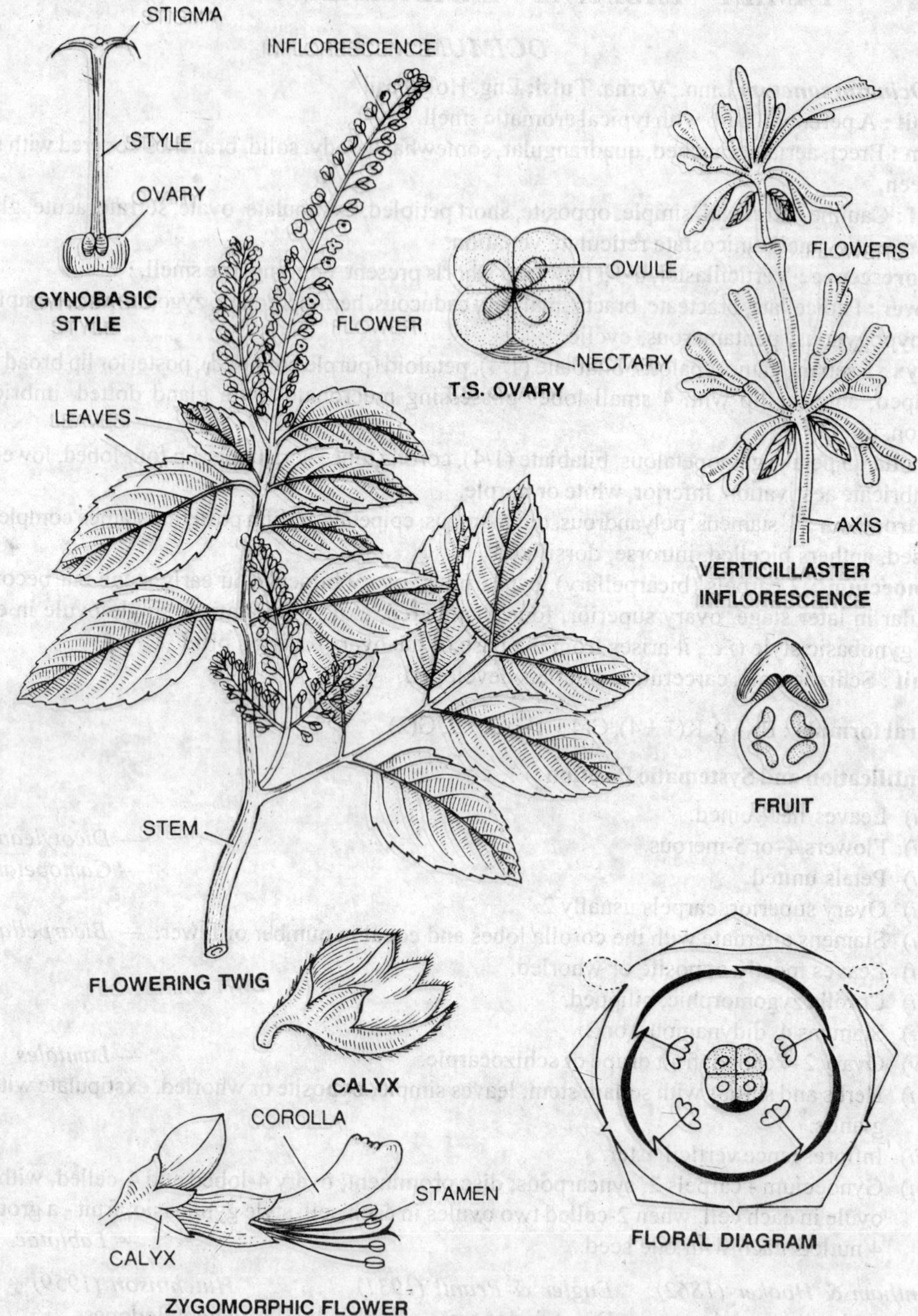

Fig. 9.80. Labiatae (Lamiaceae). *Ocimum sanctum* Linn.; Eng., holy basil; Verna., **tulsi.**

Economic value. A medicinal plant. The leaves are expectorant, stomachic, diaphoretic and aromatic; their infusion is given in malaria, gastric diseases of children and liver disorders. The leaf juice is given in chronic fever, haemorrhage, dysentery and dyspepsia; it is also used to check vomiting and as an anthelmintic.

SALVIA

2. ***Salvia officinalis*** Linn.; Verna. **Salbia sefakuss;** Eng. Sage.

Habit : An annual ornamental herb with typical aromatic smell.

Stem : Erect, branched, herbaceous, quadrangular, solid, hairy and green.

Leaf : Cauline and ramal, simple, opposite, decussate, petiolate, exstipulate, ovate, serrate, acute, glabrous, unicostate reticulate venation.

Inflorescence : Verticillaster with usually six-flowered whorls.

Flower : Pedicellate, bracteate, hermaphrodite, zygomorphic, complete, coloured, hypogynous, pentamerous, cyclic.

Calyx : 5 sepals, gamosepalous, bilabiate, 2 lobes in one whorl and 3 in the other, imbricate aestivation, inferior.

Corolla : 5 petals, gamopetalous, bilabiate, 2 lobes in one whorl and 3 in the other, imbricate aestivation, inferior.

Androecium : 2 stamens (anterior), posterior, 3 stamens absent or staminodes present, epipetalous, short filament connected to a long connective, lower end of connective is flat, short and sterile, upper end of it with a large, fertile anther lobe, anthers bicelled, introrse.

Gynoecium : 2 carpels (bicarpellary), syncarpous pistil present on secreting disc, ovary superior, bilocular when young, but becomes tetralocular in the later stage, single ovule in each loculus, axile placentation, gynobasic style; bifid stigma.

Fruit : Carcerulus; four nutets in a group.

Floral formula : Br | ⚥ K(2 + 3), $\overparen{C(2+3), A2}$, $G(\underline{2})$

Identification and Systematic Position :

(*i*) Leaves net-veined.
(*ii*) Flowers 4- or 5-merous. — *Dicotyledons.*
(*i*) Petals united. — *Gamopetalae.*
(*i*) Ovary superior, carpels usually 2.
(*ii*) Stamens alternate with the corolla lobes and equal in number or fewer. — *Bicarpellatae.*
(*i*) Leaves mostly opposite or whorled.
(*ii*) Corolla zygomorphic; bilipped.
(*iii*) Stamens 4, didynamous, or 2.
(*iv*) Ovary 2-4 celled; fruit drupe or schizocarpic. — *Lamiales*
(*i*) Herbs and shrubs with square stem; leaves simple, opposite or whorled, exstipulate with oil glands.
(*ii*) Inflorescence verticillaster.
(*iii*) Gynoecium - carpels 2, syncarpous; disc prominent; ovary 4-lobed and 4-celled, with one ovule in each cell, when 2-celled two ovules in each cell; style gynobasic; fruit - a group of 4 nutlets each with one seed. — *Labiatae.*

Other important members of the family. *Coleus ambionicus* Lour., **Pathorchur** - used for flavouring food products; *Leucas cephalotes* Spreng., **Goma** - flowers are used for cough and cold; *Melissa officinalis* Linn., used for flavouring food products; *Mentha arvensis* Linn., **Pudina** -a carminative, refrigerant and stimulant; *Lavandula officinalis* Chaix., an essential oil is obtained, which is used in perfumery.

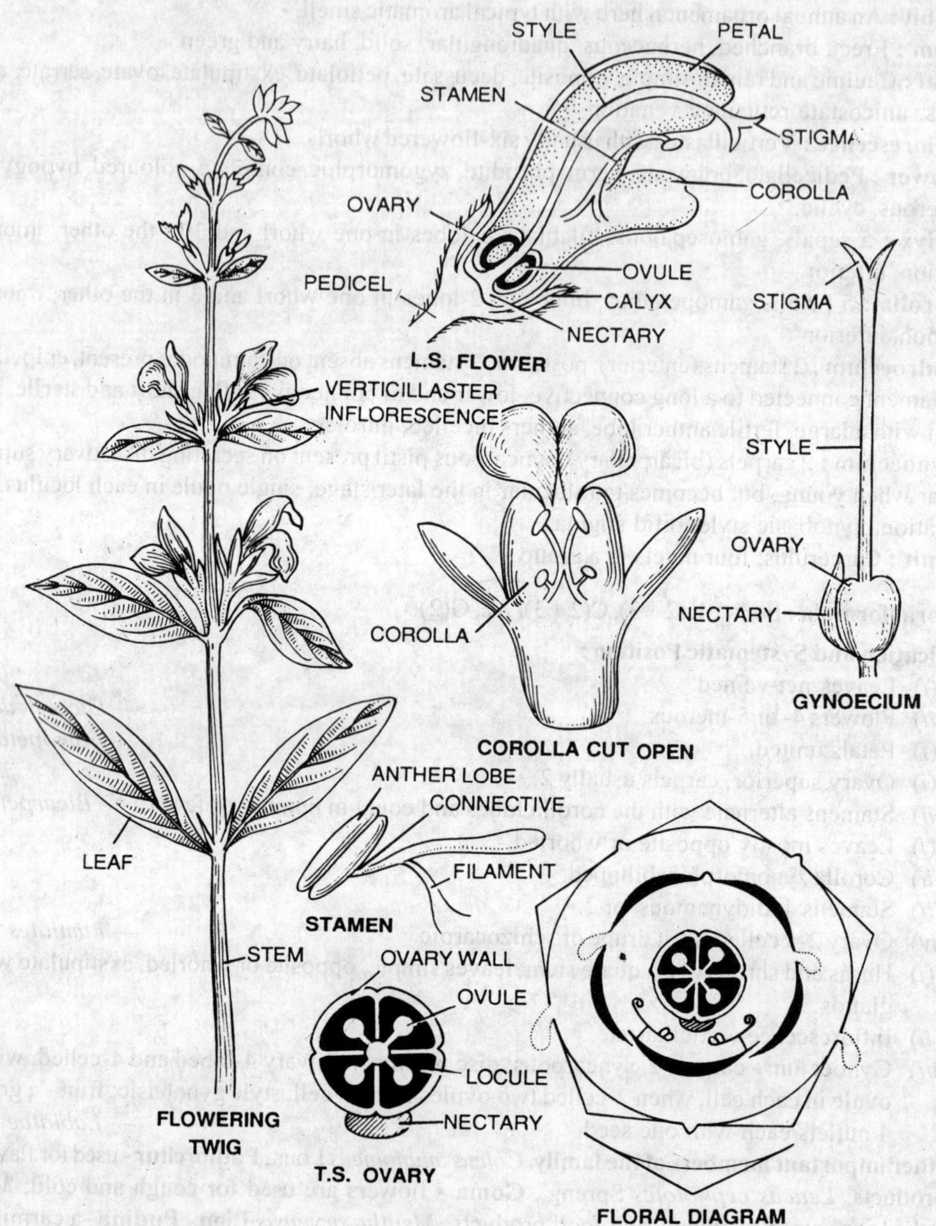

Fig. 9.81. Labiatae (Lamiaceae). *Salvia officinalis* Linn.,; Eng., sage; Verna. **salbia sefakuss.**

Economic value. Grown as an ornamental. The plant is tonic, astringent and aromatic; its infusion is used as a lotion for ulcers. Leaves make excellent gargle for relaxed throat and tonsils and for ulceration of mouth and throat.

FAMILY - NYCTAGINACEAE (four-o-clock family)

MIRABILIS

Mirabilis jalapa Linn.; Verna. **Gulabbas**; Eng. Four-o-clock plant

Habit : Large perennial herbs.

Root : Tap and branched.

Stem : Erect, aerial, herbaceous or somewhat woody, branched, cylinderical, pinkish green, swollen nodes.

Leaves : Cauline and ramal, opposite, petiolate, simple, entire, exstipulate, ovate, acute, glabrous, netveined, opposite leaves of pair unequal in size.

Inflorescence : Cymose, dichasial cyme with a tendency to become monochasial cyme in higher branches.

Flower : Pedicellate, bracteate, an involucre of 5 sepaloid bracts, hermaphrodite, actionomorphic, complete, red, yellow or white, hypogynous. In *Mirabilis,* the flowers are arranged in cymes of three, of which only the middle flower develops; there remains an involucre of five parts at its base, which really belongs to cyme, but looks exactly like the calyx of the flower.

Perianth : 5 tepals, petaloid, imbricate or twisted, contorted, connate in a funnel shaped or tubular perigone, the base of which persists and enclosing the fruit forming the *anthocarp*.

Androecium : 5 stamens, alternate to tepals, filaments unequal, anther dithecous, basifixed, introrse.

Gynoecium : Single carpel, ovary free, superior, unilocular, basal placentation, single basal erect ovule.

Fruit : An achene, enclosed within the persistent perianth, indehiscent.

Floral formula : Br ⊕ ⚥ P5, A5, $G(\underline{1})$

Identification and Systematic Position :

(*i*) Leaves net-veined.
(*ii*) Flowers 4- or 5-merous. — *Dicotyledons.*

(*i*) Flowers with simple perianth which is usually sepaloid and sometimes absent. — *Monochlamydeae.*

(*i*) Embryo curved. — *Curvembryae.*

(*i*) Herbs, shrubs, trees or climbers; leaves opposite, simple, exstipulate, opposite leaves of a pair unequal.
(*ii*) Cymose inflorescence; petaloid bracts, each flower becomes adnate at the base of each petaloid bract (*e.g., Bougainvillaea*), tepals petaloid, perianth tubular and persistent.
(*iii*) Single carpel, ovary superior, unilocular; single basal ovule.
(*iv*) Fruit achene enclosed within persistent perianth. — *Nyctaginaceae.*

Bentham & Hooker (1862)	*Engler & Prantl (1931)*	*Hutchinson (1959)*
Dicotyledons	Dicotyledoneae	Dicotyledones
Monochlamydeae	Archichlamydeae	Lignosae
Curvembryae	Centrospermae	Thymelaeales
Nyctaginaceae	Nyctaginaceae	Nyctaginaceae.

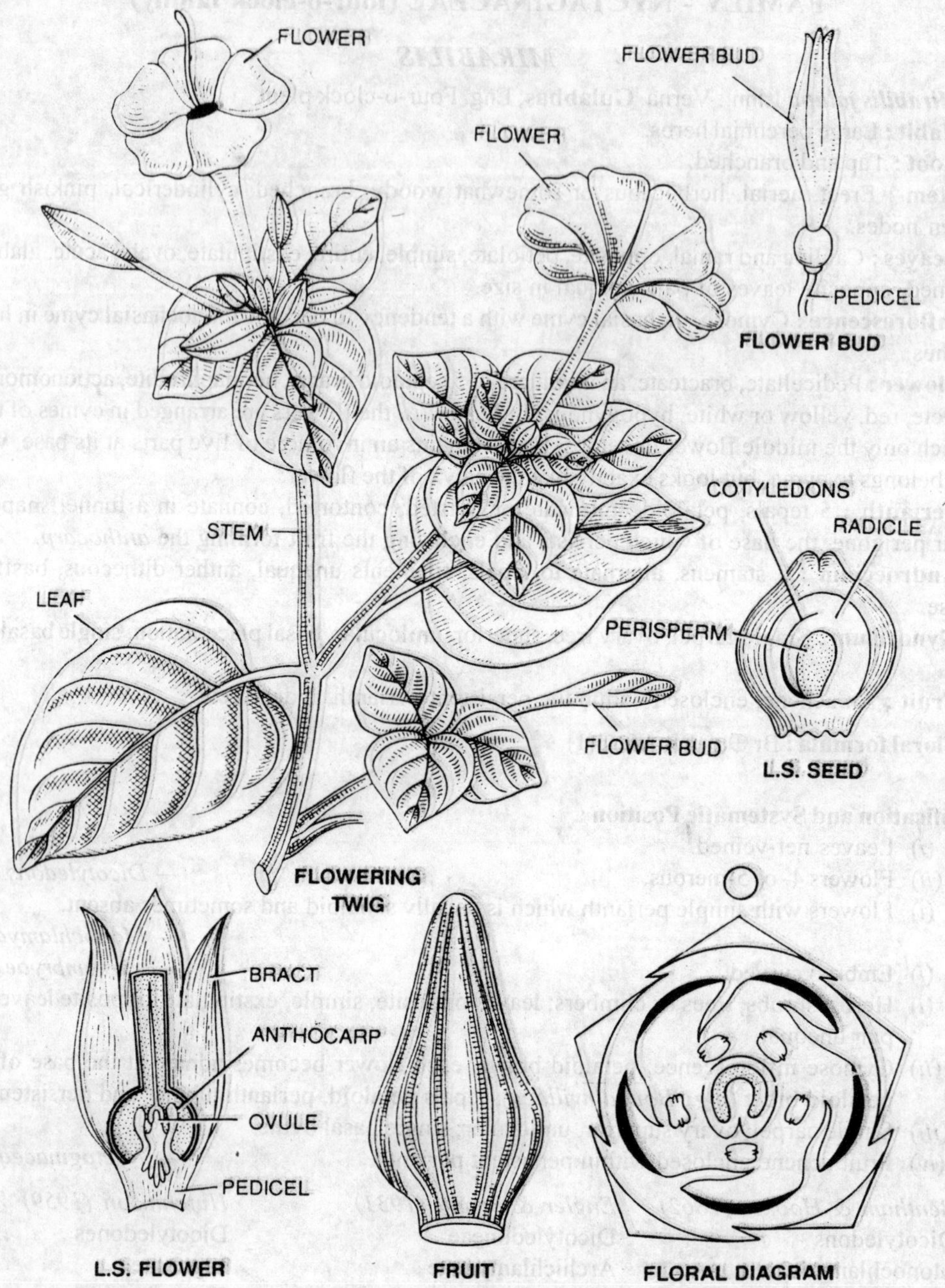

Fig. 9.82. Nyctaginaceae. *Mirabilis jalapa* Linn.; Eng. four-o-clock plant; Verna., **gulabbass.**

Economic value. The powdered seeds are used in cosmetics and the flowers are the source of a crimson dye. The leaves are edible. The root is aphrodisiac and purgative. The leaves are maturant and lessen inflammation.

Other important members of the family. *Bougainvillaea spectabilis* Willd., **Baganvilas** - an ornamental; *Boerhaavia diffusa* Linn., **Sant** - root diuretic, laxative and expectorant in asthma.

FAMILY - AMARANTHACEAE (Amaranth family)

ACHYRANTHES

1. Achyranthes aspera Linn.; Verna. **Chirchita, Latzira, Apamarg.**

Habit : Perennial herbs.

Root : Tap and branched.

Stem : Erect, herbaceous, quadrangular, branched, solid, green, pubescent.

Leaf : Cauline and ramal, opposite, exstipulate, simple, sub-sessile, ovate, entire, acute, unicostate reticulate, rough, coriaceous, hairy.

Inflorescence : Racemose, spike.

Flower : Bracteate, bracteolate, sessile, bracts and bracteoles, spinous and persistent, hermaphrodite, actinomorphic, regular, complete, pentamerous, hypogynous, cyclic.

Perianth : 5 tepals, polyphyllous, dry, membranous, white or coloured, hairy.

Androecium : 5 stamens, antetepalous, stamens alternated by fringed outgrowths, anthers, dithecous, introrse, dehiscing longitudinally.

Gynoecium : 2, bicarpellary, syncarpous, ovary unilocular, superior, single basal ovule, style short, stigma bifid.

Fruit : Dry, utricle.

Floral Formula : Br Brl ⊕ ⚥ P5, A5, G$\underline{(2)}$

Identification and Systematic Position :

(*i*) Leaves net-veined.
(*ii*) Flowers 4- or 5- merous. — *Dicotyledons*

(*i*) Flowers with simple perianth which is usually sepaloid and sometimes absent. — *Monochlamydeae.*

(*i*) Embryo curved. — *Curvembryae.*

(*i*) Herbs, shrubs with opposite or alternate exstipulate leaves.
(*ii*) Mostly the small flowers in dense fascicles; usually the flowers are bracteate, bracteolate, hermaphrodite (rarely unisexual), actinomorphic and hypogynous.
(*iii*) Perianth of 4-5 tepals, usually sepaloid.
(*iv*) 2-3 carpels, syncarpous; ovary unilocular superior.
(*v*) 4-5 stamens, situated opposite the perianth leaves. — *Amaranthaceae.*

Bentham & Hooker (1862)	*Engler & Prantl (1931)*	*Hutchinson (1959)*
Dicotyledons	Dicotyledoneae	Dicotyledones
Monochlamydeae	Archichlamydeae	Herbaceae
Curvembryae	Centrospermae	Chenopodiales
Amaranthaceae	Amaranthaceae	Amaranthaceae.

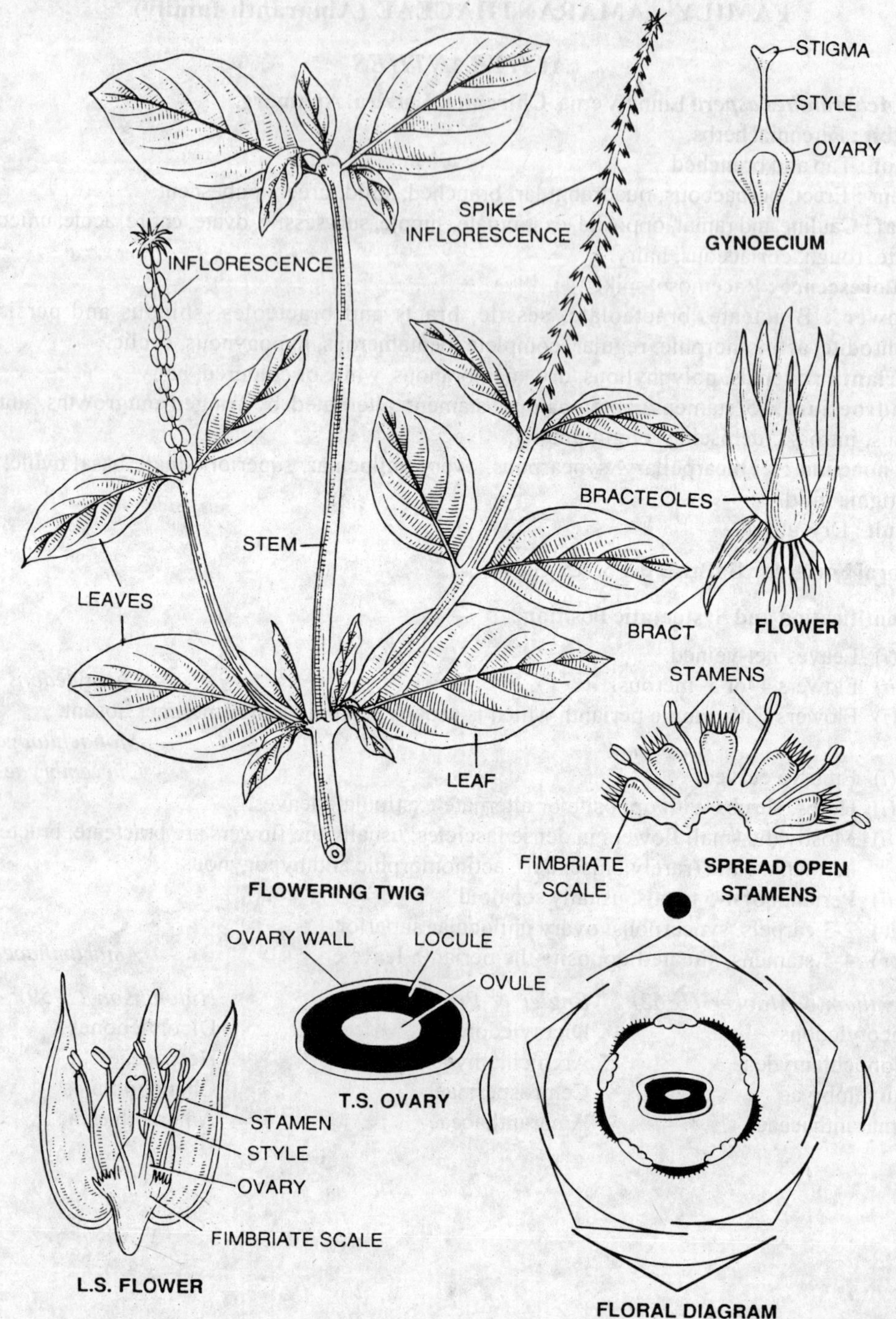

Fig. 9.83. Amaranthaceae. *Achyranthes aspera* Linn.; Verna. **Chirchita, latzira, apmarg.**

Economic value. The plants are used medicinally for piles, colic, boils, etc. It is pungent, purgative, diuretic and astringent. Roots are used for pyrrhoea. Also used in cough and fevers.

AMARANTHUS

2. Amaranthus spinosus Linn.; Verna. **Jangli chaulai.**

Habit : A spiny herb.

Root : Tap and branched.

Stem : Erect, aerial, branched, herbaceous, terete, solid, smooth, green.

Leaf : Cauline and ramal, exstipulate, alternate, simple, petiolate, ovate, entire, acute, unicostate reticulate; 2 spines present in the axil which represent the modified axillary branch.

Inflorescence : Spike.

Male flower : Bracteate, bracteolate, sessile, actinomorphic, unisexual, incomplete, staminate, cyclic.

Perianth : 5 tepals, polytepalous, quincuncial aestivation, membranous.

Androecium : 4-5 stamens, polyandrous, anteposed, filaments long, dithecous, versatile, introrse.

Gynoecium : Absent.

Floral formula : Br, Brl ⊕ ⚥ P5, A4 or 5, G0

Female flower : Bracteate, bracteolate, sessile, unisexual, incomplete, pistillate, actinomorphic, cyclic.

Perianth : 5 tepals, polytepalous, quincuncial, membranous.

Androecium : Absent.

Gynoecium : 2 carpels (bicarpellary), syncarpous, ovary superior, unilocular, single basal ovule, style short, stigma bifid and hairy.

Fruit : Utricle.

Floral formula : Br Brl ⊕ ⚥ P5, A0, G($\underline{2}$)

Identification and Systematic Position :

(*i*) Leaves net-veined.
(*ii*) Flowers 4- or 5-merous. — *Dicotyledons.*
(*i*) Flowers with simple perianth which is usually sepaloid and sometimes absent. — *Monochlamydeae.*
(*i*) Embryo curved. — *Curvembryae.*
(*i*) Herbs, shrubs with opposite or alternate exstipulate leaves.
(*ii*) Mostly the small flowers in dense fascicles; usually the flowers are bracteate, bracteolate, hermaphrodite (rarely unisexual), actinomorphic and hypogynous.
(*iii*) Perianth of 4-5 tepals, usually sepaloid.
(*iv*) 2-3 carpels, syncarpous; ovary unilocular superior.
(*v*) 4-5 stamens, situated opposite the perianth leaves. — *Amaranthaceae.*

Other important members of the family. *Amaranthus blitum* Linn., **Sadanatiya** -plant cooling, emollient, astringent; *A. blitum* Linn. var. *oleracea* Duthie, **Marasa** - cooling, stomachic, used in biliousness; *Celosia cristata* Linn., **Morshikha** - an ornamental; *Digera muricata* (Linn.) Mart., **Latmahuria** - tender twigs are eaten as vegetable.

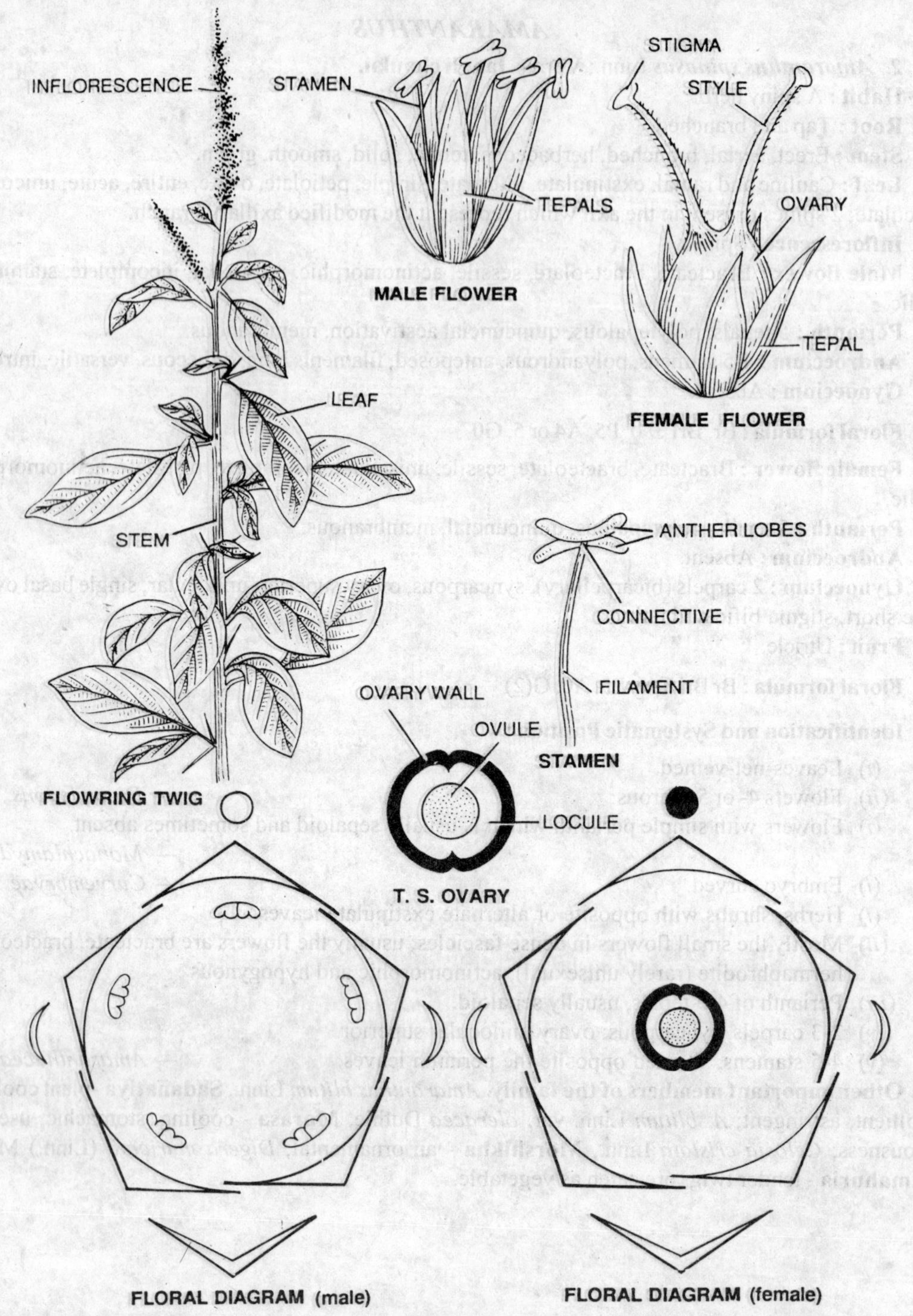

Fig. 9.84. Amaranthaceae. *Amaranthus spinosus* Linn.; Verna., **jangli chaulai.**

Economic value. The root is used in eczema and colic. The boiled leaves and roots are given to children as laxative and applied as emollient poultice to abscesses, boils and burns. Plant is also used in snake-bite.

FAMILY - CHENOPODIACEAE (Pigweed family)

BETA

*1. **Beta vulgaris*** Linn.,; Verna. **Chukandar;** Eng. Beet root.

Beta vulgaris is cosmopolitan in distribution. The roots and leaves are used as vegetable. In European countries the roots are used as main source for the manufacture of sugar.

Habit : Annual or biennial herbs.

Root : Tap and branched; swollen, possessing dark-red juice.

Stem : Herbaceous, erect, branched, solid, cylinderical, pubescent, purplish green.

Leaves : Cauline and ramal, alternate, exstipulate, simple, petiolate, entire, elliptic lanceolate, unicostate, reticulate, coriaceous.

Inflorescence : Cymose, condensed cyme.

Flower : Bracteate, sessile, complete, actinomorphic, hermaphrodite, pentamerous, peri or epigynous.

Perianth : Tepals 5, polyphyllous, sepaloid; imbricate aestivation.

Androecium : 5 stamens; antetepalous, situated on a disc; anthers dithecous, introrse, dehiscing longitudinally.

Gynoecium : 3 carpels (tricarpellary), syncarpous; ovary half-inferior or inferior; unilocular with a single basal campylotropous ovule.

Fruit : A nut or achene enclosed in the perianth.

Seeds : Albuminous with a curved embryo.

Floral Formula : Br ⊕ ⚥ P5, A5, G(3)

Identification and Systematic Position :

(*i*) Leaves net-veined.
(*ii*) Flowers 4- or 5-merous. — *Dicotyledons.*
(*i*) Flowers with simple perianth which is usually sepaloid and sometimes absent. — *Monochlamydeae.*
(*i*) Embryo curved. — *Curvembryae.*
(*ii*) Flowers small axillary; uni- or bisexual, actinomorphic, hypogynous.
(*iii*) Perianth lobes 3-5, imbricate, persistent.
(*iv*) Stamens usually 5, opposite tepals.
(*v*) Ovary 1-celled, 1-ovuled; stigmas 2-5; fruit a membranous utricle. — *Chenopodiaceae.*

Bentham & Hooker (1862)	*Engler & Prantl (1931)*	*Hutchinson (1959)*
Dicotyledons	Dicotyledoneae	Dicotyledones
Monochlamydeae	Archichlamydeae	Herbaceae
Curvembryae	Centrospermae	Chenopodiales
Chenopodiaceae	Chenopodiaceae	Chenopodiaceae.

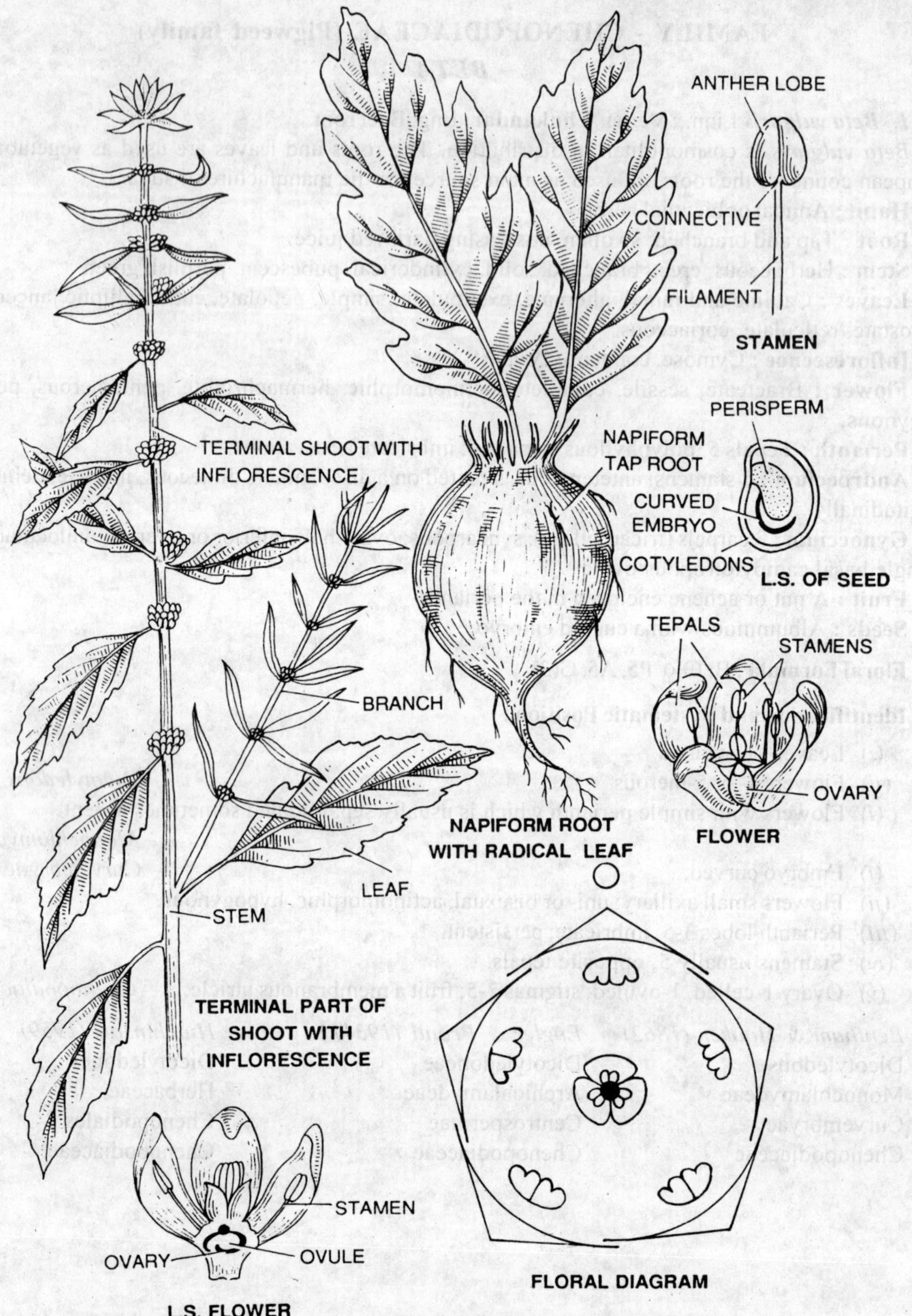

Fig. 9.85. Chenopodiaceae. *Beta vulgaris* Linn.; Eng., beet root; Verna. **chukandar.**

Economic value. Beet root is used in vegetable salad. Refreshing juice is extracted. Sugar is manufactured from juice in European countries. The seeds are cooling and diaphoretic. Leaves are applied to burns and bruises. Beet greens contain more iron and are richer in vitamins, particularly vitamin A.

CHENOPODIUM

2. *Chenopodium album* Linn.; Eng. Pigweed, lambs-quarters; Verna. **Bathua.**

Habit : An annual herb.

Root : Tap and branched.

Stem : Erect, aerial, herbaceous, branched, angular, solid, hairy, reddish green or green.

Leaf : Cauline and ramal, exstipulate, petiolate, alternate, simple, elliptic-lanceolate, coriaceous, unicostate reticulate.

Inflorescence : Cymose, condensed cyme.

Flower : Bracteate, sessile, actinomorphic, hermaphrodite, complete, pentamerous, hypogynous, cyclic.

Perianth : 5 tepals, polytepalous, quincuncial aestivation, sepaloid.

Androecium : 5 stemens, polyandrous, anteposed, filament long, dithecous, basifixed, introrse.

Gynoecium : 2 carpels (bicarpellary), syncarpous, ovary superior, unilocular, single basal ovule, style short, stigma bifid.

Fruit : Utricle.

Floral formula : Br ⊕ ⚥ P5, A5, G$(\underline{2})$

Identification and Systematic Position :

(*i*) Leaves net-veined.
(*ii*) Flowers 4 or 5-merous. — *Dicotyledons.*

(*i*) Flowers with simple perianth which is usually sepaloid and sometimes absent. — *Monochlamydeae.*

— *Curvembryae.*
(*i*) Embryo curved.

(*ii*) Flowers small axillary; uni- or bisexual, actinomorphic, hypogynous.
(*iii*) Perianth lobes 3-5, imbricate, persistent.
(*iv*) Stamens usually 5, opposite tepals.
(*v*) Ovary 1-celled, 1-ovuled; stigmas 2-5; fruit a membranous utricle. — *Chenopodiaceae.*

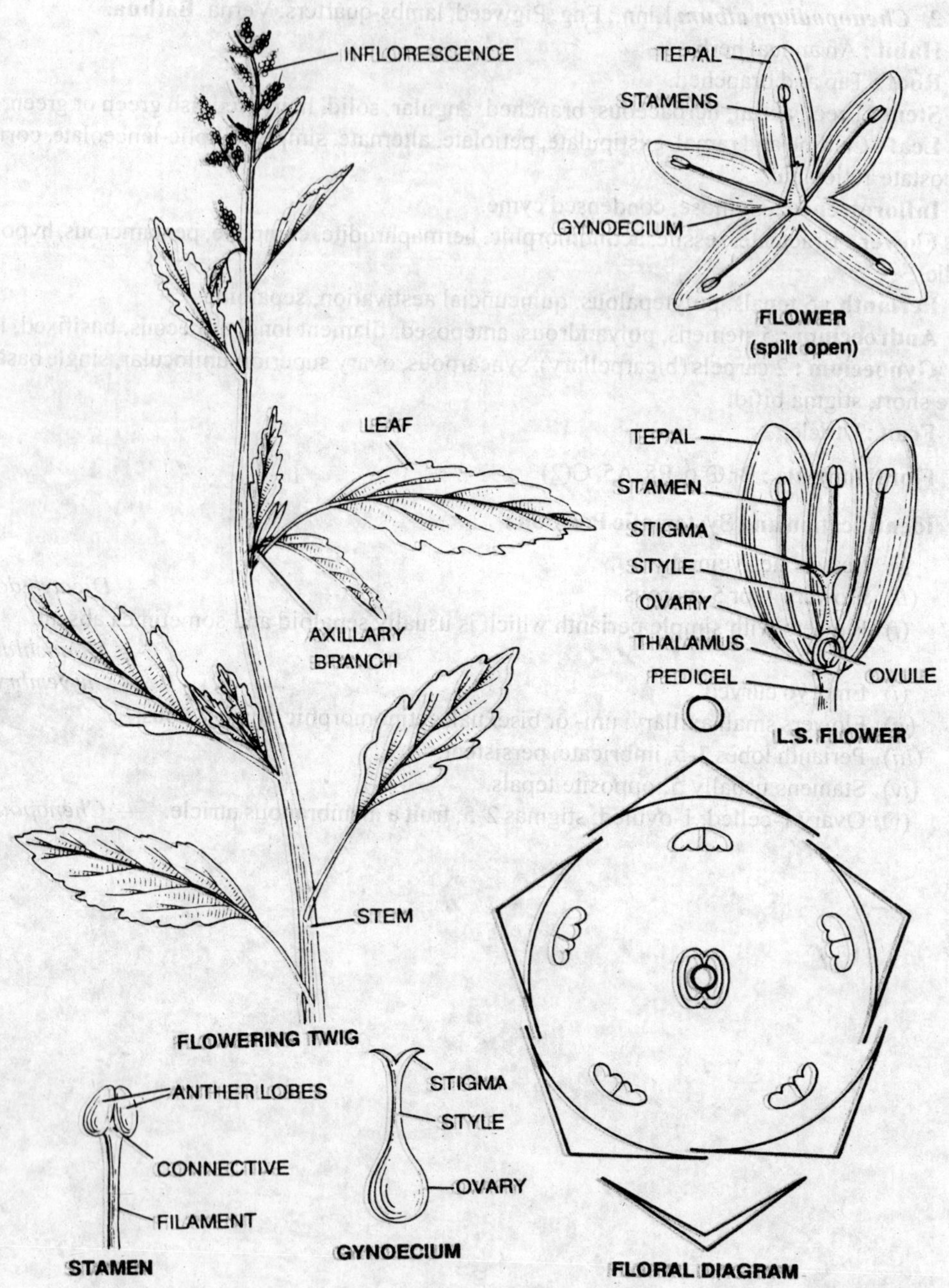

Fig. 9.86. Chenopodiaceae. *Chenopodium album* Linn.; Eng., pigweed, lambs-quarters; Verna., **bathua.**

Economic value. The tender twigs are used as vegetable and fodder. The plant is laxative and anthelmintic.

FAMILY - POLYGONACEAE (Buckwheat family)

POLYGONUM

*1. **Polygonum barbatum*** Linn., Verna. **Narri, Bekhunjubaz**.

Polygonum is world-wide in distribution and found in all the five continents. They are found in moist places.

Habit : Annual herb.

Root : Tap, branched.

Stem : Erect or prostrate, branched, herbaceous, cylinderical, glabrous, solid, conspicuously swollen at nodes, purple.

Leaf : Simple, alternate, sessile, cauline, stipulate, ochreate stipules (short and fimbriate), linear, lanceolate, unicostate reticulate venation, entire, acute.

Inflorescence : Axillary, 2 or 3 flowers in axil of leaf (*e.g.*, *P. plebejam*); flowers of *P. orientale* are found to be arranged in panicled racemes.

Flower : Pedicellate, short pedicel, pedicel jointed under perianth, bracteate, bract membrane like, complete, hermaphrodite, actinomorphic, pink, hypogynous, small.

Perianth : 5, polyphyllous, perianth leaves short, broad and rounded, rarely two outer ones acute, pink, quincuncial aestivation.

Androecium : 8, stamens arranged in two whorls, 5 in outer whorl and three in inner, anthers of outer five introrse and inner three extrorse, filaments flat at base, basifixed anthers.

Gynoecium : 3, syncarpous, ovary superior, unilocular, single ovule, basal placentation, 3 angled, nectar secreting disc present below ovary.

Fruit : Three sided nut.

Floral formula : Br ⊕ ⚥ P5, A 5 + 3, G($\underline{3}$).

Identification and Systematic Position :

(*i*) Leaves net-veined.
(*ii*) Flowers 4- or 5-merous. — *Dicotyledons.*

(*i*) Flowers with simple perianth which is usually sepaloid and sometimes absent. — *Monochlamydeae.*

(*i*) Embryo curved. — *Curvembryae.*

(*i*) Herbs with alternate leaves, and sheathing stipules.
(*ii*) Flowers axillary, in heads, spikes or cymes, bracteate, hermaphrodite; perianth 4-9 cleft, often coloured, imbricate, persistent.
(*iii*) Stamens 4-8, perigynous.
(*iv*) Gynoecium superior, unilocular with one basal ovule; fruit 3-gonous or biconvex nutlet. — *Polygonaceae.*

Bentham & Hooker (1862)	*Engler & Prantl (1931)*	*Hutchinson (1959)*
Dicotyledons	Dicotyledoneae	Dicotyledones
Monochlamydeae	Archichlamydeae	Herbaceae
Curvembryae	Polygonales	Polygonales
Polygonaceae	Polygonaceae	Polygonaceae

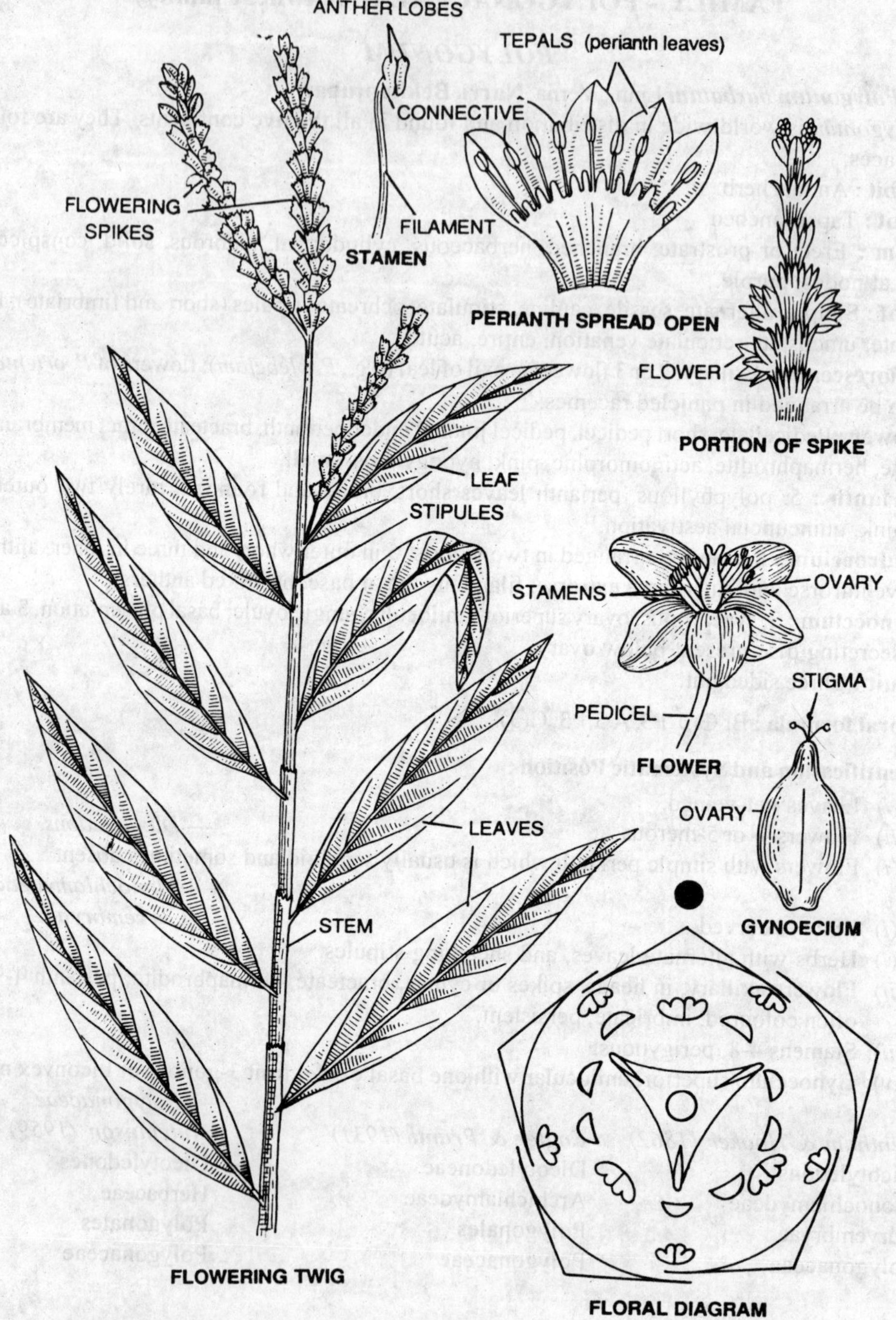

Fig. 9.87. Polygonaceae. *Polygonum barbatum* Linn.; Verna., **narri, bekhunjubaz.**

Economic value. The plant is used medicinally. The seeds are used to relieve gripping pains of colic. The root is astringent and cooling.

RUMEX

2. *Rumex dentatus* Linn., Verna. **Lalbibi, Jangli palak.**

Habit : Annual herb.

Root : Tap, branched.

Stem : Erect, aerial, herbaceous, branched, angular, solid, glabrous, green.

Leaf : Cauline and ramal, exstipulate, petiolate, alternate, simple, elliptic-lanceolate, undulate, acute, smooth, unicostate reticulate venation.

Inflorescence : Panicled racemose clusters.

Flower : Ebracteate, pedicellate, actinomorphic, hermaphrodite, trimerous, hypogynous, complete, cyclic.

Perianth : 6 tepals in two whorls of three each, polyphyllous, valvate, sepaloid, persistent.

Androecium : 6 stamens in two whorls of three each, the stamens of outer whorl are opposite to tepals of outer whorl and that of inner whorl are opposite to tepals of inner whorl, polyandrous, dithecous, basifixed, introrse.

Gynoecium : 3 carpels (tricarpellary), syncarpous, ovary superior, unilocular, basal placentation, style short, stigma 3 hanging downward.

Fruit : Nut.

Floral formula : ⊕ ⚥ P3 + 3, A 3 + 3, G($\underline{3}$).

Identification and Systematic Position :

(*i*) Leaves net-veined.
(*ii*) Flowers 4- or 5-merous. — *Dicotyledons.*
(*i*) Flowers with simple perianth which is usually sepaloid and sometimes absent. — *Monochlamydeae.*
(*i*) Embryo curved. — *Curvembryae.*
(*i*) Herbs with alternate leaves, and sheathing stipules.
(*ii*) Flowers axillary, in heads, spikes or cymes, bracteate, hermaphrodite; peianth 4-9 cleft, often coloured, imbricate, persistent.
(*iii*) Stamens 4-8, perigynous.
(*iv*) Gynoecium superior, unilocular with one basal ovule; fruit 3-gonous or biconvex nutlet. — *Polygonaceae.*

Other important memoers of the family. *Antigonon leptopus* Hook. & Arn., an ornamental; *Muehlenbeckia platycladus* Meissn., an ornamental; *Polygonum fagopyrum* Linn., **Kutu** - the seeds are edible; *Fagopyrum tataricum* (Linn.) Gaertn., **Kaspat, Paphra** - grains are used as food; *Rheum emodi* Wall., **Revand chini** - the roots and rhizomes yield a drug which is used as a laxative, tonic and purgative.

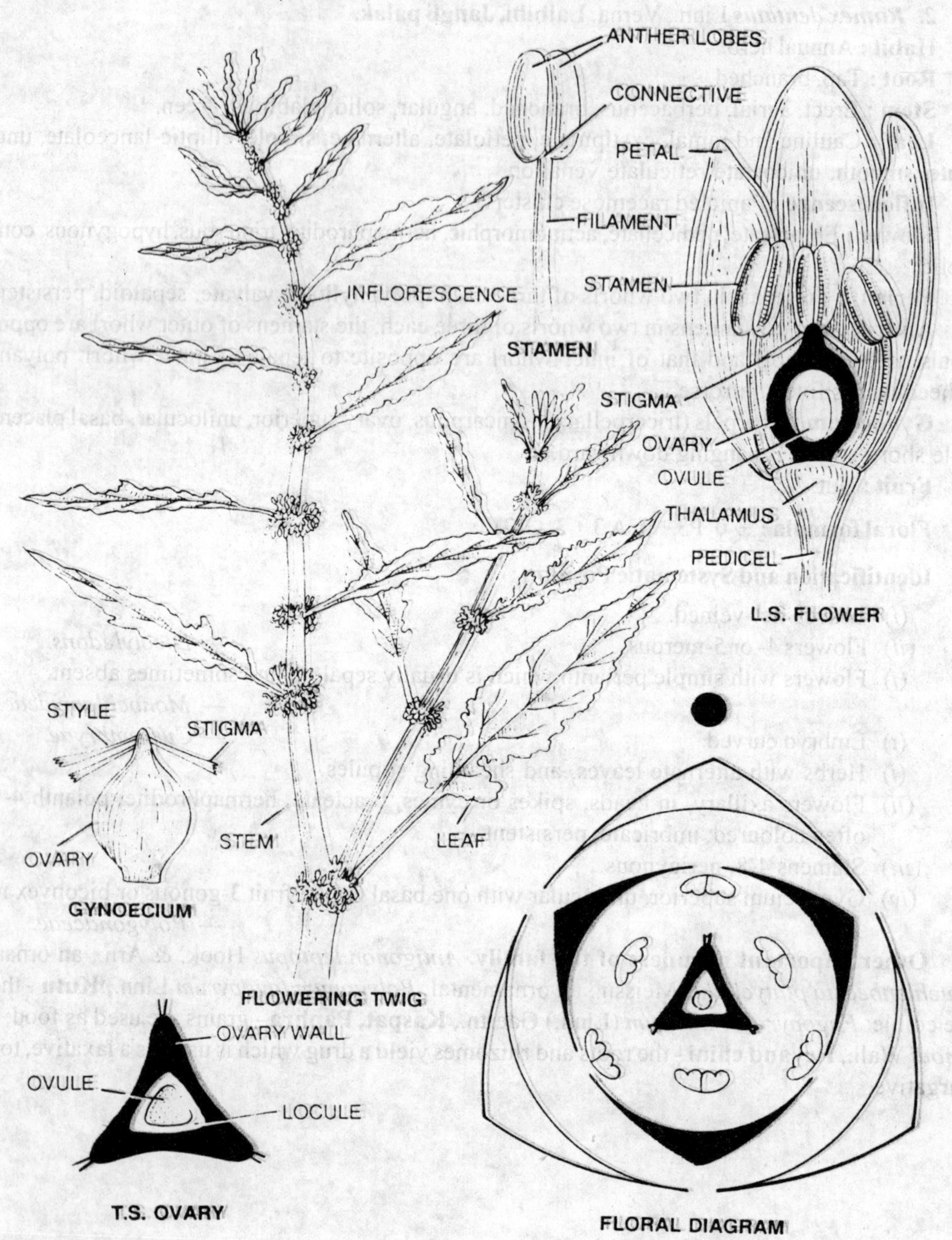

Fig. 9.88. Polygonaceae. *Rumex dentatus* Linn.; Verna., **Lalbibi, jangli palak.**

Economic value. The roots yield a red dye. The root is used as astringent application in cutaneous disorders.

FAMILY - EUPHORBIACEAE (Spurge family)

RICINUS

1. ***Ricinus Communis*** Linn.; Eng. Castor oil plant; Verna. - **Arand.**

Habit : Tall annual or perennial shrub or small tree.

Root : Tap, branched.

Stem : Erect, cylinderical, branched, fistular, glabrous.

Leaf : Alternate, simple, petiolate, broad, palmately lobed, lobes usually 7-9, serrate, multicostate reticulate venation.

Inflorescence : Terminal panicled cyme.

Flower : Pedicellate, bracteate, unisexual, monoecious, male flowers towards lower portion, female flowers towards apical portion of inflorescence, actinomorphic, incomplete, hypogynous.

Male flowers :

Calyx : 5 or 4, membranous, polysepalous, green, inferior, valvate aestivation.

Corolla : Absent.

Androecium : 5 stamens, each stamen profusely branched, anther cells borne on ultimate branchlets, anthers basifixed.

Female flowers :

Calyx : 3 to few or more, membranous, caducous, spathaceous, valvate aestivation.

Corolla : Absent.

Gynoecium : 3 carpels (tricarpellary), syncarpous, ovary superior, trilocular, covered with spiny outgrowths, axile placentation, single large ovule in each locule, three styles, three bifid stigmas.

Fruit : A schizocarpic capsule or regma, splitting into three cocci, spiny outgrowths on fruit.

Floral formula :

Male : Br. ⊕ ⚥ K5, C0, A5, (branched)

Female : Br ⊕ ⚥ K3, C0, G($\underline{3}$).

Identification and Systematic Position :

(*i*) Leaves net-veined.
(*ii*) Flowers 4- or 5-merous. — *Dicotyledons.*

(*i*) Flowers with simple perianth which is usually sepaloid and sometimes absent. — *Monochlamydeae.*

(*i*) Flowers unisexual, hypogynous actinomorphic.
(*ii*) Calyx present, rarely absent; petals rarely present.
(*iii*) Axile placentation; 1-2 ovules in each carpel. — *Unisexuales.*

(*i*) Trees, shrubs or rarely annual herbs.
(*ii*) Leaves simple, alternate, with latex.
(*iii*) Stamens indefinite to one, free or monadelphous, or branched.
(*iv*) Ovary superior, tricarpellary, syncarpous, axile placentation, seeds endospermic. — *Euphorbiaceae.*

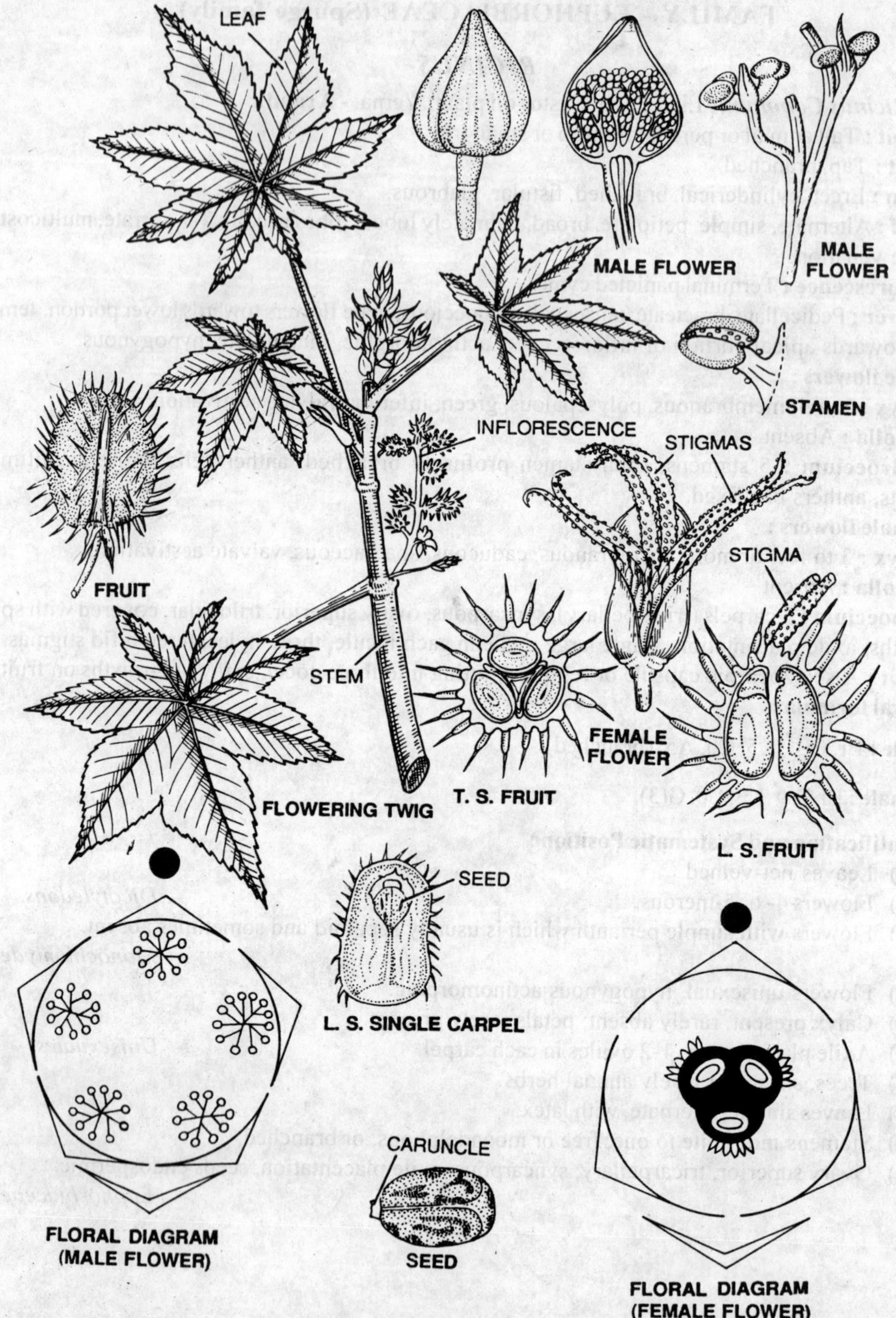

Fig. 9.89. Euphorbiaceae. *Ricinus communis* Linn.; Eng., castar - oil plant; Verna., **arand.**

Economic value. The seeds are the source of castor-oil, which is used as a lubricant and as a purgative. It is also used for transparent soap, textile-soap, typewriter-inks, perfume aromatics, varnishes and paints. The seed-cake is used as a fertilizer.

EUPHORBIA

*2. **Euphorbia hirta*** Linn.; Verna. **Dudhi.**

Habit : Annual wild herb.

Stem : Erect, usually unbranched (sometimes branched), herbaceous, cylinderical, solid, covered with yellow crisped hairs.

Leaf : Simple, opposite, superposed, sub-sessile (short petiole), acute, oblong, lanceolate, serrulate, stipulate, stipules caducous, unicostate reticulate venation.

Inflorescence : Large number of cyathia densely crowded and arranged in peduncled axillary cymes.

Flower : Pedicellate, unisexual, monoecious, enclosed within minute involucre of bracts forming cupular structure.

Male flowers :

Perianth : Absent, naked flower.

Androecium : Single stalked stamen representing male flower, bracteate, anthers 2-celled dehiscing longitudinally.

Female Flowers :

Perianth : Absent, naked flower.

Gynoecium : A single stalked, bracteate, tricarpellary pistil represents female flower, it remains surrounded by male flowers (stalked stamen), ovary superior, three-chambered, single ovule in each loculus, axile placentation, three styles, three bifid stigmas.

Fruit : A capsule.

Floral formula :

Male : Br ⊕ ⚥ K0, C0, A1.

Female : Br ⊕ ⚥ K0, C0, G($\underline{3}$).

Identification and Systematic Position :

(*i*) Leaves net-veined.
(*ii*) Flowers 4- or 5-merous. — *Dicotyledons.*

(*i*) Flowers with simple perianth which is usually sepaloid and sometimes absent. — *Monochlamydeae.*

(*i*) Flowers unisexual, hypogynous actinomorphic.
(*ii*) Calyx present, rarely absent; petals rarely present.
(*iii*) Axile placentation; 1-2 ovules in each carpel. — *Unisexuales.*

(*i*) Trees, shrubs or rarely annual herbs.
(*ii*) Leaves simple, alternate, with latex.
(*iii*) Stamens indefinite to one, free or monadelphous, or branched.
(*iv*) Ovary superior, tricarpellary, syncarpous, axile placentation, seeds endospermic. — *Euphorbiaceae.*

Bentham & Hooker (1862)	*Engler & Prantl (1931)*	*Hutchinson (1959)*
Dicotyledons	Dicotyledoneae	Dicotyledones
Monochlamydeae	Archichlamydeae	Lignosae
Unisexuales	Geraniales	Euphorbiales
Euphorbiaceae	Euphorbiaceae	Euphorbiaceae

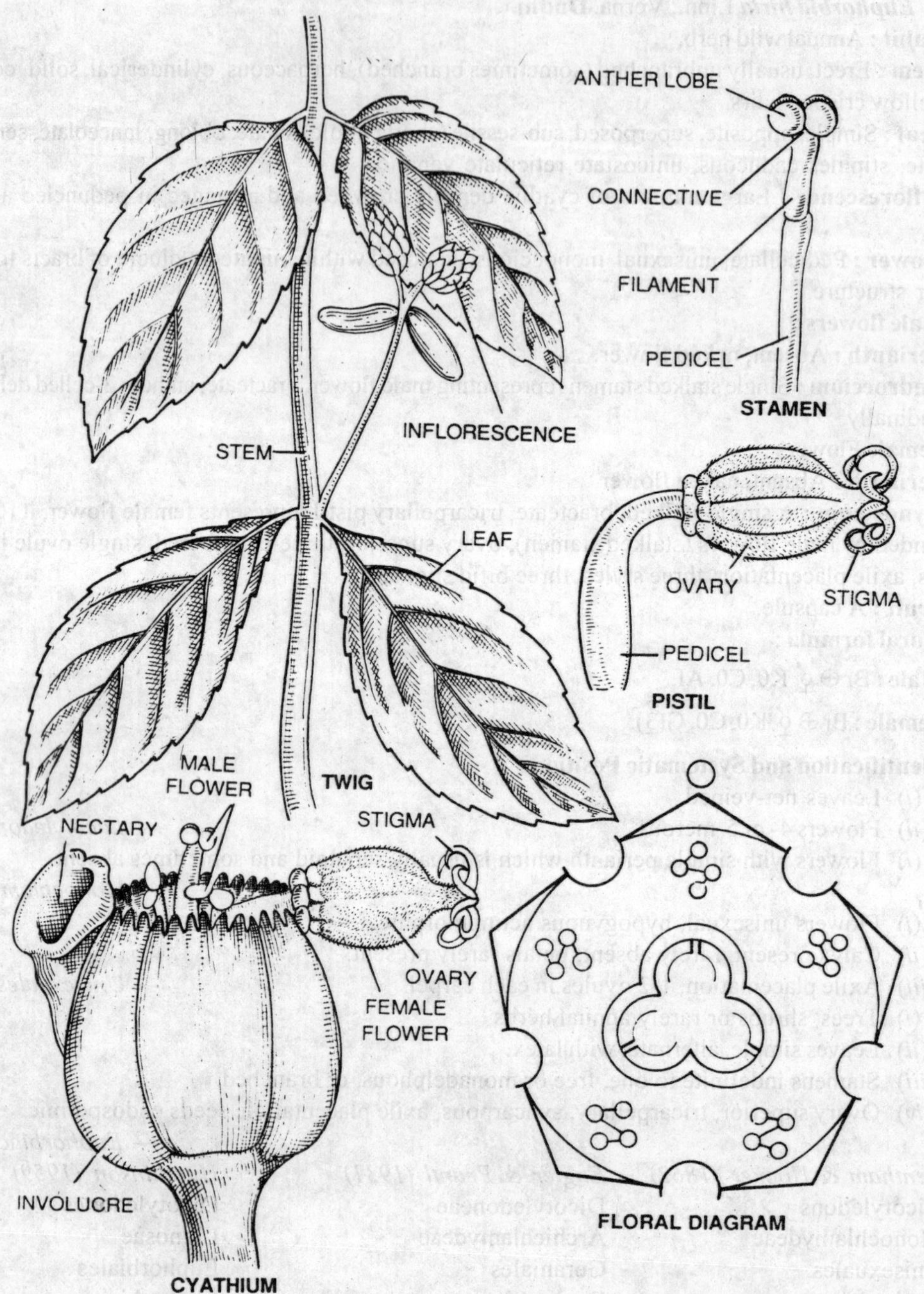

Fig. 9.90. Euphorbiaceae. *Euphorbia hirta* Linn.; Verna., **dudhi.**

Economic value. The plant is used in diseases of children in worms, bowel complaints, cough, etc. The juice of plant is used in dysentery and colic. Decoction of plant is given in bronchial affections and asthma. The latex of plant is used as application for warts.

CROTON

3. Croton sparciflorus.

Habit : Annual wild herb.

Stem : Erect, herbaceous, branched, rough, latex present, solid, cylinderical.

Leaf : Alternate, simple, petiolate, exstipulate, serrate margin, acute, rough, unicostate reticulate venation.

Inflorescence : Racemose, raceme, male flowers on the upper portion, female flowers on the lower portion of inflorescence.

Flower : Pedicellate, bracteate, unisexual, monoecious plant, actinomorphic, incomplete, hypogynous, glands present.

Male flowers :

Calyx : 5 sepals, polysepalous, persistent, imbricate.

Corolla : 5 petals, polypetalous, 5 glands opposite sepals, valvate aestivation.

Androecium : Stamens many, inserted on the receptacle, filaments free, incurved in bud, anthers adnate.

Female flowers :

Calyx : As in male flower.

Corolla : Absent.

Gynoecium : 3 carpels (tricarpellary), syncarpous, 3 styles ending in 3 bifid stigmas, ovary superior, three chambered, single ovule in each loculus, axile placentaiton.

Fruit : Indehiscent capsule.

Floral formula :

Male : Br. ⊕ ⚥ K5, C5, A ∝.

Female : Br ⊕ ⚥ K5, C0, G($\underline{3}$).

Identification and Systematic Position :

(*i*) Leaves net-veined.
(*ii*) Flowers 4- or 5-merous. — *Dicotyledons.*
(*i*) Flowers with simple perianth which is usually sepaloid and sometimes absent. — *Monochlamydeae.*

(*i*) Flowers unisexual, hypogynous, actinomorphic.
(*ii*) Calyx present, rarely absent; petals rarely present.
(*iii*) Axile placentation; 1-2 ovules in each carpel. — *Unisexuales.*
(*i*) Trees, shrubs or rarely annual herbs.
(*ii*) Leaves simple, alternate, with latex.
(*iii*) Stamens indefinite to one, free or monadelphous, or branched.
(*iv*) Ovary superior, tricarpellary, syncarpous, axile placentation, seeds endospermic. — *Euphorbiaceae.*

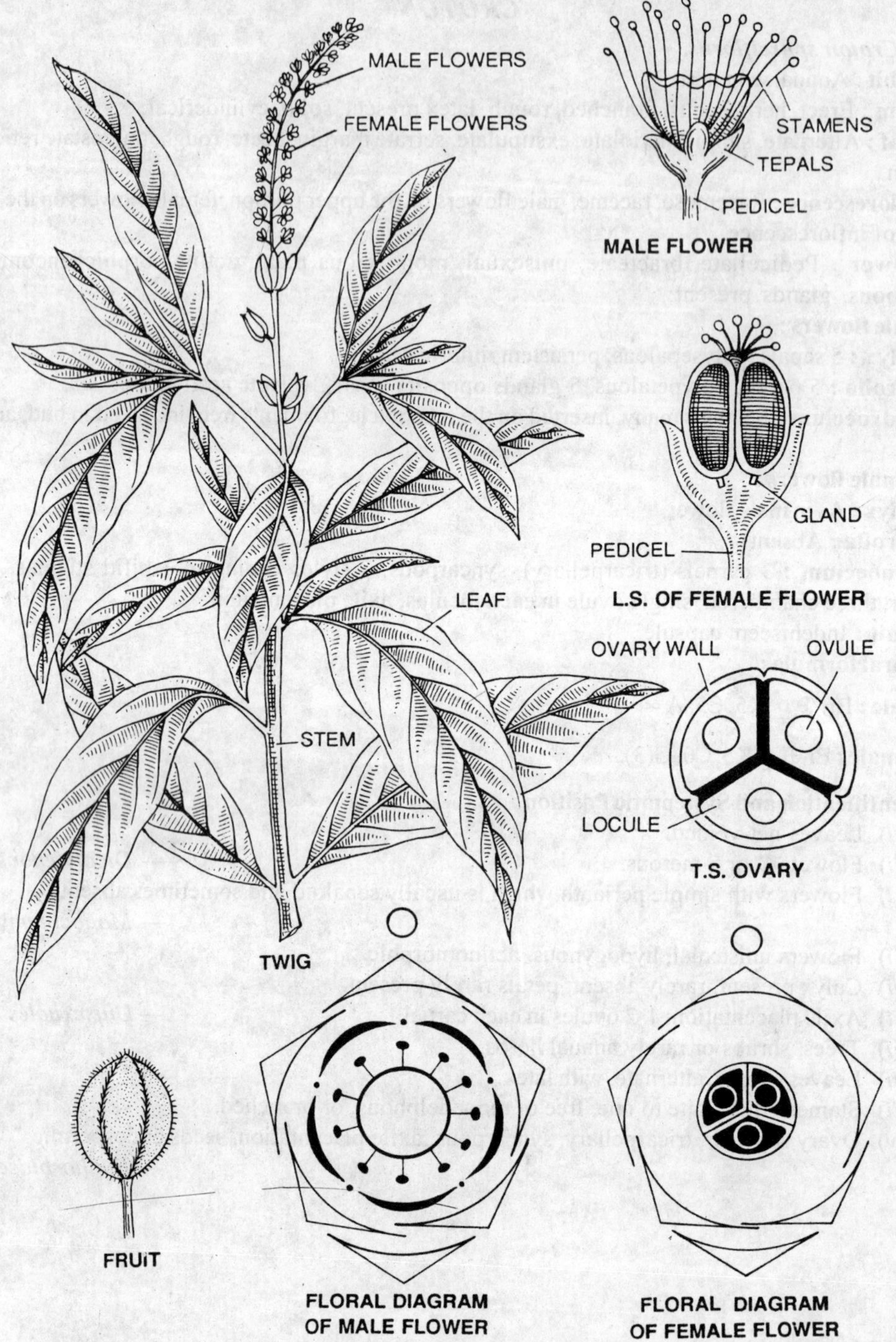

Fig. 9.91. Euphorbiaceae. *Croton sparciflorus.*

PHYLLANTHUS

4. ***Phyllanthus reticulatus*** Poir.; Verna. **Panjoli**.

Habit : An annual herb.

Stem : Erect, branched, herbaceous, green, solid, cylinderical, ½ to 2 feet in height.

Leaf : Simple, alternate, sub-sessile, elliptic-oblong, rounded obtuse, glucous beneath, stipulate, distichous, often resembling pinnate compound leaves 1/4 - 1/2 inch long.

Inflorescence : Axillary flowers.

Flower : Minute, unisexual, trimerous, actinomorphic, bracteate, shortly pedicellate.

Male flowers :

Perianth : 5 tepals, (perianth leaves), arranged in two whorls of three each, polyphyllous, sepaloid, imbricate aestivation, disc of minute glands inside the perianth.

Androecium : 3-4 stamens, polyandrous, filaments short, borne on a short column.

Female flowers :

Perianth : As in male flower.

Gynoecium : 3-4 carpels (tri-or tetracarpellary), syncarpous, ovary superior, three chambered, each loculus having two ovules, axile placentation, stigma trifid.

Fruit : Schizocarpic regma.

Floral formula :

Male : Br ⊕ ⚥ P5, A3 or 4

Female : Br ⊕ ⚥ P5, G($\underline{3}$) or ($\underline{4}$).

Identification and Systematic Position :

(*i*) Leaves net-veined.
(*ii*) Flowers 4- or 5-merous. — *Dicotyledons.*

(*i*) Flowers with simple perianth which is usually sepaloid and sometimes absent.
— *Monochlamydeae.*

(*i*) Flowers unisexual, hypogynous, actinomorphic.
(*ii*) Calyx present, rarely absent; petals rarely present.
(*iii*) Axile placentation; 1-2 ovules in each carpel. — *Unisexuales.*

(*i*) Trees, shrubs or rarely annual herbs.
(*ii*) Leaves simple, alternate, with latex.
(*iii*) Stamens indefinite to one, free or monadelphous, or branched.
(*iv*) Ovary superior, tricarpellary, syncarpous, axile placentation, seeds endospermic.
— *Euphorbiaceae.*

Other important members of the family. *Manihot esculenta* Crantz, **Shakarkand, Maravuli,** the tapioca tubers are used for making starch, sago, semolina and flour; *Hevea brasiliensis* (H.B. & K.) Muell. - Arg., **Rabar** - the latex obtained from the bark of the tree is used for preparing rubber; *Emblica officinalis* Gaertn., **Amla** - fruits are a very good source of vitamin C, and are used in diarrhoea and dysentery; *Putranjiva roxburghii* Wall., **Putranjiva** - the nuts are made into rosaries, which are placed around the neck of the children, for keeping them in good health.

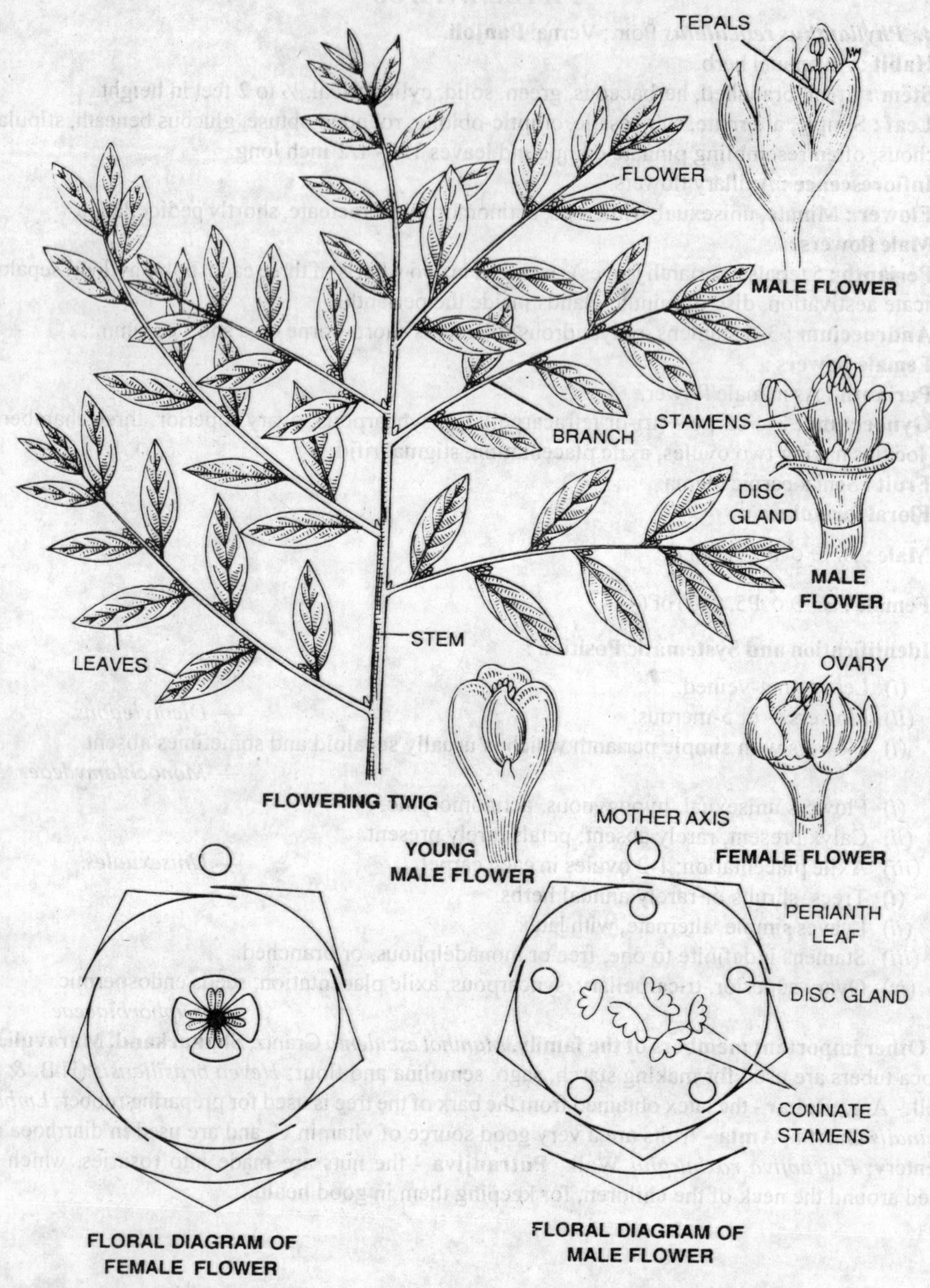

Fig. 9.92. Euphorbiaceae. *Phyllanthus reticulatus* Poir. Syn. *Karganelia reticulata* (Poir) Baillon.; Verna. **Panjoli.**

Economic value. The roots are the source of a red dye. The leaves are diuretic and cooling. Juice of leaves is used for diarrhoea in infants.

FAMILY - MORACEAE (Mulberry family)

MORUS

*1. **Morus australis*** Poir.; Verna. **Sahtoot**; Eng. Common Mulberry.

Habit : Tree, cultivated.

Root : Tap and branched.

Stem : Erect, woody, aerial, cylinderical, branched, smooth, green.

Leaf : Cauline and ramal, petiolate, simple, alternate, stipulate, ovate, serrate, acute, smooth, unicostate reticulate venation.

Inflorescence : Racemose, catkin.

Male flower : Ebracteate, sessile, unisexual, incomplete, actinomorphic, staminate (male), tetramerous, cyclic.

Perianth : 4 tepals, in 2 whorls of 2 each, polyphyllous.

Androecium : 4 stamens, antetepalous, filaments long, anthers dithecous, basifixed, introrse.

Gynoecium : 0.

Floral formula : ⊕ ⚥ P2 + 2, A4, G0.

Female flower : Ebracteate, sessile, unisexual, incomplete, actinomorphic, pistillate (female), tetramerous, cyclic, hypogynous.

Perianth : 4 tepals, in 2 whorls of 2 each, polyphyllous.

Androecium : 0.

Gynoecium : 2 carpels (bicarpellary), syncarpous, ovary superior, unilocular with one pendulous ovule, styles short, stigmas 2.

Fruit : Sorosis.

Floral formula : ⊕ ⚥ P2 + 2, A0, G$(\underline{2})$.

Identification and Systematic Position :

(*i*) Leaves net-veined.
(*ii*) Flowers 4- or 5-merous. — *Dicotyledons.*

(*i*) Flowers with simple perianth which is usually sepaloid and sometimes absent. — *Monochlamydeae.*

(*i*) Flowers unisexual.
(*ii*) Tepals sepaloid, much reduced or none. — *Unisexuales.*

(*i*) Stamens as many as tepals and antetepalous.
(*ii*) Catkin inflorescence or hypanthodium.
(*iii*) Fruit sorosis or syconus.
(*iv*) Ovary 1-2 celled, cells 1-ovuled. — *Moraceae.*

Bentham & Hooker (1862)	*Engler & Prantl (1931)*	*Hutchinson (1959)*
Dicotyledons	Dicotyledoneae	Dicotyledones
Monochlamydeae	Archichlamydeae	Lignosae
Unisexuales	Urticales	Urticales
Moraceae	Moraceae	Moraceae

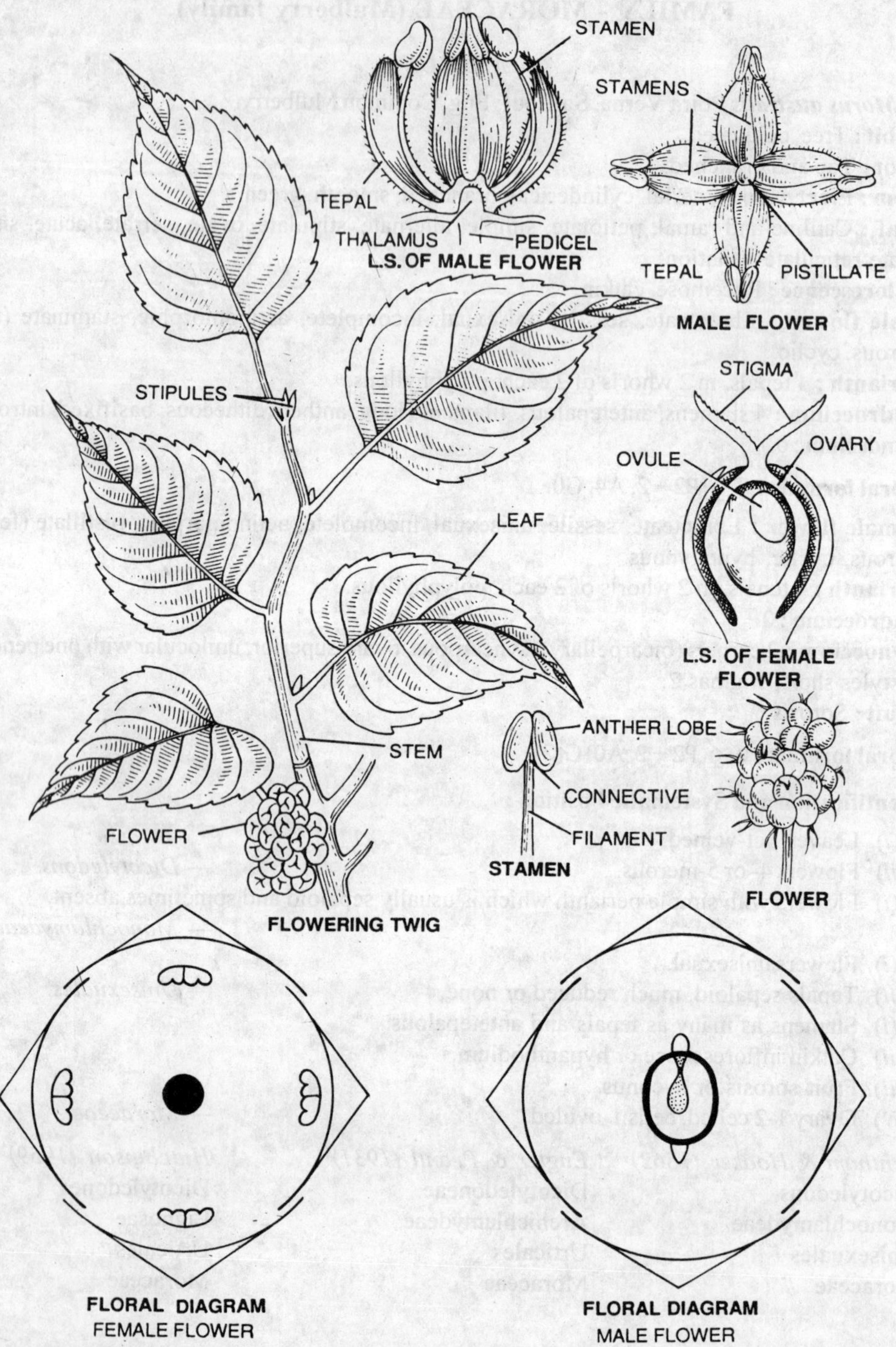

Fig. 9.93. Moraceae. *Morus australis* Poir. Syn. *M. indica;* Eng., common mulberry; Verna. **sahtoot.**

Economic value. The leaves are the source of food of silkworms and the fruits are edible.

Other important members of the family. *Artocarpus heterophyllus* Lamk., **Kathal;** *A. lakoocha* Roxb., **Barhal,** *Ficus benghalensis* Linn., **Bargad;** *F. elastica* Roxb. **Bor.**, *F. glomerata* Roxb., **Gular;** *F. religiosa* Linn., **Pipal;** *Morus alba* Linn., **Tut.**

MONOCOTYLEDONS

FAMILY - ORCHIDACEAE (Orchid family)

VANDA

*1. **Vanda roxburghii*** R. Br.; Verna. **Rasna.**

Habit : Epiphytic herbs.

Root : Adventitious aerial roots, the aerial roots are characterized by a special development of the epidermis to form the **velamen,** other roots serve as anchorage organs.

Stem : Leafy or scapose, monopodially branched, the main axis grows year after year and bears flowers at the axil of leaves, the axis continuously produces new leaves apically.

Leaves : Simple, alternate, exstipulate, fleshy, linear, distichous, leaf sheath present which surrounds the stem, the axis is very short and the leaves appear to come out from the substratum; margin entire, apex acute to obtuse, parallel venation.

Inflorescence : Racemose, raceme.

Flower : Pedicellate, bracteate, hermaphrodite, medianly zygomorphic, irregular, epigynous, trimerous, colourful.

Perianth : 6 tepals arranged in two whorls of three each, outer whorl calyx-like, inner whorl makes corolla, polyphyllous, imbricate, tepals of each whorl are different in size, shape and even in colour from the lateral segments; one of the tepals of inner whorl becomes much enlarged, the **labellum**; labellum prolonged backward into a spur which collects nectar.

Androecium : 6 in two whorls of 3 each, never all stamens present; in *Vanda* one stamen present which unites to an extension of the gynoecium forming a **column**; anthers bicelled, introrse, dehiscing by longitudinal slits; pollen grains granular and bound up by elastic threads of viscin forming two **pollinia**; the viscin extends into a columnar organ, the **caudicle,** at its lower end.

Fruit : Capsule.

Seeds : Numerous, very minute.

Floral formula : Br | ⚥ P3 + 3, A1, G(3).

Identification and Systematic Position :

(*i*) Leaves usually parallel-veined.
(*ii*) Flowers usually trimerous.
(*iii*) Embryo with single cotyledon. — *Monocotyledons.*
(*iv*) Fibrous roots.

(*i*) Ovary superior or inferior; tricarpellary.
(*ii*) Seeds very minute and many.
(*iii*) Inner tepals petaloid. — *Microspermae.*

(*i*) Herbs often epiphytic.
(*ii*) Stamen usually 1, confluent with the style in a column.
(*iii*) Ovary 1-celled, with 3 parietal placentas, usually twisted. — *Orchidaceae.*

Bentham & Hooker (1862)	*Engler & Prantl (1931)*	*Hutchinson (1959)*
Monocotyledons	Monocotyledons	Monocotyledones
Microspermae	Microspermae	Corolliferae
Orchidaceae	Orchidaceae	Orchidales
		Orchidaceae

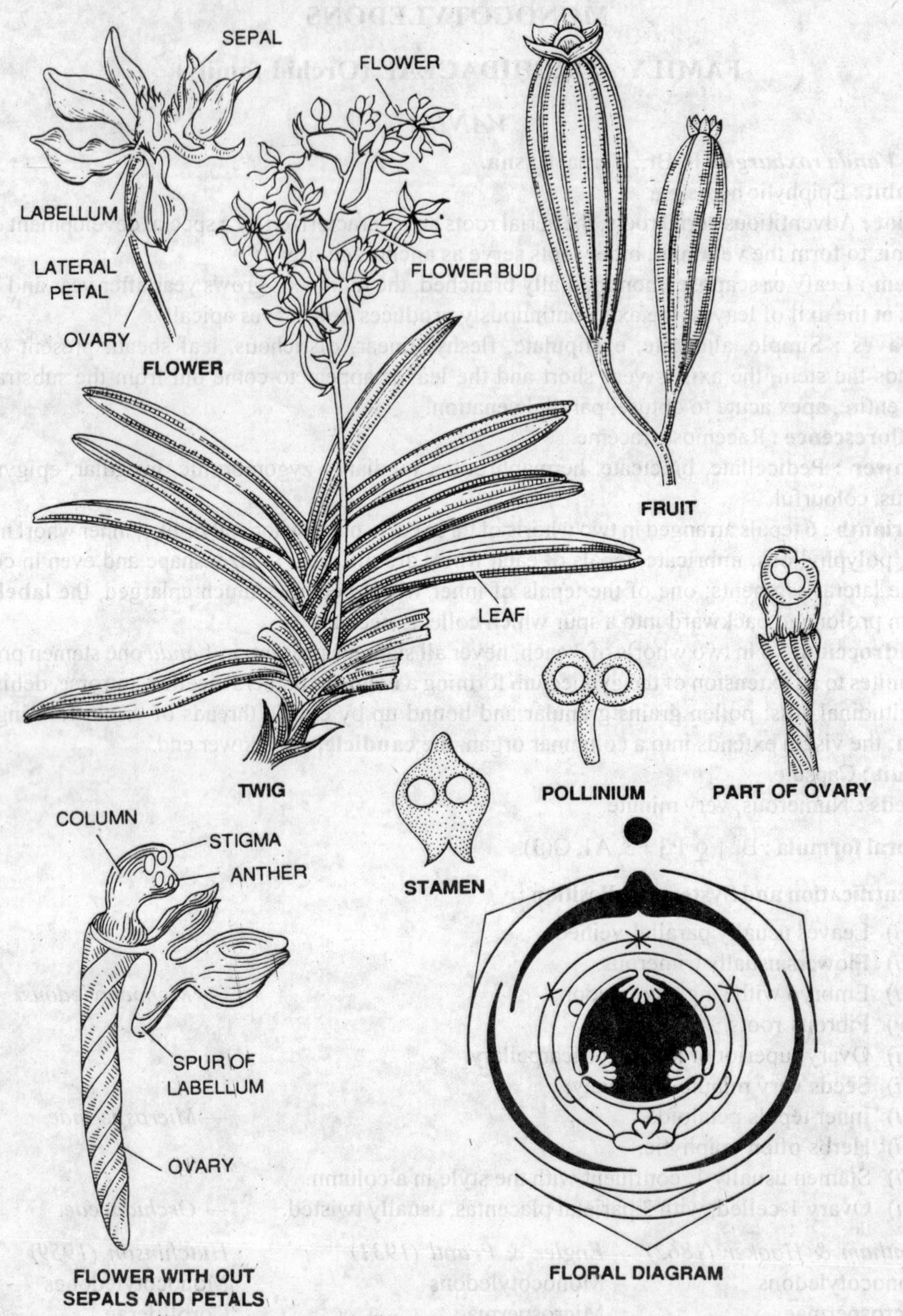

Fig. 9.94. Orchidaceae. *Vanda roxburghii* R. Br.; Verna., **rasna.**

Economic value. An epiphytic herb with beautiful purple flowers. Grown as an ornamental. The root is useful in rheumatism. The paste of leaves is applied to the body during fever.

Other important members of the family. *Orchis latifolia* Linn. **Salap** - tubers edible; *Vanilla planifolia* Andr., pods are used for flavouring purposes; *Vanda spathulata* Spreng., flowers given in asthma and mania.

FAMILY - MUSACEAE (Banana family)

MUSA

1. Musa paradisiaca Linn.; Verna. **Kela;** Eng. Banana.

Habit : Perennial gigantic herb, sometimes 15 feet high, cultivated or wild.

Root : Adventitious.

Stem : Underground rhizome, also present a false erect aerial stem formed by the long, stiff and overlapping leaf sheaths, apparent aerial stem known as **shaft.**

Leaf : Simple, large sometimes six feet long or more, entire, glabrous, apex obtuse, with a strong midrib and parallel venation, petiolate, with long and thick petiole, exstipulate, lamina tears between the veins and often makes its appearance like caducous and red in colour.

Inflorescence : A terminal spike covered by red bracts arranged in three spiral lines round the floral axis, each bract covers many unisexual flowers, bracts are caducous and red in colour.

Flower : Sessile, monoecious, unisexual, zygomorphic, epigynous, male flowers occur above the female, in the bracteate inflorescence, bisexual flowers also found within the middle bracts.

Perianth : Six perianth leaves (tepals), arranged in two whorls of three each, three outer and two inner anterior perianth leaves unite to form a tube like structure, inner perianth leaf (tepal) is free, petaloid.

Androecium : Six stamens, five stamens perfect and one (posterior) rudimentary (staminode), sometimes the sixth stamen altogether absent, stamens free, anthers bicelled and basifixed.

Gynoecium : Three carpels, syncarpous; ovary inferior, trilocular; axile placentation; each loculus with many ovules, in *Musa paradisiaca* and *Musa sapientum* the ovules are very short and do not develop in seeds, and therefore, the fruits are seedless; style simple, filiform; stigma with three branched lobes.

Fruit : An elongated berry. The mesocarp is edible.

Seeds : Undeveloped, if present exalbuminous.

Generic characters : Apparent aerial stem 'shaft' is present; inflorescence terminal spike with large, leathery and reddish bracts; six stamens, five stamens perfect, one staminode; ovules do not develop in seed; fruit an elongated berry.

Floral formula : Br | ⚥ or ⚥ or ⚥ P(2 + 3) + 1, A5 + 1, G(3).

Identification and Systematic Position :

(*i*) Leaves usually parallel-veined.
(*ii*) Flowers usually trimerous.
(*iii*) Embryo with single cotyledon.
(*iv*) Fibrous roots. — *Monocotyledons.*

(*i*) Ovary inferior.
(*ii*) Perianth in two series; petaloid.
(*iii*) Ovary 1-3 celled. — *Epigynae.*

(*i*) Perennial large herbs.
(*ii*) Inflorescence compound spadix with large coloured bracts.
(*iii*) Perianth two seriate; petaloid.
(*iv*) Flowers irregular, hermaphrodite.
(*v*) Gynoecium tricarpellary, syncarpous, ovary inferior; fruit berry or capsule.
—*Musaceae.*

Bentham & Hooker (1862)	*Engler & Prantl (1931)*	*Hutchinson (1959)*
Monocotyledons	Monocotyledonae	Monocotyledones
Epigynae	Scitamineae	Calyciferae
Musaceae (Scitamineae)	Musaceae	Zingiberales
		Musaceae

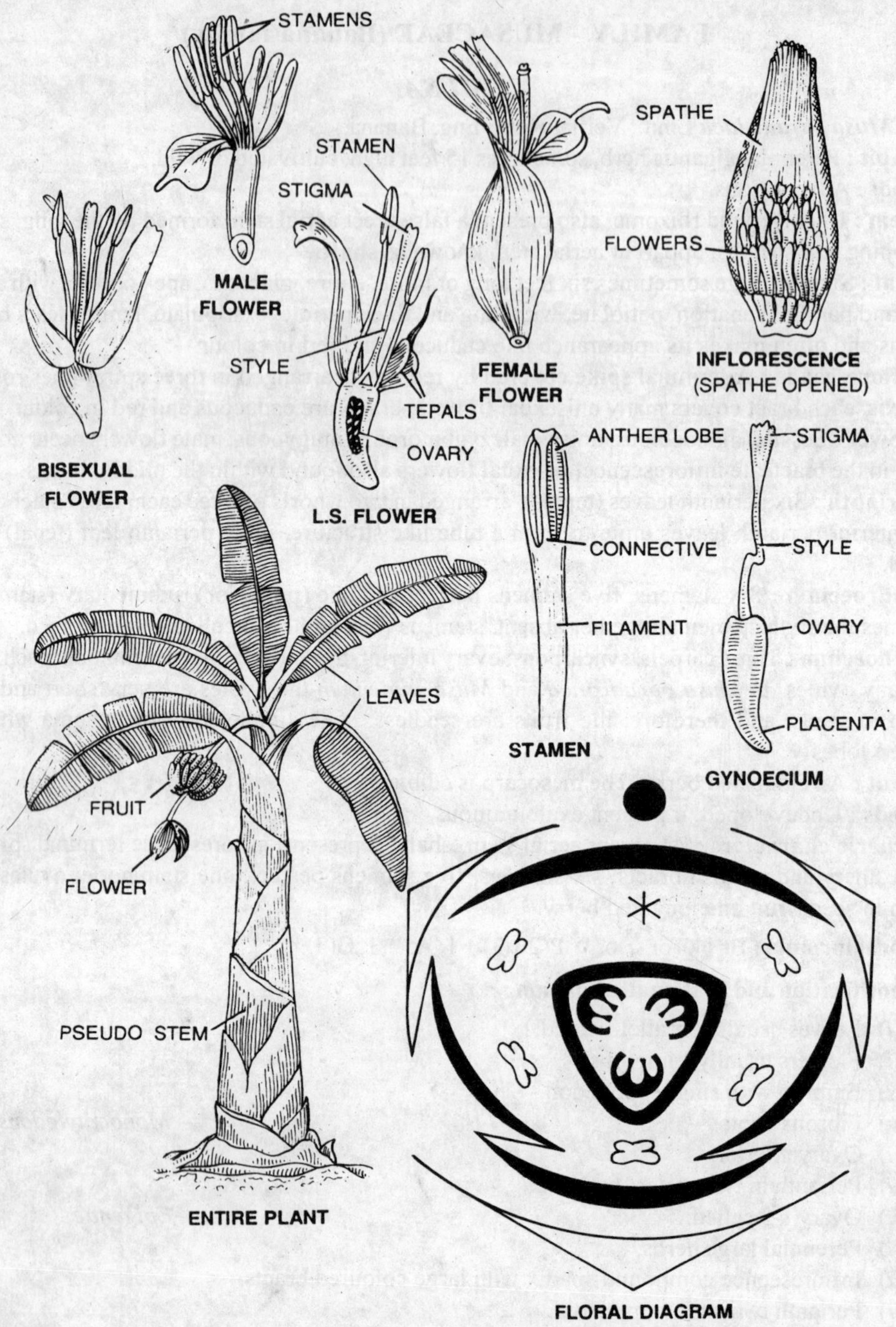

Fig. 9.95. Musaceae. *Musa paradisiaca* Linn.; Eng. Banana; Verna. **Kela.**

Economic value. The fruits are edible. They have a high content of carbohydrates with some fats and proteins. Their food value is three times that of wheat. Green bananas may be cooked and eaten as vegetable. Banana powder can be used as baby food and in the manufacture of chocolate and biscuits. The leaves are commonly used as plates on festive occasions. The root is anthelmintic. The flowers are astringent. The juice of stem is used in otalgia and haemoptysis.

FAMILY - CANNACEAE (Canna family)

CANNA

Canna indica Linn,; Verna. **Keli**; Eng. Indian shot.

There is only one genus containing about fifty species in this family.

Distribution : The species of *Canna* are chiefly found in the warmer parts of America. Several species are cultivated for their beautiful flowers. *Canna indica* (Indian shot; Verna. - **Keli**) is commonly grown in parks and gardens in our country and cultivated throughout the warmer parts of the world.

Habit : The species of *Canna* are perennial herbs.

Stem : The plants persist by means of a rhizome. The aerial stem is also found. The scape bears the inflorescence.

Leaves : The aerial stem bears large pinnately veined leaves. The leaves are large, foliaceous, oblong to broadly elliptical, parallel venation.

Inflorescencc : The inflorescence is terminal, forming a spike; sometimes it is branched, and therefore, each bract found on the main axis subtents a two-flowered cincinnus, instead of a single flower.

Flower : The flowers are hermaphrodite, zygomorphic, bracteate, bracteolate, showy, trimerous and epigynous.

Perianth : The perianth consists of two trimerous series, the outer consisting of sepals and the inner of petals.

The sepals are free, small, herbaceous, greenish purple, showing imbricate aestivation.

The petals are united into a tube below, large than the sepals, coloured, subequal, imbricate.

Androecium : The androecium consists of six stamens, sometimes reduced to four. All stamens are petaloid, showy and slightly connate at the base. The outer three stamens are always sterile, out of which, the **labellum** is rolled back on itself. The remaining part of the androecium consists of a petaloid stamen bearing a half-anther on one edge.

Gynoecium : 3 carpels, syncarpous, ovary inferior, trilocular, axile placentation. The anatropous ovules are being arranged in two series at the inner angle of each loculus. The style is petaloid; the stigma is terminal and oblique.

Fruit : The fruit is a warty or spinose trilocular many seeded capsule.

Seed : The seeds are roundish, containing a hard white perisperm, and a well developed straight embryo.

Floral formula : Br, Brl •|• ⚥ K3, C(3), A1, G(2).

Identification and Systematic Position :

(*i*) Leaves usually parallel-veined.
(*ii*) Flowers usually trimerous.
(*iii*) Embryo with single cotyledon.
(*iv*) Fibrous roots. —*Monocotyledons.*

(*i*) Ovary inferior.
(*ii*) Perianth in two series; petaloid.
(*iii*) Ovary 1-3 celled. —*Epigynae.*

(*i*) Perennial herbs possessing rhizomes; scape present.
(*ii*) Inflorescence scapiferous, terminal.
(*iii*) Stamens petaloid, showy, connate at base.
(*iv*) 3 carpels; syncarpous; style petaloid; fruit spinose, trilocular, many seeded capsule.
—*Cannaceae.*

Bentham & Hooker (1862)	*Engler & Prantl (1931)*	*Hutchinson (1959)*
Monocotyledons	Monocotyledoneae	Monocotyledones
Epigynae	Scitamineae	Calyciferae
Cannaceae	Cannaceae	Zingiberales
		Cannaceae

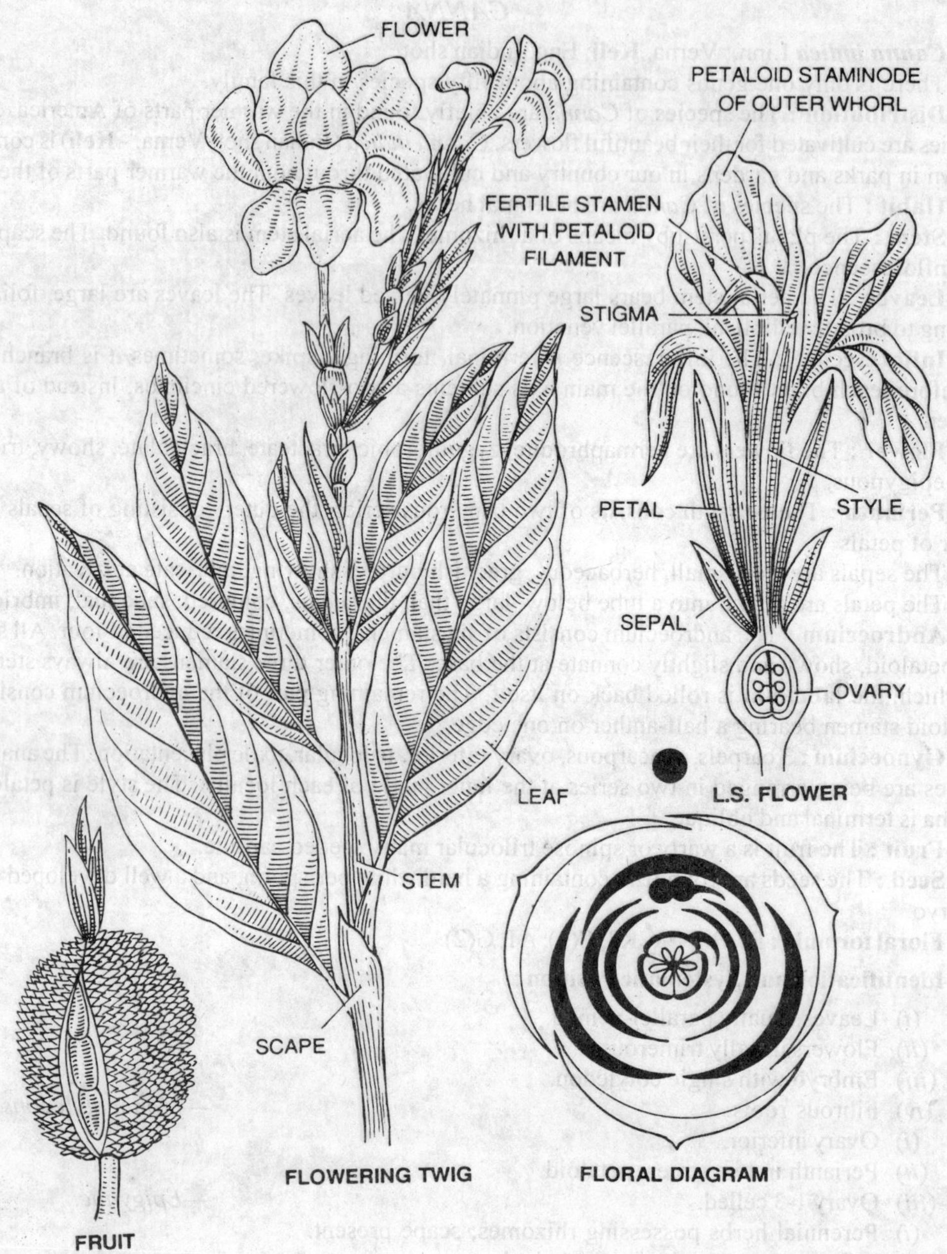

Fig. 9.96. Cannaceae. *Canna indica* Linn.; Eng. Indian shot; Verna. **Keli**.

Economic value. An ornamental herb. It is grown in the gardens for its beautiful variously coloured flowers. The tuberous rhizomes are cooked as vegetable. Root is diaphoretic, diuretic in fevers and dropsy, demulcent, stimulant.

FAMILY - LILIACEAE (Lily family)

ASPHODELUS

Asphodelus tenuifolius Cav.; Verna. **Piazi**.

Habit : Annual weed.

Root : Adventitious and fibrous.

Stem : Very small bulb.

Leaves : Radical, slender, erect, semi-terete, fistular, glabrous and pointed.

Inflorescence : Racemose, raceme.

Flower : Pedicellate, bracteate, small, actinomorphic, regular, hermaphrodite and hypogynous.

Perianth : Six tepals, leaves in two whorls of three each; white; free or united at the base.

Androecium : Six stamens in two whorls of three each; epiphyllous; filaments broad at the base and surround the ovary; anthers dithecous, basifixed or versatile, introrse, brown.

Gynoecium : Three, tricarpellary, syncarpous; ovary superior, trilocular, each loculus bearing two ovules; placentation axile; style short, stigma three-lobed.

Fruit : Small capsule.

Seeds : Albuminous with straight embryo.

Floral formula : Br ⊕ ⚥ P(3 + 3), A3 + 3, G($\underline{3}$).

Identification and Systematic Position :

(*i*) Leaves usually parallel-veined.
(*ii*) Flowers usually trimerous.
(*iii*) Embryo with single cotyledon.
(*iv*) Fibrous roots. — *Monocotyledons.*

(*i*) Ovary superior; 3-celled.
(*ii*) 6 tepals in two whorls; petaloid. — *Coronariae.*

(*i*) Perianth petaloid; 6 tepals free or connate below.
(*ii*) Ovary 3-celled; 2 or more ovules per cell, fruit 3-celled berry or capsule.
(iii) Stamens 6 in two whorls; epitepalous. — *Liliaceae.*

Bentham & Hooker (1862)	*Engler & Prantl (1931)*	*Hutchinson (1959)*
Monocotyledons	Monocotyledoneae	Monocotyledones
Coronariae	Lilliflorae	Corolliferae
Liliaceae	Liliaceae	Liliales
		Liliaceae

Other important members of the family. *Lilium candidum* Linn., an ornamental; *Gloriosa superba* Linn., **Kalihari** - an ornamental; *Asparagus officinalis* Linn., **Satmuli,** shoots are used as vegetable; *Aloe barbadensis* Mill., **Ghikanvar** - the succulent leaves yield a drug which is used in liver disorders.

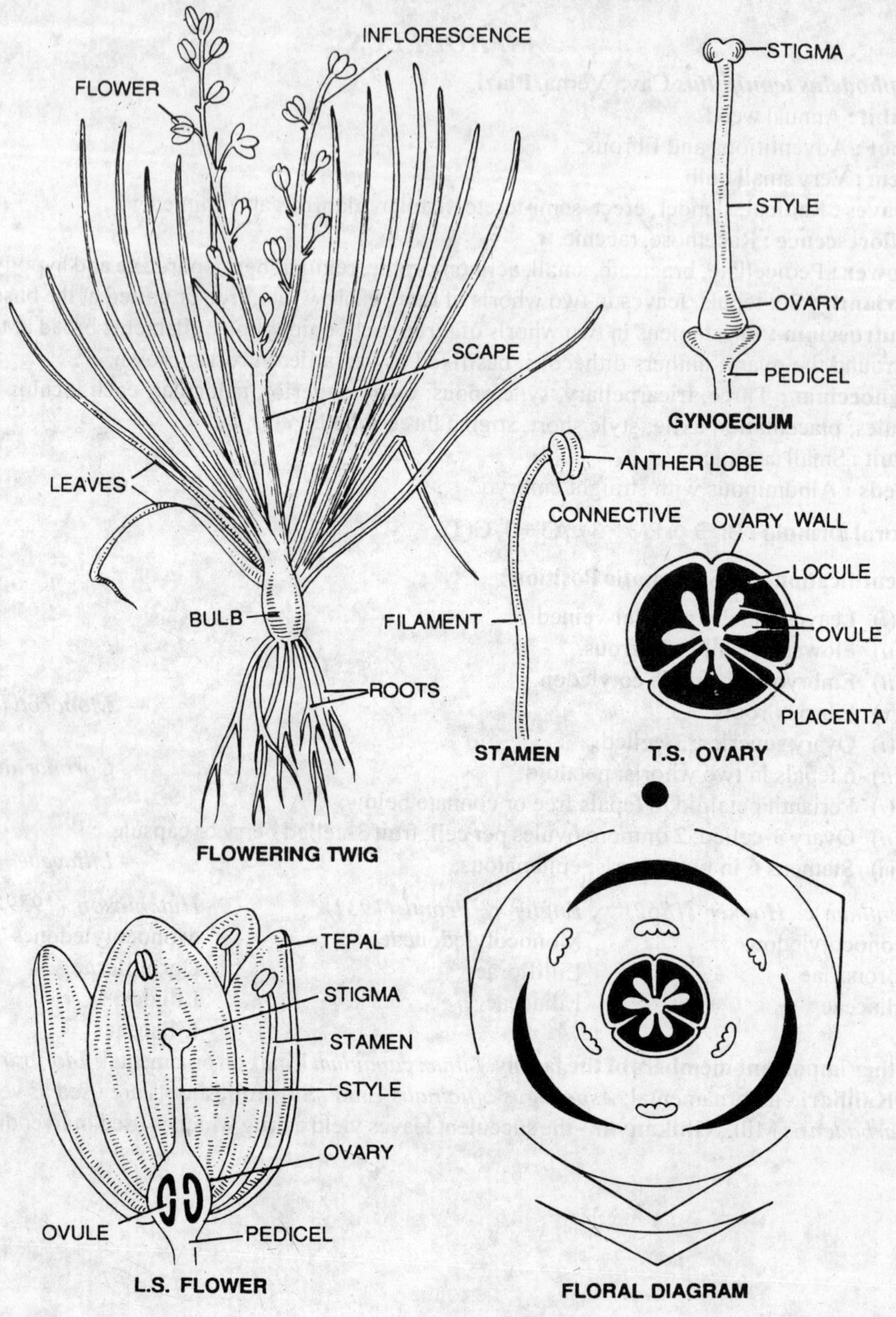

Fig. 9.97. Liliaceae. *Asphodelus tenuifolius* Cav.; Verna. **piazi.**

Economic value. The seeds are diuretic and applied externally to ulcers and inflamed parts.

FAMILY - PALMAE - ARECACEAE (Palm family)

BORASSUS

Borassus flabellifer Linn.; Verna. **Tar;** Eng. Palmyra palm.

Habit : Tree

Stem : Erect, aerial, woody, cylinderical, covered with persistent bases of petioles, unbranched, solid, rough, brown.

Leaf : Cauline, arranged in terminal crown; exstipulate, petiolate, petiole long and stout, glabrous, multicostate parallel venation.

Inflorescence : Spadix.

Male flower : Bracteate, sessile, incomplete, actinomorphic, unisexual, staminate, trimerous, hypogynous, cyclic.

Perianth : 6 tepals, arranged in two whorls of 3 each.

Androecium : 6 stamens, in two whorls of 3 each, polyandrous, filament short, dithecous, dorsifixed, introrse.

Gynoecium : 0.

Floral formula : Br ⊕ ♂ P3 + 3, A3 + 3, G0.

Female flower : Bracteate, sessile, incomplete, pistillate, unisexual, actinomorphic, trimerous, hypogynous, cyclic.

Perianth : 6 tepals, in two whorls of 3 each, imbricate or valvate.

Androecium : 0.

Gynoecium : 3 carpels (tricarpellary). syncarpous, ovary superior, 3-locular, single ovule in each locule; style absent, stigma short.

Fruit : Berry.

Floral formula : Br ⊕ ♀ P3 + 3, A0, G($\underline{3}$).

Identification and Systematic Position :

(*i*) Leaves usually parallel-veined.
(*ii*) Flowers usually trimerous.
(*iii*) Embryo with single cotyledon.
(*iv*) Fibrous roots — *Monocotyledons.*

(*i*) Ovary superior.
(*ii*) Perianth inconspicuous, sepaloid, stiff or herbaceous. — *Calycineae.*

(*i*) Flowers mostly 1-sexual; small, yellowish.
(*ii*) Perianth 6-lobed in two series.
(*iii*) Stamens 6 on base of perianth segments; anthers versatile,
(*iv*) Ovary 1-3 celled; one ovule in each locule.
(*v*) Shrubs or trees, armed or not, stem with fan-like leaves.
(*vi*) Inflorescence at first enclosed in woody or coriaceous spathe. —*Palmae.*

Bentham & Hooker (1862)	*Engler & Prantl (1931)*	*Hutchinson (1959)*
Monocotyledons	Monocotyledoneae	Monocotyledones
Calycineae	Principes	Corolliferae
Palmae	Palmae	Palmales
		Palmae (Palmaceae/Arecaceae)

Other important members of the family. *Areca catechu* Linn., **Supari**; *Cocos nucifera* Linn., **Nariyal**; *Caryota urens* Linn., **Mari**; *Metroxylon sagu* Rott.; **Sago**; *Phoenix dactylifera* Linn., **Pindkhajur**; *P. sylvestris* (Linn.) Roxb; **Khajur.**

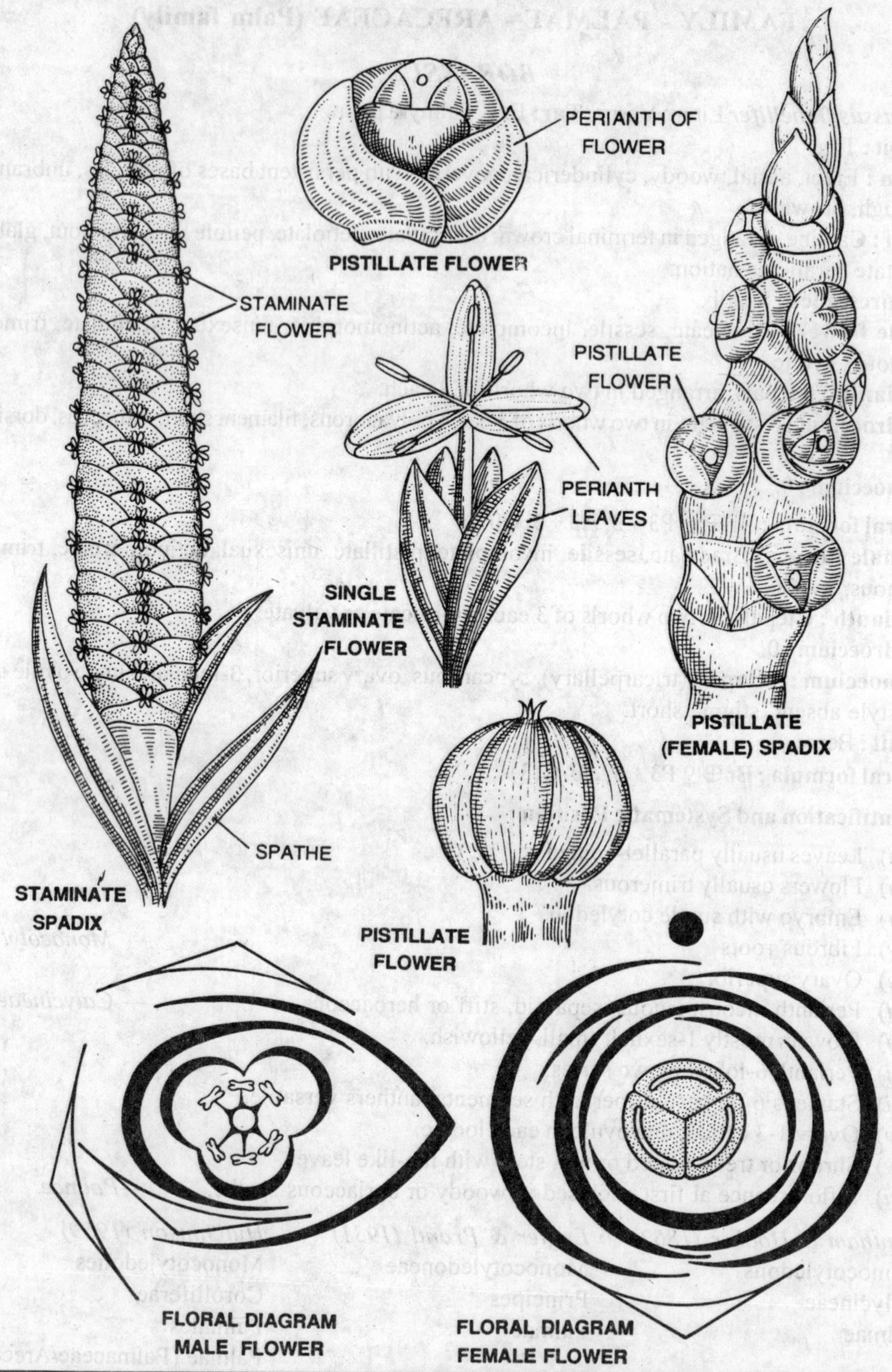

Fig. 9.98. Palmae (Arecaceae). *Borassus flabellifer* Linn.; Eng., palmyra palm; Verna., **tar.**

Economic value. A palm, which yields toddy, nira, palm jaggery, fruit and fibre. The fibre is used for preparing brushes and brooms and the leaves for making fans, umbrellas, baskets and mats. Root is cooling and restorative. Juice of plant is diuretic, stimulant, useful in inflammatory affection and dropsy.

FAMILY - ARACEAE (Arum family)

ALOCASIA

*1. **Alocasia indica*** Schott.; Eng. Giant Taro; Verma. **Mankanda**.

Habit : Annual herb, either grown for its beautiful foliage in the gardens or it is cultivated for its edible rhizomes.

Root : Adventitious; some are aerial

Stem : Usually rhizome, but sometimes rises a considerable distance above the ground.

Leaves : Usually large, entire, peltately attached or not to the long petiole, more of less ovate and cordate or sagittate, venation parallel, petioles are well developed and swollen at the base.

Inflorescence : Spadix, which is covered by a leafy bract known as spathe, which is tubular at the base but spread above, spadix free, somewhat shorter than the spathe. Female flowers are arranged towards the top of the spadix while male flowers on the lower side. In the gap between males and females the neuters are present.

Perianth : Absent in *Alocasia*.

Androecium : 3 to 5 stamens arranged in a single whorl; the filaments are united throughout their length forming a **synandrium,** anthers are dithecous (2-celled), dehiscence by pores.

Gynoecium : Two to four carpels, syncarpous, ovary ovoid one celled (unilocular), with few to many basal orthotropus ovules; style short; stigma 2-4 lobed.

Fruit : Berry, almost spherical, red, few seeded, enclosed by the accrescent tube of spathe.

Seeds : Albuminous, roundish, with thick smooth testa and axile embryo.

Generic characters : Fruit a berry, enclosed by the accrescent tube of spathe; perianth absent; inflorescence spadix, monoecious female flowers above, males below; synandrium is formed by the fusion of the filaments of the stamens; stem usually rhizome.

Floral formula : ⚥, ♂ or ♀, P0, A3 to 5, G$\underline{(2-4)}$.

Identification and Systematic Position :

(*i*) Leaves usually parallel-veined.
(*ii*) Flowers usually trimerous.
(*iii*) Embryo with single cotyledon.
(*iv*) Fibrous roots. — *Monocotyledons.*

(*i*) Ovary superior.
(*ii*) Perianth absent or reduced to scales. — *Nudiflorae.*

(*i*) Flowers small, mostly 1-sexual, in a monoecious spadix with female flowers below; spathe herbaceous.
(*ii*) Perianth 0.
(*iii*) Anther 2-4 celled, free or connate; synandrium.
(*iv*) Ovary sessile, 1-3 celled; fruit a berry.
(*v*) Terrestrial or aquatic herbs with radical leaves. —*Araceae.*

Bentham & Hooker (1862)	*Engler & Prantl (1931)*	*Hutchinson (1959)*
Monocotyledons	Monocotyledoneae	Monocotyledones
Nudiflorae	Spathiflorae	Corolliferae
Aroideae (Araceae)	Araceae	Arales
		Araceae

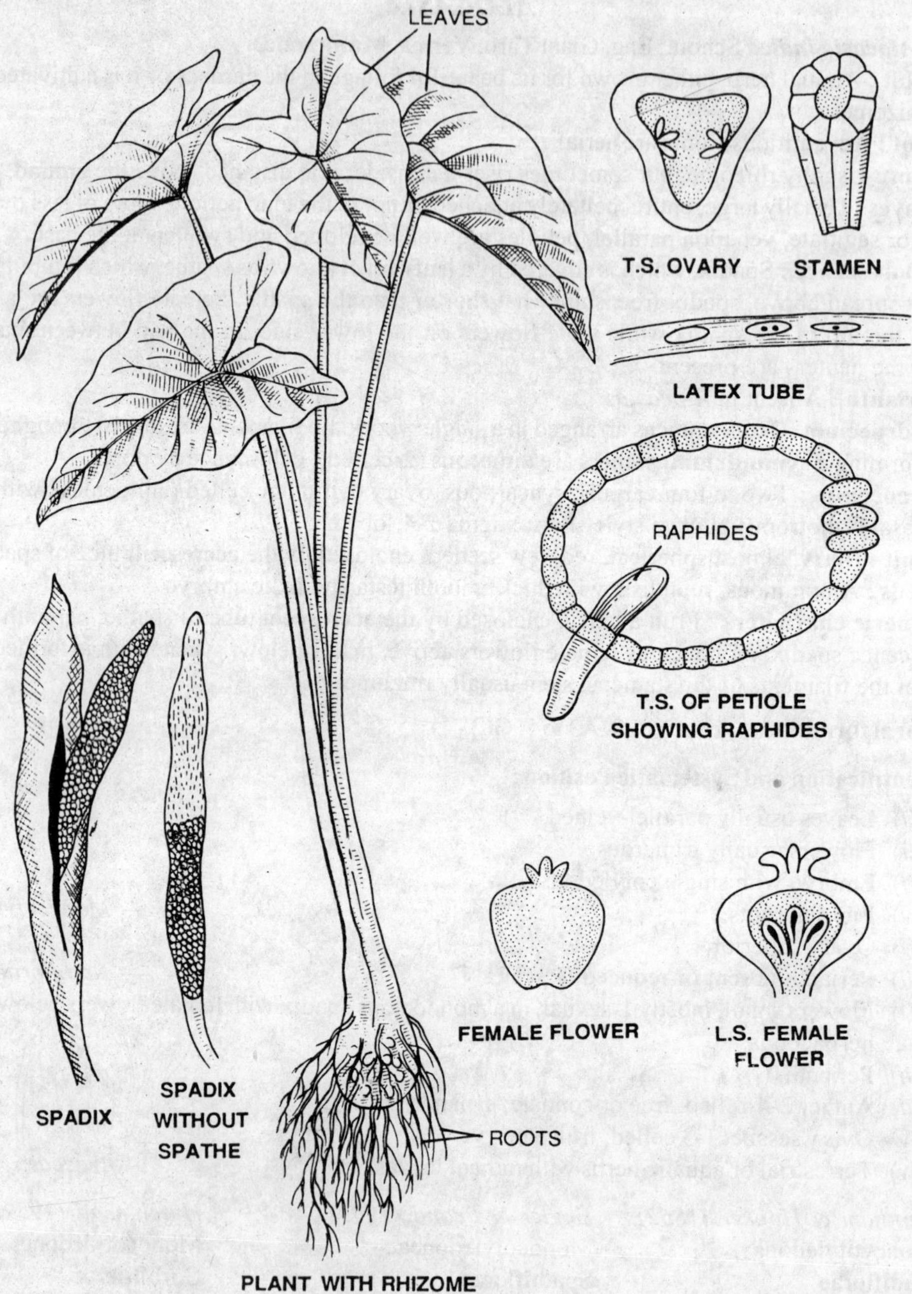

Fig. 9.99. Araceae. *Alocasia indica* Schott.; Eng., giant taro; Verna., **Mankanda.**

Economic value. The plant is grown as an ornamental. The stems and root-stocks are eaten as vegetable only after cooking. The leaves are styptic and astringent. The tuber is used in piles and constipation.

PISTIA

2. ***Pistia stratiotes*** Linn.; Verma. **Jalkhumbhi.**

Habit : Aquatic herb, free floating.

Root : Adventitious, root caps absent, root pockets present.

Stem : Stolon, prostrate on the water surface, cylinderical, herbaceous, containing water juice (latex), sap is acrid with pungent odour, spongy, green.

Leaf : Simple, sessile, large, entire, clustered, radical, coriaceous, spongy, parallel veined.

Inflorescence : Spadix enclosed in spathe.

Flower : Sessile, small, bracteate, actinomorphic, regular, unisexual, monoecious, male flowers towards the apex of spadix, female flowers below, neuter or suppressed male flowers are present in between.

Perianth : A cupular structure, 4-6 scaly tepals, connate.

Androecium : The male flower is reduced to two anthers, which unite to form a synandrium.

Gynoecium : One carpel, ovary superior (embedded) in spadix, unilocular, many ovules in each locule; basal placentation, style short, stigma disc-like or lobed.

Fruit : A berry.

Seeds : Endospermic in each berry one to many seeds.

Floral formula : Br ⊕ ♂ or ♀, P4 - 6, A2, $G\underline{1}$.

Identification and Systematic Position :

(*i*) Leaves usually parallel-veined.
(*ii*) Flowers usually trimerous.
(*iii*) Embryo with single cotyledon.
(*iv*) Fibrous roots. — *Monocotyledons.*

(*i*) Ovary superior.
(*ii*) Perianth absent or reduced to scales. — *Nudiflorae.*

(*i*) Flowers small, mostly 1-sexual, in a monoecious spadix with female flowers below; spathe herbaceous.
(*ii*) Perianth 0.
(*iii*) Anther 2-4 celled, free or connate; synandrium.
(*iv*) Ovary sessile, 1-3 celled; fruit a berry.
(*v*) Terrestrial or aquatic herbs with radical leaves. —*Araceae.*

Other important members of the family. *Amorphophallus campanulatus* (Roxb.) Blume ex Dcne., **Zamin-kand**- tuberous roots eaten as vegetable; *Arisaema tortuosum* (Wall.) Schott, **Samp-ki-kumb**-tubers used as insecticide; *Acorus calamus* Linn., **Safed bach**-rhizomes used medicinally as carminative, stimulant and tonic, *Colocasia esculenta* (Linn.) Schott, **Arvi, Kachalu** - starchy, tuberous rhizomes eaten as vegetable after cooking.

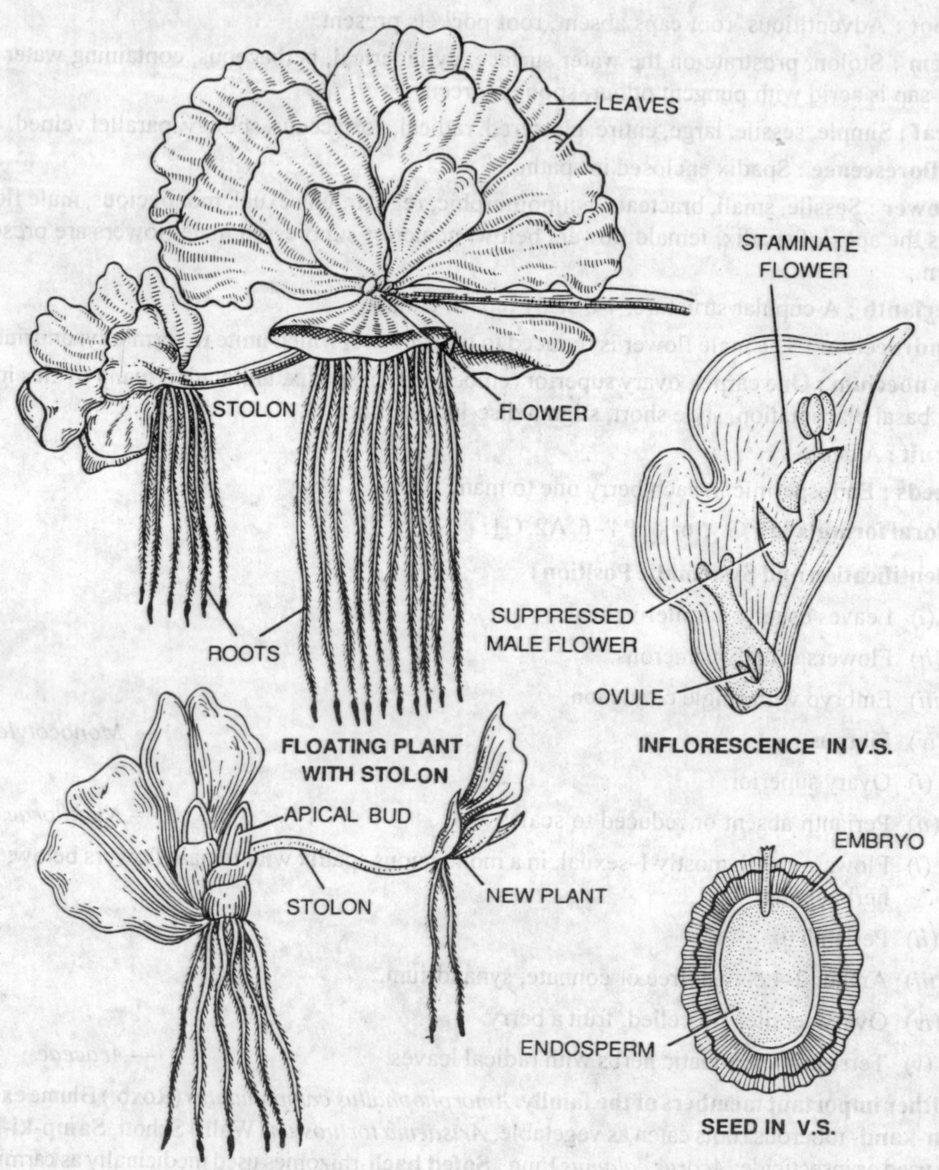

Fig. 9.100. Araceae. *Pistia stratiotes* Linn., Verna., **jalkumbhi.**

Economic value. The plant is demulcent, refrigerant and given in dysuria; used to destroy bugs. The root is emollient, laxative and diuretic. The leaves are made into poultice and applied to haemorrhoids. The ashes are applied to ringworm of the scalp. The juice of leaves boiled with coconut oil is used externally in chronic skin diseases.

FAMILY - GRAMINEAE-POACEAE (Grass family)

TRITICUM

*1. **Triticum aestivum*** Linn.; Verna. **Gehu**; Eng. Wheat.

Habit : Annual cereal, in India all wheats are winter grown.

Root : Adventitious, fibrous.

Stem : The 3 to 4 feet in height, erect, cylinderical, sometimes furrowed, and either glabrous or scabrous, nodes 5 to 7, average number six, nodes swollen and solid, internodes hollow, internodes are covered by the leaf-sheaths, branching by tillers.

Leaves : Divisible into two parts, the leaf-sheath and leaf blade (lamina), possesses two accessory organs, the ligules and the auricles; sheath inserted on the node and envelops stem, leaf sheath usually thicker than the leaf blade with thin transparent margins, surface either glabrous or hairy; leaf blade is long, narrow, lanceolate, acuminate with parallel venation, sometimes hairs also present along the veins, thin membranous **ligule** encircles stem, colourless and hairy; two claw-like appendages near ligule region are prominent, these are known as **auricles**, hairy and pale green.

Inflorescence : Spike of spikelets, compound spike bearing two rows of lateral spikelets on its axis and a single terminal, short internodes, each internode is narrow at base and broad apex, one side of internode convex, other side concave or flat, concave alternates with convex side and axis has a *zig zag* appearance, spikelets sessile and arranged alternately.

Spikelets : Solitary and sessile flowers (florets) arranged on a short, jointed axis, the **rachilla**, flowers alternately placed at the base of each spikelet 2 glumes, one glume overlaps the other, normal glume boat shaped with a thick main nerve, dividing it in two unequal halves, base of glume rounded, sometimes the nerve extends in an awn 2 to 5 cms., long, glabrous or hairy, usually two grains, sometimes three, and very rarely four, mature in a single spikelet.

Flower : Sessile, bracteate, two bracts - a lemma (inferior palea) and a palea (superior palea), opposite to each other, **lemma** boat-shaped, with many nerves, upper margin is notched and ends in awn, lemma greenish white, or pink, **palea** thin membranous bract just opposite lemma, slipper-shaped with two prominent nerves, small, zygomorphic, hermaphrodite, hypogynous, incomplete, irregular and not showy.

Perianth : 2 membranous lodicules, colourless, narrow, scale-like, hairy.

Androecium : 3 stamens, filaments long, slender scale-like, free; the anthers are bicelled and versatile.

Gynoecium : Monocarpellary, ovary superior, unilocular, hairy, triangular, two styles, stigma feathery, single ovule, basal placentation.

Fruit : Caryopsis, seed coat firmly united to the ovary wall.

Seeds : Albuminous.

Floral formula : Br •|• ⚥, P2(lodicules), A3, G($\underline{1}$).

Identification and Systematic Position :

(*i*) Leaves usually parallel-veined.
(*ii*) Flowers usually trimerous.
(*iii*) Embryo with single cotyledon.
(*iv*) Fibrous roots. — *Monocotyledons.*

(*i*) Ovary single celled, single ovuled.
(*ii*) Flowers in spikelets or heads.
(*iii*) Perianth scale-like. — *Glumaceae.*

(*i*) Flowers in spikelets of glumes; 1 - 2 sexual.
(*ii*) Perianth of 2 minute lodicules or 0.
(*iii*) Stamens 3, anthers versatile.
(*iv*) Ovary superior with one ovule, styles 2, stigmas feathery; fruit caryopsis.
(*v*) Stem terete or compressed; leaves narrow; ligule present at the junction of leaf blade and leaf sheath. — *Gramineae.*

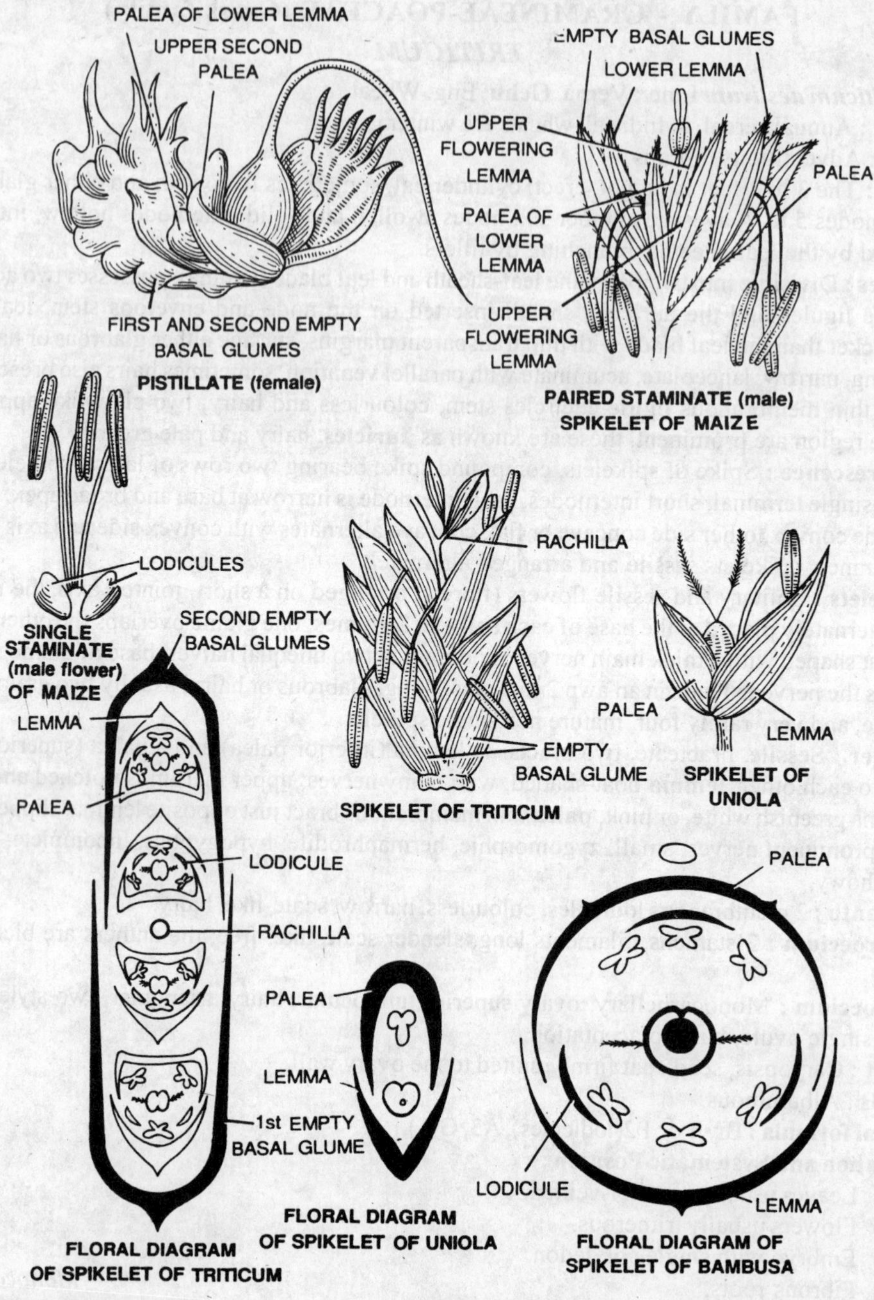

Fig. 9.101. Gramineae (Poaceae). *Zea mays; Triticum; Uniola; Bambusa*, etc.

Bentham & Hooker (1862)	*Engler & Prantl (1931)*	*Hutchinson (1959)*
Monocotyledons	Monocotyledoneae	Monocotyledones
Glumaceae	Glumiflorae	Glumiflorae
Gramineae	Gramineae	Graminales
		Gramineae (Poaceae).

Economic value. Cereals and millets : They constitute the most important group in the food plants of India. The cereals and the millets are the members of family Gramineae. They are : rice, wheat, maize, barley, sorghum, pearl millet, etc. They contain carbohydrates, proteins and fats.

ORYZA

2. ***Oryza sativa*** Linn.; Verna. **Dhan;** Eng. Paddy (rice).

Habit : Annual herb, cultivated in lowland humid areas.

Root : Root system divided into two parts, seminal or primary and adventitious or secondary roots; adventitious roots arise from the lower nodes, fibrous and branched.

Stem : Erect, cylinderical, hollow except at nodes, 6 to 8 mm., thick, nodes and internodes conspicuous, the number of internodes may vary from 10 to 20, branching by tillers.

Leaf : Emerge from nodes, number of leaves on axis equal to the number of nodes, possesses leaf sheath, ligule, auricles and leaf blade (lamina). Leaf sheath encircles internode, leaf sheath splits at base, finely ribbed, glabrous; ligule well developed, membranous, colourless or pink auricles well developed, sickle shaped 3 mm in length, present at the junction of the sheath and the leaf blade; long, narrow, lanceolate, acuminate, pubescent, parallel venation with a distinct midrib, uppermost leaf, thc flag shorter than lower leaves.

Inflorescence : Terminal panicle; partly covered by leaf sheath, rachis of panicle slightly angular, glabrous, somewhat hairy at nodes; erect or curved; one to many branches given out from each node, compact or loose.

Spikelets : Spikelets borne either single on the ends of the branches or in clusters of 2 to 7, number of spikelets on a panicle varies from 50 to 500, each spikelet short pedicelled, generally single flowered, very rarely two flowered, apex of pedicel enlarged and oblique and termed **facet,** on facet two glumes one outer and the other inner, glumes small, lanceolate, shiny, coriaceous, equal in size, coloured or colourless.

Flower : Bracteate, a large conspicuous bract, the **lemma,** lemma boat shaped, 5-nerved and hairy on the nerves; apex pointed and prolonged into an awn; on each side of the apex or awn two tooth like projections, lemma usually pigmented, **palea** situated just opposite the lemma, boat shaped and 3-nerved; flower is zygomorphic, hypogynous, irregular, incomplete and sessile.

Perianth : The perianth is represented by two broad, thick and fleshy lodicules.

Androecium : Six stamens, arranged in two regular whorls, filaments long, slender and free; anthers bi-celled, versatile.

Gynoecium : Single carpel (monocarpellary); ovary superior, unilocular, longer than broad, single, ovuled, anatropous ovule; basal placentation; ovary surmounted by two long styles with feathery stigmas.

Fruit : A caryopsis.

Seeds : Albuminous.

Floral formula : Br ·|· ⚥, P2(lodicules), A3 + 3, G$\underline{1}$.

Identification and Systematic Position :

(*i*) Leaves usually parallel-veined.
(*ii*) Flowers usually trimerous.
(*iii*) Embryo with single cotyledon.
(*iv*) Fibrous roots. — *Monocotyledons.*

(*i*) Ovary single celled, single ovuled.
(*ii*) Flowers in spikelets or heads.
(*iii*) Perianth scale-like. — *Glumaceae.*

(*i*) Flowers in spikelets of glumes; 1-2 sexual.
(*ii*) Perianth of 2 minute lodicules or 0.
(*iii*) Stamens 3, anthers versatile.
(*iv*) Ovary superior with one ovulc, styles 2, stigmas feathery; fruit caryopsis.
(*v*) Stem terete or compressed; leaves narrow; ligule present at the junction of leaf blade and leaf sheath. — *Gramineae.*

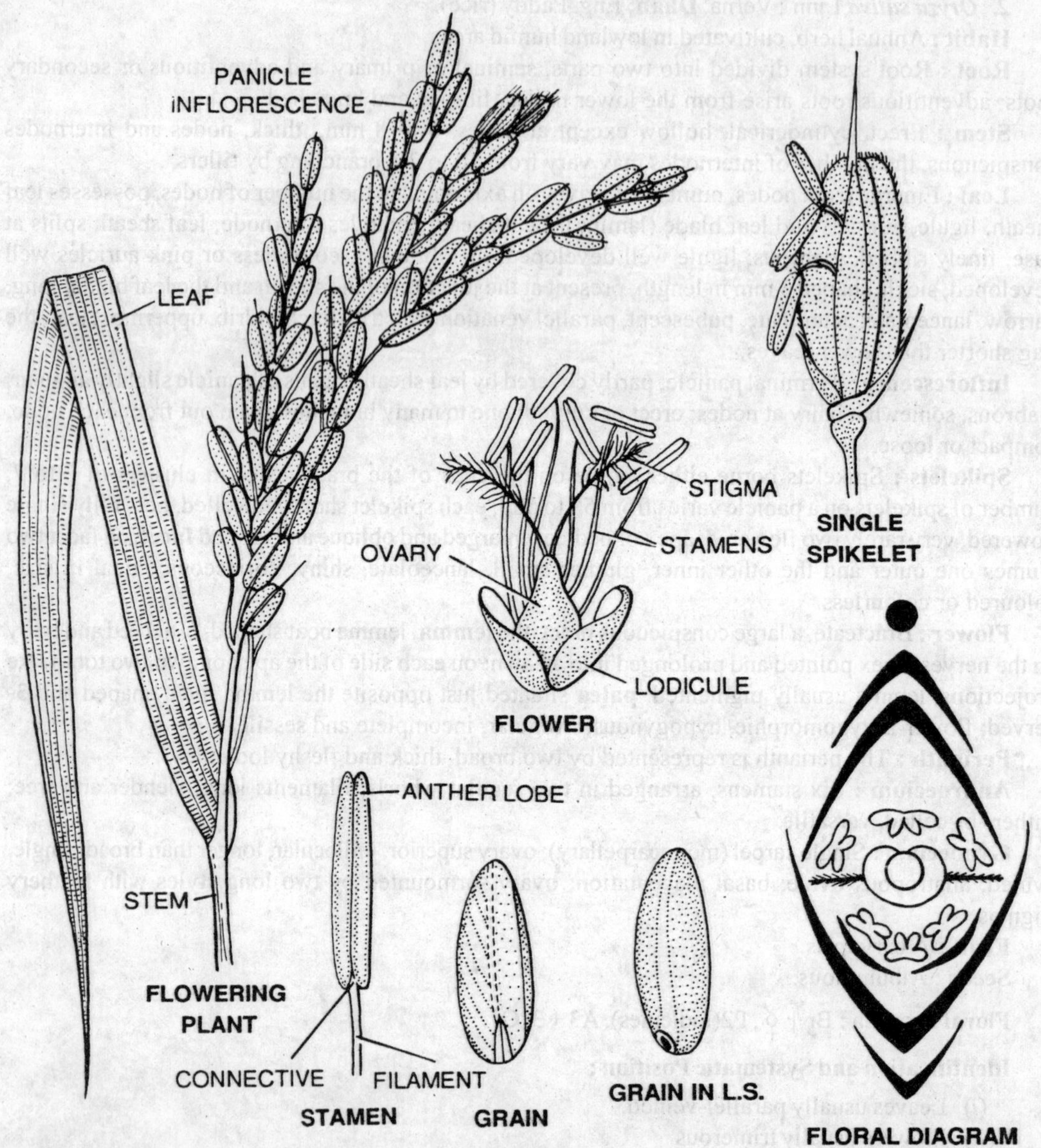

Fig. 9.102. Gramineae (Poaceae). *Oryza sativa* Linn. Eng., paddy, rice; Verna., **dhan, chaval.**

Economic value. Grown as a food crop. The rice is generally eaten with pulses or some other food rich in proteins. The rice straw is used for making straw boards, paper and mats. Rice bran oil is used for making soaps and cosmetics. Important beverage of Japan, *Sake* is prepared by fermenting rice.

Other important members of the family. *Triticum aestivum* Linn., **Gehu**; *Hordeum vulgare* Linn., **Jau**; *Sorghum vulgare* Pers., **Jawar**; *Pennisetum ityphoides* (Burm f.) Stapf C.E. Hubb., **Bajra**; *Panicum miliare* Lamk., **Sawa**; *Zea mays* Linn., **Makka**; *Setaria italica* (Linn.) Beauv., **Kangni**; *Eleusine coracana* (Linn.) Gaertn. **Mandua**; *Saccharum officinarum* Linn., **Ganna**; *Bambusa arundinacea* (Retz.) Willd; **Bans**; *Cynodon dactylon* (Linn.) Pers., **Doob**, etc.

UNIT–2

STRUCTURE, DEVELOPMENT AND REPRODUCTION IN FLOWERING PLANTS

10

CHAPTER

Plant Physiology Experiments

Everything that the organism does is due to the activity of the cells of which it is made up of. In order to understand how an organism as a whole functions it is necessary to study the physiology or functions of an individual cell of a plant. The functions of plant cell are *absorption, metabolism* (that includes *synthesis of foods, food storage, assimilation, digestion*), growth and cell reproduction. All these processes and many others which go on within the plants are the manifestations of life, and it is the object of **plant physiology** to study and analyse all the life processes of the plants, to study the effect of various factors upon these life processes, and if possible, to solve the nature of life itself. This involves a study of functions of the various plant organs and tissues.

The plant physiology experiments on water relations, photosynthesis, respiration, growth and movements are given in subsequent pages.

GENERALASPECTS

EXERCISE 1

Object : To prepare suspension.

Requirements : $BaCl_2$ solution, H_2SO_4, test tube.

Experiment : In a test tube the solution of $BaCl_2$ is taken and then some amount of H_2SO_4 is added to it. On shaking the suspension of fine particles of $BaSO_4$ is obtained. Now the test tube is left as such for a little while.

Observation : The precipitate gradually settles down. In the suspension the particles remain dispersed.

EXERCISE 2

Object : To prepare suspensoid.

Requirements : Sulphur, 95% ethyl alcohol, water bath and a conical flask.

Experiment : Take about 25 ml. 95% alcohol in a conical flask and add a small pinch of sulphur to it. Now boil this mixture on the water bath and then cool it.

Observation : The suspensoid of sulphur is formed. Here the solid phase of sulphur acts as dispersion medium.

EXERCISE 3

Object : To prepare emulsion.

Requirements : Olive oil, water and a test tube.

Experiment : Take water in the test tube and add three or four drops of olive oil to it. Now shake it vigorously and then put it as such undisturbed.

Observation : After shaking the test tube the particles of olive oil get dispersed in the water and form and emulsion.

EXERCISE 4

Object : To Prepare an emulsoid.

Requirements : Castor oil, 90% ethanol, water and a test tube.

Experiment : Take a few drops of castor oil in a test tube and add some 90% ethanol to it and shake vigorously. Now pour this solution in a flask of water.

Observation : Here a fine emulsion is formed in which the two liquid phases can not be separated. It is called an emulsoid.

EXERCISE 5

Object : To prepare a reversible gel.

Requirements : Agar-agar, conical flask, water, spirit lamp.

Experiment : Take some water in the conical flask and add a little agar-agar powder to it. Now put this solution on the spirit lamp with a continuous stirring. After some time a fine homogeneous solution is obtained.

Observation : This experiment suggests that on boiling the agar-agar with water a solution is formed which on cooling sets to the gel form. If this gel is warmed again it will get converted into sol and this sol on cooling will get converted to gel. Therefore this change is termed as a reversible one.

EXERCISE 6

Object : To demonstrate the Tyndall Phenomenon.

Requirements : Glass tank or beaker, arsenious sulphide solution, condensing lens and a candle.

Experiment : The solution of arsenious sulphide is taken in a glass tank or beaker. Now a source of light is placed at a distance from it. The light rays are focussed through a condensing lens. This whole experiment is done in a dark room.

Observation : When the light falls through a condensing lens on the beaker of arsenious sulphide solution, a cone like structure is formed. It is known as Tyndall cone.

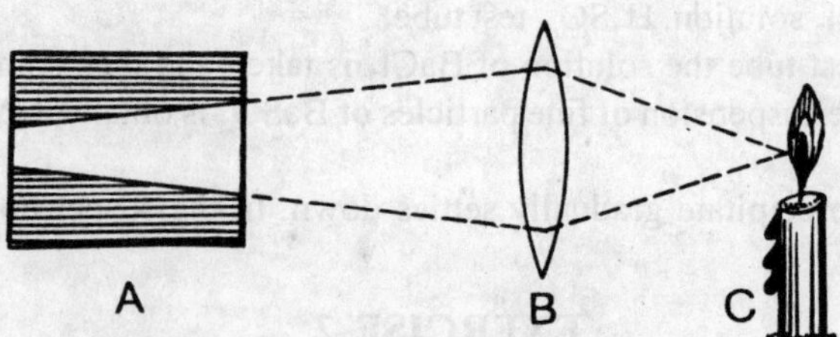

Fig. 10.1. Showing Tyndall phenomenon

Explanation : This is due to scattering of light by the particles of the dispersed phase. These particles thus visible and appear in the form of a bright cone.

Note : This phenomenon may easily be seen in a closed room when a beam of light is passed through a small hole.

EXERCISE 7

Object : To demonstrate Brownian movement.

Requirements : Latex of any plant, water, slide.

Experiment : Take a drop of latex on the slide and dilute it with the addition of few drops of water. Now place a cover slip on it and observe under microscope.

Observation : Under the high power of microscope it is observed that there are rapid, oscillatory movements performed by solid colloidal particles in the *zig zag* direction. Robert Brown (1827) first told about this movement so it is termed as Brownian movement (Fig. 10.2).

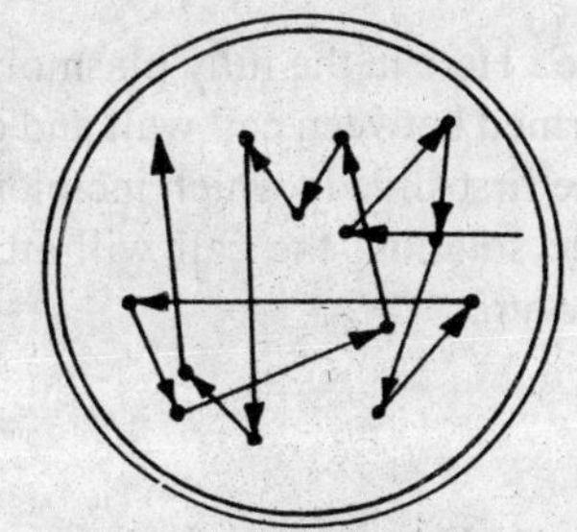

Fig. 10.2. Showing Brownian movement.

WATERRELATIONS PLASMOLYSIS

EXERCISE 8

Object : To demonstrate plasmolysis.

Requirements : Red coloured *Tradescantia* leaves. Water, sugar solution, slide and microscope.

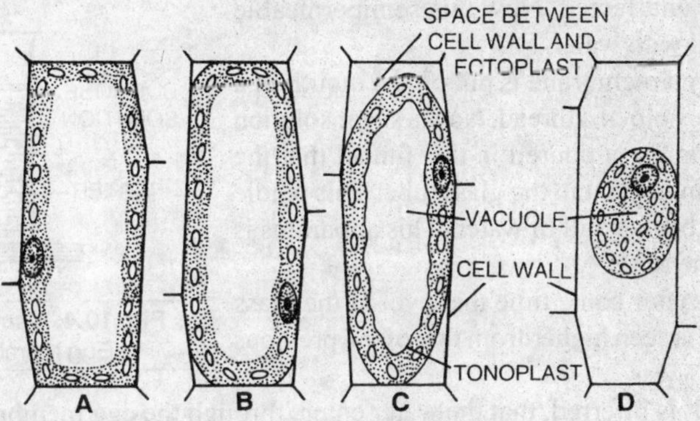

Fig. 10.3. Plasmolysis, a, turgid cell; b-d, successive stages in the shrinkage of protoplasm from the cell wall.

Experiment : To demonstrate plasmolysis, red coloured *Tradescantia* leaves are taken. With a sudden jerk a small segment can be peeled off from the lower surface of leaf. Cut this piece of peel into two parts. First part is put in a drop of water on a slide, second part is put in a drop of sugar solution on another slide. Now both slides are observed under the microscope respectively.

Observation : In first slide the cell structure is seen clearly. Almost most of the cells are turgid. Another slide shows that the cell contents have been separated from their cell walls and so a space is being formed nearer the cell wall.

If the sugar solutions are used with higher concentrations, then the cell contents of the cells will shrink continuously.

Explanation : First slide represents the normal condition. Only a slightly inflated condition may be observed after a considerable time.

The second slide shows the separation of cell contents from the cell wall. It is due to loss of water from the cell. Here so-called space shows the beginning of the plasmolysis and so it is called as incipient type of plasmolysis.

When the concentration of outer medium is increased, the space becomes more widen due to complete loss of water from the cell. This condition is of complete plasmolysis.

Note : Here in the fully plasmolysed cell the hypertonic solution, *i.e.*, the sugar solution fills the space formed between cell wall and cell contents.

If the first slide in which incipient plasmolysis has been completed, is provided by pure water or hypotonic solution, the cell will attain its normal position of turgidity. This process is known as *deplasmolysis.*

OSMOSIS

EXERCISE 9

Object : Demonstration of osmosis by Egg Membrane Osmoscope.

Requirements : An egg, thistle funnel, dil. HCl, water beaker, sugar (sucrose) solution, stand, etc.

Experiment : To set this experiment, an egg is taken. One small hole is made at one end of the egg. The yolk and albumen are taken out of the egg shell through this hole. Now the egg shell is kept in dil. HCl for some time, with the result the hard egg shell of calcium carbonate dissolves in the dil. HCl and the semipermeable egg membrane adhering to the shell remains unaffected. Now this semipermeable membrane is washed with water.

Thus the prepared membrane is put on the mouth of a thistle funnel with the help of a thread. Now a sugar solution of suitable concentration is poured in this funnel that the level of it rises to some extent in the glass tube. This whole apparatus is put in a beaker full of water. This apparatus is kept as such for some time.

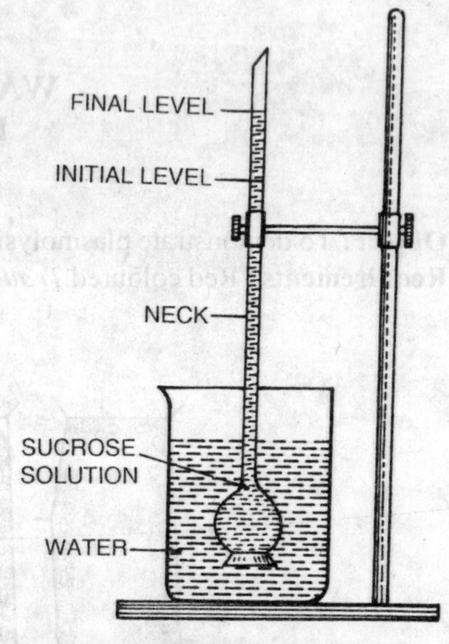

Fig. 10.4. *Osmosis*, demonstration by Egg Membrane Osmoscope.

Observation : After some time the level in the glass tube of thistle funnel is seen higher from that of the previous one.

Explanation : It is inferred, that the water enters through the egg membrane, and the level of the liquid inside the tube rises sufficiently. The density of the inner liquid is greater than that of outer, and in between two, there is semipermeable membrane, and therefore, the outer fluid enters inside through this membrane. This process is called *endosmosis.* In the same way, if the fluids are reversed, the fluid of lower density sweeps out, and the process is called *exosmosis.*

EXERCISE 10

Object : Demonstration of Osmosis by Potato Osmoscope.

Requirements : Potato, sugar solution, water and beaker.

Experiment : A peeled potato is made flat on its one end, and towards other end a cavity is made. This cavity must be sufficiently deep and broad, so that this may reach to the bottom, and the walls may not remain thick. Now, fill up this cavity with concentrated sugar solution and place this potato in a beaker filled up with water. The level of the outer and inner solutions must be same. After some time it is observed, that the level of the fluid inside the potato cavity rises sufficiently.

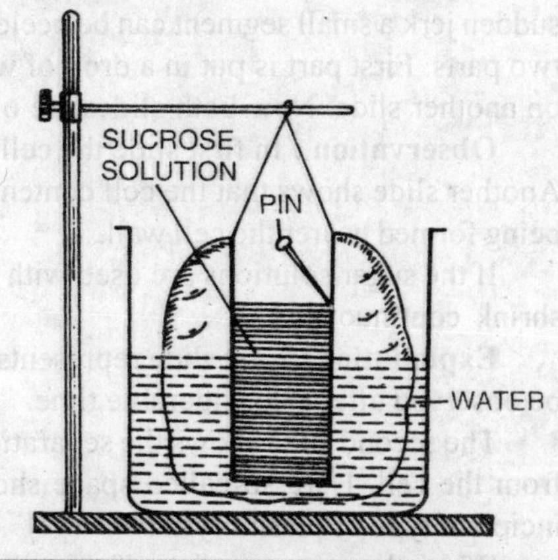

Fig. 10.5. *Osmosis*, demonstration by Potato Osmoscope.

Explanation : This happens, because of *endosmosis.* The density of the sugar solution is greater than that of water, and the potato tissues collectively act as semipermeable membrane, and thus the water moves in from outside.

Note : If sugar solution is placed in the beaker and water is placed in the cavity of potato, the result will be reversed. It happens because of *exosmosis, i.e.*, water moves out from the inside.

IMBIBITION

EXERCISE 11

Object : Demonstration of phenomenon of imbibition.

Requirements : Gram seeds, water and watch glasses.

Experiment : Take some gram seeds in the water in the water glasses. Keep them for some time.

Observation : After some time the seeds got swollen.

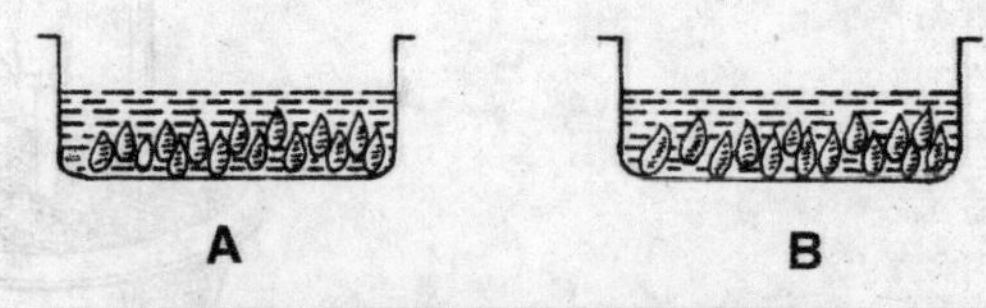

Fig. 10.6. *Imbibition,* demonstration of the phenomenon.

Explanation : Here no cell membrane is involved in this process. The pectic or proteinaceous surface attracts the water molecules by intermolecular forces. These pectic substances are hydrophilic in nature. As the diffusion pressure of dry seeds is zero, therefore, the water is absorbed in the seeds. This process remains continued till the diffusion pressure of the seeds and water becomes equal. Thus the seeds get swollen here.

EXERCISE 12

Object : Demonstration of developing pressure during imbibition.

Requirements : A corked jar, a disc fitting in it, a round scale and a pointer attached with the disc, stand, experimental gram seeds and water.

Experiment : Take seeds and water in the jar as directed in the figure 10.7. Fit the disc over these seeds. To this disc attach the pointer indicating initial reading at zero on the round scale. The whole apparatus should be airtight. Let this adjustment put as such for few hours.

Observation and explanation : After few hours the pointer moves down showing an upward movement of disc in the jar. Here the gram seeds swell considerably due to imbibition process. These seeds cause a pressure known as imbibition pressure.

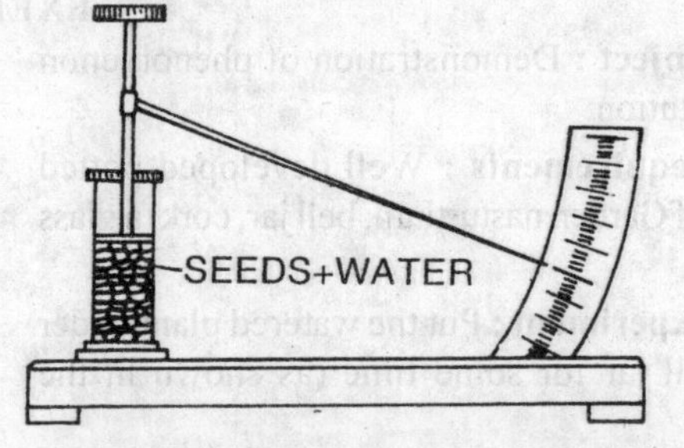

Fig. 10.7. Demonstration of developing pressure during imbibition.

ROOT PRESSURE

EXERCISE 13

Object : Demonstration of root pressure.

Requirements : A potted balsam plant, a rubber tubing, a glass tube and a U-shaped manometer.

Experiment : The stem of a healthy balsam plant is cut a few inches above the ground level in the morning time and set up the apparatus as shown in the figure. With the help of rubber tubing a glass tube is fitted just above the stem is not dried up. A U-shaped manometer, partially filled up with mercury is connected to the glass tube. The whole apparatus must be air-tight.

Observation : When again observed the apparatus after few hours, the mercury is found on the higher level in the open tube of the manometer, and simultaneously the quantity of water is also increased in the glass tube.

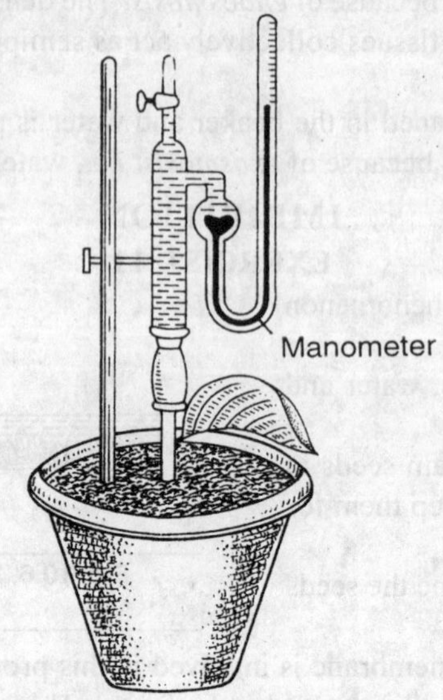

Fig. 10.8. Demonstration of root pressure.

Explanation : Due to accumulation of water in the glass tube, the pressure is exerted on the mercury, and it is pushed upwards in the open glass tube of manometer. This water exudates, because of root pressure from the cut end of the stem and accumulates in the glass tube fitted just above the cut end of the stem. This is also proved by this experiment that root pressure helps the ascent of sap.

GUTTATION

EXERCISE 14

Object : Demonstration of phenomenon of Guttation.

Requirements : Well developed potted plant of Garden nasturtium, bell jar, cork, a glass tube.

Experiment : Put the watered plant under the bell jar for some time (as shown in the figure).

Observation : After some time water droplets are observed at the tip of veins near the margin of leaf.

Explanation : It is due to the fact that the rate of water absorption by roots is higher than that of transpiration. As a result of which the excess amount of water collected in the veins of leaf which is forced to come out at their tip in the form of water droplets. The oozing out of the water in the form of water droplets from uninjured part of leaf is known as guttation. These so-called uninjured parts are called hydathodes or water stomata.

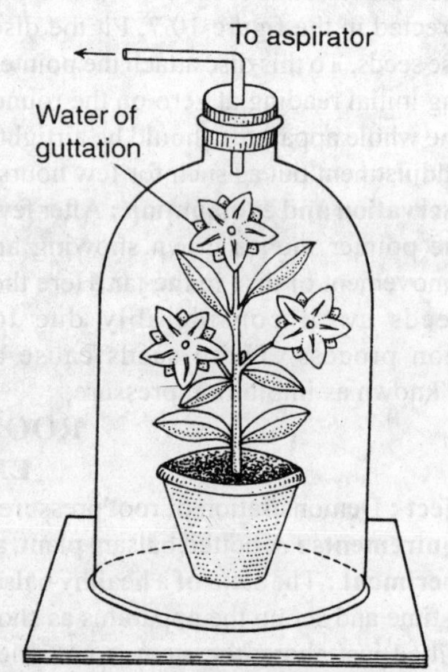

Fig. 10.9. *Guttation,* demonstration of the phenomenon.

MOVEMENT OF WATER THROUGH XYLEM

EXERCISE 15

Object : Demonstration of movement of water through xylem.

This may be shown in various ways. Some important ones are given here.

(*i*) Requirements : Balsam plant, water safranin, microscope.

Experiment : The stem of the Balsam plant is cut under the water. Now, to make the water red coloured, a few drops of safranin or euosine are added in the beaker full of water. Thereafter, the balsam stem, cut under the water is kept in this coloured water. After some time the stem is cut into transverse sections at various levels, and the sections are studied under the lens of the microscope.

Observation : Here, we find that only the vessels and tracheids are red stained. This way, this experiment proves, that water rises in the stem through the vessels and tracheids only.

(*ii*) Requirements : Plant of *Arundo donax,* vegetable ghee, coloured water in a beaker.

Experiment : Two white and linear leaves of *Arundo donax* are taken. The vessels of one of the leaves have been blocked by applying the melted vegetable ghee at its base; the other leaf is kept without blocking its vessels. Now, both the leaves are kept in the beaker full of coloured water.

Observation : After a few hours, it is observed that the leaf with blocked base is as before, and the veins of the leaf with unblocked base have become coloured. This indicates the rising of water through the veins (xylem vessels).

(*iii*) Requirements : Two twigs of a plant, vegetable ghee, two beakers of water, etc.

Experiment : We take the two twigs of plant cut under water. The base of one of the twigs is blocked with melted vegetable ghee whereas of the other twig is not blocked. These twigs are kept in two separate beakers full of water.

Observation : After sufficiently a long time, it is observed that the leaves of the twig with blocked end have been wilted and drooped whereas the leaves of the other twig are turgid and fresh. In the second twig, the water rises through the vessels, as they are not blocked by melted vegetable ghee.

(*iv*) The Ringing Experiment :

Requirements : A twig, a sharp scalpel, beaker full of water, etc.

Experiment : A twig with few leaves cut under the water is taken. In the middle part of the twig, with the help of sharp scalpel, the cortex and phloem are removed, and a ring is formed. The central xylem strand is kept intact. This twig is kept in a beaker full of water.

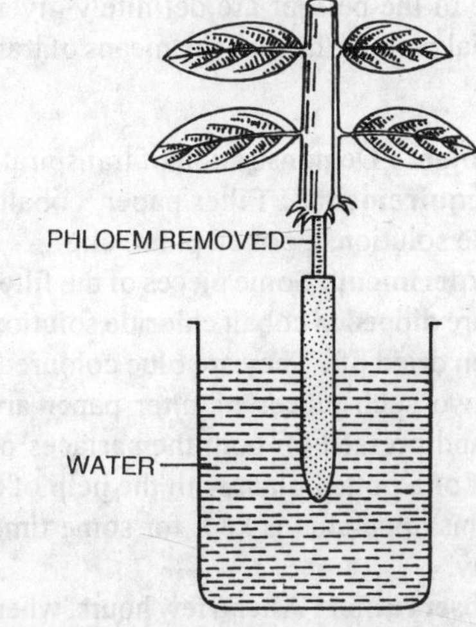

Fig. 10.10. *Movement of water through xylem, demonstration of phenomenon.*

Observation : It is observed, even after a long time that the leaves of the twig are turgid and fresh. The water supply of the leaves is not cut as the xylem strand is intact. This experiment proves that the water rises in the plant through xylem vessels.

The above given experiments indicate clearly that the pathway of the ascent of sap in the plants is through the xylem vessels and the tracheids.

TRANSPIRATION

EXERCISE 16

Object : Demonstration of transpiration by keeping a plant under a bell jar.

Requirements : A potted plant, rubber sheet, water, bell jar, glass plate, vaseline.

Experiment : A healthy potted plant is taken for this purpose. Now, the soil surface of the pot is being covered by the rubber sheet so that there is no evaporation of water from the moist surface of the soil. Thereafter the potted plant is kept on a glass plate is being covered over by a bell-jar. The margins of the bell-jar are vaselined, so that the atmospheric air may not enter the bell-jar. Now the covered potted plant is kept at room temperature.

Observation : After some time, the droplets of water appear on the inner surface of bell-jar.

Explanation : As all the precautions have been taken for checking the entrance of any moisture from out-side, and the release of moisture from the soil surface, these droplets of water adhered to the inner surface of the bell-jar are definitely given off from the aerial parts of the plant by means of transpiration.

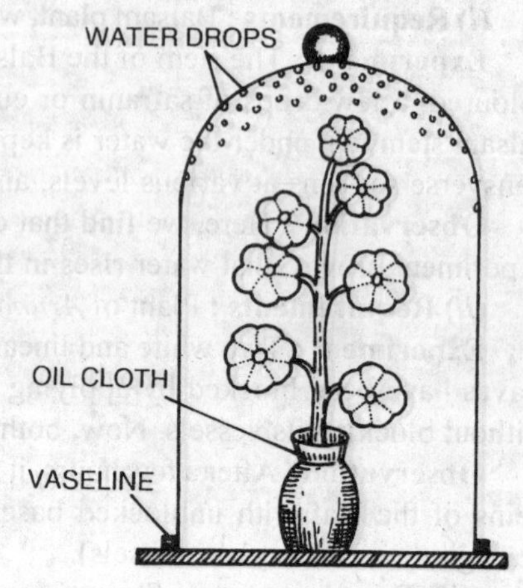

Fig. 10.11. *Transpiration,* demonstration of the phenomenon.

EXERCISE 17

Object : Demonstration of transpiration by cobalt-chloride screen.

Requirements : Filter paper, cobalt-chloride solution, a potted plant, clip.

Experiment : Some pieces of the filter paper are dipped in cobalt chloride solution and then dried off. They are blue coloured. Now, two such pieces of filter paper are taken and pressed on both the surfaces of the leaf of a potted plant with the help of a clip. This apparatus is kept for some time this way.

Observation : After a few hours, when it is observed, the cobalt chloride paper of the lower surface of the leaf becomes pink coloured.

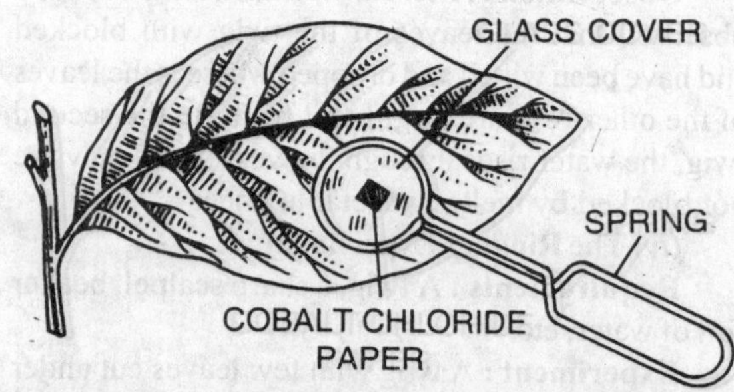

Fig. 10.12. *Transpiration,* demonstration of phenomenon. (Cobalt-chloride method).

Explanation : The dried blue coloured cobalt chloride paper turns red as it becomes moist. The stomata are confined mostly on the lower surface of the leaf, and therefore the cobalt chloride paper of that surface becomes moist and turns red. The paper of the upper side of the leaf may also become pink to some extent, as few stomata are found on this side.

EXERCISE 18

Object : Demonstration of transpiration by weighing method.

Requirements : A wide mouthed bottle, a twig, rubber cork, melted wax, balance, etc.

Experiment : A wide-mouthed bottle is taken. A twig with few leaves cut under the water is entered the bottle through the hole of the rubber cork. With the help of melted wax the apparatus is made air-tight. Now, this apparatus is weighed on a pan balance. Thereafter the apparatus is kept under normal conditions for transpiration. After few hours, the apparatus is weighed again. This time weight reduces to some extent.

Observation :

First weight = 87.3 gms.
Second weight = 86.9 gms.
Loss/Gain = 0.4 gms. loss.

Explanation : Here, it is quite clear, that the weight reduces, because of the transpired water from the aerial parts of the twig.

EXERCISE 19

Object : Demonstration of transpiration by Four Leaves Experiment.

Requirements : Four leaves, vaseline and a string.

Experiment : To demonstrate the transpiration from the leaf surface, four banyan leaves are taken. Both the surfaces of the A leaf, lower surface (with stomata) of B leaf, upper surface (without stomata) of C leaf are vaselined. The vaseline is not applied on the D leaf. Now, as shown in the figure the leaves are hanged so that they may transpire freely.

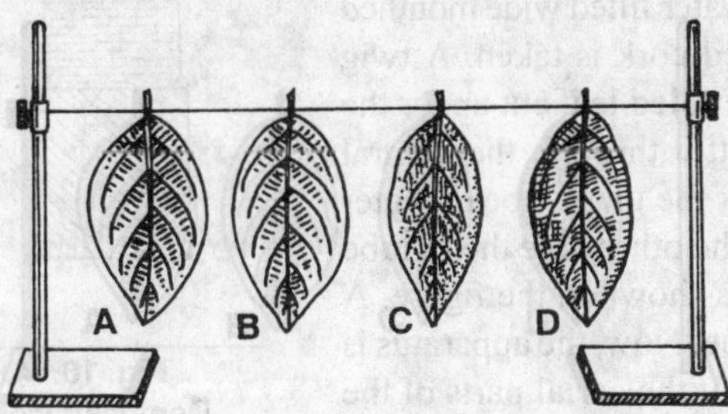

Fig. 10.13. *Comparison of Transpiration,* demonstration by four leaves.

Observation and Explanation : When the observations are taken after a day or two, they are as follows - the A leaf, which is vaselined on its both the surfaces, looks fresh and green, as no surface transpires. The B leaf is vaselined on its lower surface (with stomata), and transpiration takes place only from the upper surface which is negligible. This leaf also remains turgid and green like the A leaf. If few stomata are present on the upper surface of the leaf, then it shrivels to some extent. The C leaf is vaselined on its upper surface, which contains less number of stomata or no stomata. The transpiration takes place from the lower stomatal surface, and the leaf shrivels to a large extent. The D leaf is not vaselined and both the surfaces transpire freely releasing much water. The leaf wilts completely in this case. This experiment proves that the rate of stomatal transpiration is fairly higher than the cuticular transpiration.

Rate of Transpiration : The rate of transpiration is measured by potometer. There are many types of potometers which are designed by various scientists from time to time. These potometers are after the names of Farmer, Ganong, Garreau and Bose.

EXERCISE 20

Object : Demonstration of rate of transpiration by potometers.

Requirements : Farmer or Ganong or Bose Potomer, water, plants, vaseline, stop watch, etc.

Experiment : (*i*) Farmer's Potometer - This type of potometer consists of a wide mouthed bottle, fitted with a three-holed rubber cork. The glass tube of water reservoir passes through one of these holes situated on one side. As shown in the figure another bent glass tube finds its way through another hole situated on the other side of the rubber cork. The central hole of the rubber cork bears a twig with few leaves cut under the water. The apparatus is completely filled up with water, and as shown in the figure the other end of the horizontal glass tube is dipped in the beaker full of water. The complete apparatus is air tight. The apparatus is kept in this position for some time. The water transpires from the surface of leaves, and to fulfil the vacuum the water rises in the horizontal glass tube. To demonstrate this process clearly, an air bubble is entered with the help of a dropper from the other end of the horizontal tube.

***(ii)* Ganong's Potometer** - The mode of action of this potometer resembles to that of Farmer's potometer. The apparatus is completely filled up with water. A twig with few leaves cut under the water is entered in the wide mouthed bent tube on one side through the hole of the rubber cork, like that of Farmer's potometer. There is a water reservoir, from which the water may be taken inside the apparatus when needed. The horizontal tube of the potometer is well marked. The bent end of the horizontal tube remains dipped in the beaker containing water.

***(iii)* Bose's Potometer** - We set the apparatus as shown in the figure. The water filled wide mouthed bottle fitted with three holed cork is taken. A twig with few leaves or a long petioled leaf cut under the water is inserted in the bottle through the central hole. In one hole of the cork the glass tube of water reservoir is inserted and in the other hole the U-tube with two bulbs is inserted as shown in the figure. A drop of oil is put in the U-tube. Now, the apparatus is kept in such condition so that the aerial parts of the twig transpire freely.

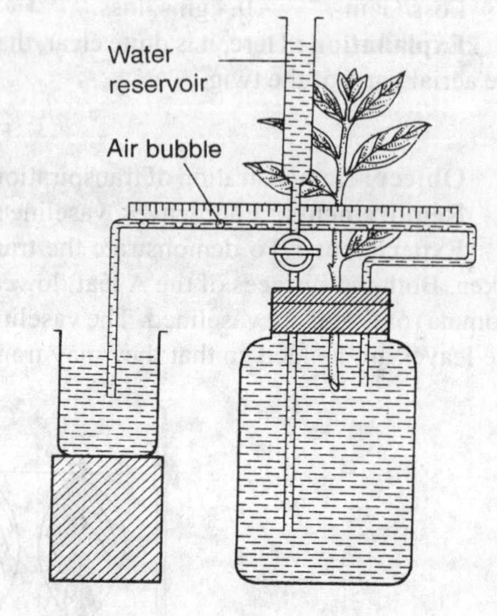

Fig. 10.14. *Rate of Transpiration,* Demonstration by Farmer's Potometer.

Observation : (*i*) As water transpires, the air-bubble moves towards the bottle along with water. This air-bubble may be brought back by adding the water in the bottle from the reservoir which is controlled by a stop cock. There is a scale behind the horizontal tube. With the help of a stop watch, the time may be noted, which is consumed in the travelling of the airbubble from one particular mark to another particular mark on the scale. Several readings may be taken in different conditions. The

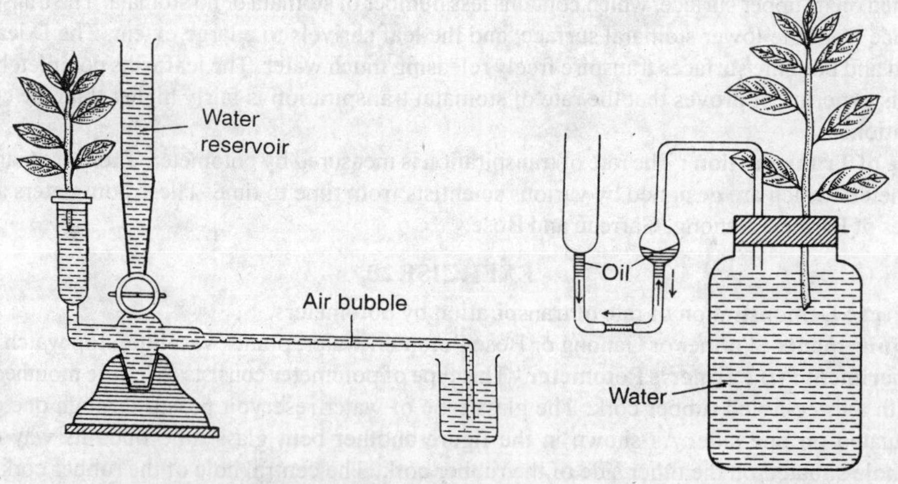

Fig. 10.15. *Rate of Transpiration :* Ganong's Potometer and Bose's Potometer.

rate of transpiration may easily be calculated, if, one knows the actual volume of water in between two particular points on the horizontal tube.

(*ii*) As the leaves transpire, the water flows towards the twig in the horizontal tube. At the end of the bent horizontal tube there is a sub-terminal hole. With the help of a dropper or otherwise an air bubble is entered through this hole in the tube. As the leaves transpire the water from the beaker rushes towards the twig in the horizontal tube along with air bubble. The time spent in the travel of the air bubble from one particular mark to another on the horizontal tube may be noted. The air bubble may be brought back on the first mark in the tube by releasing water from the reservoir. Several observations may be taken in different transpiring conditions and the rate of the transpiration may be calculated. The apparatus must be completely air-tight.

(*iii*) The vacuum develops within the bottle because of the transpiration, and the oil drop gradually rises up in the U-tube towards the twig. As the oil drop reaches the inner bulb, it bursts and goes back again in its original position. The time taken in rising and bursting of the oil drop is being noted. Several such readings may be taken in different conditions. The apparatus must be completely air-tight.

Various modifications for transpiring plants : (1) Potometer kept in atmosphere of high humidity. (2) Potometer kept under the fan. (3) Potometer kept in higher temperature. (4) Potometer kept in dark.

(1) Potometer kept in atmosphere of high humidity : Here the air bubble moves with a slow speed. Stomatal transpiration is caused by the diffusion of water vapours from the intercellular spaces of the mesophyll cells into the outer atmosphere through the stomata. This condition is only possible when outer atmosphere possesses less humidity or less vapour contents. Here in the given condition the outer atmosphere is of higher humidity, so the loss of water from the leaves is negligible and consequently the transpiration is lowered. Therefore higher the humidity of air, lower is the transpiration.

(2) Potometer kept under the fan : Here the air bubble will move with a greater speed. The running fan causes to increase the rate of transpiration by sweeping away the water vapours that are present in the vicinity of transpiring plant. Therefore in this area the humidity of air becomes lower and the rate of transpiration is promoted.

(3) Potometer kept in higher temperature : Here the air bubble moves with a faster speed.

Temperature has an indirect influence on the rate of transpiration. Increase in temperature causes the following effects :

(A) Stomata get widen with the increase in temperature. So the loss of water is more, increasing the rate of transpiration.

(B) A rise in temperature decreases the relative humidity of surrounding air. The drier the air, the more rapid is transpiration.

(4) Potometer kept in dark. The air bubble does not move at all. It is due to fact that the stomata get closed when it is dark. Lowering of pH value (pH - 5) favours in closing of stomata. In dark the reducing osmotically active sugars change into the osmotically inactive starch. So the pH value lowers to 5 and the stomata are closed. On closing the stomata, no transpiration takes place, hence, the air bubble remains stable.

EXERCISE 21

Object : Comparison of rate of transpiration from both the surfaces of leaf by Garreau's Potometer.

Apparatus : Garreau's potometer, stand, leaf, etc.

Experiment : *Garreau's Potometer* - With the help of this apparatus, the comparative study of the transpiration from both the surfaces of the leaf is being done. This apparatus consists of two small bell-jars, which are kept together in close contact as shown in the figure. A leaf of a potted plant is kept in between these two bell-jars. In each of these bell-jars a small test tube is kept. Each small test tube contains equal amount of anhydrous calcium chloride ($CaCl_2$). The apparatus is made air-right, applying vaseline where they press the leaf in between. There are two manometers at the two ends of the bell-jars. They are partially filled with oil. These manometers, however, maintain the vapour of the bell-jars. If the surface of the oil, within the manometers changes, then it indicates that the apparatus is not airtight or the vapour released from the leaf surface is not completely absorbed by calcium chloride. The complete apparatus is fitted upon a vertical stand. After few hours, the calcium chloride tubes are taken out and weighed again. This way, the water transpired from both the surfaces of the leaf may be known.

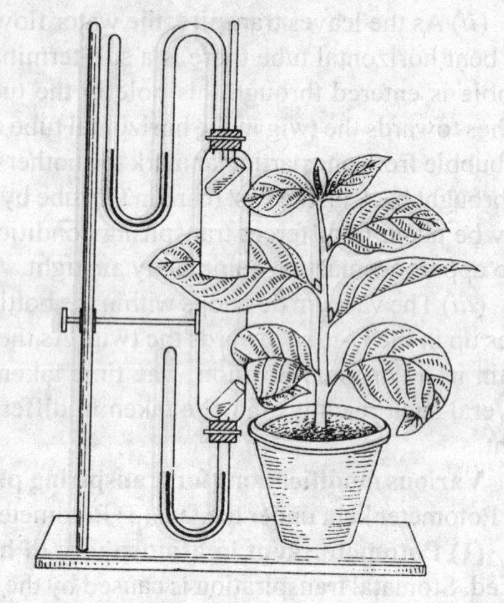

Fig. 10.16. *Garreau's Potometer.* Measurement of relative transpiration from two surfaces of a leaf.

Observation and Explanation : The amount of water transpired from the lower surface (stomatal surface) of the leaf is always greater, as it bears large number of stomata. The cuticular transpiration takes place from the upper surface of the leaf, which is very much less.

STOMATAL OPENING

EXERCISE 22

Object : Demonstration of the stomatal opening by Darwin's porometer.

Requirements : Darwin's potometer, water or mercury, a potted plant, stop watch, etc.

Experiment : This apparatus functions on the principle that the stomatal apertures govern the rate of flow of water. Cement the glass cup to the surface of the leaf by an adhesive (durofix, etc.) and immerse the vertical arm of tube in water or mercury. Open the clip and suck the water to a predetermined height in the vertical arm, close the clip.

Observation : Two possibilities occur here ;

(A) The water level in arm remains unchanged.

(B) The water column begins to fall.

Explanation : On the closing of the clip, the air inside the potometer undergoes a reduced pressure.

(A) If the stomata under the cup are closed, the water level in the arm will not change.

(B) If the stomata under the cup are open, the air will find its way through them and water column in the arm will begin to fall.

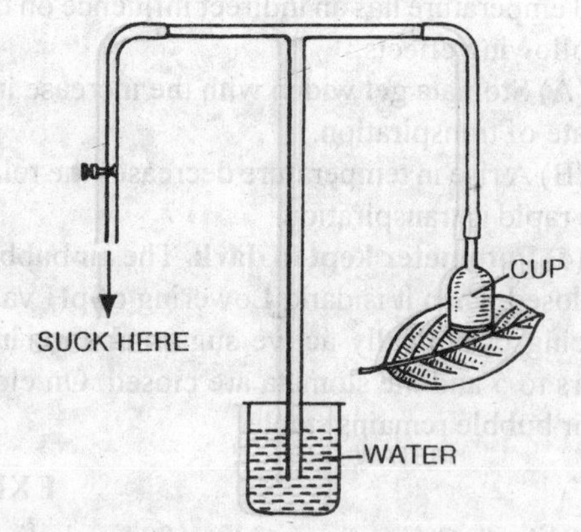

Fig. 10.17. Darwin's potometer.

RELATION BETWEEN TRANSPIRATION AND ABSORPTION

EXERCISE 23

Object : Demonstration of relation between Transpiration and Absorption.

Requirements : A bottle with a side tube, cork, a plant, oil, balance, etc.

Experiment : Here, the apparatus must be completely filled up with water and air-tight. In the side marked tube of the apparatus some oil drops are being added so that the water may not evaporate. The cork is fitted in the wide mouth of the bottle in the way that the aerial part of a complete plant remains outside of it and the root system or the plant remains within the bottle. Now the apparatus is weighed on a pan balance to note its weight and thereafter it is kept for few hours in such a place where sufficient transpiration from the aerial parts of the plant takes place. In the end the apparatus is weighed once again and the difference from that of the original weight may be calculated.

Observation : This way the quantity of transpired water is known in grams. The oil drops present on the surface of water in the marked side tube travel somewhat downward and we know the actual quantity of absorbed water in c.c. by the roots. By comparison, it is noted that the quantity of absorbed water is always greater than the transpired water because some of the water is used in other metabolic activities.

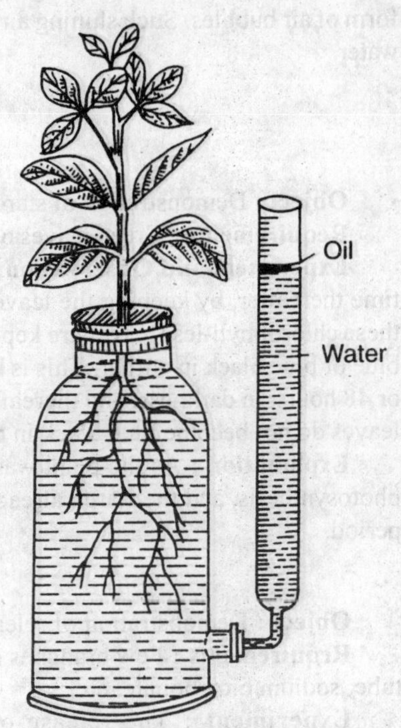

Fig. 10.18. *Relation between Transpiration and Absorption,* demonstration of the phenomenon.

AERATION SYSTEM

EXERCISE 24

Object : Demonstration of aeration system in plants.

Requirements : A wide mouthed bottle, a cork with two holes, glass tube and a long petioled leaf.

Experiment : The presence of aerating system may easily be demonstrated by the apparatus shown in the figure. For this purpose one wide mouthed bottle fitted with two holed rubber cork is taken. The bottle is partially filled up with water. Through one hole of the cork a long petioled leaf is being inserted. The petiole of the leaf is partially dipped in the water. The complete apparatus is made air-tight. Now, the air within the jar is pumped out through the side tube with the help of a suction pump fitted to it.

Observation and explanation : With the result a negative pressure develops within the jar, and the air from the outer atmosphere enters through the stomata situated on the leaf lamina, and through the cortical region of the petiole, it comes out in the water in the form of air-bubbles, which are easily visible.

Note : This way the presence and continuity of aerating system is assumed. If we keep the leaf lamina within the jar in the water and the petiole outside of it and pump to oust

Fig. 10.19. *Aeration System in plants,* demonstration of the phenomenon.

the air, then the air enters through the cut end of the petiole, and comes out through stomata in the form of air bubbles. Such shining air bubbles may easily be seen on the lower surface of the leaf in the water.

PHOTOSYNTHESIS

EXERCISE 25

Object : Demonstration of starch test.

Requirements : Green leaves of a plant, burner, water, 70% alcohol, dilute iodine solution.

Experiment and Observation : The green leaves of any healthy plant may be boiled in the day time thereafter, by keeping the leaves in 70% alcohol, the chlorophyll is extracted from them. Now these chlorophyll-less leaves are kept for some time in dilute iodine solution. The leaves become deep blue or blue black in colour. This is known as 'starch test'. If the plant is kept for a long time, *viz*., 24 or 48 hours, in darkness, and thereafter the leaves are tested for starch test, it is always negative. The leaves do not become blue black in colour.

Explanation : As the plant was kept in darkness continuously for a long period, there was no photosynthesis, and the starch already prepared was shifted to the lower part of the plant during this period.

EXERCISE 26

Object : Demonstration of release of oxygen during photosynthesis.

Requirements : Few branches of an aquatic plant, *i.e.*, *Hydrilla*, etc., beaker, glass funnel, test tube, sodium bicarbonate, etc.

Experiment : The release of oxygen during photosynthetic process may be proved experimentally. A few branches of an aquatic plant, *Hydrilla* are kept in a big beaker full of the same pond water. Thereafter, the branches are covered with a glass funnel, and a test tube full of water is inverted at the end of the funnel as shown in the figure. If required, a small quantity of sodium bicarbonate may be added in the water, so that the supply of carbon dioxide may become adequate for the photosynthesis. Now, the apparatus is kept in the sun light.

Observation : The gas bubbles may be observed from the ends of the *Hydrilla* branches kept under the glass funnel in the beaker. These gas bubbles are accumulated in the end of the test tube inverted over the end of the funnel, and the water within the tube goes downward. On test the gas is to be proved oxygen.

Note : To test the gas, the pyrogalol solution is taken in a beaker, and with the help of the thumb the tube partially filled with gas is kept inverted in the pyragalol solution. The solution enters the test tube and the tube again fills up completely because the pyragalol is soluble in oxygen.

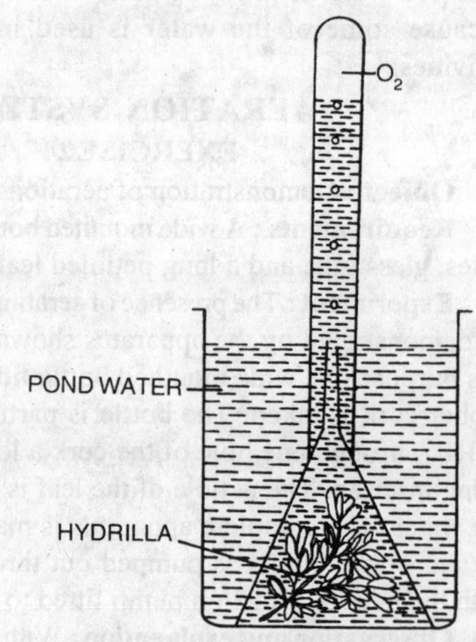

Fig. 10.20. *Liberation of oxygen in photosynthesis*, demonstration of the phenomenon.

Various modifications for this experiment :

(1) When the pond water of beaker is replaced by boiled or distilled water.

(2) When the above experiment is covered by a black cloth.

(3) When the *Hydrilla* twigs are replaced by terrestrial plants.

(1) When pond water of beaker is replaced by boiled or distilled water : If the pond water in the beaker is replaced by boiled or distilled water, the gas bubbles are not released from the ends of the *Hydrilla* branches kept under the glass funnel in the beaker. Why ? The reason is quite clear, that during distillation or boiling of the water, the dissolved carbon dioxide goes out, which is necessary factor for photosynthesis. The photosynthesis does not take place. With the help of this modification of the experiment, the necessity of the carbon dioxide for the photosynthesis of water plants may be proved.

(2) When the above experiment is covered by a black cloth : If this apparatus is covered with black cloth, or kept in darkness, the gas bubbles are not released showing that the light is one of the essential factors for the photosynthesis in the case of water plants.

(3) When the *Hydrilla* twigs are replaced by terrestrial plants : Here the photosynthesis is completely checked. Only hydrophytes may absorb CO_2 from the water, the terrestrial plants, being of different habitat, fail to absorb CO_2 from water, and therefore, the photosynthesis is stopped here.

EXERCISE 27

Object : Demonstration of comparison of rate of photosynthesis under different conditions.

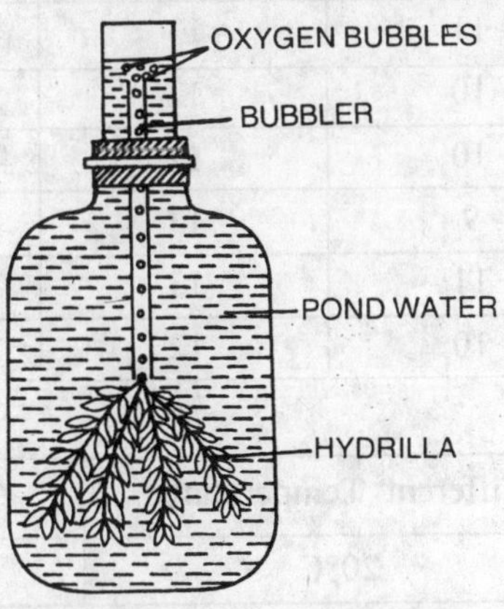

Fig. 10.21. *Willmott's Bubbler.*

(A) Different concentrations of CO_2 (by sodium bicarbonate)
(B) Reaction of sun light and shade.
(C) Reaction in red, green and blue coloured-light.
(D) Reaction of different temperatures.

Observations :

A.

S.No.	Conc. of $NaHCO_3$	Bubbles coming out in definite time
1.	0.4 gm.	14
2.	0.45 gm.	22
3.	0.5 gm.	23
4	0.5 gm.	23
5.	0.5 gm.	23
6.	0.5 gm.	25

B.

S.No.	Sun/Shade for definite time-intervals; (5 Seconds in this case)	Bubbles coming out
1.	Sun	9
2.	Shade	5
3.	Sun	9
4.	Shade	4
5.	Sun	10
6.	Shade	4

C.

S.No.	Time	Bubbles coming out in Sunlight	Bubbles coming out in Red light.	Bubbles coming out in Blue light	Bubbles coming out in Green light
1.	10 Minutes	11	13	11	7
2.	-do-	10	12	10	6
3.	-do-	10	12	9	6
4.	-do-	9	13	10	7
5.	-do-	11	13	11	5
6.	-do-	10	12	9	6

D.

S.No.	Different Temperatures	Bubbles coming out
1.	20°C	9
2.	30°C	11
3.	35°C	14
4.	40°C	15
5.	45°C	18
6.	50°C	21

Requirements : Willmott's bubbler, *Hydrilla* plant, sodium bicarbonate, different coloured papers, burner, thermometer, pond water, stop watch, etc.

Experiment : Willmott's Bubbler : It can easily be prepared in the laboratory. Take a wide mouthed bottle and fix a cork in it. Pass wide glass tube through this cork. Another narrow glass tube having a jet at its one end is introduced in the former one. Fill this apparatus with pond water and tie the twigs of *Hydrilla* at the lower end of narrow glass tube as shown in the figure.

For different conditions the following factors are provided here :

(A) Add sodium bicarbonate to the water of the bottle and count the bubbles coming out in each case in definite time.

(B) Put the apparatus as such in sun and shade respectively for definite intervals and count the bubbles coming out in each case.

(C) Put the apparatus in double walled bell jar providing different coloured papers. Count the bubbles coming out in each case for definite time intervals.

(D) Take another beaker of hot water and put the apparatus in it at definite temperatures. Count the bubbles coming out in each case for definite time intervals.

Explanation : (A) With the increasing concentration of $NaHCO_3$, the rate of photosynthesis increases. This rate of photosynthesis goes on increasing till light or some other factor acts as a limiting factor.

(B) The readings shown that the rate of photosynthesis is more in sun.

(C) The readings show that the rate of photosynthesis is the highest in red light and lowest in green.

(D) This experiment shows that photosynthesis occurs at a rapid rate from 10°C to 35°C, provided other factors are not limiting.

EXERCISE 28

Object : Demonstration of measurement of photosynthesis by Ganong's photosynthetometer.

Requirements : Ganong's photosynthetometer, green leaf, water, KOH, Kipp's apparatus, etc.

Experiment and Observation : With the help of this apparatus, the quantity of released oxygen, and the quantity of utilized carbon dioxide during photosynthesis in a green leaf may easily be detected. This way, the photosynthetic quotient O_2/CO_2 may be known.

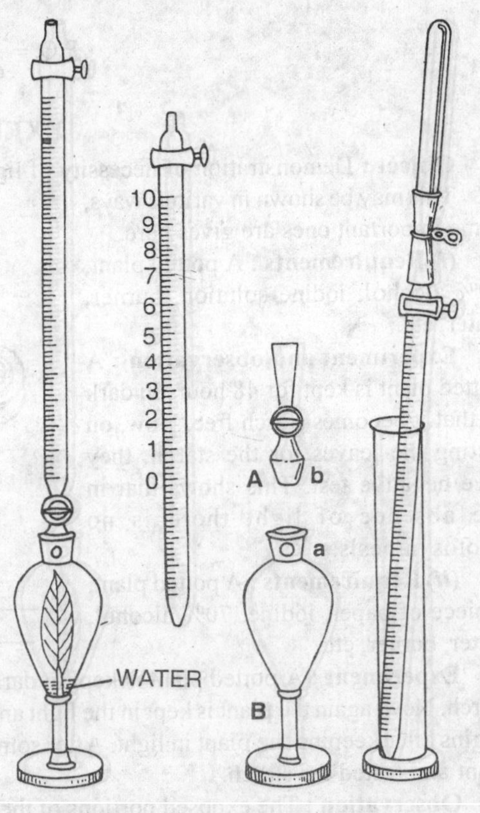

Fig. 10.22. Ganong's Photosynthetometer.

This apparatus consists of three parts A, B, and C as shown in the figure. It consists of a bulb C, a measuring graduated tube A and a terminal stop cock B. The photosynthetic material to be utilized in the experiment, *viz*., about 2 c.c of green leaves of garden nasturtium, etc., are kept in the bulb. The graduated tube is inverted, the stop-cock is closed and filled up with water up to that mark as much as the carbon dioxide is required. The graduated tube is closed by the hollow stopper. The hollow portion of the stopper is also filled up with water. Now, this end of the tube is to be closed with the help of the hand, and inverted in the trough full of water. Thereafter, it is clamped this way that the level of water remains at par to the level of the hole of the stop-cock. Now, the stop-cock of the lower end is opened and the upper end of the graduated tube is connected with the Kipp's apparatus to receive the carbon dioxide. The upper stop-cock is opened carefully, the carbon dioxide enters the tube, this is closed again, when the water of the tube is replaced by carbon dioxide, and its level becomes at par of the level of the outer water. Now, both the stop-cocks are being closed, and the complete tube is attached to the bulb with photosynthetic material. Now, the lower stop-cock is opened, and the carbon dioxide diffuses in the bulb containing photosynthetic material. This apparatus is kept for 3 or 4 hours in sunlight and after noting the time the lower stop-cock is closed and the tube is pulled out from the bulb. Now, this is placed in the trough filled with water, and by keeping it in the water, the hollow stopper is removed. Now, the zero mark of this measuring graduated tube is kept at par of the water level, and gradually the stop-cock of the upper end is opened and make the water rise up to the zero mark of the tube.

Now a test tube is filled up with 30% caustic potash (KOH) solution and this tube is connected with the graduated tube with the help or rubber tubing. Thereafter, this apparatus is taken out from the water and removed the clamp and let the caustic potash solution enter the graduated tube. The graduated tube is shaken thoroughly and the caustic potash solution is again transferred to the test tube and the rubber tube is clasped. The end of the graduated tube is kept in water by keeping the zero mark at the water level, and the test tube is removed. Now, in the graduated tube that much amount of water rises, as much carbon dioxide is absorbed by caustic potash solution. This way, the volume of carbon dioxide is known which has been used by the leaf in the process of photosynthesis. If this experiment is furnished by filling the test tube with alkaline pyragalol solution the released oxygen is absorbed.

Explanation : The reduction in the volume of carbon dioxide and addition in the volume of oxygen indicate the volume of utilized carbon dioxide and released oxygen during photosynthesis. There values are usually identical and this way, the photosynthetic quotient is usually one.

$$P.Q. = \frac{6O_2}{6CO_2} = \frac{6}{6} = 1$$

EXERCISE 29

Object : Demonstration of necessity of light for photosynthesis.

This may be shown in various ways, some important ones are gives here.

(*i*) Requirements : A potted plant, 70% alcohol, iodine solution, burner, water, etc.

Experiment and observation : A potted plant is kept for 48 hours in dark so that it becomes starch free. Now, on testing the leaves for the starch, they give negative test. This shows that in the absence of light there is no photosynthesis.

(*ii*) Requirements : A potted plant, a piece of paper, iodine, 70% alcohol, water, burner, etc.

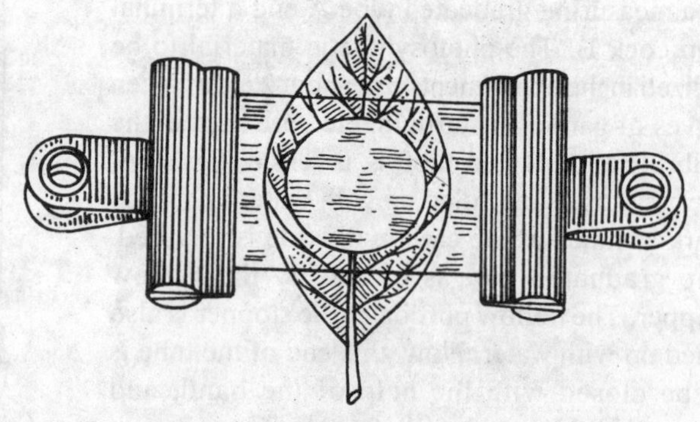

Fig. 10.23. *Ganong's Light Screen*

Experiment : A potted plant is kept in dark continuously for 48 hours, to make it free from the starch. Now, again the plant is kept in the light and one of its leaves as in the figure. The photosynthesis begins after keeping the plant in light. After some time the partially covered leaf is detached from the plant and tested for starch.

Observation : The exposed portions of the leaf give positive test and the covered portion of the leaf gives negative test. This experiment shows that the photosynthesis takes place only in those portions of the leaf which were exposed to the light and not in covered portions.

(*ii*) Ganong's Light Screen Test.

Requirements : A potted plant, a Ganong's Screen, 70% alcohol, burner, iodine, water, etc.

Experiment : A potted plant is kept in darkness for about 48 hours, so that its leaves become starch free. A small Ganong's light screen is attached to a leaf of the plant as shown in the figure. The Ganong's light screen partially covers the leaf. There is proper arrangement in the screen for the aeration of the leaf. Now, the plant along with light screen is kept in the light for photosynthesis. After 3 or 4 hours, the leaf is detached from the plant and tested for starch (see Fig. 10.23).

Observation : The portion of the leaf exposed to light gives positive starch test, *i.e.*, it becomes deep blue in iodine solution, whereas, the covered portion of the leaf gives negative starch test and does not become blue-black in iodine solution. This experiment proves the necessity of light for photosynthesis.

EXERCISE 30

Object : Demonstration of necessity of CO_2 for photosynthesis.

Requirements : Two small sized potted plants, two bell jars, KOH solution in a petri dish, water, 70% alcohol, iodine, water, burner, etc.

Experiment : Two small sized potted plants are taken. They are kept in the darkness at least for 48 hours, so that their leaves become starch free. Now, these potted plants are kept under two separate bell-jars. A petri dish partially filled up with KOH solution is kept under bell-jar 'A' and another petri dish partially filled with water is kept under bell-jar B. Now the apparatus is kept in sunlight for photosynthesis. After some time (3 or 4 hours), the leaves from both the potted plants are tested for starch by extracting their chlorophyll and keeping them in iodine solution.

Observation : The leaf detached from the plant kept under bell-jar, does not give positive test for starch when kept in iodine solution, whereas the leaf detached from the plant kept under bell-jar B gives positive starch test and becomes blue-black in colour, in iodine solution.

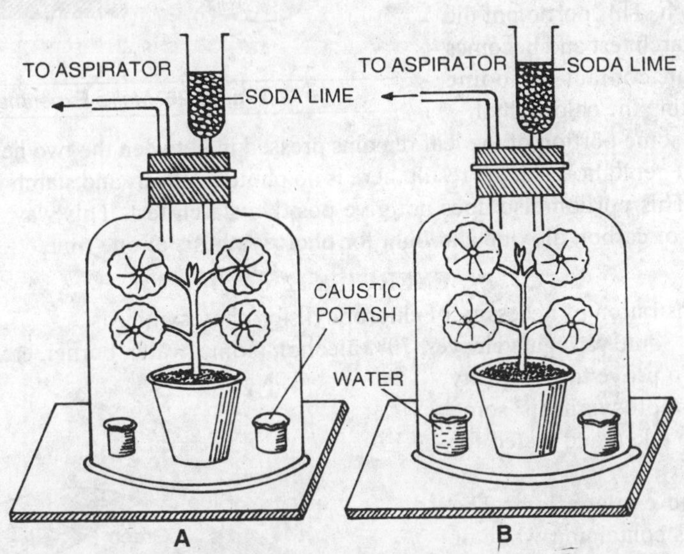

Fig. 10.24. *Necessity of CO_2 for photosynthesis*, demonstration of phenomenon.

Explanation : The KOH solution kept under bell-jar 'A', absorbs all the carbon dioxide, ceases the process of photosynthesis and starch formation. This experiment proves the necessity of the carbon dioxide for photosynthesis.

EXERCISE 31

Object : Demonstration of Moll's Experiment.

Requirements : A wide mouthed bottle, a split cork, conc. KOH solution, a leaf, water, beaker, wax, etc.

Experiment : A wide mouthed bottle with a split cork in two equal halves is taken. The bottle is partially filled up with concentrated caustic potash (KOH) solution. A leaf detached from the plant previously kept in darkness at least fro 48 hours is pressed in between the two halves of the cork of the bottle so that half the leaf remains within the bottle and the other half outside the bottle. The petiole of the leaf remains outside which is kept in water filled beaker, so that the leaf may not become dry soon. The apparatus is made air-tight by applying melted wax so that the atmospheric air may not enter the bottle. Thereafter the apparatus is kept in the sunlight for photosynthesis.

Observation : After few hours the leaf is tested for starch by extracting its chlorophyll and keeping it in iodine solution. The portion of the leaf which remained inside the bottle gives negative test, *i.e.*, this does not become blue-black.

Explanation : The carbon dioxide within the bottle is absorbed by caustic potash (KOH) solution and in the absence of carbon dioxide, the photosynthesis does not take place and the starch is not formed. The portion of the leaf which remained out side the bottle could receive all the necessary factors for photosynthesis and the photosynthesis did take place in this portion forming starch. This portion of the leaf gives positive starch test and becomes blue when comes in contact of iodine solution after extracting the chlorophyll.

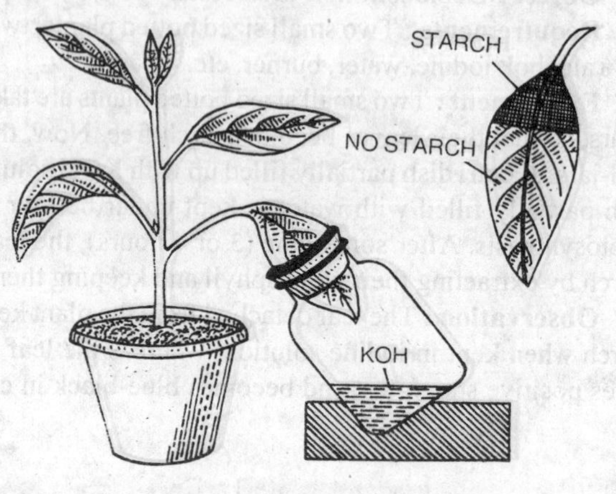

Fig. 10.25. *Moll's Experiment.*

In addition to it some portion of the leaf remains pressed in between the two halves of the cork. This portion does not get light. With the result there is no photosynthesis and starch formation in this portion of the leaf. This portion also does not give positive starch test. This way, this experiment proves the necessity of carbon dioxide and light for photosynthesis at one time.

EXERCISE 32

Object : Demonstration of necessity of chlorophyll for photosynthesis.

Requirements : Some variegated leaves, 70% alcohol, iodine, water, burner, etc.

Experiment : To prove the necessity of chlorophyll for photosynthesis some variegated leaves are taken and tested for starch as usual.

Observation and explanation : The portions of the leaves containing white or yellow spots do not give positive starch test. They do not become blue when brought in contact of iodine solution. This experiment proves that the photosynthesis takes place only in the green coloured portion of the leaves (fig. 10.26).

EXERCISE 33

Object : Demonstration of importance of light's colour for photosynthesis in land plants by Ganong's big light screen.

Requirements : Ganong's big light screen, a potted plant, 70% alcohol, iodine solution, water, burner, etc.

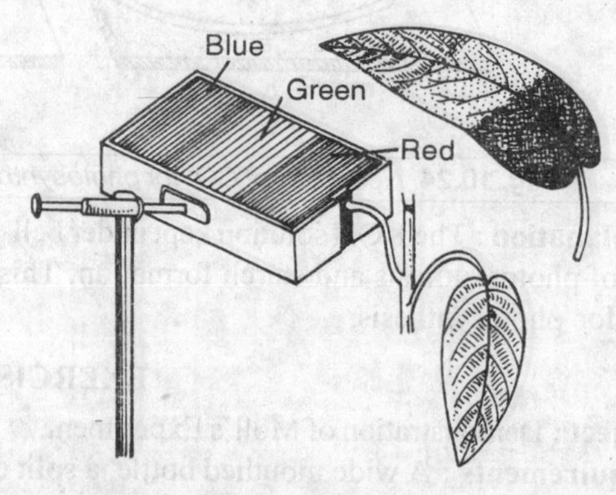

Fig. 10.26. Importance of light's colour for photosynthesis. (*Ganong's big light screen*)

Experiment : The Ganong's big light screen is taken as shown in the figure. This consists of red, green and blue coloured glass screens. A long leaf is detached from a potted plant, previously kept in darkness for 48 hours and the leaf is kept under the 3 coloured screen for three or four hours in sun light so that the photosynthesis may take place. Thereafter the leaf is tested for starch. (See Fig. 10.26)

Observation : The portion of the leaf remained under red-coloured screen gives the positive starch test with deep blue colour. The portion of the leaf remained under the blue coloured screen also give positive starch test, but with fade blue colour. The part of the leaf remained under green-coloured screen either gives negative starch test or very less formation of the starch.

Explanation : This way, this experiment proves that the red and blue coloured rays are absorbed to the utmost by the chlorophyll. The absorption of the green rays by the chlorophyll is the lowest. The rate of photosynthesis is the highest under red screen and lowest under green screen. (Fig. 10.26)

EXERCISE 34

Object : Demonstration of an increase in the mass of leaves due to formation of photosynthetic products by Ganong's leaf-area cutter.

Requirements : Ganong's leaf-area cutter, green leaves, an oven, balance, etc.

Experiment : Take two green plants. Put one in the light and another in dark. Now pick some leaves from each of the plants after putting them in their respective conditions for few hours. Using the Ganong's leaf-area cutter, cut few circular discs from respective sets of leaves. Now put these sets in an oven and heat. After heating, they are weighed properly by a balance. (See Fig. 10.27)

Observation : The weight of the set (leaves from the plant kept in light) is found much enough than that of another set (leaves from the plant kept in dark).

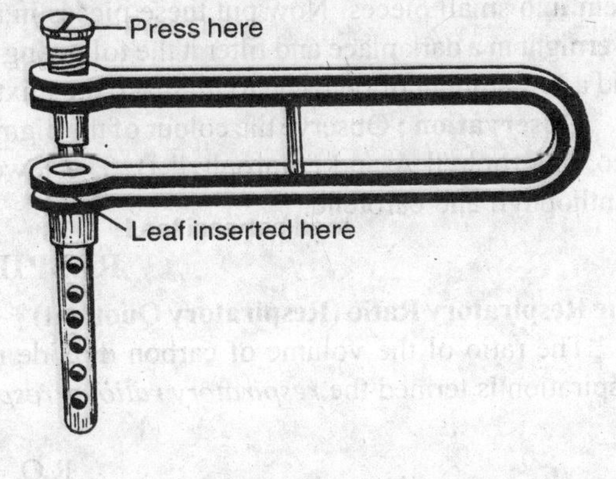

Fig. 10.27. *Ganong's Leaf Punch.*

Explanation : This simple experiment shows that there is a rise in dry weight of leaves which is due to accumulation of photosynthetic products.

EXERCISE 35

Object : Demonstration of separation of chlorophyll by paper chromatography.

Requirements : *Tecoma* leaves, mortar and pestle, acetone, petroleum ether, beaker, tube, etc.

Experiment : Take about 10 gm. of *Tecoma* leaves in a mortar and crush them by a pestle. Add about 12 to 15 ml. of acetone to it and filter in a beaker. This so obtained filtrate is being concentrated by heating. Take a paper strip and sketch a pencil line 2 cm. above the base of it. Point out the centre of it and pour the acetone filtrate on it drop by drop. The size of spot on the paper strip should bc small. Now, add a few drops of petroleum ether in a separate tube and place the above paper strip in a vertical position in this tube. Close the tube tightly.

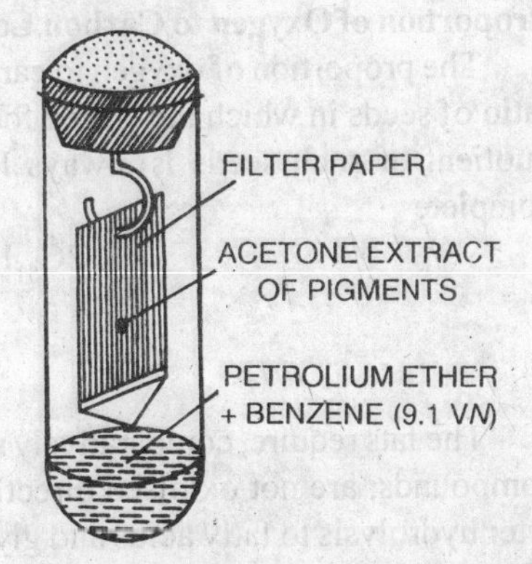

Fig. 10.28. Paper chromatography, strip filter paper method

Observation : Observe the paper strip after some time. The level of solvent, *i.e.*, petroleum ether and different colours should be pointed out by a pencil. Here the pigment may be identified by their different colours (Fig. 10.28).

Colour	Name of pigment
Blue green	Chlorophyll A
Yellow green	Chlorophyll B
Orange	Carotenes
Yellow	Xanthophyll

EXERCISE 36

Object : Demonstration of extraction of chlorophyll by chemical method.

Requirements : Green leaves of spinach, 95% ethyl alcohol, distilled water, benzene, beaker, etc.

Experiment : Boil about 50 gm. green leaves of spinach for some time. Dry these leaves and chop them into small pieces. Now put these pieces in a test tube containing 95% alcohol. Place this tube overnight in a dark place and filter it the following day. Dilute the filtrate with some distilled water and add a few amount of benzene to it. Shake the mixture and stand it for some time.

Observation : Observe the colour of the pigments. The upper layer is of green pigments, these are two, chlorophyll A and chlorophyll B. The lower layer is of yellow pigments, these are also two xanthophyll and carotene.

RESPIRATION

The Respiratory Ratio (Respiratory Quotient)

The ratio of the volume of carbon dioxide released to the volume of oxygen absorbed in the respiration is termed the *respiratory ratio or respiratory quotient* (R.Q.)

$$\text{R.Q.} = \frac{CO_2}{O_2}$$

When a carbohydrate is respired, the R.Q. is equal to one.

$$C_6H_{12}O_6 + 6O_2 \rightarrow 6CO_2 + 6H_2O$$

$$\text{R.Q.} = \frac{CO_2}{O_2} = \frac{6}{6} = 1.$$

Proportion of Oxygen to Carbon Lower than in Carbohydrates

The proportion of oxygen to carbon is invariably less in fats than in carbohydrates. The respiratory ratio of seeds in which the stored foods are mostly in the form of oils have shown that the respiratory quotient of such seeds is always less than one. The following summary equation represents the complete

$$2C_{51}H_{98}O_6 + 145O_2 \rightarrow 102CO_2 + 98H_2O$$

$$\text{R.Q.} = \frac{CO_2}{O_2} = \frac{102}{145} = 0.7.$$

The fats require, comparatively more oxygen for complete oxidation. Actually fats, being insoluble compounds, are not oxidised directly as indicated in the above equation. The fats are oxidised only after hydrolysis to fatty acids and glycerol. Here, the sequence of reactions will require the absorption of oxygen in excess of the quantity of carbon dioxide released. The summation effect of the reactions involved in the respiration of fats will be a respiration quotient (R.Q.) of less than one.

Similarly oxidation of the hydrolytic products of the proteins results in a respiratory ratio of less than one (usually 0.8 – 0.9) since the proportion of oxygen to carbon in such compounds is less than in carbohydrates.

Proportion of Oxygen to Carbon Higher than in Carbohydrates

When respiratory substrates are rich in oxygen the value of respiratory quotient is greater than one. This is found in the case of organic acids. The equations for the respiration of malic, tartaric and oxalic acids are :

$$C_4H_6O_5 + 3O_2 \rightarrow 4CO_2 + 3H_2O \text{ malic acid}$$

$$R.Q. = \frac{CO_2}{O_2} = \frac{4}{3} = 1.3$$

$$2C_4H_6O_6 + O_2 \rightarrow 8CO_2 + 6H_2O \text{ tartaric acid}$$

$$R.Q. = \frac{CO_2}{O_2} = \frac{8}{5} = 1.6$$

$$2(COOH)_2 + O_2 \rightarrow 4CO_2 + 2H_2O \text{ Oxalic acid}$$

$$R.Q. = \frac{CO_2}{O_2} = \frac{4}{1} = 4.$$

Oxygen Liberation or Utilization without Consumption of CO_2

When the seeds containing fats attain maturity, simple carbohydrates are converted into fats. Oxygen is eliminated during the process without any corresponding utilization of carbon dioxide, since the molecules of the fats contain much less oxygen in proportion to the carbon and hydrogen present that in the molecules of sugars. The internally freed oxygen is being transferred to other molecules in respiration. The volume of oxygen absorbed by seeds from the outer atmosphere during this period will be less, and the respiratory ratio is greater than one. The R.Q. of maturing flax seeds is about 1.22.

During the germination of fatty seeds essentially the opposite situation prevails in which very low respiratory quotients sometimes prevail after several days. The respiratory ratio of germinating castor bean seeds is as low as about 0.3. Murlin (1934) explained this finding on the assumption that transformation of fat to sugar, *i.e.*, an oxygen consuming process where no carbon dioxide is released is proceeding much more rapidly than oxidation of sugar.

Similar situation is found in many succulent species where incomplete oxidation of sugars to organic acids takes place. For example, in the species of Crassulaceae and Cactaceae, some of the sugar present is often incompletely oxidized to malic acid :

$$2C_6H_{12}O_6 + 3O_2 \rightarrow 3C_4H_6O_5 + 3H_2O \text{ malic acid}$$

$$R.Q. = \frac{CO_2}{O_2} = \frac{0}{3} = 0$$

As a result of similar respiratory process other organic acids are formed in succulent plants. The synthesis of such compounds requires absorption of oxygen for which there is no corresponding evolution of CO_2. In such cases the R.Q. is less than unity.

The leaves of *Bryophyllum* and some other species make direct use of carbon dioxide absorbed in the dark in the synthesis of organic acids. The effect of the occurrence of the process will give such leaves an apparent respiratory quotient of less than unity.

Respiration in the Absence of Oxygen

In anaerobic respiration, the release of carbon dioxide takes place without any corresponding utilization of atmospheric oxygen.

R.Q. values for different respiratory substrates

R.Q.	Respiratory substrate
> 1.0	Carbohydrate with some anaerobic respiration. Carbohydrate synthesized from organic acids. Organic acids.
1.0	Carbohydrates
0.99	Proteins with NH_3 formation
0.8	Proteins with amide formation
0.7	Fats, *e.g.*, tripalmitin
0.5	Fats with associated carbohydrate synthesis
0.3	Carbohydrates with associated organic acid synthesis

Such anaerobic respiration occurs in higher green plants under certain conditions. Sometimes, when the oxygen supply is deficient, both aerobic and anaerobic respiration occur simultaneously in a plant tissue. In such cases, some cells respire anaerobically while other aerobically. Under these conditions the volume of carbon dioxide evolved may be very large in proportion to the volume of oxygen absorbed, and the respiratory quotient (R.Q.) is much greater than one.

$$C_6H_{12}O_6 \xrightarrow{\text{zymase}} 2C_6H_5OH + 2CO_2$$

$$R.Q. = \frac{CO_2}{O_2} = \frac{2}{0} = 2$$

EXERCISE 37

Object : Measurement of R.Q. by Ganong's Respirometer.

Requirements : Ganong's Respirometer, respiratory substrate, etc.

Experiment : The respiratory quotient may easily be measured by Ganong's respirometer. In Ganong's respirometer the amount of oxygen absorbed and carbon dioxide released out during respiration are determined simultaneously. The respirometer consists of a bulb with a graduated side tube. The volume of the apparatus is about 102 c.c. The stopper and neck of the bulb are each provided with hole. The stopper may be turned to bring the two holes opposite each other so that the air inside the bulb may communicate with the outer air and is at the atmospheric pressure. The side graduated tube is connected with a levelling tube by a rubber tubing.

For the determination of respiratory quotient the manometer is filled with mercury or a saturated solution of common salt. The water cannot be used since carbon dioxide dissolved in it. Carbon dioxide is slightly soluble in salt solution and therefore, best results can be obtained when mercury is used.

Two c.c. of plant material, the R.Q. of which is to be measured is being placed inside the bulb. In the beginning the air of the graduated tube is kept in direct

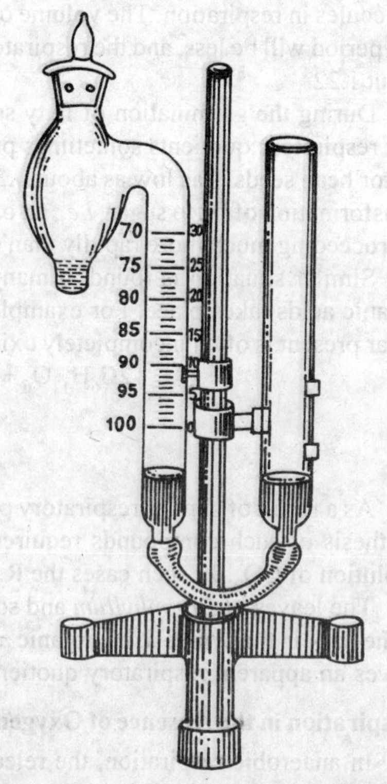

Fig. 10.29. *Ganong's Respirometer.*

communication with the atmospheric air at the atmospheric pressure. The mercury in both the tubes is brought to the same level by raising or lowering the levelling tube. Now the stopper in the neck of the bulb is turned so that the two holes get apart and the air in the apparatus is cut off from the outside air and respiration proceeds in closed chamber.

Observation and Explanation : The initial level of mercury in the graduated tube is noted. The level is again noted after about an hour. If the respiratory substrate kept in the bulb is carbohydrate, the amount of carbon dioxide released during respiration will be equal to the amount of oxygen absorbed and therefore, there will be neither a rise and nor a fall in the mercury level. If caustic potash (KOH) is now added to the apparatus, the accumulated carbon dioxide, will be absorbed, and hence a rise in the mercury level, and thus the amount of carbon dioxide can be measured. The volume of oxygen absorbed will be equal to the volume of carbon dioxide measured. Hence the R.Q. is unity.

When the respiratory substrate is a fat, the respiratory quotient is less than one. Here the amount of carbon dioxide released is less than the amount of oxygen absorbed and therefore, a vacuum is created in the closed chamber. This results in the rise of mercury level. The rise of mercury level is denoted by V_1 c.c. that is equivalent to the excess oxygen. Now the caustic potash (KOH) is added and there is a further rise of mercury level. The second rise in the mercury level is denoted by V_2 c.c. this represents the volume of carbon dioxide liberated. This way, the total amount of oxygen absorbed is equal to $V_1 + V_2$ c.c. the respiratory quotient will therefore, be less than one.

$$\text{R.Q.} = \frac{CO_2}{O_2} = \frac{V_2}{V_1 + V_2}$$

When the respiratory substrate is such that the carbon dioxide released is more than the volume of oxygen absorbed during respiration, the mercury level falls. The fall in the mercury level is denoted by V_1 c.c. that is equivalent to the excess carbon dioxide. Now the caustic potash is added to the tube. It absorbs the total amount of carbon dioxide and therefore, the mercury level rises. The rise is denoted by V_2 c.c. that is equivalent to the total amount of carbon dioxide. The total volume of oxygen absorbed is then $V_2 - V_1$ c.c. The respiratory quotient will, therefore, be more than one.

$$\text{R.Q.} = \frac{CO_2}{O_2} = \frac{V_2}{V_2 - V_1}$$

EXERCISE 38

Object : Demonstration of release of CO_2 during respiration.

Requirements : Germinating seeds, a bottle, a bent tube, two holed cork, water reservoir, beaker, etc.

Experiment : Inside the bottle some germinating seeds are placed. The bottle is closed with the help of a two-holed cork. Here one of the holes is provided by glass tube bent twice at right angles. Another hole possesses a water reservoir which remains closed by a stop-cock. The free end of bent glass tube is dipped in a beaker of water which also acts as a seal. Now this apparatus is left undisturbed for a while.

After some time the water of beaker is replaced by lime water and the stop-cock of reservoir is opened. The water runs in the bottle and so it drives out the air of bottle in the beaker through the bent glass tube.

Observation : The lime water turns milky.

Explanation : The germinating seeds undergo the respiration releasing CO_2 in this process. The CO_2 passes through the bent glass tube making the lime water milky.

***(ii)* Requirements :** Germinating seeds, a conical flask, a single holed cork, caustic potash in a test tube, a bent glass tube, water beaker, etc.

Experiment : Inside the conical flask some germinating seeds are placed. The bottle is closed with a single-holed cork through which a glass tube bent twice at right angles is inserted. Another free end of this tube is put in a beaker of water. A test tube of Caustic Potash is hung inside the conical flask. Now this apparatus is put as such for some time.

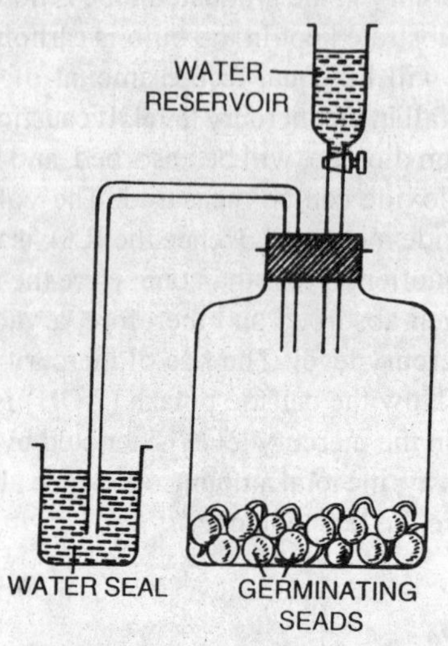

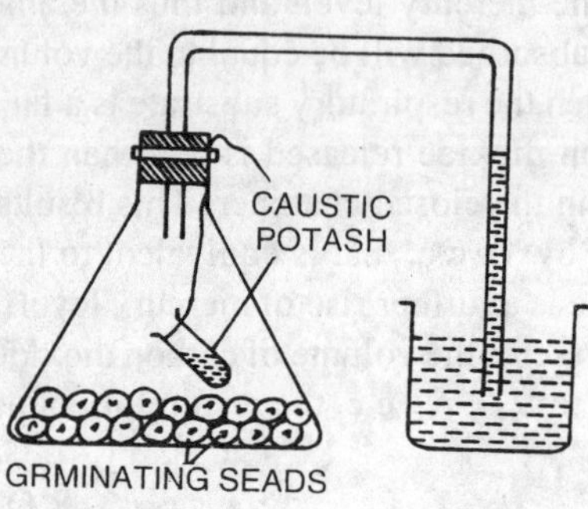

Fig. 10.30. *Release of CO_2 during Respiration, demonstration of the phenomenon.*

Fig. 10.31. *Release of CO_2 during respiration, demonstration of the phenomenon.*

Observation : Water rises in the far end of glass tube from the beaker.

Explanation : Germinating seeds undergo the anaerobic respiration, releasing CO_2 gas which is absorbed by the Caustic Potash. So a vacuum is created inside the conical flask and consequently water rises in the tube to fulfil it.

Note : The experiment should be performed in dark in case the green leaves are used as the respiratory substrate.

EXERCISE 39

Object : Demonstration of utility of oxygen in respiration.

Requirements : A conical flask, a bent tube, germinating seeds, caustic potash in a small container, a mercury dish.

Experiment : Germinating seeds are taken in a conical flask in which a container of caustic potash is also put. The mouth of this conical flask is closed by a single-holed cork through which a glass tube bent twice at right angles in inserted. The far end of this tube is put in the mercury dish. Now this apparatus is left undisturbed for some time.

Observation : The mercury in far end of bent glass tube rises to a height of 15 cm.

Explanation : The germinating seeds undergo aerobic respiration so they use the oxygen available inside the conical flask. As whole of the oxygen is used up by the germinating seeds, the pressure inside the flask is decreased. So consequently the mercury level rises in the far end of the bent glass tube. This level reaches only a height of 15 cm. in the glass tube. As this level is about one-fifth the air. As oxygen constitutes one fifth of total composition, it is reasonable to infer that the seeds have used this gas of the air in respiration.

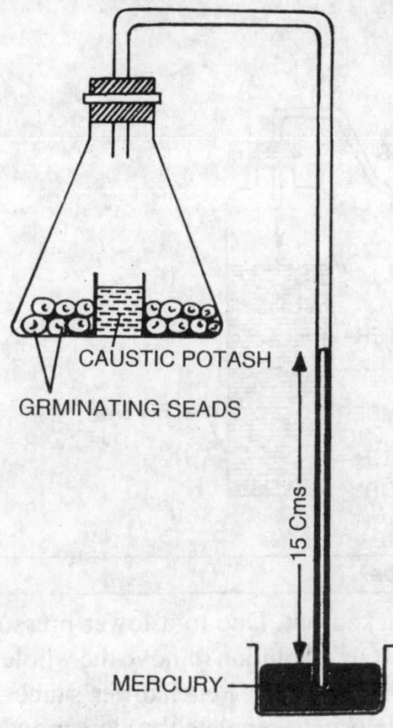

Fig. 10.32. *Utility of O_2 in respiration, demonstration of the phenomenon.*

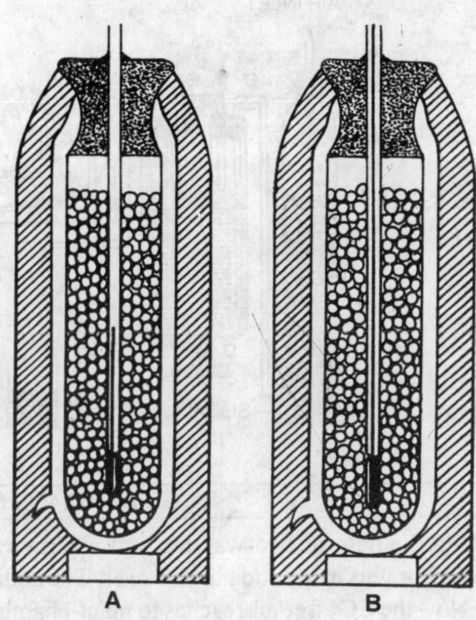

Fig. 10.33. *Production of heat in respiration, demonstration of the phenomenon.*

EXERCISE 40

Object : Demonstration of production of heat in Respiration.

Requirements : Two thermos bottles, germinating seeds, dry seeds, corks with a single hole, two thermometers.

Experiment : Half fill both the thermos bottles with germinating and dry seeds respectively. Now close their mouths with the help of single-holed corks through which a thermometer passes respectively. Put this experiment for about 24 hours.

Observation : There is a rise in temperature in the thermometer which is placed in the thermos bottle of germinating seeds. Another thermos bottle shows no change in previous temperature.

Explanation : The dry seeds or physiologically died seeds do not undergo respiration so there is no change in temperature. But the germinating seeds are going to make respiration where energy also releases alongwith CO_2 gas. So this energy causes a higher temperature in another thermos bottle. This release in energy is due to many biological activities going on stepwise with a gradual release of energy.

EXERCISE 41

Object : Demonstration of release of CO_2 by Pettenkoffer's gas stream method.

Requirements : Pettenkoffer's tube, soda lime, $Ca(OH)_2$, passing tubes, rubber tubes, respiratory tissue, aspirator, water, $Ba(OH)_2$, plant chambers, etc.

Experiment : The experiment is set as follows :

Firstly, there is a soda lime tower which is open to air by a tube. This tower is connected by passing tubes to the bottles of $Ca(OH_2)$ solution. Usually two bottles are used in the experiment. The second bottle is connected to the plant chamber by another passing tube. Pettenkoffer's tube is put between the plant chamber and aspirator by some rubber tubing connections. A two-way tap is also connected to the Pettenkoffer's tube. This tube is filled with $Ba(OH)_2$ solution.

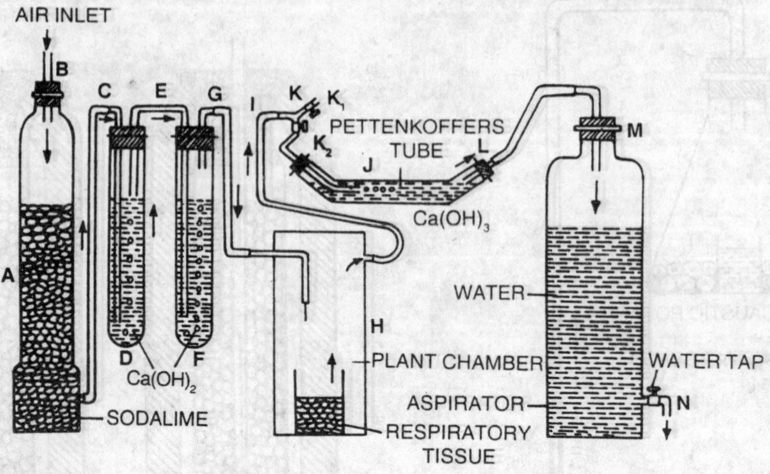

Fig. 10.34. *Pettenkoffer's Tube.*

With the help of two-way tap and aspirator the air is sucked out. Due to a lower pressure, a current of air gets in the soda lime tower. The soda lime and $Ca(OH)_2$ solution remove the whole CO_2 of air. Now the CO_2 free air reaches to plant-chamber from which it gets in the Pettenkoffer's tube. Here the $Ba(OH)_2$ solution is turned turbid. The aspirator is set in the way to regulate the slow movement of air in the form of bubbles.

After some time the turbid solution of Pettenkoffer's tube is titrated by using N/10 HCl and phenolpthalin-indicator.

Observation and explanation : The turbidity of the solution of Pettenkoffer's Tube is due to formation of $BaCO_3$. The plant tissue respires releasing CO_2 gas. The CO_2 gas reacts with $Ba(OH)_2$ solution forming $BaCO_3$.

EXERCISE 42

Anaerobic Respiration

Object : Demonstration of anaerobic respiration.

Requirements : Germinating seeds, a test tube, mercury, KOH crystals, petri dish, etc.

Experiment : The mercury is filled in the test tube up to the rim. Take a petri dish full of mercury and put the mercury filled test tube in the inverted condition with the help of thumb. The thumb is removed inside the petri dish. Now introduce some seeds (germinating or soaked) in the test tube with the help of a forceps. Let this apparatus be put as such for some time.

Observation : After some time the mercury level in test tube goes down. Now introduce some KOH crystals in the above test tube. After a little while the mercury level will go up to the former position.

Explanation : The lowering of mercury level in test tube indicates that some gas has been released by germinating seeds. Only CO_2 gas is

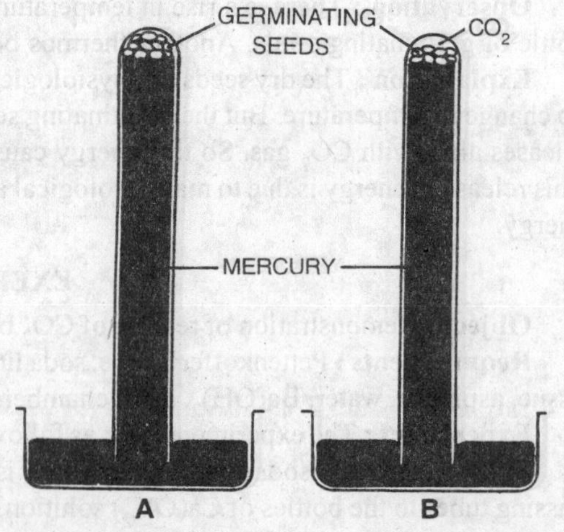

Fig. 10.35. *Anaerobic Respiration,* demonstration of the phenomenon.

it which may be absorbed by KOH crystals. We see that with the introduction of KOH crystals the level of mercury goes high, so the seeds have released CO_2 under the anaerobic conditions.

EXERCISE 43

Object : Demonstration of "Alcoholic-Fermentation" by yeast cells.

Requirements : Kuhne's fermentation tube, glucose or sucrose solution (10% aqueous solution), yeast power (Baker's yeast), beaker, etc.

Experiment : Take some glucose solution in beaker and add 1 gm. yeast powder to it. Now fill the Kuhne's fermentation tube with this solution. The half of the bulb and complete vertical tube is filled with the solution. The open end of the bulb is plugged with some cotton.

Observation : There is a consequent fall in the level of solution in vertical tube.

Explanation : The gas produced in vertical tube is proved to be CO_2 with the help of caustic potash. At the same time ethyl alcohol is also liberated :

$$C_{12}H_{22}O_{12} \xrightarrow{\text{yeast Invertase}} \underset{\text{Glucose}}{C_6H_{12}O_6} + \underset{\text{Fructose}}{C_6H_{12}O_6}$$

$$C_6H_{12}O_6 \xrightarrow{\text{Fermentation}} 2C_2H_5OH + 2CO_2 \uparrow$$

Alcohol may also be tested 'by Iodoform test'.

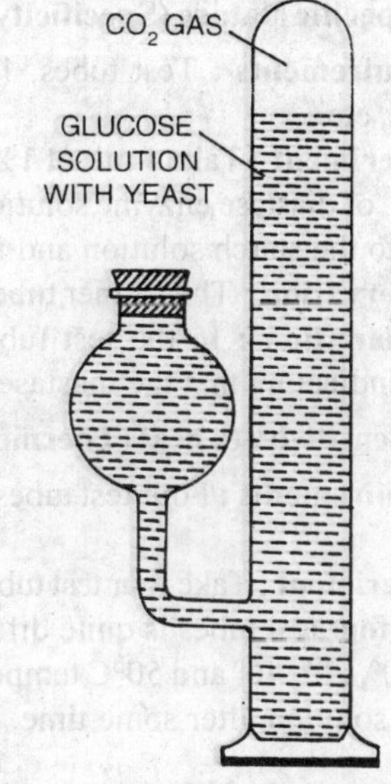

Fig. 10.36. *Kuhne's Fermentation tube*

BIOCHEMISTRYEXPERIMENTS

Biochemistry (Greek, *bios* = life) is a science concerned with the chemical nature and chemical behaviour of living things, or it may be defined as a discipline in which biological phenomena are analysed in terms of chemistry. With the advancement of knowledge, many new disciplines, such as enzymology, neurobiochemistry, molecular biology, pharmacology, endocrinology, agricultural biochemistry, etc., have emerged out from the parent biochemistry.

Biochemistry includes the following :

1. Study of chemical constituents of the cell and chemical substances produced by living things.
2. Functions and transformation of these substances in biological systems.
3. Chemical and energetic changes associated with these transformations in the course of the activity of protoplasm.

Precautions. For any biochemical experiment the following precautions may be taken :

1. All the glass ware, etc. be clean and dry.
2. Acids, alkalies and other corrosive chemicals be handled with care.
3. While preparing solutions, the chemicals be taken out carefully from the bottles or packages avoiding any contamination of one chemical with the other. After weighing, the bottles and packages should be immediately closed and not left open.
4. While pipetting, care be taken, not to suck any chemical into one's mouth. Moreover, one pipette be used for one chemical to avoid mixing and contamination, and the same principle be used for other glass ware.
5. After completing the experiment, the glass ware, etc., be washed and the table be left neat and clean.
6. Precision is the key to success in any biochemical experiment.

ENZYMES

EXERCISE 44

Object : Demonstration of properties of enzyme : (*i*) specificity; (*ii*) thermolability and (*iii*) colloidal nature.

***(i)* Specific Nature (Specificity) :**

Requirements : Test tubes, 1% starch solution, castor oil, diastase enzyme solution, Iodine, Sudan III, etc.

Experiment : Take 1 ml. of 1% starch solution in a test tube and in other tube 1 ml. of castor oil. Add 2 ml. of diastase enzyme solution to each test tube. After about 5 minutes add few drops of iodine solution to the starch solution and few drops of Sudan III to castor oil.

Observation : The former tube shows no test of starch while in the latter castor oil is turned red.

Explanation : In the test tube of starchy solution the diastase enzyme has hydrolysed this solution indicating that the diastase enzyme is specific for starch in action.

***(ii)* Sensitivity to heat (Thermolability) :**

Requirements : Four test tubes, diastase enzyme solution, beaker, water, starch solution, Iodine, etc.

Experiment : Take four test tubes and pour diastase enzyme solution in each of it. The temperature for these four test tubes is quite different, *i.e.*, 0°, 20°, 40° and 50°C respectively. Four beakers with water of 0°, 20°, 40° and 50°C temperature are used here to obtain the required condition. Add 10 c.c. of starch solution after some time. Now take few drops from each test tube and treat it with iodine solution.

Observation : Solution gives no colour at about 40°C.

Explanation : It shows that the rate of enzymatic reaction is optimum at this temperature. In other cases the positive iodine test is obtained.

***(iii)* Colloidal Nature :**

Requirements : NaCl solution, enzyme solution, thistle funnel, beaker, $AgNO_3$, parchment membrane.

Experiment : A mixture of NaCl solution and enzyme solution is taken in a thistle funnel covered by the parchment membrane. Immerse it in a solution of starch. Test the filtrate with $AgNO_3$.

Observation : A white ppt. of AgCl is obtained here.

Explanation : Due to colloidal nature the enzyme molecules are large. Here only NaCl molecules are diffused through the parchment membrane, while the colloidal particles are held back on the parchment membrane.

EXERCISE 45

Object : Assay of invertase.

Requirements : Commercial yeast, distilled water, 3% sugar solution, Fehling's solution.

Experiment :

***(i)* Extraction of Invertase :** Take 5 gm. of commercial yeast in a dish. Powder it and add about 100 ml. water to it. After sometime filter the yeast in a beaker. The filtrate contains invertase in solution form.

***(ii)* Test :** Take 3% sugar solution. Add 10 c.c. of each of the solutions in a test tube. Pour some Fehling's solution in this test tube.

Observation : No colour develops here. Put the enzyme sugar (sucrose) solution for an hour and test it again with Fehling's solution. Here red colour appears.

Explanation : Sucrose (sugar solution) is not a reducing agent so no change appears in the beginning. After some time (about an hour) it has broken down into reducing hexoses which give the test.

$$\underset{\text{Sugar solution}}{C_{12}H_{22}O_{12}} \xrightarrow[\text{Enzyme}]{H_2O} C_6H_{12}O_6 + C_6H_{12}O_6$$

Note : Assay is a test of biologically active substance which is done by a living material.

EXERCISE 46

Object : To prepare the enzymes from wheat or rice seeds.

Requirements : Rice or wheat seeds, water, mortar and pestle, centrifuge, phosphate buffer at pH 6.9, ice bucket, etc.

Method : Take rice or wheat seeds soaked and germinated for 0, 24 and 48 hours. Place 50 seeds in a mortar and pestle with a little bit of 10 ml. phosphate buffer at pH 6.9. Now grind seeds adding more fluid to extract thoroughly until 35 ml. has been added. Now this process may be repeated with each set of seeds (for 0, 24 and 48 hours). Allow the homogenate to stand approximately for 10 minutes in the ice bucket. After doing so, centrifuge the debris, starch grains and other major organelles at 15,000 g for 10 minutes. Use the supernatant as enzyme source.

GROWTH

EXERCISE 47

Object : Measurement of growth in plants.

Requirements : Auxanometers : (*i*) Arc auxanometer (*ii*) Pfeffer's automatic auxanometer.

(*i*) Arc auxanometer : It consists of a vertical stand with a pulley to which is attached a long thread and a needle or pointer movable over a graduated arc. One end of the thread is tied with the growing point of the plant and another is stretched with a suitable weight.

(*ii*) Pfeffers automatic auxanometer : It consists of a vertical stand with two pulleys. One of these two pulleys possesses a thread carrying two weights at either ends to keep it stretched. This thread on one side is also attached with a fine scratching pointer which touches a smoked drum. Another pulley is also provided with a thread of which one end is tied with the growing point of plant and another is stretched with a suitable weight.

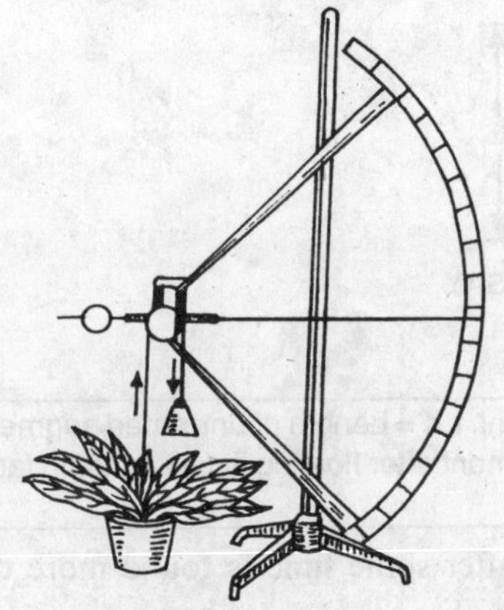

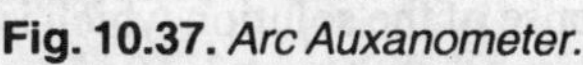

Fig. 10.37. *Arc Auxanometer.*

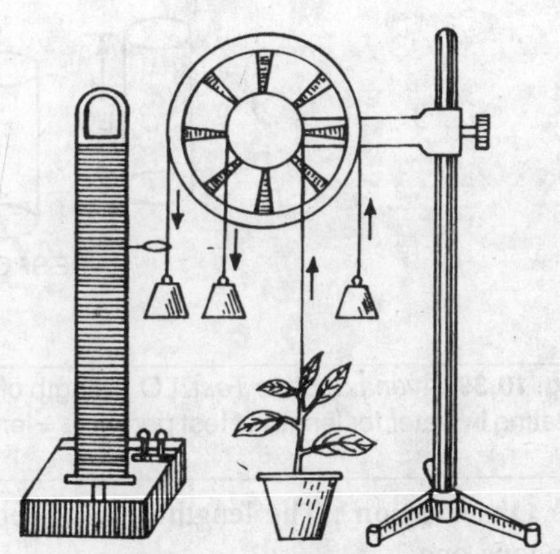

Fig. 10.38. *Pfeffer's Auxanometer*

Observation and Explanation : (*i*) With the growth of plant, the weight moves the thread down and the movement of needle can be read easily on the scale.

There exists a notable ratio between the size of pulley and the needle. If pulley is 4 inches with the needle 20 inches from the centre of the disc of pulley, growth will be magnified ten times on the scale. It can easily be illustrated by an example :

If indicator moves 4 cm. in 8 hours and the magnification is 10 times, then the actual growth is:

∵ Growth in 8 hours = 4/10 cm.

= 0.4 cm. or 4 mm.

∴ Growth in one hour = 4/8

= 0.5 mm./hour

(*ii*) With the growth of plant first pulley makes moving the another which in turn moves the pointer. This pointer moves downwards and traces a spiral on the rotating smoked drum. Thus the growth for a certain period is recorded.

PLANT HORMONES

EXERCISE 48

Object : Demonstration of effect of auxin by *Avena* section test.

Requirements : Coleoptiles, distilled water, auxin solution, Petri dishes.

Experiment : Take some germinating *Avena* seedlings. Cut the coleoptiles, 25-30 mm. in length. Remove the tip of coleoptile and sections 3-5 m.m. in length of each coleoptile. Put all the sections for an hour in distilled water and then transfer them into other petridishes containing auxin solution. Remain the experiment as such for a day or two.

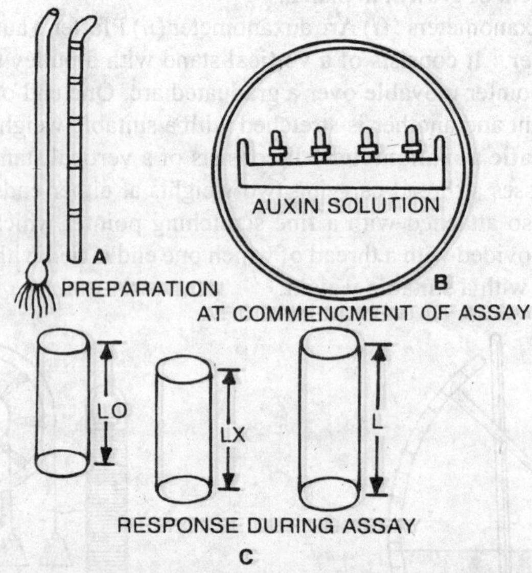

Fig. 10.39. *Avena Section Test.* LO = length of freshly cut segment. LX = Length of untreated segment after floating in water for length of test period; L = length of treated segment after floating in test solution far length of test period.

Observation : The length of each section, measured after some time is found more than the previous one.

Explanation : This experiment explains the growth response of the solution which is found to be directly proportional to the logarithm of the concentration of auxin used.

EXERCISE 49

Object : Demonstration of effect of gibberellic acid GA_3 on elongation.

Requirements : Prepared aqueous solutions of GA_3 having 0.01, 0.1, 1.0, 10.0 and 1000.0 mg/ml, young plants of dwarf and tall varieties of peas, distilled water.

Experiment : Take ten dwarf variety plants and ten tall variety plants. Apply 1 ml. of a GA_3 solution to a young leaf of each of the plants. Do this application again after one week. Distilled water is applied as a control in separate plants. Measure the height of each daily for fifteen days.

Observation and Explanation : Each time there is a clear elongation in the plant height. The growth response in dwarf variety increases with the increase of concentration of GA_3.

EXERCISE 50

Object : Demonstration of effect of kinetin of senescence.

Requirements : Solutions of kinetin containing 0, 0.001, 0.01 and 100.0 mg./litre of hormone, mature fresh leaves of radish, sterile distilled water, petri dish, filter paper, etc.

Experiment : Take mature fresh leaves of radish plant and wash them with sterile distilled water. Keep them in petri dishes on moist filter paper. Apply 0.5 ml. of one of the kinetin solutions per leaf. Examine the leaves daily for a week.

Observation and Explanation : The leaves turn yellow after a week. This is due to disappearance of chlorophyll and degradation of proteins.

MOVEMENTS

EXERCISE 51

Object : Demonstration of geotropism by clinostat.

Requirements : Clinostat apparatus and a potted plant.

Experiment : The potted plant is fitted in the clinostat apparatus in a horizontal position.

(*i*) The clinostat is rotated with an even and slow speed.

(*ii*) The clinostat is stopped in a particular direction after some definite intervals.

Observation : (*i*) The shoot and root do not represent any curvature.

(*ii*) Here the stem goes high or against the gravity while the root moves down or towards the gravity.

Explanation : Here in first case the plant possesses a simultaneous and equal effect of gravity so no curvature is seen here.

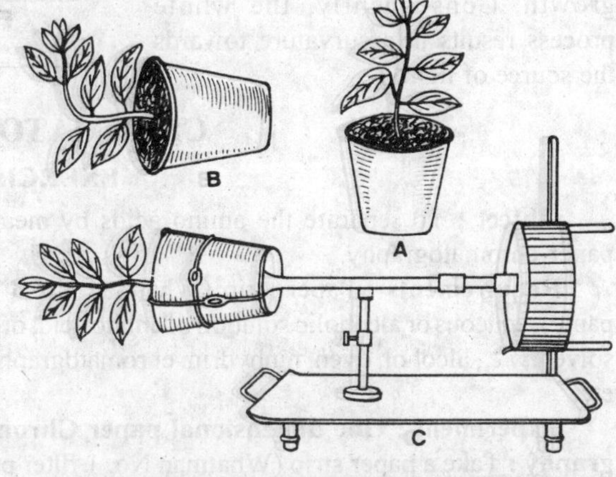

Fig. 10.40. *Clinostat Apparatus.*

In second case the definite intervals possess some special effects of gravity on the plants. So the shoot represents the negative geotropism (*i.e.*, goes against the force of gravity) while the root represents the positive geotropism (*i.e.*, goes down towards the force of gravity).

Note : Geotropism is caused mainly due to optimum concentration of auxins. The optimum concentration of auxin for stem growth is higher than for root growth. The increased concentration of auxin at lower part of stem causes the growth of that side so the stem goes upwards. The optimum concentration for root growth is much lower. The increased concentration of auxin at lower side of root exceeds the optimum, so the growth of that side is retarded and consequently the root goes downwards.

EXERCISE 52

Object : Demonstration of phototropism.

Requirements : A box of black inner surface with a hole on one side, a potted plant.

Experiment : Take a potted plant and keep it under the box for 3 or 4 days. Here the light gets in through the hole of box.

Observation : Observe the plant after 3 or 4 days. It gets bent towards the hole of the box from which light is getting in. So the stem curves towards the source of light.

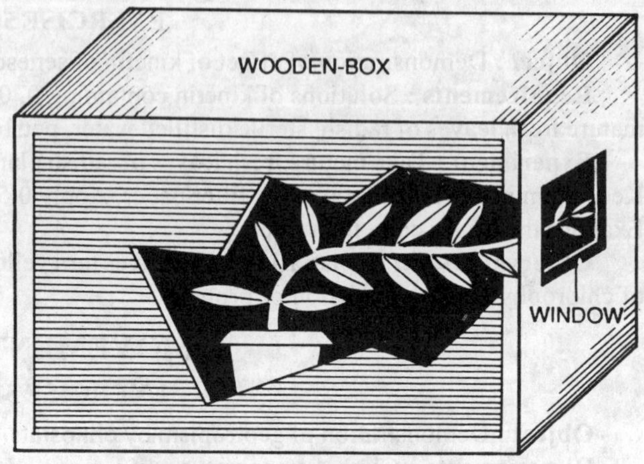

Fig. 10.41. *Phototropism*, demonstration of the phenomenon.

Explanation : The growth-curvature of plants caused due to stimulation by unilateral light source is known as phototropism. This phototropism occurs due to unequal distribution of auxin on the two sides of the stimulated stem. The concentration of auxin is more on the side which is away from the light so this far off area of stem shows the maximum growth. Consequently, the whole process results in a curvature towards the source of light.

CHROMATOGRAPHY

EXERCISE 53

Object : To separate the amino acids by means of paper-chromatography.

Requirements : Paper strip (Whatman No. 1 filter paper), aqueous or alcoholic solution of amino acid, organic solvent, *i.e.*, alcohol, oven, ninhydrin, chromatography jar, etc.

Experiment : One dimensional paper Chromatography : Take a paper strip (Whatman No. 1 filter paper) and mark a pencil dot near the bottom of it. Now put a small drop of alc. or aqu. solution of amino acid on it. (The amino acid is obtained by grinding imbibed germinating seeds in 80% ethyl alcohol. It is filtered and the filtrate is dried. The dried solid is dissolved in few drops of distilled water). Place this strip of filter paper in the chromatography jar so that the bottom of strip is being dipped into any one of following solvents.

Solvent	Ratio by Volume
(*i*) Alcohol : Water Ammonium hydroxide	80 : 20 : 1
Or	
(*ii*) Butanol : Acetic acid : water	4 : 1 : 1

(Mostly the (i) solvent is preferred for this experiment).

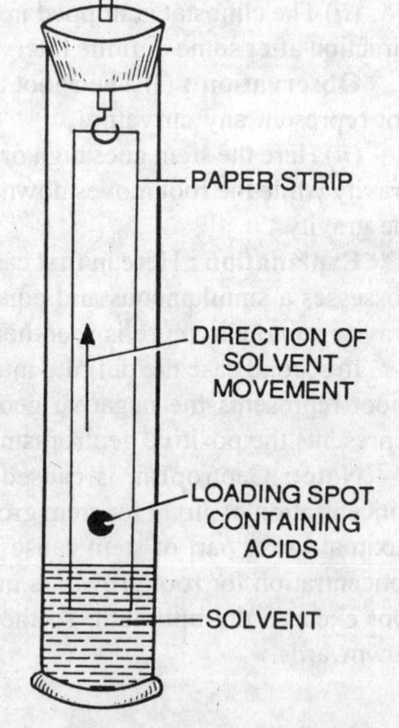

Fig. 10.42. Apparatus for one dimensional paper chromatography.

The solvent flows through the paper strip by capillary action passing over the amino acid drop. The amino acid having more solubility in the solvent that of in water goes along with the solvent. Each amino acid travels a specified distance under the similar conditions. After a sufficient amount of time the paper strip is taken out and put in the oven. Spray this dried strip with ninhydrin that will produce a certain colour for a certain amino acid. Up to now the paper strip has attained some coloured spots and it is called as the Chromatograph.

Fig. 10.43. Two dimensional paper chromatography.

Two dimensional paper Chromatography : It is done with two different solvents in order to separate the substances having the same Rf value. Turn the filter paper at 90° to the first plant and another rechromatograph is obtained with another solvent. The new solvent travels at right angles to the direction of the first one.

Observation : Here the partition co-efficient or Rf value in a chromatograph may be obtained as

$$Rf = \frac{\text{Distance travelled by the compound from the origin}}{\text{Distance travelled by the solvent from the origin}}$$

EXERCISE 54

Object : To separate the amino acids by TLC (thin layer chromatography) method.

Requirements : Silica gel (Kieselgel G or H), distilled water, slides, oven, amino-acids (glycine and aspartic acid), 80% phenol solvent, beakers, 0.1 per cent ninhydrin, capillarity pipette, atomiser, etc.

Method : Weigh 2 gm. of silica gel and put it in a test tube, filled with 10 ml. of distilled water. Stir the suspension. Now pour the suspension over 3 to 4 slides and allow the gel to set at least of 15 minutes. Activate the slides by heating them in an oven at 120°C, for about 30 minutes. Thereafter take out the slides and allow them to cool. After this, repeat the procedure as mentioned in exercise 52. Make a scratch on the margin of slide, and dip the slide in beaker filled with 80 per cent phenol solvent.

This method is supposed to be better than the method given in exercise 52 (*i.e.*, of paper chromatography).

COLOURTESTS

EXERCISE 55

Object : To perform colour test for carbohydrates (reducing sugars).

Requirements : Fehling's solution, measuring glass or pipette, test tubes, glucose solution, spirit lamp and Bendict's solution.

Fehling's solution. (*a*) Dissolve 34.65 gm. of $CuSO_4.5H_2O$ in water and make up to 500 ml. (*b*) Dissolve 125 gm. of KOH and 173 gm. of Rechelle salt in water and make up to 500 ml. Mix (*a*) and (*b*) in equal volumes immediately before use.

Method : *Fehling's test* — Warm about 2.3 ml. of Fehling's solution in a test tube and add a few drops of glucose solution and boil.

Result. A brownish red precipitate is formed on boiling.

Bendict's solution. (*a*) Dissolve 173 gm. of sodium citrate and 100 gm. of sodium carbonate in 800 ml. of water by warming and make up to 850 ml. (*b*) Dissolve 17.3 gm. of $CuSO_4.5H_2O$ in water and make up to 100 ml. Add (*b*) to (*a*) slowly with constant stirring.

Bendict's test — To 5 ml. of Bendict's solution add about 1–2 ml. of the glucose solution, and boil the mixture vigorously.

Result. A red yellow or green precipitate is formed.

EXERCISE 56

Object : To perform Lugol's iodine test for carbohydrates (non-reducing sugars).

Requirements : Iodine solution, 1% starch, conc. HCl, Na_2CO_3 or $NaHCO_3$, distilled water, spirit lamp, measuring glass or pipette, etc.

Iodine solution. Prepare a 2% solution of potassium iodide and add sufficient iodine to colour it a deep yellow.

1% Starch solution. Dissolve 1 gm. of soluble starch in 10 ml. of boiling distilled water and make up to 100 ml.

Method : Starch, sucrose and other non reducing sugars can be tested by first of all hydrolysing them to yield the non-reducing sugars. The hydrolysis may be carried out by adding an equal volume of conc. HCl to the sugar solution and boiling the mixture for 5 minutes. The resulting solution after neutralisation with Na_2CO_3 or $NaHCO_3$, is then subjected to the test for reducing sugars.

Result : Starch or sucrose gives a blue-violet colour with iodine.

EXERCISE 57

Object : To perform colour test for lipids.

Requirements : Castor oil, Sudan III, test tube, measuring cylinder or pipette.

Sudan III. Dissolve 0.1 gm. (100 mg.) Sudan III in 50 ml of 95% ethyl alcohol and then stir 50 ml. of glycerol into the solution.

Method : To few ml. of castor oil add few drops of Sudan III.

Result : A red colouration is produced which shows the presence of lipids in castor oil.

EXERCISE 58

Object : To perform colour test for proteins.

Requirements : Protein solution, conc. HNO_3, spirit lamp, test tubes, alkali (NaOH, KOH, etc.), Biuret reagent, Millon's reagent, measuring flask or pipette, etc.

Proteins. Egg albumin solution - Egg albumin solution may be prepared by either of the following two methods :

(*i*) 1% solution of egg albumin crystals in water, or

(*ii*) beat egg white with 6-10 volumes of water, filter as the egg albumin solution.

Biuret reagent. (Welker's) (*a*) 1% $CuSO_4$ solution. (*b*) 40% NaOH solution.

Add few drops of (*a*) to (*b*) till a deep blue colour is obtained. The blue solution is the Biuret reagent.

Millon's reagent. (*a*) Digest 1 part by weight of mercury (Hg) with 2 parts by weight of conc. HNO_3. Dilute the digest with two volumes of water.

(*b*) 10% $HgSO_4$ in 10% H_2SO_4.

Method : The procedure for colour test is as follows :

1. *Biuret test.* To 2 – 3 ml. of protein solution add an equal volume of Biuret reagent. In a few minutes a violet colour is produced.

2. *Millon's test.* Take 5 ml. of the protein solution in a test tube. Add 2–3 drops of Millon's reagent in the test tube. Mix and boil the solution over a flame of spirit lamp. On doing so a precipitate forms which dissolves on further heating to yield a red solution.

3. *Xanthoproteic test.* To 2 – 3 ml. of protein solution add 1 ml. of conc. HNO_3. A white precipitate forms, which on heating turns yellow and dissolves to give a yellow solution. On addition of excess of alkali the colour deepens into orange.

SEPARATIONOFCHLOROPHYLLPIGMENTS

EXERCISE 59

Object. To separate four pigments, chlorophyll *a*, *b*, carotene and xanthophyll by paper chromatography.

Method. Five grams of spinach leaves are grinded in a medium of about 60 ml of 80 per cent acetone by a mortar and pestle. After this slurry is filtered and residue discarded. The filtrate has all the pigments, that are required. Now on a piece of Whatman no. 1 filter paper, *i.e.*, 9 × 3", a drop of filtrate is placed as the loading point. Dry it and apply again and again the filtrate drop, so that, the loading point become concentrated. But after every drop the point is dried by electric heater or any other means. Before this loading, draw a fine line with pencil parallel to and 1 inch from one edge of the strip. This line indicates the bottom of the chromatogram. On this line, draw a circle and a drop of filtrate is put in this circle. Now strip is fixed and inserted in rectangular jars in such a way that loading point should not be dipped in a solvent mixture (*i.e.*, petroleum ether and acetone mixed in 100 : 12 volume). Close the jar by lid and allow to remain as such for some time. Paper strip should not touch the wall of the jar. When the solvent has risen within 1 inch from the top of the paper, strip is removed, and let it dry.

Observation. We see that solvent rises up along the paper and carrying along with it the different pigments depending on their solubility in solvent, to different heights. Position of various pigments on the strip is marked and by calculating Rf or simply by seeing colour of the spots, identification can be made.

Four different pigments are seen on the paper and their colours, Rf are as follows :

$$\text{Rf (Resolution front)} = \frac{\text{distance movement of compound from origin on paper}}{\text{distance of movement of solvent from origin on paper}}$$

ELECTROPHORESIS

EXERCISE 60

Demonstration of seed proteins separation by disc electrophoresis.

Electrophoresis. The movement of charged particle in an external electric field toward the oppositely charged electrode is called **electrophoresis.** This was developed by Tiselius in 1937, and is used in isoelectric point and electrophoretic mobility of proteins.

Proteins migrate in an electric field except at the isoelectric point, which is the pH where net positive (+) charge equals the net negative (–) charge. Since a protein's net charge varies with pH, two proteins with different isoelectric points will have different mobilities and so could be separated by the technique of **electrophoresis.** This technique is most effective when the protein solutions are buffered and at a known pH. For most proteins (whose isoelectric points are below 7), the pH is made alkaline (7.5 – 8.0) to give them a maximum net negative (–) charge. Solution is then placed in the bottom of a U-tube and a buffer solution of the same pH is carefully placed on the top of it. Electrodes are placed in two arms of the tube and electric current is turned on. The negatively (–) charged proteins will move upward in the arm containing positive (+) electrode and downward in the arm containing the negative (–) electrode.

CHAPTER 11

Anatomy of Angiosperms

KEY FOR IDENTIFICATION

It is root

(*i*) The vascular bundles are radial and exarch.
(*ii*) The endodermis is quite conspicuous and ring-like.
(*iii*) The epidermal hairs are unicellular and tubular.

It is stem

(*i*) The vascular bundles are conjoint, collateral and endarch.
(*ii*) The endodermis is inconspicuous and may or may not present.
(*iii*) The epidermal hairs are multicellular.

It is dicot root

(*i*) Xylem bundles vary from 2 to 6 (di-to hexarch), rarely more.
(*ii*) Pith is small or absent.
(*iii*) The cambium appears later.

It is monocot root

(*i*) Xylem bundles are numerous (12-20), polyarch, rarely limited in number.
(*ii*) Pith is large and well developed.
(*iii*) The cambium is altogether absent.

It is dicot stem

(*i*) The vascular bundles are conjoint, collateral and open (*i.e.*, cambium present).
(*ii*) The vascular bundles are arranged in a ring ; generally they are uniform is size ; no bundle sheath.
(*iii*) Phloem is represented by sieve tubes, companion cells and phloem parenchyma.
(*iv*) Cortex and pericycle are well marked and differentiated ; usually hypodermis is collenchymatous.

It is monocot stem

(*i*) The vascular bundles are conjoint, collateral and closed (*i.e.*, cambium absent).
(*ii*) Vascular bundles are scattered and many ; the larger bundles are towards the centre and smaller towards periphery ; usually each bundle is surrounded by a sclerenchymatous bundle sheath.
(*iii*) Phloem is represented by sieve tubes and companion cells only.
(*iv*) The ground tissue is present ; it extends from periphery to centre ; usually hypodermis is sclerenchymatous.

N.B. The points for identification and special characters if any should be mentioned in the end of the description of the transverse section of the particular organ (i.e., root, stem, etc.) of the plant.

ANATOMY OF ROOT

The root is the descending portion of the plant axis which develops from the radicle of the embryo. They serve to absorb water and nutrients from the soil with the aid of unicellular root hairs. The most outstanding and distinctive anatomical characters of the root are as follows :

1. The epidermis may be called epiblema or piliferous layer covered with numerous unicellular root hairs. The stomata and cuticle are not found on it.

2. The cortex is very well developed and consists of many layers of thin walled parenchyma. Sometimes leucoplasts also develop in them. The intercellular spaces are well developed in this region. Collenchyma is altogether absent.

3. The innermost layer of the cortex is the endodermis. It is a definite ring like layer, often with radial and inner walls thickened and possessing Casparian strips. The passage cells are also seen.

4. The outermost layer of the stele is a single layered pericycle usually consisting of thin walled parenchymatous cells, without intercellular spaces among them.

5. The xylem is exarch, *i.e.*, protoxylem lies towards outside and metaxylem towards the centre. The xylem is always centripetal in its development. Phloem bundle consists of sieve tubes, companion cells and phloem parenchyma. Protoxylem consists of annular and spiral vessels and metaxylem of reticulate and pitted vessels.

6. The parenchyma found in between xylem and phloem bundles is called conjunctive tissue.

7. Pith may be large, small or absent.

From the point of view of the study of their internal morphology, the selected examples of dicotyledonous and monocotyledonous roots are to be studied separately.

DICOTYLEDONOUS ROOTS

The most outstanding anatomical characters of the dicotyledonous roots are as follows :

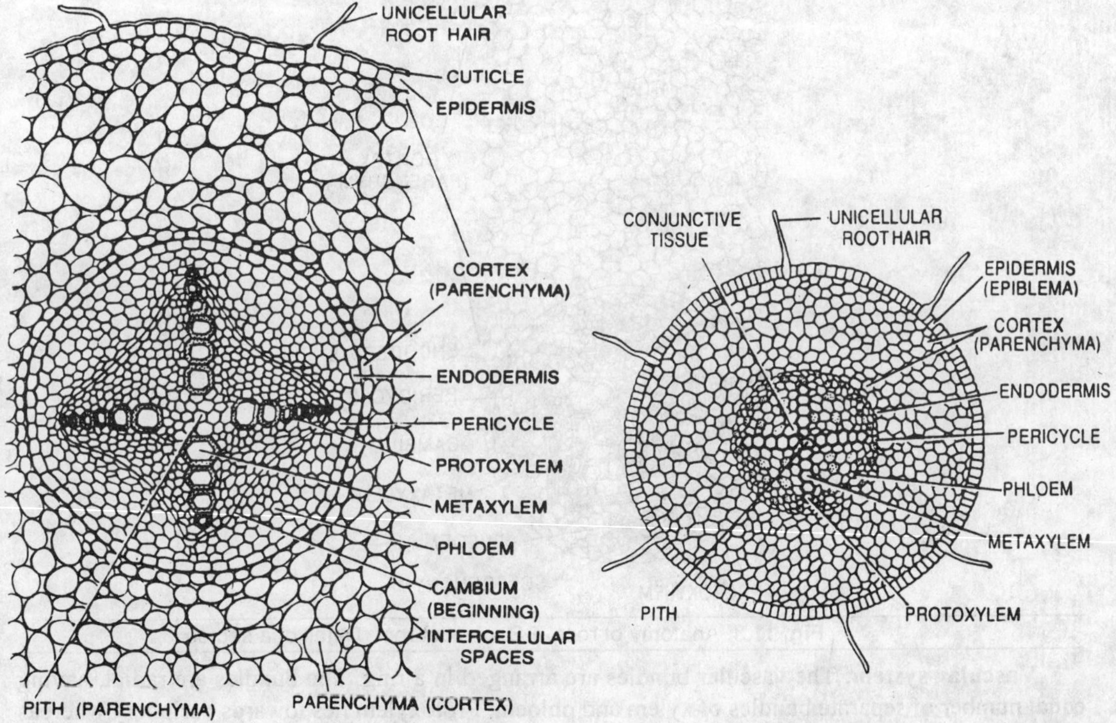

Fig. 11.1. Anatomy of root. Secondary growth. T.S. of dicotyledonous root, showing secondary growth (later stage).

Fig. 11.2. Anatomy of root. T.S. of dicot root. Detail.

1. The xylem bundles vary from two to six, they may be diarch, triarch, pentarch or hexarch.
2. The pericycle gives rise to lateral roots and secondary meristems, *i.e.*, cambium and phellogen (cork-cambium).
3. The cambium appears later as a secondary meristem.
4. The pith is very small or altogether absent.

A few typical dicotyledonous roots have been selected for the study of internal morphology.

1. Root of *Phaseolus radiatus* (Dicot)

Epiblema or piliferous layer. It is a single outermost layer of thin walled cells, the outer walls of most of these cells extend outwards in the form of unicellular root hairs. Usually this wall functions as absorbing wall of water and solutes and possesses no cuticle.

Cortex. It is multilayered and consists of thin walled rounded or polygonal cells with numerous intercellular spaces. Usually the cells contain leucoplasts and store starch.

Endodermis. The innermost layer of the cortex is endodermis. This circular layer consists of barrel-shaped cells which are closely arranged without intercellular spaces. The radial walls of endodermis are often thickened. The endodermis surrounds the stele. Sometimes a few thin walled cells in this layer, usually opposite the protoxylem, are present which are passage cells.

Pericycle. The pericycle is single layered and consists of thin walled parenchymatous cells containing abundant quantity of protoplasm.

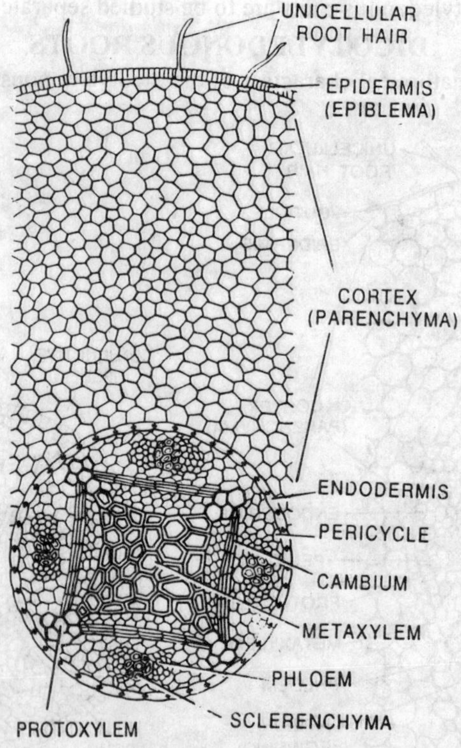

Fig. 11.3. Anatomy of root. T.S. of dicot root. Detail of a sector.

Vascular system. The vascular bundles are arranged in a ring. The bundles are radial, having equal number of separate bundles of xylem and phloem. Protoxylem lies towards periphery whereas metaxylem towards pith. This type of arrangement of xylem is said to be 'exarch'. The number of xylem and phloem bundles is equal, *i.e.*, four (it varies from two to six.) The cambium appears only in later stages. Phloem bundle consists of sieve tubes, companion cells and phloem parenchyma.

Xylem bundle consists of protoxylem which lies towards periphery and metaxylem which lies towards centre. Protoxylem consists of annular and spiral vessels which are narrow and metaxylem of bigger vessels which are reticulate and pitted. Sometimes metaxylem vessels meet in centre and total obliteration of pith takes place.

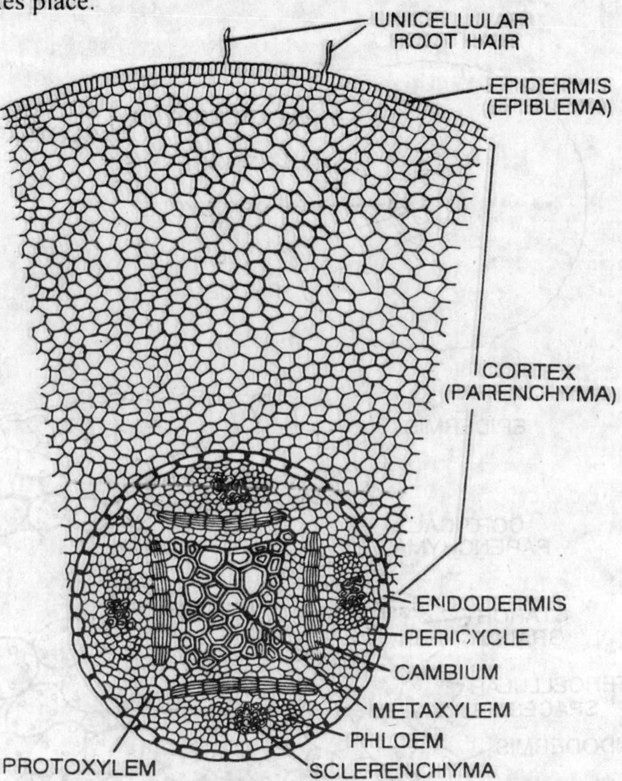

Fig. 11.4. Anatomy of root. T.S. of dicot root showing beginning of secondary growth. Details of a sector and central stele.

Conjunctive Tissue. In between xylem and phloem bundles, parenchyma is found which is known as conjunctive tissue.

Pith. This occupies a very small area in the centre and consists of thin walled parenchymatous cells with intercellular spaces. Sometimes due to development of metaxylem vessels it is altogether obliterated.

2. T.S. of Root of *Ranunculus repens* (Dicot)

Epiblema or Pilferous Layer. It is the uniseriate outermost layer with usually unicellular root hairs.

Cortex. The cortex is massive and consists of thin walled rounded or polygonal parenchyma cells having sufficiently developed intercellular spaces among them. Usually a multilayered exodermis also develops immediately below the epidermis or epiblema. The parenchyma cells of the cortex contain abundance of starch grains in them. Innermost layer of the cortex is called the **endodermis.** It consists of a row of barrel shaped cells with Casparian bands or thickenings. The thin walled passage cells are also found in the endodermal layer which lie against the protoxylem groups.

Stele. Immediately beneath the endodermis lies a central cylindrical stele. The stele consists of a single layered outermost pericycle and vascular bundles. The vascular bundles are radially arranged. Here in *Ranunculus* root, four xylem strands (tetrarch) alternate with equal number of phloem strands. Xylem is exarch, *i.e.*, protoxylem lies towards periphery and metaxylem towards the centre. Protoxylem consists of annular and spiral vessels and metaxylem of reticulate and pitted vessels. Phloem bundle consists of sieve tubes, companion cells and phloem parenchyma. The parenchymatous conjunctive tissue also occurs between xylem and phloem, the pith is altogether absent.

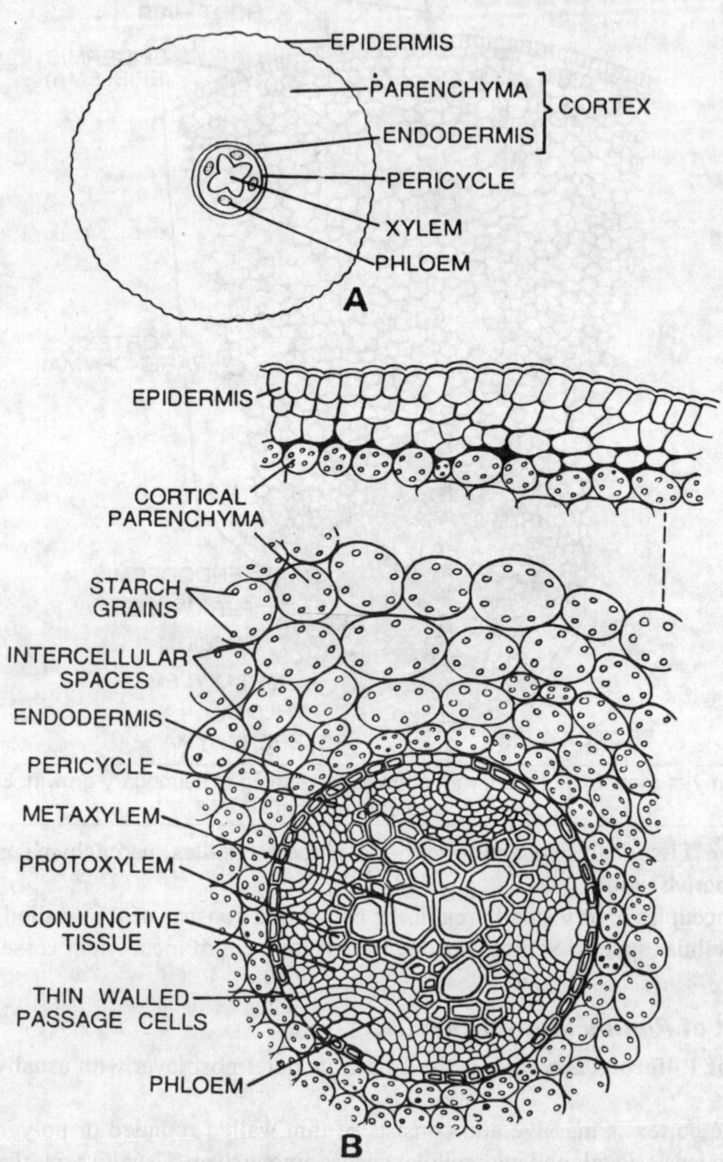

Fig. 11.5. Anatomy of root. T.S. of root of *Ranunculus* (dicot). A, diagrammatic ; B, detail.

3. T.S. of Banyan Root (*Ficus benghalensis*) — Dicot

The transverse section of the aerial root of *Ficus benghalensis* reveals the undermentioned structure

Rhizodermis. The outermost limiting layer of the root is represented by rectangular cells. A thick cuticular layer may also be seen.

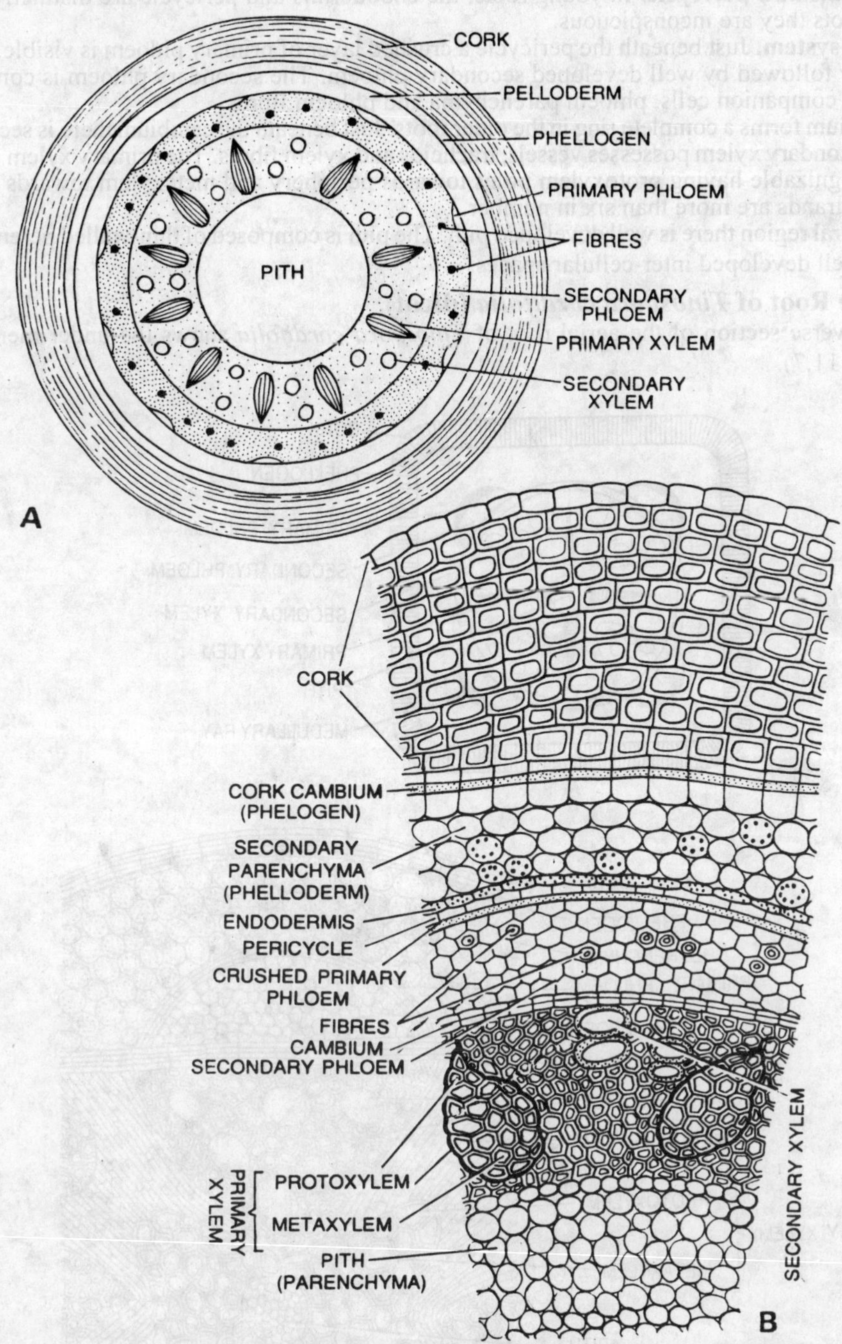

Fig. 11.6. Anatomy of root. T.S. of *Ficus* (dicot) root. A, diagrammatic ; B, detail of a sector.

Cork. Just beneath the rhizodermis there are several layers of cork cells. These cork cells somewhat rounded, suberized and having intercellular spaces.

Phellogen. The phellogen or cork cambium is found beneath the cork cells. The rectangular cells of cork cambium divide tangentially forming cork cells towards the outer side and secondary cortex towards the inner side. The secondary cortex is composed of a few layers of parenchyma cells.

Endodermis and pericycle. In young roots, the endodermis and pericycle are distinctly clear, but in older roots they are inconspicuous.

Vascular system. Just beneath the pericycle a crushed layer of primary phloem is visible, which is immediately followed by well developed secondary phloem. The secondary phloem is composed of sieve tubes, companion cells, phloem parenchyma and phloem fibres.

The cambium forms a complete ring in the older roots. Just beneath the cambium there is secondary xylem. The secondary xylem possesses vessels, tracheids and xylem fibres. The primary xylem strands are easily recognizable having protoxylem poles towards periphery and metaxylem towards centre. The vascular strands are more than six in number.

In the central region there is well developed pith. The pith is composed of thin-walled perenchyma cells having well developed inter-cellular spaces.

4. T.S. of the Root of *Tinospora cordifolia* (dicot).

The transverse section of the aerial root of *Tinospora cordifolia* shows the under mentioned structure (Fig. 11.7).

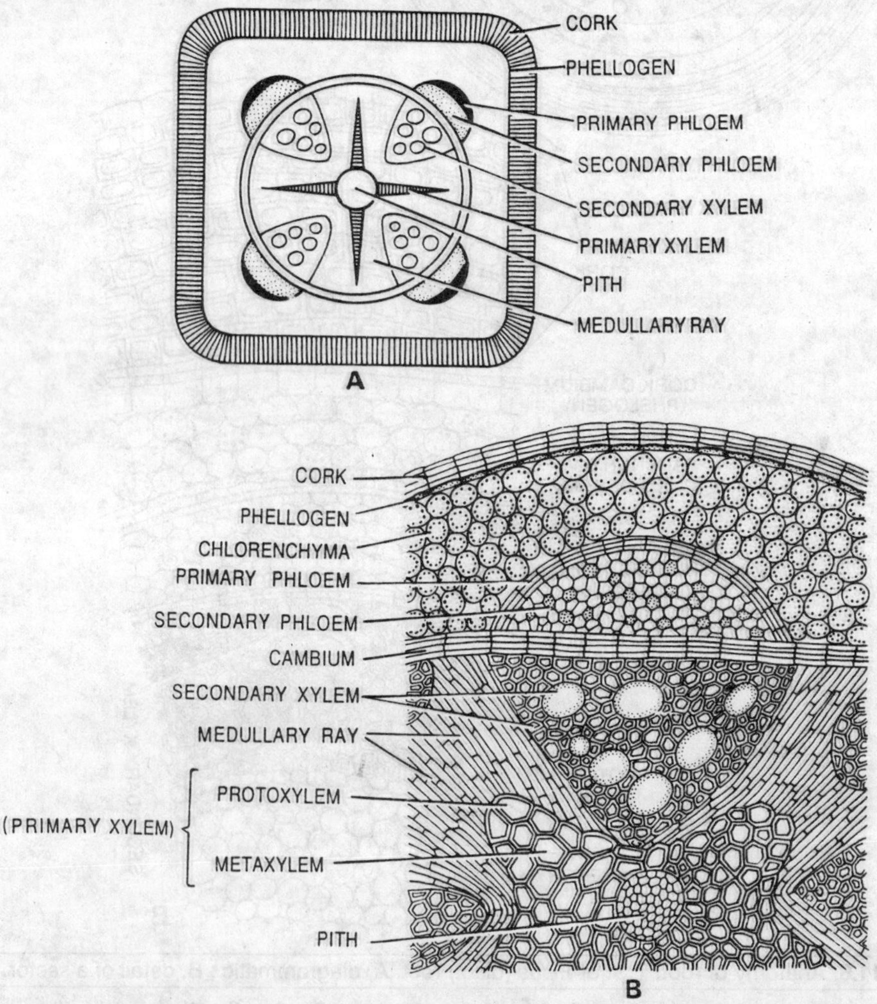

Fig. 11.7. Anatomy of aerial root of *Tinospora cordifolia* (dicot). A, T.S. of root, diagrammatic ; B, T.S. of root, detail of a sector.

Rhizodermis. The outermost limiting layer of the root is represented by rectangular cells.

Cork. Just beneath the rhizodermis there are few layers of rectangular cork cells. The cork cells are arranged in radial rows.

Phellogen or cork cambium. The phellogen is found beneath the cork. The cells of phellogen divide tangentially forming cork towards the outer side and secondary cortex (or chlorenchyma) towards inner side.

The endodermis and pericycle are inconspicuous.

Vascular system. The crushed primary phloem is found beneath the secondary cortex (chlorenchyma). Next to crushed primary phloem there is secondary phloem. The secondary phloem is composed of sieve tubes, companion cells and phloem parenchyma. In between secondary phloem and secondary xylem. The secondary xylem has large vessels. The primary xylem strands are easily recognisable possessing protoxylem poles towards periphery and metaxylem towards centre. There is tetrarch condition. Scanty pith is present in the centre. The medullary rays of parenchyma are visible.

MONOCOTYLEDONOUS ROOTS

The distinctive anatomical characters of the monocotyledonous roots are as follows :

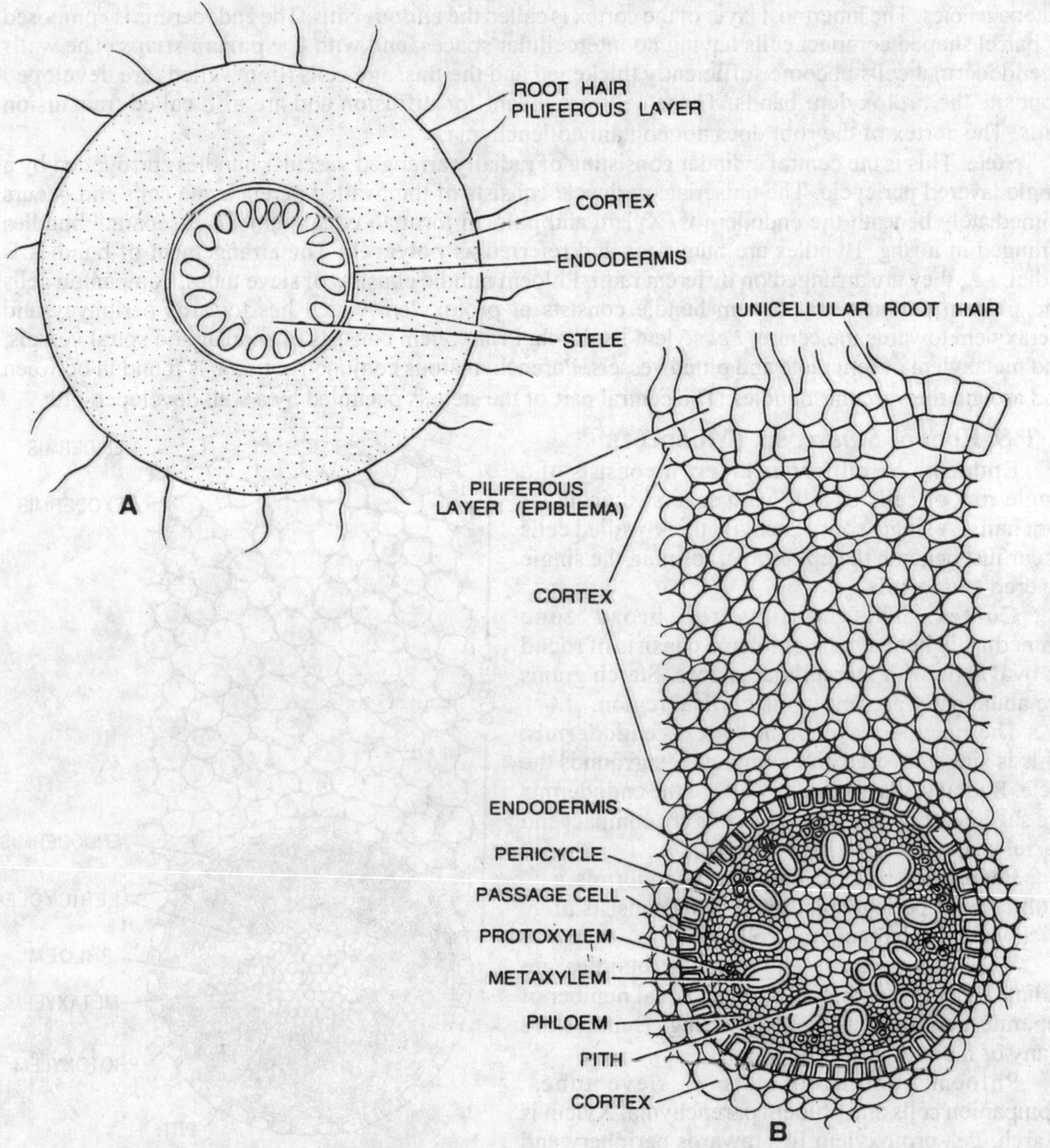

Fig. 11.8. Root. T.S. of monocotyledonous root (*Iris*). A, diagrammatic ; B, detailed structure.

1. The xylem bundles are numerous (polyarch and vary from twelve to twenty in number.)
2. The pericycle gives rise to lateral root only.
3. The cambium is altogether absent as there is no secondary thickening in such roots.
4. The pith is large and well developed. Sometimes it becomes sclerenchymatous.

5. T.S. root of *Zea mays* maize (monocot).

Epiblema or piliferous layer. The epidermis or outermost layer is commonly known as **epiblema** or piliferous layer. It is uniseriate and composed of compact tubular cells having no intercellular spaces among them. The unicellular root hairs are also present on this layer.

Cortex. Immediately beneath the epidermis a massive cortex lies consisting of thin walled parenchyma cells having sufficiently developed intercellular spaces among them. Usually in an old root a few layers of cortex immediately beneath the epiblema undergo suberisation and give rise to a single or multilayered zone **exodermis.** This is a protective layer which protects internal tissues from outer agencies. The innermost layer of the cortex is called the **endodermis.** The endodermis is composed of barrel shaped compact cells having no intercellular spaces, and with **Casparian strips.** The walls of endodermal cells become sufficiently thickened and the **passage cells** (thin walled) are developed opposite the protoxylem bands. These cells are meant for diffusion and are also called transfusion cells. The cortex of the root does not contain collenchyma.

Stele. This is the central cylinder consisting of radially arranged vascular bundles surrounded by a single layered pericycle. The uniseriate pericycle consists of thin walled parenchyma cells and occurs immediately beneath the endodermis. Xylem and phloem form an equal number of separate bundles arranged in a ring. Bundles are numerous and referred as **polyarch.** The arrangement of bundles is radial, *i.e.*, they are arranged on different radii. Phloem bundle consists of sieve tubes, companion cells and phloem parenchyma. Xylem bundle consists of protoxylem which lies towards periphyey and metaxylem towards the centre, *i.e.*, xylem is exarch. Protoxylem consists of annular and spiral vessels, and metaxylem of reticulate and pitted vessels. Parenchymatous conjunctive tissue is found in between and around the vascular bundles. The central part of the stele is occupied by a well developed pith.

6. T.S. Root of *Smilax* sp. (Monocot).

Epiblema or piliferous layer. It consists of a single row of cells usually with several unicellular root hairs. A single row of heavily thick-walled cells occur just beneath the epidermis, forming the single layered **exodermis.**

Cortex. This multilayered broad zone immediately beneath the epiblema consists of round or oval cells with inercellular spaces. Starch grains are abundantly present in the cortical region.

The innermost layer of the cortex is **endodermis.** This is single layered and completely surrounds the stele. Radial walls and inner walls of the endodermis are sufficiently thickened. The cells are compact and barrel shaped.

Pericycle. Just beneath the endodermis a multilayered pericycle is found. This consists of thick walled sclerenchyma cells.

Vascular system. The vascular bundles are radial. Xylem, and phloem form an equal number of separate bundles, arranged in a ring. Bundles are many or more than six (polyarch).

Phloem bundle consists of sieve tubes. Companion cells and phloem parenchyma. Xylem is exarch, *i.e.*, protoxylem lies towards periphery and metaxylem towards pith. Metaxylem consists of broad, reticulate and pitted vessels.

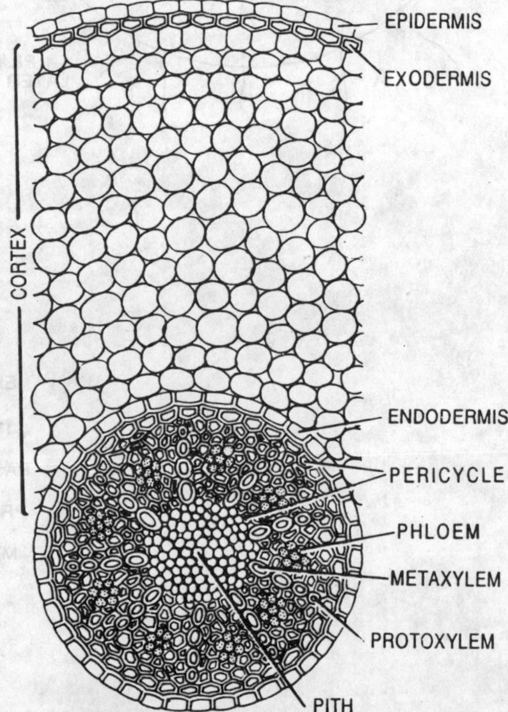

Fig. 11.9. Anatomy of root. T.S. of monocot root, of *Smilax*, detail of a sector and central stele.

Pith. It is well developed and found in the central region. It consists of thin walled parenchyma cells with intercellular spaces among them. In few cases the pith becomes thick walled and lignified, *e.g.*, in *Canna*.

7. T.S. of Epiphytic Root of *Dendrobium orchid* (Monocot).

The orchids are epiphytes. Usually they possess certain absorbing roots hanging in the air. The anatomy of their aerial roots is somewhat different from normal monocot roots in having the dead velamen region towards outside to absorb water and carbon dioxide from atmosphere. The cells of velamen are quite big in size, containing air and water. The cell walls develop fibrous thickenings.

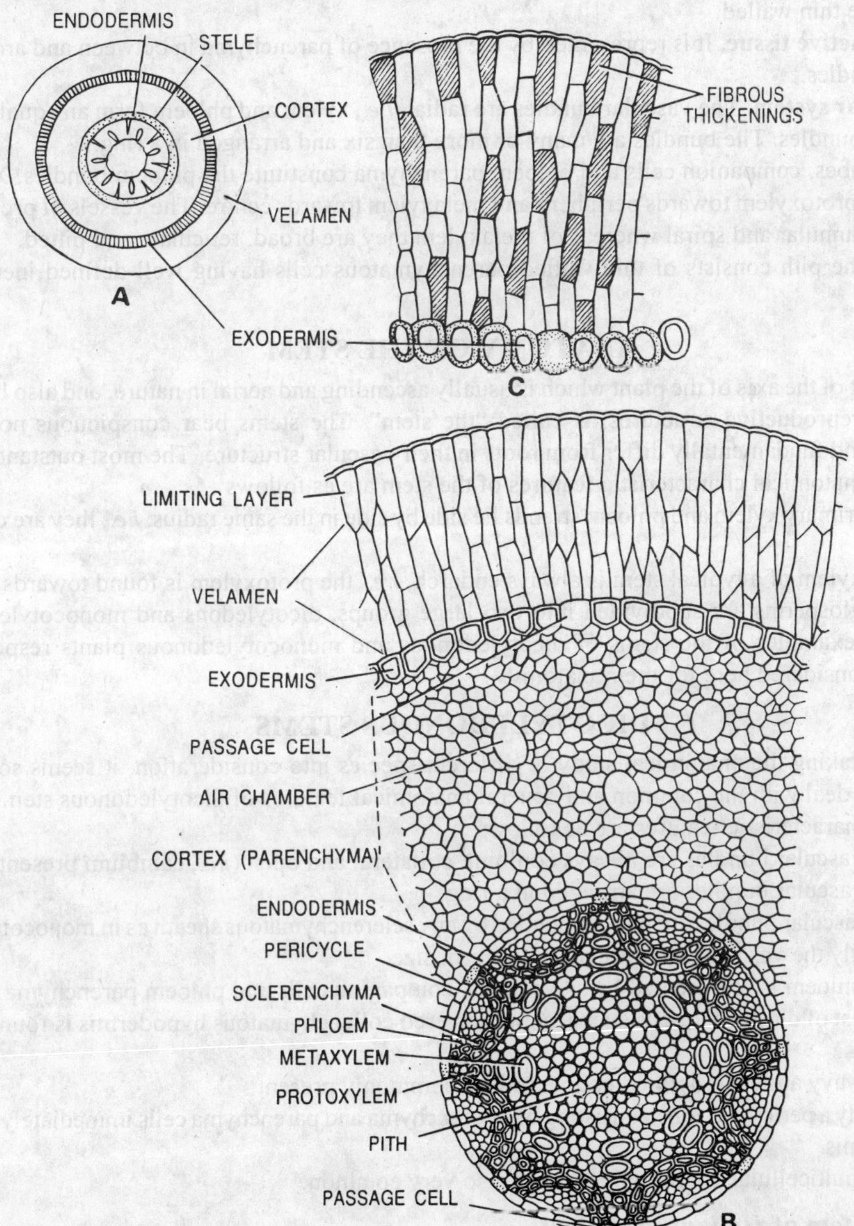

Fig. 11.10. Anatomy of orchid root (monocot). A, diagrammatic ; B, detail of a sector and stele ; C detail of velamen.

Exodermis. In orchid roots the outermost layer of the cortex is exodermis. It consists of a single row of cells with thickened outer and lateral walls except certain passage cells which remain thin walled.

Cortex. The main cortical region consists of thin walled parenchymatous cells having intercellular spaces among them. The innermost layer of the cortex is endodermis which consists of compact barrel shaped cells usually having starch grains in them. The endodermis completely surrounds the stele.

Pericycle. Immediately below the endodermis a single layered pericycle is found. The cells of this layer are thin walled.

Conjunctive tissue. It is represented by the presence of parenchyma in between and around the vascular bundles.

Vascular system. The vascular bundles are radial. *i.e.*, xylem and phloem form an equal number of separate bundles. The bundles are many or more than six and arranged in a ring.

Sieve tubes, companion cells and phloem parenchyma constitute the phloem bundles. Xylem is exarch, *i.e.*, protoxylem towards periphery and metaxylem towards centre. The vessels of protoxylem are narrow, annular and spiral whereas of metaxylem they are broad, reticulate and pitted.

Pith. The pith consists of thin walled parenchymatous cells having well defined inercellular spaces.

ANATOMY OF THE STEM

The part of the axis of the plant which is usually ascending and aerial in nature, and also bears the leaves and reproductive structures, is called "the stem". The stems bear conspicuous nodes and internodes and fundamentally differ from roots in their vascular structure. The most outstanding and distinctive anatomical characteristic features of the stem are as follows :

1. The primary xylem and phloem strands lie side by side in the same radius, *i.e.*, they are conjoint. collateral.

2. The xylem of a typical stem is always endarch, *i.e.*, the protoxylem is found towards centre.

The angiosperms are subdivided into two large groups, dicotyledons and monocotyledons. A few typical examples of the stems of dicotyledonous and monocotyledonous plants respectively. have been considered here for their anatomy.

DICOTYLEDONOUS STEMS

Before taking the anatomical study of different species into consideration, it seems somewhat necessary to deal with the common and general anatomical features of dicotyledonous stems. These distinctive characteristic features are as follows :

1. The vascular bundles are always conjoint, collateral and open (*i.e.*, cambium present).
2. The vascular bundles are arranged in a ring.
3. The vascular bundles are not surrounded by any sclerenchymatous sheath as in monocotyledons.
4. Usually the vascular bundles are of uniform size.
5. The phloem is represented by sieve tubes, companion cells and phloem parenchyma.
6. In most of dicotyledonous stems, a multilayered collenchymatous hypodermis is found below the epidermis.
7. The wavy and well defined endodermis is commonly present.
8. Usually a pericyclic zone consisting of sclerenchyma and parenchyma cells immediately beneath the endodermis.
9. The multicellular epidermal hairs are also very common.

8. T.S. of Stem of *Helianthus* (Dicot)

1. Epidermis. The outermost layer consists of a single row of cells, arranged very closely to each other, flattened tangentially with well defined, cuticle. Some of the epidermal cells extend into multicellular hairs. A few stomata are also visible, but no chloroplasts. However, the guard cells of the stomata, contain chloroplasts.

2. Cortex. The cortex region is found just below the epidermis, which consists of peripheral collenchyma, central parenchyma and endodermis or starch sheath.

(*a*)Collenchyma. It lies just beneath the epidermis and consists of four or five layers of cells. The cells are specially thickened at the corners by the deposition of cellulose and pectin and thus the intercellular spaces are obliterated.

(*b*)Parenchyma. The central region of the cortex consists of a few layers of thin walled parenchymatous cells. There are well defined intercellular spaces in this region.

(*c*)Endodermis. The last layer of the cortex is endodermis which consists of single row of barrel shaped compact cells having no intercellular spaces. The endodermis contains starch grains and therefore it is also known as starch sheath.

3. Pericycle. The pericycle consists of semilunar patches of sclerenchyma lying in between the endodermis and vascular bundles. The sclerenchymatous patches are intervened by parenchymatous tissue. This type of sclerenchymatous patches associated with phloem of vascular bundles are termed as hard bast fibres.

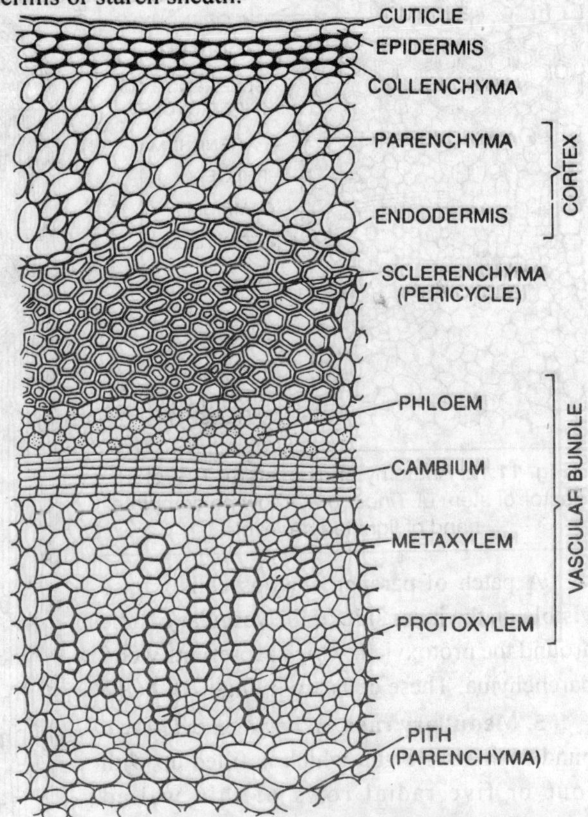

Fig. 11.11. Anatomy of a stem. T.S. of *Helianthus* (dicot) stem. Detail of sector.

4. Vascular bundles. The vascular bundles are conjoint, collateral, open and arranged in a ring. Each bundle consists of phloem cambium and xylem.

(a)Phloem. The phloem consists of sieve tubes, companion cells and phloem parenchyma. The sieve tubes are narrow and each sieve tube is associated by a small companion cell. The rest of the phloem represents phloem parenchyma. The phloem cells are living and help in translocation of carbohydrates.

(b) Cambium. In between xylem and phloem of the bundles a cambium strip is found. The cells of the cambium strip are thin walled, living, rectangular and arranged in radial rows. In young stems the cambial strips are confined only to vascular bundles but as the stem becomes older the interfascicular cambium also develops.

(c)Xylem. The xylem consists of xylem vessels, tracheids, wood fibres and wood parenchyma. The xylem vessels are represented by metaxylem and protoxylem. The bigger, preripheral and wide cavities represent metaxylem while the narrow cavities, towards pith indicate protoxylem. The metaxylem consists of reticulate and pitted vessels whereas protoxylem consists of annular, spiral and scalariform vessels. The walls of the vessels are always thick and lignified.

Sometimes around the metaxylem vessels some small thickwalled tracheids are also found.

The wood fibres are also found which are somewhat irregular, polygonal, thickwalled and lignified cells.

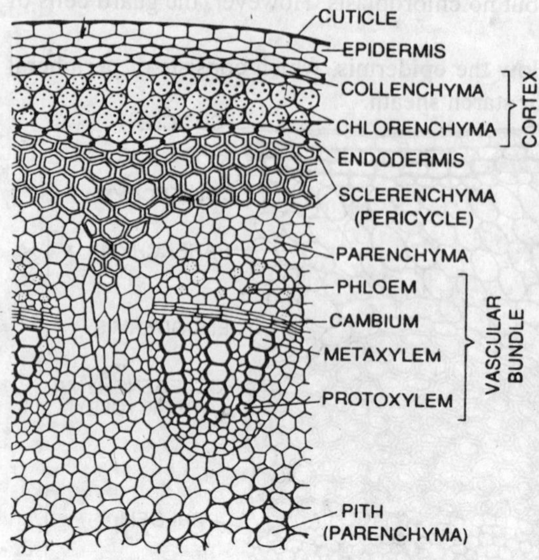

Fig. 11.12. Anatomy of dicot stem. T.S. of a sector of stem of *Tinospora*, showing complete band of lignified pericycle.

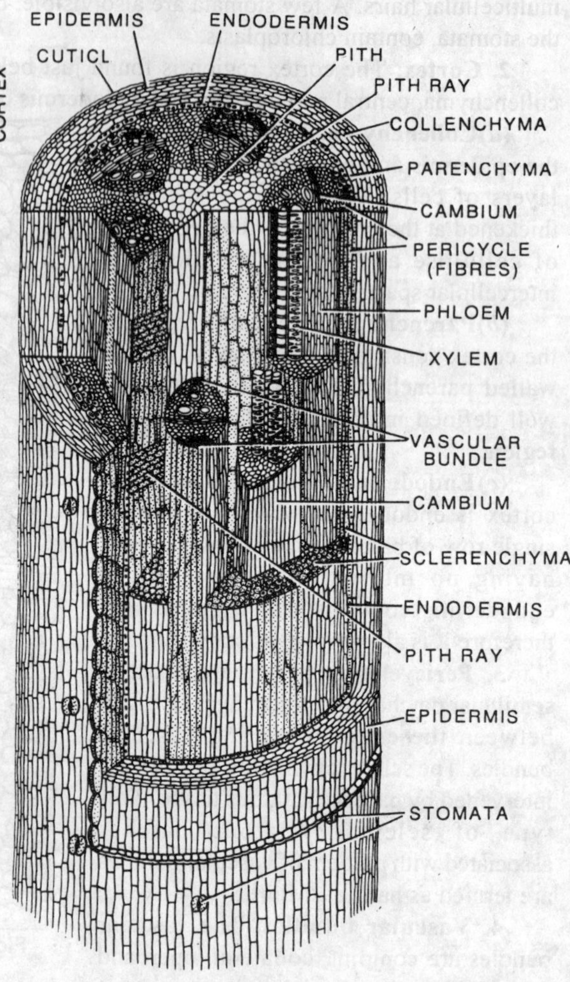

Fig. 11.13. Three dimensional diagram of a portion of an internode of a dicot stem to show transverse, radial and tangential sections.

A patch of parenchymatous cells is also visible on the inner side of the vascular bundle around the protoxylem which represents wood parenchyma. These cells are living.

5. Medullary rays. In between every two bundles there is a gap which is filled up with four or five radial rows of thin walled parenchymatous cells, which represent medullary rays.

6. Pith. The central region of the stem which is filled up with thin walled, round or polygonal parenchymatous cells, represents pith. The pith occupies the major portion of the stem. The intercellular spaces in this region are very conspicuous.

9. T.S. of Stem of Xanthium (dicot)

(1) Epidermis. The epidermis consists of a single row of compact cells, the cuticle extends over it and many epidermal cells give rise to multicellular epidermal hairs.

(2) Cortex. The cortex is sufficiently broad and consists of, collenchyma, parenchyma and endodermis.

The outer region of cortex consists of a few layers of collenchymatous cells having deposition of cellulose at their corners, usually no intercellular spaces. Below the collenchyma a multilayered parenchymatous region having thin walled, oval or rounded cells with intercellular spaces is present. The last wavy layer of the cortex is endodermis which consists of barrel-shaped compact cells, containing starch grains and having no intercellular spaces.

(3) Pericycle. It lies in between the endodermis and the vascular bundles, and consists of lignified sclerenchymatous patches associated with the vascular bundles, and the intervening strands of parenchyma.

(4) Vascular bundles. The vascular bundles are conjoint, collateral, open and arranged in a ring. Each vascular bundle consists of phloem, cambium, and xylem. The phloem lies externally to the vascular bundle and consists of sieve tubes, companion cells and phloem parenchyma. In between phloem and xylem a cambial strip is found having living rectangular cells arranged in radial rows. In young stem the cambial strips are confined only in the vascular bundles, but as the stem becomes older, the interfascicular cambial strip also develops. The xylem lies internally with protoxylem towards centre and metaxylem towards periphery. The metaxylem consists of bigger vessels whereas protoxylem of narrow vessels. Protoxylem consists of annular, spiral and scalariform vessels and metaxylem of reticulate and pitted vessels. Their walls are thick and lignified. Around the metaxylem certain tracheids are also present. Xylem parenchyma is also found in the inner region of the vascular bundle.

(5) Medullary rays. The medullary rays, having thin walled rounded or polygonal, parenchymatous cells ; multilayered and found in between the vascular bundles.

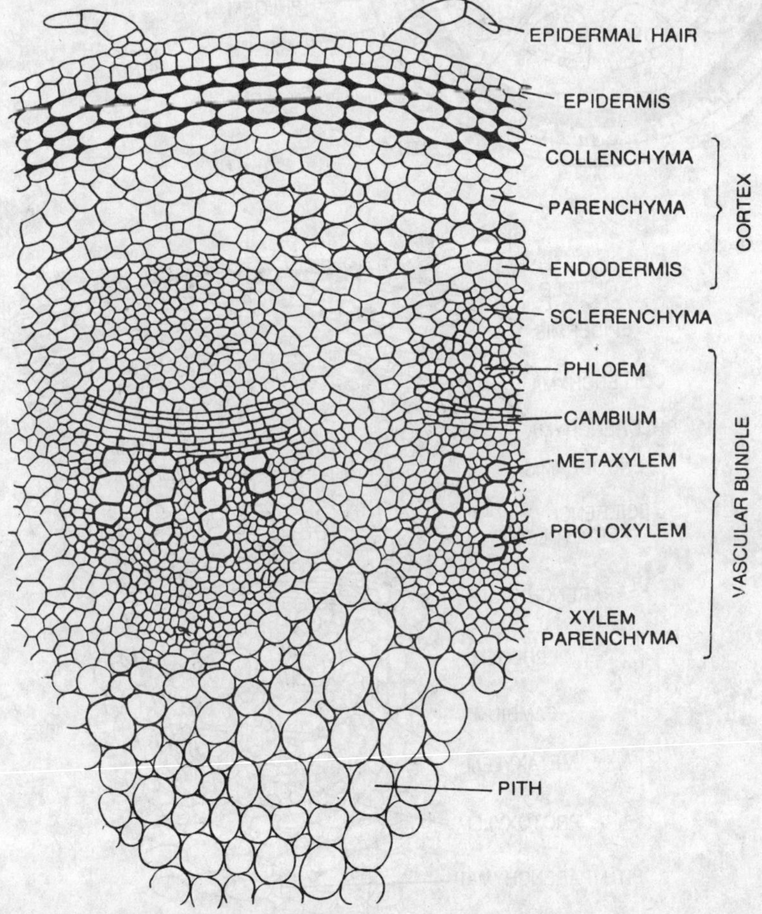

Fig. 11.14. Anatomy of stem. T.S. of (dicot) stem of *Xanthium*. Detail of a sector.

(6) Pith. It is very well developed and occupies the main central region of the stem. The pith consists of thin walled, parenchyamatous cells with intercellular spaces.

10. T.S. of stem of *Aristolochia* (young stem)-Dicot.

1. Epidermis. The epidermis consists of a single layer of cells and is the outermost layer of the stem. The outer cell walls are thickened and cutinized. Usually multicellular epidermal hairs also develop.

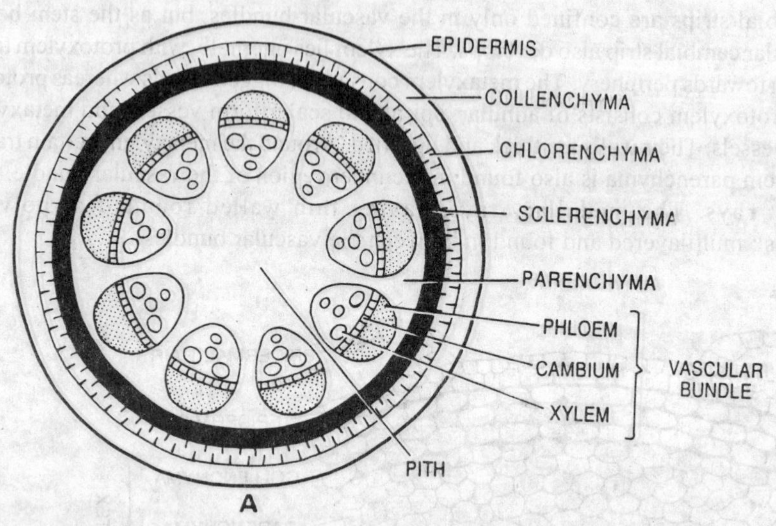

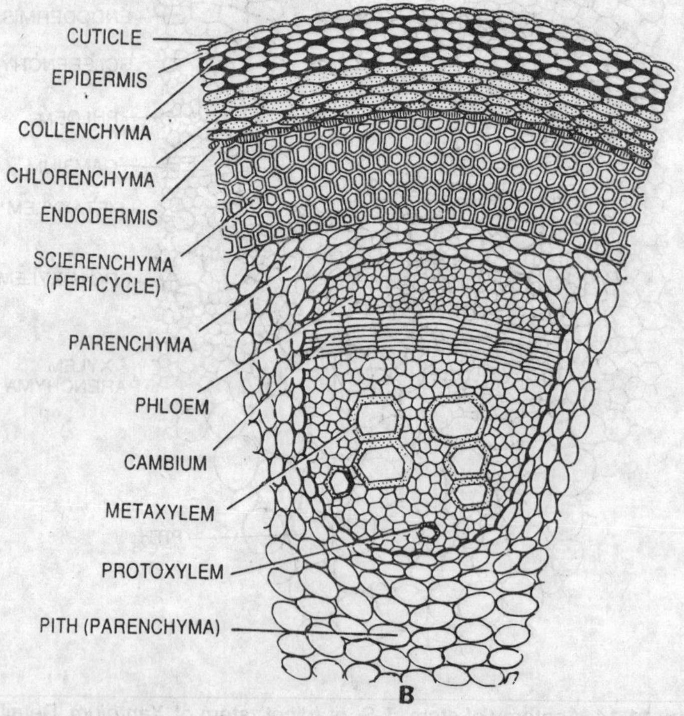

Fig. 11.15. Anatomy of stem. T.S. of young stem of *Aristolochia* (dicot). A, diagrammatic ; B, detail of a sector.

2. Cortex. The region that lies next to the epidermis is the cortex. It consists of a few layers of collenchyma, parenchyma and single layered endodermis.

Collenchyma is usually found in the form of a multilayered continuous band just beneath the epidermis. The cells of the collenchyma are modified parenchymatous cells with thickened cellulose walls at the angles. The cells are living and contain a moderate amount of protoplasm. Usually below the collenchymatous cells, the parenchyma cells of the cortex are found. Parenchyma cells are usually regular, thin walled and with protoplasm. Due to the exposition of these cells to the light they develop chloroplasts and are known as chlorenchyma cells. Chlorenchyma cells perform the function of photosynthesis. The innermost layer of the cortex is the endodermis which consists of barrel shaped, elongated, compact, cells, having no intercellular spaces. Usually the cells contain starch grains and the endodermis is known as starch sheath.

3. Pericycle. In young stem of *Aristolochia,* usually the pericycle consists of wide, closed rig of sclerenchyma, but fibers split up into separate strands in old stem.

4. Vascular bundles. The vascular bundles are conjoint, collateral, open and separated from each other by wide, parenchymatous medullary rays. Each vascular bundle consists of phloem, cambium, and xylem.

The phloem lies externally to the vascular bundle and consists of sieve tubes, companion cells and phloem parenchyma. The sieve tubes consist of thin walled elongated cells arranged in vertical rows. Each sieve tube is accompanied by a companion cell which is smaller in size. A single mother cell gives rise to one sieve tube and one companion cell. The phloem also contains parenchymatous cells whose structure is more or less similar to that of other parenchymatous cells. They are known as phloem parenchyma.

In between the external phloem and inner xylem there is a strip of cambium having thin walled rectangular cells arranged in radial rows. The cells of cambial zone are meristematic. In young stem the cambial strips are confined to the vascular bundles whereas in old stem the inter-fascicular cambium also develops with the result of secondary thickening.

The innermost part of the vascular bundle is represented by xylem which consists of xylem vessels, tracheids, wood fibres and xylem parenchyma. The xylem with wide vessels and towards periphery is metaxylem and the xylem with narrow vessels and towards pith is protoxylem. Around the metaxylem certain tracheids are also found which are narrower than the true vessels. Parenchymatous cells in the xylem represent wood or xylem parenchyma.

5. Medullary rays. In *Aristolochia,* the medullary rays are broad, so that the vascular bundles are widely separated from each other.

6. Pith. The wide central region of the stem consists of thin walled rounded or polygonal cells with intercellular spaces represent medulla or pith.

11. T.S. of stem of *Ricinus* (dicot)

1. Epidermis. It is the outermost layer, and consists of a single row of cells having cuticle.

2. Cortex. The region that lies next to the epidermis is the cortex. It consists of a few layers of collenchyma, parenchyma and single layered endodermis. The cortical region is sufficiently wide in *Ricinus.*

Collenchyma lies just below the epidermis and consists of four or five layers of cells. Collenchymatous cells are thickened at the corners against the intercellular spaces due to deposition of cellulose and pectin.

The central region of the cortex consists of a few layers of thin walled, large, oval or rounded parenchymatous cells with intercellular spaces.

The endodermis is the innermost layer of the cortex and consists of barrel shaped, compact cells, having no intercelluar spaces. It is very conspicuous in early stages. It almost contains starch grains and is also known as the starch sheath.

3. Pericycle. The pericycle is represented by small groups of sclerenchyma, usually intervened by regular parenchyma. The sclerenchymatous cells are lignified and thick walled whereas parenchyma cells are thin walled, polygonal and with small quantity of protoplasm.

4. Vascular bundles. The vascular bundles are conjoint, collateral, open, arranged in a ring, and separated from each other by broad, thin walled, and parenchymatous medullary rays. Each vascular bundle consists of phloem, cambium and xylem.

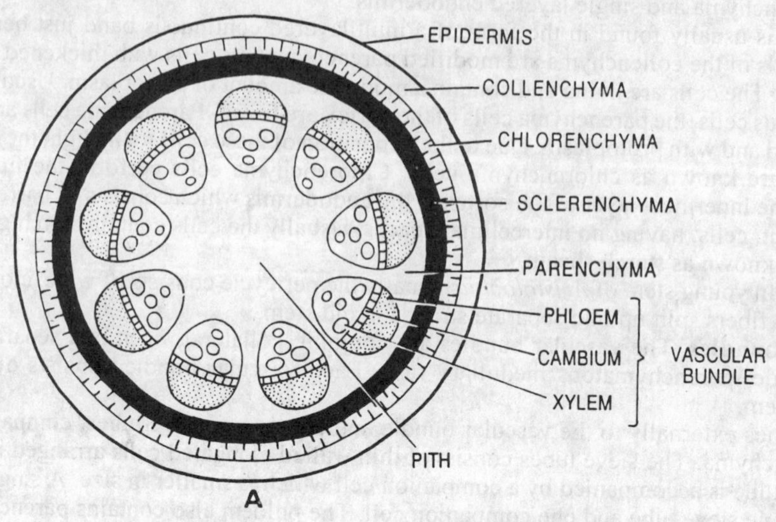

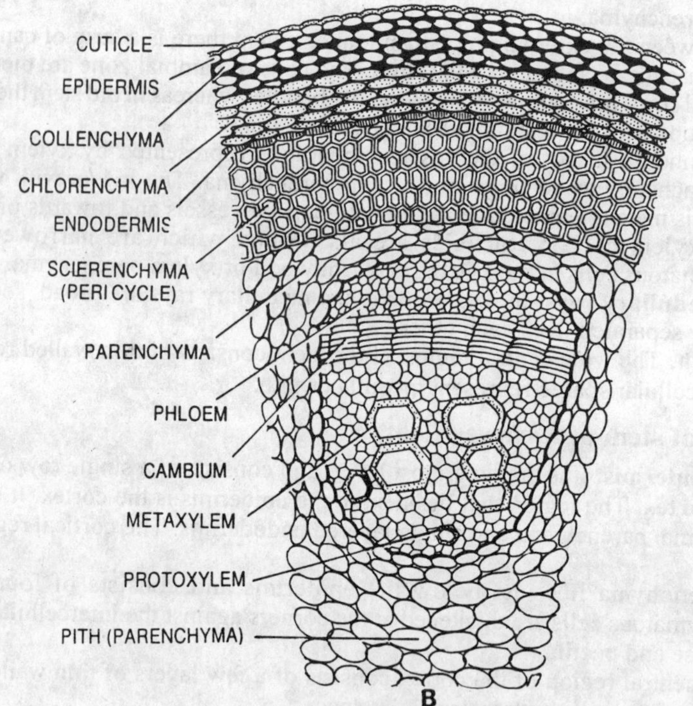

Fig. 11.16. Anatomy of dicot stem. A, diagrammatic ; B, T.S. of a sector of stem of *Ricinus communis*.

The phloem lies externally in the vascular bundle and consists of sieve tubes, companion cells and phloem parenchyma. The central zone of cambium is composed of thin walled rectangular cells arranged in radial rows and confined to vascular bundles only in early stages. The xylem consists of primary xylem, xylem fibres and xylem parenchyma. The metaxylem with wide vessels is found towards periphery whereas protoxylem with narrow vessels is found towards pith region.

5. Medullary rays. The vascular bundles are intervened by wide, parenchymatous medullary rays.

6. Pith. The central part of the stem which represents medullary or pith region consists of large thin walled and parenchymatous cells. The intercellular spaces are quite conspicuous.

12. T.S. of stem of *Cucurbita* (dicot.)

1. Epidermis. The epidermis is single layered possessing a thin cuticle and barrel shaped compact cells. Some of the epidermal cells are elongated into multicellular epidermal hairs.

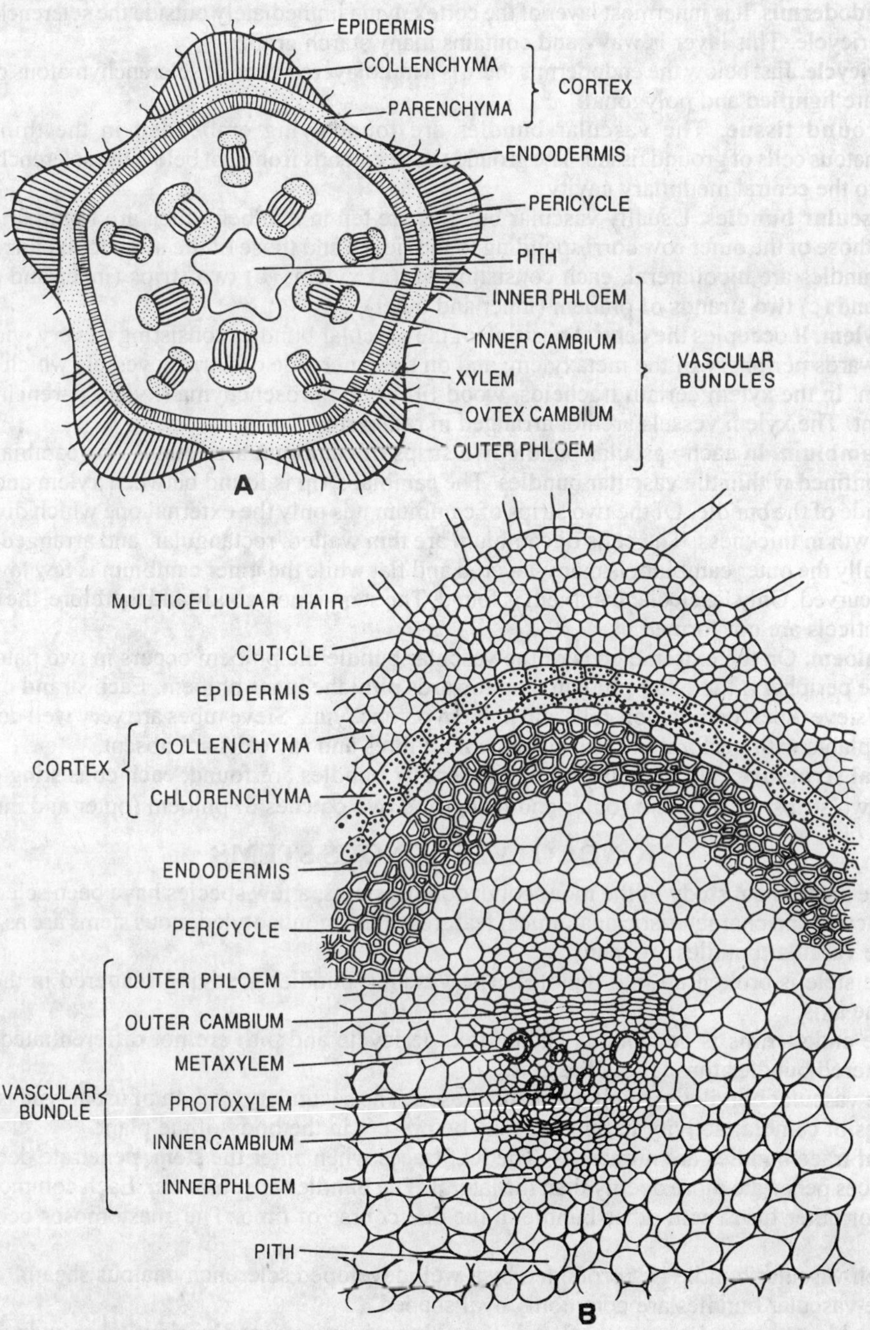

Fig. 11.17. Anatomy of stem of *Cucurbita* (dicot.) A, T.S. of stem, diagrammatic ; B, T.S. of same, detaii of a sector.

2. Cortex. This region consists of external collenchyma, chlorenchyma (photosynthetic tissue) and endodermis.

***(a)* Chlorenchyma.** It lies just beneath the epidermis and consists of many layers of cells in the ridges, whereas in the furrows it is only few layered or sometimes altogether absent.

***(b)* Chlorenchyma.** Just below the collenchyma two or three layers of parenchyma containing chloroplasts (chlorenchyma-photosynthetic tissue) present, which help in the process of assimilation.

***(c)* Endodermis.** It is innermost layer of the cortex, lying immediately outside the sclerenchymatous zone of pericycle. This layer is wavy and contains many starch grains.

3. Pericycle. Just below the endodermis there is a multilayered zone of sclerenchymatous pericycle. The cells are lignified and polygonal.

4. Ground tissue. The vascular bundles are found lying embedded in the thin walled, parenchymatous cells of ground tissue. The ground tissue extends from just below the sclerenchymatous pericycle to the central medullary cavity.

5. Vascular bundles. Usually vascular bundles are ten in number which are found arranged in two rows, those of the outer row corresponding to the ridges and those of the inner to the furrows. The vascular bundles are bicollateral, each consisting of, (a) xylem, (b) two strips (inner and outer) of cambium and (c) two strands of phloem (inner and outer).

***(a)* Xylem.** It occupies the central position of the vascular bundle, consisting of very wide, pitted vessels towards periphery of the metaxylem, and on the inner side of narrow vessels which form the portoxylem. In the xylem certain tracheids, wood fibres and prosenchyma (xylem parenchyma) are also present. The xylem vessels are not arranged in radial rows.

***(b)* Cambium.** In each vascular bundle two strips of cambium are found. The cambial activity remains confined within the vascular bundles. The cambial strip is found between xylem and phloem on either side of the bundle. Of the two strips of cambium it is only the external one which divides and causes growth in thickness. The cells of cambium are thin walled, rectangular, and arranged in radial rows. Usually the outer cambium is many-layered and flat while the inner cambium is few layered and somewhat curved. Only fascicular cambium is found. The stem is not woody and therefore, the periderm and the lenticels are not formed.

***(c)* Phloem.** On the extreme ends of the vascular bundle the phloem occurs in two patches, and towards the periphery, the outer phloem, and towards pith, the inner phloem. Each strand of phloem consists of sieve tubes, companion cells and phloem parenchyma. Sieve tubes are very well developed. The sieve plants with perforations are also visible. Fibres and ray cells are absent.

Special structure. The bicollateral open vascular bundles are found, each consisting of xylem (central), two strips of cambium (outer and inner) and two patches of phloem (outer and inner).

MONOCOTYLEDONOUS STEMS

For the anatomical study of the monocotyledonous stems, a few species have been selected. The most distinctive and characteristic anatomical features of the monocotyledonous stems are as follows :

1. The vascular bundles are many.

2. The stele is broken up into bundles. The vascular bundles are lying scattered in the ground tissue of the axis.

3. The endodermis is not found. The cortex, pericycle and pith are not differentiated because of the scattered bundles throughout the axis.

4. The vascular bundles are collateral and closed. The secondary growth of usual type is lacking, but vestiges of cambial activity in bundles may be present in the body of the plant.

5. Leaf trace bundles are numerous. The leaf traces when enter the stem, penetrate deeply. The median traces penetrate more deeply than the lateral. The bundles are common. Each common bundle somehow or other fuses with other bundle in the due course of time. The anastomoses occur at the nodes.

6. Each vascular bundle is surrounded by a well developed sclerenchymatous sheath.

7. The vascular bundles are commonly oval shaped.

8. The phloem parenchyma is not found. The phloem is represented by sieve tubes and companion cells only.

9. The pith is not marked out.

10. Usually sclerenchymatous hypodermis is present.
11. Usually epidermal hairs are not present.

13. T.S. of stem of *Zea mays* (monocot).

1. Epidermis. The outermost layer epidermis consists of a single row of compact cells. It is covered with a thick cuticle Epidermal hairs are altogether absent.

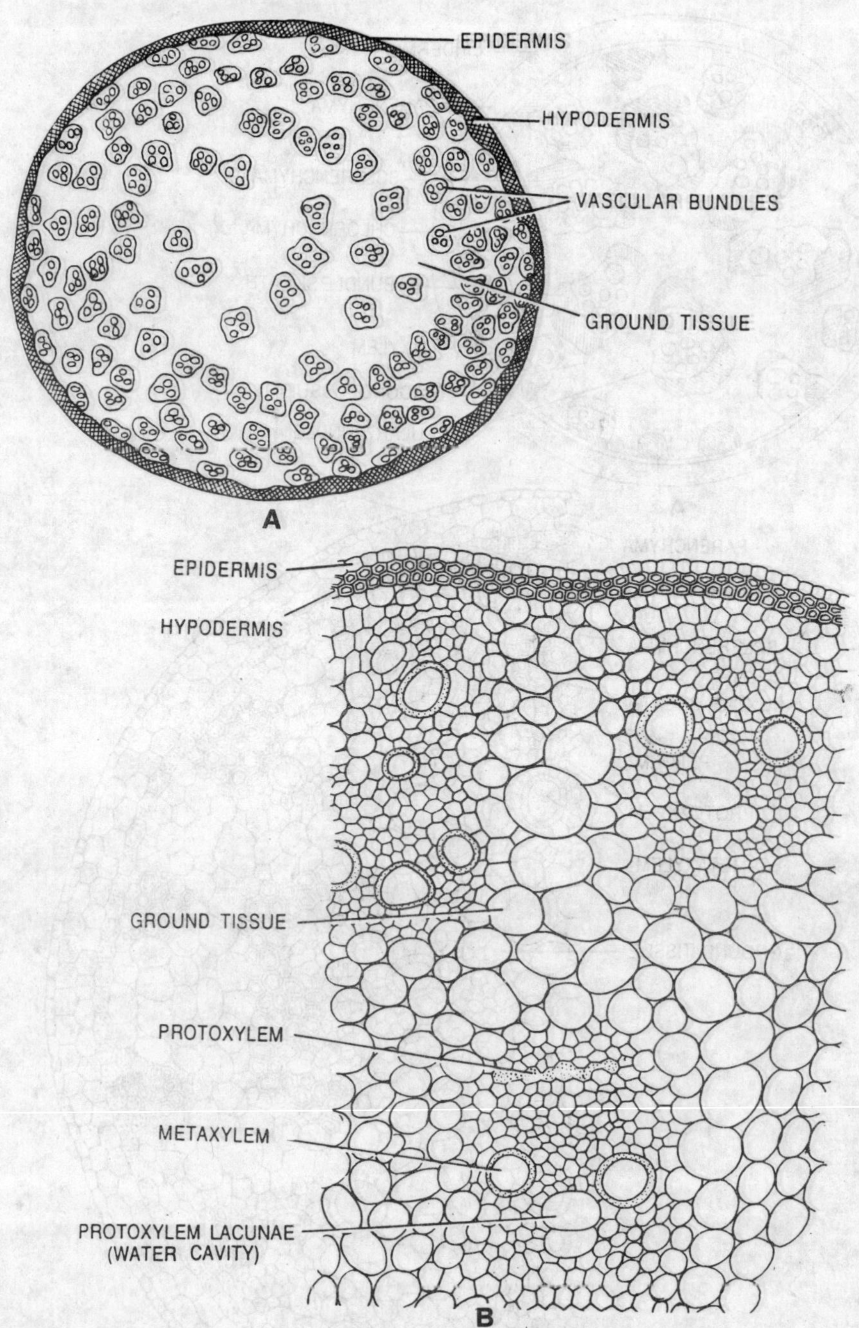

Fig. 11.18. The monocotyledonous stem. T.S. of maize stem, showing sclerenchymatous hypodermis, parenchymatous

Hypodermis. Below the epidermis, usually two or three layers of sclerenchyma represent hypodermis.

2. Ground tissue system. It consists of thin walled parenchymatous cells, having well defined intercellular spaces among them. This tissue extends from below the sclerenchyma (hypodermis) to the centre. It is not differentiated into cortex, endodermis, pericycle, pith, etc.

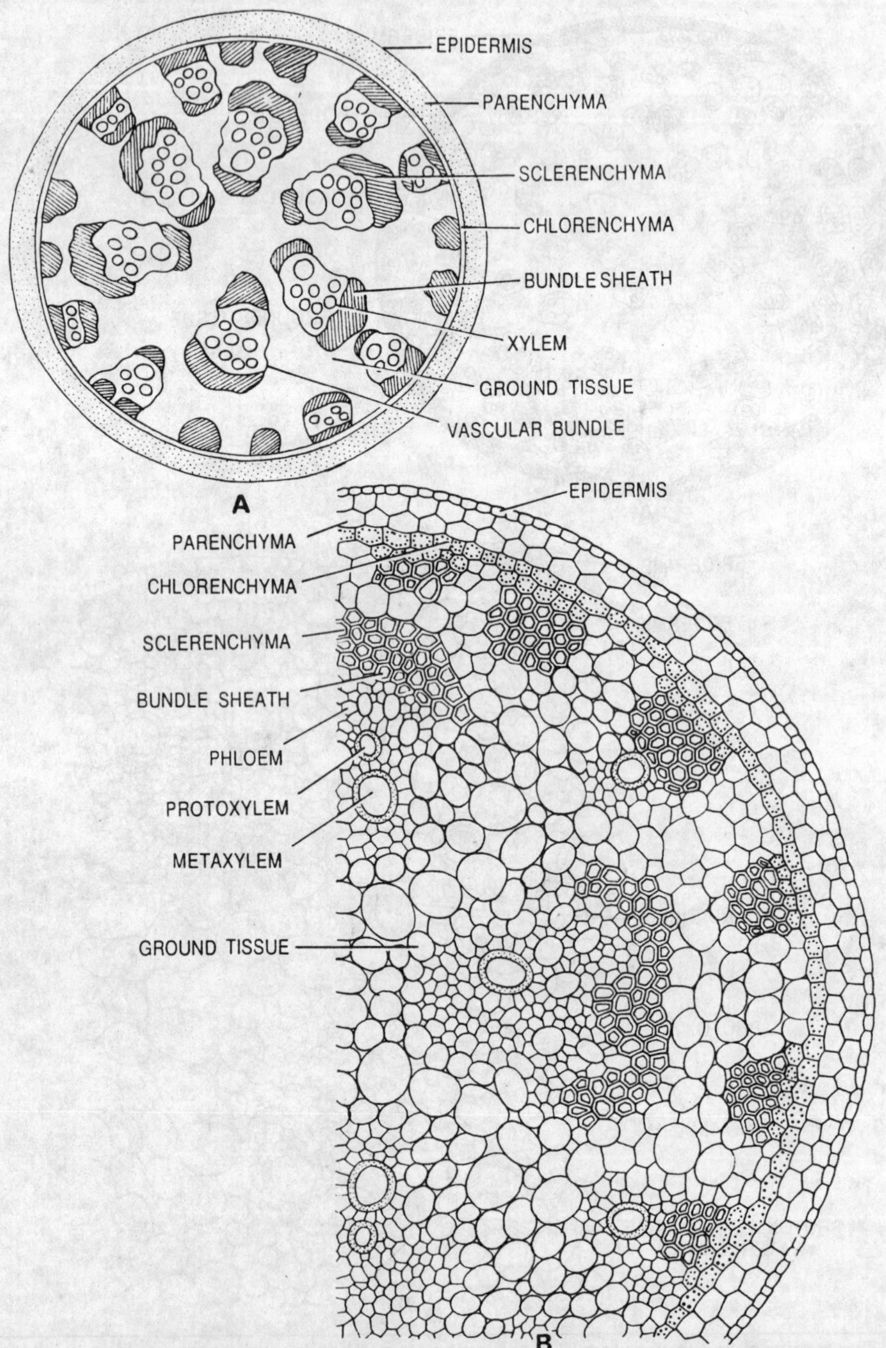

Fig. 11.19. Anatomy of stem. T.S. of *Canna* (monocot stem) A, diagrammatic ; B, detail of sector

3. Vascular system. This consists of many collateral and closed vascular bundles scattered in the ground tissue. The vascular bundles lie towards periphery in greater number than the centre. Comparatively the peripheral bundles are smaller in size than the central ones. Each bundle is more or less surrounded by a sheath is more conspicuous towards upper and lower sides of the bundle. The bundle consists of two parts, *i.e.*, xylem and phloem.

Usually the xylem is Y shaped and consists of pitted and bigger vessels of metaxylem and smaller vessels (annular and spiral) of protoxylem. In between metaxylem vessels, small pitted tracheids are also fond. Around the lysigenous or water cavity wood parenchyma is present. The lysigenous cavity is formed by the breaking down of the inner protoxylem vessel.

Phloem consists of sieve tubes and companion cells. Phloem parenchyma is altogether absent in most of monocotyledonous stems. The outer phloem which is a broken mass may be called as protophloem and inner portion is metaphloem. Sieve tubes and companion cells are quite conspicuous.

14. T.S. of scape of *Canna* (monocot.)

1. Epidermis. It is the outermost uniseriate layer consisting of small, polygonai cells with cuticularized outer walls.

2. Ground tissue system. Just beneath the epidermis a few layers of parenchyma occur forming small cortical region. The cells of cortex are sufficiently large and polygonal. Immediately below the cortex, a single layered chlorophyllous tissue is found consisting of chloroplast bearing cells. The sclerenchyma patches remain attached to the chlorophyllous tissue here. The rest of the portion consists of a continuous mass of large, thin walled, parenchymatous cells having sufficiently developed intercellular spaces among them. It is called the ground tissue.

3. Vascular bundles. They are many of various sizes, lying scattered in the ground tissue. The bundles are closed and collateral. Each bundle is incompletely surrounded by a sheath of sclerenchyma called bundle sheath. The outer sclerenchyma patch of the bundle is more distinct and cap like whereas inner patch is not so developed. Each bundle consists of xylem and phloem. The xylem is situated on the inner side and the phloem towards outer side. The xylem consists of a large spiral vessel with one or two smaller vessels of same nature; phloem consists of sieve tubes and companion cells.

15. T.S. of stem of *Asparagus* (monocot).

1. Epidermis. It is outermost uniseriate layer composed of approximately rounded cells with cuticularized outer walls.

2. Ground tissue system. Just beneath the epidermis a few layers of parenchyma are found which contain chloroplasts in them. This may be called **cortex.** The inner most layer of the cortex consists of compact cells and called the **starch sheath.** Below sheath a multilayered complete band of sclerenchyma occurs, which gives mechanical support to the stem. The rest of the portion is ground tissue which consists of thin walled parenchymatous cells having well developed intercellular spaces among them. The vascular bundles remain scattered in the ground tissue.

3. Vascular bundles. The vascular bundles remain scattered in the ground tissue. The central bundles are comparatively large than the peripheral ones. They are always collateral and closed. Each vascular bundle consists of xylem and phloem. The xylem is Y shaped. The metaxylem vessels form the arms of Y and protoxylem, the base. Phloem consists of sieve tubes and companion cells. Bundle sheath is not found (see Fig. 11.20).

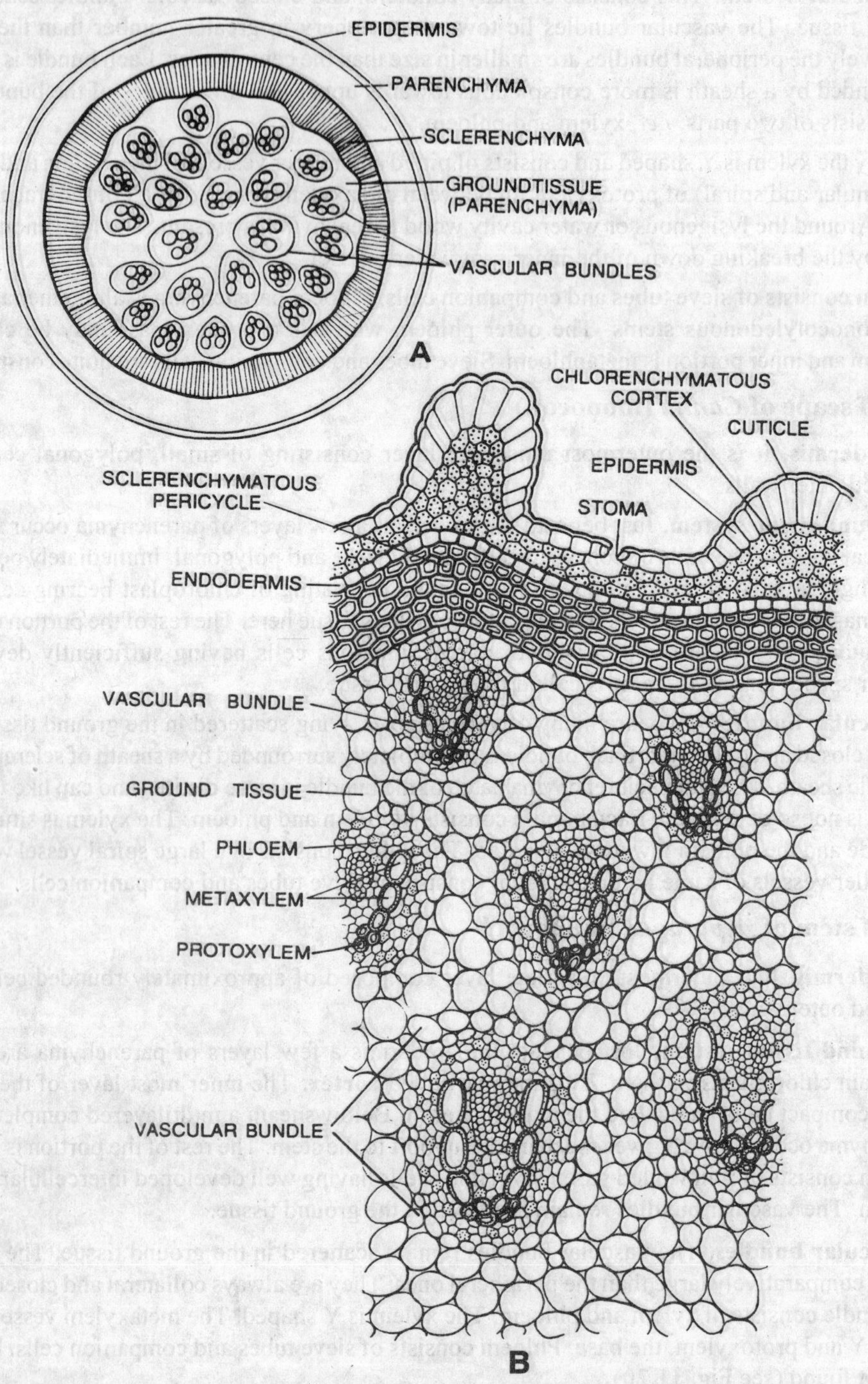

Fig. 11.20. Anatomy of monocotyledonous stem. A, T.S. of *Asparagus* stem ; B, T.S. of a vascuiar bundle of *Asparagus*, lacking secondary growth. Crushed protophloem and protoxylem are also seen.

16. T.S. of stem of *Cynodon dactylon* (monocot.)

1. Epidermis. It is the outermost uniseriate layer, usually composed of compact tablet cells with cuticularized outer walls.

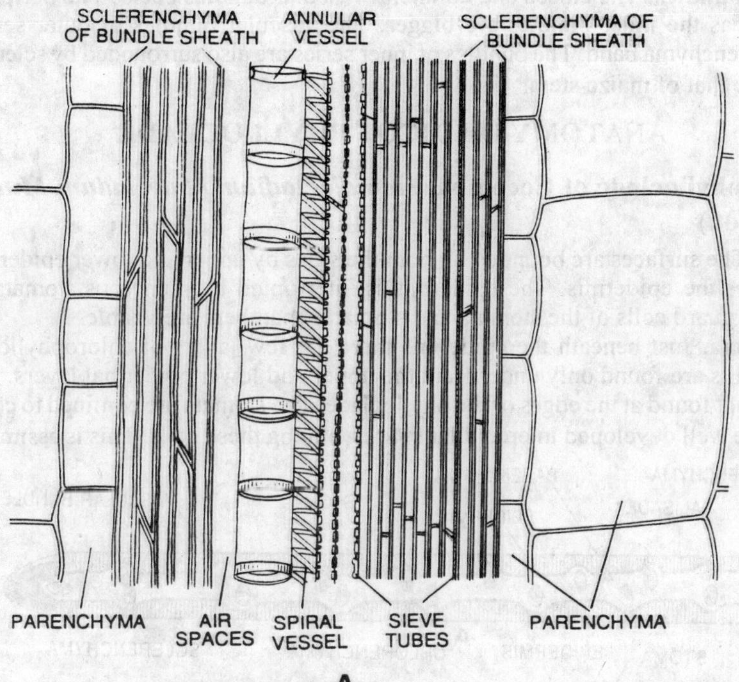

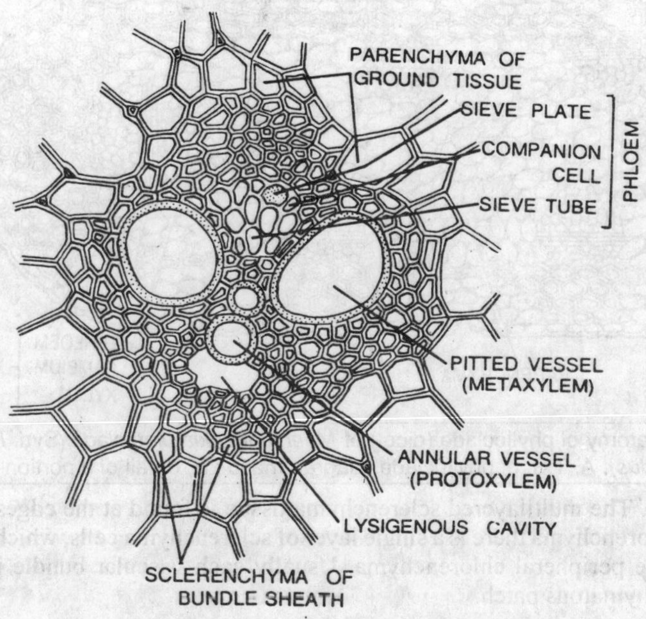

Fig. 11.21. Anatomy of monocot stem. A, L.S. of a vascular bundle of *Saccharum officinarum* (sugar cane); B, a vascular bundle.

2. Ground tissue system. Just beneath the epidermis a few layers of chlorenchyma cells occur. It is followed by a few layers of sclerenchyma cells. The rest of the ground tissue consists of thin walled rounded or oval parenchyma cells having sufficiently developed intercellular spaces among them.

3. Vascular bundles. The closed and collateral vascular bundles occur. The peripheral bundles are smaller whereas the inner bundles are bigger. The vascular bundles of outer series are lying embedded in sclerenchyma band. The bundles of inner series are also surrounded by sclerenchymatous bundle sheath like that of maize stem.

ANATOMY OF DICOT PHYLLOCLADE

17. T.S. of the phylloclade of Cocoloba (*Homalocladium platycladum-Muehlenbeckia platyclada* - dicot.)

Epidermis. The surfaces are bounded on both the sides by upper and lower epidermal layers. A thin cuticle covers the epidermis. The epidermis is interrupted by numerous stomata on both the surfaces. Distinct guard cells of the stomata and stomatal chambers are visible.

Chlorenchyma. Just beneath the epidermis there are few layers of chlorophyllous cells. The chlorophyllous cells are found only underneath the upper and lower epidermal layers. However, the chlorenchyma is not found at the edges of the phylloclade. The stomata are confined to chlorophyllous regions. There are well developed intercellular spaces, among these cells. This is assimilatory tissue.

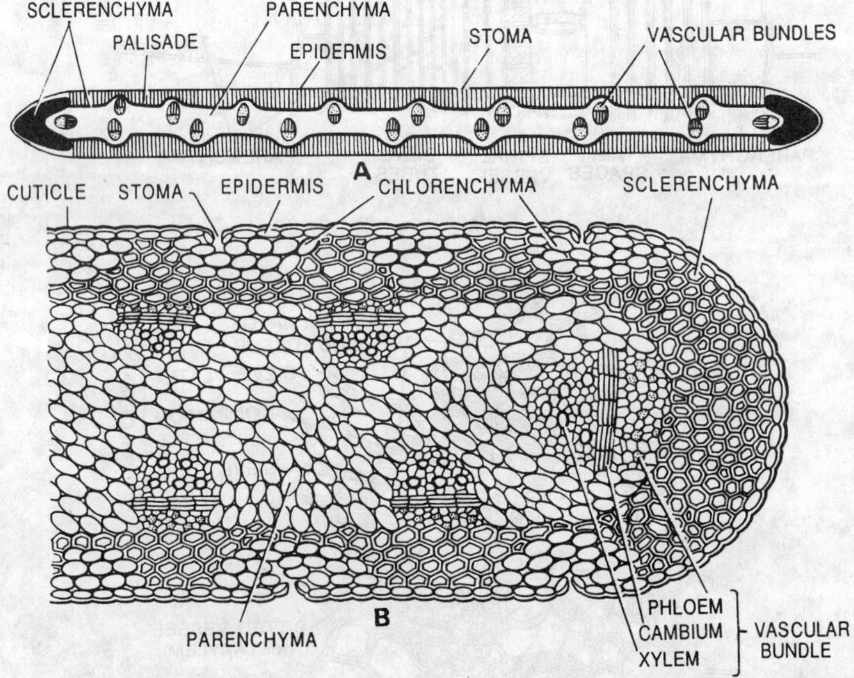

Fig. 11.22. Anatomy of phylloclade (dicot) of *Muehlenbeckia piatyclada (*Syn. *Homalocladium platycladus).* A, T.S. of phylloclade, diagrammatic ; B, detail of a portion of same.

Sclerenchyma. The multilayered sclerenchyma tissue is found at the edges of the phylloclade. Just beneath the chlorenchyma there is a single layer of sclerenchyma cells, which delimits the central parenchyma and the peripheral chlorenchyma. Usually each vascular bundle is capped by a well developed sclerenchymatous patch.

Vascular bundles. Around the central parenchyma the vascular bundles are found to be arranged in the peripheral region. The vascular bundles of the two corners are bigger in size than the remaining ones. Each vascular bundle is capped by a sclerenchymatous patch, and is composed of xylem, phloem and cambium. The xylem consists of metaxylem and protoxylem groups. The xylem parenchyma is also present. The phloem is composed of sieve tubes, companion cells and phloem parenchyma. In between xylem and phloem strands there lies the cambium. The cambium is confined to the bundle.

Parenchyma. The central region is occupied by parenchyma. It is composed of thin walled rounded or oval, living cells having well developed intercellular spaces. This is storage tissue.

ANATOMY OF MONOCOT PHYLLOCLADE

This is a modified stem which has taken the general appearance and functions of a leaf. *Ruscus* is monocotyledonous phylloclade having the anatomy of monocot stem with few alterations.

The phylloclade becomes flattened and leaf like, and possesses two surfaces, upper and lower. The most characteristic anatomical features of the phylloclade are as follows :

1. The stem becomes flattened and leaf-like.
2. The upper and lower epidermis are present (leaf character).
3. The bulges are present in the central region on both upper and lower surfaces (leaf character).
4. The chlorenchyma tissue is present (leaf character).
5. The stomata are present (leaf character).
6. The vascular system consists of amphivasal vascular bundles (stem character)
7. The phloem strands are not found towards lower surface (stem character).

18. T.S. of phylloclade of *Ruscus* (monocot).

1. Epidermis. The upper epidermis consists of a single row of radially elongated epidermal cells. At certain places the stomata are found. Sub-stomatal chambers and guard cells with chloroplasts

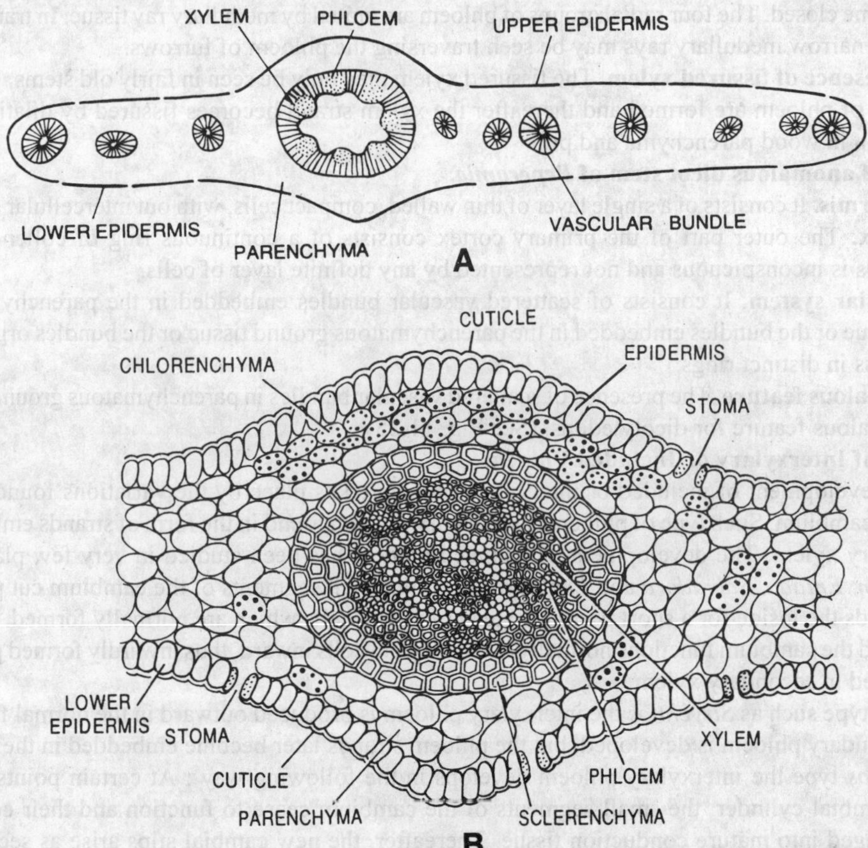

Fig. 11.23. Anatomy of phylloclade (monocot) of *Ruscus*. A, T.S. of phylloclade, diagrammatic ; B, detail of central part of same.

are well defined. The surface becomes somewhat bulged in the central region. The lower surace in the central region becomes somewhat angular, otherwise anatomy of epidermis is same as in upper epidermis.

2. Chlorenchyma. Immediately below the epidermis few layers of chlorenchyma are found having rounded or oval cells with chloroplasts and intercellular spaces among them. Parenchyma is also well developed.

3. Vascular system. It is well developed and represented by many amphivasal (phloem surrounded by xylem) vascular bundles. Phloem consists of only sieve tubes and companion cells.

ANATOMY OF THE STEMS OF ANOMALOUS ANGIOSPERMS

19. T.S. of *Bignonia* stem (dicot)

The most interesting anatomical feature in *Bignonia* of Bignoniaceae is the occurrence of anomalous secondary thickening. This type of anomalous thickening is as follows :

A. Presence of phloem wedges in the xylem. The young stems which exhibit this type of structure when mature are provided with a normal ring of vascular bundles. The vessels of the young stem are narrow in diameter. The wood formed in later stages contains wider vessels. As soon as this stage is reached four fur- rows at four equidistant points appear in the xylem, extending almost to the pith. The cambium is situated on the inside of the furrows and gives rise to the phloem in the furrows. However, the cambium is not found on the radial surface. The phloem increases in bulk and the tissues slide along the lateral surfaces of the furrows. Later on, because of the development the furrows again become closed. The four radial groups of phloem are united by medullary ray tissue. In transverse section the narrow medullary rays may be seen traversing the phloem of furrows.

B. Presence of fissured xylem. The fissured xylem may only be seen in fairly old stems. First of all wedges of phloem are formed and thereafter the xylem strand becomes fissured by dilation and cell division in wood parenchyma and pith.

20. T.S. of anomalous dicot stem of *Peperomia.*

Epidermis. It consists of a single layer of thin walled, compact cells, with out intercellular spaces.

Cortex. The outer part of the primary cortex consists of a continuous ring of collenchyma. Endodermis is inconspicuous and not represented by any definite layer of cells.

Vascular system. It consists of scattered vascular bundles embedded in the parenchymatons ground tissue or the bundles embedded in the parenchymatous ground tissue or the bundles organized more or less in distinct rings.

Anomalous feature. The presence of scattered vascular bundles in parenchymatous ground tissue is an anomalous feature for dicotyledons. (See Fig. 11.25)

Presence of Interxylary or Included Phloem

The development of included or interxylary phloem takes place by the variations found in the activity of cambium. Such type of phloem is secondary phloem found in the form of strands embedded in secondary xylem. The development of included phloem has been studied in very few plants. In *Combretum, Entada, Salvadora* and *Leptadenia* certain small segments of the cambium cut phloem cells towards the inside for a short period, instead of xylem cells which are normally formed. After a short period the cambium functions normally and cut xylem cells inward, thus inwardly formed phloem is embedded in secondary xylem.

In the type such as *Strychnos* the interxylary phloem is produced outward in the normal fashion, as the secondary phloem is developed, but the phloem strands later become embedded in the xylem. In *Strychnos* type the interxylary phloem develops in the following way : At certain points of the general cambial cylinder, the small segments of the cambium cease to function and their cells are being changed into mature conduction tissue. Thereafter, the new cambial stips arise as secondary meristems either in the phloem or in the pericycle. Later on these newly formed cambial strips unite

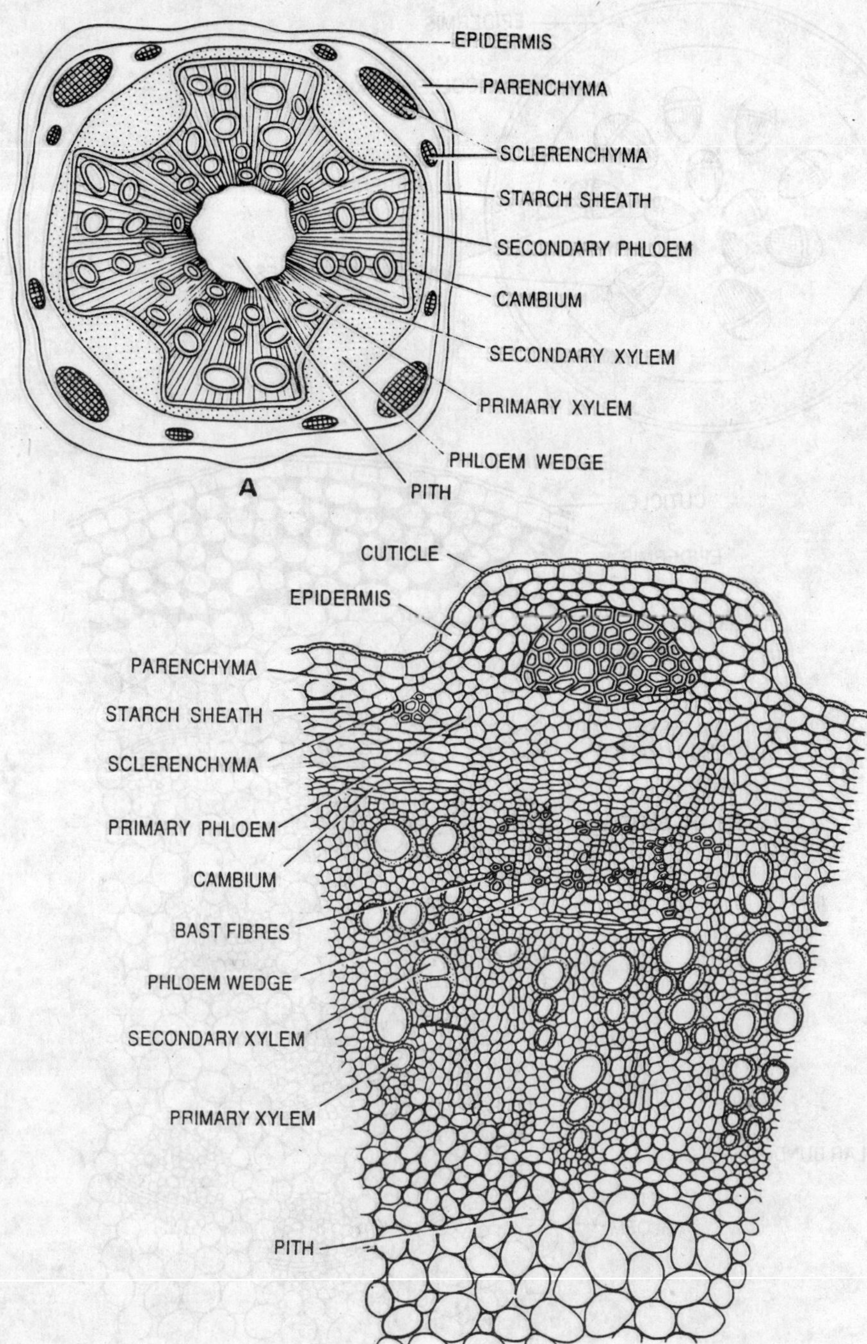

Fig. 11.24. The stem, anomalous structure. T.S. of stem of *Bignonia* (dicot). A, diagrammatic ; B, detailed structure.

with the edges of the segments of the general cambium. Thus a wavy cambium cylinder is formed. Soon after this camnial cylinder becomes stretched. The normal activity of the cambium is resumed and thus the phloem cells are engulfed in the secondary xylem. This process is repeated in other parts

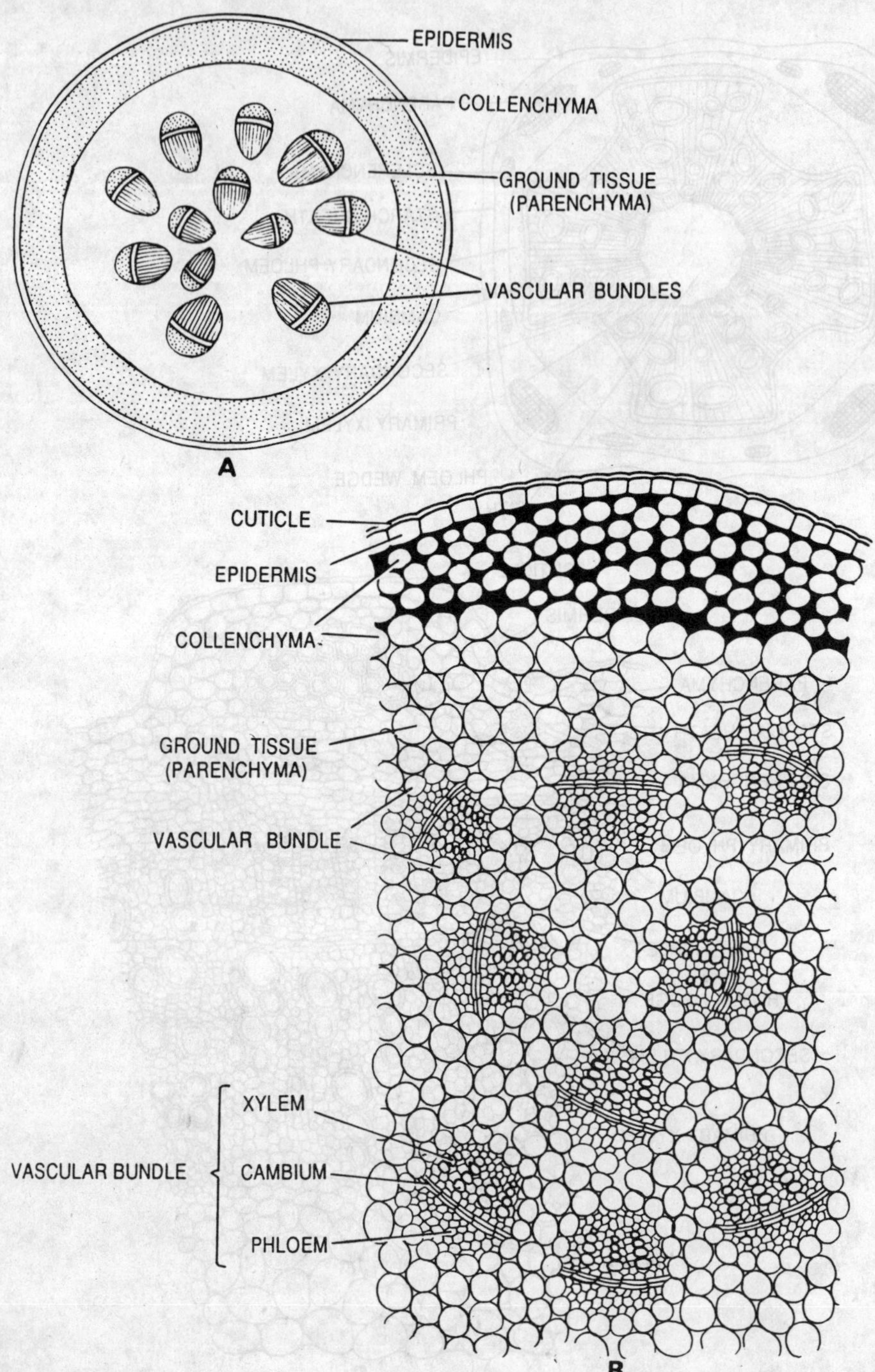

Fig. 11.25. Anatomy of anomalous stem. T.S. of *Peperomia* (dicot stem.) A, diagrammatic ; B, detail of a sector.

of the cambium and this way several phloem patches are engulfed in the secondary xylem. These are interxylary phloem patches which are secondary in origin. The interxylary phloem occurs in many families, *e.g.*, Nyctaginaceae, Onagraceae, Asclepiadaceae, Salvadoraceae, Amarantaceae, Loganiaceae and many others.

21. T.S. of anomalous dicot stem of *Leptadenia*.

Epidermis. The outermost layer epidermis consists of single row of compact cells, and is covered with a thick cuticle.

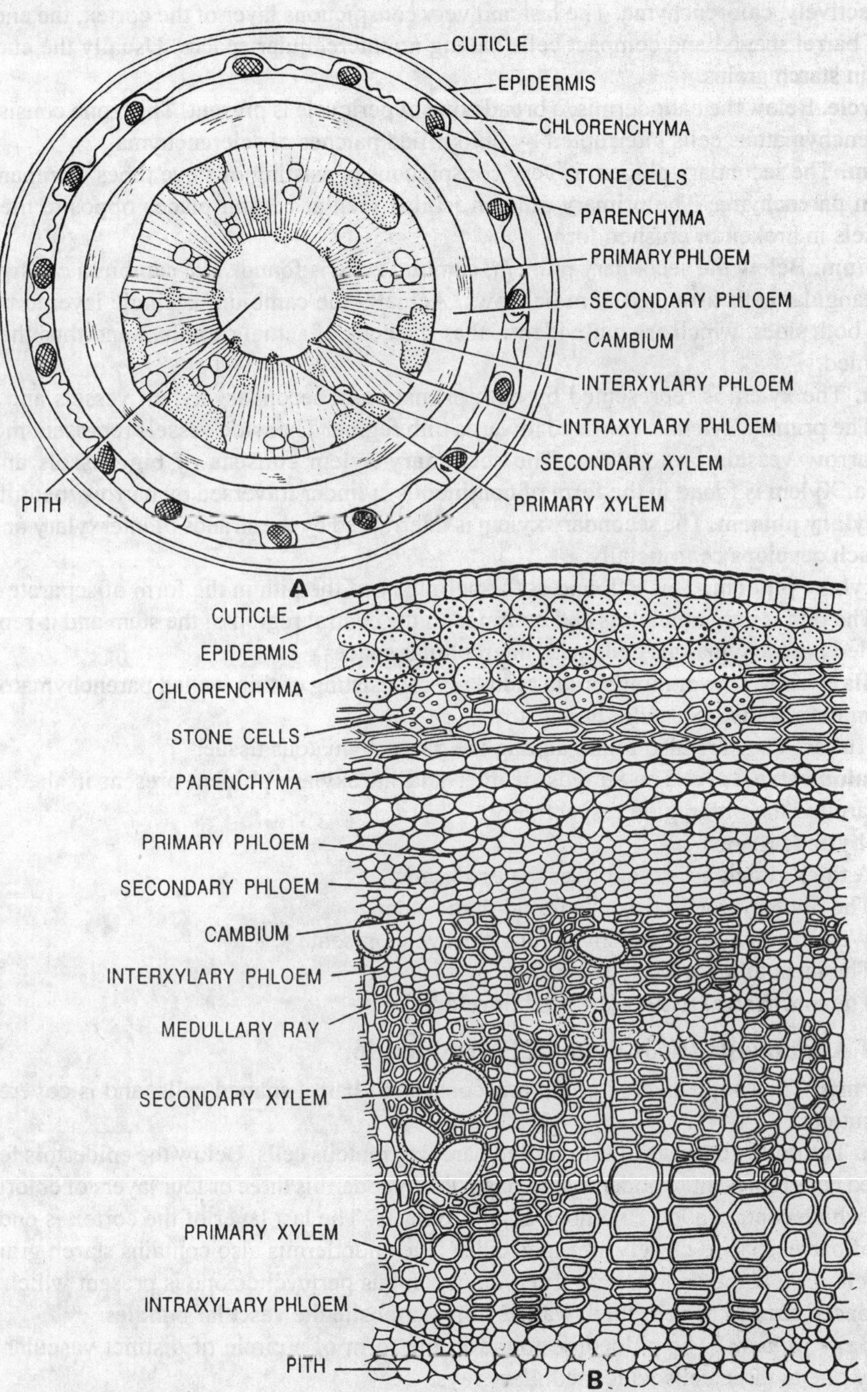

Fig. 11.26. Anatomy of anomalous stem. T.S. of *Leptadenia* (Asclepiadaceae - dicot) stem. A, diagrammatic ; B, detail of a sector.

Cortex. This region consists of hypodermis, chlorenchyma and endodermis. The hypodermis consists of one or two layers of thin walled parenchymatous cells. Below the hypodermis few layers of parenchymatous cells are present containing a large number of chloroplasts, these cells may be called collectively, chlorenchyma. The last and very conspicuous layer of the cortex, the endodermis consists of barrel shaped and compact cells having no intercellular spaces. Usually the endodermal cells contain starch grains.

Pericycle. Below the endodermis, a broad zone of pericycle is present. This zone consists of thin walled parenchymatous cells interrupted by unlignified patches of sclerenchyma.

Phloem. The secondary phloem is very conspicuous consisting of sieve tubes, companion cells and phloem parenchyma. The primary phloem is also seen at certain places opposite the primary xylem vessels in broken or crushed form.

Cambium. Below the secondary phloem, cambial zone is found. The cambium consists of thin walled rectangular cells arranged in radial rows. Actually the cambium is single layered but it cuts cells on its both sides, which are quite identical as the cells of actual cambium and thus the cambial zone is formed.

Xylem. The xylem is represented by both primary and secondary xylem vessels and vascular tracheids. The primary xylem is confined towards pith region. The wide vessels represent metaxylem whereas narrow vessels protoxylem. The secondary xylem consists of big vessels and xylem parenchyma. Xylem is found in the form of continuous cylinder traversed by narrow medullary rays.

Interxylary phloem. The secondary xylem is interrupted by the strands of interxylary or included phloem which develops centripetally.

Intraxylary phloem. This is found at the periphery of the pith in the form of separate strands.

Pith. The pith is very much less and confined to the central region of the stem and is represented by thin walled parenchymatous cells with intercellular spaces.

Medullary rays. Uni-or multiseriate radial rays consisting of thin walled parenchymatous tissue and found in between two vascular bundles.

Latex tubes. They are also found among the parenchymatous tissue.

Anomalous structure. The strands of inter-and intraxylary phloem present in the secondary xylem and around the pith region respectively.

Xerophytic features.

(*i*) A thick cuticle is present over the epidermis.
(*ii*) The photosynthetic tissue is found in the stem.
(*iii*) Well developed sclerenchymatous pericycle present.
(*iv*) The latex tubes are also found.
(*v*) The mechanical tissues, are well developed.

22. T.S. of Anomalous Dicot Stem of Salvadora sp.

Epidermis. The single layered epidermis consists of barrel shaped cells, and is covered with a very thick cuticle.

Cortex. The cortex consists of thin walled parenchymatous cells. Below the epidermis few layers of thin walled cells represent hypodermis. Beneath the hypodermis three or four layers of chlorenchyma are present which contain a large number of chloroplasts. The last layer of the cortex is endodermis consisting of barrel shaped closely arranged cells. The endodermis also contains starch grains.

Pericycle. Below the endodermis a very conspicuous pericyclic zone is present which consists of widely spaced strands of very thick walled fibres opposite the vascular bundles.

Secondary phloem. The phloem is found in the form of a circle of distinct vascular bundles separated by one to three cells wide medullary rays.

Xylem. Both primary and secondary xylem strands are quite conspicuous. The primary xylem may be easily recognized by the presence of wide vessels of metaxylem and narrow vessels of protoxylem arranged in radial rows. The xylem is found in the form of a complete circle of vascular bundles separated by medullary rays. The secondary xylem is represented by xylem parenchyma and wide vessels.

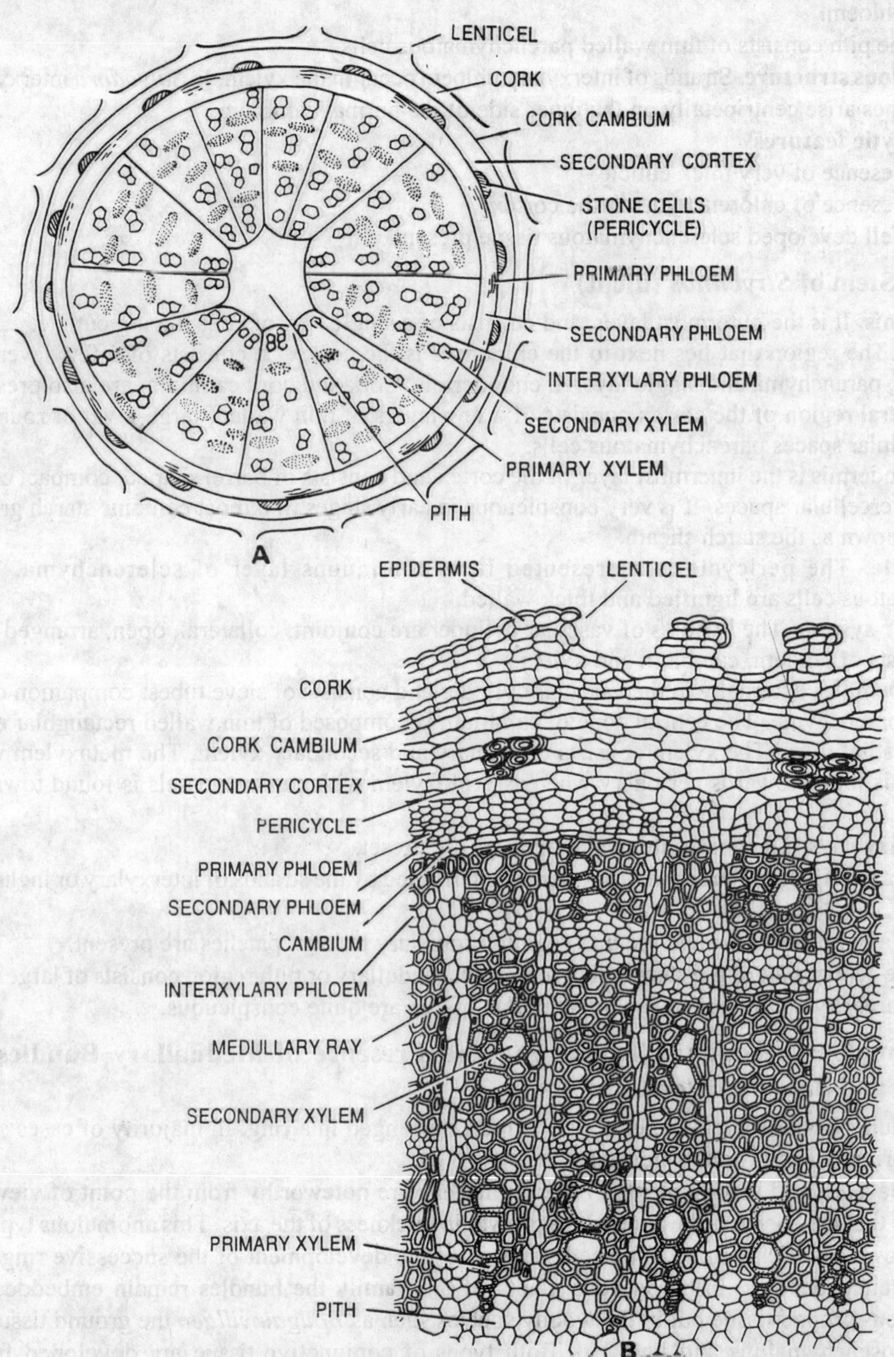

Fig. 11.27. Anatomy of anomalous stem. T.S. of *Salvadora* (Salvadoraceae dicot) stem. Detail of a sector.

Cambium. Both xylem and phloem are interrupted by a cambial zone. The cells of cambium strip are usually rectangular and found in radial rows.

Interxylary phloem. The secondary xylem in interrupted by the presence of the strands of interxylary phloem.

Pith. The pith consists of thin walled parenchymatous cells.

Anomalous structure. Strands of interxylary phloem occur in the xylem. In *Salvadora* interxylary phloem patches arise centripetally on the inner side of the normal cambium.

Xerophytic features.

(*i*) Presence of very thick cuticle.

(*ii*) Presence of chlorenchyma in the cortex.

(*iii*) Well developed sclerenchymatous tissue present.

23. T.S. of Stem of *Strychnos* (dicot)

Epidermis. It is the outermost layer, and consists of a single row of cells having cuticle.

Cortex. The region that lies next to the epidermis is the cortex. It consists of a few layers of collenchyma, parenchyma and single layered endodermis. Cork and cork cambium are also present.

The central region of the cortex consists of a few layers of thin walled, large, oval or rounded with intercellular spaces parenchymatous cells.

The endodermis is the innermost layer of the cortex and consists of barrel shaped, compact cells, having no intercellular spaces. It is very conspicuous in early stages. It almost contains starch grains and is also known as the starch sheath.

Pericycle. The pericycle is represented by a continuous layer of sclerenchyma. The sclerenchymatous cells are lignified and thick walled.

Vascular system. The bundles of vascular cylinder are conjoint, collateral, open, arranged in a ring. It consists of phloem, cambium and xylem.

The phloem lies externally in the vascular cylinder and consists of sieve tubes, companion cells and phloem parenchyma. The central zone of cambium is composed of thin walled rectangular cells arranged in radial rows. The xylem consists of primary and secondary xylem. The metaxylem with wide vessels is found towards periphery whereas protoxylem with narrow vessels is found towards pith region.

Medullary rays. The uniseriate medullary rays are preset.

Interxylary phloem. The secondary xylem is interrupted by the strands of interxylary or included phloem.

Intraxylary phloem. Around the pith region intraxylary phloem patches are present.

Pith. The central part of the stem which represents medullary or pith region consists of large thin walled and parenchymatous cells. The intercellular spaces are quite conspicuous.

24.25. Anomalous Secondary Thickening and Presence of Meduallary-Bundles in *Boerhaavia* and *Bougainvillaea.*

The medullary bundles may be either scattered or arranged in a ring. In majority of cases such bundles are primary and originate normally.

The herbaceous and woody plants of Nyctaginaceae are noteworthy from the point of view of their anatomy that they possess the anomalous growth in thickness of the axis. This anomalous type of secondary growth in thickness takes place by means of the development of the successive rings of collateral vascular bundles. In herbaceous plants of this family the bundles remain embedded in parenchymatous ground tissue but in the woody species such as *Bougainvillaea* the ground tissue is somewhat prosenchymatous and lignified. Both types of conjunctive tissue are developed from successive cambia. In the woody species there is no clear differentiation between the xylem and the conjunctive-tissue and therefore, sometimes in transverse sections of the axis the phloem is seen in the form of islands. In certain other cases the strips resembling medullary rays are also seen in the conjunctive-tissue.

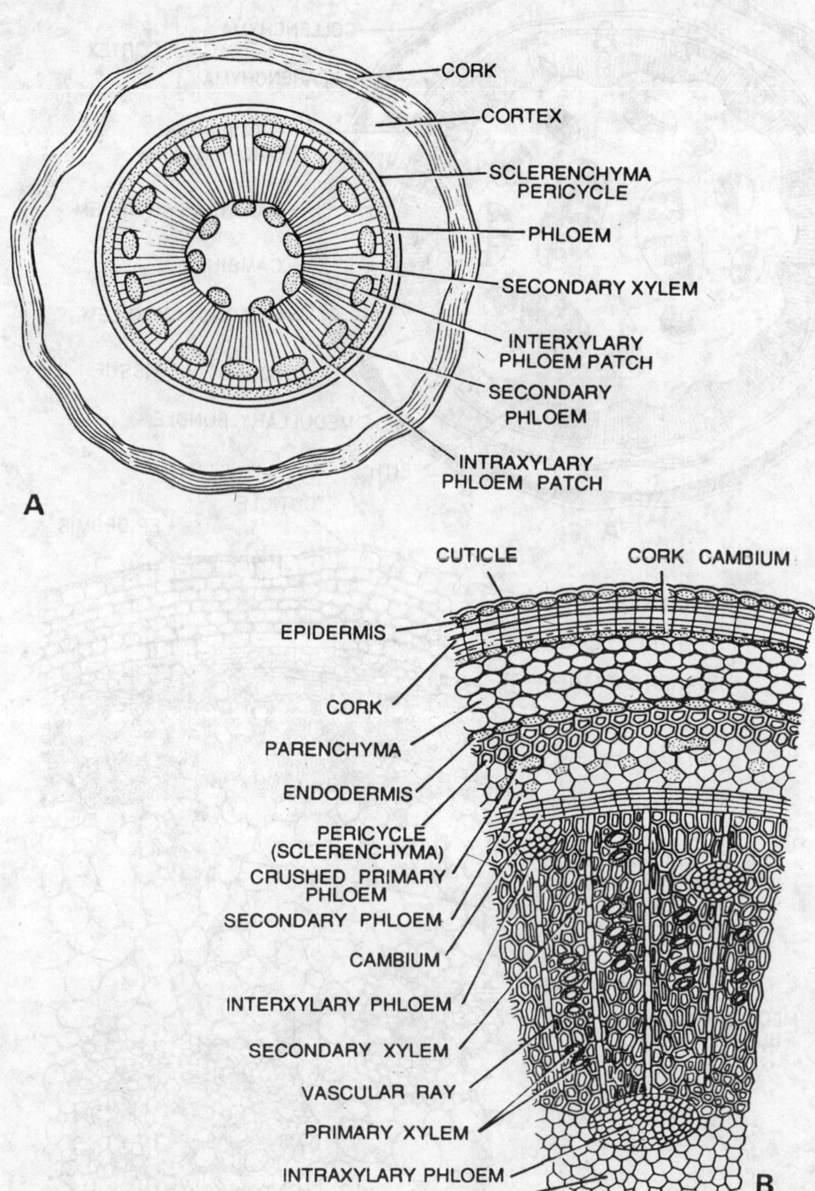

Fig. 11.28. Anatomy of anomalous stem of *Strychnos* (dicot), A, T.S. of stem, diagrammatic ; B, T.S. of stem, detail of sector.

In *Boerhaavia*, *Bougainvillaea* and *Mirabilis* the anomalous secondary thickening occurs in the form of succession of rings of vascular bundles. In the members of family Nyctaginaceae the secondary vascular bundles remain embedded in parenchymatous, prosenchymatous or lignified conjunctive tissue, as the case may be. In *Bougainvillaea glabra* a robust herbaceous or slightly woody species the inner bundles remain embedded in parenchyma and the outer bundles in the prosenchymatous

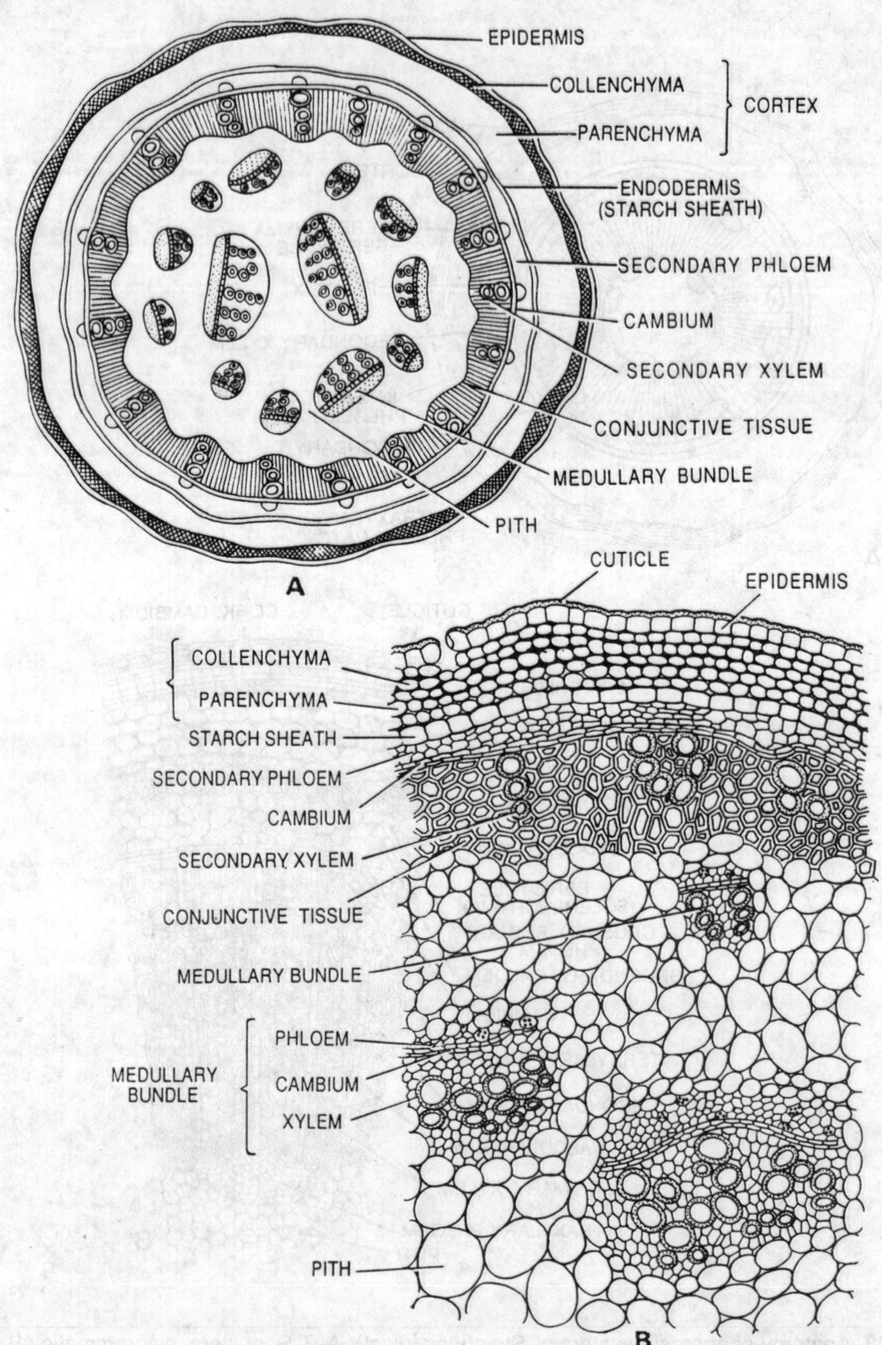

Fig. 11.29. The stem-anomalous structure. A, T.S. stem-diagrammatic ; B, T.S. of a sector of stem of *Boerhaavia diffusa* showing periderm, anomalous secondary growth, thick-walled conjunctive tissue, and medullary bundles.

gound tissue. Sometimes, in certain species the narrow radial strips resembling normal medullary rays are also seen traversing the conjunctive tissue. In *Beorhaavia* thin walled lignified groups of parenchyma are associated with the phloem ; the phloem groups and adjoining ground parenchyma occasionally appear as concentric annular or band shaped strips of tissue. In *Bougainvillaea, Mirabilis,* etc., the innermost part of the conjunctive tissue, formed by the secondary meristem resembles true pith and thus causes the innermost secondary bundles to appear as if they are medullary in origin. The development of vascular system in *Boerhaavia diffusa* is as follows :

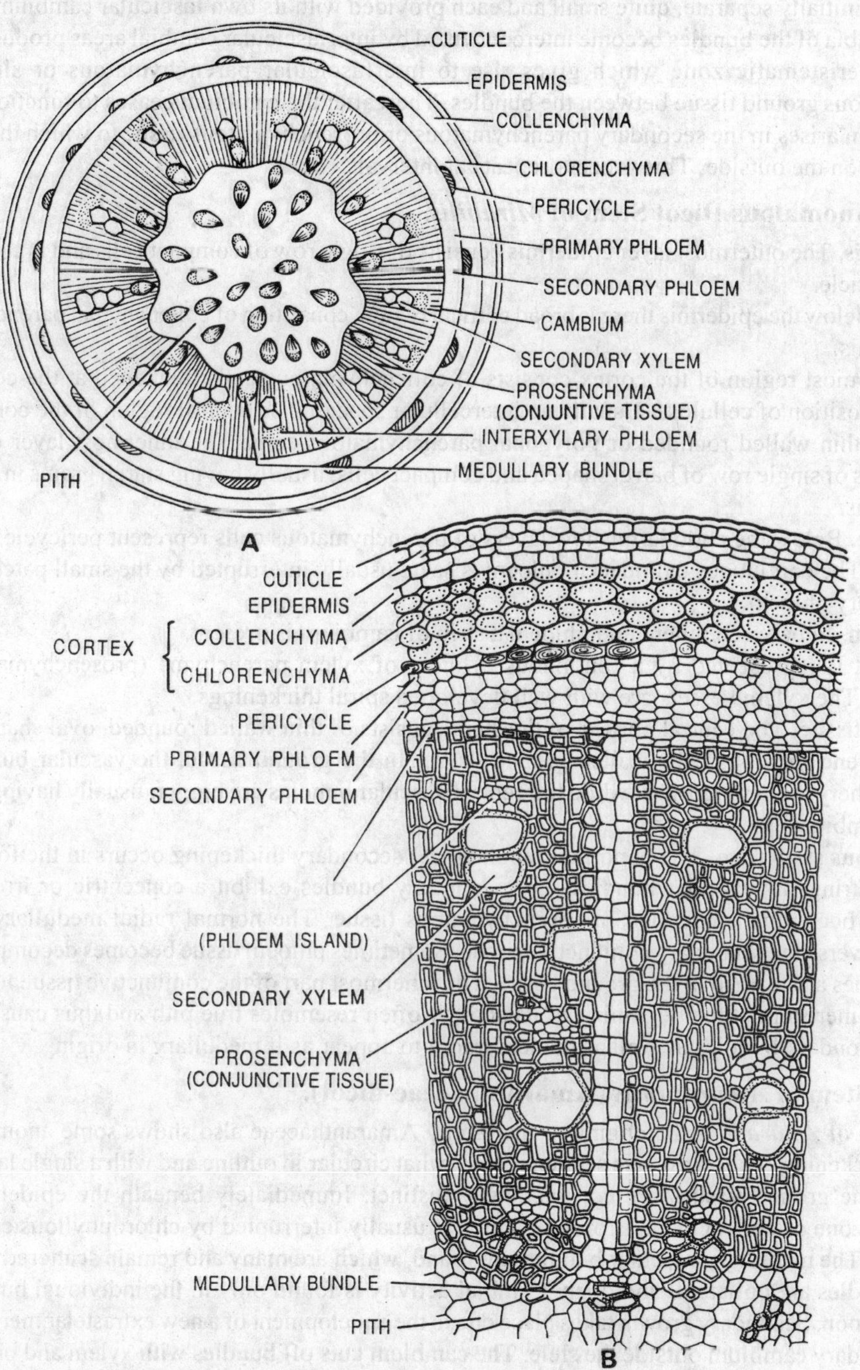

Fig. 11.30. Anatomy of anomalous stem. T.S. of *Bougainvillaea* (Nyctaginaceae - dicot). A, diagrammatic; B, detail of a sector.

The transverse sections through the young stem of *Boerhaavia diffusa* show two medullary bundles, a middle ring of 6 to 14 bundles and another ring of 15 to 20 or more small bundles. The bundles of the middle ring increase in thickness to a limited extent by a fascicular cambium. The bundles of the outer ring are initially separate, quite small and each provided with its own fascicular cambium. The fascicular cambia of the bundles become interconnected by interfascicular cambial areas producing a cylindrical meristematic zone which gives rise to interfascicular parenchymatous or slightly prosenchymatous ground tissue between the bundles. Thereafter the cambium ceases to function and a new meristem arises in the secondary parenchymatous or prosenchymatous tissue to which the first has given rise on the outside. This process repeats at intervals.

26. T.S. of Anomalous Dicot Stem of *Mirabilis*.

Epidermis. The outermost layer epidermis consists of single row of compact cells and is covered with a thin cuticle.

Cortex. Below the epidermis there is broad cortical region, consisting of collenchyma, parenchyma and endodermis.

The outermost region of the cortex consists of collenchymatous cells thickened at the corners due to the deposition of cellulose. Usually no intercellular spaces. The central region of the cortex is composed of thin walled rounded or polygonal parenchymatous cells. The innermost layer of the cortex consists of single row of barrel shaped and compact cells, usually having starch grains in them, the endodermis.

Pericycle. Below the endodermis few layers of parenchymatous cells represent pericycle.

Phloem. The continuous cylinder of phloem is seen, usually interrupted by the small patches of crushed primary phloem.

Cambium. In between xylem and phloem a strip of cambium is present.

Xylem. It is represented by a continuous cylinder of xylem parenchyma (prosenchyma) and xylem vessel. The xylem vessels are with well developed spiral thickenings.

Ground tissue. The central portion of the stem consists of thin walled rounded, oval shaped of polygonal parenchymatous cells, called ground tissue. In the ground tissue, the vascular bundles, towards periphery are small in size, while the central vascular bundles are bigger, usually having well developed cambium.

Anomalous structure. The abnormal (anomalous) secondary thickening occurs in the form of succession of rings of vascular bundles. The secondary bundles exhibit a concentric or irregular arrangement, becoming embedded in parenchymatous tissue. The normal radial medullary rays sometimes traverse the secondary conjunctive tissue. Sometimes phloem tissue becomes decomposed, and thus cavities are formed in the ground tissue. The innermost part of the conjunctive tissue formed by secondary meristem at the beginning of its activity often resembles true pith and thus causes the innermost secondary bundles as well as the leaf traces to appear as if medullary in origin.

27. T.S. of Stem of *Amaranthus* (Amaranthaceae-dicot).

The stem of *Amaranthus* belonging to the family Amaranthaceae also shows some anomalous secondary thickening. The transverse section is somewhat circular in outline and with a single layered epidermis. The ground tissues are conspicuously distinct. Immediately beneath the epidermis a multilayered zone of collenchyma is present which is usually interrupted by chlorophyllous cells at many places. The medullary vascular bundles are found, which are many and remain scattered in the pith. The bundles are collateral and open. Cambial activity is found only in the individual bundles, and it ceases soon. Secondary growth takes place due to the development of a new extrastelar meristem, *i.e.*, the secondary cambium outside the stele. The cambium cuts off bundles with xylem and phloem on the inner side. The secondary bundles remain embedded in the conjunctive tissue found around the region.

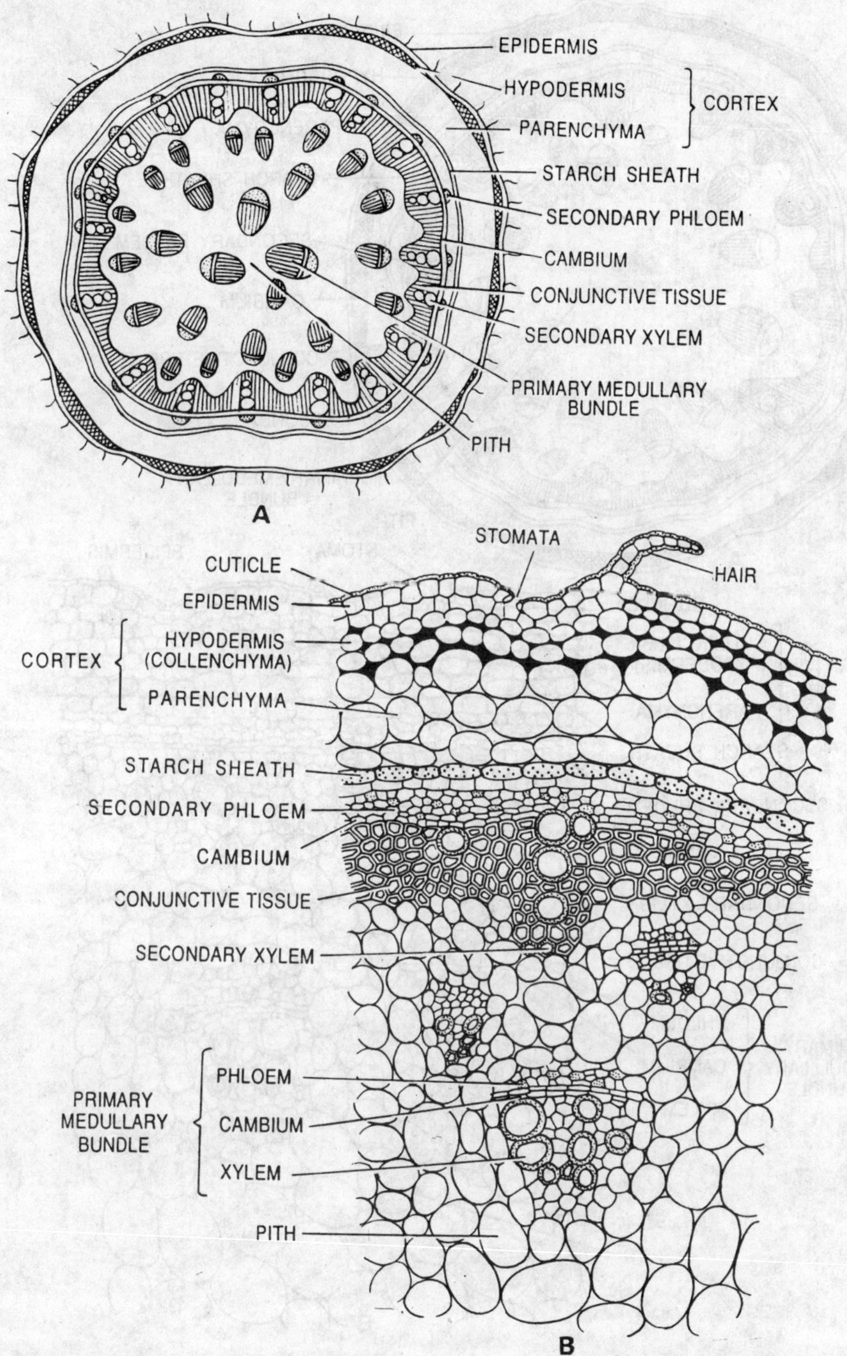

Fig. 11.31. Anatomy of anomalous stem of *Mirabilis* (Nyctaginaceae - dicot). A. T.S. of stem, diagrammatic ; B, detail of a sector of same.

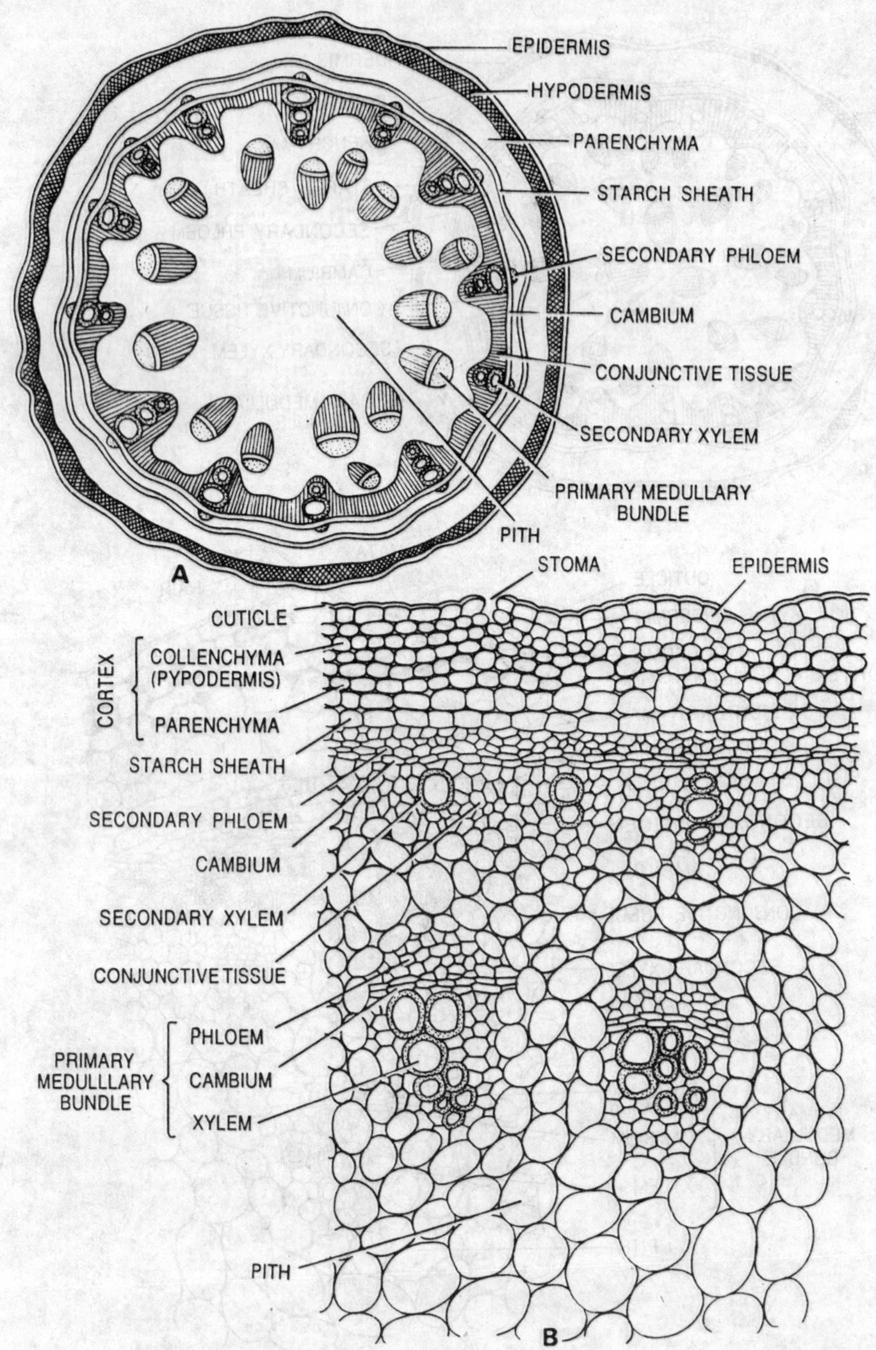

Fig. 11.32. Anatomy of anomalous stem of *Amaranthus* (dicot). A, T.S. of stem, diagrammatic ; B, detail of a sector of same.

28. T.S. of Stem of *Nyctanthes arbortristis* (dicot).

In the stem of *Nyctanthes,* apart from normal vascular bundles which occur in a ring in the central region, there are four inversely oriented cortical bundles found at the ridges of the stem. These cortical bundles are also collateral and open. (Fig. 11.33).

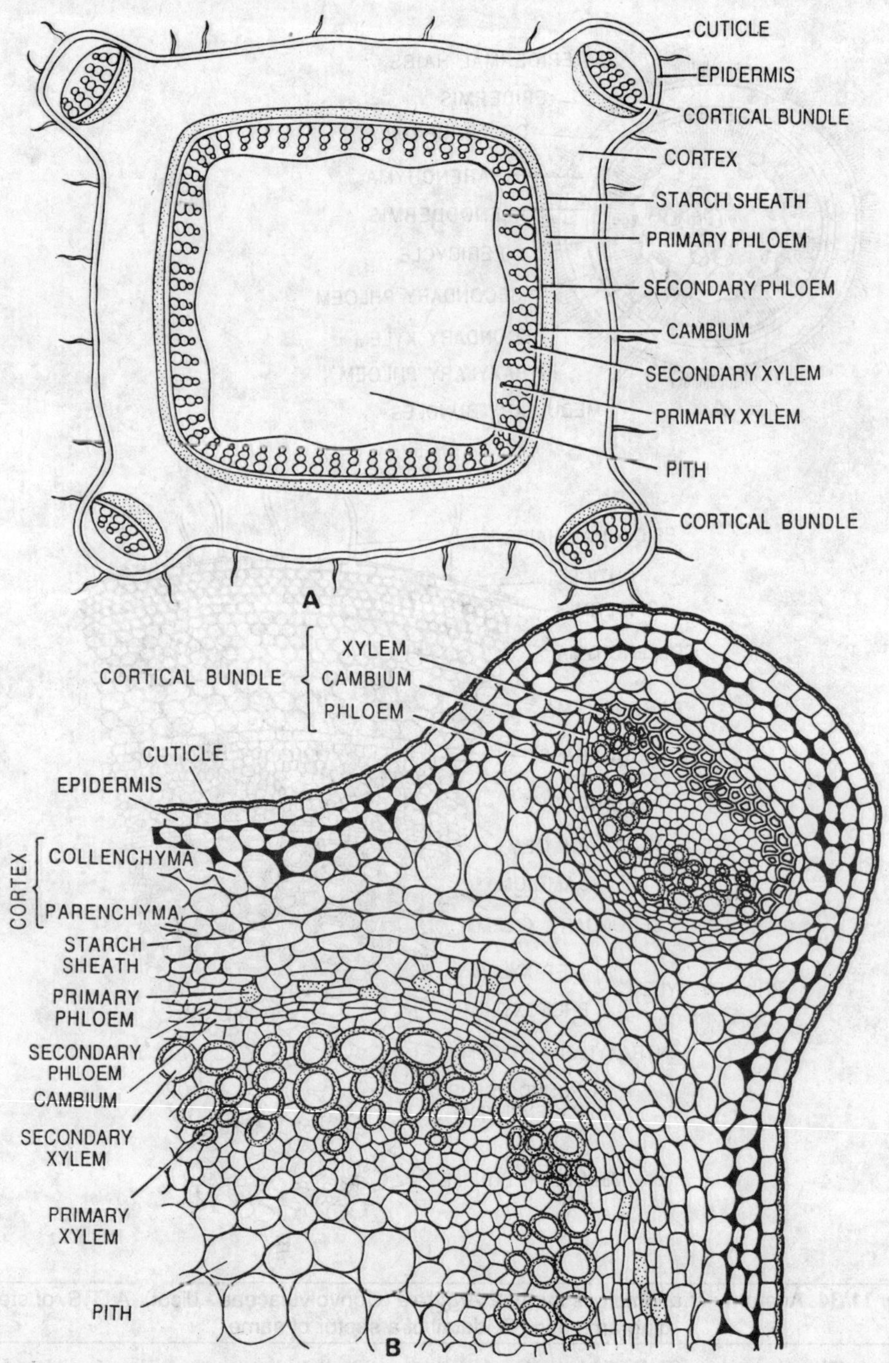

Fig. 11.33. Anatomy of anomalous stem. A, T.S. of *Nyctanthes arbortrists* (Oleaceae-dicot) stem, diagrammatic ; B, T.S. of a sector of same, detail.

29. T.S. of Stem of *Argyreia* (Convolvulaceae - dicot)

Epidermis. The epidermis consists of a single row of compact cells, the cuticle extends over it and many epidermal cells give rise to multicellular epidermal hairs. The hairs possess short stalk cells.

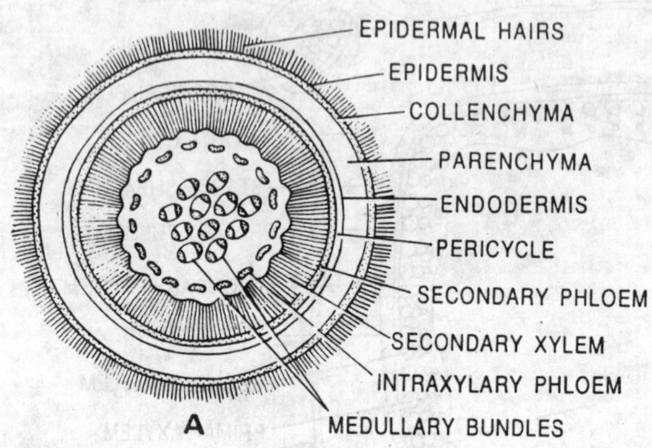

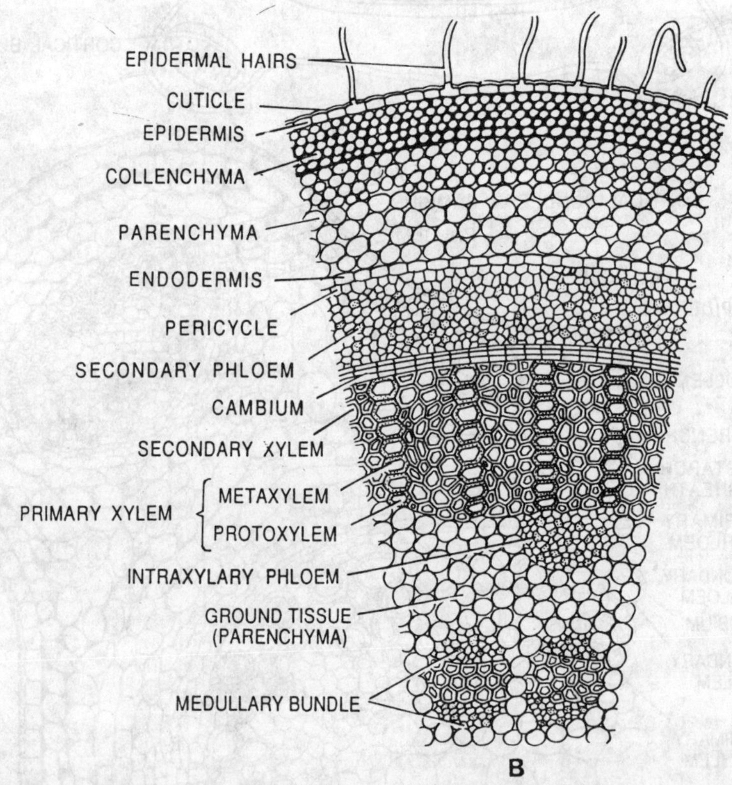

Fig. 11.34. Anatomy of anomalous stem of *Argyreia* (Convolvulaceae - dicot). A, T.S. of stem, diagrammatic ; B, detail of a sector of same.

Cortex. The cortex is sufficiently broad and consists of, collenchyma, parenchyma and endodermis. The outer region of cortex consists of a few layers of collenchymatous cells having deposition of cellulose at their corners, usually no intercellular spaces. Below the collenchyma a multilayered parenchymatous region having thin walled, oval or rounded cells with intercellular spaces is present. The last wavy layer of the cortex is endodermis which consists of barrel-shaped compact cells, containing starch grains and having no intercellular spaces.

Pericycle. It consists of parenchyma. It is single layered and inconspicuous.

Vascular system. The vascular bundles are conjoint, collateral, open and arranged in a ring. The vascular cylinder consists of phloem, cambium and xylem. The phloem lies externally the vascular cylinder and consists of sieve tubes, companion cells and phloem parenchyma. In between phloem and xylem a cambial strip is found having living rectangular cells arranged in radial rows. The xylem lies internally with protoxylem towards centre and metaxylem towards periphery. The metaxylem consists of bigger vessels whereas protoxylem of narrow vessels. Protoxylem of annular, spiral and scalariform vessels and metaxylem of reticular and pitted vessels. Interxylary phloem patches are present. Several medullary bundles are present in the pith region.

Vascular Bundles arranged in a Ring in Monocots.

In *Tamus communis (*a monocot), the vascular bundles are arranged in a ring around large pith. The vascular bundles are also arranged in ring in hollow monocots *e.g., Triticum.*

30. T.S.of anomalous Monocot Stem of *Tamus.*

Epidermis. It consists of a single layer of compact, barrel shaped cells having no in tercellular spaces. A thin cuticle may be also found.

Cortex. Of course, the presence of cortex is in abnormal character in monocot stem. The cortex is well developed and consists of thin walled rounded or oval parenchymatous cells having well defined intercellular spaces among them. The innermost layer of the cortex is endodermis. It is very conspicuous and consists of barrel shaped cells.

Pericycle. Immediately beneath the endodermis multilayered sclerenchymatous pericycle is found. This constitutes a complete cylinder of sclerenchyma around the stem.

Ground tissue. It is represented by large, thin walled, rounded or oval parenchymatous cells having intercellular spaces.

Vascular system. It consists of many vascular bundles arranged in a ring (anomalous feature). Usually they are arranged in two rings (outer and inner). Each vascular bundle consists of xylem and phloem. The bigger vessels (pitted) towards outside constitute metaxylem whereas narrower vessels (annular and spiral) towards centre form protoxylem. Phloem consists exclusively of sieve tubes and companion cells. Phloem parenchyma is altogether absent in monocot stem. Secondary growth or cambium formation never occurs.

Pith. The central region is represented by thin walled, rounded, parenchymatous cells with sufficiently developed intercellular spaces, may be called pith.

Anomalous features.

(*i*) Well developed cortex and conspicuous endodermis are present.
(*ii*) The sclerenchymatous pericycle is present.
(*iii*) The vascular bundles are arranged in a ring.
(*iv*) The central region is represented by pith.

Normal Characters of Monocot Stem :

(*i*) The vascular bundles are many.
(*ii*) The xylem vessels are rounded.
(*iii*) Phloem consists exclusively of sieve tubes and companion cells ; no phloem parenchyma.
(*iv*) Ground tissue is present.
(*v*) No cambium formation.

Cambium Formationin in Monocots :

Secondary growth occurs in some monocotyledons, *e.g., Yucca, Dracaena*, etc.

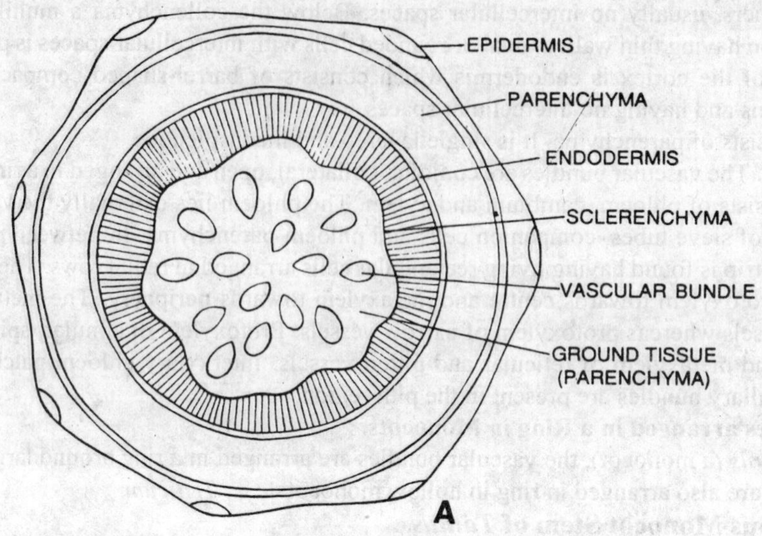

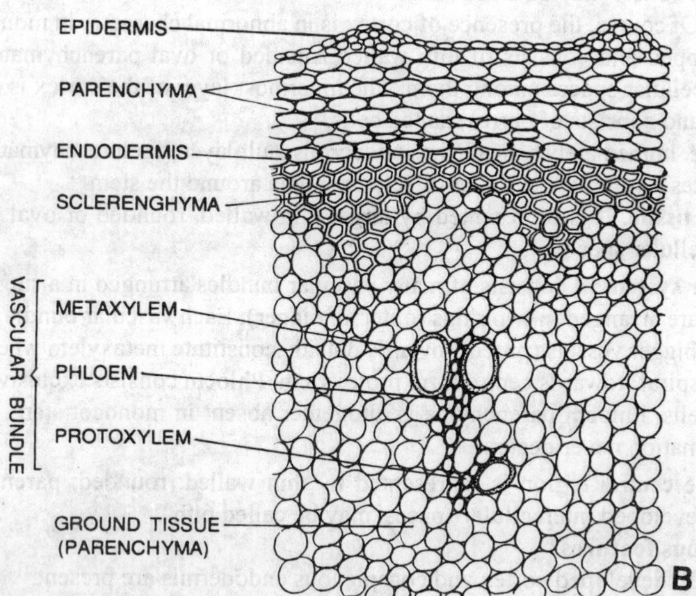

Fig. 11.35. Anatomy of anomalous stem. T.S. of *Tamus communis* (monocot) stem. A, diagrammatic ; B, detail of a sector.

31. T.S. of Anomalous Monocot Stem of *Dracaena.*

(*i*) The outermost layer, epidermis is cutinized (cuticle well developed) single layered and with compact barrel shaped cells. The lenticels are also found on the epidermis.

(*ii*) Beneath the epidermis, the cork cambium arises which gives rise to the cork.

(*iii*) Below the cork cambium, well developed, parenchymatous secondary cortex is present.

Anomalous structure. *Dracaena* possesses a form of anomalous secondary thickening. In the primary condition the stem shows the scattered arrangement of closed, common bundles. But later on a secondary meristem develops in the parenchymatous region outside the outermost vascular bundles. This newly formed cambium cuts cells both externally and internally. The tissue developed on the inner side of the cambium differentiates into vascular bundles are separated by lignified tissue, sometimes these tissues remain unlignified and thin-walled. The cells formed on the outer side of the cambium produce parenchymatous secondary cortex.

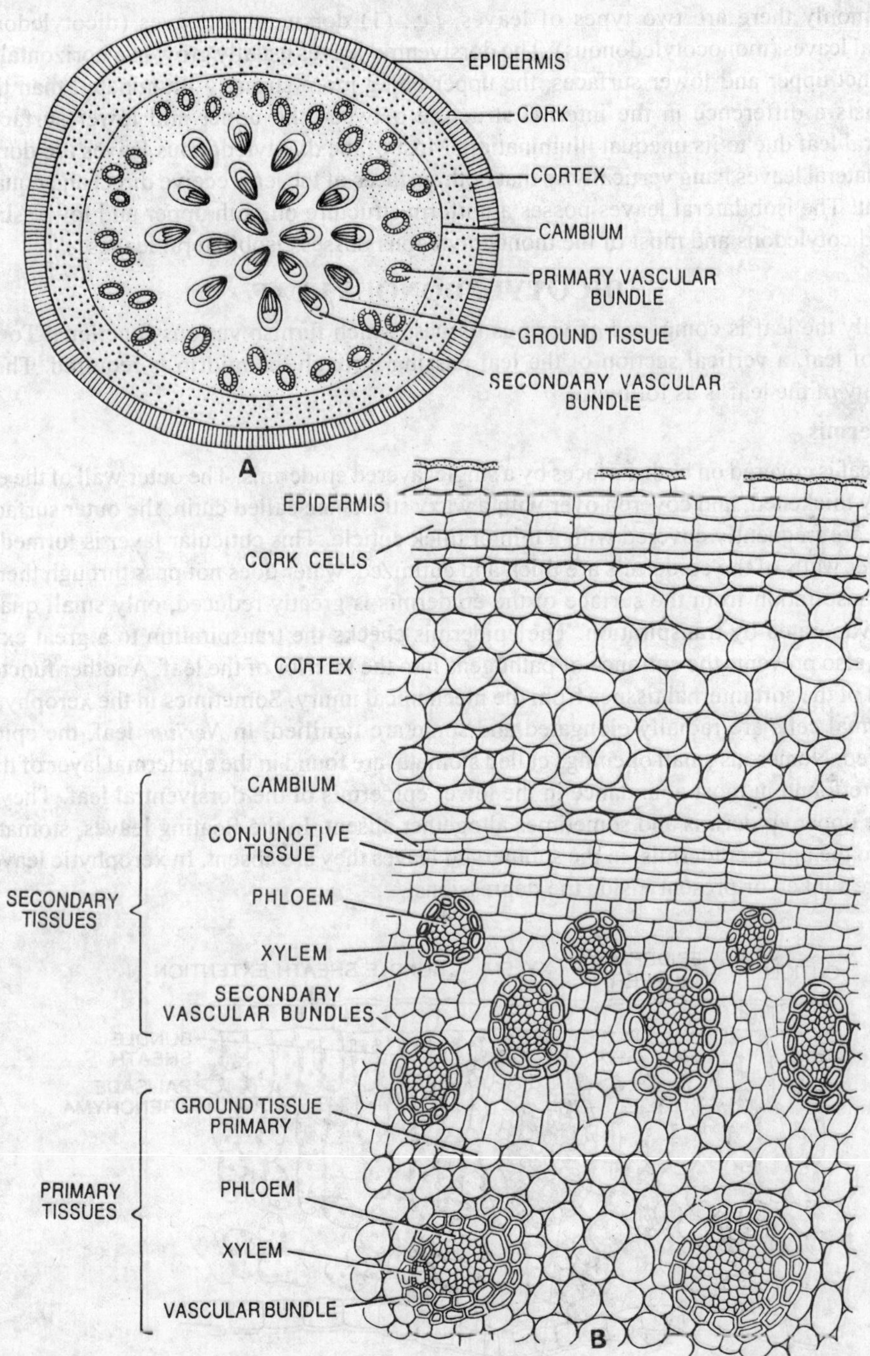

Fig. 11.36. Anatomy of anomalous stem. T.S. of *Dracaena* (monocot) stem. A, diagrammatic ; B, detail of a sector.

The secondary bundles are concentric. A small amount of phloem surrounded by xylem (amphivasal) in each bundle. The bundles are scattered throughout in ground tissue.

ANATOMY OF LEAF AND PHYLLODE

Commonly there are two types of leaves, *i.e.*, (1) dorsiventral leaves (dicotyledonous) (2) isobilateral leaves (monocotyledonous). The dorsiventral leaves usually grow in a horizontal direction with distinct upper and lower surfaces, the upper being more strongly illuminated than the lower. There exists a difference in the internal structure between the upper and lower surfaces of the dorsiventral leaf due to its unequal illumination. Most of the dicotyledonous leaves are dorsiventral. The isobilateral leaves hang vertically so that both surfaces of the leaf receive direct and equal amount of sunlight. The isobilateral leaves posses a uniform structure on both upper and lower surfaces. A very few dicotyledons and most of the monocotyledons possess isobilateral leaves.

DICOTYLEDONOUS LEAF

Usually the leaf is composed of various tissues, which furnish various functions. To study the anatomy of leaf, a vertical section of the leaf passing through the midrib is required. The internal morphology of the leaf is as follows.

Epidermis

The leaf is covered on both surfaces by a single layered epidermis. The outer wall of the epidermis are usually thickened, and covered over with a waxy substance called cutin, the outer surfaces of the epidermis are frequently covered with a thin or thick cuticle. This cuticular layer is formed of cutin. As the outer walls of the epidermis are thick and cutinized, water does not pass through them rapidly and the transpiration from the surface of the epidermis is greatly reduced, only small quantities of water is evaporated by transpiration. The epidermis checks the transpiration to a great extent. The epidermis also prevents the entrance of pathogens into the interior of the leaf. Another function is the protection of the soft internal tissues from the mechanical injury. Sometimes in the xerophytic leaves the epidermal cells are radially elongated and some are lignified. In *Nerium* leaf, the epidermis is multilayered. Numerous small openings called stomata, are found in the epidermal layer of the leaves. Stomata are found in most abundance in the lower epidermis of the dorsiventral leaf. They are very few on the upper epidermis and sometimes altogether absent. In the floating leaves, stomata remain confined to the upper epidermis; in the submerged leaves they are absent. In xerophytic leaves either, stomata are sunken or present inside the depressions.

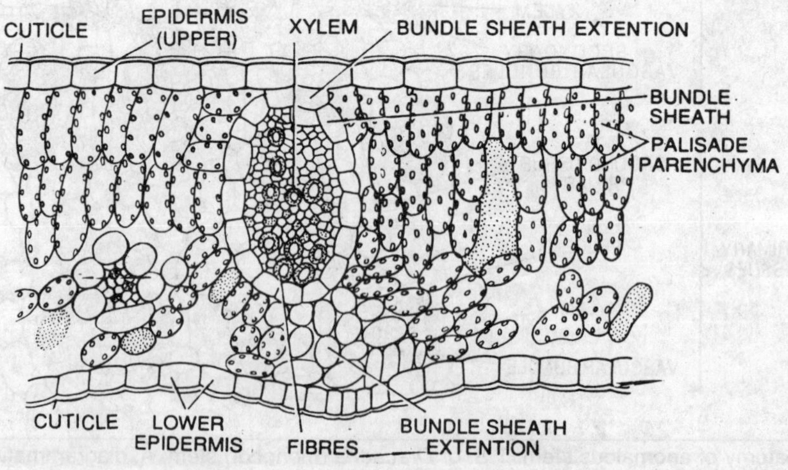

Fig. 11.37. Anatomy of bifacial leaf. T.S. of pear leaf (dicot). Detail of a portion.

Each stoma is surrounded by two semilunar guard cells. The guard cells are living and contain chloroplasts, they regulate opening and closing of stomata. Sometimes the guard cells are surrounded by two or more **accessory cells** in addition to epidermal cells. The stomata are found in scattered condition.

Usually the stomata are used for interchange of gases between the plant and the atmosphere. To facilitate the diffusion of gases in proper manner, each stoma opens internally into a respiratory cavity or substomatal chamber. The evaporation also takes place through stomata and the plants get rid of the surplus water.

Mesophyll Tissue

The tissue of the leaf that lies between the upper and lower epidermis and between veins consists of typically thin walled parenchyma known as **mesophyll.** This tissue forms the major portion of the inner of leaf. Commonly the cells of mesophyll are of two types. The palisade parenchyma, or palisade tissue, and the spongy parenchyma tissues. The mesophyll tissue always contain chloroplasts in them.

The palisade parenchyma is generally composed of elongated and more or less cylindrical cells which are close together with their long axis of the cells perpendicular to the epidermis. In transverse sections the cells appear to be arranged quite compact, are really separate from each other having intercellular spaces among them. The palisade tissue may consist of a single or more layers. These cells are arranged near to the upper surface of the leaf, where they receive sunlight and facilitate to carry the function of photosynthesis. Sometimes the leaves hang vertically, (*e.g. Eucalyptus*) so that both surfaces of the leaf are equally illuminated. In such leaves the palisade parenchyma may occur on both sides. The compactness of the palisade parenchyma depends upon light intensity. The leaves which receive direct sunlight develop more compact parenchyma in comparison to the leaves which develop in shady places.

The lower portion of the mesophyll, in the leaf is known as spongy parenchyma or spongy tissue. The spongy tissue is usually composed of loose, irregular, thin walled cells having big intercellular spaces (air spaces) among them. The cells of spongy parenchyma also contain chloroplasts and carry on photosynthesis. But in comparison to palisade parenchyma less chloroplasts are developed. Due to the presence of large air spaces in the spongy tissue they are more adaptable to the exchange of gases between the cells and the atmosphere.

Both spongy and palisade parenchyma contain discoid chloroplasts arranged in parallel rows in the cells. As the chloroplasts are more dense in the palisade tissue than the spongy tissue the upper surface of the leaf appears to be deeper green than the lower surface.

Mechanical Spport in the Leaf

The functions of the midrib and the lateral veins are to give mechanical support in leaf. Usually the midrib consists of the following tissues, *i.e.*, collenchyma, sclerenchyma, turgid parenchyma and woody xylem, etc.

Collenchyma. The collenchyma of the midrib of the leaf possesses the cells much thickened at the corners against the intercellular spaces. The cells, look circular, oval or polygonal in the vertical section of the leaf, the cells are thickened due to the deposition of cellulose impregnated with pectin. Though the cells are thickened yet not lignified. The cells are living. They are flexible also, and give strength to the leaves. These cells are more or less turgid and also give mechanical support to the leaf in this way.

Sclerenchyma. Usually the sclerenchyma or the fibres are associated with the vascular tissues of the leaves. They occur usually as bundle caps adjacent to the phloem. Sometimes the fibres are found on both the sides of the large vascular bundles of the leaves. Usually these cells are thick walled, dead and lignified. These are strengthening cells and give support to the leaf lamina.

Turgid parenchyma. The turgid parenchyma cells also give mechanical support to the leaf during its developmental stages.

Xylem. Usually the vessels of xylem conduct water, but due to their thick walled nature they also give mechanical support to the leaves. The xylem elements are also composed of lignified and dead cells.

Orientation of Vascular Tissue

In the leaf traces of flowering plants, before they leave the stele, the phloem is always found towards the outside of the stem. The leaf traces after their entrance in the petiole and lamina, also maintain the relative position of the xylem and phloem, *i.e.*, the phloem is always found towards the lower side and the xylem towards the upper side in leaf. Sometimes the xylem ring is surrounded by a ring of phloem. The phloem occurs only below the xylem or rarely both above and below it.

Conducting system

The tissues which constitute the conduction system are situated near or at the centre of the midrib. The system may have various shapes, *e.g.*, the form of a ring, a crescent shaped ring, a crescent or scattered patches. In the ring shaped conducting system parenchyma cells are usually found in the centre of the ring. The inner part of the ring is composed of xylem (towards lower surface).

Xylem is composed of various kinds of vessels, tracheids, wood fibres and wood parenchyma. Specially the vessels are annular and spiral. Xylem conducts water, raw food material and also gives mechanical support to the leaf. The phloem consists of sieve tubes, companion cells and phloem parenchyma. The phloem serves for the translocation of prepared food material from the mesophyll of the leaf.

Veins. The structure of large veins is more or less similar to that of a midrib. As they pass from the base of a leaf blade towards the apex or margin of the leaf, they get reduced in size, and simple in structure. The small veins consist of only of few conducting cells. The xylem is always found towards the upper surface and phloem towards lower even in very small veins.

The bundle sheath. Usually the vascular bundles of leaves are surrounded by a structure known as the bundle sheath. Around the vascular bundles of petioles and large veins usually sclerenchymatous sheath is found. The cells of the sheath are thin walled, fibrous and add to the strength of vascular bundles. The sclerenchyma may completely surround each vascular bundle or it may be restricted in the form of caps to the upper or lower side of as one or two separate patches.

Sometimes the bundle sheath consists of parenchyma cells. These cells are thin walled, elongated and found parallel to the vein axis, and joined laterally in such a fashion as to surround the vascular tissue with a compact sheath resembling an endodermis. In some species these cells consisting the bundle sheath may contain chloroplasts in them. The bundle sheath cells are in direct contact with the conducting cells of the vascular bundle or parenchyma and on the outer face with the mesophyll tissue.

32. T.S. of Leaf of *Dalbergia* (Dorsiventral Dicot Leaf).

Epidermis. There are two epidermis layers called upper and lower epidermis found on upper and lower surfaces of the leaf.

The upper epidermis is uniseriate and consists of barrel shaped cells having no intercellular spaces. A cuticle is also extended over this layer. Usually the stomata are not found on this layer.

The lower epidermis is also uniseriate and consists of barrel shaped cells without intercellular spaces among them. The outer walls of these cells are cuticularized. This layer is, however, interspersed with many stomata of which the two cells contain chloroplasts. Immediately beneath each stoma there is large air chamber called respiratory cavity or substomatal chamber which helps in exchange of gases between the atmosphere and the plant body.

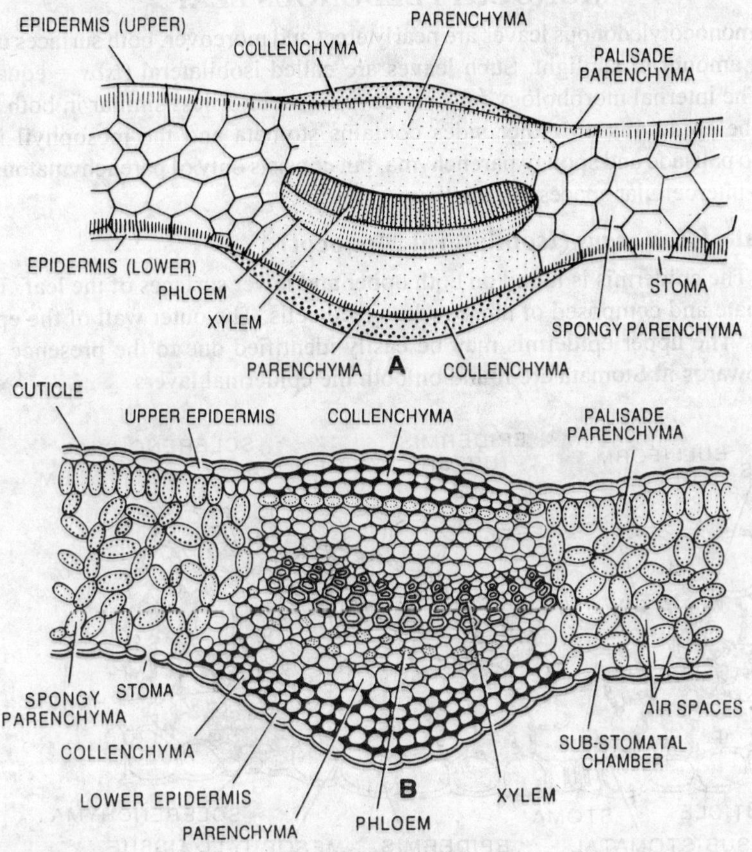

Fig. 11.38. Anatomy of bifacial dicot leaf. A, T.S. of leaf diagrammatic ; B, T.S. of leaf detail.

Mesophyll. The mesophyll tissue of a dorsiventral leaf is well differentiated into palisade tissue and spongy tissue.

The palisade tissue consists of one or two layers of elongated cylindrical cells found just beneath the epidermis. These cells contain numerous chloroplasts which are arranged along the side of the cell walls.

The spongy tissue or parenchyma is found immediately beneath the lower epidermis of the leaf, consists of oval, rounded or more commonly irregular cells arranged quite loosely and having big intercellular spaces among them. Comparatively these cells contain few chloroplasts. The chloroplasts are arranged along the sides of the cell walls.

The midrib. Usually the midrib portion is bulged towards adaxial side of the leaf. Immediately beneath upper and lower epidermis layers a few layers of collenchyma are found which give mechanical support to the leaf. Collenchyma is composed of living cells with thick walls at the angles due to deposition of cellulose.

The regions between the collenchyma cells and the main central portion of the midrib are filled up by parenchyma cells. These cells are rounded, living, thin walled and with sufficiently developed intercellular spaces.

The central portion of the midrib is occupied by a well developed crescent shaped conduction system. It consists of xylem and phloem. The xylem, which is composed of vessels is found towards the abaxial side of the leaf and phloem towards adaxial side. The phloem occurs only below the xylem. Cambium is not present.

MONOCOTYLEDONOUS LEAF

Most of the monocotyledonous leaves are nearly erect and moreover, both surfaces usually receive direct and equal amount of sunlight. Such leaves are called isobilateral (*isos* = equal ; *bi* = two ; *lateris* = side). The internal morphology of such leaves is more or less similar in both the upper and lower halves. The epidermis on either sides contains stomata and the mesophyll is usually not differentiated into palisade and spongy parenchyma, but consists only of parenchymatous cells, having chloroplasts and intercellular spaces among them

33. V.S. of Leaf of *Zea mays* (Isobilateral Monocot)

Epidermis. The epidermis is found on both upper and lower surfaces of the leaf. The epidermal layers are uniseriate and composed of more or less oval cells. The outer wall of the epidermal cells are cuticularized. The upper epidermis may be easily identified due to the presence of xylem and bulliform cells towards it. Stomata are found on both the epidermal layers.

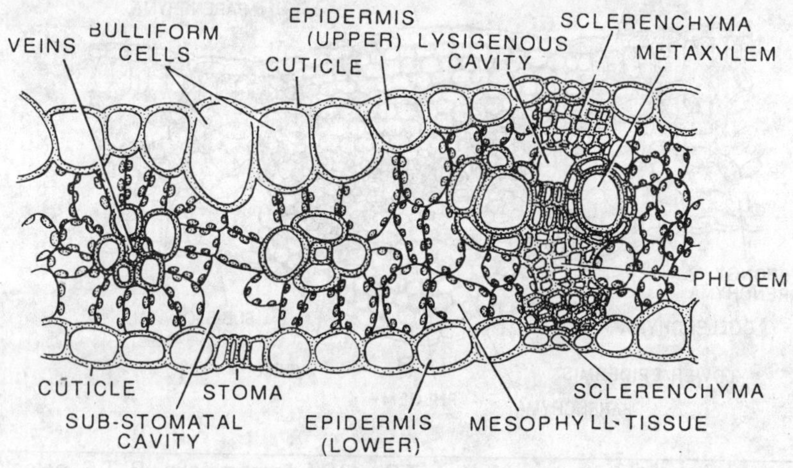

Fig. 11.39. Anatomy of a monocotyledonous leaf of *Zea mays*.

Mesophyll. As the leaf is isobilateral one the mesophyll is not differentiated into palisade and spongy tissues, and is made of compactly arranged isodiametric chlorenchymatous cells.

Vascular bundles. The vascular bundles are collateral and closed as found in monocotyledonous stems. Most of the bundles are small in size but fairly large bundles, also occur at regular intervals. The xylem is found towards upper side and phloem towards lower side in the bundles. Usually each bundle is surrounded by a bundle sheath consisting of thin walled parenchymatous cells. The cells of sheath usually contain starch grains in them. Xylem consists of vessels and phloem of sieve tubes and companion cells. Sclerenchyma cells occur in patches on both ends of the large vascular bundles which give mechanical support to the leaf.

34. V.S. of leaf of *Triticum aestivum* (Isobilateral Monocot)

Epidermis. As usual two epidermal layers on both upper and lower surfaces of the leaf are found. The epidermal layers are uniseriate and composed of more or less oval cells having no intercellular spaces among them. The outer walls of epidermal cells are cuticularized. The conspicuous big sized bulliform cells are found, in the upper epidermal layer. The stomata are found on both epidermal layers. The sub-stomatal chambers are also seen.

Mesophyll. It is composed of more or less oval chlorenchyma cells having intercellular spaces among them. The mesophyll tissue is not clearly differentiated into palisade and spongy parenchyma; though the cells towards epidermal layers are somewhat elongated and palisade like. Sub-stomatal chambers are also seen below the stomata.

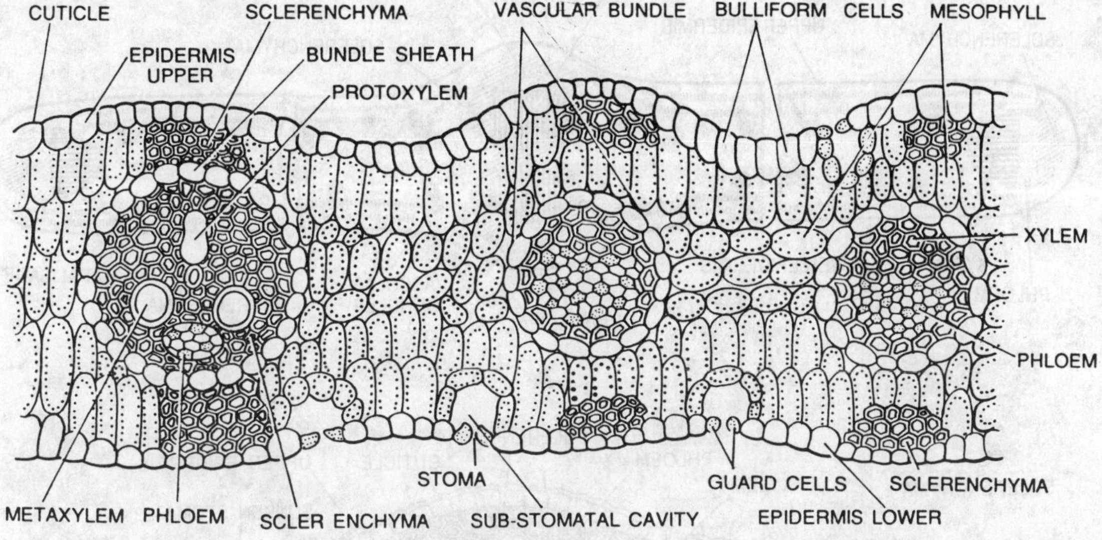

Fig. 11.40. Anatomy of isobilateral leaf. T.S. *Triticum aestivum* (monocot) leaf. Detail of portion.

Vascular bundles. The vascular bundles are collateral and closed as found in monocotyledonous stems. The bundles are arranged in parallel series. Xylem occurs towards upper surface and phloem towards lower surface. Each vascular bundle is surrounded by a bundle sheath usually consisting of thin walled parenchyma cells. The sclerenchyma strands are found on both the ends of each big vascular bundle (see Fig. 11.40).

THE PHYLLODE

The phyllode is the most interesting modification of petiole. Here the petioles become flattened and leaf-like. The flattened petioles which look like ordinary leaves are called phyllodes. Usually the phyllodes are isobilateral so that both the surfaces are equally illuminated.

35. T.S. of Phyllode of Australian *Acacia*.

Epidermis. It consists of a single row of cells covered with well developed cuticle. Sunken stomata are also present. The extreme ends of phyllode possess radially elongated epidermal cells covered with cuticle. The extreme ends of phyllode possess radially elongated epidermal cells covered with cuticle. Below each stoma there is a sub-stomatal chamber for exchange of gases.

Palisade and parenchyma. Just beneath the epidermis one or two layers of palisade tissue are present which help in carbon assimilation. In the central region, parenchyma with intercellular spaces is found.

Vascular system. Alike in petiole the vascular bundles form a ring and are arranged below the palisade tissue. The central and corner vascular bundles are sufficiently big in their size. Each vascular bundle consists of xylem and phloem. Around the central and corner vascular bundles well developed sclerenchyma is found.

Special features :

(*i*) Vascular bundles are arranged in complete ring. The central and corner bundles are bigger in size (petiole character).

(*ii*) Palisade tissue is present (leaf character).

(*iii*) Presence of radially elongated epidermal cells (xerophytic feature).

(*iv*) Presence of well developed cuticle (xerophytic feature).

(*v*) Presence of sunken stomata (xerophytic feature).

(*vi*) Well developed sclerenchyma present (xerophytic feature).

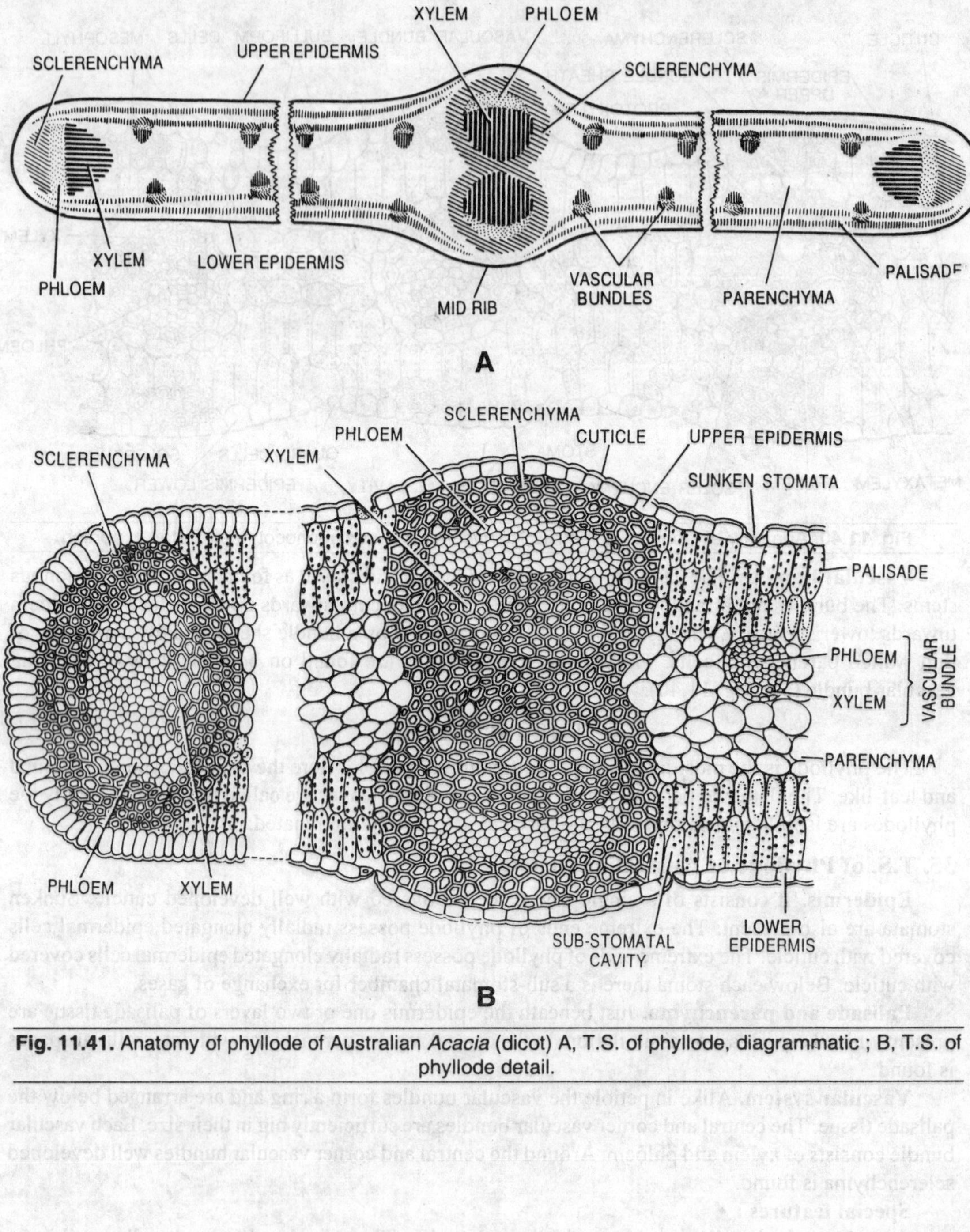

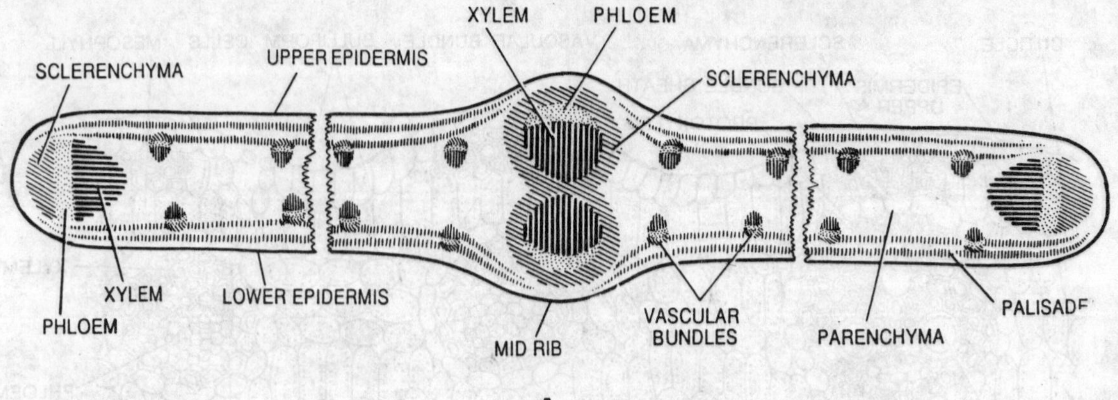

A

B

Fig. 11.41. Anatomy of phyllode of Australian *Acacia* (dicot) A, T.S. of phyllode, diagrammatic ; B, T.S. of phyllode detail.

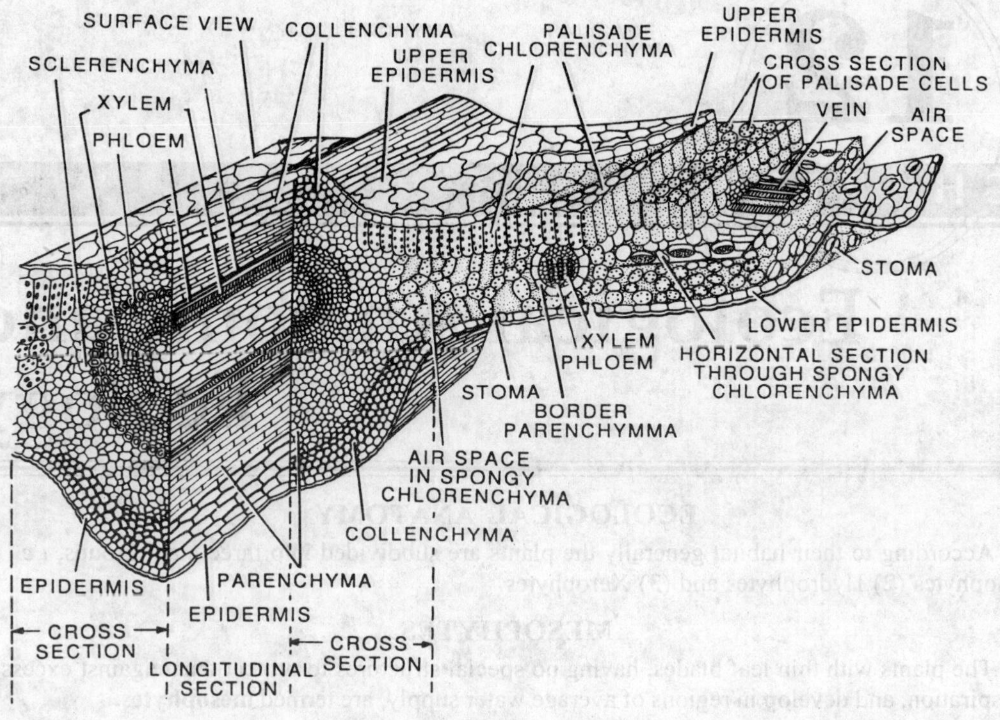

Fig. 11.42. The leaf. A three dimensional view of a midrib and a small part of the leaf blade. On the left side is a cross-section of half of the midrib, followed by a longitudinal section, and this by a cross-section of the remainder of the midrib and a portion of the blade. The leaf on the right side is dissected in various ways to show the arrangement of the tissues.

CHAPTER

Ecological Anatomy and Ecology

ECOLOGICAL ANATOMY

According to their habitat generally the plants are subdivided into three main groups, *i.e.*, (1) Mesophytes (2) Hydrophytes and (3) Xerophytes.

MESOPHYTES

The plants with thin leaf blades, having no special structures to protect them against excessive transpiration, and develop in regions of average water supply, are termed **mesophytes.**

HYDROPHYTES

The number of species of flowering plants, known as **hydrophytes,** live under extremes of water supply. The plants which are entirely submerged grow comparatively in deeper water. In submerged plants, the conducting and mechanical tissues are very poorly developed. As they float in the water, they do not need mechanical tissue to strengthen their body, and as they do not transpire, there is no need of water conducting tissue. The plants with floating leaves possess conspicuous air spaces. These air spaces serve as an aerating system of the plant and also give them buoyancy to float. The characteristic anatomical features of the hydrophytes are as follows.

Epidermis. In aquatic plants, the epidermis does not serve the purpose of protection but it absorbs nutrients and gases directly from the water. Usually the chloroplasts are found in epidermal cells of the leaves, especially when the leaves are very thin they enable the photosynthesis. The epidermis of typical hydrophytes possess an extremely thin cuticle and thin cellulose walls. In submerged plants, stomata are also not found, and exchange of gases takes places directly through the cells. The plants with floating leaves possess abundance of stomata on the upper surface of leaf.

Air spaces. Usually the aquatic plants are provided with well developed air spaces, which serve as an aerating system for the diffusion of the oxygen from the leaves to the roots. On the other hand, the air spaces make the plants buoyant to float. The air spaces are quite big in size. The tissue with many large air spaces may be termed as 'aerenchyma'. Usually the intervening walls of air spaces are constituted of thin walled cells. Sometimes sclereids or idioblasts are also seen on the uniseriate rows of thin walled cells which strengthen the plant body. Suitable examples of this type of structure are *Hippuris*; *Potamogeton*; *Nymphaea*; *Victoria regia*; *Limnanthemum; Hydrilla*, etc.

Absence of mechanical tissue. (Sclerenchyma). The submerged plants usually do not possess sclerenchymatous tissue. Instead of sclerenchyma a few star shaped sclereids or idioblasts may be formed to strengthen the general body of the plant, *e.g.*, *Nymphaea* leaf; *Limnanthemum*, etc.

Reduced vascular system. In aquatic plants the vascular system is very much reduced. The root system is also greatly reduced. The absorption of nutrients and water takes place through the leaves and stems. In the vascular tissues, the xylem is greatly reduced and sometimes in many species it is fairly developed as compared with the xylem. The endodermis is usually present around the stele but in undeveloped condition.

1. T.S. of Stem of *Hippuris* (dicot).

Epidermis. The epidermis consists of a single row of cells usually provided with a thin cuticle. The cells are radially elongated. The outer and inner tangential walls of the cells are considerably thickened whereas radial ones less.

Cortex. The region is sufficiently wide and consists of thin parenchymatous cells and big air spaces. The two subepidermal layers of cells have no big intercellular spaces, whereas rest of the cortex is permeated by large intercellular or air spaces. The air spaces or cavities being separated from one another by single layered multicellular plates. The innermost layer of the cortex is endodermis which is well defined.

Vascular system. The vascular system is very much reduced due to hydrophytic nature of the plant. The outer part consists of a narrow zone of phloem and the inner part of xylem. The vessels are small in diameter, with spiral or reticulate thickenings.

Pith. Though there is no true pith in young stems, yet according to Solereder in old stems due to obliteration of certain central vessels a pseudopith is developed.

Hydrophytic Features :

(1) The big intercellular spaces or air spaces are very much developed.
(2) No mechanical tissues are present.
(3) Very thin walled parenchymatous tissues are present.
(4) Vascular system is very much reduced.

2. T.S. Stem of *Trapa* (dicot)

Epidermis. It consists of a single row of thin walled cells.

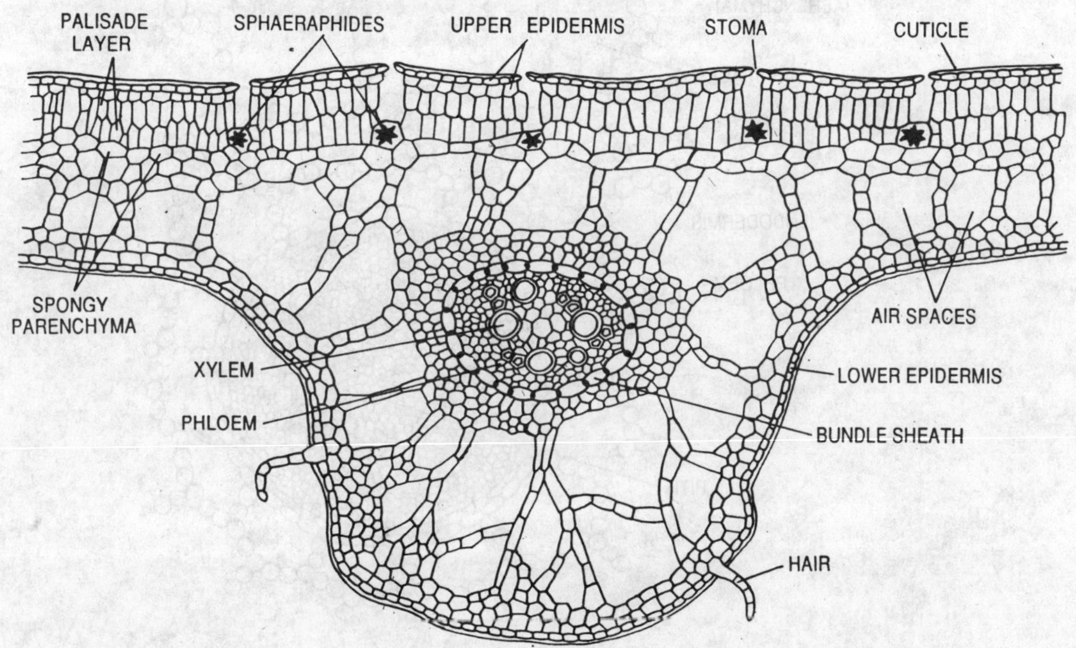

Fig. 12.1. Hydrophytic leaf. T.S. of floating leaf of *Trapa bispinosa*, showing big air spaces, the stomata confined to upper epidermis only.

Cortex. The cortex is broad and consists of multilayered subepidermal region of collenchymatous cells having no intercellular or air spaces, rest of the cortical region consists of numerous vertically elongated air cavities and parenchyma cells. Branched sclerenchymatous idioblasts or sclereids project

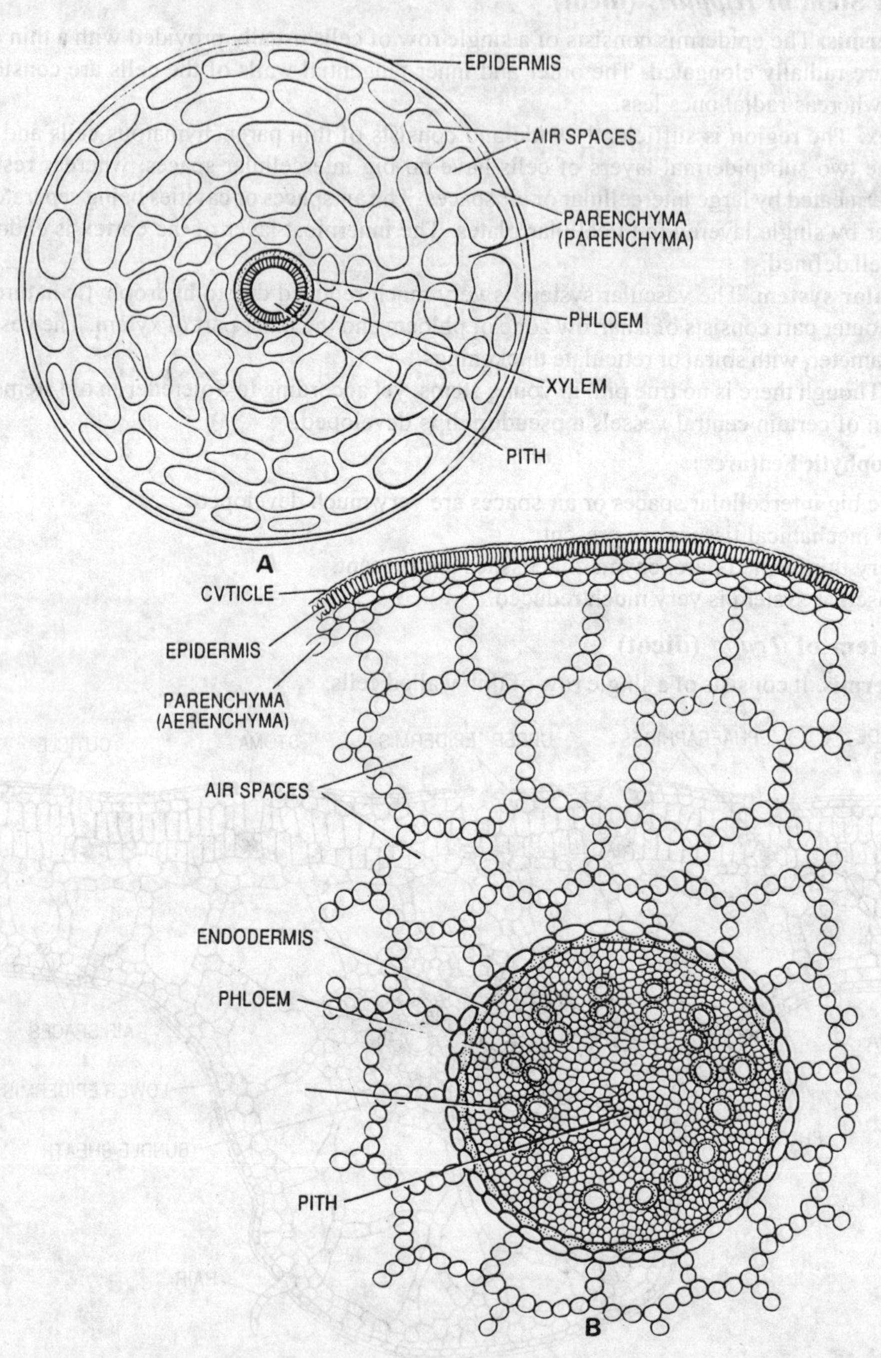

Fig. 12.2. Anatomy of hydrophytic stem. T.S. *Hippuris* (dicot) stem. A, diagrammatic ; B, detail of a sector and stele.

into the intercellular cavities from the surrounding cells. These sclereids give support in strengthening the framework of the stem. The innermost and conspicuous layer of the cortex is endodermis or starch sheath.

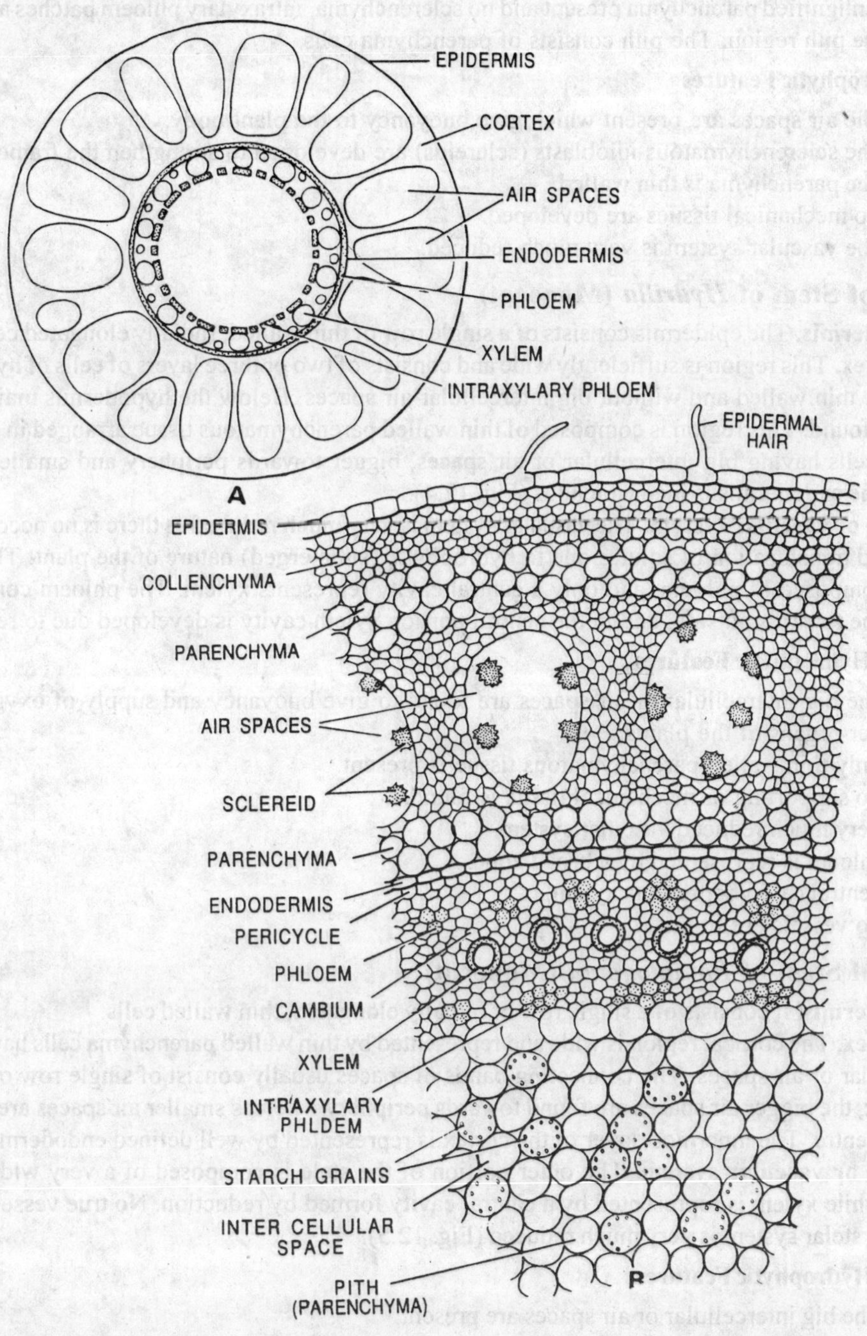

Fig. 12.3. Anatomy of hydrophytic stem of *Trapa* (dicot) A, T.S. of stem, diagrammatic ; B, T.S. of stem, detail of a sector.

Stele or vascular system. The vascular bundles are separated from each other and unconnected by an interfascicular cambium. Each vascular bundle consists of phloem, xylem and rarely cambium. Cambium, rarely develops in between xylary and phloic regions. In the inner portions of the vascular bundles unlignified parenchyma present and no sclerenchyma, intraxylary phloem patches are present around the pith region. The pith consists of parenchyma cells.

Hydrophytic Features

(1) The air spaces are present which give buoyancy to the plant body.
(2) The sclerenchymatous idioblasts (sclereids) are developed to strengthen the framework.
(3) The parenchyma is thin walled.
(4) No mechanical tissues are developed.
(5) The vascular system is very much reduced.

3. T.S. of Stem of *Hydrilla* (Monocot)

Epidermis. The epidermis consists of a single row of thin walled, radially elongated cells.

Cortex. This region is sufficiently wide and consists of two or three layers of cells of hypodermis which are thin walled and without big intercellular air spaces. Below the hypodermis main cortical region is found. This region is composed of thin walled parenchymatous tissue arranged in uniseriate rows of cells having big intercellular or air spaces, bigger towards periphery and smaller towards centre. The endodermis is inconspicuous (Fig. 12.4).

Stele or vascular system. The vascular system is very much reduced as there is no need of ascent of sap and translocation of solutes due to hydrophytic (submerged) nature of the plant. The stele is mainly composed of phloem, and only a central cavity represents xylem. The phloem consists of a broad zone towards outside, and in the central portion xylem cavity is developed due to reduction.

Hydrophytic Features

(1) The big intercellular or air spaces are found to give buoyancy and supply of oxygen to the underwater organs of the plants.
(2) Only thin walled parenchymatous tissue is present.
(3) No supporting or mechanical tissue is found.
(4) Very much reduced vascular system.
(*a*) Phloem is represented by a broad zone.
(*b*) Central cavity represents xylem.
(*c*) No vessels are found.

4. T.S. of Stem of *Potamogeton* (Monocot)

Epidermis. It consists of a single row of radially elongated, thin walled cells.

Cortex. The cortical region is wide and represented by thin walled parenchyma cells having large intercellular or air spaces. The connecting bands of spaces usually consist of single row of cells. In the cortex, the bigger air spaces are found towards periphery whereas smaller air spaces are confined towards centre. The innermost layer of the cortex is represented by well defined endodermis.

Stele or vascular system. The outer portion of the stele is composed of a very wide zone of phloem while xylem is represented by a central cavity formed by reduction. No true vessels. On the whole the stelar system is very much reduced (Fig. 12.5).

Hydrophytic Features

(1) The big intercellular or air spaces are present.
(2) Only thin walled parenchyma is present.
(3) No sclerenchyma or mechanical tissues are met with.
(*a*) The phloem is well developed.
(*b*) The xylem is represented by a cavity.
(*c*) No true vessels are found.

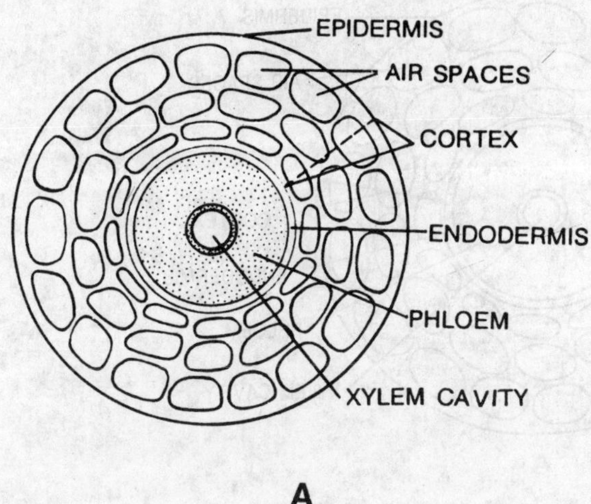

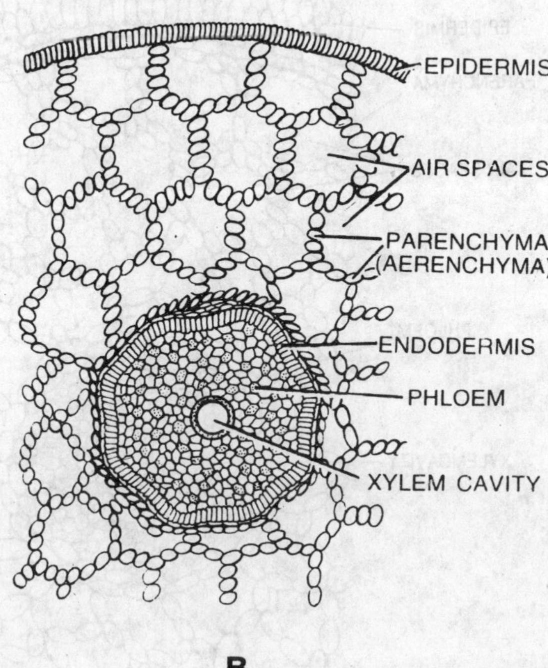

Fig. 12.4. Anatomy of hydrophytic stem of *Hydrilla* (submerged - monocot T.S. of stem). A, diagrammatic; B, detail of a sector and central stele.

5. V.S. of Leaf of *Potamogeton* (Monocot)

This is a dorsiventral leaf having two distinct faces (*i*) upper and (*ii*) lower.

Epidermis. The upper epidermis consists of a single row of thin walled cells arranged tangentially and having stomata at various places. Distinct substomatal chambers are found below the stomata.

The lower epidermis also consists of a single row of tangentially arranged thin walled compact cells, having no stomata, as the lower epidermis remains in direct contact of water.

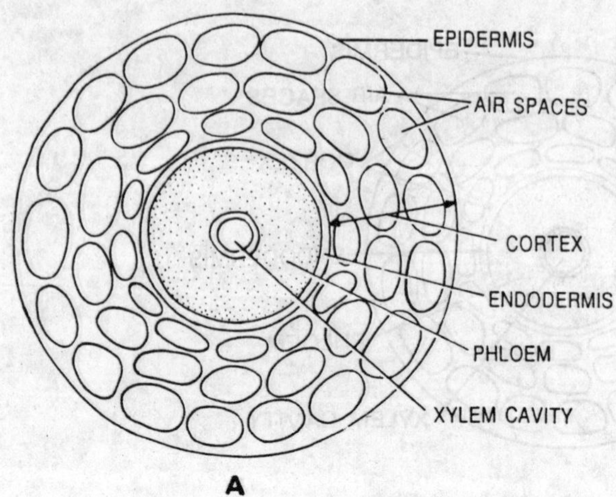

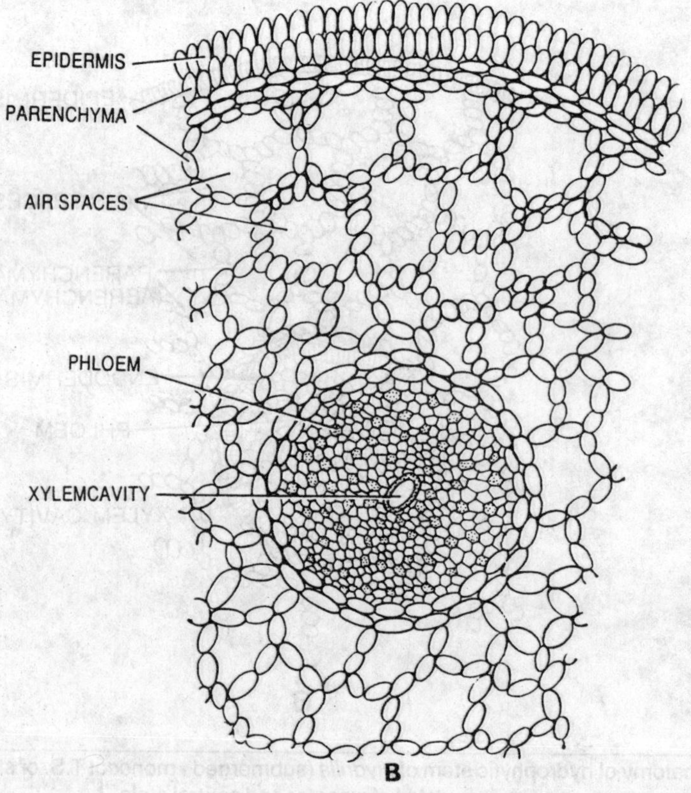

Fig. 12.5. Anatomy of hydrophytic stem. T.S. of stem of *Potamogeton* (monocot). A, diagrammatic; B, detail of a sector.

Palisade. Below the upper epidermis one or two layers of well developed palisade tissue are found. These cells contain abundance of chloroplasts.

Parenchyma. The general body of the leaf is composed of thin walled parenchyma arranged in uniseriate rows of cells and having large intercellular or air spaces.

Midrib or Vascular System

In the central region of the leaf the midrib is found. It consists of xylem and phloem. The xylem is found towards the upper epidermis and phloem towards lower epidermis. The vascular system is much reduced (Fig. 12.6).

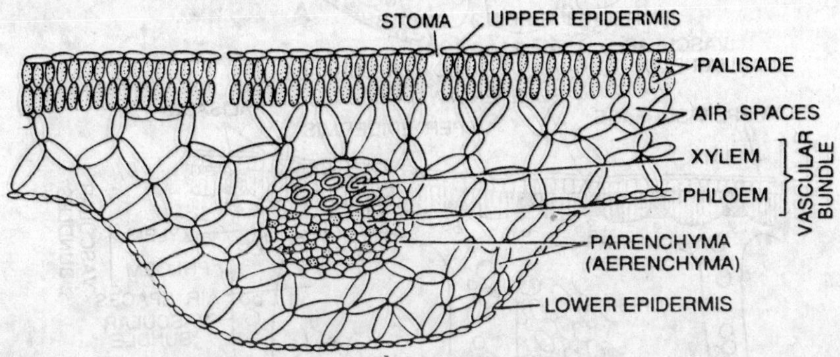

Fig. 12.6. Anatomy of hydrophytic leaf. T.S. of *Potamogeton* (monocot) leaf. Detail of central portion.

Hydrophytic Features

(1) The large air spaces are found.
(2) The stomata are confined on upper epidermis.
(3) The palisade is present towards upper side.
(4) No mechanical tissues are found.
(5) The vascular system is very much reduced.

6. V.S. of leaf of *Typha* (Monocot)

It is a dorsiventral leaf having two surfaces. It remains in direct contact of water.

Epidermis. The upper epidermis consists of a single row of cells. The stomata are confined to the upper surface. The lower epidermis is also single layered, and having no stomata.

Palisade. Just beneath the upper epidermis a few layers of palisade tissue are found having abundance of chloroplasts.

Spongy tissue, idioblasts and air spaces. The general body of the leaf consists of spongy parenchyma with large air spaces. Minute crystals of calcium oxalate are found, projecting in the intercellular spaces from the connecting parenchymatous strands. The walls of idioblasts are pitted wherein contact with adjacent cells. Diaphragms are present in large air spaces.

Vascular system. The vascular system is poorly developed and represented by closed bundles. Normally towards upper and lower side double or mixed inversely oriented bundles are found. Each vascular bundle consists of phloem and póorly developed xylem. True vessels are altogether absent.

Hydrophytic Features

(*i*) The air spaces are present.
(*ii*) The raphides are present to give support to the framework of thin walled spongy parenchyma.
(*iii*) Stomata are present only on the exposed (upper) surface.
(*iv*) No mechanical tissues are developed.
(*v*) Very much reduced vascular system.
(*vi*) True vessels are absent.
(*vii*) Phloem is much developed in comparison to the xylem (Fig. 12.7).

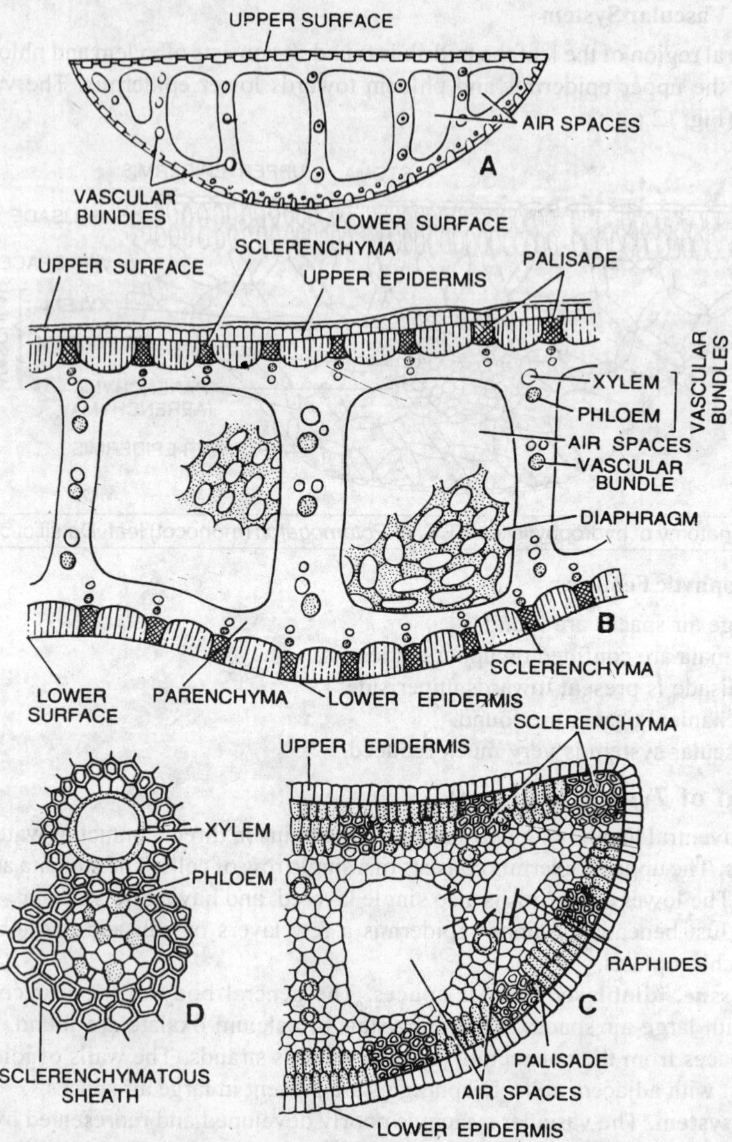

Fig. 12.7. Anatomy of aquatic leaf of *Typha* (monocot). A, T.S. of leaf, diagrammatic; B, T.S. of leaf, semidiagrammatic; C, T.S. of leaf, showing detail of a corner; D, a vascular bundle.

3. XEROPHYTES

At the other extreme of plant association, plants are known as xerophytes. The term, however, is applicable to a great number of plants, which vary in their structural peculiarities to adapt them to live under the conditions of water. Some plants live in very dry situations while on the other hand some are found living in conditions of fairly reasonable supply of water. The plants growing in dry situations develop a large and deeply penetrating root system capable of efficient absorption. Some plants develop in marshy places, which possess higher osmotic concentration and due to this higher concentration within plants, the absorption of water from the marshy soil takes place (*e.g. Molinia*). Usually the xerophytic plants possess succulent and small leaves having less surface exposed to wind gusts. Sometimes the leaves contain abundance of mucilage, which tends to reduce transpiration.

In addition to these morphological adaptations, the plants possess many anatomical xerophytic features. They are as follows :

Epidermis and thick cuticle. In the xerophytic plants, the epidermis becomes somewhat specialised. Usually the epidermal cells become cutinized and radially elongated. Sometimes it becomes multilayered, *e.g.*, *Nerium* leaf. The cuticle varies in its thickness from species to species. Sometimes it is slightly thicker than normal, as in semixerophytic plants and on the other hand, in extreme xerophytes the cuticles may be as thick as, or thicker than the epidermal cells. Sometimes a waxy substance is produced on the cuticle, *e.g.*, *Calotropis*.

Hypodermis. Many xerophytic plants possess single or multilayered hypodermis immediately beneath the cutinized epidermis. Sometimes the hypodermis becomes lignified. In many plants, the mucilage, gums and tannings are common in this layer.

Structure of stomata. The stomata are very minute openings formed in the epidermal layer in green aerial parts of the plant. The stomata are used for interchange of gases, and evaporation of the surplus water. They are most abundant in the lower epidermis of dorsiventral leaf. In the isobilateral leaves, they are usually evenly distributed on all sides. Some of the xerophytic plants possess less stomata, either by reduction of leaf surface or of stomatal number per unit area. The reduce excessive transpiration, usually the stomata in pits are produced. Commonly these stomata may be termed 'sunken stomata'. They occur in *Hakea, Agave,* etc. In the oleander (*Nerium*) and *Banksia* the stomata are found in groups and in irregular depressions on the leaf surface. Usually the depressions contain hairs in which also protect the stomata from direct attack of wind gusts, *e.g.*, *Banksia, Nerium*, etc.

Sclerenchyma. The xerophytes commonly have a large proportion of sclerenchyma in their leaf structure than the mesophytes. This tissue is either found in groups or in continuous sheets. The sclerenchyma layers check excessive transpiration to some extent and also strengthen the plant body. The xerophytes which possess heavy sclerification of the leaves may easily by called **sclerophyllous,** *e.g.*, *Dasylirion.*

Hairs. Many xerophytes, especially of alpine heights, possess a matting of hairs on the epidermis. These hairs mostly confined on the lower surface of leaves. Hairs may also be abundant over the entire aerial part of the plant. They prevent rapid evaporation through stomata. Xerophytes, which possess abundance of hairs, are called **trichophyllous.**

Rolling of leaves. Many xerophytic grasses have the stomata confined to ventral surface, and when there is a deficiency of water the leaves roll up so that all stomata are on the inner surface of the rolled leaf. The air enclosed in the rolled leaf soon becomes saturated with water and the outward diffusion of water stops. *Ammophila arenaria* or sand dune grass is a good example of rolling leaf.

Reduced leaf surface. Many xerophytes possess very reduced needle like or scaly leaves, *e.g.*, *Casuarina*, etc. Here the reduction is because of the relatively small total surface of the leaf. Xerophytes, with reduced leaves are termed '**microphyllous**'.

Water storage tissue. Many fleshy xerophytes possess water storage tissue in them. The xerophytic plants possess succulent stems or leaves, which consist largely of special parenchymatous tissue used for water storage. The examples are *Cactus, Aloe, Opuntia,* etc. These plants possess spread type of root system. In rainy season water is quickly absorbed and stored and then expanded slowly during the period of drought.

Abundant palisade. In the stems of many xerophytes, the palisade tissue is found (*e.g.*, *Capparis*). In the leaves the palisade is compact and found in abundance.

Latex tubes. In many xerophytic stems and leaves the laticiferous canals are found. Due to viscosity of latex the transpiration is checked up to a certain extent.

Vascular system. It is well developed in xerophytes.

7. T.S. of Stem of *Calotropis* (Dicot)

Epidermis. The epidermis consists of radially elongated epidermal cells and covered with very thick cuticle. A thin waxy layer is also found above the cuticle.

Parenchyma. Below the epidermis, multilayered parenchyma is present. The cells are thin walled, rounded and isodiametric. Intercellular spaces are very common.

Endodermis. The last layer of the cortex is endodermis containing starch grains. The cells are barrel shaped and arranged tangentially quite close to each other.

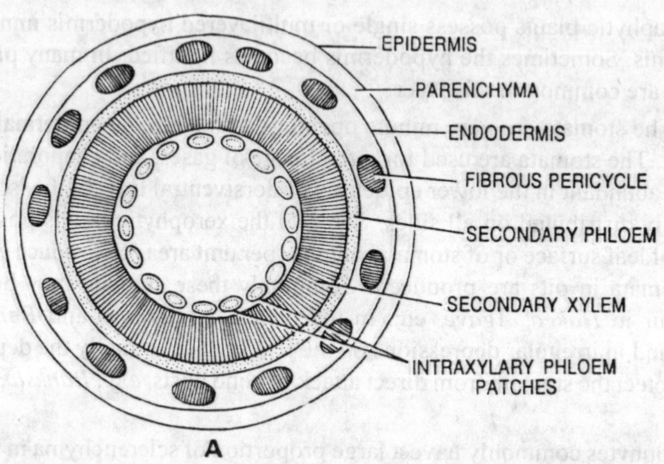

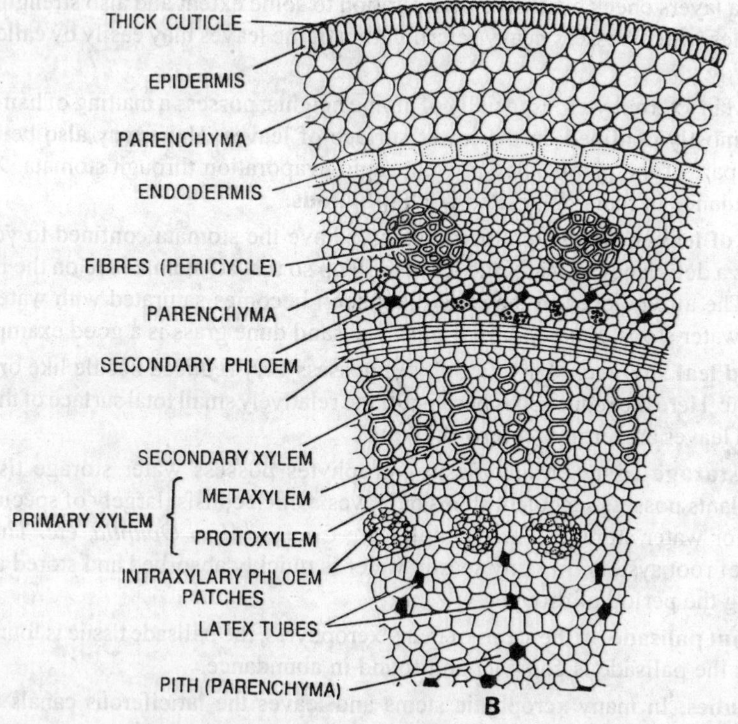

Fig. 12.8. Anatomy of xerophytic stem. T.S. of *Calotropis* (Asclepiadaceae-dicot) stem. A, diagrammatic ; B, detail of a sector.

Pericycle. Beneath the endodermis a parenchymatous zone of pericycle is present which is interrupted by unlignified group of fibres. The cells of parenchyma are polygonal and thin walled.

Secondary phloem. Just below the pericycle region, secondary phloem is present. The secondary phloem is found in the continuous strand around the axis; sieve tubes, companion cells, and phloem parenchyma present. Sometimes at certain places crushed primary phloem is also visible.

Cambium. Beneath the secondary phloem cambium zone is found. The cambial strip is found in continuous strand round-about the whole axis.

Xylem. Below the cambium a continuous strand of secondary and primary xylem is present. The primary xylem consists of wide metaxylem and narrow protoxylem vessels, whereas secondary xylem is represented by xylem parenchyma (prosenchyma,) which are lignified tissue.

Intraxylary phloem. The patches of intraxylary phloem are also found around the pith region.

Pith. The central region of the stem is filled up with thin walled, polygonal, parenchymatous cells, which represent the medulla (pith).

Latex tubes. The latex tubes or laticiferous canals are also visible in different parenchymatous regions.

Anomalous Structure

The intraxylary phloem strands are present around the periphery of pith region.

Xerophytic Characters

(*i*) Very thick cuticle with waxy layer is present on the surface of the stem.
(*ii*) The epidermis consists of radially elongated epidermal cells.
(*iii*) The latex tubes are present.
(*iv*) The sclerenchymatous tissue is well developed.

8. V.S. of Leaf of *Agave* (Monocot)

Epidermis. The leaf is isobilateral and approximately possesses the same type of anatomy on both the sides. Towards the upper surface, the upper epidermis is found whereas towards the lower surface, the usual lower epidermis is present. The anatomy of both upper and lower layers of epidermis is same. It consists of radially elongated and compact epidermal cells having no intercellular spaces.

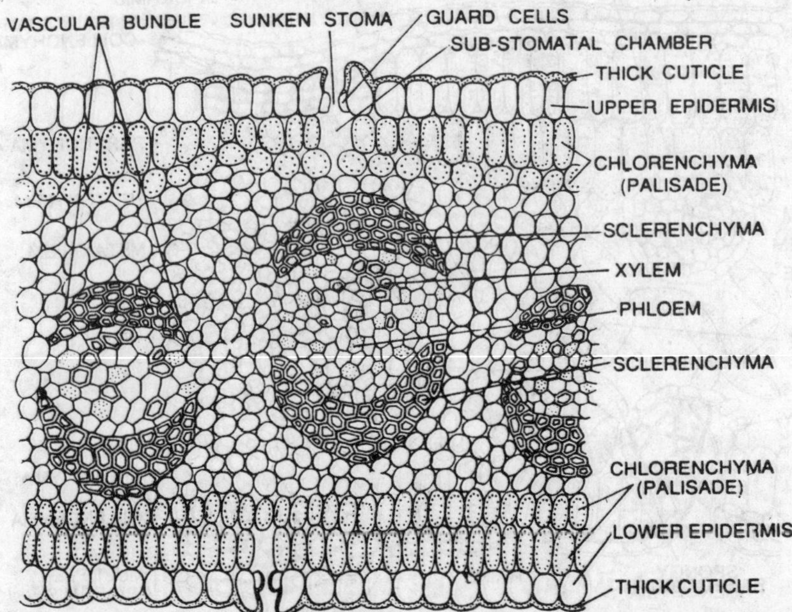

Fig. 12.9. Anatomy of xerophytic leaf. T.S. of *Agave* (monocot) leaf. Detail of a portion.

The epidermis on both the sides is covered with a thick cuticle. The sunken stomata are present. The guard cells contain many chloroplasts. Below each stoma sub-stomatal chamber is always found which helps in exchange of gases.

Chlorenchyma. Just beneath the epidermis (on both sides) one or two layers of chlorenchyma are present usually having elongated or oval cells containing chloroplasts with well defined intercellular spaces.

Parenchyma. The ground tissue of the leaf consists of thin walled, rounded parenchymatous cells having well defined intercellular spaces.

Vascular system. The vascular system is well developed and consists of many vascular bundles. The central bundle is bigger than the rest. The fibers are found on both the sides of each vascular bundle. The xylem is found towards upper side whereas the phloem towards lower side.

Xerophytic Features

(*i*) The thick cuticle is found on both the surfaces.
(*ii*) The epidermis consists of elongated epidermal cells.
(*iii*) The sunken stomata are present on both surfaces.
(*iv*) The sclerenchyma is developed.

9. V.S. of Leaf of *Nerium* (dicot)

Epidermis. The leaf is dorsiventral and consists of upper and lower epidermis. The upper epidermis is multilayered and usually consists of two or three layers of barrel shaped compact cells having no intercellular spaces among them. The outermost layer is covered with a well defined, thick cuticle. Generally the stomata are not found on the upper surface. The lower epidermis consists of a single row of barrel shaped cells, arranged closely to each other, and protected with a well defined cuticle. At certain places the irregular depressions are formed due to incurve of the lower epidermis. The stomata are found in the depression which are commonly protected with trichomes (hairs) growing around the sides. Due to the presence of these hairs, the rate of transpiration is sufficiently reduced as the stomata are not attacked by the direct gusts of wind.

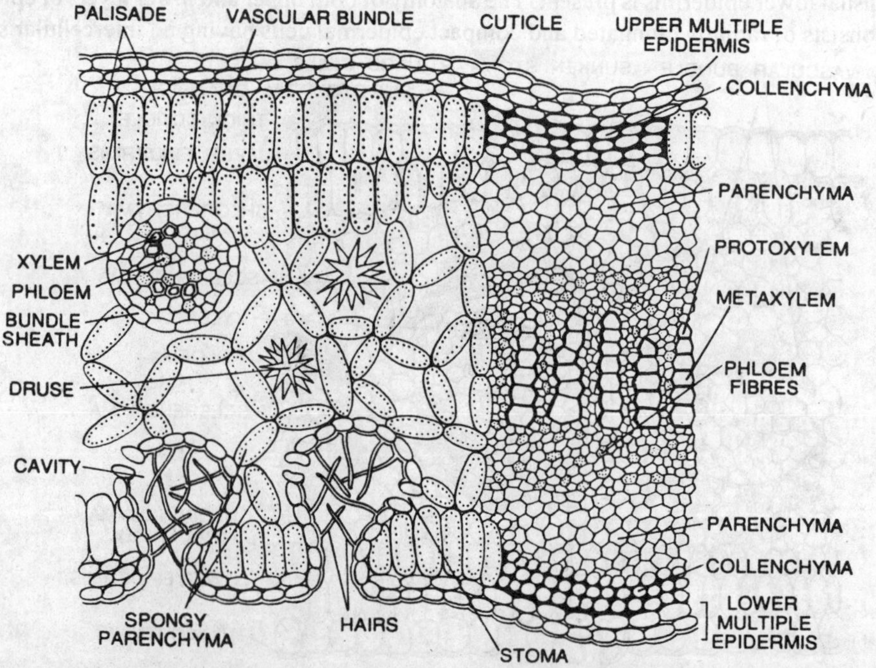

Fig. 12.10. Anatomy of xerophytic leaf. T.S. of *Nerium* (dicot) leaf, detail of a portion.

Mesophyll. It is distinguished into palisade and spongy tissue. Immediately beneath the upper epidermis one or two layers of palisade are found, containing abundance of chloroplasts. Towards lower surface, the spongy tissue is well developed. The intercellular spaces among spongy tissue are well developed and quite big in size. The cells contain abundance of chloroplasts but comparatively lesser than those of palisade tissue.

Vascular system. It is very well developed and consists of mid-rib and lateral veins. The phloem is always found towards lower side and xylem towards upper side.

Xerophytic Features

(*i*) The thick cuticle, is present on upper and lower epidermis.

(*ii*) A multilayered upper epidermis is found to check excessive transpiration.

(*iii*) The stomata are found in the depressions which are confined on the lower surface of leaf. They are also protected with hairs to check the direct attack of wind gusts.

(*iv*) The vascular system is well developed.

10. V.S. of Rolled leaf of *Ammophila arenaria* (monocot).

Epidermis. The lower or exposed epidermis is composed of radially elongated epidermal cells and is covered over with a very thick cuticle. The upper epidermis is found over the ridges and furrows of the leaf. The cells are thin walled and stomata are confined only to this surface. Some epidermal cells of the ridge are extended in the form of hairs. The epidermal cells of depressions or furrows are comparatively bigger and thin walled and may be termed as **hinge** or **motor cells**. The stomata are found on the lateral sides of the ridges.

At the time of active transpiration the leaf loses water more actively. The thin walled motor cells found in the furrows lose water more quickly than rest of the cells, and contract. Due to the contraction of motor cells the leaf tends to roll inwards, and the lower epidermis is exposed. Very soon, the air enclosed by the rolled leaf becomes saturated with water, and excessive stomatal transpiration is checked.

The hairs, which are found on the ridges also protect the surface from exposition to wind, and thus help in checking the excessive transpiration.

Sclerenchyma. The sclerenchyma is very well developed and found throughout the leaf in the form of a continuous cylinder. These tissues are also extended in the ridges.

Xerophytic Features

(*i*) Very thick cuticle is present to protect the exposed (lower) epidermis from the factors affecting rate of transpiration.

(*ii*) The epidermis consists of radially elongated epidermal cells which also check excessive transpiration.

(*iii*) The ridges and furrows are found on the unexposed (upper) surface.

(*iv*) The thin walled epidermal cells (motor cells - hinge) are also found which help in rolling the leaf inwards.

(*v*) The hairs are present which protect the stomata from exposition.

(*vi*) The well developed sclerenchyma is found throughout the lamina.

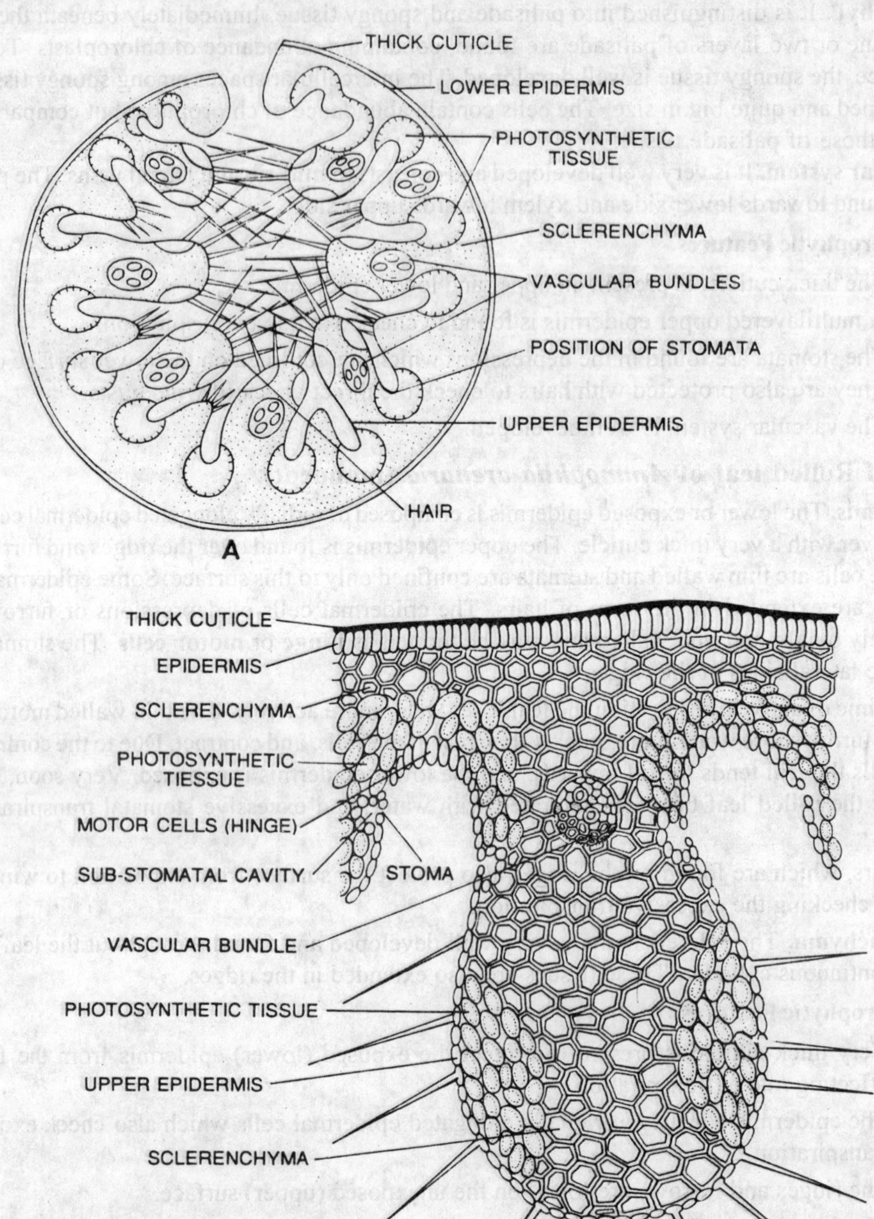

Fig. 12.11. T.S. of a xerophytic rolled leaf of *Ammophila arenaria* (monocot). A, diagrammatic ; B, detail of a sector.

11. T.S. of Stem of *Casuarina* (Dicot)

Epidermis. The epidermis is composed of a single row of closely arranged barrel shaped cells. It is covered over with a sufficiently thick and silicified cuticle. Ridges and furrows are found all around the stem. Usually the stomata are present in the furrows sometimes covered with hairs.

Sclerenchyma. Beneath the epidermis one or two layers of sclerenchyma are usually found.

Palisade. Usually in the ridges of the stem few layers of palisade tissue are present. These are loose, elongated and with a large number of discoid chloroplasts.

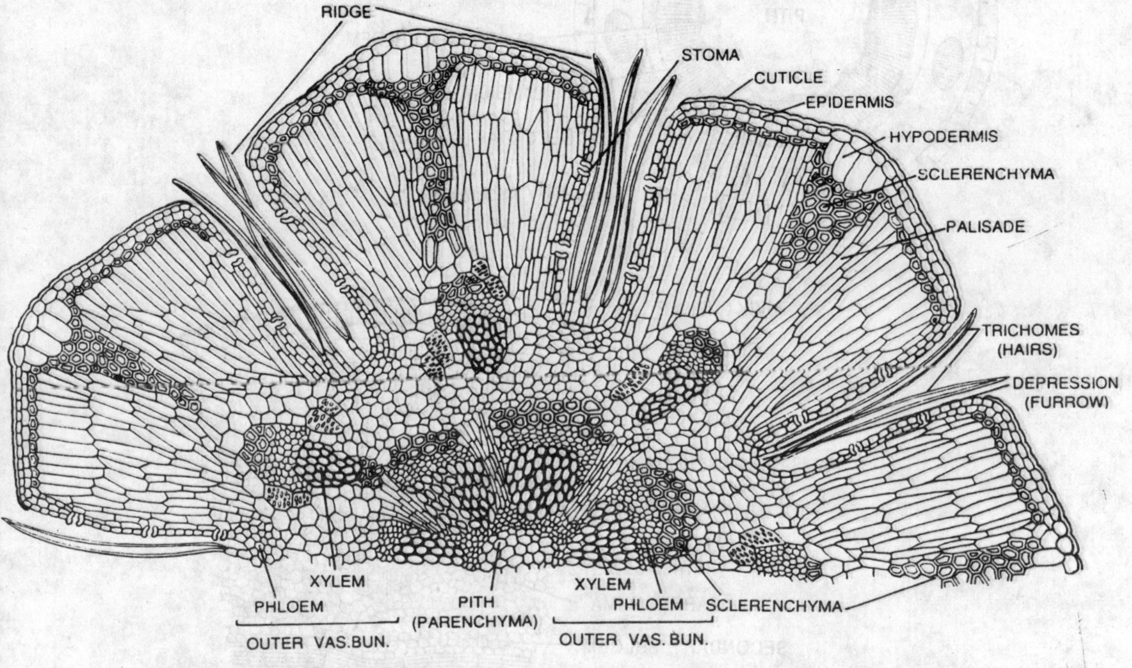

Fig. 12.12. Xerophytes. T.S. of a xerophytic stem (*Casuarina equisetifolia*), a dicot.

Xerophytic Features

(*i*) A thick cuticle is present above the epidermis.

(*ii*) The stomata are found in the depressions.

(*iii*) Usually hairs are present in the furrows which protect the stomata.

(*iv*) The palisade tissue is found even in the stem.

(*v*) The vascular system is well developed.

(*vi*) The mechanical tissues are developed.

12. T.S. of Stem of *Capparis* (Dicot)

Epidermis. The epidermis consists of radially elongated epidermal cells, arranged very close to each other, having no intercellular spaces. The epidermis is covered with very thick cuticle. These two devices are meant to check excessive transpiration — a xerophytic character.

Palisade. Below the epidermis two or three layers of palisade tissue are found which contain a large number of chloroplasts. These tissues help in carbon assimilation. In *Capparis aphylla* the leaves are altogether absent and the phenomenon of photosynthesis is completed by the palisade tissue of the stem-a xerophytic character.

Endodermis. The last but one layer of the cortex is endodermis which consists of thin walled and barrel shaped cells.

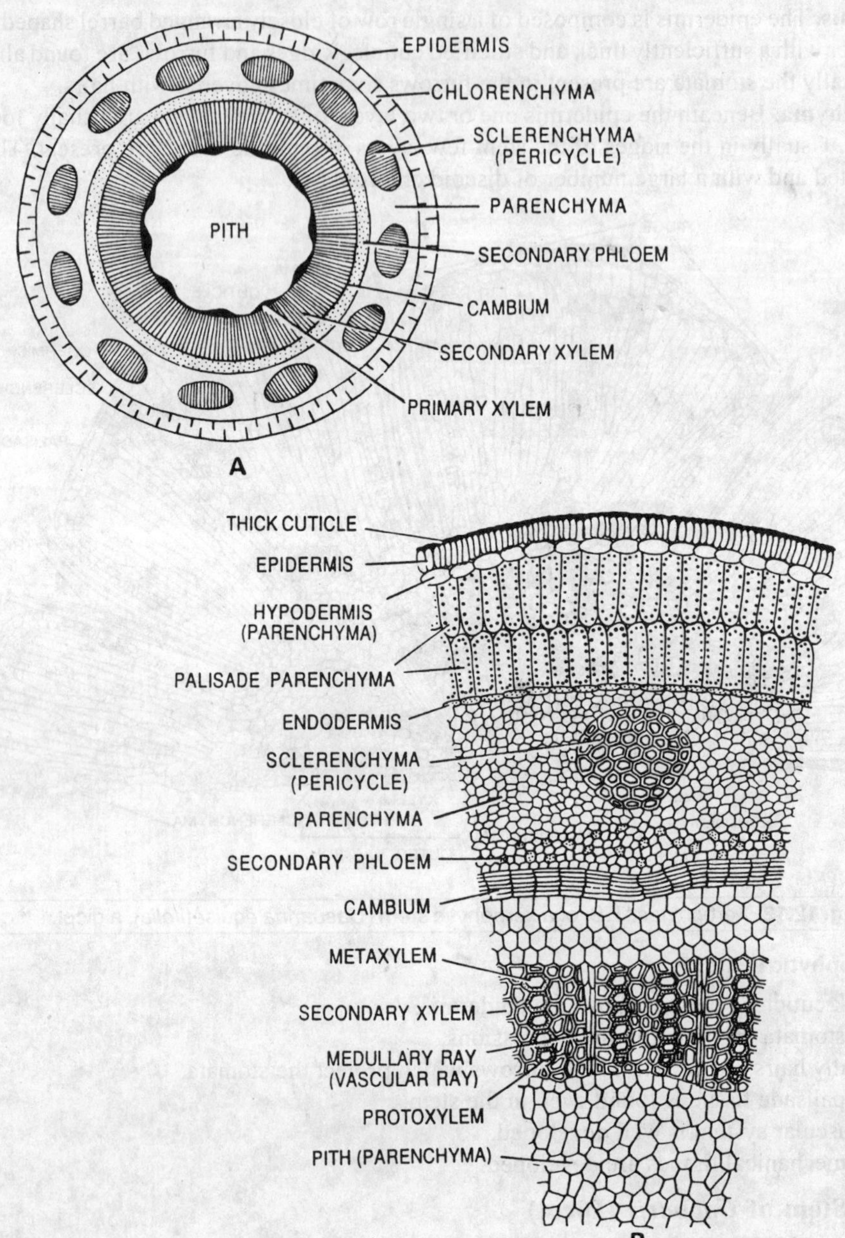

Fig. 12.13. Anatomy of xerophytic stem. T.S. of *Capparis* (dicot) stem. A, diagrammatic ; B, detail of a sector.

Pericycle. The sclerenchymatous pericycle in patches is found just below the endodermis. These patches are alternated with thin walled parenchymatous cells.

Secondary phloem. Beneath the sclerenchymatous pericycle and parenchyma secondary phloem in continuous ring is present. The phloem is represented by sieve tubes, companion cells and phloem parenchyma.

Cambium. Below the phloem multilayered cambial zone is found. The cells are thin walled, rectangular and arranged in radial rows.

Xylem. The xylem may be divided into primary and secondary xylem. The primary xylem consists of large cavities of metaxylem and narrow vessels of protoxylem which are arranged in radial rows. The secondary xylem is represented by xylem parenchyma (prosenchyma).

Medullary rays. The medullary rays are usually two or three layered. The cells are arranged radially. These rays connect the pith with outer tissues and are usually found in between the vascular bundles.

Pith. In the central region of the stem pith is found which consists of thin walled parenchymatous cells.

Xerophytic Characters

(*i*) A very thick cuticle is found over epidermis.
(*ii*) Epidermis consists of radially elongated epidermal cells. The stomata (sunken) are also found on the epidermis.
(*iii*) The palisade tissue is found in the outer cortical region of the stem.
(*iv*) The mechanical tissue (sclerenchyma) is well developed.

EPIPHYTES

Certain plants, commonly the orchids, grow on branches of trees. Such plants are known as epiphytes. They never take their nourishment from supporting plant as do the parasites. They often develop aerial roots. These are adventitious roots which hang down into the air. Each hanging root is surrounded by a spongy tissue, called **velamen.** With the help of this velamen, the roots absorb moisture from surrounding atmosphere. *Vanda* and *Dendrobium* are common examples of orchids. Many epiphytic plants possess special water absorbing hairs. The common example is *Tillandsia.*

PARASITES

The plants, which grow upon other living plants and absorb their food material from them are called 'parasites'. To absorb food material from host plant parasite develops special roots, called sucking roots or haustoria. There are different types of parasites found in nature. Some are total parasites and other partial parasites. The total parasites are never green in colour and obtain all their nourishment from host plant while the partial parasites develop chlorophyll and to some extent also manufacture their food. The parasites may live either on stem or on roots, and accordingly they are called stem parasites or root parasites. *Cuscuta* is a very common example of total stem parasite. *Viscum* is a partial stem parasite. *Orobanche* and *Santalum* are total and partial root parasites respectively.

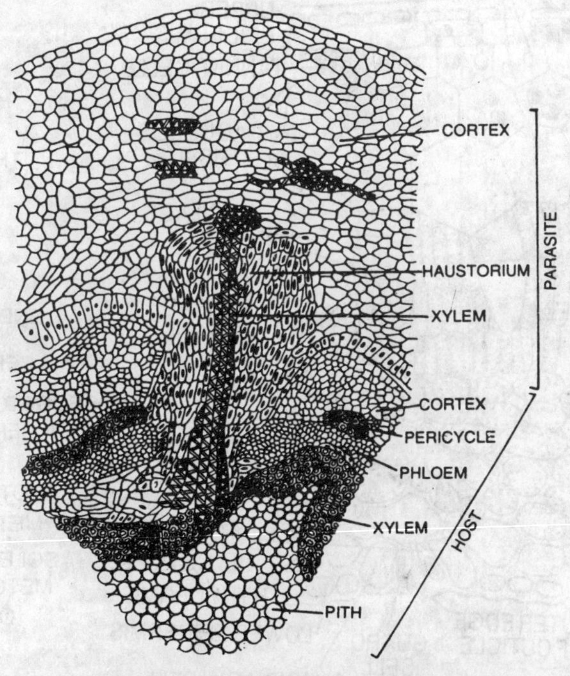

Fig. 12.14. Anatomy of host and parasite. Section through haustorium and portion of host of *Cuscuta*. The cells of the haustorium are between xylem and phloem of the host. The xylem of parasite is in contact with that of the host.

HALOPHYTES

These plants grow in saline soil or water, where there is abundance of salt in the soil; hence halophytes show some special characters. Most of halophytes have succulent leaves and some possess succulent stems. Halophytes growing in marshy places near the sea-shore, form a special vegetation known as the *mangrove.* In many cases, in addition to the stilt roots special roots, called *respiratory roots* or *pneumatophores,* are also produced, such roots develop from underground roots. These roots are provided with numerous pores, through which exchange of gases for respiration takes place. Typical examples of mangrove plants are *Rhizophora, Sonneratia, Ceriops,* etc. In the following paragraph, the anatomy of stem, leaf and root of *Rhizophora* is given :

GENUS – *RHIZOPHORA*

T.S. of Stem

Epidermis. The epidermis is composed of variously shaped cells appearing conical in transverse section. The epidermis frequently consists of more than one layer, but a true hypodermis of 3 — 7 layers is also common. The cork in young stems generally arises superficially, usually in the hypodermis. The young stem has a very thick cuticle.

Cortex. The primary cortex is lacunar. H-haped sclerenchymatous idioblasts are present. The cells of cortex possess pitted walls and are of tannin and oil. Calcium oxalate crystals are also present. The inner cortex has groups of branched sclereids which give mechanical strength to the lacunate cortex. The sclereids are lignified thick walled cells with narrow lumina. The endodermis is conspicuous. The endodermal cells possess starch grains.

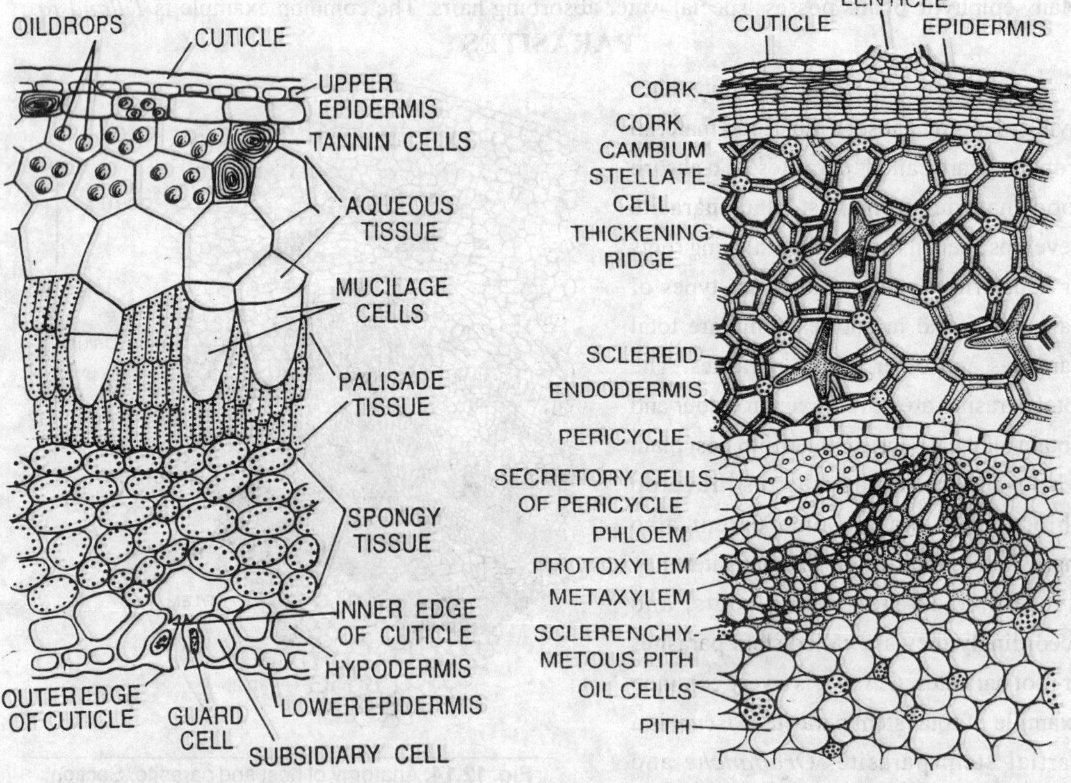

Fig. 12.15. *Rhizophora mucronata.* V.S. of leaf showing detailed structure.

Fig. 12.16. *Rhizophora mucronata.* T.S. of a portion of young stem.

Pericycle. It consists of a subcontinuous composite ring of sclerenchyma consisting of 3 - 4 layers of cells.

Vascular bundles. The vascular bundles are conjoint, collateral, endarch and open.

Xylem. The xylem is traversed by rays 2-3 cells wide in *Rhizophora mucronata.* The vessels possess scalariform perforation plates.

Crystals. The crystals are generally clustered.

Secretory elements. Vertically elongated secretory cells containing tannin and/or oil present in the cortex and the pith.

Anatomy of leaf. The leaves are usually dorsiventral. Hairs are mostly unicellular with thick or thin walls. The cuticle is well developed and often quite thick on both the leaf surfaces.

Cork warts. Occur as small black spots on the lower side of the leaf. The **epidermis** is single layered and consists of rectangular cells. The cells of upper epidermis possess some rod-shaped and cubical crystals of calcium oxalate. The **hypodermis** towards the upper surface is 2 or more layered. The **stomata** are confined to the lower surface. They are depressed and often provided with a front cavity. The **mesophyll** consists of palisade and spongy tissue. Palisade tissue consists of 1 - 4 layers. Spongy tissue usually possesses large intercellular spaces. Aqueous tissue and muclilage cells are also present beneath the upper epidermis. H-shaped sclerenchymatous idioblasts occur in the palisade tissue, and variously branched ones in the spongy mesophyll.

Anatomy of root. The well-known breathing roots (pneumatophores) of members of the Rhizophoraceae inhabiting mangrove swamps have large intercellular spaces of the spongy cortex which facilitate gaseous exchange in the special habitat in which the plants grow. The **cork** consists of suberized cells. The cork layer remains interrupted by lenticels at several places. In some cases the cork consists of alternating layers of suberized and ordinary parenchymatous cells in the aerial portion. Next to the cork there lies a thick **cortex** containing abundant, large, intercellular spaces, arranged radially around the stele. Intercellular spaces are large in the subterranean than in the aerial parts of the roots. The cortex may be subdivided into two portions -the secondary cortex and the primary cortex. The **secondary cortex** consisting of few layers is found just beneath the cork. The primary cortex lies next to the secondary cortex. The primary cortex is broad and lacunar. The primary cortex in the terrestrial part of the root is composed of cells of two kinds - (*a*) radially elongated cells connected with one another tangentially by short lateral arms; (*b*) rows of vertically elongated cells which show small, circular lumina in transverse section. Sclerenchymatous **idioblasts** also occur in the cortex. H-shaped sclerenchymatous idioblasts project into the cortical intercellular spaces in the aerial part of the root, but are less numerous below ground.

The endodermis is conspicuous. Numerous secretory cells are found in the pericyclic region. The xylem is well formed and strongly lignified. The outer pith is sclerenchymatous whereas the central region of pith is parenchymatous. Several oil cells are present here and there in the pith region.

ECOLOGY EXERCISES

Exercise. 1. To study the communities by 'Quadrat Method' by working out frequency, density and abundance.

The structure of a plant community can be studied in quantitative terms through vegetational analysis of small sample units dispersed widely. This may be done in small sample area by quadrat method. **Frequency, abundance** and **density** for different species can be worked out by the formulae given below;

Frequency. This is described as the % of Quadrats occupied by a given species.

$$\%F = \frac{\text{No. of Quadrats in which it occurred}}{\text{Total No. of Quadrats studied}} \times 100$$

Density. This is described as the number of individuals per unit area.

$$D = \frac{\text{Total No. of individuals}}{\text{Total No. of Quadrats studied}}$$

Abundance. No. of individuals per quadrat of occurrence.

$$A = \frac{\text{Total No. of individuals}}{\text{No. of quadrats of occurrence}}$$

Materials. Quadrat (or four nails), meter scale, string, field note book or data sheet.

Method. Lay a quadrat in the study area and record the name and number of individuals of a species occurring there. Lay another quadrat at random anywhere else and record the same data for it and so on. Minimum 10 quadrats should be taken for frequency, density and abundance. The data should be tabulated as given in the table.

Plant species	No. of individuals Quadrat Number 1 2 3 4 5 6 7 8 9 10	Total No. of segments occurrence	Total No. of segments studied	Total No. of individuals	F	D	Abundance
A							
B							
C							
D							
E							
F							
G							
H							

(Size of the Quadrant = 50 cm. X 50 cm.)

Calculations. Calculate Frequency, Density and Abundance from the data by the above given formulae.

Exercise 2. To measure the temperature of soil and air. (Fig. 12.17)

Method. Use ordinary thermometer and soil thermometer for air and soil respectively, on surface and 10 cm. depth in sun and shade.

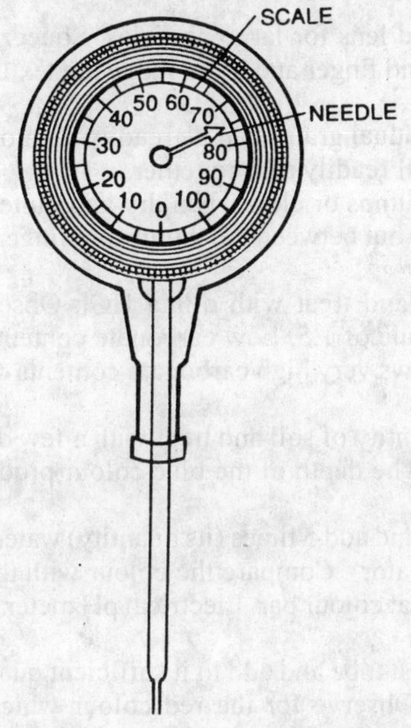

Fig. 12.17. Soil Thermometer. An apparatus to measure the soil temperature.

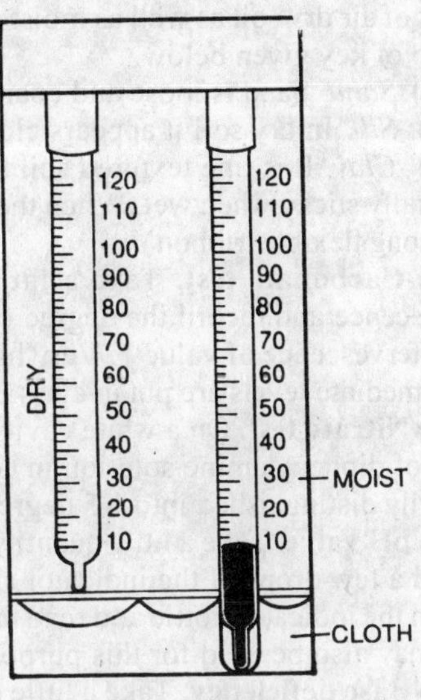

Fig. 12.18. Psychrometer (thermo-hydrograph). An apparatus for measuring humidity.

Exercise 3. To measure Humidity and Light Intensity. (Fig. 12.18)

Method. Humidity can be measured by wet and dry bulb thermometer, or thermohydrograph (which records continuously temperature and humidity) Measurement of *light intensity* is carried out in Lux unit, at different places by means of photometer or Lux-meter (Fig. 12.19)

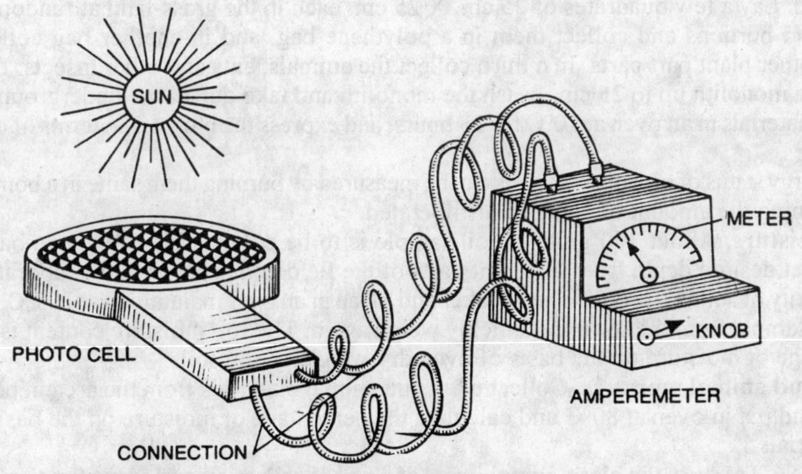

Fig. 12.19. Luxmeter (photometer). An apparatus for measuring light intensity. The unit of light intensity is lux (1 lux = 1 lumen per m^2 = approximately 0.1 foot candle ; 1 foot candle = 1 lumen per ft^2).

Exercise 4. To determine soil texture; presence of carbonate and nitrate; pH value and base deficiency including spot test.

Method. (1) *Soil texture.* Examine the soil under hand lens for large particles. Squeeze small amount of air dry soil as well as moist soil between thumb and finger and try to judge the texture with the help of key given below.

(A) *Sand.* Sand is loose and coarse grained. The individual grains can be readily seen or felt.

(B) *Silt.* In dry soil it appears clotty. When wet the soil readily runs together.

(C) *Clay.* It is fine textured soil that forms very hard lumps or clots when dry and quite plastic and usually sticky when wet. When the moist soil is pinched out between the thumb and finger, it will form a long flexible 'ribbon'.

(2) **Carbonate test.** Take a little soil in a test tube and treat with dilute HCl. Observe for effervescence and record the degree of effervescence in scale of 1.5. Low carbonate contents show poor effervescence of value 1. Very high effervescence shows very high carbonate contents of value 5. Intermediate levels are put in class 2, 3 and 4.

(3) **Nitrate test.** On a white cavity tile take a small quantity of soil and treat with a few drops of 0.02% of diphenylamine solution in concentrated H_2SO_4. The depth of the blue colour produced is arbitrarily distinguished into 1.5 degrees.

(4) **pH valve.** Take a little quantity of soil in a test tube and add 5 times (its quantity) water, shake and add a few drops of the indicator (BDH Universal Indicator). Compare the colour with the chart fixed on the indicator bottle and read the pH given against that colour bar. Electrical pH meter and pH paper may also be used for this purpose.

(5) **Base deficiency.** Take a little quantity of soil in a test tube and add to it sufficient quantity of colourless alcoholic solution of ammonium thiocyanate. Observe for the red colour which is on account of Fe (ic) ions, then add a few drops of hydrogen peroxide and observe any further red colouration, because of the conversion of Fe (ous) ion into Fe (ic). The total red colouration recorded in the scale of 1 to 5 gives base deficiency idea, while the difference on account of the addition of H_2O_2 gives the reductivity of the soil.

Exercise 5. To demonstrate and determine the Biomass, Percentage of Moisture in soil, plants and animal material.

Biomass. The quantity of living material in unit area of land is called the *Standing crop.* This can be expressed in terms of number or weight. The standing crop in terms of weight is also called the *biomass.* Biomass is usually expressed in terms of dry weight at any one time.

Method. Lay a few quadrates of 25 cm. X 25 cm. each in the grass-land at random. Clip all the above ground portions and collect them in a polythene bag, and in another bag collect the fallen leaves and other plant part parts. In a third collect the animals, ants and other insects. Dig the soil in the form of a monolith up to 25 cm., wash the monolith and take out all the underground plant parts. Dry all the materials in an oven at 70°C for 24 hours, and express the biomass in terms of dry weight per square metre.

The energy status of organic materials can be measured by burning them same in a bomb calorimeter and determining the amount of energy thus liberated.

Soil moisture. About 100 gms. of soil sample is to be collected in polythene bags each from surface and at desired depth from different parts of the field and brought to the laboratory. Weigh a certain quantity of soil in a pre-weighed beaker and place in an over maintained at 105°C. After 8 hours remove the sample from the oven and quickly weigh again. The soil moisture content is calculated as the percentage of moisture on the basis of oven dry weight of the soil.

Plant and animal moisture. Collect plant and animal materials from the area in polythene bags separately and put in oven at 80°C and calculate the percentage of moisture on the basis of oven dry weight materials.

Exercise 6. To study the biotic components of a pond; collection and identification of plants and animals.

Materials. Collection nets with different meshes, specimen tubes, glass jars of different sizes, hand lens, plant grappler, metre-scale, iron chain, scissors and forceps, centrifuge.

Method. The hydrophytes of the pond margin or marsh and shallow regions can be hand picked or lifted and collected in polythene bags. Iron hooks tied to long string can be used to drag submerged plants of deeper area. For plankton special type of plankton bottle with nylon net and long handle-rod is used. The plankton net is wielded several times as to obtain a concentrated collection of microorganisms. Identify the collection with the help of suitable key or literature for plants and animals and list them in sequence.

The biomass of macro-producers and macro-consumers per unit can also be estimated by suitable sized quadrat (preferably 25 cm. square) and can be expressed in fresh weight as well as dry weight as described in gm./m^2 or gm./cubic meter.

For microproducers and microconsumers collect the sample without much disturbance of the sampling of site in some glassware. Take about 10 ml. of this sample in test tube and centrifuge it. Drain out the water and take fresh and dry weights. Express in gm./litre.

Exercise 7. To study the environmental factors of a pond.

A. To determine the pH of pond water.

Method. The same techniques employed for measuring the pH of the soil can be used. Samples should be collected at different times and at different places. Along with this the temperature of the sample should also be recorded.

B. To measure the transparency of the pond water.

Method. Use *Sechi* disc and note the depth up to which the disc colour can be distinguished at different regions of a pond and in water of different ponds. This depth is noted and used as an index of turbidity. The greater the depth the lower will be the turbidity value.

C. To measure the light intensity available in the pond.

Method. Use photometers specially sealed in water-tight containers with glass window for free interplay of light on the photosensitive disc. Measure the light intensity at different depths.

D. To record the temperature of the pond at the surface and at different depths.

Method. For temperature recording at situations where fluctuations are sharp thermocouples are used. The principle is that when two dissimilar metal wires meet at their ends, a difference of electrical potential is set up which is directly proportional to the temperature of the function. One such instrument with a little modification is the *thermister*. Use thermister and measure the temperature at different depths of the pond.

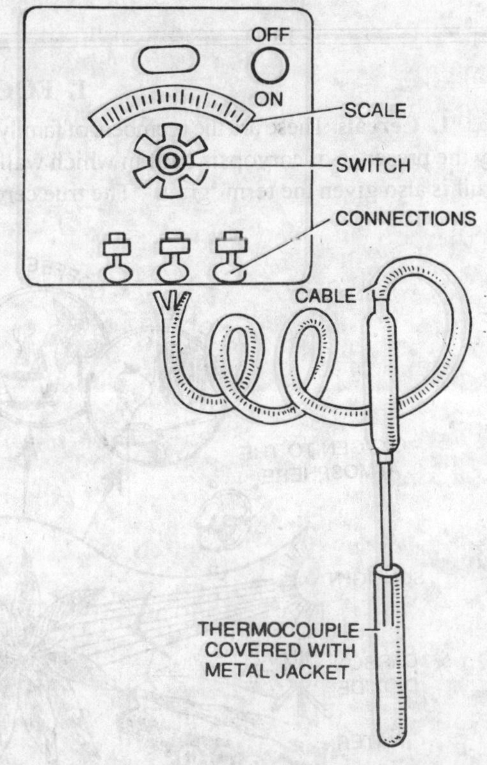

Fig. 12.20. Thirmister. An apparatus to measure the temperature of water of a pond.

Exercise 8. To undertake a comparative study of plants and animals in relation to water availability.

Method. Visit, pond, dry areas and moist places. Collect the plants and animals. Study the morphological features specially suited to aquatic and arid life in different species and list them in some sequence. Anatomical features can also be studied in plants. Group the species into different morpho-ecologic classes, *e.g.*, free floating, submerged rooted and floating, marshy plants in the case of hydrophytes and ephemerals, and succulents and non-succulent perennial plants in the case of xerophytes.

CHAPTER

Economic Botany

1. FOOD PLANTS

1. Cereals. These are the members of family Gramineae (grass-family). The cereals are characterised by the presence of caryopsis fruit in which wall of seed is fused with the ovary to form the husk. This fruit is also given the term 'grain'. The true cereals are the following :

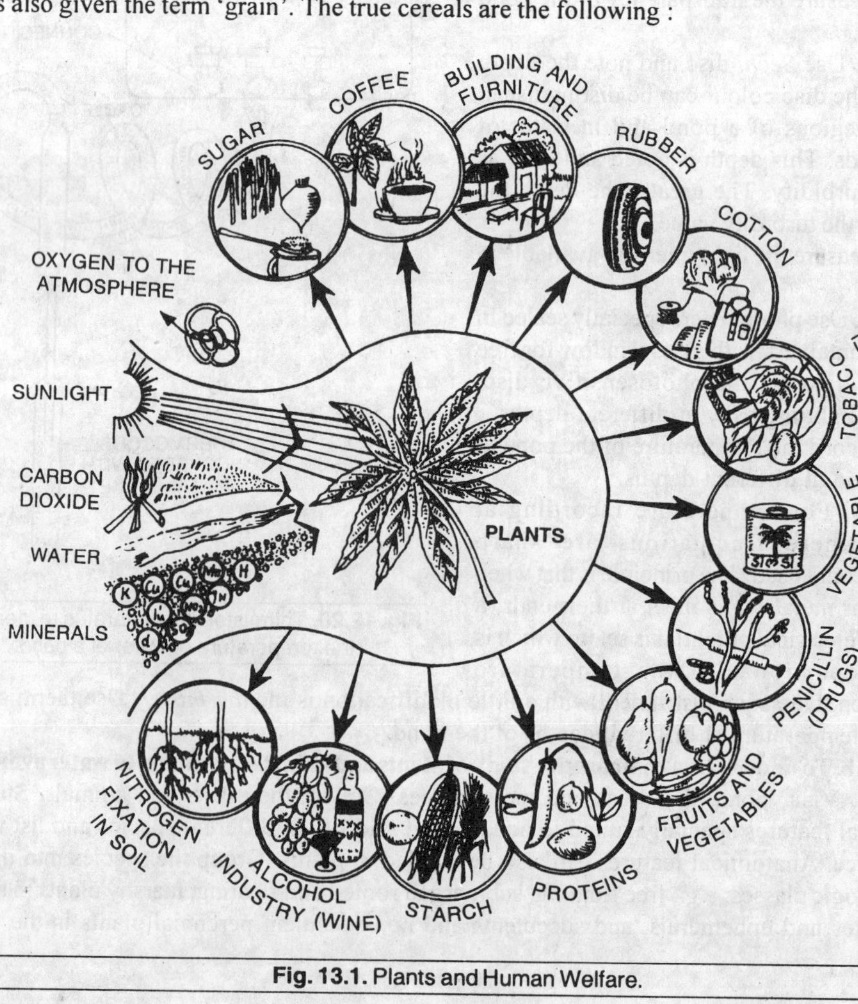

Fig. 13.1. Plants and Human Welfare.

(1) Barley, (2) Maize, (3) Rice, (4) Wheat, (5) Oats.

Two groups of cereals have been formed :

(A) Major cereals, (B) Minor cereals and millets.

(A) Major Cereals. (*i*) Wheat; Verna. **Gehun** (*Triticum aestivum*). Family Gramineae. It is the chief cereal of temperate region. The important varieties grown in India are Lerma Roja, Sonara 64, Sonalika, Sharbati Sonara, etc. It is an annual grass and the inflorescence is a terminal spike consisting of 15—20 spikelets.

Uses. (1) It is used mostly for human consumption. The flour is chiefly used for making bread, biscuits, etc.

(2) Other edible products are puffed wheat, macaroni, bran flakes, etc.

(3) Wheat is used in the manufacture of beer and other alcoholic beverages and industrial alcohol, especially *Bodka* of Russia.

(4) It is an excellent feed for livestock.

(5) A special variety of wheat is grown for preparation of starch which is used in the sizing of textile fibres.

(6) Wheat straw is used in making seating of chairs, stuffing mattresses, strings, baskets and straw carpets.

(7) Wheat straw is used in packing and thatching.

(8) Wheat plant is also a valuable source of fodder.

(*ii*) **Maize**, Verna. **Makka** (*Zea mays*). Family Gramineae. Maize is the largest of the cereals, a tall annual grass which attains a height of 1—5 meters. At the top of the stem, the staminate flowers are found while the cob with the pistillate flowers is produced lower down on the stem. Here each ovary possesses a long silky style which is also called as the corn silk. In India common varieties grown are Amber, Jawahar, Sona, Vijay, etc.

Uses—(1) About one half the crop is used as a food for livestock.

(2) The cobs are eaten raw or after cooking.

(3) Maize is used in making corn starch from which many derivatives are obtained such as corn syrup, corn sugar, dextrins, and industrial alcohol.

(4) Corn oil may also be extracted from the embryo of maize.

(5) Leaves and stalks are used as cattle feed.

(6) The fibres in stalks have been used for making yarn and paper.

(7) With the help of maize protein, now-a-days, some special type of artificial fibers are being made.

(8) Grains are widely used in making corn flakes which is an important breakfast food.

(*iii*) **Rice; ** Verna. **Chaval** (*Oryza sativa*) ; Fam. Gramineae. Rice is the most important cereal of tropical climate. Rice plant is an annual grass attaining the maximum height of 2 to 4 feet. It produces a panicle, an inflorescence composed of a number of fine branches, each terminating in a single grain surrounded by a husk. In this condition it is called as paddy. Recent varieties cultivated in India are Ganga, Kavery, etc.

Uses—(1) The chief use of rice is as a food.

(2) Now a days, the use of polished rice is increasing, though it is much less nutritive.

(3) Straw is used as a livestock feed.

(4) Alcoholic beverages are also made from the grain of rice, *e.g.*, sake of Japan.

(5) Recently from the husk, an oil is extracted which can be used as cooking oil.

(B) Minor Cereals. (*i*) Barley; Verna. **Jau;** (*Hordeum vulgare*). Fam. Gramineae. Barley is an annual plant. It seldom reaches more than 3 ft. in height. The inflorescence is a dense head with three sessile spikelets.

Uses. (1) Chiefly used as a feed for livestock.

(2) 20 to 25% crop is used as a source of malt to be used for alcohol, beer and whisky.

(3) Barley is also used as a crop for killing the weeds.

(4) Barley straw is used for stock feeding purposes too.

***(ii)* Oat**; Verna. **Jai** (*Avena sativa*). Fam. Gramineae. This plant varies in height from 2 to 5 feet. The inflorescence is one-sided or spreading panicle which may be either erect or drooping. At the upper end of the oat caryopsis some fine hairs are also found.

Uses. (1) Due to its high fat, protein and mineral contents it is one of the most nutritious cereals for human use.

(2) Oats constitute the chief grain food for horses and other domestic animals except pigs.

(3) It is also grown for green forage.

(4) It is used in cakes, biscuits and breakfast food.

***(iii)* Sorghum**; Verna. **Jowar** (*Sorghum vulgare)*. Fam. Gramineae. It is an annual plant of an average height from 3 to 15 feet resembling with maize in habit. The inflorescence is a dense panicle.

Uses. (1) In India it is used as a food for man.

(2) As fodder.

Millets. Usually the cultivated grasses with very small seeds are put in this class, some important millets are:

***(i)* Italian millet. Kangni**. (*Setaria italica*). Fam. gramineae. It is somewhat smaller plant than the other cultivated grasses. Here the inflorescence is a dense spike, with innumerable long or short bristles.

Uses. (1) It is used for human food after boiling or parching.

(2) It is also an important forage crop.

(3) It is much used in crop rotation.

***(ii)* Pearl millet**; Verna. **Bajra**. (*Pennisetum typhoides*) Fam. Gramineae. It grows from 6 to 15 feet in height. Here the inflorescence is very compact with three to eight cylindrical spikes.

Uses. (1) It is widely used as food for poor people.

(2) The flour made from it is used in making bread and cake.

(3) It has an enormous yield of forage too.

2. Legumes. These are next to cereals as source of human food. Due to a good amount of proteins, the nutritive value of these legumes is very high. All the legumes or pulses belong to the family Leguminosae, which is characterized by a special kind of fruit, a legume, which opens along the both sutures after the ripening of the seeds. The roots of legumes possess some swollen structures called nodules. These root nodules contain nitrogen fixing bacteria—*Rhizobium,* etc. These bacteria convert the atmospheric free nitrogen into nitrogenous substances which in turn get converted into amino acids that constitute the proteins. Besides proteins, some carbohydrates, minerals and Vitamin B are also present in these legumes.

(*i*) **Pea;** Verna. **Matar** (*Pisum sativum*) Family-Papilionaceae. Peas are annual, herbaceous, tendril bearing plants with an height of 2 to 4 feet Here the pods are about 2 to 3 inches long containing four to nine seeds. The seeds may be rounded or wrinkled with yellow or white colour.

Uses. (1) In India the peas are variously used. These are eaten fresh, canned, curried or dehydrated.

(2) These are used as green fodder.

(3) In Burma, vinegar is also manufactured by it.

(4) Famous plant breeding experiments were also made on this pea by Gregor Mendel.

(*ii*) **Chick Pea** or **Gram**; Verna. **Chana** (*Cicer arietinum)* Family-Papilionaceae. It is a plant of warm semi-arid conditions. This annual herb possesses branched, bushy and hairy stems. Here the seeds are globular with wrinkled appearance.

Uses. (1) In India it is used very widely. It is eaten both by man and animals.

(2) The flour is used in biscuit preparation.

(3) It is used in its plant form as a fodder after drying.

(4) 'Kabuli Chana', a special variety is used as human food which is very nutritious.

(5) The leaves are used as vegetable.

(iii) Soybean (*Glycine max*) Family-Papilionaceae. The plant is small, bushy, erect or prostrate annual. It has richest protein content in the plant kingdom, *i.e.*, 40—60% protein.

Uses. (1) Seeds are used green, dry or sprouted.

(2) Various edible preparations are made from it such as Soya milk, Soya sauce, Soya cheese, etc.

(3) Soya bean oil is extensively used in textile industry.

(4) Due to very low starch content it is a very fine ingredient of food for diabetic people.

(5) Soya flour is used in bakery, meat industry and in manufacture of ice cream.

(6) Soya protein is also used in paper industry as an important sizing material.

(iv) Green Gram; Verna. **Mung** (*Phaseolus aureus*): Family Papilionaceae. It is an annual plant, bushy in appearance. Warm climate is suitable for its cultivation. Here the pods are somewhat hairy enclosing the seeds within them.

Uses. (1) Green pods are eaten as vegetable.

(2) Seeds are used as dal which contain 20—25% protein.

(3) Plants are used as green manure.

(4) Plants after harvesting are used as cattle feed.

(v) Black-Gram; Verna. **Urd** (*Phaseolus mungo*) Family Papilionaceae. It is an annual with white or coloured flowers and slender pods.

Uses. (1) Used as human food in form of split pulse or dal.

(2) After harvesting the plant body is used as fodder.

(3) Woody parts are also used as fuel after drying.

(vi) Lablab; Verna. **Sem**. (*Dolichos lablab*) Family Papilionaceae. The plant body is woody. It is a perennial climber.

Uses. (1) Both the pods and seeds are eaten.

(2) Plant is also used as forage, chiefly for horses.

(vii) Red Gram or **Arhar** (*Cajanus cajan*). Family Papilionaceae. It is an annual or perennial herb grown mostly in warm and moist climate.

Uses. (1) Split dal is used as human food.

(2) Old woody parts are used as fuel.

(3) After harvesting, the plant body is also used as fodder.

(4) Stalks are used for basket making.

(5) In Indian villages the dried plants are vastly used for roof thatching.

(*viii*) **Ground Nut**; Verna. **Mungphali** (*Arachis hypogea*). Family Papilionaceae. It is a true legume rather than a nut. The plant is a creeping annual bush. Here fruits ripe under the ground. It is very nutritious.

Uses. (1) The nuts or seeds are used after roasting for making peanut butter. The seeds are roasted then ground to a paste which is converted into the peanut butter.

(2) Peanut oil is used as a fine cooking medium.

(3) Vegetable ghee is also prepared from peanut oil.

(4) The oil cake is fed to the livestock.

(5) Now-a-days the peanut protein is also being used in the manufacture of ardil, a synthetic fibre.

Potato. Verna. **Aloo** (*Solanum tuberosum*) Family Solanaceae. It is an annual plant with 1 to 2 feet long stem. Tubers are modified stems found in different shapes-round, oval, cylindrical, etc. Important Indian varieties are Phulwa, Kufri, Safed and Pahari.

Uses. (1) The tubers are rich in starch and used as vegetable.

(2) The tubers are used in the manufacture of alcohol.

(3) Starch and industrial food preparations are made from potato tubers.

(4) Tubers are also feed to livestock.

(5) In India the tubers are also used in making potato chips and potato pickles.

Sugarcane. Verna. **Ganna** (*Saccharum officinarum*). Family Gramineae. It is a perennial grass which attains a maximum height of 4 m. It grows usually in clumps. The stem is solid which contains 80% of juice, the sugar content of which varies greatly. Juice also contains sucrose, proteins, gums, acids, etc. Sugar Cane Research Station, Coimbatore has produced many varieties of sugarcane among which Co 312, Co 5510, Co351 are under cultivation now-a-days. Here inflorescence is branched plume-like panicle.

Uses. (1) Sugar industry fully depends on the sugarcanes.

(2) Several by-products are obtained from this sugar industry, *e.g.*, begasse and molasses.

(3) Begasse are used as fuel and fodder. It is also used in paper industry.

(4) Due to rich fermentable contents, the molasses are used as manure, fuel and also in making alcohol, carbon dioxide, etc.

(5) A mixture of begasse and molasses is a valuable cattle food.

Common Edible Fruits

English name	*Botanical name and family*	*Type of fruit*	*Edible part*
Apple	*Malus sylvestris* Rosaceae	pome	thalamus
Banana	*Musa pardisiaca* Musaceae	berry	mesocarp and endocarp
Cashew-nut	*Anacardium occidentale* Anacardiaceae	nut	peduncle and cotyledons
Coconut	*Cocos nucifera* Palmaceae	fibrous drupe	endosperm
Cucumber	*Cucumis sativus* Cucurbitaceae	pepo	mesocarp, endocarp and placentae
Custard apple	*Annona squamosa* Annonaceae	etaerio of berries	fleshy pericarp of individual berries
Date palm	*Phoenix sylvestris* Palmaceae	one seeded berry	pericarp
Fig	*Ficus carica* Moraceae	syconus	fleshy receptacle
Jack fruit	*Artocarpus heterophyllus* Moraceae	sorosis	bracts, perianth and seeds
Grape	*Vitis vinifera* Vitaceae	berry	pericarp and placentae
Guava	*Psidium guava* Myrtaceae	berry	thalamus and pericarp
Indian plum	*Zizyphus jujuba* Rhamnaceae	drupe	mesocarp and epicarp
Litchi	*Litchi chinensis* Sapindaceae	one-seeded nut	fleshy aril
Wheat and other cereals	*Triticum aestivum* Poaceae	caryopsis	starchy endosperm
Mango	*Mangifera indica* Ancardiaceae	drupe	mesocarp
Melon	*Cucumis melo* Cucurbitaceae	pepo	mesocarp
Orange	*Citrus aurantium* Rutaceae	Hesperidium	juicy placental hairs
Papaw	*Carica papaya* Caricaceae	berry	mesocarp
Pea	*Pisum sativum* Papilionaceae	legume	cotyledons
Pear	*Pyrus communis* Rosaceae	pome	fleshy thalamus
Pine-apple	*Ananas comosus* Bromeliaceae	sorosis	outer portion of receptacle bracts and perianth
Pomegranate	*Punica granatum* Punicaceae	special (balusta)	juicy testa
Strawberry	*Fragaria vesca* Rosaceae	etaerio of achenes or nuts	succulent thalamus
Tomato	*Lycopersicon esculentum* Solanaceae	berry	pericarp and placentae
Wood apple	*Aegle marmelos* Rutaceae	berry	mesocarp, endocarp and placentae

2. FIBRES

The fibre plants are second to rank to food plants in their usefulness to man, the tropics supply world's fibre requirement.

The fibres serve as a skeleton of plant as they are made up of sclerenchymatous cells which may be obtained from different parts of plant body, *e.g.,* vessels, tracheids, pericycle, phloem, etc. Usually the fibres are long, thick walled with a small cavity and pointed ends. They are strongly lignified but contain cellulose too. The strength and durability of the fibres are due to presence of cellulose. Some chief fibre yielding plants are :

(1) **Cotton**. Verna. **Kapas** (*Gossypium* sp.). Family Malvaceae. Cotton is the world's chief fibre plant. It is an annual or perennial shrub. Fibres are produced by the seed coat so it is also called as **the surface fibre.** When separated from the seed the fibres are termed as "lint". Four main species of *Gossypism* are referred of great commercial importance.

Gossypium barbadense (Egyptian cotton).

G. hirsutum (American upland cotton) New World species.

G. abroreum

G. herbaceum Old World species.

Fruit. The cotton fruit is called as boll. It is ovoid leathery capsule.

Seed. The seed is an ovoid more or less pointed structure; the testa of which bears hairs of two kinds; long thickened, white-lint and short white or coloured fuzz which is attached to the seed coat. The fuzz may not be produced by some varieties.

Fibre. The fibre is translucent, hollow some convolutions within it. The main constituent of this fibre is cellulose with some other protein, pectic substances, sugar, wax, etc.

Uses. (1) Almost whole textile industry fully depends on this fibre.

(2) Cotton is used in stuffing the pillows, cushions, etc.

(3) It is used in making the rubber tyres.

(4) Carpets, blankets and cordages are made from this cotton.

(*ii*) **Jute** (*Corchorus* sp.) Family. Tiliaceae. It is a **soft fibre.** The plant is a tall, slender and annual shrub. It is most valuable and useful fibre and is second in use to cotton.

Fibre. Jute is the best of the loose bast fibres obtained from the secondary phloem of two species of *Corchorus* :

(*i*) *C. capsularis* (round pods)

(*ii*) *C. olitorius* (long pods).

The fibres are very long (about 6 to 10 feet) and pale-yellow coloured. They are considerably lignified with silk appearance.

Uses. (1) It is chiefly used for rough weaving and gunny wool bags.

(2) Fibre is used for making carpets, curtains and rough clothes.

(3) Ropes and strings are also made from this fibre.

(*iii*) **Sunn Hemp** (*Crotalaria juncea*); Family Papilonaceae. It is an important Asiatic fibre plant. This plant is a shrub from 6 to 12 feet in height. It is an annual legume with yellow flowers.

Fibre. Here the fibres are obtained from phloem. It is a yellow fibre 1 to 1.5 meter long, more durable and stronger than jute fibre.

Uses. (1) It is vastly used in making ropes, nets, mats, cordages, etc.

(2) Cigarette paper is also made from it.

(3) India earns a great foreign currency by exporting it every year.

(*iv*) **Hemp.** Verna. **Bhang** (*Cannabis sativa*). Family Cannabinaceae. The plant is a stout and branched annual shrub varying 5 to 7 feet in height.

Fibre. Here the fibre develops in pericvcle and can be obtained from the bast (phloem). The fibre varies from 3 to 15 feet in length.

Uses. (1) It is used for making ropes, twine, carpets, bags and webbing.

(2) Hemp waste is sometimes used in making paper.

(*v*) **Coir.** These are short, coarse and rough fibres which make the greater part of husk of coconut palm (*Cocos nucifera*). Family Palmae. It is only prominent fibre obtained from fruits. Here the fruit develops from spadix inflorescence.

Fibre. The fibre is obtained from the mesocarp of the fruits. This fibre is very light and elastic, and exceedingly resistant to water.

Uses. (1) It is used for making bristles of brushes.

(2) Doormats, floor coverings, sacks, coarse textile, etc., are also made from it.

(3) Also used as a substitute for jute.

3. Oils

The oils are complex compounds having tri-ester-glycerides with long chain organic acids, chiefly palmitic, stearic and oleic acids.

The oils are of two kinds;

(*i*) Essential oils; and (*ii*) Fatty oils,

The Fatty Oils

Also called as fixed oils as they are nonvolatile and cannot be evaporated. Chemically these fatty oils are very close to the animal fats. They consist of glycerin with the combination of a fatty acid. Generally these are liquid at ordinary temperature and usually contain oleic acid. These are insoluble in water but soluble in various organic solvents. On hydrolysis with alkali, they give soap.

Fatty oils are produced in many families of plants, both tropical and temperate. Some important fatty oils are :

(*i*) **Linseed oil (Alsi Ka Tel).** Oil is extracted from the seeds of *Linum usitatissimum* belonging to the family Linaceae.

Oil. It is a **drying oil** as it may absorb oxygen and also gets dried on exposure in the form of a thin elastic film. The seed contains 32 to 43 per cent oil. Usually it is extracted by pressure with heat or by the use of solvents. The colour of oil is yellow to brownish and has acrid taste and smell.

Uses. (1) It is used chiefly in making paints, varnishes, linoleum, soft soap and printer's ink.

(2) Oil cake is used as cattle feed.

(3) Also used as food purposes when obtained by cold process.

(*ii*) **Soybean oil**. Oil is extracted from the seeds of *Glycine max* belonging to the family Papilionaceae.

Oil. It is a **drying oil** as it may absorb oxygen and also gets dried on exposure in the form of a thin elastic film. The seed contains 19—22 per cent oil. Usually it is extracted by hydraulic or expeller process. The colour of oil is yellow to light brown.

Uses. (1) Over 50 different food products have been made from it, principally margarine.

(2) It can be used as a cooking oil after refining.

(3) A number of commercial products are made from this oil as candles, soaps, linolium, paints, greases, rubber substitutes, etc.

(4) Oil cake has 40 to 48 per cent protein so it is a valuable cattle feed and also a source of soya flour.

(5) It is also used in making adhesives, plastics, spreaders, fertilizers, a synthetic textile fibre and many other products.

(*iii*) **Cotton seed oil.** Oil is extracted from the seeds of *Gossypium* species belonging to the family Malvaceae.

Oil. It is a **semidrying oil** as it absorbs oxygen very slowly and in limiting amount and forms a soft film only after long exposure. The seeds contain 30—40 per cent oil. Oil is extracted through hydraulic or expeller process.

Uses. (1) It is used for salad or cooking purpose.

(2) Oleomargarine and lard substitute (fat of pig) are made from it.

(3) The raw oil is used for making soap, artificial leather, insulating materials, washing powders, oil cloth, etc.

(4) Oil cake is used as a livestock feed and also as a manure.

(*iv*) **Sesame oil (Til Ka Tel)**. Oil is extracted from the seeds of *Sesamum indicum* belonging to the family Pedaliaceae.

Oil. It is a **semidrying oil** as it absorbs oxygen very slowly and in limiting amount and forms a soft film only after long exposure. The seeds contain 50 to 57 per cent oil. The clean oil is clear yellow coloured with a characteristic smell.

Uses. (1) The refined oil is used for cooking.

(2) The raw oil is used in making soap, cosmetics, medicinal purposes, etc.

(3) Also used as an illuminant.

(4) Oil cake is used as cattle feed and as fertilizer.

(*v*) **Mustard Oil (Sarson Ka Tel)**. Oil is extracted from the seeds of *Brassica campestris* belonging to family Cruciferae.

Oil. Purified oil ranks midway **between semidrying and nondrying oils.** The seeds contain 30—40 per cent oil. The crude oil is yellowish or light brown in colour with a definite taste and odour.

Uses. (1) It is an excellent cooking medium.

(2) It is used for greasing and burning in the lamps.

(3) It is also used in making soaps, rubber substitutes and tempering steel plates.

(4) Oil cake is a cattle feed.

(*vi*) **Sunflower oil**. Oil is extracted from the seeds of *Helianthus annuus* belonging to the family Compositae.

Oil. It is a drying oil as it may absorb oxygen and also gets dried on exposure in the form of a thin elastic film. The seeds contain 32-45 per cent oil. The oil is extracted by expression method. Oil is pale yellow in colour.

Uses. (1) The oil is used as a cooking medium.

(2) It is used in the manufacture of paints, soaps and cosmetics.

(3) Oil cake is an excellent cattle feed.

(4) Margarines and lard substitutes are also made from it.

(*vii*) **Olive oil (Jaitun Ka Tel)**. Oil is extracted from the fruits of *Olea europaea* belonging to the family Oleaceae.

Oil. It is a **non-drying oil** at ordinary temperature, it remains liquid and do not form a film. The colour of oil is golden yellow and is clear and odourless.

Uses. (1) The oil is used as a cooking medium.

(2) It is widely used as a medicine.

(3) Inferior grades have a greenish tinge and are used for soap making and as lubricants.

(4) Olive oil is used greatly as a food oil.

(5) Oil cake is a cattle feed and fertilizer.

(*viii*) **Castor Oil**. Oil is extracted from the seeds of *Ricinus communis* belonging to family Euphorbiaceae.

Oil. It is a **non-drying oil** as at ordinary temperature they remain liquid and do not form a film. The characteristically marked seeds contain 35—55% oil. Oil is colourless or greenish.

Uses. (1) It is vastly used as a medicine in the form of a purgative.

(2) It is an excellent lubricant for aeroplanes.

(3) It is water resistant so also used in coating fabrics and as protective covering for aeroplanes.

(4) It is used for making soaps, links, plastic, etc.

(5) It is used as an illuminant.

(6) Oil cake is used as a fertilizer

(7) When hydrated, it gets converted into drying oil and used in paint and varnish.

(*ix*) **Peanut Oil (Mungfali Ka Tel).** Oil is extracted from *Arachis hypogea* belonging to family Papilionaceae.

Oil. It is a **non-drying oil** as at ordinary temperature they remain liquid and do not form a film. The seeds contain 40% oil. It is extracted by hydraulic pressure. The oil is yellow in colour.

Uses. (1) It is an excellent cooking medium.

(2) After hydrogenation, Vanaspati Ghee is made from it.

(3) Inferior grades are used to form soaps and lubricants.

(4) It is used as an illuminant.

(5) Oil cake is a good cattle feed.

(*x*) **Coconut oil (Nariyal Ka Tel)**. Oil is extracted from the endosperm of the fruits of *Cocos nucifera* belonging to family Palmae.

Oil. It is a **vegetable fat.** Here the yield is 65 to 70 per cent. The oil is pale yellow or colourless, and solidifies below 74° F.

Uses. (1) Refined oil is edible. Margarine, candy bars and similar type of confectionery are made from it.

(2) Best kind of soaps, shaving creams, cosmetics, shampoo, etc., are made by it.

(3) It is only oil used in marine soaps.

(4) Oil cake is used as cattle feed and fertilizer.

4. DRUGS

(*i*) **Opium**. Opium poppy (*Papaver somniferum*). Family Papaveraceae. It is an erect, annual herb with ovate oblong amplexicaul leaves. The flowers are large, bluish with a purple base. The capsules are large globose. Opium poppy is cultivated for the production of opium.

Opium is the dried juice or latex obtained from unripe capsules. Crude opium is a brownish material containing as many as 25 alkaloids, the most important and most powerful of which are morphine and codeine.

Uses. (1) It is narcotic and sedative.

(2) Its derivatives are used to relieve pain, induce sleep and relax spasms.

(3) Mainly the alkaloids morphine and codeine are used in form of medicine.

(*ii*) **Rauwolfia**. *Rauwolfia serpentina.* Family Apocynaceae. It is an erect, ever green annual under shrub with leaves in whorls of three. The inflorescence is cyme of white or pinkish flowers. The fruit is a purplish black drupe.

Here the medicinal value of roots is very high. The dried roots of *R.serpentina* are an important source of an alkaloid reserpine. Other alkaloids are—serpentine, ajmalinine, etc.

Uses. The alkaloid reserpine is used as a very effective drug as it produces sedation, lowering of blood pressure and increases uterine contractions. The juice of its leaves is used for removal of opacities of cornea of the eyes.

Solanum. *Solanum viarum*; Family-Solanaceae. It is a wild perennial herb, with a woody stem, of about 2 feet in height, nearly whole body of the plant is covered with yellow hairs. The stem bears two types of prickles, hooked and straight. Leaves deeply lobed, hirsute and bear only straight prickles. Flowers are white in colour. Berry is about an inch in diameter.

Uses. The berries contain the alkaloid *Solasodine.* It is a glycon which is used by pharmaceutical companies for the preparation of many important drugs. It is a good source of *sapogenin.* Sapogenin is used as a base for the preparation of *Cortisone* and allied products.

Cortisone, a steroidal hormone prepared from solasodine, is found to be effective in the treatment of acute stages of rheumatoid arthritis, chronic cases of asthma, leukemia obesity and many skin diseases.

Digitalis. *Digitalis purpurea* Linn.; Eng. Common foxglove; Family-Scrophulariaceae. An annual cultivated herb. Cultivated in Kashmir, Darjeeling and the Nilgiris.

Uses. The leaves are used for certain conditions of the heart mainly as a cardiac stimulant and tonic.

Leaves contain several glycosides of which digitoxin, gitoxin and gitalin the principal glycosides to which its physiological activity is due ; digitoxin is most potent of digitalis glycerides ; tannins, inosital, luteolin and many acids and fatty matter are also present; a new cardiotonic glucoside digicorin is isolated from leaves.

Belladonna. *Atropa belladonna* Linn. of family Solanaceae. This is a tall-erect herb.

Uses. The roots are used as sedative, stimulant and antispasmodic. It is used externally to relieve pain and internally to check excessive sweat, cough, etc.

Quinine. *Cinchona calisaya* Wedd.; *C. officinalis* Linn. of family Rubiaceae. It is a tree.

Uses. Quinine is one of the most important drugs known, and it is the only adequate cure for malaria. It is obtained from the bark of the tree. The most important constituent of Cinchona bark is quinine, a very bitter white, granular substance. In addition to its use in the treatment of Malaria, It is a valuable tonic and antiseptic. It is also used in the treatment of other fevers. Some 29 other alkaloids have been isolated from the bark, including cinchonidine, cinchonine, and quinidine, all of which are useful in medicine.

5. TIMBERS

Large branches of trees sawed are called as Timber. Apart from food and clothing timber is most widely used commodity.

Due to activity of cambium both in Angiosperms and Gymnosperms, the secondary tissue wood is produced. This wood is made up of heterogenous tissue, which are responsible for mechanical strength of the tree. Wood may be porous or non-porous as in angiosperms and gymnosperms respectively. Some important trees producing wood are :

(*i*) **Teak or Sagwan** (*Tectona grandis*) ; Family Verbenaceae. It is a large deciduous tree and good resistant to decay and termites.

Wood. Here the wood is porous. The pores are partly filled with tyloses. Sap wood is white while heart wood when cut is green possessing a fragrance and a beautiful golden yellow colour which on seasoning soon darkens into brown mottled with dark streaks. The timber retains its fragrance for a long time. It is hard, durable, strong and also takes good polish.

Uses. In India it is used for making furniture, building, sleepers, etc. Ships and bridges are also made by the use of this timber.

(*ii*) **Sal** (*Shorea robusta*). Family Dipterocarpaceae. Here the tree grows in a gregarious habit.

Wood. It is porous with heavily plugged tyloses. The sap wood is distinct which is small in amount, whitish and not durable. Heart wood is brown, finely streaked with darker lines, hard, strong and cross grained structure. The fibres run obliquely. It does not season well. It has good strength, elasticity and durability.

Uses. (1) It is used for poles, beams, planking and railing for bridges, doors and window parts of houses.

(2) It is used to make cart bodies, railway sleepers.

(3) In Assam it is favourite wood for boat building.

(*iii*) **Shisham** (*Dalbergia sissoo*). Family Papilionaceae. It is a large deciduous tree found in plains throughout India.

Wood. It is also porous. The sap wood is small and white. Heart wood is brown with longitudinal veins, grained, season well and hard. Annual rings are not distinctly marked. Wood is durable and does not warp or split.

Uses. It is vastly used for making naves of wheels, sleepers, ship building, furniture, etc.

Deodar. *Cedrus deodara* Loud.; Eng. Deodar; Verna. *Deodar, diar*; Family Pinaceae. A tall evergreen tree found in the North-Western Himalayas.

Wood. It is of light yellow-brown colour and possesses distinctive odour. It is a medium weight wood which is very sturdy in use and durable. It is usually even-grained and of medium to fine texture, but the presence of large knots is a common feature. It is the strongest of the Indian conifers. Its weight is 20% less than teak and its strength is also about 20% less. It is an easy timber to saw and work to a smooth finish.

Uses. The timber is used for construction work and for railway sleepers, packing cases, furniture and in match industry.

Pine. *Pinus roxburghii* Sar.; Eng. Longleaved pine; Verna. *Chir, Salla,* Family Pinaceae. An evergreen coniferous tree, found in the western and Eastern Himalayas.

The wood is used for construction work, railway sleepers, packing cases, furniture and in match industry.

Pinus merkusii. Jungh & de Vries. A tree. The wood is very resinous with reddish brown heartwood and yellow sap wood. It is used for building purposes and general carpentry.

Pinus wallichiana A.B. Jackson; Eng. Indian blue pine; Verna. *Kail, Cail.* A coniferous tree. The wood is used for pencils, penholders, splints, match boxes, construction work, railway sleepers, and furniture. Also used for shingles, packing cases, constructional work and house fitments. It is a good wood for pattern making, cores for laminboards, drawing boards and plane tables.

Embryology of Angiosperms (Sexual Reproduction)

THE FLOWER AND ITS PARTS

The flower is a highly specialized reproductive shoot. Each typical flower consists of four distinct types of members arranged in four separate but closely set whorls, one above the other, on the top of a long or short stalk. The lower two whorls are called *accessory* whorls, and the upper two *essential* or *reproductive* whorls because only these two are directly concerned in reproduction. The essential whorls consist of two kinds of sporophylls—microsporophylls or *stamens* and megasporophylls or *carpels.* Both kinds of sporophylls may be present in a flower (hermaphrodite flower), or only one (unisexual flower) may be seen in some types.

PARTS OF A FLOWER

The flower is commonly borne on a short or long axis. This axis consists of two regions, *viz*, the *pedicel* and the *thalamus.* The pedicel is the stalk of the flower. It may be short or long or even absent. The thalamus is the swollen end of the axis, to which the floral leaves are attached. These floral leaves are sepals, petals, stamens and carpels, and the respective whorls consisting them— calyx, corolla, androecium and gynoecium.

Calyx. This is the first or the lowermost whorl of the flower or the first accessory whorl of it and, is composed of a number of green leafy *sepals.* The primary function of the calyx is to enclose the flower in its bud and protect it from sun and rain.

Corolla. This makes the second whorl of the flower or the second accessory whorl of it, and consists of a number of usually brightly coloured *petals.* The main function of the petals is to attract insects for *pollination.* In the bud stage of the flower the corolla encloses the essential organs-stamens and carpels, and protects them from external heat and rain.

Androecium. (*andros* = male). This is the third or male whorl of the flower. It consists of *stamens* or *microsporphylls* which are regarded as the male organs of the flower. Each stamen consists of three parts—*filament, anther* and *connective.* The anther filament is the selender stalk of the stamen, and the anther is the expanded head borne by the filament at its tip. Each anther consists usually of two lobes connected together by a sort of mid-rib, the *connective.* The anther bears four chambers or *pollen sacs* each filled with *pollen grains* or *microspores.* Pollen grains are produced in large quantities in the pollen-sacs.

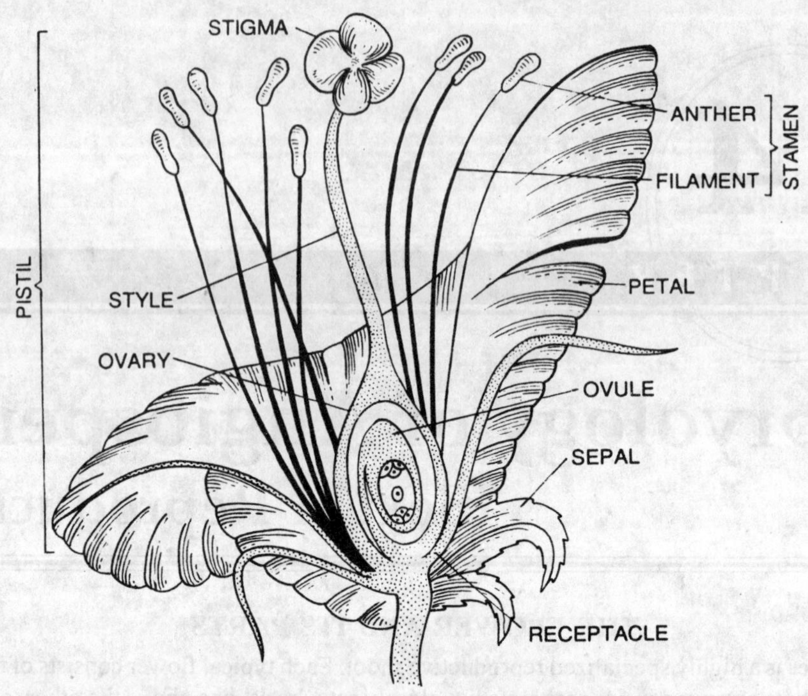

Fig. 14.1. Flower. Sectional view (L.S.) of typical flower.

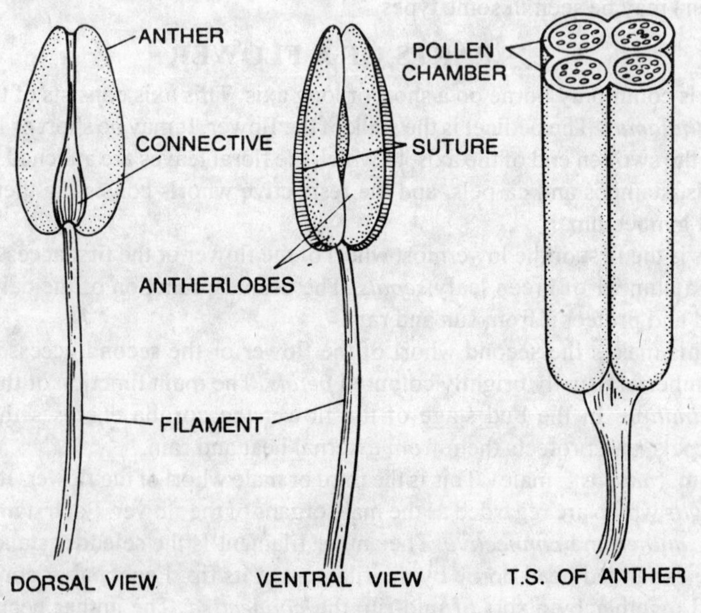

Fig. 14.2. Anther-dorsal view; ventral view; T.S. of Anther.

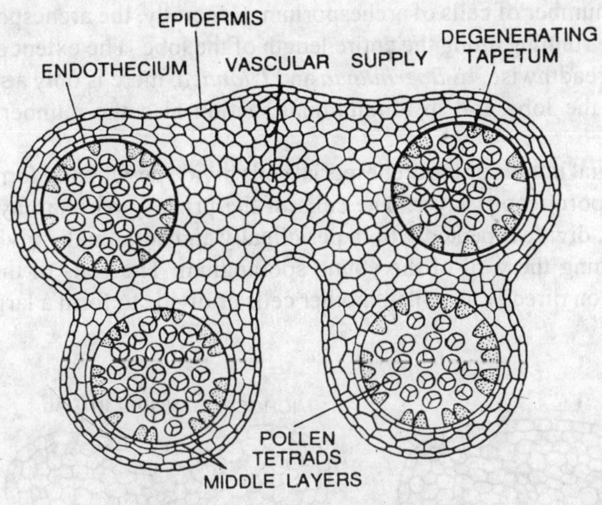

Fig. 14.3. Anther. T.S. of an anther showing tetrads of pollen grains.

ANTHER OR MICROSPORANGIUM (POLLEN SAC)

Each stamen arises as a small papillate outgrowth of meristematic tissue from the growing tip of the floral primordium. It grows actively and soon gets differentiated into an apical broader portion, the anther, and the lower slender part, the filament.

The cross-section of a very young anther consists of a homogeneous mass of meristematic cells surrounded by an epidermal layer. Further growth of the anther makes it four-lobed.

Development of microsporangium (pollen-sac)

In each lobe a few cells in the hypodermal region become differentiated by their large size, radial growth, dense cytoplasm and conspicuous nuclei. They make the *archesporium*. There is

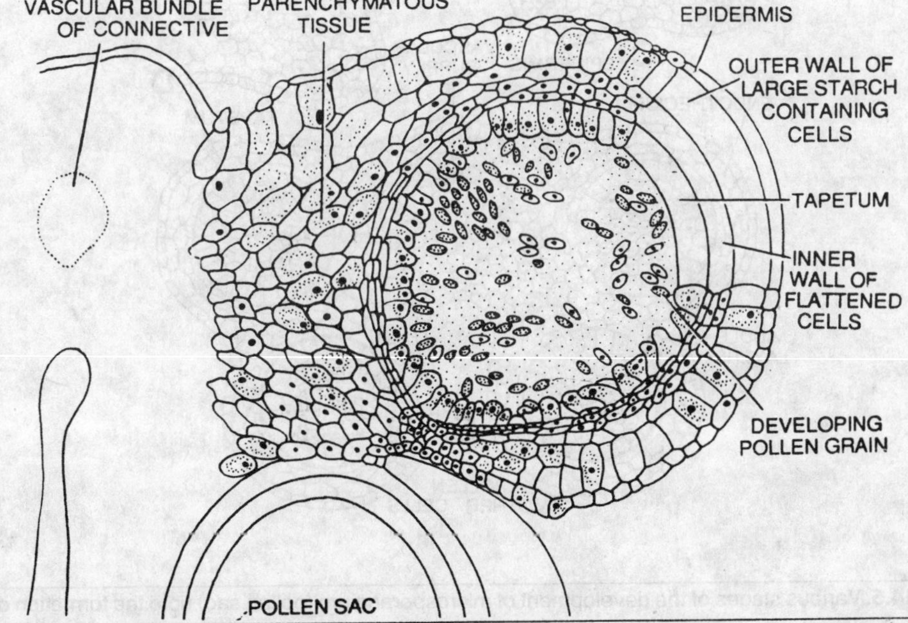

Fig. 14.4. The stamen. Transverse section of anther of *Lilium*.

much variation in the number of cells of archesporium. Generally, the archesporium consists of a two to three cell wide plate running along the entire length of the lobe. The extent of archesporium varies both lengthwise and breadthwise. In *Boerhaavia* and *Dionaea,* there is only a single archesporial cell in a cross section of the lobe and in longitudinal section also the number is only two and one respectively.

The microsporangial initials or the archesporial cells divide periclinally forming a primary parietal layer and a primary sporogenous layer. The cells of the primary parietal layer, lying immediately beneath the epidermis, divide repeatedly both periclinally and anticlinally giving rise to three to five concentric layers forming the wall of the young sporangium. The cells of the primary sprogenous layer may either function directly as pollen mother cells or divide to form a large number of cells.

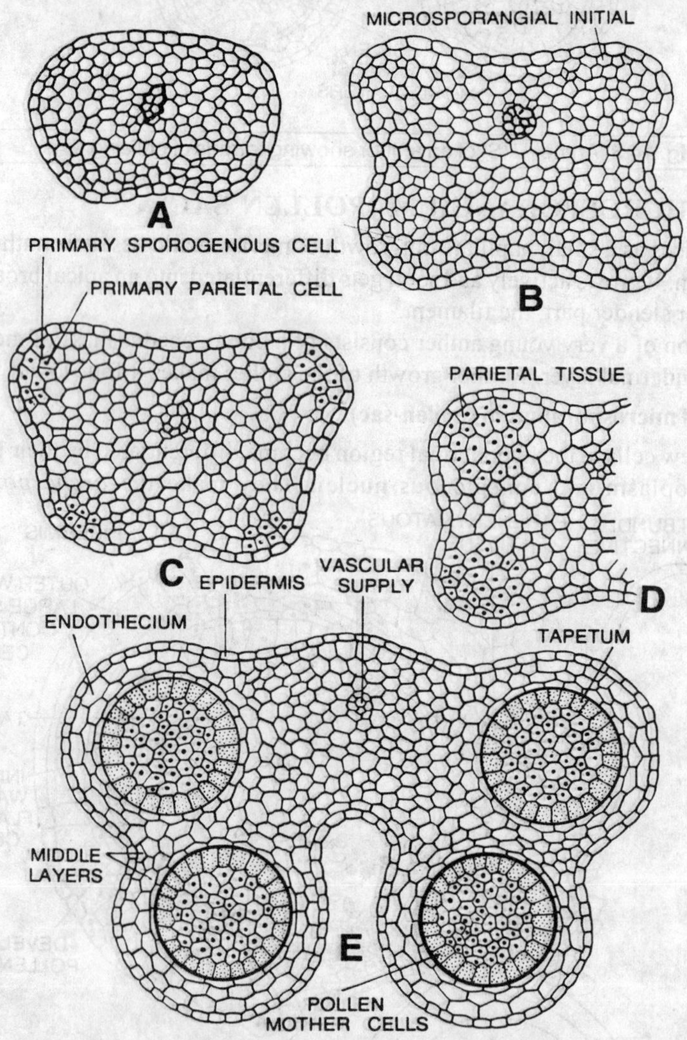

Fig. 14.5. Various stages of the development of microsporangium (pollen sac) upto the formation of pollen mother cells.

SPOROGENOUS TISSUE

In the meantime the primary sporogenous layer cells give rise to the *microspore mother cells* or *the pollen mother cells.* The sporogenous cells in normal way divide several times mitotically before functioning as pollen mother cells. In certain cases the primary sporogenous cells may either show packed but as the anther enlarges in size, the pollen sac also increases in size, the microspore mother cells also enlarge in size, become spherical in shape and get loosely arranged. In many cases, some of the sporogenous cells are non-functional and serve as the food material for the functional microspore mother cells.

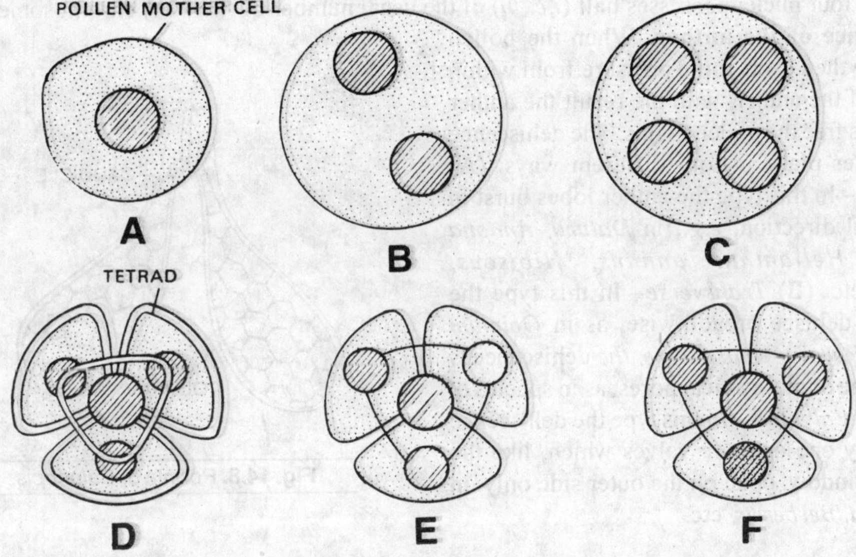

Fig. 14.6. A—F, stages showing development of pollen grains from pollen mother cell.

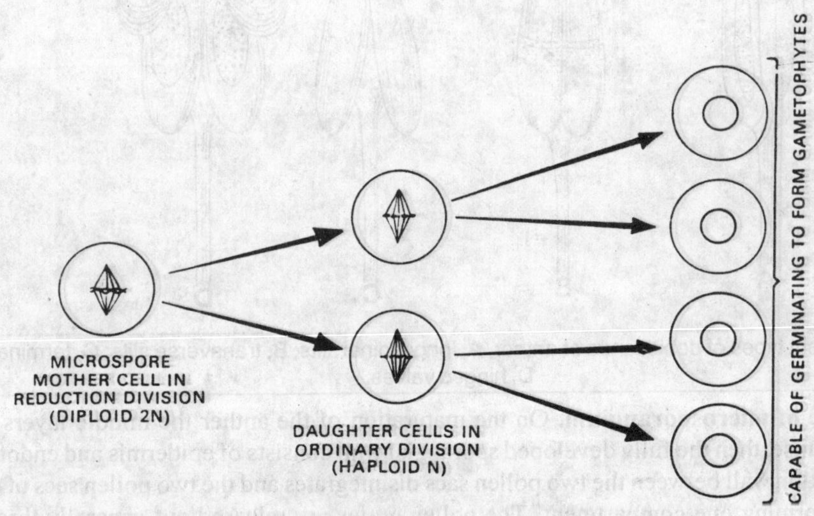

Fig. 14.7. Formation of microspores from microspore mother cells.

MICROSPOROGENESIS

The microspore mother cells (pollen mother cells) which are at first polygonal and closely packed gradually become rounded and loosely arranged in the rapidly enlarging microsporangium (pollen sac). Although all the mother cells in an anther are capable of giving rise to pollen grains but some of them may degenerate and serve as food material for the remaining cells which give rise to pollen grains. Each functional spore mother cell produces four microspores or pollen grains. The nucleus of each spore mother cell divides twice to form four nuclei, the first division being the reductional one (*i.e.,* meiosis I) and the second division being an ordinary mitotic one (*i.e.*, meiosis II). With the result each of these four nuclei possesses half (*i.e.*, n) of the usual number of (*i.e.*, $2n$) chromosomes.

Dehiscence of the anther. When the pollen grains mature they exert some pressure from within on the wall of the anther, with the result the anther bursts and sets free the pollen grains. The dehiscence of anther takes place in four different ways: (A) *Longitudinal*—In this type the anther lobes burst in a longitudinal direction, *e.g.*, in *Datura, Annona squamosa, Helianthus annuus, Hibiscus, Gossypium,* etc. (B) *Transverse*—In this type the anther lobes dehisce breadthwise, as in *Ocimum sanctum* (C) *Porous—In this type, the* dehiscence is effected by one or more apical pores, as in species *of Solanum,* (D) *Valvular— In* this type the dehiscence takes place by one or more valves which, like the shutter of a window, open on the outer side only, in *Cinnamomum, Berberris,* etc.

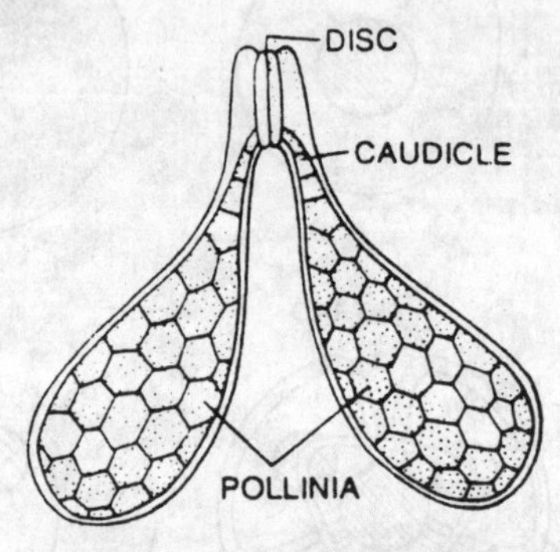

Fig. 14.8. Pollinia of *Calotropis.*

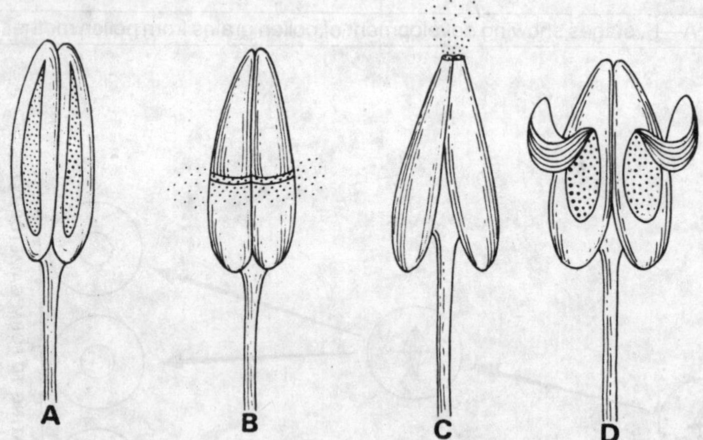

Fig. 14.9. Different types of dehiscence of anther, A, longitudinal slits; B, transverse slits; C, terminal pores; D, hinged valves.

Dehiscence of microsporangium. On the maturation of the anther the middle layers and the tapetum disorganise, then the fully developed sporangial wall consists of epidermis and endothecium. The sterile partition wall between the two pollen sacs disintegrates and the two pollen sacs of one side unite together forming one compartment. The pollen grains are released out generally through the stomium.

THE POLLEN GRAINS

The pollen grains or microspores are the male reproductive bodies of a flower, and are contained in the pollen sac or microsporangium. They are very minute in size, and are like particles of dust. Each pollen grain consists of a single microscopic cell, possessing two coats — the *exine* and the *intine*. The exine is tough, cutinized layer, which is often provided with spinous outgrowths are reticulations of different patterns and sometimes smooth. The intine, is a thin, delicate, cellulose layer laying internal to the exine. The exine possesses one or more thin places, known as *germ pores*. The pollen tubes make their way through these germ pores, when the pollen grains germinate. The pollen grains germinate on the stigma, and each forms a selender tube, called *the pollen tube,* which elongates through the tissue of the gynoecium carrying the two male gametes in it.

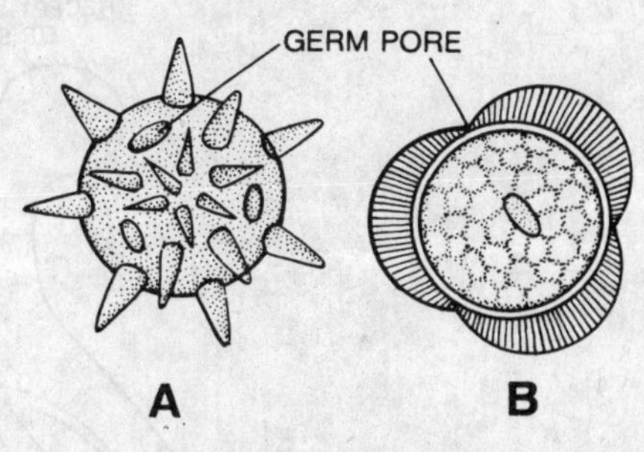

Fig. 14.10. Pollen grains-A, sculptured pollen grain, B, sectional view.

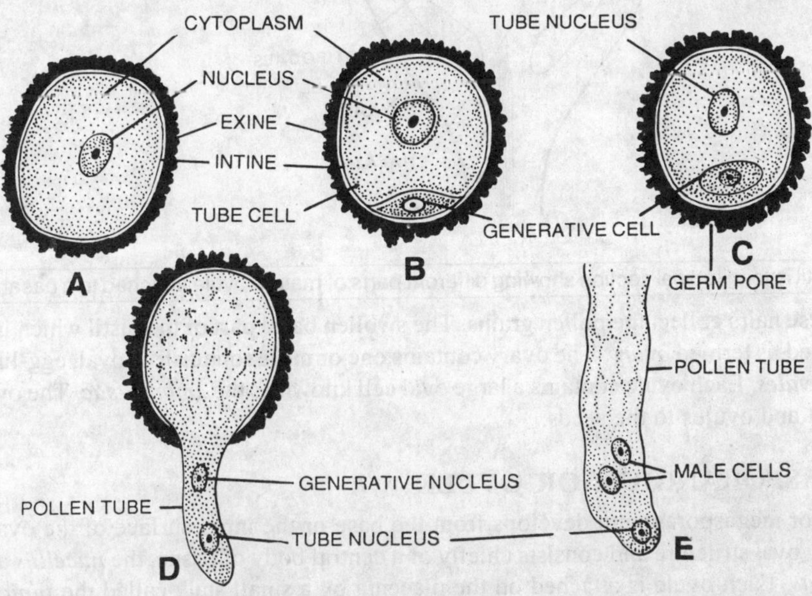

Fig. 14.11. Pollen grain and its germination. A, pollen grain: B—E different stages in the development of male gametophyte.

CARPEL OR MEGASPOROPHYLL

Gynoecium or *pistil* is the female reproductive whorl of the flower. It is composed of one or more *carpels*. The carpels are modified leaves which bear the ovules, and are also called the *megasporophylls*. When the pistil consists of only one carpel (*e.g.*, in pea flower), it is known as *simple*, and when it consists of two or more carpels, the pistil is said to be *compound*. The compound pistil may be *apocarpous* (free carpels) or *syncarpous* (united carpels). Each carpel consists of *three* parts—*stigma, style* and *ovary*. The *stigma* is the terminal end of the style upon which the pollen grains fall, and is generally knob-like and sticky. The *style* is the slender projection of the ovary and bears stigma at its terminal end. The surface of the style may be smooth or covered with hairs. In

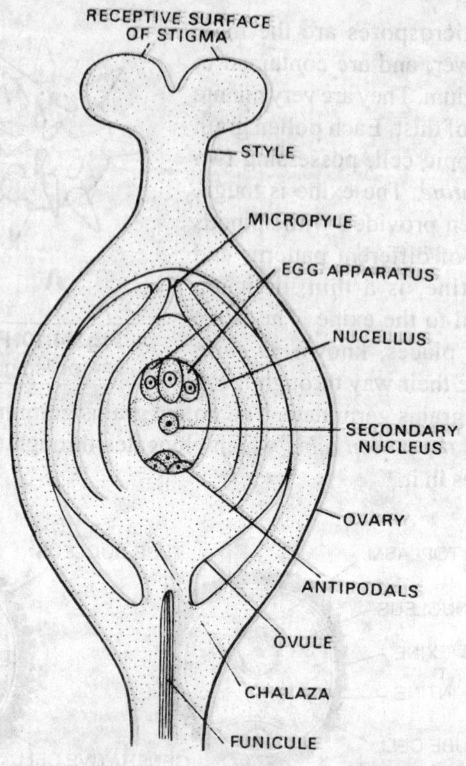

Fig. 14.12. Pistil in longitudinal section showing different parts of mature ovule attached to a basal placenta.

many cases these hairs collect the pollen grains. The swollen basal part of the pistil which is single or many chambered, is termed *ovary.* The ovary contains one or more roundish or oval, egg-like bodies, known as the *ovules.* Each ovule contains a large oval cell known as the *embryo-sac.* The ovary-gives rise to the fruit and ovules to the seeds.

THE MEGASPORANGIUM OR OVULE

An ovule or megasporangium develops from the base or the inner surface of the ovary. It is a small generally oval structure and consists chiefly of a central body of tissue, the *nucellus* and one or two *integuments.* Each ovule is attached on the placenta by a small stalk called the *funiculus.* The place of attachment of the stalk with main body of the ovule is called the *hilum.* In an inverted ovule, the runicle fuses with the main body of the ovule, forming a sort of ridge, known as the *raphe.* The upper end of the raphe which is the junction of the integuments and the nucellus is called the *chalaza.* The nucellus makes the main body of the ovule, which is made up of parenchyma tissue. Nucellus is the megasporangium proper, and it is surrounded by two coats the *integuments.* In Compositae and few other families of Gamopetalae there is only one integument. In *Santalum* and *Dendrophthoe* there are no integuments. A small opening is left at the apex of the integuments; this is called the *micropyle.* When there are two integuments then the inner integument is formed first and followed by the formation of the outer integument. A large oval cell lying embedded in the nucellus towards the micropylar end is the *embryo sac.* This makes the most important part of the mature ovule. It is the embryo sac, which bears the embryo later on.

Development of ovule. The ovule primordium appears as a small protuberance on the surface of the placenta. It grows rapidly and develops into a prominent conical structure with rounded tip.

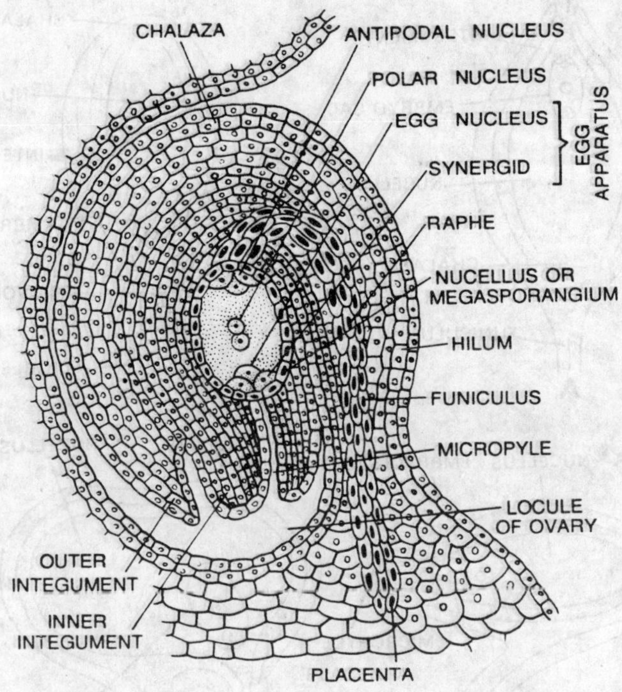

Fig. 14.13. Ovule, L.S.. of a typical ovule of angiosperm.

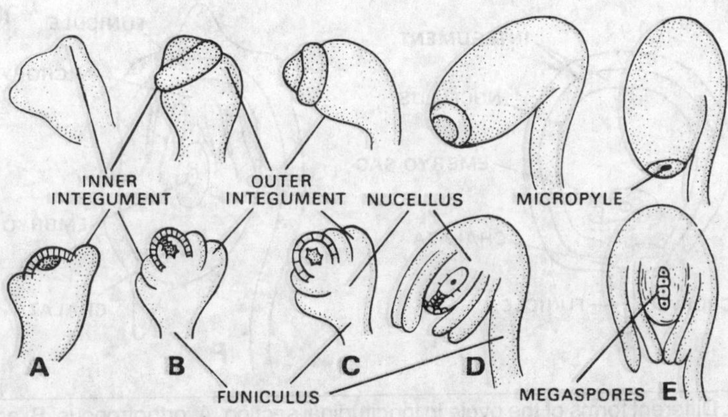

Fig. 14.14. Various stages of the development of anatropous ovule (A-E).

This rounded tip is the fore runner of the nucellus. It gradually develops into a projecting mass of tissue by the growth and division of its cells. As the development continues either one or two layers of the tissue develop from the base of the nucellus forming the integuments. The inner integument develops first and thereafter the outer one develops. The growth of the integuments is much faster than the nucellus and thus they completely enclose the nucellus except for a narrow opening, the *micropyle.*

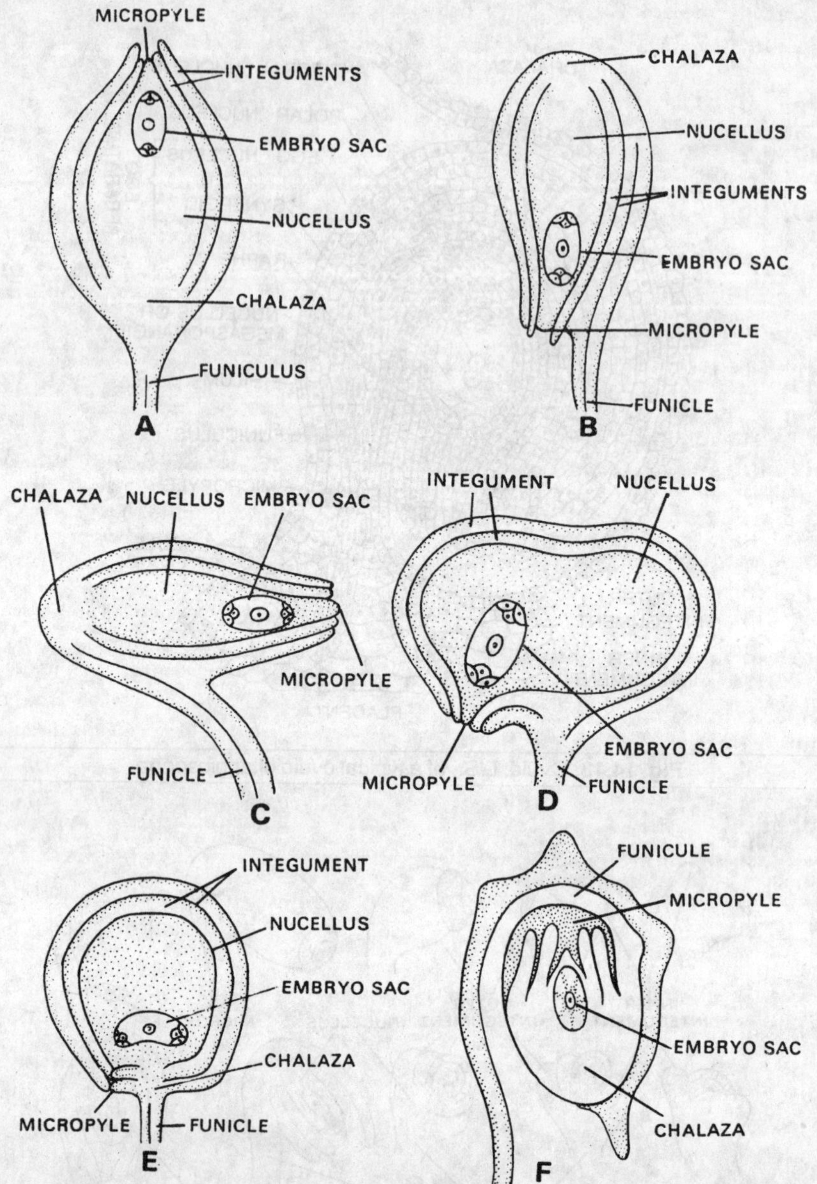

Fig. 14.15. Different forms of the ovule in longitudinal section. A, orthotropous; B, anatropous; C, hemianatropous; D, campylotropous; E, amphitropous; F, circinotropous.

FORMS OF OVULES

On the basis of the relative position of the micropyle, chalaza and funiculus the mature ovules can be categorized as follows:

(A) **Orthotropous or straight.** In this type the ovule is erect or straight so that the funicle, chalaza and micropyle lie in one and the same vertical line, as in members of Polygonaceae (*e.g.*, *Polygonum, Rumex,* etc.) and Piperaceae (*e.g.*, *Piper nigrum, Piper betle*).

(B) **Anatropous or inverted.** In this type the ovule bends along the funicle so that the micropyle lies close to the hilum. The chalaza lies at the other end. This is the commonest type of ovule found both in dicots and monocots.

(C) **Amphitropous or transverse.** In this type the ovule is placed transversely at a right angle to its stalk or funicle, as found in *Lemna.*

(D) **Hemitropous or hemianatropous.** In this type the body of the ovule is straight but twisted in such a way that it is placed transversely at right angle, and so the chalazal micropyle line is at right angle to the funiculus. It is found in *Ranunculus.*

(F) **Campylotropous or curved.** In this type the transverse ovule is bent round like a horse-shoe so that the micropyle and the chalaza do not lie in the same straight line, as in *Capparis,* Cruciferae, Gram, *Mirabilis jalapa,* etc.

(G) **Circinotropous.** In this type the nucellus and the axis remain in the same line in the beginning but due to rapid growth on one side, the ovule gets inverted. This curvature continues and thus the ovule turns completely and once again the micropyle faces upwards. This type is found in *Opuntia* and *Plumbago..*

FEMALE GAMETOPHYTE OR MEGAGAMETOPHYTE

The megaspore (n) makes the beginning of the megagametophyte (female gametophyte) generation. The nucleus of the megaspore divides and develops into the female gametophyte or the embryo sac. The female gametophyte of angiosperms is very much reduced and totally dependent for its nutrition upon the tissue of the sporophyte.

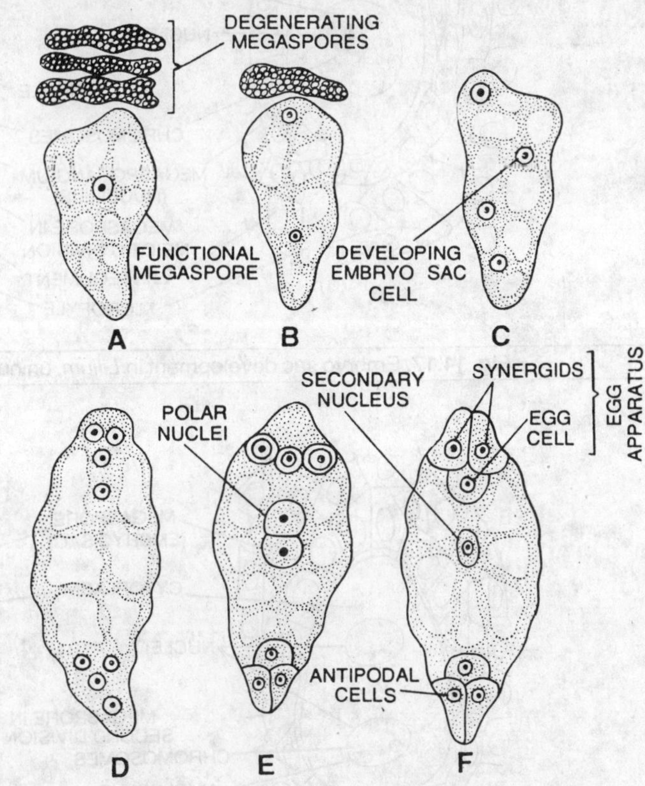

Fig. 14.16. Female gametophyte. A — F, development of the embryo sac (female gametophyte) of normal type (*Polygonum* type.)

Depending on the number of megaspore nuclei taking part in the development, the embryo sacs (female gametophytes) of angiosperms may be classified into three main categories; *monosporic, bisporic* and *tetrasporic.* In monosporic type, only one of the four megaspores takes part in the development of the female gametophyte (embryo sac). In bisporic type, two megaspore nuclei take part in the development of the female gametophyte. However, in the tetrasporic type, all the four megaspore nuclei take part in the development of female gametophyte. They have been further subdivided into *ten* types on the basis of the number of nuclear divisions taking place between the time of megaspore formation and the type of differentiation of the egg, and the total number of nuclei present in the gametophyte at the time when such organization takes place.

Polygonum **or normal type.** In the development of 8 nucleate embryo sac the nucleus of the functional megaspore divides to form two nuclei: the primary micropylar and the primary chalazal nuclei. These nuclei again divide so that the number is increased to four. Each of these nuclei divides again so that altogether eight nuclei are formed in the embryo-sac, four at each end. The female gametophyte (embryo sac) increases in size. Now one nucleus from each end or pole passes inwards, and the two polar nuclei fuse together somewhere in the middle of the embryo sac, forming the *secondary nucleus* (2n). The remaining three nuclei at the micropylar end, each surrounded by a very thin wall, form the *egg apparatus.* The other three nuclei at the opposite or chalazal end, lying in a group, often surrounded by very thin walls; from the *antipodal cells.*

This type of embryo sac is the most common or generally known as the *normal type.* It has also been called *Polygonum type,* because for the first time in 1879, this type was reported in *Polygonum divaricatum* by Strasburger.

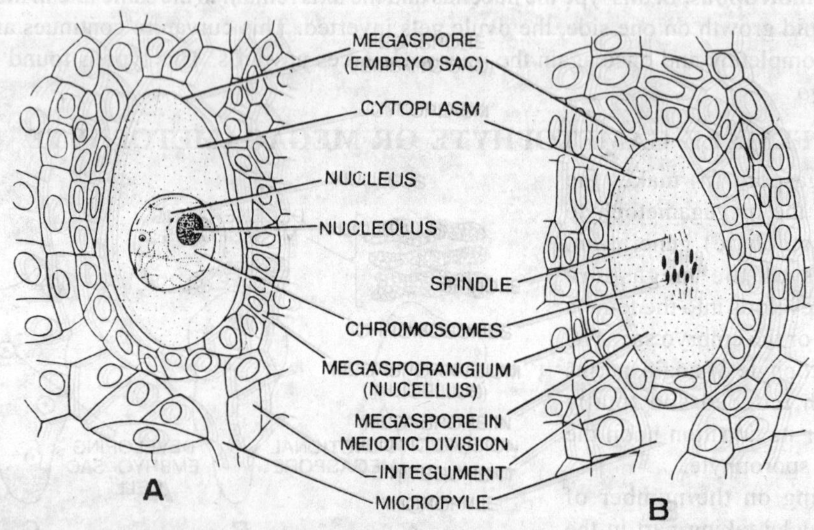

Fig. 14.17. Embryo sac development in *Lilium,* uninucleate stage, B, first division.

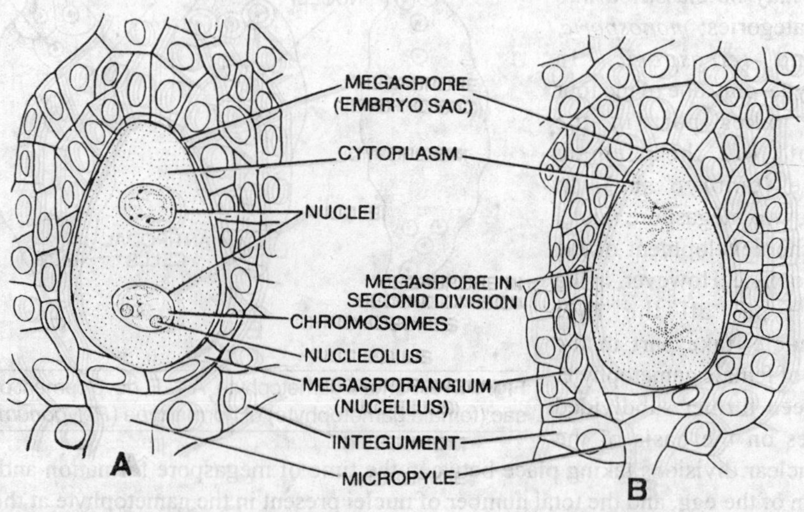

Fig. 14.18. Embryo-sac development in *Lilium.* A, first two-nucleate stage; B, second division.

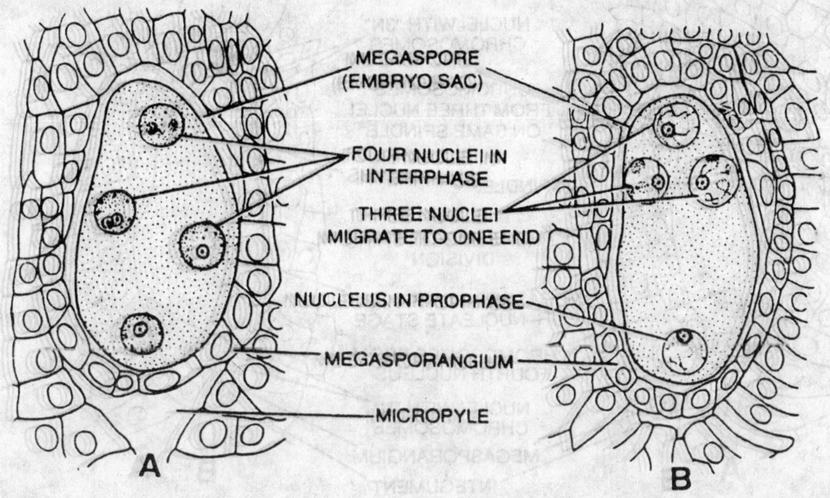

Fig. 14.19. Embryo-sac development in *Lilium*. A, first four-nucleate stage; B, migration of three nuclei.

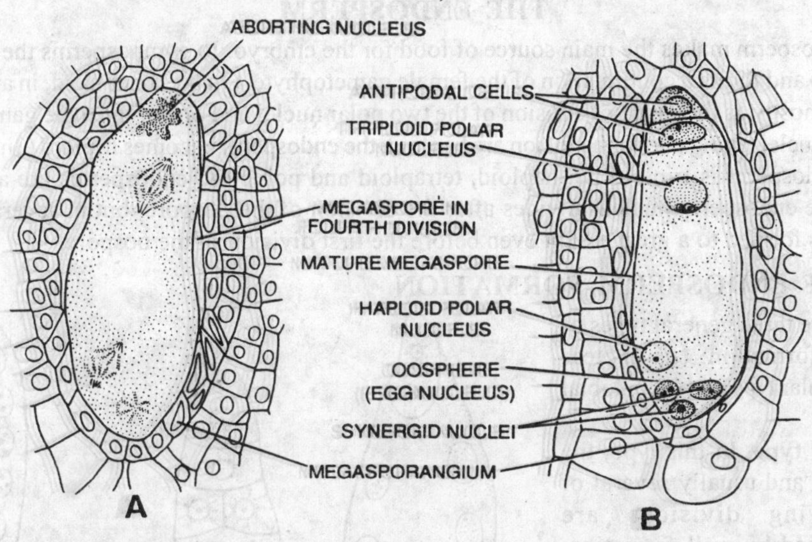

Fig. 14.20. Embryo-sac development in *Lilium*. A, fourth division, B, immature female gametophyte.

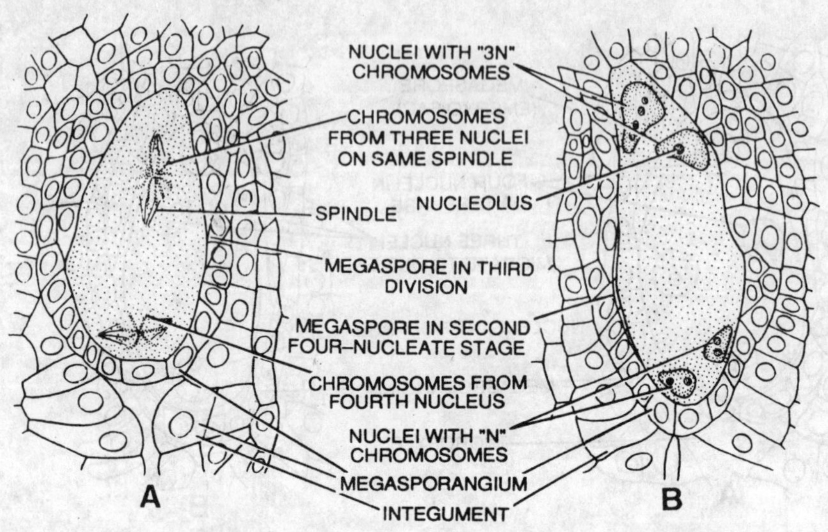

Fig. 14.21. Embryo-sac development in *Lilium.* A, third division; B, second four nucleate stage.

THE ENDOSPERM

The endosperm makes the main source of food for the embryo. In gymnosperms the endosperm is haploid (n) and forms a continuation of the female gametophyte. On the other hand, in angiosperms it is formed mostly as the result of a fusion of the two polar nuclei and one of the male gametes. Since all the three nuclei taking part in the fusion are haploid, the endosperm becomes triploid (3n). In normal cases the endosperm is triploid but haploid, tetraploid and polyploid endosperms are also known. Generally the endosperm nucleus divides after the division of the oospore, but in several cases the endosperm is formed to a great extent even before the first division of the oospore.

TYPES OF ENDOSPERM FORMATION

There are three general types of endosperm formation: (*a*) nuclear type, (*b*) cellular type and (*c*) helobial type.

Nuclear type. In this type, the first division and usually several of the following divisions are unaccompanied by wall formation. The nuclei may either remain free or in later stages they may become separated by walls.

As divisions progress, the nuclei are being pushed towards the periphery, thus a large central vacuole is formed. Often the nuclei are specially aggregated at the micropylar and chalazal ends of the sac and form only a thin layer at the sides. Generally the endosperms nuclei in the chalazal part of the

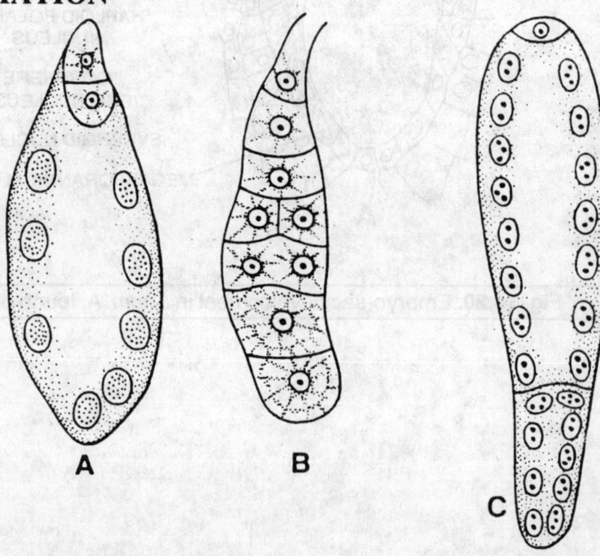

Fig. 14.22. Development of endosperm. A, nuclear type; B, cellular type and C, helobial type.

embryo sac have been observed to be larger than those in the micropylar end. The number of free nuclear divisions varies in different plants. In *Primula, Malva, Juglans,* etc., several hundred endosperm nuclei are formed which are seen lining the wall of the embryo sac. In *Trapaeolum, Melastoma,* etc., there is no wall formation. In *Asclepias, Calotropis, Rafflesia*, etc., the wall formation occurs at a very early stage when only 8 or 16 nuclei are formed, and in *Coffea* at the 4-nucleate stage. The wall formation generally progresses from the periphery of the embryo sac towards the centre or from its apex towards the base.

Cellular type. In this type, the first and most of the following divisions are accompanied by wall formation, and thus the sac is divided into several chambers, some of which may contain more than one nucleus. The first wall is usually transverse but sometimes vertical or oblique, and in some other cases the plane of division is not constant.

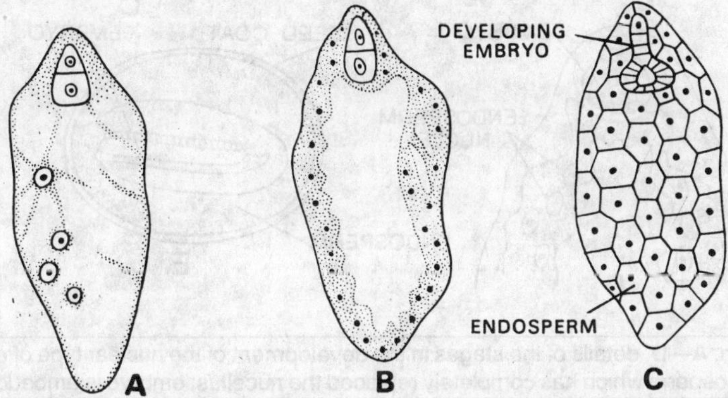

Fig. 14.23. Embryosac showing formation of nuclear type of endosperm. Developing embryo is also seen.

Helobial type. This type is frequently found in the members of the order Helobiales. This type is intermediate between the *nuclear* and the *cellular* types. In this type the first division is followed by a transverse wall resulting in a micropylar and chalazal chamber. Further divisions are generally free nuclear an d may take place in both chambers, but the main body of the endosperm is formed by the micropylar chamber only.

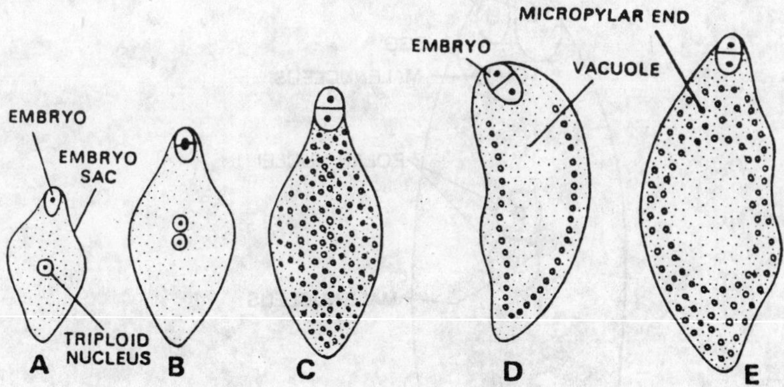

Fig. 14.24. Endosperm. Some more stages of the development of nuclear type endosperm from a triploid nucleus.

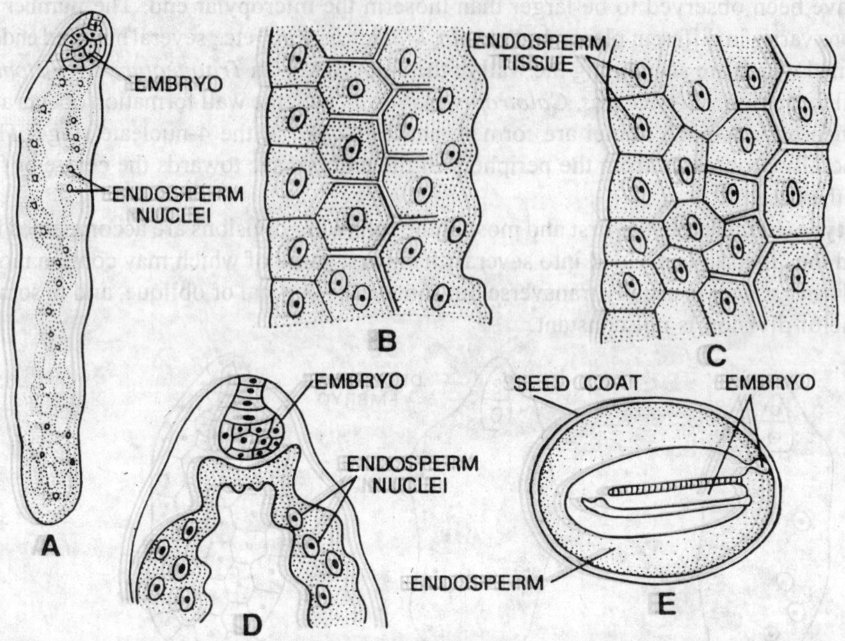

Fig. 14.25. Endosperm. A—D, details of the stages in the development of the nuclear type of endosperm; E, fully formed endosperm which has completely replaced the nucellus; embryo is embedded in it.

MATURE EMBRYO SAC

The structure. It lies embedded in the nucellus towards the micropylar end and consists of the following parts :

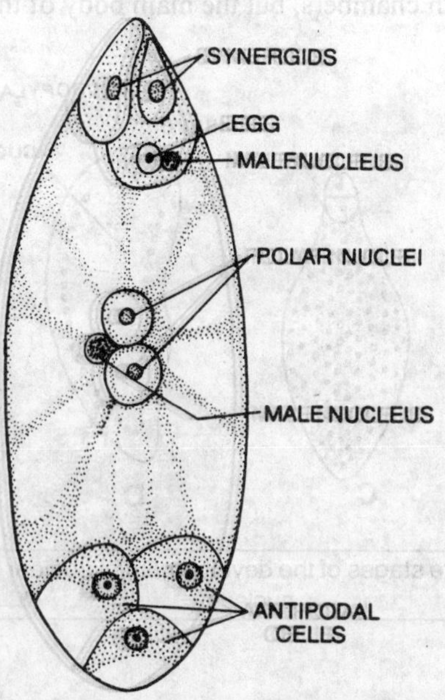

Fig. 14.26. The embryo sac. Eight nucleate stage.

(1) Synergids. Usually the pair of synergid cells is apparently equivalent and similar. The upper ends of this pair are attached with the wall of embryo sac while lower ends of the cells protrude into the cavity of the sac. Here in lower round end of each synergid has a large vacuole. Here the walls of synergids are made of cellulose.

(2) The oosphere. The egg apparatus comprises of two parts, two synergids and an egg (oosphere), the former has been just described above. Normally this oosphere is found attached with the synergids. At the time of fertilization it seems somewhat large in size. This oosphere is supposed to be metabolically inactive and so it receives its nourishment from the synergids.

(3) The central cell. It is the largest cell of the embryo sac. The nuclei of it are termed as polar nuclei. The number of polar nuclei in an embryo sac is not definite but it varies from species to species. The polar nuclei unite either before, during or after the entry of the pollen tube into the embryo sac and the product is called the secondary nucleus.

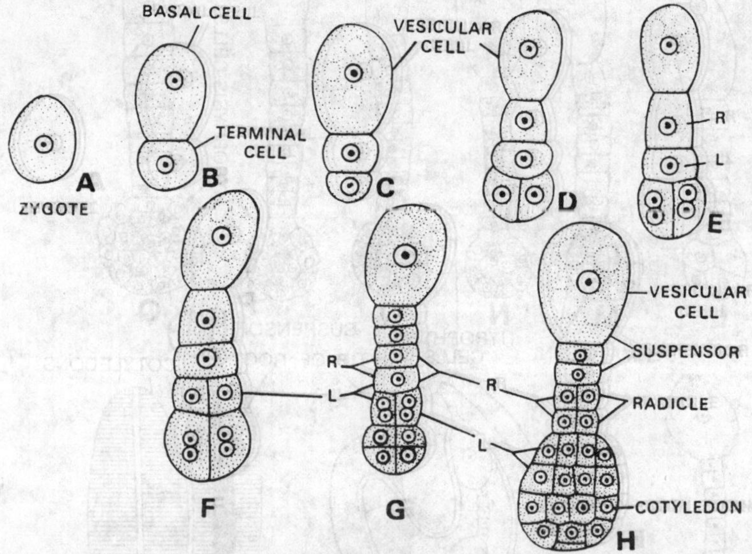

Fig. 14.27. Stages in the development of a typical monocot embryo (A-H).

(4) The antipodal cells. These are short lived cells and possess great variation in their size, number and durability. Generally these cells are found in a group of three cells separated by delicate cell walls.

EMBRYO

The structure :

Dicot embryo. The mature embryo consists of a short axis with two cotyledons. The portion which lies above the point of attachment of cotyledons is called as plumule or epicotyl while the lower portion of this attachment is called as radicle. As the seed germinates, the plumule becomes the stem system of new plant and me radicle becomes the root system. The transitional zone between plumule and radicle is called as hypocotyl. Normally for a germinating seed the cotyledons function as food storage organ. Sometimes a filamentous suspensor is also found with the embryo.

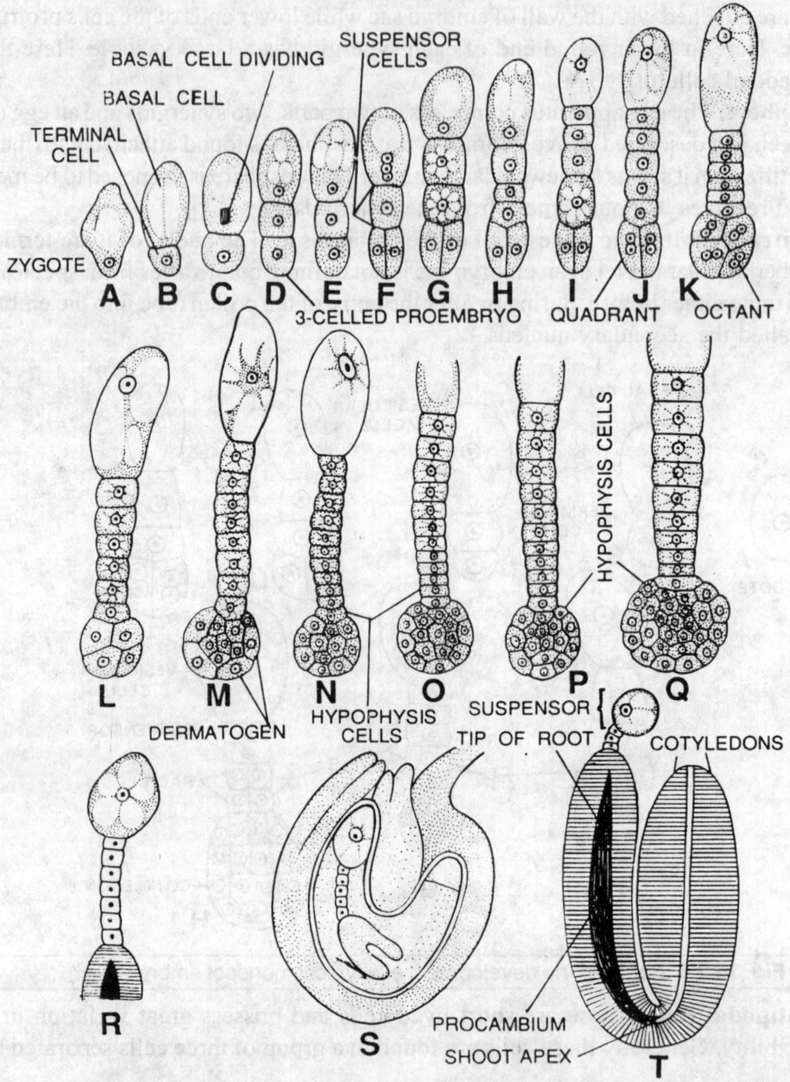

Fig. 14.28. Stages in the development of a typical dicot embryo in *Capsella bursa-pastoris*.

Monocot embryo. This embryo comprises of only a single cotyledon. Here the plumule arises as a depression midway between the base of the cotyledon and the axis of the embryo. So here the plumule occupies a lateral position. Suspensor may also be available here but with some variations. Plumule lies just next to the radicle, *i.e.*, it occupies the lower portion of the embryo.

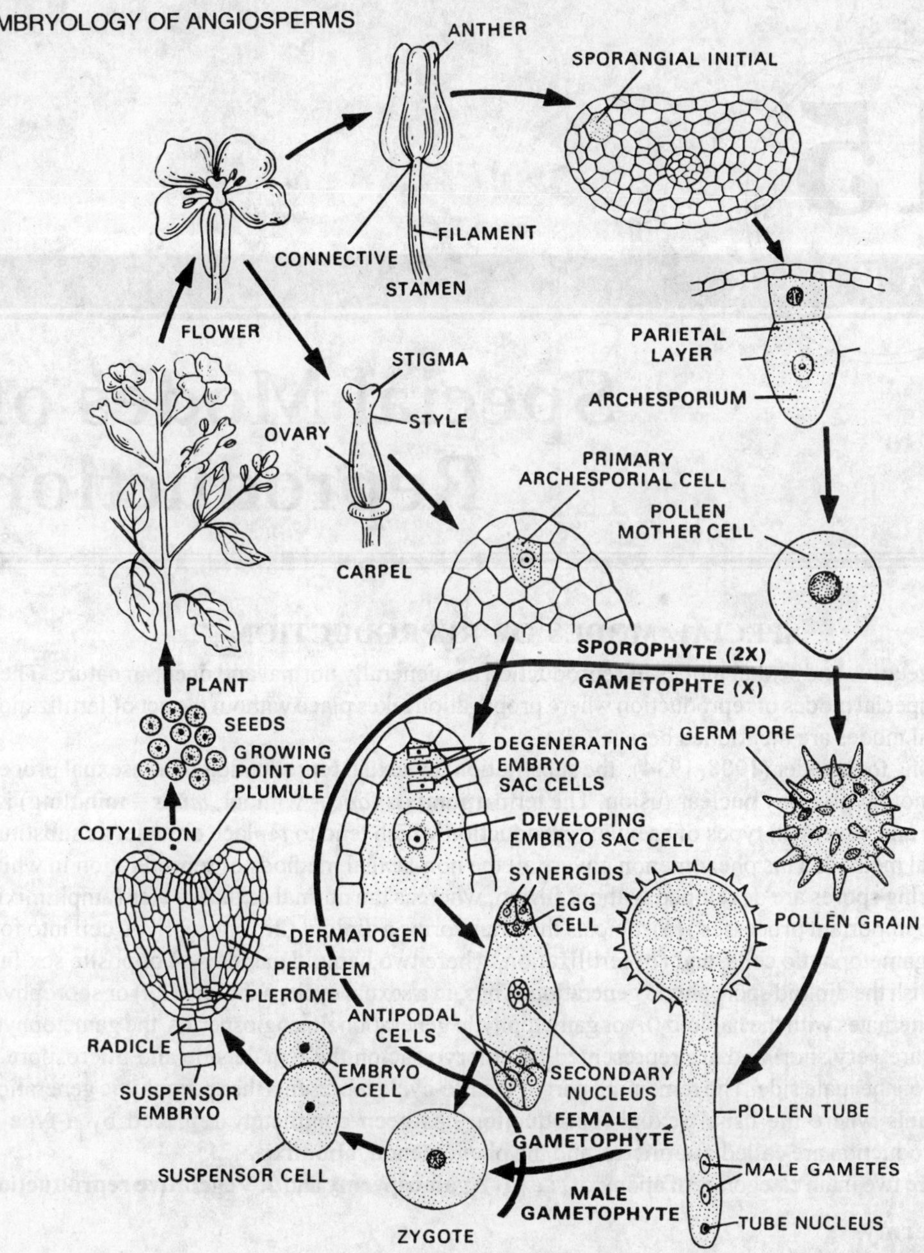

Fig. 14.29. Life-cycle of an angiosperm.

CHAPTER 15

Special Modes of Reproduction

SPECIAL MODES OF REPRODUCTION

The vegetative and sexual modes of reproduction are generally normal and occur in nature. There are cases of special modes of reproduction where propagation takes place without the act of fertilization. Some special modes are mentioned here :

According to Winkler (1908, 1934), the substitution for sexual reproduction of as asexual process which does not involve any nuclear fusion. The term **apomixis** (*apo* = without, *mixis* = mingling) is a general one, and covers all types of asexual reproduction which tend to replace or to act as substitute for the sexual method. This phenomenon covers all the non-sexual methods of reproduction in which the reproducing spores are developed without fusion, whereas the normal sexual cycles (amphimixis) involves two important processes : (a) meiosis that transforms a diploid (2n) sporophytic cell into four haploid (*n*) gametophytic cells, and (*b*) fertilization, where two haploid gametes of opposite sex fuse and re-establish the diploid sporophytic generation. Thus, in a sexual cycle, a diploid (2*n*) or sporophytic generation alternates with the haploid (*n*) or gametophytic generation. In angiosperms, the gametophytic generations are very short and are represented by embryo sac on the female side and microspore or pollen grain on the male side. The remaining part of the life-cycle represents the sporophytic generation.

The plants where the usual sexual reproduction has been completely replaced by a type of asexual reproduction are called **apomictic,** and the phenomenon, **apomixis.**

There are two main categories of apomixis, *i.e.*, **1. Agamospermy** and **2. Vegetative reproduction.**

Agamospermy

In this category of apomixis the plants have retained seed as the agent of propagation but the embryo is formed by some process in which normal meiosis and syngamy have been eliminated. This phenomenon is known as **agamospermy.** There are three different types of agamospermy.

1. Adventive embryony. In this type of agamospermy, embryos arise directly from the diploid sporophytic cells either of nucellus or integuments. The sexual embryo sac develops in normal way and the zygotic embryo either degenerates or competes with the apomictic embryos.

2. Diplospory. In this type of agamospermy, a diploid embryo sac is formed from a megaspore mother cell, without a regular meiotic division (*e.g.*, in *Aerva tomentosa*). In this type an archesporium differentiates, but the megaspore mother cell develops into an unreduced embryo sac. The embryo is formed by the unfertilized egg, *i.e.*, parthenogenesis or some other cell of the embryo sac, *i.e.*, apogamety.

3. Apospory. This phenomenon was reported in angiosperms for the first time by Rosenberg (1907). Here a somatic cell in the nucellus directly forms an unreduced embryo sac, and the diploid egg parthenogenetically develops into embryo. Here the megaspores gradually degenerate and the aposporic embryo sac may develop from a functional megaspore mother cell.

However, for the sake of convenience Dr. P. Maheshwari (1950) has sub-divided apomixis into three types, *i.e.*, (*i*) nonrecurrent apomixis, (*ii*) recurrent apomixis, and (*iii*) adventive embryony.

1. Non-recurrent apomixis. In this type the megaspore mother cell undergoes the usual meiotic divisions and a haploid embryo sac is formed. Here the embryo arises either from the egg (*i.e.*, **haploid parthenogenesis**) or from some other cell of the gametophyte (*i.e.*, **haploid apogamy**). The plants produced by this method are, haploid and generally sterile and do not reproduce sexually any more. This type of apomixis has been seen in several species such as *Solanum nigrum, Lilium, Bergenia, Erythraea centaurium. Orchis maculata, Nicotiana tabacum,* etc.

2. Recurrent apomixis. In this type, the embryo sac generally arises either from an archesporial cell (*i.e.*, generative apospory) or from some other part of the nucellus (*i.e.*, somatic apospory). Here all the nuclei of the embryo sac are diploid, and there is no meiotic division. The embryo arises either from the egg (diploid parthenogenesis) or from some other cell of the gametophyte **(diploid apogamy).** Generative apospory has been observed in *Eupatorium glandulosum, Parthenium argentatum*, etc. Somatic apospory has been reported in *Hieracium excelens. H. flagellare* and *H. auraniacum.*

3. Adventive embryony. This type of apomixis is also known as **sporophytic budding.** Here, the developed embryo sacs may be haploid or diploid, but the embryos do not arise from the cells of nucellus or the integument. There is no alternation of generations, because the diploid tissues of the present sporophyte directly give rise to the new embryo. Adventive embryo has been frequently reported in *Citrus, Euphorbia dulcis, Capparis frondasa, Mangifera indica* and *Hiptage madablota.*

Significance of apomixis. The most important apomictic crop plants are citrus, mango, mangosteen and black berries. As a reproductive system, it offers the possibility of the indefinite propagation of specially favourable biotypes, which may be highly heterozygous or sexually sterile. In obligate apomixis, this advantage is served at the expense of the long term evolutionary flexibility which is the gift of sexuality. However, in facultative apomixis, where sexual and apomictic members co-exist, the phenomenon is of special significance.

Vegetative Reproduction

In this type of apomixis, the new individual arises from a group of undifferentiated or differentiated cells, where neither embryo nor seed are produced. This type of reproduction takes place by means of bulbs, bulbils, tubers, runners, suckers, etc. Such propagules are formed by the sporophyte only. Gustafsson (1946) has distinguished three types of vegetative reproduction in angiosperms : 1. In this type, the propagules are formed outside the floral regions; though the sex organs are formed, yet no fertilization or seed setting takes place, *e.g.*, in *Agave americana* and *Elodea canadensis.* 2. In this type, the propagules are formed outside the floral regions, and the plants are sexually sterile, as found in *Fritillaria imperialis* and *Lilium bulbiferum.* 3. In this type, the propagules are formed on the floral branches either in addition to the flowers or in place of them. This phenomenon is commonly known as **vivipary.** This term is also used for those plants (*e.g.*, mangrove vegetation), in which sexually formed seeds germinate on the mother plant. Here the term vivipary will be used as **vegetative vivipary.** The vegetative vivipary is commonly found in grasses, *e.g.*, *Festuca, Poa,* and in *Allium.* The vegetative vivipary is actually an adaptation for the multiplication of a genotype under a set of environmental conditions which prevent or check to some extent the opportunity for normal pollination. However, most of the vegetative viviparous races have not lost the capacity for flowering and normal seed setting, *e.g.*, a grass, *Desciangsia caepitosa* is sexually reproducing in Sweden, while growing by vegetative vivipary in California.

Apospory

The apospory (*apo* = without) is the development of the gametophyte from a cell of the sporophyte without the intervention of a spore. In angiosperms, this phenomenon was for the first time reported by Rosenberg (1907) in *Hieracium* spp. Here the megaspore mother cell undergoes the usual meiotic divisions and forms a tetrad. In the angiosperms it is sometimes seen that an embryo may be formed from the diploid cells of the nucellus, as in *Citrus, Mangifera, Opuntia,* etc. or even from those of integument, as in *Allium cepa.* The embryo thus formed is pushed into the embryo sac during the course of its development. Since the nucellus or the integument belongs to the sporophyte, the production of the embryo from the tissue of the sporophyte without intervention of the spore is a case of apospory.

In the aposporic members of the Asteraceae, only one nucellar cell acts as the mother cell and gives rise to a normal 8- nucleate embryo sac, while in the grasses, more than one sporophytic embryo sac may develop in the same nucellus, and the organization of mature embryo sac is 4-nucleate.

Parthenogenesis

The development of the zygote from the egg-cell without the act of fertilization, or in other words, formation of embryo from an unfertilized egg is called **parthenogenesis.** In some species of angiospems, the embryo develops parthenogenetically. In such cases the embryo may develop from haploid egg-cell or diploid egg-cell. In apomicts of Asteraceae and Rubiaceae, the development of embryo is independent of the pollination stimulus. However, in many other apomicts, the embryo develops only after pollination, and the phenomenon is known as **pseudogamy,** *e.g.*, many apomictic grasses. According to Heslop-Harrison (1972) there are three roles of pollination in pseudogamy: (*i*) to activate the growth of ovary and ovule, (*ii*) *to* supply the male nucleus for the development of the endosperm, and (*iii*) to stimulate the parthenogenesis.

In most of grass apomicts, the egg may divide parthenogenetically but the proembryo ceases to grow unless and until the endosperm develops. Here, the development of endosperm occurs only after the fusion of the male nucleus with the polars, and therefore, a mature apomictic embryo in these plants is formed only after pollination.

Significance of parthenogenesis. The role of parthenogenesis in nature is severely limited; the zygogenesis and other methods of reproduction are predominant. The reason is thought to be that parthenogenetic species are not adaptable enough. In ameiotic parthenogenesis, genetic variability is practically nil. In meiotic parthenogenesis, individuals tend to become homozygous, and cause the accompanying disadvantage of this condition.

The advantages of this phenomenon are several fold. In meiotic parthenogenesis which applies to homozygous genotypes, advantageous combinations of genes are maintained instead of dispersed by meiosis as in zygogenetic species. Well adapted forms thus spread rapidly, as long as the environmental conditions remain unchanged. As Peacock (1961) reports, the existence of hardly triploid organism becomes possible in ameiotic parthenogenesis.

Parthenocarpy

In certain cases of angiosperms the ovary normally develops into a fruit without pollination and fertilization. This type of free development of fruit is known as **parthenocarpy.** Such fruits (parthenocarpic fruits) are always seedless. Sometimes the fruit formation may be induced by artificial pollination by foreign pollen from another species, but without subsequent fertilization. The parthenocarpy may also be induced by the spraying of growth promoting substances, such as naphthalene acetic acid NAA. This is called **induced parthenocarpy.** The examples of parthenocarpy are commonly found in banana, papaya, pineapple, guava, grapes, apple, *Thalictrum, Alchemilla,* etc.

In modern days, a lot of work has been done to produce seedless fruit on seeded varieties by controlling pollination and applying certain chemical substances to the pistil. Thimann (1934) suggested that many pollen grains possess considerable quantities of growth substances. Gustaffson (1938) used several growth substances, such as IAA, IBA, α-NAA and phenylacetic acid mixed in the lanolin paste of about 0.5 to 1 per cent strength and smeared on the stigma to produce parthenocarpic fruits. Among the species where the fruits can be set by auxins are tomato, tobacco, pepper, figs and blackberry. Here, the fruits which have been set by treating unpollinated flowers are seedless. Nitsch and other, workers used α-NAA in aqueous form to induce parthenocarpy by atomizer. Crane (1964) induced parthenocarpy is tomatoes, apples and pears by gibberellins. Cytokinins have also been used in the induction of parthenocarpy in certain fruits.

In addition to induced parthenocarpy, the natural parthenocarpy may occur is certain species. Many horticultural varieties of bananas, pineapples, cucumber, tomatoes and figs exist, where seedless fruits are normally produced without the need for any exogenous hormone. In some species, the fruits are formed without pollination while in others, pollination is necessary but fertilization does not occur, in still others fertilization occurs but the embryos abort before the fruits mature. It is not understood clearly how the growth of these parthenocarpic fruits is controlled, but it is thought that in some cases maternal tissues, such as the placentae may produce auxin in the absence of normal embryos. It has been noticed that the ovaries of unopened flowers of parthenocarpic varieties of orange and *Vitis vinifera* (grape) possess a higher auxin content than those of normal seeded varieties.

Polyembryony

The occurrence of more than one embryo in the seed is known as **polyembryony.** Polyembryony is quite common among conifers (gymnosperms), but many species both of dicots and monocots (angiosperms) exhibit this phenomenon. Usually there are two main types of polyembryony, *i.e.*, 1. **true polyembryony** and 2. **false polyembryony.**

1. True Polyembryony

The true polyembryony may be subdivided into two types : (*i*) **cleavage polyembryony,** where the embryos arise within as embryo sac, either by a cleavage of the egg, or from the synergids, antipodals or endosperm; (*ii*) **adventive polyembryony,** where the embryos arise from the tissues living outside the embryo sac, *i.e.*, the cells of the nucellus or the integuments, but generally they come to lie within the embryo sac.

2. False Polyembryony

Sometimes the polyembryony occurs due to the presence of multiple embryo sacs within the ovule. They may arise from : (*a*) the derivatives of the same megaspore mother cell; (*b*) from two or more megaspore mother cells, or (*c*) from nucellus cells (*i.e.*, apospory).

Importance of Polyembryony

This phenomenon plays an important role in plant breeding and horticulture. Nucellar adventive polyembryony is of great value in horticulture, where the nucellar seedlings of *Citrus* have been proved to be better clones of orchard stock than cuttings. On the other hand, the nucellar embryos are supposed to be free from disease, and the nucellar seedlings rejuvenate the vigour that is generally lost after continued cutting propagation. The advestive polyembryony is much useful in the propagation of the fruit trees, such as *Citrus* and *Mango*. The application of adventive embryos is also important for providing genetically uniform seedlings in fruit trees.

The haploids can be used for the development of homozygous diploid, which are of much value. Due to the practical value of haploids in plant breeding, the methods have been recognized for the artificial production of these embryos from the eggs or synergids.

16

CHAPTER

Vegetative Reproduction and Micropropagation in Flowering Plants

VEGETATIVE REPRODUCTION

In vegetative propagation, any part of the plant, *i.e.*, stem, root, leaf or even buds are capable to give rise to new plants. The most striking example of such reproductive capacity is seen in the leaves of *Bryophyllum*. Like other leaves they too carry on photosynthesis, their usual function, but in addition they have the capacity to produce one or more plants from the notches in their margins. If one keeps a leaf of *Bryophyllum* on damp soil, within a day or two the buds appear in the notches of the margin of leaf. These buds would later form new plants, complete with roots, leaves and stem.

More often the capacity for vegetative propagation resides in roots, *e.g.*, in sweet potato asparagus and dahlia, or stems, *e.g.*, in ginger, turmeric, banana, potato, onion, sugarcane and canna. In all these cases the plant parts possess the power of **regeneration,** which means that a part of the plant can either replace its lost portion or bring forth a new adult plant.

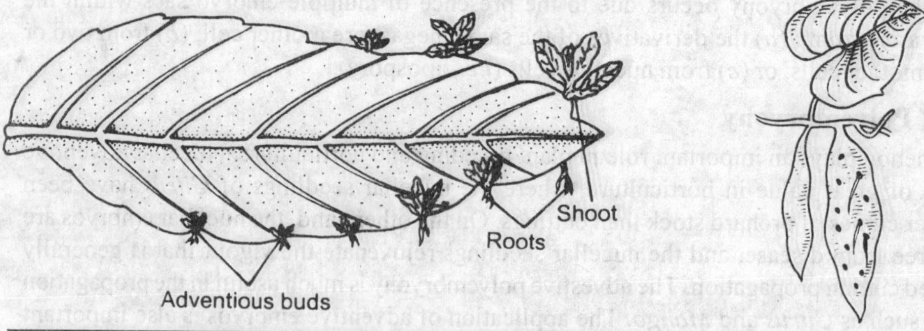

Fig. 16.1. *Bryophyllum.* Buds on margin of leaf. **Fig. 16.2.** Tuberous roots of sweet potato.

The capacity for regeneration is quite common in most higher plants and has been put to great use by mankind since time immemorial. Thus, rose, coleus, pathos and glory of garden (*Bougainvillaea*) are generally propagated by placing their stem cuttings is moist soil. The cuttings soon strike roots and grow into new plants.

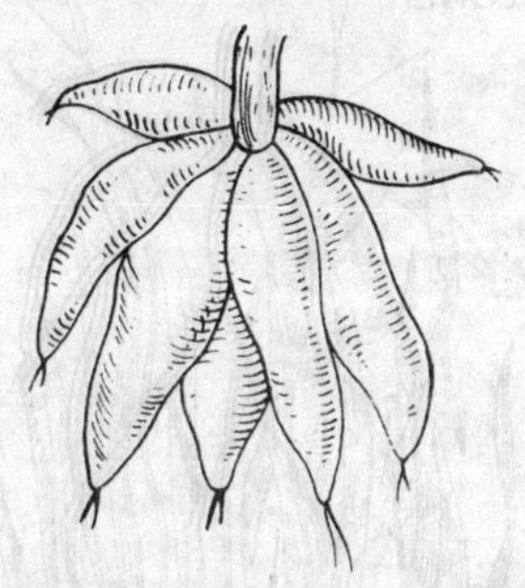

Fig. 16.3. Fasciculated tuberous roots of *Dahlia*.

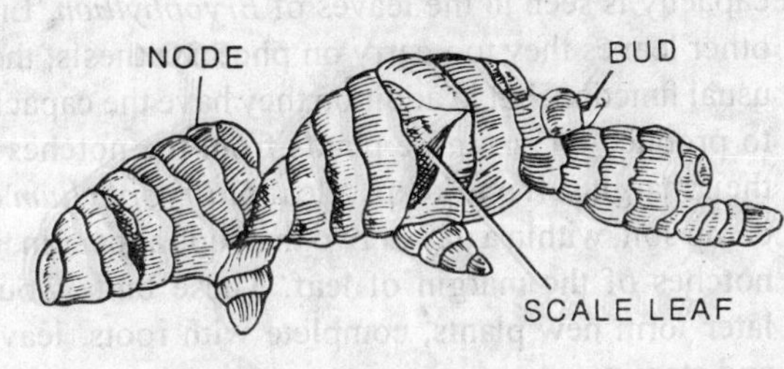

Fig. 16.4. Underground modified stem rhizome of ginger with bud.

Cutting, grafting and layering are generally referred to as artificial methods of vegetative propagation. The resulting offspring are normally identical, and resemble the parent forms in almost all respects. Gardeners generally use these methods for getting plants of same types.

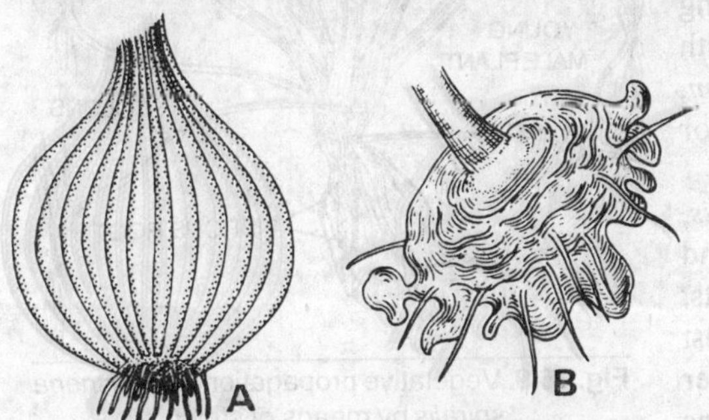

Fig. 16.5. Underground modified stems.

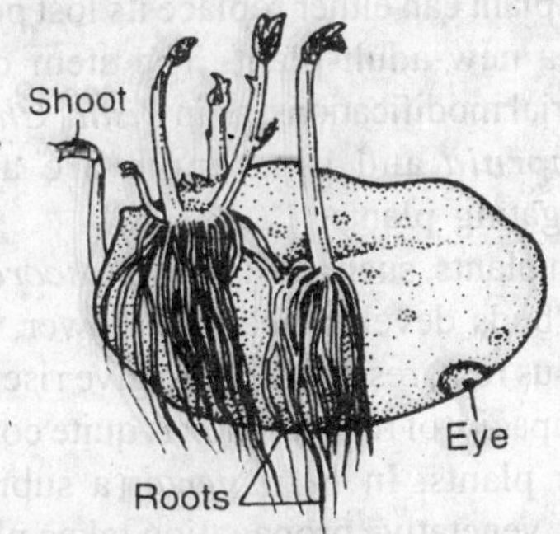

Fig. 16.6. Underground modified stem of potato.

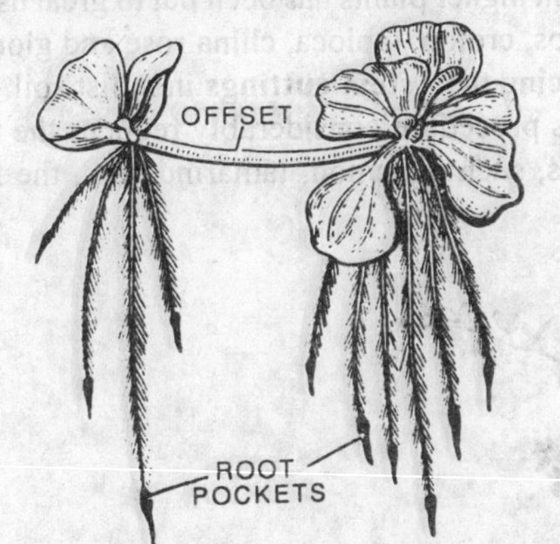

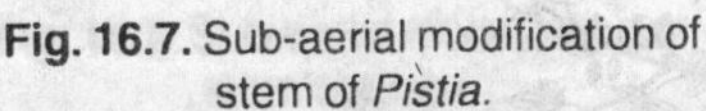

Fig. 16.7. Sub-aerial modification of stem of *Pistia*.

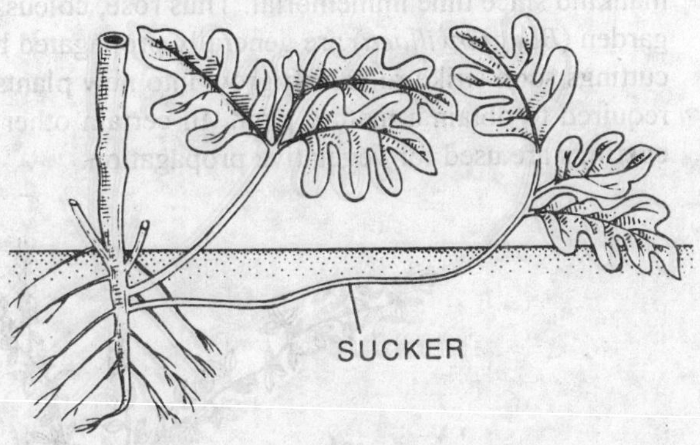

Fig. 16.8. Sub-aerial modification of stem of *Chrysanthemum*.

The methods of vegetative reproduction may be grouped into two categories, *i.e.*, (*i*) natural methods and (*ii*) artificial methods.

1. Natural methods. In such methods of vegetative propagation, a portion of the plant gets detached from the mother plant and develops into a new independent plant under suitable environmental conditions. The detached parts may be roots, stems, leaves or flowers.

The most striking example of such reproductive capacity is seen in the leaves of *Bryophyllum*. Like other leaves they too carry on photosynthesis, their usual function, but in addition they have the capacity to produce one or more plants from the notches in their margins. If one keeps a leaf of *Bryophyllum* on damp soil, within a day or two the buds appear in the notches of the margin of leaf. These buds would later form new plants, complete with roots, leaves and stem.

More often the capacity for vegetative propagation resides in roots (*e.g.*, in sweet potato, asparagus and dahlia) or stems (*e.g.*, in ginger, turmeric, banana, potato, onion, zamikand, sugarcane and canna). In all these cases the plant parts possess the power of regeneration, which means that a part of the plant can either replace its lost portion or bring forth a new adult plant. The stem of plants with subaerial modifications, as in *Pistia, Chrysanthemum*, *Eichhornia* and pine apple are also used for propagating plants.

In plants, such as *Agave, Dioscorea* and *Oxalis*, small buds develop near the flower, leaf, axil and tuberous root, respectively, to give rise to new plants. The capacity of regeneration is quite common in most higher plants. In *Vallisneria* (a submerged water plant), vegetative propagation takes place by means of stolons.

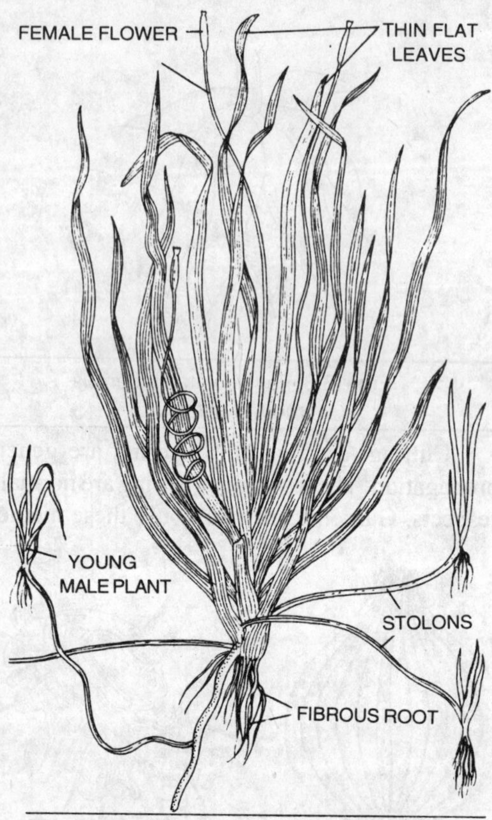

Fig. 16.9. Vegetative propagation in *Vallisneria spiralis* by means of stolon.

2. Artificial methods. The capacity for regeneration in higher plants has been put to great use by mankind since time immemorial. Thus rose, coleus, pothos, croton, tapioca, china rose and glory of garden (*Bougainvillaea*) are generally propagated by placing their **stem cuttings** in moist soil. The cuttings soon strike roots and grow into new plants. This procedure considerably reduces the time required to obtain a mature plant. In certain other plants, such as lemon, tamarind, etc., the **root cuttings** are used for vegetative propagation.

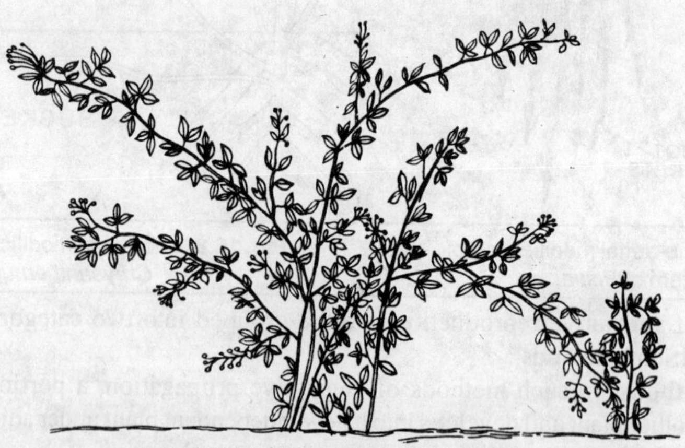

Fig. 16.10. Vegetative propagation. Tip layering in Raspberry.

As the process of vegetative propagation involves simple cell division, the qualities of the parent plant are faithfully reproduced in the offspring. Some very useful plants like banana and certain varieties of oranges are sterile and do not produce any seeds. Propagation by cuttings is the only method of attaining more of these plants.

Horticulturists have evolved several other methods to produce new plants in a short time. The methods are as follows :

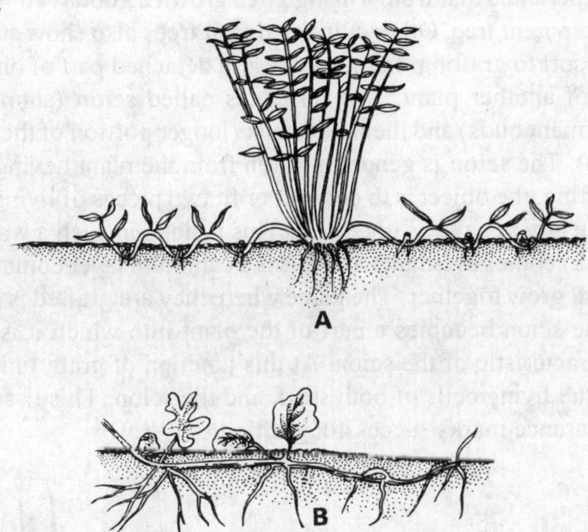

Fig. 16.11. Layering. A, serpentine layering; B, trench layering.

Layering. This is one of the most common methods used for propagating plants such as rose, jasmine, grape vine, lemon, rhododendrons and magnolias. .

Layering is the development of roots on a stem while it is still attached to the parent plant. The stem or branch that develops adventitious roots while still attached to the parent plant is called a **layer.** This is a natural means of reproduction in black raspberries and trailing blackberries. Layering can be artificially induced in many plants. It can be induced by bending the branch to the ground and covering a medium portion of it below the soil. The apical portion of the branch is left exposed to the air to form the leaves. The part below the soil develops adventitious roots. Now the connection of the layered branch can be cut from the parent plant and grown independently.

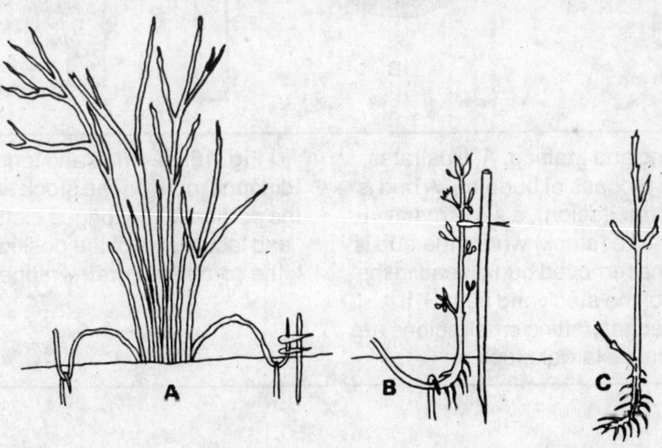

Fig. 16.12. Common method of layering. A, the branches of the plants are bent and buried under the soil; B, buried part, after it develops roots; C, the cut part is separately planted.

Grafting. This is another method in which man has remarkably exploited the regenerative capacity of higher plants. It is generally practiced in plants which do not root easily or have a weak root system. It is an art of joining parts of two plants of the same or allied species in such a way as to bring about an organic union or fusion of the tissues. This method is practiced in mango, apple, pear, citrus, guava, rose and rubber plant.

It is a common experience that from a mango tree grown a good seed will not always bear fruit of the same quality as the parent tree. Other cultivated fruit trees also show such variations. Under such conditions one may resort to grafting. In this process, a detached part of one plant is inserted into the stem or root system of another plant. The former is called **scion** (short place of detached shoot containing several dormant buds) and the latter stock (longer portion of the plant which is fixed to the soil by its root system). The **scion** is generally taken from the plant having superior characters.

In successful grafting, the object is to connect or fit two pieces of living plants in such a way they will unite and subsequently behave as one plant. This is done in such a way that the cambium tissue of both (scion and stock) comes in contact and forms a cambium layer common to both. Consequently, the two **scion** and **stock** grow together. The place where they are grafted is covered with grafting wax to avoid infection. The scion becomes a part of the plant into which it is grafted. This plant bears flowers and fruits characteristic of the scion. At this junction of graft, union a mass of parenchyma tissue develops from the living cells of both stock and the scion. This tissue heals the wound and is called **callus.** Its appearance marks successful grafting.

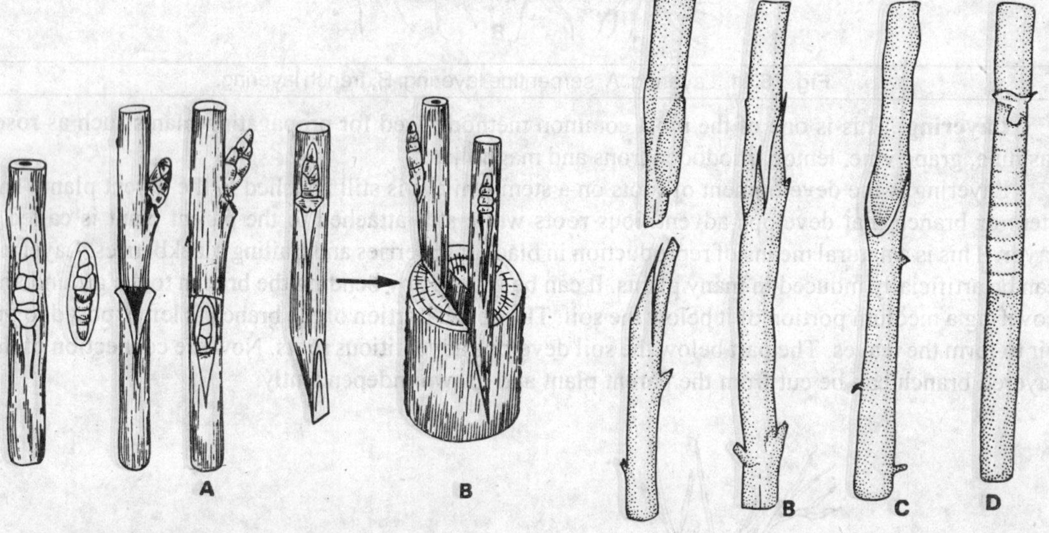

Fig. 16.13. Budding and grafting. A, Illustrates three stages in the process of budding. A bud is removed from the tree (scion), a slit is made in the bark of another tree (stock) where the bud is to be planted and the removed bud placed in the slit in the bark of the stock and tied; B, it illustrates cleft or wedge grafting small scions are grafted into a larger stock.

Fig. 16.14. Whip and tongue grafting. A, the diagonal cuts on the stock and the scion showing the portion of the tongue cleft. B and C are the side and face views of the positioned components; D, the completed graft wrapped with nurserv tape.

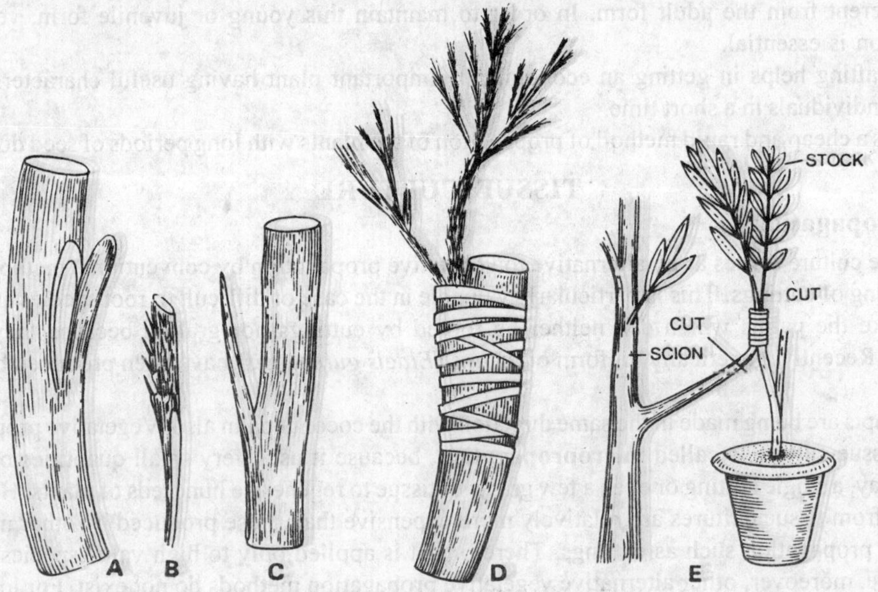

Fig. 16.15. Side grafting, A and C illustrate the position of the cut on the understock; B, scion prepared for insertion; D, complete graft; E, spliced grafting.

Gootee. This method is usually employed for vegetative propagation of lemon, orange, guava and litchi during rainy season. In this process, a healthy and woody branch is selected and the bark is sliced off in a ring form of about 3-5 cm in length. A thick plaster of grafting clay is wrapped up with rag and tied around the debarked portion. The 'grafting clay' is prepared by mixing cow-dung, finely cut hay and water. The tied up portion is kept moist by suitable supply of water. In about 2 or 3 months the roots come out and 'gootee' is ready to be cut below the tied rag for propagation.

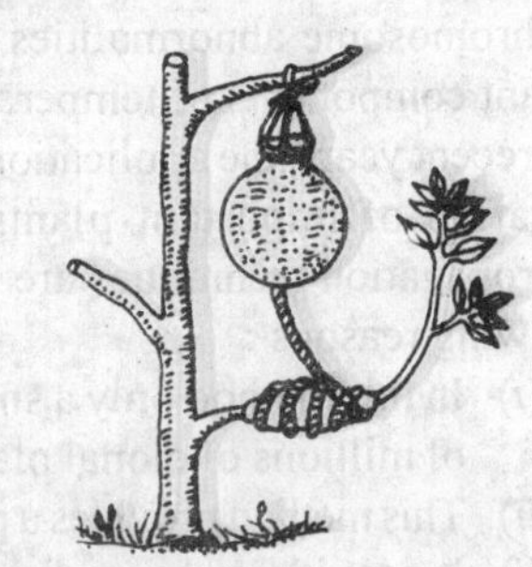

Fig. 16.16. Gootee. Method usually employed for vegetative propagation of lemon, orange, litchi, etc.

Significance of Vegetative Reproduction

1. Plants in which useful characters of parents have to be maintained, are propagated vegetatively.

2. The plants which do not produce viable seeds are propagated by this method.

3. Plants with reduced power of sexual reproduction, long dormant period of seed or poor viability are multiplied easily through this method.

4. The plants which are unable to produce seeds as a result of self-pollination cannot breed true. Such plants bear flowers that are only cross-pollinated and thus there is always mixture of characters. Such plants cannot produce seeds that will germinate to give rise to plants exactly like the parent. In such cases, vegetative propagation is the only method to get true to type plants.

5. Vegetative reproduction also helps in removing common infections from the parent plant.

6. Plants raised through vegetative propagation from a single plant constitute a genetically uniform population, the **clone.** Whereas plants developed from seeds may show variations due to genetic recombination and segregation thus by propagating plants through vegetative means a large stock of selected strains can be built up and maintained without losing the desirable characters.

7. It helps to perpetuate particular form of plants. In some individuals young stage of plants is

quite different from the adult form. In order to maintain this young or juvenile form, vegetative propagation is essential.

8. Grafting helps in getting an economically important plant having useful characters of two different individuals in a short time.

9. It is a cheap and rapid method of propagation of the plants with long periods of seed dormancy.

TISSUE CULTURE

Micropropagation

Tissue culture serves as an alternative to vegetative propagation by conventional methods, such as by rooting of cuttings. This is particularly valuable in the case of difficult to root species and those species like the palms which can neither be rooted by cuttings nor grafted because they lack a cambium. Recently, genetically uniform oil palms (*Elaeis guineensis*) have been produced by tissue culture.

Attempts are being made in the same direction with the coconut palm also. Vegetative propagation through tissue culture is called **micropropagation,** because it uses very small quantities of starter material, say, a single cutting or even a few grams of tissue to regenerate hundreds of plants. However, seedlings from tissue cultures are relatively more expensive than those produced by other means of vegetative propagation such as cuttings. Therefore, it is applied only to high value species like oil palm where, moreover, other alternative vegetative propagation methods do not exist. For low value species such as *Eucalyptus* rooted coppice shoot cuttings are still used commercially. Plants raised from tissue cultures require a longer hardening period before they become fit for transplanting, especially in harsh forest environments. Genetic instability of callus cultures is another drawback. Thus chromosome abnormalities are common in tissue cultures of Gymnosperms which constitute important components of temperate and arboreal forests.

In recent years, the application of micropropagation techniques as an alternative means of asexual propagation of important plants has increased the interest of workers in various fields. The micropropagation techniques are preferred over the conventional asexual propagation methods due to following reasons :

(*i*) In this method only a small amount of tissue is needed as the initial explant for regeneration of millions of clonal plants in a year.
(*ii*) This method provides a possible alternative method for developing resistance in many species.
(*iii*) It provides a mean for international exchange of plant materials, hence the problem for introduction of disease can be solved in quarantine.
(*iv*) Stock can be quickly proliferated *in vitro* as it is not season dependent.
(*v*) Valuable germplasm can be stored for a long time.

Application in horticulture and forestry. Regeneration of plantlets in cultured plant cells and tissues has been achieved in many trees of high economic value. Many of the studies are aimed at large scale micropropagation of important trees yielding fuel, pulp, timber, oil or fruits. Hence, clonal forestry and horticulture are gaining an increasing recognition as an alternative for tree improvement. However, strategies for transferring cultured plants *in vitro* to field conditions are based on relatively higher priced horticultural species rather than agricultural and forestry species.

Regeneration of plantlets in cultured tissue has been described by Murashige (1974) into three undermentioned stages:

(*i*) Establishment of explant aseptically.
(*ii*) Multiplication of propagules by repeated subcultures on a specific nutrient medium.
(*iii*) Rooting and hardening of plantlets and planting into soil.

Later on Fossard (1987) has described the following four stages of micropropagation:

(*i*) Selection of a suitable explant and inoculation into nutrient medium.
(*ii*) Multiplication and growth of culture which takes about two months, followed by repeated subcultures.

(*iii*) Cultures are obtained by changing the medium to planting out.

(*iv*) This is 'planting out' stage where plantlets are aseptically removed from test tube environment to natural and harsh environment. At this stage, roots should be fully functional in potting mix, the soil where plantlets are transplanted.

However, at planting out stage, the plantlets fail to survive due to sudden change in the environment and invasion by soil microbes. Scientists have suggested that the 'regenerates' should be transferred first to green house and then to field. The humidity should be controlled by covering the plants with transparent polyethylene sheets. This acclimatization requires several weeks which should be followed by potting into sterile peat or soil.

In recent years, the interest has created in commercialising the *in vitro* propagation of forest trees. For betterment and improvement of tree plants of high economic value, a breakthrough in forestry research has come with production of artificial seeds in *Eucalyptus*, and genetic transformation and *in vitro* regeneration in conifers. Moreover, micropropagation has been successfully done in many trees.

Advantages of Micropropagation (Tissue Culture)

Micropropagation, an essential component of plant biotechnology, has been proved to be means of producing millions of identical plants by culturing plant tissues or organs under aseptic conditions. The advantages of micropropagation over conventional methods, of a sexual reproduction are as follows:

(*i*) Greater output

(*ii*) Economy of time and space

(*iii*) Freedom from seasonal constraints

(*iv*) Multiplication under disease-free conditions.

Hence, this technique is ideal for the species where :

(*i*) Traditional methods of propagation are inadequate to meet the demand for planting material

(*ii*) Marked variability exists in the natural population and productivity can be significantly increased by cloning of superior individuals.

(*iii*) Virus can be eliminated by culturing the shoot meristem, thus pathogen-free stock can be maintained by routine micropropagation.

In the modern days, tissue culture has been successfully employed for the multiplication of orchids and many other ornamental plants. In the developed countries, tissue culture is a routine method of multiplication while in developing countries, the techniques are largely used for producing plants for export markets.

The Department of Biotechnology (DBT), Government of India, set up two pilot-scale national facilities for large scale production of elite planting material of forest trees through tissue culture, one at the Tata Energy Research Institute (TERI), New Delhi, and the other at the National Chemical Laboratory (NCL), Pune.

INCOMPATIBILITY

In nature, the stigma receives a variety of air-borne or insect-carried pollen but not all pollen that reach the stigma succeed in effecting fertilization. The pistil allows the pollen of only the right mating type to function normally, others are discarded. Thus, incompatibility is the inability of certain gametes, even from genetically similar plant species, to fuse with each other. If a pistil carrying functional female gamete fails to set seed following pollination with viable and fertile pollen, capable of bringing about fertilization in another pistil, the two are said to be incompatible.

Incompatibility is also called **intraspecific incompatibility, self-sterility** or **self-incompatibility.** The phenomenon of self-incompatibility is generally due to the prevention of some physiological or morphological mechanisms. This involves many complex mechanisms associated with interactions of pollen and stigmatic tissues.

Self-Incompatibility

A large number of flowering plants are successfully fertilised only by the pollen of other plants and not by their own. Such flowering plants are called **outbreeders.** In nature different floral adaptations, such as dichogamy, herkogamy and unisexuality have evolved to prevent self-pollination but the most widespread and effective natural device in such plants is self-incompatibility, which refers to the inability of a plant producing functional male and female gametes to set seeds when self-pollinated.

Depending on the origin of factors determining the mating types on the pollen side, two categories of self-incompatibility have been recognised :

***(i)* Sporophytic incompatibility.** Where the incompatibility is due to the genotype of the sporophytic stigmatic tissues; *e.g.*, *in* Asteraceae, Brassicaceae, etc.

***(ii)* Gametophytic incompatibility.** Where the incompatibility is due to the genotype of pollen, *e.g.*, in Poaceae, Liliaceae, Solanaceae, etc. This may be due to prevention of pollen germination, retardation of growth, deorientation of pollen tube, or even failure of nuclear fusion. It is controlled by genes with multiple alleles (S-allele). Usually, it develops with the maturation of stigma.

Biological significance of incompatibility. In nature a balanced breeding of the plants is regulated by incompatibility. Extensive selfing of the plants leads to highly homozygous individuals which have a very low survival value. To overcome this, nature has imposed self-incompatibility.

Despite the natural value, incompatibility may turn out to be a serious hurdle in a plant improvement programme. For example, before the introduction of anther culture technique selling was one of the chief methods to obtain homozygous individuals. For several plants where anther culture has failed to yield haploids, self-pollination continues to be an important approach to achieve this. In this context, self-incompatibility is a serious problem.

Germination of Non-Dormant and Dormant Seeds

DORMANCY OF SEEDS

All the viable seeds have capacity to germinate if placed under suitable conditions necessary for germination. While in certain plants such seeds will immediately germinate after harvest, in others they **fail to germinate for sometime** even if placed under such conditions that are ordinarily favourable for germination either due to some **internal factors** or due to specific requirement for some environmental factors. During this period the growth of the seeds remains suspended and they are said to be in rest stage or dormant stage and this phenomenon is called as dormancy of seeds.

FACTORS CAUSING DORMANCY OF SEEDS

Dormancy of seeds results from one or a combination of several different factors which are described below :

(1) Seed Coats Impermeable to Water

The seeds of certain plants especially those belonging to the families Leguminosae, Malvaceae, Chenopodiaceae, Convolvulaceae, and Solanaceae have very hard seed coats which are impermeable to water. The seeds remain dormant in the soil until the impermeable layer of testas decay by the action of soil micro-organisms.

(2) Seed Coats Impermeable to Oxygen

In many plants such as cocklebur (*Xanthium*), many grasses and some members of the family Compositae the dormancy of seeds results from the impermeability of the seed coats to oxygen. However, during the period of dormancy the seed coats gradually become more permeable to oxygen so that they may germinate afterwards.

(3) Mechanically Resistant Seed Coats

The seeds of certain weeds such as pigweed (*Amaranthus*), shepherd's purse (*Capsella*), water plantain (*Alisma*) etc., remain dormant because their hard seed-coats prevent any appreciable expansion of the embryo. This dormancy may persist up to periods as long as 30 years in case of pigweed if the seeds remain saturated with water. However, if the seed coats become dry and then again saturated with water, they are no longer able to resist the expansion of the embryo. The seed coats rupture and germination takes place. At higher temperatures (above 40°C) also the seed coats in pigweed become less resistant to pressure developed by the imbibitional forces in the embryo so that seed germination may take place.

(4) Immaturity of the Embryo

In many plants, *e.g.*, certain orchids, *Ginkgo biloba, Anemone nemorosa, Fraxinus excelsior,* etc. the seed dormancy results from the immaturity of the embryos which fail to develop fully by the time the seeds are shed. In such cases the seeds germinate only after a period of rest during which the development of embryo inside the seeds is completed.

(5) Need for After-Ripening in Dry Storage

In many plants, *e.g.*, barley, oats, wheat, etc., the seeds though containing fully developed embryos are dormant when they are harvested. They require no special treatment to overcome this dormancy and germinate if kept under dry storage conditions at normal temperatures for about a few weeks to several months. During this period probably due to certain physiological changes in the embryo, the seeds develop the capacity to germinate which is called as after-ripening. The nature of these physiological changes during after-ripening is not clear.

The dormancy of the cereal seeds, however, may be removed either by storing them at 35°C to 40°C for 2 to 4 days or removing their seed coats.

(6) Germination Inhibitors

Sometimes, the dormancy of seeds results due to the presence of certain germination inhibitors either in some parts of the seeds such as testa, endosperm, embryo or in structures surrounding them such as the juice or the pulp of fruit (*e.g.*, in tomato) and glumes (*e.g.*, in oats). The molecular structures of some of the common natural germination inhibitors are given in Fig. 17.1.

(7) Chilling (or Low Temperature) Requirement

In certain plants such as apple, rose, peach, etc., the seeds remain dormant after harvest in the autumn because they have a low temperature or chilling requirement for germination. In nature this requirement is fulfilled by the winter temperatures. In such case the seeds remain dormant throughout the winter season and germinate only in the following spring.

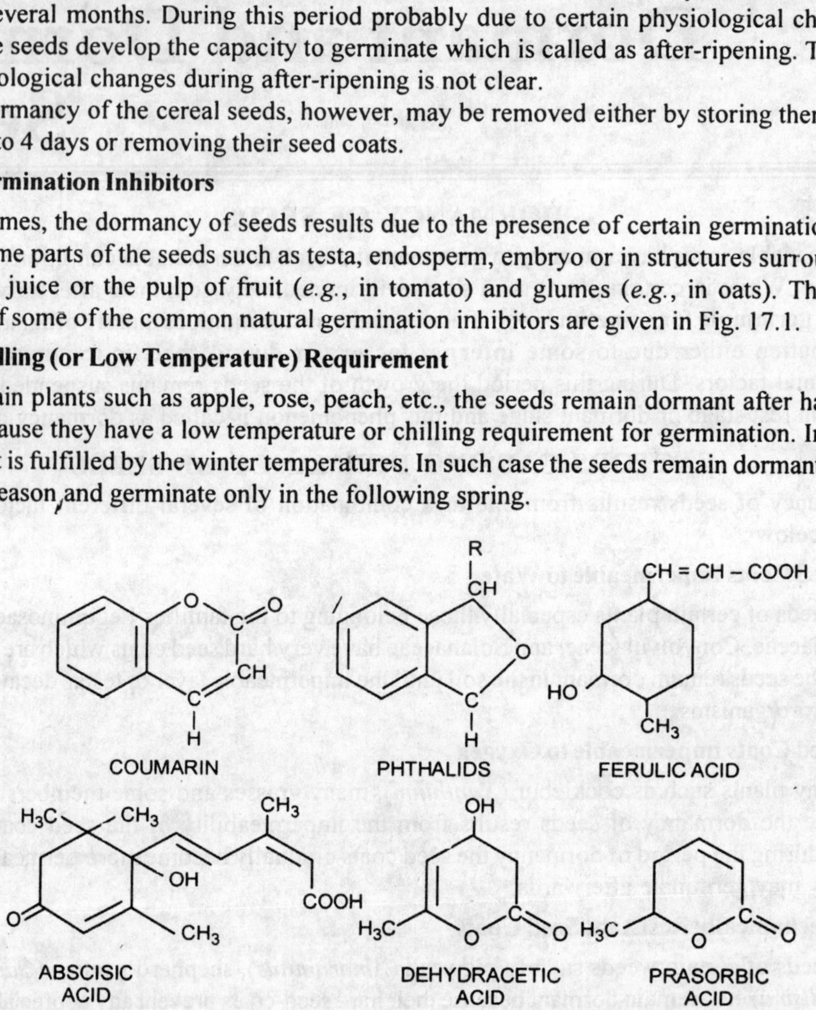

Fig. 17.1. Molecular structures of some of the common germination inhibitors.

(8) Light Sensitive seeds

In many species the germination of the seeds is affected by light resulting in seed dormancy. Such light sensitive seeds are called **photoblastic.** The seeds of certain plants *e.g.*, lettuce (*Lactuca sativa*), Shepnerd's purse (*Capsella bursa pastoris*), peppergrass (*Lepidium vigrinicum*), tobacco (*Nicotiana tabacum*), tomato (*Lycopersicum esculentum*), etc., are **positively photoblastic** and germinate only after they have been exposed to light. On the other hand, the seeds of certain plants, *e.g. Helleborus niger, Nigella damascena, Silene armeria*, etc., are **negatively photoblastic** and their germination is inhibited by light.

The light sensitivity of many photoblastic seeds declines with age if they are kept in dark under dry storage conditions.

SECONDARY DORMANCY OF SEEDS

Sometimes, the seeds which are capable of germinating immediately after harvest become dormant if kept in environment in which at least one of the factors essential for germination is unfavourable. This induced dormancy is called as **secondary dormancy of seeds.**

For instance, if the seeds of *Brassica alba* are exposed to high concentration of CO_2, they become dormant and will not germinate for a long time even after the removal of CO_2 from the environment which is otherwise favourable for germination.

However, the secondary dormancy of the seeds can be overcome by low temperature or other treatments.

ARTIFICIAL METHODS OF BREAKING THE DORMANCY OF SEEDS

Various methods are employed for breaking the dormancy of seeds depending upon its cause and the particular plant species.

(1) Scarification

The process of rupturing or weakening the seed coats by mechanical or other means is called as scarification and is employed in those cases where the dormancy of seeds results due to their resistant or impermeable seeds coats. The scarification can be done either mechanically by thrashing the seeds by machines or by hands, or chemically by treating them with strong mineral acids. Care should be taken during scarification so that the embryos are not damaged.

(2) Pressures

In certain plants, *e.g.*, sweet clover (*Melilotus alba*) and alfalfa (*Medicago sativa*) the germination of seeds can be improved by 50-200 percent if the seeds are subjected to hydraulic pressure of 2000 atm. at 18°C for about 5-20 minutes. This effect of pressure on germination results due to changes in the permeability of the testas to water.

(3) Low Temperatures

In many species seed dormancy resulting from chilling requirements can be overcome if the seeds are treated in moist medium at low temperature (5-10°C) for sufficient period of time. This process is called **stratification.** Artificial stratification is done by alternating the layers of seeds with layers of wet *Sphagnum* (peat moss), sand or some other suitable material and keeping them at low temperatures.

Low temperatures are also known to overcome the dormancy of certain light sensitive seeds such as lettuce.

(4) Alternating Temperatures

An alternation of low and high temperatures (the difference of the two being not more than 10°C or 20°C) greatly improves the germination of seeds in certain plants such as *Poa pratensis*.

Alternating temperatures of 15°C and 25°C daily can also overcome the dormancy of certain positively photoblastic seed such as *Rumex crispus*.

(5) Light

• The dormancy of positive photoblastic seeds can be broken by exposing them to red light (most effective near 660 mμ) or white light.

• Within limits the germination response depends upon the quantity of light received.

• The effect of red light is reversed by far-red light (maximum inhibition is near 735 mμ).

• Inhibitory effect of the far-red light declines if the far-red irradiation is delayed.

• The inhibitory effect of far-red irradiations can in turn be reversed by subsequent red irradiations.

• This promotion of germination by red-light and inhibition by far-red light probably involves the operation of a proteinaceous pigment called phytochrome. This pigment occurs in two forms, one red absorbing and the other far-red absorbing. Both these forms are photochemically interconvertible. The red absorbing from (P_R) after absorbing the red light is converted into far-red form (P_{FR}). The latter absorbs the far-red light and is converted back into red absorbing form of the pigment.

$$P_R \underset{735\ m\mu}{\overset{660\ m\mu}{\rightleftharpoons}} P_{FR}$$

It is considered that in positively photoblastic seeds, *e.g.*, pepper grass, lettuce, etc., the far-red absorbing form of the pigment is stimulatory to seed germination while red-absorbing form is inhibitory to seed germination.

(6) Germination Stimulating Compounds

The effects of kinetin and gibberellins in inducing certain positively photoblastic seeds such as tobacco, lettuce, etc., even in dark is well known. Besides them, a number of other chemical compounds are also known to possess germination stimulating capacity in certain seeds. Most common of these are KNO_3,, thiourea and ethylene.

ADVANTAGES OF DORMANCY OF SEEDS

(*i*) In temperate zones the dormancy of seeds helps the plants to tide over the severe colds which may be injurious for their vegetative and reproducing growth.

(*ii*) In tropical regions the dormancy of seeds resulting from their impermeable seed coats ensures good chances of survival.

(*iii*) Dormancy of seeds in many cereals is of utmost importance to mankind. If these seeds would germinate immediately after harvest in the field, they will become useless to man for consumption as food.

DORMANCY OF BUDS

In most of the woody trees growing in temperate regions the buds are formed either in the late summer or autumn and remain dormant throughout the winter period. They resume their further development and growth in the following spring season.

It has been observed in many plants that during the dormant period the level of endogenous growth inhibitor **abscisic acid** increases in the buds while there is a decrease in the level of endogenous gibberellins.

The dormancy of buds in woody trees can be broken artificially by (*i*) low temperature or chilling treatment (at 1-10°C for 10-40 days), (*ii*) exposure to long-day conditions, (*iii*) treatment with chemical substances such as **thiourea, ethylene-chlorhydrin,** or **gibberellic acid.**

Besides woody trees, the dormant buds are also formed by many herbaceous plants. One such example is **potato** where the eyes (buds) do not sprout immediately after they have been formed on the tuber and remain dormant for considerable period of time. This dormancy which is overcome during storage period can also be broken by treatment with thiourea, ethylene-chlorhydrin or gibberellins.

However, certain synthetic auxins like α-naphthalene acetic acid prolong the dormancy of buds in potato tubers and are very useful in preventing the 'eyes' to sprout during storage.

PHYSIOLOGY OF SEED GERMINATION

All the viable seeds which have overcome dormancy (if any) either naturally or artificially will readily germinate under suitable environmental conditions necessary for seed germination, *i.e.*, water, O_2, temperature and in some cases light. Such seeds which just wait for suitable environmental conditions to germinate are said to be **'quiescent'.** In most cases these seeds germinate if placed on moist substrate.

The process of seed germination starts with the imbibition of water by seed coats and emergence of growing root tip of embryo. It ends when the embryo has developed into a seedling which is out of bounds of seed coats and has its own photosynthetic system. Before describing the physiological and biochemical changes accompanying the seed germination, it is better to evaluate the physiological state of seed immediately before germination.

PHYSIOLOGICAL CONDITION OF QUIESCENT SEED

Before germination seed is a dry structure with various metabolic activities reduced to a minimum. It has dry, comparatively hard seed coat consisting of usually non-living cells. This seed coat and the cells of endosperm when present form a barrier to the outward growth of the embryo. Moreover, in certain seeds the seed coat is impermeable to water and O_2 and acts as barrier between embryo and these substances. Therefore, the cells of the seed coat and endosperm (when present) must become permeable to water and oxygen, also these must become penetrable to the growing root tip of the embryo if germination is to occur.

Most part of the embryo (excluding cotyledones) consists of potentially meristematic cells. But still these cells do not divide and enlarge and have minimum respiration rate in dry seed. It is chiefly due to the following reasons : —

(*i*) In absence of sufficient amount of water, these cells are unable to maintain turgor so that their growth is checked.

(*ii*) These cells do not have sufficient amount of soluble respirable food. The reserve food stored in cotyledones or endosperm is in insoluble form and is not available to these cells.

(*iii*) Aerobic respiration in embryo cells is at its minimum. It is because seed coat acts as barrier to O_2. Oxygen uptake in dry seeds is reduced to about 0.05 μ1//g tissue/hr.

(*iv*) Seed coat may contain inhibitors which check growth of these cells.

(*v*) The concentration of hydrolytic enzymes is low in dry seeds.

(*vi*) Hard seed coat forms a physical barrier to the growth of embryo.

All these above conditions are admirably overcome if seeds are placed under suitable conditions essential for germination and in most cases seed germination begins just by placing the dry seeds on a moist substrate.

PHYSIOLOGICAL, BIOCHEMICAL AND OTHER CHANGES ACCOMPANYING SEED GERMINATION*

Water Uptake. Seed germination, as mentioned earlier, starts with the **imbibition of water by** dry seed coat which is purely a physical process. Various hydrophilic groups such as —NH_2, —OH, —COOH, etc., of proteins, polymeric carbohydrates, etc., found in the seed coat attract dipolar water molecules and form hydrated shells around them resulting in the swelling of these substances. This water uptake by swelling is followed by intensive water uptake associated with germination. Due to imbibition of water the seed coats become (*i*) more permeable to O_2 and water and (*ii*) less resistant to outward growth of the embryo.

Respiration. The uptake is accompanied by rapid increase in respiration rate of embryo. Initially there may be anaerobic respiration but it is soon replaced, by aerobic one due to availability of O_2. As compared to dry seeds, the uptake of O_2 in germination seeds may rise in case of cereals from 0.05 μ 1/g tissue/hr to 100 ml/g tissue/hr within very short period after germination when water content has reached about 40%. Sucrose is probably the respiratory substrate at this stage which is provided by endosperm.

Mobilization of Reserve Materials. As germination progresses there is mobilization of reserve materials to provide (*i*) building blocks for the development of embryo, (*ii*) energy for the biosynthetic processes, and (*iii*) nucleic acids for control of protein synthesis and overall embryonic development. Changes in these components during seed germination are described below:

(*i*) **Nucleic Acids.** In monocots during the imbibition stage of seed germination there is rapid decrease of DNA and RNA content in the endosperm with a simultaneous increase in the embryonic axis probably due to their transportation as such. Appreciable amount of RNA appears in the **aleurone layer** after about 16 hours which is probably due to its *de novo* synthesis. Higher concentration of RNA (and also protein) in the embryonic axis precedes cell division. Due to more cell divisions the DNA content is increased.

(*ii*) **Carbohydrates.** Insoluble carbohydrates like starch are the important reserve food of cereals in the endosperm. During germination starch is hydrolysed first into maltose in the presence of α-*amylase* and β-*amylase* and then the maltose is converted into glucose by *maltose.* The glucose is absorbed by the **scutellum,** converted into soluble sucrose and transported to growing embryonic axis.

During germination the embryonic axis secretes **gibberellic acid** into the aleurone layer which causes *de novo* synthesis of α-*amylase.* This enzyme is not found in ungerminated seeds. Removal of gibberellic acid during this period results in rapid fall of α-*amylase* synthesis. The latter can be restored by supplying external gibberellic acid. The gibberellic acid induced synthesis of α-*amylase* is countered by **abscisic acid.**

In contrast to α-*amylase,* β-*amylase* is already present in the seed in **inactive form** which gets activated curing germination. The activity of the enzyme *maltase* is also regulated by gibberellic acid.

(*iii*) **Lipids.** Many plants like castor bean, peanut, etc., store large amount of neutral lipids or fats as reserve food in their seeds. During germination the mobilization of these fats is brought about by hydrolysis of fats to fatty acids and glycerol by *lipases* and β-oxidation of fatty acids to **acetyl-CoA.** The activity of *lipases* is greatly stimulated by imbibition and in some cases there may even be *de novo* synthesis of these enzymes which is probably triggered by gibberellic acid. Some of the acetyl-CoA is converted into sucrose via the **glyoxylate cycle** and is transported to the growing embryonic axis. Synthesis of the two key enzymes of glyoxylate cycle (*i.e.*, *isocitratase* and *malate synthetase*) takes place *de novo* during the early stages of germination. Their concentration is increased during the stage when fats are being actively converted into sucrose. They disappear when all the stored fat has been consumed and the seedling has developed the photosynthetic system. .

(*iv*) **Proteins.** Some plants store proteins as reserve food in their seeds in the form of **aleurone grains.** Mobilization of these proteins involves their hydrolytic cleavage into amino acids by *peptidases.* These enzymes, in part, are synthesized *de novo* as the germination starts in the same way as α-*amylase* is synthesized in cereals. The amino acids may either provide energy by oxidation after deamination or may be utilised in the synthesis of new proteins.

During seed germination there is active synthesis of enzymes and other proteins and also the formation of different RNA species for their synthesis. For the synthesis of these proteins **polysomes are involved.** It is not definite whether these are already present in the seed or are synthesized during germination. Moreover, it is also not certain whether polysomes are synthesized *de novo* or from pre-existing m-RNA.

(*v*) **Inorganic Materials.** A number of inorganic materials such as phosphate, calcium, magnesium and potassium are also stored in seeds in the form of **phytin.** These materials which may activate a number of important enzymes are liberated during germination due to the activity of various phosphatases including *phytase.*

Emergence of seedling out of the seed coat. All these changes described above gradually result in splitting of seed coat and emergence of the growing seedling. First, the radicle comes out and grows downward, then plumule comes out and grows upward. Due to continued growth of this seedling, the latter comes out of the soil, exposed to light and develops its own photosynthetic apparatus.

The splitting of seed coat may take place either (*i*) by imbibitional pressure or (*ii*) by internal pressure created by the growing primary root or (*iii*) by hydrolytic enzymes which act on cell wall contents of seed coat and digest it *e.g.*, *cellulase, pectinase*, etc. Sometimes the seed coat may be extensively rotted by the activity of micro-organisms in the soil.

GLOSSARY

CYTOLOGY AND ANATOMY

Abaxial. That surface of any structure which is remote or turned away from the axis.

Absciss. Layer of meristematic cells just outside cork layer, which causes fall of leaves, floral parts, fruits and certain branches.

Abscission. The separation of parts.

Abscission layer. Layer at base of leaf stalk in woody dicotyledons and gymnosperms, in which the parenchyma cells become separated from one another through dissolution of middle lamella before leaf fall.

Accessory bud. An additional axillary bud; a bud formed on a leaf.

Accessory cells. Auxiliary cells.

Acicular. Like a needle in shape; sharp pointed.

Acrogenous. Increasing in growth at summit or apex.

Acropetal. Development of organs in succession towards apex, the oldest at base, youngest at tip, *e.g.,* leaves on a shoot.

Acuminate. Drawn out into long point; tapering; pointed.

Adaxial. Turned towards the axis.

Adenine. A compound occurring in many cells; $C_5H_5N_5$.

Adventitious. Tissues and organs arising in abnormal positions; secondary.

Aerenchyma. Cortex of submerged roots of certain swamp plants; aerating cortical tissue in floating portions of some aquatic plants.

Aerial. Roots growing above ground, from stems.

Aerophyte. A plant growing attached to an aerial portion of another plant; epiphyte.

Agranular. Without granules.

Air-cells. Air spaces in plant tissue.

Alburnum. Sap wood or splint-wood, soft white substance between inner bark and true wood; outer young wood of dicotyledon.

Aleurone. Protein grains found in general protoplasm, and used as reserved food material.

Aleuroplast. Colourless plastid, storing protein.

Alkaloid. Basic nitrogenous organic substance with poisonous or medicinal properties produced in certain plant species as caffeine, morphine, nicotine, etc.

Ameiosis. Occurrence of only one division in meiosis instead of two.

Ameiotic. Parthenogenesis in which meiosis is suppressed.

Amino acids. Compounds containing amino (NH_2) and carboxyl (COOH) groups, constituents of proteins, synthesized in autotrophic organisms.

Amitosis. Direct cell-division and cleavage of nucleus without thread-like formation of nuclear material.

Amphicribral. Amphiphloic.

Amphicribral bundle. Concentric bundles are amphicribral, when phloem surrounds xylem, *e.g.*, in some ferns.

Amphiphloic. With phloem both peripheral and central to xylem.

Amphivasal. With primary xylem surrounding or on two sides of centric phloem, vascular bundle; amphixylic, perixylic. Opp. amphicribral, amphiphloic, periphloic.

Amphivasal bundle. Concentric bundles are amphivasal, when xylem surrounds phloem, *e.g.*, in *Dracaena*.

Amyloplast. A leucoplast or colourless starch forming granule in plants; amyloplastid.

Amylum. Vegetable starch.

Anaphase. A stage in mitosis during divergence of daughter chromosomes; the stages of mitosis upto division of chromatin into chromosome; kataphase.

Anatomy. The science which treats of the structure of plants and of animals, as determined by dissection.

Angienchyma. Vascular tissue.

Angiosperm. Having seeds in a closed case, the ovary.

Angular. Collenchyma with cell-walls thickened in the angles of the cells.

Annual ring. One of the rings, seen in transverse sections of dicotyledons, indicating the secondary growth during a year.

Annular. Ring-like, certain vessels in xylem, owing to ring-like thickenings in their interior.

Anomaly. Any departure from type characteristics.

Anthocyanin. One of the blue, reddish or violet pigments of flowers, leaves, fruits and stems.

Anticlinal. Line of division of cells at right angles to surface of apex of a growing point.

Apical. At tip; cell at tip of growing point; meristem.

Apical meristem. Growing point (zone of cell division) at tip of root and stem in vascular plants, having its origin in a single cell (initial), *e.g.*, Pteridophyta, or in a group of cells (initials), *e.g.*, Spermatophyta.

Apposition. The formation of successive layers in growth of a cell wall.

Aquatic. Living in water. An aquatic plant.

Arachnoid. Consisting of fine entangled hairs.

Artefact. An appearance, or apparent structure, due to preparation and not natural.

Articulate. Jointed; articulated.

Astrosclereid. A multiradiate sclereid or stone cell.

Autoplast. Chloroplast.

Axial. Axis or stem.

Axillary. Growing in axil, as buds.

Axis. The main stem or central cylinder.

Bark. The tissues external to the vascular cambium, collectively; phloem cortex and periderm; outer dead tissues and cork.

Bast. The inner fibrous bark of certain trees.

Bicollateral. Having the two sides similar, *e.g.*, vascular bundle with phloem on both sides of xylem, as in Cucurbitaceae and Solanacae.

Bifacial. Leaves with distinct upper and lower surfaces; dorsiventral.

Bilateral. Having two sides symmetrical about an axis.

Blind pit. A cell wall pit which is not backed by a complementary pit.

Biometry. Application of mathematics to the study of living things.

Bordered pit. A form of it developed on walls of tracheids and wood-vessels, with overarching border of secondary cell-wall.

Botany. The branch of biology dealing with plants, phytology.

Brachysclereid. A stone-cell.

Branch gaps. Gaps in the vascular cylinder of a main stem, subtending branch traces.

Branch traces. The vascular bundles connecting those of a main stem to those of a branch.

Brownian movements. (R. Brown. Scottish botanist). The passive vibratory movements of fine particles when suspended in a fluid.

Bud. A rudimentary shoot, or flower.

Bulbous. Like a bulb.

Bulliform. Thin walled cells which cause rolling, folding or opening of leaves by turgor changes.

Bundle-sheath. A layer of large parenchymatous cells surrounding vascular tissue of leaf-vein.

Callose. An occasional carbohydrate or periodic component of plant cell walls; as on sieveplates.

Callus. Tissue that forms over cut or damaged plant surface; deposit of callose on sieve plates.

Cambial. Pertaining cambium.

Cambiform. Similar to cambium cells.

Cambium. The tissue from which secondary growth arises in stem and roots.

Canada balsam. Gum commonly used, dissolved in xylene, for making permanent microscopical preparations. The object is placed in a thin layer of balsam solution between cover-slip and slide. The balsam dries hard, and because its refractive index is like that of proteins and other constituents of biological objects, it makes them very transparent.

Capitate. Swollen at tip.

Carbohydrates. Compounds of carbon, hydrogen and oxygen, aldehydes or ketones constituting sugars, or condensation products thereof.

Carotene. A yellow pigment synthesized by plants.

Carotenoids. Pigments occurring in plants, including carotenes, xanthophylls and other fat-soluble pigments.

Casparian band. (R. caspary. German botanist). A cork or wood-like strip encircling radial walls or endodermis cells; Casparian strip.

Cauline. Vascular bundles not passing into leaves.

Cell. A small cavity or hollow; a unit mass of protoplasm, usually containing a nucleus or nuclear material; originally, the cell-wall.

Cell division. Division of cell, both cytoplasm and nucleus, into two.

Cell lineage. Developmental history in terms of descent by cell division of later cells from earlier cells. The cell lineage of an organ traces the succession of cells, from the zygote onwards, which culminates in the group of cells, constituting that organ.

Cell membrane. A bimolecular layer of lipoids and proteins enveloping the protoplasm of a cell; plasma membrane; ectoplast and tonoplast of a plant cell.

Cell plate. Equatorial thickening of spindle fibres from which partition wall arises during division of plant cells.

Cell sap. Fluid in vacuoles of plant cell.

Cell theory. Theory, initiated by Schleiden and Schwann, 1838-39; that all animals and plants are made up of cells and their products, and that growth and reproduction are fundamentally due to division of cells.

Cellular. Consisting of cells.

Cellulose. A carbohydrate forming main part of plant cell-walls. $(C_6H_{10}O_5)x$.

Cell-wall. Investing portion of cell.

Cement. A uniting substance, as between cells or animals.

Central body. Centrosome.

Central cylinder. Stele.

Centrifugal. Turning or turned away from centre of plants or axis.

Centriole. The central particle of the centrosome; the centrosome itself.

Centripetal. Turning or turned towards centre of axis.

Centromere. The part of the chromosomes located at the point lying on the equator of the spindle at metaphase, and dividing at anaphase controlling chromosome activity.

Centrosome. A cell-organ, the centre of dynamic activity in mitosis, consisting of centriole and attraction-sphere.

Chitin. Nitrogen-containing polysaccharide with long fibrous molecules, forming material of considerable mechanical strength and resistant to chemicals. Present in cuticle.

Chlorenchyma. Tissues collectively, or stem tissue, or mesophyll, containing chlorophyll.

Chlorophyll. The green colouring matter found in plants and in some animals.

Chloroplast. A minute granule or plastid containing chlorophylls a and b, bound in plant cells exposed to light.

Chloroplast pigment. Chlorophylls, carotene, and xanthophyll.

Chondriosomes. Mitochondria, chondriomites, chondrioconts, chondriospheres, chondrioplasts.

Chromatid. A component of tetrad in meiosis; a half chromosome between early prophase and metaphase in mitosis, or between diplotene and second metaphase in meiosis.

Chromatin. A substance in the nucleus which contains nucleic acid, proteids, and stains with basic dyes.

Chromatophore. A coloured plastid of plants and animals; a colourless body in cytoplasm and developing into a leucoplast, chloroplast or chromoplast.

Chromomere. One of the chromatin granules of which a chromosome is formed and which corresponds to a gene.

Chromoplast. A coloured plastid or pigment body; coloured plastid other than a chloroplast; chromoplastid.

Chromosome. One of deeply staining bodies, the number of which is constant for the cells of a species, into which the chromatin resolves itself during karyokinesis and meiosis.

Cluster-crystals. Globular aggregates of calcium oxalate crystals in plant cells; sphaeraphides.

Collateral. Side by side; bundles with xylem and phloem in the same radius.

Collenchyma. Parenchymatous peripheral supporting tissue with cells more or less elongated and thickened, either at the angles or on walls adjoining intercellular spaces, or tangentially.

Colloid. A gelatinous substance which does not readily diffuse through an animal or vegetable membrane.

Columnar. Cells longer than broad.

Companion cell. A narrow cell, retaining its nucleus, derived, from a cell giving rise also to a sieve-tube element, in phloem of angiosperms.

Complementary. Non-suberized cells loosely arranged in cork tissue and forming air passages.

Concentric. Having a common centre.

Concentric bundle. The vascular bundle, with one tissue surrounding the other, *i.e.*, amphicribral and amphivasal.

Conjunctive. Tissue, mesocycle and pericycle in a stele.

Cork. A tissue derived usually from outer layer of cortex in woody plants.

Cork-cambium. Phellogen.

Corpus. Body; core of apical meristem within the tunica.

Cortex. The extrastelar fundamental tissue of the sporophyte.

Cortical. Pertaining the cortex.

Cristae. Folds of the inner membrane of a mitochondrion.

Crystalloids. A protein crystal found in certain plant cells.

Crystal sand. A deposit of minute crystals of calcium oxalate, as in Solanaceae.

Cuticle. An outer skin or pellicle.

Cuticularisation. Cutinisation in external layers of epidermal cells.

Cutin. A mixture of substances associated with cellulose, found in external layers of thickened epidermal cells of plants.

Cutinisation. The deposition of cutin in cell-wall, thereby forming a cuticle.

Cyanin. The blue pigment.

Cystolith. A mass of calcium carbonate occasionally of silica, formed on ingrowths of epidermal cell in some plants.

Cytokinesis. In an dividing cell, division of cytoplasm as distinct from division of nucleus.

Cytology. Study of cells.

Cytoplasm. Substance of cell-body exclusive of nucleus.

Cytosine. A cleavage product of nucleic acids $C_4H_6N_3O$.

Deoxyribose nucleic acid, DNA. Stable nucleic acid component of kinetoplasts, chromosomes, bacterial cells and phages, which consists structurally of two spirals linked transversely and constitutes a pattern or template for replication.

Dermatogen. The young or embryonic epidermis in plants.

Dextrose. Grape sugar or glucose, the end product of starch digestion, $C_6H_{12}O_6$.

Diakinesis. The later prophase state of meiosis. Between, diplotene and prometaphase; movement of chromosomes between metaphase and telophase.

Diarch. With two xylem and two phloem bundles; root in which protoxylem bundles meet and form a plate of tissue cross cylinder with phloem bundle on each side.

Diastase. An enzyme which acts principally in converting starch into sugar.

Dicotyledon. A plant with two seed-leaves.

Dictyosome. Unit of Golgi apparatus several of which occur as discrete bodies in cells of plants.

Dictyostele. Amphiphloic siphonostele that is broken up by crowded leaf gaps into a net work of distinct vascular strands (meristeles), each surrounded by a endodermis. Present in stems of certain ferns.

Diploid. Having the *2n* number of chromosomes.

Diplotene. Stage in meiosis at which bivalent chromosomes split longitudinally.

Discoid. Flat and circular, disc-shaped.

DNA. Deoxyribonucleic acid, a compound consisting of a large number of nucleotides attached together in single file to form a long strand.

Dorsiventral. With upper and lower surfaces distinct; bifacial.

Duct. Any tube which conveys fluid or other substance.

Duplication. A translocated chromosome fragment attached to one of normal set.

Dynamic. Producing or manifesting activity.

Ecology. Study of the relations of plants, particularly of plant communities, to their surroundings.

Ectoplast. The protoplasmic film or plasma membrane just within the true wall of a cell.

Elaioplast. A plastid in a plant cell, which forms or helps to form oil globules.

Embryo. A young organism in early stage of development.

Emergence. An outgrowth from sub-epidermal tissue.

Endarch. With central protoxylem, or with several surrounding a central pith.

Endodermis. Innermost layer of cortex in plant; layer surrounding pericycle.

Endoplasmic reticulum (ER). Complex mesh work of tubular channels, often extended into slit like cavities (*cisternae*) together with more or less flattened vesicles, all bounded by unit membranes, occurring in the cytoplasm of many eucaryotic cells; usually only visible by electron microscopy.

Enzyme. A catalyst produced by living organism and acting on one or more specific substrates.

Epiblema. The outermost layer of root tissue; piliferous layer.

Epidermis. The outermost protective layer of stems, roots and leaves.

Epiphyte. Plant which lives on surface of other plants.

Epithelium. Layer of cells living schizogenously formed secretory canals and cavities, *e.g.*, in resin canals of pine.

Ergastic. Life-less cell inclusions, as fat, starch.

Ergastoplasm. Endoplasmic reticulum.

Essential oils. Volatile oils, composed of various constituents and contained in plant organs, with characteristic odour.

Eumeristem. Meristem composed of iosodiametric thin-walled cells.

Eumitosis. Typical mitosis.

Exarch. With protoxylem strands outside metaxylem, or in touch with pericycle.

Excentric. One sided.

Exodermis. A specialized layer below the piliferous layer.

Extracellular. Occurring outside the cell.

Extracortical. Not within the cortex

Extranuclear. Situated outside the nucleus.

Extrastelar. Occurring outside the stele.

Extraxylar. On the outside of the xylem.

Fibre. Elongaated plat cell for mechanical strength.

Fibre tracheids. Fibres of a nature intermediate between that of libriform fibres and of tracheids.

Fibrous. Composed of fibres.

Fibrovascular. Bundle of vascular tissue surrounded by non-vascular fibrous tissues.

Filaments. A thread-like structure.

Flower. Specialized reproductive shoot, consisting of an axis (*receptacle*), on which are inserted four different sorts of organs.

Fructose. Fruit sugar.

Gland. Superficial discharging secretion externally, *e.g.*, glandular hair, nectary, hydath-ode; or embedded in tissue, occurring as isolated cells containing the intercellular space (secretory cavity) into which secretion is discharged, *e.g.*, resin canal of pine.

Gland cell. An isolated secreting cell.

Glandular. With glands.

Glandular tissue. Tissue of single or massed cells, parenchymatous and filled with granular protoplasm, adapted for secretion of aromatic substances in plants.

Globoid. A spherical body in aleurone grains, a double phosphate of calcium and magnesium.

Globose. Spherical.

Globule. Any minute spherical structure.

Glucose. The grape sugar, dextrose.

Glycogen. A carbohydrate storage product of plants.

Golgi apparatus or complex. (C. Golgi, Italian, histologist). Cell-constituents, localised or diffused, often consisting of separate elements, the Golgi bodies, batonettes, dictyosomes or pseudochromosomes, containing lipoprotein, and concerned with cellular synthesis and secretion.

Grana. Minute particles consisting of a pile of thin double platelets, probably containing chlorophyll, in chloroplasts.

Granum. Singular of grana.

Ground tissue. Conjunctive parenchyma.

Growing point. A part of plant body at which cell-division is localised, generally terminal and composed of meristematic cells.

Guanine. A purine base found in some plants; $C_6H_5ON_5$.

Gurad cells. Two cells surrounding stomata of aerial epidermis of plant tissue.

Gum. An exudation of certain plants and trees; vegetable mucilage.

Hair. Any epidermal filamentous outgrowth consisting of one or more cells, varied in shape.

Halophyte. A shore plant; plant capable of thriving on salt impregnated soils.

Haploid. Having a single set of unpaired chromosomes in each nucleus.

Haustorium. Specialized organ of parasitic plant, *e.g.*, *Cuscuta,* which penetrates into and withdraws food material from tissues of host plant.

Heart-wood. The darker, harder, central wood of trees; duramen.

Helix. A spiral.

Hemicellulose. One of several polysaccharides, chemically unrelated to cellulose. Occurring as cell-wall constituents in cotyledons, endosperms, and woody tissues, and serving as reserve food.

Herb. Plant with no persistent parts above ground, as distinct from shrubs and trees.

Herbaceous. Being a herb.

Hereditary. Transmissible from parent to offspring, as characteristics.

Hexarch. Having six radiating vascular strands; *e.g.*, roots.

Hilum. Nucleus of starch grain.

Hinge-cells. Large epidermal cells which, by changes in turgor, control rolling and unrolling of a leaf.

Histogens. Tissue producing zones or layers; plerome, periblem, dermatogen, and calyptrogen.

Histology. The science which treats of the detailed structure of animal or plant tissues; microscopic morphology.

Histone. A basic protein constituent of cell nuclei.

Homologous. Resembling in structure and origin; chromosomes with the same sequence of genes.

Hormones. Substances normally produced in cells and necessary for the proper functioning of other distant cells to which they are conveyed and of the body as a whole.

Hydathode. An epidermal structure specialized for secretion, or for exudation of water; water stoma.

Hydrophyte. An aquatic plant.

Hypocotyl. Part of seedling stem below cotyledons.

Hypodermis. The cellular layer laying beneath the epidermis.

Idioblast. Plant cell containing oil, gum, calcium carbonate or other product and which differs from the surrounding parenchyma.

Intercalary. (Of a meristem) situated between regions of permanent tissue, *e.g.*, at base of nodes and leaves in many monocotyledons.

Intercellular. Among or between cells.

Interfascicular. Situated between the vascular bundles.

Internode. The part between two successive nodes or joints, as of plant stem.

Interphase. Resting stage between first and second mitotic divisions; interkinesis.

Interxylary. Between xylem strands; interxylary phloem.

Intracellular. Within a cell.

Intrafascicular. Within a vascular bundle.

Intrastelar. Within the stele of a stem or root; ground tissue, bundles.

Intraxylary. Within wood or xylem.

Inulin. A carbohydrate occurring in rhizomes and roots of many plants; dahlia starch; $(C_6H_{10}O_5)x$.

Invertase. A plant enzyme which converts cane sugar into dextrose and laevulose.

Irritability. *e.g.*, Protoplasmic movements. A universal property of living things.

Isobilateral. A form of bilateral symmetry where a structure is divisible in two planes at right angles.

Isobilateral. A form of bilateral symmetry where as structure is divisible in two planes at right angles.

Isolateral. Having equal sides; leaves with palisade tissue on both sides.

Karyokinesis. Indirect cell-division; mitosis.

Karyolymph. Nuclear sap.

Kataphase. The stages of mitosis from formation of chromosomes to division of cell; anaphase.

Lacunate. Collenchyma with cell-walls thickened where bordering intercellular spaces.

Lamella. Any thin plate.

Latex. A milky, or clear, sometimes coloured, juice or emulsion of diverse composition found in some plants, as in spurges, rubber trees.

Laticifer. Any latex containing cell, series of cells or duct.

Laticiferous. Conveying latex; cell, series of cells or duct.

Laticiferous. Conveying latex; cells, tissue, vessels.

Leaf-gap. Gap in vascular cylinder of stele, a parenchymatous region associated with leaf-traces.

Leaf trace. Scar making position where a leaf was formerly attached to the stem.

Leaf scar. Vascular bundles extending from stem bundles of leaf-base.

Lenticel. Ventilating pore in angiosperm stems or roots.

Leptotene. Stage in early prophase of first division of meiosis.

Leucoplastids. Colourless plastids from which amylo-, chloro and chromoplastids arise.

Leucoplasts. Colourless granules of plant cytoplasm.

Lianes. Climbing plants found in tropical forests, with long woody rope like stems of anomalous anatomical structure.

Libriform. Resembling base.

Lignification. Wood formation; thickening of plant cell-walls by deposition of lignin.

Lignin. A complex substance which, associated with cellulose, causes the thickening of plant cell-walls, and so forms wood.

Lipoid. Resembling a fatty substance.

Lumen. Central cavity of a plant cell.

Lysosomes. Particles in cytoplasm, smaller than mitochondria, consisting of a membrane enclosing several enzymes.

Macerate. To wear away or to isolate part of a tissue or organ.

Macrosclereids. Relatively large columnar sclereids, as in coat of certain seeds.

Matrix. Ground substance of connective tissue.

Medullary. In region of medulla.

Medullary rays. A number of strands of connective tissue extending between pith and pericycle.

Meiosis. Process of reduction division of germicell chromosomes from diploid to haploid number at maturation.

Meristeles. See *dictyostele*.

Meristem. Tissue formed of cells all capable of diversification, as found at growing points; meristematic tissue.

Meristematic. Consisting of meristem; tissue, cells of growing point.

Mesarch. Xylem having metaxylem developing in all directions from the protoxylem, characteristic of ferns.

Mesophyll. The internal parenchyma of a leaf.

Mesophyte. A plant thriving in temperate climate with normal amount of moisture.

Messenger RNA. RNA molecule that conveys from the DNA the information that is to be translated into the structure of a particular polypeptide molecule.

Metabolic. Chemical changes occurring in the living organism.

Metabolism. The chemical change, constructive and destructive, occurring in living organism.

Metaphase. The stage in mitosis or meiosis in which chromosomes are split up in equatorial plate.

Metaphloem. The phloem of secondary xylem.

Metaxylem. Secondary xylem with many thick walled cells.

Micron. One thousandth part of a millimetre symbol : μ

Microscope. The ordinary microscope of the laboratory is a compound microscope with two sets of lenses (objective and eye-piece) which magnify the object in two steps.

Microtome. Machine for cutting extremely thin sections of tissue (usually 3 to 20 μ).

Microtomy. The cutting of thin sections of objects, as of tissues, or cells, in preparing specimens for microscopic or ultramicroscopic examination.

Middle lamella. The layer derived from the cell plate, and covered on both sides by cellulose in formation of the wall of a plant cell.

Mid-rib. The large central vein of a leaf, continuation of the petiole.

Mitochondria. Granular, rod shaped, or filamentous self-replicating organelle in cytoplasm, consisting of an outer and inner membrane containing phosphates and numerous enzymes, varying in different tissues and functioning in cell respiration and nutrition; chondriosome.

Mitochondrion. Singular of mitochondria.

Mitosis. Indirect or karyokinetic nuclear division, with chromosome formation, spindle formation, with or without centrosome activity.

Mitotic. Produced by mitosis.

Monocotyledonous. Having one cotyledon.

Morphogenesis. The development of shape; origin and development of organs or parts or organisms.

Morphology. The science of form and structure of plants and animals, as distinct from consideration of functions.

Mucilage. A substance of varying composition, hard when dry, swelling and slimy when moist, produce in cell-walls of certain plants.

Mucilaginous. Composed of mucilage.

Mycorrhiza. Association of fungal mycelium with roots of a higher plant.

Nectar. Sweet substance secreted by special glands, nectaries, in flowers and certain leaves.

Nectary. A group of modified subepidermal cells of no definite position in a flower, less commonly in leaves, secreting nectar, a nectar gland.

Nodal. Pertaining a node or nodes.

Node. The knot or joint of a stem at which leaves arise.

Nuclear membrane. Delicate membrane bounding a nucleus, formed from surrounding cytoplasm.

Nuclear sap. Karyolymph.

Nuclei. Plural of nucleus.

Nucleic. Acids containing phosphorus, found in nuclei of cells.

Nucleolus. A dense rounded mass in a cell-nucleus, consisting of protein and ribonucleic acid granules, and functioning in RNA and protein synthesis controlled by a special region or nucleolar organiser in the chromosome; plasmosome or a karyosome.

Nucleoplasm. Reticular nuclear substance; karyoplasm.

Nucleoprotein. A compound of protein and nucleic acid, a constituent of cell nuclei.

Nucleotide. Compound formed from sugar (with 5 carbon atoms) phosphoric acid, and a nitrogen-containing base (purine or pyrimidine).

Nucleus. Complex spheroidal mass essential to life of most cells.

Obtuse. With blunt or rounded end.

Oil gland. A gland which secretes oil.

Oil immersion objective. Objective of light microscope, space between which and the cover slip over the object examined is filled with drop of oil of same refractive index as glass; system used for highest magnification with the light microscope.

Ontogeny. The whole course of development during and individual's life-history.

Organ. Multicellular part of a plant which forms a structural and functional unit, *e.g.*, leaf.

Organelle. A persistent structure with specialized function forming part of a cell, *e.g.*, a mitochondrion.

Osteosclereid. A sclereid with both ends knobbed.

Oxalates. Salts of oxalic acid, occurring as metabolic by-products in various plant tissues.

Pachytene. Stage in prophase of first division of meiosis, follow zygotene.

Palisade. Tissue, the layer or layers of photosynthetic cells beneath the epidermis of many foliage leaves.

Papain. A proteolytic enzyme in fruit juice of the tree *Carica papaya.*

Parasite. An organism living with or within another to its own advantage in food or shelter.

Parenchyma. Plant tissue, generally soft and of thin walled relatively undifferentiated cells, which may vary in structure and function as pith, or mesophyll, etc.

Parenchymatous. Pertaining or found in parenchyma; a kind of cell.

Passage-cells. Thin-walled endoermal or exodermal cells of root, which permit passage of solutions.

Pectic. Substances in cell walls and cell sap of plants, including pectic acid and its salts, pectin and pectase; enzymes; pectosinase, pectase, and pectinase, which hydrolyse pectic substances.

Pectose. A carbohydrate constituent of plant cell-walls, converted into pectin and cellulose by action of pectosinase.

Pedicel. Stalk of individual flowers of an inflorescence.

Pentarch. With five alternating xylem and phloem groups.

Periblem. Layers of ground or fundamental tissues between dermatogen and plerome of growing points.

Periclinal. System of cells parallel to surface of apex of a growing point.

Pericycle. The external layer of stele, the layer between endodermis and conducting tissues.

Periderm. The outer layer of bark; phellogen, phellem and phelloderm collectively; epiphloem.

Permanent tissue. Tissue consisting of cells which have completed their period of growth and subsequently change little until they lose their protoplasm and die.

Permeability. Of membrance, extent to which molecules of a given kind can pass through it.

Phellem. Cork; cork and non-suberized layers forming external zone of periderm; phellem.

Phelloderm. The secondary parenchymatous suberous cortex of trees, formed on inner side of cork cambium.

Phellogen. The cork-cambium of tree stems arising as a secondary meristem and giving rise to cork and phelloderm.

Phloem. Bast tissue; the soft bast of vascular bundles, consisting of sieve-tube tissue.

Phloem parenchyma. Thin walled parenchyma associated with sieve tubes of phloem.

Phloem sheath. Pericycle, together with inner layer of a bundle sheath later consists of two layers.

Phloic. Pertaining phloem.

Photosynthesis. In green plants, synthesis of organic compounds from water and carbon dioxide using energy absorbed by chlorophyll from sunlight.

Phylloclade. A green flattened or rounded stem functioning a leaf as in *Cactus*; flattened axillary bud, as in *Ruscus*; flattened axillary bud, as in *Ruscus*; phyllocladium, cladode, cladophyll.

Phyllode. Winged petiole with flattened surfaces placed laterally to stem, functioning as leaf.

Phylogency. Evolutionary history.

Physiology. Study of the processes which go on in living organism.

Pigment. Colouring matter in plants.

Pigment cell. A chromatophore.

Piliferous. Bearing or producing hair; outermost layer of root of epiblema which gives rise to root hairs.

Pit. A depression formed in course of cell-wall thickening of plant tissue.

Pit chamber. The cavity of a bordered pit below the overarching border.

Pit-fields. Areas of depressions in primary cell-walls.

Pith. Central part of an organ of plant; central core of usually parenchymatous tissue in those stems in which the vascular tissue is in the form of a cylinder.

Pit memrane. Middle lamella of plant cell-wall forming floor of pits of adjacent cells.

Plasmalemma. Plasma membrane (external plasma membrane in plants).

Plasma membrane. The membrane forming the surface of cytoplasm and consisting of a bimolecular phospholipid layer between an inner and outer layer of protein molecules.

Plasmodesma. Cytoplasmic threads penetrating cell wall and forming intercellular bridge; plural plasmodesmata.

Plastid. A cell-body other than nucleus or centrosome.

Plastidome. In a cell, the plastids as a whole; cytoplasmic inclusion which give rise to plastids.

Plastochondria. Mitochondria.

Plerome. The core or central part of an apical meristem.

Polyarch. Having many protoxylem bundles.

Pore. A minute opening or passage, as of sieve plates, stomata, etc.

Primary. First; principal; original.

Primary meristem. Ground meristem, procambium and protoderm.

Procambium. The tissue from which vascular bundles are developed.

Promeristem. Meristem of growing point, and primary meristem.

Prometaphase. Stage between prophase and metaphase in mitosis and meiosis.

Prophase. The perparatory changes, the first stage in mitosis, or in meiosis.

Proplastid. An immature plastid, as in meristematic cells.

Protein. A nitrogenous compound of cell protoplasm; a complex substance characteristic of living matter and consisting of aggregates of amino-acids, and generally containing sulphur.

Protoderm. The outer cell layer of apical meristem; primordial epidermis of plants; superficial dermatogen.

Protophloem. The first phloem elements of a vascular bundle.

Protoplasm. Living cell substance; cytoplasm and karyoplasm.

Protoplasmic. Pertaining or consisting of protoplasm.

Protoplast. Protoplasm of a plant cell.

Protoxylem. Primary xylem lying next to pith of stems.

Pteridophyta. Division of plant kingdom comprising ferns, horsetails, club-mosses, etc.

Purine. Bases-adenine and guanine.

Pyrimidine. Bases-thymine and cytosine.

Quantasome. Regularly arranged sub-units observed by electron microscopy in thylakoid lamellae. Estimated each contains about 300 chlorophyll molecules which are believed to function as photosynthetic units in absorption of light quanta.

Quiescent centre. Inactive or passive region of cells.

Raphides. Needle shaped crystals of calcium oxalate occurring in bundles in certain plant cells.

Radial. Pertaining radius.

Ray. A parenchymatous band penetrating from cortex towards centre of stem.

Replication. Duplication of a molecule or aggregate by copying from a pre-existing molecule or structure of the same kind of mitochondria, chloroplast, etc.

Reticulate. Like network; thickening of cell-wall.

Rhizome. Underground stem, bearing buds in axils of reduced scale-like leaves.

Rhytidome. The outer bark.

Ribonucleic acid. RNA, a nucleic acid containing adenine, guanine, cytosine and uracil, in nucleolus, mitochondria, and ribosomes, and taken part in cytoplasmic protein synthesis.

Ribosomes. Spherical granules or microsomal particles containing ribo-nucleic acid, on nuclear membrane and membranes of endoplasmic reticulum, and taking part in protein synthesis.

RNA. Ribonucleic acid, a molecule consisting of a large number of nucleotides attached together to form a long strand one nucleotide thick. Each nucleotide contains the sugar ribose, and one of the four different bases found in DNA except that uracil replaces thymine.

Root. Descending portion of a plant, fixing it in soil, and absorbing moisture and nutrients.

Root-cap. A protective cap of tissue at apex of root.

Root-hairs. Unicellular epidermal outgrowths from roots, of protective and absorbent function.

Rosette. A cluster of crystals, as in certain plant cells.

Saprophyte. The plant that obtains organic matter in solution from dead and decaying tissues of plants or animals, *e.g., Monotropa.*

Saprophytic. A plant which lives on dead and decaying organic matter.

Sap-wood. The more superficial, softer wood of trees; alburnum.

Scalariform. Ladder-shaped; vessels or tissues having bars like a ladder.

Scalariform thickening. Internal thickening of wall of a xylem vessel or tracheid, in the form of more or less transverse bars, suggestive of ladder rungs.

Scape. Leafless flowering stem arising from ground level, *e.g., Canna.*

Schizogenous. Cavity origninating by separation of cells, *e.g., Citrus.*

Sclereid. Any cell with a thick lignified wall; a sclerenchymatous cell; a stone cell.

Sclerenchyma. Plant tissue of thickened end of the hard cells or vessels.

Scleroid. Hard.

Sclerotic. Containing lignin.

Secondary. Arising not from growing point, but from other tissue.

Secondary cortex. Phelloderm.

Secondary growth. Development of secondary meristem of cambium producing new tissue on both sides, as in woody dicotyledons.

Secondary meristem. Phellogen. Region of active cell division.

Secondary wood. Wood formed from cambium.

Sepal. One of the parts forming calyx of dicotyledonous flowers.

Septum. Partition of wall.

Shoot. Stem of a vascular plant derived from the plumule.

Sieve area. Perforated area of cell wall of sieve elements, with groups of pores surrounded by callose.

Sieve cell. A phloem cell having perforated areas of cell-wall; a cell of sieve tubes.

Sieve elements. The conducting parts of phloem; sieve cells and sieve tube cells.

Sieve plate. Part of the wall of a sieve cell, containing simple or compound sieve areas; the perforated and thickened end of a sieve tube cell.

Sieve tubes. Phloem vessels, long slender structures consisting of elongated cells placed end to end, forming lines of conduction.

Somatic cells (soma). The cells of an organism, other than the germ cells.

Spermatophyta. Seed plants. Division of plant kingdom providing dominant flora of present day, including most trees, shrubs, herbs, grasses, etc.

Spindle. A structure formed of a chromatin fibres during mitosis.

Spiral. Thread-like appearance of nuclear chromatin during prophase of mitosis.

Spongy. Parenchyma of mesophyll.

Sporophyte. Phase of life-cycle of plants which has diploid nuclei, and during which spores are produced.

Stamen. Organ of flower which produces pollen grains.

Starch. The common carbohydrate formed by plants and stored in seeds. $(C_6H_{10}O_5)x$.

Starch sheath. Endodermis with starch grains,

Stele. A bulky strand or cylinder of vascular tissue contained in stem and root of plants, developed from plerome.

Stellate. Star shaped hair.

Stem. Main axis of a plant.

Steroids. Complex hydrocarbons, chemically similar, occurring in plants and animals.

Sting. Stinging hair and cell.

Stoma. A small orifice; minute openings with gurad cells, in epidermis of plants, especially on under surface of leaves, or, the stomatic pores only.

Stomata. Plural of stoma.

Stone cells. Sclerotic cells are rounded sclerenchymatous elements, as found in pear; brachysclereids.

Suberisation. Modification of cell-walls due to suberin formation.

Suberin. The waxy substance developed in a thickened cell-wall characteristic of cork tissues.

Subsidiary cells. Additional modified epidermal cells lying outside guard cells.

Substomatal. Hypostomatic.

Sucrose. Cane sugar $C_{12}H_{22}O_{11}$.

Sulcate. Furrowed, grooved.

Superficial. On or near the surface.

Tabular. Flattened, as certain cells.

Tannins. Group of astringent substances of wide occurrence in plants, dissolved in cell sap particularly common in the bark of trees, unripe fruits, leaves and galls. Complex organic compounds containing phenols, hydroxy-acids, or glucosides.

Tap root. Root system with a prominent main root, directing vertically downwards and bearing smaller lateral roots.

Taxonomy. Study of the classification of organisms according to their resemblances and differences.

Telophase. Termianl stage of mitosis or meiosis during which nuclei revert to resting stage.

Terminal. Situated at the end, as terminal bud at end or twig.

Tetrarch. With four protoxylem bundles.

Thylakoid. In photosynthetic organisms, vesicle, wall of which bears photosynthetic pigments. Thylakoids vary in form arrangement in different groups of organisms.

Tissue. The fundamental structure of which animal and plant organs are composed; an organization of like cells.

Tissue culture. A technique for maintaining fragments of animal or plant tissue or separated cells alive after their removal from the organism.

Tonoplast. A vascular membrane; a plastid with distinct vacuole walls; a special form of vacuole-producing plastid.

Torus. Thickened centre of a bordered pit membrane.

Trachea. Spiral or annular vascular tissue of plants; wood vessel.

Tracheid. One of the cells with spiral thickening or bordered pits, conducting water and solutes, and forming wood tissue.

Tracheophyta. Division including all vascular plants (Pteridophyta and Spermatophyta).

Transection. Cross section; transverse section.

Transfer RNA. A relatively small molecule of RNA, whose function is to place the amino acids that will be linked into a polypeptide molecule in the specific sequence specified by a molecule of *Messenger RNA*.

Transfusion tissue. Tissue of empty cells with pitted and occasionally, internally thickened walls, and protein containing, parenchyma cells, accompanying vascular tissue in leaves of most gymnosperms, lying on either side of the vascular bundles of the single vein.

Triarch. Having three xylem bundles uniting to form the woody tissue of root.

Trichoblast. A cell, of plant epidermis, which develops into a root hair.

Trichome. An outgrowth of plant epidermis, either hairs or scales; a hair tuft.

Tunica. Apical mertistematic cell giving rise to protoderm.

Tunica corpus concept. An interpretation of the shoot apex which recognizes two tissue zones in the promeristem, *tunica* consisting of one or more peripheral layers, in which the planes of cell division are predominantly anticlinal, enclosing *corpus,* or central tissue of irregularly arranged cells in which the planes of cell division vary.

Tylosis. Development of irregular cells in a cell cavity; a cell cavity; a cellular intrusion into vessel through pit of parenchyma cells.

Ultrastructure. Structure, at the molecular or electron microscopical level.

Unciform. Shaped like a hook or barbed.

Uncinate. Unciform; hook like.

Unit membrane. The common form, as seen in the electron microscope, of the membranes of the cells, *i.e.*, of the plasma membrane and of the membranes organelles such as mitochondria, nucleus and endoplasmic reticulum.

Vacuole. One of spaces in cell protoplasm containing air, sap, or partially digested food.

Vascular. Containing, or concerning vessels.

Vascular bundle. A group of special cells consisting of two parts, xylem or wood and phloem or bast portion; many have in addition a thin strip of cambium separating the two parts.

Vascular cylinder. Stele.

Vascular plant. Plant possessing vascular system, member of Tracheophyta. (Pteridophyta and Spermatophyta).

Vascular system. Plant tissue consisting mainly of xylem and phloem which forms a continuous system throughout all parts of higher plants. It functions in conductio of water, mineral salts, and synthesized food materials and form mechanical support.

Vascular tissue. Specially modified plantcells, usually consisting of either tracheae or sieve cells for circulation of sap.

Veins. Strands, vascular tissue of leaf.

Velamen. A specialized moisture absorbing tissue.

Ventral. Situated on lower surface.

Vesicle. Small globular or bladder-like air space in tissues.

Vessel. Any tube or canal with properly defined walls.

Water stomata. Pores on surfaces of leaves for excretion of water; hydathodes.

Wax. A substance soluble in fat solvents.

Wood. The hard substance of a tree stem, xylem of vascular bundles.

Wood vessel. An element of tracheal tissue, a long tubular structure formed by cell-fusion.

Xanthophylls. Yellow or brown carotenoid pigments found in plastids.

Xerophyte. A plant growing in desert or alkaline or physiologically dry soil.

Xylary. Pertaining xylem.

Xylem. Woody tissue; lignified portion of vascular bundle.

Xylem-parenchyma. Short lignified cells surrounding vascular cells or produced other xylem cells towards the end of the growing season.

Xylem-ray. Ray or plate of xylem between two medullary rays.

Zygotene. Stage in prophase of first division of meiosis following leptotene, in which pairing (synapsis) of homologous chromosomes occurs with formation of bivalents.

MEDICAL TERMS

Abortifacient. An agent that produces abortion.

Alterative. A drug which corrects disordered process of nutrition and restores the normal function of an organ or of the system.

Amenorrhoea. Abnormal suppression of menses.

Anaemia. A deficiency of blood or of red blood-cells.

Angina pectoris. A disease of the heart marked by severe constricting pains in the chest.

Anodyne. A drug that relieves pain.

Anthelmintic. A drug that kills intestinal worms.

Anthihydrotic. A drug which checks sweating.

Antilithic. A drug which counteracts the development of stone.

Antipyretic. A drug which reduces fever.

Antiscorbutic. A drug which cures scurvy.

Antispasmodic. A drug which counteracts spasmodic disorders.

Aphrodisiac. A drug which promotes sexual desire.

Aromatic. A drug which is fragrant, spicy and mildly stimulant.

Asthma. A chronic disorder of the bronchial tubes.

Astringent. A drug which checks secretion or bleeding.

Beriberi. A deficiency disease caused by lack of vitamins especially B_1.

Bronchitis. An inflammation of the air passages.

Calculus. A hard and solid concretion formed in the body, especially in the urinary organs; it may be sand, gravel or stone.

Cancer. Any malignant growth.

Caries. Decay of teeth.

Carminative. A drug which relieves flatulence.

Cathartic. A drug which induces active movement of the bowels.

Cholagogue. A drug which promotes flow of bile.

Colic. Pain due to spasmodic contraction of the abdomen.

Congestion. An abnormal collection of blood in the blood vessels of any organ or part of the body.

Conjunctivitis. Inflanmation of the conjunctiva, the mucous membrane covering the eyeball and lining the eyelids.

Dandruff. An inflamed condition of the scalp characterized by the presence of white scales in the hair due to the exfoliation of the horny cells of the scalp.

Demulcent. An agent having a soothing effect on the skin and mucous membranes.

Deobstruent. A drug that removes an obstruction to secretion or excretion by opening the natural passages or pores of the body.

Diabetes. A wasting disease of metabolism; abundant sugar is present continuously in the urine.

Diaphoretic. A drug that induces copious perspiration.

Diuretic. A drug which increases the secretion and discharge of urine.

Dropsy. A disease marked by an excessive collection of a watery fluid in the tissues or the cavities of the body.

Dysentery. An infectious disease of which the chief symptoms are acute diarrhoea and discharge of mucous and blood.

Dysmenorrhoea. Usually painful and difficult menstruation.

Dyspepsia. Indigestion.

Eczema. A skin disease accompanied by swelling, redness and exudation of lymph.

Elephantiasis. A disease of the skin caused by a tiny worm and attended with hypertrophy of the affected parts.

Emetic. A drug which induces vomiting.

Emmenagogue. A drug which promotes menstruation or regulates the menstrual periods.

Emollient. A drug which allays irritation of the skin and alleviates swelling and pain.

Enteritis. Inflammation of the intestines.

Epilepsy. A chronic nervous disorder marked by attacks of unconsciousness or convulsions.

Expectorant. A drug that promotes the removal of catarrhal matter and phlegm from the bronchial tubes.

Febrifuge. An agent used from reducing fever.

Flatulence. A disorder in which there is an excessive collection of the gas in the stomach.

Galactagogue. An agent that promotes secretion and glow of milk.

Gleet. A chronic discharge from the urethra.

Goitre. A chronic enlargement of the thyroid gland.

Gonorrhoea. An infectious venereal disease marked by an inflammatory discharge from the genital organs.

Haemoptysis. Spitting of blood from the lungs or bronchial tubes.

Heartburn. A burning feeling in the regions of the chest and stomach, generally due to indigestion.

Hepatitis. Inflammation of the liver.

Hysteria. A disease in which a physically healthy patient has lost control over acts and feeling and suffers from imaginary ailments.

Intermittent fever. Fever which is marked by intervals of normal temperature between periods of rise of temperature.

Jaundice. A diseased condition in which there is a yellowish staining of the tissues and excretion with bile.

Lactagogue. Galactagogue.

Laryngitis. Inflammation of the larynx.

Leprosy. A chronic wasting disease caused by a germ; the disease generally results in mutilations and deformities.

Leucoderma. A condition of the skin in which there is loss of pigment wholly or partially.

Lithontriptic. A drug used for removing calculi or stones formed in the urinary system.

Malaria. A recurrent disease marked by bouts of shivering, sudden rise of temperature and general aching of the body.

Narcotic. A drug which induces deep sleep.

Nausea. A feeling that vomiting is about to take place.

Nephritis. Inflammation of the kidney.

Neuralgia. Pain felt above a nerve.

Opthalmia. Conjunctivitis.

Orchitis. Inflammation of the testicles.

Paralysis. A disease in which there is loss of power of voluntary movement in any part of the body.

Pectoral. A drug to cure disorders of the chest.

Pharyngitis. Inflammation of the pharynx.

Phythisis. Consumption; tuberculosis of the lungs.

Piles. An inflamed condition of the veins in the rectal region.

Pneumonia. Inflammation of the lungs.

Prophylactic. An agent that prevents disease.

Refrigerant. A drug which relieves feverishness or produces a feeling of coolness.

Rheumatism. An indefinite term used for pains in the muscles, joints and certain tissues.

Rubefacient. A mild counter-irritant,

Scabies. An itching skin disease caused by a mite.

Scorbutic. Suffering from scurvy.

Scurvy. A deficiency disease due to lack of vitamin C.

Sedative. A drug which reduces excitement, irritation and pain.

Sialagogue. A drug which promotes salivation.

Soporific. A drug that induces sleep.

Stomachic. A drug that strengthens the stomach and promotes its action.

Styptic. An agent which checks bleeding

Syphilis. A chronic venereal disease.

Tetanus. An infectious disease, marked by painful contraction in the muscles.

Tonsillitis. Inflammation of the tonsils.

Ulcer. An open sore of the skin.

Vermifuge. A drug which expels intestinal worms.

Whooping chough. An acute infectious disease of coughing.

NOTES

NOTES